LYLE E. BOURNE, JR.
University of Colorado
BRUCE R. EKSTRAND

Third Edition
PSYCHOLOGY

Its Principles and Meanings

HOLT, RINEHART AND WINSTON

New York   Chicago   San Francisco
Dallas   Montreal   Toronto
London   Sydney

Senior Acquisitions Editor	Richard C. Owen
Developmental Editor	Johnna Barto
Assistant Editor	Charlyce Jones
Managing Editor	Jeanette Ninas Johnson
Senior Project Editor	Françoise Bartlett
Photo and Cartoon Researchers	Jo-Anne Naples
	Mili Ve McNiece
Production Manager	Victor Calderon
Text Designer	Robert Kopelman
Cover Designer	David Epstein

Library of Congress Cataloging in Publication Data
Bourne, Lyle Eugene, 1932–
Psychology: Its Principles and Meanings.
  Bibliography: p. 586
  Includes indexes.
  1. Psychology.   I. Ekstrand, Bruce R., joint author.
II. Title.
BF121.B62   1979   150   78–21605
ISBN 0–03–021486–6

For permission to use copyrighted materials, the authors are indebted to the following:

Chapter 1

Photo, p. 1, by Richard Kalvar, © Magnum Photos, Inc.
News story, p. 3, reprinted courtesy of *The Denver Post.*
Figure 1–1, p. 4, photo by Baron Hugo van Lawick, © National Geographic Society.
Photo, p. 5, by Ellis Herwig, Stock, Boston.

News story, p. 6, © *The Washington Post.* Reprinted by permission.
News story, p. 9, reprinted by permission of Associated Press.
News story, p. 15, reprinted by permission of *TIME,* The Weekly Newsmagazine; Copyright Time Inc. 1976.
News story and table, pp. 16–17, reprinted by permission of *TIME,* The Weekly Newsmagazine; Copyright Time Inc. 1971.

(Continued on p. 595)

Contributors

Douglas Bernstein
University of Illinois, Champaign-Urbana
Chapter 9

Roger Dominowski
University of Illinois, Chicago Circle
Chapter 6

Lewis O. Harvey, Jr.
University of Colorado
Chapter 3

William Hodges
University of Colorado
Chapters 11 and 12

Steven F. Maier
University of Colorado
Chapter 4

Neil Salkind
University of Kansas
Chapter 8

Charles Tart
University of California, Davis
Appendix D

Michael Ziegler
York University, Toronto
Chapter 10

Acknowledgments

Because of their large number, it is impossible for us to name everyone who assisted us in producing this book. Several people, however, deserve special mention because of the importance of their contributions. Foremost among them are the eight professors of psychology, each a teacher of college-level introductory psychology, who served as subject-matter experts and who drafted initial versions of several chapters in this edition. These psychologists are listed above as Contributors. To each of them we owe thanks and apologies—thanks for telling us in written form about current developments in special areas of psychology and apologies for editing and revising their work in ways that may have distorted both their intentions and their scholarship.

In addition to the Contributors, several others made substantive contributions to sections of various chapters. Among these we would name, in particular, Murray Camazine, University of Colorado; David Dodd, University of Utah; Philip Groves, University of Colorado; Don Johnson, University of Colorado; Ellin Scholnick, University of Maryland; and Rita Yaroush, National Jewish Hospital, Denver.

The book has materially benefited from the comments and reactions of many reviewers. We would like to recognize the thorough, intelligent, and critical essays on our efforts provided by the following: James F. Alexander, University of Utah; Robert M. Arkin, University of Missouri, Columbia; Herbert H. Bell, University of Tennessee, Nashville; Jacob Beck, University of Oregon; Douglas Bernstein, University of Illinois, Champaign-Urbana; Sharon A. Brehm, University of Kansas; James Bryan, Northwestern University; Edward Caldwell, West Virginia University; Charles N. Cofer, University of Houston; Diane DeArmond, University of Missouri, Kansas City; Kenneth Deissler, Embry-Riddle Aeronautical University; Terry L. DeVietti, Central Washington University; John J. Duda, Gannon College; Karen Edwards, University of Tennessee, Nashville; Robert Eisenberger, State University of New York, Albany; Morton P. Friedman, University of California, Los Angeles; James B. Garrett, Innerspace Research Institute; Andrew Gilpin, University of Northern Iowa; Mitchell Glickstein, Brown University; Gary Greenberg, Wichita State University; Anthony Greenwald, Ohio State University; Don E. Hamachek, Michigan State University; Albert A. Harrison, University of California, Davis; Richard H. Haude, University of Akron; Douglas L. Hintzman, University of Oregon; Morton Hoffmann, Metropolitan State College; James Howell, Portland Community College; Wayne L. Hren, Los Angeles Pierce College; William A. Johnston, University of Utah; Raymond Kesner, University of Utah; John Knight, Central State University; Joel F. Lubar, University of Tennessee; Colin MacLeod, University of Toronto; Leslie Patrick McGovern, State University of New York, Buffalo; W. Wade Martin, Catholic University; Richard E. Mayer, University of California, Santa Barbara; Ronald Mayer, San Francisco State University; Roger N. Moss, California State University, Northridge; Benjamin H. Newberry, Kent State

University; Cecil B. Nichols, Miami Dade Community College, North; Gary M. Olson, University of Michigan; Thomas M. Ostrom, Ohio State University; Robert Pagano, University of Washington; Louis Penner, University of South Florida; Michael H. Phillips, Fordham University at Lincoln Center; David Pomeranz, State University of New York, Stony Brook; Richard H. Price, University of Michigan; D. W. Rajecki, University of Wisconsin; Freda Rebelsky, Boston University; Robert E. Remez, Indiana University; Kenneth Ring, University of Connecticut, Storrs; Dwight R. Riskey, Mount St. Mary's College; Donald A. Robinson, Indiana University; Alexander J. Rosen, University of Illinois, Chicago; Duane Rumbaugh, Georgia State University; Edward Stricker, University of Pittsburgh; Richard C. Teevan, State University of New York, Albany; Barry Unger, Fordham University; Michael Wertheimer, University of Colorado; Bond Woodruff, Northern Illinois University; Addison Woodward, Jr., Governors State University; Max Zwanziger, Central Washington University.

Many ideas and suggestions were contributed by those colleagues who prepared ancillary materials for the text. We would like to thank: Ruth de Bliek, University of Connecticut, Hartford, and Virginia Quinn, Northern Virginia Community College, for the *Student Workbook;* Arthur Gutman, Georgia State University, and John Karpicke, Valparaiso University, for the *Unit Mastery Workbook;* and Patricia Lunneborg and Vicki Wilson, University of Washington, for the *Instructor's Manual.*

Also, there are the long-suffering companions who worked with us on many and varied tedious chores throughout this project. Their support and encouragement, typing and proofreading, ideas and stimulation, technical and emotional help, are too great to recount in detail. We are, however, eternally grateful to Françoise Bartlett, Johnna Barto, Victor Calderon, Mary Ann Gundel, Jeanette Ninas Johnson, Charlyce Jones, Robert Kopelman, Mili Ve McNiece, Jo-Anne Naples, Richard Owen, Suzanne Reissig, and Roger Williams.

Finally, we owe special thanks to Norma for her continuing support.

L.E.B., Jr.
B.R.E.

Preface

Our purpose in writing this book was to provide a useful text for the first course in psychology. The book treats a selection of major topics in psychology in some depth. Of course, not all topics that might be covered are included. We did not want to write a superficial survey. The coverage we selected proved to be quite adequate for most instructors, so that in the second edition we concentrated mainly on updating the material and improving the general readability of the text. In this third edition, we have tried to improve readability even more, and we have introduced new material into every chapter. We have strived to make the book informative, interesting, and readable.

The book consists of 12 chapters and 4 appendices. The first chapter is an introduction and is followed by 11 chapters covering basic topics in psychology: biopsychology, perception, conditioning, human learning and memory, cognition, motivation, development, personality, social psychology, psychopathology, and psychotherapy. The appendices cover statistics, neurophysiology, testing, and altered states of consciousness and may be used as supplementary reading.

We continue to employ the two most unique features of our book which have been so well received by students and instructors. First, each of the substantive chapters is divided into two parts, one dealing with the basic knowledge in a particular area (what do we know?) and the other dealing with applications of that knowledge (what does it mean?). In this edition the "What Does It Mean?" sections have been set off at the end of the main body of the chapter so that they can more easily be assigned separately. The second feature centers around the use of newspaper articles and cartoons to illustrate many aspects of psychology. Users of the first two editions have found these materials to add greatly to their enjoyment and understanding of psychology.

Some particular changes in the third edition are especially worth bringing to your attention. The chapter on perception is completely new, with an increased emphasis on the sensory end of the information-processing continuum. There is much more material on the senses other than vision and a unique section on music perception.

The very long chapter on learning and memory from the previous editions has been divided into two chapters in this edition, one on conditioning and one human learning and memory. The conditioning chapter has benefited greatly from the revision work of Professor Steven Maier, one of the discoverers of the learned-helplessness phenomenon. In the cognitive chapter, we have significantly expanded the coverage on language and on intelligence, and we have simplified and reduced in size the treatment of concept formation.

In the motivation chapter are new sections on sexual motivation and sociobiology and new material on facial expression in emotions. The discussion of social development has been expanded and new material on adult development and aging has been added in the developmental chapter. The altered states of consciousness chapter has been condensed into an appendix.

In various chapters we have included new material on sex-role development, attribution theory, discrimination by age, and psychosomatic medicine, among other topics. We have also changed most of the cartoons and clippings. Our purpose has been to move steadily away from the typical cryptic clipping to more and more well-written and informative news stories and articles. Almost all of the clippings now contain factual information about human behavior—which can be and should be tested for on your exams.

Finally, we have tried to keep the book short as introductory psychology texts go. To do this meant that for just about every new item we added, some old material had to be deleted. In some cases—in fact in most cases—what was deleted was material that we would rather have kept in the book. We apologize for those instances where you might disagree with our deletions, but we hope you agree with our choices for new material. It is our hope that you will enjoy reading and using the book in your introductory course.

Boulder, Colorado   L.E.B., Jr.
November 1978   B.R.E.

Contents

DEAR READER . . .

November 4, 1978

Last night's local paper (The Daily Camera, Boulder, Colorado) had the following stories:

A woman pushed four of her children off an 11th-floor balcony and then jumped with three other children to her death. Her husband had recently committed suicide--he had been described as a religious fanatic.

A Boulder resident has become the first woman in the country to receive a doctoral degree in astro-geophysics.

Children of age 2 are being taught to play the violin using a method developed by a Japanese music teacher.

A 73-year-old woman, who has been hitchhiking for 50 years, says she began hitchhiking when she was 21 in an effort to find her first husband who had run off with another woman. She has been at it ever since and has no plans to quit.

Dr. Robert Baker of the Department of Psychology at the University of Kentucky is featured in an article about dreaming.

A woman writes to "Dear Abby" and tells her that she lied to her husband about her age when they were married and now has to tell the truth on her passport application.

Patricia Hearst wants her seven-year bank-robbery sentence overturned on the grounds that her lawyer, F. Lee Bailey, was tired, shaky, and taking "hangover" medicine.

NBC is being sued for $11 million, the charge being that a TV movie ("Born Innocent") led to a sexual attack on a 9-year-old girl in California.

A study has found that serious marital discord, centering around sex, can develop when one of the partners loses a great deal of weight using a surgical procedure known as an intestinal bypass.

In one way or another, all of these stories are about human behavior. Behavior makes news. Imagine what the newspaper would be like if it couldn't report on behavior. We are all fascinated by behavior, and at least when it comes to our behavior, we are all amateur psychologists.

Psychology is the science of behavior. The goals of this science are to measure and describe behavior, to predict and control it, and to understand and explain it. While you have all been students of behavior, this book will introduce you to the study of behavior as a scientific enterprise and as a formal academic discipline. Our goal is to provide you with an overview of the field of psychology today.

A very large part of understanding psychology has to do with understanding variations in human behavior. There are two types of variation that must always be kept in mind: (1) variation within the same individual from one time to the next, as in, "Why did I eat more than I usually do last night?" and (2) variation between individuals, as in, "Why does Ralph always drink so much--Harry never does that?"

In seeking answers to questions about variation in behavior from one person to the next, or from one time to the next, we think that generally the answers can be found in one of four general concepts or aspects of behavior: (1) biological capacity--behavior varies because people have different biological equipment to work with, or the biological state of their bodies differs from one time to another; (2) knowledge--people's behavior will differ if their knowledge differs, as, for example, when some people unknowingly eat high-cholesterol foods while others don't; (3) competence or skill, as when some people can ride a bicycle and others can't; and (4) intention or motivation, as when some people want to lose weight and others don't. The variations in behavior we observe are variations in people's performance--it is the performance, the overt behavior that is observable, which the science of psychology must explain. The explanations will involve variations in biological capacity, knowledge, skill, and motivation. These concepts are crucial in understanding behavior, and we will refer to them repeatedly throughout the book.

We have emphasized two basic aspects of psychology in this book. First we have tried to present the basic knowledge about behavior-- the facts, principles, and "laws." We have tried to present answers to the question: "What do we know about behavior?" Second, we have attempted to spell out the significance of this knowledge--how it can be applied, its implications for the future. We have tried to present answers to the questions: "What does this knowledge mean?" Accordingly, with the exception of Chapter 1, each of the chapters has been divided into two parts, the first telling what we know about a particular aspect of behavior, such as memory or motivation, and the second attempting to describe the impact this knowledge had or may have on our lives. We have not hesitated to speculate about the potential usefulness and application of present knowledge. We apologize for sometimes letting our imaginations run away. We do not apologize, however, for attempting to make psychology look important, exciting, and fascinating, and of great applied significance, because it is all that and more.

We hope that this book will convey to you what psychology is about. Psychology, like other sciences, has become highly specialized and diverse, and we can hope only to cover the highlights. To give you an idea of the diversity of specific problems that psychologists are interested in, consider the following sample:

Ralph is a 27-year-old salesman for a large insurance company. He has a promising career with the company, has a good income, and is married with two children. Yesterday he tried to commit suicide. Why?

Mary is undergoing an operation for removal of a brain tumor. She has received only a local anesthetic, and while her skull is open and her brain exposed the neurosurgeon stimulates her brain with a tiny electrical current. Mary reports seeing and hearing a past experience happening again. Has her brain recorded her entire life of experiences? Is everything we have ever done stored in our brains? How can we tap our stored memories more efficiently?

Johnny is in the sixth grade but reads at only a third-grade level. In one study of college students, less than half could read and comprehend at a level necessary to understand their introductory psychology text. How do the eyes perceive the words on this page, and how are these words understood by the reader? Can research on visual perception lead to better methods of teaching people to read?

In the heart of a New York City residential area, a woman is attacked by a man. She screams loudly many times, begging for help. Many residents hear her screams, but no one even bothers to call the police, much less come to her aid. How can we understand this?

Psychologists devise tests of just about everything--IQ, ability to assemble pickup trucks, personality, and so on. There are tests to predict your success in college or in various occupations and tests of your current state of mental health. Bill is a young black high school graduate looking for a job. He just finished taking a whole battery of tests as part of a job interview at the local steel factory. He thinks that tests discriminate against blacks. Is there any truth in his belief?

Gene is the successful mayor of a large city. His backers want him to challenge the incumbent governor in the upcoming primary election. Gene wants to see the outcome of a local newspaper poll before deciding. Will the poll be of any use to him in predicting his chances of winning? Can psychologists help him to be a more persuasive speaker, a more attractive candidate? Can psychology help him win the election?

As children grow up, do they acquire knowledge in different ways? Should the method of teaching change as children get older? Are there natural stages in the development of a child that make it impossible to teach some things, such as reading, until the child is at least, say, 6 years old? How do people learn anything? Why can't we learn while we are sleeping? Why can't we learn faster? Why are some things easy to learn and others difficult? Why do people forget what they once learned?

Throughout the book you will see more examples of what psychology is about. Many have been drawn from newspapers and magazines. We present you with these clippings, not because we believe everything that is said in each clipping, but because they are thought-provoking, interesting, exciting, and sometimes depressing. You should not accept them as proven facts. Clippings are not a good source of scientific information or of psychological principles. They are however, a fair reflection of what psychology must address. Use your common sense and think about the ideas being expressed in the clippings--do not hesitate to challenge the "facts" as well as the ideas. And, incidentally, this applies as much to what we say in the text as it does to what others are saying in the newspapers and magazines.

We hope that you will maintain an open mind as you read. When you finish with the book we hope that you'll be asking for more--more facts and less speculation, more precise knowledge and less oversimplification, and more real answers to your questions about behavior. If so, we will be satisfied with the book.

The book has 12 chapters. The first chapter is an introduction, telling you in general what psychology is all about and including a little historical background. The next 11 chapters cover basic content areas in psychology: biopsychology, perception, conditioning, human learning and memory, cognitive processes, motivation and emotion, development of behavior, personality, social psychology, psychopathology (the study of deviant behavior), and finally psychotherapy (the treatment of disordered behavior). We have tried to select those topics we feel are most important for the beginning student. With a good foundation of principles and applications in these 11 areas, we feel that you will be able to move on to more advanced study.

We hope that you enjoy reading this book. We aren't promising that you won't be able to put it down, but we will be satisfied if it turns out that when you do put it down, you will at least occasionally be thinking about what you read in it. And when you have finished with it, we hope you will have a better understanding and appreciation of psychology.

Sincerely,

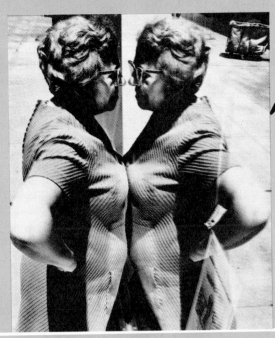

The Nature of Psychology 1

We are all psychologists. Every one of us practices psychology every single day, for in the most general sense psychology is the study of human and animal behavior. Because we are all interested in and affected by the behavior of other people, we must be psychologists, at least on an informal level.

In an academic or professional sense, psychology is the systematic, scientific study of behavior and the knowledge that results from that study. The field covers an enormous range of topics: practically everything you experience in daily life—all forms of behavior—have come or will come under the scrutiny of psychologists. The techniques of study that psychologists use vary greatly, ranging from simple observation to complex experimental manipulations. Therefore, to give a fair and accurate picture of what psychology is will be a difficult task.

One useful way to begin, however, is to describe some of the things that psychologists do. This is the primary focus of the first chapter. But we will also consider the most important goals of psychology, look briefly at the history of the field, and take a look into the future of psychology.

WHAT PSYCHOLOGISTS DO

All psychologists study the behavior of living organisms. As in other fields, however, there are many different specialties within psychology (Table 1–1) and thus many different types of psychologists (Table 1–2). These differences can be described in terms of three dimensions: (1) the particular behavioral issues or areas of research examined, (2) the research methods used, and (3) the kinds of employment circumstances under which the study is conducted. Table 1–1 summarizes these dimensions, which we will now discuss in some detail.

Areas of Research

There are literally thousands of different problems being systematically investigated within psychology today. The list in Table 1–1 is a crude classification of these areas of research, arranged in ascending order of complexity. It begins with the basic study of human beings as biological organisms in an environment of physical stimuli and culminates in topics that relate to the "whole person," interactions with other people, and some abnormal aspects of behavior. People's actions are limited by their biological equipment and by the nature of their environment, and an understanding of these limitations provides a necessary background for further psychological analysis. The deeper, more complex questions have to do with how people use their biological equipment and operate within their physical circumstances.

Table 1–1 is arranged so that the areas of research at one level provide much of the background for understanding problems at higher levels. We must understand the basics of psy-

chology before considering the complexities of behavioral interactions; therefore, the chapters in our book reflect this ordering.

TABLE 1-1   What Psychologists Do

Areas of Research

1. Relations between behavior and nonpsychological factors, such as chemicals (drugs), the physical properties of stimulation, genes, and the nervous system (Chapter 2)
2. Perception of stimulation from one's environment, the first psychological step in most behavioral episodes (Chapter 3)
3. Learning and memory: processes in the acquisition and retention of knowledge and skill (Chapters 4 and 5)
4. Using one's knowledge and skill for purposes of problem solving, creativity, and other forms of thinking (Chapter 6)
5. Motivation, arousal, and intention, the driving forces behind our actions (Chapter 7)
6. The development, with age and experience, of perception, learning, thought, motivation, and other behavioral phenomena and processes (Chapter 8)
7. Personality traits and behavior patterns that make each of us unique and individual (Chapter 9)
8. Social interaction: the processes by which we influence each other's behavior (Chapter 10)
9. Unusual or abnormal behavior patterns, behavior pathology, its causes and its treatment (Chapters 11 and 12)

Methods

1. Individual case study
2. Naturalistic observation
3. Tests, interviews, and surveys
4. Experiments

Employment

1. Colleges and universities	40%
2. Elementary and secondary schools	12%
3. Clinics	11%
4. Industry	6%
5. Government	14%
6. Private practice	6%
7. Other	11%
Total	100%

**Lady of 22 Identities Recalls
43 Years of Personality Changes**

Terry Anderson

For 43 of her 48 years Chris Sizemore coexisted with two or more personalities; for more than 20 years her husband, Don, never knew when he left home for work in the morning just who would greet him at night.

Would it be "the purple lady?" Or "the strawberry girl?" The "retrace lady?" After all, she had a repertoire of 22 personalities from which to choose over the years. . . .

"Since the age of two, I coexisted with two or more personalities but none of them has come back to haunt me for over two years now," she said.

"At the age of two, I became aware that I was receding into a vacuum and someone else was taking my place," she said about her first split with herself. "But, as a girl it didn't bother me. I thought it was just the way people were. But, I was ostracized by my peers."

Throughout her childhood she went through periods of amnesia when she would assume different personalities. Her tone of voice would change, she displayed different skills and facial expressions—even talents.

Then, as a teen-ager, headaches began, each signaling the coming of another identity. Some identities lasted hours, others weeks or months.

After she became a wife and mother for the first time, she sought help and was under a doctor's care for nearly three years beginning in 1952. At the time she was not only Eve White but also Eve Black and Jane, the three personalities portrayed in the movie [*The Three Faces of Eve*].

As Jane, doctors thought she had achieved a cure and she married Don, her second husband. But she was married for only six months before the next personality came on the scene. . . .

Most of her personalities came in groups of three but, with the death of each personality, Sizemore suffered and grieved over them as if she had lost a member of her own family.

Doctors convinced her that writing a book about her experiences might help provide a cure.

Over the past three years, Sizemore has gained confidence. She speaks to college students and other groups, not only to promote her book but also to promote a better understanding of mental health. . . .

The Denver Post
September 13, 1977

A case of multiple personality—Chris Sizemore, alias "Eve," has now written her own case history.

Methods

Progress in psychology depends upon discovering new facts about the behavior of organisms. But knowledge does not materialize out of thin air. To find out about behavior, psychologists have invented new methods or adapted old methods of inquiry from other fields. Although learning scientific methods may require hard work, it is very important, because these methods are indispensable to the progress of psychology. You need to know something about methodology to decide between fact and fiction. The methods of psychology differ in both the kind of information about behavior they yield and the types of behaviors to which they are best suited. We will discuss four major approaches to the study of behavior, as listed in Table 1–1.

Individual Case Study

The case study or case history method is perhaps the simplest and most direct form of psychological investigation. One individual is examined intensively to find out as much as possible about a certain problem, question, or issue as it relates to that individual. A combination of procedures might be used, including biographical data on the individual, administering psychological tests, and interviewing him or her extensively.

The case study procedure is most often used to investigate abnormal behavior patterns. Perhaps the best-known clinical case history in psychology is that of a woman with three different personalities, popularized in the movie *The Three Faces of Eve*. Such case histories can have great impact because of the detail of description they provide and the unusual behavior they are concerned with. One of the earliest and most famous clinical case studies, reported by Sigmund Freud, concerned a patient, Anna O., who was paralyzed without apparent cause. By composing a detailed case history from a variety of sources, Freud was able to piece together the critical events in Anna O.'s life that contributed

TABLE 1–2   **Kinds of Psychologists**

Experimental psychologist.   Uses scientific methods to carry out experiments designed to develop a basic understanding of such processes as learning, memory, motivation, sensation, and perception in human beings and lower animals.

Biopsychologist.   Studies the contribution of biological factors—such as heredity, the sensory and nervous systems, drugs, and species differences—to various kinds of behavior.

Social psychologist.   Uses a variety of scientific methods to study the behavior of people in social situations, that is, in the presence of at least one other person.

Developmental psychologist.   Studies normal behavioral development from infancy to adulthood, including the development of learning, perception, social behavior, and motivation.

Educational psychologist.   Studies the educational process with the hope of developing better educational systems and is responsible for implementing these systems.

Personality psychologist.   Studies the whole person in an effort to discover the basic underlying dimensions of behavior, such as introversion-extroversion, and to find means of measuring and describing individuals on those dimensions.

Clinical psychologist.   Generally focuses on abnormal behavior in an effort to understand, diagnose, and change such behavior.

Counseling psychologist.   Offers expert advice for solution of personal or educational problems when there is no sign of serious mental disorder—for example, in marriage counseling and in student counseling and guidance.

Industrial psychologist.   Usually works for a business enterprise, applying psychological knowledge to such areas as personnel policies, working conditions, production efficiency, and decision making.

Educational Background

Most psychologists have a Ph.D (Doctor of Philosophy) degree, which requires 4 to 5 years of graduate study (beyond a bachelor's degree) in a specialty area. Most were psychology majors as undergraduates, although psychology graduate programs often take nonpsychology majors. There are also numerous graduate programs that lead only to the master's degree, usually requiring about 2 years of graduate study. Master's-level psychologists can be employed in most of the same jobs as Ph.D.-level psychologists, although the salary, responsibility, and opportunities for advancement are usually not as great.

Figure 1–1
Chimpanzee searching for termites

© *National Geographic Society.*

One of psychology's best-known naturalistic studies was conducted by Jane van Lawick-Goodall on the behavior of chimpanzees in their natural African habitat. Contrary to the generally accepted idea that only human beings are capable of tool making and tool using, Goodall's observations established that chimps can construct crude tools. In this photograph, a female chimp is using a blade of grass as a "fishing rod" for termites. Evidence taken from animals in zoos or laboratories gives a quite different and more limited picture of the abilities of infra-human animals.

to her neurotic behavior. The results of this one case also had tremendous impact on Freud's theory.

Naturalistic Observation

As the name would suggest, naturalistic observation is a systematic method for observing and recording events as they naturally occur in the real world. It is used in those cases where artificial probes or manipulations might destroy some or all of the basic characteristics of the phenomenon in question or where there is no way of making a more controlled observation. Suppose we were interested in the mating or maternal behavior of wild elk. Any kind of human intervention, no matter how subtle, might disrupt the basic behavioral pattern. Therefore, some animal psychologists use unobtrusive observational procedures, getting close enough to the animals in their natural habitat to be able to observe (with the help of equipment) but far enough away so that their presence goes undetected. Similar techniques are often used to observe human behavior as well, for example, the observation of peer interaction among children from behind a one-way mirror. The idea is to observe behavior without influencing it. The observations, of course, are recorded as objectively as possible, for example, with tape recorders and cameras.

Naturalistic observation is also the best technique in cases where ethical considerations may prevent the scientist from creating the phenomenon in the laboratory. For example, all of us are concerned with relationships between countries and between races. From a scientific point of view, the psychologist would like to know how these relationships develop and how more cooperative relationships might be arranged. Some by-products of these relationships are destructive and unpleasant—for example, wars between nations and race riots. Because both wars and riots are part of the basic phenomenon of interpersonal relationships, they must be examined by the scientist. On the other hand, the scientist is in no position to influence the occurrence of either kind of tragedy. To investigate such behavioral phenomena psychologists have to observe, record, and try to understand the events as they occur naturally.

Tests, Interviews, and Surveys

Psychological tests have been developed and standardized for just about any aspect of be-havior you can imagine. Many of us have had some experience with such tests in school or at work. There are tests of general ability, called intelligence tests, and there are tests of specific traits, such as anxiety or leadership ability. All of these tests consist of a number of questions, and the pattern of answers people give is thought to reveal something about their level on the trait or ability being measured. The sum total of a person's answers gives a composite score that is considered a fair reflection of that person's typical behavior in everyday circumstances.

The psychological interview is often used in the case study method. In that context, the interview is usually free-floating and unstructured. Its direction is guided by the responses of the individual being examined and any hypothesis that the examiner might have about the underlying rationale of these responses. But interviews can also be highly structured, consisting, much like psychological tests, of a series of items to which the individual is asked to respond. A structured interview is more often used to collect data from a group of people that will lead to general conclusions about that population, rather than to do an intensive study of a single individual.

Surveys fall somewhere between structured interviews and psychological tests. Again, they consist of a series of questions to which indi-

Tests for intelligence, aptitude, creativity, and other abilities are administered mainly in order to predict educational or vocational success.

"Contrary to the popular view, our studies show that it is real life that contributes to violence on television."

Playboy, February 1977. Reproduced by special permission of PLAYBOY Magazine; copyright © 1977 by Playboy.

Correlation Does Not Mean Causality

If two variables are correlated with each other, there is a tendency to conclude that one variable causes the other. On the strength of a correlation between the amount of TV violence and real-life violence, some people conclude that TV violence makes people more violent in their everyday behavior. We cannot draw such a causal conclusion from correlations. As the cartoon suggests, the causal connection may be in the opposite direction. Still another alternative is that a third factor, for example, the increased stress of modern living, causes both TV and real-life violence.

The only way to establish the existence and direction of a causal relationship between two variables is to use the experimental method.

Women Workers Waste Less Time on Job

WASHINGTON — Women workers waste less time on the job than men do.

Women generally also spend more time each day primping and on "personal hygiene" than do men—but just barely. Working women spend an average of 59 minutes a day on their appearance, housewives 52 minutes and men 46 minutes.

These are among the discoveries of a University of Michigan survey just released, a survey based on diaries kept by 1,500 individuals for six weeks in 1975.

The survey was one of a series of Michigan studies on the American use of time that have involved 5,000 subjects over the last 10 years.

The survey found that men watch more television than women. Men watch, on the average, an hour and 39 minutes a day; housewives, 3 minutes less than that and working women an hour and two minutes.

At work, it was found that the average woman wastes 35 minutes in a typical day, compared to 52 minutes for the average man.

According to the study, the coffee-break factor translates into an increase in the gap between men's and women's pay. Men making $7 an hour and spending 52 minutes of each day not earning it are really making $8.48 an hour. Women paid an average $4.34 an hour are really earning $4.86 an hour when the coffee-break factor is computed.

The Use-of-Time Project was funded by a $500,000 grant from the National Science Foundation.

The series of studies, which have been going on since 1965, has culminated in a book written by one of the researchers, John P. Robinson, a communications professor at Cleveland State University.

"It seems employers are getting a lot more out of women's work investments than men's," he said.

That's not all. When working women go home, according to the study, things get worse.

The average working wife spends 25 hours a week doing housework—in addition to her job.

Boulder (Colo.) Daily Camera
August 20, 1977

Surveys, opinion polls, and interviews are important research tools for the psychologist. Here is a recent example that may interest you.

viduals are asked to respond. The purpose of the interview is to determine general opinions, attitudes, or feelings on a specific issue. A candidate for political office, for example, might want to determine the general attitude of the public toward a particular issue in order to decide whether his or her campaign should stress or minimize that issue.

Testing, interviewing, surveying, and sometimes naturalistic observation are often combined under the general heading of a **correlational approach**[1] to psychological issues. In general, this approach is used to discover the degree of relationship between two or more **variables.** A variable is any characteristic of an object, event, person, or whatever, that can take two or more values. A psychologist might hypothesize, for example, that the position people take on welfare issues (one variable) is highly related to their annual income (a second variable). In general, the more income a person has, the less likely he or she is to favor welfare payments to needy people. To check on this hypothesis, the psychologist would try to find data reflecting both income and attitudes toward welfare. Interviews or surveys of a cross section of the population at large might be conducted. For each person in the study, there would be two scores, one for annual income and one reflecting both direction and degree of attitude toward welfare proposals, ranging from strongly opposed to strongly favorable.

To find out how strong a relationship there is between these variables, the psychologist would compute a numerical value, or statistic, called the **correlation coefficient** (see Appendix A). The correlation of zero signifies no relationship at all between the two variables. In the above example, a correlation of zero would mean that amount of income is not related to a person's attitude toward welfare plans. A positive correlation means that the two variables are related: The higher the value of one score, the higher the value of the other. A positive correlation in this example would mean that the more money a person makes each year, the more likely that person is to favor welfare plans. This, of course, would not confirm the original hypothesis. A negative correlation implies a relationship between the two variables that is op-

[1] Terms appearing in boldface type are defined in the Glossary.

What's Wrong with This Experiment?

A psychologist is interested in the effects of divorce upon children. The hypothesis is that children raised in fatherless homes will be adversely affected such that they will be less successful as adults. From a large pool of subjects, a group of 30 adults (15 men and 15 women) raised in fatherless homes as a result of divorce is randomly selected. A matching group of 15 men and 15 women raised in homes where both parents were present until the child reached age 18 is also selected. Success is measured in terms of annual salary.

The results show that the average annual salary in the group with fatherless rearing is $11,275, while in the other group it is $17,500. The psychologist concludes that being raised in a fatherless home results in psychological damage, which ultimately causes the child to become less motivated toward achievement (resulting in a lower-paying job as an adult).

---

posite, or inverse: As the value of one variable increases, the value of the other decreases. In the example, a negative correlation would mean that the more people earn, the less likely they are to favor welfare—and vice versa. Thus, a negative correlation *would* be consistent with the original hypothesis.

The Experimental Method

Case studies, naturalistic observation techniques, and the various correlational methods all suffer a major drawback. While they provide information about relationships among psychological variables, they do not allow for a determination of direct or cause-effect relationships. For example, a case study of a psychologically disturbed person might reveal a difficult childhood, but this does not mean that unhappy early experiences *necessarily* lead to abnormal behavior. Any number of other factors might also be involved. The fact that elk are observed to mate more frequently after a spring rain can-

Two Common Pitfalls in Psychological Research

The Placebo Effect

The placebo effect refers to the fact that any kind of treatment may produce a behavioral change, perhaps due to suggestion. For example, suppose the hypothesis is that Drug A will relieve depression. The experimenter gives Drug A to a group of depressives and finds that they improve, leading to the conclusion that Drug A is effective. This conclusion may be wrong—giving these depressives any kind of treatment might have resulted in equal improvement. The experimenter should have included a **placebo-control group** in the experiment. This group would have received a "fake," or placebo, "drug," one that contains no active ingredients. In order to conclude that Drug A is effective, the experimenter must demonstrate that it results in greater improvement than treatment with the placebo. Of course, subjects in the experiment must not know whether they are receiving the real drug or the placebo. In such cases the subjects are said to be *blind* to the conditions of the experiment.

Experimenter Bias

While it is obvious that the subjects should be "blind" to the treatment they receive,

it may also be important that the experimenter be uninformed about which group receives the placebo and which the real treatment. If both the subjects and the experimenter are blind, the study is called a **double-blind experiment.** You should be cautious about believing the results of treatment studies that are not double-blind.

Robert Rosenthal has demonstrated that, in several different types of experiments, experimenters, if they know how the results are supposed to come out, can influence them in that direction. The most startling demonstration of this was Rosenthal's study showing that teachers can influence their pupils' scores on intelligence tests (IQ scores). Rosenthal told a group of teachers that certain students in their classes had high intellectual potential as judged by psychological tests. Actually these students were randomly selected. At the end of the year, these pupils showed a much larger IQ gain than students not identified as high in potential. The teachers (the experimenters) expected these children to improve and probably took steps along the way, often unconsciously, to make sure that they did. We will have more to say about this phenomenon in Chapter 10.

not be taken as evidence for a causal relationship between humidity and the mating instinct. Perhaps spring rains tend to occur in the late afternoon, the time of day the elk prefer to get together. The fact that high income tends to be *correlated with* opposition to welfare does not necessarily imply that if someone's income were suddenly to double, his or her opinion of welfare would become more negative. The fact is that opinions toward welfare are commonly formed even before an individual has achieved permanent employment. Observational procedures are important, but the establishment of direct, cause-effect relationships requires a dif-

ferent method of investigation, namely, the experimental method.

In addition to observing, experimental psychologists attempt to manipulate and control their subject matter. They bring the phenomenon at issue into the laboratory, where conditions of interest can be manipulated with precise equipment and procedures, and where all extraneous and distracting variables can be ruled out. Experimental psychologists set up simplified versions of what goes on in the outside world and examine these phenomena under conditions in which only one thing at a time is changed. If the changed condition is associated

Cancer Patients Aided by Dummy Pills

AP

CHICAGO — Dummy pills brought pain relief for a large percentage of cancer patients, particularly among very self-sufficient persons, a Mayo Clinic study shows.

The study demonstrated there can be a psychological element in pain relief in cancer, as has been shown in other diseases in experiments using inactive or dummy pills.

Researchers at the Rochester, Minn., institution compared the effects of orally administered pain relievers with those of a placebo, or dummy pill, given to 288 cancer patients. The patients did not know they were being given dummy pills.

The researchers reported in the February issue of Mayo Clinic Proceedings, a medical journal, that 112 — or 39 per cent — said they had 50 per cent or greater pain relief with the dummy medications, made of milk sugar. The other patients reported less than 50 per cent pain relief.

These patients also had a greater response rate to the active drugs and more instances of reported central nervous system side effects to the placebo, such as dizziness, sedation and impaired thinking.

They found that those who responded most to dummy pills were the highly educated, farmers, professional workers, women working outside the home and patients who were widowed, separated or divorced.

Those who had a low response were the poorly educated, unskilled workers, housewives, smokers and married women without children.

The researchers theorized that response to sugar pills was a type of self-hypnosis, resulting from extreme dependency needs.

Rocky Mountain News, *Denver*
March 20, 1976

The placebo effect can be quite powerful. The existence of such an effect is one reason placebo control groups are necessary in designing experiments to test the effectiveness of new treatments. The placebo effect also indicates that psychological factors play a significant role in illness.

---

with a change in behavior, then the experimental psychologist can be certain that there is a direct cause-effect relationship between the changing variable and the behavior in question.

For example, suppose we want to know whether a person should study in relatively short periods over the course of, say, two weeks preceding an examination or whether it would be better to concentrate all study time into the evening before the exam. If we were merely to observe the study habits of people who happen to be available, we might have difficulty drawing a precise conclusion. The person who distributes study time over two weeks preceding an examination might actually be studying more in terms of total time than the individual who concentrates effort on the evening before. Furthermore, the person who crams might be a psychologically different type of individual, more secure about his or her ability to perform on a

test or less intelligent than the individual who distributes study time. The observations would tell us something, but they might not make all of the effective variables entirely clear.

An experimental approach to the question would be different. First, we would probably construct a simplified version of the problem for investigation in the laboratory. We might select a set of materials to be learned, similar though not necessarily identical to the kind of material a person might study for an examination. Suppose the test is to cover knowledge of foreign language vocabulary. A simplified version of this might be a list of about 12 to 20 pairs of words that a subject would try to memorize in such a way that given the first word of the pair he or she could respond with the second.

We want to find out how fast people learn these materials under different study condi-

"NOW I WANT YOU TO RELAX COMPLETELY!"

12-8 © 1974 Gahan Wilson
The Register and Tribune Syndicate, Inc.

Gahan Wilson Sunday Comics reprinted courtesy of The Register and Tribune Syndicate, Inc.

The equipment or techniques that psychologists use can affect the behavior they are trying to measure. In such cases the measurements are said to be *obtrusive*. The scientist in the cartoon is obviously using obtrusive techniques to study relaxation. But developing *unobtrusive* methods for observing behavior is not always easy.

tions. We therefore decide to have two timing conditions. In one condition, effort is concentrated. The pairs are presented to the subject at a rate of 5 seconds per pair for study; immediately after presentation, the first member of each pair is shown and the subject is tested for ability to respond with the second. Then the pairs are presented once again, followed by a second test. This procedure—study followed immediately by test, followed immediately by study, and so on—is repeated for, say, 20 trials. In the second study condition the same procedure is used, with the exception that the subject is allowed to rest for 30 seconds between each test and the following study period. The same number of trials will be given and the same amount of study time will be allowed, but practice is spread out over a longer period of time.

Independent and Dependent Variables

When observations of a subject's performance are taken within the laboratory or some other well-controlled situation, psychologists are in a position to hold constant most variables that might affect performance. All subjects perform as closely as possible under the same circumstances except for the variable the experimenter manipulates. A good investigator will try to control or hold constant all but the variable

of interest. The variable of interest is the one that the experimenter manipulates and is called the **independent variable.** In our vocabulary-learning example, the independent variable is the time between the study and test periods, and there are two levels of this variable, 0 and 30 seconds. That is, half the subjects will learn while getting 0 seconds rest between study and test, and half will learn with a 30-second rest period. The experimenter then measures the subjects' performance to find out whether it is changed in any way by the difference in the independent variable. The measure of performance is called the **dependent variable.** The experimenter tries to determine whether the dependent variable depends in any way on the independent variable. In our example, the dependent variable might be the number of correct responses made by the subject on each test trial. Thus the point of our illustrative experiment is to determine whether number of correct responses (the dependent variable) is influenced by the timing conditions during learning (the independent variable).

Random Selection

Suppose performance by the spaced practice group (30-second rest condition) is better than performance by the concentrated practice group (0-second rest). What is there to assure us that subjects in our spaced practice condition are not, in general, smarter than subjects in our concentrated practice condition? Unwanted effects in the experiment might be attributable to the fact that a different group of subjects participates under each of the two experimental conditions.

Our main assurance of unbiased effects comes from the way subjects are selected for the various groups or conditions in the experiment; this is an important aspect of *experimental control.* Experimenters cannot hold individual differences among people constant in the same way they can control other variables operating in the laboratory situation. But they can take the following steps in order to equalize the groups: (1) select all subjects randomly from the population to which they wish to generalize the results; (2) assign subjects randomly to the various experimental conditions; (3) use a large enough number of subjects in each group to average out random variations; and (4) take all possible precautions to avoid biasing subjects in any way. When experimenters follow these simple steps, they should obtain comparable groups of subjects participating in each condition.

Testing the Hypothesis

Having no reason to believe otherwise, an experimenter might guess that the way people distribute their study time has no effect on performance on a test, if the total amount of time spent in study is comparable. A hypothesis stated in this form is called a **null hypothesis.** It is the prediction that the variable being manipulated, the independent variable, will have no effect on the behavior being measured, the dependent variable.

The results of the experiment provide a test of this hypothesis. If at the end of 20 study trials both groups of subjects perform the same on their test, the experimenter would conclude that distribution of study time has nothing to do with the degree of learning. The null hypothesis would not be rejected. If, on the other hand, a relationship of some sort is observed, then the null hypothesis would be rejected. For example, if performance improves with increasing amounts of rest between study periods, the experimenter would conclude that distribution of study time has a favorable effect on learning.

The key advantage of the experimental method is that it allows for direct cause-effect conclusions from the data. If all of the variables have been properly controlled, and it is observed that the dependent variable changes when the independent variable is changed, the experimenter can conclude that the relationship is *causal.* Because of this logic, psychologists have a distinct preference for experimental techniques over nonexperimental techniques in the study of behavior. The assumption is that understanding behavior eventually comes down to knowing what causes what, and the experimental method is our chief means of finding out.

The experimental method is the only technique available that allows us to determine the causes of behavior. Unfortunately, there are many behavioral situations in which it cannot be employed. For example, in the first box entitled "What's Wrong with This Experiment," the study described was really not an experiment at all, not in the strict sense. The investigator did not *manipulate* the variable of fatherless homes versus homes with fathers, but simply

What's Wrong with This Experiment?

An experimenter hypothesizes that watching *Sesame Street* on TV will increase children's general knowledge. Twenty-five children are randomly selected to participate in the experiment. In September, with a special test, the experimenter measures the general knowledge of each child and finds that the average score is 67. Then every weekday for the next 9 months the parents bring the children to the laboratory, where they all sit and watch the 1-hour program. In early June, after the children have seen close to 200 different *Sesame Street* programs, the experimenter gives them the general knowledge test again. Now the children score an average of 77, which is significantly higher than the 67 average back in September. The experimenter concludes that watching *Sesame Street* results in increased general knowledge, and that all parents should make their children watch the program.

selected families according to that characteristic. Thus it cannot be concluded that the differences found in money earned were *caused* by differences in father presence. Many other things are correlated with the father being absent, and any of these could have caused the difference in earnings. To do the experiment properly, the investigator would have to take a group of babies and randomly assign them either to a home with a father or to one without a father. Obviously such an experiment is impossible in our culture. Many experiments that would in fact reveal important causes of behavior are impossible for ethical, moral, religious, financial, or other reasons. In such cases, we have to rely on information gained from nonexperimental methods such as the correlational approach. This means that we may not be completely sure about cause-effect relationships. Nevertheless, some problems are so important that we must go ahead with research and make guesses about the cause, accepting the fact that we may be wrong. If we were unwilling to act without com-

The Control Group

The simplest and most common experimental design involves two groups, *the experimental group* and *the control group*. The control group provides a baseline against which to compare the experimental group. Suppose the experimenter wants to know if a particular treatment (treatment X) for mental illness is effective in helping patients. An experimental group of patients is given treatment X, and the experimenter observes their behavior and sees that there is marked improvement. At this point, it might be concluded that treatment X is beneficial. But perhaps the patients would have improved anyway.

The experimenter needs a control group of patients that is treated the same way as the experimental group (same meals, same hospital, same diagnoses, etc.) with the *single* exception that no control patient is given treatment X. If the experimenter then observes greater improvement in the experimental group than the control group, it can safely be concluded that the difference in improvement between the two groups must have been caused by treatment X, since treatment X was the only thing on which the two groups differed. Many experiments fail because the experimenter did not run an appropriate control group.

The following experiments should provide you with a better understanding of the need and use of control groups in psychological research.

1. A physiological psychologist surgically destroys a particular part of the brain, the hypothalamus, to see if this particular brain structure is important in controlling eating. A control group of animals who undergo brain surgery procedures (anesthesia, cutting open the skull, etc.), but who do not have their hypothalamus destroyed or have some other area of the brain destroyed is required. If the hypothalamus is uniquely involved in controlling eating, the investigator should find greater eating disturbances in the experimental animals than in the control animals.

2. A psychologist wants to know if hypnotic suggestions can cause you to make your body become so stiff and rigid that it can be suspended between two chairs. A control group of subjects who are asked

plete proof of a cause, we might never be able to apply psychological knowledge to many real human problems.

Employment

Research areas, methods, and focus all have something to do with where and how psychologists are employed, that is, with the nature of their jobs. Table 1–1 lists six primary kinds of employment and the percentage of psychologists in each, according to the *National Register of Scientific and Technical Personnel*. Psychologists in colleges and universities are usually concerned with the full range of research areas outlined in Table 1–1. A well-rounded academic psychology department tries to provide training in each of these areas with as much depth as possible. Furthermore, psychologists engaged in teaching try to train new people to be competent in all research methods. Psychologists in colleges and universities are generally more concerned with basic knowledge than with practical applications. They assume that given basic knowledge and skills in the methods, a psychologist can engage, when necessary, in psychology on a more practical level.

Other areas of employment, however, put a

to do the task without the induction of hypnosis is required. Both groups of subjects should receive the same instructions about their ability to accomplish this feat if they try hard. The control subjects should be treated by the same experimenter, under the same conditions. The only difference between experimental and control subject should be whether or not a hypnotic induction procedure is used.

3. An industrial psychologist thinks that he or she can improve production at a factory by making the surroundings more pleasant—brightly colored rooms, better lighting, and music. So the psychologist sets up such a production line in a special room at the factory and selects a random group of workers to come and work on this line. It is observed that production is higher in this setting than at the regular line in the factory and it is concluded that the lighting, colors, and music were responsible. The psychologist needs a control group of workers selected from the regular lines and also asked to work in a "special" room, but this special room duplicates the regular working conditions.

"Four years of research, and now you tell me you forgot which is the control group!"

G. Spitzer, APA Monitor, August 1971.

Merely being selected to work in a special room as part of an experiment may make people work harder, if only because they assume that someone is watching their work more carefully.

greater premium on practical application. In elementary and secondary schools, psychologists are concerned with learning and motivational processes and with student guidance and counseling. In hospitals, clinics, or private practice, the psychologist is usually involved in diagnostics and therapy. That is, he or she is concerned with trying to find out, by testing, interviewing, or general case study method, what is wrong with a particular individual and why. Then, the psychologist can administer corrective or psychotherapeutic measures if required. Industries employ psychologists to answer particular questions about products, services, or personnel,

such as how to design a product for efficient operation or improve employment conditions.

THE GOALS OF PSYCHOLOGY

Because of the varied activities of psychologists, it is difficult to single out a simple set of goals. But remember our definition of psychology—the scientific study of behavior and the systematic application of behavior principles. With this definition in mind, we can identify three basic goals: (1) to measure and describe, (2) to predict and control, and (3) to understand and

What's Wrong with This Experiment?

A psychologist believes that hypnosis can help people stop smoking, or at least help them cut down. A group of 25 heavy smokers is selected for treatment with hypnosis. Each smoker comes to the laboratory for four hypnosis sessions. In each session, the smoker is hypnotized, told the dangers of smoking, asked to repeat them aloud while in the trance, and given a list of 10 things to think or do when the urge to smoke a cigarette gets strong.

Aware of the necessity for control groups, our psychologist selects a control group of smokers who are given no treatment whatsoever. They check in at the beginning of the experiment to report how much they are smoking and again at the end of the experiment. This group should tell the psychologist how much people would have cut down (or how many would have quit) anyway, without treatment. There are thus a total of 50 smokers in the experiment. The smokers are randomly assigned to the two conditions.

The results show that after six months, the average number of cigarettes smoked per day was 12 in the hypnosis group and 21 in the control group. The psychologist concludes that hypnosis is a successful technique for reducing smoking.

explain behavior. Let us consider each of these goals in more detail.

Measurement and Description

Before we can understand or manipulate a phenomenon, we must first be able to describe and measure it. Much of a psychologist's work involves measuring and describing behavior. All the so-called psychological concepts and processes mentioned in the preceding pages—IQ, anxiety, learning, attitudes, abilities, depression, and more—must be measured. A major goal, therefore, is to develop tests or techniques for

measuring. Each measuring device must possess two characteristics: First, it must have **reliability,** which means that a person's score should not change much with repeated testing. A scale that registered a different weight each time you got on it would be unreliable, and therefore not useful. Likewise, a test of intelligence that gave you a different score each time you took it would be worthless. But reliability is not enough. A test must also have **validity,** which means that it must measure what it is supposed to measure. If we measured your IQ by applying a tape measure to the circumference of your head, we might get the same score each time (indicating reliability), but the measuring technique would have little to do with intelligence.

The questions of reliability and validity of measurement and description apply to all techniques developed by psychologists for the assessment of behavior. You should keep these two criteria in mind when examining the experiments, surveys, observations, and clinical assessments reported in later chapters. These criteria are considered in greater detail in Appendix C.

Prediction and Control

The second goal of psychology is to be able to predict and thereby to control behavior. Success in this effort relies heavily on measurement. Indeed, as correlational methods imply, psychologists typically use present or past measurements of behavior as a primary basis for predicting what a person will do in the future. We can predict a student's performance in school with increased accuracy if we know the student's general intellectual ability. From the factory worker's score on a mechanical aptitude test, we should be able to predict his or her success on an assembly line. College entrance exams help to determine who is admitted to college, and aptitude tests help the personnel director decide whom to hire. Many prediction efforts assess interests rather than abilities. Vocational counselors give their clients tests to find out what kind of work might interest them most. An ability to predict your future bill-paying behavior would help a credit agency decide whether or not you are a good risk for a loan. Psychological predictions affect the lives of just about every American. If you have been excluded from medical school or denied a job or credit, it is difficult to think kindly of the psychologist who produced these tests.

Prediction goes hand in hand with behavior modification and control. Assume that the knowledge necessary to predict mental illness existed. We certainly would not want to stop there; good predictions alone would not satisfy us. Psychologists would want to try to change or modify the behavior of the potentially mentally ill person in a way that would help that person. Indeed, behavior change is often the practicing psychologist's primary aim. The psychotherapist tries to change the patient's behavior; the industrial psychologist is commonly engaged in an effort to modify the behavior of employees; the marriage counselor attempts to modify the behavior of husband and wife; and the prison psychologist tries to control and modify the behavior of criminals. In all of these cases, an effort is made to improve the present or future circumstances of the individual in question and of society.

Many techniques of behavior modification that have been developed are remarkably successful, allowing the possibility that someone who has mastered them may control others for his or her own ends. This necessitates that appropriate safeguards be used to ensure the ethical use of successful techniques. A drug that can control cruelty or aggression does not exist now. Consider the problems that may arise if such a drug were discovered. Who would decide when and where techniques and treatments of this sort would be used? What would be the role of society, the government, and the individual on whom it would be used?

Understanding and Explanation

The final goal of psychology is to *understand* and *explain* behavior, that is, to isolate the reasons for what is observed. This process involves the formulation of the theories, which organize the known facts, and the development of hypotheses about relationships that are yet to be proved. A good theory helps us make reasonable guesses when we do not know the correct answer.

Some people have argued that explanation is really what basic research in psychology is all about. The psychologist may be able to describe and measure anxiety, to make predictions from these measurements about the likelihood of a

Coke–Pepsi Slugfest

THE DAY COCA-COLA BEAT COCA-COLA blared the strange headline in a recent newspaper ad in Dallas. Starkly pictured beneath the message was the soft drink's familiar hourglass bottle flanked by two glasses, one marked M, the other Q. Thus opened what is becoming one of advertising's most bizarre feuds. It pits the nation's leading soft-drink maker, Coca-Cola, against its closest ranking competitor, Pepsi-Cola. . . .

The whole thing began more than 15 months ago, when Pepsi decided to challenge Coke's 3-to-1 sales lead in the Dallas area. (Nationally, Coke is estimated to hold 26.2% of the market, compared with Pepsi's 17.4%.) Pepsi concocted a promotion supposedly showing that more than half the Coke drinkers tested preferred Pepsi's flavor when the two colas were stripped of brand identification. During the test, Coke was served in a glass marked Q and Pepsi in a glass marked M. Within a year Pepsi had whittled Coke's sales lead in Dallas to 2 to 1. Irritated, Coke officials conducted their own consumer-preference test—not of the colas but of the letters. Their conclusion: Pepsi's test was invalid because people like the letter M better than they like Q. Chicago Marketing Consultant Steuart H. Britt theorizes that Q is disliked because of the number of unpleasant words that begin with Q (quack, quitter, quake, qualm, queer . . .).

No Studies

To make its point, Coke put its own cola in both glasses—those marked M and those marked Q. Sure enough, most people tested preferred the drink in the M glass (hence the "Coke beat Coke" headline). Pepsi then revised the letters on its test glasses to S and L—and again consumers preferred Pepsi, which was always in the L glass. Again Coke executives cried foul, contending that just as people preferred M to Q, they liked L better than S. Questioned about this, Dr. Ernest Dichter, a motivational research expert, reported that he knew of no studies indicating a bias in favor of the letter L. . . .

Time
July 26, 1976

Here's a real-life example of how not to design a study. If you understand the information in this chapter, you should be able to plan much better experiments than the ones described in this article.

Rating Life Changes

Life Event	Value	Life Event	Value
Death of spouse	100	Son or daughter leaving home	29
Divorce	73	Trouble with in-laws	29
Marital separation	65	Outstanding personal achievement	28
Jail term	63		
Death of close family member	63	Wife beginning or stopping work	26
Personal injury or illness	53		
Marriage	50	Beginning or ending school	26
Fired at work	47	Revision of personal habits	24
Marital reconciliation	45	Trouble with boss	23
Retirement	45	Change in work hours or conditions	20
Change in health of family member	44		
		Change in residence	20
Pregnancy	40	Change in schools	20
Sex difficulties	39	Change in recreation	19
Gain of new family member	39	Change in social activities	18
Change in financial state	38	Mortgage or loan less than $10,000	17
Death of close friend	37		
Change to different line of work	36	Change in sleeping habits	16
Change in number of arguments with spouse	35	Change in number of family get-togethers	15
Mortgage over $10,000	31	Change in eating habits	15
Foreclosure of mortgage or loan	30	Vacation	13
Change in responsibilities at work	29	Minor violations of the law	11

The Hazards of Change

Any great change—even a pleasant change—produces stress in man. That is the implication, at least, of a study recently reported to the American Association for the Advancement of Science by Dr. Thomas Holmes, professor of psychiatry at the University of Washington in Seattle. Furthermore, Holmes found that too many changes, coming too close together, often produce grave illness or abysmal depression.

In the course of his investigation,

---

person's suffering mental illness, and to intervene and modify the person's behavior in hopes of preventing the illness—all with little or no understanding of why these techniques work. In principle, almost anyone with reasonable intelligence and the necessary books can diagnose and treat a disease without knowing what causes the disease or why the prescribed medicine works. Science is motivated by a desire to know and to understand, that is, to discover the causes or reasons for phenomena.

Psychologists seek to understand the most complex part of the world—human behavior. This enterprise promises both excitement and reward, and the potential for great practical achievement. Basic psychology attempts to understand in detail many significant issues, such as mental illness, the fundamental knowledge and skill involved in reading, and the basis of interaction between motivation and performance. Achieving adequate explanations for these and other psychological phenomena has far-reaching implications.

ETHICS IN PSYCHOLOGY

The activities of psychologists directly affect the private lives of other human beings. Whether in educational research or in clinical work, psychologists are almost always concerned with and in a position to influence the experiences of

Holmes devised a scale assigning point values to changes that often affect human beings *(above)*. When enough of these occur within one year and add up to more than 300, trouble may lie ahead. In Holmes' survey, 80% of people who exceeded 300 became pathologically depressed, had heart attacks, or developed other serious ailments. Of scorers in the 150–300 range, 53% were similarly affected, as were 33% of those scoring up to 150.

A hypothetical example: John was married (50); as he had hoped, his wife became pregnant (40), stopped working (26), and bore a son (39). John, who hated his work as a soap-company chemist, found a better-paying job (38) as a teacher (36) in a college outside the city. After a vacation (13) to celebrate, he moved his family to the country (20), returned to the hunting and fishing (19) he had loved as a child, and began seeing a lot of his congenial new colleagues (18). Everything was so much better that he was even able to give up smoking (24). On the Holmes scale, these events total an ominous 323.

To arrive at his scoring system, Dr. Holmes assigned an arbitrary value of 50 to the act of getting married and then asked people in several countries to rank other changes in relation to marriage. For example, a person who thought that pregnancy represented a greater change than marriage was to assign to pregnancy a number higher than 50. To correlate change and health, Holmes kept a watch on 80 Seattle residents for two years and then compared their personal-change histories with their physical and mental ailments.

Built-In Danger

To be sure, a method of predicting such ailments may well have a built-in danger; a self-rater using the scale could become depressed at the very prospect of depression. But Holmes is confident. Physical and emotional illness can be prevented, he says, by counseling susceptible people not to make too many life changes in too short a time.

Time
March 1, 1971

An example of prediction. The investigator devised a means for predicting the likelihood that a person will develop emotional or mental disorder. Since there is a shortage of mental health professionals in many areas, efforts have been made to reduce the caseload by getting help to those who need it most *before* serious illness occurs. Accurate prediction can help prevent later behavior problems.

others. Psychology aims to contribute positively to the welfare and betterment of humankind, of course, but there is always the potential for negative effects. Psychologists have an ethical responsibility to protect their subjects and clients from these undesirable effects.

Throughout the years of its existence, the major national organization of psychologists, the American Psychological Association, has been concerned with the ethical practice of psychology. Any evidence of unethical practice, whether in research or clinical work, is grounds for dismissal from the organization. Furthermore, the organization has published and periodically revised a book entitled *Ethical Principles of Psychologists,* which prescribes the obligations of psychologists to the human beings with whom they deal.

With regard to research, these principles assert that the psychologist will take all necessary steps to protect the confidentiality of the records of any individual, will not knowingly use any procedures that will result in harm or injury to the person, will fully disclose the purpose, procedures, and results of any study in which an individual participates, and prior to any interaction, will obtain from the individual his or her fully informed voluntary consent to participate. Clinical psychologists are obliged to follow much the same rules, but, in addition, must ensure that any testing performed on the client is fair to that individual and that any

More than any other field of psychology, psychotherapy raises many ethical issues—this one on sexual intimacy being by far the most controversial. Ethical guidelines of the American Psychological Association call for conflicts of interest always to be resolved in favor of the client's welfare, not the therapist's.

therapeutic steps are designed to ensure the welfare of the individual.

Ethical considerations in psychology are important but complex. There are many borderline cases. All reputable psychologists know that there must be no exceptions to the rule that the ethics of the profession must be adhered to in every professional interaction in which they engage.

PSYCHOLOGY IN HISTORICAL PERSPECTIVE

From as far back as historical records go, it is evident that people have been curious about themselves. This curiosity was almost entirely speculation, however, until psychologists adopted a scientific approach to their subject matter in the nineteenth century. From that point forward, the field took on a new form, which was essentially empirical and had biological underpinnings and an experimental superstructure. We will now briefly review some of the landmark achievements of the "new" scientific psychology. We must have some acquaintance with the history of psychology in order to appreciate what psychology is today.

The new psychology had rather modest beginnings. The problems addressed were simple, perhaps even naive, in comparison with the psychological issues that face people and scientists today. Early psychologists, for example, studied the sensations aroused by simple physical stimuli. They were curious about how fast the human hand could react to a stimulus, and how small a difference between two pure tones the human ear could detect. By modern standards these early experiments in psychology were crude. The new discipline of "psychology" that emerged in the late 1800s as an offshoot of philosophy and physiology lacked coherence and organization. The few scholars who were interested in psychological problems established their own individual schools of thought, and there were very few psychological principles that everyone agreed on. The impact of early scientific psychologists should not be minimized, however. Their accomplishments triggered many significant developments evident in the field today.

The activities of psychologists from approximately 1880 through 1940 were governed by

Weber's Law

One of the fundamental laws in psychology is known as Weber's Law, after its discoverer, Ernst Weber. It is called a psychophysical law because it describes a relation between physical and psychological events. Weber's Law states that the amount of increase in stimulation that is just noticeable by a human observer is a constant proportion of the starting level of stimulation. For example, suppose you determine that someone carrying a 50-pound load can detect the addition of 1 more pound to the load. Additions less than 1 pound are not noticed. So we say that the *just noticeable difference,* or *jnd,* is 1 pound. This is also called the *difference threshold.* It takes a change of 1 pound in 50 to produce a jnd, so the ratio is:

$$\frac{1}{50} = .02 \text{ or } 2\%$$

Weber's Law says that regardless of the starting weight, it will take a 2 percent increase in weight to be just noticeable. So if you were carrying 25 pounds, we would have to add 2 percent of 25, or 0.5 pounds, before you would notice the increase in weight. If you were starting with 100 pounds, we would have to add 2 pounds, and if you were starting with only a 1-pound box of candy, we would only have to add 0.02 pounds for you to detect it.

Weber's Law appears to hold quite well for middle ranges of values, but breaks down somewhat at extreme values—when the starting weights are extremely small or extremely large. It also applies to just about every dimension you can think of, including judging the height of a building, the loudness of a radio, the number of people in a crowd, and probably the price of merchandise. You could easily get away with a 10-cent increase in the price of a new car, but increasing the price of a roll of Life Savers by 10 cents would quickly be detected or noticed by customers.

The fraction above, 1/50 for weights, is called the *Weber fraction,* and it is a measure of how sensitive we are in various judgments. The smaller the fraction, the more sensitive we are. A fraction of 1/25 would mean we could detect a 4-percent change. Below are some actual Weber fraction values for different sense modalities. Note that the real Weber fraction for lifting weights is, more accurately, 1/53.

Dimension	Weber Fraction	Percent Change Needed to Notice a Difference
Pitch	1/333	0.3
Deep pressure	1/77	1.3
Brightness of a light	1/62	1.6
Lifted weight	1/53	1.9
Loudness of a tone	1/11	8.8
Smell—amount of rubber smell	1/10	10.4
Pressure on the skin surface	1/7	13.6
Taste—amount of salty taste	1/5	20.0

Weber's Law states that within a dimension the fraction is a constant, independent of the starting value. Between dimensions, however, the fraction can differ and represents how sensitive that sensory system is —the table shows that your sense of pitch change is much better than your sense of change in salty taste. Thus, by this measure, your ears are more sensitive than your tongue.

Figure 1–2
Wilhelm Wundt

The founder and leader of the structuralist movement felt that psychology should be concerned with studying the contents of conscious experience. By the method of introspection, he concluded that the mind consists of three basic elements—sensations, images, and feelings—from which our experience is compounded.

a number of diverse viewpoints and beliefs about (1) the proper subject matter of psychology, (2) the basic questions to be asked about that subject matter, and (3) the appropriate methods for answering these basic questions. We examine now some of the schools of thought that evolved around these issues, because they are the ideas that have shaped and continue to shape psychology today.

Structuralism

The first major theoretical school of psychology was **structuralism,** primarily a product of the work of Wilhelm Wundt (1832–1920), a professor of philosophy who founded the first formal laboratory of psychology at the University of Leipzig, Germany, in 1879 (see Figure 1–2).

Wundt proposed that the subject matter of psychology was **experience,** the experience or knowledge one has of the content of his or her own conscious mind. Influenced by the rise of modern physical and medical science, Wundt argued that the fundamental approach of science, namely, analysis, should be applied to psychological phenomena. To understand any problem, we need to break it down into its smallest component parts and then examine the parts themselves as fundamental building blocks. Structuralism, therefore, was an attempt to compartmentalize the mind into its basic parts, the so-called mental elements. Wundt believed that the existence of these elements were well established by philosophical study and examination, but he wanted to identify them *empirically* through a method called **introspection.** Introspection, according to Wundt, requires observers who can objectively examine and verbally report what is going on in their minds. These verbal reports could then be analyzed and categorized in an effort to determine the number

Figure 1–3
William James

Stream of consciousness

One of the earliest and foremost American psychologists, William James founded the first laboratory of psychology in this country. For James the mind was a continuous, ongoing "stream of consciousness" that could not be analyzed into elementary building blocks.

and kinds of basic elements in the mind. Wundt's studies led him to conclude that there are three basic elements, which he called **sensations** (the direct products of external stimulation), **images** (sensationlike experiences produced by the mind itself), and **feelings** (the affective or emotional components of an experience).

The major fault of structuralism was its failure to relate the concept of mind to human action. Psychology is still concerned today with mental activities, but its emphasis is on the way these activities influence performance. Psychologists attempt to explain the *hows* and *whys* of behavior, not just what is going on in the mind. To do this, they must observe how people act, as well as how they think and feel. In addition, structuralism deals primarily with *private* experience. Later psychologists argued convincingly that private experiences alone can never

be studied objectively. That being the case, private experiences cannot provide the data of a scientific field, which by definition must be public and openly observable to all. What people *do* or how they perform is publicly observable and can therefore legitimately be the subject matter of scientific psychology.

Functionalism

Partly because of its strong tradition in philosophy and partly because it was the first theoretical school of thought, structuralism dominated psychology for years, both in Europe and the United States. But it was not without critics or competition, and after the turn of the century three new schools of thought became strong competitors. The first was **functionalism,** primarily the product of American psychologists.

Stimulus-response relationships are important to behaviorists. Sgt. Snorkel believes in using a stimulus that elicits the desired response.

Among the foremost functionalists were William James of Harvard University (1842–1910). James Cattell of the University of Pennsylvania (1860–1944), John Dewey of the University of Chicago (1859–1952), and E. L. Thorndike of Columbia University (1874–1949).

Structuralists were concerned with what the mind is composed of, that is, the elements of consciousness. Functionalists, in contrast, studied *why* and *how* the mind works. Strongly influenced by the evolutionary principles of Darwin, functionalists argued that the mind is a human being's most important organ for adaptation to the environment. They emphasized the *use* of the mind rather than its contents. Functionalists did not reject mind and consciousness as important concepts in psychology, but they took these concepts a step beyond the structuralists' position on them. They recognized the connection between mind and behavior and were determined to study mind-body interactions. They examined how a person's mind, envisioned as a sort of master biological organ, controls other bodily organs in a never-ending struggle to cope with and adapt to the circumstances in the person's life. Rather than studying momentary glimpses of the structure or content of the mind, they proposed to investigate the continuous stream of consciousness that characterizes large segments of human life (see Figure 1–3). They did not reject introspection as a legitimate scientific method, but they did point out its limitations, especially in comparison with more objective observations of people functioning in the real world.

The functionalists were among the first to see that a person's most important way of adapting to the environment is through **learning**— the acquisition of facts and skills. This ability is in large measure what sets human beings apart from lower animals and allows us, despite our relatively feeble physiological equipment, to adapt to so many environments. The functionalists were among the first psychologists to examine learning scientifically.

Behaviorism

Functionalism was a loose general orientation toward psychology. Functionalists studied a variety of psychological processes but never developed a coherent general psychological theory. In contrast, **behaviorism,** the first truly American school of psychology, had a definite and explicit theoretical point of view. Behaviorism was primarily the work of John B. Watson (1878–1958). Although trained as a functionalist, Watson argued that private mental states, those we presumably study through introspection, cannot be the subject matter of a science. Only public events—that is, actions, responses, or performances that can be objectively observed and measured—fulfill the requirements of a scientific discipline. These events he called behaviors. Responses or behaviors, according to Watson, are affected by specifiable stimuli in the environment (see Figure 1–4). Therefore, the major goal of psychology is to identify those stimulus-response relationships that are lawful and predictable.

Figure 1-4
John B. Watson

For John B. Watson, the founder of behaviorism, behavior consisted of learned responses to external stimuli that are perceived by the senses. He rejected the concept of "mind," believing it was useless to speculate on the question of whether such a thing existed. In his behavioral system, Watson substituted a "black box" or empty head for the mind and put exclusive emphasis on observable stimulus-response relationships. His was the first stimulus-response psychology, abbreviated as S-R psychology.

During the same period of time in Russia, Ivan Pavlov (1848–1936) provided an impressive demonstration of the use of stimulus-response analysis in his famous description of classical conditioning. In the course of his physiological studies of digestion, Pavlov observed that his experimental subjects, dogs, came to salivate at the sound of a neutral stimulus—say, a bell—if food and bell were repeatedly paired together. Both Pavlov and Watson saw this conditioning phenomenon as evidence of the importance of learning and of stimulus-response connections in behavior. Watson saw Pavlov's research as confirmation of the lawful nature of behavior and of the possibility that all behavior, no matter how complex, can be reduced to learned stimulus-response units. Watson believed that *all behavior was learned,* that no aspect of it was inherited. He once boasted that he could make any healthy baby into any kind of adult—doctor, lawyer, or thief—merely by controlling the conditioning of the child. Today we know, of course, that heredity is also an important determinant of behavior.

Behaviorism sees the subject matter of psychology as stimulus-response relationships. These relationships are to be studied and understood by objective experimental and observational methods. A verbal report may be treated as an objective behavioral response (talking), but its status as a description of private mental experience is rejected. For behaviorists, the problem of psychology is to predict what responses will be evoked by what stimuli.

Figure 1–5
Max Wertheimer

Max Wertheimer was the founder of Gestalt psychology. His guiding principle was that mental content and behavior are different from the sum of their parts.

Gestalt Psychology

Gestalt psychology was a different kind of reaction to structuralism. The Gestalt movement began in Germany in the early part of the twentieth century, about the same time as behaviorism began to dominate American psychology. Gestalt psychology is a broad, research-oriented point of view toward behavior. It is not to be confused with a recent innovation in psychotherapy called Gestalt therapy (see Chapter 12). The German word *Gestalt* has no exact English translation. Roughly speaking, it means form or organized whole, reflecting the emphasis of this school on organizational processes in behavior. Whereas the focal problem of behaviorism was learning, Gestalt psychologists chose primarily to work with perceptual problems and sought to prove Wundt wrong in the very area that Wundt himself chose to emphasize. As a result, Gestalt theory is often identified as a theory of perception—although its principles are logically applicable to a broad range of psychological issues.

Behaviorists, like the structuralists, accepted the basic scientific idea that complex phenomena had to be analyzed into their simpler parts before they could be understood. The main proponents of Gestalt psychology, Wolfgang Köhler (1887–1967), Kurt Koffka (1886–1941), and Max Wertheimer (1880–1943), opposed the structuralists' efforts to reduce experience to a small set of fundamental component parts. They seized on other ideas from physical science, particularly the notions of field theory in physics, arguing that the whole of a phenomenon is different from the sum of its parts (see Figure 1–5). For example, from a series of still pictures, you perceive continuity of action in a movie. There is movement even in the neon lights on a theater marquee. Both of these effects are based on the phenomenon of *apparent movement*, identified by early Gestalt psychologists. Figure 1–6 shows another example of how perception of a whole can differ from perceptions of its parts.

Gestalt theory can be applied to nearly all important forms of behavior. Köhler, for example, argued that learning and problem solving, like perception, are largely a function of organizational processes. How to behave in a particular situation may elude subjects until they see the various components of the task in their appropriate relationship. The situation is a problem primarily because the correct or necessary relationship among the elements is not easily seen. The subject's behavior may take the form of overt trial and error or covert "thought." But the subject must take a variety of perspectives on the situation until the correct one emerges. When it does emerge, the subject experiences a "moment of insight." Finally the problem is solved and, in a flash, the subject knows what to do. Notice the persistent use of terms related to perception, such as "seeing," "perspective," and "experience," in the foregoing description. This is a consistent theme within Gestalt explanations of behavior. Note also the implication that learning and problem solving are "all-or-none," insightful processes. This is another major principle that distinguishes Gestalt psychology from other theoretical attempts to deal with learning.

From many examples like those given above, the Gestalt school argued against the utility of describing integrated human action by a mere analysis of component parts. They were concerned with the completeness, the continuity, and the meaningfulness of behavior as a whole.

Psychoanalysis

Psychoanalysis, the theoretical point of view identified with Sigmund Freud (1858–1939), was less a reaction to structuralism than an effort to apply science and medicine to the study and treatment of abnormal behavior. (Several portraits of Freud appear on page 353 in Chapter 9.) Psychoanalysis has been called the third great intellectual blow to human pride. First, we human beings found that we are not at the

Figure 1–6
The Gestalt approach to perception

Panel A: rim light

Panel B: center light

Panel C: combination (theory)

Panel D: what subjects actually see

Here is an interesting perceptual effect that demonstrates one of the basic Gestalt principles of perception. It suggests that we do not perceive an event merely by adding up the perceptions that we have of the separate parts. A wheel is rolled from left to right across a table in a dark room. In the top panel, a light is attached to the rim of the wheel and the dashed line indicates what subjects perceive. The second panel shows our perception of a light attached at the center of the wheel. Panel C indicates what the geometric sum of the motions of the rim light and center light should look like. Panel D is what subjects *actually* perceive.

center of the universe; then, we discovered that we are descended from apes; and, finally, Freud argued that we are basically controlled by impulses, many of which are buried in the unconscious, below the level of awareness. The view that human beings are rational and in conscious control of their behavior was weakened when Freud described the behavioral impact of early childhood experience, anxiety, and conflicting unconscious motives.

Freud, whose theory we will discuss in detail in Chapter 9, described the personality structure of a human being as consisting of three forces: the pleasure-seeking **id,** composed of basic biological impulses; the realistic **ego,** reacting to the stresses and strains of everyday life; and the idealistic **superego,** representing the dictates of one's conscience. Unlike structuralism, functionalism, and the other schools we have discussed, the primary method of psychoanalysis was detailed case study, and its primary focus was abnormal behavior. Indeed, psychoanalysis is primarily identified today with a method of psychotherapy for mental illness.

CONTEMPORARY TRENDS IN PSYCHOLOGY

Our review of historical events has been sketchy, but it illustrates some of the major trends in psychological thought. The schools of thought just described no longer exist intact, but they are not without impact on contemporary thinking.

Structuralism, in its original form, never recovered from the penetrating criticisms raised by other schools. Few psychologists would refer to themselves today as structuralists. Yet the concepts of structuralism have not entirely disappeared. Jean Piaget, the famous Swiss developmental psychologist, has written volumes on changes in the structure of the human mind with age. American experimental psychologists study the way knowledge is organized and refer extensively to the structure of our current memory of past events. The principles of association, originally applied by structuralists to the formation of complex mental events out of simpler elements, are still the basis of some learning theories. So structuralism is also present in modern psychology.

Functionalism was never a coherent school, nor did it center on the thinking of any one psychologist. It was, rather, a vaguely stated set of principles about the pragmatic—that is, functional—significance of the mind. But, while there was no strong theoretical commitment, functionalism left a significant legacy in its emphasis on learning as humanity's most important adaptive process.

In a sense, psychoanalysis has been the most persistent school of psychological thought. Strongholds of adherents can still be found. While its influence as a pervasive theory of human behavior has decreased, it still has considerable importance in some areas of clinical psychology and personality theory, and it forms the basis of a widely used psychotherapeutic technique.

Behaviorism and Gestalt psychology have probably had the greatest role in shaping modern psychology. The basic ideas that both groups formulated and explored are clearly evident in contemporary psychology, though there are few psychologists today who identify themselves as behaviorists or as Gestaltists in the traditional sense. The behaviorists' emphasis on the role of learned responses as building blocks of behavior is a predominant principle in modern psychological theory. B. F. Skinner has developed both a theory and a technology for changing behavior based on observable responses and their subsequent rewards and punishments. We will have a good deal more to say about Skinner's ideas in our discussions of learning (Chapter 4) and personality (Chapter 9). Mentalistic ideas, rejected by Watson, are admitted into some modern versions of behaviorism (called neobehaviorism), though often disguised as implicit (nonobservable) responses. The insistence of Gestalt psychologists on the importance of organizational processes and continuity in behavior, as opposed to a simple analysis of content, persists in a lively form. The issue of content versus process analysis has a bearing on many aspects of contemporary psychology, perhaps the most important of which is learning. These relationships will appear throughout the book.

Schools of psychology have disappeared because, as psychologists examine the issues more closely, they have discovered that explanations cannot logically take the simple form offered by narrow versions of structuralism, behaviorism, or any other school. Psychologists have come to realize that it takes a *mixture* of mental and performance concepts and both innate and experiential processes to give a complete description of human activity. There are differences in emphasis and opinion in psychology today, but extremist thinking and close-minded groups are fortunately becoming rare.

Cognition and Information Processing

One perspective on behavior today is widely shared by psychologists across a broad range of interests. This is a position that views the human being as an active information processor. This perspective recognizes that human beings are constantly interacting with their environment and that they bring cognitive or mental capacities to bear on all such interactions. Such a viewpoint has been used by psychologists in the analysis of all levels of behavior, ranging from simple conditioning to abnormal behavior and therapeutic attempts to correct it.

A brief description of the information-processing framework is as follows. Information enters the human processing system through various sensory receptors. It proceeds through a succession of stages, which includes the conversion of physical energy into a psychological or mental form. There are various kinds of memory in the system, each with its own characteristics. We can remember an event accurately, but only for a brief time in what is called sensory memory. Somewhat more durable is the information placed in short-term memory, the memory store that allows you to retain a new telephone number just long enough to dial it. The most important information usually gets placed in long-term memory, where it resides until needed at a later time.

In addition to its various memories, our information-processing system also allows for the selectivity of attention, the experience of consciousness, the ability to make inferences and form concepts from incoming data, problem solving and decision making, and the establishment of action patterns for overt behavior.

The complex information-processing system called a human being is impossible to summarize in a few short paragraphs. Because the information-processing view is becoming increasingly important in psychology today, we will refer to it repeatedly throughout later chapters, especially those dealing with perception, learning and memory, and cognition. We will try to make it clear how this particular perspective attempts to make sense of the variety of behaviors people exhibit.

Want To Be Healthy? Change Lifestyle

AP

NEW HYDE PARK, N.Y. — "We are caught in the 'lifestyle' diseases," says Dr. Mary McLaughlin, Director of Community Medicine at Long Island Jewish-Hillside Medical Center.

"Heart disease and accidents, two major killers, can be traced to a great degree to lifestyle," she explains. "One's mode of living is probably primary in the case of emphysema, cirrhosis of the liver and at least two types of cancer. It is also a basic factor in venereal disease, in alcoholism, in obesity, in the ills resulting from drug abuse."

Lifestyle plays a primary or contributory role in chronic illnesses such as mental illness, ulcer, diabetes, and, in the case of stroke, it is an important element, she adds. . . .

Dr. McLaughlin cites a study of 7,000 adults who were followed for over five years. After that period of time, the health status of those in the group who consistently observed seven prescribed health rules was roughly the same as people 30 years younger who did not follow any special health regimen. . . .

The study concluded, Dr. McLaughlin says, that people can add a decade or more to their life expectancy by adopting these simple health habits:

Eat three meals a day at regular intervals. Don't substitute snacks for meals.

Have breakfast every day.

Exercise moderately by walking, biking, swimming, gardening or the like. Take this exercise two or three times a week.

Sleep seven or eight hours a night.

Don't smoke.

Maintain moderate weight.

Don't drink or, if you must, drink in moderation. . . .

Boulder (Colo.) Daily Camera
September 21, 1977

There is now general agreement in the medical professions that the best answers to many medical problems can be found in the field of psychology—in the study of behavior. Understanding such things as why we smoke, overeat, and drink too much and figuring out ways to get people to change their behavior will contribute significantly to longer and happier lives.

Mixing Humanism and Science "Ruins Both," Says Hebb

Humanistic psychology "confuses two very different ways of knowing," said a veteran Canadian brain researcher recently. "Combining the two ruins both."

In the view of McGill University psychologist Dr. Donald Hebb, efforts to marry humanism and science stem from a fundamental misunderstanding of "what psychology is about"—the title of his invited address at APA's 81st Annual Convention.

Scientific psychology will "always be incomplete" in its understanding of man and "has little to tell us about how to live wisely and well," cautioned Hebb at the August meeting in Montreal. For answers to these questions he referred his audience to Shakespeare, Conrad and Mark Twain.

"A science," he explained, "imposes limits on itself, and makes its progress by attacking only those problems that it is fitted to attack by existing knowledge and methods. Psychology has made much progress in this century, and the rate of progress is accelerating, but it is limited, and must be if it is to continue its progress. Limited in the questions it can ask, but sure of its results."

In these days of journal articles "that haven't an idea anywhere about them" it's easy to lose sight of such fundamentals. The 69-year-old professor noted that most of the graduate students entering a seminar he teaches "have no clear ideas about the relation of mind to body, or about consciousness, or what thought is, or free will."

A good check against "talking nonsense," said Hebb, is to regard psychology as a biological science concerned with man's mind and thought, and then to proceed on the following assumptions:

The mind and the brain are one.

Thought is the "integrative activity of the brain."

Free will is simply the control of behavior by the thought process.

Thought, along with other behavior, is shaped by heredity and environment.

Hence, one can believe in free will and still be a determinist.

For those "dualists" who persist in believing that consciousness is not produced by the brain, Hebb prescribes the work of Dr. Roger Sperry on split-brain patients: "Today no one, psychologist, philosopher, neurologist, or humanist, is entitled to an opinion on the mind-body question if he is unfamiliar with the split-brain procedure and its results in human patients."

Still, Hebb acknowledged, speculative ideas are the stuff of science—so long as they spring from such an "objective-biological-psychological approach." . . .

APA Monitor
November 1973

Some distinguished psychologists doubt that a humanistic approach has anything to contribute to the science of psychology. But the debate between humanistic and mechanistic psychology is far from settled.

The Mechanistic versus the Humanistic View

A characteristic of most psychological theories, both historical and contemporary, is their mechanistic view of human behavior. These theories, like the information-processing theory just described, assume that we are unable to control our fate. They assume that we are at the mercy of the stresses and strains imposed by the environment and by processes built innately into our nervous system and other biological structures. Stimuli are thought to impinge on a person much as they might impinge on an electronic computer or some simpler machine. According to the mechanistic point of view, what a person does with these stimuli is a function of the way the machine is wired and what information has been stored from the past. Overt responses are programmed by earlier events in the sequences, and human reason exerts little influence.

This assumption is not a logical requirement of psychological theory. It is only one form of theorizing, yet most psychologists have accepted it uncritically. Quite possibly this position may be misleading and inadequate. Contemporary research is beginning to indicate that this kind of theory is too simple. A somewhat more humanistic view of the person may be in order. In fact, one of the major contemporary movements in psychology is basically a reaction against the mechanistic conception. This movement, usually referred to as *humanistic psychology*, has grown out of the writings of such noted psychologists as Carl Rogers, Abraham Maslow, Rollo May, and Fritz Perls. Briefly, this view holds that each of us is unique and can determine our own fate by conscious exertion of our free will. The exercise of our reason and intuition may be more important than environment and biology in determining the course of our development. You will read more about the ideas of humanistic psychology in later chapters.

This school of thought presents a growing challenge to the prevailing psychological model of the person as machine. We shall not adopt any particular view of the person in this book. We do wish to alert you to this issue, however, and to request that you keep an open mind before committing yourself too thoroughly to any particular point of view.

THE FUTURE OF PSYCHOLOGY

It is difficult to forecast where any rapidly developing field will be five or ten years from now. Compared with most sciences, psychology is in its infancy—at best, its history goes back only about 100 years. But it has grown rapidly, and its progress shows no signs of tapering off in the near future.

Mike Smith, a British psychologist, asked 50 experts, including university professors, basic and applied researchers, and practitioners of psychology, what they expected psychology to accomplish in the future and when. Certain developments in applied psychology commonly envisioned by some laypersons were rejected outright as impossibilities by the panel of experts. For example, none of the experts expects a convincing demonstration of thought transference with animals or any reliable application of extrasensory perception. But there are some interesting possibilities. Toward the end of this century the experts expected a breakthrough in understanding the biological bases of behavior, beginning with the practical use of drugs to reduce specific, unwanted behavioral tendencies. Society will replace prison control with drug control. Thus, we should be able to reduce the sexual impulses of a sex offender, for example, without interfering with other aspects of the offender's life. Chemicals may begin to be used to advance or to retard learning.

Our knowledge of biopsychological processes may be so advanced by the middle of the twenty-first century that we may have biological methods for selectively erasing memories. People whose happiness is affected by unfortunate emotional memories may be able to have them erased by a short and simple process. Psychology may develop a series of self-manipulative procedures, or "experience packages," which will enormously expand the functions and lifestyles of individuals. Bright children from the worst slums could, for example, elect to undergo a self-manipulative program that would enable them to hold their own in any social situation.

By the turn of the century conscious attempts may be made to use psychology to design cultures and social systems. In the more distant future, more bizarre aspects of this trend may arise. Do-it-yourself pleasure centers may become technically possible. Self-stimulation of certain centers in the brain could well make sex, alcohol, gambling, and eating obsolete as modes of human gratification.

You should, of course, be skeptical of many of these possibilities. There is a huge margin of error surrounding them. Nonetheless, it is interesting to know what experts in the field think will be happening in psychology in the future. Make your own list of future possibilities, then make another list after you have read the next eleven chapters.

SUMMARY

1. All psychologists study behavior, yet they use a variety of approaches to a wide range of issues. There are many different kinds of psychologists, including experimenters, clinicians, counselors, and social, educational, and industrial psychologists.

2. One way to describe the diversity within psychology and among psychologists is in terms of the issues studied, the methods used, and the employment of the psychologist.

3. Areas of research in psychology range from those aspects of the physical organism that affect behavior, such as the genes, to the diagnosis and treatment of complex abnormal behavior patterns.

4. Psychology employs a variety of methods in its attempt to find out the whats, whys, and hows of behavior. Among them are (a) the case study, the intensive examination of one individual; (b) naturalistic observation, an investigation of interacting psychological processes as they occur in everyday circumstances; (c) surveys, tests, and interviews, which are techniques that are employed to find out what relationships exist between measurable variables and how strong these relationships are; and (d) experimentation, the establishment of arbitrary models of psychological situations in the laboratory and the examination of how manipulated independent variables affect the dependent variables (performance) in these situations under controlled circumstances.

5. Psychologists in basic science are employed primarily at colleges and universities. Applied psychologists work in industry, government, hospitals, clinics, schools, and private practice.

6. Psychology is described as a science that studies behavior and systematically applies behavior principles. Three goals of psychology are: (a) measurement and description, (b) prediction and control, and (c) understanding and explanation of behavior.

7. Highlights of the history of psychology include the formation of various major schools of psychological thought and theory during the late 1800s and the early 1900s, namely, structuralism, functionalism, behaviorism, Gestalt psychology, and psychoanalysis.

8. Few of these early schools of thought have survived intact, but contemporary psychology was shaped by them. Psychologists have come to realize that to give a complete description of human activity they must consider both mental and performance concepts.

9. Today many psychologists take an information-processing perspective on human behavior. They view the human being as an active information processor, receiving sensory information from the environment, converting it into a mental form, and storing it for future use.

10. Psychology is a young science but it is developing rapidly through basic and applied research. But by the year 2000, many experts expect significant practical accomplishments in the understanding and the control of human behavior.

RECOMMENDED ADDITIONAL READINGS

For more on the methods of research psychology:

Anderson, B. F. *The psychology experiment,* 2d ed. Belmont, Calif.: Brooks/Cole, 1971.

Arnoult, M. D. *Fundamentals of scientific method in psychology.* Dubuque, Iowa: W. C. Brown, 1972.

Plutchik, R. *Foundations of experimental research,* 2d ed. New York: Harper & Row, 1974.

For more on the history of psychology and an analysis of basic issues:

Chaplin J. P., and Krawiec, T. S. *Systems and theories of psychology*, 4th ed. New York: Holt, Rinehart and Winston, 1979.

Wertheimer, M. *A brief history of psychology*. New York: Holt, Rinehart and Winston, 1970.

If you are considering a career in psychology write to the American Psychological Association for a copy of their booklet: *A career in psychology*. American Psychological Association, 1200 17th St., N.W., Washington, D.C. 20036.

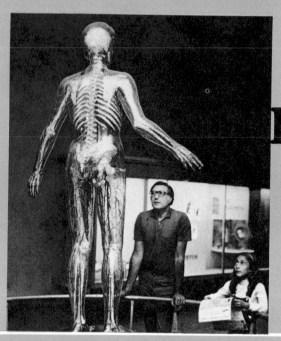

Biological Foundations of Behavior 2

Ray has suffered from severe attacks of epilepsy since childhood. During his attacks, he often becomes violent, unreasonable, and even homicidal. He was finally committed to a state institution where several brain researchers became interested in his case. They first tried to control the epilepsy with drugs, a treatment found to be ineffective in Ray's case. The doctors then decided on a new experimental treatment.

Small electrodes were surgically implanted into Ray's brain. These electrodes were attached to a stimulator small enough so that Ray could carry it with him wherever he went. He was instructed to press a button on the stimulator whenever he felt an attack coming on. Since the operation, Ray has not suffered from a single complete attack. He has been able to eliminate his violent obsessions by simply pressing a button and sending small electrical impulses to the right part of his brain.

At birth, Mr. and Mrs. J's daughter was diagnosed as suffering from an inherited disease known as phenylketonuria (PKU). This condition is caused by a single gene, and children suffering from this disease, if not treated from birth, may grow up mentally retarded due to a malfunctioning brain and nervous system. Upon the recommendation of Mrs. J's attending physician the child was immediately placed on a special diet deficient in a particular amino acid. The child now has a very good chance of growing up to lead a more-or-less normal life.

These two cases have something in common—they involve the operations of the nervous system. They are representative of the infinite number of ways in which the brain is involved in all aspects of our behavior.

People have long been intrigued by the question of how a mass of organic material such as the human brain is capable of generating consciousness and behavior. How does the brain translate its language of electrical and chemical signals into conscious perceptions, thoughts, and voluntary movements? How is it that the glands, through chemical secretions called hormones, affect almost all aspects of our behavior? How is it that genes by controlling metabolic processes in cells can influence our behavior? These questions are statements of the classical "mind-body" problems which many people consider the ultimate question in the search for the biological foundations of behavior.

The examples above raise many questions about the relation between the brain and behavior. For instance, what makes us violent, and which parts of the brain are involved? Answers to questions such as this one are unknown. However, a good deal has been learned about how the nervous system is involved in "psychological" processes such as sensory perception and learning. The purpose of this chapter is to present an overview of what is known about the physiological underpinnings of behavior. We will also discuss some of what is known about the relation between hormonal secre-

tions and behavior. Finally, we will present some of the findings in the new field of behavioral genetics and conclude with a discussion of recent and potential applications of knowledge gained in these areas of research.

THE NEURON

If we want to understand behavior from a biological point of view, then we must first understand the physiology of the nervous system. Similarly, if we are to understand the physiology of the nervous system, we must first understand the functioning of its elementary unit, the nerve cell, or **neuron** (see Appendix B).

While there is no accurate count, our nervous system contains at least 10 billion nerve cells. Although there are many types of nerve cells that are specialized in structure and function, all consist of three basic structural units. These are the **soma, dendrites,** and **axon.** These parts of the nerve cell are illustrated in Figure 2–1 (see also Figures B1–2 in Appendix B). The cell body, or soma, contains the nucleus of the nerve cell, which controls all cellular activities such as oxygen utilization and energy production. One cellular activity that nerve cells do not carry out is reproduction. But neurons do die. It has been estimated that human beings lose as many as 10,000 nerve cells each day, a loss that tends to increase with age.

The dendrites are short "fibers" or processes

Figure 2–1
The basic parts of a neuron

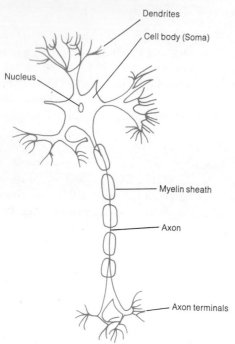

Dendrites

Cell body (Soma)

Nucleus

Myelin sheath

Axon

Axon terminals

Most vertebrate nerve cells consist of three basic parts—the dendrites, the cell body (soma), and the axon. The axon ends in the so-called axon terminals which make contact with another cell, another nerve cell, a muscle, or a gland. Many axons are encased in a myelin sheath which increases the cell's rate of conduction and its action potential.

extending from the soma. They act like receiving stations which pick up signals from other neurons. A nerve cell may have just a few or several hundred dendrites, all of which conduct information toward the cell body.

Each neuron has a single longer fiber, the axon, extending from the soma, the cell body. In some cases the axon may divide into several branches after leaving the soma. Some axons are quite long, measuring several feet in length; others are very short. Axons conduct information away from the cell body. They end in terminal branchings, each of which is referred to as an *axon terminal*. These axon terminals are located near other dendrites and somas of other neurons, and the signals generated by the neuron are transmitted along the axon to its terminals, and then to the dendrites or soma of the next neuron.

The region where an axon makes a functional connection, where it comes closest to a dendrite or cell body of the next neuron, is known as the **synapse.** However, the axon terminals do not actually touch the dendrites or

soma of the next neuron in the communication chain. There are small spaces between adjoining neurons known as *synaptic spaces,* or *clefts.* A nerve impulse travels down the axon, invading the terminals, where it causes the release of **chemical transmitter substances,** sometimes called neurotransmitters. These chemical transmitters travel the small distance across the synaptic space to the dendrites or soma of the next neuron. In this way nerve impulses are communicated from one neuron to the next and on to distant parts of the body.

We know a great deal about the generation and transmission of nerve signals, which are called **action potentials.** Much of this information is presented in Appendix B for the student who wishes to study these processes more intensively.

Coding Information

We can think of the nervous system as a very large communication system which transmits information from one part of the body to another. For example, when we "see" something, information is transmitted from the eye to the brain over a neural communication system, the optic nerve. When we "hear" something, information is transmitted from the inner ear to the brain over the auditory or acoustic nerve.

The nervous system has evolved a number of ways of coding the information it transmits. Before we discuss how the nervous system codes information, you should know that most neurons emit impulses or action potentials every once in a while even when nothing is happening —this is called the base rate of firing. A neuron can signal that an event has occurred by increasing its rate of firing (turning the signal system on) or by decreasing its base rate of firing (sometimes turning completely off). In other words, the neuron can signal with either "on" or "off" responses. Consider what happens when we shine a light into the eye of a human observer: While sitting in the dark the subject's optic nerve is firing at its base rate. Then, when the stimulus light is turned on, some of the neurons of the optic nerve might increase their rate of firing. The brightness of the light might then be coded by the magnitude of change—a dim light would be coded as a small increase in the rate of firing and a bright light as a larger increase in the rate of firing.

Curing the Mind

Thirty-five-year-old Brian suffered his first nervous breakdown at age 22. He has since been given psychotherapy and anti-psychotic drugs to combat feelings of anxiety and the imaginary voices he heard. But this summer, a few days after he was injected with a substance known as beta-endorphin, his family said Brian became "his old, salty self again." After a second round of beta-endorphin, Brian wept "for the first time in years" because he was happy. Brian said he realized his happiness when he heard the song "Yesterday" on the radio. "I knew yesterday was over," he explained.

Brian is one of the first psychiatric patients to be treated with beta-endorphin, a substance produced by the pituitary gland. In a newly disclosed study, beta-endorphin relieved depression or schizophrenia in five of six patients. But the authors caution that more intensive research will be necessary and that the cost of beta-endorphin—$3,000 per injection—is prohibitive.

First Smile

In the tests, Dr. Nathan S. Kline, director of research at the Rockland Research Institute in Orangeburg, N.Y., gave six adult male patients injections over a period of 21 days. The most immediate results were seen in two depressed patients. Hours after receiving the injection, a 63-year-old depressive who had attempted suicide in 1975 and had electro-shock therapy without benefit, became animated and voluble. The patient's mother said that it was "the first time in three years that he had smiled." After six hours, however, the patient's depression returned. All three of the schizophrenics tested experienced a lessening or disappearance of their symptoms, but these effects were often delayed until several days after the injections were given.

Prior to the beta-endorphin, each patient was given a placebo solution to insure that changes in his mood were not caused by his expectations. To determine beta-endorphin's effect on normal persons, Dr. Edward Laski, a co-author of the study, took an injection. After four hours he suddenly felt sleepy and retarded; seven hours later these symptoms rapidly disappeared.

Open Door

Researchers are not sure how beta-endorphin works within the brain, and it may be some time before they find out. The molecule of which beta-endorphin is a part was first isolated in 1965 by Dr. Choh Hao Li, of the University of California, a co-author of the study. At first, Dr. Li extracted the substance from animal pituitaries, but he later discovered a way to synthesize it in the laboratory. Producing beta-endorphin in pure form, however, is expensive and time-consuming, which accounts for the high cost of a single injection.

Scientists now know beta-endorphin can be safely tested on a large scale, and that could lower the cost of individual injections. "It may be that we have opened a door that will lead us to a cure for schizophrenia and depression," said Dr. Kline cautiously. "But it is also possible that the results we obtained were actually the result of other factors. We shall have to wait, experiment further, and see."

Newsweek
August 29, 1977

A newly discovered class of proteins in the brain seems to relieve pain and alter various mental states when administered to human beings. These substances—known collectively as endorphins—are thought to be neurotransmitters. It has been suggested that they play a role in drug addiction and schizophrenia.

In addition, the neural code for brightness might involve the number of neurons that change their rate of firing as a function of the intensity of the stimulus. A dim light might trigger a change in the firing rate of only a small number of neurons, whereas a bright light might trigger a change in a large number of neurons.

Another way of coding information concerns *which* neurons are firing. For example, a visual stimulus causes a change in the firing rate of neurons in the optic nerve; a tone causes a change in the firing rate of neurons in the acoustic nerve. This principle also applies within a given sensory system. For example, within the eye it makes a great deal of difference *which*

Figure 2–2
The structural organization of the nervous system

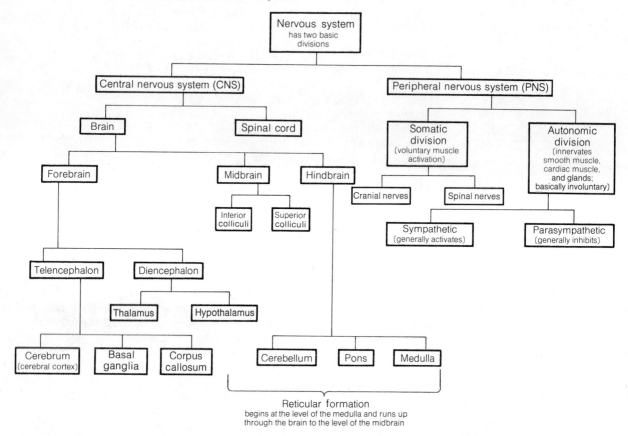

Reticular formation
begins at the level of the medulla and runs up
through the brain to the level of the midbrain

neurons of the optic nerve are activated, because these neurons code for the location, color, and other characteristics of the stimulus we are observing. It has also been shown that tones of different pitch stimulate different neurons; in other words, one of the neural codes for pitch is which nerves are firing. Most amazing of all is the relatively recent discovery that specialized cells in the visual system (and perhaps in other sensory systems as well) respond to particular types of stimuli and not to other very similar types. For example, there are cells in the visual system that respond with an "on" signal to a vertical line, but do not respond if a horizontal line is flashed before the eye (see Chapter 3). If this neuron produces an "on" response, a vertical line of some sort has been "seen."

There are three major factors that character-ize the way neurons transmit and code information about what is happening to the organism: (1) The rate of firing impulses, (2) the number of neurons responding, and (3) which particular neurons are firing. All three factors convey information about the nature and location of sensory stimuli.

THE ORGANIZATION OF THE NERVOUS SYSTEM

The nervous system can be divided into the **central nervous system** (CNS), which is contained within the skull and a bony spinal column; and the **peripheral nervous system,** comprised of all the nerves connecting the muscles, glands, and sensory receptors with the central nervous system (see Figure 2–2). The central nervous system—the brain and spinal cord—may be viewed as the integrating center for all bodily functions and behavior, while the peripheral nervous system brings information into and out of the central nervous system.

Neurons are organized into specialized groupings that constitute the main structures of the nervous system. Cell bodies of neurons usually cluster together in one place. Such clusters of somas are called **nuclei** when they occur within the central nervous system and **ganglia** when they occur in the peripheral nervous system. In similar fashion, the axons of neurons tend to cluster together and travel in large bundles. Such bundles of axons are often called **tracts** when they occur in the central nervous system and **nerves** when they occur in the peripheral nervous system.

The Peripheral Nervous System

The peripheral nervous system is divided into two major parts—(1) the **somatic nervous system,** which includes the sensory nerves that bring all sensory information into the central nervous system plus the motor nerves that control the activity of the skeletal muscles concerned with voluntary bodily movements; and (2) the **autonomic nervous system** that directs the activity of smooth (involuntary) and cardiac (heart) muscles and of glands.

The Somatic Division

The somatic nervous system consists of both the cranial and spinal nerves. There are 12 pairs of cranial nerves and 31 pairs of spinal nerves. As their names imply, the cranial nerves enter and leave the nervous system at the level of the brain, and the spinal nerves enter and exit from the spinal cord.

The cranial nerves carry sensory information to the brain from all the sense organs of the head, such as the eyes, ears, and nose. The optic nerve is an example of a cranial nerve; it carries information about the visual world from the eyes to the brain. The cranial nerves also carry information from the brain to control the muscles of the face and neck. (See color Plate 10.)

Those nerves that carry sensory information into the central nervous system are called **sensory,** or afferent, nerves. Those that carry information from the central nervous system to

Figure 2–3
The organization of peripheral nerves and their relationship to the spinal cord

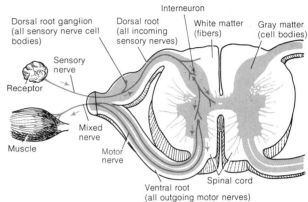

Only one-half of the cross section of the spinal cord is fully illustrated, but the arrangement is duplicated on both sides.

peripheral structures such as muscles and glands are called **motor,** or efferent, nerves. Many nerves contain both sensory and motor fibers and are referred to as mixed nerves.

You will recall that the spinal nerves enter and exit from the spinal cord. Information can easily be channeled up and down from higher parts of the nervous system by connecting fibers found within the spinal cord. Although the spinal nerves contain both sensory and motor fibers, these segregate on entering the spinal cord into two branches or roots. Sensory fibers enter the spinal cord in the dorsal root. The cell bodies of these sensory fibers are found in groups outside the spinal cord but running parallel with its length. These aggregations of nerve cell bodies are called the dorsal root ganglia. Motor, or efferent, fibers which leave the spinal cord to send information to the muscles and glands exit from the spinal cord by the ventral root. The cell bodies of these motor fibers are located in the lower portion of the spinal cord. The details of this spinal anatomy are illustrated schematically in Figure 2–3.

It is extremely important to understand the difference between the functions of the dorsal and ventral roots. Damage to the dorsal (sensory) roots in the lower part of the spinal cord, for example, will produce a lack of sensation in the lower part of the body. Damage to the ven-

Parts of the Nervous System

Many of the terms in the section on the anatomy of the nervous system may be new and unfamiliar to you. Below is a listing of the most important parts of the nervous system. These are the basic terms you need to know to understand the biological foundations of behavior.

The Neuron

A. The cell body (soma)
B. The dendrites for receiving information
C. The axon for sending information on to other neurons; a nerve is basically a bundle of axons from many neurons

The Brain

A. The cerebral hemispheres
   1. Sensory cortex: receiving area for information from sensory systems
   2. Motor cortex: area that initiates motor responses
   3. Association cortex: the undifferentiated remainder of the cortex that underlies all higher mental functions
   4. Corpus callosum: the band of fibers that connects the two cerebral hemispheres and constitutes a pathway for interhemispheric communication
B. Thalamus: the preliminary-processing and relay station for incoming information
C. Hypothalamus: a complex structure involved in regulating a wide variety of emotional and motivational behaviors
D. Medulla: involved in regulating involuntary behavior
E. Cerebellum: controls motor coordination
F. Reticular formation: regulates arousal level

The Spinal Cord

A. Dorsal roots — collects information coming into the spinal cord
B. Ventral roots — disperses information going out from the spinal cord

The Peripheral Nervous System

A. Somatic division: the nerves that serve voluntary muscles
B. Autonomic division: the nerves that serve involuntary muscles
   1. Sympathetic division: generally activates our bodies, as in emergencies
   2. Parasympathetic division: generally inhibits or slows down involuntary functioning

tral (motor) roots will produce paralysis, since the ventral roots carry commands to the muscles responsible for movement. Cutting all of the ventral roots would, therefore, produce complete paralysis below the neck, including paralysis of the breathing muscles — artificial respiration would be necessary to prevent death.

Certain simple kinds of behavior are controlled by the nerves of the spinal cord. The behaviors controlled by these spinal nerves are called reflexive behaviors. An example of a reflexive behavior is that which results when you put your hand to a hot plate. The heat from the hot plate stimulates receptors located in the skin. This information is passed on into the spinal cord through the sensory neurons which enter by the dorsal root. These sensory fibers make contact through an interneuron with efferent nerves within the spinal cord. Commands are then sent to the muscles by way of these motor nerves and the limb is withdrawn. All of this happens very rapidly.

The Autonomic Division

The second major division of the peripheral nervous system is divided into two parts, the **sympathetic** and **parasympathetic** divisions. (See Figure 2–4.) Many of the body's organs and glands are supplied with nerves from both branches of the autonomic nervous system. In general, the two systems produce opposite effects. For example, the sympathetic system acts to speed up the heart, whereas the parasympathetic division acts to slow it down. The same principle applies to many other structures including the stomach, the gastrointestinal system, the pupils, tear glands, and sweat glands. Under normal conditions, the two branches of the autonomic nervous system maintain a balance, enabling normal body functions to operate smoothly.

These two branches of the autonomic nervous system are especially important in controlling emotional behavior (see Chapter 7). For example, activation of the sympathetic division prepares an organism for emergencies. You may have felt this sympathetic activity if you have ever been in an automobile accident or other frightening situation. Your *adrenal glands* are activated, your heart speeds up, your pupils dilate, and gastrointestinal activity is inhibited. The adrenal glands respond by secreting a hormone called **epinephrine (adrenalin).** Epinephrine is carried all over the body by the bloodstream, producing effects very similar to the activity of the sympathetic nervous system itself. Therefore, this hormone reinforces the activity of the autonomic nervous system. The sympathetic nervous system also diverts blood from the internal organs to the muscles, preparing them for action.

The parasympathetic nervous system is particularly important in controlling certain vegetative functions, for example, digestion, and in the conservation of energy. The activity of the parasympathetic nervous system stimulates the gastrointestinal system and also slows down the heart.

The Central Nervous System

The central nervous system (CNS) is the collecting, integrating, and output center for all bodily activity. Some functions are controlled at a single level of the CNS, while others are controlled by interconnecting circuits at various levels of the brain. The human brain (Figure 2–5) may be viewed in three parts: (1) the hindbrain—the lowest level of the brain, immediately above the spinal cord; (2) the midbrain—lying just above the hindbrain; and (3) the forebrain—including the most highly developed parts of the human brain, the cerebrum, or **cerebral cortex.**

The Hindbrain

The major components of the hindbrain (Figure 2–5) are the medulla, pons, and cerebellum.

The *medulla* is the part of the brain lying closest to the spinal cord. All the fiber tracts that connect the spinal cord with the rest of the brain pass through the medulla. The medulla also contains some very important nuclei. Several of these nuclei serve as relays for the activities of certain cranial nerves, while others are important in controlling vital bodily functions. The medulla contains nuclei that, in part, control heart rate and respiration. Damage to the medulla can impair breathing, heartbeat, and other vital functions. Damage to the ascending and descending fiber systems that relay information from the spinal cord to the brain might cause loss of sensation or result in partial or complete paralysis.

The **pons** lies just above the medulla and also contains many of the ascending and descending fibers that connect higher and lower levels of the CNS. It contains important nuclei controlling respiration, as well as several sensory and motor nuclei of the cranial nerves. The pons also relays information on body movement from the cortex to the cerebellum.

Contained within the central core of the medulla, the pons and a region of the midbrain, is the reticular formation, a lengthy network of small neurons that we will discuss later. Also running along the lower hindbrain is a pair of structures called the raphé nuclei. These nuclei, located near the midline of the brain stem, contain rich supplies of the neurotrans-

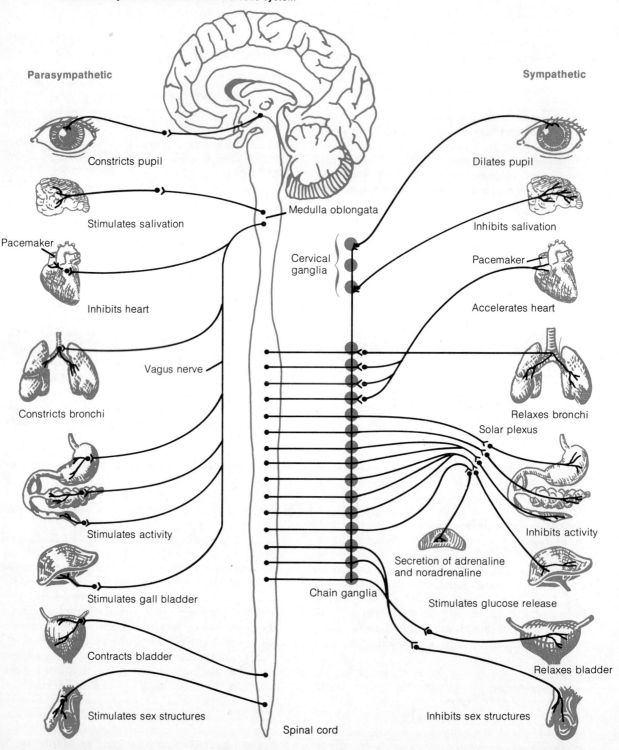

Figure 2–4
Schematic layout of the autonomic nervous system

Parasympathetic

Sympathetic

Constricts pupil

Dilates pupil

Stimulates salivation

Inhibits salivation

Medulla oblongata

Pacemaker

Pacemaker

Cervical ganglia

Inhibits heart

Accelerates heart

Vagus nerve

Constricts bronchi

Relaxes bronchi

Solar plexus

Stimulates activity

Inhibits activity

Secretion of adrenaline and noradrenaline

Stimulates gall bladder

Chain ganglia

Stimulates glucose release

Contracts bladder

Relaxes bladder

Stimulates sex structures

Inhibits sex structures

Spinal cord

The sympathetic division is schematized on the right. The neurons are located in clusters or ganglia that are lined up like a chain alongside the middle portion of the spinal column. In the parasympathetic system (shown on the left), communication with the spinal cord is at the top and bottom of the spinal column, and there are neuron cell bodies in the periphery (away from the spinal cord), often distributed near the organs affected by this system. Each organ is "serviced" by two systems—the sympathetic and parasympathetic—with opposite effects.

Figure 2–5
The lateral surface of the human brain is shown above, and a midline section below; the major subdivisions of the brain are indicated

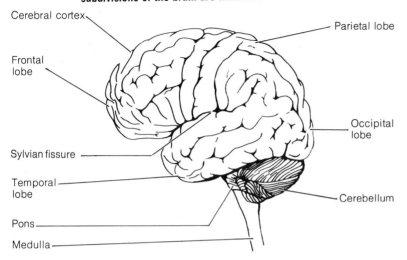

Cerebral cortex
Frontal lobe
Sylvian fissure
Temporal lobe
Pons
Medulla
Parietal lobe
Occipital lobe
Cerebellum

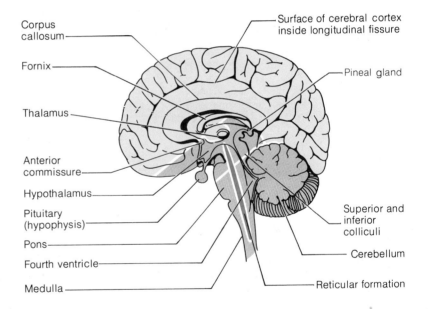

Corpus callosum
Fornix
Thalamus
Anterior commissure
Hypothalamus
Pituitary (hypophysis)
Pons
Fourth ventricle
Medulla
Surface of cerebral cortex inside longitudinal fissure
Pineal gland
Superior and inferior colliculi
Cerebellum
Reticular formation

mitter serotonin, which is thought to be important in producing sleep.

The **cerebellum** lies on top of the pons. It consists of two large connected lobes. The cerebellum is involved in the control of motor behavior. Damage to the cerebellum may result in disturbances of balance, movement, and muscle tone, the severity depending on the extent and location of the injury.

The Midbrain

This structure is located immediately above the hindbrain. It too contains important fiber tracts and nuclei. Extending throughout the core of the hindbrain, and well into the midbrain and beyond, is a network of thousands of nerve cells collectively called the **reticular formation** (Figure 2–6). Extensive study has shown this structure to be involved in sleep, wakeful-

Figure 2-6
Diagrammatic representation of the role of the reticular formation in the brain

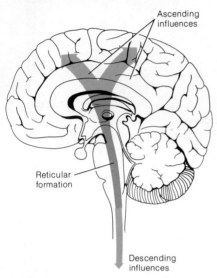

Ascending influences

Reticular formation

Descending influences

The reticular formation can influence higher structures, such as the cerebral cortex, by its "ascending projections," and it can influence the spinal cord by its "descending projections." The ascending influences of the reticular formation are thought to be intimately concerned with arousal and sleep, while the descending influences seem concerned primarily with the excitability of reflexes and other types of movement.

ness, and attention. Damage to the reticular formation of animals may render them permanently comatose, exhibiting all the behavioral and physiological signs of sleep (see Appendix D). Electrical stimulation of the reticular formation awakens sleeping animals. Many of the anesthetic and sedative drugs produce their affects by suppressing ongoing neural activity in this structure. Alcohol is also thought to produce many of its effects by its action on this structure.

Overlying the midbrain are the inferior and superior colliculi. They appear as four bumps on the surface of the midbrain and in front of the cerebellum. The inferior and superior colliculi are parts of the auditory and visual systems, respectively. The superior colliculus is primarily involved in eye movements and eye reflexes. The inferior colliculus plays a similar role in hearing, but also serves as a major relay station for auditory information.

The Forebrain

This part of the brain consists of two parts. The first is the diencephalon—which is divided into the **hypothalamus** and the **thalamus.**

THE HYPOTHALAMUS The hypothalamus is a very small but important structure. It contains nuclei involved in a wide range of behavioral functions, including eating and drinking, sexual behavior, reproductive cycles, activity cycles, temperature regulation, sleep, the expression of aggression, and many others. The hypothalamus has intimate anatomical and functional connections with the **pituitary gland** and controls many of its hormonal secretions which regulate metabolism, reactions to stress, and sexual development and behavior. Many of the hormones secreted by the pituitary gland are manufactured within the hypothalamus itself. This important interrelation between the hypothalamus and the endocrine system is an active area of research. (See color Plate 11.)

THE THALAMUS Lying above the hypothalamus and shaped like two joined footballs, the thalamus contains important nuclei classified into two groups—the specific sensory relay nuclei and the nonspecific nuclei of the thalamus.

The best understood of these nuclei are the sensory relay nuclei. The visual, auditory, and somatosensory (touch and position) systems all have relay nuclei in the thalamus. The information brought from receptors and lower relay stations to the thalamus is projected by fibers from the thalamus to appropriate destinations in the cerebral cortex. For example, visual information from the retina is brought to a specific relay nucleus in the thalamus (see Chapter 3) from which it is projected to a specific part of the cerebral cortex, the primary visual cortex. The thalamus performs a very important relay function (Figure 2-7).

Relaying neural information is not the only function of the thalamus. Many thalamic nuclei project to parts of the cortex not classically defined as sensory areas, and many have been implicated in the control of sleep and attention, probably in collaboration with the reticular formation, pons, and other areas of the brain.

The second part of the forebrain consists of the telencephalon, which contains such struc-

Figure 2-7
The functions of the thalamus

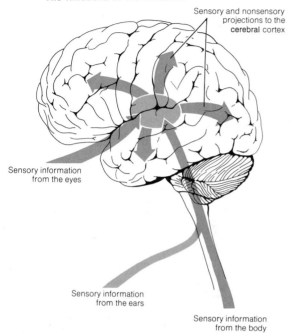

Sensory and nonsensory
projections to the
cerebral cortex

Sensory information
from the eyes

Sensory information
from the ears

Sensory information
from the body

The functions of the thalamus include receiving sensory information from the receptors and their central relay stations and projecting it to the cerebral cortex. The thalamus also projects other information to the cerebral cortex, particularly to the association areas.

Figure 2-8
The corpus callosum

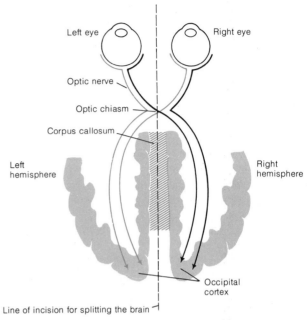

Left eye

Right eye

Optic nerve

Optic chiasm

Corpus callosum

Left
hemisphere

Right
hemisphere

Occipital
cortex

Line of incision for splitting the brain

This view looking down on the top of the brain shows the bundle of fibers called the corpus callosum connecting the two cerebral hemispheres. Studies have been done on the localization of brain functions by severing the corpus callosum and optic chiasm, or crossing, in experimental animals. The split-brain operation is performed on human beings in some cases of epilepsy. Amazingly little ability is lost when just the corpus callosum is severed.

tures as the **basal ganglia,** the **cerebral cortex,** and the **corpus callosum.**

THE BASAL GANGLIA   The basal ganglia consist of a group of nuclei buried deep within the cerebral hemispheres. They are called basal ganglia by convention, although you will recall that in general the word "ganglion" refers to the aggregations of nerve cell nuclei outside the central nervous system. The basal ganglia contain three major nuclei on each side: the caudate nucleus, the putamen, and the globus pallidus. The basal ganglia are important in the control of movement, and their degeneration has been implicated as a factor in Parkinson's disease, a disorder characterized by jerky, uncoordinated movements. Degeneration of the basal ganglia is also a symptom of Huntington's chorea, a heritable disease also characterized by jerky (choreic) movements and mental deterioration.

THE CEREBRAL CORTEX   In most higher mammals, including human beings, the cerebral hemispheres are the largest and most prominent part of the brain. Complex behaviors such as language, numerical ability, and abstract thought are mediated by cerebral hemispheres.

The cerebral hemispheres consist of an outer cortex of cell bodies—the cerebral cortex—and an inner core of white matter made up of myelinated axon fibers (see Appendix B) that connect the hemispheres with each other and with other parts of the brain, including the projections of the thalamus.

The two cerebral hemispheres are connected by a great band of fibers running between them called the corpus callosum, the major communication link between them (Figure 2-8). Surgical severing of the corpus callosum is called a

The Two Brains

Most people know that the actions of the right hand and the rest of the right side of the body are controlled by the left hemisphere of the brain, while the left side reacts to orders from the right hemisphere. Because nineteen people out of every twenty are right-handed, and because studies on patients with brain damage have shown that the faculty of speech is largely centered in the brain's left hemisphere, that side of the brain has long been regarded as dominant in controlling human actions.

But a series of research projects on brain-damaged subjects and normal people is revealing that a host of specialized functions, such as perception and artistic skill, are actually seated in the right hemisphere of the brain. This knowledge is contributing to a new picture of the human brain as an organ housing two entities—largely separate but equal—that think in different ways and can be applied preferentially to any task at hand.

In normal people, the brain's two hemispheres are linked by a large bundle of nerve fibers, known as the corpus callosum. The first scientific studies of differences between the hemispheres started

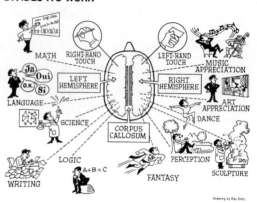

HOW THE BRAIN DIVIDES ITS WORK

MATH · RIGHT-HAND TOUCH · LEFT HEMISPHERE · LEFT-HAND TOUCH · RIGHT HEMISPHERE · MUSIC APPRECIATION · LANGUAGE · ART APPRECIATION · SCIENCE · DANCE · CORPUS CALLOSUM · LOGIC · PERCEPTION · A+B=C · FANTASY · SCULPTURE · WRITING

Drawing by Ray Doty

about a decade ago, using as subjects patients who had had their corpora callosa surgically severed to alleviate epilepsy. Such patients behave perfectly normally except for one thing: their left hands literally don't know what their right hands are doing. One man in this condition, for example, attacked his wife with his left hand while trying to rescue her from the attack with his right hand.

At the California Institute of Technology, psychologist Roger Sperry has used

split-brain operation. The effects of this operation have important implications for understanding how the brain works. For example, under certain conditions the two sides of the brain are able to function independently, as if there were two brains. (See the article entitled "The Two Brains.")

The human cerebral cortex is highly convoluted, with as much as two-thirds of the area of the cortex buried within its own fissures. In lower organisms, such as rats, the cerebral cortex has far fewer fissures. Convolutions are obviously an evolutionary adaptation to increase the surface area of the cerebral cortex. As one ascends the evolutionary scale, convolution of the cerebral cortex becomes more and more pronounced with corresponding changes in the complexity of behavior.

The human cerebral cortex may be arranged into functional areas (Figure 2–9). The three major functional groups are the **motor cortex,** the **sensory cortex,** and the **association cortex.**

The motor cortex Cerebral cortex that engages in the control of movement is referred to as motor cortex. Removal of the motor cortex in human beings results in a loss of muscle tone and the ability to perform fine and skilled movements. However, injury to the motor cortex seldom results in complete paralysis. Many other a number of simple tests on such patients to determine the functional difference between their two hemispheres. In one, the subject is told to describe a pencil he is holding behind a screen, out of his sight. When he holds the pencil with his right hand he has no trouble, but when the pencil is in his left hand he is totally unable to describe it in words—his left hand is connected with his right hemisphere, which has virtually no capacity for speech. However, if the subject is then given a selection of objects and asked to select by feel the one he had previously held, he unerringly chooses the pencil.

These tests, and others showing that split-brain patients can draw much better with their left hands than with their right after the operation, suggest strongly that analytical skills such as language and arithmetic ability are based in the left hemisphere, while intuitive talents such as orientation in space, creative ability and appreciation of music lie in the right hemisphere.

In recent months, some brain researchers have tried to extend these findings to normal people. At the Langley Porter Neuropsychiatric Institute in San Francisco, for example, Drs. David Galin and Robert Ornstein are measuring the brain waves from both hemispheres as their subjects attempt a variety of analytical and intuitive tasks.

Alpha

In one experiment, scientists instructed their subjects first to show their analytical ability, by writing or mentally composing a letter, and then to exhibit their intuitive talent, by arranging colored blocks to match patterns and finding matches for specific shapes from a number of alternatives. The results provided clear proof that the specialization of the hemispheres in split-brain patients is shared by normal people. During the analytical tasks, the subjects' left hemispheres all showed electrical traces typical of mental activity, while their right hemispheres showed alpha waves, indicating total relaxation. On the tests of intuition, this was completely reversed, with the left hemispheres producing alpha. In effect, the hemisphere not called on to exhibit its specialist skills simply idled, leaving the other to do the work. . . .

Newsweek
August 6, 1973

parts of the brain are concerned with motor movements and can, to some degree, take over the functions of the motor cortex.

The motor cortex gives rise to the pyramidal tracts. The axons of these fibers descend all the way down into the spinal cord where they contact motor nerves which control the activity of the voluntary muscles. These axons, which form the pyramidal tract, cross over at the level of the medulla, the right motor cortex controlling the muscles of the left side of the body, and vice versa. It is for this reason that a stroke involving the right side of the brain will result in paralysis of the left side of the body, and vice versa.

There is a good deal of localization of function in the motor cortex. Different areas of the motor cortex control different muscles of the body. Some groups of muscles are represented by large amounts of the motor cortex, others by relatively smaller areas. In general, the greater the area of motor cortex devoted to controlling the musculature of a particular structure, the finer the degree of control we can exercise over that structure. For example, the tongue, relative to its size, has a very large area of the motor cortex devoted to its control. It is for this reason that we can move our tongues in so many directions, movements which are necessary for the production of speech.

Figure 2-9
The cerebral cortex

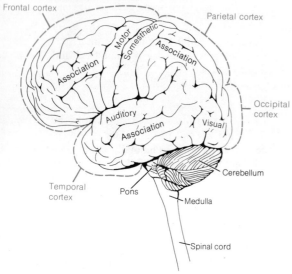

The cortex is often grossly described as consisting of four major lobes or areas: frontal, parietal, occipital, and temporal. Each of the major sensory systems feeds information to the cortex and to a specific receiving area in the cortex. This information is sent to the central nervous system from the peripheral nervous system. Once in the brain or spinal cord, the information is relayed from point to point until it reaches the primary sensory receiving area in the cortex. The figure shows the location of the receiving areas for vision, audition, and somesthesis (touch, pain, temperature). There is also a primary motor area responsible for the initiation of motor movements, located just in front of the somesthetic cortex. Stimulation in the motor area causes a movement of muscles, and stimulation in the sensory receiving areas causes the subject to report that he or she saw or heard or felt something, depending on which primary sensory area was stimulated. Note that most of the cortex is association cortex.

The sensory cortex   The sensory portions of the cortex are so named because they can be regarded as the terminal receiving stations for the classical sensory systems (vision, audition, and somesthesis). A great deal of research has been done on these sensory areas of the cerebral cortex, and much is known about its organization.

We know, for example, that each of the sensory systems is represented by at least one—and in some cases several—topographically orga-

nized areas of the sensory cortex. Topographic organization means that each point of the receptor surface is represented by a specific portion of the sensory cortex. For example, the receptors in the fovea of the eye are connected to specific points in the visual cortex; receptors in the periphery of the eye are connected to other specific points in the visual cortex. Specific receptors on the surface of the skin, which mediate the sensation of touch, are connected to specific regions of the sensory cortex.

In addition to such point-for-point organization found in all sensory modalities, there are other features common to all areas of sensory cortex. For example, within each sensory system there exist cells that respond only to particular aspects of the appropriate sensory stimulus. In the auditory system there are cells that respond only to sounds of a particular frequency, while other cells respond only to combinations of tones. In the visual system there are cells that respond only to light which forms a line of a particular orientation. Other cells in the visual cortex respond only when we look at two edges that form a particular angle. These kinds of data suggest that the responses of different groups of cells might be an important means by which the brain codes and stores sensory information. We will discuss this matter in greater detail in Chapter 3. Evidence suggests that many of these characteristic modes of response by individual cells are present at birth, which indicates that the neural mechanisms necessary to perceive many aspects of our sensory environment are present from the very beginning.

The association cortex   Those parts of the cerebral cortex that are neither sensory nor motor in function have been termed association cortex. These areas occupy by far the largest part of the cerebral hemispheres in human beings. They are involved in the more complex forms of behavior, including perception, language, and thought. There appears to be some degree of localization of function within the association cortex. For example, damage to specific parts of the association cortex produces a loss in the ability to speak or understand language (**aphasia**). In addition, speech and language areas of the association cortex appear to be localized in the dominant hemisphere, which is usually the left one.

Other regions of the association cortex are involved in mathematical ability and other cognitive functions. The challenge to understand the complex functions of the association cortex is immense. Some interesting experimental studies with people have demonstrated that certain kinds of electrical and chemical events are correlated with learning and thought. But the correlations needed to establish a theoretical basis for language, reason, and abstract thought are still uncertain. This much we do know: there is a correlation between the amount of association cortex, relative to other cortex, and apparent learning ability. In other words, there is an evolutionary trend in the development of association cortex; humans have the most, while other organisms tend to have less.

The limbic system The limbic system is not a specific area but a circuit covering many areas and their interconnections (see Figure 2–10). It includes the hypothalamus, the amygdala, portions of the cerebral cortex such as the hippocampus, and a number of other nuclei and pathways. The limbic system has been implicated in a number of functions, including motivation and emotion. Stimulation of certain parts of the limbic system may produce eating, drinking, or aggression. Damage to areas of the limbic system may produce docility and other emotional changes.

The limbic system in human beings seems to be closely associated with certain aspects of memory storage. Removal of the hippocampus, undertaken to alleviate the symptoms of severe epilepsy, can produce particularly striking memory deficits. Such individuals are capable of remembering information they acquired before the operation and can carry on normal conversations and other functions that require only short-term retention of information. However, they are incapable of remembering new information for more than a few seconds. Such individuals are no longer able to store information over long periods. Deterioration of parts of the limbic system due to **alcoholism** provides additional evidence for the importance of the limbic system in memory and other mental activities.

Pleasure centers Stimulation of certain areas of the limbic system and some areas connected with it can produce extremely pleasurable sensations. This important discovery was made by James

Figure 2–10
The major structures within or associated with the limbic system; this system is particularly involved in arousal, motivation, and emotion

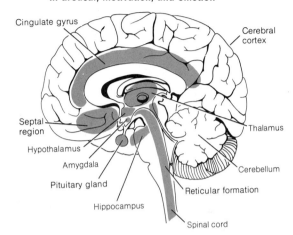

Olds and Peter Milner in 1954, when they showed that experimental animals could be made to press a lever, or learn other responses, when rewarded with electrical stimulation to these "pleasure centers." In some cases rats quite literally starved to death when given a choice between pressing a lever for food or for electrical stimulation. Animals rewarded in such a way will cross electrified grids, swim through water, and undergo extreme exertion. Humans who have been stimulated in these areas report that the experience is extremely pleasurable, and some have equated the sensations to sexual orgasms.

These fascinating findings suggest that these regions of the brain may be involved in reinforcement and reward, powerful methods for controlling behavior (see Chapter 4). Recently, theories have been proposed which postulate that certain types of abnormal behavior, particularly depressive states, may result from functional abnormalities in these reward systems.

THE ENDOCRINE SYSTEM

We can conceive of all bodily activities, including behavior, as being regulated by two interacting systems, the nervous system and the endocrine system. The **endocrine system** con-

Figure 2–11
The endocrine glands and their products (hormones)

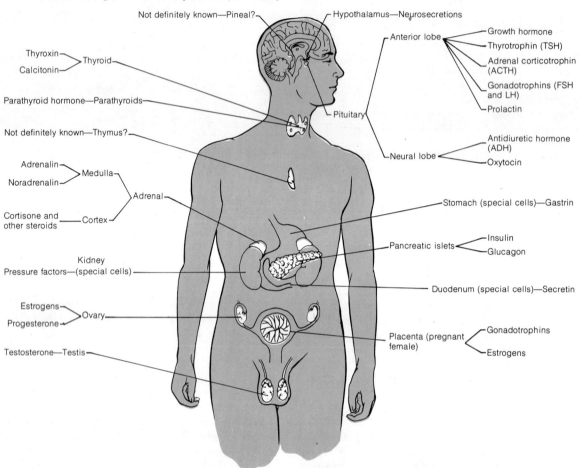

sists of a number of endocrine **glands** located throughout the body (Figure 2–11). Endocrine glands are defined as organs that secrete certain chemicals, namely, **hormones,** into the general circulation. They are distinguished from so-called exocrine glands, which also secrete chemical substances but not into the general circulation; the salivary glands, which secrete saliva into the mouth, are an example of an exocrine organ.

The hormones secreted by the endocrine system function as "chemical messengers" in that they affect the activity of other organs. It is not possible to discuss the endocrine system in any great detail here, but we will mention a few of the major glands, the hormones they secrete, and some of the effects they produce.

The Pituitary Gland

Often referred to as the master gland, the pituitary gland secretes hormones that control the activity of many other endocrine glands located elsewhere in the body. In reality, the pituitary gland, often called the hypophysis, consists of two separate organs, the adeno-hypophysis and the neurohypophysis. The anatomy of the pituitary gland, and the hormones it secretes, are illustrated in Figure 2–12.

The adenohypophysis secretes several kinds of hormones. These include (1) the thyroid-stimulating hormone, (2) the growth hormone, (3) the adrenocorticotrophic hormone, and (4) the gonadotrophic hormone, of which there are three—follicle-stimulating hormone, luteinizing

Figure 2–12
The pituitary gland and its major hormones

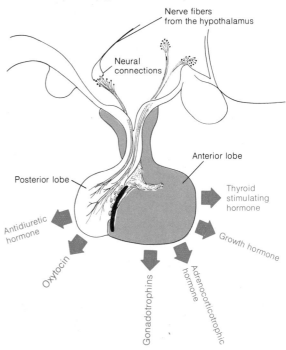

hormone, and luteotrophic hormone. Let us briefly consider the actions of each of these hormones.

The thyroid-stimulating hormone, as the name implies, acts on the thyroid gland to stimulate the production and secretion of thyroxin. Thyroxin is then carried to all parts of the body by the circulation and increases the rate of metabolism of all cells.

The growth hormone serves a number of metabolic functions involved in growth and the maintenance of the body, including the rate of growth of bones and soft tissues. Overproduction of the growth hormone may lead to grotesque increases in weight and body features. This hormone has recently been implicated in the control of sleep.

Adrenocorticotrophic hormones act on the **adrenal cortex** (the outer portions of the adrenal gland) to stimulate the secretion of its hormones, in particular cortisol. Cortisol is then carried to all parts of the body and increases the rate of energy production in cells. This

hormone is particularly important in mobilizing the body's defenses during periods of stress.

The final category of hormones secreted by the adenohypophysis are the gonadotropins: the follicle-stimulating hormone, luteinizing hormone, and luteotrophic hormone. The follicle-stimulating hormone acts on the ovaries to stimulate the development of the follicle that contains the developing egg of the female (see box on "Ovarian Cyclicity"). In males this hormone stimulates the production of sperm. The luteinizing hormone also acts on the ovaries to stimulate the development of the corpus luteum, the small tissue that develops from the follicle after the release of the egg. The luteotrophic hormone also stimulates the mammary glands to produce milk for the potential newborn.

The Control of the Adenohypophysis

The secretion of hormones by this endocrine gland is under the control of the hypothalamus.

The Cyclical Nature of the Ovaries

In females of most species the ovaries function in a regular cycle which begins at puberty and persists until menopause. This ovarian cyclicity can be traced directly to hypothalamic activity. Beginning at puberty, the hypothalamus starts to signal the pituitary to secrete hormones that trigger regularly occurring estrous cycles. These estrous cycles can be divided into two phases, a follicular phase and a luteal phase. Upon hypothalamic command the pituitary gland secretes large amounts of follicle-stimulating hormone (FSH), which results in the secretion of estrogens by the ovaries. FSH and estrogen together cause the eggs to mature, and other physiological and behavioral changes take place that prepare the female for copulation. Estrogen acts on the pituitary, causing it to secrete large amounts of luteinizing hormone (LH); this hormone, in turn, stimulates ovulation and the secretion of progesterone by cells that line the egg follicle. The luteal phase of the estrous cycle now begins; the corpus luteum begins to function as an endocrine organ, secreting large quantities of progesterone. The progesterone depresses further estrous cycles and prepares the uterine wall for implantation. If fertilization does not occur, the lining of the uterus is absorbed and the corpus luteum regresses, signaling the beginning of another follicular phase.

In human beings and some other primates a slightly different pattern has evolved. In these species the uterine wall which has been prepared for implantation is not reabsorbed. Rather, it is sloughed off, in the process called menstruation. In animals that exhibit a menstrual cycle female receptivity is not tied as closely to hormonal events as in animals that exhibit an estrous cycle. Some female monkeys accept males even when they are non-ovulatory, although such behavior has been interpreted as appeasement of male aggression. Attempts to correlate human female sex drives with the stages of the menstrual cycle have not been very successful.

Nerve cells within the hypothalamus produce hormones called releasing factors that are carried to the pituitary gland by a blood system connecting the hypothalamus above the adenohypophysis below. These releasing factors—and there are many different kinds—act on cells within the adenohypophysis, causing them to secrete their respective hormones.

The neurohypophysis, the posterior pituitary, secretes two hormones: antidiuretic hormone (ADH) and oxytocin. ADH acts on certain cells of the kidney to decrease the amount of water passed on to the bladder. Thus, urine is concentrated and the body conserves water. ADH has an important role in regulating drinking behavior (see Chapter 7). Oxytocin has two effects: First, it acts on mammary tissue, resulting in the ejection of milk. Second, it acts on the smooth muscles of the uterus, causing them to contract; this hormone may function in the process of birth.

The Control of the Neurohypophysis

Neither of the two hormones secreted by the posterior pituitary gland is manufactured in this organ. Rather, both antidiuretic hormone and oxytocin are produced by cells within the hypothalamus. From there they are transported to the pituitary along (or in) the nerve fibers that connect these two structures (see Figure 2–12). The hormones are then stored in the cells of the neurohypophysis. The release of these hormones is triggered by nerve impulses transmitted to the pituitary cells along these same nerve fibers.

The Thyroid Gland

In most species the **thyroid gland** is located in the neck, consisting of two lobes shaped like the capital letter H. The function of this gland is to secrete thyroxin, production of which is triggered by the thyroid-stimulating hormone. Thyroxin has a variety of functions, including (1) stimulation of metamorphosis in certain amphibians, (2) stimulation of growth, including the eruption of teeth and the growth of antlers and horns, (3) effects on the nervous system, and (4) effects on the pituitary gland.

An underproduction of thyroxin during development results in a smaller brain with fewer neurons. This may result in a condition referred to as **cretinism,** the symptoms of which include dwarfism and mental retardation. Another condition produced by malfunctioning of the thyroid gland is goiter, which results from an insufficiency in iodine, one of the constituent parts of thyroxin. Goiter was historically treated with burnt seaweed, a plant extremely rich in iodine. In some parts of the world we avoid this condition altogether by seasoning our food with iodized salt.

Thyroxin, as we have already indicated, also has an effect on cells of the pituitary gland, inhibiting the production of thyroid-stimulating hormone. This is an example of a negative feedback loop, one endocrine gland affecting the activity of another. Without such negative feedback the thyroid gland might produce too much thyroxin, causing hyperthyroidism.

The Adrenal Glands

This endocrine organ, located just above the kidneys, consists of two distinct anatomical parts, an inner portion called the **adrenal medulla** and an outer part called the **adrenal cortex.**

The adrenal medulla derives embryologically from nerve tissue, a fact reflected in the hormones it produces, namely, epinephrine (adrenalin) and norepinephrine (noradrenalin). The effects of these two secretions are to prepare the body for emergencies by increasing blood pressure, diverting blood from internal organs to the voluntary muscles, and increasing blood sugar levels. The release of these hormones is controlled by direct neural innervation of the adrenal medulla.

Brain's Opiate

In little more than 20 years, the population of U.S. mental hospitals has been cut from 560,000 to 170,000, and a million or more patients have been restored to bearable, often productive life. This mental-health revolution was brought about by a group of drugs, mostly phenothiazines (best-known: Thorazine). But like all potent medications, these have severe long-term side effects in some patients (for example: muscular spasms of the tongue, mouth or limbs).

Two of the men who introduced drug treatment for mental illness into North America, Dr. Nathan S. Kline, director of New York's Rockland Research Institute, and Dr. Heinz Lehmann of Montreal's McGill University, now report highly promising results with a substance that occurs naturally in the human body.

The substance is beta-endorphin, classed as a hormone, tested by medical researchers as a painkiller and hailed as "the brain's own opiate." Actually it originates in the pituitary gland but seems to exert its effects in the brain. Because camels have a notoriously high tolerance for pain, the University of California's master hormonologist, Choh Hao Li, imported more than 500 camel pituitaries from Iraq and identified and synthesized the active segment—beta-endorphin—of a larger molecule he had identified in 1965.

Kline and Lehmann first thought beta-endorphin might be most effective against depression, but tried it on schizophrenics with auditory hallucinations and victims of severe neuroses. So far, they have treated only 14 patients with a total of 40 injections because the cost is forbidding: $3,000 for one 10-mg. dose. But the effects in treatment-resistant patients have been startlingly good, sometimes lasting for weeks. Schizophrenics have stopped hearing voices, and most patients were, at least temporarily, partially restored to their preillness personalities.

Beta-endorphin works best when patients are taken off phenothiazines. But the average dose of phenothiazines and similar medications costs only a few dollars a week, so these will probably remain the primary treatment until an inexpensive synthesis of beta-endorphin or a comparable substance is achieved.

Time
January 23, 1978

Are Androgens the Libidinal Hormone?

We know that hormones are involved in mediating sexual behavior. In animals of most species castration of the male results in a marked decrement in sexual behavior, even though the ability to copulate may not be impaired. The administration of testosterone to such animals restores sexual behavior to normal levels. Similar observations have been reported for human males in whom gonadal malfunctioning has been known to decrease sexual desire, resulting in less frequent coitus. Replacement therapy—the administration of androgens—restores normal desire and behavior fairly rapidly. These results suggest that the male sexual desire, or libido, is somehow mediated by androgens.

In human females the situation is obviously different. The removal of the ovaries, which reduces levels of estrogen, has no measurable effect on sexual desire or behavior. Neither does the onset of menopause. In fact, some data suggest that sexual drive is increased as estrogen levels decrease. What then mediates libido in human females?

The answer seems to be that androgens perform this function in females as well as in males. For example, when female patients are given androgens for medical reasons, there is an increase in sexual desire. Removal of the adrenal glands, which are the main source of androgens in females, results in a decrease in sex drive. Data such as these have raised the interesting possibility that the androgens function as the libidinal hormone in humans of both sexes.

The adrenal cortex secretes as many as 20 different hormones, collectively called adrenal cortical steroids. These substances regulate many metabolic processes, including metabolism of carbohydrates, balancing of sodium and potassium in body fluids, and influencing the reproductive organs. The secretions of the adrenal cortex are stimulated by adrenocorticotrophic hormone, secreted by the pituitary gland.

The Gonads

The last endocrine glands we will consider are the gonads, or the reproductive glands, the **ovaries** in the female and the **testes** in the male. These structures secrete a variety of hormones that maintain and regulate sexual cycles and accompanying behavior; sexual characteristics; and the functions that accompany mating and reproduction, such as the estrous and menstrual cycles, lactation (milk secretion), and the maintenance of the uterus. Research into the endocrine bases of sexual behavior (see the box on androgens) may well provide clues to explain many normal and abnormal sexual behaviors.

The endocrine system is clearly important in the regulation of many behavioral processes. Some of the effects of the endocrine glands on behavior are direct, but many others are indirect. The hormones secreted by endocrine glands frequently produce their effects by acting on the central nervous system or other endocrine glands. The effects of endocrine functions go far beyond their biological significance. The development of secondary sexual characteristics, body form, and growth, have an obvious impact on the development of an individual's personality and attitudes.

BEHAVIORAL GENETICS

This field of study is concerned with the *degree* and *nature* of those aspects of behavior that are inherited. Behavioral genetics can be said to have begun with the studies of Sir Francis Galton, who studied eminence (genius) among families. His research led him to conclude that genius "runs in families," that is, that the trait is heritable (influenced by heredity). Galton's studies, though not as rigorous as later experiments, suggested that behavioral traits are determined, at least in part, by genetic factors. Since Galton an extensive research literature has accumulated which suggests very strongly that many behaviors are determined by interacting genetic and environmental factors.

"I'll tell you why you're bald and I'm not. It's the genes. I read up on the genes, and, boy, do I know my genes! Take me. I got <u>good</u> genes."

The New Yorker, November 17, 1975. Drawing by Ross; © 1975 The New Yorker Magazine, Inc.

Figure 2–13
Paired human chromosomes

Males and females cannot be distinguished by the first 22 pairs of chromosomes (called autosomes). In pair 23 males and females differ. Females possess two similar chromosomes for pair 23, both called X chromosomes; thus the female genotype is XX. Males have two different types of chromosomes in the 23rd pair, one X and one Y chromosome, and thus have an XY genotype. Note pair 21. Sometimes instead of a pair there are three chromosomes at this position. This "trisomy" results in a form of mental retardation: Down's syndrome, or mongolism.

Genetic Structures

Within the last 30 years scientists have discovered that the structures transmitted from parents to offspring are genes that consist of large molecules of deoxyribonucleic acid (DNA). The genes are carried on **chromosomes,** which are organelles found within the nucleus of all cells. Each chromosome carries a large number of genes. Through the process of cell division called meiosis, human sperm and ova (eggs) are each provided with 23 chromosomes. The combination of the egg and sperm, called fertilization, results in a cell with 23 pairs of chromosomes. Each pair is distinct from all other pairs, and the two chromosomes of any given pair are referred to as homologous chromosomes, one homolog being of maternal and the other of paternal origin. The genes carried on these chromosomes direct the development and growth of all other cells in the body, and they control all metabolic processes within cells. The chromosome complement of normal human males and females, as well as an abnormality in chromosome number, are illustrated in Figure 2–13.

Genetic Functions

The genetic material, DNA, has two functions: it codes for the synthesis of more DNA and for the synthesis of another large molecule, ribonucleic acid (RNA). RNA is transported from the nucleus of the cell into the cytoplasm where it functions to code for the synthesis of proteins.

One class of these proteins, enzymes, controls the metabolism of all cells.

Although we know a great deal about how DNA functions, we do not yet understand the mechanisms by which the genetic material directs the course of development and behavior. Recent research, however, has provided some clues as to how this might take place. For example, some forms of mental retardation are caused by the lack of specific genes and others by the absence of whole chromosomes.

One disorder resulting from the lack of a

The Cruelest Killer

One day in the 1950s, Marjorie Guthrie noticed that her husband, the celebrated folk singer Woody Guthrie, was walking "a little lopsided." Later, she observed that his speech was a bit slurred. She didn't become alarmed, however, until he suddenly flew into a towering rage, even though he hadn't been drinking his usual cheap wine. "Woody," she said, "you're sick."

Just how sick, slowly became apparent. At first, the doctors told the balladeer that he was an alcoholic. But over the next five years, his symptoms gradually worsened. Most notably, the tantrums became increasingly intense. Finally, one young doctor made the correct diagnosis. Woody was suffering from Huntington's disease, one of the cruelest and most devastating neurological disorders of all. Gradually, Woody lost all ability to talk, read or walk. He could communicate with his wife and children only by pointing a wildly flailing arm at printed cards marked "yes" and "no." In 1967, after fifteen years of emotional and physical suffering, Woody Guthrie died in a state hospital.

Huntington's disease is an inherited degenerative disorder of the central nervous system, first described by Dr. George Huntington, a Long Island, N.Y., physician in 1872. It is caused by a dominant gene. This means that everyone who happens to inherit the gene from one of his parents will inevitably develop the disease—and every child of an HD victim has at least a 50 per cent chance of inheriting the gene. What makes HD especially cruel is that the symptoms usually don't appear before the age of 35. A victim unaware of a history of the disease in his family may unwittingly pass it on to his children before he knows he has it. The children of an HD victim must grow up with the terrible knowledge that they, too, may be doomed.

The Guthrie family provides an illustration of the tragic scope of Huntington's disease. Woody's mother had died of it, but at the time some doctors said the malady afflicted only females and that her son was safe. Two of Woody's children by a previous marriage have since developed HD, and the shadow of the disease now hangs over Marjorie's children—Arlo, 29, a brilliant folk singer in his own right (and already the father of three), as well as Joady, 27, and Nora, 26.

Newsweek
September 27, 1976

single gene is a disease known as phenylketonuria (PKU). PKU is transmitted as a *recessive gene,* which means that parental carriers transmit the condition to one-quarter of their offspring. The disease results from an inability to metabolize an important dietary building block, phenylalanine, because the victim does not possess the enzyme that transforms phenylalanine in normal individuals. Severe mental retardation is one symptom. Although we don't know the cause of this symptom, it seems likely that the excess phenylalanine or some abnormal phenylalanine byproduct is toxic to the nervous system and prevents normal development of intellectual functioning. Identification of the mechanism that results in PKU has made early diagnosis possible; newborns are tested for high levels of phenylalanine in their blood. Early diagnosis has also resulted in the development of a treatment technique. Children with PKU are placed on a special diet low in phenylalanine, which helps, although it may not provide a complete cure.

Huntington's chorea is another disease with behavioral symptoms transmitted as a single gene defect. Huntington's chorea is transmitted as a single *dominant gene,* which means that an affected individual transmits the condition to half of the offspring. The tragedy of this inherited disease in a famous family is discussed in the clipping entitled "The Cruelest Killer." Other conditions with behavioral symptoms are caused by abnormalities of whole chromosomes, either autosomes or sex chromosomes.

Genetic Methods

The methods used by behavioral geneticists are quite varied and depend, to a great extent, on the species of organisms used in the research. Of course, certain kinds of breeding experiments we can perform on animals are impossible with human subjects. Research methods used with human subjects include twin comparison, family correlations, and adoption studies. For example, experiments of this type have provided evidence that IQ test scores have a genetic component (see Chapter 6 for a more detailed discussion of this topic). Identical twins are more similar with respect to IQ than are normal siblings. This is the case even when twins are separated at birth and reared in different homes. Twin research has also provided

Schizophrenia Is Hereditary, Says Psychiatrist Citing Study

Bill Bucy

SALT LAKE CITY — A psychiatrist who has just completed a study of the inheritance factor says schizophrenia is hereditary and not produced by environment.

"Just as tall parents have tall children, schizophrenic parents produce schizophrenic children," Dr. Paul Wender said in an interview.

Dr. Wender, professor of psychiatry at University of Utah College of Medicine, said his study of adopted children in Denmark deals a serious blow to the idea that schizophrenia — one of the most common mental illnesses — is caused by environmental factors.

"This study may get psychiatrists and social workers off the backs of parents with mentally ill children," Dr. Wender said. "For years they have been blaming parents for destroying the mental health of their children.

"This attitude is incorrect, cruel and hurts the chances of the children for getting treatment."

Wender and four other doctors began the study in 1963, using former mental patients in Denmark as test subjects. The Scandinavian country keeps detailed records of persons hospitalized for mental disorders and the team chose 79 parents who showed symptoms of schizophrenic disorders.

The research team located, interviewed and tested offspring of these patients who had been placed for adoption as infants. The study found definite evidence of schizophrenia among these children — even if they had been reared by normal parents.

The study then looked at 30 children who had normal natural parents, but who had been reared by schizophrenic adoptive parents. The results showed that those children were no more psychologically ill than children whose natural and adoptive parents were psychologically healthy.

And, he said, the results remained the same when the team studied adults, both schizophrenic and normal, who had been adopted as children.

Dr. Wender defined the chronic schizophrenic as "the typical state hospital psychotic," who has a history of social maladjustment, exhibits periods of confusion and often suffers from delusions and hallucinations.

He said these severe cases usually can be treated, "but they seldom get back into the mainstream of society." However, he said, studying the schizophrenic may help to identify the "borderline" schizophrenic.

"This could be of considerable importance because so-called borderline schizophrenia affects between 5 and 10 per cent of the population," he said.

He said the borderline schizophrenic is often considered eccentric, has trouble relating to others and suffers from chronic mild depression.

"But if we can identify these people through the study of records and relatives, we may be able to help them before they become really schizophrenic," he said. . . .

The Denver Post
August 20, 1974

While most investigators believe heredity plays a significant role in schizophrenia, few are willing to rule out environment as a crucial factor.

---

strong evidence for a genetic connection in certain types of mental disorders, particularly schizophrenia.

Behavioral geneticists who work with organisms other than human beings have used selective breeding and inbred strain comparison studies extensively. Selective breeding is a technique in which animals are chosen for reproduction on the basis of how much of a particular trait they exhibit. Consider this classic selective breeding experiment reported by Robert Tryon of the University of California at Berkeley. Tryon measured learning in rats with a complicated maze. Those animals that made few errors in learning this maze were mated with similar animals, and rats that made many errors were mated with rats that also made many errors. Two strains were established, and the "brightest" and "dullest" animals *within* each strain were mated for many generations. In due course two strains were established which differed substantially in the number of errors they made in learning this maze; Tryon called the strains maze-bright and maze-dull. Given these names, many people conclude that "generally" bright and dull rats had been created. In fact, this is not true. Maze-bright and maze-dull animals behave as predicted when tests are conducted in mazes similar to the one used for selection. In other learning situations maze-bright rats are not necessarily superior to maze-dull animals. Nevertheless, the fact that animals can be selected for this behavior indicates that learning ability is determined, at least in part, by hereditary factors.

Other examples of selective breeding for behavioral traits have been reported. The important concept to remember is that if a trait can be selected for, then it must be influenced by genetic factors. If a trait cannot be influenced by selective breeding, then there is little evidence that it is differentially influenced by the genes.

Another technique in behavioral genetic studies with animals is the use of inbred strains. Inbred strains are developed by mating related animals. As animals are inbred for successive generations, their genetic variability decreases until animals within an inbred line are essentially identical in genetic make-up, just as identical twins are. There are many such inbred strains, some having been inbred for hundreds of generations. When one animal in an inbred line differs significantly from another, the most important determining factor must be environmental. On the other hand, when animals from two or more different inbred strains are reared and maintained in identical environments yet consistently differ in their behavior, one can confidently conclude that the behavior in question is influenced by genetic variables.

Genetic versus Environmental Influences

Modern work of behavioral genetics, however, leaves little doubt that heredity plays an important part in behavior. This should hardly be surprising, since behavior is a function of living organisms whose genetic make-up must be taken into account if we are to understand individual differences in behavior. But we must never overlook the importance of the environment. Rather, we should consider behavior the product of interacting genetic *and* environmental factors.

Psychologists have usually been more interested in environmental than genetic effects on behavior. One reason for this emphasis is the feeling that we can do something about the environment, that it is more susceptible to experimental control and manipulation, whereas the genetic endowment of an animal is fixed. Consider the following example: You raise rats in different environments, one of which is enriched with "toys" to play with—ladders to climb, swings to swing on, platforms to climb and jump off, and so on. The other environment is impoverished—the cages are empty, provided only with food and water. Several studies have shown that rats reared in these conditions differ in behavior; rats reared in enriched conditions are superior, as adults, in learning ability to animals reared in impoverished environments. Not only are these animals different in their behavior, but animals reared in enriched environments also have thicker and heavier layers of cerebral cortex than do animals reared in impoverished environments. These differences are clearly the result of different environments. Recall, however, the two strains of maze-bright and maze-dull rats developed by Tryon. Research has shown that an enriched environment in infancy can compensate for a maze-dull heredity. Enriched maze-dull rats can catch up and perform as well as maze-bright rats. In short, we must remember that the behaving organism always has an environmental history as well as a biological or genetic constitution. An adequate understanding of behavior requires careful consideration of both heredity and environment.

SUMMARY

1. The study of the biological foundations of behavior encompasses an understanding of the nervous system, the endocrine system, and the inherited aspects of behavior. Many basic physiological processes underlie behavior and are studied by biological psychologists.
2. The neuron, although it can assume many different shapes, consists of three basic elements—the soma, dendrites, and axons. The neuron is the building block of the nervous system and is specialized to conduct and transmit information.

3. Conduction is accomplished by the all-or-none action potential. Transmission occurs at functional contacts between neurons — the synapses. It involves the release of chemical neurotransmitter molecules.

4. Transmission of information from one neuron to the next may result in excitation or inhibition of the next cell. All nervous activity — and thus behavior — may ultimately be understood in terms of the balance between neural excitation and inhibition.

5. The nervous system is composed of an enormous number of nerve cells and nonneural elements and is organized into a number of functional circuits and divisions.

6. The peripheral nervous system includes all nervous tissue outside the skull and spinal cord. Sensory and motor fibers of the peripheral nervous system bring information to and from the central nervous system.

7. The somatic division of the peripheral nervous system is involved in skeletal movement and bodily sensations. The autonomic division of the peripheral nervous system is involved in emotional responses and controls the smooth (involuntary) muscles and glandular activity. The autonomic nervous system is organized into the parasympathetic and sympathetic branches.

8. The central nervous system may be divided into three major components:
   a. The hindbrain — the most posterior part of the generalized vertebrate brain — contains the medulla, pons, and cerebellum.
   b. The midbrain — lying above the hindbrain — includes two important visual and auditory reflex centers, the superior and inferior colliculi.
   c. The forebrain — consisting of the diencephalon and telencephalon — is most highly developed in primates. The diencephalon contains the hypothalamus, which controls sleep and wakefulness, eating, drinking, and many other motivated behaviors, and the thalamus, which serves as an important relay center for sensory information. The telencephalon contains the cerebral cortex and several important motor nuclei, such as the basal ganglia.

9. In human beings, the cerebral cortex has become extremely enlarged and convoluted so that it very nearly covers the rest of the brain. An understanding of the functions of the cerebral cortex will make it possible to understand the higher mental functions such as language and thought.

10. The endocrine system is composed of the various endocrine glands. These glands secrete chemical messengers called hormones which influence many aspects of physiological and behavioral functioning.

11. The close relationship between the endocrine system and the nervous system is illustrated by the neural control of the master gland — the pituitary — by the hypothalamus at the base of the brain.

12. A branch of biological psychology called behavioral genetics investigates the heritable causes of behavior. Using the techniques of genetics, including twin comparisons, strain comparison, selective breeding, and so forth, investigators in this area are discovering that inheritance plays an extremely important role in many behavioral characteristics.

RECOMMENDED ADDITIONAL READINGS

Gazzaniga, M. S. *The bisected brain.* New York: Appleton, 1970.

Hebb, D. O. *A textbook of psychology.* Philadelphia: Saunders, 1966.

Milner, P. M. *Physiological psychology.* New York: Holt, Rinehart and Winston, 1970.

Thompson, R. F. *Introduction to biopsychology.* San Francisco: Albion, 1973.

Valenstein, E. S. *Brain control.* New York: Wiley, 1973.

what does it mean?

Although our understanding of the brain, endocrine system, and genetics and their relationships to behaviors is far from complete, there are attempts even now to apply research findings to the modification and control of behavior. Some of the methods used to study the nervous system have been successfully applied to the control of behavior, including surgery to cause brain lesions, electrical and chemical stimulation, and electrical recording techniques. Similarly, our understanding of the role of hormones in behavior has been applied in practical ways. The recent findings of behavioral genetics have also had clinical application. The use of these techniques and findings provides great hope for the elimination and control of unwanted behavior, but it also raises the possibilities of misuse and abuse. There are many questions about the biological control of behavior for future students to consider.

PSYCHOSURGERY

The use of surgery to control behavior dates back to ancient civilizations. The Egyptians and Peruvians used trephining, a technique in which the skull is opened and the brain is exposed, to rid patients of suspected demons believed to cause abnormal and irrational behavior. More recently, particularly during the 1940s and 1950s, an operation in which the frontal cortex was either removed (lobectomy) or its connections with the rest of the brain were severed (lobotomy), was used extensively in an attempt to alleviate certain emotional conditions, particularly extreme anxiety. Although these procedures sometimes resulted in improvement, as often as not they produced human "vegetables."

Such extreme procedures are no longer used widely in medical practice. However, newer techniques of psychosurgery are being used in many hospitals on a more or less experimental basis. For example, surgical techniques have been used in attempts to control violent aggressive behavior and abnormal sexual behavior. In these operations an attempt is first made to locate that part of the brain presumed to be malfunctioning. Electrodes are placed into the suspected area, and the brain is stimulated with low-voltage electric current. If this produces violent behavior, the surgeon can then produce the lesion by simply increasing the current passing through the electrode. Structures that mediate aggressive and violent behavior are often a part of the limbic system, and surgical removal of parts of this system have produced favorable results in approximately 40 percent of the cases. Lesions of certain parts of the hypothalamus have been produced in patients who have committed a succession of violent sex crimes; recall that the hypothalamus is involved in controlling certain aspects of sexual behavior.

Some psychiatrists and surgeons believe that brain surgery should never be used. First,

Psychosurgery Decline Reported

AP

WASHINGTON — Surgery to destroy some of the brain to relieve psychological problems was performed last year on an estimated 300 to 375 persons in the United States, a federal commission has been told.

Political pressure and public criticism have led to reductions in the number of such operations from earlier in this decade, it was reported.

Another 180 such cases of psychosurgery occur each year to relieve "intractable pain" usually caused by some physical ailment, Dr. Eliot S. Valenstein of the University of Michigan has calculated. A third of those patients were cancer victims.

Another study for the commission examined 27 persons who had had the surgery. It found about an even split between beneficial results and no benefits four to five years later.

Valenstein presented his findings to the Commission for Protection of Human Subjects of Biomedical Research, meeting at the National Institutes of Health.

The commission is charged by law with recommending rules to regulate all medical experimentation on humans. It contracted with Valenstein for the first national estimates on how much psychosurgery actually is performed.

Valenstein's survey found that 25 per cent of the psychosurgery is performed by surgeons who do such operations fewer than three times a year. This is "a serious problem" because those doctors may have the poorest results and may not report to their colleagues through medical journals, he said. . . .

Valenstein estimated that from 1971 through 1973, between 400 and 500 psychosurgical operations were performed each year.

But "with the heat on, there are probably 25 per cent fewer operations," he said. "Some young surgeons say they wouldn't touch one with a 10-foot pole. They say, 'You have to go through committees to do it and then be castigated in the press. Who needs it?'"

That "heat" is precisely what led to the commission's formation by Congress.

One member of both groups, Rep. Louis Stokes, D-Ohio, argued at the meeting that the surgery must be prohibited because "it has no therapeutic value," it is impossible for patients to give informed consent before the surgery and it has "awesome potential as a tool for social and political repression of minority groups, political dissenters and the poor."

Psychiatrists, neurosurgeons and neuroscientists who appeared before the commission, however, said that the patients generally are middle-income, paying patients, not the poor. They also discounted the use of psychosurgery as a tool of repression.

The Denver Post
June 13, 1976

Psychosurgery, the destruction of brain tissue to alleviate behavioral problems, has always been a controversial method of treatment. Legal controls on its use, designed to protect patient rights, are increasing.

they point out that the procedures, once applied, produce irreversible results. Second, undesirable side effects, such as irreversible personality changes, are sometimes produced. Other physicians believe that psychosurgery should be used as a treatment of last resort and attempted only after all other methods of treatment have failed. Third, there is always the danger that brain surgery can be used indiscriminately to control unwanted behavior. Clearly, much more research is needed before psychosurgery can be used with any degree of confidence. There are also ethical and moral considerations which must be discussed publicly.

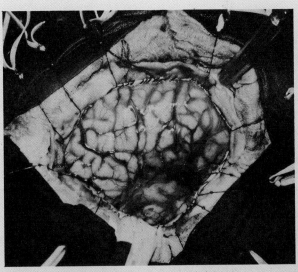

View of exposed human brain during neurosurgery.

BRAIN STIMULATION

Electrical stimulation of the brain has also been used to control behavior. A dramatic example of the effectiveness of this technique has been provided by José Delgado. This neuroscientist stopped a charging bull dead in its tracks by remote-control electrical stimulation of a particular part of the animal's brain. Similar results have been observed in human beings. Electrodes are implanted into the brain, and the patient presses a button to stimulate the brain whenever a violent attack is felt to be coming on. The electrical current calms the patient and the attack is prevented. Electrical stimulation procedures have also been used with some success to produce relief from extreme pain.

Electrical stimulation of the brain has also been used to "program movements." Experimentally, this is done as follows: First, the motor cortex of monkeys is destroyed, and stimulating electrodes are implanted into lower centers of the animals' nervous system. By means of a computer, electrical signals are generated that mimic the normal influence of the motor cortex on these lower brain structures. Thus, monkeys are programmed to move limbs paralyzed by loss of the motor cortex. Similar procedures have been used in an attempt to aid people who are deprived of sensory input. Small computers are programmed to "pick up" certain features of the visual environment. This computer input is converted into small electrical impulses that are used to stimulate the visual cortex. With these procedures blind individuals "see" certain aspects of the visual environment and can avoid objects in their path.

ELECTRICAL RECORDING

For many years it has been possible to monitor and record the electrical activity of the brain by means of surface electrodes attached to the skull. Perhaps the best-known form of recorded electrical activity is the **electro-encephalogram** (EEG) (Figures 2–14 and 2–15). As mentioned earlier, the EEG displays definite patterns during different stages of wakefulness and sleep, and it has been used extensively in sleep research. The EEG is also extremely useful as a diagnostic instrument to detect the specific location of brain injuries. It is used to pinpoint epileptic foci, tumors, or other abnormalities of the brain, such as those caused by accidents. Thus, the EEG is useful not only in detecting brain damage, but in localizing and characterizing the injury.

Another type of electrical activity that can be recorded is the so-called evoked potential. An evoked potential is an electrical signal recorded from the brain in response to sensory stimulation. Within the last decade it has become possible—by means of computer techniques—to record evoked potentials with electrodes placed on the surface of the scalp. The electrodes are relatively far away from where the evoked potentials are generated, which interferes with the recording. However, devices called averaging computers are capable of taking many small and unclear responses and reconstructing them so that, added together, they look like the responses that might have been recorded directly from the surface of the brain.

Several applications of these new experimental methods have already been attempted. For example, evoked potentials have been used as a diagnostic tool to identify hyperkinetic children. Hyperkinetic children have numerous problems, particularly in school, because their hyperactivity prevents them from concentrating on their schoolwork. Evoked responses to auditory stimulation have been observed to be less frequent and lower in amplitude in hyperkinetic children than in a control group of normal children. Drug treatment for hyperactivity has been fairly successful, but therapists have long felt the need for a test capable of screening large numbers of children to identify hyperkinesis, and the evoked response technique offers hope of becoming such a test.

**Figure 2-14
Recording the EEG**

The EEG is recorded by small electrodes glued to the scalp that pick up the tiny electrical potentials generated by the brain. The EEG machine is basically a system for amplifying these potentials and converting them into a written record. The left panel shows a subject wired for a sleep recording. The wires from the electrodes are connected to a "terminal box" in the bedroom, which in turn is connected to the EEG machine in the next room. The right panel shows the EEG being printed out by the pens of the EEG machine.

**Figure 2-15
Normal EEG records showing different patterns of electrical activity for different stages of sleep and wakefulness.**

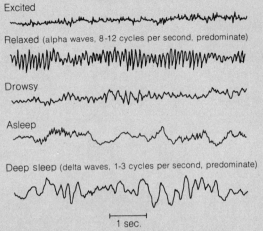

Note that for each level the EEG shows a characteristic frequency (the number of waves occurring during each unit of time) and amplitude (the height of each wave).

PSYCHOPHARMACOLOGY

The number of investigations into how drugs affect behavior has increased and has given rise to a new discipline called psychopharmacology, or behavioral pharmacology. Many processes that take place in the nervous system are based on chemical events, and we can learn a good deal about the functioning of the brain from an understanding of how drugs affect behavior. The potential applications of psychopharmacology are enormous. A recent president of the American Psychological Association has called for the development of drugs to control violence, and he would have the leaders of the world take these drugs to reduce the threat of war. Drugs, as we shall see, have been used with some success to control obesity, insomnia, and sleep. And why

stop there? What about the possibility of producing drugs to increase intelligence, improve memory, increase creativity, and stop criminal behavior?

Research in psychopharmacology has also increased our understanding of the factors involved in addiction, tolerance, and dependence with respect to the so-called drugs of abuse. Examples of drugs of abuse are the narcotics, alcohol, the barbiturates, and the amphetamines. In the case of alcohol, there is clear-cut evidence that heredity plays a major role in alcoholism, and similar suggestions have been made in the case of narcotics addiction. This evidence suggests that there are physical bases for these disorders, over and above the role played by environmental circumstances in the life of addicts. For example, alcoholism may be mediated, in part, by deficiencies in certain enzymes necessary for the metabolism of alcohol, and this lack may contribute to an increased vulnerability

From Joy to Depression

Maggie Scarf

The past 10 to 15 years have witnessed an explosion of research into mood disorders. Now, an accumulation of evidence suggests that a particular class of substances, called the biogenic amines, are central to the regulation and maintenance of mood. The most important of these delicate compounds, as far as moods are concerned, are serotonin and norepinephrine. Both are present at certain critical receptor sites in the brain, and are most highly concentrated in areas associated with such drives as hunger, sex and thirst.

The evidence so far suggests that it is the balance between these compounds at the nerve-cell synapses—what Harvard psychobiologist Gerald L. Klerman likens to "a particular carburetor mix" —that is most decisive in the maintenance of normal mood states. Too much of one or more of them may correlate with spiraling mania; too little of one or more of them may create the conditions for acute despair. And it is possible that the mood drugs achieve their sometimes-miraculous results by reversing an "imbalance" that has somehow occurred in this biochemical system. . . .

Many scientists now think the critical factor is some balance of norepinephrine, serotonin and perhaps other, lesser known, biogenic amines—that crucial "carburetor mix." This suggestion is an attempt to explain the puzzling effects of the drug lithium, which is not only useful in calming and preventing manias, but also works to counteract the "down" phases of manic-depressive patients. How can lithium do two opposite things at the same time?

It may be that lithium restores levels of serotonin in relation to norepinephrine at the synapse. Animal studies have recently shown that lithium does promote synthesis, or manufacture, of brain serotonin. And a current notion, first posited by Dr. Seymour Kety, is that serotonin's role might be that of a modifier, a counterbalance of sorts, at both emotional poles. "The idea is," Kety told me, "that serotonin might have nothing to do with the mood states *per se,* but may be acting to keep those norepinephrine fluctuations within certain bounds at *both* ends of the mood-scale . . ." If one visualizes serotonin as having such a "stabilizing" role, it is easy to see why a mood might go haywire either in the happiness or misery direction— and why one medication might be useful in treating both disturbed states. . . .

Will a growing sophistication in drugs trumpet the downfall of the "talking" types of therapy? Probably not. If a depression is due to a traumatic experience and the individual's adjustment to it, conventional psychotherapy would still be the most valuable approach (perhaps combined with drug treatments). But for the major types of emotional disorders—such as manic-depressive illness or the kind of depression that arises from within and appears unrelated to life crises—drug treatments will continue to offer the most effective relief (with psychotherapy perhaps playing a secondary role).

"Thinking" alone can alter brain chemistry; biochemical processes can alter thinking and feeling. Psychological and biological factors constantly interact within our brains to produce the very human experiences we call mood.

The New York Times Magazine
April 24, 1977

to this drug. Individuals who become narcotics addicts may have inherited nervous systems with unusually large numbers of receptors sensitive to these addicting drugs, resulting in an increased susceptibility to addiction.

We are also beginning to understand the bases for certain types of tolerance. Tolerance is defined as the phenomenon that occurs with repeated use of a drug so that previously effective doses no longer produce an effect. It is important to understand that the phe-

nomenon describes a response to a particular effect. For example, tolerance to the sedative effects of the barbiturates develops fairly rapidly; however, tolerance to the respiratory depressant effects of these drugs develops much more slowly, if at all. Undoubtedly, the tolerance phenomenon is responsible for many of the cases of overdose that are reported for this category of drugs.

An interesting theory with respect to the development of physical dependence is the disuse theory. After repeated use of a drug, its abrupt discontinuance results in gross, sometimes life-threatening, withdrawal symptoms. The disuse theory is based on evidence that prolonged periods of disuse of a muscle results in the muscle's becoming supersensitive. Similar findings have been reported for nervous tissue. Prolonged inactivity of a nerve may result in its becoming so highly sensitive that when activity is restored, the nerve may over-respond to the stimulation. Since we know that many of the drugs which result in dependence are central nervous system depressants, their use may produce prolonged "disuse" of major parts of the nervous system. When the drugs are then withdrawn, the nervous system may be so supersensitive that smooth transmission of nerve impulses is impossible. This results in terrible withdrawal symptoms.

Drug research also promises to contribute to our understanding of mental illness. Certain drugs, when taken in large amounts, can induce a reaction which resembles that of psychosis. A basic understanding of the way drugs produce these symptoms may contribute to our understanding of the psychoses themselves. Finally, we should point out that drug development and drug research have already produced major changes in the treatment of mental illness. The major and minor tranquilizers (drugs used in the treatment of psychoses and neuroses, respectively) have quite literally revolutionized the treatment of these illnesses and have also contributed much to our understanding of the underlying causes of these diseases. For example, there is now good evidence to suggest that some disturbance in chemical transmission mediated by dopamine and norepinephrine may be responsible for the symptoms associated with certain psychoses.

BEHAVIORAL GENETICS

The work in behavioral genetics has far-reaching theoretical and practical implications. It seems likely that at some time in the future we will have techniques which will allow us

"I have to take one three times a day to curb my insatiable appetite for power."

The New Yorker, April 25, 1977. Drawing by Dana Fradon; © 1977 The New Yorker Magazine, Inc.

Not long ago Kenneth Clark, then president of the American Psychological Association, suggested that research in psychopharmacology might some day lead to drugs that could be given to world leaders to curb their motivations for power and their tendencies toward violence, in hopes of promoting world peace. Some day that may be possible, scientifically speaking, but do you think it will ever actually be done?

to manipulate the genes that determine physical and psychological processes. In the future we may have techniques for actually affecting chromosomes in ways designed to eliminate such problems as mental retardation, schizophrenia, and alcoholism. To reach these goals, behavioral geneticists pursue programs designed to reveal the genetic contributions to various psychological disorders; the hope is eventually to develop techniques that will contribute to their eradication. We can also envision genetic engineering designed to produce offspring with more adaptive characteristics, such as great intelligence. Obviously, such research and the knowledge derived from it will create new moral and ethical issues concerning their application.

There is little doubt that behavioral genetics will have an enormous impact on our future lives. It has already changed our view of behavior, from a simplistic belief in environ-

Nature's Sleeping Pill?

As much as half the adult population of the U.S. suffers from some degree of insomnia, which is one reason why the overuse of habit-forming barbiturate sedatives is a serious problem. But two Baltimore researchers have shown promising evidence that a substance called l-tryptophane, found naturally in many foods, may overcome sleeplessness without the risk of addiction.

L-tryptophane is one of the amino acids essential in human nutrition. It occurs plentifully in meat, milk and cheese. Over the past few years, several researchers, including Dr. Ernest Hartmann of Boston's Tufts-New England Medical Center, have suggested that l-tryptophane may act as a natural sedative if taken in a sufficient dose.

To test this theory further, Dr. Clinton Brown of Johns Hopkins and Dr. Althea M.I. Wagman of the Maryland Psychiatric Research Center chose twelve women who frequently spent up to an hour getting to sleep. Over a period of two weeks, the volunteers reported to the center in Catonsville, where their sleep patterns could be electronically monitored. Before going to bed, they were given tablets containing up to 3 grams of l-tryptophane or an inert placebo. The study showed that volunteers who took the largest dose of the amino acid went to sleep on the average in only half the time they normally took to get to sleep—and that they slept 45 minutes longer. Both Brown and Wagman warn that their research to date has involved only a small sample of subjects, and that it has not yet included hard-core insomniacs who have trouble getting any sleep at all.

Just how l-tryptophane works isn't known. But biochemical studies of the volunteers suggest that it may increase the production of serotonin, a brain chemical suspected of playing a role in sleep. Interestingly, the fact that dairy products contain large amounts of l-tryptophane may explain why many people find they sleep better if they drink a glass of warm milk before bedtime. The most important advantage of l-tryptophane over barbiturates or other sedatives is that it is naturally metabolized by the body and won't cause coma or death if taken in heavy doses.

Newsweek
October 13, 1975

mental determinism to a realization that behavior results from interacting environmental and genetic factors.

POSSIBLE USES OF BIOPSYCHOLOGICAL KNOWLEDGE

The potential areas of application of biopsychology are unlimited. Here are two examples.

Obesity

Consider the control of obesity. Research has determined that certain nuclei of the hypothalamus are responsible for the control, both starting and stopping, of eating behavior. It is possible that some day certain types of people with chronic overweight problems will be helped by drugs acting specifically on the hypothalamus.

Sleep

Insomnia is one of the most common problems in the U.S. population. Since biopsychology has uncovered much of the neurological basis for control and regulation of sleep and wakefulness, there is little doubt that help for the insomniac is just around the corner. This could take the form of new drugs that affect the sleep system, without producing the unwanted side effects of barbiturates. Or there may be electrical devices for stimulating the brain in such a way as to produce sleep. Such devices are already in the experimental stage and may some day eliminate the problem of insomnia.

Although sleep research is progressing at a feverish pace, we do not yet know why we need sleep. The most commonly held conception is that sleep is a time of rejuvenation during which certain waste products are eliminated. When we discover the real need for sleep, we can expect the immediate development of procedures that will make sleep less necessary, or perhaps unnecessary. Consider the fact that we all spend about one-third of our lives asleep. Think of the implications of such discoveries.

Alcoholic Tendency Inherited?

Edward Edelson

BAR HARBOR, Me. — There is growing evidence that some people are born with an inherited tendency to alcoholism, an expert in human genetics said.

The geneticist, Dr. Gilbert S. Omenn, Jr. said he has already warned some parents who came to him for counseling that their children ran a high risk of becoming alcoholics.

"If I have a family where several people are clear-cut alcoholics, I tell them that they are well advised to tell their children not to drink," Omenn said.

Prevention is possible because there is no such thing as an "alcoholism gene" that dooms an individual to having a drinking problem, Omenn said.

Rather, alcoholism is the result of a combination of factors, some social, some genetic, he said.

The evidence for a genetic factor in alcoholism is similar to that linking inheritance to other behavior disorders, such as schizophrenia, Omenn said.

The genetic factor in schizophrenia is well established, he said. While only 1 per cent of the general population has schizophrenia, 10 per cent of close relatives of schizophrenics have the disease, he said.

There are comparable statistics for alcoholism. If one parent is an alcoholic, there is a 10 per cent risk of a child being alcoholic. The risk rises to about 30 per cent Omenn said, when both parents are alcoholic.

Boulder (Colo.) Daily Camera
August 10, 1976

Sensation and Perception

3

Ayoung couple is sitting on the ground watching the moon rise over the distant horizon. It is a huge golden-yellow globe, a breathtaking sight. Its large size is so dramatic they decide to photograph it. Later in the evening, when the moon is higher in the night sky, it seems much smaller and far less dramatic. And when the film is developed and printed, the moon appears disappointingly small. What has happened?

A commercial pilot is making the final approach for landing a jet airliner. The night is clear and moonless. The city lights twinkle in the distance, and the unlit countryside below the plane is ink-black. Everything seems normal as the pilot guides the plane in, watching the runway lights draw nearer and nearer. Suddenly, without warning, the huge jet crashes into the ground several miles short of the end of the runway and bursts into flames. What went wrong?

These questions are answered by psychologists who study perception. In this chapter, we will see how the processes of perception work and what consequences they have in our daily lives.

WHAT IS PERCEPTION?

This question has been the subject of philosophical debate since the time of Plato and Aristotle. In trying to find answers, philosophers quickly became involved in answering other equally difficult questions, such as "How do we know what we know?," "What is the nature of reality?," and "What is the difference between sensation and perception?." Experimental psychology developed in the nineteenth century in an attempt to answer many of these questions.

After more than 100 years of research on the nature of perception we can define it in this way: Perception is the process by which the brain constructs an internal representation of the outside world. This internal representation is what we experience as "reality," and it allows us to behave in such a way that we survive in the world. We are forever prevented from directly knowing or directly experiencing the outside world; we know or experience only what our perceptual processes create for us. Normally, these processes work so well that we are unaware that what we are experiencing is an internal construction and not the world itself. Under certain circumstances, however, the perceptual processes fail to operate properly — with a high fever, with sensory deprivation, in schizophrenia, or with hallucinogenic drugs, the internal representation constructed by the perceptual processes is "distorted" and "unreal." People who are basing their behavior on these versions of "reality" say or do inappropriate things which may lead to hospitalization, injury, or death.

The construction of the internal representation is a dynamic process. It is continuously on-going in time and is continually changing. This internal representation is the basis for answers to two important questions: "What is out there?" and "Where is it located relative to me?" Sensory information, memory, beliefs, and expectations all contribute to the exact nature of the internal representation that is constructed at each moment in time.

While reading this chapter, keep four kinds of concepts clear in your mind: physical, physiological, behavioral, and experiential (see Figure 3–1). Physical concepts are used to describe the

Figure 3–1
Relationship among four types of concepts used in perception and how these concepts apply to a real-life example

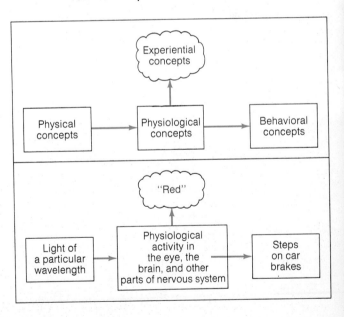

physical characteristics of the outside world. The physical characteristics of light include wavelength and intensity. Sound is described by frequency and amplitude. Physiological concepts are used to describe the behavior of cells, especially nerve cells in the peripheral and central nervous system. Two such concepts are excitation and inhibition, the increase and decrease in the activity of a nerve cell. Behavioral concepts are used to describe the behavior of a complete organism. For human beings, they include what people say and what people do. In a simple detection experiment, one might measure how many times a person said "Yes, I saw that light."

The fourth kind of concept is used to describe the nature of subjective experiences. Unlike the other three concepts, experiential concepts cannot be directly observed. They are private for each individual. If you look at the setting sun and say that it looks green to you, one cannot test directly whether or not you are telling the truth. What is observed is what you *said*, not what you experienced. The goal in the study of perception is to understand the relationships among physical stimulation, neural activity, what a person says and does, and what experiences are generated. We know much about these matters now, yet compared with what there is yet to learn, we know very little. The study of perception is important, for if we can understand how perceptual processes operate, we will have taken a huge step toward understanding ourselves fully. We hope that some of you reading this book today will some day contribute to that understanding.

The Five Senses

Aristotle classified our sources of information about the outside world into the five senses: sight, hearing, taste, smell, and the skin senses (touch, warmth, cold, and pain). These sensory systems work by means of receptors. A receptor is a specialized nerve cell that converts physical stimulation into electrical information. This electrical information is then transmitted to the brain by additional nerve cells connected to the receptors. Receptors can be stimulated in only two ways, either chemically—as in taste, smell, and vision—or mechanically—as in touch and hearing. The senses transform this variety of physical stimulation into electrical signals which the brain can understand and use in its construction of a representation of the world.

Table 3–1 lists some of the characteristics of each sensory system.

VISUAL PROCESSING

The visual system takes light energy and transforms it into patterns of neural activity in the brain. This transformation is not a simple one, but during the past 50 years progress has been made toward understanding it. Stop reading for a moment and look around you. Notice the various objects both near and far from you. Look at their visual appearances and consider that all of them are creations of your perceptual processes. We will now look at the physical, physiological, and perceptual processes that create these experiences. (See color Plate 12.)

The Nature of Light

Light is composed of packets of energy called quanta or **photons.** The physical property of a photon may be described in any one of three different ways: as the energy per photon in Joules, as the frequency of the photon in cycles per second, or as the wavelength of the photon in meters. In this book we will describe light by its wavelength, using a unit very much smaller than a meter, the nanometer (1 nm = 10^{-9} meters). One quantum of 500 nm light has a wavelength of 0.0000005 meters, a frequency of 599,600,000,000,000 cycles per second, and an energy of 0.000 000 000 000 000 000 397 Joules! A 50-watt incandescent light bulb radiates approximately 3,800,000,000,000,000,000 quanta of visible light per second (see color Plate 1). The range of wavelengths that our visual system can convert into neural signals is incredibly small, extending from approximately 400 to 700 nm.

A light source has two important characteristics—the intensity of the light (the number of quanta per second) and the wavelength distribution of the quanta (the number of quanta per second at each wavelength). The quanta that leave a light source travel in a straight line until they strike an object. If the object is transparent, most of the quanta are transmitted through the object. If the object is opaque, some of the quanta are absorbed by the object and the remainder are reflected from it. The ratio of the

TABLE 3–1   Characteristics of Our Sensory Systems

Sense	Stimulus	Receptors	Minimum Stimulus	Equivalent Stimulus
Vision	Electro-magnetic energy, photons	Rods and cones in the retina	1 Photon absorbed by one rod	Candle flame viewed from a distance of 48 km (30 miles)
Hearing	Sound pressure waves	Hair cells on basilar membrane of the inner ear	0.0002 dynes/cm²	Ticking of a watch in a quiet room 6 m (20 ft.) away
Taste	Chemical substances dissolved in saliva	Taste buds on the tongue	Several molecules (depending on the substance)	1 Teaspoon of sugar dissolved in 2 gallons of distilled water (1 part in 2000)
Smell	Chemical substances in the air	Receptor cells in the upper nasal cavity	Several molecules (depending on the substance)	1 Drop of perfume in a three-room house (1 part in 500,000,000)
Touch	Mechanical displacement of the skin	Nerve endings in the skin	0.1 μ (0.00000001 mm) (depending on the part of the body)	The wing of a bee falling on your cheek from a distance of 1 cm (0.39 in.)

number of quanta reflected from a surface to the number of quanta falling onto a surface is called the reflectance of the surface. The *reflectance* may be different for different wavelengths. For example, a surface might reflect all wavelengths equally; it might reflect only long wavelengths or only short wavelengths, or it might reflect wavelengths in various combinations. Thus the exact nature of the reflectance greatly influences the appearance of a surface.

Only light that enters the eye can be converted into neural activity by the receptors of the eye. Because our eye is not equally sensitive to all wavelengths, equal number of quanta at different wavelengths will not cause equal neural activity. In order to measure the intensity of light leaving a surface and at the same time to compensate for the unequal sensitivity of the eye to different wavelengths, the unit of luminance is used. The international unit of luminance is the candela per square meter (cd/m²). All things being equal, two lights having equal luminance, regardless of their wavelength composition, are supposed to appear equally intense when viewed under daylight conditions.

The Eye

The eyeball is an optical instrument much like a camera. Its function is to form an image of the outside world on the **retina**—the network of neural cells at the rear of the eye. It is in the retina that quanta of light are converted into nerve activity. The various parts of the eye are shown in Figure 3–2. The optical system of the eye has two major components, the **cornea** and the **lens.** Take a close look at a friend's eye. The curved transparent surface on the front of the eye is the cornea. Behind the cornea you can see the **iris,** the colored part of the eye. Notice that the size of the opening (the **pupil**) in the middle of the iris is constantly changing. The iris helps control the amount of light entering the eye. The pupil becomes as large as eight mm in diameter in the dark and constricts to two mm in bright light.

Behind the iris is the lens, which you cannot see without a special instrument, called a slit lamp, used by eye doctors. The lens can change

Figure 3–2
The eye

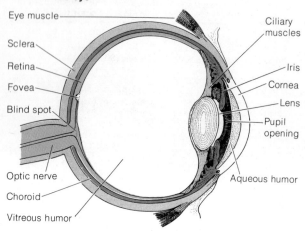

The eye is a complicated structure with many parts. Its purpose is to present an optical image of the world to the retina, where that image is transformed into nerve impulses.

Figure 3–3
The process of accommodation

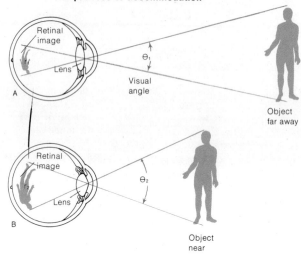

Two examples of optic arrays from objects with their retinal images. Only lines from the extremities of the objects are illustrated. In (A) the object is far away, so the visual angle is small with a correspondingly small image projected on the retina. Notice that the lens inverts the image. In (B) the object is closer, so there is a larger visual angle and a larger retinal image. To provide a sharp focus on the retina the lens has to change its curvature—a process called *accommodation*—so that it is thicker for near objects and thinner for distant ones.

its shape, becoming thinner and thicker in order to keep the image of objects focused on the retina. This process of focusing the image is called accommodation and occurs automatically. People who do not accommodate properly must wear glasses or contact lenses to compensate (see "What Does It Mean?"). Figure 3–3 illustrates the process of accommodation. Notice in the figure that the size of the image on the retina depends not only on the physical size of the object but also on the distance the object is from the eye. For example, if two people, both six feet tall, are standing at different distances from you, the retinal image of the farther person will be smaller than the retinal image of the nearer person. This fact plays an important role in the phenomenon of "size constancy," to be discussed later. The object at a distance is known as the "distal" stimulus, while the retinal image of that object is called the "proximal" stimulus.

The Retina

Once photons from objects enter the eye through the pupil and fall on the retina, they are converted into electrical signals by the photoreceptors. There are two basic types of

photoreceptors in the human retina, the **rods** and the **cones,** named for their distinctive shapes. Actually there are three different kinds of cone receptors. The rods and the three kinds of cones have an important characteristic: they are more likely to absorb quanta of some wavelengths than of others. Figure 3–4 indicates the relative sensitivity to different wavelengths of the three kinds of cones and the rods. In the figure notice that the R-type cone is maximally sensitive to 570 nm light, the G-type cone to 535 nm light, and the B-type cone to 445 nm light. The rod receptors are maximally sensitive to 510 nm light. Also notice that rods are more than 1000 times more sensitive to middle wavelength light than are the cones and that all of the receptors have some sensitivity to all the visible wavelengths.

Since rods are so much more sensitive than cones, rods control our vision at night (scotopic

Figure 3-4
Relative sensitivity of cones and of rods in the retina

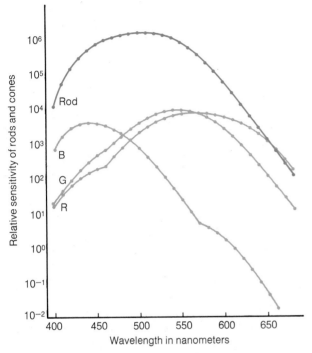

The retina contains three types of cone receptors and one kind of rod receptors. The graph shows the sensitivity of each type of receptor to different wavelengths of light. Notice that each receptor is sensitive to all wavelengths, but in different degrees. Each receptor can be characterized by the wavelength to which it is *most* sensitive.

Figure 3-5
An enlargement of a section of the retina showing photoreceptor connections

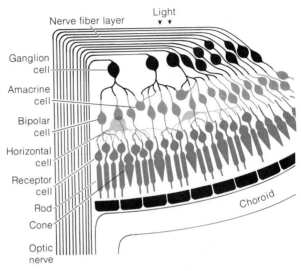

The rod and cone receptor cells are linked with the cerebral cortex by an intricate chain of neural interconnections.

vision). During the day the less sensitive cones take over (photopic vision). Because of the neural circuitry connected to the cones, our vision during daylight is marked by color experiences and the ability to see fine detail. Rod vision, on the other hand, creates only black, gray, and white experiences, with much loss of fine detail. We will discover why there is this difference between scotopic and photopic vision in the section on color vision.

The electrical signal generated by a rod or cone depends only on the number of quanta of light absorbed per second. Once a quantum is absorbed, the signal generated is the same regardless of the wavelength of the quantum. There are about 120 million rod receptors and about 8 million cones in the retina. Of the

three types of cones, there are about 5,225,000 R-type, 2,600,000 G-type, and 1,600,000 B-type. The cones are concentrated in the foveal region of the retina (Figure 3-2), while the rods are completely missing from the central **fovea** and are found in the peripheral retina. An elaborate network of neural connections, involving the horizontal, bipolar, and amacrine cells, connects the 8 million cones and the 120 million rods to 1 million ganglion cells (Figure 3-5). The axons of these 1 million ganglion cells leave the eye and form the optic nerve, which transmits information to the visual areas of the brain.

There are many receptors and few ganglion cells. Consequently, many receptors connect—via bipolar, horizontal, and amacrine cells—to each of the ganglion cells. These ganglion cells send nerve impulses to the brain constantly, even in the absence of light. The base firing rate of a ganglion cell in the dark might be as high as 20 or 30 spikes (action potentials; see Chapter 2 and Appendix B) per second.

Each ganglion cell is indirectly connected to a circular region of receptors. This circular region is called the receptive field of the ganglion

Figure 3–6
Dark adaptation

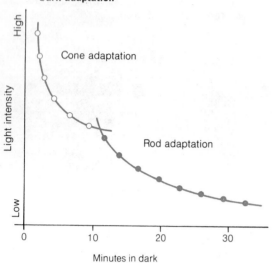

Dark adaptation is measured in terms of the lowest intensity of light that can be seen at a given time. As time in the dark passes, the lowest perceivable level decreases. A laboratory test shows that the process of dark adaptation takes a total of about 45 minutes. Adaptation of the cones produces an increase in sensitivity (shown by a drop in the curve) during the first 10 minutes. Subsequent sensitivity changes are due to adaptation of the rods.

cell. The circular area is divided into a central region and a surrounding region. The effect of these two regions of the **receptive field** on the activity of the ganglion cell is opposite. For half the ganglion cells in the retina, shining light in the center of a cell's receptive field will excite the ganglion cell (increase its neural activity), and shining light in the surrounding area will inhibit the cell (decrease its neural activity). Such a cell is said to have an "on-center, off-surround" receptive field. The other half of the ganglion cells in the retina have receptive fields with just the opposite characteristics ("off-center, on-surround"). An important effect of this functional organization of the input to each ganglion cell is that the activity of a ganglion cell is not much affected by a uniform light filling its entire receptive field because the excitatory and the inhibitory influences tend to cancel out. What is very effective in changing the signal sent to the brain by a ganglion cell is a different amount of light falling on the center than on the surround of the receptive field. Thus, it is

Visual Experiences in the Absence of Stimulation by Light

Your visual system is always active. Even when no light is being absorbed by visual receptors, the nerve cells in the eye and visual areas of the brain are generating signals and creating visual sensations. The following exercise will permit you to experience these visual sensations.

Sit quietly and close your eyes. Notice that although you cannot see any objects, your visual field is filled with speckle-like flashes of light. Now cup your hands over your eyes, shutting out as much light as you can without putting pressure on the eyes themselves. What do you experience? Although the sensation is one of greater darkness, notice that the unevenness and speckled appearance is still there. Finally, go into a room without windows (such as a bathroom or a darkroom). Turn off the lights and sit quietly for 5 or 10 minutes. Pay attention to your visual experiences. Notice that your visual field is filled with an ever-changing gray, and that there are light and dark gray patches that come and go. These experiences are called visual noise and are the result of the constant activity in your nervous system. Visual noise makes the detection of very weak visual stimulation quite difficult.

often said that ganglion cells function as difference or contrast detectors rather than as absolute detectors of light. Later in this chapter we will learn how the organization of the receptive field has dramatic consequences for what we see.

Limits of Visual Performance

When you first enter a darkened room from the bright outdoors, you cannot see at all, and then slowly you recover your vision. This increased sensitivity to light as you remain in the dark is called **dark adaptation**. Figure 3–6 shows the amount of light required for detection as a function of the time spent in the dark. You can see that there are two parts to this function — the cone branch and the rod branch of the curve. After 10 minutes in the dark, the cones become as sensitive as they can. At this point the more sensitive rods take over. Then, after about 45 minutes in the dark, the rods reach their maximum sensitivity. This maximum sensitivity is truely fantastic. Careful measurements have shown that if a single rod absorbs a single quantum of light, the change in the electrical activity of the ganglion cells is enough to generate a very faint sensation. Since some of the quanta from a stimulus are reflected from the surface of the cornea and lens, some are absorbed by the fluids within the eye, and some are not absorbed by rods, about 100 quanta need to reach the eye to assure that one is absorbed by a rod. This sensitivity is equivalent to seeing a single candle flame more than 30 miles away!

Our knowledge about light and dark adaptation can be used to aid persons who function in changing conditions of light and dark. For example, a soldier on patrol at night needs to be dark-adapted enough to see where to walk, yet occasionally must use a brighter light in order to read a map. If an ordinary flashlight is used, the soldier will have to go through the process of dark adaptation all over again. This problem was solved during World War II. Notice in Figure 3–4 that the R-cones (the ones that are most sensitive to long wavelength light, that is, red light) are just as sensitive as rods in long wavelength light, and that compared with their peak sensitivity, rods are relatively insensitive in long wavelength light. What these facts mean is that if the soldier puts a red filter over the flashlight and uses it to read the map, the cones will be sufficiently stimulated to give good visual acuity, but the rods will remain fairly well dark-adapted. This principle is also used by people who must go in and out of photographic darkrooms; if they wear red goggles in the light, they will be able to see more quickly when they return to the dark.

Detection and Threshold

What must happen in the nervous system in order to detect a faint light in the dark? Since even in the absence of light the ganglion cells are constantly sending signals back to the brain,

Fire-Engine Yellow

It may well be difficult to picture a black and white Dalmatian perched atop a screaming fire engine of bright lime yellow, but that peculiar color combination is beginning to appear in fire departments around the nation. Thanks to extensive research by such men as Dr. Stephen Solomon, an optometrist and a member of the Port Jervis, N.Y., volunteer fire department, more and more fire chiefs have been made aware of a stark physiological fact: people are red-blind at night. Says Dr. Solomon, who has published a number of articles on color research: "The color red is one of the least visible colors and rates next to black for getting attention."

Fire chiefs have seen the consequences of this principle. Chief Bernie Koeppen of Wheeling, Ill., has changed to lime yellow, even for the department's ambulance. "In accident after accident involving red wagons," he notes, "all you hear is, 'I didn't see it. I didn't see it.'" Adds Chief Ed Underwood of St. Charles, Mo.: "The majority of fire fighters killed or wounded catch it on their way to fires. Red is dead. Lime yellow is the coming color."

Fire engines have been red for so long (for no visible reason) that the switchover may create problems. Ted Haberman, manager of Pueblo West, Colo., points out that automobile drivers are accustomed to red as the danger color, and that since many Americans ride in air-conditioned cars with the windows rolled up, they may not hear the siren from approaching, unfamiliar lime yellow wagons. Simple tradition may also militate against a wholesale switch from red. But as Dr. Solomon accurately observes: "Firemen have one tradition that is stronger, and that is to stay alive."

Time
July 10, 1972

Here's a case in which the inability to see red in the dark may be dangerous.

the light falling on the retina must change this activity enough to be noticed. The act of detection involves two separate processes — a sensory process (in this case the visual areas of the brain) and a decision process (its location in the brain is not known). The job of the sensory process is to create visual experiences from the activity

Figure 3-7

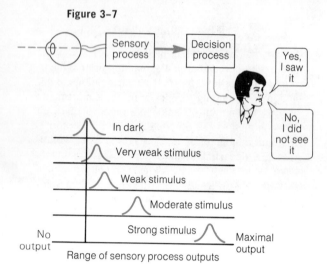

The sensory process converts physical light energy into nerve signals and experiences of brightness. There is some variability or "noise" in this process. The exact output of the sensory process at any moment depends on the intensity of (1) the stimulus and (2) the noise.

of the ganglion cells. The job of the decision process is to decide whether or not a particular visual experience resulted from light being absorbed by the retina or from random activity in the retina (see Figure 3-7) and then to control your behavior such that you decide to say "yes, I saw that light" or "no, I did not see the light." It is important to note that the decision process has access only to the output of the sensory process and not to the world directly.

As Figure 3-7 shows, when a very weak light is being detected, the range of sensations generated by the sensory process does not differ much from the sensations generated randomly in the dark. It is therefore impossible to detect a very weak light with 100 percent accuracy. That is, if you were being tested, you would often say that you saw a light when there was none and that you did not see a light when in fact it was really there.

When the physical intensity of the light is made stronger, the sensations created by the sensory process are likewise stronger and vary more from the sensations created by random activity. It is therefore possible to distinguish the presence of the light more accurately. For lights

of even greater intensity, the sensations produced by the sensory process are so different from those produced by random activity that you could correctly detect the light 100 percent of the time.

A **threshold** is the amount of physical stimulus required to achieve a certain level of correctness in a detection task. We often use the stimulus intensity necessary for 75 percent correct as threshold, but this choice is arbitrary, and other values are sometimes used. We want to emphasize the point that a threshold is arbitrarily defined. If a stimulus is below threshold, it is detected less often; if it is above threshold, it is detected more often. Very precise experiments in vision and hearing have failed to find a stimulus intensity below which the stimulus is *never* detected. There is always a very low percentage of detection even with the weakest stimuli possible.

The absolute threshold is the minimum amount of stimulus energy detectable in the dark. It represents the best performance the the visual system can muster. The relative threshold (or differential threshold) is the amount of stimulus energy required for detection of a light against a background of a fixed light intensity. For example, how intense does a spot of light have to be in order to detect it 75 percent of the time when it is presented on a uniformly lit wall? The answer depends on the luminance of the light on the wall itself. The more intense the light on the wall, the more intense the spot has to be in order to be detected. At higher, daylight levels of intensity, detecting the spot follows Weber's Law (see box on p. 19).

The detection process described here (Figure 3-7) illustrates how our knowledge of perception requires knowledge in the four conceptual areas mentioned at the beginning of the chapter. Light (a physical concept) consists of quanta of various wavelengths. These are absorbed by photoreceptors in the eye resulting in excitation and inhibition of ganglion cell activity (physiological concepts). The sensory process creates visual experiences and sensations (experiential concepts) from the nerve activity. The decision process decides what behavior is appropriate and carries it out by saying something or making some other kind of response (behavioral concepts).

The resolution threshold—the ability to dis-

Figure 3–8
Visual acuity as a function of light intensity

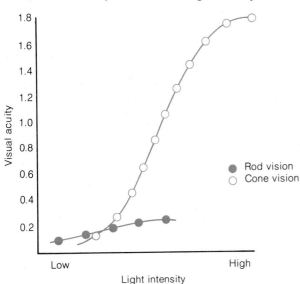

Visual acuity depends upon the intensity of light. Our acuity is much better in daylight than at night.

Figure 3–9
Grating patterns used in laboratory measurements of visual resolution

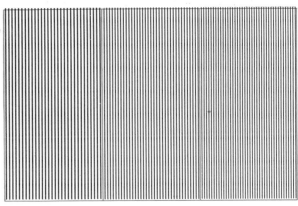

criminate fine details—is a threshold very important in our daily lives. We usually express the resolution threshold in terms of **visual acuity**—the lower the threshold, the better the visual acuity. A person with poor visual acuity has difficulty reading, sewing, or doing other tasks that require the perception of fine detail. The ability to perceive fine detail depends on the focus of the eye (see "What Does It Mean?") and on the nature of ganglion cell receptive fields. When light levels are low, and rods are operating, receptive fields are large with little excitation or inhibition from the surround region. As the light levels increase, and cones begin to operate, the ganglion cell receptive fields grow smaller, more precise, with much interaction between the center and surrounding regions of the receptive field. These conditions allow the ganglion cell to detect very small differences in the amount of light falling in the two regions. As you know, our visual acuity is very poor under low light conditions and steadily improves with increases in illumination, as shown in Figure 3–8. Like the dark-adaptation function (Figure 3–6), the increase in acuity shown in Figure 3–8 has two branches: a lower one, corresponding to rod vision, and

an upper one, corresponding to cone vision. The level of illumination at which your eye switches from rods to cones is the level of light cast by the full moon on a clear night.

Under ideal conditions the resolution of our visual system is remarkable. Experiments have found that persons with normal vision can detect a fine black line with an angular width of 0.5 seconds of arc. Such resolution is equivalent to detecting a ¼-inch black wire against the bright sky from more than a mile and a half away!

In the laboratory, visual acuity can be measured by discovering the finest grating pattern in which a person can just detect the lines 75 percent of the time (threshold). Such gratings are shown in Figure 3–9. In a well-lit room, find the distance between your eyes and this page at which the right-hand grating (the finest) is just visible. As you move the page away, this grating will disappear, although the others remain visible. Repeat the measurement in a dim room and notice how much closer you have to be in order to see the lines. In the dim light, the grating must be coarser in order to see it.

When you visit an optometrist or ophthalmologist (eye doctors) to have your eyes checked, he or she will first measure your visual acuity. The doctor will not use gratings for this purpose, but probably a letter chart like the one shown in Figure 3–10. Nevertheless, the doctor will measure your threshold—the size letter you can read with 75 percent accuracy. Tests have determined the size letter the average person

Figure 3–10
Visual acuity tests

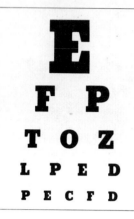

Above are two patterns commonly used for clinical tests of visual acuity. The Snellen letters (on the left) use lines and spaces that become progressively smaller as one reads down the chart. The Landolt C pattern (on the right) requires the viewer to locate the position of the gap—up, down, right, or left. The viewing chart consists of a series of C patterns of decreasing gap size. This test is somewhat more sensitive than the Snellen test, because the perceiver might be able to name a Snellen letter correctly even though only part of it was seen.

can read on the eye chart while standing 20 feet away. If, standing also at 20 feet from the chart, you are just able to read that size print with about 75 percent accuracy, your visual acuity is 20/20, which is considered normal. If you are able to read finer print, which a person with normal vision could read only by standing 15 feet from the chart, your visual acuity is 20/15, better than normal. On the other hand, if you can read print standing at 20 feet that a normal person is able to read standing at 40 feet, your acuity is 20/40, which is below normal.

Representation of Visual Qualities: Color Perception

Look around you for a moment. One of the important functions of the sensory processes is to create experiences associated with the surfaces of the objects in your internal representation of the world. Of these different experiences, the most important is the experience of color.

In daylight vision, the sensory processes are able to create a wide variety of color experiences that better enable you to tell one object from another. Color is a descriptive name for a set of experiences; color is not a physical property of light. Today a lot is known about color vision and the mechanisms that create it. Certain individuals do not have normal sensory mechanisms and do not, therefore, have normal color vision. Such people are (incorrectly) called color blind.

The experiences we call color experiences are actually composed of three separate and independent experiences (psychological dimensions): hue, saturation, and brightness. **Hue** is the dimension of color experience to which we give different qualitative names, like red, violet, blue, yellow, purple, and green. The second dimension of color experience is called **saturation,** which is a description of how much hue there is in a particular color experience. For example, white light is a completely unsaturated color experience. Pink is a partially saturated color experience, while red is a deeply saturated experience. The third dimension of color is **brightness,** an experience that ranges from light to dark. Black and white form the two extremes of the experience. Navy blue, for example, is relatively dark compared with powder blue. Since any color experience may be described by its hue, saturation, and brightness, all possible colors may be represented in a three-dimensional color solid (color Plate 2).

How do our sensory processes create color experience from the light absorbed by receptors? Color Plate 3 presents a schematic diagram of the color mechanism along with a representation of the various hues and saturations the mechanism can create. The nervous system creates colors by comparing the rate at which the three kinds of cone receptors are absorbing quanta. Figure 3–4 shows how the three types of cones differ in their sensitivity to different wavelengths. The three types of cones, called R-, G-, and B-types, are believed to contain different kinds of photopigments. The only thing a receptor can do is to give an electrical signal that is proportional to the number of quanta absorbed. If light falling on the retina contains mostly long wavelength quanta, then the R-cones will give the largest signal. Light containing mostly short wavelengths will cause the B-cones to be most active. Light containing equal amounts at all the visible wavelengths will cause equal activity in all three types of cones.

The outputs of the three cones are only the beginning. Next, neural mechanisms, called opponent processes, compare the activity of the cones with each other. There are two of these channels. The activity of these two channels is combined to form the color experiences of hue and saturation. The first channel, the R/G channel, compares the activity in the R-cones with the activity in the G-cones. If the two are equal, the R/G channel does not change its resting signal to the brain. If, however, the R-cone is getting more quanta than the G-cone, the R/G channel increases its activity. If, on the other hand, the G-cone is absorbing more quanta than the R-cone, the R/G channel decreases its activity.

The second color channel, the Y/B channel, compares the activity of the B-cones with the summed activity of the R- and G-cones (R + G). If the light falling on the retina contained mostly short wavelength quanta, the B-cone would be most active, and the Y/B channel would decrease its activity. If the R- and G-cones were absorbing more quanta than the B-cones, the Y/B channel would increase its activity.

Color experience is created in the brain by different combinations of signals from the R/G and Y/B channels. These possible combinations are represented in color Plate 3 as a color surface (a slice through the color solid in Plate 2). The exact color, hue, and saturation you experience depends on the place on the color surface that is stimulated by the activity of the two color channels. For example, if the two channels are both signaling at their resting level, the color experience you have is colorless (white or gray), as shown in the middle of the surface. High activity on the R/G channel combined with medium activity on the Y/B channel creates the perception of red. A medium activity on the R/G channel and a high activity on the Y/B channel create the perception of yellow. A low activity on both channels creates the perception of purple.

Also shown on color Plate 3 are the color experiences generated by light of single wavelengths (monochromatic light). These experiences are as far away from the white center as possible and are therefore the most saturated experiences possible. It is not possible to create color experiences that are more saturated than those created by monochromatic light. Notice that the experience of purple cannot be created by light of a single wavelength. In order to experience purple, the color mechanism must be presented with several wavelengths simultaneously—in this case, long and short wavelengths.

Another feature of the color space shown in Plate 3 is that it predicts what color you would experience if two lights were mixed together. For example, if you mixed monochromatic light of 400 nm wavelength with 700 nm light, the color perceived in the mixture would be one of the colors that falls along the straight line connecting these two points. The exact color depends on the relative amounts of each light. If the straight line connecting two colors passes through the point marked "white," the two colors are said to be complementary. Two complementary colors, when mixed together in the right proportions, will produce an experience lacking a hue (white). (See color Plates 4, 5, and 6.)

There is a third mechanism in the perceptual process shown in color Plate 3. This channel, the Brightness-channel, signals the total activity of the R-, G-, and B-cones. The activity in the Brightness-channel is used to code the perceptual experience of brightness. We will consider some of the properties of brightness perception shortly. To summarize, there are three channels: R/G and Y/B working together tell us about the hue and the saturation of a light; the Brightness-channel tells us about the brightness of a light.

Color Blindness

Some people do not have normal color mechanisms. These people are missing one or more of the three types of cones. The most common type of color deficiency is red-green blindness caused by the lack of either the R-cones or the G-cones. These two types of red-green defective mechanisms are shown in Figure 3–11. An example of a test for red-green blindness is shown in color Plate 7. Such people are called red-green blind because they are unable to distinguish between colors a normal person experiences as red and green. The term "color blind" is not really appropriate, however. Although the R/G color channel does not work properly in these defective mechanisms, the Y/B channel is almost completely normal. Careful experiments

Figure 3–11

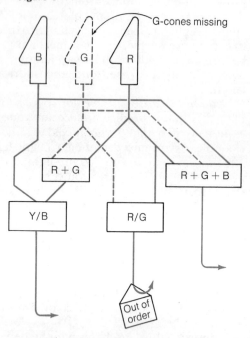

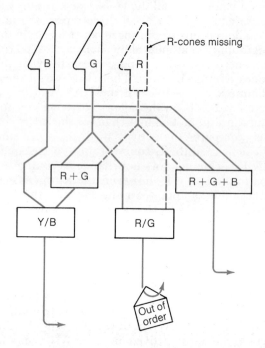

Two conditions are responsible for red-green blind-ness: a lack of G-cones (left) or a lack of R-cones (right). In both cases the missing cones affect the R/G color channel but not the Y/B color channel.

with people who are red-green blind in one eye, yet have normal color vision in the other eye (a very rare condition—fewer than 50 cases have ever been found), have shown that a red-green color blind person experiences the world in colors consisting of blue and yellow hues. Color Plate 8 attempts to represent the color experiences of various types of color-defective people.

We saw earlier that both rods and cones are connected to ganglion cells. At daylight levels of light intensity, the cones are able to function, and therefore the signals that are sent to the brain by ganglion cells reflect cone activity. At night, however, the cones do not function and the rods take over. Ganglion cell signals to the brain reflect rod activity. Take a good look at the color model in Plate 3. In order to operate properly, the opponent mechanisms need to get input from cones with different spectral sensitivities to wavelengths. At night the three different types of cones are replaced by one type of rod, and the opponent color mechanisms now receive identical inputs. The result of this condition is that the R/G and the Y/B channels

send signals to the brain indicating that all receptors are absorbing equal numbers of quanta, the condition that creates the perception of white.

The next time you are outside at night, look carefully at the colors of objects around you. You will notice that your perceptual experience consists only of shades of gray. Objects appear as lighter or darker shades of gray, but there are no hue experiences. These experiences of shades of gray are a consequence of the rods being connected to the opponent channels. These channels, regardless of the wavelength composition of the stimulating light, always signal the same message to the brain—equal activity in all receptors—and this message creates the experience of white and shades of gray. The only channel that can give different signals to the brain is the Brightness-channel, the one used to code brightness.

Brightness Perception

Look around the room. Notice that objects have various brightnesses, ranging from the white of the paper of this book to the black of the ink. The perceptual experience of brightness is created by your perceptual mechanisms and depends upon the relative intensities of light coming from objects to your eye. Actually, the brightness of an object is closely related to its reflectance. For example, the white sheet of paper in front of you reflects about 80 percent of the light falling on it, while the ink reflects about 5 percent (a 16 to 1 ratio for the paper over the ink). Because of the way ganglion cells are connected to receptors (circular, center-surround receptive fields), the signal sent to the brain is based on the relative stimulation (a ratio) of adjacent retinal regions, not upon the absolute levels. When you look at this page, the receptors receiving light from the white page are absorbing about 16 times as many quanta per second as the receptors receiving light from the black letters. This ratio (16 to 1) remains constant regardless of the level of illumination on the page.

The ganglion cells signal this ratio to the perceptual processes where it is used to create the perception of black and white. It is for this reason that objects keep their relative brightness in the bright sunlight and in a darkened room. A lump of coal will look black in your cellar or in daylight because in both cases it reflects less light to your eye than other objects around it.

The ability of your perceptual processes to create brightness perception over a wide range of light levels is called **brightness constancy.** It is one of a number of constancies and reflects a general principle of the perceptual processes: properties of objects remain constant in spite of widely changing viewing conditions. Think how unstable the world around you would be if a piece of paper, for example, changed in appearance from black to white when you went from a darkened room to bright sunlight.

The creation of the experience of brightness is not as simple as we have outlined. The brightness of a particular object depends not only on the activity of ganglion cells stimulated by the image of that object but also on the kind of stimulation in adjacent retinal regions. Figure 3–12 contains two small squares that are reflecting equal amounts of light into your eye. Yet the squares do not appear equally bright. The square on the right, surrounded by a white field, appears darker than the one on the left,

**Figure 3–12
Brightness contrast**

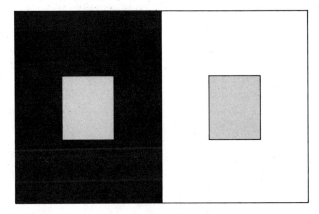

Even though the two center squares reflect exactly the same amount of light to your eye, the one on the right appears darker because of the contrast effect with the white surrounding area.

surrounded by a black field. This phenomenon is called **brightness contrast** and is based on the fact that the retinal areas adjacent to the central squares are not being stimulated equally.

Figure 3–13 shows other examples in which the perceived brightness of a surface does not correspond to the luminance of the light coming from the surface, but is influenced by the luminance of adjacent areas as well. Although each of the strips in the left figure reflects light uniformly (that is, the left side of each strip reflects exactly as much light as the right side of the strip), they do not appear to be at all uniform in brightness. This perceptual effect is a consequence of the ability of the visual system to enhance edges. The dark and light strips at each edge are called Mach bands. In the same manner, in the drawing on the right, the Hermann grid, the light reflected from the white areas is uniform in all places, yet in the regions of the four black corners, light gray spots appear. These spots are creations of your perceptual system and do not correspond to a lower light intensity coming from these regions. Both of these perceptual phenomena are a consequence of the circular, center-surround organization of ganglion cell receptive fields. Because these cells respond to the difference between the light falling in the center and the light falling in the surround of their receptive fields, they best respond to edges and not to uniform light.

Figure 3-13
Brightness perception as a consequence
of the receptive fields of ganglion cells

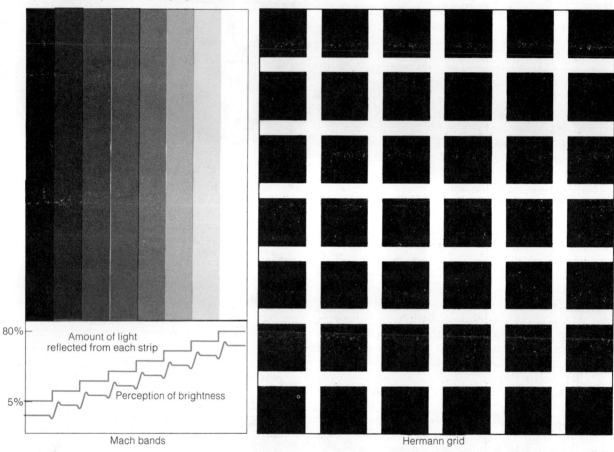

80%

Amount of light
reflected from each strip

5%

Perception of brightness

Mach bands

Hermann grid

PERCEPTION OF OBJECTS

The perceptual processes constantly answer two important questions: "What is out there?" and "Where is it?" Our internal representation of the world is filled with objects. Our perceptual processes rarely fail to successfully create objects out of physical input to the visual system. Even if the physical stimulus is ambiguous, an internal representation of an object will be created. This fact leads different people, exposed to the same stimulus, to experience entirely different things (see Chapter 6 for a discussion of eye-witness testimony). Since very little is known about the physiological processes involved in object perception, we will examine this area first.

Role of the Visual Cortex in Object Perception

Many of the retinal ganglion cells send their signals to the visual cortex of the brain through the lateral geniculate body (see Chapter 2). There is an orderly relationship between a region of the retina and a region in the visual cortex. It has been known for a long time—from studies of patients with strokes and soldiers wounded on the battlefield—that injury to a restricted region of the visual cortex causes blindness in a restricted region of the visual field. Figure 3-14 shows the extent of vision (the visual fields) of the left and right eyes of a normal person. Normally there is a blind area in each eye (the dark black area on each field) where the

Figure 3-14
Normal vision field

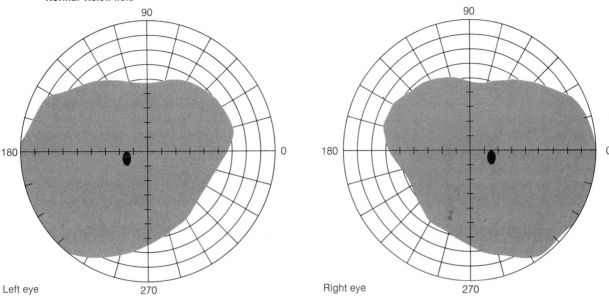

Left eye

Right eye

Figure 3-15
Blind spot demonstration

Do you find this person annoying? Make him disappear by positioning his image on the blind spot of your right eye. Close your left eye and fixate the cross with your right eye. At a viewing distance of about 14 inches, the face will disappear but the vertical lines will not.

blood vessels and the optic nerve enter the eye (Figure 3–15). Each eye is able to see more than 100 degrees to the outside, about 60 degrees on the nasal side, and about 60 degrees up and down. Figure 3–16 is a photograph of a soldier shortly after surgical removal of most of the left visual cortex, which had been extensively damaged by shell fragments. This patient was completely unable to detect objects in his right visual field and suffered blindness in regions of his left

Figure 3–16
Soldier after battlefield injury prior to cosmetic surgery

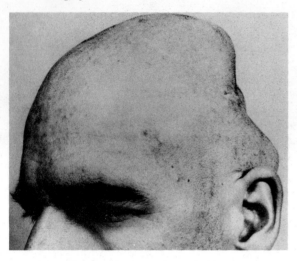

Figure 3–18

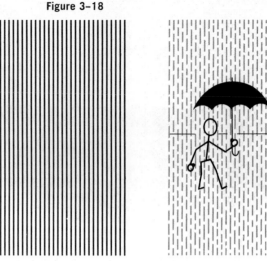

Look at the center of the left panel for two minutes, then look at the right drawing. The rain disappears for a few seconds. Two minutes of staring causes a fatigue in the detectors so that they cannot detect the rain.

Figure 3–17
Mapping the receptive field of a cell in the visual cortex

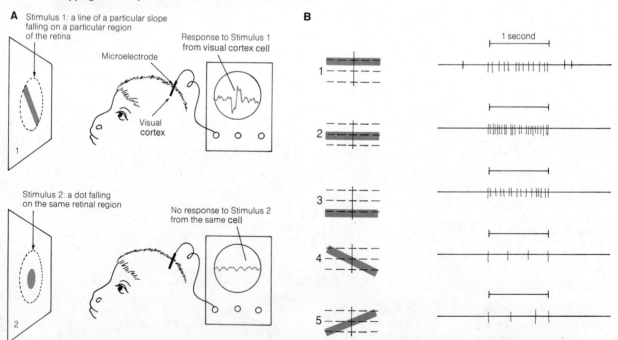

A Stimulus 1: a line of a particular slope falling on a particular region of the retina

Microelectrode

Response to Stimulus 1 from visual cortex cell

Visual cortex

Stimulus 2: a dot falling on the same retinal region

No response to Stimulus 2 from the same cell

B

1 second

Mapping the receptive field of a cell with a microelectrode implanted in the cortex. Panel A shows that single cortical cells are sensitive to stimuli of a particular type and from a particular area of the retina. In this case, only the slanted bar, and not the dot, elicits a cortical response. The responses of a single cortical cell to five different bar stimuli are shown in panel B. Note that the cell responds mainly to the horizontal bar and hardly responds at all to the slanted bars. Note too that the cell is also somewhat sensitive to location—it fires maximally when the horizontal bar is in the center of the field and responds less when the bar is higher or lower in the visual field. The bar was present for 1 second, indicated by the line above each of the five records.

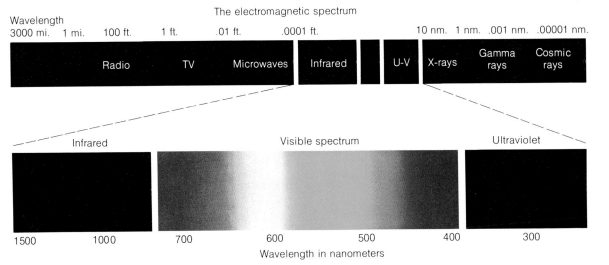

The electromagnetic spectrum

Wavelength											
3000 mi.	1 mi.	100 ft.	1 ft.	.01 ft.	.0001 ft.		10 nm.	1 nm.	.001 nm.	.00001 nm.

Radio · TV · Microwaves · Infrared · U-V · X-rays · Gamma rays · Cosmic rays

Infrared   Visible spectrum   Ultraviolet

1500	1000	700	600	500	400	300

Wavelength in nanometers

Plate 1   The electromagnetic spectrum

The full spectrum of electromagnetic radiation, of which the human eye can see only the narrow band extending from 400 to 700 nanometers in wavelength. A nanometer (abbreviated nm.) is a very small unit of length equivalent to 1/1,000,000,000 meter (a meter is 39.37 inches).

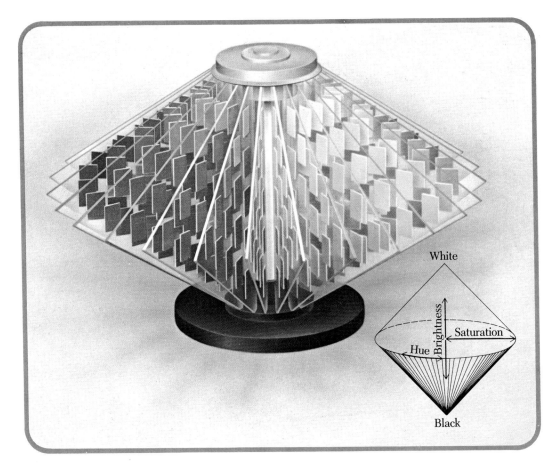

Plate 2   Color solid

Three dimensions of color sensitivity—hue, brightness, and saturation—can be seen in this color solid. The gradual change in brightness from black to white along the central axis is illustrated by the diagram.

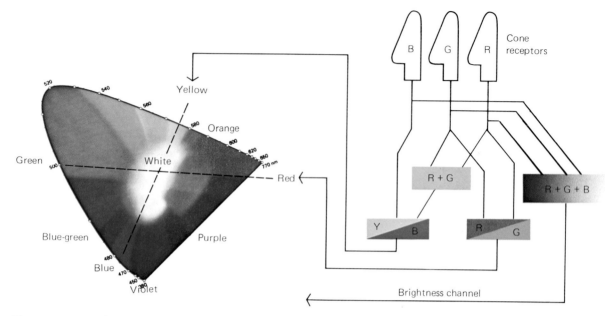

Plate 3   Internal representation of color spectrum
The standard chromaticity diagram (left) and its relationship to the internal
representation of color experience (right)

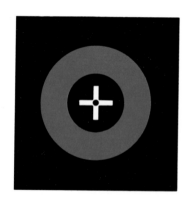  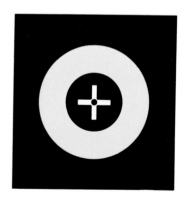

Plate 4   Negative afterimage
Look steadily for about 20 seconds at the dot inside the blue circle, then
transfer your gaze to the dot inside the gray rectangle. Now do the same with
the dot inside the yellow circle. What you see is a negative afterimage. Each
afterimage is the complementary color of the color you stared at.

Plate 5 Additive color mixture

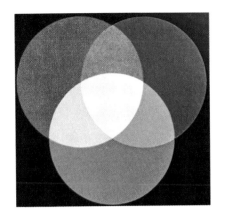

If a *light* of a single wavelength is shined onto a white surface, the perceived color will correspond to that wavelength, because the surface reflects only that wavelength to the eye. Now if two lights of different wavelengths are shined on the surface together, the resulting perceived color will be an *additive* mixture. The surface will reflect both wavelengths, and they will add together to produce a color sensation. As is shown in Plate 5, it is possible to produce the complete spectrum of colors by additive mixture if you mix three properly chosen lights in the correct proportions.

Plate 6 Subtractive color mixture

In contrast to mixing lights, when paints are combined the resulting perceived color is produced by subtraction. For example, a yellow paint absorbs (subtracts) primarily non-yellow wavelengths. If you mix a yellow paint with a blue paint (which absorbs primarily non-blue wavelengths), the result is a subtraction which leaves wavelengths between yellow and blue, namely green. Plate 6 illustrates how you can produce a variety of colors by subtractive mixture given three appropriately chosen paints.

Plate 7 Tests for colorblindness

People with normal vision see a number 6 in the top plate, while those with red-green color blindness do not. Those with normal vision see the number 12 in the bottom plate; those with red-green color blindness may see one number or none. These two illustrations are from a series of 15 color-blindness tests necessary for a complete color recognition examination.

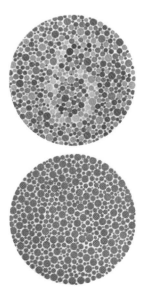

(Man Ray, "The Rope Dancer Accompanies Herself with Her Shadows," 1916. Oil on canvas, 52" x 6'1⅜". Collection, The Museum of Modern Art, New York. Gift of G. David Thompson.)

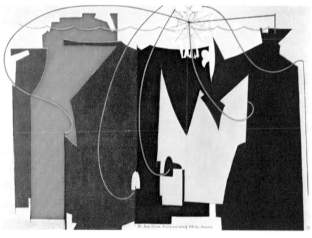 

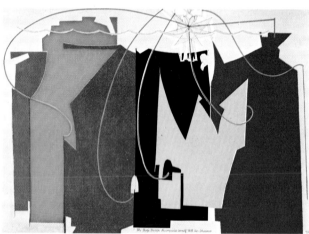 

Plate 8   Colorblindness

The painting in the upper left panel appears as it would to a person with normal color vision. If you suffered from red-green blindness, the same picture would be seen as it is in the upper right panel. Similarly, the lower left and lower right panels show how the picture would look to persons with yellow-blue or total color blindness, respectively.

A.

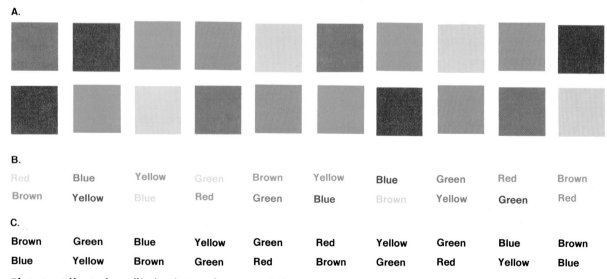

B.

Red	Blue	Yellow	Green	Brown	Yellow	Blue	Green	Red	Brown
Brown	Yellow	Blue	Red	Green	Blue	Brown	Yellow	Green	Red

C.

Brown	Green	Blue	Yellow	Green	Red	Yellow	Green	Blue	Brown
Blue	Yellow	Brown	Green	Red	Brown	Green	Red	Yellow	Blue

Plate 9   Effect of conflicting internal representations

The Stroop Color Naming Test illustrates the effect of interference by "irrelevant stimuli." For A, name the color of each patch as rapidly as possible. For B, name the colors of the words, ignoring the meaning of the words. For C, read the color names. Try A, B, and C on your friends, timing each task.

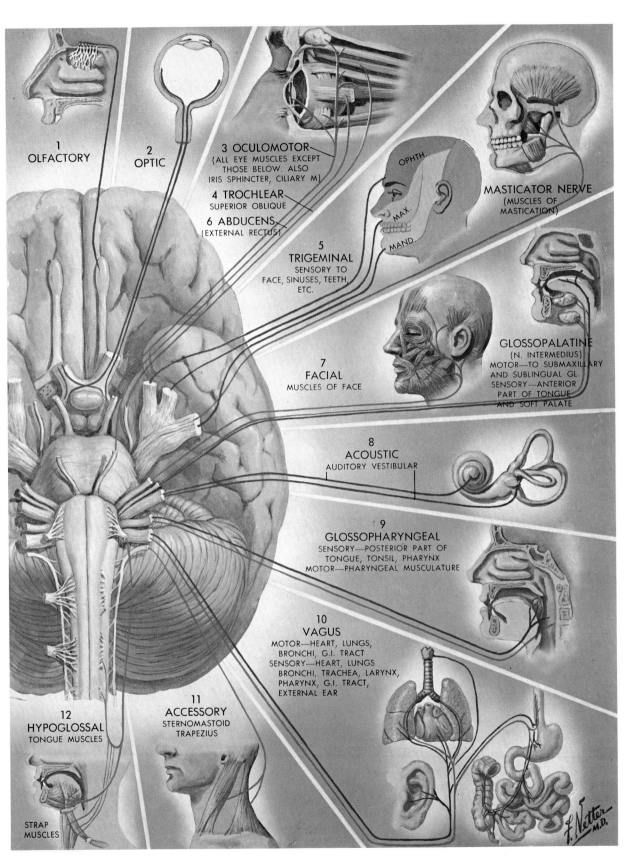

Plate 10   Cranial nerves

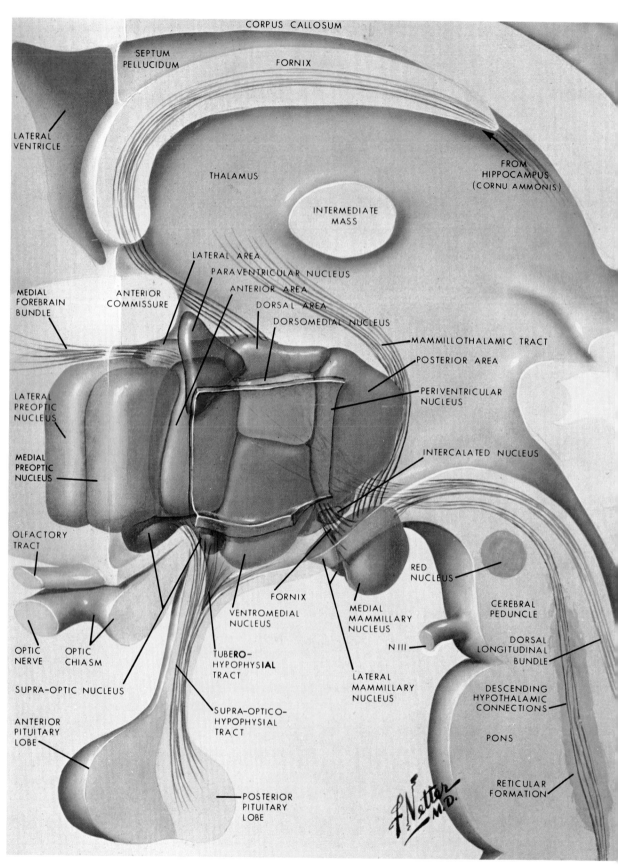

CORPUS CALLOSUM

SEPTUM
PELLUCIDUM

FORNIX

LATERAL
VENTRICLE

THALAMUS

FROM
HIPPOCAMPUS
(CORNU AMMONIS)

INTERMEDIATE
MASS

LATERAL AREA

PARAVENTRICULAR NUCLEUS

ANTERIOR AREA

MEDIAL
FOREBRAIN
BUNDLE

ANTERIOR
COMMISSURE

DORSAL AREA

DORSOMEDIAL NUCLEUS

MAMMILLOTHALAMIC TRACT

POSTERIOR AREA

PERIVENTRICULAR
NUCLEUS

LATERAL
PREOPTIC
NUCLEUS

MEDIAL
PREOPTIC
NUCLEUS

INTERCALATED NUCLEUS

OLFACTORY
TRACT

RED
NUCLEUS

CEREBRAL
PEDUNCLE

FORNIX

OPTIC
NERVE

OPTIC
CHIASM

VENTROMEDIAL
NUCLEUS

MEDIAL
MAMMILLARY
NUCLEUS

N III

DORSAL
LONGITUDINAL
BUNDLE

TUBERO-
HYPOPHYSIAL
TRACT

SUPRA-OPTIC NUCLEUS

LATERAL
MAMMILLARY
NUCLEUS

DESCENDING
HYPOTHALAMIC
CONNECTIONS

ANTERIOR
PITUITARY
LOBE

SUPRA-OPTICO-
HYPOPHYSIAL
TRACT

PONS

POSTERIOR
PITUITARY
LOBE

RETICULAR
FORMATION

F. Netter M.D.

**Plate 11   Schematic reproduction of hypothalamus
(three-dimensional)**

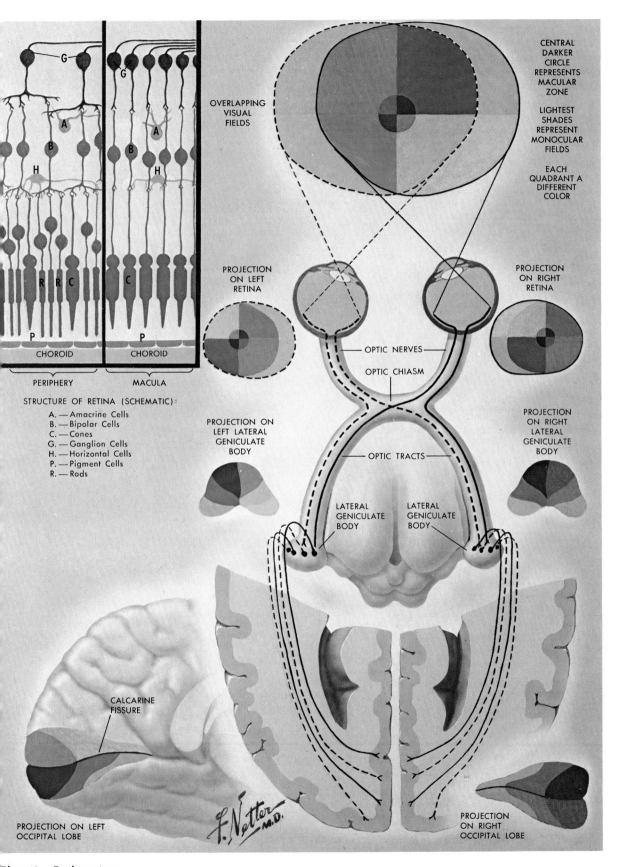

CENTRAL DARKER CIRCLE REPRESENTS MACULAR ZONE

LIGHTEST SHADES REPRESENT MONOCULAR FIELDS

EACH QUADRANT A DIFFERENT COLOR

OVERLAPPING VISUAL FIELDS

CHOROID

CHOROID

PERIPHERY

MACULA

STRUCTURE OF RETINA (SCHEMATIC):

A. — Amacrine Cells
B. — Bipolar Cells
C. — Cones
G. — Ganglion Cells
H. — Horizontal Cells
P. — Pigment Cells
R. — Rods

PROJECTION ON LEFT RETINA

PROJECTION ON RIGHT RETINA

OPTIC NERVES

OPTIC CHIASM

PROJECTION ON LEFT LATERAL GENICULATE BODY

PROJECTION ON RIGHT LATERAL GENICULATE BODY

OPTIC TRACTS

LATERAL GENICULATE BODY

LATERAL GENICULATE BODY

CALCARINE FISSURE

PROJECTION ON LEFT OCCIPITAL LOBE

PROJECTION ON RIGHT OCCIPITAL LOBE

F. Netter M.D.

Plate 12   Optic system

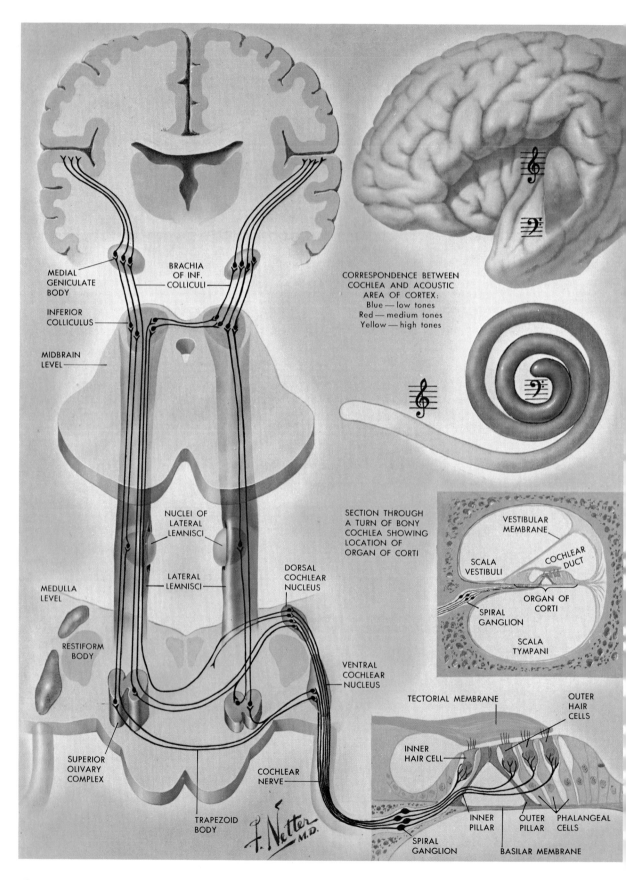

MEDIAL GENICULATE BODY

BRACHIA OF INF. COLLICULI

INFERIOR COLLICULUS

MIDBRAIN LEVEL

CORRESPONDENCE BETWEEN COCHLEA AND ACOUSTIC AREA OF CORTEX:
Blue — low tones
Red — medium tones
Yellow — high tones

NUCLEI OF LATERAL LEMNISCI

LATERAL LEMNISCI

MEDULLA LEVEL

DORSAL COCHLEAR NUCLEUS

RESTIFORM BODY

SECTION THROUGH A TURN OF BONY COCHLEA SHOWING LOCATION OF ORGAN OF CORTI

VESTIBULAR MEMBRANE

SCALA VESTIBULI

COCHLEAR DUCT

ORGAN OF CORTI

SPIRAL GANGLION

SCALA TYMPANI

VENTRAL COCHLEAR NUCLEUS

TECTORIAL MEMBRANE

OUTER HAIR CELLS

INNER HAIR CELL

SUPERIOR OLIVARY COMPLEX

COCHLEAR NERVE

INNER PILLAR

OUTER PILLAR

PHALANGEAL CELLS

TRAPEZOID BODY

F. Netter M.D.

SPIRAL GANGLION

BASILAR MEMBRANE

Plate 13   Acoustic system

visual field as well, due to some additional damage to his right visual cortex. Incidentally, this man now lives a normal and productive life in spite of these visual handicaps.

Why are the cells in the visual cortex so important to our perception of objects? Researchers are trying to answer this question, but there is much disagreement about the answer. About 20 years ago, the studies of cell function in the visual cortex carried out by D. H. Hubel and T. N. Wiesel revolutionized our thinking about the visual cortex. These investigators made two exciting discoveries. The first is that each cell in the visual cortex does not "look" at a single point on the retina or in visual space, but has a receptive field that is relatively large— in some cases more than five degrees of visual angle. This means that each visual cortex cell "analyzes" a region of visual space. The second important discovery made by Hubel and Wiesel was that each cell is very particular about the kind of visual stimulus that changes its activity. A given cell responds only to an edge or a bar of a specific orientation (Figure 3–17). Hubel and Wiesel found that different cells are sensitive to different specific orientations. Thus it seems that cells in the visual cortex function as edge or orientation detectors.

When you look at a vertical line or an edge, only the cells in your visual cortex sensitive to vertical orientations are wildly active; the cells sensitive to other orientations are relatively quiet. If the line is rotated from the vertical, a whole different set of cells—those sensitive to the new orientation—become active. In humans, there is evidence that it is possible selectively to fatigue a set of neurons sensitive to one particular orientation (Figure 3–18). Just how and if these cortical orientation detectors create our perception of objects is subject to much discussion and argument. But without the visual cortex, our ability to perceive objects disappears (see "What Does It Mean?").

Principles of Object Perception

The objects we experience have properties we describe as shape, size, texture, color, distance, and location. These properties are constructed by our perceptual processes, and the principles by which this construction takes place were first described by the Gestalt psychologists in the first two decades of this century. The fundamental principle of perceptual organization is called **Prägnanz,** or "goodness of figure." This principle states that the perceptual processes form internal representations of objects by grouping visual elements together in the simplest manner possible. What is represented by the two elements labeled 3 in Figure 3–19A? Most people would say that there are two rectangles, one behind the other. The principle of Prägnanz predicts this perception because it is simpler to perceive two rectangles, one blocking part of the other, than it is to perceive a rectangle with a second figure cut out to fit in the manner shown in Figure 3–19B. Figure 3–20 illustrates some other Gestalt principles: **proximity, similarity,** and **closure.**

Sometimes the information in a stimulus is ambiguous and does not permit a unique perceptual organization. Look at the left-hand portion of Figure 3–21. It is possible to perceive the drawing as a vase or as two faces. As your perceptual processes try to determine which is "better," your experience of the drawing alternates between the two. It does not seem possible to perceive both the faces and the vase at the same time. As soon as we provide other information, the perceptual experience becomes more stable as either the vase (Figure 3–21B) or the faces (Figure 3–21C). Here you experience perception in action.

Depth Perception

An important aspect of object perception has to do with where objects are relative to each other and to you. The ability to construct a representation of distance and depth in your internal representation of the world is called **depth perception.** Two sources of information are used by your perceptual processes to construct depth representations—information extracted from the retinal image of either eye alone (monocular cues to depth) and information that requires both eyes simultaneously (binocular cues to depth). The most important **monocular cues for depth** are partial overlap, size, shading (attached and cast shadows), texture gradients (Figure 3–22), linear perspective, and motion parallax. *Motion parallax* is the relative motion of objects created when your head moves from side to side. When you look out the side window of a moving train or car, notice that distant objects seem to move slowly while closer objects move faster. The difference in the motion, caused by the objects resting at

Figure 3–19
Depth perception

A

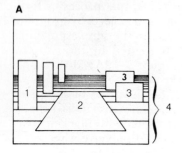

B

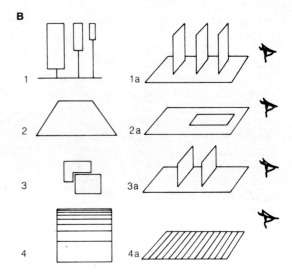

The Prägnanz principle of organization as applied to perception of depth. (A) is a drawing of a surface that can be seen either as stretching away from the eye (in depth) or as a flat, two-dimensional surface. Parts (A1–A4) illustrate monocular depth cues. In (A1) the three posts could have been due to (B1) or (B1a). Which seems simpler? In (A2) the shape could be a trapezoid (B2) or a square (B2a). Which seems simpler? In (A3), one rectangle could be missing a corner (B3) or be behind the nearer one (B3a). Which seems simpler? In (A4) the textured surface could be progressively finer near the top of the picture (B4) or could be stretching away (B4a). Which seems

simpler? In each case, organizing the scene in depth permits the objects to be simpler in form; the posts are all the same size, the shape on the floor is regular, the two rectangles are the same, and the textured floor is uniform. For these reasons, the flat scene is perceived as three-dimensional, because that is the simplest perception.

Figure 3–20
The Gestalt principles

```
xx  xx  xx  xx  xx  xx  xx  xx
```

Proximity.

```
x   o   x   o   x   o
x   o   x   o   x   o
x   o   x   o   x   o
x   o   x   o   x   o
x   o   x   o   x   o
```

Similarity.

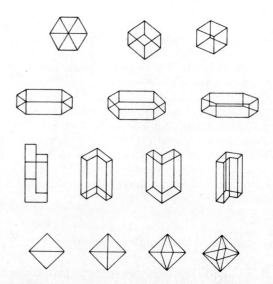

Closure.

According to the Prägnanz principle, the first member of each series of ambiguous drawings is perceived as two-dimensional and the others as three-dimensional, because these are the simplest ways of perceiving the drawings.

Figure 3–21
Figure-ground perception

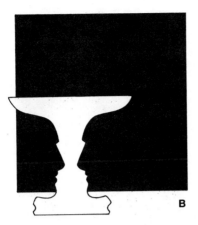
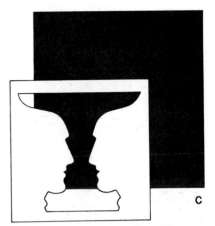

A

B

C

The Rubin vase, a reversible figure, is often used to point out the distinction between *figure* and *ground* in perception. In A the figure-ground relationship is ambiguous. Do the lines mark the edges of the center shaded space, in which case we see a vase, or do they mark the right and left edges of the white space, in which case we see two facing profiles? In the first case, the vase is figure and the surrounding white space is ground. In the second case, the shaded space in the center, which once was seen as figure, is now seen as background for the two faces. In B the ambiguity is reduced to accent the organization of the vase, and in C the profiles are accented.

Figure 3–22
Monocular depth cues

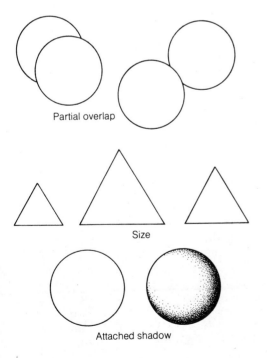

Partial overlap

Size

Attached shadow

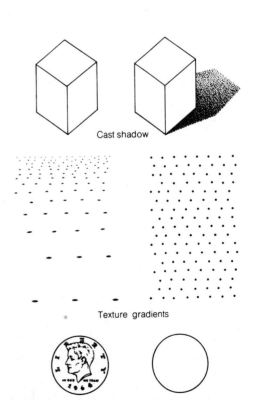

Cast shadow

Texture gradients

The two circles are actually identical in size, yet the filled circle may appear both larger and closer as a function of the fact that the space is filled.

Figure 3–23

Monocular cues to depth can fool us and make a two-dimensional object, in this case a painting, look like a three-dimensional dome.

different distances, is called motion parallax. Our visual system is very sensitive to this motion, and only a slight amount is needed to provide information about the relative depth of objects.

The monocular cues to depth were discovered by artists during the Italian Renaissance (fourteenth century) who used them to portray three-dimensional scenes on a flat canvas. Figure 3–23 is a sophisticated example of their skill. The ceiling on the left seems to have a large dome in it. This dome, however, is merely painted on a flat ceiling and appears realistic only when viewed from exactly the right position. When viewed from a different position

(right side of Figure 3–23), the dome appears terribly distorted. The artist achieved this effect by carefully painting a picture on the flat ceiling, which when viewed from one particular spot below forms a retinal image exactly like the retinal image a real dome would form. When you view the dome from the "wrong" viewpoint, the retinal image, compared with the retinal image of the rest of the ceiling, makes no sense. In this case, our perceptual processes create the perception of a highly distorted painted dome rather than a real dome. By very careful consideration of the cues used by our perceptual processes, modern artists like Maurits Escher

Impossible But Perceivable Shapes

Psychologists and artists have been especially ingenious at drawing forms that have impossible relationships among the components. Figure 3–24 illustrates three of these. None of these drawings could be translated into touchable three-dimensional objects, but their interest resides in how perceivers can be fooled when looking at them as two-dimensional line drawings. Actually, of course, we are not fooled. We see the drawings as impossible. But it is hard to do so, because if we look at any

one place on one of them, the information is quite consistent. It is as if we expect them to be a certain way based on one view, and then when we move our eyes to look at some other part, it is inconsistent with our expectations. Although nobody has fully explained how these are perceived, again we seem to have a case in which our expectations are important in telling us what we perceive and how to construct it. When these expectations are not met, then we are fooled.

Figure 3–24
Two-dimensional drawings of impossible three-dimensional forms

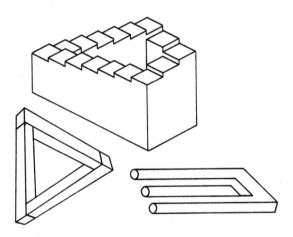

M. C. Escher, *Relativity*, collection Haags Gemeentemuseum—The Hague.

have been able to draw on flat surfaces pictures of "impossible" three-dimensional objects (Figure 3–24).

The binocular information about depth is extracted by a perceptual process called **stereopsis** which operates on the fact that the two eyes are separated horizontally in the head. Each eye views the world from a slightly different position, and therefore the retinal image of various objects at different distances from you falls on very slightly different positions in the retinal

images of the two eyes. This difference in the retinal position of the image of an object in the left and right eyes is called **retinal disparity.** In the brain (probably in the visual cortex) are mechanisms that are very sensitive to this retinal disparity. These stereoscopic mechanisms extract the retinal disparity information and use it to create the experience of objects at different distances.

When you look at a painting that uses monocular cues to portray depth, or when you view

Heredity and Eyesight

The continuing debate over the relative importance of heredity and environment in shaping human behavior extends even to how well people see. Not long ago, Canadian researchers demonstrated that North American Indians see diagonal lines better than white city-dwellers do, and attributed the difference to the fact that the Indians had grown up in a world of slant-walled tepees. But researchers at the Massachusetts Institute of Technology have now tipped the nature vs. nurture scales in the opposite direction, with evidence that visual acuity for diagonal—as well as for vertical and horizontal—shapes is genetically determined.

Experimental psychologist Richard M. Held and his associates studied non-Indian babies as young as two weeks of age, and therefore not likely to have acquired a visual preference for any shape through experience alone. Assuming that a baby would automatically look at the figure he saw best, they placed the infants before two screens. One screen displayed a pattern of vertical or horizontal lines, the other showed diagonals. Consistently, the babies preferred to peer at the horizontals and verticals, rather than the diagonals. This preference, the researchers conclude, is genetically programed.

Held and his co-workers are applying their findings to the study of astigmatism, a condition in which vision is blurred along the horizontal, vertical or diagonal axis.

Newsweek
September 27, 1976

The work of Hubel and Wiesel, discussed in the text, indicates that the visual cortex contains cells that detect lines of various orientations. Some cells detect (respond most to) vertical lines, others horizontal, and others various degrees in between. The number of cells of each type is probably related to our ability to detect these types of visual stimuli. Genetics may partly determine these numbers, but there is also evidence that early environmental stimulation affects the number of cells of each type. As usual, environment and heredity working simultaneously determine our behavior, even our eyesight.

a photograph with monocular depth information, your stereoscopic processes negate the monocular depth cues by providing information that the scene is "really" a flat surface. Your experience of depth in such paintings or photographs can be considerably enhanced if you view them with one eye (to eliminate stereopsis) and hold your head very still (to eliminate motion parallax). When viewed under these conditions, many paintings and photographs produce surprisingly realistic depth experiences. Of course, the ultimate way to trick the perceptual processes is to combine all the monocular and stereoscopic cues, as is done in a 3-D movie. Under these circumstances, the internal representation is so similar to real-life conditions that your behavior may actually be influenced by it (while watching such movies, people often duck to avoid flying objects shown in the film)! This "tricky" quality of our internal representation is so good that our behavior in everyday life is largely based on it, and we are usually unaware that it is being constructed by our perceptual processes.

Perceptual Constancy

One of the most impressive capacities of our perceptual processes is their ability to maintain a stable internal representation of objects when the physical stimulus is constantly changing. We have already discussed brightness constancy as an example of this property. Look around you again. Notice that windows look rectangular regardless of the angle at which you view them. The top of a glass looks circular even though its retinal image is elliptical. This ability is called **shape constancy**—the ability of the internal representation to maintain a constant shape of an object despite different viewing angles and distances.

Size constancy is the ability of the perceptual processes to represent an object as a constant size even though its retinal image may change drastically. Look at the two drawings in Figure 3–25. The person standing between the rails in the left picture is 100 feet away from the observer in the foreground. In the right-hand picture the person is 500 feet away. If you measure with a ruler the size of the image of the person on the left, you will find that it is five times as large as the image of the person on the right. The drawings simulate the retinal image of the observer under the two conditions. That is, the image of the farther person is one-fifth the size of the image of the closer person. Yet in our internal representation of the size of the person, the size remains

Figure 3–25
Size constancy

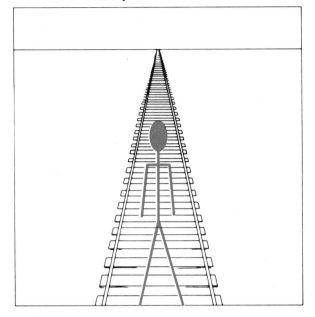
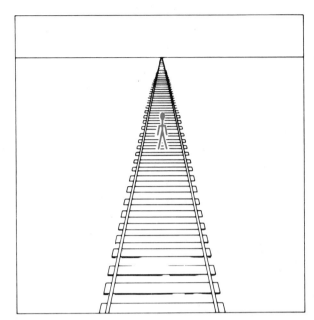

unchanged despite these changes in the size of the retinal image. We "know" that the person remains the same size in spite of the different viewing distances. This knowledge, based on our internal representation, is called size constancy.

What is the basis of this ability? Previous knowledge certainly plays a role, at least for familiar objects like people, but it is not necessary for size constancy. Careful measurements using unfamiliar objects as test stimuli have shown that our perceptual systems can construct reasonably accurate representations of the true size of objects at distances as great as three-quarters of a mile! How do the perceptual processes manage to do this?

The size constancy ability is based on two types of information: the size of the retinal image of an object and its distance from the observer. Size constancy seems to involve two separate processes, illustrated in Figure 3–26. The input from both eyes goes through the first process where both binocular and monocular information are analyzed. Out of this process come two internally represented magnitudes: the size of the retinal image and the distance of the object. As you can see from the lower draw-

Figure 3–26
Processing of binocular and monocular information

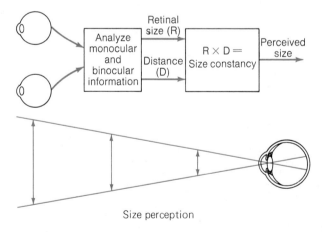

Size perception

ing in Figure 3–26, knowing only the size of the retinal image does not yield very much information about the physical size of an object, since a given retinal image size may correspond to a relatively small object close up or to a larger object farther away.

The estimate of the retinal image size is useful only in conjunction with an estimate of the

What you expect to see often determines what you do see. Most motorists passing the Illinois state line didn't see anything wrong with this sign.

Your perceptual processes play an important role in helping interpret real size. Considering distance and size constancy, you can accurately perceive the cars in the background as actually being larger than the people in the foreground.

distance of the object. This distance is the other piece of information coming out of the first process and is obtained using all the monocular and binocular cues discussed above. These two pieces of information are fed into the second process, the size constancy process. The size constancy process calculates an estimate of the real size of the object by multiplying the estimated retinal image size by the estimated distance of the object. The result of this multiplication is the representation of the real size of the object in your internal representation of the world. If the output of the first process indicates that object A is half the retinal size of object B, but is twice as far away as object B, then the result of the size constancy calculation is that objects A and B are the same physical size. If, however, objects A and B were estimated by the first perceptual process to have the same size retinal image, with object A being at two times the distance of object B, then the result of the size constancy process would indicate that object A is twice as large as object B.

Notice in Figure 3–26 that the accuracy of the size constancy representation of the size of an object is only as good as the accuracy of the estimations of the retinal size and the object distance. The size of the retinal image is registered with relative accuracy since it is measurable directly on the retina. But the estimate of the distance of the object is another matter, depending upon the quality of the monocular and binocular cues for depth. In other words, if the first perceptual process in Figure 3–26

Figure 3–27
Filled and unfilled space

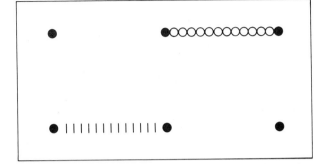

In each example, do the dots seem equally spaced?
Measure them with a ruler. This is an example of
filled and unfilled spaces.

"Excuse me for shouting—I thought you were farther away."

Playboy, January 1972. Reproduced by special permission of PLAY-BOY Magazine; copyright © 1971 by Playboy.

If you were a giant and thought everyone else was too, then the simplest perception in this case would be that the man on the left is a giant who is far away.

could be "tricked" into giving an inaccurate estimate of the object distance, then the perception of the object size would also be inaccurate.

Many visual illusions are thought to be a consequence of the size constancy process being fed inaccurate distance information. The most famous illusion, one that has fascinated people for centuries, is the moon illusion: The moon appears considerably larger when it is at the horizon than when it is overhead. This effect is not an optical or a physical effect; it is a perceptual effect. Let's look more closely at what goes on.

The reality of the moon is that it is a ball 2000 miles in diameter located 289,000 miles from the earth. Our perceptual processes are not equipped to represent internally sizes and distances of such magnitude. We have never experienced a size so large by walking up to it or holding it in our hand. It is outside the range of our perceptual experience. Nor have we ever walked a distance so far. There is no way for the mechanism that estimates distance to represent accurately 289,000 miles. So the distance estimate from the first perceptual process is completely dependent on factors other than the true distance of the moon. When the moon is overhead, there is absolutely no information the perceptual process can use to estimate its distance. There are no other objects nearby, no texture gradients, no stereoscopic cues. Under these circumstances, the judged distance

coming out of the perceptual process is underestimated. When the moon is near the horizon, its distance can be estimated relative to objects in the field of vision, to the texture gradients of the ground, and to the interposition of the horizon itself. The message from the perceptual process is that the moon is at least as far away as the horizon. This difference between the estimate of distance over space that is filled with objects (to the horizon) and the estimate of distance over unfilled space (overhead) is a well-known phenomenon (see Figure 3–27).

Filled spaces are judged to be longer than unfilled spaces. In one experiment subjects were asked to estimate the distance of airplanes. When the airplane was flying close to the horizon at a distance 10,000 feet from the observer, it was estimated to be at a distance of 15,800 feet. When the plane flew overhead, again at a distance of 10,000 feet, it was estimated to be only 6,200 feet away.

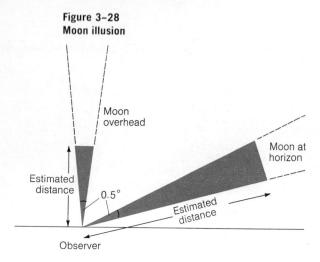

Figure 3–28
Moon illusion

Moon overhead

Moon at horizon

Estimated distance

0.5°

Estimated distance

Observer

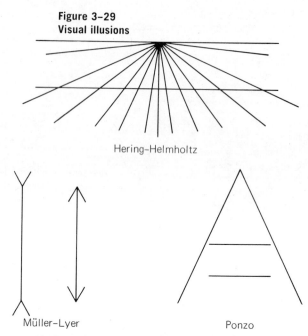

Figure 3–29
Visual illusions

Hering-Helmholtz

Müller–Lyer

Ponzo

Three types of visual illusions thought to be due to a "misapplication" of distance cues.

The retinal image size of the moon is 0.5 degrees of visual angle, regardless of where the moon is in the sky. You can verify this for yourself by taking a picture of the moon at the horizon and overhead. You will find that the photographic size of the moon is the same in both conditions. The reason for the moon illusion should now be quite clear. The first perceptual process estimates a constant retinal image size of 0.5 degrees. But the estimate of the distance of the moon is highly dependent on the position of the moon in the sky. When the moon is at the horizon, the perceptual process estimate of its distance is from 2.5 to 4 times its estimate when the moon is overhead. Consequently, the size constancy mechanism calculates an estimated "true" size that is from 2.5 to 4 times larger for the horizon moon than for the overhead moon (see Figure 3–28).

Figure 3–29 illustrates some of the better-known visual illusions. Although these illusions are drawn on a flat piece of paper, some psychologists think that the effect in some of the illusions is caused by the perceptual processes signaling false information about distance, which is then used by the size constancy process to calculate perceived sizes that are not in accord with the physical sizes of the objects. This theory is still subject to much argument and research. Can you think of ways that the size constancy theory could explain the illusions shown in Figure 3–29? We will not fully understand perception until we are able to understand these illusions.

AUDITORY PROCESSING

Although our most accurate information concerning objects comes from visual perception processes, the auditory processes contribute a large amount of important information to our internal representation of the world. Since many of the principles in audition are similar to those in vision, we will examine auditory perception more briefly. (See color Plate 13.)

Auditory Stimulus

The air around us is composed of various molecules. Sound waves are disturbances in the uniform pressure of these molecules caused by vibrating objects. As a vibrating object moves back and forth, it alternately compresses and rarifies the air around it. These waves of compressions and rarefactions then spread out through the air at a rate of about 760 miles an hour.

The simplest kind of sound is the sound produced by a tuning fork. Such a sound is called a pure tone and is shown on the left in Figure 3–30. The time that a sound wave takes

Figure 3–30
Pure and complex tones

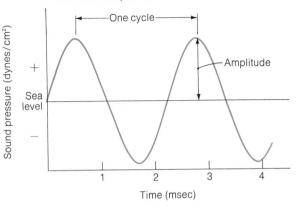

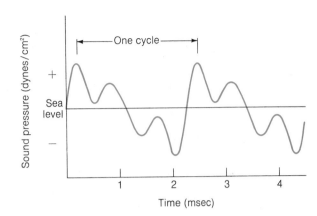

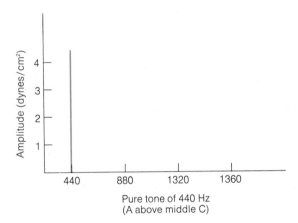

Pure tone of 440 Hz
(A above middle C)

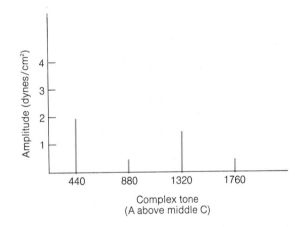

Complex tone
(A above middle C)

to complete one cycle of compression and rarefaction is called its period. The period is usually measured in milliseconds (1000 msec = 1 sec). The more common way to express the time aspect of a sound wave is by its frequency —the number of cycles completed in one second. Our auditory processes are sensitive to auditory frequencies ranging from 20 cycles per second (abbreviated Hz for Hertz) all the way up to 20,000 Hz. A second aspect of a simple tone is its *amplitude*—the amount of pressure change away from the average atmospheric pressure. This amplitude is expressed in pressure units, dynes/cm². The atmospheric pressure at sea level is about 10,000,000 dynes/cm². Under ideal conditions we can detect sound pressure changes away from this average pressure of about 0.0002 dynes/cm². In other words, if the atmospheric pressure changed from

10,000,000.0002 to 9,999,999.9998 dynes/cm² a thousand times per second, we would be able to detect a tone! The most intense sound pressure we can hear without doing physical damage to the ear is about 200 dynes/cm², a pressure range of 1 million to 1.

It is common to use the *decibel* (dB) to express sound amplitude. The decibel scale avoids the necessity to use very small numbers (like 0.0003). The lowest intensity on the decibel scale that we can hear is 0 dB, and the highest intensity we can stand is about 120 dB. Figure 3–31 gives the intensity of common sounds in decibels.

The simple tone on the left in Figure 3–30 is called a *sine wave tone*, because of the mathematical nature of its shape. Most of the sounds in nature, however, are not simple sine waves in shape. The sounds produced by the vocal

Figure 3–31
The decibel scale

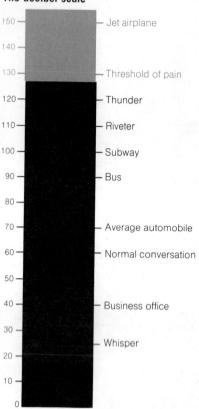

The intensities of various common sounds in decibels (dB). The take-off blast of the Saturn V moon rocket, measured at the launching pad, was approximately 180 dB. For laboratory rats, prolonged exposure to 150 dB causes death.

Figure 3–32
The major parts of the ear

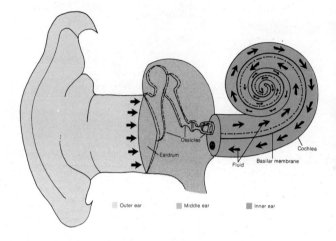

cords, by birds and insects, and by musical instruments have complex wave forms, like the one shown on the right in Figure 3–30. Like the simple tones, the complex sounds are also periodic; that is, they repeat a complete complex cycle at regular time intervals. The time that it takes to complete one complete cycle is called the period of the sound. Both wave forms shown in Figure 3–30 have the same period (2.27 msec).

A complex tone may also be described in terms of its frequency. Instead of having just one frequency, a complex tone may have many frequencies. The lowest frequency of a complex sound is called its fundamental frequency, and it corresponds to the number of complex cycles the sound completes in one second. The simple and the complex waves shown in Figure 3–30 have the same fundamental frequency, 440 Hz. In addition, the complex sound contains other frequencies, called harmonics or overtones. The second harmonic has a frequency twice that of the fundamental, the third harmonic has a frequency three times that of the fundamental, and so on.

The number and amplitude of the harmonics of a complex tone determine the complexity of the tone. A very complex tone will have up to 20 or 30 harmonics, while a less complex tone will have only a few. Of course, the simplest tone has only the fundamental frequency. The lower half of Figure 3–30 illustrates the harmonic content of the simple and the complex wave forms shown.

The Ear

Sound pressure waves are converted into nerve impulses in the ear. The ear actually consists of three major parts, shown in Figure 3–32. Sounds enter the *outer ear* and cause the eardrum, a flexible membrane separating the outer and the middle ears, to vibrate in the same manner as the sounds themselves. These vibrations of the eardrum are transmitted to the *inner ear* by the three bones (ossicles) of the *middle ear*. These bones, the smallest in the human body, are called, because of their shapes, the malleus (hammer), incus (anvil), and stapes (stirrup).

Figure 3–33
Map of the basilar membrane

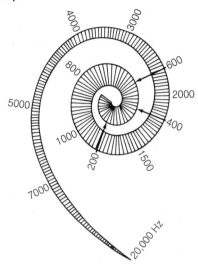

The location on the basilar membrane that receives maximum stimulation depends upon the frequency of the sound.

Electronic amplification is used to increase the loudness of rock music. However, extreme levels of loudness can damage your ear and affect your ability to hear. (See What Does It Mean section, p. 109.)

It is in the inner ear that the sound vibrations are transformed into nerve signals which are then sent to the brain. The inner ear is a 34 mm long tube called the **cochlea,** because it is curled up like the shell of a snail. The cochlea is filled with fluid and is divided down its length by a flexible membrane, the **basilar membrane.** Sound vibrations transmitted to the inner ear distort the basilar membrane. The exact place where the distortion is maximum is determined largely by the frequency content of the sound. Figure 3–33 shows a map of the basilar membrane indicating that low frequencies (200 Hz) stimulate the basilar membrane at one end while high frequencies (20,000 Hz) stimulate it at the other end. The sine wave tone shown on the left of Figure 3–30 would stimulate the basilar membrane maximally at the place corresponding to 440 Hz (Figure 3–33), while the complex tone shown on the right of Figure 3–30 would stimulate the basilar membrane in four different places simultaneously (at the places corresponding to 440, 880, 1320, and 1760 Hz). Georg von Békésy was awarded the Nobel Prize for figuring out exactly how the basilar membrane works.

Along the length of the basilar membrane are thousands of tiny receptor cells, called **hair cells** because stiff hairs protrude from their top surface. These hair cells are very sensitive to the bending of the basilar membrane and are connected in such a way that they give a signal which indicates how much the basilar membrane is being distorted at each point along its length. Each hair cell is connected to an auditory nerve fiber that sends a neural signal to the brain. In human beings, there are about 31,000 such fibers from each ear. The nerve activity in each of these 31,000 nerves from each ear is the input to the auditory processes and is the basis for the construction of our auditory experience. As in vision, the primary purpose is to construct an internal representation that answers two questions: "what" and "where?"

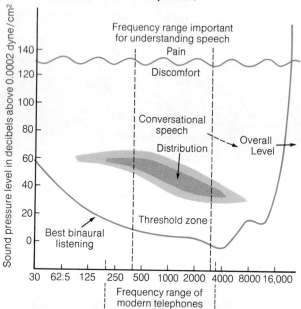

Figure 3–34
Frequencies of sound pressure

Limits of Auditory Performance

Our ears are not equally sensitive to all sound frequencies. Figure 3–34 shows how much sound pressure (in decibels) is required just to detect sounds of various frequencies. The lowest frequency that our auditory system is able to transform into an auditory experience is about 20 Hz. Frequencies below 20 are felt as vibrations against the body, rather than heard. The upper limit is about 20,000 Hz, although this figure depends upon age (see "What Does It Mean?"). Notice in Figure 3–34 that although you can just detect a sound of 1000 Hz at a pressure level of 0 dB, you will need 60 dB of pressure to barely detect a sound of 30 Hz (60 dB is 1000 times the pressure of 0 dB).

For human beings, perhaps the most important function of hearing is that it makes possible communication by speech. In Figure 3–34 the levels and frequencies of normal conversational speech are shown. In order to comprehend speech the ear must be able to hear these frequencies (see "What Does It Mean?"). There is a limit to the sound pressure the ear can receive without risking physical damage to the

basilar membrane and the receptor hair cells on it. At these high levels we experience discomfort and then pain. The pressure levels that can damage the ear are those above about 130 dB. Recall that a riveter produces a noise of about 110 dB.

Dimensions of Psychological Experience

The perceptual processes create auditory experiences for us that differ on three major psychological dimensions—loudness, pitch, and timbre. People describe their experiences of different **loudness** using words like "loud" and "soft," and in music, *forte, fortissimo, pianissimo,* and *piano.* The loudness dimension is primarily one of quantity or magnitude. The loudness of a tone depends, of course, on the physical intensity of the sound; but that is not all. Loudness also depends on the frequency and the complexity of the tone. As you can see in Figure 3–34, a 30 dB tone would be clearly audible if its frequency were 1000 Hz, but would be inaudible if its frequency were 125 Hz. Remember that intensity, frequency, and complexity are physical properties of sound, while loudness, pitch, and timbre are dimensions of psychological experience. There is not a one-to-one relationship between the physical properties and the psychological experiences.

The second psychological dimension of sound experience is that of **pitch.** It is the property that is described by words like "high" and "low." Musical scales are constructed out of tones having different pitches. When you sing "do, re, mi, fa, so, la, ti, do," you are singing different pitches arranged in ascending order. Sounds that evoke a strong sense of pitch are said to be musical. Other sounds, like the rustling of leaves, do not evoke an experience of pitch and are said to be unmusical. Complex tones, containing a fundamental frequency and a number of harmonics (Figure 3–30), create a strong sense of pitch. The pitch corresponds to the frequency of the fundamental of the complex tone. Four tones—all having a fundamental frequency of 440 Hz, for example, but differing in the number and intensity of their harmonics—will be perceived as having the same pitch. There is much controversy about the nature of the perceptual mechanisms that create the sensation of pitch. One thing is clear though. Our

Skillful violinists are prized among musicians and composers because they can obtain a wide range of timbres by using different bowing techniques. Different bowings change the amplitude of the harmonics in the musical tone.

perception of pitch depends on the pattern of stimulation on the basilar membrane.

The third major psychological dimension of sound is **timbre.** Timbre is the psychological experience that allows you to distinguish a violin from an oboe when the two are playing exactly the same pitch at the same loudness. Timbre is a qualitative dimension that is not well represented by words in our language. Some sounds are said to have a nasal timbre while others are described as being rich or full. The nature of our experience of timbre seems to depend largely on the physical complexity of sound, that is, the number and intensity of the harmonics in a sound. A simple sine wave tone, for example, sounds dull and lifeless, while an organ note can sound rich and full. The organ note contains many harmonics, while the simple tone has only its fundamental frequency.

Perception of Music

One of the most creative of human activities has been the making of music. Although music has been created for centuries, only within the last 100 years has there developed a theoretical basis for understanding the effects of music. All music made in all cultures is based on the different psychological experiences created by the sequential (melody) and simultaneous (harmony) sounding of musical tones. Some of these combinations are experienced as pleasant while others are experienced as unpleasant. The degree to which musical experiences are found to be pleasant is influenced by culture, but the quality of the experience is determined by the perceptual mechanisms that produce pitch, loudness, and timbre. A skillful composer creates music by carefully combining pleasant and unpleasant musical sounds in particular sequences to create a satisfying experience.

Ancient musicians discovered that certain notes or tones when sounded at the same time created very special psychological experiences. Western music is based on a sequence of eight notes arranged to form an ascending scale. Letter names are used to describe each note in the scale: C, D, E, F, G, A, B, and C. This is the C-major scale, one of many possible scales. These are the notes that are sounded by hitting the white keys of the piano. Notice on the scale that there are two notes called C (actually there are eight different C's on the entire range of musical notes, from a very low-pitched C to a very high-pitched C). These notes have the same name because something about them sounds the same in spite of their having different pitches. Why should the first note on the musical scale (called the tonic note) and the eighth note on the scale (called the octave note) sound so similar?

To answer this question, we need to look at the sounds that are produced by musical instruments playing these two notes. Musical instruments produce complex sounds, consisting of a fundamental frequency and as many as 20 har-

TABLE 3-2   The Frequency of Each of the First 10 Harmonics of Each Note on the Natural C-Major Scale

	Natural Musical Scale							
	Tonic C	Second D	Third E	Fourth F	Fifth G	Sixth A	Seventh B	Octave C
Harmonics								
1	264	297	330	352	396	440	495	528
2	528	594	660	704	792	880	990	1056
3	792	891	990	1056	1188	1320	1485	1584
4	1056	1188	1320	1408	1584	1760	1980	2112
5	1320	1485	1650	1760	1980	2200	2475	2640
6	1584	1782	1980	2112	2376	2640	2970	3168
7	1848	2079	2310	2464	2772	3080	3465	3696
8	2112	2376	2640	2816	3168	3525	3960	4224
9	2376	2673	2970	3168	3564	3960	4455	4752
10	2640	2970	3300	3520	3960	4400	4950	5280

monics. By international agreement, the note A above middle C is defined by a complex tone whose fundamental frequency is 440 Hz. Table 3–2 gives the frequency of the first 10 harmonics of each note of the C-major natural scale beginning with middle C. Notice that the fundamental frequency of the octave is exactly twice the fundamental frequency of the tonic. Furthermore, each harmonic of the octave is exactly the same frequency as every other harmonic of the tonic. So when two musical instruments play these two notes, the basilar membrane is stimulated in the same places by the harmonics, which blend smoothly together.

The fifth note on the musical scale (G on the C-major scale) was also singled out by musicians long ago for its special sound when played with the tonic note. A look at Table 3–2 indicates why. Although their fundamental frequencies are different, the second harmonic of the G is the same frequency as the third harmonic of the C, and the fourth harmonic of the G is the same frequency as the sixth harmonic of the C, and so on. When these two notes are played together they stimulate the basilar membrane at some of the same positions. These note combinations produce very pleasant or consonant sounds.

Listening to music containing only pleasant sounds, however, would be like having a diet of only candy. Musicians deliberately produce unpleasant, or dissonant, sounds as well. For example, look at Table 3–2 to see what will happen when the tonic C is played at the same time as the second note of the scale, D. Notice that only the eighth harmonic of the D and the ninth harmonic of the C have the same frequency. The result is that the basilar membrane is stimulated in many different places that do not overlap, producing a very dissonant sound.

Modern musical instruments are not tuned to exactly the natural scale frequencies shown in Table 3–2. For technical reasons that allow musicians to play a much wider variety of music (in different keys, for example), all the notes except A above middle C are slightly mistuned by three or four Hz. This modern musical scale is called the well-tempered scale and is in universal use for playing Western music written since the eighteenth century. In this scale the fundamental frequency of middle C is 261.63 Hz and not 264 Hz. Even in the well-tempered scale, however, the frequencies of the octave are exactly twice the frequencies of the tonic note, and the pleasantness or unpleasantness of note combinations still depends upon the pattern of stimulation on the basilar membrane.

Spatial Localization

The auditory system also helps locate objects in space. Two sources of primary information take advantage of the fact that the ears are located on opposite sides of the head. Because of this, a sound source that is not located straight ahead will stimulate the two ears with slightly different intensities and with a slight time delay. For example, if a sound is located to the left, the left ear will receive more intense stimulation than the right, which is in the "shadow" of the head. In addition, the sound will arrive at the left ear a bit earlier than at the right ear.

The perceptual mechanism that measures the time delay between the two ears is so sensitive that it can reliably detect a difference of only 5 microseconds (0.000 005 sec)! The combination of intensity difference and time difference between the two ears is used by the auditory localization mechanism to create the perception of the sound being located somewhere to the left, straight ahead, or to the right.

Location of objects on the basis of sound is especially important to a person without vision. Blind individuals can learn to localize quite accurately on the basis of sound alone, even to the extent of making sounds that then echo back from objects in front of them. In one experiment it was shown that a blind person can detect large obstacles in his or her path at a distance of 10 to 15 feet in a large room. A person with sight who puts on a blindfold is initially poor at object localization, but improves with practice. This finding suggests that the remarkable performance of a blind person depends upon considerable practice and experience in exploring the environment acoustically. The blind person's ability to navigate successfully through a room with several barriers is greatly reduced if there is carpeting on the floor (because the sound of the footsteps, which reflect off objects, is reduced) or if earplugs are worn.

TASTE AND SMELL

Taste and smell are perceptual experiences created by mechanisms much like the auditory and visual mechanisms. Compared with hearing and vision, however, very little is known about how the taste and smell processes transform the absorption of molecules (the physical stimuli) into perceptual experiences.

Taste

The receptors for taste are grouped together in the taste buds visible on the surface of the tongue. Each bud contains about 10–15 individual receptor cells, and there are about 10,000 buds on the tongue. Individual receptor cells are sensitive to and absorb certain specific molecules of substances tasted. Each receptor, however, lasts only about four days before it wears out and is replaced by a new receptor from those constantly being created in the taste bud.

The experience of taste is often described in terms of four dimensions: salty, sweet, bitter, and sour. There are different sensitivities to the different types of tastes over different regions of the tongue. The back surface of the tongue is very sensitive to bitter-tasting substances like quinine, while the sides of the tongue are more sensitive to salty and sour substances. The tip of the tongue is most sensitive to sweet substances like sugar. Verify this difference for yourself. Compare your experience of a bit of salt at the tip of your tongue with your experience of salt on the side of the tongue. Repeat the experiment using sugar. Although there do seem to be specific receptors related to each of these taste substances, efforts to develop a simple model of taste experience have failed so far.

Our experience of a specific substance is no doubt a result of the combined activity of many different receptors. It is possible to modify your taste experience by knocking out certain of the receptors. For example, artichoke hearts contain a chemical that reduces the sensitivity of all receptors except those sensitive to sweet substances. After eating an artichoke heart most substances taste sweet. Try this experiment. Take a sip of water and swirl it around in your mouth, concentrating on the taste. For most people, water will taste neutral or slightly bitter. Now eat a piece of artichoke heart, chewing it thoroughly. Once again take a sip of water and concentrate on its taste. You will experience a sweetness in the water not experienced before.

Smell

The receptors for smell lie in the upper part of the nasal cavity. There are about 30 million of these receptors in each nostril, resulting in an extraordinary sensitivity to odors. Human beings are able to detect smells consisting of only 100 or so molecules.

The most prominent theory of smell receptor function is that the receptors are sensitive to certain molecule shapes (stereochemical theory). These different shapes result in seven basic types of smell experiences: pepperminty, ethereal, floral, camphoraceous, musky, pungent, and putrid. How these smell experiences are created by perceptual processes has puzzled

Army Ants on the March

Few jungle horror tales have become quite so much the stuff of legend as those that recount the ravenous activities of South America's army ants. Army ants, so the tall tales have it, regularly create vast ribbons of wasteland, blindly devouring every creature, plant or vegetable in their path. But entomologists have long known that army ants are in fact far less destructive than their reputation would have it—and now University of Connecticut researchers, working in the Ecuadorian forest, have learned a great deal about just how discriminating, not to say fastidious, army ants are in their tastes.

The staple of the army ants' diet, it turns out, is other insects. Indeed, Ecuadorian villagers often welcome the arrival of a column of the ants, because once they have passed through, they will have stripped the village of other insect pests. . . .

The ants carry out their foraging in regular army fashion. Each day, columns of hundreds of thousands of female ants travel as much as a hundred yards from the colony's main base, flanked by scouts that move in all directions from the line of march to search for food. When individual scouts discover likely prey, according to researchers Ruth Chadab and Carl Rettenmeyer, they use a unique combination of tactile and chemical clues to bring their comrades to the site as quickly as possible.

Bait

At one point in the research, the scientists used a wasp's nest as bait to capture individual ants. They marked the individuals with a spot of paint and placed them back near the column. Each marked individual quickly made her way back to the main body of ants, laying a chemical trail from her abdomen on the way. On reaching the main column, the "recruiter" ran up and down the line of march, touching the other ants with her antennae and her body. The result of the contact was immediate. "Within 30 seconds after the recruiter reached the raid column," Chadab and Rettenmeyer report in Science magazine, "ants were diverted from the column and followed the recruitment trail. . . . And if those ants found the prey, they too returned to the column and started recruiting in the same way.

This method of communication is extremely efficient in getting large numbers of ants to a source of food in a short time, the two entomologists explain. . . .

Newsweek
June 23, 1975

Chemicals that are produced by animals for purposes of communication by smell are called pheromones.

and eluded investigators for years, and today there still does not exist a satisfactory model of these perceptual processes.

Smell seems to have two major functions in animals—evaluation of food and communication. For the first function, smells combine with taste to create an internal representation of the edibility of food substances. Much of what we experience as taste is really mediated through smell. When we suffer a cold and our nasal passages are blocked, food seems dull and tasteless; an onion and an apple even have the same taste! The differences between them are due entirely to smell. Try this experiment for yourself. Cut a small piece of apple and an equally small piece of onion (about a quarter-inch cube). Holding your nose with one hand, put one piece in your mouth and chew it for a moment; then put the other piece in your mouth. As long as none of the smell reaches your nose, the apple and the onion taste the same.

Two important uses of smell in animal communication are territorial marking and sexual attraction. Chemicals produced for the purpose of communication by smell are called **pheromones.** Many animals have special glands that produce territorial pheromones; other animals secrete these chemicals in their urine. You may have noticed that dogs often urinate at the far corners of a yard. What the dog is really doing is marking its territory with its own scent. Other dogs coming into the yard immediately recognize the smell and tend to stay away.

When a female animal is sexually receptive, she gives off a special pheromone that attracts males of the species. Gypsy moths are extraordinary in this regard. The male gypsy moth is able to detect a receptive female gypsy moth several miles away by means of sexual pheromones. When a female cat or dog is in heat, she gives off sexual pheromones that attract male cats or dogs, often from quite a distance.

Whether or not human beings give off or use pheromones is a controversial question. The evidence for pheromones is indirect. Women, for example, differ in their sensitivity to certain musky smells at different times in their menstrual cycle. The sensitivity to these smells is highest just before ovulation and is minimum during menstruation. Since these musky smells are related to male sex hormones, this cyclical variation may indicate a pheromonelike function. A further piece of evidence suggesting the possibility of human pheromones comes from a study by marriage counselors. This study found that the most common complaint among couples seeking marriage counseling was that one or both partners found that the other "had bad breath" or simply "had a bad smell." We conclude that smells have a profound effect on human interpersonal behavior and that much of this effect exists at a nonverbal and emotional level.

Touch and Feeling

Objects that come in contact with the skin have four separate qualities. They may yield sensations of warmth, cold, touch, and pain. Each of these qualities appears to arise from electrical impulses triggered in a particular kind of receptor cell. Thus, an anatomical examination of regions just beneath the skin reveals a variety of different sensory cells and nerve endings. Some of these, when stimulated, yield a sensation of warmth, others a sensation of cold, still others the sensation of touch or feel, and finally some yield the sensation of pain. Most objects that we come in contact with produce a combination of sensations, not just one. Consider, for example, what it would "feel" like to touch, in the dark, a refrigerator, a cabinet, the arm of another person, or a hot stove. These objects are discriminable on the basis of touch alone because they give unique combinations of tactual sensations.

ATTENTION

Our perceptual processes are marvelous in their ability to create a rich and complex internal representation of reality, yet this ability is not without limits. There are a limited number of processing mechanisms, and these can construct a detailed representation in only one small proportion of the world at any one time. The processes by which the mechanisms are selectively allocated to a specific portion of the internal representation is called attention.

In visual processing the attention mechanisms are closely related to the anatomy of the visual system. As we saw earlier, the fovea of each retina has a dense concentration of cones. But in addition, the brain mechanisms devoted to analyzing the fovea are disproportionately large. For example, the fovea occupies only

Attention Is a Right-Sided Function

Patients acting like the stereotypic drunk—overactive and unable to concentrate—frequently are not intoxicated, but suffer from damage to the right side of the brain. Norman Geshwind and Marek-Marsel Mesulam of Harvard Medical School presented evidence that the complicated ability to pay attention is localized in the brain's right hemisphere.

In humans, lesions (usually caused by a blocked blood vessel) of the left side of the brain seldom cause severe, persistent loss of attention. However, lesions of the right hemisphere can lead either to general inattention or to particular inattention to stimuli on the left side. Geshwind hypothesizes that normally the right hemisphere scans both sides of space and applies criteria for shifting the focus of attention. If the attention-directing regions (the inferior parietal lobules) of the right hemisphere are destroyed, the left hemisphere eventually begins to monitor its own half of space (the right side), but not the other. In animals, damage to either hemisphere generally produces inattention to stimuli from the opposite side.

Science News
February 25, 1978

about ¹/₆₀₀₀ of the total visual field, yet fully ¹/₃ of the visual cortex of the brain is devoted to the fovea. This fact means that the visual system can construct a detailed internal representation of the world only for a part seen by the fovea. For vision, then, the chief mechanism for directing attention is eye movements. Our eyes point at the things we want to attend to. When we are looking at something, other objects in our visual field cannot be represented in as great detail.

In hearing, the attention mechanisms operate rather differently. When you are at a party with many people talking at once, the sounds from a number of different voices all enter the ear together. Your internal representation of the voices consists of different voices, male and female, each with a characteristic timbre and located at a particular place in the room. But in terms of the meaning, the language content of the voices, you can process and represent only one voice sound at a time. This limitation shows that you have only one perceptual process sophisticated and complex enough to carry out

a language and meaning analysis of the voice sounds. Your attentional processes can shift or allocate this language process to whichever voice it chooses, but to only one voice at a time. Careful studies have shown that when you try to listen to two voices at once, you always miss some of both. If you fully attend to one of the voices, about the only thing you can detect is if the speaker is replaced by a speaker of the opposite sex. In fact, the second voice can even start to speak another language, and this change will go undetected.

Even though there seems to be only one language-processing mechanism, specific simple stimuli can be detected in unattended voices. For example, when you fully attend to the language content of one voice, your attention is attracted by a second voice if that voice says your name. Another example is that of a sleeping mother who is often awakened by a soft cry from her baby, but not by other, louder noises. Exactly how a person allocates visual and auditory processing capacity is largely determined by motivation and needs at each moment.

SUMMARY

1. Perception is the process by which a person constructs an internal representation of the outside world. This internal representation is the basis for our behavior. Perceptual processes provide the answers to the questions: "What is out there?" and "Where is it?" The study of perception involves the study of physics, physiology, behavior, and subjective experience.
2. Sensory receptors convert physical energy such as light, sound, heat, and pressure into nerve impulses, signals that the brain can understand.
3. The human eye is sensitive to a narrow range of electromagnetic wavelengths, ranging from about 400 to 700 nm. This energy is called light because the eye can convert it into nerve impulses.
4. The eye is constructed much like a camera, forming an inverted image of the world on its rear surface, the retina. The retina contains four kinds of photoreceptors. The rods are very sensitive and function at low levels of light (scotopic vision). There are three types of cones. They function at daylight levels of light (photopic vision) and form the basis of color vision.
5. Rods and cones are connected to ganglion cells in the retina by means of a complex network of horizontal, bipolar, and amacrine cells. Each ganglion cell receives input from many rods and cones. The area of the retina that influences a given ganglion cell is called the receptive field of that ganglion cell. These fields are circular and consist of a central region and a surrounding region.

6. Because of the way receptive fields are shaped, ganglion cells function as contrast detectors, not absolute light detectors. The activity of a ganglion cell is determined by comparing the amount of light falling on the center of the receptive field with the amount of light falling on the surround.

7. Visual acuity is the ability to see fine detail. Generally as the average light intensity increases, our visual acuity improves.

8. Color is one of the basic experiences created by our perceptual processes. The neural activity of the three types of cones is combined in the retina to form three neural channels of color information: an R/G channel, a Y/B channel, and a Brightness-channel. All our color experiences result from various combinations of activity of these three channels.

9. The experience of color has three psychological dimensions: hue, saturation, and brightness. Hue is the qualitative nature of the color, saturation is the intensity of the color, and brightness is the description of color ranging from black to white.

10. Our perception of brightness is closely related to the relative amount of light reflected from objects rather than the absolute amount of light. Thus a piece of white paper looks white and a lump of coal looks black when viewed in bright sunlight or in a dim room.

11. The cells in the visual cortex of the brain provide the first stages of pattern and object perception. These cells are primarily sensitive to bars, gratings, and edges of specific orientations. Different cells are sensitive to different orientations.

12. Gestalt principles describe how stimuli on the retina are formed into objects by the perceptual processes. The basic principle is called Prägnanz, or "goodness of figure." Other Gestalt principles are proximity, similarity, and closure.

13. There are two types of cues used to perceive depth: those requiring both eyes (binocular cues) and those requiring one eye (monocular cues). Skilled artists can use monocular cues to give a realistic perception of depth.

14. Size constancy is the process of maintaining a stable internal representation of the size of objects when we move around and view them at different distances. This process uses two types of information: the size of the retinal image and the distance of the object.

15. The stimulus for hearing is sound pressure waves traveling in the air. Physical sound is described by its intensity, frequency, and complexity. Our hearing covers a range of frequencies from 20 Hz to 20,000 Hz. We can hear sounds as faint as 0 dB and as loud as 120 dB.

16. The inner ear analyzes complex sound waves into its sine wave (harmonic) components. The basilar membrane of the inner ear is stimulated at different places by different frequencies of sound.

17. Experience of sound varies on three principal psychological dimensions: loudness, pitch, and timbre. Timbre is the quality that allows you to tell the difference between a violin and flute playing the same musical note. The pleasantness of various musical notes played in combination is a function of the place on the basilar membrane where the harmonic components of the notes stimulate.

18. Taste and smell are interrelated senses that depend on the absorption of chemical molecules by receptors on the tongue and in the nose. Taste experiences are often described as salty, sweet, bitter, and sour. Smell experiences are likewise described as pepperminty, ethereal, floral, camphoraceous, musky, pungent, and putrid. Smell plays an important role in animal communication and sexual attraction.

RECOMMENDED ADDITIONAL READINGS

Gregory, R. L. *Eye and brain,* 2d ed. New York: McGraw-Hill, 1972.

Held, R., & Richards, W. (Eds.) *Recent progress in perception.* San Francisco: Freeman, 1976.

Lindsay, P. H., and Norman, D. A. *Human information processing,* 2d ed. New York: Academic Press, 1977.

Schiffman, H. R. *Sensation and perception: An integrated approach.* New York: Wiley, 1976.

what does it mean?

The perceptual mechanisms that construct internal representations of reality allow us to behave in appropriate ways. Scientific knowledge is part of our internal representation of reality, and much of it can be used in our everyday lives. Sometimes the usefulness of a discovery is not apparent for many years, while sometimes its utility is obvious. Knowledge gained in the study of perception and perceptual processing has had—and continues to have—a strong impact on our culture.

EYE GLASSES

One of the first applications of knowledge about the formation of the retinal image was in the prescription of eye glasses. The eye is supposed to focus a sharp image on the retina. This image is then analyzed by neural processes. If the image is not sharp the information obtainable from it is reduced, and an internal representation adequate for getting around in the world may not be possible.

There are two types of focusing problems found today. In the first type, called near-sightedness, or myopia, the eye has too much optical power. As a result, the eye forms an image of distant objects in front of, instead of on, the retina, and these distant objects are experienced as blurred. A near-sighted person can clearly see objects close to the eye, where the additional optical power is needed. The method used to allow a near-

sighted person to see distant objects is to cancel the excessive optical power of the eye by using a negative lens in front of the eye (see Figure 3-35). A negative lens is one that is thicker at the edges than in the center.

The second type of focusing problem is called far-sightedness, or hyperopia, and results when the eye does not have enough optical power. A far-sighted person can see

Figure 3-35
Two types of focusing problems

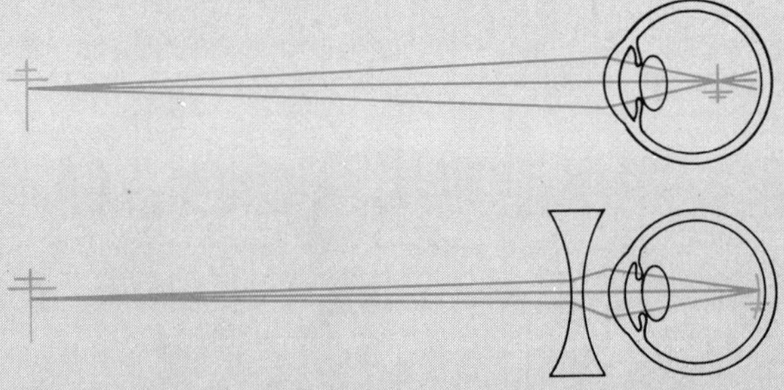

Near-sightedness corrected by a negative lens

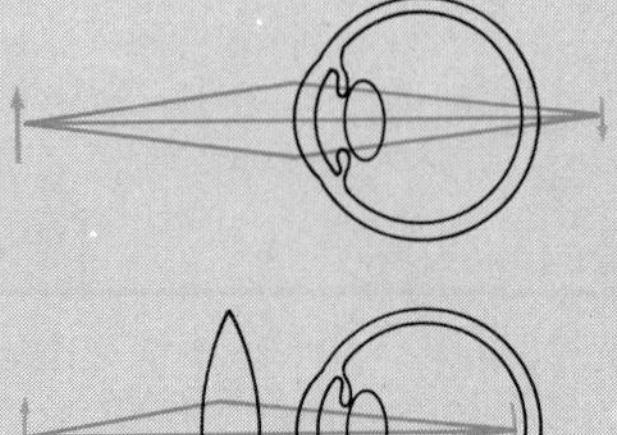

Far-sightedness corrected by a positive lens

Landing an aircraft requires skill, experience, and accurate interpretation of all visual cues.

Light for the Blind

The need is plain enough—of the estimated 350,000 legally blind persons in the U.S., fewer than 20 per cent read Braille and a scant one in ten can get about with a cane or Seeing-Eye dog. For the past four years, Dave [a 43-year-old electronics technician in Salt Lake City who has been blind for the last 28 years as the result of congenital eye defects] and Doug, a 28-year-old graduate student blinded by a land-mine explosion seven years ago in Vietnam, have been active collaborators in a program to devise a system of artificial vision at the University of Utah's Institute for Biomedical Engineering. Preliminary experiments—in which the volunteers could perceive spots and even patterns of light—are reported by biophysicist William H. Dobelle and computer scientist M. G. Mladejovsky and their colleagues in the journals *Science* and *Electronics*. . . .

Dobelle and his co-workers are now at work de-signing a miniaturized system that may produce useful vision, but they warn that its development is years away. The system would consist of a glass eye containing a lens and subminiaturized camera that would be placed in the eye socket and attached to the eye muscles. Through a wire leading out of the eye socket, the camera would transmit electronically various levels of light to a tiny computer built into an eyeglass frame. The computer—like the large one used in the experiments—would translate the light into electric current, which would then be carried through receivers in the wearer's scalp to electrodes permanently planted in the brain. Such a device, Dobelle emphasizes, would not reproduce normal vision. But it would hopefully permit a blind person to perceive objects, including faces, and allow him to read. . . .

Newsweek
February 11, 1974

distant objects clearly, but does not have enough optical power to focus on close objects. In this case the method used to correct the focus is to place a positive lens—one that is thicker in the center than at the edges—in front of the eye. Now when the far-sighted person looks at a close object, the image of that object is focused on the retina, not behind it (see Figure 3–35). Lenses are like crutches; they are aids, but they do not correct the problem itself. They only allow a person to get along in the world. Perhaps in the future someone will discover methods that allow a near- or far-sighted person to see clearly without the use of optical crutches.

VISUAL ILLUSIONS

We read earlier that many visual illusions, the moon illusion, for example, are caused by our perceptual processes creating an internal representation based on inaccurate and misleading information. These illusions are fun to experience, but in real-world situations, such as flying an airplane, the consequences of the illusions may be tragic. Modern technology has developed ways to extend our behavioral capacities beyond all but the wildest dreams. It is not surprising that these new behavioral abilities can sometimes outstrip the ability of our perceptual mechanisms to provide an adequate basis for this behavior. For example, our own perceptual mechanisms evolved without having to support the ability to fly. Fortunately, modern technology has also developed ways to extend our sensory and perceptual information through instrumentation. Today, pilots of large airplanes use instrumentation in many situations where to rely on perceptual mechanisms alone would be to invite disaster. The psychologist Conrad Kraft discovered a common flying situation where the visual input causes pilots to overestimate their altitude, thus creating the danger of a crash. Pilots in this situation have learned to resist the strong temptation to rely solely on perceptual information and use aircraft instruments instead.

Sociological Problems Haunt Victims of Dyslexia

UPI

SANTA BARBARA, Calif. — At least 10 per cent, possibly more, of children in elementary schools suffer from dyslexia—a perceptual disorder which blocks their ability to read, spell, or write legibly. It could turn them into delinquents later on.

Recent federal studies indicate a deep sociological problem results from dyslexia with 80 per cent or more of the prison population in the United States affected by it.

Dyslexia, which may be inherited, scrambles symbols—letters and numbers—in the brain and also can cause a similar effect in hearing.

A dyslexic child may see the word "dog" as "god," may confuse concepts such as "floor" for "ceiling" and "hostile" for "hospitable." A "b" changes into a "d" or a number series such as "1-2-3" may come out "2-1-3."

Experts say many dyslexic children are of superior intelligence but often are lumped with retarded children or others with multiple learning disabilities because the disorder is not widely understood and there are no programs available within the public education system. . . .

Beth Slingerland of Seattle, a teacher and national consultant on dyslexia, told the Orton Society meeting that dyslexic children are "perfectly normal, intelligent children with no brain damage and no primary emotional problems."

"But they may have emotional problems due to academic failure and behavioral problems which may clear up when they get a taste of learning. . . .

Many eminent people have suffered from dyslexia including Vice President Nelson Rockefeller. . . .

President Woodrow Wilson and Albert Einstein also suffered from dyslexia, but overcame the difficulty.

Rocky Mountain News, *Denver*
December 21, 1975

Disorders of our perceptual systems can cause severe problems in functioning. You cannot easily learn to behave appropriately in a world you cannot perceive accurately. It is hoped that perception research will help us solve or cure such disorders as dyslexia.

Ambient Vision Lets
Blind Person 'See'

AP

STATE COLLEGE, Pa. — The person with "eyes in the back of his head" may be more common than not, a Pennsylvania State University professor says.

Dr. Herschel Leibowitz, a professor of psychology, said his research with the blind shows human beings have two types of sight — normal vision allowing them to see, and an ambient vision that subconsciously tells them where they are in relation to surroundings.

Thus, a blind person whose ambient vision hasn't been destroyed is capable of avoiding walls despite not being able to see them, Leibowitz said.

Because the two systems originate in different parts of the brain, a person may lose one type of vision but not the other in some cases of brain injury, Leibowitz said. Focal vision, as Leibowitz calls that used for reading and recognizing objects, is controlled by the visual cortex in the outer portion of the brain. Ambient vision, he said, originates inside the midbrain.

Leibowitz said the explanation for ambient vision is found in the interaction of fibers from the peripheral retina of the eye with vestibular fibers of the inner ear that are stimulated by gravity. That gives a person a sense of equilibrium, he said, an effect evident through motor activity rather than consciousness.

Experiments at the Neurological Clinic of the University of Freiburg, Germany, with a neurologist, Dr. Johannes Dichgans, confirmed this past year that people, like animals, have the two types of vision, Leibowitz said.

"Focal vision can be improved with glasses. It has to do with the 'what' of perception," Leibowitz said.

"Ambient vision is the 'where' of perception," he said. "It permits us to move about freely and orient ourselves in space. . . ."

The Denver Post
October 13, 1977

Can you think of ways to test Professor Leibowitz's hypothesis that there are actually two types of vision?

People with a deficiency in one sensory system usually develop increased abilities in other senses. The blind concentrate on the tactile sense by using braille. This student is using a braille map to study campus geography.

BLINDNESS

Blindness can result from any disruption of the visual system. A person may become blind because of interference with the optics of the eye, such as in cataracts. Another cause of blindness is damage to the retina or to the optic nerve. In these cases blindness results because information is prevented from reaching the brain. There is no input out of which to construct an internal representation. When damage occurs in visual areas of the brain, however, our visual ability may not be completely destroyed. As the article on "Ambient

Figure 3–36
Hearing loss associated with aging

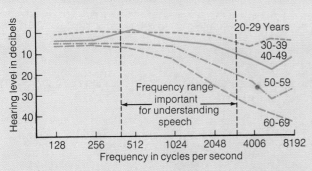

As we age, we progressively lose sensitivity to high-frequency sounds, including some of the sounds important for understanding speech. Each curve represents the reduction in sensitivity at different frequencies for the indicated age groups.

Figure 3–37
Hearing loss associated with environment

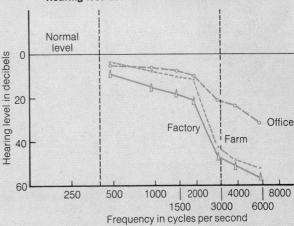

Unless precautions are taken, continuous exposure to loud sounds causes a permanent loss of sensitivity, especially at high frequencies. The graph shows that farm and factory workers (noisy environments) suffer more hearing loss than office workers (quiet environments). To avoid such damage, ear protectors should be worn during exposure to loud noises.

vision" suggests, perhaps those people who have damaged the visual cortex and are "blind" as a result have damaged only the perceptual mechanisms that supply answers to the question "what is out there?," leaving the "where is it located?" mechanisms intact. Might it not be possible to train such "blind" people to use these intact mechanisms more fully? Only further research will tell.

When blindness is caused by information not reaching the brain, it may be possible to supply the brain directly with the needed information. One approach is to stimulate the visual cortex directly with electrical signals derived from a tiny TV camera mounted on eye-glass frames. This approach has not been very successful so far, but with our increased understanding of the functions of cells in the visual cortex, perhaps this approach will soon enable the blind to see again.

DEAFNESS

The loss of the ability to hear some or all of the auditory spectrum is a serious problem for many people, especially older ones. Loss of hearing can result from mechanical changes in the middle or inner ears or from damage to the neural mechanisms. Some loss of sensitivity to high frequencies seems to occur as a function of the aging process. Figure 3–36 shows this trend. After the age of 30, people become progressively deaf to frequencies above about 1000 Hz. By the age of 70, the loss is severe enough that it interferes with speech understanding. This loss contributes to the feeling of isolation experienced by many older people in our society.

Much of this loss of sensitivity may be due to the exposure to loud noises prevalent in our environment. Figure 3–37 shows the effect of different occupations on deafness to high frequencies. People working in noisy environments (farm and factory workers exposed to loud machinery) show a much more severe loss than do office workers. Noise may have additional effects, such as mental depression.

As in the area of vision, scientists are also trying to restore the hearing of deaf people by electrical stimulation of the auditory nerve. It is hoped that electrical signals from a microphone can be transformed to stimulate the

Help for Deaf Babies

Matt Clark with Dan Shapiro

About one in every 2,000 babies in the U.S. is born with a significant degree of deafness. But diagnosis with conventional audiometric testing is difficult in such cases because a baby can't describe how noises sound to him. At the University of California in San Diego, however, a team of neuroscientists is detecting hearing problems in infants by measuring the electrical impulses produced by sound as they travel from the ear to the higher auditory centers of the brain.

The team's leader, Dr. Robert Galambos, says there are two main types of deafness in children: first, conductive hearing loss, often involving damage to the bones of the middle ear that conduct sound waves from the eardrum to the inner ear; second, sensory-neural deafness, caused usually by a lack of hairlike cells in the cochlea of the inner ear that carry sound to the auditory nerve.

Many of these hearing problems can be corrected—by surgery, medication or the use of hearing aids. But because of the difficulty of testing hearing in small children, deafness often isn't detected until the child is around 2. Deprived of normal hearing perception for such a period, Galambos says, a child will suffer a lag in the development of speech and language skills that may lead to a permanent handicap—even after the hearing disorder is eventually diagnosed.

The new test was developed by Galambos and his colleagues at several other laboratories over the past eight years. It involves the measurement of electrical activity generated in response to sound by the brain stem, a short structure between the top of the spinal cord and the base of the cerebral cortex to which the auditory nerve is connected.

Signals

By means of earphones, the infant is presented with a series of clicking sounds that stimulate the auditory nervous system. The electrical activity evoked by the sounds in the brain is picked up by electrodes placed behind each ear and on top of the head. These electrical signals are amplified, fed into a computer and printed out in the form of waves on a graph.

Within 12.5 milliseconds of a click, the graph of a normal baby will show seven distinct peaks, each representing a point along the path the sound has taken from the auditory nerve to the hearing centers of the cerebral cortex. For a baby with impaired hearing, the peaks take longer to appear. Different types of hearing defects, moreover, will produce wave patterns that deviate from the normal in characteristic ways. For example, absence of all seven waves indicates total sensory-neural deafness, which is usually untreatable. In conductive deafness, on the other hand, wave patterns will emerge if the intensity of the sound is increased. Hearing aids are frequently sufficient to correct this problem. . . .

Newsweek
December 8, 1975

auditory nerve of a deaf person, resulting in relatively "normal" input to the brain. So far only limited success has been achieved with this technique. But the knowledge gained from these first steps may enable deaf people 50 years from now to hear once again.

SUBLIMINAL ADVERTISING

Several years ago advertising agencies claimed that rapidly presented verbal messages, superimposed on a regular movie, could be used to make people hungry or thirsty without their being aware of the message itself. This technique was called subliminal advertising and was based on the (incorrect) notion that there existed a threshold above which stimuli were detectable and below which they were not. Today these claims are largely discredited. There is no evidence that it is possible to present an effective verbal message without its being clearly detectable.

It may be possible to evoke feelings, both positive or negative, through the use of nonverbal, visually suggestive material. There is very little experimental evidence relevant to these claims. Little is known about the es-

Our environment shows evidence of sensory extremes as well as physical and chemical excesses.

Modern urban areas often produce unpleasant, and sometimes painful, noise pollution.

See Sex in a Box of Crackers? That's Subliminal Ad at Work

Michael Dixon

CHICAGO — When you look at a magazine or television advertisement, you see more than you think you do—only you don't know it. But media-watcher Wilson Bryan Key does.

When Key looks at the picture on the box of a nationally known brand of crackers, or at the crackers themselves, he sees a pattern of the word "SEX" embedded in both.

In a TV commercial for a drain opener, Key sees the word "SEX" in the sink, formed as the water gurgles down the drain. Key even sees those "SEXes" on the arms of a cute little baby in a toothpaste ad.

No, Wilson Bryan Key isn't a twisted personality who sees sex everywhere. He says everybody can see the messages about sex and death that are present in advertising, just as he does. He'll point them out to you, and you'll see them, too. It's all right there for your subconscious to take in and, if pointed out, for the naked eye.

The cracker, drain opener and toothpaste ads are examples of subliminal advertising. By definition, the word subliminal is a psychological term refer-ring to the use of stimuli that operate below the threshold of consciousness. The messages in those ads aren't perceived by the conscious eye, unless told they exist.

But the subconscious mind does perceive the information immediately, and stores it. So the next time you see the brand of cracker, drain opener or toothpaste in a store, you probably will opt for it over other brands.

Wilson Brian Key may have seen more of those unconscious messages than anyone. He has served as a professor of journalism at four universities and written two books, "Subliminal Seduction" and . . . "Media Sexploitation". . . . Both books and Key's work with the Medaprobe Center for the Study of the Media, his San Diego-based company, all revolve around the exploration of the use of subliminal techniques in media. . . .

"Almost 98 per cent of subliminal ads have themes related to either sex or death," Key explained. "We know that the brain picks up information and retains it largely based on its emotional content. Since most people respond strongly to sex, that's what's used most often. But a lot of subliminal themes revolve around death. . . ."

The Denver Post
July 28, 1977

111

Honesty Being Stressed
with Subliminal Message

AP

ATLANTA — A subliminal, taped message that says "I will not steal" is being tested on shoppers in "a large Eastern Seaboard city" to see whether it will cut down on shoplifting.

The words "I will not steal," "I am honest" and others are "embedded" in background music, according to Dr. Hal Becker, a behavioral scientist at Tulane University. "To the best of my knowledge, it is not in use anywhere except in our field test," he said.

The Denver Post
April 14, 1978

thetic nature of perceptual experiences. What makes certain visual stimuli—paintings, for example—pleasing and certain others unpleasant? This is an area that is ripe for good experimental research.

PERCEPTUAL CONFLICTS

Our internal representation is based on information from all the sensory systems, and there is usually no conflict between them. But what happens if the brain receives conflicting information? One of two things usually happens: either processing continues normally by ignoring one of the sources of conflicting information or processing is greatly slowed down by the conflict.

The first possibility is to ignore one kind of information. The most common occurrence of this, called visual capture, is when visual information overrules other sources. The ability of a ventriloquist depends on visual capture. On the one hand an observer's auditory localization mechanism is signaling that the source of the dummy's voice is the ventriloquist's mouth, but on the other hand, the observer's visual system is correlating the movement of the dummy's mouth with the speech sounds. Since the visual system indi-

cates that the ventriloquist's mouth is not moving and the dummy's is, the experience created by the perceptual mechanisms is that of a speaking dummy. Ventriloquists do not "throw" their voices, they depend on the visual capture effect. If you close your eyes when watching a ventriloquist act, you will experience both the "dummy's voice" and the ventriloquist's voice as coming from the same location in space.

The other possibility in the case of conflict of information is to disrupt processing. A good example of such disruption is shown in color Plate 9, where the names of colors are printed in ink of different colors. Both kinds of information, the color experience of the letters and the color name represented by the word itself, are coming in through the visual system. It is quite difficult to ignore one in order to process the other rapidly. Test yourself on this demonstration. Look at the top section of the plate and name the color of each patch as fast and as accurately as you can, timing yourself with a second hand. Now name the *colors* of the letters below, ignoring the meaning of the words they form. You will find that your speed is considerably slowed down. Now read the words printed in black ink below. Your speed will return to normal because no conflict exists. It is as if, when reading the color names printed in different colored inks, both color names compete for access to the verbal processes, and since we cannot say two different words at the same time, our reading time is greatly slowed.

Another dramatic example of conflict between two types of perceptual information is evidenced in motion sickness. The brain has two major sources of information about body motion: the visual system and the vestibular system, located in the inner ear. Normally, the two systems signal the same information. But picture this situation. If your entire room, with you in it, were tilted 30 degrees to one side, how would you know it? Well, from the visual point of view, you would not know it because, visually, everything would be the same. But the vestibular system would be signaling that everything had tilted. When you are on a ship, especially below deck in a cabin, as the ship rocks back and forth, the vestibular system is constantly telling the rest of the brain that you are rocking back and forth. But the visual system has no information about your movement, since as your body moves, so does the whole cabin. So your visual system tells the rest of the brain that the body is stationary. This situation, for reasons not well understood, causes intense nausea and may lead people to vomit.

To prevent sea sickness or eliminate it when you begin to feel sick you must restore the agreement between the visual and vestibular information. If you fixate the horizon or an object on land as your body rocks back and forth, the visual system is able to sense the motion by comparison with the stationary land or horizon. It then signals the brain — in agreement with the vestibular system — that the body is rocking. The symptoms of nausea will rapidly disappear. Seasoned sailors adapt to the disagreement between the two systems so that nausea is not a problem. Such persons, when they go ashore, report that there is a short period of time when the stable ground feels as though it is rocking!

Basic Principles of Learning

4

When we look for basic explanations of behavior, we have two places to turn—heredity and environment. Throughout most of the history of psychology, environment has been the preferred explanation, although modern work on behavioral genetics (see Chapter 2) has made it clear that heredity is also crucial. Both heredity and environment are involved in behavior.

To understand the effects of environment on behavior, we must talk about learning. Psychologists have asked: Do children learn prejudicial attitudes from their parents? Can we learn while sleeping? Are personality traits of adults learned when they are children? Is stuttering a bad habit that children learn? What is the best way to learn to speak a foreign language? Can we learn how to think? Have we all learned bad living and eating habits which affect our health? Do people who are mentally ill really suffer from having learned maladaptive ways of coping with the stresses of life? On and on the list could go. Every branch of psychology, indeed all areas of human concern, deal in a fundamental way with learning (see Table 4–1).

Since learning is one of the most important factors in behavior, we will take the next two chapters to examine the elements of learning. In this chapter we will concentrate on basic learning processes, commonly referred to as conditioning principles. In Chapter 5 we will discuss the more complex forms of learning with emphasis on human learning and memory.

LEARNING AND BEHAVIOR

For our present purposes, we will define learning as a relatively permanent change in behavior potential, traceable to experience and practice. Learning is closely related to knowledge, skill, and intention. Knowledge and intention are usually thought to be acquired through experience, and skill through practice. A teacher might tell his or her class that Columbus discovered America in 1492, and from then on, as long as they remember, the students *know* and can respond to that fact. After an experience of pleasure from an event or activity, such as eating ice cream or drinking good wine, these activities become the objects of one's wants and *intentions*.

TABLE 4–1   The Central Role of Learning in Psychology

Branch of Psychology	Sample Concerns Dealing with Learning
Physiological psychology	1. What changes take place in the nervous system when a person learns? 2. Are there physiological defects in the learning mechanism of mentally retarded individuals? Are there any drugs that speed up the learning process or correct physiological defects?
Educational psychology	1. Will learning be improved or impaired in school buildings with no walls separating the classrooms? 2. What is the best way to teach reading? Why do so many children fail to learn to read in school?
Developmental psychology	1. As a child grows, are there changes in the manner in which the individual learns that teachers should be aware of? 2. Are there periods of readiness for learning (for example, reading readiness) before which attempts at teaching the child will be useless?
Industrial psychology	1. What is the best way to train employees to be safety conscious? 2. What is the best way to retrain employees for jobs requiring new skills?
Social psychology	1. How do people learn attitudes? 2. Will social facilitation (being in groups) speed the learning process?
Clinical psychology	1. How can a therapist teach a client not to be afraid of catching a fatal illness from the "germs" in the person's own home? 2. What kind of reward or pleasure does a "peeping Tom" get from looking into his neighbors' windows?
Experimental psychology	1. What factors are important in determining the rate of learning? 2. Does learning take place faster with rewards, punishments, or both? 3. What is the best way to memorize (learn) a set of important facts?

Figure 4–1
Pavlov's work on classical conditioning

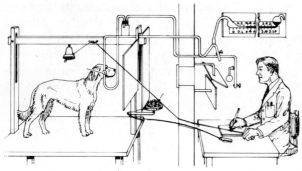

Pavlov's experimental set-up for measuring saliva flow in dogs. Food elicits saliva, measured by a tube connected to a cup placed over one of the salivary glands. The bell serves as the neutral stimulus.

Some activities, such as driving an automobile or playing baseball, involve *skills* as well as knowledge and intention. Repetition of these activities, or practice, leads to an improvement in skill. Note that each of these cases fits our definition of learning.

The relationship between learning and performance (the observed behavior in a particular situation) is important. Most learning theories, indeed most theories of behavior, note this special relationship, drawing a strong distinction between the two. Traditionally, it is argued that learning is never really observed directly. In many theories, learning is given the status of an **intervening variable,** a variable that stands between (intervenes) and provides a relationship between some stimulus in the environment and some response or performance on the part of a person. Learning is not observed directly but is inferred from observation of a change in **performance.**

Thus learning and performance are closely related but distinct concepts pertaining to behavior. Too often the distinction is not maintained, and performance is taken to be a direct and accurate measure of how much a person has learned. This implies that if learning occurs, performance should improve; and if learning is reduced—for example, by forgetting—performance should get worse. But performance is not always an accurate reflection of the amount learned. Consider the basketball team that does well throughout the season, only to be humiliated in the state tournament. The team performed poorly, but not because the players forgot how to play or lost any of their skill. Other factors, such as tension or distraction, prevented them from performing at the level of their true ability. Schoolteachers frequently report that students do not perform up to their capabilities. The students may have the necessary knowledge and skill, but for some reason these are not reflected in their performance. Their poor performance is often attributed to lack of motivation.

Because learning is such a fundamental concept, let us consider carefully the two main types of conditioning. Most instances of learning can be categorized into these basic types: **classical conditioning** and **instrumental** or **operant conditioning.** Indeed, some investigators suggest that there are just two types of learning. Incidentally, we could just as readily refer to these as classical and instrumental "learning" if it were not for a historical precedent favoring the term "conditioning."

CLASSICAL CONDITIONING

Pavlov's Work

Ivan Pavlov, the Nobel Prize–winning Russian physiologist, was among the first to report classical conditioning. During his studies of digestion, he examined the characteristics of dogs' salivary flow, a reflex response to food in the mouth. Pavlov's experimental method was to present food to the dog and measure the amount of saliva (see Figure 4–1). In the process he discovered that if a neutral stimulus, one that did not automatically elicit saliva, such as a bell, was paired repeatedly with the food, the dog would gradually "learn" to salivate at the sound of the bell alone, without any food. Learning to respond to a formerly neutral stimulus, because that stimulus is paired with another stimulus that already elicits a response, is the essential characterization of classical conditioning.

The importance of Pavlov's work cannot be overestimated. Not long after it became known, some psychologists began to argue that all behavior is based on classical conditioning. Al-

Pavolv's early experiments at the Soviet Military Medicine Academy.

though this extreme view is no longer popularly held in America, Russian psychology is still dominated by theories based on the principles of classical conditioning. It is agreed, at any rate, that a significant portion of our behavior can be better understood by noting the influence of classical conditioning.

Stimuli and Responses

The conditioning situation involves four events, two pertaining to the stimulus and two to the organism's response. There is a neutral stimulus that, prior to conditioning, does not elicit the desired, to-be-learned, response. This is the **conditioned stimulus** (CS), the bell in our example from Pavlov. The second stimulus is the **unconditioned stimulus** (UCS). Prior to conditioning it reliably elicits the desired response. Presentation of meat, the UCS, elicits saliva flow before conditioning. The salivary response to the UCS is known as the **unconditioned response** (UCR). This is the response that occurs before any conditioning has taken place. The response that begins to happen as a result of conditioning is called the **conditioned response** (CR)—a salivary response to the bell alone in the absence of meat.

Conditioning occurs as the two stimuli are presented contiguously (close together in space and time) and repeatedly. Usually the UCS is presented just after the CS. Gradually, after several pairings of the CS and UCS, the CS begins to elicit the flow of saliva. Whenever this happens, the animal has made a CR. The once-neutral CS (bell) is now capable of eliciting

A Cough for Pavlov

"Saint Ildefonso used to scold me and punish me lots of times. He would sit me on the bare floor and make me eat with the cats of the monastery. These cats were such rascals that they took advantage of my penitence. They drove me mad stealing my choicest morsels. It did no good to chase them away. But I found a way of coping with the beasts in order to enjoy my meals.

"I put them all in a sack, and on a pitch black night took them out under an arch. First I would cough, and then immediately whale the daylights out of the cats. They whined and shrieked like an infernal pipe organ. I would pause for a while and repeat the operation—first a cough, and then a thrashing. I finally noticed that even without beating them, the beasts moaned and yelped like the very devil whenever I coughed. I then let them loose. Thereafter, whenever I had to eat off the floor, I would cast a look around. If an animal approached my food, all I had to do was to cough, and how that cat did scat!"

Thus, in free translation by the University of Connecticut's Professor Jaime H. Arjona, runs a story from *El Capellán de la Virgen (The Virgin's Chaplain)*, reprinted in the current *American Psychologist*. No clearer exposition of the principle of conditioned reflexes has ever been written. As every Russian schoolboy knows, reflex conditioning was unknown until it was discovered by Russian Physiologist Ivan Petrovich Pavlov (1849–1936). *El Capellán de la Virgen*, a play about the life of Saint Ildefonso (606–667), Archbishop of Toldeo, was written by the Spanish Dramatist Lope de Vega about 1615.

Time
January 23, 1956

Classical conditioning was known and used long before Pavlov.

saliva flow by itself. (See Table 4–2 for a summary of the events of classical conditioning.)

A situation commonly used in the study of classical conditioning in human beings is the reflex action of blinking the eyes. The UCS is a puff of air (delivered to the subject's eye) that regularly and forcefully elicits a blink (the UCR). Experimenters use an apparatus that

TABLE 4–2   Basic Features of Classical Conditioning (Illustrated by Salivary Conditioning)

Before Conditioning		
Meat or ⟶ UCS	saliva flow by reflex action, called the UCR	UCS = unconditioned stimulus, in this case the meat. The UCS already elicits the specific response of saliva flow.
Bell or ⟶ neutral stimulus	no saliva, only an "orienting response" (looking, pricking up ears, etc.)	UCR = unconditioned response made to the UCS, in this case saliva flow when meat is presented.

During Conditioning	
Bell (UCS) + meat (now CS) ⟶ saliva flow	Bell and meat are presented together for several trials.

After Conditioning	
Bell or ⟶ CS	saliva flow or CR	CS = conditioned stimulus, in this case the bell. CR = conditioned response to the CS, saliva flow when the bell is sounded and no meat is present.

both delivers the air puff and measures the amplitude, latency (time to respond), and other characteristics of eye blinks. The eye-blink response can be conditioned to a neutral stimulus, for example, the word "psychology." Conditioning begins by pairing the CS (*psychology*) with the UCS (air puff). Usually it is arranged so that the CS occurs slightly in advance of the UCS, for research has shown that a 0.5-second interval between the two stimuli (the *CS–UCS interval*) will yield most rapid conditioning of the eye-blink response. Periodically, the experimenter tests for the occurrence of a CR, a blink in response to the word "psychology" alone. On test trials the UCS might simply be omitted, or the experimenter might carefully observe records of eye movements to determine whether the subject begins to blink before the air puff is presented. If the eye blink occurs following the CS (and before the UCS), conditioning has occurred. The subject blinks to a formerly neutral stimulus and has acquired (learned to make) a CR.

If we introduce a longer time interval between the CS and UCS, conditioning is more difficult to produce, and if the CS–UCS interval becomes very long, no conditioning at all will take place except under very special circumstances. The best interval for conditioning varies with the response being conditioned. The interval tends to be around 0.5 second for quick responses such as eye blinks, but is longer for more slowly occurring and longer-lasting responses such as fear. The conditioning of fear to a neutral stimulus proceeds best with CS–UCS intervals of around 10 seconds and is not prevented by intervals as long as several minutes. In other words, normally it is necessary for the CS and UCS to be contiguous—close together in space and time—for conditioning to take place. This principle is embodied in the *law of contiguity*.

The Law of Contiguity versus Prepared Learning

The law of contiguity states that any two stimuli experienced together in space and time become associated with each other by the experiencing organism. It is often heralded as the most fundamental law of learning and the basic explanation of classical conditioning. In Pavlov's conditioning studies the CS and UCS were experienced close together in space and time; that is, the bell and food were spatially and temporally contiguous.

But what happens if the CS is separated from the UCS by a long interval? For example, suppose the bell is sounded but the food is not presented until 30 minutes later. The food, of course, elicits salivating in the dog, but even after several trials in which both food and bell are presented, the dog does not salivate to the bell alone. Conditioning does not occur with such a long delay. Thus the law of contiguity seems well supported.

However, conditioning has in fact been demonstrated when the interval between the CS and the UCS was even as long as 7 hours. S. H. Revusky (1968) did such an experiment using X-ray radiation as the UCS and a sweet solution as the CS. Earlier studies had shown that X-rays elicit the UCR of being sick (radiation sickness), which can be conditioned to the solution. Rats that drank the sweet solution while being radiated developed a firm dislike for the solution, which normally they enjoyed. Eventually the animals became sick at the sight, taste, and smell of the solution, even when no X-rays were given. Thus the rats had developed a conditioned aversion to sweets, as the law of contiguity would predict.

Revusky tried the same conditioning procedure, except that he changed the CS–UCS interval to 7 hours, so the stimuli were no longer contiguous. The rats drank the sweet water and were radiated 7 hours later. Yet even with such a long delay, the rats developed a dislike for the solution (Figure 4–2). Either Revusky's demonstration is not an instance of classical conditioning or the law of contiguity is not the only explanation of why conditioning occurs.

A possible explanation of this phenomenon is that some organisms have a built-in conditioning system, genetically based, that quickly associates certain kinds of stimuli. Thus there might be a special system that relates food stimuli, through taste perception, with feeling sick. Such a system would have survival value for the species because it would underlie the organism's ability to avoid eating things that might be poisonous. Such learning has been called **prepared learning.**

The concept of prepared learning is nicely illustrated in an experiment performed by Garcia and Koelling (1966). Rats were exposed to a stimulus consisting of a sweet taste, a light, and a noise. This was done by turning on the light and sounding the noise whenever the rat licked at a tube containing the sweet solution. For some rats the exposure to the "sweet bright noisy water" was followed by exposure to an illness-inducing agent. For other rats the exposure to the sweet bright noisy water was followed by electric shock delivered to the paws.

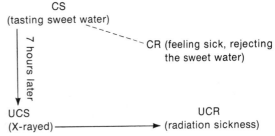

Figure 4–2
It looks like classical conditioning, but is it?

CS (tasting sweet water) ----→ CR (feeling sick, rejecting the sweet water)

7 hours later

UCS (X-rayed) ————→ UCR (radiation sickness)

The rats were then tested to determine whether they had formed an aversion to the sweet taste or to the light and the noise.

The results were dramatic. The rats that had experienced illness following the sweet bright noisy water formed an aversion to the sweet taste but not to the light or the noise. That is, they would not drink a sweet solution but readily drank unsweetened water when the light and noise were present. In contrast, the rats that had experienced electric shock to the paws following the CS formed an aversion to the light and noise rather than to the taste. They drank the sweet solution but would not drink it in the presence of the light and noise. This suggests that rats preferentially associate gastrointestinal consequences (illness) with taste stimuli and exteroceptive consequences (shock to the paws) with external stimuli such as lights and sounds. Such a mechanism would be very adaptive, since in nature illness is usually caused by something that has been eaten, and external pain is usually caused by an external event (a predator, a fall, and so on). Thus this sort of prepared learning should allow organisms to learn quickly to avoid the likely cause of a dangerous event.

Prevalence of Classical Conditioning

Examples of classical conditioning abound in the everyday life of animals and human beings. One important example is the conditioning of emotional responses. Some psychologists have argued that anxiety—perhaps the most common symptom of emotional disorder—is a case of classically conditioned fear. Suppose a person experiences terror from a wild automobile drive that ends in a crash and painful injury. The fear

Figure 4-3
Classical conditioning of fear

A baby develops fear of an animal because that animal has become associated with a fear-eliciting stimulus. In panel 1 the rabbit is approached by the child, who shows no signs of fear before conditioning. Then the rabbit is presented contiguously with a loud noise that scares the child (panel 2). Panel 3: After conditioning, the rabbit alone is capable of eliciting fear in the child. Panel 4: Worst of all, the child may now be afraid of all furry things, such as rats, stuffed animals, or even a man with a beard. The fear, originally conditioned to the rabbit, has now generalized to similar stimuli. Can you identify the CS, UCS, CR, UCR, and the generalization test stimuli? How might a child or even an adult learn to be afraid of policemen? of doctors and dentists? of strangers? of high places? of taking examinations?

TABLE 4-3   Diagrams of Classical Conditioning

Basic pattern	CS ⟍	
	UCS ⟶	⟶ UCR
Sight of a car provokes anxiety following automobile accident	Sight of automobile ⟍	
	Automobile crash and injury ⟶	⟶ Fear
Child cries at sight of baby-sitter before parents leave	Baby-sitter arrives ⟍	
	Parents leave child ⟶	⟶ Crying
Seeing a cat elicits wheezing before any dander could contact the body	Sight of a cat ⟍	
	Cat dander ⟶	⟶ Allergic reaction such as wheezing
Constant worrying about one's job, even when not on the job, leads to stomach ulcers	Thinking or worrying about the job ⟍	
	Tension or anxiety (on the job) ⟶	⟶ Secretion of acid in stomach

examples of classical conditioning are diagramed in Table 4-3.

INSTRUMENTAL OR OPERANT CONDITIONING

The second basic type of learning is called **instrumental** or **operant conditioning.** The term "operant" is used to emphasize the work required of the learners (they must "operate" on their environment), while the term "instrumental" indicates that learners have some control over their own circumstances (what they do is instrumental to what happens to them). Thus instrumental conditioning involves more activity on the part of the learner than classical conditioning does. Whenever a person behaves so as to gain reward or avoid punishment, that behavior is an example of instrumental action. The emphasis in this form of behavior is on

and pain (UCRs) have been elicited in the context of, and thus could become conditioned to, "automobile" stimuli. The mere sight of a car may elicit the vague emotional feeling of fear in the person following recovery. While the feeling of physical pain would be absent, "mental pain" or conditioned fear might occur. Some psychologists have argued that fear conditioned to specific neutral stimuli is the essence of anxiety (see Figure 4-3). This and other everyday

Reprinted by permission of Newspaper Enterprise Association.

intention and achievement; the learner acts intentionally in a particular manner to bring about a specific state of affairs.

Key words in this type of conditioning are *contingency* and *consequences.* Instrumental learning involves learning about the consequences of behaving in a certain way—learning that if a particular response is made it will be followed by a particular stimulus event. For example, a little boy might learn that if he cries, his mother will pay attention to him and comfort him, perhaps even giving him some candy to "make you feel better." The basic idea is simple: Learning consists of discovering that a particular response (R) is followed by a particular stimulus event (S) or consequence (Table 4-4).

Another way of looking at this kind of learning is in terms of contingency learning. The learner discovers that in order to make a particular consequence occur (say a piece of candy), he will have to make a particular response (perhaps crying). In such a case, we would say that getting the candy is contingent upon crying. The stimulus consequence is contingent upon the learner's making a particular response. In short, responses have consequences; and if we

want to produce particular consequences, we have to make particular responses because the consequences are contingent upon the responses. A young boy might have to take out the garbage and mow the lawn in order to get his allowance; his behavior of taking out the garbage and mowing the lawn is an example of instrumental behavior. The consequences of doing his chores consist of getting his allowance, having his parents praise and thank him, and so on. Getting his allowance is contingent upon completing his chores.

Whenever the occurrence of a particular stimulus consequence is contingent upon the organism's behavior, or whenever a particular response leads to a particular set of consequences, we have the basic instrumental learning situation. This response-reward contingency is, of course, not present in classical conditioning. For example, in classical eye-blink conditioning, the air puff (UCS) is delivered regardless of whether the subject blinks when the CS is presented. Of course there is also a contingency in classical conditioning, but it is a contingency between two stimuli (the CS and the UCS). In contrast, instrumental conditioning involves a contingency between a response and the subsequent stimulus consequence (the reinforcer). The reinforcer (the boy's allowance, for example) is contingent upon the prior occurrence of a particular response (mowing the lawn).

Historical Antecedents

Whereas classical conditioning is associated with the name of Pavlov, instrumental conditioning

TABLE 4-4   The Basic Features of Operant Conditioning

The subject emits a response	which leads to or produces	a stimulus consequence
R	$\longrightarrow$	S
Hungry rat presses a bar		experimenter presents food
R	$\longrightarrow$	S

B. F. Skinner

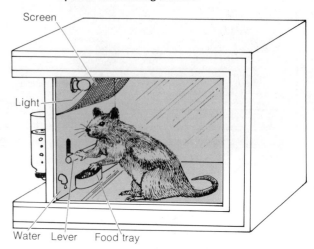

Figure 4–4
Operant conditioning chamber

Screen

Light

Water   Lever   Food tray

The experimental chamber often called a Skinner box is used for many studies of operant conditioning. When the rat pushes the lever, a pellet of food automatically drops into the food tray.

is associated with the names of E. L. Thorndike and B. F. Skinner (see Chapter 1). Thorndike was the first to perform laboratory experiments using instrumental conditioning. His work led him to formulate the **law of effect,** which is the forerunner of the contemporary principle of reinforcement (see below). But it is Skinner who has made operant conditioning famous. He has studied the behavior of pigeons, rats, and human beings, including his own children. His work has led to the identification of the basic elements and laws of operant conditioning. He is the leading figure in the field of operant conditioning and almost singlehandedly has been responsible for the recognition of the importance of this type of learning in analyzing, predicting, and controlling behavior. His pioneering efforts have led to the development of an entire philosophy of behavior known as *functional analysis* because of its emphasis on the functions (and the consequences) of behavior. His discoveries have been the foundation for a whole new technology of **behavior modification** that is still in its early stages, but nevertheless has already had enormous success in its application and has been one of the most controversial developments in the history of psychology.

Reinforcement

A **reinforcer** is a stimulus event (a consequence) that increases the likelihood of any response

with which it is associated. Reinforcement is the effective stimulus that makes learning instrumental responses possible. Skinner used a device now known as the Skinner box to investigate the relationship between the events of instrumental conditioning. He placed a rat inside a glass box that contained a lever and a food tray (see Figure 4–4). The animal was allowed to explore the box freely. If it happened to press down on the lever, a pellet of food automatically dropped into the tray. A timer connected to the bar recorded the number of presses the rat made while in the box. Pressing the bar was the response to be learned (the operant response), and the food pellet was the stimulus consequence (or reinforcement). Skinner discovered that by rewarding the rat with food each time it pressed the bar, the rate of presses increased dramatically. The rat learned the instrumental response by being reinforced.

The term "reinforcement" is used to describe the fact that a response increases in frequency when the occurrence of the response is followed by the reinforcing stimulus. There are two basic ways to produce increases in response frequency involving two basic types of reinforcement, positive reinforcement and negative reinforcement.

Punishment Is Not the Same as Negative Reinforcement

Punishment: an unpleasant stimulus is *delivered* contingent on the occurrence of a particular *undesired* behavior. This punishing stimulus terminates at some point in time, but the termination is in no way related to the behavior of the organism being punished.

Examples:
1. A child spills his or her milk and the parents administer a spanking.
2. A prisoner spits in the face of his or her captor and is beaten with a club.

Negative reinforcement: an unpleasant stimulus is *terminated* contingent on the occurrence of a particular *desired* behavior. The beginning of the unpleasant stimulus is in no way related to the occurrence of any particular behavior.

Examples:
1. A prisoner of war is tortured until he or she makes responses desired by his or her captors, such as confession; the torture is then terminated. This process strengthens the response of saying what the enemy wants to hear.
2. A rat is shocked continuously until it jumps over a barrier, at which point the shock is terminated. This strengthens the response of jumping.

In most everyday situations, punishment and negative reinforcement occur together and so are easily confused. The same stimulus event is used to punish one response and negatively reinforce another.

Example:
A little boy comes home and throws his coat on the floor. The parent yells at the child until he picks up the coat and hangs it in the closet, at which point the yelling stops.

Here the yelling is serving once as a punishment and once as a negative reinforcer. It is a punishment for throwing the coat on the floor because it is an unpleasant stimulus that is delivered contingent on the coat being thrown on the floor. It is a negative reinforcer because it is continuously being delivered until the child picks up the coat and hangs it up, at which point the shouting is all over. The parent has *punished* throwing the coat on the floor and *negatively reinforced* hanging the coat in the closet. So you can see that punishment is used to *decrease* the rate of an undesired response, while negative reinforcement is used to *increase* the rate of a desired response.

In positive reinforcement, the response frequency or response strength is increased by delivering a pleasant stimulus when the organism makes the desired response. Thus, rewarding the rat with a food pellet when it makes the response of pressing the lever is an example of positive reinforcement—the frequency of bar pressing increases.

The second basic type of reinforcement—negative reinforcement—also results in *increased* rates of response. However, it is accomplished by arranging a negative contingency—making a particular response leads to the termination or removal of an unpleasant stimulus. For example, if the floor of the rat's cage is electrified so that the rat is being continuously shocked in the cage, and if the shock is terminated for a period of time each time the rat presses the lever, we will observe that the rate of lever pressing increases. Lever pressing is being reinforced, but it is being negatively reinforced. Lever pressing leads to the termination of the shock (an unpleasant stimulus). In contrast, in the case of positive reinforcement, lever press-

**"Mommy, we keep saying 'go home, kitty-cat'—
but she just keeps hanging around here!"**

Reprinted courtesy of The Register and Tribune Syndicate, Inc.

If there is one thing that is certain about the behavior of animals and people, it is that they will repeat responses that lead to rewards. The cat will undoubtedly keep coming back as long as rewards are available. Likewise, assuming that the children like the cat and have fun (a reward) when they are feeding it, they will keep on bringing more food.

ing leads to the presentation of a pleasant stimulus (a piece of food). Both cases involve increased rates of responding and are thus instances of reinforcement; however, two opposite ways of increasing the response are used.

The opposite effect of reinforcement on response rate would occur in a situation in which a contingency is arranged that results in a *decreased* rate of response, eventually to the point where the organism completely withholds the response. One such contingency is known as punishment. In punishment, an unpleasant stimulus is delivered if the response is made. For example, if we took a rat that had learned to press a lever in the box because of positive reinforcement and then started to punish the rat with electric shock each time it pressed a lever, we would observe a decrease in the rate

of lever pressing, to the point that the rat would cease to press the lever at all.

Secondary Reinforcement

The kinds of reinforcement we have considered thus far are automatically effective. The subject does not need prior experience with reinforcers like food or electric shock for them to have the effect of increasing the subject's responses. Reinforcers like food for the hungry animal, water for the thirsty, and painful shock are all examples of "innate" or "unlearned" reinforcers. Technically they are referred to as **primary reinforcers.**

Other stimuli are capable of becoming reinforcers if the organism learns that they are associated with primary reinforcers or that they can be used to obtain primary reinforcers. Once the subject learns about them, they become **secondary reinforcers.** The most potent example of a secondary reinforcer for human beings is, of course, money. Consider the dollar bill and ask yourself why it is that we all learn and perform the extraordinary tasks that we do in order to get money. The dollar cannot be eaten or drunk. It becomes a reinforcer only because we have learned that money can buy food, drink, and many other things; that is, money will buy primary reinforcers (see Figure 4–5).

In our society, secondary reinforcers are extremely important. Most people are not starving or thirsty or lacking oxygen. To be sure, the promise of sexual reinforcement may control a portion of human behavior, but, sex aside, most of our activity does not need to be motivated by primary reinforcement. Psychologists of all persuasions have postulated the existence of many learned secondary reinforcers. In addition to money, obvious examples are prestige, fame, security, and approval. There is, of course, a heavy emphasis on social factors in this list, implying the existence of a strong learned need to be liked by others. This, in turn, tends to make us dependent on the people who can deliver these reinforcers.

While it seems rather obvious that human beings, in general, are social animals with a strong need to be liked by other members of the species, it is not necessarily the case that this is based on learning. A new emerging field that is getting a great deal of publicity these days, sociobiology (see Chapter 7), would suggest that much of this type of behavior is innate to the species. It is also true that learned secondary reinforcers, when acquired in controlled laboratory situations, do not work well unless they are rather continuously paired with primary reinforcers. In technical terms, secondary reinforcers extinguish rapidly if they are not repeatedly paired with primary reinforcers. This fact leads many people to conclude that human behavior cannot be easily explained by saying it is controlled by secondary reinforcers, since these reinforcers (such as prestige, fame, approval) are paired only with primary reinforcers (food, water, sex, and so on) in extraordinarily indirect ways. So this leaves the door open for other explanations of socially based rewards, the most obvious of which is that evolution has created a species (human beings) that is innately social in character. In other words, the social rewards could be viewed as primary reinforcers, not secondary ones based on learning. It is an interesting point to consider.

Many secondary reinforcers seem to develop through classical conditioning. The most important source of secondary reinforcement for a child is the parents. One or the other parent is almost always associated with the delivery of the infant's primary reinforcement—food, diaper changes, water, and comfort. Thus the mere sight of a child's parents becomes rewarding, and the child will work (crawl around) just to maintain sight of them.

Unfortunately, parents can inadvertently reinforce a bad habit merely by paying attention to the child at the wrong time. Suppose a little boy is playing with a friend and his mother overhears him saying or doing something "bad." Running to him immediately constitutes secondary reinforcement of the undesired behavior, even if she scolds him when she gets there. Because attention has such a powerful effect, many psychologists recommend that a child's minor bad habits be ignored, at least as a first attempt at solution. Ignoring the child when he engages in "bad" behavior is a form of withdrawing reinforcement and should result in extinction of those habits. The picture is not this simple, of course, since attention is not the only reinforcer that is effective with children. In fact, it is important for anyone concerned with the rapid extinction of a response to remember to withhold not only primary reinforcement but also any secondary reinforcers that may be a natural part of the original learning situation.

Figure 4–5
Secondary reinforcement

Like human beings, chimpanzees can be trained to work for money (secondary reinforcement) that can be exchanged for primary reinforcement. The chimp shown here is about to put its money (a poker chip) into a "chimp-o-mat," which will dispense bananas or grapes. Chimps can be trained to work all day for poker chips if they have first learned that the poker chips can be used to obtain food.

Identifying Reinforcers

In order to institute instrumental reward training, one must identify those objects or events that the learner values. Obviously, candy and other favorite foods can be used with children, but there are side effects that may be

Table 4–5 Basic Instrumental Conditioning Situations

A. No cues available				B. Discriminative cues present		
	Train to elicit	Train to withhold			Train to elicit	Train to withhold
Use pleasant stimuli	Reward training	Omission training		Use pleasant stimuli	Discriminated operant	Discriminated omission
Use unpleasant stimuli	Escape training	Punishment training (passive avoidance)		Use unpleasant stimuli	Active avoidance	Discriminated punishment

detrimental. What other reinforcers will be effective is sometimes hard to know. One general principle that may be helpful for the identification of reinforcers has been suggested by David Premack. The *Premack principle* is that given two behaviors that differ in their likelihood of occurrence, the less likely behavior can be reinforced by using the more likely behavior as a reward. For example, given free choice, many children will spend more time watching TV than studying. Watching TV is a more probable behavior. The Premack principle states that the amount of studying can be increased by making TV time contingent on study behavior. Again, children are more likely to eat candy than to do odd jobs, given free choice. Thus candy can be used to encourage work. In a prison, playing softball is more probable than learning a new skill, given free choice. To induce skill acquisition, the prison administration might use access to the softball field as a reinforcer. Thus from observation of an organism in a free-option environment, one can develop a list or hierarchy of preferred behaviors.

Types of Instrumental Conditioning

We can derive four basic types of instrumental conditioning. We can try either to increase or decrease the rate of response. To accomplish this increase or decrease, we can use either a pleasant stimulus (such as food) or an unpleasant stimulus (such as electric shock). This gives us four combinations: (1) if we increase the rate of response using a pleasant stimulus, we have a positive reinforcement situation called *reward training;* (2) if we decrease the rate of response using a pleasant stimulus, we have a situation called *omission training;* (3) if we increase it by using an unpleasant stimulus, we have a negative reinforcement situation called *escape training:* and (4) if we decrease it by using an unpleasant stimulus, we have *punishment training* (Table 4–5).

Let us now discuss each of the four basic types: (1) In reward training positive reinforcement is used to elicit a desired response—a pleasant stimulus is contingent upon the occurrence of a particular response. Getting your allowance if you take out the garbage is an example of reward training. (2) In omission training, pleasant stimuli (usually called rewards) are used to get the learner to withhold a response that is not desired. For example, you make the purchase of a new car for yourself contingent on giving up cigarette smoking. The rewarding consequence is contingent on *not* making a particular response. (3) In escape training negative reinforcement is used to increase the frequency of a desired response. If the learner gives the desired response, the consequence is that an unpleasant stimulus will be terminated. For example, you could train a dog to jump over a fence by giving it an electric shock until it makes the jumping response. Turning off the shock is contingent on making the jump. Telling a convict that he can have "time off for good behavior" is an example of escape training—he can escape imprisonment if he produces "good behavior." (4) Finally, the fourth basic case is punishment training (also known as *passive avoidance*), and it is used to make the learner stop performing an undesired response. If the undesired response is made, the consequence is that an unpleasant stimulus is presented, and so the subject learns to withhold the response. Telling children that you will spank them if they say "dirty" words is an example; so is putting people in jail for breaking the law.

"I'm getting him conditioned beautifully — every time I run through the maze, he throws me a bit of cheese."

© Punch (Rothco).

Discriminative Stimuli (Cues)

Suppose a young girl is punished by her parents for saying "dirty" words. We might expect that she would never say them again. But the child can be punished only if her parents are there to hear her say the words; that is, the punishment can be delivered only when a certain stimulus (her parents) is present. If the stimulus is absent, the response can be made without the threat of punishment. Thus whether or not the child says dirty words depends upon whether or not her parents are present. The child can discriminate between the presence or absence of her parents, and she learns to make her behavior of saying dirty words contingent on this discrimination. There is a stimulus (the parents) that now controls whether or not the child says dirty words. This process is known as **stimulus control,** and the controlling stimulus is called a **discriminative stimulus** or *cue.*

In stimulus-control situations, a cue or stimulus is presented to the learner to indicate that reward or punishment will take place contingent on his or her behavior. Reward or punishment is contingent on behavior only when this discriminative stimulus is present. When the criti-

Experimental Diet Shocking

AP

MIAMI, Fla. — Several overweight Miami women have discovered that the best way to take it off is to plug in.

A team of Miami psychologists is helping patients diet by attaching a portable electric "shocker" to their forks to discourage rapid eating.

"We're aiming for a change in eating behavior and we're even doing things like timing the intervals between forks to the mouth and the number of chews of food," said Dr. Michael S. Stokols of the Center for Psychological Services Inc.

"We may ask a patient to bring a portion of her usual dinner right here to our office and then we hook her up with electrodes and the shocking mechanism," he said. "One of us may sit opposite her and eat ourselves. If the patient picks up the fork too soon, she will get a shock."

Stokols said the psychologist sets a timed waiting interval for the patient after analyzing her eating behavior.

The patient soon begins to "chain together" non-eating behavior to take up time at the table instead of simply eating.

"She may take a sip of water, dab her mouth with a napkin, speak to us, instead of wolfing down the food," he explained. .. .

"We're not shocking the eating itself — just rapid eating. And often we shock only when the patient eats the 'wrong' thing — maybe cake, ice cream and so forth," he said.

The weight loss itself is usually the principal "reinforcer" to change the eating behavior, the psychologist said, noting that some women patients have lost as much as 80 pounds using the center's technique.

And in case a patient begins to backslide into her old "food addiction" approach, there are even portable shockers available. .. .

Boulder (Colo.) Daily Camera
June 13, 1972

Here is an example of the use of punishment training to control eating behavior.

cal stimulus is not present or some other stimulus is present, no rewards or punishments are delivered regardless of what the learner does.

These cued situations are thus different from noncued situations, where reward or punishment is always available and contingent on behavior.

Stimulus-control learning (also called discriminative learning) can be demonstrated in the laboratory by training a rat to press a lever for food (reward) when a buzzer is sounded (cue present) and not to press when the buzzer is off (cue absent). The rat learns to stop pressing the bar as soon as the buzzer stops and to start pressing again as soon as the buzzer comes back on. Its pressing is then said to be under the (stimulus) control of the buzzer. In a real sense, its behavior is controlled by the buzzer.

Each of the four basic learning situations we have discussed has its counterpart involving a discriminative cue (see Table 4–5B). The rat's bar pressing for food only when the buzzer sounds is an example of a *discriminated operant.* Teenagers who do not smoke *only* when their parents are around to reward their abstention exemplify the *discriminated omission* response. Convicts who work hard *only* when a guard is watching exemplify *active avoidance* (they actively produce desired responses to avoid punishment from the guard). The child who omits dirty words from her vocabulary *only* when her parents are present to punish her exemplifies the process of *discriminated punishment.*

Shaping

Because the desired response may be uncommon or difficult, the individual using operant training procedures may want to use an auxiliary technique called **shaping.** Shaping consists of learning in graduated steps, where each successive step requires a response that is more similar to the desired performance. It is often known as the method of successive approximations.

Suppose an experimenter wanted to train a pigeon to peck an illuminated response button. He or she might start by reinforcing the pigeon just for turning its head toward the response button. After the animal begins to orient toward the button consistently, the experimenter may then require it to move toward the button before rewarding it. When the bird is trained to stand near the response button, the experimenter may withhold reinforcement until the animal makes slight head movements toward it.

In the next stage, the animal may be reinforced only if it actually contacts the response button with its beak. Finally, the animal is reinforced only when it hits the button with sufficient force to trip an automatic switch that controls the delivery of pigeon feed. After the bird has been shaped to peck forcefully at the button, the experimenter may introduce colored illumination as a discriminative cue.

INTERACTION OF CLASSICAL AND INSTRUMENTAL CONDITIONING

Thus far we have discussed classical and instrumental conditioning as though they were two entirely separate processes, some learning situations being an instance of one and some being an instance of the other. However, many learning situations involve both. This is because most instrumental reinforcers also serve as effective UCSs (eliciting a reflexive response) for classical conditioning. Even relatively simple examples that are thought to involve only one could really involve both. For example, take a simple discriminated operant situation in which a rat receives food reinforcement for pressing a lever in the presence of a tone, but does not receive food for pressing the lever in the presence of a light. Instrumental learning occurs when the organism learns a contingency between a response and an outcome of that response. Thus our example certainly involves instrumental learning, since there is a contingency between pressing the lever and food reward. However, our example also contains a contingency between stimuli, as in classical conditioning. Food is presented during the tone but not the light. Thus the tone is paired with the presence of food and the light with the absence of food. Therefore, classical conditioning (for example, salivation to the tone) as well as instrumental conditioning should occur, and it does.

Autoshaping

We have seen that classical and instrumental conditioning can occur together and that one can partially control the other. It is therefore possible to confuse a classically conditioned response for an instrumental one, and vice versa. Consider a frequently studied instrumental learning situation in which a hungry pigeon is

BEETLE BAILEY

given food for pecking a button or key when the key lights up. Because the pigeon is given food only if it pecks the illuminated key, we might assume that the pecking of the key is learned instrumentally. However, it is obvious that this situation contains a CS-UCS contingency (classical conditioning) as well as a response-reinforcer contingency (instrumental conditioning). Food occurs only when the key is illuminated. Thus the key is paired with food. The pigeon's UCR to a food UCS does include pecking, so it is possible that the pecking of the key is really a classically conditioned response.

If pecking the key is a classically conditioned response, it should occur even if there is no contingency between pecking and the occurrence of food. That is, pecking should develop if we simply pair the illumination of the key with the delivery of food even if the peck does not make the food come any sooner. Pecking of the key does indeed develop under such circumstances, and this phenomenon is called **autoshaping.**

This does not mean that pecking is always classically conditioned but only that it sometimes is. We must be very careful when determining the origins of different behaviors. In general, organisms seem to approach classically conditioned CSs for positive UCSs (for example, food) and withdraw from CSs for negative UCSs (for example, shock). Such approach and avoidance reactions often appear to be instrumental responses but are really classical in nature.

Two-Process Theory

Since both classical and instrumental conditioning frequently occur in the same situation, how does one process influence the other? A theory called **two-process theory** was developed by O. Hobart Mowrer and Richard L. Solomon to explain how the two different learning processes interact. They argued that emotional states become classically conditioned. They also argued that the occurrence of these classically conditioned states motivates instrumental responses and that the termination of these states reinforces instrumental responses.

To understand this view we will apply it to active avoidance learning (see p. 126). In avoidance learning a warning signal precedes the occurrence of some painful event such as electric shock. The occurrence of a response (for example, pressing a lever) in the interval of time between the onset of the warning signal and the scheduled time of the shock terminates the warning signal and avoids the shock. If no response is made during this interval, the shock is presented. It should be obvious that no responses will occur on the first few experiences the organism has with the warning signal-shock sequence since no learning will yet have occurred. This would mean that the warning stimulus is consistently followed by shock. Two-process theory argues that this should lead to the classical conditioning of fear to the warning signal. Thus on later trials the onset of the warning signal should produce this classically conditioned fear, and two-process theory asserts

BC by permission of John Hart and Field Enterprises, Inc.

The dinosaur is responding to a discriminative stimulus—the verbal command "sit." This is not the most elementary form of operant conditioning. In the fundamental form the dinosaur would be rewarded whenever it sat down. From there we might progress gradually—the procedure known as shaping—to the situation where it sits only on command and does not sit if we say "roll over" or if we say nothing.

that this fear state motivates the avoidance response. Further, the avoidance response terminates the warning signal in addition to avoiding the shock. The offset of the warning signal (now an unpleasant stimulus) should terminate the fear that it produces, and two-process theory argues that this should negatively reinforce the avoidance response.

The implication of this discussion of avoidance learning is that classically conditioned responses can control or modulate instrumental responses. The onset of the classically conditioned fear response is said to motivate the avoidance response; and its termination is said to reinforce the response. Two-process theory holds that much of instrumental learning is directly governed by such classically conditioned states rather than by primary reinforcers.

EFFECTS OF CONDITIONING

Conditioning is a multifaceted phenomenon, and it has many effects on the subsequent behavior of the organism. In this section we will discuss several of the more important effects and by-products of conditioning.

Extinction and Spontaneous Recovery

Extinction is a process that takes place when (in classical conditioning) the UCS is no longer paired with the CS or when (in instrumental conditioning) reinforcement of a learned response is withdrawn. The response frequency declines toward zero. In classical conditioning, as the CS is repeatedly presented alone, it gradually loses its power to elicit the CR. In instrumental conditioning, extinction is brought about by eliminating reinforcement. An example of the value of extinction might be the elimination of a bad habit. Habits, good or bad, are usually learned because a person has achieved something, reinforcement, for his or her action. By identifying the reinforcer of a bad habit and removing it, the habit can be extinguished and should disappear. Can you apply this principle to the elimination of temper tantrums in a child?

There is a process, however, that makes complete extinction difficult, if not impossible. This process is called **spontaneous recovery.** To illustrate, suppose a rat is trained to run a maze for food. On a certain day extinction is begun by removing food from the maze. The rat continues to run the maze, trial after trial, until finally it quits running. At this point, you might think that the rat will never again run the maze unless food is reinstated. But you would be wrong. If the rat is put back in the maze after a day, it will run again for a few trials. Although it is given no food, its attraction to the goal box seems to recover without intervening training, that is, spontaneously. If the goal was to eliminate the running response, spontaneous recovery has worked against extinction.

Spontaneous recovery is likely to occur after each of several successive extinction sessions.

Figure 4–6
Extinction-spontaneous recovery sequence

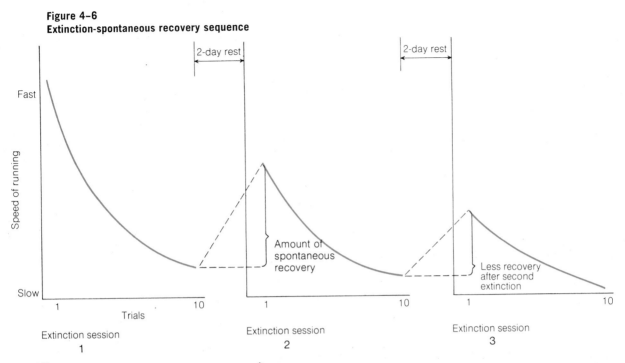

The three curves show the course of extinction of a maze-running habit in three successive extinction sessions, with a two-day rest between sessions. Note that the strength of the habit increases between the end of one session and the start of the next. This is called spontaneous recovery.

Total extinction is likely to take a long time, as shown in Figure 4–6, and may never be attained. Spontaneous recovery is one reason that we all find it so difficult to eliminate bad habits. Ask anyone who has tried to stop biting his or her nails. One way to forestall spontaneous recovery is to overextinguish the habit by carrying the extinction sessions on long after the response has ceased.

Partial Reinforcement and Extinction

During learning, reinforcement might not be presented for each and every response that the learner makes. That is, the learner's responses are only partially reinforced. **Partial reinforcement,** a reinforcement schedule in which less than 100 percent of all correct responses are rewarded, is a valuable aid in teaching new habits. For one thing, you save money and effort if you do not have to give your dog a biscuit every time it brings your newspapers or slippers. At the outset of training, you would probably want to use *continuous* (100 percent) *reinforcement.* Once the animal is performing reasonably well, however, you can reduce the percentage gradually with the surprising effect that there is no deterioration in performance. In fact, there is some evidence that the partially reinforced subject actually comes to make the response faster and more vigorously than the continuously reinforced subject.

Now, suppose you institute extinction—no more rewards for the animal ever again. The effect here is also surprising. It will take much longer to extinguish an animal who has been trained on partial reinforcement than one trained on continuous reward. On an intuitive level, it is as if the partially reinforced animal does not realize that extinction has begun. The animal is used to not getting rewarded on some trials. In contrast, the continuously rewarded animal experiences an abrupt change in its circumstances on the first trial of extinction.

Any habit learned instrumentally under par-

Schedules of Reinforcement

There are four major types of partial reinforcement schedules that can be viewed as a 2 × 2 combination of two variables (see diagram below). First, the schedule can depend upon how many responses the subject makes (called ratio schedules), or it can depend upon how much time has passed since the last reinforcement (interval schedules). Second, the number of responses in the case of ratio schedules, or the time in case of interval schedules, can be fixed and invariable, or it can be random and highly variable. This gives us the four basic combinations shown and described below.

	Ratio	Interval
Fixed schedules	Fixed ratio (FR)	Fixed interval (FI)
Variable schedules	Variable ratio (VR)	Variable interval (VI)

1. *Fixed ratio:* You reward after a fixed number of responses have been emitted. For example, you reward your dog every fourth time it performs the correct response.

2. *Fixed interval:* You reward the first response that occurs after a fixed amount of time since the last reinforcement. You might reward a rat for the first bar press emitted after 1 minute has passed since the last reward. Pressing during the 1-minute delay would do the rat no good. Note that getting paid every Friday is like a fixed-interval schedule.

3. *Variable ratio:* You reward such that, *on the average,* a reward is given after the fourth response, for example. Sometimes it is given after 1, sometimes after 6, after 3, after 9, and so forth on a random basis, the average being some specified value. The payoff schedule of a Las Vegas slot machine is a good example.

4. *Variable interval:* You reward the first response after *an average time interval* of, say, 1 minute. Sometimes only 5 seconds has to elapse, sometimes 2 minutes, sometimes 45 seconds, and so on, but the average time interval is set at a specific value. Have you ever tried hitchhiking? Is that a good example?

In general, the variable schedules (variable interval and variable ratio) lead to much higher rates of performance. They also lead to much greater resistance to extinction. Pigeons and rats have been trained to perform at very high levels over very long periods of time for very little in the way of reward, provided the rewards are scheduled properly. They also will continue to perform for very long periods of time after you have ceased giving rewards altogether.

tial reinforcement will be difficult to extinguish (this phenomenon does not appear strongly for classically conditioned habits). Partial reinforcement is a pervasive phenomenon for human beings. Not every cigarette tastes good, only some of them; even the best gambler does not win on every play; temper tantrums do not always result in "getting your way." Because of partial reinforcement, we can expect our good habits to persist even in the face of adversity. But our bad ones will, too, and simple extinction is probably not the answer to getting rid of them.

Punishment and Extinction

An important but unusual observation is that a response that has been learned in the presence of mild punishment is often more difficult to

"Oh, for goodness' sake! Smoke!"

The New Yorker, April 14, 1962. Drawing by Saxon; © 1962
The New Yorker Magazine, Inc.

If you are trying to quit smoking, *extinction* would involve simply stopping, whereas *counterconditioning* would involve substituting a new habit for the old one. In general, counterconditioning is a better procedure for eliminating bad habits, provided, of course, that the substitute habit is not worse than the original one.

Figure 4–7
Punishment and extinction

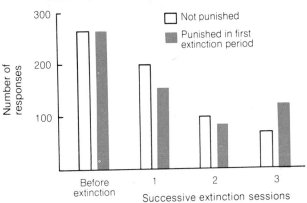

The data shown may cause you to think twice before using punishment as a means for facilitating extinction. Rats punished during the first of three extinction sessions made fewer responses during the first session; but by the third extinction session, they were responding *more* than animals not punished. If punishment is used in extinction, it should be carried out through the entire extinction, not just delivered early in extinction.

extinguish than one learned on the basis of reward alone. In the laboratory, this can be demonstrated by training rats in a simple maze. Suppose the rat has to learn to choose between turning right or left. During training food is put on the right side and the rat is given a mild shock after it has turned right, just before it gets the food. The shock has to be mild enough, of course, that the rat still goes forward in the maze and gets its reward. After training, the food is switched to the left side. A rat that has learned under combined reward and punishment takes longer to learn the new response of turning left than does a control rat that did not experience punishment.

Remember the mother who ran to punish her child for being nasty to a friend. The attention of the mother is a reward for the child,

and it is coupled with punishment, which the mother inflicts when she gets there. The inappropriate behavior of the child may be strengthened rather than weakened under these circumstances. A juvenile delinquent commonly gets both rewarded and punished by his or her activities. So does a cigarette smoker, a sex offender, a neurotic with a phobia, and so on. This fact may make these bad habits even more difficult to extinguish or to replace than they otherwise might be. The routine of replacing one habit with another, rather than simply extinguishing a habit without replacement, is called **counterconditioning.** Research shows that counterconditioning is a better procedure than mere extinction for eliminating unwanted responses, particularly if the new, substitute response is incompatible with the undesired response.

An obvious alternative to extinction and counterconditioning for the elimination of a habit is severe punishment, probably the most popular, everyday method of response elimination. The use of punishment has been criticized frequently by psychologists on the grounds that punishment itself has undesirable side effects.

TABLE 4-6   Principles for the Effective Use of Punishment

1. *Avoid inadequate punishment.*
   If the punishment is not strong enough to eliminate the behavior, the response is also being rewarded, and fixation on that response may develop. Too small a fine for air polluting may in fact encourage pollution.

2. *If at all possible, the punishment should suit the crime.*
   The punishment should by itself elicit a response incompatible with the undesired response. A jail sentence for a burglar is not necessarily incompatible with future crimes, because he or she may use the time to learn more efficient techniques and to develop better plans.

3. *At least require an incompatible escape response.*
   The person should be required to make an incompatible response to terminate the punishment. Jail sentences should be for indeterminate lengths—until the person has been rehabilitated or, in the case of vandalism, until the damage has been repaired.

4. *If at all possible, punish immediately.*
   Since part of the punishing effects are a result of classical conditioning, and since classical conditioning is most effective with short intervals between CS and UCS, one should try to punish immediately after the undesired response has been emitted. Even better is to deliver the punishment just as the subject is about to make the undesired response, but, of course, this is often impossible.

5. *If punishment cannot be delivered immediately, try to reinstate the circumstances.*
   A child can be told or reminded about a past indiscretion that is now being punished. Even better is to "return to the scene of the crime." Make the subject repeat the offense or simulate a repetition, which can then be punished immediately. If you are employing counter-conditioning, make the subject reenact the behavior sequence and perform the counter or incompatible response. If you walk into a party and immediately ask to borrow a cigarette when you are trying to quit smoking, go back outside and come in again with your hands in your pockets.

6. *Avoid rewards after punishment.*
   If you feel sorry for your child after punishing him or her and then proceed to offer affection and ice cream, the punishing stimuli will become secondary rewards (they become associated with rewards and are no longer effective). Masochism is a condition in which a person *wants* to be punished. It may result from always experiencing reward following punishment so that the punishment itself becomes rewarding.

7. *Always provide an acceptable alternative to the punished response.*
   If a very strong drive is motivating the behavior, punishment will prevent the satisfaction of this drive, which leaves the subject in a state of strong conflict—wanting to satisfy the drive but knowing punishment will follow. Prolonged conflict in important drive areas (for example, sexual drive) can lead to neurosis. In such cases try to provide an alternative mechanism by which the drive can be reduced.

Fitting the Crime

One night last winter, after drinking in a Miami tavern, 20-year-old Joe Fales drove to the home of an interracial couple and fired a rifle shot at the house. Fales was captured, pleaded guilty and faced a five-year prison term. But he has never spent a day in jail. Instead, every Saturday morning for six months, the young meat cutter traveled to St. John's Institutional Baptist Church in the heart of Miami's black ghetto. Once there he breakfasted on eggs, grits, sausage and homemade biscuits with a group of ministers. On other days, Fales would help children in a predominantly black Head Start program.

Fales was sentenced by Miami Judge Alfonso Sepe to spend his Saturdays in the ghetto program. Judge Sepe thinks that punishment should fit the crime. "He didn't seem like a bad boy," says the judge. "He was just misguided, and going to church was the best way to cure him. He can learn that there is no reason to hate anybody, something he wouldn't have learned in prison." Prisons, as penologists know, tend to turn young people and first offenders into hardened criminals—and at best a prisoner is a drain on the public till. Accordingly, law officers across the nation are groping for ways to combine punishment with rehabilitation and service.

When Phoenix, Ariz., physician Patrick Lorey was convicted of selling $40,000 worth of liquid amphetamine to a state undercover agent, he faced a life prison term. Instead, Lorey was sentenced to spend seven years practicing medicine in Tombstone, Ariz., which had not had a doctor of its own for four years. "He's a great asset to the town," says Mayor Jack Hendrickson, who doubles as keeper of the Lucky Cuss Saloon. "In Tombstone, what a man does before he comes doesn't matter a whit. It's what he does after he gets here that counts." . . .

Newsweek
December 23, 1974

To take an extreme example, your child may develop an aversion to you or even a neurosis if you use punishment excessively to control behavior. There is some experimental evidence that punishment during extinction may not accelerate the process. Punishment might cause an early suppression of undesired behavior, giving the impression that it is effectively extinguishing the behavior. The total time for complete extinction, however, may not be affected at all (see Figure 4–7). Still, there are some situations in which punishment does work, particularly if the punishment is not overly severe. Frank Logan (1970) has summarized the available evidence into seven statements concerning the effective use of punishment, which are given in Table 4–6. As Logan himself cautions, his conclusions are not meant to encourage the use of punishment but rather to provide guidelines for its appropriate application.

Generalization and Discrimination

The importance of two key learning processes, **generalization** and **discrimination,** has been implicit in the foregoing discussion. There are two kinds of generalization, response generalization and stimulus generalization. In response generalization, a person who has been trained to make a particular response sometimes makes a similar response if the originally learned behavior is somehow blocked or interfered with. Stimulus generalization pertains to the occurrence of a learned response under circumstances that are similar to but discriminably different from the original training situation.

As an example of response generalization, consider training a rat to press a bar in a Skinner box for food pellets. The first successful bar press might be quite accidental. Let's say the animal strikes the bar with sufficient force with its left paw while exploring the cage. The immediate delivery of a food pellet reinforces the left paw response. The animal will have a tendency to make that same response again. With successive responses and reinforcements the response gains strength. But usually that strength will not be limited to left paw presses just because the animal began that way. Rather, response strength will generalize to other similar responses.

Now if the intention was to train an animal to press a bar with its tail only, a different pro-

The New Yorker, March 4, 1961. Drawing by Opie; © 1961 The New Yorker Magazine, Inc.

Merely paying attention to someone's behavior can be reinforcing, particularly if the person is "starved for attention." Withdrawal of the reinforcing attention results in the elimination of the behavior.

Figure 4–8
Gradient of stimulus generalization

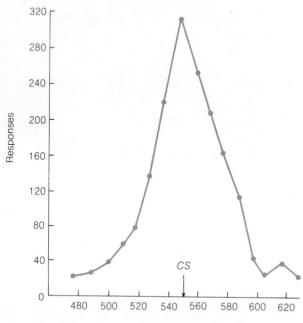

The gradient of stimulus generalization is shown for a group of pigeons trained to peck a button illuminated with a light of 550 nm and then presented with test buttons of several other colors, ranging from 480 to 620 nm. The graph shows that the closer the test stimulus was to the training stimulus of 550, the more the birds pecked.

cedure would have to be used. The animal would be rewarded only when it pressed with its tail and never when it pressed with its paw or nose; this method would effectively extinguish all responses except the tail press. The procedure would be called **response discrimination** or **differentiation,** resulting in a highly specific, stylized response—pressing only with the tail.

There are many examples of response generalization and response differentiation in human behavior. For example, in athletics, there is generally only one best way (or a very few ways) to perform a desired act, say high jumping or pole vaulting. Even slight deviations from the ideal, the response generalization phenomenon, may result in failure when jumping in a competition event. An athlete must undergo

years of training in response differentiation until he or she can make the ideal response over and over again with little variation. Consider the problem of response differentiation as it pertains to playing a concerto on a piano, cutting a diamond, or disarming a bomb.

Stimulus generalization is likewise an important phenomenon and has received a great deal of attention from both experimental and theoretical psychologists. In this phenomenon, a response learned in one stimulus situation tends to occur in other similar situations. For example, a child's fear of dogs after being bitten may generalize to similar stimuli, such as other animals or even stuffed animal toys. Experimenters frequently construct a **gradient of stimulus generalization** to indicate the degree of generalization to various stimuli. Suppose a group of pigeons were trained to peck a button illuminated with a light of 550 nm (a greenish-yellow color). Then, by testing the strength of their response to buttons of other colors, the experimenter can determine the gradient of generalization (see Figure 4–8). It is known that the more similar a test stimulus is to the original training stimulus, the greater the likelihood that the organism will respond to it in the way it has been trained. Thus it is no surprise that the curve in Figure 4–8 shows the greatest number of responses by the pigeons to buttons of illumination close to 550 nm.

Stimulus generalization can have both positive and negative consequences. On the positive side, note that it is unnecessary to teach an organism a desired response in each and every stimulus situation it will encounter. After training it to respond in one or at most a few situations, we can expect it to be able to respond in almost any similar situation. For example, a parent who has toilet-trained a little boy at home can reasonably expect him to generalize both his control and the appropriate behavior to the schoolroom, the neighbor's child's birthday party, his trip to the zoo, and just about everywhere else.

Negative effects of stimulus generalization are possible whenever the response in question is an undesired one, such as stuttering. Many speech pathologists believe that stuttering is a learned response arising in parent–child interaction situations, especially when the parent is overly concerned with the child's speech behavior. Once stuttering is learned, however, the child stutters in almost all situations regardless of whether the parents are present. Problems arise also when we try to extinguish undesired behavior. It may be possible to extinguish stuttering in some situations but not all. Compounding the problem is some experimental evidence suggesting that the generalization gradient is heightened and broadened under conditions of anxiety. Since the extinction of undesirable responses is often accompanied by considerable frustration and anxiety, stimulus generalization may make extinction more difficult.

Many responses are acceptable in one situation but not in another. In these cases, stimulus generalization may cause mistakes that result in punishment. Thus it becomes necessary to learn a **stimulus discrimination** essentially the opposite of stimulus generalization. The learner must be trained to discriminate among stimuli such that he or she responds to some but not to others. An essential aspect of learning to drive a car, for example, is learning to apply the brakes at the sight of a red light and not at the sight of a green one.

In the laboratory, discrimination learning is usually studied by training a subject to respond to one stimulus by rewarding him or her and not to respond to others by withholding the reward if a response is made. For example, a rat could be given food for pressing a lever when a tone is sounded but not when a light is on.

The combination of stimulus generalization and differentiation can lead to quite complex learning tasks. Suppose a pigeon is taught to peck at a green response key as rapidly as it can, and after extensive training the response button is suddenly changed to yellow. If the response of pecking the yellow button is not reinforced, the pigeon will gradually stop pecking (extinguishing the response) and begin to form a discrimination. The green button is called the positive stimulus and the yellow the negative. The simplest theory of discrimination learning says that an organism, in this situation, builds up an approach or *excitatory tendency* to the positive stimulus and a corresponding avoidance or *inhibitory tendency* to the negative stimulus. Because of stimulus generalization, excitatory and inhibitory tendencies will generalize to other, similar stimuli. The net tendency to respond to a particular stimulus is determined by the difference between the excitatory and the inhibitory tendencies to that stimulus.

Chaining and Higher-Order Conditioning

Larger habits tend to be compounded of a number of smaller ones. In instrumental situations the compounding process is called response **chaining,** and in classical conditioning the corresponding process is **higher-order conditioning.**

Suppose a rat is trained to press a bar to get food. At this point the opportunity to press a bar should be secondarily reinforced because of its association with food. With further training, the rat can be taught to step on a pedal in order to open a door to the compartment where the bar is. Moreover, once it has learned to step on a pedal to get to the bar, the pedal should become a secondary reinforcer so that the rat can then be trained to stand on its hind legs before stepping on the pedal. By successive steps, working backward from the goal, a chain of responses can be built up that might consist of licking a spout that turns on a light, bumping the light to gain access to a string, pulling the string to produce a pedal, stepping on the pedal to open a door, running through the door to confront a bar, and finally pressing the bar to obtain food. Psychologists have made the rat do a lot of work for one small pellet of food. The relation to human behavior is obvious. Generally, we are not rewarded for each response that we make. Rather, we are taught long chains of responses that eventuate in reward.

Higher-order conditioning is related to response chaining. Suppose a dog is trained to salivate at the sight of a light. Because the light now elicits saliva, it can be used as a UCS. Then a tone is presented, followed in half a second by the light, which elicits saliva because of initial training. Gradually, the tone comes to elicit saliva. When saliva is evoked by the original CS, the light, the response is called a first-order CR. When the tone elicits saliva, as a result of being paired with the light, the response is called a second-order CR. Next, the tone could be paired with a touch on the back of the animal. If the touch came to elicit saliva, it would be a third-order CR. It should be noted that higher-order conditioning is difficult to produce, even in the laboratory, and probably is not as powerful as chaining in human behavior.

Obviously, both response chaining and higher-order conditioning are dependent on secondary reinforcement. These and other examples stand as strong testimony to the crucial role played by secondary reinforcement in all behavior, human and animal.

Learned Helplessness

Thus far we have discussed what happens when an organism has control over the occurrence of the reinforcer. If the organism makes the designated response, the occurrence of the reinforcing stimulus is made more probable; if the organism refrains from making the designated response, the reinforcer is made less probable. For example, if a rat is given food for lever pressing it can make food more likely by pressing. If a rat is punished for lever pressing by the administration of shock, it can make the occurrence of shock less likely by not pressing.

But what happens when reinforcing stimuli (rewards or punishments) occur independently of behavior? That is, what happens when a rewarding or punishing stimulus occurs and is unrelated to the behavior of the organism? What happens when the organism does not have control of important events that are occurring? This is an important question because we are frequently exposed to events over which we have no control. Consider the death of a child's mother or father. This is an intensely aversive event, but the child has no control over it whatsoever. Alternatively, consider the child who is given presents and privileges regardless of whether he or she is behaving appropriately. Here the child receives rewards no matter what he or she does.

The behavioral consequences of exposure to aversive events that cannot be controlled have been investigated by Steven F. Maier and Martin E. P. Seligman. They gave one group of dogs electric shocks that the dogs could control. These dogs were able to terminate the shock (escape) by pressing a panel. A second group of dogs was given an identical series of shocks, but they had no control over shock. Each dog in this group was paired with a dog from the first group. Each shock began at the same time for both dogs, and the shock terminated for

both dogs whenever the dog in the first group pressed the panel. Thus the dog in the first group could escape shock by responding, but the dogs in the second group had no control.

Both sets of dogs were later placed in a different situation in which shock could be escaped by jumping over a hurdle. Now escape was possible for all dogs. However, Seligman and Maier found that only the dogs which had initially experienced escapable shock learned to escape in the new situation. The dogs that had first experienced shock which they could not control failed to learn to escape even though they were now in a new situation. Maier and Seligman called this the **learned helplessness** effect.

Seligman and Maier developed a view called the learned helplessness hypothesis as an explanation of the later failure to learn produced by exposure to inescapable shock. In essence, they argued that the dogs exposed to inescapable shock learned that shock termination and responding were independent, that shock could not be controlled. They further argued that such learning should have two effects on the organism. First, it should reduce the organism's motivation to try to escape when later confronted with shock in a different situation. Second, it should interfere with the formation of an association between the escape response and shock termination should the dog make the correct response.

The learned helplessness hypothesis suggests that certain kinds of experiences should prevent the learned helplessness effect from occurring. Exposure to escapable shock *before* receiving inescapable shock should interfere with learning that shock cannot be controlled and thus prevent the inescapable shock from producing a later failure to learn. Seligman and Maier showed that such an "immunization effect" does indeed occur. In addition, the learned helplessness hypothesis suggests what kinds of procedures might eliminate learned helplessness once it exists. If the subjects fail to learn because they expect the shock to be inescapable, forcibly exposing them to the fact that shock is now escapable should counteract this expectation and thus eliminate the failure to learn. This can be accomplished by physically forcing the subject to make the response that terminates shock. Seligman and Maier showed that this does produce successful therapy.

Exposure to uncontrollable aversive events

also has physiological consequences. Jay M. Weiss has shown that subjects exposed to inescapable shock exhibit a much greater stress reaction than do subjects exposed to equal amounts of escapable shock. Rats that had no control over shock developed severe stomach ulcers; rats that had control of shock did not. Thus the effects of controllability are quite wide ranging and seem to have important influences on both behavior and physical health.

PROCESSES THAT AFFECT CONDITIONING

What is responsible for producing a CR to the CS after the CS and UCS have been presented together? After all, the food does not come any sooner if the dog salivates to the bell. So why does the dog salivate in response to the bell?

Pavlov himself suggested an answer. He believed that the presentation of any stiumulus to which an organism is sensitive activates an area in the brain responsive only to that stimulus. The contiguous presentation of the CS and the UCS should lead to the CS and UCS areas in the brain being active at the same time. Pavlov argued that the simultaneous existence of activity in two areas of the brain should form something like a connection between them. Presentation of the CS by itself after the CS and UCS have been paired together a number of times should, as always, activate the area of the brain that corresponds to that stimulus. However, Pavlov argued that this should also produce activity in the UCS area, since the CS and UCS areas became connected as a result of their prior contiguous occurrences. Activation of the UCS area should produce the UCR, since the UCR was said to be a reflex response to the UCS. Thus it was Pavlov's view that the CR is simply the UCR, but activated by means of a learned connection between the CS and UCS areas of the brain.

Clearly, the physiological aspects of Pavlov's theory cannot be maintained in light of present-day knowledge. However, the psychological aspect is important. What Pavlov proposed is that a connection between the CS and the UCS is learned or acquired as a result of CS-UCS pairings. The CR is not really learned or conditioned, but occurs because the CS and UCS have been connected. This is why Pavlov's theory has been called a stimulus-stimulus or S-S theory.

Pavlov's views were quickly challenged by a number of the early behaviorists in the United States, most notably John B. Watson. Watson maintained that because the CS and UCS areas in the brain could not be observed directly, connections between them should not be offered as an explanation. He argued that the contiguity of the CS and the UCR—both observable events—established a connection between them. Here, the CR is again viewed as the same as the UCR, but now elicited because the CS and UCR have become connected rather than because the CS and UCS have become connected. For obvious reasons this position came to be called a stimulus-response or S-R view.

Much research has examined this issue. Although not all of the evidence is consistent, the trend supports Pavlov's S-S view. Conditioning seems to be a process in which the CS and UCS become connected in some fashion. However, we still have to explain why the CR occurs. As noted above, Pavlov believed that the CR was merely the UCR elicited through a learned connection between the CS and UCS areas of the brain. That is, the CR was seen as the reflex response to the UCS transferred to the CS. This view requires that the CR and UCR be identical, or at least very similar. Unfortunately, this is often not the case. Moreover, not all behavior that occurs in response to a CS is reflexive. An organism will not only salivate at the appearance of a light that has been paired with food but will also approach the light and direct behaviors at the light that would normally be used in food seeking and ingestion. It is difficult to categorize these behaviors as reflexes.

Memory Representations of the UCS

We have seen that the CR is not directly connected to the CS and that the CR is hard to describe as a transferred reflex. Thus it is still not clear why the CR occurs. Perhaps the basic process involved is one in which the organism acquires an anticipation or expectation of the UCS in the presence of the UCS. Along these lines, Robert A. Rescorla has suggested that the CS comes to evoke a *memory representation* of the UCS as a result of the pairings of CS and UCS. That is, after the CS and UCS have been paired a number of times the occurrence of the CS produces an **image** of the UCS in memory. The CR might simply be the organism's reaction to having the memory of the UCS called forth. The advantage of this position is that an image of the UCS allows for motivated behaviors such as approaching the food source, and it could also produce more reflexive responses such as salivation. In addition, the CR and UCR do not here have to be identical, since one's reaction to a stimulus and to the memory of that stimulus do not have to be the same.

Rescorla has provided evidence for this view with what is called the UCS inflation experiment. If the CR is a reaction to the memory image of the UCS, it ought to be possible to change the CR by altering only the memory representation of the UCS without changing the connection between the CS and the image. Rescorla began by pairing a tone CS with an electric shock UCS. In the next phase of the experiment the subjects were presented with even more intense shocks, but no tones occurred. The occurrence of these shocks should not have affected the association between tone and shock since no tones occurred. However, the presentation of more intense shocks should have altered the organism's image of shock to the image of a more intense shock. If the tone were now presented, it should produce the image of a more intense shock than before. If the CR is really a reaction to the calling forth of the image of the UCS, the CR to the tone CS should now be larger than it was before the intense shocks occurred. Remember that the more intense shocks were not paired with tones, so we would not ordinarily expect this outcome. However, this was the result obtained. The presentation of more intense shocks in the absence of the tone augmented the CR to the tone. This constitutes support for the idea that the conditioning process does involve a memory representation or image of some sort.

Inhibition, Contingency, and Contiguity

The preceding section suggests that the crucial relationship in conditioning is between the CS and the UCS. Before we discuss this relationship further, we must describe a form of conditioning not yet encountered.

Thus far, all examples of classical conditioning we have discussed have involved situations in which the CS is quickly followed by the UCS. Here the CS comes to evoke a CR. This is called *excitatory conditioning* because the CS comes to excite a response as a result of its pairing with the UCS. Conditioning also occurs when the CS is followed by the absence of the UCS, when it is followed by nothing. However, here the CS does not come to elicit the CR but rather acquires the capacity to suppress or inhibit responding. This is called *inhibitory conditioning.*

For example, assume that one CS, which we will call CS+ (say a tone), is followed by meat powder injected into a dog's mouth, and another CS, which we will call the CS− (say a light), is not followed by meat powder. The CS+ will come to elicit salivation and the CS− will not. However, the CS− will not merely come to produce no salivation but will actually inhibit the occurrence of salivation. Thus if a stimulus that produces salivation is present, a CS− will suppress that salivation if it is presented.

Inhibitory conditioning is hard to interpret within the traditional view that the pairing or contiguity in time between CS and UCS is the crucial aspect of the CS-UCS relationship. The CS is followed by the nonoccurrence of the UCS in inhibitory conditioning, so what is it paired with? One suggestion is that the *contingency* between CS and UCS—rather than the pairing of CS and UCS—is the most important feature determining conditioning.

By contingency we mean that there is some relationship between the occurrence of the CS and the occurrence of the UCS. The contingency can be either positive or negative. The contingency is positive when the UCS is more likely to occur in the presence of the CS than in the absence of the CS. The contingency is negative when the UCS is more likely to occur in the absence of the CS than in the presence of the CS. In the first case, the occurrence of the CS predicts that the UCS will soon occur, and in the second case it predicts that the UCS will not occur. The contingency view says that it is these informational relationships between the CS and UCS that determine conditioning and that excitatory conditioning should occur when there is a positive contingency between CS and UCS, and inhibitory conditioning should occur when the contingency is negative. Here prediction of what will happen rather than the contingency of events is crucial. In fact, excitatory conditioning takes place when the UCS is more likely to occur in the presence of the CS than in its absence; and inhibitory conditioning seems to result when the UCS is more likely in the absence of the CS than in its presence. Thus conditioning seems to be bipolar, excitatory conditioning resulting when the CS predicts an increased likelihood of the UCS and inhibition resulting when the CS predicts a decreased likelihood of the UCS. These relative likelihoods appear more important than the simple pairing or contiguity between events.

Factors That Determine When These Processes Occur

We have seen that conditioning involves the formation of a connection between the CS and the memory image of the UCS and that the contingency between the CS and UCS is responsible for that connection. However, we would not expect organisms to form connections between all contingent events in the environment. This would be very inefficient, since many of these events are not important to the organism. Only some relationships should be learned about or internalized. What determines when such learning takes place?

The Blocking Experiment

An experiment performed by Leon Kamin suggests that organisms do not condition to all stimuli involved in a contingency. Kamin studied the conditioning of fear. A CS was paired with electric shock and the amount of fear conditioned to the CS measured. In the initial experiment one group of subjects received a compound CS composed of a tone and a light paired with shock. The amount of fear conditioned to the tone and the light was measured separately, and strong fear was conditioned to each. A second group of subjects was first conditioned to the tone and the shock, and then to the tone-light compound with shock. When the tone and the light were tested after their pairings with shock, subjects showed no fear of the light but only of the tone. That is, no conditioning occurred to the light even though the tone-light compound was paired with shock. This means that the prior conditioning of fear to the tone blocked or prevented conditioning of fear to the light. Fear was conditioned to the light when the tone-light pairings with shock were not preceded by the pairing of the tone by itself with

Figure 4–9
The blocking experiment

	Phase I	Phase 2	Test Light
Group 1	–	Tone + light → shock	Strong conditioning
Group 2	Tone → shock	Tone + light → shock	Weak conditioning

shock. However, conditioning to the light was not successful when tone-light conditioning was preceded by tone conditioning. This experiment is shown diagramatically in Figure 4–9.

This blocking experiment is important because it illustrates a case in which conditioning does not occur even though the organism is exposed to a contingency between an adequate CS and UCS. We know the CS and UCS were adquate because strong conditioning to the light occurred in the first group, and the light, tone, and shock were the same for both groups. The only factor that differed between the groups was whether or not conditioning had already occurred to the tone. This means that the mechanisms that produce conditioning are not always brought into play when an organism is exposed to events, and so some process must decide when a relationship is to be internalized or learned.

Rehearsal

Kamin speculated that a contingency is learned only when the occurrence of the UCS is unexpected and thus surprises the organism. He argued that the occurrence of an important unexpected event like electric shock causes the organism to scan backward through its memory in order to find the stimuli that preceded or predicted the important event. This process of scanning backward through memory was believed to be responsible for conditioning. If the occurrence of an important event is expected and thus not surprising, no backward scan of memory—and thus no learning—occurs. In the blocking experiment, the shocks that followed the tone-light stimulus were not surprising since the tone alone predicted the occurrence of shock. This is so because the tone had previously been paired with shock. Thus the shock should not have provoked a backward scan through memory, and so no relationship between light and shock was learned by the organism.

Allan R. Wagner has recently related Kamin's suggestions to the process of *rehearsal*. Rehearsal means going over something again and again in one's memory. Wagner argued that CS-UCS relationships are learned only if they are rehearsed, and perhaps only surprising or unexpected UCSs promote rehearsal. It is commonly assumed that an organism cannot rehearse many different things at once. (To satisfy yourself that this is true, try to say a number of different things to yourself over and over all at the same time.) This means that if surprising events are rehearsed, and if conditioning requires rehearsal, the occurrence of a surprising event shortly after a conditioning trial should interfere with conditioning. If only a small number of things can be rehearsed at once, rehearsing the surprising event that occurs after the trial should reduce the organism's ability to rehearse the CS-UCS episode that occurred during the conditioning trial. This conditioning should be weak. To see this clearly just assume that only one thing can be rehearsed. If the event after the trial is rehearsed, the events during the trial cannot be.

Wagner, Rudy, and Whitlow (1973) began by following one CS, which we will call CS_1 with a UCS and another CS—CS_2—with no UCS. In the second phase of the experiment a new CS—CS_3—was followed by the UCS, and conditioning to CS_3 was measured. For some subjects the CS_3-UCS pairings were quickly followed by a surprising event, CS_1 followed by no UCS. This would be surprising, since the UCS had followed CS_1 in the past. For some subjects the CS_3-UCS pairings were followed by a nonsurprising event, CS_2 followed by no UCS. This should not be surprising, since CS_2 had never

been followed by the UCS. The result was that the occurrence of the surprising episode interfered with conditioning to CS_3, whereas the occurrence of the nonsurprising episode did not. This means that surprising events do command rehearsal and that rehearsal of the CS-UCS sequence is involved in the conditioning process.

This discussion of the processes that affect conditioning should help you understand the role of classical conditioning in aiding organisms to adapt to the environment. That is, it should help you understand why classical conditioning is a useful process. It allows you to picture which events in your environment predict biologically significant events like UCSs. Accurate predictions of this sort should increase your chances of acting adaptively and dealing with those UCSs. If an important event occurs and is surprising, that means that you didn't know it was going to occur. Here rehearsal is brought into play and learning occurs. If you are not surprised, this means that you knew the event would occur. That is, you already have an accurate prediction. Here rehearsal and learning do not occur, for it would be wasteful to use a mechanism on something you already know if that mechanism can be used only on one thing at a time. It would be better to keep it available to be used on new information for which you do not already have an accurate representation.

The view of classical conditioning we have just elaborated holds that the CR is the organism's reaction to the occurrence of the memory of the UCS. However, the CR itself may have adaptive significance. It may aid in coping with the UCS that is to follow. An eye blink to a puff of air might make the puff less harmful, and salivating before eating food might make the food easier to digest. Such adaptiveness will be discussed further on page 144.

SUMMARY

1. Learning is defined as a relatively permanent change in behavior potential traceable to experience and practice.
2. Many instances of learning can be classified into two basic types: classical conditioning (based on the work of Pavlov) and instrumental or operant conditioning (identified mainly with the work of Skinner).

3. In classical conditioning, a neutral stimulus (CS) comes to elicit a response (CR) that, prior to conditioning, was elicited as a response (UCR) only by some other stimulus (UCS).

4. Classical conditioning is thought to be mainly a function of the contingency between the CS and UCS during the learning trials.

5. In operant or instrumental conditioning, the subject must emit a response or withhold a response, this behavior being "reinforced" by the delivery of rewards or punishments contingent on what the subject does.

6. The technique known as shaping (reinforcing successively closer approxima-mations to the desired response) is also frequently used in operant training of a subject.

7. Several learning phenomena take place both in classical and operant learning situations: extinction, spontaneous recovery, generalization (both stimulus and response), discrimination, and chaining of responses (or higher-order conditioning in the case of classical conditioning).

8. Extinction is the process of eliminating a learned response. Partial reinforce-ment during learning retards extinction. Punishment can also make it more difficult to extinguish a response.

9. Learned helplessness is a phenomenon that occurs when response and rein-forcement are independent, that is, when the subject cannot control reinforc-ing events in the environment.

10. Among the various processes that have been implicated in conditioning are (a) memory representation, that is. an image of the UCS, (b) expectancy or surprise, and (c) rehearsal, all of which are cognitive in nature.

RECOMMENDED ADDITIONAL READINGS

Hill, W. F. *Learning: A Survey of psychological interpretations,* 3d ed. New York: Crowell, 1977.

Logan, F. A. *Fundamentals of learning and motivation.* Dubuque, Ia: William C. Brown, 1970.

Mackintosh, N. J. *The psychology of animal learning.* London: Academic Press, 1975.

Skinner, B. F. *Walden two.* New York: Macmillan, 1948.

what does it mean?

Classical and operant conditioning techniques are widely applied. Although the applications are sometimes called inhumane or degrading, these techniques have brought about many behavioral changes that have benefited individuals and society. Problems could, of course, develop if someone with a great deal of power decided to use these techniques to his or her own advantage. Misuse of them could be detrimental to humanity.

We have only begun to apply learning principles. The future possibilities demand an informed public understanding of the benefits and dangers involved.

CLASSICAL CONDITIONING

Phobias

A phobia is an overpowering and intense fear a person can do little about. Classical conditioning is often implicated in phobias. Take the case of someone with a phobia of heights. Perhaps the person as a child experienced an aversive event following exposure to a high place. Perhaps the person fell off a high stool as an infant. This might have conditioned fear of heights.

But phobias do not have the same characteristics as classically conditioned responses. Classically conditioned responses usually do not develop in one trial, usually extinguish rapidly, and generally form to arbitrary events like tones and lights. Phobias do develop in one trial. Someone who has a snake phobia does not repeatedly have a bad experience following exposure to a snake. Phobias do not extinguish readily. Someone who has a snake phobia receives an extinction trial every time he or she sees a snake, but the phobia does not disappear. The extinction trial results when the person sees the snake (CS) but does not experience the hypothesized aversive consequence of exposure to the snake (UCS). Thus the CS is presented without the UCS, but the phobia remains. Perhaps you think the fear which follows seeing the snake is a UCS that maintains the phobia. But this is different from classical conditioning. If a tone and shock are paired, the tone by itself produces fear; but presenting the tone by itself extinguishes this fear.

Finally, phobias do not develop to arbitrary objects. Common human phobias are associated with such stimuli as animals, fire, heights, open spaces, closed spaces, and so on. Phobias do not commonly develop to lights, tones, electric outlets, cars, and so on. From a classical conditioning point of view phobias to light sockets should be more common than those to snakes. More children have a negative experience (electric shock) following exposure to light sockets than to snakes (particularly in cities), yet phobias are much more common to snakes.

Examination of things to which phobias commonly develop suggests that they tend to be things that have been important in human evolution. They are all things that it would have been adaptive for prehistoric human beings to be afraid of. For example, it would have been adaptive for an early human being to avoid open spaces if a tiger had been encountered the first time he or she ventured onto an open plain as a child. However, tigers do not exist in all locations, so it would not have been useful for people to be automatically afraid of open spaces. The most useful mechanism would have been for human beings to be sensitive to a pairing of open spaces with bad consequences.

This line of reasoning led Martin E. P. Seligman to argue that phobias are an example of prepared classical conditioning (see p. 142). He argued that phobias are caused by the same sort of mechanism responsible for the rat's peculiarly sensitive association of tastes and poisons. Such associations form in one trial, do not extinguish readily, and do not form to arbitrary events like tones and lights. Also, the association of taste and poison makes adaptive and evolutionary sense.

This position views phobias as the normal consequences of a normal mechanism. A phobia is what *should* result if exposure to an open space in infancy is followed by an aversive consequence. Such phobias may once have been highly adaptive but now seem abnormal in the context of modern-day society. Perhaps other behavioral problems are manifestations of mechanisms no longer adaptive.

Morphine Tolerance

Learning is often a factor in phenomena not thought to involve learning. Drug tolerance may be one example. Tolerance refers to the fact that a given amount of a drug has less and less effect with repeated usage. This means that more and more of the drug must be used to obtain the same effect. Most explanations of tolerance focus on the cellular effects of the drug in question. For example, tolerance to morphine has typically been explained by proposing that repeated stimulation with morphine either prevents the drug

from gaining access to morphine receptors in the brain or decreases the sensitivity of these central receptors.

Shepard Siegel has recently provided strong evidence that physiological factors such as these are not sufficient to account for tolerance to morphine and that learning is involved. You will remember that the CR which develops to a CS as a result of classical conditioning is often different from the UCR to the UCS. In fact, when the UCS is a drug, the CR is often the opposite of the UCR. For example, insulin (UCS) decreases blood sugar (UCR). However, a stimulus repeatedly paired with insulin (for example, the injection procedure) frequently increases blood sugar (CR) when presented by itself. That is, the injection of an inert placebo (say saline) produces increases in blood sugar if the subject has had previous injections of insulin.

What if this is true of morphine? As the person repeatedly encounters morphine, conditioning should occur to those stimuli that precede morphine. These stimuli are the injection ritual. The CR should be opposite to the effect produced by morphine and should thus oppose the action of morphine. If the CR is relatively long lasting, it should take away from the action of morphine, since it is the opposite of the morphine reaction.

Morphine is an analgesic; it reduces sensitivity to pain, and tolerance develops to this effect of the drug. That is, a given dose of the drug will have less and less pain-reducing effect with repeated injections. Siegel has argued that this occurs in part because an increased sensitivity to pain develops as a CR to the injection procedure and cancels some of the pain-reducing effect of the morphine. This view predicts that tolerance should be decreased or eliminated if the morphine is given without the stimuli that usually accompany it. The opposing CR should not occur if the stimuli to which it is conditioned are not presented. Clearly, theories that hold tolerance to be only a cellular phenomenon would not expect stimuli preceding morphine administration to make a difference. In fact,

New Psychotherapy for Drug Addiction

Jerry V. Williams

New treatments for drug addiction and schizophrenia were disclosed Friday to 150 psychologists and psychiatrists attending the fifth annual meeting of the Society for Psychotherapy Research at the Cosmopolitan Hotel.

Presenting papers on the new treatments were Dr. Charles O'Brien of the University of Pennsylvania School of Medicine and Dr. Loren Mosher of the National Institute of Mental Health.

In an interview, Dr. O'Brien said he has experienced some success in combatting drug addiction through what he described as "extinction trials" in conjunction with more traditional forms of therapy.

O'Brien said there is a heavy "conditioning" aspect of drug addiction, in which a person gets "conditioned" to compulsive drug use. Many drug users experience "highs" through the simple process of going through their shooting routine.

He termed these individuals "more needle freaks than anything else." With the advent of heavier law enforcement, particularly, resulting in more diluted supplies of heroin, some addicts continue "shooting up" and may even be provoked to the act through stimulation by their environment, O'Brien said.

Studies of addicts treated at the medical school, he noted, showed 20 per cent to be "pseudoaddicts" and another 20 per cent to have "very mild addictions."

Obviously, he explained, treatment with methadone—the only method now available—would create true physical dependence in these individuals. An alternative was needed.

The alternative O'Brien came up with involved the use of an experimental narcotic "antagonist" to neutralize any intake of drug the addict might take.

Extinction trials were undertaken in which the addicts, having been given the antagonist, were given several syringes containing measured amounts of a saline solution or a narcotic. The addicts then were allowed to inject the contents of one or the other of the syringes, after which measurements were made of their physical reactions and they were required to fill out a series of tests.

The first three to five injections showed no difference in the amount of "high" obtained, O'Brien said, whether the saline or narcotic was injected.

After this first plateau, the addicts developed a dislike for the needle routine when the results were no longer maintained.

Reporting on 20 cases with an eight-month followup, O'Brien said six of the 20 are drug-free and another four are on a methadone program and "doing well." The remainder are either "back on the street" or not doing well.

O'Brien estimated the technique would be applicable to only about 30 per cent of the addict population—always in connection with other forms of therapy such as job counseling—because of the degree of motivation required for use of the narcotic antagonist. . . .

The Denver Post
June 16, 1974

Siegel has shown that tolerance is greatly reduced if the usual stimuli that precede the morphine are not presented with the morphine. The pain-reducing effects of morphine were restored simply by presenting new stimuli before the morphine.

This view concerning tolerance has important implications. Consider the heroin addict who habitually takes the drug in a given setting, say with a particular group of people in a particular place. These stimuli should come to elicit a CR opposite in effect to the heroin and counteract it. This leads to bigger and bigger doses to maintain the same effect. What might happen should the person take this large dose with different people in a different place? Could this be one of the causes of overdose death?

The phenomenon of opposed CR and UCR can help us better understand the adaptive value of classical conditioning. It allows the body to defend itself against repeatedly encountered stimuli that produce bodily changes. Such a mechanism would help the organism maintain a balance and cope with events that alter its functioning.

Bedwetting

Principles of classical conditioning have been used to cure children of bedwetting (called **enuresis**). Bladder tension is usually the stimulus that awakens us in the middle of the night, but the bedwetting child has not learned the response of waking up. To stop the child from wetting the bed requires conditioning the awakening response to the stimulus of bladder tension. The UCS would be a stimulus that would awaken a person, such as a loud buzzer or bell. After repeated pairings of the bell with the CS of bladder tension, bladder tension alone should be sufficient to elicit awakening.

In practice, though, how do parents know when a child's bladder is full so they can sound the bell? Obviously the bladder is full at the time the child first starts to wet the bed, but how do parents know when the child is wetting the bed? A psychologist has devised an apparatus that consists of a special sheet equipped with wires that detect urine the moment it starts flowing. The detection apparatus closes an electrical circuit that in turn sounds the bell to awaken the child. After a short period of training with this device, the child begins to awaken himself in anticipation of the release of urine. Indeed, the unit works so well that some companies sell or lease it at extraordinarily high prices to desperate parents. A functional unit, however, can be purchased for a small amount of money from most large catalogue companies (see Figure 4–10). Classical conditioning principles have also been applied to toilet training through the use of a buzzer circuit built into training pants.

Conditioning Taste Aversions

Coyotes kill sheep. As a consequence sheep ranchers have taken up arms against them. The slaughter of coyotes has, in turn, become a matter of concern to environmentalists and naturalists. Thus a controversy has developed, and there is need for a solution that will be satisfactory to both naturalists and ranchers.

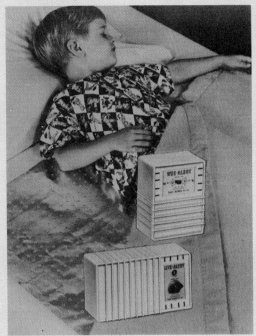

Figure 4–10
Conditioning cure for bedwetting

Children's Bedwetting Alarms

Helps keep sleeper dry by conditioning him to stop bedwetting. Each bedding pack has 2 foil pads with separate sheet between. Moisture passes from top pad to bottom . . . alarm goes off almost instantly. Units can't shock . . . use low voltage batteries. Not for organic disorders or baby training.

The principles of classical conditioning have been used effectively to cure bedwetting. This device is sold by Sears.

A direct application of long-delayed conditioning has been made to the problem by Gustavson, Garcia, Hankins, and Rusiniak (1974). Using principles derived from laboratory studies on conditioned aversions, these psycholo-

When It Comes to Behavior Modification, the Professor Knows the Score

Rick Ratliff

KALAMAZOO, Mich. — See the hairy, bearded man with the wire-rimmed glasses? Check out the bands on his wrists.

"These are golf counters," Richard Malott explains. "I'm trying to manage my own behavior." His right arm rises. "On this one I enter negative remarks, and this one is for nutritional points."

His left arm rises. "This one is for NRTs—nonrecurring tasks."

Malott wants to stop making negative remarks about people; so whenever he makes one, he clicks his remarks' counter. He wants to eat sensibly, so after each meal, he clicks his nutrition counter a few times. He wants to stop procrastinating, so after he finishes a tedious job, he rewards himself with a click of the NRT counter.

Behavior modification is what Malott is all about. Malott, 41, a psychology professor at Western Michigan University here, has helped shape the entire psychology curriculum around behavior modification. He also teaches students how to use it, and he uses it himself. Malott knows of no other program like it in the country. "We're not just 9-to-5 behavior modifiers," he says.

Behavior modification (mod for short) has become a fashionable way to lose weight, stop smoking, or curb other vices. At Western, Malott has tried to help students approach behavior mod as a philosophy. . . .

Behavior modification involves principles advanced by the controversial psychologist B. F. Skinner of Harvard. Namely, that behavior is affected by positive and negative reinforcement. . . .

Other forces that affect behavior include bills and parking tickets, pats on the back, kicks in the shins, angry criticism, soft approval, and exam grades.

Ah, grades.

There's the key to lots of behavior mod at Western, according to Barb Fulton, who assists Malott and calls herself an education technologist.

From the beginning, she explains the stress in psychology courses at Western is on "contingency management" in which "everything for the student is specified and up front: what to read, when they will be tested, when the deadlines will be, and what the consequences are."

The system is immediately rewarding, Malott explains. "We don't want to give people a chance to cop out. What's more," he says, "we play down competition." Rather than grading on a relative scale, or bell-shaped curve, "we have people compete to an absolute standard." Students know from the start that so many accumulated points will earn an A, so many a B, and so forth. . . .

Students learn how to manage themselves and others through positive and negative reinforcement. A student-run program, for example, enables students to help other students complete two years of psych courses in one. . . .

Chicago Tribune
January 28, 1978

gists reasoned that coyotes could be conditioned to avoid killing and eating sheep flesh.

The basic laboratory procedure consisted of feeding coyotes "free" sheep meat laced with lithium chloride, a chemical that makes the coyotes very sick. Despite the long delay between the CS (tasting the meat) and the UCR (getting sick), coyotes so treated develop an immediate dislike for the kind of food containing the poison. Only one or two "treatments" are needed to inhibit the coyotes' desire for the sheep. Gustavson and his associates showed that this treatment did not affect the coyotes' willingness to eat rabbit or other kinds of meat. The treatment results in a specific dislike for sheep. The authors concluded that a method based on their laboratory procedures could stop coyotes from killing sheep and yet not deprive them of other prey. Sheep-meat baits, laced with a nondeadly but illness-producing chemical, could be distributed around the territory where the coyotes are known to prey on sheep. A coyote who happens on the trap would eat the sheep meat and automatically develop an instant aversion to sheep. It would then stop killing sheep but continue to prey on less-valued species.

Classical and Instrumental Conditioning Usually Work Together

Novel Treatment

UPI

ENGLAND — Doctors have found a novel way to stop compulsive gambler David Smith from putting his money where his mouth is, Smith says.

"I pick out horses twice a day," Smith said of his treatment. "Then they let me listen to the race broadcast. When I get excited a doctor or nurse presses a button which gives me an unpleasant electric shock through the arms."

"It brings me down to earth every time," he said. "Already I am getting to hate racing and all that goes with it."

The Events

Listening to the races ⟶ getting

excited causes therapist to present

Shock ⟷ pain, discomfort

Classical Conditioning Component

CS (listening to the races)

UCS (shock) ⟶ UCR (pain and discomfort)

Results: Eventually the CS alone (listening to the races) should elicit a CR similar to the UCR — the subject will feel anxious (conditioned fear) whenever he hears the races.

Instrumental Conditioning Component

R (getting excited) ⟶ S (shock)

Results: The subject learns that the consequences of getting excited are unpleasant. To avoid shock he learns to avoid making the "excitement response," which of course means that he would say he no longer enjoys (gets excitement from) listening to the races.

In most behavior modification situations, the therapy consists of a component centering on classical conditioning and another component involving instrumental conditioning. Usually, one of the two components is more obvious than the other (and perhaps more important), but both components are usually present.

INSTRUMENTAL CONDITIONING

Biofeedback

Psychologists have discovered how to use conditioning techniques to control physiological responses that are under the automatic control of the nervous system. Take the control of blood pressure, for example. To instrumentally condition blood pressure we need a device that will continuously monitor and inform the subject of his or her relative blood pressure at all times. To use the operant conditioning technique, we would construct a device that would sound a tone whenever blood pressure rose above a specified level. The subject would be instructed to prevent the tone in any way possible.

A shaping technique might be used. At the start the critical blood pressure level would be set fairly high and in such a way that only slight reductions would terminate the tone. The tone offset tells the subject that the pre-

TABLE 4-7 Some Examples of Behavior Modification

1. Elimination of crying episodes of a preschool boy by having the teacher ignore him when he cried and pay attention to him when he talked. Previously, the teacher had usually done just the opposite.
2. Elimination of the psychotic responses of a female schizophrenic who always talked about the "royal family" and called herself Queen. The nurses were instructed to reward her with social attention and cigarettes when she talked normally and to ignore her when she talked about her delusions of royalty.
3. Elimination of a patient's obsessive thought about strangling his wife by having the patient punish himself whenever he had the thought. He did this by wearing a thick rubber band around his wrist that he snapped vigorously to inflict pain until the thought went away.
4. Reinforcement of standing and walking in a child who usually crawled around the classroom by having the teacher praise the child when she walked and ignore the child when she crawled.
5. Elimination of a child's tantrums and severe crying episodes at bedtime simply by having the parents stay out of the bedroom after the child was put to bed. Previously the child had cried and screamed until a parent returned to his room, and the parents had developed a pattern of staying with the child until he fell asleep.
6. Getting a patient to feed herself, instead of demanding spoon feeding by a nurse. The patient wanted to stay clean and neat, so the nurse was instructed always to spill some food on the patient during spoon feeding. In effect, the patient was taught, "If you want to stay neat, you will have to feed yourself." If self-feeding occurred, the nurse reinforced this with praise and social attention.

ceding behavior was beneficial to blood pressure level. Those activities, whatever they might be and whether or not they are conscious, are reinforced. When repeated, they are reinforced again. Gradually the subject learns to keep the tone off most of the time.

When the subject has learned to stay below the critical level, the setting is adjusted, making the subject reach for an even lower blood pressure level. Gradually the critical level is reduced to an acceptable range.

With advanced technology, we can expect to see an even greater reliance on bioelectric feedback devices in the control of undesired physiological responses. Use of these techniques will contribute to longer and healthier lives.

Behavior Modification

The treatment of behavior defects through the application of operant conditioning procedures has come to be known as **behavior modification.** Operant techniques have been successfully applied to such unwanted behaviors as stuttering, temper tantrums, poor study habits, smoking, excessive eating, and other problems (see Table 4-7).

Teachers are being trained to use operant techniques for handling problem students. For example, withdrawn children often get reinforced for playing alone, because the teacher attends to them in an effort to interest them in group activities. Instead, the teacher should reinforce them with her attention only when they show signs of participating in group activities. The teacher who does not know or fails to apply reinforcement principles often encourages misbehavior and class disruption by his or her attention to it. Ignoring these activities in their initial stages is a much better cure.

Psychologists used operant conditioning procedures in an unusual task during World War II. They trained pigeons to guide missiles to their targets. The pigeon was placed in the nose cone of a rocket. As the missile approached the target, the pigeon would peck on a key, sending out signals that modified the direction of the rocket, until the pigeon's actions indicated that the missile was on target.

Pigeons have also been trained to function as quality control inspectors. A company that manufactures gelatin capsules for drugs had a problem spotting defects difficult for the human eye to detect. Moreover, the inspection task was boring to human inspectors. Pigeons, who have remarkable eyesight, were shaped to respond to defects. Their work was superior to that of human inspectors. Nonetheless, the company decided not to use pigeons. Can you guess why?

The Token Economy Reward training, derived from the principles of operant conditioning, has been applied on a large scale to shape the

Why Not Provide Positive Reinforcement in Welfare?

William Raspberry

WASHINGTON — Human beings seem to need opportunities to set themselves apart in ways that are considered positive.

We know that, of course, and we act on that knowledge in countless aspects of our lives. We pass out gold stars and other rewards to children who do their school work uncommonly well. We give bonuses to workers who show themselves to be unusually useful.

We sponsor testimonials, award honorary degrees and name public buildings for people who demonstrate uncommon devotion to the public good. We are forever devising ways to satisfy the human urge to be set aside as special.

But somehow this instinct — so effective in reinforcing and encouraging those attributes we believe to be in the public interest — abandons us when it comes to social welfare.

We create all sorts of potentially useful programs for the needy among us — public housing, financial assistance, job training, special educational projects. But instead of using these programs to reinforce and encourage good things, we do just the opposite.

The one overriding criterion for access to any of these programs is: failure.

You have to be a failure to get into the housing projects (you're kicked out if you show signs of overcoming). You have to be virtually without resources, financial and otherwise, to qualify for public assistance payments. You have to be an academic failure to gain entry into a whole host of special education programs.

In general, we reward those things we wish to see repeated. But in social welfare, we reward those things which most distress us, and we are endlessly surprised when people react negatively to the things we offer as rewards for their negative attributes. . . .

I have a feeling we'd all be better off if we turned the thing on its head. Suppose, for instance, that in addition to sheer need — a negative criterion — we established positive criteria for, say, public housing eligibility. We could require, for instance, that public-housing applicants commit themselves to being responsible for the upkeep of both their apartments and, on a rotating basis, such common areas as halls and lawns.

Suppose these families, by exemplary fulfillment of their assigned duties, could earn merit points toward more desirable public housing and, if their economic situation improved a bit, assistance toward home ownership. (The other side of that coin, of course, would be demerits for poor behavior, an accumulation of which would render the family ineligible for public housing altogether.)

My guess is that we would thereby not only greatly diminish the amount of vandalism and other evidences of contempt for public assistance, but also greatly increase the number of families "graduating" into self-sufficiency. In addition, it might have a salutary effect on the ability and inclination of the families to discipline their children. . . .

Rocky Mountain News, *Denver*
February 23, 1978

Can the principles of instrumental conditioning work at the level of society? Here's one man's opinion.

behavior of groups of patients living together in mental hospitals. The goal is to teach the patients to behave more in accord with the definition of normal behavior. The hospital staff and patients devise a miniature society based on a token economy. Tokens (poker chips) are used, like money, as secondary rewards. The patients can earn tokens for certain behaviors and redeem them for special privileges.

At the outset the patient may earn points for only the slightest modification of behavior. Gradually the requirements are increased until the patient must behave normally to achieve rewards. In one project, tokens could be earned for the following behaviors: getting up quickly and at the right time every morning; good personal hygiene habits, such as bathing and wearing clean clothes; performing clean-up chores around the ward; and working at off-the-ward jobs, such as gardening or doing the laundry. The tokens could then be

The A–B–A Design and Operant Control of Vomiting

Laura was a nine-year-old child in an institution for retarded children. While she was enrolled in a class at the institution, she began to vomit in the class, and soon vomiting was an everyday occurrence. When she vomited on her dress, the teacher had Laura sent back to her residence hall. No medical cause for the vomiting could be found and no medication seemed to help. Perhaps her vomiting was not a reflex action, but a response Laura was emitting (*operant* behavior) because of its consequences (she could get out of the class).

In order to test this hypothesis, it was decided to measure Laura's vomiting under three conditions: (A) extinction— the reinforcement is eliminated; Laura had to stay in class regardless of vomiting; (B) reinstatement—the original reinforcement is reinstated; Laura was returned to her residence hall if she vomited; and (A again) a second extinction session; vomiting was not rewarded by allowing Laura to leave class.

The results were quite dramatic. During the first extinction period Laura vomited a lot at first, but gradually the vomiting declined in frequency until it reached a zero level. Then reinstatement began (she could leave if she vomited). It was quite some time before she finally vomited again, but when she finally did,

she was allowed to leave. In no time her vomiting reappeared; she vomited once a day and left class. Finally, during re-extinction, she was again forced to stay in class despite her vomiting. Again, at first she vomited a great deal, but the vomiting gradually decreased to zero.

This case (Wolf, Birnbrauer, Lawler, and Williams, 1970) illustrates the application of operant conditioning to a behavior problem—once the reinforcing event is discovered, its elimination can be used to terminate the undesired behavior. The case also illustrates the A–B–A design (the reversal design) that operant psychologists use to make sure they have discovered the relevant reinforcers for a behavior. The design involves three stages, where the first and third stages are the same (hence A–B–A). Going from one stage to the next involves a reversal of the contingency thought to be reinforcing the behavior. In this case, the design involved going from reinforcer absent to reinforcer present and then back to reinforcer absent. The ability to reverse the behavior (bring back the vomiting and then make it go away a second time) eliminates the alternate interpretation that Laura might have quit vomiting without any change in the reinforcement contingencies.

used to purchase a bed with an innerspring mattress to replace a cot, an opportunity to watch TV, and entrance to a fancy dining room rather than the customary undecorated hall.

Token economy programs have been extremely successful. Many long-term patients adopt model ward behavior, and sometimes

the entire ward completely changes character. Follow-up studies are still in progress, but, on the basis of what is known so far, there is every reason to believe that techniques of this sort speed up the reeducation process for patients and produce more rapid discharge from hospitals. The program provides rewards to patients working on their own problems and encourages them to develop new skills that can be used upon release. The reaction to token economies, however, is not entirely positive. Many lay people and experts alike feel these programs dehumanize patients, training them like lower animals. This reaction is not unfounded, but it must be considered in light of patients' behavioral changes in the direction of what is socially acceptable.

LEARNED HELPLESSNESS

When we discussed learned helplessness, we indicated that animals exposed to aversive events they cannot control show symptoms of severe physical stress and later fail to learn to escape the aversive event. Learned helplessness is not limited to animals. Human subjects also later fail to learn to escape aversive events if they are first exposed to uncontrollable aversive events. In fact, they are even debilitated when faced with solving problems such as anagrams if they are first given insoluble anagrams. An insoluble problem is analogous to an event that cannot be controlled. No solution occurs regardless of how hard the subject tries. Like rats, people exposed to uncontrollable aversive events show more signs of stress than do people exposed to controllable aversive events. It has been shown that loud noises over which an individual has no control is more stressful than equivalent amounts of controllable noise.

Research on learned helplessness has been extended to a variety of problems of human adaptation. The most extensive work has been done by Seligman. He has proposed that learned helplessness is a model of reactive depression. Some depressions seem to be induced by environmental events and others seem to occur cyclically without any environmental cause. Seligman has argued that learned helplessness is a model of the first kind. He feels that the cause of learned helplessness is the same as the cause of depression, that the symptoms are the same, and that cure and prevention are similar for both. He argues that depression is not caused directly by bad events but by the occurrence of bad life events over which the person has no control. Successful therapy should occur if the person is forcibly exposed to the fact that life events are controllable.

This view of depression has a great deal of intuitive appeal because depressions do seem to be brought on by uncontrollable events. Events such as the death of a spouse, marital

Unlearning Pain

For twenty years after a back injury had been healed, a San Francisco salesman named John Herbert suffered from pain so severe that he underwent eighteen major operations in a vain attempt at relief. Unable to return to his job, Herbert began to vegetate in bed most of the day and quickly became dependent on round-the-clock doses of potent painkillers. But today, thanks to an innovative rehabilitation program at the University of Washington School of Medicine in Seattle, John Herbert walks 4 miles every day, plays golf — and is permanently off medication.

John Herbert's dramatic recovery is typical of those experienced by some 150 chronic-pain victims who have enrolled in an eight-week training program run by clinical psychologist Dr. Wilbert E. Fordyce. The aim of the program is to help the patient "unlearn" a pain response that once had a genuine organic basis but over the years has become little more than habit. The pain habit persists, argues the 50-year-old Fordyce, because it tends to be positively reinforced by the patient's normal environment, which provides attention, concern, medication — and time off from work.

To reduce pain behavior, Fordyce and his colleagues try to eliminate the positive consequences of the patient's pain reaction and to reward what they term "well" behavior, such as exercise and work. But first, they must determine to what degree the cause of each patient's pain is organic. "If a patient reports experiencing pain, we have no reason not to believe that," says Fordyce.

"The key question is, what are the factors that influence the pain behavior?"

One of the main factors, Fordyce has observed, is often the patient's spouse. (About 80 per cent of the Seattle patients are women, most of whom are in their 40s and 50s.) "Some husbands pay attention to their wives only when they hurt," the psychologist points out. On the other hand, he adds, some wives use pain as an excuse for avoiding their husbands' sexual advances.

Once the staff has determined that the patient is experiencing more pain than her organic condition warrants, she is given an intensive course in behavioral conditioning. She undergoes rigorous physical and occupational therapy — such as exercising with a weighted leg pulley or operating a heavy printing press — in order to restore muscle tone and body energy. Each patient regularly receives a "pain cocktail," a solution of cherry syrup containing an antipain drug, but the cocktail is served when the patient is not experiencing severe pain — thereby depriving it of any reinforcement value. Although the patient knows that her painkilling medication is being gradually reduced until nothing remains but the syrup, she is not told by the doctors at what point the cutbacks will occur. . . .

Fordyce emphasizes that learned pain is not imaginary and that it cannot simply be wished away. But after participating in the "unlearning" program, he reports, only one patient in twenty has had to return to the clinic for a refresher course.

Newsweek
August 20, 1973

separation, loss of a job, and aging frequently precede severe depression. More important, Seligman has provided experimental evidence for his assertions. His experiments show that depressed people and nondepressed people given insoluble problems behave similarly in a variety of circumstances. He has also shown that depressed people tend to view events to which they are exposed as uncontrollable. Nondepressed people view these same events as controllable. Seligman has provided good preliminary support for the idea that learned helplessness is a model for depression.

Carol S. Dweck has argued that many instances of chronic failure in school are attributable to learned helplessness. The young child may accidentally be taught that success in school is not attainable no matter how hard he or she tries (independent of responding), and so the child stops trying. Dweck found that forced exposure to the escape contingency had a pronounced positive impact on many children who were chronic failures in

'Learned Helplessness' Cited in Wives Accepting Beating

Rykken Johnson

Women who put up with beatings by their male mates might be yielding to "learned helplessness," according to a psychologist at Colorado Women's College in Denver.

Battered women who refuse to leave their assailants behave much like dogs and rats which have been conditioned in laboratory experiments into passivity, said Dr. Lenore Walker, assistant professor of psychology at CWC. . . . Walker referred to studies by Martin Seligman at the University of Pennsylvania that provide the basis for her hypothesis. . . .

"Battered women behave like subjects in Seligman's experiments on learned helplessness," Walker said in her paper.

"They believe no one can help them and neither can they stop man's violence," Walker stated. "They have a negative cognitive set, behave in a passive manner and believe they are powerless in their home life."

Ironically, the paper contended, many battered women have responsible jobs and "exciting careers." However, Walker wrote, "There is great reluctance to leave their relationship. They have difficulty learning to take control of their lives." . . .

Walker is quick to emphasize that she doesn't feel women "ask for it" or are at any way at fault for their beatings. . . .

Instead, she said, battered women learn to adapt to their particular situations and that they can't stop the "bashing." Walker said she knew of one battered wife who knew another beating was coming, could feel "tension" around her home, had an important social gathering coming up, and "provoked a fight . . . to get it out of the way" before the gathering.

But Walker strongly suggests that battered women leave an abusive situation. "My advice has been, 'Run, don't walk away from it.' Women don't realize the acuteness of their situation," she said. . . .

The Denver Post
September 13, 1976

Passivity in human beings may result from experiences from which helplessness has been learned as a behavioral strategy.

school. Her procedure involved showing them that they were not trying hard enough when they failed to solve math problems rather than telling them they were stupid or that the problems were insoluble.

Finally, it has been proposed that much of the stress involved in urban living is due to the uncontrollability (e.g., noise, crowds, crime) of the things that happen. It has even been argued that crowding has negative consequences for individuals because they have less control in crowded circumstances. The next few years will no doubt see extensions of these ideas.

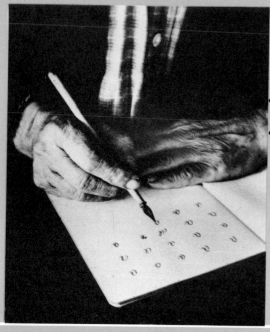

Human Learning and Memory

C an you imagine what life would be like if we could not read, write, or talk? Without our unique verbal capacities, human beings could not communicate with each other or perhaps even learn simple tasks that are necessary for survival such as securing food and finding shelter. In short, we would be very much like wild animals. When our distant ancestors developed a way of communicating with each other through spoken sounds, they made a great evolutionary advance. In addition to making communication possible, language enabled human beings to learn more easily and to store what they learned for future use.

COMPLEX HUMAN LEARNING

Human beings learn and perform many behaviors according to the principles of classical and instrumental conditioning we discussed in the preceding chapter. But another realm of learning, unique to human beings, is based on our capacity for language. For example, at this moment you may be learning for the first time that Sigmund Freud had a daughter named Anna. You learned that from reading the last sentence, using your language capacity. It is hard to imagine that the learning involved CS-UCS combinations, as in classical conditioning, and it is not easy to see how the learning could be viewed as involving a response followed by reinforcement, as in instrumental conditioning. Learning about Anna Freud hardly seems like dogs salivating to bells or like pigeons pecking for grain rewards. A vast amount of what we have learned, of what we know, has been learned through our verbal abilities. As a result, investigators of human learning have focused on verbal learning, and their most recent theories don't resemble the principles of classical and instrumental learning. In this chapter we will consider the basic principles of verbal learning and memory.

Despite the fact that verbal learning seems very unlike classical or instrumental conditioning, much of its history has been dominated by a theoretical position that has used conditioning as a fundamental, underlying concept. This position is called *associationism*, because its basis is the concept of an association. Furthermore, it was assumed that the principles of classical and/or instrumental conditioning applied to verbal associations. Hardly anyone believes this today, and yet the concept of verbal association is still extremely important in analyses of verbal learning. We all possess a complex memory system that contains an enormous amount of information; and, in our storehouse of memories and knowledge, there are complex associations among the various pieces of information. These associations make it possible to get from one place to another as we use our knowledge and memories in everyday behavior. Associations

are thus crucial to our functioning. In the last five to ten years, however, it has been demonstrated that much more is involved in verbal learning than learning associations. Applying what we already know and remember to a new problem involves much more than applying old associations to learning in new situations. Perhaps this seems obvious to you, but it was traditionally felt that we should start with basic elements (associations) and construct theories of more complex tasks by using these elements as building blocks. It was believed that complex learning could be understood by inventing complex association networks composed of many simple associations and that these simple associations could be studied by looking at the most fundamental type—the CS-UCS association in classical conditioning.

One of the major difficulties of this associative tradition stems from the fact that such theories have little or no room in them for any activity on the part of the person doing the learning and the behaving. Basically, they were passive theories—the learner didn't *do* anything. But suppose you were given a list of facts to memorize and told that your ability to recall them would be tested in a few weeks or months and that how you did on the test might affect your admission to medical school. You would do something—you would actively engage in behavior designed to learn the material. Even so simple a task as looking up a phone number and remembering it for a few seconds until you dial it involves doing something—you would probably rehearse the phone number, repeating it to yourself. If you got distracted while you were rehearsing, you would probably have to look the number up again or you might dial a wrong number. In any case, you do things when you learn and recall verbal materials. Several different processes and stages are involved, and associations, though important, are only a part of the picture.

The Information-Processing Approach

In order to develop models of what kinds of processes and stages are involved, psychologists

Our information-processing system operates most efficiently if we focus on only one mental task at a time.

have turned to an important analogy with the computer, particularly the computer program and flow chart. This analogy has given birth to one of the most significant developments in modern psychology—the information-processing approach, which was introduced in Chapter 1. First, this approach is characterized by the fact that it breaks up the learning process into components or stages and examines what happens to incoming information as it progresses through these stages. At each stage processes are at work or are applied to the information. These processes affect the information in some way—the information is extracted, rehearsed, or transformed in some way, leading to the next stage in which different processes operate. We thus have *stages* and *processes* as critical components. For example, we have already mentioned rehearsal as a process—this keeps the information (the phone number) "alive" in short-term memory (the stage).

The second major aspect of information-processing analyses of learning and memory is known as the *limited-capacity assumption*. It is assumed that the system for learning and memory can handle only so much information at a time in each stage. We can't do too many things at once or the system will become overloaded and break down. Again, if you are distracted (say by a blaring TV commercial) while you are rehearsing that phone number to keep it alive in your short-term memory, you may start processing information from the TV and forget the number.

The third aspect of the information-processing analogy is the postulation of a control mechanism to oversee the whole process. This control mechanism governs the overall flow and analysis of the information that is impinging upon the system, usually trying to overload the system. The control system has higher-level processes that it can employ to govern the overall operation. Examples might be the setting of overall goals or the application of various strategies. Consider the phone number—the control mechanism will determine how the information is processed according to some plan with a goal. If you just want to remember the number long enough to dial it, and you don't expect to use the number again, rehearsal will be the primary process employed. But suppose it is the new phone number of the pizza parlor you call at least once a week. The control mechanism will call upon different processes or strategies (for example, make a word with some of the numbers) designed to produce a more permanent memory (called long-term memory). Sometimes you get outside help with such matters. In Denver, if you want to order hockey tickets you call 534-PUCK which is a preprocessed version of 534-7825. We know very little about the operation of the control mechanism; indeed we will hardly mention it again in the current discussion. We do know that such a mechanism is necessary to govern the overall operation of the learning and memory system.

The Fundamental Memory System

Any system that must do all the things we do with our brains and language capacity has to be incredibly complicated. It is beyond the scope of this book to outline such a complex system in detail. We will present only the most simpli-

Figure 5–1
The Memory System

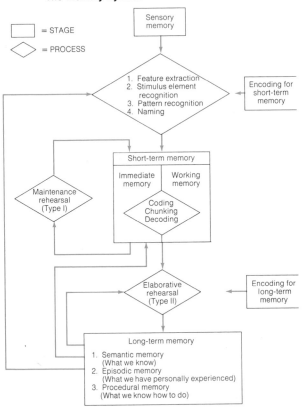

"Let me just make a little note of that. I never seem to get anything done around here unless I make little notes."

The New Yorker, January 6, 1975. Drawing by H. Martin; © 1975 The New Yorker Magazine, Inc.

Could this be a case of brain damage similar to that of patients studied by Brenda Milner?

fied version possible, but enough to give you the flavor of current thinking in this field.

There are three basic memory stages that most investigators agree are useful concepts in describing how information flows through the system. These are (1) sensory memory, which persists for a very brief period; (2) short-term memory, which may be conceived of as the information that you are consciously aware of at any given time; and (3) long-term memory, which consists of your knowledge and memories of your experiences, not currently conscious but capable of becoming conscious if the information stored there can be retrieved. We can diagram these three memory systems as in Figure 5–1, but you should remember that this analysis is based on an analogy with computers. Information *flows* through the system in a continuous fashion. The information does not jump from one "memory box" to another. It is just easier

to think about the information flow in this way. We use the boxes as a way of simplifying our thinking about the system without necessarily maintaining that the boxes have a real location in the brain.

There is, however, some evidence from studies of brain-damaged individuals that can be used to support the separate box distinction between short- and long-term memory. Brenda Milner has studied such individuals and described a syndrome that appears in some individuals with brain damage in the hippocampus region (see Chapter 2). Such people have short-term memories, but they can remember something new only if they keep rehearsing it. Their long-term memories are apparently unaffected by the brain damage—they remember quite well things they knew before the brain injury. The problem is that they can't seem to get any new information into long-term memory. In order to function, they have to write everything down before they forget it and carry these notes around with them. Such evidence makes it rea-

Everybody Has a Photographic Memory (Well, Almost)

There is now ample evidence that our brain continues to "see" a stimulus for some time after the stimulus has been physically removed. Unfortunately, this representation is viewed for only a fraction of a second. This memory system is called sensory memory, or short-term visual store.

George Sperling devised an important method for studying visual sensory memory. Subjects were shown three rows of four symbols (numbers and letters):

7 H T 9
P D 3 1
2 K 8 G

The matrix of symbols was briefly flashed (for less than 1/10 of a second), and then the subjects were asked to report what they saw. Presumably they would start reading off what they saw, reading from left to right and top to bottom. One subject might say, "7, H, T, 9, ah . . ." and fail on the remaining symbols because the sensory image had disappeared. But if the subject really had an image of the whole matrix, he or she should be able to report any row, as long as it was reported first,

before the image disappeared. Sperling demonstrated that if at the time of the flash he inserted an arrow pointing to the row to be reported first, the subject could report any row he asked for. This must mean that the subject had some kind of image of the array after it had gone off. Sperling's method is called *cued partial report*, because the subject is given a cue (the arrow) and asked to report only part of the array (the row the arrow points to). For example, the subject would see:

8 9 M F
⟶ 1 J 7 W
X V 6 2

Naturally, reporting was best if the arrow came on before the subject saw the array, because the person could then focus attention on the crucial row. But the subjects could report any row, even when the arrow came on *after* the array, provided it was immediately after. If presentation of the arrow was delayed until the image had faded, the subjects could not report very well. So our visual perceptual system has a brief memory capability, located, most probably, in the rods and cones themselves.

sonable to make a qualitative distinction between short- and long-term memory.

Other evidence also suggests that short- and long-term memory are truly separate stores, but most of it is subject to different interpretation or has been refuted. For example, some have argued that the representation of an item (its encoding) in short-term memory is only acoustic (based only on its sound), whereas representation in long-term memory is semantic (based on its meaning). While this would have been a neat basis for distinguishing between the two memory stores, it is now clear that both acoustic and semantic information is available in both short- and long-term memory.

Sensory Memory

This component of the memory system is based on sensory processes that allow the effect of a stimulus on the sensory system to persist for a very brief time after the stimulus itself has been removed. For visual stimuli, it is as though we have a very brief photographic memory that provides us with a sensory photograph of the stimulus that quickly fades away. So information is first registered in the sensory component, but it is quickly lost without additional processing.

The additional processing of the contents of sensory memory leads eventually to that information being encoded into short-term memory in some form. These additional processes first involve attention and filtering of the information. The sensory "photograph" contains a massive amount of information. The attentional and filtering processes determine what "gets through" to the next stage in which additional processes determine what has been presented. This determination constitutes the encoding that is entered in short-term memory. For example, if the stimulus is the word "Freud," there will be (1) feature-extraction processes that analyze the lines, angles, and curves, allowing (2) the stimulus-element recognition process to determine some or all of the letters that have occurred, (3) a pattern-recognition process that after some time will identify the overall pattern that has occurred, and (4) with the help of the information that is stored in long-term memory the pattern may get named. It is with these processes that we determine the word "Freud" has occurred, and this information is then entered into short-term memory.

A key thing to remember here is that not all of the information contained in the sensory memory will make it through all this analysis. The analysis takes time and there is limited capacity. The sensory memory fades rapidly, and much of the information is lost before it can be analyzed by all these processes and will thus never make it into short-term memory. For example, "Freud" may make it into short-term memory, but information such as where the word was located on the page, the exact shape of the letter "r," and the size of the letters may not. Only a small portion of the information in the sensory photograph will get further processing, and the rest of the information will be lost. So, the attentional/filtering processes determine what gets the further processing necessary for encoding into short-term memory.

Short-Term Memory

Short-term memory is the intermediate stage between sensory memory and long-term memory. Short-term memory is a part of the continuum of which we are consciously aware. It is convenient to think of it as divided into two compartments called (1) immediate memory and (2) working memory.

Immediate memory contains information that

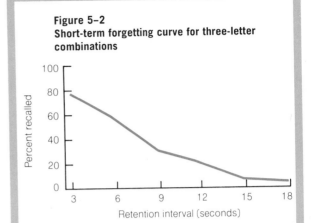

Figure 5–2
Short-term forgetting curve for three-letter combinations

Short-Term Forgetting

Do you think you can remember a single three-letter combination (for example, HMK) for a period of 30 seconds? Of course you can if you rehearse the letters over the 30-second retention interval. But what if you could not rehearse? Suppose we do the following: We give you a syllable (XTK) and then immediately give you a number (291). You must start with 291 and count backward by three's (291, 288, 285, 282, and so on) until the 30 seconds are up. Then we ask you what the syllable was. A pioneering experiment by Peterson and Peterson (1959) on retention of three-letter combinations used retention intervals of 3, 6, 9, 12, 15, and 18 seconds. As you can see in Figure 5–2, the startling results show that college students cannot remember a three-letter combination for 18 seconds, much less 30.

can be immediately recalled or directly "read out." *Working memory* processes information in some way that changes its nature (changes its encoding). Roberta Klatzky has suggested an analogy with a workbench in a carpentry shop. The carpenter has his or her materials piled up immediately at hand on part of the bench (immediate memory). The rest of the bench is the area where the carpenter works on the materials with his or her tools to create something that wasn't there to begin with. How much space the carpenter devotes to each aspect is variable and changes from job to job. Some jobs require large amounts of work space, leaving little room for having materials immediately at hand. Other jobs require little work space, allowing a lot of space for the materials. In short-term memory we can devote much space to immediate memory and therefore keep the maximum amount of information immediately available, but this leaves little room to work on the information. As soon as a task requires considerable working space, we have to take space from immediate memory, meaning that we are unable to have as much information at hand. We are confronted by limited capacity.

It has been shown that immediate memory can handle about seven "chunks" of information when no work must be done on the information. For example, in the memory-span task, subjects are read a series of digits (1398756, say) and simply asked to repeat them (no work on them is required). Memory-span experiments show that people have a capacity of seven plus or minus two items. George Miller's research has made this number (7 ± 2) famous. However, when subjects are required to work on this information entering short-term memory, the number of items that can be kept immediately available drops, because the resources must be shifted to working memory.

Recall that we said seven *chunks*—not seven pieces—of information. A **chunk** is a unit of immediate memory that may contain many pieces or "bits" of information. For example, the word "Freud" contains five letters. This word may be one chunk among the seven. You might be able to handle seven five-letter words and remember them all immediately, which would be the same as remembering 35 letters. If you were tested on a string of letters that you could not chunk into words (BRHSKQM, say), you could remember only about seven different letters. Since we can handle only about seven chunks, we try to squeeze as much information into each chunk as possible to maximize our memories. Consider the following sequence of letters: TVF—BIJ—FKY—MCA. It has 12 letters and is thus beyond the span of immediate memory. You might chunk

it into the four groups of three letters presented above, but these chunks don't form words. Consider the same letter sequence chunked in a different way: TV—FBI—JFK—YMCA. Now it becomes easy to remember the 12 letters because they have been chunked (recoded) into meaningful units, each unit containing more than one letter, making the overall capacity larger than seven letters. Chunking information into larger and larger units is one of the most important kinds of work we can do with our working memories.

The reverse of chunking or recoding is called *decoding*, and it is something we must also be able to do in working memory. If you are presented with the sequence of letters BOKGLSRNGBLT, you might first recode to something like BOK—GLS—RNG—BLT and then from there to book-glass-ring-belt. You have then coded and recoded a 12-letter sequence into four words. At recall, you will probably be able to remember the four words, but you will have to decode from the words to get back the correct letter sequence. With a sequence like this you could make errors because of decoding mistakes.

A final process of short-term memory is called rehearsal. Investigators have found it useful to distinguish between two types of rehearsal. *Type I rehearsal* (also known as *maintenance rehearsal*) is like repeating the item to yourself to keep it from disappearing from short-term memory. The item is not transformed at all, but simply repeated to keep it "alive" in memory. At one time it was thought that if an item were rehearsed in this way enough times, it would automatically be passed on for storage in long-term memory; and it was believed that the more the item was rehearsed, the stronger it became in long-term memory. Now it is believed that Type I rehearsal does not automatically result in long-term memory. In Type I rehearsal the item is merely repeated, not worked on in any fashion. For the item to be entered or encoded into long-term memory additional processing may be necessary—it certainly will be helpful to do additional work on the item.

This type of work is called *Type II rehearsal* (or *elaborative rehearsal*). Type II rehearsal is necessary to encode an item into long-term memory. Type II rehearsal relates the item to information that is already in long-term memory. This may be done in many different ways. You might think of things associated with the item, or you might try to fit the item into a category of other items already stored in memory, or you might conjure up a mental image of the item. The word "Freud" might make you think of "couch" or "dreams" or "Oedipus." You might categorize it in some way, such as "famous Viennese physician," or you might imagine how Freud looked. All this involves relating the presented word to things or information already stored in your memory.

Experiments have shown that the amount and type of elaborative rehearsal performed drastically influences the amount of information that gets out of short-term memory into long-term memory. Much of this work has been done within a theoretical framework known as *levels-of-processing theory*, developed by Fergus Craik and R. S. Lockhart. These authors focus on the quality and quantity of the processes applied to information in memory. They distinguish among various levels, arguing that some items get superficial treatment (shallow level of processing) while others get processed much more deeply. Their basic assumption is that the depth to which an item is processed determines the ease with which it can be remembered or recalled from long-term memory. Depth is much more important than simply repeating an item over and over to yourself (Type I rehearsal). Presumably there is a depth-of-processing continuum. At one end are the shallow processes related to the sensory aspects of the stimulus (how it sounds as it is repeated, what it rhymes with). At the deep end of the processing continuum are processes that deal with the semantic aspects of the stimulus (what it means). The word "Freud" is processed at a shallow depth if you merely think of a word that rhymes with it. If on the other hand you think of words that are associated with the word "Freud," deep processing is required. Many experiments have shown that words processed deeply (semantically) are better remembered than words processed minimally (see the Box on p. 182).

Long-Term Memory

Information reaching long-term memory has been processed thoroughly and deeply and is *available* for use for a relatively long time.

Having the information available, however, does not mean that we have access to it. There is a distinction between *availability* and *accessibility* in memory. Accessibility means that we can get to the information when we want it — this process of getting to the information is called *retrieval*. We can fail on a memory test for two reasons: (1) the information is not available in long-term memory; that is, it was never learned or stored, or if it was stored, it was somehow removed; and (2) we cannot retrieve the information; it is in there, but we can't get to it. When we say that something is on the tip of our tongue, we are saying that we feel sure the information is available, but we just can't retrieve it at the moment.

Some investigators have speculated that unlike other components of the overall system, long-term memory has essentially unlimited capacity — it cannot be overloaded. There is room for all the information the system can process through the earlier stages — old information is not pushed out as new information comes in. Another astounding speculation is that information is never lost from long-term memory. This view is controversial and difficult to test. In order to test this speculation, we would have to devise a memory test that could distinguish between availability and accessibility. After a failure a subject might be provided with retrieval hints (for example, "his name begins with F"). Studies using these retrieval cues show that much more information is available than is accessible, but they can't prove that everything we have learned is still available. Opinion remains divided. Some believe information is lost from long-term memory, while others say it is never lost, but gets harder to retrieve.

Endel Tulving also makes a distinction between semantic memory and episodic memory. Semantic memory roughly corresponds to our knowledge, to what we know about the world and about the meaning and grammar of our language. Episodic memory roughly corresponds to personal memory of things we have actually experienced in our life. Semantic memory contains the information that Freud was a famous physician who founded psychoanalysis. Episodic memory contains the information that we read about Freud having a daughter named Anna a few pages ago. This distinction is

Figure 5–3
A simple hierarchy in semantic memory

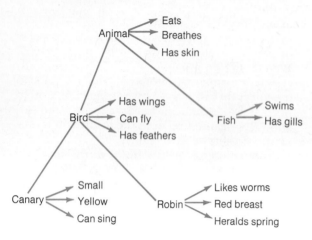

thought to be important because different processes might be involved in storing and retrieving information between these two systems. At present, however, there seem to be only conceptual distinctions between the two — no clear-cut experiments demonstrate different processes.

ORGANIZATION IN LONG-TERM MEM-ORY   Because we are able to retrieve so much information from long-term memory, the information must be highly organized. Just how information is stored and organized in long-term memory is a question several psychologists have tried to answer. Their theories are incredibly complex. New models are being developed at a rapid pace as older ones are tested and found deficient. Because of their complexity, we will not consider any of these models here. Suffice it to say that developing such models is one of the most challenging and exciting tasks facing the psychologist who studies memory.

We all have an enormous amount of information stored in our long-term memories and we keep adding new information to the store all the time. Figuring out how we have all this information organized or structure so that we can get to it when we need it, and get to it

quickly, is going to take a great deal of creative theorizing and experimentation. To give some feel for the task, consider how one type of model, called a network model, would deal with only the simplest of chores: answering a question, "Do canaries have skin?"

Network models assume that the information in semantic memory is arranged in a vast, highly organized network consisting of nodes (locations) and connections among nodes. Furthermore, the network is arranged in a hierarchy with more general or abstract information higher in the hierarchy than the more specific information (see Figure 5–3). For example, there would be a node in semantic memory corresponding to the concept *canary*. Extending from this node would be connections leading to other nodes. Information about each concept is stored at a node, with connections specifying its properties. Looking at Figure 5–3, we see that at the canary node there are three properties or features stored about canaries: they can sing, they are small, and they are yellow. We also see a connection leading upward in the hierarchy from canary to the more general concept *bird*. At the bird node additional information is stored which is true of birds in general; they have wings and feathers and can fly. Moving upward again, we get to the animal node where we find information concerning skin. To answer our question we would have to enter the network at the canary node specified in the question and then move upward first to the bird node and then to the animal node. It is like saying to ourselves, "A canary is a bird, and a bird is an animal, and animals have skin; therefore, canaries have skin." And so we answer yes to the question. If the question were, "Do canaries have feathers?" we would only have to move up one node to find the answer because "has feathers" is stored at the bird node. In fact, research has shown that we answer the question about feathers faster than we answer the question about skin, which gives support to the hierarchy notion (Collins and Quillian, 1969). It suggests that "has skin" is stored higher in the hierarchy than "has feathers." Network models such as this are only one type of theory, although perhaps the most popular type at the moment. Just imagine the size and complexity of a network capable of containing all the information we know!

LEARNING AND TRANSFER

Learning Variables

In this section we will describe the three major variables research has identified as affecting the speed and ease with which we learn verbal materials. We will consider: (1) the meaningfulness of the material, (2) the similarity of the material to other things we have learned or are learning, and (3) the degree to which the material can be processed using mental imagery. But before we examine these variables, we must look at the methods psychologists use to test subjects on learning and memory abilities.

Verbal-Learning Methods

There are four commonly used learning and memory tasks. The first of these is called **memory span.** In this task we test subjects' immediate memory capacity. The subject is presented with a string of items—usually digits—and is asked to repeat them back immediately after presentation. The string is increased in length until the subject fails, and we have then determined the subject's memory span. Research shows the span is usually about seven items (plus or minus two).

The second task is known as **free recall.** Here the subject is presented with a list of items that is usually much longer than the memory span. After seeing all the items, the subject is asked to recall as many as possible in any order. The subject is usually unable to recall all of them, so the items are presented again for another study trial, and then another test trial is given. Subjects alternate between study and test trials until they can recall all the items on the list.

One of the most interesting facts about free-recall learning is that even though subjects are free to recall items in any order, they don't seem to take advantage of this freedom. Across trials subjects tend to adopt a fixed order for recalling the items, a phenomenon known as *subjective organization.* The theoretical interpretation of this phenomenon is that since the list is too long to handle with immediate memory, the subjects must recode the items into larger chunks, with the items arranged in order within each chunk. Close examination of the order of

item recall across trials enables the experimenter to see the chunks developing and increasing in size as the subject recodes more and more information into each chunk. The number of chunks that can be handled at one time is limited, so the best memory strategy is to cram as much information as possible into each chunk.

The third task is known as **serial learning.** It is much the same as free recall except that in serial learning the subject must recall the items in exactly the same order as they were presented.

The fourth task is known as **paired-associate learning.** In this task the subject is confronted with a list of pairs of items. For example, there might be 12 pairs of words (Freud–Anna could be a pair) in the list. After subjects are exposed to all the pairs on a study trial, they are tested by the experimenter who presents the first item in a pair as a stimulus and the subject attempts to recall the item that was paired with it on the study trial. Study and test trials alternate until the subject has learned all the pairs. This method is used to study the process of association.

Meaningfulness

Obviously, it is easier to learn meaningful than nonmeaningful materials. To take an extreme example, the pair JQM–ZJR is considerably more difficult to commit to memory than is the pair CAT–SKY. Why and how does meaningfulness affect learning? What is meaningfulness, and how can it be measured? Several explanations have been offered.

1. The more similar an item is to an English word, the more meaningful it is. Note that JOK, while not an English word, is so much like one that it is easily connected with one. Other things being equal, this item would probably be easier to memorize than JQM.

2. Meaningfulness correlates with the frequency with which an item has been experienced in the past. The more familiar an item, the greater its meaningfulness. The letters JOK have been experienced many more times by each of us than the combination JQM.

3. Meaningfulness depends on the number of mental associates elicited by an item. Highly meaningful items elicit many associates, while

Serial Position and the "Isolation" Effect

When studying textbooks, students often underline important points they want to remember, usually with brightly colored "magic markers" that make the important points stand out. Of course, some students emphasize so much that entire pages be-become yellow or pink or orange. Do you think the underlining helps? Is there a limit to how much underlining is bene-ficial?

Here's a simple verbal-learning experi-ment you can try on your friends. At right is a list of 11 nonsense syllables. Copy each one onto a note card so that you have a set of "flash cards" to show your subjects. Make three sets of cards: (1) none of the syllables are placed in a border of colored magic marker; (2) the middle or sixth syl-lable is isolated by surrounding it with a colored border; (3) all 11 syllables are sur-rounded with a colored border. Now test some people on each of the three sets, say three or four subjects on each set. Show them the cards one at a time at a reason-ably slow rate. Say nothing about the bor-ders; just ask them to learn the syllables in any order. After this study trial, hand them a slip of paper and ask them to write down as many of the syllables as they can in any order. Then tally the results and see which group remembered the most syllables alto-gether and which group did best on the middle syllable. In the second group with only one isolated item, was there any recall of the item before the isolate and the item after the isolate? Draw a graph, called a *serial-position curve*, in which you plot the

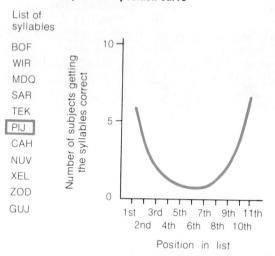

Figure 5-4
Sample serial-position curve

List of syllables

BOF
WIR
MDQ
SAR
TEK
PIJ
CAH
NUV
XEL
ZOD
GUJ

number of people who recalled the syllable at each position. A sample curve is shown in Figure 5-4. In it you can see a **primacy effect** (syllables near the beginning of the list are remembered well) and a **recency effect** (syllables near the end of the list are also remembered well). Did you find these two effects in your serial-position curve? This is a study dealing with what is known as the *von Restorff effect*. The von Restorff effect refers to better retention of an iso-lated item—in our example the single item surrounded with a colored border—than of other items around it. Was PIJ recalled better when it was isolated (in condition 2) than when it was not (conditions 1 and 3) in your experiment? If so, you demon-strated the von Restorff effect.

items low in meaningfulness suggest absolutely nothing to you. JOK may elicit funny, comic, prank, and so on. But unless JQM happened to be your initials, the combination would probably suggest little or nothing. Moreover, highly

meaningful items are more likely to produce images (JOK → an image of a TV comic) than are items low in meaningfulness.

4. In connection with verbal items, pro-nounceability also clearly relates to meaningful-

ness. JOK is easily pronounced, while JQM requires three separate responses, J-Q-M.

Perhaps the best way to think about the effect of meaningfulness is in terms of the processing work already done on the information. The more meaningful the material is to begin with, the more it has been preprocessed into a form the system can deal with. Meaningful material is preprocessed into larger chunks. For example, the phone number for hockey tickets in Denver (534-PUCK) is a more meaningful stimulus than seven digits because PUCK is one chunk that can be decoded easily into four numbers. It is much easier to relate the material to the already existing contents of memory if the material is meaningful. PUCK can easily be related to what we know, but what can you do with 7825? Meaningful information is processed through the memory system more rapidly—leading to faster learning and better recall—simply because much of the processing has already been done for meaningful items.

Meaningfulness facilitates learning, so a good technique for learning is to make material to be learned more meaningful than it is on the surface. For example, if you are faced with the task of learning the item JQM, you might use the letters to make up a sentence: "*J*ohnny *q*uivered when *M*ary touched him." Under these circumstances, JQM becomes more meaningful. This technique is called *coding.* You code JQM to "*J*ohnny *q*uivered when *M*ary touched him," and, when asked to recall what you have learned, you decode from the sentence back to JQM. The more meaningful you can make the material, the easier it will be to learn. Three simple steps to faster learning and better memory are: (1) familiarize yourself with the material over and over again; (2) pronounce each item until you can say it easily and identically every time; (3) invent associations for the material, including silly sentences or funny visual images.

Similarity

There is a close relationship between similarity and generalization. When you learn a response to a stimulus, you simultaneously develop a tendency to make that same response to other similar stimuli. Therefore, when the stimuli of a paired-associate list are similar to

Meaningfulness Facilitates Learning: A Simple Test

Here are three lists of nonsense syllables that differ in rated meaningfulness. The rating procedure was to have the subject indicate whether or not a given syllable made him or her think of something—an association. If 100 percent of the subjects get an association to the syllable, the association value for that syllable is 100 percent, and so on. To prove that meaningfulness facilitates learning, ask a few friends to practice each of these three lists for a few trials of serial learning. Which one is easiest?

100%	*53%*	*7%*
NAR	NOH	NUX
CUS	CEG	CEJ
MEX	MIQ	MIB
HON	HUJ	HUC
BEC	BOZ	BOF
WOM	WOB	WOJ
PUF	PIV	PIW
DAR	DUP	DAQ
REG	RIK	XEZ
JUS	JIR	JEQ

each other, the learning task is more difficult because of interpair generalization. You will have trouble learning which response goes with which of the very similar stimuli, even though the responses themselves may be easily discriminated.

Like meaningfulness, similarity is a multidimensional variable. Some of the contributing factors, illustrated in Table 5–1, are formal similarity, semantic similarity, and conceptual similarity. *Formal similarity* is based on physical features of words. There are two primary types: *orthographic similarity,* which means that the items to be learned share some number of identical letters; and *acoustic similarity,* which means that the items contain letters that sound alike, for example, T, B, C, D, E, G, P, V, and Z. A serial list of nonsense syllables that is high in

TABLE 5-1   Different Kinds of Similarity

Formal similarity
The items to be learned are in some sense physically similar.

Orthographic similarity: They are similar because of identical letters.

High similarity:		Low similarity:	
	JZH		JZH
	ZJQ		MVQ
	QHJ		KPL
	HQZ		XTZ
	QJZ		BGN

Acoustic similarity: They are similar in sound when pronounced letter by letter.

High similarity:		Low similarity:	
	BIM		BIM
	TYN		XAF
	EPV		HUW
	GBQ		LOR
	DTU		SXB

Semantic similarity
The items are not physically similar, but they have similar or closely related meanings in English.

High similarity:		Low similarity:	
	large		black
	tremendous		hard
	gigantic		involved
	big		lovable
	whopping		quiet
	massive		distant

Conceptual similarity
The items are not physically similar nor do they mean the same or similar things. Rather, they are instances of the same general concept.

High similarity:		Low similarity:	
	maple		maple
	oak		tango
	elm		diamond
	ash		doctor
	cherry		canary
	poplar		snake
	birch		priest
	aspen		valley
	pine		martini

orthographic similarity is practically impossible to memorize. Try the list given in Table 5-1 on yourself or your friends. Formal similarity, especially of nonsensical material, makes both response learning and the associative process of connecting these responses to different stimuli extremely difficult.

Semantic similarity refers to the fact that two words may have the same or similar meanings. Unlike formal similarity, semantic similarity may be used to facilitate the response-learning component of a paired-associate task. For example, if all responses of a list have something

to do with "largeness," they will be easy to learn. Trouble may arise, however, when the learner attempts to associate these responses with their corresponding stimuli. Suppose the response *big* is paired with the stimulus *green*, and the response *large* is paired with the stimulus *dog*. It will be easy to learn the two required responses, *big* and *large*, but hard to remember which one goes with *green* and which one goes with *dog*. If you learn *green–big*, response generalization may introduce a tendency to say *green–large*. Semantic similarity, then, might facilitate response learning while inhibiting associative learning. In a paired-associate list, therefore, there should be little or no effect when the semantic similarity of responses is manipulated. The positive and negative effects tend to cancel each other out. On the stimulus side, however, we see only the negative effect, due to stimulus generalization. Thus, in this case, semantic similarity retards learning.

Conceptual similarity derives from the fact that the items in question are interrelated as instances of a general concept, for example, names of animals, trees, birds, or professions. Conceptual similarity and semantic similarity have about the same effects on learning—they facilitate response learning but inhibit associative learning. Note that because conceptual and semantic similarity facilitate response learning, free-recall lists of items with high levels of these variables should be more easily learned. Moreover, if you want to memorize a list of names of objects, it will definitely help to begin by organizing the list into conceptual or semantic grouping. When similarity is likely to inhibit, you should try to develop a memory code for the material that minimizes this effect of similarity.

Imagery

Another factor influencing verbal learning is the imagery value of words. Imagery is generally correlated with how concrete or abstract words are. Abstract words lack physical referents and typically fail to arouse images of any sort. Examples of abstract words are *injustice, envy hate, moral,* and *peace.* Concrete words, on the other hand, refer to physical objects, for example, *table, book, door,* and *grass.* Concrete words readily evoke images for most people. Not all abstract words, however, are necessarily low in imagery value. *Peace,* for example, has frequently been symbolized by the dove, and dove may be the image aroused by that word. Imagery and abstractness are highly correlated, but the correlation is not perfect.

Imagery facilitates learning. In paired-associate learning the facilitating effect is large when the stimulus rather than the response items are high in imagery. Consider the pair *football-happy.* Suppose the stimulus term *football* elicited the image of a large stadium, while *happy* elicited no image at all for the subject. A learning strategy might be to imagine the stadium filled with whatever kind of thing the response term could be used to refer to, in this case, *happy* spectators. When the memory is eventually tested for this pair, presentation of the stimulus term *football* should arouse this image, enabling the subject to think of the response term *happy.* The imagery of the response term is not nearly as important as that of the stimulus term, because the response is not a cue or stimulus for recall, but is the word to be recalled.

Subjects taught to make up strange visual images of the material to be learned perform at a much higher level than subjects who do not use images. For hundreds of years, memory experts have relied heavily on visual images to improve their performance. If you want to remember a list of objects, you might try to imagine the items in a stack, one thing on top of another. Try to visualize what the stack would be like. Another technique is to contrive a picture to go with the words to be remembered. In the spinal cord there is a nucleus called the *substantia gelatinosa,* a difficult name for most people to remember. But imagine a midget sitting on your spinal column at the locus of this nucleus eating a *substantial* bowl of *gelatin,* and you may never again forget the name of this nucleus.

Why does imagery facilitate learning? The prevailing interpretation is that human beings have two primary modes for remembering: a verbal mode and a pictorial, or visual, imagery mode. If we learn something in both modes of presentation, as is more likely for high-imagery words, the chances for later retention are better than if we learned only in one mode. Another factor is that we can chunk or record a lot of information into a single image that takes up less space in memory.

Imagery techniques are not only powerful, they can be fun. They not only improve your

Imagery and Learning: A Simple Experiment

Here are two lists of words, one high in imagery value (concrete words) and one low in imagery value (abstract words). Look at each list for 30 seconds and then try to write down as many of the words as you can remember. You should find that imagery facilitates learning.

High-Imagery Concrete Words	Low-Imagery Abstract Words
nail	injustice
cloud	envy
house	happiness
tire	institution
ball	education
fence	fashion
cigar	modesty
rock	motive
truck	contempt
dress	depth
book	thought
table	void
milk	agreement
telephone	society
bed	temper

learning speed but they take some of the boredom out of what otherwise might be a dull memorization task.

Transfer of Training

When we learn something new, some knowledge or skill, we usually do so with the intent to use it at a later time. In some cases we are later asked to recall or remember the exact information we learned, as in a final objective examination in a college course. In such cases, we are concerned with *memory,* which will be covered in the next section. Closely related to memory is the phenomenon of **transfer of training,** which refers to the effect of prior learning on the subsequent performance of a different task. Driving a new car is an example of transfer. While the responses required are similar to those you've learned in earlier driving ex-

TABLE 5-2   Transfer of Training

Experimental group ⟶ learns Task 1 ⟶ learns Task 2

Control group ⟶ does nothing ⟶ learns Task 2

1. If the experimental group does *better* on Task 2 than the control, there is *positive transfer*.

2. If the experimental group does *worse* on Task 2 than the control, there is *negative transfer*.

3. If the experimental group and the control group do not differ, there is *zero transfer*.

Why does a fireman wear red suspenders?
A. ☐ **The red goes well with the blue uniform.**
B. ☐ **They can be used to repair a leaky hose.**
C. ☐ **To hold up his pants.**

The New Yorker, March 25, 1974. Drawing by D. Fradon; © 1974 The New Yorker Magazine, Inc.

The multiple-choice test is a test of recognition memory. One theory is that this test is easier than a fill-in-the-blank test (recall memory) because recall requires retrieval of the correct answer and recognition of the fact that it is correct, whereas no retrieval is required on a recognition test because the correct answer is right in front of you. In short, this theory says that different processes are involved in the two types of test.

periences, they are not exactly the same. You may find it necessary to adapt old habits or learn some new ones. You may even find some of your old habits interfering with the smooth operation of the new car. The point is that there will be some effect of prior learning and that is what is called transfer of training.

To demonstrate transfer effects in the laboratory, we might construct two different paired-associate tasks. Two groups of subjects are used: (1) the experimental group, which learns Task 1 and then transfers to Task 2 and learns it; and (2) a control group, which has to learn the second task without the prior learning of Task 1. The control condition is similar to learning to drive a car for the first time, without any prior experience. We examine the performance of the two groups on Task 2 and ask which group did better. If the experimental group performed better than the control group, we assume that something about Task 1 benefited their performance—the prior learning of Task 1 transferred positively to the learning of Task 2. This would be a case of *positive transfer*. If the experimental group did worse than the control group on Task 2, we would have an instance of *negative transfer*—the prior learning of Task 1 actually hindered performance on Task 2. Finally, if there were no difference between the two groups on Task 2, we would have *zero transfer*. Zero transfer might mean that Task 1 learning has no effect whatsoever on Task 2 learning, or it might mean that learning Task 1 produces both positive and negative transfer effects on Task 2 that cancel each other out. The operations for measuring transfer are shown in Table 5-2.

The most important variable in transfer of training is the similarity of the two tasks. If Tasks 1 and 2 are highly similar, we can expect

positive transfer. If they require opposite or conflicting habits, we can expect negative transfer. Suppose Task 1 is to memorize several pairs of words like *book–happy* and Task 2 is to memorize pairs like *book–glad*. *Happy* and *glad* are similar responses to the stimulus *book*, so similar that learning one is almost like learning the other at the same time, and positive transfer would result. If the subject has learned *book–happy* and is transferred to *book–dirty*, there might be interference. During Task 2, the stimulus *book* will elicit the competing response *happy*, which will slow down the rate of learning of the correct response, *dirty*. Negative transfer would probably result in this case, especially if there were a number of such pairs to learn. Finally, when the two tasks are completely unrelated—*book–happy* and *grass–old,* for example—we would expect zero transfer.

Even if two tasks are related, we might find zero transfer because there is a combination of positive and negative transfer effects that cancel each other out. Analyses of transfer phenomena have suggested that this is usually the case. Transfer is usually a mixture of positive and negative effects, the particular balance determining whether the net transfer is positive, negative, or zero. The analysis of transfer has thus concentrated on breaking down the different tasks into various components and showing how, within the same task, some components transfer positively and other components transfer negatively. To maximize positive transfer and minimize negative transfer, you would teach only those components that show positive transfer.

FORGETTING

Most of us are plagued at one time or another with failing memory. We learned something last semester but cannot remember it now. After cramming the night before, on the exam we are frustrated by an inability to recall the things we studied. Just as interesting are cases of complete recall after many years. We have fairly vivid recollections of some events from childhood. A poem or verse memorized in grade school may reassert itself verbatim when, as adults, we come across the title or author. These are the problems of memory. Why do we forget? Why do we selectively remember?

Storage, Retention, and Retrieval

We can break the memory process into three phases: (1) learning or storage, (2) retention, and (3) retrieval. Storage is the assignment of information to be remembered to some hypothetical memory system. Retention is holding items in storage for later use. The interval between initial storage and eventual recall is referred to as the **retention interval.** The retrieval stage refers to the extraction of items, heretofore stored and retained, for use on some task. Memory failures can be traced to any one or all of these three processes. Information may be improperly stored or not stored at all. Assuming proper storage, information might somehow be lost through the passage of time. Finally, the information might be stored and retained, but for some reason unretrievable when needed; it is available but not accessible.

Have you ever forgotten where you parked your car?

Two commonly used tests for memory are the *recognition test* and the *recall test*. In a recognition test the subject is presented with the correct response along with distractor responses, and he or she merely has to recognize which of the responses is correct. Does this remind you of a multiple-choice test? In a recall test, the subject has to produce the correct response, as in a fill-in-the-blank or essay test. As you know, recognition is normally easier than recall. Recognition tests eliminate the retrieval stage of memory because the response is provided in the test. The subject does not have to retrieve it from memory as in a recall test. Compare the following two tests:

1. What were the names of the two robots in the movie *Star Wars?* _____
2. Which of the following was the name of the computer in the movie *2001: A Space Odyssey?*
   a. Alex
   b. Eliot
   c. Hal
   d. Henry

In the first item, you can fail because you never stored the names or because you have failed to retain them since you learned them, or because you cannot retrieve them. In the second item,

Sleep Must Follow Period of Studying

Sleep helps us remember only when sleep follows a period of study, says Psychology Today. It doesn't seem to make much difference whether a person sleeps immediately after learning or waits a few hours before going to sleep. What is important is the sleep.

In fact, a short nap before studying can seriously increase forgetting, according to Bruce Ekstrand of the University of Colorado.

Says Ekstrand: "Everyday examples of this are common: a person is awakened by the telephone in middle of the night, talks for a while, goes back to sleep, and remembers nothing of the call the next morning.

"Don't sleep before you study unless you allow yourself a period of time of being awake before you start studying seriously," concludes Ekstrand. "And allow for an undisturbed period of sleep."

Pueblo (*Colo.*) Chieftain
June 22, 1977

Memory is improved if you sleep between the time of learning and recall. However, sleep *immediately* before learning can decrease subsequent memory.

the name has already been retrieved for you, so a failure is probably due to poor storage or retention.

Why Do We Forget?

There are two basic reasons for forgetting: (1) the information is not available, or (2) the information is not accessible. In the first case, we have what is called **trace-dependent forgetting.** Some psychologists believe learning sets up physiological *traces* in the brain. Forgetting is then seen as resulting from the fact that the traces are not available at the time of recall. The information just is not available anymore.

The second reason we forget involves what is called **cue-dependent forgetting.** Here the forgetting is mainly a retrieval failure—the cues present at the time of learning are not present at the time of recall; or competing, interfering cues are also present and block memory. The

traces are still in the brain, but the cues are not appropriate for "getting at" the traces, so we have cue-dependent forgetting. This is the same as saying the information is not accessible. The three memory theories we are about to describe each involve one or the other of these processes.

Consolidation Theory

Corresponding to the first stage of our memory scheme—storage—is the theory of memory **consolidation.** This theory postulates that every experience sets up some kind of trace. The trace may be thought of as a small electrical circuit formed in the brain, the circuit somehow coding the experience. According to the theory, this circuit must "consolidate" in order for the experience to be permanently stored. When the circuit is first set up, it is not very stable and is subject to easy disruption. The "neuroelectricity" (or whatever it is that underlies storage) must travel around the circuit many times (a process called **perseveration**) in order to consolidate the circuit, making it final and lasting. During the period between the end of learning and the completion of consolidation, the circuit is easily destroyed. Once the circuit is consolidated, however, it has been stored in long-term memory and is difficult to destroy. According to the consolidation theory, a major factor in forgetting is that memory is partly destroyed before it is consolidated. This theory focuses on the storage of information and maintains that memory failure can be a consequence of inadequate storage.

What kinds of events could affect the storage or consolidation process? Most research has studied the effects of electrical shock delivered to the brain shortly after learning. The shock is called **electroconvulsive shock** (ECS) whenever it is strong enough to produce a convulsion in the subject. ECS has been used as a treatment for severe depression in human beings. Patients who receive ECS report a complete memory loss for events shortly preceding the ECS, a phenomenon known as **retrograde amnesia.** Their long-term memory, however, remains completely intact. The same is true for someone knocked unconscious by a blow on the head; he or she may not remember the events just prior to the blow. Effects of this sort support the consolidation theory. The strong electric shock or the blow on the head disrupts the

"Partial amnesia, Doc. Doesn't know his name, but remembers the Alamo."

The New Yorker, May 3, 1976. Drawing by Handelsman; © 1976 The New Yorker Magazine, Inc.

Amnesia usually involves forgetting of things learned just before the amnesia-producing event (e.g., a blow on the head). Material learned long before is usually unaffected. This is called retrograde amnesia.

memories that are consolidating at the time. Events that occurred earlier remain unaffected.

Another side of the consolidation theory is even more interesting. Consolidation is the process of laying down a permanent memory; therefore, if consolidation could be facilitated, memory would be facilitated. Lengthening the time that preservation continues might facilitate consolidation, and certain drugs, including strychnine, picrotoxin, and metrozal, are thought to have just this capability. These drugs excite the brain and might very well produce faster, more efficient, and more permanent memory storage. Administration of these drugs to animals after each trial of a learning task does result in more rapid learning. This effect is strong support for the consolidation theory.

This theory may eventually lead to the solution of problems related to mental retardation.

Certain kinds of mental retardation may be caused by an inherited defect in the memory consolidation system. If drugs can be discovered that correct this defect or substitute for the chemicals that might be missing, it would be a fantastic development. Preliminary work is underway on this project.

Decay Theory

Given that an item of information has been properly stored, what might account for its loss during the retention interval? **Decay theory** postulates a process by which stored information "wears out," or decays, over time. According to some versions of the theory, a biological process, metabolic or otherwise, produces the hypothesized decay and consequent forgetting.

There is a built-in circularity to decay theory. The theory states that forgetting is due to a process that breaks down stored memories. The only proof that such a decay process takes place, however, is that we forget. Since the physiology of the hypothesized decay process is not known, it cannot be directly manipulated (that is, the rate of decay cannot be changed) to test the effect on forgetting. The only variable that can be manipulated is the length of the retention interval.

Decay theory sheds little light on forgetting. Still, the theory has great intuitive appeal. Future investigations may indeed reveal the physiological correlates of memory, which may lead to an understanding of the physiological bases of the decay process, why it occurs, and how to prevent it.

Interference Theory

The most popular and best-developed theory of forgetting is based on the notion of **interference.** This theory deals primarily with the third aspect of memory—retrieval—and interference with the retrieval process. Interference theory focuses on certain interactions among different items of previously learned information. Failure to recall a particular item of information is attributed to the influence of other, usually similar, items of stored information.

To see how this works, let us call items of information that the subject is to recall the *originally learned* items. Prior to the time of original learning the subject may have learned one or more other things that are similar. Call

Figure 5–5
Interference theory

	Interpolated learning causes retroactive	
Prior learning causes proactive inhibition	Original learning	Recall of original learning
	inhibition	
	Retention interval	

Time A   Time B

Material learned at Time A is tested for recall, after a retention interval, at Time B. Material learned prior to Time A (prior learning) produces proactive inhibition; things learned between Times A and B (interpolated learning) produce retroactive inhibition.

TABLE 5–3   Proactive and Retroactive Inhibition

Proactive Inhibition

Experimental group

learns Task B   learns Task A $\xrightarrow{\text{retention interval}}$ recalls Task A

Control group

- - - - - rests - - - - -   learns Task A $\xrightarrow{\text{retention interval}}$ recalls Task A

Here is the operational definition of proactive inhibition. The experimental and control groups both learn and recall Task A. But the experimental group also does some prior learning, Task B, while the control rests. The control group remembers more of Task A than the experimental group, an indication of proactive inhibition.

Retroactive Inhibition

Experimental group   learns Task A   learns Task B   recalls Task A

Control group   learns Task A $\xrightarrow{\hspace{1cm}\text{rests}\hspace{1cm}}$ recalls Task A

Here is the operational definition of retroactive inhibition. The experimental group learns and recalls Task A, but must do the interpolated learning of Task B. The control group only learns and recalls Task A. The control group remembers more, which is evidence of retroactive inhibition.

this *prior learning.* If prior learning interferes with recall of the original learning, it is called **proactive inhibition.** Another source of interference arises from the subject's experiences between original learning and recall. Anything learned during the retention interval is designated as *interpolated learning.* When interpolated learning interferes with recall of original learning, the process is called **retroactive inhibition** (see Figure 5–5). Interference theory postulates that forgetting is produced by one of two factors: (1) proactive inhibition from materials learned prior to original learning or (2) retroactive inhibition from things learned during the retention interval (see Table 5–3).

Laboratory studies have provided strong support for the basic notions of interference theory. While it is very clear that interference *can* produce forgetting, it is not certain that *all* forgetting is due to interference. Empirically, we know that subjects remember more if they sleep during the retention interval than if they are awake. Since we don't learn interfering material while asleep, this observation supports an interference theory. There are alternative interpretations, however. Sleep might facilitate memory by slowing down the decay process, or it might facilitate the consolidation of materials learned just before going to sleep. While the explanation of this experimental finding is vague, its practical implication is quite clear. It is better to go to sleep after studying for a test than to study for some other test, watch TV, or engage in any other waking activity (other than more studying for the test, which would be best of all).

How does interference operate to produce forgetting? Two fundamental ideas have been proposed. Consider the subject learning two successive paired-associate lists. The first is designated as a series of A–B associations in which the A terms are the stimuli and the B terms are the responses. The second list consists of the same stimuli but different responses. Therefore, this list is called A–C. After subjects have learned the A–B list followed by the A–C list, their memories are tested for A–B by presenting the A terms and asking them to guess or remember what the responses were from the first list. Failure to remember has been attributed both to (1) *response competition* and to (2) *unlearning.* Each A term should elicit two responses, the correct response B and the interfering response C. B and C compete with each other, and the subject may be confused about which one to say. When A is presented, the subject attempts to retrieve the correct answer and comes up with two equally strong possibilities that compete (cue-dependent).

In addition, the correct response, B, may have been "unlearned" during A–C trials. If so, it is no longer available to the subject (trace-dependent). At recall, A is presented and the subject attempts to retrieve the correct answer and finds nothing but C. It is as if B had been removed from storage. Response competition and unlearning are not mutually exclusive alternatives. Empirical evidence suggests that both contribute measurably to the forgetting process.

Context and State-Dependent Learning

Memory is best when the conditions of recall are identical to those at the time of learning. This is called the **context effect.** If you are going to take an exam (recall facts) in a particular lecture hall, it would be to your advantage to study the material in that lecture hall as opposed to studying in the library or in your room. This is closely related to stimulus generalization—the more similar the recall context to the learning context, the better the recall.

Context, of course, refers to one's surroundings at the time of learning and recall—the size and shape of the room, the color of the walls, the amount of noise, and so on. More recently this idea has been expanded to include the physiological state of the learner at the time of learning and recall. One's own body is, in some sense, a part of his or her context. Thus, for best performance, one's bodily state should be as similar as possible at the time of learning and recall. To take a whimsical example, if you are drunk when you learn something, you might be able to recall it better at some future time under the influence of alcohol. There are anecdotal reports of alcoholics who hide things when drunk and are unable to remember their location when they sober up. This phenomenon has a special name—**state-dependent learning.** Laboratory work on this kind of learning has typically used drug-induced states. Experimenters have found, for example, that if a rat is taught to run a maze under the influence of amphetamines, it performs better if given amphetamines just before the recall trial.

Some writers have included state-dependent learning in a list of dangers involved in drug usage. Almost all learning takes place in the normal, nondrug state. If a person takes a psychoactive drug and enters a different state, some of this information may become unavailable. He

Earn an 'A' with Beer, Study Hints

Jon Van

College students who sip beer while studying should have a few drinks before taking their exams, scientific studies suggest.

Tests conducted on U.S. Army volunteers indicate that material learned under the influence of some drugs is best remembered under the influence of the same drugs, Dr. Ronald C. Petersen reported . . . to the Federation of American Societies for Experimental Biology meeting at McCormick Place.

Dr. Petersen said past tests indicate that alcohol produces the memory phenomenon, and his most recent studies indicate that other drugs have the same effect.

Petersen, working in the Biomedical Laboratory at the Aberdeen Proving Ground in Maryland, used 28 Army volunteers for his tests. The men studied material after being given scopolamine, a drug included in several pharmaceutical preparations, including Contac and Sominex.

They were then tested for memory, once without using the drug and then with its use. The men were also given material to study without using the drug and then were tested with and without the drug.

Dr. Petersen found that the men tended to remember better when they were tested under the same drug conditions that existed when they studied the material.

He speculated that when a person studies particular material, his memory may store additional information, including his state of mind and drug condition. When that person tries to recall the information, it is easier to do so if his mental state and drug condition are the same as when he learned the material.

Aside from giving college kids an excuse for drinking before examinations, Dr. Petersen said his research may enhance the understanding of psychotherapy.

Chicago Tribune
April 9, 1977

To maximize memory, the conditions of recall (or test) should be as similar as possible to the conditions of learning. When applied to the mental or physiological state of the person, this principle is known as state-dependency.

Encoding Specificity
(Recognition Is Not Always Easier Than Recall)

Normally, recall is aided by clues, that is, material closely associated with the material to be remembered. This is particularly true if the clues were present at the time of learning. For example, when you have forgotten someone's name, mention of the person's first name should help you remember the last name. But, amazingly, Endel Tulving has demonstrated that under some circumstances what should be very strong clues does not benefit recall.

Tulving's experiment confronted the subject with a list of to-be-remembered (TBR) words, each of which was paired with a *weak* clue, a weak associate of the TBR word. A few such pairs would be:

Weak clue words	TBR word
train	black
leather	chair
nose	cold
tiger	paper

The subjects were told that trying to relate each TBR word to its clue word would help them learn the TBR words. Then, at the time of recall, the weak clues were removed and strong clues were substituted. For example, *white* was substituted for *train* as a clue for *black*. *White* is so closely associated with *black* that you would think the subjects would still recall the TBR word, *black*, very well, but in fact they did poorly. Apparently *black* was coded into memory as being related to *train*, the weak clue. This code was so specific to *train* that white

would not "break the code" and result in recall of *black*. This is called *encoding specificity*.

Most dramatic was the following demonstration by Tulving. After the subjects had failed to recall *black* when presented with *white*, he gave them a list of the strong clue words (hot, table, white, pencil) and asked them to free-associate to each one—to write down the first three or four words that came to mind. With these instructions, many subjects did in fact write down the word *black* (a TBR word) when free-associating to *white*. Then Tulving asked them to go back and circle any of the free associates that might have been TBR words. Believe it or not, most subjects failed to circle the TBR words that were staring them in the face. After their failure to recognize the TBR words in the presence of the strong clues, Tulving presented them with the weak clues, the clues that had been present during learning and that were used for coding the TBR words into memory. Presented with the word *train*, the subjects were now able to recall the word *black*, whereas they could not even recognize *black* when it was presented with *white* as the clue.

Apparently memories are coded in specific ways, and at the time of recall we must decode in the same "language" used during learning. Again we see that if the context, in this case the clue words, present at recall is not the same one that was present during learning, recall may suffer.

or she might, for example, "forget" how to drive an automobile or cope with anxiety or "forget" the laws of gravity. Consequently, we are perhaps better able to explain such drug-induced behaviors as forgetting to yield the right of way to oncoming traffic, committing suicide, jumping from a third-story window yelling "up, up, and away." Attributing these behaviors to state-dependent learning may be an exaggeration. Nonetheless, there is no doubt that this phenomenon does sometimes occur in drug-induced behavior.

Memory as Reconstruction

Most of what we have said so far about memory implies an underlying model that treats the brain as a copying machine. We learn something (copy it) and store it away in memory for later recall (retrieval and "read out" of the copy). But, it is undoubtedly true that much of memory is not consistent with such a model, but instead is more in line with a **reconstruction** model. We do not simply copy events and store the copies; rather, we store abstract representations of the events. In trying to recall an event, we retrieve the abstract representation and try to deduce (reconstruct) what the event must have been from this representation. This is perhaps most obvious when we try to remember a conversation or something we read in a book or newspaper. We do not have word-for-word copies of the conversation or the prose stored in our memory; what we have are general ideas or facts about what was said or read.

This type of model makes it clear that an additional source of memory distortion can take place at the time of storage when we have to abstract the general idea of a conversation or a prose passage. We might misinterpret the incoming information and thus store general information that was not present in the conversation or passage. Consider the following passages and the distorted or elaborated information that might be stored by someone hearing the passages:

1. John was trying to fix the birdhouse. He was pounding the nail when his father came out to watch him and to help him do the work.
2. It was late at night when the phone rang and a voice gave a frantic cry. The spy threw the secret document into the fireplace just 30 seconds before it would have been too late.

In the first example, you would probably store the general idea that John was using a hammer to fix a birdhouse with the aid of his father, when in fact the sentence does not say that a hammer was involved. In the second example, you would probably store the general idea that the spy burned a secret document just in time, when in fact the sentence says nothing about burning. Johnson, Bransford, and Solomon (1973) asked subjects who had heard these examples if they had heard the following two test sentences:

1'. John was using the hammer to fix the birdhouse when his father came out to watch and to help him do the work.
2'. The spy burned the secret document just 30 seconds before it would have been too late.

The subjects incorrectly judged that they had heard 1' and 2' when in fact they had heard only 1 and 2. Presumably, they incorrectly interpreted 1 and 2 and stored general information, not word-for-word copies. At the time of the test they retrieved the general ideas (which included *hammer* and *burned*) and reconstructed from this information some notion of what it was they must have heard. This reconstruction was then similar enough to 1' and 2' that the subjects were fooled into believing that they had heard these exact sentences.

In short, memory is probably rarely based on exact copies of the original experience. When we learn and store information, we are not passive copy machines filing away perfect reproductions for later retrieval. Instead, we actively interpret information as it is received (we think as we learn) and may file away only general abstract representations of this information. Later, if necessary, we can retrieve the general idea and reconstruct the original experience. As a result, our memories can be inaccurate because we misinterpreted the information in the first place, or because we did not retain sufficient general information to make a very accurate reconstruction, or because we commit errors in the reconstruction process itself.

Memory psychologists are only just beginning to explore the reconstructive aspects of memory in a systematic fashion. It has proved difficult to develop carefully controlled procedures and tasks that involve this type of memory. In the next few years we anticipate research that will shed much new light on this important and crucial aspect of memory.

THE RELATIONSHIP BETWEEN BASIC AND COMPLEX FORMS OF LEARNING

In Chapter 4, we examined fundamental learning processes. In this chapter, we consider more complex learning phenomena which are peculiarly human and involve the use of language.

Can You "Remember" Something You Never Experienced?

Can we *remember* things we've never learned? A recognition-memory study by John Bransford and Jeffery Franks demonstrated just such an effect. Instead of the usual word list, Bransford and Franks used a group of sentences on a related topic. When we think of recognizing a sentence or a prose passage in a book, we seem not to recognize the exact words, but rather the general theme or the "whole idea" expressed in the sentences. Theories of memory, however, have emphasized memory of specific words or elements, as if we memorized each word instead of learning an abstract "idea" that we "pull out of" the prose as we read it. The results of the Bransford and Franks study, however, mean that memory theories will now have to account for this abstraction process.

The group of sentences used in this study could be presented as a single sentence with four elements expressing a "whole idea."

Whole idea: The rock that rolled down the mountain crushed the tiny hut at the edge of the woods. *Four components:* (1) the rock rolled down the mountain; (2) the rock crushed the hut; (3) the hut was tiny; (4) the hut was at the edge of the woods.

During the study phase, the subjects never saw the sentence containing all four elements; they never saw or experienced the whole idea. Instead they saw sentences containing only one or two or three of the elements. For example, a three-element sentence would be: "The rock crushed the tiny hut at the edge of the woods." A two-element sentence would be: "The tiny hut was at the edge of the woods." And a one-element sentence would be: "The rock rolled down the mountain." Several sets of sentences were mixed together for the study phase.

At the time of the test, the subjects were presented with several different kinds of sentences: three-, two-, and one-element sentences they had actually seen before; four-, three-, two-, and one-element sentences they had never seen before; and finally, some sentences that were unrelated to the earlier materials. The basic finding was that the more elements of the whole idea a test sentence contained, the more confident the subjects were of having seen it before. They were most confident of having seen the four-element "whole idea," which had never occurred, as can be seen in Figure 5–6.

Figure 5–6
Degree of confidence that a sentence had been seen before

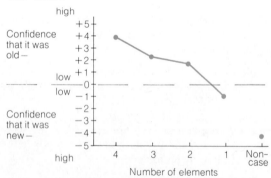

The results of the Bransford and Franks study strongly suggest that during learning, while hearing three-, two-, and one-element sentences, the subjects were actually abstracting the whole idea and storing it, even though it had never been presented in its entirety.

We should not think of these two categories of learning as separate and determined by different processes. We use the same brain to learn both simple stimuli and complex verbal materials. Obviously, some of the same processes are involved in both sorts of learning. Further, when thinking about learning in different animal species we need to remember that the human brain is evolved from and has much in common with the brains of lower species. It would be surprising if many processes were not common to human beings and other species.

As we saw in Chapter 4, recent evidence indicates that the processes underlying classical conditioning are very similar to the memory processes. For example, Allan R. Wagner has proposed that classical conditioning between a CS and a UCS is produced by the joint rehearsal of representations of the CS and UCS in short-term memory. Only such rehearsal forms an association between them. After the CS and UCS representations have been rehearsed together a number of times, presentation of the CS induces retrieval of the UCS representation from long-term memory into immediate memory and produces a CR as a concomitant of the retrieval process. We have already seen that rehearsal is important in complex learning, Type I rehearsal maintaining information in short-term memory and Type II rehearsal helping to transfer information into long-term memory.

Do factors that influence memory processing have a similar effect on classical conditioning? Experiments have been performed that lend support to this position. For example, it is known that forgetting from short-term memory is at least partly produced by new incoming information pushing out old information from memory. Such an effect follows directly from the fact that short-term memory has a limited capacity. If short-term memory is full, there is only one way for something new to get in. We also know that all incoming information does not produce the same amount of interference with short-term memory. Surprising unexpected information produces the most interference with short-term retention. It has been shown that exactly the same considerations hold for classical conditioning. The occurrence of surprising unexpected events shortly after a conditioning trial interferes with conditioning (see Chapter 4). CS and UCS representations are displaced from short-term memory and conditioning does not occur. Expected events do not have such an effect. So, here is an instance in which memory and conditioning are similarly affected by the same factor. Many other examples of this general correlation have also been shown. Thus we can conclude that the same factors which operate in the one case operate in the other. The processes that produce complex verbal learning also seem to produce conditioning.

SUMMARY

1. Studies of human learning have focused mainly on learning of verbal materials. Research has employed four major learning tasks: memory span, free-recall, serial, and paired-associate learning.
2. The information-processing approach uses a computer analogy to help explain learning and memory. That is, incoming information is processed in stages.
3. Our basic memory system has three stages: sensory memory, short-term memory, and long-term memory. Important memory processes include coding, chunking, and recoding; and two types of rehearsal (Type I, or maintenance rehearsal, and Type II, or elaborative rehearsal).
4. The meaningfulness, the similarity level, and the imagery level (abstractness versus concreteness) of the material are three factors that strongly affect the ease of learning. Context and prior training are also important.
5. Forgetting may be analyzed into two types: trace dependent (is the information still intact in the memory system?) and cue dependent (are the recall cues sufficient to retrieve the stored information?).

6. Memory is often conceived of as involving three basic steps: storage of to-be-remembered information, retention of the information over time, and retrieval of the information at the time of recall.
7. Three major theories of memory and forgetting are interference, decay, and consolidation. Memory is better when the conditions at the time of recall are similar to the conditions at the time of learning, including the physiological state of the learner (state-dependent learning).
8. Much of memory undoubtedly involves processes of reconstruction based on a stored abstract representation rather than a "verbatim" copy.
9. Some of the same underlying processes are involved in both simple and complex learning. In fact, recent research indicates a similarity in the processes of classical conditioning and memory.

RECOMMENDED ADDITIONAL READINGS

Cermak, L. S. *Improving your memory.* New York: McGraw-Hill, 1976.

Ellis, H. C. *Fundamentals of human learning, memory, and cognition,* 2d ed. Dubuque, Ia: William C. Brown, 1978.

Horton, D. L., and Turnage, T. W. *Human learning.* Englewood Cliffs, N.J.: Prentice-Hall, 1976.

Klatzky, R. L. *Human memory.* San Francisco: Freeman, 1975.

what does
it mean?

Study of the underlying processes involved in learning and memory can do more than simply satisfy intellectual curiosity. Application of these basic principles can help to solve some of our everyday problems and enhance the quality of our lives. By properly employing this knowledge we can achieve such goals as increasing our studying efficiency and improving our memory.

STEPS TO A BETTER MEMORY

While there are no magic formulas for improving the ability to remember (newspaper ads to the contrary notwithstanding), research on verbal learning does suggest some steps you can take.

1. Maximize the degree of original learning, which is the single most important variable in memory. The better you learn the material initially, the more resistant it is to forgetting. Slow learners do not forget more than fast learners if the degree of original learning is equal. A slow learner might take 30 minutes to reach the same degree of learning a fast learner attains in 15 minutes, but given that they have learned the material equally well, they will remember equally well.

2. Use visual imagery and other coding techniques during the learning process. Make up bizarre and interesting images to relate the items of information to be retained. When learning someone's name, pick out some feature of the face or body to relate to the name. If Mr. Bumstead has a nose like a ski jump, think of him as a "steady ski bum" and imagine olympic skiers leaping off his nose.

3. Return to the scene of the "crime." That is, reinstate the context and learning cues at the time of recall. Study in the place where you will have to perform. Practice under conditions similar to those under which you will have to perform. A basketball coach should always make the players practice under "game conditions."

4. Try to provide yourself with retrieval cues at the time of original learning. Select retrieval cues you know will be present at the time of recall. Mr. Bumstead's nose is a retrieval cue. It will be present at the time you have to recall his name and so should be used in memorizing his name. In the case of an examination, try to find cues in the examination room to use as "pegs" or "memory hooks" for the material you are learning. For example, there may be "no smoking" signs, a chart of chemical elements, or a map in the room. Try to form images relating these items to the material you are learning. Of course, while this technique may help you on the examination, you run the risk of being unable to remember certain items outside the examination room.

5. Practice repeatedly recalling the material. After studying a section, recite the important points to yourself or a friend. Get

Levels of Processing: Deep Processing Improves Memory

The levels-of-processing theory of learning maintains that learning is chiefly a product of the type of processing applied to the information to be learned. Shallow processing leads to poor learning and recall compared to deep processing. Deep processing forces subjects to attend to the semantic (the meaning) aspects of the information. Shallow processing involves nonsemantic aspects such as the sound of words. The basic demonstration used to support this theory involves exposing subjects to a list of words. They are not told they will have to recall them. One group of subjects is asked to perform a task with the words that requires only shallow processing, and a second group is given a task that requires deeper processing. After all the words have been exposed and processed, the subjects are given an unexpected recall test. Subjects given the deep-processing task recall considerably more of the words.

Try this experiment for yourself on some friends. Below is a list of 20 words that you should print on a set of index cards. For one group of friends, present each word and ask them to think of another word that rhymes with it (a shallow-processing task). For the other group, ask them to think of a word that means the same thing as the word (a deep task requiring subjects to process meaning). Don't tell either group that you are going to test their memories for the 20 words. You should find that recall is better for the group asked to think of synonyms than for the group asked to think of rhymes. Should you control for the time the words are presented?

Word List			
fast	shoe	rug	ticket
cold	cook	play	car
book	steal	walk	toy
chair	right	mad	stamp
lost	drink	kick	house

together with friends and test each other on the material. You must be able to retrieve what you have learned. If you do not practice retrieving, you risk knowing more than you are able to show on an examination.

6. Do not take drugs to keep awake so that you can study. With drugs you run the risk of state-dependent learning, unless, of course, you also take the drugs just before the exam. In that case, unwanted side effects, such as anxiety or confusion, may interfere with your examination performance.

These are just a few techniques that should improve your memory. The basic consideration throughout is type and degree of original learning. You should try to learn as completely and with as many retrieval cues as possible.

MEMORY AIDS (MNEMONICS)

1. The Peg System

Memorize a set of "memory pegs" in advance of learning. A convenient peg system consists of numbers and words that rhyme with the numbers. The rhyme helps you retrieve the word when given the number. For example:

one is a bun
two is a shoe
three is a tree
four is a door
five is a hive
etc.

Suppose you want to memorize a shopping list. Each item to be purchased is "hooked"

© 1966 United Feature Syndicate Inc.

on to one of the memory pegs by using an interactive image involving the item and its peg word. If the first item is *milk,* you hook *milk* on to the *bun* peg by conjuring up an image of a giant bottle of milk voraciously devouring a hot dog bun. Next, you hook, say, *peanuts* on to the *shoe* peg, perhaps by imagining a shoe with peanuts erupting from it like a volcano. You continue hooking each food item onto the next peg. When you get to the store, you recite the pegs to yourself, and each peg word should then call forth the image that contains the desired item.

2. The Method of Loci (Locations)

This system is also a peg-type device, but the pegs consist of a sequence of locations that can always be recalled in order. For example, you might imagine yourself on a long walk from your home to a particular place in your city. Along the way, you will encounter locations, places, objects in a fixed order; and each of these becomes a peg on which you hang one of the items to be remembered. For example, you first might walk to the corner where there is a mailbox, so this mailbox is then used as a peg for, say, *milk* — you imagine the mailbox opening its "mouth" and spewing forth milk on innocent pedestrians. When it comes time to recall your shopping list, you just retrace your walk in your mind, stopping at each location to recall the desired material. Another set of loci can be developed using the rooms and various objects in the rooms of your home or apartment — you develop a "walk" through your home, stopping at no-

table locations or objects which then become the pegs on which you hang the material to be learned.

3. Verbal Elaboration

In this method, also known as narrative chaining, you make up a story centering on the items to be remembered. For example, Gordon Bower has suggested the following narrative for use in trying to remember the names of the 12 cranial nerves:

At the *oil factory* (olfactory nerve) the *optician* (optic nerve) looked for the *occupant* (oculomotor) of the *truck* (trochlear). He was searching because *three gems* (trigeminal) had been *abducted* (abducens) by a man who was hiding his *face* (facial) and *ears* (acoustics). A *glossy photograph* (glossopharyngeal) had been taken of him, but it was too *vague* (vagus) to use. He appeared to be *spineless* (spinal accessory) and *hypocritical* (hypoglossal).

4. Coding Numbers to Letters

This is a system that, unlike the others, can be helpful in remembering numbers such as dates and street addresses. Each of the digits from zero to 9 is assigned a consonant, and you memorize this code. For example:

0 = B	5 = H
1 = C	6 = J
2 = D	7 = K
3 = F	8 = L
4 = G	9 = M

A.C.R.O.N.Y.M.
AROUSED CITIZENS
REPRESENTING OPPRESSED
NEW YORK MINORITIES

The New Yorker, June 3, 1974. Drawing by D. Fradon; © 1974 The New Yorker Magazine, Inc.

An acronym is a mnemonic device based on abbreviation. The idea is to condense a lot of information into one chunk.

The number is then coded into the letters, and vowels are inserted to make meaningful words, the theory being that meaningful words are easier to remember than meaningless numbers. An address of 2908 Maple might be encoded into DMBL, which is turn becomes DUMBEL. Try this with your own telephone number. Can you turn the digits into one or two words?

Texas Professor Teaches Mental Processing Strategies

Joan Temple Dennett

If you have trouble remembering things, it may just be that you never learned to be an efficient learner. This is one conclusion of a recent University of Texas study on how people "process information"—that is, learn things.

Calire E. Weinstein, a Texas professor of educational psychology, summed up past viewpoints. She said, "We just assumed that because you're born, you know how to learn. We didn't think about mental processing strategies as something one acquires. We assumed that they were there, that they got better as you grew older as a function of natural development."

But, for her own studies of people who are successful learners, Dr. Weinstein has gathered a variety of learning strategies—strategies that she believes can be taught to other people.

Basically, these learning strategies fall into three groups: mental imagery, meaningful elaboration, and grouping.

Mental imagery requires you to conjure up some pictures in your mind. For example, Dr. Weinstein's group of junior high students decided on an iron hand to serve as the mental image of dictatorship. Some students extrapolated this mental image to "everybody in chains crawling along the city." . . .

The second technique of learning is called meaningful elaboration. That means associating the new to-be-learned information with knowledge, attitudes, or experiences that you already have. . . .

The third technique, grouping, is a way to gather categories of information based on common attributes or features. Once you have collected the new information into groups, you might then want to use one of the previous techniques of imagery or meaningful elaboration.

Town and Country *(Boulder, Colo.)*
November 30, 1977

Cognitive Processes

6

Cognitive processes refer to the things you do in your head—mental activities or thinking. These processes include selecting information from the environment, modifying that information, and using it to meet the demands of the task at hand. In the preceding two chapters we discussed the processes by which people acquire knowledge and skills. Cognitive processes involve using knowledge and skills in new situations.

•   •   •   Consider the following problem: Without lifting your pencil, draw four continuous straight lines through the dots in the margin so that at least one line passes through each dot. Solution of this task requires no knowledge or skills you don't already possess. You might have to modify what you know, or use it

•   •   •   in a new way, but you don't really need to learn anything new. If you find the problem difficult, consider the possibility that you are not attending to all the information that has been given. Are you being restrictive or overly selective in your approach? If you haven't solved it yet, turn to page 188 where the

•   •   •   solution is found. Upon first glance, the solution probably seems obvious. You have what it takes to understand the solution. You could have done it yourself if you had interpreted the problem correctly. In fact, the problem is really a problem only because it "fools" your cognitive processes.

Cognition is primarily *problem-solving activity*. Of course, some cognitive processes are not well organized, clear, and problem directed. Dreams, fantasies, and hallucinations, for example, seem to be aimless activities with no specific purpose. Yet even these processes can represent problem-oriented activity, though of an ill-directed and inefficient sort. There is evidence that the tendency to daydream is correlated with the severity and frequency of everyday problems. People caught in conflict show an increase in daydreaming, especially when their overt attempts to solve the conflict have failed. In severe cases, unresolved conflict can lead to fantasy or hallucination as a means of reducing the conflict or temporarily shelving the problem. Moreover, numerous people have reported that the solution to an important problem occurred to them during sleep. Thus it is possible that such apparently aimless mental activities as dreaming might fulfill a problem-solving function.

THEORIES OF COGNITION

Stimulus-Response Theory

One of the first examinations of cognition emphasized the basic concepts of stimulus and response. According to this theory, all knowledge and skill are the result of connecting particular stimuli with particular overt actions. That is, whenever a stimulus occurs, it provokes the response with which it has been associated. If the stimulus is new, it tends to provoke a response identical or similar to the response provoked by a similar stimulus. Thus all behavior is derived from conditioning and related processes, although in some cases these processes are very involved and string together a large number of responses.

Motor Theory

An early version of stimulus-response theory was the **motor theory** of thinking proposed by John B. Watson and other behaviorists. In their

view, all behavior—be it thinking or walking—is equated with movement (muscular or glandular activity). They maintained that pure mental activity without movement does not exist. Sometimes movements are so fast or slight that special instruments are needed to record them, but, according to the motor theorists, if there is real thought, there is also real movement. Watson believed that most human thought was basically subvocal activity—that the thinker speaks to himself with usually imperceptible movements of the muscles of the voice apparatus.

Some ingenious experiments were devised by the behaviorists to support their position. Surface electrodes, placed on the skin above the muscles of the voice apparatus in the throat, characteristically record bursts of electrical activity (reflecting implicit movement) when people are instructed to think about a particular problem or situation. This muscular activity is the substance of their thought, according to Watson. Another experiment involved instruct-

The New Yorker, December 9, 1974. Drawing by Herbert Goldberg; © 1974 The New Yorker Magazine, Inc.

ing a person whose forearms were covered with electrodes to think of being struck twice on the right arm with a hammer. Under these conditions, the subject shows two bursts of electrical activity in the right forearm and nothing in the left. Again, the thought has a definite muscular component.

Despite the supporting evidence and its attractive simplicity, the motor theory is no longer widely accepted. There are too many loopholes in the theory. Most important is the fact that there are other ways to account for the evidence that has been used to support motor theory. The muscular activity recorded in the experiments cited above could quite possibly be an incidental by-product of thinking. Or it might be an overflow that results from activities in the brain that occur during thinking, the brain being so active during thinking that signals "spill over" to the muscles through motor pathways (see Chapter 2). There is also evidence that both learning and thought do occur in the absence of any recordable muscular activity, as, for example, when the body has been completely paralyzed by a drug. The motor theory simply cannot account for this finding.

Mediational Theory

A direct descendant of the motor theory is the **mediational theory** of cognition. As with the motor theory, the emphasis here is on learning and on stimuli and responses. But in mediational theory, the important stimuli and responses occur internally—in the head.

Basically, mediational theory asserts that as overt stimulus-response connections are formed

"I'm learning to think not only with my mind but with my entire body."

The New Yorker, February 7, 1977. Drawing by Charles Saxon; © 1977 The New Yorker Magazine, Inc.

According to the motor theory of thinking, there is no such thing as purely mental activity. Thinking is accompanied by muscle activity, which means, theoretically at least, that you can think with your entire body.

during learning, miniaturized versions of these stimuli and responses, called *mediational stimuli* and *responses,* may develop inside the organism. Mediational events provide a connecting link between the environment and the way one responds to it. They come about mainly through experience. Once a young boy, say, has learned several appropriate ways of responding overtly to his environment, he develops corresponding mediational processes that guide his actions in subsequent situations. When he encounters a new situation somewhat similar to one he has experienced previously, a number of mediational events may occur, representing ways in which he might behave. The child will select one

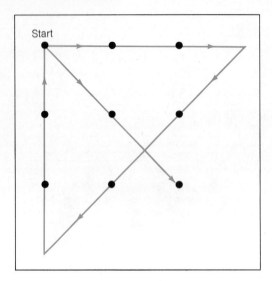

Start

Solution to the dots problem.

Hypothesis Theory

In contrast to the passiveness of the human organism suggested by stimulus-response theories, *hypothesis theory* views the organism as quite active. In learning a task or solving a problem, the individual is seen as forming and testing various ideas or hypotheses about what is happening in the environment and what is the most appropriate response. Hypothesis theory suggests that we solve problems by thinking of possible solutions (to the hypotheses) and then proceed to test the hypotheses until we determine the correct one. In the debate between proponents of hypothesis theories and stimulus-response theories, two questions arose quite early: Do hypotheses exist? Do we gain understanding by viewing organisms as hypothesis testers? The answer appears to be yes in both cases. Hypothesis theorists strove to demonstrate the existence of hypotheses in patterns of responses. For example, suppose a person is presented with a series of pairs of stimuli and is asked to guess which one is the correct member of each pair. Here are four possible pairs:

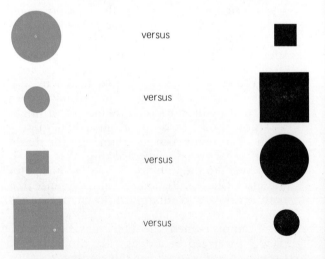

versus

of these ways, generally on the basis of its relative strength, and respond accordingly.

As the child grows, experiences the world, and practices new skills, his collection of mediational responses increases. Consequently, hierarchies of mediators begin to be formed. Any particular stimulus might elicit a number of possible responses ranked in the hierarchy by their strength. The theory allows for both **divergent hierarchies,** in which a single stimulus elicits many responses, and **convergent hierarchies,** in which clearly different external stimuli all elicit the same response. The divergent hierarchy is the basis for problem solving because most problems require that we think of a variety of possible solutions. The convergent hierarchy supplies a basis for forming concepts that organize many different objects, such as tables, into the same category.

One weakness of both the motor theory and the mediational theory is that they view the human organism as essentially passive and subject only to the influence of physical stimuli, whether external or internal. The purposeful aspects of performance, the ability of human beings to form and use rules, and the importance of language in thought are not adequately dealt with by these theories. Thus alternative theories of cognition have been proposed.

Before reading any further, guess the one in each pair you think is the correct one. When you made your choices did you have a hypothesis in mind about the correct answers? Most people do, and their hypotheses are reflected in the pattern of their choices. If you chose the left-hand member of the first pair, the right-hand member of the second pair, the right-hand member of the third pair, and the left-hand member of the fourth pair, you were probably using the "pick the large figure" hypothesis. Now, suppose the selections were left, left, right, right. Can you deduce a person's hypothesis from this pattern? Using procedures like this one, researchers have shown that organisms from rats to human beings frequently exhibit patterns of responding based on hypotheses, not just random guessing. Of course, with human beings, a fairly easy way to identify hypotheses is to ask people if they have any and what they are—people usually find such questions easy to answer and are often eager to offer hypotheses on everything from the best length for dresses to the energy crisis.

Hypothesis theory has led to considerable research on how organisms form and test hypotheses. Many questions have been explored: To what extent do individuals follow one hypothesis at a time as opposed to trying several hypotheses at once? How will an individual who is considering several hypotheses actually respond when forced to make a choice? How does an organism's confidence in his or her hypotheses change as a result of feedback given? We don't have absolute answers to these questions, but some interesting insights have been achieved. For example, it has been found that people tend to monitor several hypotheses at once only in simple situations; when the situation is more complex, they fall back on trying one hypothesis at a time. It has also been found that when given feedback consistent with their hypotheses, people tend to conclude rather quickly that their hypotheses are correct even though the feedback may be consistent with other hypotheses as well.

A criticism of hypothesis theory is that behavior is not *always* as neat and well organized as the theory might suggest. Organisms do not always approach situations by immediately forming and testing hypotheses. In addition, hypothesis testing is only a part of thinking. The basic ideas of hypothesis theory have, however, been included in a somewhat broader approach to cognitive processes, which we will now consider.

Information-Processing Theory

So long as psychology was under the influence of strict behaviorism, mental concepts such as memory, inference, reasoning, and others commonly used in reference to cognition were con-

Copyright © 1972 The Chicago Sun-Times. Reproduced by courtesy of Wil-Jo Associates, Inc., and Bill Mauldin.

The information-processing approach to cognition, based heavily on the principles of computer science, promises to have significant impact on our lives. Already there are very sophisticated programs for solving logic problems, playing bridge and chess, and even for directing psychotherapy. Computers will play an increasing role in teaching people how to think, reason, and solve problems in just about any area of knowledge. For example, computers are being used to teach medical students how to make diagnoses according to the principles used by specialists.

sidered unscientific and therefore improper in psychological theory. With the advent of the electronic computer, most psychologists began to realize that one could speak of these processes without being accused of mysticism. After all, it was clear that the computer could remember, calculate, make inferences, and solve problems, to the point of doing these things in some ways better than people. The computer was also built by people whose knowledge of science could hardly be criticized. If one could talk scientifically about the "mentalistic" processes in the

Talking Inhibits Thinking

Dr. Leonard Reiffel

In spite of its wonderful capabilities, the human brain has some definite limitations. There can be serious interference if two simultaneous tasks require the brain's attention, like trying to think and listen at the same time.

A scientific experiment on this subject was done recently in England. The tasks involved were trying to read something with an understanding of whether or not the material was correct and, at the same time, repeating a sentence that had been memorized. The sentence was familiar and didn't have significant information content. Thus, the simple act of talking and its effect on how accurately one could judge whatever he was reading, was studied.

Two groups of students from 19 to 26 years of age were asked to check off the correctness or incorrectness of a series of simple sentences. One group did so while repeating "Mary had a little lamb"; the other group did so silently. Various precautions were taken to mix the questions and the groups to avoid experimental errors.

The results were rather spectacular. The students who remained silent while they were doing these tests got about 28 correct answers on the average. Those who were speaking only got 17 correct answers. It was obvious, therefore, that the seemingly trivial act of verbalizing something like "Mary had a little lamb" slowed down the thinking ability of the people who were talking.

Psychologists have known for some time about the limited channel capacity of the human brain. They have known that a small load, even in a separate "output" channel such as speaking, can make a great difference in performance in another channel, like reading.

The psychologists who performed this test observed, however, that there are important applications. According to this experiment, compelling people to chant slogans would appear to be an excellent way of inhibiting and reducing their higher mental processes and judgements. Think about it. Doesn't it seem that the tyrants of the world have known this psychological fact for years? When people are busy chanting slogans, they can't think very well.

Boulder (Colo.) Daily Camera
November 17, 1970

The mental requirements of two different tasks may be more than our limited capacity to process information can handle. Thus it is often impossible to do two things at once.

computer, why couldn't one talk scientifically about mental processes in people?

As we discussed in Chapter 5, theories based on the flow of information through a series of internal stages are commonly known as information-processing theories. Such theories, as you know, are based on an analogy with the electronic computer. They refer to the way people receive information from their environment, operate on it, transform it, integrate it with information already available in memory, and use the product as a basis for deciding how to perform. Today information-processing theories encompass nearly all levels of psychological phenomena, from basic sensory and perceptual activities to human personality. Among these theories are some that apply to human thought and cognition.

One method for constructing a theory of this sort is as follows. Take a situation in which it is generally agreed that thought is involved, for example, playing a game of chess or solving logic problems. Write a program that will guide the computer in this activity, and then have the computer and one or more human beings solve a series of problems of the type in question. Compare the activities of the computer, as they are printed out, with the activities of the human beings, as they talk aloud during the problem-solving process. Compare also the eventual solutions obtained by the computer and by the human beings. If it is impossible to discriminate the output of the computer from the output of human beings, we say that the computer simulates human behavior. If, however, there are discrepancies between the computer output and human behavior, the computer program is adjusted in hopes of getting a better approximation. The computer program is the theory.

The information-processing approach to cognition has been adopted by many researchers who do not actually employ the technique of writing computer programs. Indeed, the view that cognitive processes are information-processing activities characterizes a great deal of research on such topics as memory, problem solving, and reasoning. Attempts are made in these and other areas to describe in some detail the particular processes people employ when working on a variety of tasks. An example that you should recall from Chapter 5 is the distinction between the two types of rehearsal processes—maintenance and elaborative. Researchers concentrate on the kinds of mental processes people exhibit, in contrast to the strict attention of the stimulus-response theorists to behavior. Recent findings have led to the identification of some fundamental characteristics of human information processing that affect behavior in many different situations.

Limits of Human Cognition

One aspect of human cognition that theorists must make allowances for is the fact that human beings have a severely limited capacity for remembering and processing information. The mind can handle only a fairly small amount of information at any given time. Limits on short-term memory were noted in Chapter 5. In addition, there are limits on what can be done with information in short-term memory. Different kinds of information processing make different demands on this limited capacity. Some mental operations can take place simultaneously—"in parallel" (that is, without mutual interference)—while others must be performed one at a time in a sequential fashion. One way to study this limited capacity is to have people attempt to "do two things at once."

If doing one task interferes with the performance of the other task, then we can assume that both tasks must be making use of some common information-processing system that is incapable of handling them both at the same time. On the other hand, if the addition of a second task has no effect on the performance of a first task, then presumably the two tasks involve different systems. For example, the process of identifying a familiar stimulus (a letter, say) does not seem to affect a person's reaction time to an auditory signal. Whatever processing is required by these two tasks can be done simultaneously. However, most mental tasks do seem to interfere with each other. A person's reaction to a signal will be considerably slower if he or she

"Oh, you press the button down.
The data goes 'round and around,
Whoa-ho-ho-ho-ho-ho,
And it comes out here."

The New Yorker, December 31, 1973. Drawing by Lorenz; © 1973 The New Yorker Magazine, Inc.

Information-processing models of thinking are based on the computer as an analogue for human thinking processes.

is mentally adding numbers when the signal is presented.

This limited capacity affects our performance in many cognitive tasks, several examples of which should be very familiar. If you have just looked up a telephone number and are trying to remember (rehearse) it long enough to dial it, you are likely to ignore a question asked of you during your task, or else forget the phone number. One of the difficulties in attending to lectures is that the need to attend to the new information the lecturer is presenting competes with the activity of rehearsing or noting the just-presented information for later study. If you ask people to add the numbers 569, 148, and 452, they are very likely to reach for pencil and paper because they will be unable to remember what the numbers are, perform the arithmetic operations, and keep track of any subtotals at the same time without the help of written notation. When a listener says, "You lost me," it is often because the speaker has produced a long, complicated sentence that requires the listener to hold on to too many pieces of information before the idea expressed by the complete sentence is formed.

Psychologists study thinking by examining the behavior of people attempting to solve problems of the kind mentioned in the cartoon, and by manipulating the characteristics of the problem, the problem solver, and the nature of the information given to the subject (such as hints or strategies).

PROBLEM SOLVING

A great deal of what we know about cognition comes from observations of what people do in well-structured problem situations. In this section we will present some of the generally accepted principles of problem solving. But first let's look at the stages involved in solving virtually any kind of problem.

Stages of Problem Solving

Although different people have proposed varying descriptions of the stages of problem solving, we shall concentrate on the proposal made by Donald M. Johnson. According to Johnson, the stages of problem solving are (1) *preparation,* (2) *production,* and (3) *judgment.* Preparation refers to those activities designed to determine exactly what the problem is, what information is available, and what constraints are imposed on its solution. Production involves thinking of possible solutions. Judgment is the evaluation of alternatives. For certain simple problems, these stages might boldly follow each other in a neat, simple order. For example, in solving the problem of which movie to see one evening, your preparation might consist simply of buying a newspaper to determine which films of interest to you are being shown at nearby theaters. This preparation might produce only two films as alternatives. And your mood might lead to your judgment in favor of the comedy. But for more complex problems, it may be necessary to reexamine the problem for new information, to repeat stages of production for different parts of the solution, or to evaluate possible solutions several times in the light of new information. Imagine the recycling through the three stages necessary for the solution of a problem such as how to achieve racial balance and equal opportunity in public schools. A diagram of the possible interplay among these stages is given in Figure 6–1.

Most studies of simple problem solving emphasize the production stage. The researcher usually tries to prepare the solver completely by giving instructions. Because the problem is uncomplicated, solution attempts can be readily evaluated as either correct or incorrect. Consequently, the time a person spends in solving the problem reflects primarily the production of solution attempts, and the process the researcher seeks to describe is the process of generating alternative solutions. Other, more complex problems can involve different emphases. For example, in trying to solve the problem of selecting the best move in a game of chess, a considerable amount of effort is devoted to evaluating the consequences of a particular move.

Tasks requiring creative solutions involve all three stages in a fairly obvious fashion. Such a problem is likely to be somewhat ambiguous, which means that the statement of the problem is subject to different interpretations and that no obvious "answer" can be readily identified. Suppose that a number of people are given the task of deciding "how to improve the distribution of wealth in the country." This problem is subject to many interpretations.

One person might assume that the best distribution of wealth is one in which wealth is most closely tied to achievement, whereas another person might assume that the desired goal is to distribute wealth evenly throughout the

Figure 6-1
**The possible interplay among preparation, produc-
tion, and judgment in problem solving. Note the
similarity to the flow chart of a computer program.**

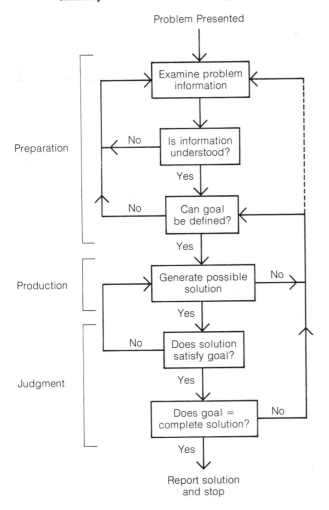

fourth stage of problem solving called **incubation.** This stage allows for the temporary (or in
some cases permanent) withdrawal by a person
who has worked on a problem for some time
without finding a solution. In severe cases this
withdrawal process may involve pathological
symptoms such as delusions or excessive daydreaming. Usually, however, it is simply a matter of doing something else for a while. When
the person returns to the problem, he or she
sometimes finds the elusive solution quite easily.
One suggested explanation for this incubation
effect is that while people are away from a problem, they continue to work on it unconsciously.
Another suggestion is that a rest period allows
a person to "clear the mind," to overcome any
shortsighted or repetitious behavior that is preventing a solution to the problem.

There is, however, no generally accepted
explanation for incubation, in part because
incubation does not always occur, and in part
because researchers have had difficulty demonstrating incubation effects in laboratory studies
of problem solving. Certainly a rest period is
no guarantee of a solution, but if you find yourself in a situation you cannot master, you have
little to lose, and perhaps much to gain, by taking some time off, putting the problem out
of your mind, engaging in some other activity,
and only later returning to work on the problem.

Perceptual Influences

Some simple problems emphasize the principles
of perceptual organization discussed in Chapter 3. Solving this kind of problem is often a
matter of being able to visualize alternative
solutions in the mind's eye. For example, consider this problem:

Given the following array of 16 matches, move 3
and only 3 matches to change the array into a 16-
match array of 4 squares all the same size.

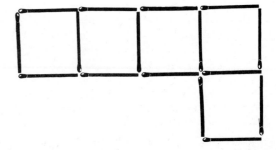

population. Furthermore, two people working
toward the same goal can make different assumptions regarding the constraints imposed on
a solution—one might try only solutions allowable within the existing social-political framework, while the other might assume that modifying the form of government is an allowable
alternative. The judgment of any proposed
solution is likely to be very complicated, and
people often do not agree on the relative importance of various facets of the evaluation. We
shall have more to say about these issues when
we discuss creative problem solving.

A number of psychologists have proposed a

Arriving at the solution to this problem (shown on page 201) depends on the ability to visualize different arrangements of the match sticks. Imagery, especially visual imagery, is an important problem-solving thought process in perceptual problems. Misperception of the situation contributes greatly to an inability to solve problems of this sort.

Perception also influences problem solving in more subtle ways. For example, one problem that has been extensively studied requires the person to discover that a match box tacked to a wall can serve as a platform for a candle. The difficulty of this problem depends critically on how the tacks and match box are arranged when the problem materials are first presented to the subject. If the tacks lie loose on the table and the match box lies empty, the problem seems trivial and the solution is easily seen. But if the match box contains the tacks when presented, the problem is seen as fairly difficult. Seeing the match box full of tacks, people often either have difficulty thinking of the match box serving any different function or don't notice it at all. When asked to describe the materials in front of them some people who have difficulty with the problem don't even mention the match box; they simply say "there are some tacks."

Although perceptual abilities play an important role in problem solving, the solution to many problems relies more on verbal or more abstract skills. Some word problems require special knowledge and skills to solve them. Consider the following sample problem:

The ages of a man and his wife are together 98 years. He is twice as old as she was when he was the age she is today. What are their ages now? (Johnson, 1944)

Finding the answer to this problem (see p. 201) depends on a knowledge of algebra and the techniques for solving simultaneous equations. Without that knowledge, it is unlikely that a person could arrive at an adequate solution except by trial and error or a lucky guess.

The Role of Past Experience

The major behavioral emphasis in experiments using simple problems is not on learning something new but rather on utilizing the products of past experience and practice. The object is

"If only he could think in abstract terms. . . ."

Imagery is a way of coding and remembering our perceptions of the world and our experiences. As such, imagery plays an important role in cognition. Often we solve problems "in our heads" by imagining the various aspects of the problem; it is obviously much easier to conjure up images of concrete objects such as tables, chairs, and elephants than of abstract things such as love, mortality, and nth roots. Problem solution may be helped by translating abstract terms into concrete ones that can easily be visualized. Psychologists like to do this, for example, by devising mechanical models of psychological processes, as when cognition is treated as a computer program.

to put together what you already know and are able to do in some simple but nonobvious way in order to bring about a solution. Of course, if a problem of this sort is new to you, you do learn something when you solve it. You experience the solution and how to derive it. Once you have experienced the solution, you will generally remember it, without further practice, for a certain amount of time.

Some investigators, such as the early Gestalt theorists, believed that a good deal of the problem-solving process was built into the organism. Finding a solution was thought to be mostly a matter of seeing things in the right way. Experience played a role, but a relatively minor one. Supporting this assumption were some studies showing insightful problem solving on the part of captive chimpanzees.

In one study, a chimp was presented with

the problem of obtaining a banana hanging from the ceiling of his cage, out of reach. There were several boxes inside the cage that could be stacked so as to provide a platform from which the banana could be reached. Wolfgang Köhler, the psychologist who conducted this study, observed that the chimp engaged for a while in overt trial and error behavior without success. Characteristically, he then would retreat from the problem and enter a kind of incubation period. The solution finally appeared to come in a moment of insight, as if the animal realized all at once how to accomplish the goal. At that point, the animal would leap up, stack the boxes, and climb them to reach the banana.

It appeared that Köhler's chimp solved his problem basically with insight, with little help from past experience. Köhler concluded that this problem-solving behavior occurs because of innate processes that force the animal (or person) to take different perceptual perspectives until, in a moment of insight, the solution automatically appears.

Later and more thorough examinations of this behavior, however, have revealed that it rarely, if ever, takes place in the absence of appropriate previous experiences. Animals who have had no experience with stackable boxes rarely, if ever, solve this kind of problem "insightfully." Indeed, the more opportunity the animals have to play with boxes, examine them, and use them for one purpose or another before the experiment, the more likely they are to solve the problem in this manner.

From these data and data of his own, Harry Harlow formulated a theory of problem solving in which prior experience is the *only* essential variable. Indeed, Harlow's point is that animals and people *learn* to think. According to Harlow, the ability to think is developed gradually through a process involving the acquisition of certain principles and skills that can then be applied to novel but similar problems.

For example, studies have shown that monkeys can gradually acquire the ability to solve problems for which the solution principle is the same from problem to problem. A typical task used in these studies is the "oddity problem." The monkey must select one object from an array of three or more objects. All objects are identical except for one, the odd one. The odd member is always the "correct" choice. At the

The New Yorker, September 28, 1968. Drawing by W. Steig; © 1968 The New Yorker Magazine, Inc.

One long-standing issue in the psychology of cognition deals with the question of whether problem solution occurs gradually, through a process of *trial and error,* with the learner getting closer and closer to solution all the time, or whether it occurs suddenly, as if the solver had *insight* into the solution. This cartoon is a takeoff on the famous study by Köhler, who found that chimpanzees could solve problems on an insight basis—they could stack boxes and climb the stack to reach the bananas. However, it turns out that *prior experience* with the problem materials is important in determining whether chimps will solve the problem.

outset, inexperienced monkeys solve these problems slowly and with much trial and error. After experience with a number of problems of the same type, however, the animal's problem-solving behavior is immediate and "insightful." On each new problem thereafter, most animals are able to select the correct stimulus on the very first attempt.

Functional Fixedness

Previous experience does not always facilitate problem solving, however. A special case of past experience getting in the way of effective problem solving is **functional fixedness.**

Figure 6–2
The Maier two-string problem

This is perhaps the most famous task ever used in laboratory studies of problem solving. The subject is required to figure out a way to tie two strings together, even though when he is holding onto one string the other is out of reach. A variety of objects are available for use in the solution of the problem, such as a chair, tissue paper, a pair of pliers, and some paper clips. The solution involves tying the pliers to the string and setting it in motion like a pendulum so that it can be reached while the subject is holding onto the other string.

Speedy, a 10-year-old orangutan, focuses a borrowed camera on Tiga, his 9-year-old pinup, after an afternoon's work at a Tampa, Fla., attraction. Speedy's behavior was spontaneous and unrehearsed. Would you call it insight? Could it have been learned by trial and error? What about the possibility of imitation or observational learning (see Chapter 9)? Do animals think?

In this situation the function of a particular object is fixed, or determined, by its use in a particular way just before the problem is presented. As a result, the problem solver tends to overlook how the object can be used in a different way to solve the problem. Under these circumstances, the problem is more difficult than it ordinarily would be.

Functional fixedness is often demonstrated with a simple mechanical problem called the pendulum or two-string problem. To solve this problem, the subject must tie together the ends of two strings suspended from the ceiling. The strings are sufficiently far apart, however, that the subject cannot reach the second while holding onto the first. The solution is to select a weighty object, from a variety of possibilities lying on a table, attach the object to the end of one string, set it in motion like a pendulum, and then, while holding onto the other string, grab the pendulum at the nearest point on its arc (see Figure 6–2).

Suppose that prior to attacking the pendulum problem the subject was given the task of wiring a simple electrical circuit, and as part of that activity, he was required to use a pair of pliers. Subsequently, in the pendulum problem, the subject would be less likely to use the pliers as a pendulum weight, even though they are obviously the best object for that purpose.

A stimulus generalization function, like those discussed in Chapter 4, applies to this phenomenon. Quite interestingly, if instead of the pliers used in the wiring task, a new but identical pair of pliers is placed on the table, subjects show somewhat less resistance to using them as a pendulum bob, and more subjects eventually arrive at the solution. If instead of an identical pair of pliers, a similar but different pair is placed on the table, an even greater percentage will choose pliers to solve the pendulum problem. Finally, if a pair of scissors, similar to the original pliers, is available on the table, there will be an even greater tendency to use them to weight the string.

In other words, functional fixedness begins with a response identified primarily with a particular tool or object. The effect spreads, however, to other objects that bear some similarity to the initial one. Only when an object is sufficiently dissimilar is it recognized by most subjects as suitable for playing a second role.

There are many similarities between functional fixedness and other cases of learning described in Chapter 5. Indeed, it is possible to conclude that functional fixedness is learned and, as such, is an example of the importance of past experience in the problem-solving process.

Mental Set

Sometimes, after solving a series of similar problems, we fall into the use of certain procedures that might not be very efficient or might fail if even a simple change in the problem occurs. Consider the following problem, based on the classic work of Abraham Luchins. You have three empty jars and a water tap to work with. The jars, labeled A, B, and C, hold 10, 32, and 7 quarts, respectively. Your task is to use these jars in such a way as to measure out exactly 8 quarts of water. After some experimenting, the proper solution becomes clear. You fill the second container, pour off 10 quarts into the first, leaving 22, and then fill the third container twice, throwing out 7 quarts each time for a total of 14. This leaves you with 8 quarts in the second container. This is a relatively simple problem that requires knowledge and skills available to most of us.

Now, for further practice, solve successively Problems 1 through 5 as given in Table 6–1. You will find that each of them is solved by precisely the same formula: $B - A - 2C$. After you recognize the formula, the solutions are easy. Once you develop the **mental set,** that is, the tendency to use this formula, answers can be generated automatically. But there is a potential disadvantage to developing a set way of solving problems. Sets are sometimes hard to break, and if a problem cannot be solved by the formula, you have more difficulty with it.

TABLE 6–1 Jar Problems

Problem Number	Three Jars Are Present with the Listed Capacity			Obtain Exactly This Amount of Water
	Jar A	Jar B	Jar C	
1	21	127	3	100
2	14	163	25	99
3	18	43	10	5
4	9	42	6	21
5	20	59	4	31
6	23	49	3	20
7	10	36	7	3

Source: Abraham S. Luchins and Edith H. Luchins, *Rigidity of Behavior.* Eugene: University of Oregon Press, 1959, p. 109.

For example, continue with Problems 6 and 7 in Table 6–1. Problem 6 is easily solved by the old familiar formula given above. Problem 7, however, may give you some difficulty, for the old formula will not work. Indeed, in a typical experiment, some subjects fail to solve Problem 7 within a reasonable working period, say three minutes. Actually, the solution to Problem 7 is easier than the formula that applies to the other problems. All you have to do is subtract Jar C from Jar A to get the right amount of water. In addition, if you look back to Problem 6, you will see that the simpler formula works there also, although most people overlook it.

This example illustrates the potentially negative effects of a mental set. Sometimes we get so caught up in a particular way of doing something that we overlook other simpler ways that may also work. Our perspective on the problem becomes too narrow for us to see alternative possibilities. There are many examples of mental set acting as a blinder on our activities in everyday life. Imagine your annoyance if you were to discover that the tedious and time-consuming method of balancing your checking account you had used each month for years involved several unnecessary steps. Can you think of other examples of mental set?

In this example we again see the relevance of learning to the process of human thought and problem solving. The effect of training or practice on the first five problems is similar to the phenomenon of interference discussed in Chapter 5. A particular way of responding is built up that then interferes with alternate ways of responding when they become appropriate or necessary. We could easily measure the *negative transfer* in this case by recording how long it takes a group to solve Problem 7 after solving

Problems 1 through 5 and comparing that time to the amount of time it takes a group that has been given a different kind of training, or no training at all, to solve the problem. As you might expect, for the untrained subjects, Problem 7 poses no difficulty whatsoever.

Solution Strategies

Although some problems can be solved if the individual simply visualizes the problem properly or retrieves the right idea from memory, many problems require extended sequences of steps for their solution. As solutions become longer and more complex, the way people organize their efforts becomes increasingly important. Getting lost down a blind alley or forgetting a part of a solution previously arrived at can cause considerable difficulty for a problem solver. For many problems, different *strategies* can be identified and evaluated. Generally, good strategies are those that keep the problem solver moving toward the solution and that minimize the amount of information which must be remembered while working on the problem. Sometimes these two ideals conflict with each other, however. An efficient, guaranteed-to-work strategy may exist for a problem but not be used because it requires too much processing and remembering of information. People are sensitive to the amount of mental labor they perform, sometimes choosing less efficient strategies because they require less cognitive effort.

Algorithms and Heuristics

Generally speaking, there are two routes to the solution of any problem. Consider the following scrambled word or anagram problems.

Make five words out of the following five sets of scrambled letters:

CHIKT _ _ _ _ _
EABLL _ _ _ _ _
OANEC _ _ _ _ _
HIGTR _ _ _ _ _
IAFAM _ _ _ _ _

There is a guaranteed route to each solution, though it is time consuming. It requires rearranging the letters in all possible combinations, of which there are 120 when 5 letters are involved. You must then look at each individual rearrangement and decide whether it is or is

not a word. When you find the first word, the problem is solved. A procedure of this sort, which will invariably pay off in a correct solution, is called an **algorithm.** Most people, however, would not use an algorithm to solve an anagram; they would adopt a simpler and less demanding approach that might shorten the solution process but is not guaranteed to work. These short-cut methods are called **heuristics.**

A common heuristic for solving anagrams is to consider only letter combinations that occur frequently, and then rule out combinations that are unlikely in ordinary English words. Thus, in the first anagram it would be appropriate to consider the combination CH or TH at the beginning of the word and CK at the end. In contrast, KC, a combination of low frequency, can be ruled out. In this case, the heuristic works. Once TH and CK are put together, the solution is almost automatic. But the solution is not guaranteed, as is perhaps best exemplified by the third anagram, where NE, a frequent combination, is not correct, while OE, an infrequent one, is (see answers on page 201).

Means-End Analysis

An heuristic of particular use in the solution of problems with well-defined beginning and end states is **means-end analysis.** This heuristic compares the current state of the problem with the desired (solution) state and tries to find means of reducing or eliminating the differences detected. This approach is useful for tasks such as solving chess problems, working through mathematical proofs, or solving the kind of water-jar problems solved earlier. Human problem solvers vary in the degree to which they use means-end analysis. Let us consider an example of means-end analysis.

Atwood and Polson (1976) gave people slightly modified versions of water-jar problems such as:

Problem 1: Given Jars A, B, and C with capacities of 8, 5, and 3 quarts, respectively, and given that Jar A is filled with water while Jars B and C are empty, achieve the goal of having 4 quarts of water in Jar A and 4 quarts in Jar B.

Problem 2: Given Jars A, B, and C with capacities of 24, 21, and 3 quarts, respectively, and given that Jar A is filled with water while Jars B and C are empty, achieve the goal of having 12 quarts of water in Jar A and 12 quarts in Jar B.

Means-end analysis compares the amounts of water in Jars A and B with the desired amounts and tries to reduce the differences. Consider this approach with respect to Problem 1. At the outset, Jar A has 4 quarts of excessive water while Jar B is 4 quarts short, a total difference of 8 quarts (between the current and desired states). There are only two possible legal moves; the water in Jar A can be poured into either Jar B or Jar C. If the water is used to fill Jar B, Jar A will then contain 3 quarts (1 quart away from the goal) and Jar B will contain 5 quarts (1 quart away), a total difference of 2 quarts. If Jar C is filled, Jar A will contain 5 quarts (1 quart away) while Jar B will remain empty (4 quarts short), for a total difference of 5 quarts. In fact, the problem can be solved by either route, but means-end analysis leads to a preference for filling Jar B because doing so results in a smaller difference between the current and desired states. In Atwood and Polson's experiment, people were more likely to fill Jar B by about a two-to-one ratio, suggesting that the majority of people were using a means-end strategy.

Further evidence that the strategy was being used came from a comparison of the relative difficulties of Problem 1 and Problem 2. Whereas Problem 2 can be solved by successively reducing the differences between the current amounts in Jars A and B and the desired amounts, Problem 1 requires two or three violations of means-end analysis. That is, in order to solve Problem 1 (but not Problem 2), the differences between the current amounts in Jars A and B and the desired amounts must sometimes be *increased.* Atwood and Polson reasoned that, if people tended to use a means-end strategy, then they should find Problem 1 harder than Problem 2, and this is precisely what happened. These and other findings illustrate two important features of means-end analysis. First, means-end analysis is a very powerful strategy for solving certain kinds of problems; generally, more efficient or sophisticated problem solvers are more likely to use it. Second, means-end analysis is a heuristic method that does not guarantee solution—Problem 1 cannot be solved by rigid application of the strategy. Third, the strategy obviously cannot work if one does not know the exact nature of the end to be achieved. For example, try to apply means-end strategy to the match-stick problem on page 193.

CONCEPT FORMATION

A concept is a scheme for organizing into categories or sequences the objects and events that make up our lives. A familiar example of a category concept is "chair." Certain objects in our environment qualify as chairs and others do not. Concepts are generally not formed on the basis of a single experience. Typically, we have to see a variety of examples and nonexamples before we obtain an idea of the meaning of a concept. It would be impossible to have a general idea of the meaning of "chair" with only the experience of a single chair. Each new experience—an armchair, a highchair, a folding chair, and so forth—provides additional information, and we gradually refine our concept. In effect, we accumulate information and integrate it with other bits of information in an effort to figure out what a concept includes and excludes.

Logical Concepts

Concepts may be defined in different ways, and there is some debate as to which way is best. A great deal of research has been done on logical concepts. These kinds of concepts are defined on the basis of certain relevant features and a rule used to determine category membership. A logical concept, once learned, can be used to categorize each of a set of objects as either belonging or not belonging to the concept. Figure 6-3 illustrates this type of concept. Figure 6-3 contains a number of geometric forms that vary in color, shape, and size. To define a concept, we must select one or more of these features, say, colored and square, and a rule. One kind of rule is a **conjunctive concept,** which says that an item must be both colored *and* square to belong to the concept. Another kind of rule is a **disjunctive concept,** which states that an item must be either colored, *or* square, *or* both colored and square to belong to the concept. Both of these examples are illustrated in Figure 6-3.

To learn such concepts, a person must determine which of the features possessed by objects are relevant to the concept (the others being unimportant or irrelevant) and what kind of rule is being used. The person uses the information contained in the examples and nonexam-

Figure 6–3
Examples of logical concepts

Stimulus Population

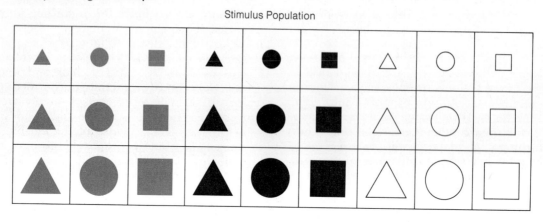

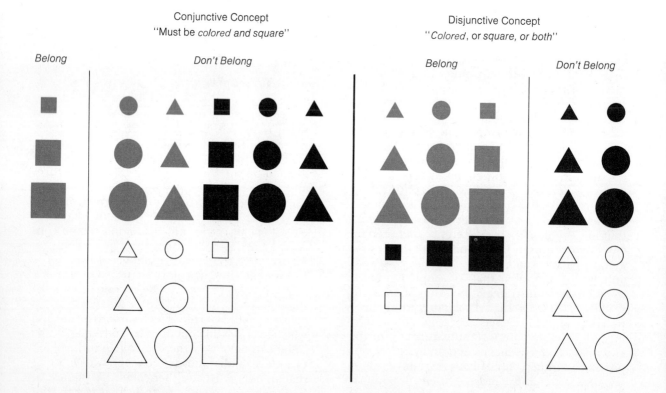

Conjunctive Concept
"Must be *colored and square*"

Belong   *Don't Belong*

Disjunctive Concept
"*Colored*, or *square*, or *both*"

Belong   *Don't Belong*

ples to figure these things out. An illustration of the kinds of experiences a person needs to use to form such concepts is shown in Figure 6–4, which uses geometric forms as stimuli. A sample of geometric forms is shown, corresponding to objects and events a person encounters in everyday life, and information is given as to whether each form does or does not belong to some unnamed concept. There is enough information in Figure 6–4 to figure out how the concept is defined—try to do it. Perhaps you will find yourself trying out various hypotheses as you explain the materials; remember that hypothesis testing is a method peo-

Figure 6–4
What is the concept?

▲ Belongs

▲ Belongs

■ Doesn't belong

△ Belongs

◯ Belongs

● Doesn't belong

▲ Belongs

■ Belongs

ple commonly use in such situations. Notice that once you figure out the concept, you are able to categorize correctly the remaining forms in Figure 6–4.

Natural Concepts

Some researchers have argued that such tightly defined, logical concepts with unambiguous examples and nonexamples do not reflect most natural concepts. Rather, they view many natural categories as having "fuzzy" boundaries and better-and-worse examples, with different items belonging "more or less" to the category. A natural category is seen as having a prototype or best example which serves as a reference point for the category. For example, many people consider chair the best example of furniture and view oranges, apples, and bananas as better examples of fruit than coconuts, tomatoes, or olives. Such ideas would not apply to a logical concept like colored square—any of the colored squares in Figure 6–3 is a good example.

In contrast to the "does or does not belong" character of logical concepts, questions of category membership arise with natural categories. For example, is a screwdriver a weapon, or an elevator a vehicle? Faced with such questions,

Answers to Problems

Match-Stick Problem

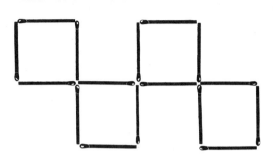

Age Problem

Let X = the man's age and Y = the wife's age

Let $Z = X - Y$, the difference in ages   [1]

Given: $X + Y = 98$ [2]

$X = 2(Y - Z)$, because the man's   [3]
age now is twice what his wife's age
was when he was Y years old

The three simultaneous equations [1], [2], and [3], with three unknowns X, Y, and Z, can be solved to yield:

$Z = 14$ years

$X = 56$ years

$Y = 42$ years

Check back to determine whether these values of X, Y, and Z satisfy the requirements of the problem.

Scrambled Words

The anagrams yield the following words:
THICK
LABEL
CANOE (did you also find OCEAN?)
RIGHT
MAFIA

people tend to hesitate and say "well, sort of," "maybe," or "sometimes," indicating the ambiguity of the situation. An essential part of the argument is that natural categories are *not* defined in terms of clear, relevant features and a neat rule. Instead, such categories are seen as containing members that share different numbers of features with each other. The prototype or best example is most similar to the other members of the same category and least similar to members of other categories. Categories of this kind are more readily learned as the similarity of features between members of the same category increases and the similarity between members of different categories decreases.

Just like logical concepts, natural concepts can be analyzed in terms of relevant and irrelevant features and sorting rules. For example, a chair must have a seat and usually has a back and four legs. It does not matter what color it is, however, or whether it's made of wood, steel, or plastic, or whether it is in the living room or kitchen. Some everyday concepts involve quite complex rules. Consider the concept of a "strike" in baseball: "A strike will be called on the batter when the pitch passes over the plate and between imaginary lines extended from the batter's knees and shoulders *or* when the batter swings at a pitch and misses *or* when the batter hits the ball into foul territory unless two strikes have already been called on him." If you have ever tried to explain the meaning of a strike to a new fan or remember your own initiation into baseball, you surely appreciate the difficulty involved in understanding this concept.

The debate about the different ways to describe concepts is likely to continue for some time. Perhaps someone will develop a new system that will allow for both tight and fuzzy, logical and natural concepts.

REASONING PROBLEMS AND LOGICAL ANALYSIS

Our most sophisticated thought processes involve reasoning and logical analysis. *Formal logic* consists of a set of rules for analyzing an argument and deciding if the argument is internally consistent or not. Typically, unless people have studied formal logic, they will not follow the laws of logic in their arguments.

That we are not an "automatically" logical species should hardly be surprising. If we were all logical, none of our arguments would ever be affected by anger or any other emotional factors.

Formal training in logic provides us with a set of intellectual skills (competence) that enables us to analyze our own and other people's arguments very thoroughly. But what about the person who has not studied logic? How does this more typical person make arguments or in general solve reasoning problems without logical precepts? In fact, studies have shown that these people do make a lot of reasoning errors, but these errors are predictable and understandable. Several factors help us understand how people usually reason. Before considering these ideas, let us examine some examples of logical problems.

Syllogisms

A logical syllogism is a three-step argument consisting of two premises, both assumed to be true, and a conclusion that may or may not follow from the premises. The task is to decide whether the conclusion is true, using only the information supplied by the two premises. Let's try some. Try to decide which conclusions are necessarily true, given the first two premises.

Syllogism 1
All As are Bs.
All Bs are Cs.
Therefore, all As are Cs.   True or false?

Syllogism 2
No As are Bs.
All Bs are Cs.
Therefore, no As are Cs.   True or false?

Syllogism 3
All As are Bs.
All Cs are Bs.
Therefore, all As are Cs.   True or false?

Syllogism 4
Some As are Bs.
Some Bs are Cs.
Therefore, some As are Cs.   True or false?

If you tried these four reasoning problems before reading on, you may be surprised to learn that only the conclusion of Syllogism 1

Figure 6-5
Diagrams of the two possible meanings of "All As are Bs"

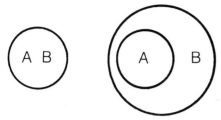

As the diagram demonstrates, "All As are Bs" does not logically imply that "All Bs are As."

Figure 6-6
Diagrams of possible meanings of Syllogisms 1–4

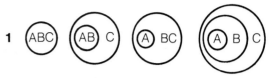

"All As are Cs" is true in every case.

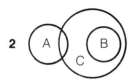

"No As are Cs" is false.

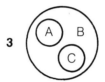

"All As are Cs" is false.

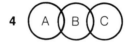

"Some As are Cs" is false.

is *logically* true. Many people will accept all four conclusions as valid. To understand how this happens, let's consider briefly the difference between formal logic and one's own personal logic. Look at the first premise in Syllogism 1. Actually, this statement is ambiguous in the sense that it can apply to two different relations between A and B. These two meanings are illustrated in Figure 6–5, using diagrams that make it easier to understand the meanings of the statements. It can be seen that "All As are Bs" might refer to a situation in which there is only one set labeled AB; that is, "All As are Bs *and all Bs are As.*" On the other hand, "All As are Bs" can also refer to the things called As being included in the larger set of things called Bs, as in "All dogs are animals." The point is this: Formal logic requires three things: (1) that each premise be considered in all its possible meanings, (2) that the various meanings of the premises be combined in all possible ways, and (3) that a conclusion is valid only if it applies to every one of the possible premise combinations. In other words, if you can find a way of interpreting the premises and combining them such that a particular conclusion does not apply, then that conclusion is not logically valid. For Syllogisms 2 to 4, ways in which the premises can be combined to yield an A-C relation inconsistent with the stated conclusions are illustrated in Figure 6–6.

Reasons for Errors in Reasoning

It would not be surprising if you found that you really had to concentrate to understand the above description of formal logic. Quite clearly,

formal logic requires a person to perform a considerable amount of information processing to analyze an argument or to solve a reasoning problem. Because we are limited information processors errors occur. One common source of error is a result of what is called **invalid conversion**. Consider Syllogism 3 again. In this case, the conclusion is not logically valid because, as shown in Figure 6–6, the premises can be combined in such a way that the conclusion is not true. However, suppose you considered only one possible meaning of each of the premises, specifically the first meaning shown in Figure 6–5 for the "All As are Bs" statement. Thus you would interpret the first premise as also meaning that "All Bs are As" and the second premise as also meaning "All Bs are Cs." Both of these are invalid conversions of the stated premises. If you make these

Did the Butler Do It?

One kind of problem used in reasoning research is the "whodunit" problem in which the subject is given information about a fairly complex set of relationships and must then determine how they fit together. Such problems can be quite difficult. Although they involve some figuring out of "what follows from what" in a fashion similar to syllogisms, their solution depends heavily on appropriate hypothesizing (about what to figure out next). Because of this need for hypothesizing, performance on whodunit reasoning problems is not strongly related to performance on syllogistic reasoning problems. Try "playing detective" for this rather unrealistic mystery.

A murder has been committed. An examination of the fatal wound established that the murderer had used a dagger that made an unusual mark on the body. There were five suspects: the doctor, butler, cook, gardener, and accountant. Each had been alone in one of the five rooms in the apartment and thus had no one to vouch for his or her innocence. The rooms lie in a line down the single corridor: bedroom, den, living room, dining room, and kitchen, in order. The additional evidence gathered from various sources, is as follows:

The butler was in the bedroom.
The man with the poison was in the room next to the man with the brown sweater.
The man with the dagger wore a gray jacket.
The man with the penknife wore a black jacket.
The cook wore a brown sweater.
The gardener was next to the dining room.
The man with the poison was in the living room.
The man with the pistol was in the room next to the man wearing the blue jacket.
The gardner had a rope.
The doctor was in the room next to the man with the black jacket.
The accountant wore a green sweater.

Sifting through the evidence, the crafty inspector deduced who the murderer was. Can you solve the crime? For the answer see page 216.

---

invalid conversions, the conclusion is true. But it is based on faulty logic. Your mistake lies in your failure to consider other meanings of the premises.

Errors can also arise from the **atmosphere effect,** the tendency to accept conclusions consistent with the "atmosphere" or context established by the premises of the syllogism. For example, a set of premises all of the form "All ____ are ____," as in Syllogism 3, establishes an atmosphere for a conclusion of the same form (see Figure 6–6). Alternatively, if one or more of the premises is negative, this sets up an atmosphere for a negative conclusion, as in Syllogism 2. Inability to ignore the atmosphere of a problem often leads to mistakes in reasoning.

Sometimes the atmosphere accords with the correct answer, as in Syllogism 1. Nonetheless, it is always important to look beyond the atmosphere of a problem if you hope to reason accurately. Atmosphere is sometimes used quite effectively in speeches to present illogical conclusions convincingly. The listener has little time for close analysis of the logic of the arguments being made, and is sometimes likely to accept the points the speaker makes without reasoning them through. Such principles have aided orators throughout history. The atmosphere effect is capitalized on by tyrants and saints alike.

Perhaps it has occurred to you that people might reason more accurately when given arguments consisting of more meaningful concepts than As, Bs, and Cs. For example, one might argue that the abstract statement "All As are Bs" is ambiguous, as indicated in Figure 6–5, but a meaningful statement like "All cats are animals" is unambiguous. Certainly it is highly unlikely that a person could interpret this statement to mean that "It is also true that all animals are cats." The fact of the matter is, however, that meaningful statements like "All cats are animals" do not always lead to more accurate reasoning.

Syllogisms containing meaningful statements allow people's judgments to be influenced by a semantic factor, namely, the factual truth or falsity of the conclusion. People will tend to accept conclusions that are factually correct or that are consistent with their beliefs, whether or not the conclusions follow logically from the premises of the argument. For example, given the premises "All cats are carnivorous" and "All tigers are carnivorous," one has a strong tendency to accept the conclusion "all tigers are cats," a conclusion that is logically invalid. This argument is in fact like Syllogism 3; if you substitute "bears" for "tigers" you will see that the conclusion does not necessarily follow.

LANGUAGE AND THOUGHT

Language is often considered our greatest intellectual accomplishment. Languages differ from culture to culture, but the language of each culture provides members of that culture with a commonly accepted way of describing and remembering their experiences and communicating them to others. In a language, both visual and auditory—written and spoken—symbols represent various objects, events, actions, and relations that make up our experiences. These symbols are combined in systematic ways to express even larger ideas. The existence of language poses several interesting questions for cognitive psychologists: What is language, and what is involved in understanding language? How is language acquired? How does language influence thinking? Most language acquisition occurs during the early years of life; this process will be described in Chapter 8. For now we will concentrate on how language is understood and how it affects our thinking.

Understanding Language

The familiar act of understanding what someone says to you is really a complicated and remarkable achievement. A speaker converts a meaningful experience into a series of vocalizations, and the listener in turn converts these vocalizations back into meaning. Let us assume that the speaker does his or her job well. Consider the task of the listener. To extract meaning from the vocalization, the listener must be able to identify the units of meaning and understand the rules underlying their organization. Travelers in foreign lands are often unable to perform this task. We are inclined to attribute this failure to inadequate knowledge of vocabulary. "How was I supposed to know that *strasse* means 'street'?"

Actually, the listener's task is much more complex than this. If you heard a language extremely different from your own, it is quite possible that you might not even understand the vocal cues that indicate units—that is, when units begin and end. In other words, you might not have any idea of how to begin processing the vocalization. A listener must be able to analyze the structure of a vocalization in order to understand its meaning. The structure of a language can be described on several different levels, each with its own units and associated rules. Ordinarily we are not aware of processing language at multiple levels because we concentrate on meaning; nonetheless, multilevel processing is taking place. Let us briefly consider what is involved.

Structural Components

Language structure can be described in terms of sounds, words, and sentences. A sentence is made up of words, and the words are made up of sounds. Let's start with the smallest unit and work our way up; in this way, you can see the complexity of processing language.

To begin, consider the fact that the *b* sound is never exactly the same each time the word "boy" is spoken, even by the same speaker. Particular sounds vary from word to word and speaker to speaker. Despite these fluctuations, certain characteristics repeatedly occur, enabling the listener to recognize the sound. Each particular *b* sound, somewhat different from every other *b* sound, is an example of a general,

At an early age children learn to make both auditory and visual discriminations among the symbols of their language.

conceptual class of sounds we recognize as "b." These classes are called **phonemes.** Each phoneme is characterized by certain distinctive features that enable us to distinguish it from other phonemes. The features are related to the way in which speech sounds are made by the speaker. For example, one basis for distinguishing phonemes is in terms of whether they are voiced (vocal chords vibrating) or voiceless. To see (or feel) this difference, make the *p* and *b* sounds (as in "pat" and "bat") with your lips. Notice that the *b* sound uses the voice box while the *p* sound does not. This is only one way in which the phonemes of the English language differ. Each phoneme can be described in terms of a distinctive bundle of such features. In effect, recognizing the sounds of a language is an important example of concept identification.

The language user deals not just in sounds or phonemes but in larger units. The smallest meaningful unit of analysis in language is the **morpheme.** The value of using the morpheme instead of the word as the unit of linguistic analysis is best understood by example. In linguistic analysis the word "bat" is a single morpheme, whereas "bats" consists of two morphemes, "bat" and "s," the second of which is the form for making a plural. Another example

is the word "sadly," which is divided into "sad" plus "ly," the latter morpheme being used to produce an adverb from an adjective.

Phonemes combine to make morphemes. The combining process follows certain rules that we use in speaking English, although we may not know them in any formal sense. We use them, however, in the sense of being able to distinguish real English words from nonsense. Thus, certain combinations of sounds are allowable and certain others are not. For example, no English word could begin with "trv." We know immediately that "trvurs" cannot be a word. On the other hand, we might have to use a dictionary to find out about "dib" or "lut." Thus you can use your knowledge of the rules for combining sounds into English to judge whether unfamiliar combinations are real words or not.

The morphemes and words produced by sound combinations are themselves combined to make sentences. Once again, the process obeys certain rules, known as the rules of grammar. These rules prescribe the ways in which words can be organized into phrases and phrases organized into sentences. For example, we recognize that "The red-haired boy threw the flat stone" is an acceptable English sentence, whereas "The stone red-haired flat threw the boy" is not. To understand language, a person must figure out how a sentence has been formed, using his or her knowledge of the rules of grammar.

The functions that such rules serve can be illustrated with ambiguous sentences. For example, "They are eating apples" is ambiguous because we cannot tell whether the verb is "are" or "are eating." The thought expressed by "They / are / eating apples" is different from that contained in "They / are eating / apples," even though the sequence of words is the same. The difficulty arises in dividing the sentence into its components. For a different example, consider "The shooting of the hunters was terrible." This sentence is also ambiguous, but its noun and verb phrases are not—it is clear that the sentence is "The shooting of the hunters / was / terrible." The ambiguity arises because "the shooting of the hunters" might have been generated by applying one set of rules to the underlying idea "the hunters shoot" or by applying different rules to the underlying idea "they shoot hunters." Such examples, by presenting us with problems of analysis, make us aware of

Semantic Differential Ratings

The **semantic differential,** developed by Charles Osgood, is one technique for assessing the connotative meaning of a word. People can be asked to rate a word on as many as 50 scales, although it is typically found that the scales can be reduced to a basic set along three dimensions: evaluation (good-bad), potency (weak-strong), and activity (fast-slow). The adjective pairs in parentheses are those best illustrating these three dimensions. Notice that ratings on certain scales, like strong-weak and heavy-light, tend to come out pretty much the same. These pairs are related to the same dimension, potency. According to the theory behind the semantic differential, the meaning of a word can be indexed according to its position along the three basic dimensions. Thus, "mother" is toward the positive end of evaluation, toward the strong end of potency, and toward the fast end of activity. The semantic differential has been used to measure the connotative similarity of words which might have quite different denotative meanings.

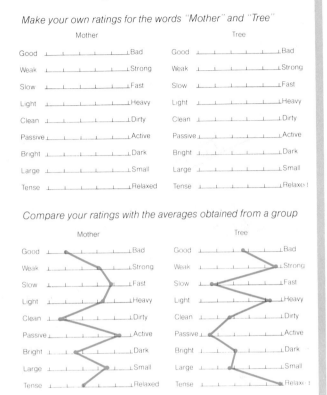

Make your own ratings for the words "Mother" and "Tree"

Compare your ratings with the averages obtained from a group

what we are constantly doing in processing language—determining the structure of the sentences we encounter.

Meaning

The primary function of language is to convey meaning, and its structural components are related to this function. One of the more difficult problems facing psychologists is the meaning of "meaning."

We mentioned earlier that morphemes and words are the smallest units of language that carry meaning. A great deal of attention has been given to the meaning of words. Actually, words have two different kinds of meaning. The **denotation** of a word is roughly its dictionary definition, a specification of the conditions under which the word may properly be used (as agreed upon by the language community). For example, it is acceptable to call some things chairs but not others, to refer to some people as uncles but not others. The **connotation** of a word refers to all the things we associate with the word but which are not part of its denotative meaning. For example, "teacher" is denotatively defined as "one who shows how to do something or gives lessons," but "teacher" might also make you think of "stern, threatening, quiet, loving, smiling" (depending on your experience). Such associations make up the connotative meanings of the word.

Many words are labels for classes of things in our experience. Certain kinds of objects are labeled wheels, certain kinds of sensory experiences are labeled red, and certain kinds of activities are labeled jumping. One theory of meaning is that words acquire meaning through consistent pairings with aspects of our experience. While this is one mechanism for acquiring meaning, it is not an all-encompassing explanation. A look at a dictionary will quickly reveal that words, standing alone, are rather ambiguous, yet we have little difficulty understanding them in context. For example, consider the difference in meaning between "the *duck* swam down the river" and "I had to *duck* under the swinging racket." Some words seem to have meaning only in sentences; what are the non-linguistic referents for "but," "neither," or "however"?

Sentences convey meanings that cannot be completely explained in terms of the meanings of the words they contain. Even though we know the words "the," "boy," "girl," and "hit," this knowledge alone does not enable us to account for the meaning of the sentence "The boy hit the girl." "The girl hit the boy" communicates an entirely different idea. Actually, we may not get the full meaning of communication from the sentence alone. Most sentences interact with our knowledge of the world, our memory for semantic meaning. Through inferences, sentences provide us with much more information than looking at the sentence alone would suggest. For example, the sentence "Babe Ruth hit a home run and drove in three runs" describes a certain action. But it implies a great deal more: that a baseball game was being played, during a particular time period, probably involving the New York Yankees, that a pitch was made, that two teammates were on base, and so on.

Usually we are unaware of how important our general knowledge is to understand language. Our ability to comprehend language is critically dependent upon this knowledge and not just on the information that is contained in the material we are trying to understand. If we are reading something and do not possess the relevant knowledge to understand it, then the passage might appear to be nonsense. Read the following passage taken from Bransford and Johnson (1973):

If the balloons popped the sound wouldn't be able to carry since everything would be too far away from the correct floor. A closed window would also prevent the sound from carrying, since most buildings tend to be well insulated. Since the whole operation depends on a steady flow of electricity, a break in the middle of the wire would also cause problems. Of course, the fellow could shout, but the human voice is not loud enough to carry that far. An additional problem is that a string could break on the instrument. Then there could be no accompaniment to the message. It is clear that the best situation would involve less distance. Then there would be fewer potential problems. With face to face contact, the least number of things could go wrong.

This passage sounds like nonsense — it is difficult to comprehend because you do not have the relevant general knowledge necessary to understand the meaning of the sentences. The meaning, then, does not reside exclusively in the words and sentences that make up the passage — if that were so this perfectly grammatical material would be comprehensible. Rather, comprehending meaning is obviously an active process in which we interpret the information contained in the words, sentences, and grammar, and this interpretation process must rely on things other than purely linguistic knowledge in order to produce understanding. To get the relevant knowledge, turn the page and look at the drawing of the "electronic serenade"; then reread the passage. Now it should be quite meaningful — easy to comprehend. This should convince you that in comprehending language, written or spoken, cognitive processes are involved in a very active way, and success is dependent upon the cognitions we have available.

Some researchers have been successful in describing the structure of paragraphs and larger portions of connected discourse. Attempts have been made to develop "grammars for simple stories." Consider the following: A particular kind of story is composed of setting + theme + plot + resolution. A setting is composed of characters + location + time. The theme specifies a goal. A plot consists of a series of episodes. An episode is composed of a subgoal, an attempt, and an outcome. This partial account of a "story grammar" indicates that stories can have a hierarchical structure above and beyond the sentences they contain. Grasping the structure of a story is critical for understanding. The full meaning of an episode depends on its relation to the plot, and the theme gives meaning to the plot. If, for example, sentences that convey the theme of a story were deleted or even moved from the beginning to the end of the story, comprehension and retention of the story would be reduced. Without information about the overall theme of the story,

Bilingualism and Information Processing

The linguistic relativity hypothesis would imply that a person's knowledge cannot be separated from his or her language. What then of the bilingual person who is fluent, say, in both English and French? One possibility is that some knowledge is stored in French and other knowledge is stored in English. A different, more nearly correct assumption is that the person's knowledge is stored centrally and is accessible to either language equally.

In one experiment, French-English speakers were asked to read various short paragraphs and then to answer questions about the information presented. A paragraph was either all in English, all in French, or in a mixture of both. An example of a mixed paragraph is given below:

His horse, followed de deux bassets, faisait la terre résonner under its even tread. Des gouttes de verglas stuck to his manteau. Une violente brise was blowing. One side de l'horizon lighted up, and dans la blancheur of the early morning light, il aperçut rabbits hopping at the bord de leurs terriers.

As long as the person could read the passage silently, it made little difference whether the paragraph was in one or two languages—for the same amount of study time, performance on the examination was the same.

Another test made use of the fact that when people see a long list of words, one at a time, and are then asked to recall as many as possible, words repeated more often in the list are recalled more frequently. The question was whether or not "repetitions" in different languages would have the same effect on recall as repetitions in a single language. The results for French-English speakers indicated that, for example, experiencing "fold" twice and its French equivalent "pli" twice had the same effect on recall as four presentations of "fold." In other words, recall was a function of frequency of exposure to the meanings or concepts, not the linguistic forms expressing those meanings. This finding suggests that the subjects were utilizing a common meaning form that is accessible to either language.

---

the plot would seem disorganized, and individual episodes might not "make sense."

The different levels of meaning interact in a circular way. Words contribute to the meaning of sentences, and sentences contribute to the meaning of stories. At the same time, stories partly determine the meaning of the sentences they contain, and sentences partly determine the meanings of their component words. Because of these complex relations, developing an adequate theory of meaning presents a tremendous challenge. The more we learn about how meaning is extracted from language, the more amazing the process seems—the everyday activity of understanding language is a marvelous information-processing accomplishment!

Cultural Differences

It is generally agreed that thought and language are closely related, but the nature of that relationship is subject to considerable debate. Is thought necessary for language? Is language necessary for thought? Is one the basis of the other? Are they identical? Do they have some material effect on each other? Psychologists do not know the answers to questions like these yet, and consequently there is a lot of room for theory and speculation.

A popular hypothesis about language and thought is the *linguistic relativity hypothesis* put forth by Benjamin Lee Whorf, which is often called the Whorfian hypothesis. It is a complex

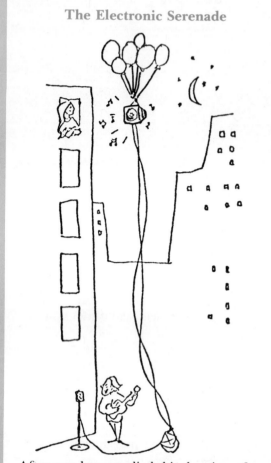

The Electronic Serenade

After you have studied this drawing of an "electronic serenade" go back and reread the passage on page 208 and see if the passage is easier to comprehend now that you have the relevant knowledge for understanding.

set of ideas, but basically the notion is that languages are organized differently, and, therefore, because language and thought are closely interrelated, speakers of these languages will think differently. Whorf argues that the way we perceive and think about the world is largely determined by the language we have for encoding the world.

Consider vocabulary richness. There is a tribe in the Philippine Islands whose language has names for 92 different kinds of rice. The Arabic language has about 6000 ways of referring to camels in their speech. Naturally, we would expect people who speak these languages to think more explicitly about rice or about camels than we can. But is this because they can think about camels or rice in ways we cannot, or is it because they just know more about camels and rice than we do? Their superior knowledge is undoubtedly due to the fact that camels and rice are more important in their culture and not that their language is different, as Whorf would argue. Most important, could they have a thought about camels or rice that we could not, in principle, have because we speak English? Basically, no, because every language can probably express anything.

The Whorfian hypothesis is an intriguing one. The evidence upon which it is based is, however, anecdotal and offers little support for the idea of linguistic relativity, that is, that language *determines* the general view we have of the world. Language does, however, determine how efficiently we can code our experiences. Eskimos talk more efficiently about snow than we can because they have many single words to represent their discriminations on the subject.

INTELLIGENCE

So far we have described a variety of cognitive processes, summarizing what psychologists have discovered about how people reason, solve problems, form concepts, and understand language. We have emphasized the role of attention, memory, and a person's knowledge and skills in these complex activities. To many people, the word "intelligence" refers to an individual's general ability to perform cognitive tasks. The belief in a general cognitive ability lies at the foundation of many intelligence tests, although some psychologists argue that intelligence refers to an amalgamation of a number of relatively separate abilities. Whether or not people are *generally* superior or inferior with regard to cognitive accomplishments is one of the major issues that has confronted research on intelligence.

The concept of intelligence has been closely tied to intelligence tests. Our society atrributes considerable importance to being intelligent, and scores on intelligence tests have often been used to make important decisions about people's

Do IQ Tests Discriminate? Judge's Ruling May Decide

UPI

SAN FRANCISCO — A U.S. District Court judge here is grappling with the question of whether standardized IQ tests should be banned from public schools.

The case specifically involves only the placement of California's black children in classes for the mentally retarded. But the decision could affect all the other 49 states because Judge Robert F. Peckham, who is sitting without a jury, is being asked to rule that the tests discriminate against minorities.

Such a decision would mean states using the tests could be in violation of federal laws and regulations.

As a result, the U.S. Justice Department has been allowed to present witnesses.

What its position will be was hinted at by Michael Thrasher, a government civil rights lawyer. At the trial's opening Tuesday he predicted testimony from experts will indicate that standardized IQ tests are culturally biased.

This is the contention of the plaintiffs, six San Francisco black children. The defendants are the California Department of Education and its superintendent, Wilson Riles.

Joanne Condas, a deputy state attorney general, said California's view was that "many facts go into the assessment process, and it would be a poorer process without this bit of information (IQ tests)."

But the plaintiffs contend the test scores overwhelm all other considerations.

So far, the plaintiffs have presented two witnesses, George W. Albee, a former president of the American Psychological Assn. and Asa Hilliard III, dean of education at San Francisco State. They testified that since the first IQ tests were devised in the mid-19th Century, they have been discriminatory.

The witnesses said current tests wrongly assume all children have the same values and experience — that of white middle-class children. But they said blacks, Indians, Spanish-speaking and others have had different experiences.

As a result, children of different backgrounds may answer questions differently, and children are vulnerable to subjective judgments by the test givers, the witnesses said. . . .

Chicago Sun-Times
October 16, 1977

Because they have been used to make important decisions about people's lives, intelligence tests have become controversial.

lives. Much controversy, not only in intellectual circles but in social and political arenas as well, has stemmed from the question of *why* people score high or low on such tests. In this section we will review the history and nature of intelligence tests and then reconsider what intelligence means. Only after understanding the concept will we consider the reasons people differ in intelligence.

Measuring Intelligence

An important point to keep in mind is the distinction between ability and achievement. A true test of ability measures a person's potential for achievement. It doesn't measure the knowledge and skills the person already has. A test of achievement, on the other hand, measures *existing* knowledge and skills independently of the person's ability or potential for future achievement. What you know now is your level of achievement. Your potential for future achievement is your level of ability. Tests of intelligence are generally considered to be measures of intellectual ability.

In practice it is extremely difficult, if not impossible, to construct a test that measures pure ability and is completely independent of a person's achievement. Thus, intelligence tests measure achievement as well as ability. This means that two people can earn the same score for different reasons, one because of high ability and low achievement, the other because of low ability and high achievement. Upon this problem centers much of the current debate concerning the fairness of intelligence tests. People with high ability may earn lower scores because of a disadvantaged background restricting their level of achievement.

The Binet Test

The first general measure of intelligence was constructed for a simple pragmatic reason. Around the turn of the century, the Ministry of Public Instruction in Paris decided it wanted to identify schoolchildren who were likely to have difficulty in school and who would benefit from special programs. The Ministry commissioned Alfred Binet, a well-known psychologist, and his colleague, Theodore Simon, to develop a test that could be used to sort these children. Since that time, the test, which for simplicity we will call the Binet test, has been repeatedly and systematically revised, and versions of it are in common use today. Most recent revisions have been undertaken at Stanford University in California and are called Stanford-Binet tests.

Binet and Simon made two basic assumptions. First, they believed that intelligence is a composite of many abilities. Therefore, intelligence tests must contain a large number of different kinds of test items. Most items used in Binet tests are based on simple everyday tasks. Binet wanted to construct a test that would not give special advantages to any particular group of children. Despite his concern and careful selection of items, however, we know that Binet's test, even in its most modern versions, is not free from environmental influence. Indeed, there is no test that is truly "culture-free," because the selection of items necessarily involves assumptions about what experiences people do in fact have. The critical point is that, if people have had unequal exposure to certain experiences assumed in a test, differences in their scores cannot conclusively be attributed to differences in their ability to learn from these experiences.

The second important assumption behind Binet tests is that the nature of intelligence changes with age. Therefore, items selected for Binet tests must be graded by age as well as difficulty. Items used for testing intelligence at age 3 are not appropriate at age 10. The same items will simply not discriminate low from high from average children at every age. Thus, Binet tests are actually a collection of subtests, one for each year of age. Some illustrative items at different age levels are presented in Table 6–2.

Binet introduced the concept of **mental age** (MA). If a child can pass the items on which the

TABLE 6–2   Test Items for the Fifth- and Twelfth-Year Scales of the Latest (1960) Revision of the Binet Test

Year 5
1. Completes a drawing of a man with missing legs
2. Folds a paper square twice to make a triangle, after demonstration by an examiner
3. Defines two of the following three words: ball, hat, stove
4. Copies a square
5. Recognizes similarities and differences between selected pictures
6. Assembles two triangles to form a rectangle

Year 12
1. Defines 14 words, such as haste, lecture, skill
2. Sees the absurdity in such items as: "Bill Jones's feet are so big that he has to pull his trousers on over his head."
3. Understands the situation depicted in selected complex pictures
4. Repeats five digits backwards
5. Defines several abstract words, such as pity, curiosity
6. Supplies the missing word in several incomplete sentences, such as: "One cannot be a hero _____, but one can always be a man."

average 9-year-old child is successful, that child is said to have a mental age of 9 years. Mental age is defined independently of **chronological age** (CA); thus, if a 6-year-old can pass the tests passed by the average 9-year-old, the child is considerably accelerated in mental development. If an 11-year-old can pass only the items passed by the average 9-year-old, his or her development is retarded. Binet felt that a dull child was retarded in mental growth and a bright child was advanced in mental growth.

It is important not to read too much into the concept of mental age, which is simply one method of scoring performance on an intelligence test. The items associated with age 7 are more difficult than those associated with age 6, which in turn are harder than those associated with age 5, and so on. Rather than earning "points" by passing items, the child earns months and years of mental age credit. Of two children tested, the child with the higher mental age has simply passed a greater number of and more difficult items on the test. Suppose a child passes all items up through age scale 7; passes 4 of 6 items, worth 2 mental age months each, on age scale 8; succeeds on 2 of 6 items on age scale 9; and fails everything on age scale 10 and above. His or her mental age score

Urban versus Rural Intelligence?

Tests of general information are commonly included in intelligence tests. They are based on the assumption that everyone has had a roughly equal opportunity to acquire such information. If so, the people who know more correct answers must be better able to learn and remember. The problems involved in devising information tests that are fair to various segments of a population are nicely illustrated in a classic study by Myra Shimberg. Two different information tests were constructed; examples of the questions on each test are shown below. Both tests seem like reasonable measures of general information for schoolchildren and contain questions much like those on standard intelligence tests.

Information Test A

1. What are the colors in the American flag?
2. What is the largest river in the United States?
3. What is the freezing point of water?

Information Test B

1. Of what is butter made?

2. Name a vegetable that grows above ground.
3. About how often do we have a full moon?

It was found, however, that the two tests had definite but subtle biases. On Test A, urban schoolchildren scored much higher than rural schoolchildren. On Test B, the situation was entirely reversed, with the rural children scoring significantly higher. Analyses of the 25 items on each test indicated that there were many questions for which the direction of the bias could not be predicted by looking at the content of the question. Nevertheless, the two tests yield radically different pictures of rural and urban performance.

This study demonstrated that items on intelligence tests can be biased in subtle ways in favor of one or another part of the population. Similar results have been obtained in other studies. Such findings indicate how difficult it is to make sure that "everyone has had an equal opportunity to acquire the information needed to pass the test."

is then 7 years plus 8 plus 4 months, or 7 years plus 12 months, or 8 years.

IQ

The most common score derived from the Binet test, and indeed any intelligence test, is the **intelligence quotient,** or IQ, which indicates how an individual scored relative to others of comparable age. Using mental age scores, one formula for the IQ is:

$$IQ = \frac{\text{mental age}}{\text{chronological age}} \times 100$$

The test is designed so that the average child earns a mental age score equal to his or her chronological age, which means the average IQ

is 100. Individuals who pass more items than the average for their age group have mental ages greater than their chronological ages and thus IQs greater than 100, while those children who do not perform as well as the average will have IQs of less than 100. Using our earlier example of the child who earned a mental age of 8 years, we can see that, if the child were 6 years old, his IQ would be

$$8/6 \times 100 = 133$$

This ratio, the IQ, thus indicates a person's achievement on the test relative to the achievement of others of comparable age.

It is not necessary to use mental age units in order to calculate an IQ. The most general

"You did very well on your IQ test. You're a man of 49 with the intelligence of a man of 53."

American Scientist, January–February 1977. Reprinted by permission of Sidney Harris.

IQ defined in terms of mental age and chronological age does not apply to adult intelligence.

formula for the IQ, using the points scored on the test, is:

$$IQ = \frac{\text{the person's score}}{\text{the average score for his age group}} \times 100$$

Whenever people score higher than the average for their age group, their IQs will be greater than 100; should they score lower than average, their IQs will be less than 100.

Wechsler Tests

Two other frequently-used tests of individual IQ are the Wechsler tests, named after their creator, psychologist David Wechsler. One version of the Wechsler test is designed for adults, the Wechsler Adult Intelligence Scale (WAIS), and the other for children, the Wechsler Intelligence Scale for Children (WISC). Items on the Wechsler tests are quite similar to those on the Binet test, but, rather than being organized into age scales, the items are combined into subscales to test different abilities. Performance on each subscale yields a score in points that can be converted directly into IQ. About half of the test is concerned with verbal abilities, involving definitions and similarities and differences among words. The other half assesses performance (nonverbal) abilities such as object assembly and picture arrangement. See Table 6–3 for examples. With the Wechsler

TABLE 6–3 Examples of Test Materials from the Wechsler Adult Intelligence Scale

Performance IQ

A. *Digit-symbol substitution*—a timed test of ability to substitute symbols for numbers
B. *Block design*—a test of ability to build specified designs with colored blocks
C. *Object assembly*—a test of ability to assemble puzzle pieces to form a common object
D. *Picture arrangement*—a test of ability to arrange pictures in order for telling a logical, coherent story (such as reassembling cartoon panels)

Verbal IQ

A. *Digit span*—a test of ability to repeat a string of digits in forward and backward order immediately
B. *Similarities*—a test of ability to say how things are alike, e.g., a bus and an airplane
C. *Vocabulary*—a test of ability to provide word definitions
D. *Arithmetic*—problems that test arithmetic ability and general problem-solving skills
E. *General information*—a test of general knowledge items like: who invented the telephone, who wrote the *Canterbury Tales*, where does oil come from?

tests, it is quite common to calculate both a performance IQ and a verbal IQ. Binet tests tend to emphasize verbal abilities more than Wechsler tests.

The Distribution of IQ Scores

An IQ score of 100 is considered average. Half the population scores within the range of 90 to 110 (see Table 6–4). At the high and low ends of the IQ distribution are exceptional people. At the high end, we speak of geniuses. Typically, people with high IQs are not only bright but also eminent. Examination of biographical information on notable historical figures has allowed psychologists to make reasonable estimates of their IQs even though no tests were available. Invariably, this informa-

TABLE 6–4 Variations in IQ Scores

Range of Scores	Approximate Percentage of People
130 and above	2
120–129	7
110–119	16
100–109	25
90–99	25
80–89	16
70–79	7
Below 70	2

TABLE 6-5 Classifications of Mental Retardation

	Preschool Age 0–5 *Maturation and Development*	*School Age 6–21* *Training and Education*	*Adult 21 and Over* *Social and Vocational Adequacy*
Profound	Gross retardation; minimal capacity for functioning in sensorimotor areas; needs nursing care.	Obvious delays in all areas of development; shows basic emotional responses; may respond to skillful training in use of legs, hands, and jaws; needs close supervision.	May walk, may need nursing care, may have primitive speech; will usually benefit from regular physical activity; incapable of self-maintenance.
Severe	Marked delay in motor development; little or no communication skill; may respond to training in elementary self-help—e.g., self-feeding.	Usually walks, barring specific disability; has some understanding of speech and some response; can profit from systematic habit training.	Can conform to daily routines and repetitive activities; needs continuing direction and supervision in protective environment.
Moderate	Noticeable delays in motor development, especially in speech; responds to training in various self-help activities.	Can learn simple communication, elementary health and safety habits, and simple manual skills; does not progress in functional reading or arithmetic.	Can perform simple tasks under sheltered conditions; participates in simple recreation; travels alone in familiar places; usually incapable of self-maintenance.
Mild	Often not noticed as retarded by casual observer, but is slower to walk, feed self, and talk than most children.	Can acquire practical skills and useful reading and arithmetic to a 3rd to 6th grade level with special education. Can be guided toward social conformity.	Can usually achieve social and vocational skills adequate to self-maintenance; may need occasional guidance and support when under unusual social or economic stress.

tion leads to estimates of IQs in excess of 125, some ranging as high as 200. The following are estimated IQ scores derived in one study: J. S. Bach, 125; Napoleon, 135; Voltaire, 170. Although these numerical values are obviously only estimates and may be off by 10 or more IQ points in either direction, it is clear that individuals who make significant contributions to society or culture often have higher than average IQs.

Biographical data of this sort have been largely substantiated by contemporary studies in which the growth and development of gifted children, those with IQs of 135 and above, have been followed throughout their life span. Contrary to common misconceptions, these children tend to be better than average in their adjustment to their environment, to enjoy good mental health, and to make use of their intellect in ways that often have a significant impact on society. Interestingly enough, however, genius is not always quick to develop. Albert Einstein did not talk until he was 4 years old, and he

was 7 before he could read. On the other hand, Mozart composed his first piece of music when he was 6.

At the opposite end of the distribution are those individuals who are in some sense mentally deficient. There are degrees, of course. The borderline ranges from about 70 to 90 IQ points, corresponding to an adult with a mental age of 12 years. These individuals are clearly deficient, though not classifiable as retarded. Below IQ 70 are the mentally retarded, who used to be classified by terms such as "moron," "imbecile," and "idiot." These terms have been replaced by adjectives describing the degree of retardation: "mild," "moderate," "severe," or "profound."

Another way of classifying the degree of mental handicap is to indicate whether the person is educable or trainable. Those classified as mildly and moderately mentally retarded can usually be taught some basic skills. The severely retarded can be trained to acquire a few habits of self-maintenance (see Table 6-5). The profoundly retarded, however, need to be cared for, typically in an institution, although today parents are being trained to provide help at home. Special local school programs have been instituted for the educable retarded, often resulting in significant increases in IQ. Other programs attempt to provide employment for the trainable retarded in "sheltered workshops" where they can work at their own pace and get paid. The hope is to provide support services so that parents will be willing to keep the child at home instead of placing him or her in an institution. Institutions for the retarded have all too often been "dumping grounds" where the retarded were kept out of sight of society. It is believed that many people classified as retarded could lead happier, more productive lives outside an institution.

The Composition of Intelligence

As pointed out earlier, there are many different opinions as to what intelligence is and the abilities of which it is composed. The tests we have examined suggest that several abilities contribute to intelligence. Some people have argued, however, that there is a single, general ability that runs through performances of all kinds. It is usually assumed that this general ability is based on heredity, while certain other individual differences in intellectual performance are attributed to special experiences that people have. At the other extreme, J. P. Guilford has proposed the possibility of as many as 120 different intellectual factors. Other investigators have argued that intelligence refers to a relatively small number of abilities. You have already seen one example of this approach in the Wechsler tests, which distinguish between verbal IQ and performance IQ. Another example is L. L. Thurstone's theory that there are seven primary mental abilities.

Attempts to determine the number of intellectual abilities have been based on examination of the *consistency* of individual differences when people are given a variety of tests. High consistency means that people who score well on one test also score well on other tests, and, conversely, that people who score poorly on one test also score poorly on other tests. If individual differences are consistent from test to test, this means that the tests, even though they may have different names and different content,

basically measure the same ability. If, on the other hand, individual differences are inconsistent, with people scoring well on some tests but poorly, average, or well in some unsystematic fashion on other tests, this suggests that the tests measure different abilities. In other words, inconsistent individual differences mean that people's scores cannot be predicted from one test to another—knowing that a person scored well on one test would not help you to predict a score on another test. The technique used to study this question is known as **factor analysis,** which is discussed in more detail in Appendix A. Briefly, factor analysis is a statistical method for finding out which kinds of measures cluster together.

Thurstone applied factor analysis to various measures of intelligence and concluded that there are seven primary abilities: number ability, word fluency (speed in thinking of the right word at the right time), verbal meaning, memory, reasoning, spatial relations, and perceptual speed (recognizing similarities and differences in visual forms). What this means is that number ability, for example, can be measured in several different ways, but individual differences will be consistent from one number-ability test to another. However, scores on number-ability tests will be less closely related to scores on, say, tests of verbal meaning, and so on. Although there is still disagreement on the number of intellectual factors and their identities, most

---

Solution to the "Whodunit" Problem

Room	Person	Clothing	Weapon
bedroom	butler	black jacket	penknife
den	*doctor*	*gray jacket*	*dagger*
living room	accountant	green sweater	poison
dining room	cook	brown sweater	pistol
kitchen	gardener	blue jacket	rope

The information given in the story can be sorted out and tabulated as shown above. The facts can then be used to deduce that the doctor, who wore a gray jacket, was in the den, had a dagger, and was the murderer.

"On second thought, let's *not* take another crack at it."

The New Yorker, January 10, 1977. Drawing by Drucker; © 1977 The New Yorker Magazine, Inc.

A creative idea must be both original and useful—relevant, practical, or feasible in some fashion. Brainstorming is a technique designed to produce large numbers of original ideas. The hope is that at least some of them will also be creative ideas. This is like saying, "Let's be original first and worry about being creative later."

The Drawing-Completion Test

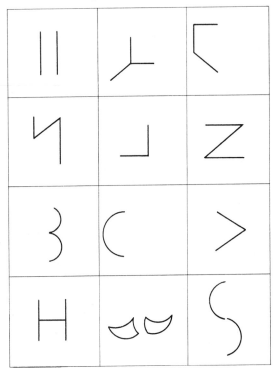

Use your pencil to elaborate on these simple figures in any way that you like. When you have finished, turn to page 219.

psychologists today are convinced that more than a single, general ability is involved.

Intelligence and Creativity

For the problems we have discussed so far, there has been one clear-cut, generally accepted answer. In contrast, there are many problems that have several "correct" solutions, some being "better" than others. The terms *originality* and *creativity* are used to refer to the behavior shown in solving such problems. It is necessary to distinguish between original and creative responses. An original response is one that is simply infrequent. The maximum degree of originality is reached when only one person produces a particular response, but there are degrees of originality. The more original a response is, the fewer people there are who produce it. A creative act is one that meets some minimum criterion of originality *and* that is also relevant, practical, or feasible in some fashion. Suppose that people are asked to think of clever titles

for a short story. If a person proposed the title "Q = Tor + WUG," this would no doubt be original, but not creative unless it also captured the sense of the story.

The distinction between original and creative behavior has two important implications. First, in any situation there are likely to be many more original responses than creative responses. Second, while originality can be defined in such a way that its measurement is straightforward and fairly reliable (one simply asks how infrequently the response is given), assessing creativity inevitably involves having someone *judge* the product. In everyday life, much of the controversy over what is creative stems from differences among judges. Two people might be looking at the same painting and agree that it is unique (original), but they might differ substantially over whether or not it expresses some idea (creative).

Although scores on standard intelligence tests are generally related to intellectual achieve-

I'M WORRIED, TIGER

WHY?

OUR TEACHER SAYS WE'RE GOING TO HAVE AN INTELLIGENCE TEST TOMORROW

...BUT OUR CLASS HASN'T EVEN STUDIED INTELLIGENCE YET!

BUD BLAKE 2-1

ment, some critics have argued that IQ tests do not tap creative thinking. They argue that IQ tests measure the knowledge and skills of individuals but have little to say about how they put them to work in novel and unique ways. Some research studies seem to support this conclusion. For example, Wallach and Kogan (1965) constructed tests of children's creativity that measure abilities different from those tapped by traditional intelligence tests. They discovered that a high IQ does not guarantee a high creativity score, nor does a high creativity score guarantee a high IQ. Many psychologists believe that creative work generally requires at least an average level of intelligence but that individuals with average intelligence may or may not be creative, depending on other factors.

On the assumption that creativity involves more than intelligence, researchers have attempted to identify other factors which influence creativity. Some psychologists have suggested that an ability to produce multiple and original ideas is involved. Earlier, when we discussed creative problem solving, we noted that the ability to evaluate one's ideas may be important. Certain personality variables may be involved, for creativity seems to require freedom from mental sets and inhibitions, allowing for the flow of unusual ideas and a playful, permissive attitude toward those ideas. In one study more creative individuals were found to be more tolerant of disorder and to be more likely to make up their own minds despite the opinions of others. Test batteries designed to measure creativity usually include tests of fluency and flexibility in thinking as well as measures of personality factors (see the discussion of personality inventories in Chapter 9).

Intelligence and Information Processing

One problem with the concept of intelligence is that research and theorizing about intelligence have *not* been closely associated with other research on cognitive processes. Remember that intelligence tests were originally developed primarily for practical reasons—to identify children who were likely to have difficulty in school. The contents of intelligence tests were thus determined on the basis of the test constructors' general ideas of what intelligence was and by considering what "worked" (that is, predicted school success). Later research on the composition of intelligence was concerned with the number of abilities involved

Sample Responses to the Drawing-Completion Test

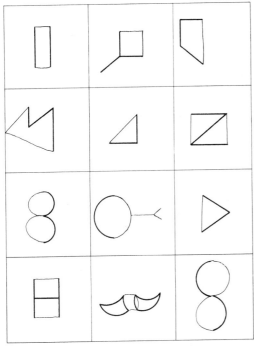

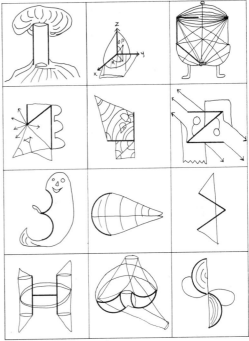

The drawings on the left illustrate the responses of the average person to the drawing-completion test, while those on the right exemplify the responses of creative individuals. The introduction of greater complexity and asymmetry is associated with creativity. Such differences are not limited to the actual production of drawings. When drawings or colored patterns of varying complexity and symmetry are shown to people, creative individuals show a greater tendency to prefer complex and asymmetrical presentations. Some psychologists have argued that a preference or "need" for complexity is an integral component of creative behavior.

in performance on intelligence tests. This research was based on examination of the consistency of individual differences from test to test rather than on a detailed analysis of the processes involved in arriving at answers to test items.

From the viewpoint of a researcher who has worked hard to identify the various processes involved in, say, short-term memory or problem solving, broad categories like "number ability" or "spatial ability" or (indeed!) "general mental ability" might seem quite vague. Detailed analysis of the process of answering an item on an intelligence test might reveal the following activities: processing language (with all its component processes), holding information in short-term memory, retrieving information from long-term memory, selecting a strategy, comparing information from long-term memory with information held in short term memory, and so on. Consequently, it can be argued that we have a very poor idea of what "intelligence" means.

In recent years several researchers have attempted to bridge the gap between work on intelligence tests and research on basic cognitive processes. For example, Hunt, Lunneborg, and Lewis (1975) compared high scorers and low scorers on a standard verbal-ability test over a variety of information-processing tasks. The idea behind their research was as follows. A verbal-ability test supposedly measures what a person knows about language (punctuation, spelling, grammar, vocabulary, and so on). Is it also true that high and low scorers on the test ("high verbals" and "low verbals") differ in how they process current information? To get some preliminary answers to this question, the researchers compared high verbals and low verbals on tasks such as short-term memory for letter strings, the speed at which they could make same-different judgments about physically identical (AA), name-identical (Aa), and different (ab) letter pairs, and make true-false judgments about whether a sentence accurately describes a picture. In general, the results were quite complex, with high verbals and low verbals differing on some tasks but not others. The findings did suggest that, compared to low verbals, high verbals could more rapidly scan short-term memory, retrieve familiar information from long-term memory more rapidly, and remember information about item-order more accurately over brief intervals.

One possible meaning of these findings is that perhaps (and only perhaps) the differences in ability to process current information had existed for a long time and were responsible for the differences in verbal knowledge. Another aspect of the results was that individual differences in some information-processing activities were not related to scores on the verbal-ability test. The researchers suggested that knowing a student's information-processing "aptitudes" might be much more useful to a teacher than a broad characterization of a student's "verbal ability." We expect to see more research of this type in the future and hope that it leads to greater understanding of individual differences in cognitive processes.

SUMMARY

1. Cognitive processes are typically studied in problem-solving situations requiring a person to select and use environmental information, along with knowledge and skills, to meet some task demand.

2. Several different theories of cognition have been proposed. Motor theory and mediational theory are based on stimulus-response ideas. Both imply that thought is action on an internal or implicit level.

3. Hypothesis theory sees the human organism as a user of environmental information to form hypotheses about what is happening. Hypotheses guide actions and are themselves tested and changed on the basis of later experiences.

4. Information-processing theory attributes to the organism a number of mechanisms capable of receiving, storing, transforming, and integrating information and of making decisions among possibilities that arise from these activities. Most contemporary research can be interpreted in terms of information-processing theory.

5. Human beings have a limited capacity for processing current information. Our inability to "do two things at once" affects behavior in many different situations.

6. The activities involved in problem solving can be categorized into stages. The preparation stage involves determining what the problem is, what information is available, and what kind of solution is required. The production stage refers to the generation of alternative possible solutions. The judgment stage involves the evaluation of the alternatives that have been produced.

7. Problems differ in the extent to which they emphasize one or another stage, and the solution of a problem can involve considerable switching from one stage to another. Sometimes there is an additional stage, called incubation, which refers to a withdrawal from active work on a problem for a period of time. Such "time off" may aid solution of a problem under some circumstances.

8. Success in problem solving can depend on arriving at an appropriate perception of the problem situation. Performance also depends on the kinds of experiences that precede attempts to solve problems.

9. Solving a series of problems with similar solutions will lead to the adoption of a mental set that can facilitate solving problems for which the set is relevant but can also prevent the solver from finding alternative, perhaps simpler, ways to solve other problems.

10. Functional fixedness occurs when experience with the ordinary use of an object prevents a person from discovering an unusual use for the object that would solve a problem at hand.

11. Solving a problem often depends on the kind of strategy a person uses to organize his or her efforts. A generally useful strategy is means-end analysis, which involves trying to reduce differences between the current situation and what is desired as a solution.

12. Concepts allow people to respond systematically to the objects and events in their environments. Difficult concepts often involve complex rules, and some concepts seem to have unclear boundaries and are hard to define in simple terms.

13. Reasoning is the process of analyzing arguments and reaching conclusions, and formal logic is typically used as the criterion of proper reasoning. People usually aren't perfectly logical but follow a kind of personal logic that sometimes leads to correct conclusions but also results in systematic kinds of errors.

14. Two characteristics of ordinary reasoning are the failure to consider all possible interpretations and a tendency to seek confirmation of arguments rather than attempting to determine if an argument can be proved false.

15. Language is a complex, flexible, highly organized symbolic system that is simultaneously something we acquire, something we know, and something we use in performing a variety of tasks. Understanding spoken language requires deciphering an utterance at each of several levels.

16. The primary function of language is to convey meaning. Although meaning can be detected in words and in sentences, full understanding of language often requires making inferences based on our general knowledge of the world.

17. Languages differ from one culture to another. One language may be better than another in providing codes for certain experiences, but there is little evidence that language in and of itself determines how people view the world.

18. Intelligence tests are used to compare a person to others of similar age with respect to whatever abilities a particular test requires. Different tests are based on different assumptions about the nature of intelligence and do not necessarily yield similar scores.

19. Although intelligence is often thought to be a general mental ability, research shows that a number of abilities are involved. The concept of intelligence is poorly related to detailed studies of cognitive processes such as creative thinking and information-processing ability.

RECOMMENDED ADDITIONAL READINGS

Bourne, L. E., Jr., Dominowski, R. L., & Loftus, E. F. *Cognitive processes.* Englewood Cliffs, N.J.: Prentice-Hall, 1979.

Cronbach, L. J. *Essentials of psychological testing,* 3d ed. New York: Harper & Row, 1970.

Mayer, R. E. *Thinking and problem solving.* Glenview, Ill.: Scott, Foresman, 1977.

Posner, M. I. *Cognition: An introduction.* Glenview, Ill.: Scott, Foresman, 1973.

Slobin, D. I. *Psycholinguistics.* Glenview, Ill.: Scott, Foresman, 1971.

what does it mean?

Various theories have been proposed to explain human cognitive processes. Although we do not fully understand these functions, we can apply our limited knowledge of how we process information to help solve problems.

"EYEWITNESS" TESTIMONY

When people listen to a number of sentences all related to a general theme, they have, under some circumstances, great difficulty distinguishing between sentences they actually heard and sentences that were not presented but "fit the theme." We also know that the context in which a given sentence is spoken has a good deal to do with its meaning and interpretation. Consequently, a person may have difficulty distinguishing between what actually happened and what he or she infers to have happened. This inferential aspect of remembering is not limited to recalling

Almost Human

Peter Gwynne with Stephen G. Michaud, James Pringle, and Peter S. Greenberg

At Stanford [University], a five-and-a-half-year-old gorilla named Koko has been taught 300 signs of Ameslan [American Sign Language] by graduate psychologist Francine Patterson. "We think that Koko knows more language than any other living ape," asserts Patterson. "She is as perceptive as a human child of the same age, although she has less linguistic ability." Koko apparently understands emotions. When asked about her feelings, she indicated in sign language: "Yes, I was sad and cried this morning."

Another communications star is Lana, a six-year-old chimp who in four years of training has mastered a remarkable computer-based lexicon at Yerkes [Laboratory, Atlanta], Lana's alphabet consists of nine geometrical symbols, which include a circle, a triangle and a vertical line. Combinations of these symbols, placed on colored keys of a keyboard, represent individual words. A triangle and a line, for instance, indicate "machine." A circle and a triangle stand for "into."

By pressing the keys in sequence, which she can do faster than any human, Lana produces grammatical sentences that answer researchers' questions—or makes requests for such treats as bananas, a slide show and M&M's. The studious chimp now commands a vocabulary of about 100 words, some of which she has coined herself. She has managed to reason her way around failures of the equipment and has demonstrated a grasp of time past and time future. So successful has this project been that officials at the Georgia Retardation Center have adapted the computer equipment, designed by bio-engineer Harold Warner, for use by severely retarded children who are unable to speak. . . .

Newsweek
March 7, 1977

Are the communications skills possessed by Lana and Koko in any way equivalent to human language?

exact sentences but can affect the recall of "facts," as has been shown in experiments conducted by Elizabeth Loftus and her colleagues.

In these studies people watched a film of a traffic accident, having been told that they were participating in a memory experiment. Subsequently, they were asked questions about what they had seen. The critical variable concerned the way in which the questions were phrased. Some subjects were asked questions like, "Did you see *the* broken headlight?" The definite article "the" implies that there was a broken headlight, with the person having to decide only whether or not he or she noticed it. Others were asked, "Did you see *a* broken headlight?" The indefinite article "a" has no implication—indeed, it raises the question of whether or not there was a broken headlight as well as the question of whether or not the person saw it.

Several questions of both forms were asked about things that had occurred in the film and things that had not. The form of the question did not affect the frequency with which people indicated that they had seen something that actually did occur. However, asking questions with "the" resulted in a much stronger tendency for people to say that they had seen something that had never occurred!

Similar effects of "suggestive questions" were reported by Loftus and John Palmer. People who had witnessed a traffic accident were asked either "How fast were the cars going when they bumped into each other?" or "How fast were the cars going when they smashed into each other?" Witnesses who were asked the first question estimated much lower speeds than those asked the second. These results are consistent with the view of memory as a reconstructive process and indicate that suggesting plausible inferences to a person at the time of recall can affect what is believed to have happened. Simply by asking the right questions, you can convince at least some people that they saw events that did not happen. The implications of such re-

How many of these witnesses would describe the auto accident in the same way?

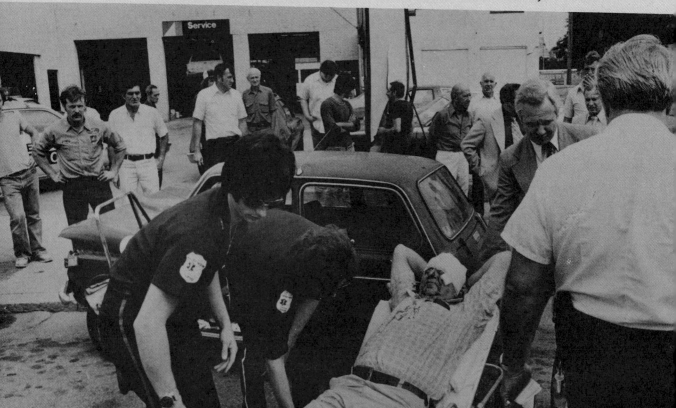

"Yes—that's the man!"

PLAYBOY, June 1973. Reproduced by special permission of PLAY-BOY Magazine; copyright © 1973 by Playboy.

sults for courtroom examinations or police investigations are fairly obvious. Such interrogations are intended to identify the "facts," with attorneys told not to "lead the witness." These findings suggest that the definition of a "leading question" may be very subtle indeed.

BIRTH ORDER

Intuitively it seems likely that birth order affects personality and intellectual development. In many ways, the oldest child has the most difficult time, especially early in life. It is more difficult for him or her to pass through the birth canal; the mother is more likely to have long labor; there is usually greater head impression during birth; the first-born is less likely to survive childbirth; and he or she weighs less at birth than later-born children. But two or three years later, the first-born tends to weigh more and to be taller than later-born children at the same age. The initial physical growth of the first-born is probably due to the fact that the parents have no one else to care for and thus provide more intensive nurturance. Differences in size tend to disappear by adulthood, because eating at

later stages of development is determined much less by parental attention.

Psychologists have studied possible relationships between birth order and personality but have found them very difficult to verify. None of these relationships is especially strong, and questions have been raised about the identification of all the factors contributing to them. Yet no one would wish to imply that birth order is completely irrelevant to any aspect of human development. Rather, it is probably the case that there are *so many* other factors involved that simple generalizations are not possible (see Chapter 8).

Consider a recent analysis of intelligence made by Robert B. Zajonc. Using data on intelligence from a study of close to 400,000 Dutchmen, Zajonc developed a model for describing birth-order effects on intelligence. First, the overall data did show a birth-order effect. The first-born child is in general slightly more intelligent than the second-born, the second-born is slightly more intelligent than the third, and so on down the line. But the data also show clearly that overall family size is a factor in this relationship. The larger the family, the lower the intellectual ability for all the children. Thus, the first-born in a family of two is likely to be brighter than the first-born in a family of three. Also, the first-born in a very large family, say, nine children, is likely to be *less* intelligent than the second-, third-, or fourth-born in a family of only four children. Thus first-borns can be *less* bright than fourth-borns *when* the family sizes differ.

Zajonc's data also showed that these effects of birth order and family size on IQ depend also upon the spacing between children, such that the closer together the children come, the lower their intelligence tends to be. Thus, a third-born child in a family of three could conceivably be more intelligent than the second-born in some other family of three if the first family spread their children over 10 years and the second family had three children in three years. One final thing Zajonc discovered was that the last-born child in a family tended to be lower in intelligence than would be predicted from factors of family size and spacing. He suggests that this is because the last child does not get the benefit of the intellectual challenge of teaching younger brothers and sisters.

Of course, there are many other factors in determining intelligence besides birth order, family size, and spacing of children. But Zajonc's analyses suggest the following for people who want to maximize the intelligence of their children: (1) keep the size of the family small—two children is best; (2) plan the family so that there are several years between children; and (3) try to find other younger children in the neighborhood for the last child to teach.

READING "AHEAD"

Reading is obviously one of the most important cognitive skills a person can acquire. In elementary school, reading instruction and practice occupy a major portion of a student's life, and tremendous attention is given to how well students can read at all levels of schooling. If test results show that reading scores are declining, educators, parents, and society as a whole express great concern and call for corrective action. Learning to read is important not just for college students, professors, or newspaper editors—reading skills must be reasonably developed in order to make one's way in society. Of course, different reading tasks require different skill levels. Understanding this textbook requires more skill than reading a traffic sign, for example.

Despite the importance of reading and the attention paid to it, we still have much to learn about what people do when they read. Compared to many other cognitive processes, reading is extremely complicated, and it has proved difficult to analyze. The complexity of the issues can partly be illustrated by considering the following "facts." Understanding *spoken* language is a complicated activity, as we have pointed out earlier in this chapter. Yet most people come to understand spoken language relatively early in their lives and without making very special efforts to do so.

In contrast, many people have trouble learning to read, which suggests that reading involves even greater complexities.

Comparisons of good and poor readers have shown that they differ in many different ways. Two characteristics of good readers are that they read rather automatically and that they *do not* read word by word. In a sense, we have known for some time that skilled reading involves taking in relatively large "chunks" of information with little conscious effort. In recent years researchers have made some progress in describing this behavior in greater detail and in developing training methods. We will describe one such effort.

Language, whether spoken or written, is redundant—that is, words and sentences are formed by rules in such a way that, in many circumstances, information about the end of a word or sentence isn't absolutely crucial because you can predict what it will be from earlier information. Consider these examples: "The cat chased the m____." "The doctor cured the ____." The first part of each sentence establishes strong constraints for how the sentence will end; "mouse" and "patient" are very likely endings. While the redundancy of language does not allow perfect prediction of later material on the basis of earlier information, it is often possible to get a good idea of what is to come. In effect, earlier information can be used to set up hypotheses or expectations about later information, and these hypotheses are frequently confirmed. It is reasonable to suppose that skilled reading involves forming and checking hypotheses in this way, rapidly and automatically. Samuels, Dahl, and Archwamety (1974) tested the idea that poor readers tend *not* to "read ahead" in this fashion and attempted to see if these readers could be taught to do so. In studies with retarded children and third-graders with reading problems, they examined the effectiveness of *hypothesis training* for improving reading performance.

Hypothesis training included practice on a number of reading subskills, but a major emphasis of the training was to encourage the children to make predictions about how sentences would end, and to do this quickly. The tasks were first given with the teacher saving part of a sentence and then asking the child to predict how it would end. When the child had learned to do this well (accurately and rapidly), *printed* versions of incomplete sentences were shown, with the child again asked to predict (quickly) how each sentence might end. For example, the child would be asked to provide an ending when the teacher said "The girl ate the ____." In a later stage of training the child was asked to read a sentence like "My mother sleeps on her ____" and provide an ending. Notice that there is no single, correct answer to the questions. In fact, any reasonable ending was accepted; it was perfectly acceptable for a child to end the sentence "The girl ate the ____" with "pizza," "sandwich," "peanuts," or any other sensible word. The emphasis was on getting the children to think about how sentences might end, and to do so rapidly.

When training was completed, tests of word recognition and reading comprehension were given. The students who had received hypothesis training performed significantly better than those who had been given ordinary reading instruction or a different, experimental training procedure. Hypothesis-trained students recognized words faster and achieved higher comprehension scores. Such findings are quite encouraging. The researchers have provided insight into what skilled reading involves and have demonstrated that positive results can be achieved from appropriate training. At the present time, a great deal of research on reading is being conducted, guided by theory and research concerning a variety of cognitive processes. There are good reasons to hope that this research will result in better understanding of reading and improved methods of reading instruction.

TEACHING MATHEMATICS

A great deal of human energy has been expended trying to teach or to learn mathematics. Many people approach mathematics

"You have a choice of three courses. You could increase speed somewhat and retain your comprehension, you could increase speed considerably and reduce comprehension, or you could increase speed tremendously and eliminate comprehension completely."

American Scientist, July–August 1977. Reprinted by permission of Sidney Harris.

Despite the claims of people trying to sell you a "speed-reading" course, there really is a trade-off between speed and comprehension. This is a real-life example of the limits on human cognition and information processing.

with considerable anxiety and view mathematical problems as insurmountable obstacles. A resounding cheer from many quarters would no doubt be heard if the ideal method of teaching mathematics were discovered. However, research on mathematics instruction suggests that the matter is not a simple one. Instead of a single method being better or worse than another, researchers have found that different instructional methods result in different *kinds* of knowledge. One kind of knowledge might be better for some purposes but worse for others.

In a study of college students, Mayer and Greeno (1972) compared two different instructional techniques. The instructional goal was to learn to use a mathematical formula that allows computation of answers to certain kinds of problems. The formula itself might seem complex to most people:

$$P(X = r/N) = \frac{N}{r} p^r (1 - p)^{N-r}$$

The two kinds of instruction were called formula training and general training.

Roughly, formula training was like a step-by-step drill in using the formula to compute answers. Instruction began with presentation of the formula, followed by identification of its terms and instruction on how to compute different parts of the answer and combine them into a final, numerical solution. In contrast, students receiving general training did not even see the entire formula until the end of instruction. With general training, emphasis was given to relating the terms in the formula to concepts that the students presumably already knew. Explanations were given of terms like "trial," "outcome," "event," and "probability," with gradual introduction of different concepts until the whole formula had been covered.

To compare the training techniques, different kinds of test problems were given after instruction. The general finding was that formula-trained students did better on some problems while generally trained students did better on others. "Familiar" test problems were just like those included in instruction and required straightforward use of the formula to compute an answer. Formula-trained students performed better on familiar problems and on test problems that were slightly different from those encountered in training. However, if the test problem required recognizing that the formula could *not* be used to arrive at a numerical solution (because "impossible" numbers or insufficient information was provided), or if questions were asked about the formula ("Can *r* be greater than *N*?"), students who had received general training were the better performers.

An important point made by the researchers is that asking whether one instructional method is better or worse than another is too simple an approach. It is not enough to ask how much a student has learned—we also need to know *what* a student has learned. The findings suggest that a teacher, in choosing a method of instruction, ought to consider carefully what the students will be required to do when instruction is over.

These findings provoke a number of interesting, related questions. Will students who receive both kinds of training be the best performers on all kinds of problems? If combined training is given, should formula training come first, or should general training precede formula training? Do some students profit more from one training scheme while others are best served by a different method of instruction? Is it possible to identify types of students ahead of time so that the most appropriate training method can then be given? These are important questions with potential application to educational practice. Research continues on these questions, although clear answers are not yet available. Research on mathematics instruction is also related to a broader issue. The findings suggest that different forms of instruction result in different forms of knowledge. Researchers are trying to understand what is meant by "different forms of knowledge." Such endeavors are related to the large and difficult question, What does it mean to know something?

INTELLIGENCE, HEREDITY, AND ENVIRONMENT

The question of whether intelligence is determined by heredity or environment has provoked considerable public interest and controversy. In recent years, this issue has resulted in heated arguments, social protests, and legal action, stimulated by Arthur Jensen's suggestion that racial differences in measured intelligence *might* be due to genetic differences and William Shockley's suggestion that some means ought to be sought to decrease child-bearing by people with low intelligence. Many commentators have observed that the issues have produced more heat than light, that people have adopted hard positions on the basis of emotions, politics, and religion, and that sensible discussion of the questions is almost impossible. We cannot possibly present a thorough discussion of these questions. The issues are tremendously complex—many books have been written on these questions without achieving a resolution. What we can do is provide a general understanding of the issues involved.

First, the heredity vs. environment issue is not meaningful when applied to any particular person. It really doesn't make sense to wonder "Is my intelligence due to my heredity or my environment?" An individual is the simultaneous product of both genetic endowment and experience; both are necessary and intertwined. If you had no genetic make-up, you wouldn't exist; similarly, you can't exist without being in an environment and having experiences. What this means is that the heredity versus environment question has meaning only when applied to differences among people, and some would argue that the question makes no sense even in this case.

The fundamental observation is that individuals differ in terms of their scores on IQ tests. Why? It has long been recognized that there is no absolute answer to this question. To what extent are differences in intelligence due to differences in heredity, and to what extent are differences in intelligence due to differences in environment (experience)? Although this question may seem more answerable, there is in fact no generally acceptable answer at present. Although we will have to oversimplify matters, let us try to understand why this is so.

Much of the controversy revolves around the concept of heritability. Roughly, heritability is the extent to which differences in some measured trait are due to differences in genetic make-up. If individual differences in the characteristic are totally due to genetic differences, heritability is 100 percent; if differences in the characteristic have nothing to do with genetic differences, heritability would be 0 percent. Values between 0 and 100 percent

"It'll bring in a lot of business until everyone learns the metric system."

"Grin and Bear It" by George Lichty. © Field Enterprises, Inc., 1977. Courtesy of Field Newspaper Syndicate.

We are so overtrained on inches, feet, and miles that converting to the easier metric system requires a great deal of cognitive effort.

indicate varying levels of relationship between the particular trait and genetic structure.

The basic evidence suggesting that intelligence has high heritability is the finding that similarity of IQ is strongly related to similarity in genetic make-up. For example, identical twins are more genetically similar to each other than fraternal twins; and, sure enough, the IQ scores of identical twins are more similar than the IQ scores of fraternal twins. This type of evidence has led some people to conclude that 70 to 80 percent of the differences in intelligence can be explained on the basis of heredity. You may be surprised to learn that other researchers examining basically the same evidence have estimated the heritability of intelligence at 45 percent or 25 percent or even 0 percent.

How can such different claims be made on the basis of the same data? For one thing, different researchers have used different methods to calculate heritability. Methods for calculating heritability estimates were developed to analyze results from breeding experiments with plants and animals (to help in determining how much a characteristic could be developed by selective breeding). The conditions of such experiments typically involved randomly (unsystematically) assigning plants

"B.C." by permission of Johnny Hart and Field Enterprises, Inc.

or animals with known genetic differences to different environments. One problem with applying heritability estimates to individual differences in IQ scores is that people are *not* randomly assigned to different environmental conditions. In brief, the conditions of ordinary human affairs do not result in genetic differences being independent of (unrelated to) the kinds of environments people live in.

A second problem is that the data on similarity of IQs among people of varying genetic similarity are not particularly reliable. If you think about it, finding identical twins, or identical twins reared separately, or aunts and nieces in order to measure their IQs is rather difficult. Consequently, the question arises as to how representative of "people in general" are those people who do participate in research on intelligence. Furthermore, the variability in findings from study to study is greater than some reports suggest. Leon Kamin has delivered the most severe criticisms of the reliability of the findings in his book *The Science and Politics of I.Q.* (1974), arguing that the available data are not trustworthy enough to justify analyses of heritability.

Even if investigators did agree about the reliability of the evidence, problems of interpretation would remain. For example, it has generally been found that identical (one-egg) twins are more similar in IQ than are fraternal (two-egg) twins. Since identical twins are genetically more like each other than are

fraternal twins, this finding is consistent with the idea that intelligence has high heritability. However, it can and has been argued that identical twins have much more similar experiences than fraternal twins. If so, the "fact" that identical twins have more similar IQs could result from their greater genetic similarity, or their greater similarity of experience, or both factors in some unknown fashion. Investigators have not yet satisfactorily disentangled genetic similarity from similarity of experiences.

Heritability estimates have also been misinterpreted in some instances; occasionally, people have reached conclusions that do not necessarily follow, given a finding of high heritability. For example, people tend to believe that if intelligence has high heritability, this means that an individual's intelligence is "fixed," and little or nothing can be done about it. This belief is incorrect. High heritability means that for a particular population of individuals in a particular set of circumstances at a particular point in time, individual differences in some trait (like IQ) are largely due to differences in genetic make-up. Finding high heritability in one population, situation, and time does *not* mean that differences in IQ in other populations, other situations, or other points in time must also be largely due to genetic differences. Furthermore, high heritability does *not* mean that a trait cannot be changed by altering the environment. To understand these issues, let

A Taint of Scholarly Fraud

The late British psychologist Cyril Burt was eminent in his profession: he held the psychology chair at London's University College, was knighted by King George VI and won the Thorndike award from the American Psychological Association. As a government adviser, he helped restructure the British educational system in the 1940s. Now, five years after his death, Burt is the object of a growing scandal. He has been accused of doctoring data and signing the names of others to reports that he wrote. . . .

Much of Burt's reputation rested on his prominent role in the debate about heredity and intelligence. His studies of identical twins who grew up apart indicated that heredity—rather than environment—explains most of the differences in IQ scores. But shortly before Burt's death in 1971 at the age of 88, there were academic murmurs that the psychologist's data were suspect. For one thing, the statistical correlation between IQ scores of his identical twins remained the same to the third place after the decimal point as more and more twins were studied—an extraordinary and highly unlikely coincidence. Yet most experts assumed it was an honest and unimportant mistake. . . .

The doubts became public knowledge when the London *Sunday Times* reported that Burt's co-authors of the later twin studies—Margaret Howard and J. Conway—are not listed in London University records and are unknown to 18 of Burt's closest colleagues. The revelation is crucial: the two women were presumably Burt's field investigators on the twin research at a time when the psychologist was becoming feeble and deaf. It thus seems increasingly possible that the women never existed, that their investigations were never carried out and that Burt invented them and their reports. . . .

Says Princeton Psychologist Leon Kamin, an opponent of Burt in the heredity-intelligence debate: "It was a fraud linked to policy from the word go. The data were cooked in order for him to arrive at the conclusion he wanted."

Burt's allies prefer to believe the psychologist was careless but honest. The suggestion of fraud "is so outrageous, I find it hard to stay in my chair," says Harvard Psychologist Richard Herrnstein. "Burt was a towering figure of 20th century psychology. I think it's a crime to cast doubt over a man's career." Professor of Educational Psychology Arthur Jensen of the University of California at Berkeley adds: "If Burt was trying to fake the data, a person with his statistical skills would have done a better job. It is a political attack. The real targets are me, Herrnstein and the whole area of research on the genetics of intelligence."

At best, Burt's methods were incredibly sloppy. The raw test sheets on the twin studies were among papers stuffed into half a dozen tea chests and later destroyed. Many of his professional articles do not give primary data, referring readers to unpublished reports. Some of those reports, says Kamin, are at least as hard to find as are Howard and Conway.

Why did Burt's work go unchallenged during his lifetime? Says Philip Vernon, a collaborator of Burt's now at Alberta's University of Calgary: "There were certainly grave doubts, although nobody dared to put them into print because Burt was so powerful." In fact, he was powerful enough to see his ideas on heredity and intelligence translated into educational policy. . . .

Time
December 6, 1976

us consider some hypothetical studies with plants.

Imagine that we plant seeds of different genetic make-up in exactly the same environmental conditions and later measure the heights of the plants. Since every plant would have exactly the same environment, any and all differences in height would be due to differences in genetic make-up; heritability would be 100 percent. Now imagine that in another experiment we plant seeds of identical genetic make-up in different environments. Under these circumstances, since all plants would be genetically identical, any and all differences in plant height would be due to environmental differences; heritability would be 0 percent. As you can see, high heritability of a trait in one setting does not mean that high heritability must be found in other settings. Consider again the first setting—genetically different plants all having the same environment. Clearly, all differences in plant heights are due to genetic differences. However, the actual heights of the plants will depend on whether or not we fertilize them. Whether we fertilize none of the plants or all of them equally, differences in height would be due to genetic differences. Of course, all the plants would probably be taller in the fertilized environment! Applied to intelligence, this means that even if individual differences in intelligence were entirely due to genetic differences, it would still be possible to make everyone more intelligent (on an absolute basis) by improving living conditions in an appropriate manner. Furthermore, if we improved the living conditions for only some of the individual's thus eliminating the condition of identical environments, heritability would decrease!

The heredity-environment issue is complicated enough when only individual differences in intelligence are considered. The question becomes even more complicated and heated when racial differences in intelligence are discussed, particularly black-white differences. It is a statistical fact that, on the average, blacks in the United States score lower on IQ tests than do whites. Why is this the case? Several years ago the mere suggestion that the black-white differences in IQ *might* be due to genetic differences between blacks and whites touched off a ferocious controversy in scientific, social, and political circles. At the heart of the issue is the question of whether or not blacks and whites have had equivalent experiences relevant to performance on intelligence tests. Those favoring the explanation of the black-white difference in average IQ in terms of environmental factors have argued that intelligence tests are biased in favor of whites and that blacks have not been afforded equal exposure to test-relevant experiences. Resolving the question is difficult. At the present time there is no clear evidence that the black-white difference in average IQ is genetically determined. There is, however, clear evidence that blacks score

A Second Opinion from Jensen

Psychologist Arthur Jensen is not widely admired among liberal intellectuals. Last winter a number of prominent professors, including Anthropologist Margaret Mead, displayed some remarkably illiberal behavior by protesting Jensen's election as a fellow of the American Association for the Advancement of Science. The reason: he believes heredity accounts for most of the difference in average IQ scores between blacks and whites.

Jensen's now famous—or notorious—article appeared in a 1969 issue of the *Harvard Educational Review* under the title "How Much Can We Boost IQ and Scholastic Achievement?" His answer: Not much. His own later study of black and white children in Berkeley (where he teaches at the University of California) confirmed his conclusion that IQ scores are 60% to 90% determined by genetics. IQ tests show blacks in the U.S. scoring, on the average, 15 points lower than whites.

Now, however, Jensen has produced an IQ study to delight his critics. As reported in the journal *Developmental Psychology*, Jensen studied 1,479 children, both black and white, in a dirt-poor town in southeastern Georgia. He compared the scores of pairs of siblings in order to test the thesis that environmental factors can produce a decline in IQ scores. His finding: unlike the blacks in relatively affluent Berkeley, whose IQs remained stable with increasing age, the rural Georgia blacks on the average showed a decrease of one IQ point each year between ages five and 18. There was no significant decrease with age in the scores of whites, who were generally from less impoverished families.

Though Jensen does not believe these results undermine his genetic theory, he thinks it proves the case for some environmental damage to black children. Says he: "You have to conclude that something is happening to those kids while they are growing up." Jensen, in fact, claims he has done a better job proving environmental damage than the environmentalists themselves. Says he: "This is one of the first rigorous studies of IQ deficit. The environmentalists just took it for granted. They never did a really careful study." . . .

Time
August 8, 1977

Heredity and Environment, But Not Race, Found to Influence Intelligence

Cheryl M. Fields

Recent studies of the IQ levels and school achievement scores of black and white adopted children indicate that both genetic background and family environment—but not race—have substantial impact on intellectual performance.

This latest chapter in the continuing, explosive controversy over what effects genes, environment, and race have on people's levels of intelligence was reported by Sandra Scarr, professor of psychology at Yale University, at the annual convention of the American Psychological Association here.

Following two adoption studies and other research while she was a professor of child development at the University of Minnesota, Ms. Scarr concluded that "the tests I have been able to make indicate that there are no substantial genetic differences between U.S. blacks and whites in IQ, personality, or any other behavior."

Adopted Children Scored Well

In the adoption research, Ms. Scarr found that in one study of black and mixed-race children adopted by 101 white, working-class-to-upper-middle-class families, the adopted children averaged 110 on IQ tests, well above the average of 90 generally scored by black children in the North Central United States.

School achievement scores provided by the children's school districts, which were scattered throughout Minnesota, also showed that in vocabulary, reading, and mathematics, the adopted children not only scored above the average scores of black and interracial children in the state's public schools, but "were scoring above the national average for white children," Ms. Scarr said.

Such above-average performance is consistent, she said, with the fact that by their desire to adopt children and by meeting the various criteria required by adoption agencies, the adoptive families "are a better-than-average" group in terms of parental IQ, income, education, occupational standing, and desire to rear children.

The lack of a racial explanation for the usual 10 to 15-point difference between blacks' and whites' performance on IQ tests also was demonstrated, she indicated, by a study of 104 white families who adopted white children. These adopted children, who were 16 to 22 years old when tested, had average IQ scores of 106—very close to the 110 scored by the adopted black children, whose average age was 7.

Parents Had Average IQ's

Data available from the state public-welfare department and adoption agencies indicated that the natural parents of the adopted children in both studies had average IQ's and levels of education, Ms. Scarr said. For example, the average IQ of the natural mothers of the white adoptees was predicted to be about 100, she said.

"We concluded that adoptive family environments have increased the scores of genotypically average groups by 5 to 15 points," she said.

"Being reared in the culture of the tests and the schools resulted in intellectual achievement for black and interracial children comparable to adopted white children in comparable families. Therefore it is highly unlikely that genetic differences between the races could account for the major portion of the usually observed difference in performance levels" between black and white groups, Ms. Scarr said.

Another study, scheduled to be published in the journal *Human Genetics* also revealed no racially based difference in intelligence, Ms. Scarr said. The study used blood groups to estimate the proportion of African and white ancestry in a group of blacks, with the estimates based on frequency and concentrations of various blood components.

Not the "Ultimate Human Value"

The study showed, she said, "that having more or less African ancestry was not related to how well one scored on cognitive tests. . . . Blacks with greater amounts of white ancestry did not score better than other blacks with more African ancestry."

In publishing their adoption studies, Ms. Scarr and a fellow researcher, Richard A. Weinberg, another University of Minnesota psychologist, cautioned that by using IQ scores they did not intend to endorse them "as the ultimate human value. Although important for functioning in middle-class educational environments, IQ tests do not sample a huge spectrum of human characteristics that are requisite for social adjustment. Empathy, sociability, and altruism, to name a few, are important human attributes that are not guaranteed by a high IQ. Furthermore, successful adaptation within ethnic subgroups may be less dependent on the intellectual skills tapped by IQ measures than is adaptation in middle-class white settings."

Although a strong environmental influence on intellectual performance, and no racial influence, would not be considered controversial findings by many psychologists, Ms. Scarr also reached what is probably a more controversial set of conclusions about the importance of genetic factors in intelligence.

In the cross-racial study, the adoptive parents also had 145 of their own, biological offspring. In the study of adolescents, the 104 adoptive families were compared with a control group of 120 non-adoptive families with children of similar ages.

The genetic impact on intelligence was shown, Ms. Scarr indicated, when the researchers tried to account for the variance in IQ scores of the adopted children—that is, why did one child score 90 and another 120? Although the adopted groups averaged IQ scores of 110 and 106, the actual scores ranged from about 75 to 150.

Complex Statistical Analyses

Essentially, the researchers found that the most "advantaged" families in terms of parental IQ's, income, education, and other indicators, did not necessarily produce the adopted children with the highest IQ's. . . .

In the cross-racial study, Ms. Scarr similarly found that in the families with both biological and

adopted children, information about education, IQ, and occupation of the parents "predicts about twice as much of the variance [in children's IQ's] if they are biologically related," than if they are adopted.

From these and other analysis, Ms. Scarr said, "it seems evident to us that the study of adoptive and biological families provides extensive support for the idea that half . . . or even more, of the long-term effect of what we call family background on children's intellectual attainment depends upon genetics, not environmental transmission."

The results, she added, suggest "that within a range of 'humane environments' from a socio-economic level of working to upper-middle class, there is little evidence for differential environmental effects" on intelligence.

Studies such as hers should permit "behavioral scientists and policy makers to sort out the important from unimportant differences in people's environments," she said. Further, such studies should lead psychologists and others to avoid pressuring everyone to follow the child-rearing practices of "the professional class," she said, when "it has not been demonstrated that variations in child-rearing practices are functionally different in their effects."

Chronicle of Higher Education
September 12, 1977

All behavior is a joint product of heredity and environment, and intelligence is no exception. This article presents recent evidence suggesting that racial differences are due to environmental variations and not to heredity.

---

higher on intelligence tests when their living conditions have improved.

We have barely scratched the surface of the heredity-environment question with regard to intelligence. You should now at least have some understanding of the issues involved and the problems encountered by researchers. More thorough treatments are provided in the books by Kamin and by Loehlin, Lindsay, and Spuhler listed in the Bibliography. The question of how much differences in IQ are due to genetic differences is very

emotional; many people consider intelligence to be extremely important. People would hardly be aroused if it were reported that 75 percent of individual differences in fingernail length result from genetic differences. Intelligence somehow seems very special. Look again at the section on intelligence and contemplate how little we really know about what intelligence is. You may then appreciate why some scientists have suggested that issues concerning intelligence ought not to be so important.

Motivation and Emotion 7

R eaders of the newspapers are routinely confronted with the following kinds of news items: (1) a couple decided not to let doctors administer insulin to their diabetic son, who subsequently went into a coma and died; (2) a city councilman was arrested for hit-and-run driving; (3) a young boy and his father designed an illegal car in order to win the Soapbox derby; (4) a religious group refused diphtheria inoculations

235

after one of their members contracted the disease and died, leaving the whole group and possibly the state vulnerable to a diphtheria epidemic; (5) three young men were arrested for a "joy killing" of a four-year-old girl; (6) a young man was hospitalized after spending 4½ days in the shower in an abortive attempt to break the world's record (more than 7 days); and on and on it goes. Why do people do such things? Another way to state this question is, "What *motivates* people to behave like this?"

This chapter is about motivation. Motivation raises the question of *why* people behave as they do. This is in contrast to *how* they do it, which is usually a question about the person's knowledge, skill, and performance. In this chapter, we assume that people have the ability to act in certain ways, and ask why they do what they do. Motivation is one of the important answers we can give. We can assume that many teenage boys know how to drive a car and to shoot a shotgun. Why would three such youths use their knowledge and skills to murder a four-year-old girl playing in her front yard? What motivates such a brutal act? Indeed, what motivates common, everyday behaviors, such as playing games, reading novels, eating, and the like? Obviously, in order to understand behavior, we will have to answer questions like these.

MOTIVATION AS AN EXPLANATORY CONCEPT

The Variability of Behavior

Different people behave differently in the exact same situation. At the same cocktail party, some people eat the available food and others don't. This is a difference in behavior *between* people. There is also variability *within* the same person. When you pass by a restaurant, sometimes you go in and eat and other times you don't. The same person behaves differently in an identical situation on different occasions—his or her behavior varies. It is this variability in behavior, both between individuals and within the same person on different occasions, that psychologists seek to understand. When we say motivational concepts help us make sense out of behavior, one important thing that we mean is that motivational concepts help to explain behavioral variability.

Circularity in Explanations

Consider a man who goes to a lot of cocktail parties. Suppose we observe that he eats lots of food at one party and nothing at the next. There is variability in the individual's behavior —he eats at one time and not at another. Moti-

vation is an obvious way to account for the difference in his behavior. We postulate the existence of a motive for food and "explain" the behavioral variability by saying that the man was hungry on one occasion and not on the other. This explanation makes sense, but note the circular reasoning involved. The only way we had of knowing that the man was hungry on the first occasion was the fact that he ate some food—the very behavior we are trying to explain. It goes like this: He eats food. Why? Because he was hungry. How do you know he was hungry? Because he ate the food.

Motivational Constructs

To get around this circularity psychologists look for *independent* ways of defining a motive. Often this boils down to defining the strength of a motive as being the length of time since the motive has been satisfied. In our example, the existence and degree of hunger is determined by the number of hours it has been since the man has eaten—the hours of food deprivation. So the hunger motive is defined not by if and how much one eats (which would be circular), but by amount of deprivation. Now the reasoning is like this: He eats food. Why? Because he was hungry. How do you know he was hungry? Because it has been five hours since he has eaten any food.

Motivational constructs, such as hunger, are powerful explanatory devices because they can account for a wide variety of behaviors without having to have a new principle for each action we observe. People go shopping at grocery stores for food, work for food, steal money for food, beg for it, grow it in a backyard garden, stand in long cafeteria lines for it, kill animals for it, and so on. There are numerous different behaviors involved, all centering on food and all understood by introducing one concept, namely motivation for food, or hunger. Instead of having a separate explanation for each of these behaviors, we can use the concept of hunger to account for all or many of them.

Motivation Is Not the Only Explanation

Motivational constructs are used in psychology because they account for some of the variability in behavior. They do so by reducing a large variety of acts to a much smaller number of motivational principles. In these aspects, motivational constructs are not different from other psychological principles. Take the concept of learning for example. We use it also to account for variability in behavior—Jane is a good bridge player and Harvey is a poor one because Jane has taken lessons and *learned* how to play. Or take heredity—Jane and Harvey differ in IQ, in part because they have different genetic backgrounds. Learning and heredity are two major concepts used to understand why people differ or vary in their behavior, but these two concepts cannot account for all the variability. Motivational principles fill in many of the remaining gaps in understanding.

How can we sort out the effects of motivation from those of learning and heredity? Consider the following example. Two rats that are known to have identical genetic make-ups (through extensive inbreeding; see Chapter 2) and an identical history of learning experiences have learned to run down a straight alley to a goal box for food. These two rats might differ greatly in the speed with which they run down the alley. Further, once they get to the goal box they might differ in the length of time before they start eating or in the amount of food they eat. We see, then, that these two rats differ

"The crew is in excellent health and seems to be suffering no ill effects, with the exception of Commander Fenwick, who reports that he is hornier than a hoot owl!"

Playboy, September 1969. Reproduced by special permission of PLAYBOY Magazine; copyright © 1969 by Playboy.

Commander Fenwick is suffering from a long period of sexual deprivation. Motives are often measured by the length of time since the person has engaged in the behavior that reduces the motive. In fact, motives are often defined by the fact that deprivation leads to increases in behavior designed to obtain the deprived object. For example, we infer the existence of a hunger motive because if we deprive people of food they will try harder and more often to get food.

Also note the variability—the other two astronauts are apparently not suffering. How would you account for the variability among these spacemen? Does Fenwick have a higher sex motive than the other two? Has he been deprived longer?

on three dependent variables—running speed, time to eat, and amount eaten. Why? The reason cannot be heredity or learning because we have used scientific techniques to equate the rats on these two important dimensions. It could be motivation. Perhaps one rat was fed all the cheese it could eat just before being put in the alley, and the other had not eaten for 24 hours. The variability in all three dependent measures would then be understood in terms of variability in one factor: motivation, or hunger in this case.

Note that we could be sure that the rats were equal in learning experience and had identical genetic make-ups only because they had been raised in the laboratory, where these factors can be controlled. In studying everyday human behavior, we can almost never be sure that two people have equivalent genetic make-ups or learning histories. Thus, behavior variability in human beings might be due to learning or heredity, not to differences in motivation. This means, obviously, that it is difficult to tell why people behave differently and difficult to conclude with any confidence that differences in motivation are responsible for behavioral variability.

BASIC CONCEPTS

Recall our example of the rats trained to run down a straight alley to a goal box containing food. The rats have learned that food is at the end of the alley. Now suppose we want to make the rats run faster—we want to motivate them to work harder. Basically, there are two ways to accomplish this. Crudely translated, they are (1) "push" the rats harder or (2) "pull" them harder.

To push them we can increase the level of their need for food, say by increasing the amount of time since they have eaten. Rats that have recently eaten will not run as fast as rats that have not eaten for 24 hours. When we do this, we say that we have increased the drive level of the animals. The *drive level* corresponds to the amount of energy available for *pushing* behavior. The fact the animal has not eaten in some time means that there is a *need* for food. This need is somehow detected or "felt" by the animal and results in an increase in its drive level. There is more energy available for pushing behavior, and thus the rat runs faster. Note that the need leads to the drive, but needs and drives are not the same thing. If you starve an animal long enough, the need for food will get very high. The drive level, or available energy for pushing behavior to get food, however, will drop off as the animal becomes too weak for the behavior needed.

The second way of increasing motivation, corresponding to pulling the rats harder, would be to increase the quantity or quality of the food reward in the goal box. Rats will run faster for a large reward than for a small one, and they too have preferred foods (such as Limburger cheese) that will cause them to run faster than they would for ordinary laboratory rat chow. By this technique we can motivate the rats by enticing or pulling them. When we do this we say that we have increased the **incentive** for the rats.

These two concepts, drive and incentive, have long dominated psychologists' thinking about motivation. If we are in a state of need, a drive is aroused that energizes and pushes or goads us into action to seek the things that will satisfy the need. Some of these things are more attractive to us than others, and so we will work harder to get them. The incentive value of each of these rewards represents their pulling power. Motivation is the combined action of drives and incentives, push and pull.

How much is push and how much is pull? Are we mainly driven to behave or enticed into it? The answer to that question reflects the history of motivational psychology. For a long time drive theory predominated as the basic explanation for motivational phenomena, while incentives were treated as merely minor "extra attractions." In the last 10 to 15 years, as our understanding of the concept of drive has grown, psychologists have become less convinced of its importance. Now the focus is on incentives. Indeed, some incentive theorists have maintained that the entire concept of drive can be discarded, although most researchers still include it in their systems, especially when talking about basic biological needs such as food and water. Let us first take a closer look at the concept of drive as the energizer of behavior.

Motivation as a Pushing Force: Drives and Energy

Drive theorists emphasize the energizing aspects of motivation. Like a machine, a person must have energy in order to behave. The theory is that the arousal of a motive provides the energy or the drive necessary for executing some behavior. High motivation means high drive, which in turn means more energy for pushing behavior, which ultimately means more behavior, more vigorous behavior, and more persistence of behavior.

According to drive theory, deprivation of

Incentive refers to the *motivational* properties of a reward. Two things, say a hug and a kiss for Lucy, might be rewards in that she would learn something in order to get either one. But the kiss might motivate her more than the hug—she would try harder for a kiss reward than a hug reward. In that case, we would say that the incentive value of a kiss was higher than the incentive value of a hug.

some needed substance such as food or water leads to a state of need, which in turn leads to increases in drive level. The result is an increase in the energy available for behaving (going to get food or water).

When someone manages to perform a "superhuman" act such as lifting a car off a child, we tend to think in terms of high drive or energy. Consider also the drug addict who will stop at nothing for a "fix" or the nicotine addict who will "walk a mile" for a cigarette—these behaviors seem best described by saying the person was driven or pushed into behavior by an addiction. As we will see in Chapter 9, Sigmund Freud believed in an energy concept and postulated the existence of sources of instinctual energy which he called *libido*. Often psychologists invoke such states as anxiety and frustration as sources of the energy needed for behavior. In short, much of our behavior gives the appearance of being pushed or driven, and this has been recognized by motivational theorists and formalized into the drive-energy concept.

According to this drive-energy formulation, the motivated organism is aroused or energized. This implies that the motivated organism should be active, an organism bubbling with energy. And indeed, many early studies indicated that hungry or thirsty or sexually deprived animals were highly active—given the opportunity they ran around a lot in an activity cage. Female rats, for example, show activity bursts just at the time of peak sexual motivation. Hungry rats will explore a maze more quickly than rats that have just eaten.

Aroused or Arousable?

The most recent available evidence questions this interpretation. Increases in activity may not be a direct, automatic result of deprivation. Several studies have shown that the animals' activity increases because they *expect* reward. The increased activity displayed when an animal is hungry seems to be more a reaction to stimuli that are associated with food than a reaction to a state of need. One study showed that hungry rats are not more active than satiated (full) rats unless there is a change in the stimulus situation. When the lights in the room were turned on (perhaps a signal that the experimenter was coming with food) or the fan was turned off, the hungry rats reacted with increased activity more than the satiated rats. But the hungry rats were not more active before the stimulus change. In another study, food odors were used as a stimulus; the hungry rats showed a great increase in activity, while the satiated rats hardly reacted at all to the smell of food. Again, when no stimuli were presented the hungry and satiated rats did not differ in their activity levels.

The conclusion is that a deprived organism *is not necessarily* a more active organism. Motivation does not directly lead to increased activity as was once thought, and this finding casts doubt on a simple energy notion. Instead, the motivated organism appears to be more *reactive* to stimuli, especially stimuli that are associated with the motive being manipulated. Instead of thinking of the motivated organism as being simply energized or active, it is perhaps more accurate to speak of higher *arousability*. The

Woman Lifts Car Off Son

AP

KENTUCKY — Mrs. Herbert Seaman, a 5-foot-5, 120-pound brunette, lifted a 2,000 pound automobile off of her trapped son following a traffic accident, then dismissed the feat as "nothing."

"I knew my boy was under the car and I had to get him out," Mrs. Seaman, 33, said. . . . "I didn't notice the weight of the Pinto."

Her son, Dana, 11, was recovering today in a hospital with head and shoulder injuries.

Mrs. Seaman, of Louisville, Ky., said she was driving home from a veterinarian's office and was distracted when the family Irish setter became sick in the front seat.

The car ran off the road and Dana was thrown out. He was trapped under the car after it hit a pole and rolled over.

"Dana was partially under the car and was complaining of his shoulder, and it was just a small car," said Mrs. Seaman, a part-time secretary.

Boulder (Colo.) Daily Camera
January 16, 1972

Motivation as a source of energy.

motivated organism is more reactive to stimuli, more sensitive, more arousable. Stimulation will arouse the organism more easily when it is deprived, especially when the stimuli are associated with the deprivation state. Thus a hungry rat appears to be more sensitive to food-related stimuli and reacts with greater arousal to such stimuli. For that reason, it gives the impression of being more active. The activity is a function of being aroused by the stimulus situation, not a direct effect of being deprived of food. We might say that the motivated organism is *predisposed* to react to certain stimuli but is not automatically more active or energized.

Motivational Functions of Stimuli

Donald O. Hebb has suggested that each stimulus can serve two functions, an arousal function and a cue function. The smell of food will arouse the hungry person (arousal function) and provide information about where to find the food (cue function). Physiological evidence indicates that the *reticular formation* (see

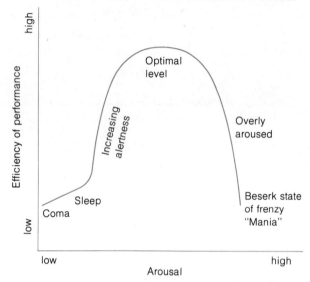

Figure 7–1
Arousal and performance: The inverted U function

Chapter 2) underlies the arousal function. Each sensory modality, such as smell or vision, involves inputs into the reticular formation, which then produces arousal of the higher brain centers. These centers then evaluate the information in the stimulus (cue function) for clues to the source of the stimulation and its significance.

Levels of Motivation

Our arousal level varies. Sometimes we are sleeping and not aroused at all; at other times we are highly excited, practically "crazy" or "climbing the walls." We cannot engage in behavior to satisfy our motives when we are sleeping, nor can we do a very good job of behaving appropriately when we are in a highly excited state. Presumably there is some optimal level of arousal for engaging in any behavior. The relationship between arousal and efficiency of behavior is an *inverted U function* (see Figure 7–1). At very low levels of arousal, such as when we are drowsy and near sleep, our performance will not be very efficient. At extremely high levels of arousal our behavior will be disorganized and inefficient to the point that people might describe us as "wild" or "berserk." Between the extremes of sleep and frenzy are the moderate levels of arousal that are presumably optimal for behavior.

Exactly where the optimal level lies depends on the task at hand. With a very easy task to perform the optimal level will be high—the task is so easy that efficiency does not suffer until extremely high arousal takes place. With a very difficult or complicated task, the optimal level will be on the low side. You should be aroused somewhat but not very much. This principle is generally known as the **Yerkes-Dodson Law** and applies to motivation in general, not just the arousal aspects of motivation. The principle says that the optimal level of motivation depends upon task difficulty—the more difficult or complex the task, the lower will be the optimal motivational point (see Figure 7-2).

In summary, motivation does not automatically mean arousal, energy, and high activity. However, we must be aroused in order to behave, and so arousal, activity, and energy are a part of motivated behavior. Increasing motivation leads to an organism that is more sensitive, more reactive, or more easily aroused. This arousal is necessary in order for the organism to react to incoming stimuli, to process the information in these stimuli, and thereby to engage in behavior that will satisfy its needs. For simplicity, in our discussion we will continue to use the term "drive," but keep in mind that high drive does not automatically energize and push the behavior of the organism. High drive will mean that the organism is predisposed or set or prepared to respond, but it will not respond in the absence of stimulation.

Motivation as a Pulling Force: Incentives

The incentive theory of motivation stresses the attracting or pulling power that rewards appear to exert on behavior. The emphasis is on rewards and the conditions of reinforcement for behaving (see Chapter 4). Incentive theory rests on the assumption that the behaving organism knows what the consequences of its behavior will be. Thus, it focuses attention on the circumstances we are attempting to obtain (positive incentives) or those we are trying to avoid (negative incentives). Incentive theory is primarily concerned with the objects, events, and states of affairs that people find rewarding or punishing and are thus motivated to achieve or avoid. The emphasis is on the goals of behavior.

Figure 7-2
The Yerkes-Dodson Law

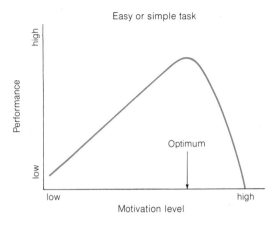

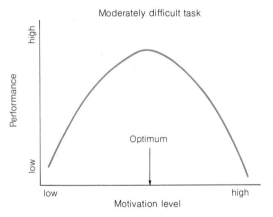

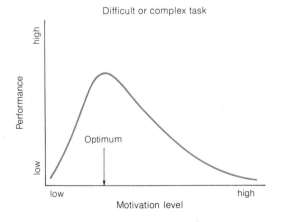

Graphs showing the effect known as the Yerkes-Dodson Law of motivation and performance. With an easy task, increasing motivation increases performance. With increasing task difficulty, the optimum motivation level (that giving best performance) decreases.

241

The New Yorker, January 7, 1974. Drawing by H. Martin; © 1974
The New Yorker Magazine, Inc.

Most of the time we are not motivated by incentives
that are staring us in the face. Rather, we are motivated by our ability to anticipate the receipt of positive incentives or the avoidance of negative incentives. We are motivated by our knowledge that certain
behaviors will lead toward positive incentives or
away from negative ones.

Such an analysis of motivation leads researchers
to study what it is that people are trying to
acquire—food, drink, love, fame, prestige,
money—and what it is they are trying to avoid—
pain, anxiety, frustration, starvation, poverty,
and the like. Incentives are not only objects to
be obtained, such as money, but may include
complicated states of affairs, such as receiving
a promotion, winning an election, feeling satisfied with one's accomplishments, earning the
respect of a colleague, and so on.

Switching the emphasis away from drives
and toward incentives is consistent with the
facts of human motivation. People do not seem
particularly driven to behave, except in special
circumstances usually centering on physical
needs of the body. For example, our behavior
with respect to getting food is usually better
described as behavior designed to prevent intense hunger rather than behavior caused by an
intense hunger drive. We engage in all sorts of
behavior aimed at preventing us from becoming hungry or thirsty. We go to the grocery
store not because we are driven by an intense
hunger drive but because we know that food is
necessary to prevent intense hunger and starva-

tion. We know the consequences of not being
able to eat, and so we arrange our behavior so
that we keep food available. Thus, our behavior
is usually best described as an attempt to achieve
certain goals. We are primarily motivated by the
consequences of our behavior. We seek positive
incentives and we avoid negative ones.

Why Incentives and Not Drives?

Many factors led to deemphasis on drives
and increased emphasis on incentives as moti-
vators. We have already mentioned one, the
fact that deprivation states apparently do not
automatically energize behavior. We have also
indicated that drive theory does not contribute
much to an understanding of human motivation
because our behavior seems more appropriately
described as a search for goals. Another major
factor came from experiments showing that
drives were not necessary to motivate behavior.
In one study it was found that animals will
work to achieve rewards that have nothing to
do with any known need state. Rats will perform
in order to get to drink a sweet saccharin solution, even though they were not deprived of
water, and the saccharin, an artificial sweetener,
does not provide any body nutrients. Monkeys
will work and learn just for an opportunity
to see out into the laboratory or to see novel
objects (see Figure 7–3). Of course, human
beings do many things that do not alleviate any
known drives—they go to horror shows, read
murder mysteries, play all sorts of games, run
nude through school cafeterias, and try to
break the world record for staying in the shower.
It seems nearly impossible to explain such behaviors as attempts to satisfy drives. Rather,
they appear to be a result of the consequences
of the behavior—excitement, pleasure, recognition, prestige, or whatever. They are motivated by incentives, not drives. A lot of research
converged on one conclusion that more than
any other led to the decline of drive theory—to
motivate behavior it is not necessary to provide
a reward that will reduce a drive. From this it
follows that the behavior was not motivated by
a drive in the first place.

Thus the emphasis, particularly in human
motivation, has shifted from drives to incentives, from push to pull, from motivation as an
attempt to reduce a drive to motivation as a
search for goals. What is needed, however, is an
understanding of how incentives produce their

Figure 7–3
The curious monkey

One major problem with drive theory became obvious when various studies showed that animals would learn and work for rewards which did not reduce any known drive. Thus, it was difficult to maintain that it was a drive which motivated them in the first place. One of these studies demonstrated that monkeys would learn to operate a lever that opened a door in the box just so they could see out into the laboratory or get to see novel objects such as a toy train. The monkey in the picture above, however, seems more interested in the photographer than in the train.

motivational effects and of how we learn the incentive values of various things. Why is one person's positive incentive another person's negative incentive?

Predisposition and Precipitation

We can think of the motivated organism as being *predisposed* or set to behave in particular ways. Further, we can imagine that there are *precipitating* circumstances—circumstances that actually result in the organism behaving in those ways. As we mentioned earlier, depriving an animal of food does not automatically cause it to become active. Instead, deprivation appears to predispose it to behave, but in the absence of any stimulation the animal does not do much of anything. The stimulation is the precipitating

factor. The animal starts behaving when it smells food or hears a noise that might be the laboratory assistant bringing food.

One can think of deprivation or drive states as one way of predisposing an organism to behave in particular ways. The hungry person is predisposed to eat or behave in ways that will result in food and eating. The female dog "in heat" is predisposed to engage in sexual behavior. Likewise, one can think of the incentives as being the primary precipitating factor in getting an organism to behave. For example, rats, even if quite hungry, will not run very fast in a maze if there is no food for them at the end; but they will start running quickly as soon as they discover that the experimenter has placed food in the goal box. Moreover, if the experimenter switches the reward from a large amount to a small amount, the rats very quickly adjust to the lower incentive by running more slowly. If the amount of reward is increased, the rats immediately start running faster. This demonstration of switching reward size emphasizes the importance of incentives in controlling motivation. Furthermore, it indicates that incentives precipitate behavior. The rats will not run without some incentive motivation.

Focusing on the concepts of *predisposition* and *precipitation* will help you organize your thinking about motivation. The advantage of these terms over *drives* and *incentives* is a matter of generality. Drive states are not the only source of predispositions, and incentives are not the only precipitators. Predispositions can come from sources other than deprivation. The most important one is learning, particularly learning of the incentive value of various rewards. Consider the person who loves to eat snails. For this individual, snails have positive incentive value; but this is the same thing as saying that the person is predisposed to behave in ways designed to get snails. Obviously this person has learned to like snails—learning was the source of the predisposition, not deprivation of snails. In fact, most of the things we find rewarding, the things that have positive incentive value for us, have achieved this status through learning.

Another source of predisposition may be heredity. For example, in Chapter 2 we mentioned that heredity probably plays a role in susceptibility to alcoholism and perhaps drug addiction. People with certain inherited physiological features are thus predisposed to behave in certain ways. For example, strains of mice have been developed that have a strong preference for drinking alcohol instead of water. They are thus predisposed to be motivated by alcohol as an incentive, and this predisposition comes from their genetic make-up. It has nothing to do with being deprived of alcohol, and so it is not an alcohol drive but a predisposition.

Later in this chapter we will see that most psychologists consider personality traits to be sources of motivation. Some people are said to be highly motivated by a trait called need for achievement. These people need to engage in behavior that will lead to recognized achievement; they have a strong desire to win, to be best at something, or to be better than the next person. Perhaps the need for achievement motivated the man who tried to set the world's record for continuous showering. Thus, one's personality can involve predispositions to behave in certain ways, to be motivated by some incentives (the opportunity to set a world's record) and not by other incentives (the opportunity to sit around and help someone else set the world's record). In turn, however, one's personality is obviously a result of other factors, especially the two we have already mentioned, learning and heredity.

One final point we need to make is that incentives themselves are not usually the immediate precipitators of behavior. Most of the time, our behavior is precipitated by our knowledge that certain behaviors will lead toward positive incentives or away from negative ones, and, of course, this knowledge is a result of our learning history. As an example, consider the laboratory rat that is motivated into activity when it hears the door open, sees the lights come on, or smells food. The activity is motivated not by the food itself but by the stimuli that serve to inform the rat that food might be forthcoming. The animal has learned that such stimuli are often followed by food, and this is the source of the action the rat displays.

Thus motivation is generated when a predisposed organism is subjected to precipitating circumstances. These circumstances result in the organism's utilizing its knowledge and skills to behave in ways designed to achieve positive incentives or avoid negative ones. Sometimes this behavior will appear to be pushed, or driven; at other times it will appear to be a matter of pulling.

MOTIVATION AND BIOLOGICAL NEEDS

We are biological creatures with bodies that require certain things to survive. The motivation for much of our behavior can be traced to this fact. We need food, water, air, sleep, and a certain amount of heat, and our behavior can often be described as an attempt to obtain these life-sustaining items. We have built-in physiological systems for regulating the intake of such things as food and water. It is because of these needs and the systems that regulate them that such items as food and water can reinforce behavior and become positive incentives. As examples, in this section we will discuss the regulation of eating and drinking, but first we must introduce the important concept of homeostasis.

Homeostasis

Complex physiological systems in our bodies determine the conditions under which a need for food or water exists, resulting in the organism's becoming predisposed to eat or drink or to engage in behaviors that have in the past led to food or water. Finally, when sufficient food and water have been ingested, the system detects this fact and the organism is no longer predisposed to eat or drink.

Basically, these physiological systems are designed to maintain a "steady state" in our bodies. As such, they are said to operate according to the principle of **homeostasis.** The best analogy for describing homeostasis is the heating system in the typical home. The system is designed to maintain a steady state, say a temperature of 70 degrees. In order to accomplish this, we have a thermostat (a homeostat for temperature) that detects the need for heat, turns on the furnace when the temperature is too low, and then turns off the furnace when the temperature has reached 70 or so again.

The physiological systems underlying our biological needs appear to operate in a similar fashion, that is, according to a homeostatic principle. Thus, we presumably have "sensors" that detect when we need food and water. When the need reaches some critical level, we become motivated to act in ways designed to obtain and ingest food or water. When we eat or drink, the system senses that the need is being reduced and modifies our behavior so that we stop eating or drinking at the appropriate time. Of course, we must remember that overlying this homeostatic system is an elaborate system of learned behaviors designed to make food and water available. We have learned to anticipate the need in order to prevent starvation or dehydration. Many of these behaviors have been learned because food and water reinforced them; part of the motivation for these behaviors stems from the fact that food and water are positive incentives. But given that we have learned how to find, buy, beg, or borrow food or water, the homeostatic systems regulate how much we consume.

Eating

We eat in order to satisfy a primary biological need. We must supply the various tissues, organs, and structures in our bodies with the nutrients required for growth and proper functioning. We have to take in such varied items as calcium, sodium, iron, protein (amino acids), and various vitamins. It is the homeostatic system that regulates the maintenance of these supplies. Eating is the behavioral component of this system that gets the food into the body where it can be utilized. The homeostatic system is very complex and we still have much to find out about it, though we know some important things about it already. First, we know that the homeostatic system works incredibly well if left to itself. Despite wide variations in our expenditure of energy, our body weight stays remarkably constant—the system obviously adjusts intake to outflow. Just imagine if the system were consistently off by as little as $1/2$ ounce per day. In a year that would amount to over 10 pounds gained or lost. Starting at age 15 with a 150-pound person, such a system would produce a 45-year-old person who weighed 450 pounds, or, if you can imagine a negative weight, a person weighing −150 pounds.

We also know that this complex system involves multiple control factors that provide

Fat people usually have an oversupply of fat cells and high levels of fat in the blood.

"fail-safe" back-up or auxiliary support should one aspect of the system fail. Thus, it is not nearly so simple as the home-heating system.

Predispositions—The Set Weight Level

Like the thermostat in the home set to a particular level, the body has a set weight level, and the homeostatic system is designed to regulate food intake in a way that maintains that level. We have little information about the exact way this is accomplished, but research to date indicates that the culprit is fat—fat levels in the blood and the number of fat cells in the body as a whole. Here we are speaking of the long-term regulation of weight, not the hour-by-hour food intake, which, as we will see later, appears to be related to the level of sugar (glucose) in the blood.

Evidence is beginning to accumulate which supports the hypothesis that the number of fat cells in the body is a crucial determinant of the set weight level. The body sets a weight level according to the number of fat cells in the body, in order to keep a relatively constant level of fat. For example, the overweight person apparently does not have bigger fat cells, stuffed to the brim or overflowing with fat, but rather *more* fat cells stuffed to the same level as the fat cells of the normal-weight person. In other words, the system regulates food intake in a way to keep a constant level of fat in the cells, but if you have more cells than the next

Figure 7–4
Hypothalamic hyperphagia

A hyperphagic rat made obese by a lesion in the ventromedial nucleus of the hypothalamus. This rat weighs 1080 grams (the indicator has spun completely around the dial and beyond). A normal rat the same age weighs less than 200 grams.

'Pre-Set' Hypothalamus Believed Weight Controller

MADISON, Wis. — Many flabby folks trying to lose weight face a hopeless prospect because their bodies are "pre-set" to certain weight levels, says a University of Wisconsin psychologist.

"People who claim to eat the same amount of food that normal-weight people eat—and yet remain obese—are probably right," concludes Professor Richard E. Keesey.

Keesey believes he has found a clue in experiments with rats as to how weight levels can vary from person to person.

The portion of the lower brain known as the hypothalamus determines the "set point" for body weight, he finds. The body staunchly defends this point, compelling heavy food intake if the point is high and lesser amounts if the set point is low.

The set point also controls the metabolic rate. "When we lose weight our body uses energy more efficiently, and if we gain weight, we use it less efficiently in an attempt to maintain the set value," he explains.

How the set point is determined isn't understood, but Keesey believes that heredity and early childhood eating habits contribute. The psychologist speculates that the hypothalamus may regulate body weight through the automatic nervous system, which controls the rate of breathing, the functions of the intestines and the secretion of glands.

The Denver Post
January 21, 1978

person, you will obviously have to eat more to keep your fat cells stuffed to the same degree. And, of course, because you have more cells for storing the fat, you will weigh more.

The hypothalamus in the brain is involved in regulating the set weight level over the long term. There is evidence that the hypothalamus may regulate fat levels in the cells by being sensitive to the levels of free fatty acids in the bloodstream.

The evidence for the important role this structure plays comes from studies on surgical destruction and electrical stimulation or activation of two areas of the hypothalamus: the ventromedial nucleus and the lateral nucleus.

Destruction of these areas is accomplished surgically by making lesions in them.

Making a lesion in the ventromedial nucleus produces an animal with **hyperphagia,** an abnormally increased desire for food. The animal overeats and becomes enormous (see Figure 7–4). But the animal does not go on eating forever and ever until it explodes. Instead, the animal levels off at a new, although very much higher, weight and then maintains that weight. It is as if the thermostat or "fatostat" has been reset at a higher level. In fact, if the animals are gorged and forced to become extremely overweight before the operation, they will not overeat after the operation but will actually eat less until they reduce down to the new weight level, which, of course, is now set higher than normal.

Making a lesion in the lateral hypothalamus produces the opposite effect, apparently resetting the "fatostat" to a lower level. Animals with this lesion exhibit **aphagia;** they will not eat at all. Such an abrupt and complete cessation of eating would normally lead to death, and so they have to be force-fed for a while. After recovery they eat on their own, but they maintain their body weight at a much lower level than normal. If the animals are gradually starved down to a very low weight before the operation, then after the operation they will eat to bring themselves up to the new weight level, which is much lower than normal but higher than the weight they were starved down to.

Electrical stimulation of these two areas of the hypothalamus produces an effect opposite to that caused by lesions. Stimulation of the ventromedial nucleus will cause a hungry animal that is eating to stop immediately. Stimulation of the lateral nucleus will cause an animal to start eating immediately even if the animal has just eaten all the food it wants (see Table 7–1).

The overall, long-term predisposition to eat thus seems to be mainly a function of the number of fat cells in the body. Long-term food consumption is designed to maintain body weight at some set level, and this seems to be quite closely regulated by structures in the hypothalamus that are sensitive to levels of body fat.

Precipitating Factors

In the short term, day-to-day food intake seems to be more a function of blood glucose (sugar) levels than of fat levels in the body. The hypothalamus also plays an important role in this phase of food-intake regulation.

Glucose is the body's basic source of energy, and when we are using it up quickly the blood glucose levels are affected. Blood glucose levels are obviously monitored by the body, because the level is closely regulated to stay within certain limits. If blood glucose levels drop, presumably we are using energy and need food. This decrease in sugar levels is somehow detected and results in our eating.

Taking insulin into the body results in decreased blood glucose levels. People who take

TABLE 7–1   Effects of Lesions (Destruction) and Electrical Stimulation (Activation) on Two Parts of the Hypothalamus

	Destruction	**Activation**
Ventromedial nucleus	Animal becomes hyperphagic and overeats	A hungry animal that is eating will stop eating immediately
Lateral nucleus	Animal becomes aphagic—it will not eat at all and will die unless force-fed	Animal will immediately start eating. even if it has just eaten all it wants

insulin injections report feeling hungry soon afterward, and animals given insulin injections will start to eat. Reversing the process works too; giving glucose injections to hungry animals will cause them to stop eating. Actually, the regulation may be more complex than simply monitoring overall glucose levels. Overall levels do not correspond very well to hunger and the amount eaten; therefore, it has been suggested that what is monitored is the *difference* between the glucose levels in the arteries and the levels in the veins. In any case, it is clear that glucose levels are critically involved.

It has been suggested that there are specialized cells (glucoreceptors) in the body to detect glucose levels and communicate the need for food to the higher centers of the brain, which then initiate eating. There may be glucoreceptors in the stomach and the liver, and it is also assumed that the hypothalamus contains these cells. At one time it was thought that this was merely a result of destroying the parts of the brain that start and stop eating, presumably because these parts monitor the glucose levels. The picture is not so simple, however, because, as we we have seen, the hypothalamus regulates not only short-term but also long-term weight level. Moreover, hyperphagic rats prone to overeating are not particularly *motivated* to eat. They overeat their favorite food if it is right under their noses, but if the food does not taste good or if they have to do the least bit of work to get it, they do not appear to be hungry.

It is perhaps the case that both the long-term weight level (based on fat levels) and the short-term system (based on glucose levels) have regulatory centers in the hypothalamus and that these two systems are complexly intertwined. As mentioned previously, the hypothalamus is only one, though evidently a crucial, part of the complex system involved in regulating food intake. The manner in which the hypothalamus plays its role in regulating food intake is not completely known at this time.

PERIPHERAL PRECIPITATORS   Blood fat and sugar levels and the hypothalamus are critical, but there are other factors that play a role, although small when compared to that of the blood and the brain. For example, consider the stomach. We have already mentioned the possibility of glucoreceptors in the stomach that would monitor glucose and send information to the brain. The stomach also monitors the amount of food: An empty stomach leads to hunger pangs, while a full stomach signals satiation to the brain. Ingested food is also monitored in the mouth by taste, smell, and muscle receptors involved in chewing and swallowing. All of this information is used by the brain to decide when to start or stop eating.

But neither mouth factors nor stomach factors alone are absolutely necessary. We can feed an animal working for food rewards by directly placing the food in its stomach, bypassing the mouth completely. The animal will regulate its weight within normal limits even though it never gets to taste or chew any of the food it has been working for. Likewise, we can surgically remove the stomach or cut the nerves from the stomach to the brain and the animal will still be able to regulate its eating. Mouth and stomach factors play a role, but they are only part of the system.

Taste seems critically involved in regulating what we eat. This is shown by experiments on *specific needs*. We can create a specific need in an animal by feeding it a diet deficient in one particular item, say salt. There appears to be a built-in system designed to detect and regulate sodium (salt) intake, and taste is critical to it. If you take a rat's favorite food and cut out all the sodium to produce a sodium deficiency, the rat, when given free access to several different foods, will immediately eat only the ones with sodium. Of course, taste is also involved in the pleasurable aspects of food, and much of human eating is centered on producing taste sensations we have learned to enjoy.

It was once concluded from these experiments on specific needs that we had specific detectors regulating the intake of all the various types of nutrients our bodies require. Thus there would be a detector for salt, for each of the vitamins and minerals we must take in, and so on. It was suggested that proper nutrition would automatically happen as a result of the control these detectors would exert on what we eat. While there may be a few such detection systems built into the system (for example, salt), it now appears that most of the results of these experiments can be explained on the basis of the novelty of the taste. If you have been specifically deprived of a particular nutrient and are offered some food with that nutrient in it, you will eat it, but probably because it has a novel and presumably more pleasant taste, since you haven't had that taste for awhile. In short, good nutrition does not happen completely automatically.

EXTERNAL PRECIPITATORS   Did you ever "stuff yourself" at dinner on the turkey and dressing and then somehow find room for the pumpkin pie with whipped cream? Did you ever eat something because it looked good, or did you ever feel hungry all of a sudden because you smelled the pizza your dormitory neighbor just had delivered? It is obvious that stimuli outside the body also play a role in getting us to eat. The sight, smell, and anticipated taste sensations of food and even the presence of other eaters can induce us to eat.

Perhaps the most amazing fact about the external factors is that we regulate our food intake so well *despite* their continued presence. But there is also some impressive evidence that external stimuli can come to play a dominant role in food consumption for some people, overriding the internal regulatory systems we have been talking about. As you might guess, these are people with weight problems, the obese or overweight. We shall consider their plight in the "What Does It Mean?" section of this chapter.

The Role of the Liver

Physiological psychologists have almost uniformly emphasized the brain, particularly the hypothalamus, in their theories about eating.

The brain and nervous system are critical in the behavioral aspects of eating, but the liver may be the key organ that monitors and sends out signals about the flow of nutrients to the body tissues and from the fat deposits. The liver obviously plays a key role in body metabolism and seems to be the central processor in the physiology of nutrients. Such processes as the conversion of amino acids into glucose, of fatty acids into ketones, and of glucose into energy (to be used) or fats (to be stored) all take place in the liver. Through the bloodstream the liver sends its various products out to the tissues to be used in cell metabolism or to be stored as fat for later use. Because of its role as central processor, the liver, we may reasonably assume, analyzes the levels of the various substances and regulates its processes accordingly. If this is true, then the liver may well be the place where the signal to eat is generated and sent on to the brain. In such a system there would be no need for glucose or fat monitors in the brain itself. Thus many psychologists may be placing too much emphasis on the hypothalamus, which may only be the place where the signals from the liver are *first* processed. We do not yet know the entire role of the liver, but it appears that this organ is far more important in regulating eating behavior than we have so far considered.

The key point about eating is that the starting and stopping of the behavior is controlled by many factors that work together in a complex way. There is regulation of fat stores and the blood glucose level and monitoring of the sensations from the stomach and mouth. The hypothalamus is critically involved in the regulation process, but it is not the only crucial brain center, and it certainly is not the simple food thermostat we once thought.

Drinking

Another primary, biologically based drive is thirst. Our bodies require water to operate. To keep bodily fluid levels within some critical range, we have developed a complex and sophisticated homeostatic system. If fluid levels are too high, the body gets rid of excess water by sweating or by excreting it in urine. If fluid levels are too low, the body takes steps to conserve the water it has by first inhibiting urine formation and then activating our motivation to search for and drink water.

As with hunger, the hypothalamus seems to play a crucial role in the homeostasis of bodily fluid, It does this by controlling two key processes: (1) drinking and (2) urine formation. When information reaches the hypothalamus that our fluid levels are too low, the system responds by motivating us to seek and drink water and by slowing down the rate of urine formation in the kidneys. The result is that we drink more and urinate less until balance is restored.

The hypothalamus detects low fluid levels in the body in two ways. First, body cells shrink in size as water levels decline, and some cells in the hypothalamus may be activated by shrinking, thus signaling low fluid levels. Second, the blood flow through the kidneys slows down, causing the kidneys to signal the hypothalamus by secreting the hormone **angiotensin.** There may also be blood-flow detectors in the walls of blood vessels which directly signal the hypothalamus by using the nervous system to communicate instead of the blood. In either case, the hypothalamus detects the low fluid levels and activates its two responses.

One response, the slowing down of urine formation, is activated when the hypothalamus signals the pituitary gland to secrete a hormone called **antidiuretic hormone** (ADH; see Chapter 2). This hormone is then carried in the blood to the kidneys where it inhibits urine formation. We form less urine and conserve water, keeping the fluid decrease to a minimum.

The second response of the hypothalamus is to activate the behavior we use when we are thirsty—we seek out and drink water or beer or whatever is handy. Exactly how this happens is not known, but obviously the behavior involves the application of knowledge and skills we possess to locate the vital fluid. Finally, as we drink receptors in the mouth and throat evidently monitor how much we consume and at the appropriate time signal the hypothalamus to deactivate the thirst system and to stop signaling the pituitary to release ADH.

In terms of the concepts we have used to analyze motivation, we can think of the biological system just described as consisting of the hypothalamus, ADH, angiotensin, and various receptors in the blood vessels and mouth which together regulate our level of predisposition to drink. Water or fluids become positive incentives for us and precipitate drinking behavior only when the level of predisposition is above some critical point. Otherwise, water and other beverages will not have positive incentive value. Of course, which particular fluids we choose to seek out and drink, whether water, beer, wine, or cola will be determined by other factors, notably taste. The pleasant or unpleasant taste effects of various fluids will contribute to (or detract from) the incentive values of these fluids. The incentive value of the fluid, combined with our knowledge of what will be required of us in the way of behavior to obtain that particular fluid, will determine, for example, whether we drink water at home or drive to the corner for a couple of beers.

We have a complete system fundamentally based on a biological need and a physiological system to monitor the need. But this system is supplemented by an incentive system based on what we have learned. The biological system predisposes us toward drinking, and the incentive system controls or directs our behavior in ways designed to satisfy the biological need and to give us pleasant experiences at the same time. We have a biological system that predisposes, and we have a cognitive system—through which we arrive at information which determines incentive—that precipitate and direct behavior.

MOTIVATION AS INSTINCT

The concept of motivation first entered psychology in the form of **instincts,** inherited patterns of behavior or predispositions to behave in particular ways. Thus, a man who fights a lot would be characterized as having a strong aggression instinct, and it is this instinct that motivates the individual to fight. The instinct conception of human motivation had its origins in the evolutionary theory of Darwin, which stressed the survival value of instinctive animal behaviors (particularly instincts centering on aggression, feeding, and reproduction) and which hypothesized that human beings are descendants of the lower animals. If animals are obviously creatures of instincts, then it followed that human beings are too. Freud also adopted an instinct-based theory of motivation. The instinct theory came to dominate psychology

around the turn of this century, when two distinguished psychologists, William McDougall and William James, adopted the concept as the central explanatory construct in their theories.

But the popularity of instincts did not last long. Instinct theories were attacked as being useless for understanding behavior, basically because of the circular reasoning problem: He fights. Why? Because of a strong aggression instinct. How do you know he has such an instinct? Because he fights. Psychologists were also indiscriminate in their use of instincts. "Everything under the sun" was viewed as being caused by an instinct. The concept of instinct "explained" everything and nothing, and so it gave way to another explanation.

What instinct gave way to was learning. Instinct theories imply that behavior is predominately a function of heredity. In the early years of this century, psychology turned radically away from such ideas, focusing instead on the concept of learning. Classical conditioning, Pavlov, Watson, and the rise of behaviorism, to a large extent, were responsible for the decline of instinct theories. Behavior came to be viewed as primarily learned, not inherited. But learning theories quickly found that a motivational principle of some kind was necessary. Instead of instinct, they adopted the concept of **drive** as the central motivational force.

Ethology and the Resurrection of Instincts

The concept of instinct lay dormant until the 1930s when it began to reappear in the writings of a small group of influential European zoologists studying animal behavior in natural settings. They called their science **ethology** and resurrected the concept of instinct in a new and scientifically acceptable form. The three most notable figures in ethology are Konrad Lorenz, Karl von Frisch, and Nikolaas Tinbergen. In 1973 they became the first scientists to win the Nobel Prize in physiology and medicine for work done strictly in the area of behavior.

Fixed-Action Patterns

For the ethologists, an instinct is defined as an invariant behavior sequence that is universally observable in and unique to the members of a single species of animals. Furthermore, there is no learning involved—the behavior is innate to members of that species. In short, an instinct is an *innate fixed-action* pattern uniquely characteristic of a particular species (species-specific). The crucial aspects of the behavior, then, are (1) it is innate, (2) it is invariant from one time to the next, (3) it is universally found in all members of the species (if you look at the right time and place and at the appropriate sex), and (4) the pattern is unique to that species.

Of course, modern ethology theory consists of much more than just saying that the behavior is an instinct. The major concepts are illustrated in Figure 7–5. First, innate fixed-action patterns do not just happen. Instead, they are triggered by stimuli known as **sign stimuli** or **releasers.** For example, the territorial defense-action pattern of the flicker is "released" by the black "moustache" of the male flycatcher trying to intrude. For the squirrel, the action pattern of burying nuts is released by any object that is hard and round. Place a steel ball bearing on a concrete floor and the squirrel will go through all the motions (the fixed-action pattern) of trying to bury it. Another example comes from Tinbergen's classic studies of a species of fish called the three-spined stickleback. Aggressive behavior in defense of territory in this fish is released by the red belly of the male intruder. Tinbergen used balsawood models of males in order to determine what would release the defensive aggression pattern. He found that a perfect replica of the male intruder would not release the pattern if the belly was not painted red, but that a very crude model with a red belly would release the pattern. Even a floating beachball would release aggression if it was red.

Action-Specific Energy

The diagram in the upper left-hand portion of Figure 7–5 shows the general model that Konrad Lorenz developed to account for fixed action patterns. It is a drive-energy model that states that members of the species inherit action-specific energies to motivate specific fixed action patterns. The energy builds up (we might say the animal is becoming predisposed to respond) and is finally released (we might say precipitated) when the sense organs perceive the sign stimuli. If no sign stimuli or releasers are encountered, the energy will continue to build up, finally bursting forth and releasing the behavior in the absence of a releasing stimulus. When

this happens, the behavior is called a **vacuum activity.**

Another principle states that competing action patterns (say both an aggressive pattern and a sexual pattern) can block each other, leading to a build-up and overflow of action-specific energy into other instinct centers, from which the energy is then released. Under these circumstances the animal is said to be engaging in displacement activity. For example, an animal that is neither aggressive nor sexy, may groom (displacement activity) because the energy from the sexual and aggressive instincts has overflowed into the grooming instinct centers. The interpretations of vacuum activity and displacement activity have been among the most controversial aspects of ethological theory. Critics say such a theory explains these behaviors only in an after-the-fact fashion.

Many ethologists have rejected the hydraulic model based on action-specific energy. This model was derived because instinctive behaviors occurred when no stimulus appeared to be present—the so-called vacuum activity just mentioned. The alternate interpretation would be that in fact there is a stimulus present, either in the environment or within the body. The vacuum activity may simply appear to be happening in a vacuum (no stimulus present) because we have not looked closely enough in the environment nor inside the body to find stimuli. To the extent that stimuli are found, vacuum activity is not an appropriate name. And this would mean, of course, that we do not have to postulate a hydraulic system with overflowing action-specific energy. In fact, we wouldn't need an energy concept at all, only the innate action patterns automatically released by a specific stimulus. If we broaden the concept of stimulus to include events or states within the body, such as the levels of various hormones, we can account for most, if not all, instinctive behavior without postulating action-specific energy. The releasing stimulus can then be seen as a specific *configuration* of various stimulus elements, including the internal state of the body. This is the trend in recent ethological theories of instinctive behavior.

Ethology and its revised treatment of instinct is not without its critics and problems. We have already mentioned the problem with displacement and vacuum activity. Another major prob-

Figure 7–5
Important ethological concepts

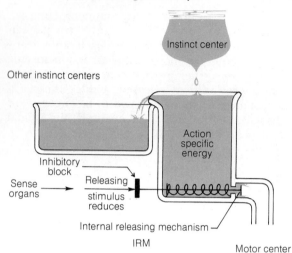

A hen searches frantically for a peeping chick she cannot see but ignores the chick in distress that she can see but not hear. Sound is the releasing signal for her maternal behavior. Can you suggest why sound rather than sight evolved as the releaser here?

Vacuum activity. Dr. Lorenz in his easy chair watching his flycatcher snap at an insect that is not there.

The male flicker's defense of territory instinct is released by the sight of another flicker in his territory provided the intruder has the black "moustache" that distinguishes the male from female. This black patch is the releaser stimulus.

Releasing stimuli are generally simple but specific and conspicuous so that in nature they would not be confused with other characteristics. For example, the herring gull's chicks peck at the red spot on the parents' bill to get food.

Displacement activity. When one instinctual center is blocked from expression its energy may "spill over" to another center to produce displacement behavior. Thus ducks show preening and gulls show grass pulling as displacement behavior.

lem has been the tendency of ethologists to generalize their findings to human beings without adequate evidence. Lorenz, for example, has written a book, *On Aggression*, that implies that aggressiveness in human beings is basically instinctive. The ethologists have been helped in this endeavor by such authors as Desmond Morris *(The Naked Ape)* and Robert Ardrey *(The Territorial Imperative)*, who have taken great liberties in applying instinctive concepts to human beings. Do we have a personal territory that we will instinctively defend against intruders? Are such instincts responsible for world problems such as the Arab-Israeli conflict and war in general? The ideas are certainly provocative and worthy of study, but at present the evidence is barely suggestive, at best.

Sociobiology

A recent theory to explain motivation comes from biology and is known as **sociobiology.** It began to receive widespread attention in 1975 when Edward Wilson, a leading proponent, published the first major text in the field. For sociobiologists, motivation is closely related to instincts in that behavior is viewed as being preprogrammed into the organism. The basic assumption is that the preprogrammed behavior has one and only one function: to ensure the survival of the DNA material which constitutes the genes. All forms of living organisms, including human beings, are seen as survival machines designed to protect and propagate the genes. The genes, in a selfish endeavor to survive. are viewed as motivating and controlling all behavior. Even social behavior in human beings is seen as automatically motivated by the genes in order to ensure their own survival. It is not the survival of the particular organism that is at stake, but of the particular genes in the cells.

Thus, sociobiology starts with the assumption that the primary motivation is purely biological, with the organism being pushed strongly and automatically to behave in ways that will protect the genes. Allowances are made for learning in the system, and human beings are seen as capable of resisting the self-preservation struggle of the genes. But neither are they given much credit in the conflict. Most human

behavior is seen as selfish, designed to protect the genes from extinction—even behavior that looks unselfish or altruistic. In its treatment of what we would call altruistic behavior sociobiology has stirred considerable controversy.

According to sociobiologists, even helping others is usually aimed at protecting our own genes. One would think that preserving the genes would be a matter of reproduction at the level of the species or of the individual organism. This is essentially the Darwinian theory of evolution through natural selection and survival of those individuals that are the fittest. Fitness, according to Darwin, would be mainly a matter of surviving and reproducing. Competition for limited resources and natural selection would "weed out" the unfit, who would not live to reproduce and pass on their genes. In the Darwinian system it is the species or the individual organism that is struggling to survive. In contrast, sociobiological theory says it is not the individual but the genes that are trying to survive. Thus survival is possible through ways other than reproduction—namely, you can help other people who have some of the same genes as you do. Fitness is not simply a matter of self-reproduction but of gene reproduction. To determine the fitness of your genes, then, we have to look not only at your reproduction but at that of all people who share your genes—your relatives. Since we have to include your relatives to determine your fitness, a key concept in the theory is called **inclusive fitness.**

Sociobiologists have relied heavily on studies of animal behavior in their attempt to show that altruistic behavior can be accounted for by the concept of inclusive fitness. In the sociobiological scheme, helping your brothers and sisters—even cousins—to survive ensures the survival of your own genes even if you give your life in helping them. Some studies, in fact, indicate that helping behavior can be predicted by kinship—the closer the kin, the greater the helping. As one sociobiologist said, "I'd give my life for two brothers or eight cousins." Each brother would have one-half his genes in common, and each cousin would have one-eighth in common. Thus saving eight cousins would be preserving the same number of genes represented by two brothers, either of which would be roughly equivalent to the biologist having two children of his own.

Child Altruism: Saving Johnny Not Mommy

What would you do if two tigers escaped from the zoo, and one leaped for your mother, the other for your best friend—and you had a gun with only one bullet? You might say it depends on how you feel about your mother and your friend, but one school of sociobiology (*SN: 11/29/75, p. 347*) says your choice is largely predetermined by genetics.

According to the "kin selection" or "kinship genetics" theory, your altruistic action would be directed toward your mother because social organisms instinctively spring to the defense of relatives before they would do so for nonrelatives. . . . Supposedly, the closer the relative, the more likely it is a person will come to his or her aid. In most cases, a non-related individual would be the recipient of aid when the costs to the benefactor are low, and when the non-related individual is not in competition with a relative's need for aid, according to the kin selection theory.

Although this view has been confirmed in field studies of animals, "To date, no empirical evidence has been gathered either in support or refutation of human altruism based on kin selection," says Harvey J. Ginsburg of Southwest Texas State University, Ginsburg, along with co-researchers Sandra Hense and Brian Bielefeld, recently tested the kin selection theory with 70 children, 3 years to 10 years of age. . . .

The children were asked to rank in order their five favorite relatives and five favorite friends. The youngsters were then given hypothetical danger situations—such as the leaping tigers—for each friend-kin pair.

"The results of the study did not fully support the sociobiological argument of kin selection as an underlying biological mechanism mediating altruistic behavior," reports Ginsburg. In fact, up to the age of 6, children more often (52 percent of the time) chose to save or help a friend rather than a relative. "There was absolutely no pattern to the decision making," Ginsburg adds. "Moms, dads and siblings were thrown to the wolves as often as cousins or other distant relatives."

In marked contrast, children older than 6 opted for saving a friend only 14 percent of the time; in the 9 and 10 year olds, that percentage dropped to near zero. . . .

The results suggest, particularly to opponents of sociobiology, that "devotion to kin is a culturally acquired process, and as such has little to do with any presumed biological origins of altruism," Ginsburg says. "They might also note that the age of the shift occurs at a time when children are entering an expanded social milieu—elementary school—adding further to the claim that loyalty to kin is a learned, reinforced process of childhood socialization and is not a biological phenomenon." . . .

Science News
November 26, 1977

This system is sometimes referred to as *kinship selection* or *kinship genetics* to indicate that relatives with shared genes must be included in the analysis of gene fitness. Kinship genetics, for example, can explain why daughters of insect queens do not themselves reproduce but devote themselves to servicing their queen mother. The genetics is such that all the daughters will have about three-quarters of their genes in common. Thus a particular daughter will reproduce more of her genes if she helps mother to give her more sisters than if she herself produces offspring that will carry only half her genes.

Despite some success with kinship genetics in animal and insect studies, the theory does not seem capable of accounting for all altruistic behavior. Robert Trivers, another leading sociobiologist, has devised the concept of *reciprocal altruism* to account for the altruism among nonrelatives. According to this notion, the individual who helps another really expects something in return, something that eventually, in one way or another, will help his or her own genes to survive. Reciprocal altruism is seen not as something that is learned but as a tendency that has been built in by the genes through natural selection over millions of years. To the extent that helping others leads a person to help in return, the helper will have improved survival chances, so natural selection can operate to pass on the genes of helpful organisms. Thus, reciprocal altruism could be genetic in origin.

Sociobiological theories are, as you can imagine, highly controversial because they cast human beings in an ultimately selfish light. Our motivation is seen as almost purely biological and purely grounded in our genes. It is worthwhile to remember that we are biological creatures with a genetic background that has been subjected to natural selection. However, it remains for sociobiology to prove that we are simply gene-survival machines. The concepts of sociobiology have been useful in understanding some insect and animal behavior, but the application to human behavior (see the article on child altruism) is likely to be limited in effectiveness, simply because it is obvious that so much of our behavior is learned. To be sure, genetics is crucial, but so is learning.

MOTIVATION AS THE SEARCH FOR OPTIMAL AROUSAL

As we have seen, for a long time psychologists emphasized the push aspect of motivation. The key concept was "drive"—our behavior was driven or pushed toward relevant goals. Deprivation led to drive, which led to arousal or energy mobilization, which pushed our behavior until we found the goal. Attaining the goal then satisfied the drive—that is, the goal object reduced the drive and with it the arousal and energy. In short, we were seen as being motivated to keep our arousal level at a minimum, to keep our drives down to nothing.

One of the main problems with this general formulation of motivation as drive is that it is perfectly clear that we do not always try to keep our level of arousal low. Much of the time we behave in precisely the opposite manner—we try to increase our arousal level. To do this, we seek rather than avoid sources of stimulation. On these occasions external sources of stimulation become positive incentives that we will work to expose ourselves to. Think of mountain climbers, daredevils, race-car drivers, and ski jumpers. Consider the things you might say you do for "fun," such as playing bridge or poker, watching TV, reading mystery stories, and playing tennis. A lot of these things have a common feature—they involve exposing yourself to external stimuli that will arouse you. These activities can hardly be described as attempts to keep your arousal level at a minimum. Obviously, then, a theory which implies that we try to keep arousal at a minimum is just plain wrong.

It took some experimental evidence to put drive theory in its proper place. Some psychologists believe that drive theory is needed to account for our biological needs, but others argue that it can be completely dispensed with. In its place has come the notion of arousal level and the crucial assumption that we are motivated to keep our level of arousal at some optimal and nonzero point. Let us take a brief look at some of the studies that support this idea.

The Need for Stimulation

There were several lines of attack on the theory that we seek to minimize stimulation and drive. First, there were the studies of curiosity in animals, mentioned earlier, that showed monkeys will learn new responses and perform old ones just to get a chance to look out of a window to see the laboratory. Drive theory tried to account for this behavior by postulating a curiosity drive, but it never was clear what it was one deprived an animal of and what this did to its body that resulted in the activation of the drive.

In other studies it was demonstrated that monkeys would work on and solve mechanical puzzles left lying around in their cages. The monkeys got no extrinsic rewards for playing with the puzzles or solving them; yet they kept on doing the latch problems over and over. Drive theory responded with the concept of a *manipulation* drive, although again there was no explanation of the manner of drive activation and the underlying source of the drive. And, of course, the only way we knew that animals had a drive to manipulate things was the fact that they manipulated things.

Next were the demonstrations of exploratory behavior. Rats will learn a new response apparently just to have the opportunity to explore. Say you have a two-choice maze in which a left turn leads the rat into another maze that is very complex and a right turn merely leads to the end of the corridor. Rats will learn to turn left apparently just for the opportunity to explore the complex maze, and if you reverse the two choices, the rat will learn to turn right to get to the complex maze. No food or water or sex or any other tangible reward is offered. Drive theory responded to these data with an exploratory drive.

But as drives proliferated, drive theory became less and less useful as an explanation.

Figure 7-6
A sensory deprivation study

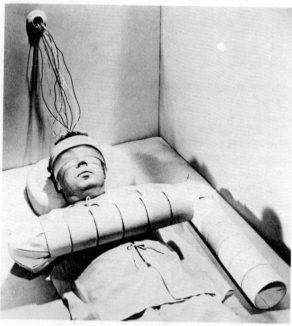

In a series of experiments at McGill University, students were paid $25 a day to stay in a room in which stimulation was reduced to a bare minimum. They wore an eyeshade that reduced vision to a dim haze and arm casts that kept their hands from feeling anything. They were placed in a soundproof room where they could hear nothing but the continual hum of a fan. Not many could stay for more than two days, and some very bizarre behaviors occurred, such as hallucinations.

People would see an organism do something and to explain it would say that there was a drive to do that thing, which explained nothing. Remember the circularity in reasoning about motivation that we discussed earlier.

There were two more, quite startling demonstrations that we are not motivated to keep stimulation at a minimum. First, James Olds and Peter Milner made an extremely important discovery while studying the effects of electrical brain stimulation on behavior. Electrodes had been embedded deep into the brains of rats during surgery, making it possible to deliver electrical stimulation to certain brain areas. What Olds and Milner discovered was that the rats liked it! The rats would work hard to have their brains stimulated in certain areas. It has since

been demonstrated that a rat will press a bar thousands and thousands of times a day to activate brain stimulation. There have been reports that, if the electrodes are in the right place, the rats will spend so much time pressing for stimulation that they do not have time to eat. Correspondingly, there are areas in the brain where the electrical stimulation is not pleasant, but extremely unpleasant. The rats will work hard to *prevent* the stimulation in these areas.

The second demonstration addressed the question of stimulation from the opposite point of view. If we are seeking to keep stimulation at a minimum, then the minimum state must be the most highly desired. What would be the consequences of being in a state of stimulus or sensory deprivation? The answer came from the work of W. H. Bexton, W. Heron, and T. H. Scott. These investigators paid undergraduate students up to $25 a day to participate in a **sensory-deprivation** experiment. Subjects were to remain in a room under conditions designed to minimize sensory stimulation (see Figure 7-6) for as long as they possibly could. The subjects, of course, had adequate food, water, oxygen, heat, and toilet facilities. But every effort was made to cut off all other sensory input. The important result was that no students lasted very long in this environment despite the high rate of pay for those days (about 1953). Some of the students reported bizarre experiences, including hallucinations, after enduring the situation for several hours. All in all, the environment was not a pleasant one. The conclusion is that an environment designed to minimize stimulus input is not something we generally seek out.

Optimal Arousal Level

Studies like those just cited have led to the notion that arousal level is crucially involved in motivation. The idea is that we are motivated to maintain an optimal, presumably moderate, level of arousal. The arousal level at any moment is a direct function of the total amount of stimulation (from both external and internal sources) impinging upon the organism. If the current arousal level is above optimum, the organism will be motivated to reduce the level of stimulation. For example, if you are terribly frightened (and thus above the optimal level of arousal) when watching a scary vampire movie, you might cover your eyes or actually leave the theater during the most frightening parts of the movie to keep the arousal level from getting too extreme. On the other hand, if the current arousal level is below optimum, the organism will be motivated to do things that will increase the level of stimulation. This is why you might have gone to see the vampire movie in the first place.

Note that what is involved here is basically a homeostatic system designed to keep the arousal level within some acceptable, moderate, reasonably optimal range. If we become over-aroused or underaroused, we are motivated to alter things until the arousal level returns to the normal range. One implication of this is that any stimulus, if it is strong enough, will be a source of motivation. It will increase the arousal level so much that the person will be over-aroused, resulting in behavior motivated to eliminate the stimulus or reduce its intensity. An extremely loud and continuous noise, for example, would motivate you to do something about it. Similarly, too little stimulation would result in the arousal level drifting below the optimal range, and you would be motivated to increase stimulation. When you are alone in your room and bored (too little stimulation), you might turn on the radio, or you might leave the room to go watch TV.

What constitutes the optimum arousal level will depend upon the task at hand, as we mentioned in the discussion of the Yerkes-Dodson Law. Listening to loud rock music on the radio might be a source of arousal that would move you toward the optimum if you were alone with nothing to do. However, the same music might move you away from the optimum if you were alone with a lot of difficult mathematics homework to do.

The incentive value of a particular external stimulus also depends on your arousal level at the moment. Listening to a tape-recorded listing of all the closing prices on the New York Stock Exchange might not be something you would want to do if you were already moderately aroused. But subjects in sensory-deprivation experiments, who are underaroused, are often quite happy to get to hear about the daily fortunes of IBM, AT&T, and GM. A quiet walk in the woods might be nice if you were troubled and worried about lots of things (overaroused),

Fireman's Holiday

In the firehouses of Norman Rockwell's bucolic America, firemen passed the hours between alarms playing checkers and showing off the polished brass and bright red trucks to wide-eyed young visitors. But for the volunteer firemen of Genoa, Texas, in suburban Houston, that was not enough. In the past three years, eight bored Genoa firemen have set about 40 fires in abandoned buildings and grass fields. As soon as the blazes were going, the arsonists would dash back to the firehouse and rush off to put out their own fires.

The Genoa firemen were quite busy until they made the mistake of setting fire to a barn owned by the brother of a Houston fire department official. An investigation of the blaze led to the Genoa firehouse, and the overeager fire fighters were exposed. Explained one of the firemen charged last week with arson: "We'd hang around the station on the night shift without a thing to do. We just wanted to get the red light flashing and the bells clanging."

Time
December 27, 1971

There is strong evidence that lack of stimulation can be a source of motivation designed to increase the level of stimulation. Here is an example of this principle in action.

but it might not be so nice if you were lonely and bored with the world.

MOTIVATION AS A PERSONALITY CHARACTERISTIC

When we think about human behavior and the factors that motivate it, we are likely to conclude that instincts, biological needs for food and water, a need for optimal stimulation levels, and related factors do not account for very much. Certainly our behavior does not look much like the fixed action patterns characteristic of instinctive behaviors. Moreover, most of us are fortunate enough to have ready access to adequate food and water. True, some of the things we do are probably motivated by these needs, but these behaviors seem to be rather minor and infrequent aspects of our behavior. Maybe we do most of the things we do largely

Figure 7–7
Measuring human motives and needs

The object in the TAT is to make up a short story about what is happening in a picture like the one above. You might try it with this picture. Tell in your story (1) what is happening and who the people are, (2) what led up to the situation shown in the picture, (3) what the people in the picture are thinking and feeling, and (4) what will happen in the future. Does your story tell you anything about yourself and your motives and needs?

for fun and excitement so as to maintain an optimal arousal level. But isn't there a lot more to human behavior than just maintaining optimal arousal?

In an attempt to answer questions about the motivation for uniquely human behaviors, psychologists have offered answers that treat the concept of motivation as a personality characteristic. Like motivation, personality is a concept that is used to account for variability in behavior, and many personality theorists have made motivational concepts central in describing personality. This is rather like saying that your personality can be described by describing your motives or, more specifically, your needs. In short, we might say, "You are what you need." If you need to be with people, we say you are friendly, extroverted, and gregarious. If you need to work hard in order to beat out the next man or woman, we say you are hard-driving or energetic. To some extent, then, a description of the things you need is a description both of your personality and your motivations. In other words, to understand human

motivation completely, we will have to understand personality.

Henry Murray's Work on Psychogenic Needs

The pioneer worker in this field was Henry Murray. For him the concept of need was central to personality, and he spent a great deal of time attempting to objectify the measurement of needs and to identify the various needs that human beings have. He is perhaps most famous for having devised the Thematic Apperception Test (TAT) with Christiana Morgan (see Figure 7–7). In this test, the subject is shown a picture and asked to make up a story about what is going on in the picture. The basic idea is that the subject "projects" into the story his or her own needs, and so a careful analysis of the stories will tell a great deal about the person who made them up. Murray also developed questionnaires for assessing needs in a more direct way. His intensive scrutiny of a small group of subjects led him to believe that there are many independent human needs. Table 7–2 lists 20 representative needs that Murray felt were present in various degrees in each of us. This list has been expanded and modified somewhat in his later writings, but it should give you a good idea of what Murray sees as the needs of humanity. The listing is primarily of the *psychogenic* (psychological or learned) *needs*, as opposed to what Murray called the *viscerogenic needs*, such as needs for food, water, and oxygen.

Murray made another important point, namely, that each person has a hierarchy of needs; some needs are more important than others, with the viscerogenic needs being most important because they are so directly tied to survival. The needs will be satisfied in order of their priority for each person—if two incompatible needs arise, the stronger need, which is higher in the hierarchy, will be satisfied first. If you need water and you need aggression, chances are you will drink first and fight later.

Finally, Murray also recognized that motivation is partly a function of environmental factors, which he called *press*. You may have, as a personality characteristic, a strong need for achievement (*n* achievement); particular environmental situations will arouse this need. For example, seeing a friend beat someone in a chess game might arouse your own achievement motive and cause you to challenge your friend.

TABLE 7–2   **Twenty Human Needs Identified by Henry Murray**

Need	Brief Definition
N Abasement	To submit passively to external force. To accept injury, blame, criticism, punishment. To admit inferiority, error, wrongdoing, or defeat.
N Achievement	To accomplish something difficult. To master, manipulate, or organize physical objects, human beings, or ideas as rapidly and as independently as possible. To surpass others and excel oneself.
N Affiliation	To draw near and enjoyably cooperate or reciprocate with an allied other. To adhere and remain loyal to a friend.
N Aggression	To overcome opposition forcefully. To revenge an injury. To attack, injure, or kill another.
N Autonomy	To get free, shake off restraint, break out of confinement. To resist coercion and restriction. To be independent and free to act according to impulse.
N Counteraction	To master or make up for a failure by restriving. To overcome weaknesses, to repress fear. To efface a dishonor by action. To search for obstacles and difficulties to overcome.
N Defendance	To defend the self against assault, criticism, and blame. To conceal or justify a misdeed, failure, or humiliation.
N Deference	To admire and support a superior. To praise, honor, or eulogize. To conform to custom.
N Dominance	To control one's human environment. To influence or direct the behavior of others by suggestion, seduction, persuasion, or command. To dissuade, restrain, prohibit.
N Exhibition	To excite, amaze, fascinate, entertain, shock, intrigue, amuse, or entice others.
N Harmavoidance	To avoid pain, physical injury, illness, and death.
N Infavoidance	To avoid humiliation. To leave embarrassing situations or avoiding conditions that may lead to belittlement. To refrain from action because of the fear of failure.
N Nurturance	To give sympathy to and gratify the needs of a helpless other. To feed, help, support, console, protect, comfort, nurse, heal.
N Order	To put things in order. To achieve cleanliness, arrangement, organization, balance, neatness, tidiness, and precision.
N Play	To act for "fun" without further purpose. To like to laugh and make a joke of everything. To seek enjoyable relaxation of stress.
N Rejection	To exclude, abandon, expel, or remain indifferent to an inferior other.
N Sentience	To seek and enjoy sensuous impressions.
N Sex	To form and further an erotic relationship. To have sexual intercourse.
N Succorance	To be nursed, supported, sustained, surrounded, protected, loved, advised, guided, indulged, forgiven, consoled. To always have a supporter.
N Understanding	To ask or answer general questions. To be interested in theory. To speculate, formulate abstractly, analyze, and generalize.

This would be a case of press for achievement (*p* achievement). Seeing a picture of a juicy steak would constitute *p* food, which, along with your viscerogenic need for food (*n* food), would motivate you to eat something. So motivation for Murray is a result of the combined action of personal needs (characteristics of people) and press (characteristics of the environment). We would classify the needs as predisposing factors and the press as precipitating factors.

The human needs we will discuss in this section are all based on a model like Murray's. During psychological development, each person acquires (learns) certain psychological needs. Different people acquire different strengths of the various needs and thus different hierarchies of needs. Initially, the psychological needs develop from the inherited, innate, biological needs, but later these needs somehow become independent of the biological needs, and the goals that satisfy these needs become ends in themselves.

For example, we begin with a biological need for food and water, which for an infant is satisfied by other people, mainly the parents. The infant is almost entirely dependent on other people and is likely to be happiest when other

Abraham Maslow and the Hierarchy of Human Needs

The psychologist most often associated with the idea of a hierarchy of needs, arranged in order of importance, is Abraham Maslow. His writings have had tremendous impact in the modern movement known as humanistic psychology. Indeed he was one of the founders of this movement. Maslow grouped the various needs (like those postulated by Henry Murray) into five categories and arranged them in the order shown in Figure 7–8. With the exception of the highest need, self-actualization, the needs are self-explanatory.

It was his concept of self-actualization that made Maslow such an important figure in the humanistic psychology movement. Self-actualization is conceived of as a need to fulfill oneself, "to become whatever one is capable of becoming." It is a need to develop and utilize one's talents, abilities, and potential fully. It is a need that very few people have ever satisfied, and Maslow spent a great deal of his time studying people (such as Eleanor Roosevelt and Albert Einstein) who he thought had become self-actualized.

The needs higher in the hierarchy will emerge only as the lower ones become satisfied. We will not need love-belongingness and self-esteem if we have not first satisfied our physiological and security needs. If we live in fear for our safety or in anxiety about where our next meal will come from, we will have no need for love and self-esteem. In our society, where safety and

Figure 7–8
Maslow's hierarchy of needs

According to Maslow's motivational theory, human needs form a hierarchy, and lower needs must be satisfied before higher needs are felt.

security and physiological needs are reasonably well satisfied for everyone, we appear to be motivated largely by needs for love and self-esteem.

Maslow felt that our inability to satisfy these needs was the major cause of neurotic psychopathology in this country. Ideally, of course, a society would provide for all the lower needs and allow for the emergence of the need for self-actualization in everyone. Although few people may ever fully satisfy this need, everyone should be striving at this level in the pyramid, free of the lower needs. In fact, for Maslow, such persons are no longer "striving" but are "being" — being themselves rather than being people who are seeking something external to themselves.

people are around, fulfilling the needs for nourishment, playing with and entertaining him or her, and so on. Because of this kind of continued exposure, the people who tend the infant become secondary reinforcers (see Chapter 4), having been continuously associated with the baby's general state of well-being. As secondary reinforcers, people then become goal objects

themselves, and the child will want to be with people and will want these people to care for and like him or her. The child will behave in ways designed to win the approval and affection of people. After a while, we might conclude that the child has developed a need to be with people and win the approval of people (*n* affiliation in Murray's list) and a need to be nursed, loved, and protected by people (*n succorance*). If the people in the child's life themselves value and reward achievement, the child may develop a strong need to achieve (*n achievement*) in order to win adult approval.

Although this is merely a speculative example, you can see how three of the human needs that Murray identified might develop and be learned by the child. Of course, different children have different experiences and different parents, who themselves have different needs and different values. Out of these differences in environmental circumstances each child learns a different set of priorities. Each child develops the human needs to various degrees or strengths and emerges into adulthood with his or her own hierarchy of psychological needs. It is this variation in the strengths of the various needs that largely accounts for the variation in adult personality, that is, for the fact that one person is a hard-driving, success-seeking fighter and another is an easygoing, introverted pacifist. We shall now turn our attention to some of the specific human needs that psychologists have found most interesting.

The Need for Achievement

Largely because of the efforts of David McClelland and J. W. Atkinson, the need for achievement (*n ach* in their shorthand) has been studied intensively. These investigators elaborated on Murray's TAT techniques for measuring needs and developed sophisticated scoring systems for the stories that subjects told in response to the carefully selected pictures. Their attention turned first to *n ach*, the need to excel, overcome obstacles, attain a high standard, accomplish the difficult. In the United States, we are so achievement oriented that for us motivation really means achievement motivation.

After developing a TAT scoring system for *n ach*, McClelland and Atkinson demonstrated that they could arouse the achievement motive (precipitate it) simply by telling subjects in an experiment that they had failed. The subjects took a group of tests and were told that they had done poorly and then were asked to tell TAT stories. The experience with failure aroused or precipitated the achievement motive, as measured by an increase in the number of achievement themes and elements in the stories. These psychologists went on to demon- strate that individuals vary in their need for achievement and that each person has a relatively stable level of *n ach* over time.

Performance Differences Due to *n* Ach

Many studies have shown that people with high *n ach* as measured by the TAT procedure do better than people with low *n ach* on a variety of experimental laboratory tasks, such as solving anagrams and doing arithmetic problems. It has also been demonstrated that high *n ach* people perform better in school than low *n ach* people with comparable intelligence. In the business world, high *n ach* people advance further than low *n ach* people with the same training and opportunity for advancement.

As suggested earlier, achievement motivation is apparently developed during childhood and is determined largely by the cultural and parental emphasis placed on achievement. These values are transmitted to the children during their socialization into the culture. One study, for example, demonstrated that mothers who themselves were high in *n ach* behaved differently toward their children than mothers low in *n ach*. High *n ach* mothers demanded that their children become independent and self-sufficient at an earlier age than low *n ach* mothers. Low *n ach* mothers were more protective of their children and placed greater restrictions on them for longer periods of time.

Success and Failure

More recently, it has been suggested that *n ach* is not a simple unidimensional personality characteristic, but a complex combination of factors. Atkinson, for example, has suggested that at least two factors are involved in achievement, a *need for success* and a counteracting *fear of failure*, and that different people have different combinations of these two tendencies. He has also stressed the importance of the situational factors operating at any given time, particularly the probability or chances of success or failure on a particular task and the incentive value of success or failure. If the task at hand is so difficult that nobody could possibly do it, then failing is nothing to be ashamed of and failing would have no negative incentive value. Likewise, if the task is so easy that anybody can do it, then achieving success is not worth much; success has little positive incentive value. Also, the goal itself (independent of the probability

Attitude Change Suggested for Women To Rise to Top

AP

ANN ARBOR, Mich. — Achievement-oriented women who still see competing against men as unfeminine cannot reach their potential as managers in business, say two management researchers in Ann Arbor, Mich.

More women need to be trained for managerial positions, but attitudes which keep women from moving ahead also must be changed, say Theodore T. Herbert and Edward B. Yost.

Herbert is an associate professor at the University of Akron and a member of the Academy of Management. Yost is a graduate student at Ohio State University.

Both sexes are strongly motivated to set and reach goals when they are at school age, the researchers say, with girls achieving more, on the average, than boys.

But by the time they enter college, women score lower in self-esteem and self-confidence than men, the authors say in an analysis in "Human Resource Management," published by the University of Michigan Graduate School of Business Administration.

Social pressure forces many women to conform to traditional roles, just because they view success as unfeminine, the researchers report.

They say this is a major reason why the number of female managers hasn't kept pace with males. The remedy, they say, is to eliminate role stereotypes through education.

Along with the slow pace of training women, the business world has been slow to accept women as managers and groom them for higher level positions, say Herbert and Yost.

"Training women in managerial skills is of little value if they aren't allowed to demonstrate their skills on the job or aren't rewarded with commensurate promotions," the researchers caution.

The Denver Post
June 1, 1978

A study conducted in 1969 by Matina Horner indicated that women are less motivated to succeed than men. The explanation offered was that women fear success because it conflicts with the traditional female role. As this clipping indicates, attitudes have changed, and more women today are achievement-oriented.

of getting it) has a positive incentive value that will determine the amount of motivation to achieve it. A person high in *n* ach will not indiscriminately attempt to achieve every conceivable goal. He or she might work very hard to achieve a goal of great value, but expend little effort to achieve a prize of no value.

A study conducted by Matina Horner (1969) produced some interesting results about success and failure. She found that women tended to be less motivated to succeed than men. One hypothesis, and a controversial one at that, is that women have a *fear of success*. The reason is that success conflicts with the traditional female role. A woman high in *n* ach may find her goal unacceptable to society. Therefore, to avoid this conflict situation, some women unconsciously shun success. Of course, times have changed (but are in need of more change; see clipping), and all women do not fear success, which is acceptable in today's world. Finally, men, we want to point out that recent research has shown that some men also display a fear of success.

The Need for Affiliation

We are social creatures who derive much of our satisfaction from other people. We join clubs, sororities, fraternities, Weight-Watchers, and Gamblers Anonymous. We try hard to make friends and often become very dependent upon them. Henry Murray would say we have a need for affiliation (*n* aff), and that like *n* ach, this functions to motivate us, making particular goals, such as being admitted to the local civic club, positive incentives. Likewise, other events, such as anything that would cause the defection of friends, will serve as negative incentives to the person with high *n* aff. Such a person will avoid hurting the feelings of his or her friends or avoid doing things that those friends would find shocking.

Elizabeth French has developed a special set of test items for measuring and distinguishing between *n* aff and *n* ach. She has shown that subjects high in *n* aff perform better on a simple task than subjects low in *n* aff under extremely pleasant and relaxed conditions designed to avoid arousing *n* ach instead of *n* aff. French concluded that the desire on the part of the high *n* aff subjects to please the experimenter, cooperate, and be friendly is what motivated them to perform better. In another

One outcome of the women's movement is that women are moving into more management jobs in business. They have learned that it is now acceptable to pursue their personal need for achievement.

experiment, French studied how people high in *n* ach and *n* aff go about picking partners to work with. People high in *n* ach choose partners who are competent at performing the task at hand (rather than choosing friends for partners), presumably because their goal is to succeed at the task. In contrast, people high in *n* aff tend to choose their friends as partners, as opposed to selecting partners on the basis of ability. When choosing sides for a game of volleyball, football, or charades, do you pick your friends for your team or the people who you believe will be the best players?

Like *n* ach, *n* aff is conceived of as a personality predisposition, presumably learned in childhood and possessed in varying degrees by different people. Like *n* ach, *n* aff is also subject to precipitation by the current circumstances. A person high in *n* aff will not be motivated by the goal of affiliating with a person or group of people who is extremely unpleasant and disliked. Instead, such people will be motivated by a friendly request to cooperate, to help out for the common good, given that the request comes from a person or group that has positive incentive value.

Finally, it has been suggested that the desire to affiliate ourselves with others is not really a need, but that instead affiliation is a goal for some other need, either our need to escape or avoid anxiety or to have others approve of us, known as a need for social approval, our next topic.

The Need for Social Approval

Perhaps the most fundamental purely psychological need is the need for social approval—the need to have others approve of us and our actions. It is obvious, for example, that the need

To Precipitate, Appeal to the Predisposition

We have emphasized in this chapter that motivation is a joint product of predisposition and precipitation. In the area of human motivation, this joint action is beautifully illustrated by an experiment done by Elizabeth G. French. From a large population, she selected large numbers of two types of people—achievers and affiliators. The achievers were selected because they scored high on n ach and low on n aff, meaning they were predisposed toward achievement but not affiliation. Just the opposite was true for the affiliators—they were high on n aff and low on n ach, meaning they were predisposed toward affiliation, not achievement.

French then set groups of four achievers and groups of four affiliators to work on a group problem-solving task that required the people to work together to get the correct solutions. The precipitating factor was introduced in the form of feedback to the groups about how they were doing. French used two different feedback techniques: (1) by telling the groups that they were working efficiently, achieving many correct responses, she could "appeal" to the achievement motive as a way to precipitate increased motivation to perform; or (2) by telling the groups that they were working well together, cooperating, she could appeal to the affiliation motive. But giving an achievement appeal should work only if the group is composed of people predisposed to achievement—it should fail with a group predisposed to affiliation. Likewise, the affiliation appeal should work only with the groups composed of people

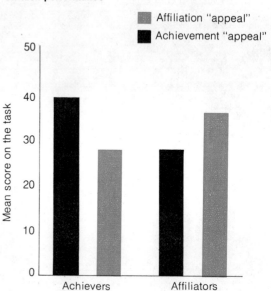

Figure 7–9
Effects of the interaction of motivation and feedback on task performance

high in n aff and not with groups with high n ach members.

Her results, shown in Figure 7–9, confirmed these predictions. When the work group was an achievement group (all people high in n ach), performance on the task was better with the achievement feedback than with the affiliation feedback. Just the opposite was true with the affiliation groups (all people high in n aff). In short, an affiliation appeal will not precipitate much behavior in someone with a low level of predisposition toward affiliation (low n aff). Likewise, an achievement appeal will not work on people who are low in n ach. The motivation is a joint function of the predisposition and the precipitation.

to affiliate with others could be based on a need for approval. Also, one could argue that the need to achieve is ultimately based on a need to win recognition and approval from others. If others did not approve of striving to achieve,

then people probably would not strive to achieve. The cross-cultural and family differences in achievement motivation suggest that approval from others is an important factor in determining the strength of the achievement motive.

There is almost no limit to what some people will do to get certain other people to approve of and therefore like them. Conversely, such people will often do anything to avoid creating the circumstances that will lead others to disapprove of and therefore dislike them.

The need for approval is an important motive for understanding much of our social behavior. Consider, for example, why people tend to be conformists, to do what others do or what they think others would do. The pioneer investigators of the need for social approval are Douglas Crowne and David Marlowe. Together these investigators have developed a test to measure social desirability, the need to be liked by others or to be socially desirable. They show that people who score high and low on the test and thus presumably have high and low motives for approval sometimes behave in vastly different ways.

In one experiment the subjects were asked to spend 25 minutes doing an incredible task: taking 12 spools and one at a time putting them into a small box, then emptying the box and starting over again. Afterward Crowne and Marlowe asked the subjects how much they enjoyed the task. Subjects with high-approval motives, believe it or not, said they enjoyed the task, more so at least than subjects with low-approval motives. In addition, high need-for-approval subjects said they learned more from the task, rated the experiment as more scientifically important, and had a greater desire to participate in similar experiments than low need-for-approval subjects. Would you pack and repack spools (and say that you enjoyed doing it) in order to gain the approval of the person who asked you to do it?

In another study Crowne and Marlowe showed subjects slides containing two clusters of dots, one clearly larger than the other. The subject was asked to indicate which cluster was larger, a very easy task indeed, except that there were other "subjects" in the room (actually not subjects but assistants to Crowne and Marlowe) who lied and said the wrong answer before the real subject could speak. The results showed that on 59 percent of these trials where the confederates lied, the high need-for-approval subjects lied also. The low need-for-approval subjects conformed and lied only 34 percent of the time. These results show that subjects with high- and low-approval motives

behave differently, and they suggest that conformity (in this case, agreeing with the judgment of others) comes from the need to win the approval of others. How much of your own behavior is motivated by a desire to be desirable?

A Final Note of Caution

The work on human motives as personality traits is very appealing and seems to contribute greatly to our understanding of human behavior. However, we must remember that there are pitfalls (see the section on dispositional theories of personality in Chapter 9). With a long list of needs, you can account for just about everything by saying that the person did what he or she did to satisfy such and such a need. It is the same problem we encountered with the long list of instincts that were once used to explain everything, or the long list of drives. A long list of needs may not be as much of an improvement as it first appears. We must remember that there will have to be independent ways of defining and measuring these needs to avoid circular explanations.

This is why we investigate ways to measure human needs with various kinds of tests, such as the TAT storytelling technique. But there is still a lot of room for improvement. The tests are not highly reliable, and they may be measuring other things besides the intended need. Another problem is that people are not as consistent in their behavior as such theories imply. For example, a person with a high need for approval does not always behave in a way designed to get approval. This may just mean that we have a long way to go in understanding the precipitating conditions for behavior; but it may also mean that it is not very useful to speak of enduring, stable traits, such as a high need for approval. Behavior may be so much a consequence of the precipitating circumstances that personality predispositions are only modestly useful in predicting what a person will do in any given situation.

Note that most of the studies we have talked about in this section are basically correlational in character. If we pick out people who are high and low in achievement motivation and see that the highs do better on some task than the lows, we merely have a correlation between *n* ach and performance. This does not mean the *n* ach

differences caused the performance differences. Perhaps high *n* ach people are more intelligent, or better coordinated, or stronger, or whatever, than low *n* ach people. If so, the performance difference could be due to that factor and not to *n* ach. It is not easy to reach unequivocal conclusions in this complex area of human motivation. Thus, we must remember to be cautious.

SEXUAL MOTIVATION

Sexual behavior, particularly human sexual behavior, is motivated in many different complex ways. Any occurrence of sexual behavior is likely to be motivated by more than one factor, and the motivating factors will change from one instance to the next. To understand sexual motivation then, we will have to borrow from all the concepts we have discussed in this chapter. Let us briefly review these factors and see how they apply to sexual behavior.

First, we talked about drives and incentives as the pushing and pulling forces, respectively, in motivating behavior. Some aspects of sexual behavior can be understood in terms of a sex drive, although it is clear that sexual deprivation does not have the same kinds of devastating effects that food or water deprivation have. From the incentive point of view, we hardly need to tell anyone that sexual behavior can be incredibly pleasurable, and thus the opportunity to engage in sexual intercourse can have enormous positive incentive value. People are motivated to do all sorts of things in order to gain access to this incentive. We feel that predisposi-

tion and precipitation more accurately capture the full range of motivational phenomena. Much of sexual behavior can be understood by looking for factors that will predispose us toward engaging in sexual behavior, and then examining the environment for the precipitating stimuli.

What about the biological basis of motivation? Sexual behavior is clearly grounded in the endocrine system we discussed in Chapter 2. However, this strong biological regulation of sexual behavior by hormone balance applies mainly to the sexual behavior of animals. Human beings have largely, although not completely, freed themselves from this regulation. Hormone therapy for sexual behavior problems serves as a good reminder to us that human sexual behavior is not all psychological. The explanation for animal sexual behavior lies primarily in the concept of instinct and in the fixed-action patterns described by ethologists. These patterns run off "automatically" when the animal is properly predisposed (probably by the endocrine balance), and the fixed-action pattern is triggered by an appropriate releasing stimulus. While human sexual behavior seems largely independent of instinctual motivation, the theory of sociobiology reminds us that many behaviors are motivated by the sexual need to reproduce and pass on one's genes. However, there is good reason to question the applicability of this theory to human sexual behavior.

Next we considered behavior as being motivated by the general need for stimulation to maintain the optimal arousal level. Sexual behavior is obviously arousing, and much of human sexual behavior may be motivated by such

"I can go two weeks without <u>water</u>, but <u>sex</u> is an entirely different matter!"

Playboy, February 1969. Reproduced by special permission of PLAYBOY Magazine. Copyright © 1969 by Playboy.

needs. Recall our discussion of the pleasure centers in the brain. The intense pleasure from sexual gratification may come about from such pleasure centers. Human sexual behavior appears to be very heavily dominated by the incentive aspects of the situation, the intense pleasure one experiences.

Finally, we turned our attention to motivation as a personality characteristic. Obviously, the need for achievement, the need for affiliation, and the need for social approval play a very important role in human sexual behavior. There clearly are situations in which sexual behavior is treated as an achievement, a game in which people try to "score" points—a rather sad commentary, but nevertheless often true. Equally questionable is the use of sexual behavior as a way of satisfying a need for approval, where sex is "handed out" as a bribe to win approval. On the more positive side, the need for affiliation brings people together to mutually enjoy each other, to fall in love, and to share the beauty and pleasure of mutual sexual fulfillment.

In summary, sexual behavior is motivated partly by a drive and partly by incentive; we are predisposed to engage in sexual behavior and there are precipitating stimuli; sexual behavior is deeply rooted in the physiology of the endocrine system and the biology of instincts and the need to reproduce. However, it is also intensely pleasurable and arousing and, in human beings, is influenced by psychogenic needs that are acquired by socialization into one's culture. All of these concepts are helpful in understanding sexual motivation.

Impotence Psychological, But Men Often Deny That

Darell Sifford

They're setting up a sleep clinic at Jefferson Medical College in Philadelphia. But it's not to teach people how to get more mileage out of their sleep. It's designed to help determine if the cause of a man's impotence is physical or psychological.

The head of the clinic, Dr. Paul Jay Fink, professor and chairman of the department of psychiatry and human behavior, says that 90 percent of all impotence is psychological but that many men deny this and insist with every breath that the problem is physical.

The sleep clinic, Dr. Fink says, helps cut through the denial mechanisms and enables appropriate treatment to be started much quicker.

In an interview Dr. Fink, 44, said men tend to want to blame their impotence on physical problems because "this removes all responsibility" from them. "If impotence is caused by diabetes, trauma, surgery or drugs, then it's not their fault. But if impotence is in the mind, then they have to take responsibility and this is frightening to the average man."

This may surprise you but, Dr. Fink says, a man is a better candidate to be cured if his impotence is psychological rather than physical in origin.

"There's an assumption that if it's 'just' organic, it can be fixed and you'll be OK. But we find that organic impotence is less fixable than psychological impotence." . . .

Dr. Fink says a lot of problems could be fixed right in the bedroom if husbands and wives had better relationships, if wives were more understanding, warmer and more seductive.

"But often what happens is that a man feels miserable about it and doesn't do anything until his wife gives him an ultimatum—either get it fixed or end the marriage." This puts added pressure on the husband and makes what could be an easy problem to solve much more difficult, Dr. Fink says.

After the sleep clinic determines if the problem is physical or psychological, then treatment can be started. For psychological impotence, Dr. Fink says, a "modified Masters and Johnson" approach is used. Basically this therapy goes to the point of learning to interact with the partner in a non-pressure, non-performing situation. . . .

Boulder (Colo.) Daily Camera
July 19, 1978

Freud's Theory

In its original form Sigmund Freud's theory of sexual development (see also Chapters 8 and 9) is based heavily on instinctual and drive-reductionistic concepts. Its basic component is the concept of ever-occurring sexual energies. Freud's theory has had and continues to have a profound impact on sexual belief, partially because it is one of the few really complete theories of sexual development and partially because of its historical position. It was presented near the end of the Victorian era (one of the most antisexual eras of history) and served as a revolutionary breakaway from the sexual attitudes of that period.

While Freud postulated a number of sources of drive-related energies, it was the sex energies or *libido* which were most powerful. This sex energy, along with hostility and aggression, account for most human motivation.

Two ideas are central to Freud's explanation of sexual behavior: unconscious mental processes and infantile sexuality. The id is composed of the basic biological drives (including the libido), and its contents are unconscious to the individual. These id drives, Freud postulated, seek a goal of pleasure. At the other end of the scale is the superego. A primarily conscious force comprised of learned moral and social concepts, the task of the superego is basically to block the pleasure-seeking id. The ego mediates between the id and the superego.

Freud's second concept, that of infantile sexuality, postulates that the instinctual id forces operate through a series of developmental stages beginning at birth and continuing through puberty. During this infantile development process a blueprint is established or "wired" into the individual for future personality and sexual patterns. In each of the three major stages of development the pleasure-seeking id forces center in a particular body area (the mouth, anus, or genitals). In each stage a particular task, usually in conflict with the id forces, must be completed. (These stages are described in detail in Chapter 9). An end product of the compromises reached among instinctual id forces and ego and superego forces, this blueprint will be activated during puberty.

Another major conceptualization of sexual motivation based in biological concepts is represented by the work of C. S. Ford and F. A. Beach, who studied sexual behavior across several cultures and species of animals. Beginning with a general thesis that a fundamental drive to act sexually exists, they then assumed that any behavior common to human beings and other animals was probably genetically based. Eventually Ford and Beach concluded that four types of sexual behaviors were probably instinctual in that they occurred among all primates, including humans. These include coitus, masturbation, homosexual activity, and methods of attracting a sexual partner.

Learning Theory

During the past two decades the increasingly predominant view has been away from biology to learning as an explanation of human sexual behavior. Research suggests that the higher up the phylogenetic scale one goes, the less evidence there is of hormonal or other biological controls in sexual patterns and the more evidence there is of learned sexual behavior. No specific theory of sexual development based on learning theory really exists. We must assume that the same general principles would apply to sexual learning as well as to other types of learning. We will not attempt to consider sexuality from all of the possible theoretical frameworks, but instead examine a few key concepts general to most learning theories as they apply to sexuality.

Consider the operant conditioning paradigm (see Chapter 4). Events become established as behavior patterns when they are associated with some form of reward or reinforcer. For instance, suppose that a child becomes sexually stimulated while pressing against an object, or perhaps climbing a tree. While the sexual feeling is not fully understood, the experience was pleasant. The child may attempt to replicate the experience, possibly using the hands. Eventually the activity is carried far enough to experience masturbation and orgasm. In each instance the pleasure obtained reinforces the activity, and a habit or pattern is established. As further learning occurs, the sexual activities become associated with particular settings (for example, darkness, being in bed) and social awareness (parental and peer attitudes).

The learning theory approach assumes that change continues throughout life even though

Liberating Women from Freud

Feminists consider Sigmund Freud one of history's leading male chauvinist pigs. No wonder. The master taught that women are far more masochistic and narcissistic than men and more prone to neurosis, that they are rigid and unchangeable by the age of 30, and unable to equal the high moral character of men. These doleful views flow from a single Freudian concept: penis envy. As Freud saw it, female identity grows from an infant girl's shocking discovery that she lacks a penis. Later, in about the third year of life, she carries this sense of castration and inferiority into the Oedipal cycle, blaming the mother for the loss of the penis, turning to the father as a love object, and converting the wish for a penis into a wish for a child. Childbearing and most of women's aspirations are thus, per Freud, attempts to compensate for the missing male organ, and penis envy becomes "the bedrock" of women's unconscious frustrations throughout life.

Despite dissent from a few of his early followers, Freud's views quickly hardened into psychoanalytic dogma. Now, under pressure from feminists, orthodox Freudians seem to be giving ground. "Anatomy is not destiny," says Psychoanalyst Robert Stoller, one of the voices for change. "Destiny is what people make of anatomy."

Doomed Castrates

Indeed, in a forthcoming special issue on female psychology, the *Journal of the American Psychoanalytic Association* reveals a willingness to revise Freud. One common refrain among the writers: male prejudice and parental expectations create many more problems for women than Freudianism has so far acknowledged. Writes Virginia Clower of Washington, D.C.: "To the extent that our society continues to educate mothers and fathers who see their female children as biological castrates doomed to inferior psychological, moral and social development, we will continue to produce women who regard themselves as second class." . . .

Though these revisions are small and perhaps arcane to the nonanalyst, they erode the idea that penis envy is the dominant, devastating factor in female experience. In fact, Clower suggests that there will be more changes when Freudians digest the mass of data accumulated in recent years about sexuality and child behavior. Says she: "Today, more than 40 years after Freud's original propositions, we are still talking about penis envy, female castration and woman's masculinity complex. Freud revised his theories many times as he accumulated new data and reached fresh insights. Contemporary analysts should do no less."   Time
January 17, 1977

---

early repeated experiences may be most influential. The general application of learning principles to sexual behavior is increased through the use of the processes of generalization and discrimination. In the process of generalization, a particular stimulus can elicit a response conditioned to a related but different stimulus. Thus learning to associate sexual feeling with one particular member of the opposite sex can generalize out to all or most members of the opposite sex. Discrimination operates in opposition to generalization and allows us to limit the objects to which we respond sexually in order not to be aroused by an ever-increasing field of stimuli.

In addition to direct experiential learning, social-learning models (see Chapter 9) suggest that we can learn vicariously what behaviors will be rewarding. Thus the media could present strong models for appropriate and rewarding sexual behavior, which are then imitated.

Most social-psychological explanations of sexual behavior tend to be minimally elaborated extensions of a particular school of personality theory, usually with a heavy emphasis on the dynamics of interpersonal relationships. Such theories see sexuality as a part of some process such as Maslow's self-actualization (see Box on p. 260) and do not explain its development. One exception to this is a fairly well-developed theory advanced by Ken Hardy which utilizes both learning theory and social-psychological concepts. He postulates that we move toward some specific sexual behavior because we have learned to expect that in so doing we will produce some positive change in our lives. And it is the expectation of positive change that is the basis of sexual motivation.

Hardy believes that young children build tentative sets of positive expectations regarding simple sexual activity such as hugging and kissing through observing apparently positive re-

Motivational Dilemmas

A person is in a state of conflict when he or she has two or more competing motives, all of which cannot be satisfied. There are two basic kinds of motives: *approach motives* refer to situations in which there is a reward or positive incentive to be gained if the person approaches the goal; *avoidance motives* refer to cases in which the incentive is negative—it is an object, event, or state of affairs that is unpleasant and is to be avoided. All cases of conflict between motives can be described in terms of approach and avoidance:

1. *Approach-approach conflict:* In this case two positive incentives exist but cannot both be attained—one or the other must be chosen. An example is trying to decide whether you should spend the evening at a movie or watching a favorite TV program. An approach-approach conflict is usually easily resolved (you can see the movie tomorrow), unless the motives for both incentives are very strong and the goals are indeed incompatible.

2. *Avoidance-avoidance conflict:* This conflict results when the choice is between two negative alternatives or incentives. For example, one may have to decide which of two dull courses to study for tonight. The most distinctive feature of avoidance-avoidance conflict is that it is usually difficult to resolve, especially if both incentives are strongly negative. Often we fail to make any decision at all, attempting instead to remove ourselves from the conflict situation, for example, by watching TV and not studying at all.

3. *Approach-avoidance conflict:* Frequently a goal or incentive has both positive and negative aspects, resulting in both approach and avoidance responses. For example, foods that you find particularly tasty may cause weight gain and cavities. In this type of conflict, "distance" from the incentive appears to play an important role. At great distances, the negative aspects do not seem as important as the positive ones, and so you move toward the goal, for example, by making a dental appointment for six months in the future. As the time for the appointment gets nearer, however, the negative aspects increase in strength and may surpass the positive ones, causing you to retreat from the goal (you break the appointment). The reaction of two different patients to this approach-avoidance conflict is shown opposite.

---

sponses to these activities in parents, older siblings, and media presentations. Children then move toward testing these simple behaviors because of their belief system, not their biology. If the initial experiences are positively reinforced (through social reinforcers), this increases the strength of the belief system. As knowledge becomes more sophisticated, a type of generalization due to positive past experience expands the expectation that more events will be positive. This in turn increases the probability that new experiences will be explored, because of the expectation of positive change. What is developed eventually, according to Hardy, is a learned appetite rather than a biological drive.

EMOTION

People love and hate. They are afraid, anxious, and sometimes terrified. They are happy and sad, angry and mad. People are emotional. They have feelings. Furthermore, there are motivational consequences associated with these emotions. People fight, we say, because they are angry and full of hate. People seek each other out because, we say, they are in love. People are

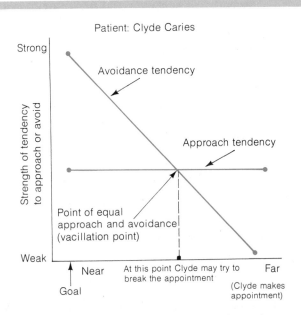

Patient: Clyde Caries

The graph diagrams the approach-avoidance conflict of a patient (Clyde Caries) who makes an appointment with his dentist a long time before he actually has to show up. There are two tendencies, one to approach (go to the dentist) and one to avoid (stay away from the dentist). In this example, the approach gradient does not change as the time for the appointment gets closer, but the avoidance tendency gets stronger and stronger (Clyde anticipates a lot of pain) as the appointment gets closer. At first, the approach tendency is stronger than the avoidance tendency, and so the appointment is made. Later, as the time for the appointment draws near, the avoidance ten-

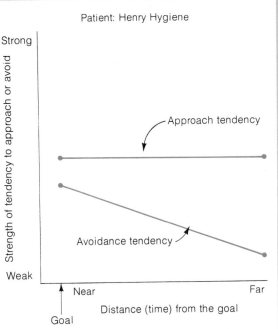

Patient: Henry Hygiene

dency gets stronger and at some time it becomes as strong as the approach tendency. This is the point of maximum conflict about what to do, the vacillation point. This is when Clyde may try to cancel or at least postpone the appointment. In any conflict situation what happens will depend on the strengths of the approach and avoidance gradients and how steep they are. For example, in the right graph, the avoidance tendency is not as strong as in the left graph because Henry Hygiene is not as afraid of the dentist as Clyde is. For Henry, the approach and avoidance tendencies never intersect, and so he does not try to cancel his appointment.

motivated to do all sorts of things in order to escape or avoid unpleasant emotional states (fear, anger, anxiety) or in order to obtain pleasant emotional states (love, happiness, joy, pleasure). Clearly emotion and motivation are closely related topics.

In psychology, the concept of emotion has proved complex and difficult to study scientifically. This is partly because so much of emotional experience is private personal experience that is not readily open to scientific scrutiny. Also, it is difficult to elicit emotions in controlled laboratory situations (particularly the positive emotions such as love, pleasure, and

joy). But although there is still a long way to go, we can say that progress is being made.

Emotions and Incentives

A great deal of effort has been expended in an attempt to devise a classification system for emotions. There are hundreds of words in our language referring to different emotional experiences. Many of these overlap in meaning, however, or refer merely to slight differences in the intensity of the emotion. There are two primary dimensions of emotions: (1) the qualitative dimension of *pleasant-unpleasant* and (2)

"I'll tell you what's missing from your game, Cowley
—hate."

*The New Yorker, October 24, 1974. Drawing by Lorenz; © 1974 The
New Yorker Magazine, Inc.*

**Emotions are generally considered to be important
sources of motivation. This is particularly evident in
athletics.**

the quantitative dimension of *intensity.* Emotional states are basically pleasant or unpleasant,
and they vary in the intensity of the feeling of
pleasantness or unpleasantness. Thus the difference between anger and rage is primarily
one of intensity, as is the difference between
happiness and ecstasy.

These two basic dimensions also determine
the motivational consequences of emotional
states. First, we can expect that unpleasant emotional states (and the things we have learned will
produce them) will act as negative incentives
(we will be motivated to avoid or escape them).
Likewise, pleasant states (and the things that
will produce them) will be positive incentives
(we will be motivated to achieve them). Because
we learn about the world, we can usually anticipate the emotional states that specific objects,
events, and states of affairs will elicit. Then we
can seek as goals those things that we expect
will elicit positive emotions and try to avoid
those things that we expect will result in unpleasant emotional experiences. Of course, we
cannot *avoid* everything unpleasant—sometimes
we accidentally encounter an overbearing bore
at a party. Under those circumstances, we will
be motivated to *escape* (the bore) because we
failed to avoid (him).

Second, we can expect that the degree of
motivation will depend upon the strength of the
anticipated or experienced state. The stronger
or more intense the emotion, the greater the
motivation to approach or avoid. In other words,
the emotional intensity will determine the
amount of incentive, and whether the emotion
is pleasant or unpleasant will determine whether
the incentive is positive (approach) or negative
(avoid).

Anxiety and Anger

Psychologists have been particularly interested
in the motivational consequences of two emotional states, anxiety and anger. Anxiety is of
interest because it appears to play a central role
in the motivation of abnormal (see Chapter 11)
as well as everyday behavior. Anger is of interest
because it is the standard emotion accompanying frustration, and it probably underlies most
acts of aggression. Together then, anxiety and
anger represent two emotional states that may
produce a great deal of undesirable behavior
in people. Understanding these emotions may
help us control or eliminate much of this
behavior.

Anxiety

Anxiety is an anticipatory fear attached to
no particular object or situation. We are anxious
when we anticipate the occurrence of a harmful
or threatening stimulus. Fear is what we experience when the threatening stimulus actually
occurs. Presumably anxiety is an unpleasant
experience with negative incentive value, meaning that we will be motivated to escape anxiety
when it develops and to avoid it if at all possible. Much of psychopathological behavior is
thought to be motivated by the desire to escape
anxiety. Behaviors that allow a person to escape
anxiety will be reinforced, and thus repeated,
and eventually will become habits for dealing
with anxiety. Similarly, objects, events, and
circumstances that we have learned will prevent
or counteract anxiety become positive incentives, and we will direct our behavior toward
achieving these goals. In some cases the anxious
person is unable to recognize the stimuli that
are anxiety provoking. This is known as *free-
floating anxiety* or *diffuse anxiety.*

The classic experiment demonstrating anxiety as a motivating force was done with rats by Neal Miller, using a shuttle box with two compartments, one black and one white. A rat was placed in the white compartment and electric shock was turned on, causing the rat to run into the black side of the box, where it escaped from the shock. This routine was repeated for several trials until presumably the fear was conditioned to the white compartment. At that point no further shocks were given. Despite the absence of shocks, the rat continued to show signs of fear when placed in the white side — the rat was "anxious." It continued to run into the black side even though it was never shocked again. The white side took on negative incentive value and the black side probably took on positive incentive value. Next, a door was put in place between the compartments, and a wheel was placed in the white compartment. This wheel, if turned by the rat, would open the door. The result was that the rats learned the wheel-turning responses to get out of the white compartment, even though shock was not administered. The rats were not escaping from real shock but from the threat of shock. They were escaping from the white compartment because it had been associated with shock. They were evidently motivated by the conditioned fear or anxiety produced by the white compartment. They may also have been motivated by the positive incentive of the black side of the box, because this side had repeatedly been associated with relief from the shock.

You might ask youself about your own behavior at this point. How much of your behavior is motivated by the desire to escape or avoid an unpleasant consequence? How often do negative incentives (like the rat's white box) influence your behavior? How often does the positive incentive value of things (like the rat's black box) stem from the fact that they allow us to escape anxiety, although many of these things may simply be temporary solutions to our anxiety? You may be anxious about a test, and instead of studying you may find yourself watching TV, a momentary relief from the anxiety. Or consider the alcoholic who may find temporary relief from anxiety in alcohol (the alcohol becomes a positive incentive). Because there are so many maladaptive ways to deal with the anxiety that is normal in life, anxiety can become a devastating state. While it can motivate appropriate behaviors such as studying for the exam, it can

Men 'Bottle Up' Emotions; Women Don't

Elaine Hooker

STORRS, Conn. — Women are more likely to give away their emotions in facial expressions but men generally keep their emotions "all bottled up," according to a psychologist who has conducted an experiment on the subject.

"I would guess it would be healthier" to express one's emotions, said University of Connecticut Prof. Ross Buck. "But I'm not going to make a value judgment."

The experiment involved 64 students — 32 women and 32 men — who were shown pictures that would evoke strong emotions. They didn't know it, but researchers were studying their facial expressions over closed-circuit television and trying to guess what type of picture the subjects were being shown.

Slides Were 'Loaded'

The "emotionally loaded" slides were scenic; sexual; pleasant, such as happy children; unpleasant, such as a patient with severe burns; or unusual, such as a double-exposed photograph.

The researchers found it much easier to tell from the women's facial expression what the picture topic was, Dr. Buck said.

He said men are "internalizers," who have been taught by society not to express emotions.

The result is that the men in the experiment reacted with a faster heart beat or increased activity in the sweat glands much more frequently than the women. These are considered reliable measurements of internalized emotions, he said.

Dr. Buck also said he has found that preschool children react differently to pictures, but not on the basis of sex. Their reactions are strictly a matter of individual personality, he said.

That means that during the process of growing up men are conditioned not to express their feelings, he said. But he doesn't know when this occurs and hopes to discover that within the next two years.

The Denver Post
December 13, 1974

also motivate behaviors that ultimately cause trouble. We will have more to say about anxiety in Chapter 11.

Stress and the General Adaptation Syndrome

"Stress" may be defined in many different ways, depending upon one's perspective.

From a physiological point of view stress may be defined as any state during which

Distress Signals

Hans Selye, M.D.

A number of manifestations of stress, particularly of the more dangerous *distress,* are not immediately evident, not constant symptoms that we should monitor throughout life. Depending upon our conditioning and genetic makeup, we all respond differently to general demands. But on the whole, each of us tends to respond with one set of symptoms caused by the malfunction of whatever happens to be the most vulnerable part in our machinery. Learn to heed these signs:

General irritability, hyperexcitation, or depression associated with unusual aggressiveness or passive indolence, depending upon our constitution.

Pounding of the heart, an indicator of excess production of adrenaline, often due to stress.

Dryness of the throat and mouth.

Impulsive behavior, emotional instability.

Inability to concentrate, flight of thoughts, and general disorientation.

Accident proneness. Under great stress we are more likely to have accidents. This is one reason why pilots and air traffic controllers must be carefully checked for their stress level.

Predisposition to fatigue and loss of *joie de vivre.*

Decrease in sex urge or even impotence.

"Floating anxiety"—we are afraid, although we do not know exactly what we are afraid of.

Stuttering and other speech difficulties which are frequently stress-induced.

Insomnia, which is usually a consequence of being "keyed-up."

Excessive sweating.

Frequent need to urinate.

Migraine headaches.

Loss of or excessive appetite. This shows itself soon in alterations of body weight, namely excessive leanness or obesity. Some people lose their appetite during stress because of gastrointestinal malfunction, whereas others eat excessively, as a kind of diversion, to deviate their attention from the stressor situation.

Premenstrual tension or missed menstrual cycles. Both are frequently indicators of severe stress in women.

Pain in the neck or lower back. Pain in the neck or back is usually due to increases in muscular tension that can be objectively measured by physicians with the electromyogram (EMG).

Trembling, nervous ticks.

Increased smoking.

Increased use of prescribed drugs, such as tranquilizers or amphetamines; or increased use of alcohol.

The Rotarian
March 1978

Anger and Frustration

Dollard, Doob, Miller, Mowrer, and Sears (1939) have suggested that all aggressive acts are caused by frustration, which is almost always accompanied by anger. This theory is known as the **frustration-aggression hypothesis.** Inflicting harm on others is a major problem in our society and the world, and so it is important to understand the motivation for this aggression. There is very strong evidence that the body tends to mobilize its resources and during which it utilizes more energy than it ordinarily would. In a general way reactions to stressful situations, by which we mean extremes of overwork, anxiety, pain, temperature, and so on, occur in three well-defined stages which Hans Selye has called the *general adaptation syndrome* (see Figure 7–10).

The Alarm Reaction

The first reaction to stress is similar to that observed during emotional states. Changes occur in heart rate, respiration, skin resistance, and endocrine activity. To give the body added energy, the adrenal glands begin to secrete large amounts of epinephrine and norepinephrine, which act on the liver to cause an increased release of stored sugar. In general, during intense stress the sympathetic nervous system is activated, whereas the parasympathetic nervous system is inhibited.

Resistance to Stress

During the second phase of the general adaptation syndrome bodily processes return to normal, and the individual endures the stress. Considerable strain has been placed on the individual, and if the stress continues, or if other stresses occur, the person may enter the third stage of the reaction.

Figure 7–10

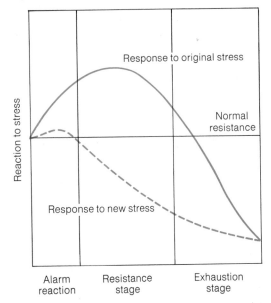

Resistance to stress increases during the alarm and resistance stages of the general adaptation syndrome. However, if the stressful situation continues for too long, or if a second stress occurs, the individual may enter the so-called exhaustion stage with very severe consequences.

Exhaustion

During this phase the individual may exhaust the resources mobilized to cope with the stress. If the stress persists, the individual may weaken to the extent that death occurs. Psychological stresses seldom reach this final stage, which is more typically observed in response to prolonged exposure to cold or heat or other extreme conditions.

frustration is sufficient to produce aggression, although it is almost impossible to determine whether frustration is also a necessary factor— that is, whether all aggression involves frustration. Consider just one study, in which a very

hungry pigeon was trained to peck a key in a Skinner box in order to get grain. After the pigeon had learned this response, an "innocent bystander" pigeon was placed in the box with the trained pigeon and simultaneously the ex-

"Can I kick it for you this time, Daddy?"

Reprinted courtesy of The Register and Tribune Syndicate.

In modern technological society machines that do not work properly are a common source of frustration, as this cartoon suggests. A common reaction, in line with the frustration-aggression hypothesis, is an aggressive act directed toward the machine. The cartoon also illustrates the fact that children can learn aggression by imitation. Presumably, the child has seen his father kick soda machines many times in the past and is already prepared to kick this one for him.

Figure 7–11
Aggression substitute

Two rats fight each other, ignoring the doll. When an appropriate object of aggression is missing, the lone rat displaces its aggression, attacking the innocent bystander. The most appropriate object for aggression is the object that is the source of the frustration. Often there are constraints against expressing the aggression against this source, as when a person is frustrated by the boss and hesitates to aggress against him or her for fear of being fired. So the aggression is displaced onto an "innocent bystander" such as his or her secretary or spouse.

perimenter stopped giving grain for pecking (extinction). During this extinction period, the trained pigeon attacked the bystander by pecking at its head, throat, and especially its eyes. There is little doubt that this was an attack reaction, apparently elicited by the frustration that was caused by the termination of the grain rewards (compare this with Figure 7–11).

The same kind of attack reactions were elicited in birds that had been reared in isolation, suggesting that there is an innate biological component to this behavior. This conclusion accords with the suggestions of the ethologists, who have argued that there is an aggressive instinct in human beings as well as in animals. However, although it may be true that there are aggressive instincts that result in predisposing us to fight when frustrated, it is clear that learning is also important. We learn aggressive tactics from seeing how others practice aggression, and

limiting such observation may be one way of exerting some control on the development of aggression. This is why, for example, so many people are concerned about the violence on television.

Issues and Theories

The Sequence of Events

When you encounter a ferocious bear in your room, at least two things are likely to happen: (1) you will run and (2) you will have an emotional experience (a feeling) that is usually called fear. Most of us would guess that we experience the fear first and run second. The first major psychological theory of emotional behavior postulated that we do just the opposite. This is known as the *James-Lange theory* after William James and Carl Lange, who independently in the late 1880s suggested that we run first and then are afraid. According to this theory, we are afraid because we observe that we are running. More specifically, the idea is that perception of the bear in the room leads simultaneously to running and to all sorts of changes in body physiology, such as increased blood pressure and heart rate. When we perceive these changes in our body, we experience the emotion (fear). This implies that we experience different emotions because the body produces a different set of physiological changes for each of the emotions. Fear is not the same thing as anger, presumably because the physiological activity in the body is qualitatively different during the experience of these two emotions. Whether or not this is true constitutes a critical issue to which we shall return shortly. For now, just remember that the James-Lange theory requires it to be true.

Other psychologists disagree with James and Lange. A prominent alternate view is commonly referred to as the *Cannon-Bard theory*, named after W. B. Cannon and P. Bard, who formulated the theory in 1915. Whereas James and Lange say, "We see the bear, we run (and our body physiology changes), and then we experience fear," the Cannon-Bard theory gives the commonsense argument: "We see the bear, we experience fear, and then we run (and our body physiology changes)." Cannon and Bard thought that the thalamus (see Chapter 2) was the "seat of emotions" (the hypothalamus would have been a better guess). According to them, when an emotional stimulus is presented, there is first strong stimulation of the thalamus. The thalamus then discharges electrical impulses upward into the brain, activating the cerebral cortex, and downward throughout the body activating the autonomic nervous system. This produces an all-over state of arousal that prepares the person for "flight or fight." It is this state that is experienced as the emotion. After this comes the observable behavior, the running. So for Cannon and Bard, emotion precedes overt behavior and consists mainly of a general state of arousal or activation. There is only one

basic physiological state in this theory, namely arousal, although obviously emotions differ in terms of degree of arousal.

Do Different Emotions Correspond to Qualitatively Different Physiological States?

The James-Lange theory required a yes answer to this question, while the Cannon-Bard theory said no, there are just differences in degree of arousal. The evidence on several fronts went against the James-Lange theory. Cannon criticized the James-Lange theory because the evidence available at the time did not show different physiological patterns for different emotions. Cannon also thought that the physiological changes out in the body's periphery took place too slowly to be the primary source of emotion. Further, in one study subjects were injected with adrenalin (epinephrine), which produces arousal in the autonomic nervous system, and yet these subjects did not report emotional experiences; the reason, according to Cannon, was that the central nervous system was not activated through the thalamus (there was no emotional stimulus). The overall picture is strongly against the James-Lange theory, although it is dying a slow death.

One reason the James-Lange theory still persists is that recent work has begun to demonstrate some differences in peripheral responses for different emotions. Most often cited is the work of A. F. Ax, who has demonstrated physiological differences between fear and anger. The adrenal glands secrete two different hormones, epinephrine and norepinephrine. Ax found that during fear epinephrine seems to dominate, while during anger both epinephrine and norepinephrine are implicated. Other studies have shown that animals which are preyed upon (and should thus be creatures of fear) secrete high amounts of epinephrine in contrast to the animals that do the preying. The preying animals (creatures of "anger"?) show predominately norepinephrine secretion. More recent work has centered on the biochemical substances that serve as neural transmitters in the central nervous system, which seem to be involved in different ways depending on the emotion. However, the evidence is not yet convincing, and so there is still a strong commitment to the notion that basically the emotional state is a general diffuse state of overall arousal or activation.

How Important Is Cognitive Appraisal of the Situation?

If the emotional state consists mainly of general arousal and there is not a different physiological state for the different emotions, how do we know whether we are happy or sad, pleased or angry? The answer probably comes from analyzing the total emotional experience into two basic parts: (1) the *general arousal* and (2) the *cognitive appraisal* or *evaluation* of the situation—such as "there is a bear loose in my room and it is about to attack me." In a simplified sense, the appraisal is designed to answer the question "Why am I aroused to this degree?" There is a continual interplay between the arousal and the appraisal, out of which emerges the emotional experience. The experience is thus a joint product of the arousal (including the degree of arousal) and the ongoing evaluation of the situation. Which comes first is not of much concern in this theory, because arousal and appraisal are constantly changing and interacting with each other. Sometimes the arousal may precede the appraisal and sometimes it may come later.

The key new element in this interpretation is cognitive appraisal. The person is appraising the situation and at the same time is looking for something that the arousal can be attributed to (the bear is an obvious choice). This part of the theory comes from the *attribution theory* of Fritz Heider (see Chapter 10) and has been investigated and elaborated by Stanley Schachter. Having something to attribute the arousal to and having a cognitive evaluation of that thing (such as "it can harm me") are crucial. Without these components there would be no emotional experience even if the arousal component has occurred. Thus, as mentioned earlier, subjects given injections of adrenalin, which produces the arousal, do not become emotional because there is nothing to attribute the arousal to other than the injection, which is nothing to be happy, sad, angry, or ecstatic about. Presumably the subjects attribute the arousal to the injection (the doctor told them they would experience arousal) and then are not emotional. On the other hand, if the subjects were misled about the injection ("this is a vitamin shot") and were told that it would not produce arousal, then when they became aroused they would need an explanation and would evaluate their predicament in seeking the explanation.

Schachter and Jerome Singer tricked subjects in just this way—the subjects received adrenalin but thought they were getting a vitamin shot. The subjects found their explanation for the experienced arousal (and thus their emotion) in the situation. Half the subjects, after receiving the "vitamin" shot, were asked to wait in a room with someone else who was pretending to be very angry. These subjects reported that they became angry. The other half waited in a room with someone who was acting very happy, and these subjects said they were happy. They thus falsely attributed the arousal they were experiencing to the situation and experienced an emotional feeling that was consistent with their evaluation of the situation.

To emphasize the back-and-forth interplay between arousal and evaluation, we can point out that there is evidence that persons evaluate the degree of arousal as well as the situation that is apparently producing the arousal. The evaluation of the degree of arousal will be fed back into the system and can affect the evaluation of the situation. In an ingenious experiment Stuart Valins demonstrated this feedback feature. Male subjects were led to believe that they were listening to their own amplified heartbeat over a loudspeaker, when in fact what they heard was a prepared tape recording. Valins then showed these men pictures of nudes from *Playboy;* for half the nudes, the fake heart rate sounds were speeded up when the picture appeared. This was designed to create the false impression in the subjects that they were especially aroused by these particular nudes. Later the subjects were asked to rate the nudes on attractiveness, and, as predicted, they rated the nudes that had been associated with increased heart rate as more attractive than the other nudes. The reasoning is that the subjects, thinking they were aroused, searched for an explanation by more closely examining the nudes to find particularly attractive features in the photographs. Having found these features, the subjects would judge the photographs more attractive.

In fact, Valins has demonstrated that the subjects still rate these nudes as more attractive after they are told that the "heartbeats" were a fake. Fake or not, they caused the subjects to discover more attractive features. It has also been shown that the "heart-rate" effect does not take place if the nude photos are presented rapidly, presumably because the subject does not have time to find the explanation for his arousal—he does not have time to find attractive features in the Playmate.

The currently most popular account of emotional experience stems from a combination of general arousal theory (similar to the Cannon-Bard theory) and attribution theory. The experienced emotion is a complex function depending on the interplay among several factors: (1) the arousal level—the degree of arousal (or more accurately the degree to which the arousal level is changed from some baseline) probably mediates the intensity dimension of emotion; (2) the cognitive evaluation of the situation producing the arousal change, which will at least partly determine the pleasantness-unpleasantness dimension; and (3) the evaluation of the arousal change, which may in turn affect the cognitive evaluation of the situation. A fourth factor is the specific physiological pattern of the arousal, which may partly determine the quality of the experience (is it fear or anger?). As yet, however, we know very little about what biochemical and physiological factors differentiate the various emotional states.

It is also possible that the degree of arousal change from the normal baseline may play a role in determining the pleasant-unpleasant dimension, in addition to determining the intensity dimension. If we assume that there is a homeostatic arousal system trying to keep arousal level in the moderate range, then we would guess that very large changes in arousal from this optimal level will, in general, be experienced as unpleasant. We might also expect that this homeostatic system will, in such cases, immediately attempt to counteract these large changes in arousal in an effort to return the arousal level to the moderate range.

The Effect of Opponent Processes in Emotions

Richard Solomon and John Corbit have proposed just such an opponent-process model: Given a large change in arousal produced by either a pleasant or an unpleasant stimulus, the homeostatic system will immediately activate an opponent process to counteract the emotional reaction. The opponent process, in general, will have just the opposite effects of the initial process, meaning that the overall experience will be a combination of the opposing processes. If the initial experience is pleasant, it will be maximally pleasant only for a short while, because the opponent process, which is by definition unpleasant, will soon be activated and begin to counteract the pleasant process. As the unpleasant opponent process gathers strength, the experience will become less and less pleasant. If the original stimulus situation that triggered the pleasant process were suddenly removed, we would experience only the opponent process in action. That is, we would experience an unpleasant emotion.

In contrast, suppose the initial state of arousal is unpleasant. Soon afterward a pleasant opponent process will be activated to counteract the arousal. Such an experience will be maximally unpleasant only in the beginning because the opponent process will begin to temper or diminish the degree of unpleasantness. If at this moment the original unpleasant stimulus situation is suddenly removed, only the opponent process will be active and we will experience a pleasant emotion.

Solomon and Corbit use this theory to account for a variety of phenomena, among which they consider the following: Immediately after hatching, the newborn duckling gives every appearance of being quite satisfied with its new circumstances, though it may emit a few cries of distress. But then, according to imprinting studies, if the duckling is exposed to a white, moving object, it will stare at it intently. All movements and vocalizations tend to disappear. If the moving object is removed, there will be a burst of distress cries that may last for several minutes before subsiding. According to the typical ethological interpretation, the moving object has suddenly established a "following behavior" released by an adequate imprinting stimulus, a white moving object.

In contrast, according to the Solomon-Corbit theory, the moving object is a stimulus that automatically releases in the duckling an affective state with pleasant emotional connotations. The stimulus-induced state is, however, opposed by an unpleasant process, of lesser intensity and designed to bring the organism back in the direction of emotional neutrality. When the triggering stimulus (the white object) is removed, only the unpleasant state remains, resulting in the distress reaction of the organism.

Another example comes from the use of drugs, such as opium. Upon first use, an individual is likely to report an intensely pleasurable

Smut Affecting Man's 'Pleasure'

CHICAGO — There was a man in Los Angeles who saw every dirty movie that came to town, and then discovered something unfortunate was happening to him.

"I don't get pleasure any more out of watching my wife undress," the man told a psychiatrist. "I'm finished with pornography."

Another California man regularly watched the violence and cruelty of bullfights on television, and finally confided to a friend:

"The other night I found myself flapping a towel at my Boxer dog and making thrusts at him with a coat hanger. No more bullfights for me."

The two stories were told in Chicago by Dr. Roderic Gorney, a California psychiatrist with new, exciting—and realistic—ideas about his life work.

Dr. Gorney found in the two cases an indication that the public may be getting a bellyful of pornography and violence in so-called entertainment.

Thousands of People

Thousands of Los Angeles people, as well as the man he quoted have had their tastes for pornography satiated, Dr. Gorney said.

He pointed out that numbers of theaters specializing in dirty films have closed.

As for the bullfights, television stations reportedly found that viewer ratings slumped as the novelty wore off.

The Denver Post

The opponent-process theory clearly predicts that you can get "too much of a good thing." If you expose yourself repeatedly to stimuli that give you a pleasant emotional reaction, the opponent process counteracting this reaction will become increasingly stronger. Eventually, the opponent process will become strong enough to completely counteract the original "pleasant" process, so that the emotion you feel (the net result of the two counteracting processes) will disappear. There will be little or no emotional feeling, and you will have had too much of the thing you once enjoyed.

feeling known as the "rush." With the passage of time, as the drug effect wears off, the user will suffer aversive pain and frightening withdrawal symptoms. There may also be a feeling of craving for the drug. Presumably, this is the opponent process in action.

Finally, consider the situation of a girl and boy falling in love. The initial state presumably experienced by both is characterized by pleasurable excitement, sexual highs, ecstasy, happiness, and, in general, good feelings. When the lovers are separated, the opponent process becomes evident. They feel lonely and depressed. Even when they anticipate reunion, loneliness may persist. Reunion does, of course, reinstate the initial stimulus circumstances and thereby overwhelm the negative opponent process.

If we are repeatedly exposed to the identical emotional situation, the character of the emotional experience changes. Solomon and Corbit suggest that this happens because the opponent process gets stronger each time it is elicited. With enough repetition the opponent process may become so strong that it overwhelms the initial stimulus-induced state and comes to dom-

inate the emotional experience. Imagine your favorite food, the thing that gives you that most pleasant taste experience. Now imagine eating that food all the time, morning, noon, and night. Do you think the pleasure would disappear?

For the examples mentioned above, consider what happens when repetition takes place. For the ducklings, if the imprinting stimulus is presented and removed several times, the frequency and intensity of distress crying by a duckling will increase (the opponent process has been strengthened). For the addict, after several weeks of opiate use, the "rush" begins to weaken, and it takes more of the drug to produce it. Moreover, the aftereffects become more intense and turn into an intensely unpleasant state of craving. Indeed, the opponent process has become so strong that the addict must take drugs all the time just to maintain his normal feelings. The drugs no longer produce the pleasant state, but just maintain the normal one, and the lack of drugs is what produces the abnormal state. Finally, consider the couple in love. After several weeks, months, or years of repeated affectionate interaction, the qualitative and quantitative aspects of their love will change. Being together is a state of "contentment," normalcy, and comfort, not the same as the excitement, joy, and enthusiasm of the young lovers. Now, separation can have highly intense aversive effects, and in extreme cases grief and severe depression. It is as if the partners have become addicted to one another; being together is "normal," not exciting, and separation will result in withdrawal symptoms.

SUMMARY

1. Motivation is an explanatory concept used to answer questions about *why* organisms behave as opposed to how they accomplish the behavior. It is used to account for observed variability in behavior both within the individual (the same person behaves differently on two occasions when the situation is identical) and between individuals (in the same situation, two different people will behave differently).

2. Motives are often defined by the length of time the organism has been deprived of some goal object, such as food, and by the observation that such deprivation leads to increased attempts to achieve the goal.

3. Two fundamental concepts of motivation are drive and incentive. Drive refers to the "push" behind behavior—the energy. Incentive refers to the goal objects that entice or pull the behavior. In practice, drive is measured by length of deprivation and incentive by the quality and quantity of the rewarding goal object.

4. In the past, most psychologists emphasized drive as the more important factor, implying we are mainly pushed into behaving by our drives. More recently, the emphasis has shifted to incentives as the most important aspect of motivation, especially in analyses of human behavior.

5. For some time it has been believed that deprivation leads to increased energy and more activity. Recent analyses, however, suggest that deprived animals are not automatically more active, but instead are more reactive to stimuli in the environment. Deprived animals are not more aroused, but more arousable when subjected to stimulation. This evidence casts doubt on the traditional drive-energy-activity concept.

6. A useful formulation for understanding motivation is based on the distinction between predisposition and precipitation. The motivated organism is predisposed to respond but will not do so until there are appropriate precipitating circumstances.

7. We have built-in physiological systems that regulate the intake of such things as food and water. These systems operate according to the principle of homeostasis, with the goal of maintaining a steady state within our bodies.

8. The homeostatic system regulating food intake is complex and involves a preset weight level determined largely by heredity and involving the monitoring of fat levels in the body. There is also a regulation of hour-by-hour intake of food, which is apparently accomplished by monitoring levels of sugar in the blood. The hypothalamus is also important in regulating weight levels and food intake. Recently attention has focused on the role of the liver in regulating eating behavior. Finally, the stomach and mouth also play a minor part in the regulation process.

9. A homeostatic system also keeps bodily fluids within a critical range. If fluid levels are too low, the body conserves water by inhibiting urine formation and then activating our behavior to find and drink water. The hypothalamus appears to play a central role in the homeostasis of bodily fluids.

10. An instinct is an inherited, invariant behavioral sequence that is unique to the species. It is a fixed action pattern precipitated by environmental "releasing" stimuli. Instinct theories were once quite popular but were not very useful in explaining behavior. Ethology has revived the concept of instinct and has used it to account for feeding, reproductive, and defensive behaviors in animals. The role of instincts in human behavior is a subject of considerable controversy.

11. Sociobiology sees human behavior as preprogrammed and having only one function—the survival of the genes. In their treatment of altruistic behavior and the concept of inclusive fitness, sociobiologists have stirred considerable controversy.

12. Much of our behavior appears to be motivated by a homeostatic system that is designed to keep our arousal level at some optimal point. We seek out sources of stimulation when our arousal level is lower than optimal, and we attempt to reduce stimulation when we become overaroused.

13. Psychologists studying human motivation often treat motivation as a personality characteristic, dealing with the psychological needs of people. These personality characteristics can be viewed as predispositions to respond to particular incentives.

14. Some of the human needs and personality characteristics that have received attention from psychologists include need for achievement, need for affiliation, and need for social approval. Each person presumably learns a set of psychological needs as he or she grows up, and these needs are of varying strengths. Variation in adult motivation is then accounted for by variation in the strengths of the needs.

15. Sexual behavior is motivated in very complex ways. In order to understand sexual motivation, we must consider such factors as drive, incentive, precipitating stimuli, physiology, personality, and social learning theory.

16. There are two primary dimensions of emotion, the qualitative dimension of pleasantness-unpleasantness and the quantitative dimension of intensity. Emotions are generally considered to be important sources of motivation—we seek positive, pleasant emotional states and strive to avoid negative states.

17. Modern analyses of emotion suggest two basic components, a general arousal and a cognitve evaluation of the circumstances that led to the arousal. There is also an evaluation of the degree of arousal, which in turn can affect the evaluation of the situation. The emotional experience is an outgrowth of the interplay between the arousal and the cognitive evaluations.

RECOMMENDED ADDITIONAL READINGS

Bindra, D., & Stewart, J. (Eds.) *Motivation,* 2d ed. Baltimore, Md.: Penguin, 1971.

Bolles, R. C. *Theory of motivation,* 2d ed. New York: Harper & Row, 1975.

Cofer, C. N. *Motivation and emotion.* Glenview, Ill.: Scott Foresman, 1974.

Cofer, C. N. & Appley, M. H. *Motivation: Theory and research.* New York: Wiley, 1964.

Lorenz, K. *Evolution and modification of behavior.* Chicago: University of Chicago Press, 1965.

Malmo, R. B. *On emotions, needs, and our archaic brain.* New York: Holt, Rinehart and Winston, 1975.

what does it mean?

INCREASING MOTIVATION

If psychological research allows for the identification of the factors that determine motivation, it should be possible to bring these factors to bear on an individual or group in hopes of increasing motivation to behave in some particular way. The focus of such an effort would probably be on increasing achievement in one way or another. In industry, for instance, it is obviously important to management that the productivity of employees be increased, that the employees increase their motivation to produce. In fact, of course, industrial psychology has concerned itself with this issue for a long time, attempting to understand how principles of motivation can be applied in a work setting. Many studies of the effects of various incentive plans on productivity have been carried out, with the goal of identifying the optimal incentive conditions for the employees.

Recently, there has been a recognition of the fact that performance in an industrial setting is dependent on other than monetary incentives. Giving praise and recognition to employees is often equally important. Consider the following case. A few years ago the management of the Emery Air Freight Corporation instituted a program to improve performance based on the motivational ideas of operant conditioning. The heart of the program consisted of setting specific goals for the employees and giving them a great deal of feedback as to how they were doing in reaching these goals. The first target for the program was shortening the time a customer had to wait for replies to questions about air freight shipments. The goal was to respond to all customer questions within 90 minutes. Although the employees thought they were meeting this goal most of the time, studies showed that in fact only about 30 percent of the time did the response to the customer come in less than 90 minutes. By keeping accurate performance records, and by praising employees for improvements found in the daily records, management was able to increase performance dramatically in a very short time—in some offices it took only one day to meet the 90-minute criterion. After three years on the program, the response rate is now so high across the entire company that 90–95 percent of all customers receive a reply within 90 minutes.

Next, the same techniques were applied to loading dock employees in order to motivate them to be more efficient in the use of "containers." The idea was to combine lots of small packages into one large package or container, which results in substantial savings in the air freight charges. If the dock workers could be motivated to increase their use of containers, the company could save a great deal of money. Again it was found that the employees thought they were making good use of the containers, but they were wrong. Containers were used in only about 45 percent of the shipments where they could be used. By keeping accurate records, management could give feedback to the

"Why, thank you, sir, and I had it in mind to tell you what a bang-up job I think you're doing."

The New Yorker, January 13, 1975. Drawing by Mulligan; © 1975 The New Yorker Magazine, Inc.

Giving praise and recognition is apparently a good way to motivate people.

workers about how they were doing and could reward them, again with praise and recognition, whenever the rate of container use went up. The result was that container use shot up from the old 45 percent figure to over 90 percent, and two years later it was still at a very high level. In one month alone the company saved $125,000 because of their container program.

Intrinsic and Extrinsic Motivation

It seems obvious that the best way to increase motivation (and thereby performance) is to increase incentives. But increasing incentives is a very tricky business and can often have effects just the opposite of those desired.

Some recent research has demonstrated that it is possible to *decrease* motivation by giving rewards for performance. The reason is that people are self-motivated to do certain things. Some tasks are interesting and enjoyable and provide their own rewards to the people doing them. If a psychologist, a teacher, an employer, or a parent offers tangible rewards to a person for doing a task he or she would do well anyway, the person may develop a more negative attitude about the task.

Where once the task seemed worth doing by itself, the new reward system makes the task take on the complexion of work. The task is now perceived as something that must be done in order to get the reward, rather than as something important in its own right. When a person does something for no obvious tangible reward, we say that he or she has *intrinsic motivation*. If, on the other hand, a person is doing something in order to receive a particular tangible reward, say a paycheck, we say that he or she has *extrinsic motivation*. If the amateur photographer decides to become a professional photographer, taking pictures may take on a different flavor and become much less fun and much more like drudgery.

Edward Deci has suggested that praise works differently than money because praise involves giving feedback to the subject about his or her competence and self-determination. Tasks that are intrinsically interesting are presumably those that, when completed, automatically give the person good feelings of competence. Perhaps this is why praise and recognition worked so well, in the case of Emery Air Freight.

In this regard psychologist Robert W. White has postulated the existence in human beings of a *competence motive* that may be the basis of intrinsic motivation. This motive causes us to interact with our environment in ways designed to master and control it, according to White's theory. We are intrinsically rewarded by demonstrating competence in the world to ourselves. White views the competence motive as basic to human nature — it is a primary drive like hunger and thirst. It can be used to explain a lot of behavior that apparently has no rewards. For example, mountain climbing can be seen as an attempt to demonstrate competence over the environment — indeed, an individual climbs a mountain "because it is there," and the climber must master it to feel competent.

It may also be the case, as the research of Deci and others indicates, that providing an external reward such as money may auto-

'Rewards' for Children Questioned

UPI

NORMAN, Okla. — Those few dollars given a son or daughter for helping with yard or housework may cause them to hate doing it, a psychology professor says.

Prof. John McCullers, University of Oklahoma Department of Psychology chairman, is conducting a research experiment to last about six years on possible bad effects of rewards.

The project applies to rewards such as bonuses for employes, gold stars for students or candy for children. The principle has been seen as "the great panacea for the past 30 to 40 years," he said.

"For years and years everyone has been talking about the good effects of reward," he said. "I think reward might be regarded as something like a drug. It has certain beneficial effects, but it's possible it may have detrimental effects."

He said rewards seem to kill the inborn motivation the person has for doing the work and to hamper his performance, possibly because he is thinking about the reward.

"A young child is just very anxious to be competent in the eyes of the parent. He wants to ride the bicycle, push the lawn mower, operate the typewriter. You can scarcely keep him away from it," he said.

"After he pesters the father enough, he says, 'I'll let you take a try with the lawnmower.' A few months later he lets him mow the grass. The next step is to offer him something for it. Shortly after that he doesn't want to do it."

McCullers began the project about two years ago and has received a $56,000 National Institute of Mental Health grant from May until mid-1978.

He conducts experiments in a laboratory in which he rewards children with a coin or candy and adults with a few dollars for performing tasks.

Rocky Mountain News, *Denver*
June 20, 1975

Providing an external reward to mow the lawn may inhibit intrinsic motivation. External rewards may get the job done — which is very likely what the parents want — but such rewards may destroy self-satisfaction as a motivating factor.

matically detract from or reduce intrinsic motivation based on competence. The main problem with White's concept of a competence motive is not that it doesn't explain much but that it could be used to explain just about everything. It could be used as a catch-all concept to "explain" behavior whenever we can't find any other motive. And it suffers from circular reasoning—"Why do they climb mountains? Because they want to be competent. How do you know they are motivated to be competent? Because I observe them climbing mountains."

Tangible external rewards will not always have the desired effect of increasing motivation, and we must pay close attention to the types of incentives we use. In the classroom, for example, we might inadvertently turn the task of learning into a chore by promising the students all sorts of rewards. Many parents and grandparents have promised children money or special privileges for good grades.

These promises may have contributed to an attitude about school that makes studying appear like work. We hope that further research in the area of motivation will allow us to discover the best ways to motivate behavior, and this includes the best ways to develop intrinsic motivation for the most important tasks of our lives.

CHANGING THE PERSONALITY ASPECTS OF MOTIVATION

As we have seen, motivation is often used as a personality concept, particularly when we are discussing human motives or needs. Earlier in this chapter we focused on achievement motivation. Is it possible to alter such personality characteristics in adults? Typically it has been assumed that once a person has reached adulthood it is quite difficult—if not impossible—to change personality character-

OKAY, SO I'M OVER-QUALIFIED —

HIRE ME AND I PROMISE TO BE AN UNDER-ACHIEVER —

PERSONNEL MGR

Washington Star Syndicate, Inc.

12-14

BRICKMAN

King Features Syndicate, Inc., 1977.

Conceptions that treat motivation as a personality characteristic imply an application of motivational research in the area of personnel selection. It is often said that a person is "overqualified" for a particular job when in fact the real problem may be that the job does not fit well with the applicant's personality needs, most obviously the need for achievement. It is hoped that personality–motivation research will lead to better techniques for matching people and jobs.

istics such as achievement motivation. However, we can expect that an understanding of the principles of human motivation might eventually allow us to manipulate or change the personality aspects of motivation. There is not a great deal of research on this topic, mainly because we do not as yet have anything like a complete understanding of human personality. But as our knowledge grows we can expect that our ability to change human motivation will increase.

As one example, consider the work of David McClelland on achievement motivation. He has used the knowledge derived from his research on the development of achievement motivation and from other areas of psychology to develop a training course designed to increase the level of need for achievement in students. He has taught this course to numerous groups of businesspersons, mainly in India, and has done careful follow-up studies of the effects of the course on students' later achievements in the business world.

The participants were thoroughly trained in the theory and measurement of achievement motivation. They all took the TAT and scored their own stories for achievement motivation. They were taught to think about everything in terms related to achievement. They analyzed the achievement motivation level in their own culture by scoring such things as books, children's stories, and customs of the culture on achievement. They also played a business game in which each person had to think in achievement terms (for example, set goals for profits and productivity) and could get fast feedback about how he was doing in running the business. The results were measured by comparing students who had taken the course with control students who had applied for the course but had not been admitted. On a number of economic measures—starting new businesses, working longer hours, increasing the number of employees in existing businesses, and so on—the students in the course did very much better than the controls. This, of course, is taken as evidence that the course did indeed succeed in increasing the achievement motivation of the participants.

McClelland's course was specifically designed to increase only achievement motivation. McClelland believes, however, that the principles he used in setting up the course would be applicable to any personality aspect of motivation. In short, his results suggest that it would be possible to design training programs or courses that would affect all of the human psychogenic needs or motives, such as the need for affiliation, the need for power, and the need for social approval. He argues that the economic growth, development, and decline of a country depends heavily on the achievement motivation of its people. If this is true and if we can develop ways of increasing achievement motivation for businessmen, then it should be possible to design ways to bring about great changes in the economic conditions of an underdeveloped country by subjecting the inhabitants to these techniques. Does this sound a little frightening to you? Wouldn't it also then be possible to destroy the economy of a rather well-developed country by systematically attempting to decrease or undermine the achievement motivation of its inhabitants?

It is hardly necessary to mention that development of techniques to change aspects of someone's personality would have important applied consequences. Many beneficial things could be done with such knowledge, such as helping people to change in ways they want to change, as when a psychotherapist tries to help clients become better adjusted emotionally. But knowledge could also be used not to help people but to control them. Some readers will already have reacted that way to the case of Emery Air Freight. Similarly, many people have strongly criticized the various types of "behavior modification" projects that have been tried in schools, mental hospitals, and prisons. The facts argue strongly for the conclusion that the people who control the incentives, whatever they may be, can use their power to control the behavior of the people who are seeking those incentives. The question is not so much whether we can apply this knowledge to affect behavior, but what kinds of behavior change are desirable and how the rights and wishes of the individual will be safeguarded.

CONTROLLING THE HAND THAT FEEDS YOU

One major area of concentration in motivation research is hunger and eating. A major application of knowledge derived from this research is body weight control. Obesity is a problem for millions of people in this country. It has been implicated as a major factor in heart disease, to say nothing of the personal pain, discomfort, and rejection that the obese person so often feels. Presently we do not have very good techniques for controlling obesity. People go on diets and lose weight, but only a small proportion of them are able to keep the weight off. Most dieters gain back later what they lost and spend much of their lives losing the same 10 pounds over and over

"I was reminded of the refrigerator by the installment I just paid on it."

Reprinted courtesy of The Register and Tribune Syndicate.

According to Schachter's theory of hunger motivation, obese people are overcontrolled by external food-related stimuli and undercontrolled by internal stimuli related to bodily needs for nourishment. Thus, the fat person is likely to eat in response to food or food-related stimuli (such as the bill for the refrigerator installment) regardless of the internal state of his body. The normal person responds to food and food stimuli more in accord with his internal cues — he tends not to eat unless "physiologically" hungry.

again. Recent research has begun to suggest reasons for this typical pattern. This knowledge may eventually lead to effective techniques for combating obesity permanently.

Numerous experiments by Stanley Schachter and his colleagues suggest that obese people have difficulty in controlling their weight because they eat mainly in response to uncontrollable external cues in their environments. This external-cue orientation manifests itself in such diverse ways as the tendency for obese Caucasians to use forks rather than chopsticks in Chinese restaurants, for overweight Air France pilots to be less disturbed by meal-time changes, for obese orthodox Jews to be less uncomfortable than those of normal weight when fasting on Yom Kippur, and for the tendency of obese individuals to give in to impulse buying in supermarkets.

Schachter's experiments showed that normal-weight people, in contrast, eat mainly in response to internal physiological cues. Nor-

Obesity Influenced by Several Factors

Judy Serrin

SAN FRANCISCO — The overweight person is not to blame for his extra pounds, according to a Yale University psychologist.

Yet, her research has shown, almost any person can learn — without using rigid diets — to lose weight and keep it lost. What has complicated weight loss so far, is a number of myths about obesity, said psychologist Judith Rodin.

"Obesity is not a matter of weak will or gluttony," Dr. Rodin said. . . .

"There could be people who are predisposed genetically, so that's no one's fault. Secondly, our environment is so full of arousal stimuli, and there are people who are more easily aroused by food cues."

For the past 10 years, Dr. Rodin, an associate professor of psychology, has studied and treated obese persons at the Yale Center for Self-Regulation.

Losing Battle

To date, she said, the battle against obesity has been primarily a losing one.

"Almost any fat person can lose weight; few can keep it off," she said.

One of the main problems in treating obesity is that it has many causes, Dr. Rodin said. Furthermore she has found that many factors people thought caused obesity are actually results of it.

For example, she said, take the matter of lack of exercise.

"Obesity makes physical activity more difficult and probably less pleasurable. With less exercise, overweight people burn fewer calories," Dr. Rodin said.

But, she said, "Decreased physical activity could not generally produce obesity."

She said a followup study of 100 patients showed that more than 70 percent increased their physical activity after losing weight.

This suggests that inactivity is a result of, not a cause of, obesity, she said.

Likewise, changes in hormones and metabolism associated with overweight come after — not before — weight gain.

And although being overweight has profound psychological consequences, people usually do not gain weight because they are unhappy and troubled, Dr. Rodin said.

Unhappy People

Rather, people are unhappy because they have gained weight. This unhappiness applies to even moderately overweight people, Dr. Rodin said.

Dr. Rodin's research identified some other factors related to obesity:

1. Obese people tend to have obese parents.
2. Overfeeding in childhood can start the growth of more fat cells than a person would normally have.
3. People in a lower social class are more often obese than those in a higher class. Although higher-class people can afford more food, Dr. Rodin said, "With increased affluence, fads and fashion exert great control on eating and weight."
4. "The longer a person's family has been in this country, the less likely they were to be obese."
5. Among religious groups, obesity is most prevalent among Jews, then Roman Catholics, then Protestants. Among Protestants, the greatest obesity is among Baptists, then Methodists, then Lutherans, then Episcopalians, Dr. Rodin said. . . .

Boulder (Colo.) **Daily Camera**
August 31, 1977

There is no single cause of overeating and therefore no simple answer to weight control. It has become clear, however, that psychological factors are as important as physical factors.

mal persons eat because their internal food-intake system "tells" them to eat, while obese persons eat whenever they encounter external stimuli that have something to do with food, such as when they walk by a doughnut shop or see a TV commercial for frozen pizza. Normal-weight persons encounter identical stimuli, but their food intake is not under external control and so they do not respond by getting something to eat. It follows that it will be easy for obese persons to lose weight if they isolate themselves from these stimuli. And indeed it is. If obese people are put into the hospital and deprived of TV, magazines,

The Chemistry of Smoking

"Don't ask me why I smoke," says the grim-looking man in the Winston cigarette ad. Columbia Psychologist Stanley Schachter, 54, agrees that it is better not to ask. The Winston man—or any other heavy smoker—would probably say he smokes for pleasure, or because it calms his nerves, gives him something to do with his hands or solves his Freudian oral problems. "Almost any smoker can convince you and himself that he smokes for psychological reasons or that smoking does something positive for him—it's all very unlikely," says Schachter, a virtual chain smoker himself. "We smoke because we're physically addicted to nicotine. Period."

Schachter reached his conclusion after conducting a series of experiments over the past four years. Like other researchers, Schachter and his team (Brett Silverstein, Lynn Kozlowski and Deborah Perlick) found that heavy smokers, given only low-nicotine cigarettes to smoke, tried to compensate: to inhale their normal quota of nicotine, they smoked more cigarettes and puffed more frequently. Even so, some were not able to make up the difference and showed withdrawal symptoms: increased eating, irritability and poorer concentration.

The researchers then went further by testing volunteers to see whether smoking eases stress. On the assumption that the more anxious a person is, the less pain he will tolerate, groups of smokers and nonsmokers were asked to endure as much electric shock as they could bear. Smokers proved to be sissies when deprived of cigarettes or given only low-nicotine brands. Those supplied with armloads of high-nicotine brands to smoke accepted a higher number of shocks—but no more than the control group of nonsmokers. Schachter's conclusion: "Smoking doesn't reduce anxiety or calm the nerves. Not smoking increases anxiety by throwing the smoker into withdrawal."

Mindless Machine

Then why do most smokers smoke so heavily when under stress? Schachter's answer: because stress depletes body nicotine, and the smoker has to puff more to keep at his usual nicotine level. The key is the acidity of urine. One result of anxiety and stress is a high acid content in the urine. Highly acidic urine flushes away much more body nicotine than normal urine does. Schachter discovered that smokers who were administered mild acids (vitamin C and Acidulin) in heavy doses smoked more over a period of days than comparable smokers who took bicarbonates to make their urine more alkaline. His tests also show that bicarbonates reduce smoking under stress. One experiment indicates that partygoing increases the acidity of the urine for smokers and nonsmokers alike. "It follows," Schachter says puckishly, "that the concerned smoker should take the Alka-Seltzer before—not after—the party." . . .

Time
February 21, 1977

Why do people smoke? Is it pleasurable? Are smokers addicted to nicotine? Is the smoker seeking to maintain a homeostatic balance of nicotine in the blood?

and any stimuli that have to do with food, they can lose large amounts of weight without great pain or discomfort. But what happens when they leave the hospital and return to the world of refrigerators, restaurants, MacDonald's hamburger stands, and 31 flavors of ice cream? Yes, indeed, they gain back what they lost.

Obese people are exceptionally sensitive to external food-related stimuli and insensitive to internal stimuli. It has been shown, for example, that normal-weight individuals report being hungry in a way that corresponds with the contractions in their stomachs, an internal stimulus. Obese people's reports of hunger do not correlate highly with stomach activity. In an ingenious experiment, Schachter and Gross showed that obese people will eat if you fool them into thinking it is dinnertime (the clock being an external stimulus), while normal-weight people will not.

Subjects were brought into the laboratory late in the afternoon. They worked in a room with a large clock that was set either to run

Researchers Discovering Emotions Can Be Lethal

Ronald Kotulak

A young Congo native was strictly forbidden by a wizard to eat wild hen. As a joke, a friend gave him some wild hen, telling him it was a different fowl. He ate it and liked it.

Two years later the friend laughingly revealed the joke. On hearing the news the young man began to tremble. He was seized by uncontrollable fear and died 24 hours later.

A 61-year-old woman accompanied her 71-year-old sister to a hospital in an ambulance. When a doctor in the emergency room told her that her elder sister had died, she clutched at her chest and fell over dead.

A 69-year-old woman who had been an invalid for 28 years lost her brother, three sisters, and a husband in rapid succession. She told her doctor that she would die in a few days. She did.

A 54-year-old man died when he met his father after a 20-year separation. The 86-year-old father then dropped dead.

These cases have sometimes been described as dying from a broken heart, loneliness, shock, voodoo hex, and even jubilation.

Often dismissed in the past as old wives' tales or superstitions, medical researchers now are taking such dangers more seriously as evidence accumulates that the mind can kill the body. . . .

Emotions can be lethal. Researchers are finding that many deaths, especially heart attacks, may be caused by the way the mind reacts to a certain situation.

Experiments with both animals and humans show that the heart is the major target of intense stress. The flood of hormones released by emotions can cause abnormal heart beats which can lead to sudden death.

But the effect of the hormonal assault is more widespread. It can suppress the body's immunological defense system and led to increased risks of dying from cancer, accidents, cirrhosis, and other diseases.

In one study of 170 emotional sudden deaths, investigators found that all had three common stress-related factors—the emotion-triggering situation was impossible to ignore, it evoked intense emotions, and the situation was one in which the person had no control. . . .

The deadly effects of loneliness and isolation are dramatically shown in a new study by Lisa Berkman, an epidemiologist at the University of California's School of Public Health in Berkeley.

The study, which followed 7,000 randomly selected people over a nine-year period, disclosed that those who were isolated with a low level of social contacts had from two to more than four times the risk of dying during the period than persons with many social ties.

The factors that led to a longer and healthier life were having good friends, family ties, and membership in social and religious groups.

A strong marriage and good friends were the best indicators for a long life but a single person with close friends did as well as a married person with few close friends. . . .

Boulder (Colo.) Daily Camera
December 20, 1977

Some psychologists think there is likely to be an emotional component in every health problem, including fatal illnesses.

faster than normal speed or slower than normal speed. When real time was 5:30, the clock was either set fast at 6:05 or set slow at 5:20. The experimenter entered the room munching on a cracker and carrying a box of crackers, which he set down on the table, inviting the subjects to help themselves. The obese students ate just about twice as much when the clock said 6:05 as when it said 5:20, while just the opposite was true for nonobese people. They ate less at 6:05 (fake time) than at 5:20, saying they did not want to spoil their upcoming dinner. In short, the obese people responded to the external stimulus of the clock by increasing their intake simply because they thought it was dinnertime. Since the real time was 5:30 in both cases, the internal stimuli were presumably the same, and if their eating were under internal control, they would have eaten the same amount regardless of whether the clock said 6:05 or 5:20.

If obese people are sensitive to external food-related stimuli, we can understand why it is so difficult for them to keep off the weight they lose. Another factor is the number of fat cells in the body and the preset weight level, which is probably controlled in the hypothalamus. These are apparently hereditary factors, which means that it will be difficult to modify them. Here we can surmise that if an obese person does lose weight, his or her internal regulating system will be signaling a food deficit and the individual will constantly be experiencing feelings of hunger and will be motivated to eat. Ultimately, research on the physiological regulation of food intake may uncover means by which we can modify the preset weight level and allow an obese person to lose weight and keep it off without suffering from constant hunger. In the meantime, we will have to use other techniques, such as behavior modification and social group pressures (for example, Weight Watchers), to modify eating habits.

CONTROLLING EMOTIONS

If we understood emotions fully we would be able to control and to express them in an appropriate fashion. Knowledge of emotion has potentially far-reaching application in the area of mental health. Many psychologists believe that inability to deal with and appropriately express emotions is the major source of psychopathology. The individual's attempt to escape anxiety is thought to be the primary motivation for pathological behavior. As we will see in Chapters 11 and 12, anxiety is a key concept for understanding mental illness, and teaching people to cope appropriately with their anxiety is a key concept in psychotherapy.

Complete knowledge of the physiology underlying emotion will also contribute to emotional control. We already have tranquilizing drugs and "mood-elevating" drugs, and as our knowledge of the physiology of emotion grows, additional techniques will be developed. As we saw in Chapter 2, there are now surgical procedures that can be used to destroy parts of the brain that control violence and aggression. The suggestion has been made that all world political leaders be given drugs to control their aggression. Perhaps we could ultimately control and eliminate all violence from from child beating to war.

The ability to control emotions would have impact on our physical health as well as our mental health. Medical science has implicated emotional factors in many diseases, the so-called psychosomatic disorders. For example, asthma and stomach ulcers are usually thought to be partially caused by emotional factors. If our knowledge of emotion were sufficient, we should be able to teach people ways to control their emotions and in turn to improve their physical health. Recently there have been suggestions that emotional factors play a role in two diseases that are major causes of death, cancer and heart disease. If this is true, then the ability to change our emotional habits could significantly prolong our lives. At the very least, it ought to be possible to identify people who because of their emotional habits are high-risk individuals. Perhaps these people could be given special medical treatment of a preventive nature.

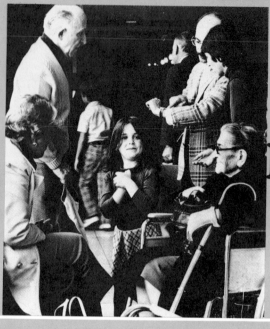

8

Developmental Psychology

Do we ever really stop growing and changing? Is there an age after which intelligence, personality, and learning ability stop developing?

What can a newborn infant do? Is the infant really helpless? Can it learn, see, and express emotions? If it cannot, how do these behaviors develop as the baby grows older?

On the first day of school some children seem calm and secure while others are anxious and unhappy. What factors contribute to these differences?

What effects do biological changes, such as voice change in males or the appearance of breasts in females, have on the behavior and feelings of 12- to 15-year-olds?

These are some of the commonly asked questions about the developmental process. Developmental psychology is the study of the changes in behavior that occur with age, as the result of biological growth, learning, and other experiences. Historically, the study of development has been both descriptive and explanatory. We strive to describe the different stages of development and to explain why these behaviors are present. Using scientific procedures, developmental psychologists attempt to understand how and why these behaviors change over the lifetime of the individual.

Traditionally, developmental psychologists have been primarily concerned with studying changes that are long-lasting and permanent. They seek to understand the processes of biological, cognitive, emotional, and social changes that take place over a period of weeks, months, or years rather than those which are typically momentary, such as changes in mood. In this chapter we will concentrate on the changes that take place during infancy, childhood, and adolescence, but we will also look at some of the major changes that occur during the middle and later years.

THE PROCESS OF DEVELOPMENT

Development is a dynamic, never-ending process that involves many complex factors. Theories help to integrate these different factors, and several different theories of development have been proposed by psychologists. Basically, these theories represent three general models: the psychoanalytic, the behavioral, and the cognitive-developmental, or organismic. Looking at the process of development from these different perspectives will help your understanding of how development is a process of change, not just a series of developmental milestones such as walking or getting married. Our interest is in the why of development as well as in the what. We are interested in both process and product.

The Psychoanalytic Perspective

Perhaps the oldest systematic theory of human development is the psychoanalytic perspective developed by Sigmund Freud during the late nineteenth and early twentieth centuries. It assumes that development is made up of *dynamic, sequential,* and *structural components.* This perspective views the human being as a passive organism whose psychological growth is initiated and maintained through internal or "intrapsychic" events.

The dynamic component involves the expression of certain **instincts** or needs. Basically, these instincts represent conflicts between opposing forces. For example, Freud identified two broad classes of instincts, one that represents life (called *eros*) and one that represents death (called *thanatos*), which he believed are present in each person at birth. These two types of instincts are involved in a never-ending but unconscious struggle with each other. The result of the individual's attempts to reduce the conflict between these opposing forces is development. These instincts are often expressed in subtle ways that are not obvious to the untrained observer. For example, a psychoanalyst might see nail-biting as the expression of a "destructive" instinct, possibly belonging to a class of instincts representing death.

The sequential component represents Freud's belief that every individual passes through qualitatively different stages of development. Each of these **psychosexual stages** is characterized by the focus of psychic energy on a different area of the body. In Freudian theory biological forces determine these stages of growth to a large extent. During the first stage, the *oral stage*, which roughly spans the

I HATED THE WAY I TURNED OUT..

SO EVERYTHING MY MOTHER DID WITH ME I HAVE TRIED TO DO THE OPPOSITE WITH MY JENNIFER.

MOTHER WAS EVASIVE. I HAVE BEEN DECISIVE.

MOTHER WAS MANIPULATIVE. I HAVE BEEN DIRECT.

NOW MY WORK IS DONE. JENNIFER IS GROWN.

THE EXACT IMAGE OF MOTHER.

© 1974 by Jules Feiffer.

to love another human being and propagate the species through sexual reproduction.

These five stages of psychosexual development take us up through young adulthood. A frequent criticism of Freudian theory is that it ignores later developmental stages. Other psychoanalytic theorists such as Erik Erikson have proposed a continuation of these stages throughout the entire lifespan, emphasizing the importance of social forces as influences on development.

Finally, Freud proposed that the mind contains structures representing different forces. The **id,** representing biological needs, is governed by the pleasure principle and seeks immediate gratification of impulses. The **super-ego** develops later in life and represents parental and societal forces that urge the child to control impulsive behavior. Finally, the **ego** acts as a mediator between the id and the super-ego and represents the forces of reality. The ego allows the id to be childish while also allowing the superego to act as its conscience. The ego constantly strives to fulfill its primary purpose, the satisfaction of need.

A major criticism of Freud's system of psychosexual development is that it is too abstract and does not often deal with observable behaviors. Yet Freud's approach is still a major force in developmental psychology.

The Behavioral Perspective

The behavioral perspective presents an entirely different viewpoint from that of Freud and his followers. While psychoanalytic theorists see human development as the result of internal conflicts, behaviorists emphasize environmental influences. Behaviorists do not believe that the concept of stages of development is a valid explanation of the developmental process. For them, development is a function of learning; experiences become organized in different ways for different people, and these differences account for the variation in individual behavior.

This emphasis on learning was thoroughly explored by a number of behaviorists, such as Ivan Pavlov and John Watson. It was the work of B. F. Skinner, however, that placed behaviorism in the forefront of modern psychology. Skinner identified two types of behaviors, re-

first 18 months of life, the most sensitive part of the body is the oral cavity. In the *anal stage,* which lasts until the end of the second year, psychic energy is focused on the organs that control the elimination of wastes. By the time children reach the *phallic stage,* they better understand the relationship between the external world and their own needs through the pleasure derived by manipulation of the genital organs. During the *latency stage,* beginning as early as the age of five in some children and lasting until adolescence, children are more interested in developing social skills and interacting with each other than in learning more about themselves. Finally, the *genital stage* is characterized by a refocus of energy on the genital area, with a strong psychological need

Work-Now-Play-Later 'Grandma's Rule' Works, Doctor Claims

Sandra Dillard

An advocate of "grandma's rule" for child-rearing, i.e., "first you work and then you play" was in Denver . . . to explain his theory to parents.

"There are better ways than nagging to accomplish things," said Dr. Wesley C. Becker, coauthor of "Successful Parenthood."

"Parents need to focus on praising their kids on things they want them to do better, rather than focusing on what's wrong," said the psychologist and educator. "And parents need to teach their children (what they want them to accomplish and how they want them to accomplish it)."

Dr. Becker feels that a warm and positive approach to "problem children" actually can change their behavior, making for happier children as well as fulfilled and successful parents.

'Most Common Mistakes'

But he also feels that parents unwittingly make mistakes that result in their getting exactly the opposite response than they had hoped for.

"The most common mistakes," said Dr. Becker, "are excessive attention to misbehavior, not teaching (social skills and behavior), and inconsistency. When you do decide it's time for a change, you demand too much. And, finally, too often parents punish by using physical force or just yelling."

The psychologist said that parents should be explicit in formulating what's expected. "Then you've got a base for checking for whether it was done or not," he said. For instance, Dr. Becker explained, a "clean your room" order is not as specific as providing a list of expected tasks to be accomplished—toys in toy box, books on shelf, dresser top clean, floor swept, bed made, etc.

He said the next step is that when a child meets a certain responsibility a parent should be behaviorally specific in praising the action.

Dr. Becker also believes in rewarding approved behavior. "A real concern that parents have is that this is bribery—that the kid should want to do it (behave well, eat properly, perform chores, etc.) on his own—but wouldn't it be better to find something that works?

"Consistent use of rewards is not bribery. There are a whole variety of possible payoffs without ever using any tangibles like food or money—a special excursion, staying up an extra half-hour, an unusual activity," Dr. Becker said.

He said that specific behavior should be encouraged "not on an 'if' but a 'when' basis. WHEN you do so-and-so, then you can do thus-and-so. This is an effective use of rewards, setting up an agreement 'When you do this, this will happen.' " . . .

The Denver Post
July 10, 1974

Here is an example of the behavioral approach—based on reinforcement principles—applied to child-rearing.

spondent behaviors and operant behaviors. Respondent behaviors (classically conditioned behaviors) are controlled by what comes before them, such as the knee-jerk reflex. These were the kinds of behaviors Pavlov and Watson studied. Operant behaviors are controlled by what follows them, and this discovery was Skinner's greatest contribution to psychology. Skinner discovered that the stimuli (or events in the environment) that follow a behavior can cause that behavior to either increase or decrease in strength. Operant behaviors are a function of their consequences. We can judge the effectiveness of an environmental force by the effects it has upon a behavior. For example, for some children being spanked is reinforcing because it represents getting attention; yet for others being spanked represents punishment.

Skinnerian psychologists view development as the result of various types of conditioning, the end product of a long sequence or "chain" of experiences. For this reason behaviorists contend that if the environment is structured in the proper way, the potential for learning (that is, development) is unbounded. For example, people classified as "vegetative idiots" can sometimes be taught new and adaptive ways of functioning.

1.

"Better not let your father see you like that. Upstairs and wash."

2.

*Ted Key, Squirrel in the Feeding Station, New York: Dutton, 1967.
Reprinted by permission of Ted Key. Copyright © 1967 by Ted Key.*

According to the behavioral perspective, the model —often a parent—is one of the most powerful influences on development. Children are more likely to do as their parents do, rather than as they say.

Another group of behaviorists believe that other factors besides environmental influences should be considered. Proponents of the **social learning theory,** such as Albert Bandura (see Chapter 9), say that although development is a function of learning, there is a reciprocal give and take relationship between the organism and the environment. It is essential to understand processes such as memory, perception, and other "mentalistic" operations in order to understand how humans acquire behaviors. The greatest contribution of these theorists has been in the area of imitation, or modeling—the process of learning new things without directly experiencing them (through vicarious learning).

In many ways the behavioral perspective is today as controversial as the psychoanalytic perspective was 70 years ago. Some people feel that the behavioral view represents development as a passive process with no input whatsoever from the organism. On the other hand, the behavioral perspective has allowed us the luxury of systematizing and understanding factors that influence behavior by the application of rigorous scientific procedures. It has also had a tremendous impact on the value of applied psychology in general. Not only are behavioral techniques used in many different therapeutic situations—such as in desensitizing people to certain fears—but they have led to such developments as *programmed instruction* which have greatly benefited education in recent years.

The Cognitive-Developmental Perspective

While the psychoanalytic and behavioral models are popular with a large number of psychologists, a major criticism of them has been that they assume the human organism is passive and contributes relatively little to its own development. In contrast, the third general model— the cognitive-developmental, or organismic— sees the human organism as playing an active role in the developmental process. The most famous proponent of this general approach is the Swiss psychologist Jean Piaget.

According to this model, development results from an interaction between what the organism knows or is capable of doing and the constant demands for change that the environment places on the organism. For example, a child might believe that all four-legged, furry animals are called dogs until he or she is told differently. Such experiences force the child to alter what cognitive-developmental psychologists call internal structures. In our example, the child will change his or her structure of animals to include dogs, or even possibly create an altogether new structure called dogs. These structures in their earliest form are simple reflexes such as sucking or grasping, but through biological growth and interaction with the environment they undergo change. Thus the developmental process is the organism's constant striving to adapt to the environment, correcting any disequilibrium that exists between its knowledge and the external world.

The cognitive-developmental model differs

from the psychoanalytic and behavioral models in three basic ways. First, it assumes that development occurs in stages. This may sound like the psychoanalytic model, but here development is primarily a function of the organism's interaction with the environment, not simply the result of internal conflicts. Second, the stages occur in a fixed sequence regardless of other influences. Third, each stage is qualitatively different from the others. For example, the way a five-year-old child learns about the world is quite different from the way a five-month-old baby comes to learn about its external environment. These different stages build upon one another in such a way that any developmental stage is more than the sum of the stages that came before it. Recall the Gestalt concept that the whole is not the same as the sum of its parts. Development from the cognitive-developmental perspective is the process of different elements coming together to form a new structure, larger and different from what existed before.

THE MAJOR ISSUES

One of the purposes of a model of human development is to use it as a tool in generating new questions for study. Sometimes these new questions present challenges to the developmental psychologist since there is no correct answer. In fact, these issues become the point of debate. We will now discuss some of the major issues of developmental psychology.

Maturation and Learning

A person's future is partly shaped at conception when the genetic material from both parents is combined to determine biological characteristics (such as hair color) and psychological characteristics (such as intelligence). But that is not the whole story. Development depends not only on hereditary factors but also on learning.

During the process of **maturation** some abilities develop in a preprogrammed way with biological growth. Although maturational changes are most obvious in behaviors that are closely tied to anatomical growth, many psychologists believe that maturation is also responsible for changes on a psychological level. These changes tend to be the same in children from various

Try Not To Interrupt When Baby Is Babbling

AP

NASHVILLE — It's not only impolite to interrupt, but if you interrupt your baby's babble, it may slow down his or her speech development, a psychologist says.

Dr. Peter Vietze, director of the infant learning program at Peabody College here, said this was one of the findings from a study of infants' learning development.

"Traditionally mothers are taught to reinforce babies—the sooner you respond, the more likely it is to have effect," Vietze said in an interview.

"One of the rules of reinforcement is that you reinforce immediately—bit it doesn't say when. What we found is that if the mother responds before the baby is finished, essentially interrupting the baby, it doesn't seem to be as beneficial as if she waits for the baby to finish."

He compared it to an adult conversation. "If you are talking with a person who continues to interrupt you, you may eventually give up trying to converse with that person."

Therefore, mothers who are more sensitive to letting their babies talk may have babies who develop language earlier than others, said Vietze.

Rocky Mountain News, *Denver*
December 5, 1975

Here is an example of developmental research that fits the cognitive model better than the behavioral one.

cultures and consequently are not dependent upon individual experiences. For example, all normal children develop some form of verbal communication we call language at approximately the same time, independent of any specific training. Psychologists who have tried to accelerate development, for example, by attempting to teach children to talk early, have not been successful.

A variety of behaviors appear to be maturational in nature, such as the ability of an infant to control eye focus. This ability develops only when the various muscles that control eye movement and the shape of the lens (see Chapter 3) have fully matured. Other examples are the ability to walk and to vocalize. Both are de-

Too-Small Kids May Be Short of Love

Robert Conn

The unloved child may unknowingly be advertising its problem for all the world to see—by being too small for its age.

There are lots of reasons why a child may not be growing as fast as its friends, and many children of devoted and loving parents may be short simply because it runs in the family.

But the most startling reason is what doctors are now terming psycho-social short stature.

According to a report in the current Medical World News, psycho-social short stature is considered the hallmark of the emotionally battered child—one who does not get enough love.

Up to a point, such short stature is reversible. If the child is removed from a home where it is not loved, and placed in a home where there is love, the child frequently grows very rapidly.

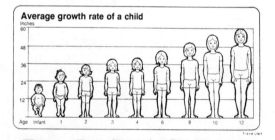

Average growth rate of a child

The Medical World News report—part of a major survey of the reasons why children are too small or too tall, cited one series of youngsters studied by Dr. Robert

M. Blizzard, chief of pediatrics at the University of Virginia Hospital in Charlottesville.

Blizzard, who specializes in pediatric endocrinology [hormones] found that the diagnosis of psycho-social short stature is provable after the fact—because it does reverse.

In 13 youngsters that Blizzard studied, growth in foster or convalescent homes was startling: The average growth rate was 0.65 inches per month [which works out to 7.8 inches a year], compared with the normal for that age range of 0.2 inches per month [2.4 inches a year].

Blizzard suspects that the emotional problems that a child experiences in his original home prevents it from eating or sleeping properly.

"The possibility that growth will be retarded [because of a social environmental factor] is much more widespread than people would have suspected," says John Money, a psychologist who has worked with children in a clinic similar to Blizzard's at Johns Hopkins University.

Money says that the diagnosis is difficult to make because the parents are the problem. He recommends that as soon as such a situation is suspected, the parents should be interviewed separately, before they've had a chance to make up a common story. . . .   Chicago Tribune
March 21, 1976

It is difficult to sort out the effects of maturation versus experience in human development. Bodily growth appears to be influenced by the social environment and by biological development or maturation.

pendent on muscular growth and a degree of organization not present at birth. Maturation, then, is a biological process in which developmental changes are controlled by internal or hereditary factors. These kinds of behaviors are characteristic of the species as a whole.

Learning, on the other hand, is a direct function of experience and refers to developmental changes that result from exercise or practice. Although the process of language development might be universal and controlled by hereditary factors, the content of the language itself is a

Healthy, active children vary enormously in their rates of development.

"When I was ready to read, they taught me to tie my shoes—when I was ready to tie my shoes, they taught me to read."

© 1979 by Sidney Harris.

Figure 8-1
Group differences, individual differences, and overlap

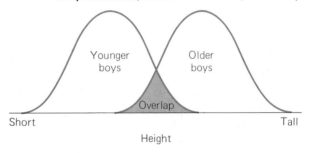

product of learning. Children of foreign-speaking parents don't speak the natural language of their parents but the language of the society or culture in which they grow up.

Group and Individual Differences

Many descriptions of behavior provided by developmental psychologists are normative, that is, the focus is on average performance on some particular task at a certain developmental level. Although the norm is a useful concept in developmental psychology, we should recognize that there are also individual differences. Norms are based on a large sample of people, all of whom do not represent the average or **mean** of a set of values. Not all of us reach puberty or attain

our intellectual peak at the same time, since variation in the rate of development is characteristic of the developmental process itself.

The importance of these differences is represented by a concept called overlap, shown in Figure 8-1. In this case the two bell-shaped, or normal, curves (see Appendix A) represent the heights of two different groups of boys. As you can see, the older group is taller in general. That is, while the average height of the older

"He's walking!"

Developmental milestones such as walking often
occur with no prior warning or indication.

Ted Key, Squirrel in the Feeding Station. *New York: Dutton, 1967.*
Reprinted by permission of Ted Key. Copyright © 1967 by Ted Key.

The Aged Adolescent

Adolescence and old age occur half a century apart,
and seem to have nothing in common. In fact, says
Psychoanalyst James Anthony of Washington University in St. Louis, the two stages are sometimes
psychologically similar; present-day youngsters,
far more often than their predecessors, show symptoms of aging long before they are out of their teens.

Among the symptoms very often shared by the
aging adolescent and the aging adult is depression,
Anthony says. "For both, the future looks black
and unappealing," and "preoccupation with death
and nothingness is frequent." Both youngsters and
oldsters "can pass days in endlessly doing nothing,
feeling that there is nothing to do." Besides, the
two groups are often alike in being "intensely self-
absorbed"; in fact, "the narcissism of old age and
the narcissism of adolescence are two peaks in the
development of human egotism." Hypochondria,
too, can peak in adolescence as well as old age—
which Anthony says "is not surprising because, in
both, profound bodily alterations are taking place."
Frequent changes in self-reliance also occur in old
and in young; both alternate between battling for
independence and leaning excessively on others.

Despite these behavioral likenesses in the age
groups, the aging adolescent has an advantage over
the aging adult: "Given a new perspective, a new
ideal, a new cause, a new hero or a new theory,"
Anthony says, he can be "rejuvenated." First,
though, he must somehow acquire something that
characterized most adolescents of an earlier generation: the intense desire to grow up.

These days, Anthony reports, "there are a growing number [of young people] who do not view
themselves as passengers in transit through a phase
of development but as persons who have arrived at
their destination and are not interested in going any
further"—certainly not in the direction set by materialistic, achievement-oriented parents who expect youngsters to perform like adults. "Nothing is
more aging than this constant pressure," Anthony
believes. The problem, then, "is to get the parent
off the adolescent's back" so he can have fun while
he is young and choose his own goals when he is
ready.

Time
May 1, 1972

Although we are usually unaware of it, there are
some strong similarities between different stages of
development.

boys is greater than the average height of the
younger boys, there are some younger boys who
are taller than some older boys. This area of
overlap, shown by the crosshatching in the figure, demonstrates how norms are important as
a point of reference for an entire group. However, unless individual differences are considered, the true picture of development might not
be clear. Norms are helpful in detecting serious
deviations from the average (see Chapter 11),
but it can be dangerous to interpret them as
characteristic of the whole group.

Continuity and Discontinuity

Psychological behavior, like maturational
changes, exhibits spurts with age. Have you
ever heard people say things like "It seems
Sarah has grown up overnight" or "Steven all
of a sudden has a new attitude about himself"?
Any dramatic change that takes place within a
short period of time suggests that development
may be a discontinuous, or stagelike, process. By
discontinuous we mean that one stage of devel-

opment is qualitatively different from a previous stage. All individuals begin life at a certain stage of development. At a later point, triggered by some events that are unspecified, but thought to be biological, the transition is made to a more mature stage.

A contradictory perspective sees psychological development as a continuous process, with change taking place in small, gradual steps; in this case the final outcome is simply "more of the same" and not qualitatively different from what preceded it. In other words, the rate of development may increase or slow down from one time to another, but there are no abrupt or discontinuous transitions from one stage to another.

As with other issues in developmental psychology, the workable answer is in the form of a compromise. Some aspects of development are probably continuous and sequential, while others unfold in spurts.

COGNITIVE DEVELOPMENT

A newborn infant is, of course, capable of some physical actions, but is psychologically immature. In five to ten years this organism will normally become an independent, social human being with the capacity for intelligent, original, and creative thought and action. This transition is in large part a matter of cognitive development, the growth and change in knowledge and competence that enables us to interact and cope successfully with our environment. We turn now to an examination of four kinds of intellectual development: perception, learning, cognition, and language.

Perception

Infant Perception

Even newborn infants exhibit certain perceptual skills. They are attracted to stimuli in the environment, can hear differences in the pitch of sounds as small as one note apart on the piano, and can differentiate among some odors and tastes.

Interestingly, the most important sense—vision—is more immature at birth than are other systems. Once an infant opens its eyes, its visual focus is relatively fixed at about 9 inches from the cornea, which is the approxi-

Figure 8-2
Measuring visual preferences in infants

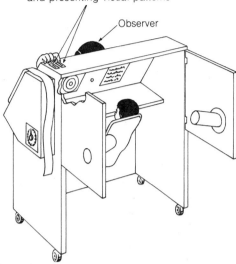

Switches for recording fixation time and presenting visual patterns

Observer

A device used to measure the interest value of different visual patterns in terms of time spent looking at them. The subject sits facing a "stage" where patterns are presented. His or her view is restricted to the inside of the illuminated chamber.

mate distance between the baby and its mother's face during feeding. The coordination of the infant's eyes is poor because the eye muscles are weak. Indeed, the newborn infant often appears cross-eyed. The retina is also immature but it responds to changes in light intensity.

Infants spend much of their waking time just looking, and they exhibit definite visual preferences. A device used to measure looking behavior and visual preferences is shown in Figure 8-2. If you present infants with a moving array of lights versus a stationary pattern, you will find that they are more attentive to the moving stimulus. One-day-old infants also spend more time looking at patterns such as a bull's-eye than at plain-colored figures like a red circle (see Figure 8-3). These preferences occur so early in a child's life that many people conclude that sensitivity to pattern is an innate phenomenon. In this connection, recall the discussion of receptive fields in Chapter 3.

One of the most interesting of the newborn's visual preferences is the human face. Infants smile more at a line drawing of a face than at

Figure 8-3
Pattern preferences in infants

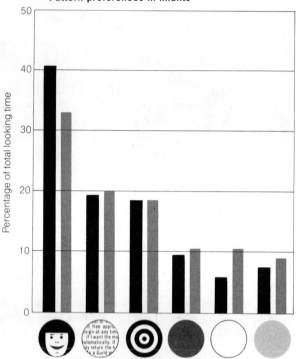

Importance of pattern rather than color or brightness is illustrated by the response of infants to a face, a piece of printed matter, a bull's-eye, and plain red, white, and yellow disks. Even the youngest infants preferred patterns. Black bars show the results for infants from two to three months old, colored bars for infants more than three months old.

"Gee, it's still just the same as when I was a little kid!"

Playboy, May 1969. Reproduced by special permission of PLAYBOY Magazine. Copyright © 1968 by Playboy.

Most parents do not realize that the world looks different to their children. Parents should try at least occasionally to see the world through their childrens' eyes and to remember what it was like to be a child.

an equally complex, nonhuman pattern. They attend more to a three-dimensional mask than to a line drawing of a face and pay more attention to real faces than to masks. After several months natural, familiar faces elicit more smiling than unfamiliar ones. Then, at about age two, the child's preference for familiar and more realistic objects tends to wane. Unusual stimuli become attractive and appear to take on the character of problems in need of solution. The child's perceptual activity develops from a period in which attention is given primarily to movement and contrast to a second period in which what is familiar and meaningful is most attractive and finally to a point in which the focus is a search for the unusual.

The perception of objects in depth, which adults take for granted, seems to develop by the time the child begins to crawl (six to eight months and possibly even before). The existence of depth perception in young children has been verified using the "visual cliff" (Figure 8-4). The illusion of a cliff is built into a level glass floor, and the child is urged to crawl across the floor over the edge of the "cliff." Babies have refused to crawl across the surface beyond the cliff even to reach their mothers. This does not mean that depth perception exists at birth, but it does suggest that it develops early in life.

Later Development of Perceptual Skills

New sensory experiences lead to changes in behavior. These changes reflect both new

Figure 8–4
The visual cliff

A mother testing her child on the "visual cliff." Above, the child eagerly crawls to the mother on the "shallow" side of the cliff, where the checkerboard pattern is placed right below the glass surface. Below, the pattern has been placed on the floor, giving the illusion of depth or of a cliff. Now the child refuses to crawl off the cliff despite the mother's inducements.

Figure 8–5
Which is writing?

Because they do not distinguish scribbles from letters, three-year-old children have trouble determining what represents writing. Even five-year-olds may have difficulty.

knowledge and new ways of gathering knowledge. Consider the following experiment. A child is blindfolded and given the chance to explore tactually a strangely contoured object. The object is then put on display with a number of other objects, and the child must identify the target object on the basis of touch only. If a three-year-old is presented with this problem, the child tends to hold the target object briefly in the palms. Contact with the object is minimal and uninformative, and the child typically fails to identify the object. In contrast, seven- and eight-year-olds run their fingers around the edges and spread the thumb and forefinger in an apparent effort to gauge the length of the object. The 10-year-old child efficiently touches just those features that are likely to distinguish the object from others. The organized search pattern of older children allows them to identify

Babies See More Than You Think

Jack Horn

The infant's world may be less egocentric than Jean Piaget's child-development theories suggest. Jerome Bruner and M. Scaife, working at Oxford, have found that children as young as two months will follow the gaze of their mother or other adults. This action—not just looking at another person, but using her as a guide to something else—indicates that even very young babies can interact with their environment in a rather complex way.

Bruner and Scaife worked with 34 infants from two- to 14-months old. They placed them in highchairs, where experimenters played with them to win their confidence, and then went through a fixed sequence of head and eye movements.

The experimenter first made eye contact with the child, then turned his or her head 90 degrees to one side, kept it there for seven seconds, and then looked back at the child. With eye contact restored, the experimenter went through the same routine, this time turning in the opposite direction. Concealed video cameras recorded the infant's reactions during the experiments.

The experimenter used the video record to score the infants' behavior as *positive* if they turned their heads in the same direction as the experimenter did, without looking elsewhere first, and appeared to be looking at something; or as *negative* if they didn't meet these criteria. Three other observers, who scored the trials independently, agreed with more than 90 percent of the experimenter's judgments.

Positive responses increased steadily with the children's age. At two to four months old, 30 percent of the babies followed the experimenter's eyes. By eight to 10 months, two thirds did so, and by 11 months, all of the children showed what the researchers call "joint visual attention."

Bruner and Scaife admit that the fact that infants turned their heads in the right direction doesn't necessarily mean they were following the experimenter's lead. But the way the older infants reacted suggests this was the reason. They would often look in the desired direction, turn back to the experimenter, and then look away again. This sequence, Bruner and Scaife reported, was even more marked when the mother was the experimenter.

The researchers point out that an infant's ability to follow his mother's lead in this way may be a basic process, useful in cognitive and social learning. . . . Human infants, they conclude, may . . . have more built-in abilities than we have supposed.

Psychology Today
July 1975

The idea that infants are helpless creatures is becoming more and more disputed as studies such as these show them to have many of the same competencies as adults.

objects more quickly and more accurately. Systematic, efficient, and thorough search patterns develop with age in all sensory systems, not just in touch.

E. J. Gibson's analysis of reading shows that what is searched for—as well as the search method itself—changes with age. When adults scan a book they use highly refined reading skills the three-year-old does not possess. Asked to identify letters, the three-year-old will correctly ignore line drawings but will incorrectly assume that unintelligible scribbles are letters. Even five-year-olds who know which marks are letters often cannot isolate words because they ignore spaces between words (Figure 8–5).

By the time the child reaches the age of 10 or 12, perceptual skills, including those involved in reading, are essentially fully developed. Significant changes occur later, such as the commonly observed deterioration in one or more sensory systems brought on by the aging process, but the peak of the fundamental abilities underlying behavior is reached at a relatively early age. Only intense specialized training can bring about significant further improvement in perception.

Learning

Learning in Infants

It was once thought that newborns could not actively learn, but with the advent of new experimental procedures researchers have begun to destroy that myth. There is even evidence that some learning takes place before birth.

A common example of early learning is the

classical conditioning of anticipatory sucking at the sight of a nipple. In one experiment Kaye (1967) sounded a tone just before a nipple was presented. Babies only three or four days old quickly learned that the tone was a signal for the subsequent appearance of the nipple. Even during extinction (when the tone was no longer paired with the nipple), many babies persisted in sucking in response to the tone alone. The conditioning of sucking responses is one of the first signs of learning that parents notice. Babies typically recognize the feeding position and begin to suck as soon as they are placed in that position.

Instrumental or operant conditioning can also be demonstrated. Siqueland and Lipsitt (1966) taught infants to turn their heads when a buzzer was sounded. Rewards were then switched so that reinforcement was given when the baby turned at the sound of a tone instead of a buzzer. Babies three days old quickly reversed their behavior. It is clear that infants are capable of learning discriminations as soon as they can be tested.

Infants also show signs of responsiveness to secondary reinforcers. For example, vocalization and smiling can be increased when reinforced by a friendly pat or a bit of baby talk; subsequent withdrawal of adult contacts produces a decrease in vocalizing and smiling.

Concept Learning in Early Childhood

At first, children's concepts are rudimentary and based on concrete, perceptual examples. Having formed simple concepts such as "dog" and "cat," they are later able to correctly classify entirely novel experiences, such as a stray dog. Although a child's repertoire of concepts increases with experience over the years, children do not develop abstract concepts until the fifth or sixth year. Young children probably learn most concepts by rote memorization. That is, they associate the same response (or category) with each of a large number of individual stimuli before the process of generalizing can occur. In contrast, the older child (seven or eight years) learns in a different way. These children can abstract the characteristics of objects, analyze each stimulus into its constituent parts, and use only those parts that define the concept. They have more sophisticated problem-solving skills.

The transition point in this developmental sequence from rote learning to analytic and abstract abilities comes at about the same time as the child is developing a command of language. This is also the period when children develop the ability to talk to themselves. Some theorists believe that this internalized speech operates as a problem-solving device and as a mechanism for guiding and regulating overt speech and other forms of behavior.

Cognition

The most detailed description of the development of cognition has been provided by Jean Piaget. Piaget divides development into four major periods: sensorimotor, preoperational, concrete operational, and formal operational.

Piaget asserts that all children progress through all of these stages in a fixed order. According to his theory, human intellect is constructed over time as the individual experiences progressively more complex interactions with the environment. Piaget believes that the initial source of development is biological but that the rate or pace of development can be influenced largely by the environment.

In Piaget's system two processes, organization and adaptation, actively operate during each of the four stages. *Organization* is the process by which different elements within a system maintain communication. For example, we have a tendency to organize basic sensory information (such as images and other experiences) in order to form more complex ideas and thought.

Adaptation consists of the complementary processes of assimilation and accommodation. These two processes are the basis for cognitive growth. **Assimilation** is the modification of external events to fit already existing schemata or underlying structures. For example, a young child might call all four-legged furry things (dogs, cats, or stuffed animals) dogs because this is the child's schema (or internal structure) for the different stimulus qualities of that experience. The child assimilates new experiences into an already existing structure (four-legged furry things). The complementary process of **accommodation** changes the internal structure to fit the demands of the environment. If a parent corrects the child by saying, "No, that is not a dog, it is a cat," the child is encouraged to adapt to the new situation by altering an existing idea. The child simultaneously integrates new experiences to old schemata or ideas (assimilation) and changes some of these old schemata when necessary (accommodation). The process is a dual one that has as its goal a state of equilibrium, or balance, between the demands of the external world and the structure of the child's mind, and it provides the motivation for further growth and development.

The Sensorimotor Stage
(Birth to Two Years)

During the first month of life (Step 1) babies appear unaware of themselves and the objects around them. They do not realize that the bottle they grasp one minute and the object they suck the next are the same object. In fact, if something drops out of sight, it literally "drops out of mind." The infant has a lack of what Piaget calls *object permanence.*

In months one through four (Step 2) babies' motor activities become more coordinated. At this point they begin to look at what is being grasped. They will move their hands to touch an object by alternating their gaze between hand and object, homing in on the object by trial and error.

Between months four and eight (Step 3), the infants' attempts to control and manipulate objects are often comical. They may hear an interesting noise and want it repeated, but since they do not know what caused the noise, they try to make the noise recur by repeating whatever they were doing when they heard the noise. Piaget calls this an example of "magical procedures to make interesting spectacles last." During this period the baby first begins to realize that objects exist when they are out of sight. If a toy is dropped, the child will search for it, but only for a short time.

In the final four months of the first year (Step 4) magical thinking gives way to more instrumental activity. By this point children have achieved object permanence (Figure 8–6). They have some interval image of the object to help them recall it and its location. Moreover, they display a sense of space and time, as exemplified by the organized and orderly actions of lifting a pillow to search for a hidden object. But the child is still quite limited intellectually. If you hide the object under one pillow and then move it in plain view to a second, the child will search under the first pillow and may or may not move to the second.

The 12- to 14-month-old (Step 5) is likely to go directly to the second pillow to find the hidden object. Piaget sees much of cognitive growth as the formulation of increasingly complex hypotheses about events and the modification of these hypotheses in the light of experience (see hypothesis testing theories in Chapter 6). For example, a child may systematically vary the position from which he or she drops a toy in order to discover where the toy will land. There are parallel developments in the infant's perceptual processes during this time.

The final stage of sensorimotor development covers the last half of the second year of life (Step 6). In the preceding six months the child appears stumped when an object is placed under one pillow and then is moved in a closed fist to another pillow. Older children are not fooled by this movement because they infer what the moving hand holds. This last stage is important because it represents the beginning of the child's ability to represent mentally objects that are no longer physically present. In essence, it is the start of abstract thought.

The Preoperational Stage
(Two to Seven Years)

The major advance made during this period is the ability to represent the external world mentally by means of arbitrary symbols that stand for objects. This is the period in which language develops and begins to reflect the child's cognitive abilities and limitations. The preoperational child is in a transitional period. His or her perspective on the world is expanding rapidly, but the child is still confused in the use of physical concepts and in evaluations of cause and effect. During this phase children make inappropriate generalizations and attribute their feelings to inanimate objects—assuming, for example, that clouds "cry" to make rain. The child's limited conception of the world is revealed in the following interview:

ADULT: Why is it dark at night?

CHILD: Because if you don't sleep, Santa Claus won't give you any toys.

ADULT: Where does the dark come from at night?

CHILD: Well, bandits. They take something or mother pulls down the blinds and then it's very dark.

ADULT: What makes it day?

CHILD: God, he says to the dark, go away.

(Laurendeau and Pinard, 1962, pp. 170–171)

Notice what Piaget would call **egocentrism** in

Figure 8–6
Object permanence

(A)

In the first four months of life an infant attends only to objects that are physically present (A). At eight months and beyond the infant knows about and attends to the location of hidden or occluded objects (B).

(B)

this example. Children seem unable to imagine the world from any perspective other than their own. They are unable to acknowledge alternative perspectives, and this inability limits the kind and amount of new knowledge the child can acquire.

**The Concrete Operational Stage
(Seven to Eleven Years)**

The concrete operational stage is characterized by the emergence of operations such as conservation. **Conservation** is Piaget's term for the idea that a property or attribute of an object

"Why did you cut my squash in half, Mommy? Now I have TWICE as much to eat."

© *1974 The Register and Tribune Syndicate*

Is this an example of conservation?

Figure 8–7
The chemical problem

The chemical problem illustrates the different stages of cognitive development described by Piaget. Children of different ages are presented with four containers of colorless, odorless chemicals and a fifth beaker (g). Next, the children are shown a glass with a combination of two chemicals (unknown to the children, these are chemicals 1 and 3). When several drops of g are added to the glass, the liquid in the glass turns yellow. The children's task is to reproduce this color.

remains the same despite some transformation that changes the appearance of the object. Piaget found that when preoperational children are shown two identical balls of clay and then see one rolled into a sausage, they may claim that the sausage contains less clay because it is thinner than the ball. The child is taking only one aspect of the situation (shape) into account. By focusing on the end state without considering how the sausage was produced, the child arrives at the wrong answer. If the child remembered that the sausage came from a ball identical to the unchanged ball, a different answer would be arrived at.

At about age seven, the child grasps the solution to conservation problems by developing three concepts that characterize **concrete operations.** The first is *compensation:* the sausage is thinner but that change is balanced by its increase in length. The second is *reversibility:* if you roll the sausage back you get the same ball you started with. The third is *identity:* nothing has been added to or subtracted from the clay, so the sausage and the ball contain the same amount of clay.

In the concrete operational period the child acquires and applies the notions of reversibility and identity across a wide variety of tasks. It is during this period that systems of classification and of number are learned. Arithmetic is

much easier when it is realized that $4 + 3 = 7$ is the same as $3 + 4 = 7$. The ability to perform these mental operations in many different situations, with many numbers in any concrete problem, eliminates the need for rote memorization. The same rules are applicable across all situations. The child gives evidence of beginning to realize that arithmetic, as well as other disciplines, are based on a system of rules.

The Formal Operational Stage

The complex, abstract, and mature logic of adults begins to manifest itself during adolescence with the systematic analysis, exploration, and solution of problems.

The following problem can be used to demonstrate how formal operational thought differs from earlier stages of cognitive development. Four similar glass containers of different colorless, odorless chemicals along with another small container containing a fifth chemical, potassium iodide, are placed on a table before the subject (Figure 8–7). A certain amount of chemical

TABLE 8–1   Contrasting Approaches to Solving the Chemical Problem

Stage	Behavior	Explanation
Sensorimotor (birth–2 years)	Child ignores the request and plays with the toys.	Lacks the vocabulary and motor skills to understand what's required to perform the task. Before 8 or so months lacks object permanence. Should one container drop from view, the child won't search for it.
Preoperational (2–7 years)	Child combines two containers at random.	Understands goal, but does not order the tests (take one jar and "g," then the next, then the third). The child cannot keep track of what has been done, and does not classify the results into combinations that produce a yellow color and those that do not. The child is likely to think an irrelevant feature like the shape of the containers or the amount of the contents determines the color.
Concrete operations (7–11 years)	Child adds the fluid from each container in a systematic fashion. Then starts to combine "g" with pairs of containers and becomes confused.	Can order tests, one container at a time, but has difficulty ordering two variables simultaneously. Can classify container combinations into those that make the yellow color and those that do not. Possesses logical operations of reversibility and identity. Understands conservation. Knows the problem has to do with the identity of the chemicals, not the shape of their containers.
Formal operations (11 years and older)	Child takes the containers and combines them with "g" one at a time, and so on. Is able to keep track of the system and identify both chemicals that make the dye and some of the others.	Possesses knowledge of permutations and combinations. Can go beyond data to describe in abstract terms the nature of his or her system of testing. Can figure out what would happen if new chemicals were introduced; can deal with hypothetical situations, laws of probability, and so on (possesses the essentials of symbolic logic).

from two of the similar containers is poured into an empty glass. The experimenter then adds several drops of potassium iodide, and the liquid, consisting of two unknown chemicals, turns yellow. The subject is asked to reproduce this color, using any or all of the containers.

Infants up to two years old pay no attention to the problem situation and merely play with their toys. Children in the preoperational stage randomly combine chemicals, making no attempt to keep track of what they have done. Between the ages of seven and eleven years children begin to combine chemicals systematically, but tend to become confused after several steps. Children over eleven, however, are able to approach the problem with a logical and complete plan. They take chemicals from the containers two at a time, keeping a record of those that do not work so they do not repeat themselves. Piaget's explanation of these chron-

ological differences in problem-solving ability is summarized in Table 8–1.

Most teenagers can deal skillfully with abstract questions or questions that are contrary to fact, like "What would have happened if the United States had not entered the Vietnam war?" The more literal, concrete operational child insists that questions of this sort are invalid because the war did take place with U.S. involvement.

During the teenage years young people realize that thoughts are private and that no one else knows what they are thinking. They value friendship and sincerity and spend much time trying to discern real motives. The formal operational thinker is more aware than the younger child that events can be interpreted in many ways and that there is no final version of truth. He or she is also more sensitive to the discrepancy between reality and ideals. Teen-

TABLE 8-2   Commonly Heard First Words

Utterance	Age (Months)	Probable Meaning
eh?	8	An interjection. Also demonstrative "addressed" to persons, distant objects, and escaped toys.
dididi	9	Disapproval (loud) or comfort (soft).
mama	10	Food, tastes good, hungry.
nenene	10	Scolding.
tt!	10	Calls animals.
piti	10	Interest(ed)(ing).

agers' knowledge of politics and attitudes toward arbitrary rules of conduct are very different from those of younger children. If a rule proves unworkable, they are likely to advocate change, while younger children recommend increasing the punishment for disobedience, as if the rule were absolutely sacred. Adolescent thinking is characterized by sensitivity to others and the abilities to handle contradiction and the logic of combinations and permutations. This mature system of thought allows the mastery of complex systems of literature, mathematics, and science. It also enables the development of abilities necessary for adult socioemotional adjustment, such as the planning of future goals and the integration of past and present into a realistic self-identity.

Language

The acquisition of language is an achievement unique to human beings, and the speed with which it occurs is remarkable. A child starts to speak intelligibly at about one year of age and goes on to master the fundamentals of language in about three years. By age four, the child has a vocabulary of well over a thousand words and can understand and produce most of the grammatical structures used. Let us now consider how this is all accomplished, taking into consideration the contributions of both maturation and learning.

Initial Speech

Sound production progresses through four periods—from crying to cooing to babbling to speaking words. The baby's first vowel-like sounds are merely accidental by-products of the business of living—breathing, digestion, crying in distress. Cooing begins at about 12 weeks when the child responds vocally to interesting sights in the environment, particularly faces. Consonants begin to emerge, and at about 6 months babbling begins. Consonants and vowels are combined into one-syllable utterances ("Ma"), and at about 8 months children begin to imitate their own speech and the speech of others, producing repeated syllables like "di, di, di, di, di." Some of the syllables heard in babbling are associated with objects or events, resulting in the child's first words at about one year of age.

Although such "words" are not, strictly speaking, part of the English language, their consistent usage as labels for objects and classes of objects makes them function like words. The meaning of the word is likely to be less precise or perhaps more flexible than the corresponding word in adult speech. "Da Da" may describe father, mother, a babysitter, or indeed any adult. Other examples of one child's first words and their meanings are given in Table 8–2.

Although the rate of vocabulary acquisition is slow for the first few months, additions occur rapidly. By 18 to 21 months the typical child's vocabulary contains approximately 200 words, by 24 months, 300 to 400 words, and by about 3 years, as many as 1000 words.

The production of speech appears to lag somewhat behind the comprehension of speech. The infant can hear the difference between *b* and *p*, although he or she cannot produce these two sounds. A lisping child may call himself "Tham" but be irked by people who fail to call him "Sam." On intelligence tests infants between 9 and 10 months are expected to respond accurately to "No" or "Where's Daddy?" although they probably will not produce these words until later.

Childhood Language Period

Between 18 months and 2 years of age the child begins to produce sentences clearly based on a grammar. Among English-speaking children the production of these sentences is systematic and regular. Some people have described the child's language at this stage as a simplified or telegraphic version of adult speech. Recent evidence, however, suggests that the child's language is unique. Its systematic nature

Interpreting Baby Talk

What do an infant's cries mean? Hunger, usually, or discomfort, or fear. But they also reveal a slow process of learning how to communicate. Within a few months the baby's noises already show signs of patterns: a cry followed by a pause to listen for reactions, then another cry.

So reports Jerome Bruner, 60, long-time Harvard psychologist now teaching at Oxford and author of such pioneering works as *A Study of Thinking* (1956) and *The Process of Education* (1960). . . .

Adult Vicars

Learning to talk is no sudden discovery, according to Bruner. It takes about two years of dogged practice—by the mother as well as the child. (Bruner means not necessarily the child's natural mother, but someone who acts as "vicar" of the adult community.) Every word the vicar uses is a lesson in what sounds and tones work best. By the age of two months, the child can make a cry that demands or one that requests, *i.e.,* one that awaits a response from the mother. "Mother talk," corresponding to "baby talk," tells the child that its request will be met and gives the child signs of the consequences of his request. Says Bruner: "Linguistic competence is developing before language proper."

In addition to making sounds, mother and child use their eyes as part of the communication process. A mother spends much of her time during the child's first four to nine months, says Bruner, simply trying to discover what the child is looking at. . . .

She begins pointing out objects and giving them names. From ten months onward, the child as well begins pointing out objects. Mothers introduce a familiar pattern: 1) pointing to an object; 2) putting the question to the child, "What (or who, or where) is that?"; and 3) labeling the object, person or place ("That's a hat," "That's Grandma," "That's the bedroom").

Without knowing it, the mother has already set in motion the process of fostering the four basic skills that Bruner considers essential for making sentences later on:

"Well-formedness," when the mother demands a closer approximation to the correct pronunciation of a word with each repetition.

"Truth functionality," generally begun after the first year, when she corrects a mistake: "That's not a dog, it's a cat."

"Felicity," which means that the manner of speech must be appropriate to the situation.

"Verisimilitude," when she allows a child to place a box on his head and pretends it is a hat, but does not encourage him to do the same thing with, say, a ball.

Step by step, in a steady series of accretions of meaning, these lessons lead toward acquiring the gift of speech. Says Bruner: "Man realizes his full heritage when he reaches language. But he is doing things along the way which are also quite remarkable."

Time
August 23, 1976

---

leads to unusual sentences that do not occur in adult speech and therefore cannot be direct imitations, for example, "All gone shoe," "Bye bye car." The following conversation between a two-year-old and his father, who has arrived home from work and is changing his clothes, illustrates how a young child combines two words to form some short sentences.

CHILD: Hi, Daddy.
DADDY: Hi, Johnny. Did Mommy buy this truck?
CHILD: This truck.
DADDY: Can you make it go fast?
CHILD: Go fast. Hat off. Shirt off. Pants off. That blue.
DADDY: Yes, my pants are blue.
CHILD: Sweater on. See Mommy. Hear Mommy.
DADDY: I'll go and help her carry in the groceries.
CHILD: Groceries. Bye-Bye. Two bag. Chicken. That red. Bag fall. Close it.
DADDY: I can't close the box so we'll have pizza for dinner.

(Palermo, 1970, p. 437)

The child's "minisentences" lack many features of adult speech, such as noun-verb or adjective-noun agreement. But the sentences are nonetheless recognizable, functional, and governed by some linguistic rules. Most importantly, they do convey meaning.

TABLE 8-3   Early Two-Word Sentences

A coat	More coffee
A celery*	More nut*
A Becky*	Two sock*
A hands*	Two shoes
The top	Two tinker toy*
My mommy	Big boot
That Adam	Poor man
My stool	Little top
That knee	Dirty knee

* Ungrammatical for an adult.

Braine (1963) observed a two-year-old child who had 14 different two-word combinations in his vocabulary. Seven months later he could produce 2500 combinations. With so many combinations learned in such a short time, it seems unlikely that the child was just memorizing each one independently. There must be a system of rules for forming sentences. Pivot words (P), although few in number, are frequently used. Words from another more variable class, called the open class (O), seem to attach themselves to pivots. Pivot words are generally adjectives, articles, and demonstration pronouns. Open words are generally nouns, and the child acquires these words rapidly. Some pivots, like "that," occur only in the first position; others, like "off," only in the second position. Pivot-open constructions are by far the most common (see Table 8-3).

For the two-year-old child studied by Braine, the grammatical system can be described by using a simple notational system (S = sentence, P = pivot word, O = open word):

S → (P) + (O)
P → a, big, dirty, little, more, my, poor, that, the, two
O → Adam, Becky, boot, coat, coffee, knee, Mommy, tinker toy, etc.

Further development occurs through word additions and new combinations of words. Children learn that "A book" is correct but not "A celery." They combine two-word sentences like "That red" and "That flower" into "That red flower." They also learn some ordering rules. When they describe the number, color, and size of trains, they say "Two large, red trains," not "Large, red, two trains." Children learn how to make themselves clear to others.

The child soon goes beyond two-word sen-

Gibberish? It's Really 'Twin Talk'

UPI

SAN DIEGO — For several years, the small twin daughters of Mr. and Mrs. Thomas Kennedy were thought to be retarded because they speak only gibberish.

But speech therapists have discovered that the 6-year-old girls actually developed their own language and are both bright youngsters.

Alexa Romain, a speech therapist at Children's Hospital, calls the language "idioglossia," or twin speech.

"Development of this kind of language has been found to occur in very rare instances among twins who have had no other contact with other children," she said. "There is very little in the medical literature about it."

English and German are spoken in the Kennedy home, but the twins could speak neither, according to the parents. Therapists have found the children understand both languages, even though they don't speak either one.

The language the girls have developed sounds like gibberish to others, but they appear to communicate well between them with their chatter.

No one—including the parents—has yet been able to translate the twins' language. Some of it sounds like this: "Dugon, haus you dinikin, duah, snup-aduh ah-wee die-dipana dihabana." . . .

Earlier this year, the twins were put in a special school class for the mentally retarded. But teachers soon realized the girls were in the wrong class, and they were sent to the state's regional center for the developmentally disabled at Children's Hospital, where authorities said the children now are learning English rather rapidly.

The Denver Post
July 23, 1977

The spontaneous development of language suggests a strong biological basis.

tences. During the second and third years, the child begins to demonstrate transformations. For example, "You went there" is a simple declarative sentence that can be transformed into a question ("Did you go there?") or a negative ("You did not go there."). The child's early speech, however, lacks transformational rules.

This progression in the direction of adult sentence structure is taken as an indication of the child's gradual acquisition of the transformational rules thought to underlie most languages. (These transformational rules are universal. If we analyzed the underlying structures of many different languages, we would find a striking similarity.)

Language and the Development of Thought

Almost all psychologists agree that language and thought are intimately related. We have noted that children's ability to use attributes or features of stimuli as mediators of their behavior probably corresponds to the ability to "think verbally." In this section we will discuss in more detail the impact of language on the development of thought.

A MENTAL MODEL OF THE WORLD There is reason to believe that, in addition to the concept of object permanence, thinking involves the development of a mental model of what the world is like. The final step in the development of this world model may depend upon the development of language.

Newborn infants have a limited world model and may be almost exclusively dependent upon and controlled by stimuli in the immediate circumstances. As children develop and experience external stimuli, they gradually acquire a more accurate, complete, and highly differentiated representation of the world.

Jerome Bruner has identified three fundamental ways human beings convert the world of immediate experience into a cognitive or mental-world model. The first to develop is called the **enactive mode** and is based upon action or movement. Within this mode the world is constructed of bodily movements. The child knows no other way to "think about" the world. For adults, familiar motor skills provide an example of how this mode works. Most of us know how to ride a bicycle and can, therefore, think about riding a bicycle (a matter of nonverbal, motor abilities). Trying to teach someone to ride a bicycle or play golf strictly by verbal instruction is difficult, if not impossible, since knowledge of these activities is so heavily stored in the enactive mode.

At a later stage of development, in the **iconic mode,** knowledge of the world is based heavily on pure sensory information stored as sensory images. Think about the arrangement of furniture in your room, apartment, or house. You can imagine the scene and "read off" your image. In so doing, you are using iconic knowledge.

The third mode involves the use of language, the **symbolic mode.** In this case words and sentences are used as symbols of objects, events, and states of affairs. Obviously, the chief milestone of cognitive development is the child's acquisition of language and his or her development of the ability to think in the symbolic mode.

Bruner illustrated a developmental sequence in modes of thought by showing how children of different ages approach a problem involving conservation of volume. A five-year-old child is shown two identical breakers filled to the same level with water. When asked which contains more water, the child replies they are the same. The water in one beaker is then poured into a third beaker that is taller and thinner so that the resulting water level is higher (Figure 8–8). Now when the child is asked which beaker contains more water, he or she selects the tall beaker. Perhaps the child is limited to the enactive mode of knowing. ("What is involved in drinking from the containers? Taller things require more drinking.") Maybe his or her thinking is bound by the stimulus situation, and he or she focuses too much on the level of the liquid.

Bruner then placed a screen in front of the beakers so that only the tops of the beakers could be seen and not the water level (the distracting feature). He studied the responses of children who were four through seven years old. Without the screen, almost all four- and five-year-olds missed the answer, and even up to half the six- and seven-year-old children responded that the taller beaker contained more water. With the screen blocking the view of the water levels, however, almost all the five-, six-, and seven-year-olds answered that the beakers contained the same amount, and even about half the four-year-olds answered correctly. When Bruner removed the screen and presented all children with the differing water levels, the four-year-olds who had answered "equal" now changed their minds and chose the taller beaker. The older children, however, stuck with their original answer. By this procedure, then, five-year-old children, who almost

Figure 8–8
Conservation of volume problem

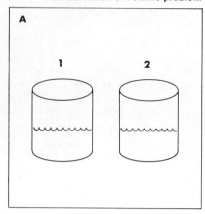
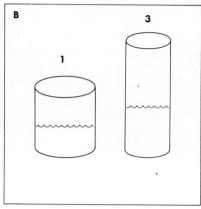
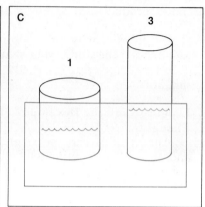

A child is shown two beakers of liquid (A) and asked, "Which contains more, 1 or 2?" A five-year-old child will say that they contain equal amounts. Then the contents of 2 are poured into 3, a taller and thinner beaker (B). The child is again asked, "Which contains more?" He or she answers, "3." The child is said to be unable to conserve volume. However, if a screen is used to block the view of the water levels, so that only the tops of the beakers show (C), the five-year-old does conserve; he or she will say that they still contain the same amount.

always fail the test under ordinary circumstances, come to answer correctly and stick with their answer.

According to Bruner, five-year-old children are capable of symbolic thought, but they are at a transition point between the iconic and the symbolic mode and feel unsure of themselves. They rely heavily on enactive or iconic information when available. The screen forces the child to use the symbolic mode and blocks the iconic by preventing distracting information about the different water levels. Four-year-olds are even less sure of their symbolic abilities and revert to the dominant iconic mode when the screen is removed.

INNER SPEECH Closely related to the symbolic mode is the development of inner speech. Inner speech is talking to oneself, or speech that has "gone underground" and has become implicit and mental. Thus inner speech guides and directs overt behavior. In young children outward speech serves the same function. Thus we see three- and four-year-old children talking to themselves while playing or otherwise engrossed in a task. According to one theory, overt speech behavior gradually breaks down, be-

comes abbreviated, perhaps is whispered until it finally becomes completely inaudible and only its indirect signs (such as minute physiological changes) are detectable. Recall the motor theory of thinking (Chapter 6) and notice how closely related to it this position is. Incidentally, it is interesting to note that implicit speech sometimes surfaces in adults when they are concentrating on a very difficult problem. You may have observed people deep in thought talking out loud to themselves without being aware of it.

Piaget has taken a different perspective. He classifies children's conversations into one of two types: (1) egocentric, in which children speak but are unable to assume the perspective of a listener (they appear to be talking out loud for their own sake and no one else's) and (2) socialized, in which the main objective of communication with someone else is achieved because the child can adopt the listener's perspective. The gradual decline of egocentric speech is considered a sign of the development of a more sophisticated mental-world model, one that is not centered exclusively on the child but allows for other perspectives. For Piaget, egocentric speech does not "go underground" to become the inner speech that controls overt per-

Language in Deaf Children: An Instinct

The acquisition of language has always been one of the more intriguing aspects of childhood development. "The child of English-speaking parents learns English and not Hopi, while the child of Hopi-speaking learns Hopi, not English," note Susan Goldin-Meadow of the University of Chicago and Heidi Feldman of the University of California at San Diego School of Medicine.

"But what if a child is exposed to no conventional language at all?" the researchers ask in the July 22 SCIENCE. "Surely such a child, lacking a specific model to imitate, could not learn the conventional language of his culture," they say. "But might he elaborate a structured, albeit idiosyncratic, language nevertheless? Must a child experience language in order to learn language?"

In attempting to answer that question, Goldin-Meadow and Feldman videotaped six deaf children in their homes for one to two hour sessions at six- to eight-week intervals. The 17- to 49-month-old children—four boys and two girls of "normal intelligence"—had not been exposed to manual sign language because their parents wanted to expose them to oral education. Yet none at that point had acquired significant knowledge from their oral education program.

The youngsters were observed and taped during informal interactions with a researcher, their mother and a standard set of toys. The researchers found that the deaf children "developed a structured communication system that incorporates properties found in all child languages. They developed a lexicon of signs to refer to objects, people and actions, and they combined signs into phrases that express semantic relations in an ordered way." . . .

"We have shown that the child can develop a structured communication system in a manual mode without the benefit of an explicit, conventional language model," the researchers conclude. They compare the findings with the "meager linguistic achievements of chimpanzees," where chimps have been shown to develop languagelike communication, but only with training. "Even under difficult circumstances, however, the human child reveals a natural inclination to develop a structured communication system," say Feldman and Goldin-Meadow.

Science News
August 20, 1977

One way to examine the relative effects of both heredity and environment on the formation of language is to study the language habits of deaf children.

formance. Instead, it disappears because it is no longer a reflection of the child's cognitive abilities.

SOCIAL DEVELOPMENT

The emotions of the newborn child appear to be expressed along only one dimension—comfort versus discomfort. While infants are very dependent on other people, and are seemingly indifferent to surrounding circumstances, most of them develop into sophisticated social beings who are able to function adequately in a complex environment. Clearly, vast changes take place in an individual's social and emotional development over the years. Many of these changes are unique to human beings, while others are universal and characteristic of development in all organisms. We focus now on social development—the long, slow process in which the dependent infant becomes a unique adult personality capable of fulfilling an active and productive role in society.

Erik Erikson's Theory of Psychosocial Development

Erik Erikson has provided a unique perspective on the study of human development which incorporates many of Freud's ideas. In its orientation, it is both psychosocial and psychoanalytic. Erikson's theory is based on the premise that psychological development is the result of an interaction between the individual's biological needs and the social forces encountered in everyday life, and it has application over the

TABLE 8–4   Erikson's Eight Stages of Psychosocial Development

Psychosocial Stage		Task or Crisis	Social Conditions	Psychosocial Outcome
Stage 1 (birth to 1 year)	Oral-sensory	Can I trust the world?	Support and provision of basic needs	Basic trust
			Lack of support and deprivation	Basic distrust
Stage 2 (2–3 years)	Muscular-anal	Can I control my own behavior?	Permissiveness and support	Autonomy
			Overprotection and lack of support	Shame and doubt
Stage 3 (4–5 years)	Locomotor-genital	Can I become independent of my parents by exploring my limits?	Encouragement to explore	Initiative
			Lack of opportunity to explore	Guilt
Stage 4 (6–11 years)	Latency	Can I master the necessary skills to adapt?	Adequate training and encouragement	Industry
			Poor training and lack of support	Inferiority
Stage 5 (12–18 years)	Puberty and adolescence	Who am I? What are my beliefs, feelings, and attitudes?	Internal stability and positive feedback	Personal identity
			Confusion of purpose and unclear feedback	Role confusion
Stage 6 (young adulthood)	Young adulthood	Can I give fully of myself to another?	Warmth and sharing	Intimacy
			Loneliness	Isolation
Stage 7 (adulthood)	Adulthood	What can I offer succeeding generations?	Purposefulness and productivity	Generativity
			Lack of growth and regression	Stagnation
Stage 8 (maturity)	Maturity	Have I found contentment and satisfaction through my life's work and play?	Unity and fulfillment	Integrity
			Disgust and dissatisfaction	Despair

entire lifespan. In fact, Erikson's work represents the first attempt in developmental psychology to account for behavior over the course of a lifetime.

Development for every individual, according to Erikson, proceeds through eight stages. At each stage the individual is confronted with a basic crisis, which can be resolved in one of two ways (see Table 8–4). As the table shows, these crises and the alternative outcomes result from particular social conditions. Erikson believed that although maturational processes might be responsible for the onset of each stage, social or cultural demands act as powerful mediating forces between biological needs and the total development of the individual. Erikson has emphasized the importance of ego strength as the adhesive that bonds the different dimensions of psychological functioning. It is through

the ego that every individual experiences each developmental or psychosocial crisis. When each crisis is resolved, the ego gains strength and progresses to the next developmental stage with its accompanying psychosocial crisis. When the ego falters and cannot deal with the crisis, development is thwarted and does not proceed successfully.

These psychosocial stages and their expected behavioral outcomes are listed in Table 8–4. As you look at the table, it is important to keep in mind, of course, that conflicts do not produce responses of one kind only; we will see that this is true as we further explore Erikson's theory.

Stage 1: Oral-Sensory

During Erikson's first stage (infancy) an individual develops a sense of basic trust or basic mistrust. A newborn child is almost en-

Baby's a Person—Don't Forget It

Ronald Kotulak

Despite the fact that we were all babies at one time, much of our knowledge about newborns is based on myths.

"Ha," you say. "There is little to know about babies because there is nothing to them." If that's what you think then answer the following questions either true or false:

1 — Babies don't have emotions, just reflexes.
2 — They are incapable of learning.
3 — They can't see or hear.
4 — They don't recognize who is taking care of them.
5 — When they cry they are hungry.
6 — All they do is eat and sleep.
7 — They really don't smile, it's gas.
8 — They are not capable of loving.
9 — They don't have anger.
10 — The infant has no way of telling you what's wrong.

If you answered any of these questions true, you are wrong. They are all false, part of the widespread misconceptions about babies that have handicapped parents as well as the medical profession, said Dr. Marcene Powell Erickson, assistant professor of nursing, Child Development Center, University of Washington, Seattle.

Because of these myths, nurses and doctors have taken notice only of obvious infant problems such as diseases or birth defects and whether the internal plumbing was working, Dr. Erickson reported. . . .

"Worse yet, we planned care based on this very fragmentary and incomplete information—a dangerous and hazardous practice to say the least," he said.

But the care of babies is undergoing drastic changes as a result of new knowledge showing newborns to be much more surprising creatures than anyone previously thought, said Erickson. . . .

It may come as a surprise to most parents but their precious bundles of joy are not as fragile as everyone treats them. Furthermore, they are capable of learning almost immediately. . . .

A baby can do many things he seldom has been given credit for, he added.

A baby has several levels of consciousness. He is capable of establishing a memory track in order to respond appropriately to different stimuli. He can maintain attention for brief periods of time.

He can see and hear. He has purposeful movements. He adapts to new environments. He senses his own needs and tries to communicate them to others. He quiets himself in stressful situations. He has different degrees of cuddling.

He initiates and terminates activity by himself. Most importantly, all newborns are not alike, said Erickson.

Chicago Tribune
February 21, 1977

tirely dependent on others for the satisfaction of basic needs. If a child receives love, care, stimulation, and consistent attention from parents, he or she develops a sense of trust. Out of this positive feeling comes a trust in oneself and in one's own ability to deal successfully with basic needs. If no one comes when the child cries for food, if wet diapers stay wet for long periods of time, if attention that is finally given is harsh and cold instead of warm and caring, the child develops a basic mistrust. If mistrust is severe, the child may become withdrawn and apathetic, and even at this early point may give up hope of achieving his or her desires. Individuals who resolve this first stage in a healthy manner carry with them into adulthood a basic trust that becomes faith in the world and in themselves.

Stage 2: Muscular-Anal

In Erikson's second stage (early childhood) the formation of autonomy or shame and doubt is the prime issue to be resolved. Children who have established a secure sense of basic trust are ready to begin to become separate entities from their parents. They start to exercise their individuality by trying to do things on their own, by asserting their will, and by developing an awareness of themselves as separate, autonomous beings rather than as extensions of their parents. During the muscular-anal stage in Erikson's system, the child begins to learn self-control of such bodily functions as bowel movements and walking. If parents encourage exploration, allow children to do some things on their own, and are reasonably tolerant of irritating negativism, a sense of separateness,

Trust versus mistrust.

© 1974 by Jules Feiffer.

independence, and individuality can develop. This is autonomy. If, however, parents constantly hover over children and do everything for them, or make harsh and unreasonable demands that cannot be met (such as in toilet training), children will begin to doubt their own ability to be free and separate persons. Such children will also begin to feel shame at their inability to meet parental expectations.

Stage 3: Locomotor-Genital

During the third stage (childhood) initiative or guilt is formed, according to Erikson. Children become more mobile and are able to move into and explore previously unreachable places. Language becomes highly functional now also, and exploration in the form of questions about everything imaginable takes place. Curiosity also leads children to explore their own bodies and to investigate the differences between male and female bodies. During this phase of infantile sexuality the child is also attracted to the parent of the opposite sex. If children are allowed to be curious and to explore their world within reasonable limitations, they develop confidence and a sense of initiative. If curiosity is generally met with "Don't bother me now," or if children are given an environment with little to explore, they may develop a basic sense of guilt. In such cases the child's need to inquire may be stifled, so that anxiety and unhappiness may be expressed in a variety of ways. Successful resolution of this childhood crisis allows the individual to meet experiences in new, flexible ways without the constricting effects of guilt.

Stage 4: Latency

In Erikson's fourth stage of development (school age) the focus is on the emergence of industry or inferiority. Children are in school now, learning to make and do things. If much of what they accomplish there is met with some success, they receive encouragement, attention, and develop a sense of industry. If, on the other hand, a child continuously experiences failure in his attempts, receiving criticism or a lack of attention for much of what is tried, he may become fearful of taking on new tasks and put little effort into work. Children in this situation may feel they are doomed to fail, regardless of how much effort they exert. In contrast, the development of a healthy sense of industry in a child produces enjoyment of work and a feeling of pride because something has been done well. This attitude is carried into adult life.

Stage 5: Puberty and Adolescence

Erikson's fifth stage begins around **puberty** (adolescence), and centers on the *identity crisis.* The outcomes are a positive identity or identity confusion. The question "Who am I?" comes to the forefront and often creates much turmoil, confusion, and anxiety. Adolescents are likely to appear fickle during this period because things that are pleasing at one time may produce quite a different response not long afterwards. At this stage the adolescent has a need for consistency and stability to offset the confusion and anxiety created by his own changing self-image. Membership in teenage gangs, political groups, social clubs, or religious organizations may well serve this need, but if the adolescent relies too heavily on others, the identity crisis may be compounded by another problem. Eventually the individual may feel anger and resentment at being forced to do things—to see people, work at a job, raise children, and so on—that don't feel personally right. The result is often a return to the identity crisis.

If, on the other hand, adolescents are given support by others but encouraged to answer their own questions and seek out what really feels best "deep down," the identity crisis begins to move toward a more enduring resolution, a stable sense of personal identity. By experiencing some of the available alternatives and discarding those that seem wrong, people begin to

Teen Suicide Blamed on U.S. 'Fairy Tale'

Timothy Harper

MILWAUKEE, Wis. — Amy, 15, had always gotten straight As in school, and her parents were extremely upset when she got a B on her report card.

"If I fail in what I do," Amy told her parents, "I fail in what I am."

The message was part of Amy's suicide note.

Dr. Darold Treffert, director of the Winnebago Mental Health Institute at Oshkosh, Wis., places part of the blame for a sharp increase in teen-age suicides on what he calls "The American Fairy Tale." . . .

He says the "fairy tale" has five themes: that more possessions mean more happiness, that a person who does or produces more is more important, that everyone must belong and identify with some larger group, that perfect mental health means no problems and that a person is abnormal unless constantly happy.

"For some, the American Fairy Tale ends in suicide or psychiatric hospitals, but for countless others, it never ends at all," Treffert said. . . .

He said millions of Americans are plagued throughout their lives by a gnawing emptiness or meaninglessness expressed not as a fear of what may happen to them, but rather as a fear that nothing will happen to them.

He said Americans must stop evaluating themselves according to what they own or what they have done and learn to accept and cope with various mental and emotional problems.

"A whole generation has come to feel that it is un-American to experience any of these emotions," he said.

He said parents should avoid trying to make their children live up to the standards of the "fairy tale," and treat them as individuals, as people rather than possessions. . . .

The Denver Post
January 22, 1975

According to Erikson, the teen years are a time for establishing identity. For some, failure to crystallize identity can have devastating effects.

find certain activities and values that fill their needs. This process can take a long time, and typically may extend into the mid-twenties. Eventually it leads to consistent answers to the question "Who am I?" and development of confidence in oneself and one's way of life.

Stage 6: Young Adulthood

In young adulthood Erikson sees the issue of developing intimacy or isolation coming to the fore. At this point the individual becomes especially concerned about developing intimate, lasting relationships with others. Persons who have established a reasonably healthy and stable sense of identity are prepared to open themselves to others and share important parts of themselves. Individuals who are unsure of their identity are less likely to be truly open and caring and may become isolated from most other people. At the extreme is the "hermit," who shies from contact with others in order to avoid being hurt. In this category too is the "pseudo-intimate," the person with many superficial friends but with none close enough for true intimacy to develop. Both of these kinds of people feel vulnerable and unsure of themselves and are thus unwilling to take the emotional risks that are involved in being close to others.

Stage 7: Adulthood

After the first phase of adulthood, development in Erikson's view focuses upon acquiring a broader sense of shared intimacy. Individuals who have progressed through the first six stages may well drift into a life characterized by complacency, stagnation, and lack of growth. During this period people need more than intimacy —they strive for productivity and a true concern for others. The crisis at this stage is the choice between generativity and stagnation. Individuals, consciously or unconsciously, put together all the virtues and wisdom acquired in order to care for and guide the next generation. By maintaining meaningful contact with others, the individual receives stimulation and new ideas that prevent him or her from becoming stagnant.

Stage 8: Maturity

The last of Erikson's stages involves feelings of integrity versus disgust and despair. If an

As an elderly person who continues to lead a fruitful and productive life, this woman has most likely developed integrity in Erikson's eighth stage.

individual can look back and feel that life has been lived with meaning, that despite mistakes life has been reasonably successful, then a sense of integrity develops. If, however, one views life as having had no meaning, as having been useless and unsuccessful, then disgust may result. Despair is a concomitant: "It's too late to change now, or too hard to change, so I'll never be any different." A healthy resolution of this crisis brings a feeling of wholeness and peacefulness as one lives out one's life.

Other important aspects of Erikson's model need to be considered. First, how we emerge from earlier stages is partly dependent upon environmental influences such as parents. Parents who are doubting and mistrusting tend to overprotect their children and insist upon doing everything for them. Such parents pass on these feelings of doubt and mistrust to their children. Second, how we emerge from earlier stages greatly affects our growth during later stages. For example, children who feel a lack of trust are likely to be so cautious that they avoid new experiences and stifle their curiosity out of fear. Third, children who progress fairly successfully through Erikson's first four stages have the best chance of resolving the identity crisis in a healthy, enduring way.

Finally, in current society it is typical for

'Emotions' Not for Women Only

Ronald Kotulak

The popular belief that women are more emotional than men is not true, according to a study of 1,205 men and women "caught in the act" of emoting.

Men experience approximately the same frequency of emotions as women except they may not show them as much, said Dr. Paul Cameron, associate professor of human development at the St. Mary's College of Maryland.

The findings "shatter the myths of greater female emotionality, something that has become lore to both professionals and laymen," he reported. . . .

The technique Cameron and his associates used to find out what people were feeling at a particular moment was to catch them unawares.

They walked up to strangers in various communities and without warning asked them if they were experiencing an emotion and what it was.

Only 27 per cent of the people interrupted in this way refused to discuss what they were feeling.

The rest related their emotional experiences. The most prevalent emotion was joy and happiness. Other common positive emotions were peacefulness and love, followed by amusement and gratitude.

The most common negative emotion was nervousness, anxiety, and confusion. Depression ranked second, followed by anger. Other negative emotions included sadness, fear, boredom, foolishness, hunger, pain, and irritability.

The 399 males and 806 females in the study reported experiencing an average of three emotions a day, equally divided between pleasant and unpleasant.

Young adults between the ages of 17 and 26 reported twice as many pleasant emotions as unpleasant ones.

Chicago Tribune
May 9, 1976

healthy individuals to experience more than one identity crisis during a lifetime. A second crisis often occurs during middle age, and a third one is often triggered by retirement or the death of a spouse in later life. Resolution of these later crises involves much the same process as resolution of the first one. There are

Boys', Girls' Behavioral Differences Mostly Myths, Authors Say

Judith Martin

WASHINGTON — What is the difference between boys and girls, anyway?

This emotion-laden question is the subject of a collection and evaluation of hundreds of studies on sex differences compiled by two Stanford University psychologists, Eleanor Emmons Maccoby and Carol Nagy Jacklin. . . .

It is full of warnings about the dangers of handling material in which everybody concerned is probably thoroughly acculturized and opinionated. . . .

After all the reservations, the authors have concluded that most beliefs about learning differences and behavioral patterns between boys and girls are "myths," but that some do exist and cannot be accounted for by socialization.

Specifically, they concluded that:

While there is a slightly greater tendency for boys to move in groups of their peers and girls in pairs or smaller groups, there is no basic difference in their sociability or social dependency.

Neither sex seems more susceptible to the influence of others.

During college years, men seem to have more of a sense of control over their fate than women, although this is not true earlier or later in life, and the self-esteem level generally is the same.

The ability to do rote learning and that of doing higher-level work that reverses previously learned responses is equally distributed in boys and girls as is analytic ability.

Boys are more vulnerable to their environment before and after birth, but in matters of learning, both sexes are affected by heredity and environment in the same fashion.

In motivation to achieve, there are either no sex differences or, in some cases, researchers have found girls to be more highly motivated; however, boys are more challenged by competition.

Responses to auditory and visual stimuli are the same in boys and girls.

Found Differences

But the authors found what they considered significant differences . . . :

Girls, from age 11 on, have better verbal skills than boys.

Boys are better at visual-spatial tasks from adolescence on, possibly because of a sex-linked gene.

Boys are "more aggressive, both physically and verbally," than girls, from age 2, a finding they say goes contrary to culturalization that tends to try to restrain boys' aggressiveness because it is considered more dangerous than that of girls.

Boulder (Colo.) Daily Camera
January 1, 1975

periods of turmoil, exploration, and inconsistency that can lead to an entirely new series of answers to the question "Who am I?"

The Development of Sex Roles

Much of psychosocial development has to do with the learning of sex roles. The differences between males and females are first of all physiological and biological. But to identify maleness and femaleness from a psychological perspective other criteria need to be applied as well. Early training and experience, for example, are both important factors in the development of sex-role identification.

Although sex-role identification was once thought to be inherited, recent evidence suggests that it results from learning. For example, in one study parents were asked to "describe your baby as you would to a close friend." Parents also filled out a questionnaire, rating the baby on 18 scales such as firm-soft, big-little, relaxed-nervous, and so on. Finally, the psychologists obtained hospital records on each baby's weight, height, muscle tone, reflexes, heart rate, and so forth. None of the hospital data showed any difference between male and female babies. Parents, on the other hand, "detected" marked differences. Parents of daughters thought their babies were significantly softer, finer featured, and smaller than did parents of boys. Fathers went further than mothers in enumerating differences between boy and girl babies in looks and behavior. Such evidence strongly suggests that sex stereotyping begins at the time parents first learn the sex of their child and is not so much a function of biology as was once thought.

Sex-role development probably takes place during the second and third years of life. By the time most children are three years old, they can distinguish themselves as boys or girls. This three-year span appears to be a critical period, because the absence of any clear sex-role differentiation by this age may be indicative of later difficulties in adjustment. Harry Harlow, for example, has demonstrated with young monkeys that unless they are exposed to certain social conditions early in life, such as adequate mothering, they are likely to develop severe problems in psychosocial adjustment and may even not know how to reproduce. Similarly, John Money has identified a critical period in the sex-role development of the young child. He has found that children who have suffered severe accidents affecting their biological gender can be treated both medically (through hormone treatment) and socially (through parent education) to orient them toward different psychosexual roles in spite of biological endowment. Very young children have not established sexual identity, and certain environmental influences during early life can have irreversible effects on later development. (Perhaps there is no such thing as permanency with regard to a specific sex role. Adults when properly counseled both medically and psychologically can undergo a sex-change process that reverses their former sex role.)

Sex Differences and Androgyny

Historically, many people have felt that men are biologically better suited for certain tasks (such as being the "provider") than women, who are destined to remain in the home as childbearers and housekeepers. People tend to employ sexual stereotypes for both males and females, and as a result, equal opportunities for both sexes have not always been provided. In their comprehensive book *The Psychology of Sex Differences*, Maccoby and Jacklin (1974) concluded that there are relatively few substantial differences be-

Traditional occupational roles based on sex are being increasingly challenged as women today play a vigorous part in every area of the work force.

tween males and females that can be supported on evidence currently available. Yet there are many implied differences that have been inadvertently reinforced in our culture and that have no basis in fact.

In a time when males and females are finding any occupational goal within reach, biological sex is no longer the important variable it once was. Gender is a convenient dimension across which individuals can be separated, but this does not mean that it is a useful one in terms of understanding behavior or the developmental process.

Recently, a new and useful perspective called **androgyny** has emphasized that biological males and females have both masculine and feminine characteristics. The word "androgyny" comes from the combination of two Greek words, *andr* meaning "male," and *gyne,* meaning "female." The truly androgynous person uses whichever behavior is most adaptive at a given time. For example, a male who is aggressive in business may be very nurturant toward his children. Figure 8–9 contrasts this perspective with the traditional view of sex differences.

This new way of viewing sex differences en-

Who Is Androgynous?

Some psychologists argue that in a world where more women are choosing to work and more men are feeling the pressure of the "rat race," new norms of masculinity and femininity need to be developed. The term given to the combination of both traits is "androgyny" (SN: 4/26/74, p. 274), and its advocates say that androgynous women are better prepared to face life outside the home, while androgynous men benefit from the softening effects of such interests as child-care.

One study, conducted by a team from the University of Kentucky, compared the sex-type characteristics of some Midwest high school students to their styles in dealing with other people. Androgynous students of both sexes tended to be "friendly-dominant" in their relationships, while masculine-typed students were "hostile-dominant" and feminine-typed students were "friendly-submissive." Students with low scores in both sex-types were "hostile-submissive." A survey of sports figures conducted by Mary E. Duquin of the University of Pittsburgh showed that professional sports attract androgynous women, but highly masculine-stereotyped men.

Science News
September 18, 1976

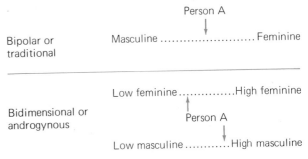

Figure 8–9
Two views of sex differences

courages young males and females to set goals and aspirations regardless of their physical characteristics. It also allows them to act in ways that are entirely natural (such as a nurturant father) but that have been discouraged up to now. As a society, we can all benefit when both males and females can contribute their skills, whether as airplane pilots or homemakers, or both. The challenge is to shake off the old stereotypical ways of thinking of males and females and begin to see people for what they are as individuals.

The Development of Morality

Morality consists of ideals or rules that govern human conduct. It also refers to one's attitudes toward social practices and institutions, and to one's judgment of what is right and what is wrong. Some system of morality is acquired early, but moral judgments usually change many times over the course of a person's life. Lawrence Kohlberg has found evidence that morality is formed by stages. To trace the development of morality in an individual, Kohlberg has devised a singular technique. He begins by telling a person a story such as the following:

A man wanted to buy a new drug that could save his wife from a fatal, incurable disease. The inventor of the drug, wanting a profit, tried to charge the husband much more than he could afford to pay. When the inventor refused to change his price, the desperate husband stole the drug.

After hearing the story, the person is asked to offer a moral judgment of the husband's act. Was it justified? Why or why not? Kohlberg found that people take different moral approaches and exhibit different attitudes depending upon their developmental level and experience.

According to Kohlberg, morality develops in stages, with each successive level representing a more mature form of moral reasoning (see Table 8–5). There are three basic levels: premoral, conventional role conformity, and self-accepted moral principles. At each level there are two steps. At level one, step 1 (early school-age), being right or wrong is judged on the basis of physical damage or punishment. One justifies the theft because the drug did not cost much to manufacture or condemns the theft because the druggist lost a lot of money. In step 2, judgment focuses on the intention that motivates the act. Selfish intentions are often condoned. Steal-

TABLE 8–5   Kohlberg's Stages of Moral Development

Level	Stage
Level one	*Premoral*
Step 1	Punishment and obedience orientation. Obey rules to avoid punishment.
Step 2	Naive instrumental hedonism. Conform to obtain rewards, have favors returned.
Level two	*Conventional role conformity*
Step 3	Good boy/girl morality. Conform to avoid disapproval or dislike by others.
Step 4	Law and authority maintaining morality. Conform to avoid censure by authorities.
Level three	*Self-accepted moral principles*
Step 5	Morality of contract, individual rights, and democratically accepted law. Conform to maintain community welfare.
Step 6	Morality of individual principles of conscience. Conform to avoid self-condemnation.

Figure 8–10
Mean percent of moral statements on Kohlberg's three levels made by boys aged 7 to 16

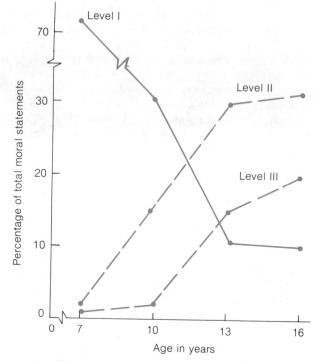

The figure illustrates the typical decrease from the first type of moral reasoning with advancing age and the accompanying increase in advanced moral judgments.

ing the drug may be judged moral because the man needs his wife's companionship, or the thief may be branded immoral because the inventor deserves a profit.

In step 3, the first step of level two, consideration of other people enters much more forcefully into the picture. Altruistic intentions are highly valued. The thief may be excused because he is unselfish and is helping his wife. Alternatively, he may be condemned because his family will be ashamed of his acts. Step 4, generally reached by age 11, reflects the concrete operational child's concern with culture and cultural rule systems. Emphasis is placed on law and order. The child says the husband must be condemned because he broke the law, or in justification of the theft, the child claims that the husband would violate his vows to protect his wife if he let her die.

The final two steps seldom appear before adolescence (see Figure 8–10). Here, a system of reciprocity that balances the rights of the individual and of society begins to be recognized. Thus, at step 5, there is an emphasis on contractual obligations and the rights of the majority. The theft is condemned on the grounds that one does not steal even when desperate because others may also be in great need. Or the theft is excused because the law was not set up for circumstances in which the

individual would forfeit a life by obeying the rules. In step 6, the individual's own conscience, based on abstract universal moral principles, acts as a guide. The man steals because it is never justified to take a life no matter what the consequences might be for stealing. Or he refrains from stealing because of the value he places on honesty. Both choices are justifiable.

The progressive stages of moral development involve changing perspectives of the role of the individual in society. A major task of adolescence is to decide how to mesh with the social order and/or how to change it, if necessary, to provide a more satisfactory life pattern. Those decisions become increasingly important as the young person reaches biological maturity and develops more complex and broader personal perspectives

TABLE 8-6 Some Relationships between Birth Order and Personality

Achievement: One of the strongest correlations between birth order and behavior is in the area of achievement. First-borns are much more likely to be prominent achievers—university professors, scientists, Rhodes scholars, research biologists, physicists, social scientists, and astronauts. First-borns are more likely to achieve better in school and be written up in *Who's Who*. It is assumed that this is the result of higher motivation, because the first-born is more adult-oriented, conscientious, and studious than later-born children.

Creativity. As with achievement, there is evidence to suggest that first-borns are more creative.

Aggression. In our society first-borns are taught to inhibit their aggression while younger siblings are taught to express it. For example, the older child is told to "pick on someone your own size," but the younger child is told to "stand up for your rights."

Sociability. It is the later-born siblings who are more often characterized as sociable, approachable, and comfortable with peers. The only child and the first-born child are characterized as being more uncomfortable in their interactions with others.

Self-esteem. Children without siblings have the highest self-esteem. In families that have more than one child, there is no relationship between birth order and self-esteem.

Psychopathology. There is no relationship between birth order and the probability of any particular child in the family being diagnosed as having emotional problems. However, if problems do occur, first-born children are likely to be timid, over-sensitive, and demanding of attention, whereas later-born children are more likely to be aggressive, negativistic, and destructive.

Favored by parents. Either the oldest or youngest child in the family is more likely to be favored by parents. Middle children are less likely, for example, to have affectionate nicknames.

Birth Order

Does birth order (first- or later-born) affect personality development? In fact, the oldest or first-born child often has the most difficult time, especially during the earlier years of development. It is more difficult for the first-born child to pass through the birth canal, and the mother is more likely to have a long labor. In addition, the first-born child weighs less at birth than later-born children. The more rapid intellectual development of the first-born child can probably be ascribed to the fact that the parents have no one else to care for. Since parenthood is new, perhaps more attention is paid to doing "what's right" or what the experts recommend.

Psychologists have studied the relationship

Why Twins Are Slow

Infant twins suffer from a sort of benign parental neglect. They get shorter hugs, less praise and fewer reprimands than singly born children, and are not spoken to as often. These findings by three Canadian scientists may help explain a fact long known but little understood: twins, in their early years, tend to have lower IQ's and pick up language more slowly than non-twins.

Using video equipment, psychologist Hugh Lytton and his colleagues at the University of Calgary taped the home lives of 46 sets of twin boys; single youngsters of the same age—about 2½—were also viewed. Computers analyzed the number of words and kinds of commands a parent used to address a child, as well as the frequency of hugs and kisses. In most cases, twins came up second best.

"The parents of twins are more harassed," says Lytton, pointing out that they have less time to devote to each child. And parents tend to assume that twins amuse each other, so they are often left alone. In the intellectual development of twins, the scientists argue, such unwitting neglect has more impact than the social and educational background of the parents.

The researchers believe their observations apply equally to twin girls. Further, they suggest, the experiment explains a puzzling discovery of the early 1970s: if one twin dies shortly after birth, the survivor develops verbal skills as quickly as single children. The slower intellectual growth of most twins, concludes Lytton, can be corrected quite simply by parents' talking more to their children—and providing more affection.

Newsweek
July 25, 1977

between birth order and personality, and we have summarized some of the generalizations that have resulted from these studies in Table 8–6. None of these relationships is especially strong, and questions have been raised as to the number of different factors involved. For example, as we discussed in Chapter 6, family size appears to be at least as important as birth order in determining intelligence. Indeed, family size probably plays a role in all the relationships listed in Table 8–6. There is need for much more research before any conclusions on birth-order effects can be stated with confidence.

OTHER PERIODS OF DEVELOPMENT

Adolescent Growth and Development

Many rapid physical changes take place during puberty as the human being becomes sexually competent. The most important of these is the appearance of secondary sexual characteristics (for example, pubic hair) and an increase in the intensity and diversity of emotional feelings. While parents want their children to become more independent, they may at the same time be reluctant to allow them to have their own way. Adolescents may also feel uncertain about their own independence. When both parents and the adolescent have uncertainties regarding the appropriateness of independence many conflicts are likely to ensue. Research indicates that both boys and girls tend to resolve most of these issues, especially those concerning moral standards, in the direction of their parents.

Physical Changes

Late in the first decade of life there is a marked increase in the production of sex hormones, leading directly to a spurt in height and a change in the reproductive organs. Other physical characteristics such as brain volume remain more or less stable, and there is even a decrease in the size of certain endocrine glands. For girls, the onset of the growth spurt is about 11 years. The next notable change occurs when the breasts begin to develop, followed by the appearance of underarm and then pubic hair (see Figure 8–11). Last comes the first menstrual period (menarche). The first ova produced are probably immature, but relatively soon after menarche a girl is fertile and essentially is able to support pregnancy.

The adolescent growth spurt in boys begins around 13 years (see Figure 8–11). Marked height changes become apparent between the ninth and fourteenth years. The average length of the penis doubles, and the volume of the testes increases tenfold between the ages of 12 and 17. Growth of the genitalia is followed in rapid succession by the appearance of pubic, underarm, and facial hair, deepening of the voice, and the first ejaculation of semen (approximately 13.5 years).

The clumsiness so often observed at the be-

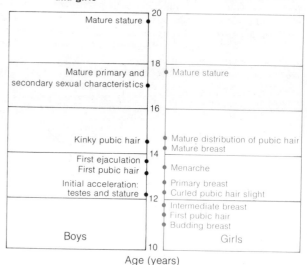

Figure 8–11

The typical sequence of sexual maturation in boys and girls

Age (years)

ginning of adolescence is not due to a lack of motor control of the new physical dimensions of the body, but rather to increased self-consciousness about bodily activities. Boys may find themselves having an erection at embarrassing or unexpected times. Girls who are not comfortable about the changes taking place in their bodies may try to hide breast growth rather than welcome these signs of maturation. While wide fluctuations in the voice tone of a teenage boy may be a source of amusement to others around him, the adolescent is typically self-conscious about these unexpected variations. Girls also go through a voice change, but the amount is not nearly so dramatic as it is in boys, and it tends to occur more gradually.

Psychosocial Changes

Parental influence tends to diminish during adolescence and is replaced by the influence of the peer group. The adolescent has a strong need to be accepted, liked, and even loved, and personal friendships are very important at this time. Mature interest in the opposite sex is also aroused at this time. The family frequently does not recognize that the boy who is now shaving and the girl who shows an interest in boys are developing new facets to their personality.

According to Piaget, adolescents experience a new type of egocentrism characterized by a failure to differentiate between what others are thinking and what they themselves are thinking. They believe that everyone else is an audience to their every move. They assume that everyone is conscious of their pimples, for example, and they constantly anticipate critical reactions from others.

Adolescent egocentrism also manifests itself in the tendency of teenagers to assume that their own feelings have a unique quality and intensity. Such overdifferentiation leads to the development of a personal fable, in which adolescents assume their experiences and emotions are entirely different from anyone else's. One reflection of this fable is the popularity of diaries, especially among girls, during early adolescence. These diaries almost always reflect the intensity and the importance the writer ascribes to her own experience.

Surprisingly, research indicates that personality is remarkably stable during adolescence. There is a sharp drop in self-esteem at the beginning of adolescence, but teenagers nonetheless tend to use the same words to describe themselves throughout this period. The amount of stress and traumatic experience in adolescence is, in all probability, overemphasized. In fact, adolescence is marked by considerable stability and conformance to the norm.

"Pop, can I have four hundred dollars to go to Fort Lauderdale and run wild?"

The New Yorker, March 18, 1967. Drawing by Lorenz; © 1967 The New Yorker Magazine, Inc.

Many adolescents face the dilemma of economic dependency on their families, yet desire social and personal independence. This conflict often leads to a breakdown in communication between teenagers and their parents and can be a source of great difficulty.

The Older Adult

Until the last 20 years developmental psychology, like child psychology, focused on the behavior changes that take place from birth through adolescence. Rarely was there a reference to the years beyond biological maturity; indeed, this practice helped to create the myth that no important changes take place during adulthood. Developmental psychology has, however, widened its scope, and in the past few years much attention has centered on the older adult, the retired person from about 65 years on.

What has been the impetus for this change of focus? It has always been easier to study certain dimensions of human development in children, since they change much more quickly than do older adults. Children also form a "captive" population that can be easily observed and studied. Schools and other child-oriented institutions such as day care centers provide consistent settings. Interestingly, a similar situation

exists in the case of the elderly who are in institutions or nursing homes.

There are at least three reasons why the study of development beyond adolescence is becoming more important. First, the myth that development is a stable process after adolescence is slowly being dissolved by empirical studies that examine development in older people. In fact, many radical changes in cognitive, physical, and social behaviors occur throughout the entire lifespan. Second, as a result of fluctuations in the birth rate, the population in general is getting older. If present trends continue, by the year 2000 half of the population of the United States will be 50 years or older, and one-third of the population will be 65 years or older. This is a direct result of the "baby boom" generation (born after World War II), entering this stage of adult development. Finally, the life expectancy of men and women (although different) is constantly increasing. A baby born in 1900 had an average lifespan of 47 years, while

Adult Life Cycles

After years of being left out of the life stages of childhood and adolescent development charted by Freud, Piaget and Erikson, over-21ers are finally being included in some newly-devised life cycles for adults.

Three important life-cycle experts—Yale psychologist David Levinson, psychiatrists George Vaillant of Harvard and Roger Gould of UCLA—all currently involved in postadolescent studies, have touched upon some interesting similarities in their findings about the adult years:

16–22

Youthful illusions about the adult world begin dissolving as young people become more peer-oriented, rather than family-oriented. Emotions tend to be held inside and friendships are easily broken.

23–28

The young adult begins to reach out toward others and is busy "mastering the world." Emotional extremes are avoided and commitments are rarely analyzed. Levinson sees this as a time for "togetherness" in marriage.

29–34

With the crisis stage generally hitting at age 30, adults are less confident, begin questioning their worth, and start finding life more difficult. An active social life starts downhill during this period, along with marital dissatisfaction. The spouse starts being viewed as an obstacle instead of an asset, and infidelity and divorce become more prevalent. Levinson detects a "wrenching struggle among incompatible drives: for order and stability, for freedom from all restraints, for upward mobility at work."

35–43

A time of instability likened by the researchers to a "second adolescence." Adults come to realize that life is not forever and time is running out. Values are confronted as the mid-lifer ponders, is there time for a change? Researchers say that the mid-life crisis, however, can yield to what Erikson calls "generativity"—nurturing, teaching and serving others.

44–50

A stable, settling down time for adults as they decide it's too late to change and decisions must be lived with. Friends and old values become more important, and money less important. Couples start turning to their spouses for sympathy and comfort as they once did to their parents.

50–Plus

During these years, adults mellow, tend to put off emotional issues and focus on the little day-to-day pleasures and annoyances, with less concern for the past or future.

While the researchers admit that their findings are far from conclusive at this stage, they predict that the "crisis 30s" and the "mellow 50s" labels will someday become as common as the "terrible twos."

APA Monitor
September–October 1975

Children aren't the only ones who go through cycles. Recent research on psychological development through the lifespan shows that human adults also pass through significant stages of development. It is hoped that understanding these stages will allow people to lead happier and more productive lives.

today it is well beyond 70. People are more educated today than ever before, and increases in technology have provided more leisure time. The four-day, 40-hour work week is not unheard of and is becoming more popular as people learn how valuable and regenerative new hobbies and activities can be during the later years. There is an increasing number of older people in our society, and we need new knowledge to understand and maximize their lives.

Changes with Aging

Most models of development that deal with old age tend to follow the decrement model in which changes in development are attributed or related to a breakdown of biological and psychological processes. This model represents a process of gradual decline and deterioration in cognitive or mental facilities, motor abilities, and biological or physiological processes. The newly developed field of gerontology addresses these

"And now to our annual vote on the mandatory retirement age. I take it we all agree it be raised by one year?"

© Punch (Rothco)

different areas and how they relate directly to the study and care of the aged. Keep in mind that individual differences between people are still very great. We have to be aware that chronological age is often not a good landmark to use in evaluating development.

Probably the major biological changes that take place during the older years of development are a change in the efficiency of the major organs. The brain consists of more fluid and less gray matter, and a decrease in the amount of blood (hence oxygen) reaching the brain may result in somewhat decreased brain efficiency. The aging process is also closely related to cardiovascular problems involving hardening of the arteries, high blood pressure, and strokes. Finally, there are dramatic changes in sexual behavior and potency.

A decline in motor abilities is also related to these biological changes. Reaction time is greatly decreased, poor visual skills make fine eye-hand coordination movements (such as handwriting) difficult, and learning new motor skills is very difficult if not impossible. In addition, the older person is much less limber than the younger person due to a hardening of the collagen or connective tissue in the skin, tendons, and elsewhere. This decline in certain abilities also has psychological effects.

Finally, cognitive capabilities also change during the later years of life. The creative thrust present in earlier life seems to diminish, and more time is required to reach the same level of learning proficiency one attained in earlier years. Is intelligence in the young adult the same as that in the older adult? Can we use the same instrument to measure creativity in both groups of people? The answer to these questions is probably no. One of the first tasks gerontologists must undertake is to shed some

Memory Doesn't Decline with Age

CHICAGO — Forget everything you've ever been told about how memory is supposed to fade with increasing age.

A University of Chicago study shows that memory does not decline with age and that a person in his 70's has as much capacity to remember things as a person in his 20s.

"The stereotype that memory is supposed to become impaired with age is just not true," said Dr. Robert L. Kahn, associate professor of psychiatry and human development. . . .

A careful study of 153 persons ranging in age from 50 to 91 at the U of C's Gerontology Clinic revealed they had normally functioning memories despite complaints that they were getting forgetful. . . .

The key factor was depression, Kahn said. Older people tend to become more depressed and their complaints about memory problems really are a "call for help" to let others know they are in the dumps, he explained.

"This is very important," he said. "Everyone, including doctors take the memory complaints at face value and don't do anything about them. When you realize that these complaints are a symptom of depression, there is something you can do to treat the depression."

The stereotype of memory impairment is so ingrained in the population that older people accept it, he said.

Actually, everyone forgets some things, he said. If you forget a phone number when you are 20 years old you laugh it off, he said. If you are 40 it doesn't bother you. But if you are 60 or 70 and you forget a number then you become afraid that your memory is slipping, he said.

An older person also has more things to forget because of his extra years of experience, Kahn said. . . .

Boulder (Colo.) **Daily Camera**
September 26, 1976

light on the relationship between performance at these two different points in life.

The later years of human life represent a dynamic and fascinating period that deserves more attention than it has been previously given. The formation of The National Institute on Aging and social groups such as the Grey Panthers testifies to the importance of this age group. It has been said that one can judge a

329

nation by the food it eats and the way it treats its older citizens. Up to now, most of us would agree that little has been done in the realm of social programs and federal priorities to award our older citizens what they rightfully deserve. We believe that more study and knowledge about this phase of development must take place.

SUMMARY

1. Developmental psychologists study changes in behavior that take place from conception through death. They describe behavior by providing normative guidelines and examine the antecedent-consequent relationships between certain influences and developmental change.

2. Three models of human development were presented: the psychoanalytic, the behavioral, and the cognitive-developmental. Each makes different underlying assumptions about the process of development which dictate different methods for studying change.

3. It is difficult to determine whether maturation or learning is more important in human development. Both operate simultaneously, and the relative contributions of each are different for different behaviors.

4. Development is both a continuous and discontinuous process. Quantitative or continuous change combines with qualitative or discontinuous change in almost every facet of development.

5. Longitudinal studies examine behavior changes, over time, while cross-sectional studies examine the behavior of individuals of different ages. Both types, however, present confounded results, and other developmental designs are now being favored.

6. According to Piaget, cognitive development can be divided into four qualitatively distinct stages: sensorimotor (birth to two years), preoperational (two to seven years), concrete operational (seven to eleven years), and formal operational (eleven years and beyond).

7. Perception depends on the development of the sensory systems, not all of which are fully mature at birth. Perceptual abilities improve dramatically during the first year of life.

8. Human children develop three forms of symbolic representation of the world. In the enactive mode the environment seems to be represented in terms of movement tendencies in the muscles. The iconic mode involves memory of the world in terms of images. In the symbolic mode the child uses words and sentences of the language to characterize objects, events, and circumstances in the world.

9. In the first two years of life the young child develops a knowledge of the permanency of objects or the ability to represent internally stimuli that are not immediately present in the environment.

10. Erik Erikson emphasized the importance of social influences on development. Each of the eight stages of development he presents is associated with some developmental crisis that must be resolved in order for development to be successful.

11. The development of sex roles is influenced by biology and the environment. There may be a critical period during which sex-role differentiation takes place.

12. Androgyny emphasizes that biological males and females have both masculine and feminine characteristics. The androgynous person uses whichever behavior is most adaptive at a given time.

13. A sense of morality is developed through a series of steps that begins with materialistic considerations of punishment and obedience and progresses through the acquisition of universal principles of conscience.

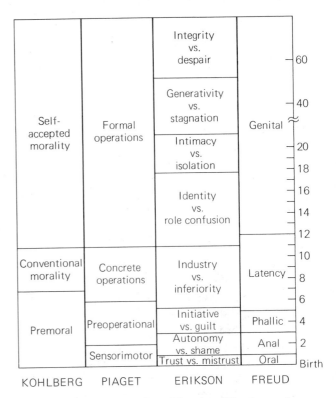

KOHLBERG	PIAGET	ERIKSON	FREUD	
Self-accepted morality	Formal operations	Integrity vs. despair	Genital	60
		Generativity vs. stagnation		40
		Intimacy vs. isolation		20 / 18
		Identity vs. role confusion		16 / 14 / 12
Conventional morality	Concrete operations	Industry vs. inferiority	Latency	10 / 8 / 6
Premoral	Preoperational	Initiative vs. guilt	Phallic	4
		Autonomy vs. shame	Anal	2
	Sensorimotor	Trust vs. mistrust	Oral	Birth

Summary of Four Stage Theories of Development

14. Not only the order of birth but other factors such as the spacing and number of children in the family seem to have some effect on an individual's personality and intellectual development.

15. Adolescence is a period of great change marked by diminishing parental influence, important physical changes including the appearance of the secondary sexual characteristics, intensity of emotion, and new social interests and expectations.

16. During adolescence adult logic and reasoning begin to appear. Adolescents can solve complex abstract problems and deal with hypothetical questions.

17. Historically, the older years of development have been ignored. New information and techniques reveal that development is as dynamic during the later years as it is at any other time during life, with the possible exception of infancy.

RECOMMENDED ADDITIONAL READINGS

Dale, P. S. *Language development: Structure and function,* 2d ed. New York: Holt, Rinehart and Winston, 1976.

McCandless, B., & Trotter, R. *Children: Behavior and development,* 3d ed. New York: Holt, Rinehart and Winston, 1977.

Munsinger, H. *Fundamentals of child development,* 2d ed. New York: Holt, Rinehart and Winston, 1975.

Mussen, P. H., Conger, J. J., & Kagan, J. *Child development and personality,* 4th ed. New York: Harper & Row, 1974.

Stone, L. J., & Church, J. *Childhood and adolescence,* 3d ed. New York: Random House, 1973.

what does it mean?

THE EFFECTS OF TELEVISION

One of the most surprising things about television is that until recently nobody cared about its effects on human development. Although television stations are licensed by the federal government, there is little supervision of program content. Considering that 25 percent of all television programs are aimed at children (sometimes called "kidvid"), that 96 percent of all U.S. homes contain at least one television set, and that one-quarter of a child's waking hours up to the age of 18 is spent watching television, it is no surprise that this medium is finally being seen as the pervasive socializing agent it really is.

One advantage of "the tube" is that it provides many valuable experiences that otherwise might not be possible. For example, many children who would otherwise never have the opportunity can see and hear a symphony orchestra or a baseball game. Television brings the world closer and provides some of the fun and entertainment necessary for healthy development. In addition, it also provides some stimulus for family discussion. Over 130 million people recently watched the TV production of *Roots*, a family-centered story of one man's search for his ancestors.

Television, of course, also has disadvantages. Children who frequently watch TV are less likely to participate in outdoor activities. Too, the content of some programs may be detrimental to healthy development, and the more TV children watch, the more likely this influence is increased. Another disadvantage is that since the primary purpose of network (not public) television is to make a profit, the main source of income is from advertisers. Advertisements (which can take almost one-third of total program time) focus on hard-sell techniques that encourage children to put pressure on their parents to purchase the latest fad in presweetened cereals or toys. Finally, TV in its selective presentation of characters and stories creates stereotypes that give the viewer a false image of the real world. For example, the white male is the predominant character in most television programs and commercials. Similarly, older people are often made to appear senile and incompetent.

Regardless of the debate over the relative advantages and disadvantages of television, children do learn from watching it. The question of how much violence children learn from watching television has been raised again and again. A recent report of the U.S. Surgeon General examined evidence concerning the effects of violence portrayed on television on the development of social behaviors in children, especially aggression. The general method for examining children's susceptibility to aggressive models is to show them a movie or tape of a person acting in a violent fashion who is either rewarded or not rewarded for that behavior. The child is then placed in a situation in which he or she is allowed to act out that modeled aggression (such as in social interaction with another

HOW DO YOU FEEL ABOUT VIOLENCE ON TV, BONNIE?

I'M VIOLENTLY OPPOSED TO IT!

© King Features Syndicate, Inc., 1977.

child). More often than not research evidence has shown that children who are exposed to an aggressive model indulge in aggressive acts to accomplish some goal. In some cases the children did not like the aggressive model, but they still copied the aggressive behavior. Knowing what we do about a young child's tendency to imitate, and the importance of imitation as a learning process, we may expect violent and aggressive modes of behavior to be learned. Considering that cartoons are the most violent of all television programs and that children watch cartoons as much as any other production, we have to assume that children are in fact exposed to aggressive models. A few studies, however, have shown that viewing television violence reduces hostility in some people. Because hostile feelings usually precede aggression, TV viewing may remove the underpinnings of aggression. On the basis of these studies, some people have theorized that viewing violence on television may be a form of release, a way of working things out, that allows people to get rid of hostile feelings without expressing them openly. On the other hand, the majority of the studies suggests that increased rather than decreased aggression is a consequence of viewing violent acts on television.

EARLY-ENRICHMENT PROGRAMS AND PLANNED INTERVENTION

Along with many other movements that characterized the "great society" of the early 1960s were the beginning attempts to eradicate the effects of poverty. A great deal of time and money were invested in programs that tried to counteract the negative effects poverty has on the development and future potential of young children. Perhaps the best-known such program is Head Start, a massive effort funded through both federal and state agencies. Another well-known enrichment or intervention program is the television production called *Sesame Street.* Both programs are aimed at stimulating children's cognitive and emotional development by expanding their experiences. Underlying each of these efforts, however, are some basic assumptions about human development that we need to examine before discussing whether the programs succeeded or failed.

We have known for many years that such factors as poor nutrition, lack of adequate housing, and an absence of important sensory and cognitive experiences early in life can have a devastating effect upon children's social and intellectual development. These findings, along with certain political and social forces, led to the creation of intervention programs that are in many ways more of a problem than a solution. For example, such questions as At what age should intervention begin? Where should these programs be offered? and How can we evaluate the results? should have been asked and answered early in the programs, yet they were often ignored. One special concern arose out of the use of such terms as "culturally disadvantaged" and "culturally deficient." Such matters are important because they reflect a world view or theoretical model. For example, if one is to assume that intervention programs are intended for the "culturally deficient," a very stong value judgment is being made regarding the quality of life in the culture. We can just as easily turn around and say that the middle-class majority in the United States is culturally deprived because all its members do not share the same experiences (such as food, music, and other customs). Others would say that "cultural differences" and not deficits should be the focus of any intervention program, and these programs should not imply that one culture is superior to another.

Study Notes 'No Harm' in Day Care

UPI

BOSTON — In a finding for working mothers, a Harvard psychologist reported that good day care centers apparently do not harm the development of young children—a reversal of his earlier position.

Only four years ago, Dr. Jerome Kagan was among those warning against taking young children from their home environment for fear the change would harm their social and intellectual development during the critical years of life.

But Kagan said that exhaustive tests into everything from language development to attention spans to relationships with other children did not find any substantial differences in children tested at age interval from 3½ to 29 months.

Five-Year Study

Kagan reached the conclusion on the basis of a five-year study that compared young children who remained home all day with those placed in a special Harvard-operated day-care center seven hours a day, five days a week.

"There were no important differences between the two groups," Kagan said in a report for a children rearing symposium at the annual meeting of the American Association for the Advancement of Science.

"The data support the view that day care, when responsibly and conscientiously implemented, does not seem to have hidden psychological dangers," he said. "I expected differences. We did not find them. It is not easy to say why. It is a bit of puzzle.

"Merely being outside the home for seven hours a day for 100 weeks does not seem to have a profound effect. There's no difference in aggressiveness, there's no difference in social play. There are just as many shy children in the day care center as there are at home," he added.

Kagan emphasized, however, that the Harvard day care center presented close to an ideal situation for the youngsters with conditions that may not be duplicated very often in centers across the nation.

He said he still believes poor day care centers can be harmful to young children, and he estimated 15 to 20 per cent of day care centers in the nation may fall in that category.

Among other things, the Harvard facility had one caretaker for every three children during their first year of life and one for every four or five toddlers. The cost of such care, Kagan estimated, would be $85 a week if it weren't subsidized.

The Denver Post
February 23, 1976

"What price day care?" Can a child who is away from his or her parents all day receive the love and attention necessary for healthy development? Current research seems to indicate that if the setting is well staffed, the answer is yes.

These strategies have had mixed results. Initial evaluation of Head Start by the Westinghouse Corporation showed the program to be unsuccessful in affecting change in young children. However, many critics of this evaluation effort came quickly to the defense of Head Start and similar programs, claiming that the evaluation was not well planned and did not reflect the true value of the program. Advocates of such programs can point to the success of the Milwaukee Project, the Bereiter-Englemann academically oriented preschool programs, and even *Sesame Street*. In addition, recent information seems to suggest that the early Head Start groups of children progressed in areas of social and emotional development not examined during the initial evaluation.

The issue of whether and how intervention is effective is unresolved. Most psychologists believe that some sort of intervention is necessary. In a review of many different programs, Urie Bronfenbrenner, a long-time advocate of children's rights, concluded that an effective intervention program should contain the following five elements: (1) effective parent education before children are born; (2) adequate provisions for basic needs such as housing and nutrition; (3) a structured program of infant-parent interaction during the early years; (4) a preschool program for children from four to six; and (5) parental support of the child's educational experiences. A potentially important sixth element is the degree to which parents are directly involved in the child's program.

Unfortunately, social policy is inextricably tied to the political arena. Too often the responsibility for the health of our country's children lies in the hands of public officials, who may be well intentioned but know little about educational matters. For this reason, psychologists have recently begun to form lobbying groups with the primary goal of educating those people in government who make the decisions that have long-range and important consequences for us all.

CHILD ABUSE

In the United States today the physical and psychological abuse of children is a serious and complex problem. In the past few incidents were reported to the proper authorities because people were afraid to become involved in lengthy legal matters. There was also little legislation in the area of child abuse that made it possible for those indirectly involved (teachers, doctors, nurses, and social workers, for example) to take effective action. Often those who did try to help became so tangled in red tape and received so many threats of retaliation by parents that they failed to pursue the issue. Only recently have state and federal laws made it mandatory for physicians (and others) to report cases of child abuse when they come to their attention.

What constitutes child abuse? When gross physical harm is done to a child, it is obvious that abuse has taken place. However, it is often difficult to prove such a case legally. Characteristically, one incident leads to another, and by the time action is taken, the child is often severely damaged. In addition, the matter of deciding when corporal disciplinary measures, such as spanking, become abuse is touchy and difficult. The issue becomes even more clouded when the abuse is

psychological. Often such abuse accompanies physical abuse. How does a concerned citizen prove that a parent is psychologically abusing a child?

Determining how much child abuse actually takes place is difficult. Estimates have been placed at between 200,000 and 250,000 cases each year in the United States. Of course, many cases are not reported to the authorities. Unfortunately, some physicians treat only the child's symptoms, ignoring problems of family conflict and pathology on the part of the abusive parent.

What are abusers of children like? First, they are often people who operate under personal stress, such as being unable to provide sufficient funds for an adequate standard of living. They may themselves be the children of abusive parents who practice what they have learned is the "right" way to deal with a child. Chronic child abusers are individuals who are emotionally ill and lack stability. Many of them say they think the abuse no more severe than the child deserves.

How can we begin to solve the problems of child abuse? First, prospective parents must be educated and encouraged to explore their own upbringing. Another step should be the involvement of personnel from all disciplines concerned with the issue, including medicine, education, law, and psychology. Parent organizations where anonymous abusers can go (or call for help) in times of crisis can also play an important role. Finally, special programs for abused children should be implemented to insure that their future development is not impaired by their past experience.

Another approach that is beginning to yield positive results involves observing the behavior of parents toward the child at birth. For example, the amount of eye contact between mother and infant might be observed. Researchers at the University of Colorado Medical Center have discovered ways to predict from early parent-child interactions those parents who are likely to abuse their children. It may become possible to prevent abuse from occurring by providing help and counseling for the parents.

EDUCATIONAL TOYS

On the market today is a variety of toys that are supposed to hasten physical, social, and intellectual development. There are toys to stimulate infants' senses, develop their eye coordination, build motor control of the limbs, and so forth. Toys for older children are designed to teach recognition of attributes, such as color and spatial relations and shapes.

There is considerable disagreement among psychologists about the value of such toys. Some claim that environments "enriched" with mobiles, mirrors, tape recordings, aquariums, and so on, may have the effect of depriving the child of normal interaction with parents—watching their faces and being held and talked to. Moreover, a child may learn as much playing with pots and pans as with expensive toys.

An elaborate educational machine called the talking typewriter has been developed to teach children how to read. These typewriters are used in some schools and institutions, often with children who need special instruction. The typewriter has a conventional keyboard except that the keys are different colors. The child's fingernails are painted in matching colors. When the child presses the key, the machine prints the letter and pronounces it. After the child has explored the device, the typewriter takes the lead. A letter is printed and spoken, and only the matching key is operable. Initially children search the keyboard, ignoring letter configurations. Eventually, however, they learn to match the key and letter. After letters come words. Most children progress rapidly with the help of this intriguing machine. Even kindergartners learn to produce and type short stories.

EDUCATIONAL INNOVATION

Jean Piaget's theory of intellectual development has sparked attempts at educational reform, especially in the open classroom tradition of the British school system. Piaget insists that children at different stages require

"This **is** the toy department, sir!"

different kinds of education. Many schools, unfortunately, instruct even the youngest children as though they were in the formal operational stage, using abstract lecture methods. Because they rely primarily on the enactive mode of symbolic representation, preschoolers learn best if they can manipulate things. According to Piaget, a six- to seven-year-old child taught on a purely verbal level learns to mimic phrases but not necessarily to understand them.

Piaget and Bruner believe that young children learn best through active discovery. Thus classrooms in the early grades might be arranged in a series of centers stocked with intriguing materials to arouse children's curiosity. In informal instructional laboratories set up to investigate discovery learning, children are allowed to manipulate things and see results. They are asked to describe outcomes and sometimes to make reports. Classmates are encouraged to question procedures and explanations, forcing children to communicate their ideas more clearly.

A curriculum based on such principles stresses new ways to organize experience rather than the mere accumulation of knowledge. Specific tasks designed to teach conservation of concepts, for example, are sometimes included in the curriculum. The development of conservation of area, for instance, might be facilitated by using the

'Best Toys Are One Step Ahead of What Child Likes'

Christine Winter

Child's play is a serious business, says Brian Sutton-Smith, a Ph.D. in child psychology, one of the nation's leading authorities on childhood development, and consultant to the Toy Manufacturers of America.

But, he urges, children should get an opportunity to play not only with toys but with their parents as well.

Parents who are "funful" and play with their children, even just clowning around once in a while, are adding significantly to their development, he says.

Of course toys have an important role too.

"Before parents go out shopping for toys, they should observe their child at play and get a feeling where their child is 'at,'" he said. "The best toys are those that are just one step ahead of what the child likes."

Parents should be careful, he warned, not to just go out and get toys that they think they would have liked or that look bigger and better than anything the neighbors have or that are large and expensive and can be bought quickly to get it all over with.

"Toys are symbols of different functions of life. They are libraries of action, thought, and feelings from which parents can check out things that will suit their own child's development." . . .

"Ideally, the toy population should match whatever children are looking for," he said. "Take dolls, for example; kids should be able to choose between rugged males, more esthetic males, rugged females and more domestic females in the doll models they want to have around and play with." The old distinctions are fading away, he added. . . .

"Children have got to learn about play," just as they have to learn about the alphabet. . . .

"Essentially, the definition of play is reversing roles, creating novelties, and doing it all in a vivid manner.

"And the child with a toy is a child in control of one small segment of the world, learning that new situations can be mastered."

As for parents joining in the fun, that's precisely what adult-child play should be.

"Parent-child play may be physical play, like rolling on the floor; verbal play, as in making jokes or just being witty; or gameplay, as in checkers or other board games. Whatever it is, it helps the child become familiar with dealing with novelty." . . .

Boulder (Colo.) Daily Camera
May 22, 1975

A learning environment should always provide some experiences that are just beyond the child's present level of development. Children are often bored by problems that aren't a challenge. On the other hand, tasks too far ahead in advance of the child's developmental level may prove uninteresting or frustrating.

linoleum squares on the floor. Children might be given 12 squares and asked to work out how many different shapes can be made from them. In this way they learn that area is independent of shape and depends on a square measurement unit. Fundamentals of arithmetic can be taught by a Dienes balance (Figure 8–12). Each side of the balance rod contains numbered hooks placed at equal intervals from the center, starting with 1 and going outward to 9. Children must figure out where to place two rings on one side to balance one ring placed at 6 on the other side. Following simple addition, they might place rings at 2 and 4 or at 1 and 5. They also discover they must multiply the number of rings

Figure 8–12
The Dienes balance

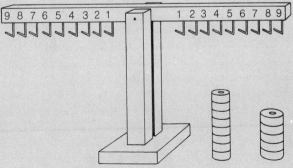

The Dienes balance uses Piagetian principles to teach arithmetic.

by the number at which each ring is placed to achieve a balance. One ring at hook 6 is balanced by three at hook 2.

Other theoretical orientations have also been applied to educational settings. As we saw in Chapter 4, application of the principles of operant conditioning has led to another approach to classroom learning. Instead of discovering concepts through free exploration and manipulation, in the operant approach the learner is led through a series of steps of increasing complexity, each building on the preceding, until the task has been learned. The structured steps may be presented by the teacher or by a programmed textbook. Whereas the Piagetian method of discovery learning involves intrinsic rewards from the pleasure of solving problems, external reinforcement (such as tokens) supply the motivation for learning in the operant approach. The two learning approaches are not necessarily incompatible. Teachers can and should use a combination of approaches in the classroom.

DEATH AND DYING

For thousands of years death has been a taboo topic. During the last few years, however, as a result of clinical research with terminally ill patients, we have become aware that death, like all developmental events, is part of an ongoing process. A better understanding of this process has enabled a new group of professionals to help terminally ill patients and their families deal with the dying process.

Perhaps the best-known examination of the stages the dying person passes through is that by Elisabeth Kübler-Ross. Through extensive interviews with terminally ill individuals, she has concluded that the dying process consists of a series of five distinct stages. The first stage, denial and isolation, is that in which the news of a fatal illness results in a denial of the fact. Kübler-Ross believes this first stage acts as a type of insulator, giving the individual time to adjust

to the shock. After a period of time denial leads to an aggressive anger in which the person (and sometimes also members of the family) is outraged that it is himself or herself (or loved one) and not some other "less valuable" person who is going to die. This resentment is often directed toward others. The third stage, bargaining, is an attempt to postpone the inevitable. It frequently takes the form of "a deal" between the individual and God. In the fourth stage—depression—the individual realizes that little can be done to change the situation.

Finally, the last stage is acceptance. At this point the patient understands the finality of the situation and begins to adjust both psychologically and emotionally. This is the time when most people who have been guided and supported through the four previous stages fully accept death with dignity. Kübler-Ross stresses that *hope* is present throughout all five of these stages. Regardless of the condition, or the stage of dying, most people hope and believe, for example, that a miracle drug might be the answer or that the dying process itself may be reversed. These are not delusions, but a form of self-support and sustenance during this difficult time.

The traditional notion that stages of development are significant only during the early years of life is losing favor. Our attempts to understand death as a process raise the question of when development stops, if in fact it does.

THE EFFECTS OF SEPARATION

With increasing frequency, and at a younger and younger age, children are spending more time away from their parents. What is the effect of separation upon the development of the child?

The work of René Spitz during the 1940s and later of John Bowlby examined the effects of institutionalization on the intellectual and social development of infants. Spitz compared children who were cared for in institutions with those cared for at home. He found

Parental Discord 'Causes' More Harm Than Divorce

UPI

WASHINGTON — A research team is reporting that discord between parents may harm children more than divorce.

Dr. E. Mavis Hetherington, professor of psychology at the University of Virginia, told at a recent symposium that the first year after divorce is difficult, but her team's findings suggest that parents who hold a troubled marriage together because of their children may do them more psychological harm than if they divorce.

"Marital discord is associated with more adverse outcomes for children than is divorce," she said, adding: "In the long run, it is not a good idea for parents to remain in a conflicted marriage for the sake of the children."

Hetherington and two associates based their conclusions on the results of a two-year study of 96 white, middle-class families with children who were 4 when the study began.

Half of the families had parents and child living together and half consisted of divorced parents in which custody of the child was granted to the mother. . . .

In the first year after divorce, the report said, children in the divorced families were functioning less well than those in high-discord families. The children in the high-discord families, in turn, showed more problems than those of families with less parental conflict.

But Hetherington said the differences were reversed during the second year after divorce, with the effect more pronounced in boys than girls.

Two years after a divorce, more aggressive and less pro-social behavior was seen in boys from intact families with high conflicts than in divorced families.

The boys in the divorced families were still not functioning as well as those in low-stress, intact families, although differences had largely disappeared in girls. . . .

The Denver Post
May 30, 1978

a high first year death rate for children in institutions, even though the care they received was good. He used the term "hospitalism" to describe the effects of institutionalization on otherwise healthy children. He found that foundling home children tended to be shorter and weigh less than the other group of children. They were also more susceptible to disease. Bowlby's comparisons of home-reared and institutionalized children yielded similar results. He also identified a separation anxiety which all children separated from their homes pass through. First these children protest their separation from their mother with a great deal of anger and rage. After these protests go unheeded, they enter a stage of despair in which they withdraw and become inactive. Finally, they become completely detached and seem to adjust. If and when the mother returns, however, they are likely to show complete rejection.

The Spitz and Bowlby findings must be examined in light of some very important considerations. The children they examined were in institutionalized settings. Because of this, it is difficult if not impossible to generalize to the normal infant or child who is separated from one or both parents for a short or extended period of time. For the modern child, separation from one or both parents is something he or she learns to expect. Recent literature seems to show that the quality of a child's life at home (including the quality of the relationship between parents) and the quality of the setting away from home are more important factors than the length of separation. Many psychologists believe that separation is important and helps to encourage healthy social and adaptive behavior. This, of course, assumes that the time away from home is spent in a stimulating and receptive atmosphere. Examinations of Israeli kibbutzim show that child care by a group of trained people can lead to healthy and full development.

With the increase in day care and other child care programs in this country, a great deal more research on child-rearing is needed.

Personality 9

I magine that, as part of a psychology experiment, you are spending an evening observing the behavior of shoppers in a large and busy supermarket. You are recording the approximate age and weight of persons who purchase candy, sour cream, and frozen pies (for later comparison with those who stick to melba toast and cottage cheese). Suddenly all the lights go out. Being an intrepid scientist, you attempt to continue your observations in the illumination provided by the store's emergency spotlights, but you find that conditions are not adequate for you to make accurate age and weight estimates. You therefore turn your attention to how individuals deal with the situation. In the produce department you spot a person calmly squeezing avocados as if nothing unusual were going on, while over by the green peppers another individual is frightened and begins to shout and scream. You arrive at the meat counter in time to see an opportunistic shopper put a standing rib roast under each arm and head for the exit. Nearby, you listen as an irate customer informs the manager that there is no excuse for this kind of situation and threatens to patronize a competitor's store in the future.

In short, you find that each individual handles the unexpected blackout differently. This is not particularly surprising; we expect great diversity in human behavior. Of course, we also expect that each individual will usually display some consistency in behavior in coping with different situations. Thus, a person who is quiet and shy at parties usually also behaves timidly and quietly in class, at public meetings, and on a date. Similarly, you expect a close friend to deal with you in a warm and interested manner in most situations and on a daily basis, not just once in a while.

How can we understand and explain these differences between individuals and consistencies within individuals, which we may take for granted as part of "human nature"? What makes people so different from each other, yet so consistent within themselves? For centuries philosophers, physicians, and religious leaders have wrestled with this basic question about people and their behavior, and in recent years psychologists have studied and theorized about it.

Over the years, the most commonly used term to describe and account for individual differences and behavioral consistencies in human beings has been "personality." In everyday situations we hear people's behavior described in terms of their personality: "He would be a nice guy if he didn't have such an aggressive personality," or "Your blind date is a bit on the heavy side but has a great personality," or "My psychology professor really knows her material but has no personality." In addition, the concept of personality is often used to explain behavior: "I think my husband's depressions are caused by his basically insecure personality," or "Her stable personality allows her to handle any situation."

WHAT IS PERSONALITY?

Even though almost everyone frequently uses the term "personality," there is little agreement on what it actually means. To get some idea of the problem, jot down your own definition (before you finish this chapter) and then ask three of your friends for theirs. You will probably find that each of them has a somewhat different conception of the term and that the three definitions you collect from others differ from your own. Such differences of opinion do not result from the fact that you and your friends are not experienced psychologists, but from the generality of the concept of personality.

Over the years, people have defined "personality" in various ways, including one's outward appearance, one's role in life, the totality of one's qualities or attributes, the way one "really" is, one's general behavior pattern, and many others. Today dozens of formal definitions exist (see Table 9-1), none of which is universally accepted. Like all definitions, those in the table reflect the interests of their sponsors: prediction

TABLE 9–1　Some Definitions of Personality

1. The dynamic organization within the individual of those psychophysical systems that determine his unique adjustments to his environment (G. Allport).
2. The more or less stable and enduring organization of a person's character, temperament, intellect, and physique that determines his unique adjustment to his environment (H. Eysenck).
3. That which permits a prediction of what a person will do in a given situation (R. B. Cattell).
4. A person's unique pattern of traits (J. P. Guilford).
5. The most adequate conceptualization of a person's behavior in all its detail (D. McClelland).
6. Each individual's characteristically recurring patterns of behavior (L. Kolb).

(Cattell), dynamics (Allport), predispositions (Eysenck), individual differences (Guilford), description (McClelland), uniqueness (Kolb). But each of these aspects is subsumed under our general definition of personality as a term used to describe (McClelland) and account (Allport) for individual differences (Guilford, Kolb) and behavioral consistencies (Cattell, Eysenck).

It is somewhat easier to define personality as an area of psychological inquiry than as a "thing" that people have. Because the concept of personality is so broad, its study involves more branches of psychology than any other specialty. A psychologist interested in personality may ask questions as diverse as: How do personality characteristics develop? Does the existence of one characteristic predict the likelihood that the person will have certain other characteristics? What role do other people play in the development of an individual's personality? When and why do different people behave similarly and given individuals behave inconsistently? How do genetic and physiological factors influence personality? What causes the appearance of "abnormal" versus "normal" personalities? Can personality be changed, and if so, how?

The study of personality can involve all facets of human behavior and can encompass aspects of developmental, social, experimental, physiological, and clinical psychology. Thus, in a sense, any psychologist who deals with human behavior can be said to be exploring some segment of personality.

THE ROLE OF THEORY IN STUDYING PERSONALITY

If, as we have seen, there is no universally accepted definition of personality, on what do psychologists base their studies of human personality? Clearly, any investigator must proceed with some sort of guidelines. The psychologist uses a **theory** of personality. The theory is important because it provides some basic assumptions about human behavior and a working definition of the concept.

For example, one could start out with the somewhat fanciful assumption that all human behavior is the result of the presence of thousands of tiny, invisible elves that reside in the pancreas. An abundance of depressed elves would produce lethargic behavior except when they were sleeping, when a smaller number of happier and more optimistic elves would take over the controls, producing less melancholy behavior. Personality could then be defined through a kind of census of the elf population in each individual. People hosting lots of anxious elves would be called neurotic, those with a preponderance of sociable elves would be labeled extroverted, and so on.

Suppose that the investigator elaborated this kind of thinking into a comprehensive set of statements or assumptions that could account for human behavior as we know it, generate accurate predictions about it, and suggest procedures through which it can be altered. He would then have a personality theory that might result in hundreds of experiments designed to test the validity of its assumptions and hypotheses. "Elf theory" would probably also foster the development of highly specialized procedures (such as extremely sensitive X-ray devices) for assessing the specific kinds of elves in each individual. In addition, the theory might suggest specific strategies for elf research.

This absurd example is meant only to make the point that, because human behavior can be interpreted in so many ways, personality can be approached, defined, assessed, and researched, from any one of a wide variety of theoretical points of view, each of which has strengths and weaknesses. Literally dozens of such theories exist. Here we shall present a description and discussion of four major classes of personality theories: dispositional theories, psychodynamic theories, social learning theories, and phenomenological theories. In considering each class of theories, you should not ask which are "right" and which are "wrong," but which come closest to providing an efficient, complete, and testable account of the development, maintenance, and modification of human behavior, "normal" and "deviant." Note that each of these four classes of theories forms what might be called a "strategy" of personality study (Liebert and Spiegler, 1974) in the sense that, like the "elf approach," they provide not only a way of thinking about personality but also a set of procedures for measuring and investigating it. With the exception of dispositional theories, each class of approaches has also generated techniques designed to produce personality change; these are discussed in Chapter 12.

DISPOSITIONAL THEORIES

When people say, "He is the nervous type," or "Kindness is one of her most outstanding traits," or "Some people are driven to work hard by their strong need for achievement," they are, usually without knowing it, adopting a *dispositional* theory of personality. Dispositional theories start with the basic assumption that personality is composed of *dispositions within the individual* to behave in certain ways. Further, they assume that these dispositions are relatively stable in time and generalize over a wide variety of circumstances. From this they conclude that if you know about people's dispositions, you can make some predictions about their future behavior. The names given to these hypothesized behavioral dispositions are different in different theories.

Personality Types

Some dispositional theories assume that there are a few specifiable personality types and that each type is disposed to behave differently. One of the earliest personality-type theorists was the ancient Greek physician Hippocrates. Working on the assumption that the human body contains four fluids, or humors (blood, phlegm, black bile, and yellow bile), he categorized peo-

Hormones Taken during Pregnancy Affect the Child's Personality

Jody Gaylin

Synthetic hormones taken by a woman during pregnancy to avert miscarriage can affect her child's personality and behavior. Psychologist June Reinisch located 34 families in which at least one pregnancy was treated with progestin (similar chemically to androgen, a male sex hormone) and/or estrogen (a female sex hormone), and at least one pregnancy was not treated with any drugs. The families had 42 children exposed to hormones (15 boys and 27 girls) and 42 unexposed siblings (18 boys, 24 girls), ranging in age from five to 18.

Reinisch found striking differences among the children in how they performed on standard personality and intelligence tests. The ones who had been exposed to progestin were consistently more independent, individualistic, and self-assured than those exposed to estrogen, who were more group-oriented and dependent. The same differences—the progestin children more individualistic and self-sufficient, the estrogen children more dependent on the group—showed up when both groups were compared with their brothers and sisters who hadn't been exposed to either drug. . . .

Reinisch believes that her study reinforces the theory that the fetal environment influences a child's behavior. No one has done long-term studies on children exposed to hormones, says Reinisch, but "the wealth of data related to early hormone influences on behavior in animals strongly suggests . . . that exposure to hormones . . . in humans should have some long term effects on . . . personality and/or temperament."

Psychology Today
October 1977

Research is beginning to suggest that personality is dependent upon biological as well as experiential factors. In addition to the prenatal effects on personality postulated in this article, the endocrine system (Chapter 2) may play a role in day-to-day personality changes.

ple into four corresponding personality types: phlegmatic (a calm, apathetic temperament caused by too much phlegm), choleric (a hot-headed, irritable temperament due to an ex-

Tricks of the Fortune-Telling Trade

I. Young girl
  A. Wild type
    1. I can't catch, or hold, my man.
    2. My conscience is bothering me.
    3. I'm in trouble.
  B. Home girl
    1. I'm afraid of men.
    2. I'm afraid of life and responsibility.
    3. I'm afraid of Mom.
  C. Career girl (usually jealous of a brother)
    1. Under twenty-five: I'm ambitious. I hate and despise men and marriage!
    2. Over twenty-five: I'm panicky. Maybe no one will marry me!

II. Mature woman (30–50)
  A. Still wild
    1. Why isn't it as much fun anymore? I'm lonely.
    2. I'm afraid of getting my face scarred, or burning to death in a fire. (This never misses)
    3. I've got to believe in something — the occult, a new religion that doesn't include morals, or you, Mr. Fortune-teller!
  B. Wife and Mother
    1. Is my husband seeing another woman?
    2. When will he make more money?
    3. I'm worried about the children . . .

III. Spinster
  A. Still presentable
    1. When will I meet him?
  B. Given up hope
    1. My best friend has done me dirt.
    2. I'm crushed — a gigolo has got my savings!

IV. Young man
  A. Wild-oats farmer
    1. Is there a system for beating the races?
    2. What do you do when you get a girl in trouble?
      a. Is she playing me for a sucker?
  B. Good boy
    1. Will I be a success?
    2. How can I improve my education?
    3. Is my girl two-timing me?
      a. She's mixed up with Type A.
    4. I'm afraid of Mom!

V. Mature man
  A. Wolf, married or single
    1. Girl trouble
      a. I can't get her!
      b. I can't get rid of her!
      c. Her male relatives are after me!
      d. Does my wife know?
  B. Businessman
    1. Where's the money going to come from?
    2. Will this deal work out?

cess of yellow bile). sanguine (an optimistic, hopeful temperament attributed to a predominance of blood), and melancholic (a sad, depressed temperament based on black bile). Hippocrates' theory is no longer taken seriously, yet it survives as a way of describing people —

you will still find his four personality types listed in your dictionary.

Since Hippocrates, several other *theories* of personality have been proposed, most of which seek to relate behavioral dispositions to physical characteristics. For example, a nineteenth-cen-

3. Did I do right in *that* deal?
4. What does my wife do all day?

VI. Elderly people
   A. Woman
      1. Will my daughter get a good husband?
      2. Will That Creature be a good wife to my son?
      3. Will the children (or grandchildren) be all right?
   B. Man
      1. Will I ever have enough money to retire on?
      2. I'm afraid to die.
   C. Both
      1. Am I going to need an operation?

VII. Wise guy
   A. Toughie
      1. Make one false move, fortune-teller, and I bust ya one! (Ease him out quick.)
   B. Defensive bravado
      1. I'm smarter than most people; I see through you. (Flatter him; he'll end by eating out of your hand.)

How can fortune tellers, palm readers, tea-leaf readers, and so on, manage to assess personality and detect problems well enough to impress many of their customers? The above outline, taken from an article on this topic entitled "Fortune Tellers Never Starve," offers some insight. By classifying a customer into one of the seven categories, the fortune teller can then deal in generalities which are likely to apply to people in that category. This fascinating article by William L. Gresham appeared in *Esquire* magazine in 1949.

"You have a strong interest in sports."

Playboy, July 1973. Reproduced by special permission of PLAYBOY Magazine; copyright © 1973 by Playboy.

Don't be too impressed with people who read palms — or tea leaves or tarot cards. They use generalities in interpreting personality—characteristics that apply to just about everyone—and they can get lots of clues from your appearance, dress, manner of speaking, and so on.

tury Italian anthropologist named Cesare Lombroso suggested that people's facial characteristics provided clues to the kinds of behaviors they would display. This "science" was called *physiognomy* and related factors such as head size, distance between the eyes, shape of the

chin, and color of the hair to personality type. Although this theory has no scientific value, it has become a part of popular thinking about people—"Criminals have small, beady eyes set close together"; "Blondes have more fun."

The most elaborate theory of personality

Figure 9–1
Extreme examples of Sheldon's body types

Physique	Temperament
Endomorphic (soft and round, overdeveloped digestive viscera; Orson Welles, for example)	**Viscerotonic** (relaxed, loves to eat, sociable)
Mesomorphic (muscular, rectangular, strong; Arnold Schwartzenegger, for example)	**Somatonic** (energetic, assertive, courageous)
Ectomorphic (long, fragile, large brain and sensitive nervous system; Don Knotts, for example)	**Cerebrotonic** (restrained, fearful, introverted, artistic)

based on body characteristics was proposed by William Sheldon, an American physician. His system involved three primary body types: endomorphic, mesomorphic, and ectomorphic (see Figure 9–1). But instead of assigning individuals to one category, he characterized each person in terms of the degree to which that person displayed features of each primary type. (This approach contains features of trait theories of personality, to be discussed later.) Sheldon then examined the relationship between people's body type and their behavior. He found that endomorphs tended to be what he called "viscerotonic" (relaxed, sociable, slow, and tolerant); mesomorphs displayed "somatonia" (an assertive, athletic, energetic, and bold temperament); and ectomorphs were "cerebrotonic" (introverted, restrained, fearful, and artistic). It is interesting to note that these relationships parallel popularly held stereotypes about physique and behavior (the jolly fat person, the bold athlete, the frail, sensitive artist). The influence of these stereotypes may account for the relationships Sheldon found, despite his use of highly trained observers. Research in social psychology and related areas has shown that, to a certain extent, people still tend to be "body-type theorists." Much of the impression we get of other people (and part of the impression we have of ourselves) is mediated by physical appearance. Sheldon's particular theory has not received strong support and is not now influential.

The convenience and simplicity of type theories have great popular appeal. It would be nice to know everything about a person by looking at his or her face, manner of dress, hair style, body type, or genetic make-up, but the behavior of human beings is just too diverse and complicated to be dealt with using a cut-and-dried, "pigeonhole" system of categories. Thus, type theories are not generally valid because they are oversimplified and inadequate descriptions of behavior. Furthermore, they can be harmful because they tend to generate or maintain prejudices about people. (See the "What Does It Mean?" section of this chapter).

Traits of Personality

Trait theories of personality seek to avoid the limitations of type systems by accounting for both the diversity of human behavior and the behavioral consistencies within the individual. They start with the basic assumption that one's behavior is controlled not by the type of person one is, but mainly by the wide variety of stable personality traits (such as dependency, aggressiveness, gentleness, thoughtfulness, and the like) which each individual has to some degree or another. Thus, just as grade-point average is determined by a student's academic performance in many separate courses, personality is determined by the combination of traits, occurring at varying strengths, that is present in each individual. The idea that many combinations of trait strengths are possible accounts for both the uniqueness of the individual and the differences among people. The idea that the individual's traits are enduring explains the relative consistency in each person's behavior over time and in many different situations.

Like type theory, the trait approach has a clear appeal; in fact, most of us employ it in describing others. If you ask a friend to tell you about her parents, for example, you will very likely be given a list of traits: "Dad is *hardworking, serious,* and *shy,* but overly *dependent* and *insecure* as well. Mom is *warm, outgoing, efficient,* and *optimistic,* but also *impulsive* and often *overbearing.*"

The danger in the casual use of this approach to personality is that trait descriptions like "Integrity is Ralph's strongest trait" can too easily be used as explanations. If we use Ralph's trait of integrity to "explain" his honesty, we end up making a statement that may be true but is not very useful in terms of understanding behavior: "Ralph is honest because he has integrity." This is like saying, "Ralph is 6 feet tall because he measures 72 inches from

© 1974 United Feature Syndicate Inc.

Phrenology, the study of head shape and its relation to behavior, was once a popular means of personality assessment. Snoopy seems skeptical, and for good reason. Head reading is no longer taken seriously in scientific circles.

head to toe." Our description of behavior cannot also be its cause. We must use trait labels carefully so that we do not fool ourselves into thinking we have explained behavior when, in fact, we have merely described it.

Over the years, there have been many scientific attempts to avoid this problem. Some early efforts, such as those of Franz Gall (1758–1828), were temporarily influential but have ultimately been discredited. Gall believed that all behavioral dispositions and abilities existed neurophysiologically in the brain and that the better developed a particular part of the brain was, the stronger the corresponding trait or ability would be. Gall and his most prominent follower, Johann Spurzheim, believed that there were 37 basic traits, and they developed a "map" of the head to locate each of them. Personality assessment then became a matter of feeling an individual's skull for bumps (well-developed traits) and depressions (poorly developed traits), a technique known as phrenology. Gall and Spurzheim traveled across Europe, feeling heads for a fee. This may be how the expression "having your head examined" got started.

Traits as Entities

Gordon Allport, one of the first and most influential of the modern personality theorists, also believed that traits actually existed within the person as "neuropsychic systems," but he went about describing them in a quite different and far more scientific way than did Gall. Allport discussed several kinds of traits, organized according to their generality: (1) *cardinal* traits, which determine behavior in the widest range of circumstances (describing someone as "a regular Albert Schweitzer" would be an example of the use of the cardinal trait of humanitarianism); (2) *central* traits, which are not as broad as cardinal traits but are still fairly general (our earlier descriptions of a hypothetical set of parents provide examples); and (3) narrow *secondary* traits which appear only in certain circumstances (for example, "She is grouchy in the morning"). Further, Allport pointed out that while some traits appeared to some extent in everyone (*common* traits), others were unique to the individual (*individual* traits) and could be studied only on an intensive, long-term case-by-case basis. Cardinal traits, in particular, apply to only relatively few people.

Allport's methods for describing common traits included asking people to tell how they would behave in certain situations. Their responses allowed him to do two things. First, he could measure the strength and stability of a trait in a single individual by determining how often and how generally a person displayed the trait. Second, he could measure the frequency of traits among people in general by totaling the answers he received from large numbers of subjects.

Allport's influence upon the development of modern trait theories has been enormous, but one of the problems with his approach is that one could spend several lifetimes describing and researching all of the 18,000 or so trait names in the English language, let alone the relationships among them. Some more efficient method of dealing with traits was needed, and a technique called factor analysis provided it.

Traits as Factors

Basically, **factor analysis** is a procedure that allows the personality researcher to look at large amounts of data relevant to the traits of many individuals and summarize what seems to "go with" what. Then the investigator can group related traits together and classify them as personality factors. An example, based on the behavior of one person, should help to clarify the general idea. Several days of close observation of a particular man might result in a long and varied list of highly specific activities, including: "places food in mouth," "rakes leaves," "plays tennis," "waxes car," "reads newspaper," "sits at desk," "chews food," "kisses wife," "drives to tennis court," "buys newspaper," "swallows food," "burns leaves," "writes reports," "sits on toilet," "removes clothes," "lies asleep for 8 hours," "washes dishes," "argues with supervisor," "sets alarm clock," "watches TV," "pets dog," and on and on. You could report on the man's behavior simply by presenting the entire list of everything he did during the period of observation (which is analogous to listing all of a person's personality traits), but this would be cumbersome and the report would be difficult to deal with.

Alternatively, you could summarize all the specific behaviors under a few categories (analogous to personality factors). You might see that certain behaviors are related to one another in some way. A group of behaviors such as "plays tennis," "pets dog," "walks to tennis court," "reads newspaper," and "watches TV" might be called "Recreation" or "Relaxation" (the name you give it is arbitrary; you could just as easily call it "Behavior group A"). Several other behaviors may be unrelated to those called "Recreation" but highly related to one another—such as "washes dishes," "rakes leaves," "burns leaves," "waxes car"—and this group might be named "Household Chores." You could follow the same grouping and name procedures with respect to all the other behaviors observed; the result might be a report saying that the person spent his time engaged in five categories of behavior: "Housework," "Occupational Pursuits," "Recreation," "Sexual Activity" (which may or may not be the same as "Recreation"), and "Body Maintenance."

Factor analysis (see Chapter 1 and Appendices A and C) allows the same kind of summaries as those in our example, but in factor analysis the relationship among specific traits is determined through sophisticated mathematical procedures, not just by human observation. We turn now to the work of one of the leading theorists who has used factor analysis in his investigation of personality traits.

Cattell's Surface and Source Traits

Raymond B. Cattell is one of the foremost proponents of factor analysis as a means of learning about personality traits. In his research on personality, Cattell has tapped three sources of information about human behavior, which he refers to as L-data, Q-data, and T-data. L-data come not directly from the person under study but from life records, generally supplied by individuals who have observed the subject and who can provide information about the individual's behavior. Q-data consist of the subject's answers to questions about himself. T-data consist of scores on standardized, objective tests. Cattell argues that one cannot obtain a complete picture of personality without using these multiple data sources.

Like Allport, Cattell recognizes that some traits are broader and more pervasive than others. His extensive research has resulted in the grouping of human behavior into about 35 **trait clusters.** Cattell calls these clusters **surface traits** because they summarize the most obvious ways in which overt behaviors are related. For example, "honest" is a surface trait which summarizes a range of related behaviors that might include "returning a lost wallet," "telling the truth," "paying a parking fine," and the like. The other end of this surface trait dimension, "dishonest," summarizes an opposite set of related behaviors.

Because they describe only the overt reactions between people, Cattell regards these surface traits more as manifestations of personality than as the basic dimensions of personality itself. In order to identify these more basic elements, the sources of personality, Cattell used factor analysis to analyze the surface traits. With this procedure he isolated 16 *source* traits. He then developed a test called the 16 PF (personality factors) to measure their relative strengths in individual subjects. Thus instead of describing personality in terms of specific behaviors or even clusters of behaviors (surface traits), Cattell provides a profile for each person in terms

© 1959 United Feature Syndicate Inc.

of his or her scores on source traits such as "reserved–outgoing," "shy–venturesome," or "relaxed–tense" (see Appendix C). Cattell views these source traits as the "building blocks" of personality and notes that they stem from either environmental influences (*environmental-mold* traits) or genetic-constitutional factors (*constitutional* traits).

Need Theory

Another kind of dispositional approach to personality views behavior as driven by the individual's needs or goals rather than by traits or personality type. This approach is exemplified by the work of Henry Murray (see Chapter 7), who postulated the existence of 12 primary human needs, such as air, water, food, sex, and 27 secondary, or psychogenic, needs, such as achievement, recognition, dominance, autonomy, aggression, affiliation, and nurturance. These needs, in combination with environmental influences (called *press*), shape the individual's personality and behavior. From Murray's point of view, measurement of personality involves assessment of both *manifest* (obvious) needs and *latent* (more subtle) needs.

Manifest needs can be measured directly by observing how often, how long, and how intensely a person engages in particular behaviors. A person who spends a lot of time pushing others around has a stronger need for aggression than a person who seldom if ever behaves assertively. Latent needs, however, are not overt —for instance, a person's latent need for affection might be expressed through romantic daydreams—and therefore they must be measured indirectly. To measure these needs, Murray developed the Thematic Apperception Test (TAT), in which the subject looks at an ambiguous stimulus, such as a picture (see Chapter 7 and Appendix C), and tells a story about it. The content of the story is seen to reflect the individual's latent needs. Tests of this type are called **projective tests** because they allow the subject to "project" aspects of his or her personality onto relatively neutral stimuli. We shall mention other projective tests in discussing psychodynamic theories in the next section.

Some Problems with Dispositional Theories

Dispositional theories have been influential in psychology and have generated massive amounts of research that has increased our ability to describe and make predictions about human behavior; but they have also been criticized on several points. For example, although dispositional theories describe personality (in terms of traits, types, or needs), they provide very little explanation of how it develops. This relative lack of attention to processes of personality development is a weakness of the dispositional approach.

In addition, one might question the assumption that personality is entirely a collection of stable, enduring, unchanging traits. Behavior and personality do not seem always to be independent of the individual's current circumstances or context—we do not always behave the same way. For instance, we may be generous most of the time, but downright stingy on occasions. Explaining the variability of behavior shown by the same person is often difficult for the dispositional theories.

Finally, dispositional theories have been criticized for their extensive use of self-report procedures in personality assessment and research. Asking someone about his or her behavior may be one of the most direct means of gaining information about personality, but it is also

© 1957 United Feature Syndicate Inc.

According to psychodynamic theory, expressive activities such as drawing may reflect unconscious feelings. As the cartoon suggests, care must be exercised in interpreting such material.

dangerous, because the data collected on a personality test may be biased or distorted in various ways. Subjects may try to present themselves in a particularly positive or negative way, or their responses may be influenced by factors such as the characteristics of the person giving the test, the situation in which they take the test, or events that occurred prior to it.

PSYCHODYNAMIC THEORIES

Psychodynamic theories are based on the assumption that personality and personality development are determined by intrapsychic events and conflicts—that is, events and conflicts which take place within the mind—and that these can best be explored and understood through careful, in-depth study of individual subjects. The foundations for this approach were set down late in the nineteenth century primarily by Sigmund Freud. A physician devoted to the principles of science, Freud evolved one of the most comprehensive and influential theories of personality ever presented.

Freud's Theory

Freud called his approach **psychoanalysis** and based his theorizing on a few fundamental principles. One of these was *psychic determinism,* the idea that human behavior does not occur randomly but in accordance with intrapsychic causes, which may not always be obvious to an outside observer or even to the person displaying the behavior. This concept, that all of our behavior "means" something, even if we are not aware of its meaning, is one of the most significant and widely known features of Freud's theory. In the psychoanalytic perspective few, if any, aspects of human behavior are accidental: Writing the word "sex" when you meant to write "six," calling your lover by another person's name, or forgetting a dental appointment could be interpreted as expressing feelings, desires, fears, or impulses of which you may not be aware.

Freud called the part of mental functioning that is out of our awareness and to which we cannot gain access the **unconscious.** Thoughts, feelings, and ideas of which we are unaware but that we can bring into the **conscious** portion of the mind are said to be **preconscious.** For example, you can easily become aware of the feelings of your tongue even though, until you read this sentence, you were probably not thinking about it. Such thoughts are preconscious. By contrast, according to Freud, if you harbor unconscious hatred toward a close friend, you would claim that no such feelings exist because you do not experience them consciously.

Another of Freud's fundamental assumptions was that human personality is formed out of the continuous struggle between the individual's attempts to satisfy inborn instincts (primarily involving sex and aggression) while at the same time coping with an environment that will not tolerate completely uninhibited conduct. In Freud's view all human beings are born with instinctual sexual and aggressive impulses which demand immediate gratification but which individuals cannot always directly express without causing themselves harm or other negative consequences. Thus, it becomes each individual's lifelong task somehow to satisfy instinctual urges while taking into account the demands, rules, and realities of the environment. For example, a man may desire sexual relations with a particular woman, but because he has been socialized by his parents and other agents of society, he knows that he cannot just walk up to her as a perfect stranger and attempt to attain his goal directly. Therefore, he may seek to meet her socially, develop a close relationship with her over some period of time, and ultimately reach his original objective. This solution to the man's problem is far more socially appropriate than a direct expression of sexual impulses and thus reflects a compromise between instinct and reality. For Freud, then, personality is a kind of arena in which what individuals want to do (instinct) conflicts with what they have learned they should or can do (morality and reason) and where some compromise is worked out.

It is important to note that Freud lived and wrote in a time of Victorian sexual repression. To argue and theorize as he did made him a rebel against society. His theory was truly dangerous to the existing social order, and his bravery in proposing such a position should not be overlooked.

Structure of Personality

As we saw in Chapter 8, Freud called the unconscious, instinctual component of personality the **id.** In the id are all of a person's inherited sexual, aggressive, and other impulses that seek immediate expression. All of the psychic energy, or **libido,** that motivates behavior is part of the id at birth. Because the id seeks to gratify its desires without delay, it operates on the **pleasure principle** (this might be translated as "if it feels good, do it"). Because it is unconscious, the id is not in touch with the world outside. As the person grows, the real world will impose more and more limitations on direct gratification of the id's instinctual impulses.

Therefore, we have seen that as a newborn child develops, a second aspect of personality, called **ego,** begins to take shape. The ego gets its energy from the id, but it is partly conscious and thus is in contact with external reality. Its function is mainly to find ways to allow satisfaction of id impulses while at the same time protecting the organism as a whole from danger. In our example of the man who wanted

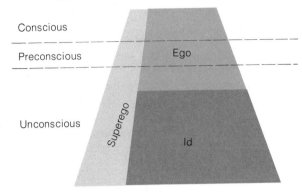

Figure 9–2
The relationship of the id, ego, and superego to levels of awareness

to have intercourse with a certain woman (id impulse), the ego planned and directed the implementation of a socially acceptable way of doing so. Because the ego takes reality into account while seeking to facilitate expression of id impulses, it operates on the **reality principle** (which might be translated as "if you are going to do it, do it quietly" or "do it later").

As the child grows, you will remember that a third component of personality develops called the **superego.** It is roughly equivalent to the "conscience" in the sense that it contains all of the teachings of the person's family and culture regarding ethics, morals, and values—how one should behave. In Freudian theory, the development of the superego actually involves internalizing these teachings so that they function not as someone else's values but as our own. Thus, this aspect of personality acts as a kind of internalized representative of society that seeks to influence us to behave in a socially acceptable fashion. Feelings of guilt are seen as the result of failing to follow the demands of the superego.

In Freud's system, then, personality is a three-part structure, partly conscious, partly unconscious (see Figure 9–2), that is constantly involved in conflicts within itself. The ego is involved in most of these intrapsychic conflicts because it must find a way to reconcile the impetuous impulses of the id, the perfectionistic demands of the superego, and the requirements of the outside world. Some examples of intrapsychic conflicts are presented in Table 9–2.

TABLE 9–2 Possible Conflicts among the Aspects of Personality

Conflict	Example
Id vs. ego	Choosing between a small immediate reward and a larger reward that requires some period of waiting (i.e., delay of gratification)
Id vs. superego	Deciding whether to return the difference when you are overpaid or undercharged
Ego vs. superego	Choosing between acting in a realistic way (e.g., telling a "white lie") and adhering to a potentially costly or unrealistic standard (e.g., always telling the truth)
Id and ego vs. superego	Deciding whether to retaliate against the attack of a weak opponent or to "turn the other cheek"
Id and superego vs. ego	Deciding whether to act in a realistic way that conflicts both with your desires and your moral convictions (e.g., the decision faced by devout Roman Catholics as to the use of contraceptive devices)
Ego and superego vs. id	Choosing whether to "act on the impulse" to steal something you want and cannot afford—the ego would presumably be increasingly involved in such a conflict as the probability of being apprehended increases

Distinct Possibility of a Freudian Slip

AP

PARIS — French Communist party leader Georges Marchais said . . . on nationwide television that French Communists would "never agree to decisions concerning . . . the future of our people and our country being made elsewhere than in Moscow."

He hastily corrected himself with ". . . in Paris."

Marchais was accusing President Valery Giscard d'Estaing during an interview of selling out France's independence.

Rocky Mountain News, *Denver*
December 10, 1975

Ego Defense Mechanisms

The result of conflict among various components of personality is **anxiety.** For example, if id impulses were to prompt a hungry person to take food from a neighboring restaurant table while waiting for his own lunch, the ego would recognize the potential danger of such action, the superego would point out that such behavior is "wrong," and the resulting feelings would be experienced as anxiety. Freud postulated that in order to prevent anxiety the ego employs a variety of unconscious tactics called **defense mechanisms,** which attempt to keep unacceptable id impulses or other threatening material from reaching consciousness.

According to Freud, one of the most basic and primitive defense mechanisms is **repres-**

sion. In repression the ego devotes a great deal of its energy to keeping a particular thought, memory, feeling, or impulse at the unconscious level. (Note that repression, an unconscious process, is not the same as suppression, a conscious means of denying an impulse one is aware of.) Thus, if a father has strong unconscious impulses to murder his children, his ego may prevent him from becoming aware of this. However, like trying to hold a fully inflated beachball under water, repression takes a lot of constant effort. At times the repressed material may threaten to surface, or actually do so.

Complete and entirely successful repression without additional help is unlikely, and the ego often employs supplementary defenses to keep unacceptable material from consciousness. One of these is **reaction formation,** in which the individual thinks and acts in a fashion directly opposite to the unconscious impulse. Our hypothetical murderous father might thus be extremely overprotective of his children and express great concern for their welfare. He might also employ (unconsciously, of course) the defense mechanism called **projection,** through which he would attribute his own taboo impulses to others. This might take the form of accusing other fathers of abusing their children. A defense mechanism called **displacement** actually allows some disguised expression of the id impulses. In this case the father who unconsciously wishes to harm his children may "take it out" on the family dog or some other target. If he justifies or explains inappropriate or unacceptable behavior toward his children without being aware of the "real" unconscious reason for it,

Figure 9-3
Sigmund Freud

Top left: Freud at 35 in 1891. At this time Freud was developing his abilities slowly and painfully. As he said, "I have restricted capacities or talents. None at all for the natural sciences; nothing for mathematics; nothing for anything quantitative. But what I have . . . is probably very intense" (Jones, 1961).

Top right: Freud at 50 in 1906, the year thought by many to mark the first recognition of Freud by English-speaking countries. Also this year Carl Jung, who later became author of his own system of personality, began a regular correspondence with Freud from Switzerland. Thus, "his researches of the past thirteen years, so scorned and despised elsewhere, were finding wider acceptance" (Jones, 1961).

Bottom left: Freud at 66 in 1922. This was one of Freud's most productive yet disappointing times. The Committee, a group of Freud's disciples which had existed for 10 years, was disrupted by dissension among its members. This event coincided with the first signs of cancer, from which Freud would eventually die. In 1920 he changed his original ideas of the unconscious and began a new theory of the ego, which is considered a great advance in the theory of psychoanalysis.

Bottom right: Freud at 82 in 1938. Because he was a Jew, Freud was forced to leave his lifelong home of Vienna, Austria, during the Nazi invasion. Here he is in England in the process of reading and writing his last work, the *Outline of Psychoanalysis*. He was still writing the manuscript a year later when he died.

he is using the ego defense mechanism called **rationalization.** Thus, he might point out that he punishes his children frequently because he loves them or "for their own good."

In Freud's view, one defense mechanism results in socially adaptive behavior. It is called **sublimation** and involves expressing taboo impulses within productive, creative channels. For instance, an individual's sexual impulses may be converted into artistic energy and result in the production of paintings or sculpture. Sublimation can provide a more or less permanent solution to the problem of protecting the person against anxiety. The other defenses, however, are less desirable alternatives that "tie up" large amounts of psychic energy and that may eventually break down, thus allowing a partial breakthrough of repressed material and forcing the

person to fall back to even more primitive lines of defense. (This is why dependence on maladaptive ego defense strategies often indicates a need for psychotherapy; see Chapter 12).

Freud believed that when adult ego defenses fail, the person may to some extent **regress,** or revert to behavior characteristics of earlier, less mature developmental stages. Partial regression may result in behaviors that are simply immature or otherwise mildly inappropriate. More profound regression can result in the appearance of severely disturbed, even psychotic behavior.

Personality Development

As we discussed in Chapter 8, Freud postulated that every human being passes through several **psychosexual stages** of development.

Each stage is named for the area of the body most closely associated with pleasure at the time. Thus the first year or so of life is the *oral stage* because eating, sucking, and other oral activities are the predominant sources of pleasurable stimulation. If, because of premature or delayed weaning, oral needs are frustrated or overindulged, the child may cling to some behavior patterns associated with the oral stage and not progress to the next stage of development. Freud called this phenomenon **fixation** because the personality fixates on some mode of gratification (in this case, oral gratification) because that is the only way it has of dealing with anxiety or frustration at the time.

As an example, consider that a baby can reduce its tension only orally (by crying and sucking). If the frustration is overwhelming to the developing ego, it will interfere with reality testing, and the personality will handle future tension (unrealistically) as it did earlier. Thus, an anxious adult may smoke cigarettes heavily. Oral stimulation might have helped the individual with childhood problems, but will smoking relieve problems at the office? Adults who depend upon patterns of behavior that are oral in nature such as smoking, overeating, or using "biting" sarcasm, may be said to have oral personalities or to exhibit some degree of oral fixation. Freud believed that the more strongly fixated an individual was at a given psychosexual stage, the more likely the person was to display behaviors typical of that stage and to regress to that stage when under stress. Thus, Freud viewed forms of psychosis in which individuals become totally dependent on others for their care and cease to speak as conditions involving almost complete regression to the oral stage.

Freud assumed that the anus and the stimuli associated with eliminating and withholding feces were central to the second year or two of a child's development, and so he called this period the *anal stage*. The critical feature of this period is toilet training, and Freud thought anal fixation resulted from either overly rigorous or overly indulgent toilet-training practices. Fixation at the anal stage is indicated in adulthood either by excessively "tight," controlled behavior or by very "loose," disorderly behavior. Individuals who are (for example) stingy, obstinate, highly organized, and overly concerned

with cleanliness and small details are characterized as anal-retentive personalities. Those who are (for example) sloppy, disorganized, or overly generous may be labeled anal expulsive.

Following the anal stage (at about age four), the genitals become the primary source of pleasure, and the child enters the *phallic stage*. As the name implies, Freud paid more attention to psychosexual development in the male than in the female. He theorized that during the phallic stage the young boy begins to have sexual desires toward his mother and wants to eliminate his father so that he will not have to compete with him. Because these desires parallel the plot of the Greek tragedy *Oedipus Rex*, Freud characterized them as the **Oedipus complex.** But the child fears that he will be castrated for having such incestuous and murderous desires, and so he normally resolves the conflict and its resultant anxiety by repressing his sexual desires toward his mother. He attempts to imitate or *identify* with his father and ultimately finds an appropriate female sex partner. Freud outlined a parallel though less clearly specified process for girls involving what is now called the **Electra complex** (after another Greek play). Here, the girl desires her father and rejects her mother. She must resolve this situation by repressing her incestuous feelings, identifying with her mother, and eventually finding an appropriate male sex partner.

Freud believed that successful resolution of the conflicts inherent in the phallic stage was crucial to healthy personality development. Identification with the same-sex parent is the beginning of superego development and the incorporation of sex-typed behaviors. But conflict resolution at this stage is extremely difficult. Freud thought fixation at the phallic stage was common and was responsible for a variety of later interpersonal problems, including aggression and various sex "deviations" such as exhibitionism.

Following the phallic stage, the child enters a sort of dormant period that lasts until the onset of puberty. This is called the *latency stage,* and is characterized by a lack of sexual interest.

During adolescence, the child matures physically and sexually and begins the *genital stage,* which lasts through the adult years. Pleasure is again focused in the genital area, but the individual seeks more than the self-satisfaction characteristic of the phallic stage. If all has gone well in the earlier psychosexual stages, the person seeks to establish stable, long-term sexual relationships that take into account the needs of others.

Freud assumed that because so much of personality operates at the unconscious level, individuals cannot be relied upon to report their own personality accurately. Thus, he and others who followed him developed special methods of assessing the unconscious aspects of personality functioning. The main problem as Freud saw it was to get around the ego defense mechanisms that prevent unconscious material from surfacing. In his early attempts to do this, he interviewed patients while they were under hypnosis. Later he employed procedures such as free association, the analysis of "accidental" behavior, and the interpretation of dreams (see Chapter 12). In more recent years, projective tests such as the Rorschach Inkblot Test and the TAT have been developed and employed as another approach to exploring the unconscious (see Appendix C).

Variations on Freud's Theory

Freud's original ideas have gone through many changes over the years since he first enunciated them. In fact, Freud himself was constantly altering, editing, and supplementing his views, so that it is possible to speak of many editions of his theory. He did cling to a few of his basic principles, however, notably the instinctual basis of human behavior (emphasizing sex and aggression); and it was on this point that many of his prominent followers ultimately broke with him. Each of them took Freud's ideas and developed them in a slightly different way. This ultimately resulted in the appearance of new psychodynamic theories as well as revisions of the basic Freudian view. These theoretical developments also prompted the evolution of a group of new therapeutic approaches and emphases. Generally speaking, early variations on Freud's theory tended to deemphasize the instinctual basis of human behavior and pay more attention to environmental factors, especially the influence of the individual's social situation. Here we will briefly consider a few of the many approaches that grew out of Freud's system (see also "Recommended Additional Readings").

Carl G. Jung

Initially Jung was a member of Freud's inner circle and, for a time, Freud's heir apparent. As a result of certain differences, however, he broke with the Viennese school and in Zurich founded his own system of **analytic psychology.** Whereas Freud considered the individual to be buffeted by instincts and fully molded by early adolescence, Jung suggested a continuing process called "individuation" leading toward harmony between the individual and the world. At the heart of his theory is his conception of the self, which he believed consists of four basic functions—thinking, feeling, sensing, and intuiting. The way these functions are carried out in the individual is influenced largely by whether the person is an introvert or an extrovert, and it was Jung who first brought this personality dimension into psychology.

Jung could not accept Freud's analysis of the unconscious as the source of all our psychic energies. Instead, he viewed the unconscious as made up of two parts—the personal unconscious, and the collective unconscious. The personal unconscious he saw in much the same way as Freud, as the repository of forgotten and repressed memories. The collective unconscious, on the other hand, contains archetypal elements that are common to the entire human race. It is an intrinsic aspect of personality that has accumulated through history and been passed from generation to generation. For Jung, the two parts of the unconscious are related in the sense that the personal unconscious contains complexes that develop out of the archetypes, or basic elements, of the collective unconscious. For example, all human beings have personal unconscious thoughts and feelings about their own mothers, but these are supplemented by the archetypical concept of "motherhood" with all its cultural and historical associations. Jung argued that the personality is heavily guided by a forward-looking, goal-directed process. In that sense, his theory is an optimistic alternative to Freud's pessimistic view of the individual.

Alfred Adler

One of the first of Freud's colleagues to reject the instinct theory of behavior was Alfred Adler. He developed instead an approach called *individual analysis,* which assumed that the most

TABLE 9–3 Horney's List of 10 Neurotic Needs (Neurotic Ways of Coping with Basic Anxiety)

1. Needs that involve moving toward people.
  a. The need for affection and approval—the person seeks to please everyone and be liked by everyone.
  b. The need for a "partner" who will take over one's life— submerges his own personality and becomes a "parasite" on someone else.

2. Needs that involve moving against other people.
  a. The need for power, mainly in order to dominate others —may seek power through intellectual superiority over others as well as through more obvious means.
  b. The need to exploit others.
  c. The need for prestige—seeks public recognition and admiration.
  d. The need for personal admiration—neurotically overestimates his own personal worth and wants admiration of this false front.
  e. The need for personal achievement—is basically insecure and truly drives himself in search of more and more achievements, overdriven to achieve goals which often are not that important to others.

3. Needs that involve moving away from people.
  a. The need for self-sufficiency and independence—the person, completely frustrated in his attempts to relate to others, essentially gives up on them and becomes the loner, the hermit.
  b. The need for perfection and unassailability—fears that others will detect his faults and mistakes and so constantly strives for the ultimate in perfection to make himself invulnerable.
  c. The need to restrict one's life within narrow borders— moves into the background, makes few demands, is overly modest and self-critical.

important factor in the development of personality is that each person begins life in a completely helpless, inferior position. Adler believed that the individual's subsequent behavior represents a "striving for superiority" (first within the family, then in the larger social world) and that the way in which each person seeks superiority constitutes the individual's style of life. He thought adaptive life-styles are characterized by cooperation, social interest, courage, and common sense, while maladaptive styles of life involve undue competition, lack of concern for others, and the distortion of reality. For Adler, maladaptive life-styles and the behavior problems they cause are due not to unresolved conflicts but to mistaken ideas or basic misconceptions that the person has about the world. For example, a child may discover

that a good way to exert control over others (and thus gain some feeling of superiority) is to be very dependent on them. Over time, the individual may develop the misconception that he or she is a "special case" who cannot deal with the world independently. Accordingly, a life-style may evolve in which the person is always sick, hurt, frightened, or handicapped in some other way and therefore demands attention and special consideration from others.

Social Influences in Psychoanalysis

The neo-Freudian personality theories are chiefly characterized by an emphasis on social factors as opposed to the Freudian emphasis on biological factors (instincts). Alder was a forerunner of this emphasis, which is brought out more fully in the theories of Karen Horney, Erich Fromm, and Harry Stack Sullivan. All of these theorists said that Freud had failed to realize the social-cultural aspects of personality development. Personality, they claimed, is shaped and influenced more by society, culture, and the other people in the life of the individual than it is by instincts. We shall use Horney's theory to illustrate this trend.

Relationships with others play a dominant role in Horney's theory of neurotic personality functioning. For Horney, the primary personality construct is called *basic anxiety*, which has its roots in childhood when the child's primary fear is of being isolated and helpless. Thus, basic anxiety stems from threats to the child's safety, security, and physiological needs, to use Maslow's hierarchy for comparison (see Chapter 7). The child develops strategies for dealing with basic anxiety, and any of these strategies can become permanent characteristics of the individual's personality.

Horney suggested that the individual's strategies for solving the problems created by basic anxiety can easily develop into irrational and maladaptive (neurotic) forms of behavior. The strategy becomes such an important part of the personality structure that it takes on all the characteristics of a drive or need. Horney identified ten *neurotic needs* that constitute three basic attitudes a person might acquire in his or her relationships with other people (see Table 9–3). The strategy might cause the person to move (1) toward other people, (2) against other people, or (3) away from other people.

The neo-Freudians stressed the principles of social psychology, the influence that the real or implied presence of other people has on behavior. They strongly believed that personality is shaped by experience—social and cultural experience—and, as a consequence, was readily subject to modification. This naturally led to a much greater realization that there were vast individual differences in people's personalities and that not everyone could be described in the same way. Perhaps most important, it led to a greater optimism about human nature and the ability of human beings to change than was present in the original Freudian notions, which were based on biological rather than social foundations.

Otto Rank

Like Adler, Otto Rank disagreed with Freud's emphasis on sex and aggression as the bases of human behavior. But while Adler emphasized inferiority and striving for superiority, Rank focused on the developing person's basic dependency and inborn potential for growth and independence. Rank thought the *trauma of birth* was very significant because it involved an abrupt transition from the passive, dependent world of the fetus where no demands are made (the unborn child does not even have to breathe) to a chaotic outside world that requires ever-increasing independence. Thus, birth provides the first example of what Rank considered to be a basic human conflict between the desire to be independent and the need to be independent. Rank felt that the appearance of behavior problems indicated that this conflict was not adequately resolved.

Transactional Analysis

Most recently, psychiatrist Eric Berne has recast many of Freud's basic notions into terms and concepts that have captured a great deal of attention. In accordance with the tendency among neo-Freudians to emphasize ego (rather than id) functions and in energizing and determining behavior, Berne described a triad of **ego states** called "Parent," "Adult," and "Child" (paralleling the superego, ego, and id, respectively). Books by Eric Berne (such as *Games People Play*) and others (such as T. A. Harris' *I'm OK, You're OK*) describe the use of **transactional analysis** to illuminate the ways in

"I've always found Freud a little tough to swallow."

Playboy, February 1972. Reproduced by special permission of PLAYBOY Magazine; copyright © 1972 by Playboy.

which ego states mediate interpersonal behavior. The lively interest shown by the public in this approach in recent years attests to the continuing influence of some of Freud's basic themes as they appear in modern form. For more detail on transactional analysis and other recent innovations in psychotherapy, see Chapter 12.

Some Problems with Psychodynamic Theories

Freud's influence is hard to overestimate. His concepts are so well known that they have become a part of our language and culture. It is not uncommon to hear people refer to "Freudian slips," unconscious motivation, the Oedipus complex, and psychoanalysis in everyday conversation. However, Freud's theory has also received strong criticism, mainly on the grounds that his concepts (such as id, ego, superego, defense mechanisms, and the unconscious) are elaborate abstractions that cannot easily be measured. The techniques designed to assess personality and personality functioning in

© 1961, United Feature Syndicate Inc.

Freudian terms have not shown themselves to be very reliable or valid. The fact that the entire basis for Freud's approach was his experiences with a relatively small number of case studies (a few patients and Freud himself) rather than experimental research has prompted the criticism that psychodynamic formulations are unscientific and do not apply to the bulk of the human population.

Critics also point out that many of Freud's assumptions about personality are difficult or impossible to evaluate because the results of any test can be interpreted according to his theory. For example, if psychoanalytic interviews or projective test results lead to the conclusion that a person harbors strong unconscious feelings of hostility toward the whole world, subsequent hostile behavior would be interpreted as evidence for the breakthrough of unconscious impulses, thus confirming the original hypothesis. But *lack* of subsequent hostile behavior could also provide evidence for underlying hostility because it could be seen as a defense mechanism (reaction formation). It has also been argued that psychodynamic personality theories make it too easy to interpret behavior as indicative of pathology and thus create problems where none existed before. For instance, a person might be called anxious and insecure if he shows up for work early, resistant and hostile if he is late, and compulsive if he is right on time.

SOCIAL LEARNING THEORIES

Instead of emphasizing intrapsychic conflicts, instincts, or dispositions (such as enduring traits), social learning theories focus on behavior and the environmental conditions that affect it. From this point of view, personality is the sum total of the individual's behavior rather than some hypothetical structure that behavior reflects. Social learning theories also assume that behavior (personality) is determined primarily through learning, which takes place in a social context. These two basic assumptions have resulted in an approach to personality that accounts for both variation and consistency in behavior. This approach explains differences among people in terms of each person's unique learning history—for example, under stress conditions such as an exam, a person who has learned to deal with problems by depending upon others may seek to cheat, while another who has been rewarded for self-reliance may not.

Social learning theories view consistencies in a particular person's behavior as a function of generalized learning—for example, a person may learn to be calm and serious in most situations if that behavior has been consistently rewarded over many years and under a wide variety of circumstances. Further, these theories seek to understand inconsistencies in a particular person's behavior and other "unpredict-able" behavioral phenomena in terms of the concept of behavioral specificity—the idea that behavior changes to fit particular circumstances. Walter Mischel summarizes this point well:

Consider a woman who seems hostile and fiercely independent some of the time but passive, depen-dent, and feminine on other occasions. What is she really like? Which one of these two patterns reflects the woman that she really is? Is one pattern in the service of the other, or might both be in the service of a third motive? Might she be a really castrating lady with a facade of passivity—or is she a warm, passive-dependent woman with a surface defense of aggressiveness? Social behavior theory suggests that it is possible for the lady to be *all* of these—a hostile, fiercely independent, passive, dependent, feminine, aggressive, warm, castrating person all in one. . . . Of course which of these she is at any particular moment would not be random and capricious; it would depend on discriminative stimuli—who she is with, when, how, and much, much more. But each of these aspects of her self may be a quite genuine and real aspect of her total being. (Mischel, 1971)

There are many social learning theories of personality. Although they often differ sub-stantially among themselves with respect to cer-tain specifics, all share several common char-acteristics: (1) an emphasis upon measurable behavior as the content of personality, (2) stress upon environmental as opposed to hereditary influences or other "givens" in personality and personality development, (3) attention to ex-perimental research on the behavior of both human and nonhuman organisms, and (4) use of scientific methods to evaluate hypotheses about behavior and personality-change tech-niques. The main differences among these the-ories are the type of learning process empha-sized (for example, classical versus instrumental; see Chapter 4) and the degree to which cogni-tion (thinking) plays a role in learning and in guiding overt behavior.

The Role of Cognition and Imitation

Modern social learning theory is primarily based on the ideas and research of Albert Bandura, although he has been heavily influenced by B. F. Skinner and other learning theorists. Bandura believes that learning theorists in general have paid too little attention to cogni-

Movie Re-enactment Turns Tragically Real

UPI

COLUMBUS, Ohio — An 11-year-old boy who was shot by his 14-year-old brother as the two re-enacted a scene from a television movie died Sunday.

The older boy is to appear in Franklin County Juvenile Court today to answer a charge of negli-gent homicide. He has been released to the custody of his parents.

Police did not release any names in the case.

Police said the two boys had watched the movie "Dirty Harry" on TV Saturday night, then began imitating the movie late Sunday morning in the bedroom of the older boy.

Homicide Detective Tom Walter said the older brother got a loaded .22-caliber two-shot derringer from his father's nightstand. A toy "Star Trek" ray gun was lying on a table near the younger brother.

Walter said the older brother, holding the der-ringer in his hand, told the younger brother: "In all the confusion, I bet you don't know if this gun is loaded."

The statement was similar to one made in the movie.

The officer said the older brother then ordered the other boy to go for the toy gun. As the younger brother did so, the older boy shot him in the chest. He said the child stumbled into the hallway and died.

Police said the boys' father was on the front porch with a friend when the shooting occurred.

Police quoted the older boy as saying they "were playing Dirty Harry."

Boulder (Colo.) Daily Camera
September 12, 1977

Social learning theories of personality put great emphasis on learning that takes place by observa-tion and imitation of the behavior of other people. The controversy about the effect of TV violence on children centers around the issue of to what extent children will imitate what they observe on the "tube." Tragic events like this one lend support to this theory.

tive and social processes in the development and maintenance of personality (behavior). Ban-dura's work stresses the idea that an enormous amount of human learning is accomplished

Figure 9–4
Learning aggression by imitation

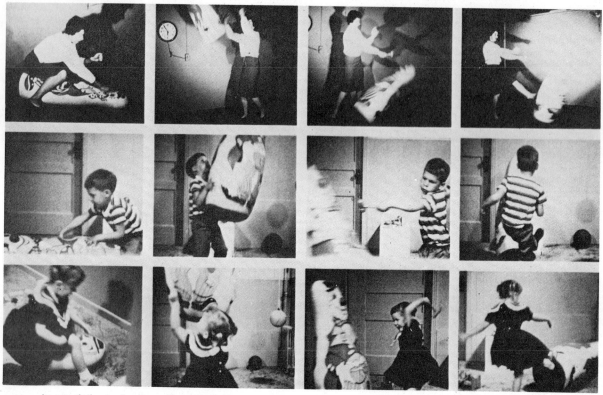

In specialized situations, there is little doubt that children will imitate the aggressive actions of adult models. Here are some pictures from a study by Bandura, Ross, and Ross (1963) that is now a classic.

In the top row an adult model exhibits four different ways to hurt a Bobo clown doll. The next two rows show a boy and a girl duplicating the model's efforts.

simply by observing the performance of others, without any obvious reinforcement or any opportunity to practice. This phenomena is called **observational learning.** According to Bandura's results, all that may be required for significant learning to occur is for the person to observe another individual—a model—engage in the to-be-learned behavior. Later, especially if the model was rewarded for his or her performance, the observer may also display the new response. For example, children may learn how to display aggression by observing someone else do so. In one well-known experiment (see Figure 9–4) Bandura and his colleages arranged for pre-school children to observe models either vigorously attacking or sitting quietly near an inflatable Bobo doll. In subsequent tests, the

children who observed aggression tended to match the model's behavior quite precisely, while those who had seen a passive model tended to be nonaggressive.

Thus, a major thrust of Bandura's theory is its emphasis upon vicarious processes or processes involving observation and imitation of others. For Bandura personality develops not only as a function of what we learn directly (through reward or punishment) but also through observation of other people's behavior and its consequences and an understanding of how those consequences could apply to us. According to Bandura, vicarious processes can result in a wide variety of behavioral effects, including acquisition of new responses, as we saw in the Bobo experiment; inhibition or dis-

**Figure 9–5
Albert Bandura**

"During the past half century, learning-theory approaches to personality development, deviant behavior, and psychotherapy have suffered from the fact that they have relied heavily on a limited range of principles based on . . . studies of animal learning or human learning in one-person situations. . . . It is necessary to extend and modify these principles and to introduce new principles that have been established and confirmed through studies . . . of dyadic [two-person] and group situations" (Bandura and Walters, 1965).

Suicide News Causing Suicides

UPI

SAN DIEGO — News stories about suicides provoke more suicides—many of which are disguised as auto accidents—according to a seven-year study by a professor of sociology at the University of California at San Diego.

The study showed that following suicide reports, the number of deaths in auto crashes jumps briefly, increasing by 9 to 18 per cent over the normal level.

"This rise apparently occurs because suicide stories stimulate a wave of imitative suicides, some of which are disguised as motor vehicle accidents," said Prof. David R. Phillips in a scientific paper.

The research covered the San Francisco and Los Angeles areas, and the results were corrected for such things as heavy holiday traffic, yearly trends or other explanations for the increase.

The average increase in auto deaths is 9.12 per cent in the week following a normally publicized suicide, he said, and 18.84 per cent in the week following a heavily publicized suicide.

Boulder (Colo.) Daily Camera
June 22, 1977

Don't make the mistake of believing that children are the only ones who learn and behave as they observe and imitate others. The principles of social learning theory apply equally to adults. This article suggests that imitation plays a role in suicide. Can you think of other explanations for the increase in suicides following news coverage of a suicide? Remember that the correlation between news coverage and suicide does not prove that the news coverage caused the increase. If this hypothesis is true, what implications does it have for the practice of journalism?

inhibition of already learned behaviors, as when a person violates a "don't walk" sign after watching someone else do so; and facilitation or prompting of behavior, as when, during gasoline shortages, a long line of cars forms at a closed station after a single prankster pulls up to the pumps.

It is important to note that although Bandura's theory emphasizes the role of observational and cognitive processes in learning, it also recognizes the importance of both social and primary reinforcement as factors influencing the continued performance of new or altered behaviors. Thus, for example, a person may learn how to meet attractive members of the opposite sex by watching others do so successfully, but unless the approach actually leads to positive consequences (once in a while, at least), it will ultimately be abandoned.

Cognition and Expectancies

The role of cognitive variables has an even stronger place in the social learning theory of Julian B. Rotter, who places strong emphasis on the importance of expectancies in the development, maintenance, and alteration of behavior. In Rotter's system, the probability that a given behavior will occur is dependent on (1) what the person expects will happen following the response and (2) the value the person places upon that outcome. Thus, a person will pay for a ticket if he or she expects that this will result in admission to a movie theater (outcome) and if the film being shown is of interest (value). Rotter assumes that the expectancies and values that influence, organize, and alter behavior (personality) are acquired through learning. Therefore, in order to "have" an expectancy about an outcome or make a judgment regarding its value, a person must have had some direct or vicarious experience with equivalent or similar situations in the past.

One of the best-known products of Rotter's expectancy-oriented theorizing has been the concept of generalized expectancies, particularly as it applies to people's perception of how events are controlled. Rotter developed a test called the Internal-External Locus of Control Scale (also known as the I-E or the LOC scale). In simplest terms, it measures the degree to which individuals generally expect the things that happen to them to be determined primarily by their own efforts (internal control) or by factors beyond their control (external control). Considerable research effort is now being devoted to an attempt to determine the importance of locus of control as a personality dimension.

Social Learning Approaches to Personality Assessment

In our earlier discussion of dispositional and psychodynamic personality theories, it was clear that the various strategies they employed to measure personality, such as paper-and-pencil tests, dream analysis, and projective techniques, assumed that a person's responses to assessment procedures provide indications or signs of underlying personality traits or characteristics. Social learning approaches to personality measurement begin with radically different assumptions. Because they view behavior and personality as virtually identical, they do not seek to learn about presumed underlying traits or constructs but focus instead on careful, systematic attempts to assess (1) how the person in question behaves and (2) the environmental and other circumstances which influence that behavior.

Thus, an individual's response to Rorschach inkblot cards would be assumed to tell us not about unconscious processes but about how that person behaves during psychological testing. In other words, the social learning approach treats responses to any sort of personality assessment procedure as a behavior sample that is useful in making predictions about future behavior in similar or related circumstances, not as a *sign* of broad, generalized personality characteristics (see Appendix C). Because of this orientation, social learning procedures tend to focus on direct observation of behavior rather than on traditional personality tests.

The questionnaires that are used tend to be direct and straightforward, asking the respondents simply to provide information about the effects of environmental stimuli on their behavior. Examples of this sort of "test" are the Fear Survey Schedule (Geer, 1965; Wolpe and Lang, 1964), which simply asks persons to rate the degree to which they fear a wide variety of objects and situations, and the Reinforcement Survey Schedule (Cautela and Kastenbaum, 1967), which asks respondents to rate the degree to which they enjoy a variety of activities, such as dancing, talking to friends, and eating. More elaborate reinforcer surveys such as the Reinforcing Event Report (MacDonald, Bernstein, and Ullmann, 1976) ask not only about what people like to do but how often they get to do it and how socially appropriate it is.

There are also several types of direct behavioral observation procedures employed by social learning theorists. Some of these ask the individual to act as his or her own observer. This is especially common when adult behaviors that typically occur in the natural environment are of particular interest. Examples include asking individuals to keep records of the number of cigarettes they smoke or the frequency and duration of sleep disturbances. A clinician who employs such assessment techniques may seek to understand a client's "depression" or "anxiety attacks" by asking that client to specify the behaviors, feelings, and thoughts that make up such states and to keep track of their frequency and the environmental conditions that precede, accompany, and follow them.

This type of personality assessment leads to precise statements about behavior (such as "This person behaves in a depressed fashion on the average of three times per week") instead of labels ("This person is a depressive"). Further, this technique can provide clues to the factors contributing to the problem. For example, a careful behavioral analysis of "depression" often reveals that episodes of discomfort tend to be associated with periods during which the client does not have access to very many enjoyable activities. An increase in such activities might thus become part of an overall treatment program.

In other forms of social learning personality assessment, specially trained personnel make systematic observations of many aspects of the behavior of children or adults. This may involve simply watching a child in a large playroom containing a wide variety of toys, games, and other materials. Recording the relative amounts of time the child spends engaged in each of the various activities available allows the observer to determine the kinds of things that interest the child (and that might thus be usable as rewards in a later behavior-change program). Notice that instead of attempting to identify the child's internal needs, traits, or motives, the social learning approach seeks to identify the external stimuli which influence behavior.

Direct observations in other settings are also used to specify the degree to which people display problem behaviors. For example, nurses, aides, and other personnel in mental hospitals often use behavior rating scales to describe with precision the nature of patients' difficulties. Typically, staff members record behaviors on a periodic basis (called time sampling); they note the presence or absence of various categories of patient behavior, such as sitting, talking to others, reading, fighting, shouting, and sleeping. The data gained from these observations, summarized in terms of the frequencies with which certain behaviors occur, may then be combined with other observations regarding the circumstances and consequences associated with the behaviors. All of this information may be used as a guide to treatment planning and,

later, as a baseline against which to measure improvement.

Some Problems with Social Learning Theories

Social learning theories of personality have been criticized mainly on the grounds that their emphasis on learning as the basis for behavior results in a narrowing of their perspective. Some critics note that these theories pay too little attention to the influence of hereditary, physiological, and constitutional factors in determining human behavior. Others point out that not all experimental evidence supports the principles of learning on which these theories are based and that therefore these principles are not as clearly established as the learning theorists would have us believe. Furthermore, even where learning phenomena in animals are well known through laboratory research, they may not be analogous to the ways in which human beings learn. A cat faced with an extremely difficult or insoluble task may display a bizarre pattern of behavior called experimental neurosis, but human neurotic behavior may not be learned in the same way.

PHENOMENOLOGICAL THEORIES

So far we have discussed personality theories that view human behavior as being primarily influenced by (1) underlying traits or needs, (2) intrapsychic events and conflicts, and (3) direct or vicarious learning. A fourth group, called *phenomenological* or *cognitive theories*, rejects many of the basic assumptions of the other three approaches and asserts that the behavior of each human being at any given moment is determined primarily by that particular person's perception of the world. In other words, phenomenological theories assume that each person is unique because his or her view of reality is just a little different from anyone else's and that each person's behavior reflects that view as it exists from moment to moment. Thus, when two people listen to the same political speech, one may react favorably and plan to vote for the speaker, while the other may decide to vote for the speaker's opponent. Phenomenologists view these divergent reactions as due not to the listener's personality traits, ego development, or reinforcement history, but to his or her individual perceptions of the candidate while he was speaking.

From this perspective, we are not passive "carriers" of personality or mere recipients of reinforcement. Rather, the emphasis is upon the active, thinking nature of human beings, upon their ability to make plans and choices about their behavior, and upon the fact that each person is ultimately responsible for his or her own actions. Although phenomenological theories recognize the existence of biological needs, these are deemphasized in considering personality and its development. Instead these theories assume that these people are born with a potential for growth that provides the impetus for behavior. Each person is seen as having an innate tendency to grow and develop into a fully mature individual, just as the seed contains the potential to be a flower. In contrast to Freud, who saw people as motivated by crude instinctual desires, phenomenological theorists view the individual as a basically good organism that will naturally strive for the attainment of love, joy, creativity, harmony, and other positive goals.

Perhaps the most important implication of the phenomenological view of personality development, assessment, and change is that no one can truly understand another's behavior unless he or she can perceive the world through that person's eyes. Accordingly, phenomenological theories, like social learning theories, reject the concept of mental illness and other pejorative labels for behavior that appears strange, unusual, or unexpected. Instead, these theories assume that all human activity is normal, rational, and sensible *when viewed from the point of view of the person being observed.* Thus, people who are violently hostile toward others are seen not as "sick" or "disordered" but as simply acting in accordance with their perception of other people.

Phenomenological theories have evolved from several sources. In part, they represent a reaction against Freud. In their rejection of the importance of instincts and their emphasis on the uniqueness of the individual and his or her conceptions of the world, Adler and Rank anticipated phenomenological theories; their writings have influenced several modern phenomenologists. Attention to the individual's perception of reality was prompted, in part, by the existential philosophies of Heidegger, Kierkegaard, Sartre, and Camus, which assert that the meaning and value of life and everything in it is not intrinsic but is provided by the perceiver. For example, a person is not "actually" beautiful or ugly; these qualities can be assigned only when someone else sees and reacts to the person in question. Thus, a different "reality" is in the eye of each beholder. This focus on the individual's view of reality was also sharpened by the writings of the Gestalt psychologists, who, as we saw in Chapter 3, emphasized that the human perceiver is an active participant in viewing the world, not just a "receiving station."

Rogers' Self Theory

Perhaps the best-known example of phenomenological approaches to personality is the **self theory** of the American psychologist Carl Rogers. Many of Rogers' basic propositions about personality are similar to those of other phenomenologists. For example, these statements from Rogers' writings are characteristic of all phenomenological theories: "Every individual exists in a continually changing world of experience of which he is the center." "The organism reacts to the field as it is experienced and perceived. This perceptual field is, for the individual, 'reality.' " "The organism reacts as an organized whole to this phenomenal field."

Rogers assumes that the one innate human motive is the tendency toward "self-actualization" and that this concept is sufficient to account for the appearance of all human behavior, from the most fundamental food seeking to the most sublime acts of artistic creativity. He has defined this innate quality as "the directional trend which is evident in all organic and human life—the urge to expand, extend, develop, mature—the tendency to express and activate all the capacities of the organism" (Rogers, 1961). Given this basic motive, Rogers views human personality (as reflected in behavior) as the efforts of individuals to actualize themselves within the world as they view it.

As the person develops and interacts with the environment he or she begins to differentiate between the environment and the self. In other words, each of us becomes aware of a part of our experience that we recognize as "I" or "me." According to Rogers, all of a person's experiences, including self experiences, are

Figure 9–6
Carl Rogers

"I have come to feel that the more fully the individual is understood and accepted, the more he tends to drop the false fronts with which he has been meeting life, and the more he tends to move in a direction which is forward" (Carl Rogers, 1961).

evaluated as positive or negative. The person thus evaluates experiences according to whether they are consistent or inconsistent with the self-actualizing tendency. Experiences are evaluated partly in terms of direct or organismic feelings, as when a child evaluates the experience of ice cream positively simply because of its taste; and partly through the influence of others, as when a young boy negatively evaluates the experience of touching his genitals even though it "feels good" because his mother told him the behavior was "bad."

Thus, the self or self-concept emerges not merely as a set of experiences but as a set of evaluated experiences, and the positive or negative value assigned to these experiences is influenced by the combination of direct evaluations and evaluations provided by other individuals.

Positive Self-Regard

Rogers postulates that human beings tend to act in ways that produce positive regard (good evaluations) from others and that this allows them to have positive self-regard. When a person's behavior results in positive direct (organismic) experiences as well as positive regard from others, there is no problem. For example, a child practices reading skills and experiences not only positive direct feelings based upon gaining competence but also positive regard from a parent, such as "I am so proud of you." The result will probably be a positively evaluated self-experience, such as "I like to read." Here, the positive direct organismic experience is in accord with, or as Rogers puts it, is congruent with, the positive self-experience, and the child accurately perceives both its own behavior and its evaluation of it.

However, as in the example given above of the boy touching his genitals, some behaviors may produce a positive organismic experience but a negative reaction from others. When this happens, and especially when it happens early in life, the evaluations of others may overwhelm the individual's direct evaluation. Then, instead of developing a self-experience like "I enjoy masturbation but mother is opposed," the person may acquire the self-experience "I do not want to masturbate" or "I should not want to masturbate." Rogers theorizes that this uncomfortable discrepancy (or incongruity) between organismic experiences and self-experiences is caused by what he calls conditions of worth—feelings that one can receive positive regard from others (and, ultimately, from the self) only on a conditional basis, that is, when one behaves in certain prescribed ways. Conditions of worth are usually set up first by parents and others, but later by the self:

If an individual should experience only unconditional positive regard, then no conditions of worth would develop, self-regard would be unconditional, the needs for positive regard and self-regard would never be at variance with organismic evaluation, and the individual would continue to be psychologically adjusted, and would be fully functioning. (Rogers, 1959)

According to Rogers, recognition that one's feelings and/or behavior do not fulfill conditions of worth results in anxiety over potential loss of positive regard. To prevent this, one may seek to reduce incongruity by distorting or mis-perceiving reality or one's own experience of it so that it fits the self-concept. For example, children are usually taught to behave in ways "appropriate" to their sex and may receive positive evaluations only when they display such behavior. Thus, when a mother scolds her little boy for displaying emotional behavior (such as crying) and praises him for unemotional "masculine" reactions, she may be setting up conditions of worth. If the child actually feels better when he expresses strong emotions than when he suppresses them, he may have to discount his experiences in order to conform to the requirements of the situation. Or he may distort his own personal reality — the fact that he feels better when expressing his emotions — by maintaining that anyone who is emotional is weak.

Rogers thinks that behavior disorders result from the individual's attempts to reduce incongruity by altering actual feelings and experiences so that they approximate the self-concept. The more incongruity and distortion, the more severe the disorder. Rogers' approach to treatment of psychological problems is aimed at helping people reduce incongruity without distorting reality (see Chapter 12).

Learning To Feel Feelings

Many of Rogers' notions about personality and personality change are similar to those associated with the Gestalt therapy of Frederick S. (Fritz) Perls. Although Perls used terms and procedures substantially different from Rogers', and although he focused more on using personality growth experiences than on articulating a formal, researchable personality theory, the basic ideas of Perls and Rogers are very similar. Perls believed that behavior problems arise when people deny or disown their feelings or experiences (that is, are incongruent, in Rogers' terms) or when they claim as their own feelings or ideas they have borrowed from others. Gestalt therapy, then, is oriented toward helping persons take responsibility for themselves and experience or "get in touch" with genuine feelings. It is assumed that when this occurs it is possible for individuals to face and resolve conflicts and internal inconsistencies of which they had been unaware. Application of the concepts and principles enunciated by Rogers and Perls (among others) prompted the widespread interest in and the rapid growth of a wide variety of encounter and sensitivity groups.

Some Problems with Phenomenological Theories

Critics of the phenomenological approach, like those of other approaches we have presented, argue that it is too narrow. They point out that by restricting attention to immediate conscious experience as the main determinant of behavior, phenomenologists fail to recognize the importance of unconscious motivation, reinforcement contingencies, situational influences, and the like. Another criticism is that phenomenological theories do not elaborate sufficiently on the ways in which personality develops; postulating an innate tendency toward growth or actualization that is assumed to "drive" the organism can account for development but it does not explain it.

This brings up a related point of criticism: Phenomenological theories provide excellent descriptions of human behavior but are not usually focused on scientific exploration of the functional causes of behavior. To say that people behave as they do because of their unique perception of reality or because they are seeking to actualize themselves is not very informative in terms of promoting understanding of the variables which are important in the development and alteration of human behavior.

Finally, critics point out that many phenomenological concepts, like psychodynamic variables, are vague and therefore difficult or impossible to measure. Indeed, many phenomenological theorists (not including Rogers) see research on human behavior as relatively unimportant compared with activities designed to promote increased individual awareness. This emphasis on experiential rather than experimental evidence has made phenomenological theories unpopular with those who favor a careful, controlled research approach. When human beings are described as "a momentary precipitation at the vortex of a transient eddy of energy in the enormous and incomprehensible sea of energy we call the universe" (Kempler, 1973), it is difficult to generate an easily testable hypothesis about their behavior.

SUMMARY

1. Personality is a broadly defined term that is used to describe and explain individual differences and stylistic consistencies in human behavior.
2. Intensive studies by psychologists over the last 100 years show that personality pervades every aspect of human behavior.
3. Many diverse theories have been proposed to explain personality. Each of them begins with a working definition of the concept and some basic assumptions about human behavior. There are many theoretical disagreements about the proper definition and the necessary assumptions.
4. These theories fall into four general classes: dispositional, psychodynamic, social learning, and phenomenological. Each approach has strengths and weaknesses, and each seeks to provide a way of understanding personality as well as a means of assessing, investigating, and changing it.
5. Some dispositional theories assume that there is a small number of personality types, each of which has a unique set of general behavioral tendencies.
6. Dispositional theories see personality as being made up of characteristics, such as traits or needs, within the person which guide the individual's behavior.
7. Psychodynamic theories derive largely from Sigmund Freud's writings about psychoanalysis. They assume that personality is shaped by events and conflicts (many of them unconscious) that take place within the mind through the action of hypothesized internal structures known as the id, ego, and superego.
8. Social learning theories base their approach on the assumption that personality is essentially the sum total of each individual's learned behaviors, and not an independent structure that is merely reflected in behavior. According to social learning theory, personality depends upon, and therefore may change with, the social context.
9. Dispositional, psychodynamic, and social learning theories differ mainly in whether they emphasize internal needs, environmental contingencies, or imitation and expectancies as major determiners of the kind of personality an individual develops. In contrast, phenomenological theories view personality as that pattern of cognitions and perceptions of reality, unique to each individual, which guides behavior. To understand someone's personality, you must be able to see things from that person's point of view.
10. Each kind of personality theory has shortcomings. No complete or universally accepted description and explanation of personality has yet been provided.

RECOMMENDED ADDITIONAL READINGS

Hall, C. S., & Lindzey, G. *Theories of personality,* 3d ed. New York: Wiley, 1978.

Liebert, R. M., & Spiegler, M. D. *Personality: Strategies for the study of man,* rev. ed. Homewood, Ill.: Dorsey Press, 1974.

Mischel, W. *Introduction to personality,* 2d ed. New York: Holt, Rinehart and Winston, 1976.

Munroe, R. L. *Schools of psychoanalytic thought.* New York: Holt, Rinehart and Winston, 1955.

what does it mean?

So far, we have looked at the ways in which psychologists of several theoretical persuasions conceive of the concept called personality. In this section, we shall examine the ways in which the concepts advanced by personality theorists affect the everyday behavior of other psychologists and the rest of society. As we shall see, personality is anything but an "ivory tower" concept. Personality theories have had significant impact on the lives on millions of people, whether they are aware of it or not.

Perhaps because some theorists conceive of personality as a collection of actually existing traits or because they talk about "personality structure" or the "distorted" or "disorganized" personality, the personality concept has achieved the status of an entity or thing in the minds of many psychologists and certainly in the minds of the general public. As noted at the beginning of this chapter, personality is commonly thought of as something that a person either does or does not possess and that he or she can turn on or off like a tap.

Of course, this view misrepresents and distorts the writings of many careful theorists, but the notion persists that we all carry around inside us a thing called personality that determines our behavior. On recommendation forms for some graduate schools, for example, there is an item asking the professor to rate the student's personality on a five-point scale from "poor" to "excellent." Presumably, this rating is thought to relate in some way to the student's potential as a graduate student. Whether they conceive of personality in terms of traits, types, or intrapsychic events, people want to assess the personality of other individuals, sometimes in order to describe them as they are and sometimes in order to make predictions about what they will do in the future.

PERSONALITY AND CLINICAL PSYCHOLOGY

In clinical treatment settings, the therapist is interested in assessing personality in order to understand his or her client more fully. Naturally, the clinician's overall approach to personality will dictate the kinds of diagnostic and treatment procedures employed (see Chapters 11 and 12). Thus, when one chooses from among several sources of psychological assistance, it is important to know the personality strategy adopted by each practitioner.

However, the importance of personality in clinical psychology goes beyond attempts to assess the characteristics of individual clients. Considerable research activity focuses on exploring more general relationships between personality and the appearance of a variety of psychological and bodily disorders. For example, about 25,000 Americans kill themselves every year; about 1000 of these are college students. Many were depressed prior to or at the time of suicide, but others apparently were not. Furthermore, countless thousands of people suffer depression but do not take their own lives. How can psychologists and others interested in suicide prevention tell who will commit suicide and who will not? Is there a "suicidal personality"?

Unfortunately, data from traditional personality tests, such as the Minnesota Multiphasic Personality Inventory (MMPI; see Appendix C), provide no clear answer. For example, one study found that in terms of MMPI scores persons who had only thought of suicide were more deviant than either those who had actually made a suicide attempt or "controls" who had never even thought of self-destruction. In another study, MMPI data collected prior to successful suicides were not significantly different from those coming from nonsuicidal individuals.

Thus, if one thinks of personality as a collection of enduring traits or characteristics, an individual's personality can tell us little about his or her suicide potential. However, if one conceives of personality in terms of overt behavior and other observable information, the accuracy of predictions about suicide increases markedly. It is known, for example, that the greatest risk of suicide occurs among males who are over 50, divorced, living alone, have a history of suicide attempts and/or talking about suicide, are depressed or stressed, have no family or friends, and have worked out a clear and lethal plan for self-destruction. Of course, the presence of *all* of these factors is not necessary to prompt suicide, but knowing about them provides some guidelines for the professional and nonprofessional workers who deal with potentially suicidal individuals. In this sense, then, there is a "suicidal personality," but it can best be described in social learning rather than in dispositional or trait terms.

In addition to being consulted about which people are likely to harm themselves, psychologists are also frequently asked to make judgments about who is likely to harm others. In a society such as ours, where the incidence of violent crime (murder, rape, aggravated assault, and so on) is frighteningly high, there

Am I Suicidal?

Can a computer predict suicide attempts? Better yet, can it do so as successfully as a therapist? On the basis of preliminary tests at the University of Wisconsin Medical School, the answer is a tentative yes.

That conclusion was reached after hundreds of depressed patients had been interviewed by a computer programmed by Psychiatrist John Greist and David Gustafson, professor of preventive medicine. In 72 of the cases, the computer predictions were compared with those made by therapists in traditional face-to-face interviews. The computer correctly identified the three patients who attempted suicide within 48 hours after their interviews. The therapists failed to predict any of the three attempts. One patient was about to be released when the computer determined that he had a gun, bullets and a precise suicide plan. In long-range predictions, covering nine months after the interviews, the computer identified 90% of the actual suicide attempters, compared with 30% for the therapists.

Greist believes it is the methodical and impersonal nature of computer interrogation that may make it more accurate. "Doctors are often reluctant to ask direct questions," he says. . . .

Patients sit at a keyboard and punch out answers to questions on the screen of a computer terminal. For the early part of the interview, the computer is programmed to cajole and compliment the user ("You're a pro at using the terminal"). But when it is time for the crucial questions, the computer is blunt ("What are your chances of being dead from suicide one month from now?" "By what method do you plan to commit suicide?"). . . .

Time
July 24, 1978

Psychologists, psychiatrists, and suicidal people are all human beings, and this may block communication about personal acts of violence. Even a professional can have trouble asking difficult and blunt questions, and a patient can have trouble giving truthful answers to another person. A "cold and impersonal" computer may be very helpful in such cases.

is an urgent need to identify individuals who are likely to commit such crimes. We seek to find personality clues that single out potentially violent people. And we look for ways to

How To Tell Who Will Kill

On a warm August afternoon in 1964, Edmund Emil Kemper III, an unusually tall 15-year-old regarded by his classmates as a well-mannered but shy lone wolf, stood outside the screen door of his grandmother's house in North Fork, Calif., and calmly shot her to death with two bullets to the head. When his grandfather returned from the grocery store, the youth murdered him in similar fashion. Then he telephoned his mother to tell her what he had done. "I just wondered how it would feel to shoot Grandma," Kemper later told authorities. After examination by a court-appointed psychiatrist, the youth was duly committed to Atascadero State Mental Hospital.

Kemper proved to be a model inmate, and after serving five years he was remanded on the advice of staff psychiatrists to the California Youth Authority. In 1970, having turned 21, he was set free and dropped into obscurity in California's Santa Cruz County. Then last September, Kemper went to court to have his juvenile murder record permanently sealed, a formality that would make his acts of violence an official secret. Two court-appointed psychiatrists examined Kemper and declared him no danger to society. "He has made an excellent response to the years of treatment," one of them reported. "I see no psychiatric reason to consider him a threat to himself or any other member of society." Accordingly the records were ordered sealed.

But the psychiatrists were to be proved tragically wrong. Late last month, Kemper called Santa Cruz County authorities, and confessed that during a year-long reign of terror he had murdered and dismembered six young girls in the Bay Area—and that just three days before, he had slain his mother with a hammer and strangled one of her friends. As it happened, one of his victims, 15-year-old Aiko Koo, was murdered only four days before he reported for the examination that found him mentally well. . . .

Most psychiatrists freely admit that the problem is almost unsolvable because specialists have no sure way of predicting antisocial behavior. "Kemper is a marvelous example of the fact that psychiatrists don't know everything," says Dr. Herbert McGrew, a staff psychiatrist at California's Napa State Hospital. "If you're right 75 per cent of the time, you're doing pretty well." For this reason, few of their colleagues would find fault with Kemper's as yet unidentified psychiatrists. "These guys weren't stupid," notes another Bay Area psychiatrist, "they were victims of the odds." "If a person appears to have changed to constructive behavior," says Dr. David Abrahamsen, a New York psychoanalyst and author of a new book on the subject, "The Murdering Mind," "you have no choice, you have to let him go." But Abrahamsen stresses that psychopaths should be followed up closely and for a protracted period after their release.

Hostility

Psychological tests like the Rorschach aren't much help in telling who will kill, most psychiatrists agree. "I get psychological test results all the time that say this guy is full of hostility and aggression," says McGrew, "so I let him go and he goes back to college and leads a perfectly normal life. The hostility and aggression are still there, and some time, under certain circumstances, they may come out. But when?"

Usually, court-appointed psychiatrists rely entirely on an interview, often cursory and seldom lasting more than an hour. And if the patient is clever enough, he can deceive the examiner. "All tests or examinations require a response," notes Dr. Bernard Diamond of the University of California, a founder of the American Academy of Psychiatry and the Law and one of the nation's outstanding forensic psychiatrists. "If a person lies or restricts his response, it may be impossible to determine whether he is mentally ill." "You develop a knack based on experience," adds Dr. Walter Rapaport, former California director of mental hygiene. . . .

Diamond criticizes Kemper's psychiatrists not for their diagnosis, but for their willingness to go beyond this and suggest that the killer is normal. While one cannot predict that a person will commit violent crime, he notes, "there is no way, ever, that a psychiatrist can say that a person is *not* dangerous. . . ."

Newsweek
June 4, 1973

Personality theory has a long way to go before it can accurately predict antisocial behavior.

predict whether a person who has already committed a crime of violence is likely to repeat that behavior. Questions such as these most frequently come from schools, courts, and other agencies responsible for making decisions about the offender's future that will ultimately affect society: Is there a risk that a certain child is moving in a criminal direction and is thus in need of special counseling or other attention? Should a nonviolent juvenile offender be put on probation or be placed in a reform school? Should an adult convicted of violent crime be imprisoned, placed in a community-based rehabilitation program, or committed to an institution for the "criminally insane"? Is a formerly violent convict ready for parole?

Some professionals who view personality from a dispositional or psychodynamic perspective employ such instruments as the Rorschach inkblot test or the MMPI in the hope that test responses will provide clues to future criminal behavior. As has been the case with suicide, however, no "criminal personality" has emerged from the use of such tests. The MMPI, TAT, Rorschach, and other objective and projective personality measures do have some value in separating *groups* of people who *may* be more likely than others to be violent, but as one expert has noted, "no structured or projective test scale has been derived which, when used alone, will predict violence in the individual case in a satisfactory manner" (Megargee, 1970). Predictions based on such tests are often incorrect and can lead to tragic consequences. Part of the problem is that a person's tendency to act violently or to inhibit violent behavior fluctuates over time and across situations. Situational factors (such as intoxication, the presence of children, and the like) are therefore often decisive and need to be taken into account for an assessment to be truly comprehensive.

Taking into consideration a person's past learning and behavior may also increase predictive accuracy. For example, the earlier in life an individual is arrested or tried for an offense, the more likely he or she is to continue criminal activity; the earlier in life an offender leaves home, the more likely the individual is to continue a life of crime; the more serious the first offense, the greater the likelihood that later crimes will be serious. The type of crime a person has committed may also provide prognostic clues. Murderers, rapists, and other violent criminals are least likely to violate parole; violations are most common among persons who have committed nonviolent crimes such as theft, burglary, or forgery.

PERSONALITY AND SELECTION

Everybody at one time or another is probably subjected to various kinds of selection procedures—for employment, military service, higher education, or other roles Personality and personality assessment play a large part in such selection efforts because it is hoped that applicants' responses to various tests and interviews will allow accurate prediction of their future behavior. Personality assessment in one form or another is employed whenever one wishes to identify individuals who will behave in a particular way.

On college campuses, for example, an informal process of personality assessment occurs continuously. In fact, one study indicated that college students *say* that they select social partners on the basis of personality, looks, and intelligence, in that order. (Tests, however, have established that height, physical attractiveness, and proximity are actually the three major factors.) Both men and women collect personality data on members of the opposite sex from various sources.

They observe the verbal and nonverbal behavior of individuals of interest by talking to them or watching them as they interact with others—Did she talk about her contraceptive pills? Did he talk about himself all the time? They listen carefully to the reports of those who know the "target" individuals—"Believe me, Jack, she is all show, no go!"; "Listen, that guy is a smooth talker but basically a real jerk." And they look for other clues, such as manner of dress, grooming habits, type of car owned, and the like. They then summarize this information in some fashion and use it to predict "target" persons' behavior and to guide decisions about initiating or accepting invitations for social contacts with them. Not surprisingly, selections made on the basis of this kind of personality assessment are not always satisfactory, especially when the predictions are based on presumably enduring personality traits. Anyone who has had to repulse unwelcome amorous advances or suffer through an evening filled with tense silences ("We always found things to talk about during class") knows that personality can be radically altered by situational factors.

Another option chosen by many (on or off the campus) is to allow a computer to collect and analyze personality data in a more formal fashion and "fix them up" with potentially compatible dates. The matching is usually based upon similarity of personality characteristics, interests, and attitudes, but at least two experiments have shown that such pairings do not result in any more satisfactory results than do random matches. The more imaginative computer dating services attempt to increase customer satisfaction by supplementing written assessment data with a videotaped interview which prospective social partners may view before deciding to spend time with the person in question. This provides an example of how the use of overt behavior samples can augment trait summaries of personality.

Selection errors in business and industry, where many decisions involving hiring and promotion are made each year, are far more costly than errors in selection of social companions. Accordingly, companies of many kinds and sizes spend significant amounts of time and money to develop employee selection procedures. Some kind of personality assessment usually plays a part in these procedures. IBM, for example, requires potential employees to have an initial interview, fill out

"He won't let me on. He says I show all the hijacker's personality traits."

© 1979 by Sidney Harris.

One application of personality research has been the development of profile assessment as an aid to detecting hijackers.

a formal application, take a variety of ability and personality tests, have a second interview, provide letters of reference, and pass a physical examination.

The personality tests most commonly employed in industrial selection procedures include projective tests like the Rorschach test (especially in executive selection, even though the evidence against their validity and usefulness is strong) and self-report inventories like the MMPI and the Guilford-Zimmerman Temperament Survey, which asks respondents to answer questions such as whether they start a new project with enthusiasm. By and large, self-report inventories of personality do not fare well in industrial settings:

A dismal history has been recorded by personality tests. There have been a few scattered successes with some modern techniques, but on the whole the typical personality questionnaire, test, or inventory has not proved to be useful. In many of them, the "right" answers . . . are so obvious that everyone comes out a model of healthy adjustment. (Barrett, 1963)

It should be noted that any test, psychological or otherwise, is only as good as the test administrator. Part of the problem in industry stems from the use of inexperienced and untrained examiners.

As usual, somewhat better results seem to come from test batteries that view personality not only in terms of traits but also in terms of overt behavior. For example, Sears, Roebuck developed a test battery for selecting executives based not on a theoretical measure of personality but on the characteristics of successful and unsuccessful executives. The company first decided how "good" executives behave, built a test that discriminated "good" from "bad" executives, and then used the test to hire or promote new executives. The results have been assessed as excellent.

As we might expect, part of the Sears test battery measures overt behavior under simulated job-relevant stress conditions. This "stress technique" is employed by other companies as well, such as AT&T, and is based on procedures developed during World War II by the Office of Strategic Services (OSS) in its officer-selection program. Candidates may be tested individually or in groups, but the common characteristic of the approach is that individuals must attempt to accomplish work, such as solving a complex problem, while under some form of pressure and while being observed by testers. One group stress-testing procedure had the following results:

Some candidates panic and disrupt the group with frequent and unhelpful reminders of the deadline, some others lose their tempers, become hopelessly confused, or refuse to abandon obsolete plans. The visible contrasts sharpen between the steadier, more flexible, and even-tempered men and those who can't operate under pressure. (Allbrook, 1968)

NFL Players Oppose Psychological Testing

AP

KEY BISCAYNE, Fla. — The National Football League Players Association called . . . for an end to personality and psychological testing of players by NFL teams because of questions involving the validity and use of such tests.

The association's board of representatives, consisting of one player from each NFL team, urged players not to participate in further testing programs.

In the cases where tests already have been given, the group's resolution asked that results be kept confidential and made available to the tested individual.

It also asked that players be given access to their entire personnel files when they leave football.

Executive Director Ed Garvey said that since professional football is such a short career, most players expect to seek other work after leaving the game.

"If there is damaging information in those files and it is available to employers or to government agencies . . . the player should have the right to see what is in that file to find out whether there are unsupported allegations against him as an individual."

Center Bill Curry of the Baltimore Colts, a member of the executive committee, said he could cite several instances in which coaches have misinterpreted information from the tests and mishandled players. He said many coaches weren't qualified to help in personality problems.

Association President John Mackey, also of the Colts, said test results should not be used to determine if a player makes a team. That should be determined by performance on the field, he said. . . .

The Denver Post
January 29, 1972

Almost every conceivable type of employer has used personality tests in an effort to improve the productivity of the organization. Basically, the idea is to select employees in a way that will maximize production by improving morale, decreasing turnover rates, decreasing absenteeism, and so forth. The factors involved for football players, of course, are different than for assembly-line workers. Because such testing procedures can have great impact on the employee, and because there is always a possibility of misuse of the techniques and results, such programs raise moral and ethical questions which are not easy to solve.

"I don't like the look of this at all."

The New Yorker, October 24, 1964. Drawing by Richter; © 1964 The New Yorker Magazine, Inc.

The purpose of this kind of personality assessment is not to make candidates uncomfortable but to identify behaviorally those who will be unlikely to handle stress well under actual employment conditions. This saves both the candidate and the company discomfort in the long run.

Personality assessment has begun to play a role in several other selection settings. For example, the personalities of prospective jurors (see Chapter 10) and even football players are sometimes assessed in order to select those whose future performances match the goals of attorneys and head coaches. Similarly, personality variables have recently been used to predict the competence of college dorm advisors, psychological counselors, and even state police. Whether this turns out to be a beneficial trend will depend largely on how carefully users of personality tests evaluate the validity and utility of their procedures. Assessment for the sake of assessment does no one any good, and because personality measurement can constitute an invasion of privacy, it should at least be restricted to spheres where it is clearly demonstrated to be useful.

PERSONALITY AND ADVERTISING

Soon after infancy children come under the influence of advertising, and its impact is more or less continuous throughout their lives. Therefore, it is important to understand that those who would have us use a particular product or service do not rely solely upon a clear presentation of its assets and benefits to sway our decision. Using some version of the dispositional or psychodynamic approach to personality, advertisers seek to understand the motives and psychological needs of their target population and to pitch their messages so that they appeal to those motives and needs. Motivational research has become an important part of the advertising industry and results in ads whose psychological aspects are subtle but often powerful. The assumptions of this approach are spelled out in a statement by a well-known motivation researcher:

Motivation research is the type of research that seeks to learn what motivates people in making choices. It employs techniques designed to reach the unconscious or subconscious mind because preferences generally are determined by factors of which the individual is not conscious. . . . Actually in the buying situation the consumer generally acts emotionally and compulsively, unconsciously reacting to the images and designs which in the subconscious are associated with the product. (Packard, 1957)

Freud's concept of the unconscious also plays a part in subliminal advertising, as noted in Chapter 3. Subliminal messages such as "Eat popcorn" have in recent years been supplemented by more sophisticated, sexually oriented efforts at unconscious persuasion. Yet in spite of advertiser conviction that this approach increases sales, no scientific evidence for its effects has yet appeared.

Another way in which advertisers seek to exploit personality concepts is to give their product a "personality" of its own. They assume that people will buy products whose "personality" matches their own actual (or desired) traits. For example, the early "personality" of Marlboro cigarettes was described as "mild as May," and the product did not sell. Changing Marlboro's "personality" to reflect masculinity, independence, and the values of

Research Labels the Beer Drinker

AP

PHILADELPHIA — Hey, Mr. Beer Drinker. Advertisers think you're a pleasure-seeking slob who lives his life with gusto and who likes to keep the little woman in line.

By knowing all this, they think they stand a better chance of whipping up an advertisement that will make you buy a product, according to Dr. Peter Bennett, a Penn State marketing professor.

This consumer profile and dozens of others like it are being drawn up in a new marketing research technique, which Bennett claims is revolutionizing advertising.

"Psychographics" or "lifestyle" research, as it is called, is being used to gather information on all types of consumers, from the fried chicken eater to the girlie magazine reader, he said.

"Advertisers are trying to crawl into consumers' skins to see how they're interpreting their worlds," Bennett said in a telephone interview from his office at State College.

The idea, he said, "is to create an advertisement that you'll pay attention to and also to help . . . make products that better fit the needs of a person." The technique is widely talked-about in the business community and is being taught in the classroom, he said.

After picking the brains of numerous beer-drinkers through questionnaires and interviews, this is the picture one company painted of a brew swigger:

"A dreamer, a wisher, a modified Walter Mitty, who's a risk-taker and pleasure-seeker, at least in fantasy. He's a sports nut because he's a hero worshipper, but he doesn't participate in sports because he's a slob; he drinks too much beer. He's probably a male chauvinist pig and not the type who attends church regularly or works for charity." . . .

A similar report generally sized up eye make-up wearers as social butterflies who would rather party and travel than clean the house or cook a pot roast. This person likes to dress up and is a stickler for appearing neat and clean, the report indicated.

Bennett said other "consumer portraits" are as closely guarded as the Mona Lisa.

In recent years, he said advertisers and marketers have developed more sophisticated techniques to probe consumer motivations and lifestyles, rather than relying on traditional information such as age, sex, income levels and place of residence.

"In many ways, it's a realization in the marketing community that really marketing is as much dependent upon psychology, that is, understanding the psyche of a consumer, as economics," he said.

Rocky Mountain News, *Denver*
January 3, 1978

Increasingly, advertisers are using psychological tools in an effort to understand the personality and buying habits of the public.

the American West placed them among the best-selling cigarettes in the country.

Advertisers point to such results as an example of getting consumers to "identify" with their products. To put it another way, the advertiser often attempts to sell you something you may not need (or that may not be any different from competitive items) by associating it with desirable personality traits or with the fulfillment of presumed needs and motives. Usually, these traits, needs, and motives are unrelated to the actual nature of the product sold. For example, food freezer ads often sell "security" by emphasizing the amount of food one can stash away. Various kinds of boxed cake mixes sell self-worth and creativity, not by telling consumers to bake the cake "from scratch" (which would be truly creative) but by telling them to put in the eggs or milk — mixes to which the consumer adds only water are not well accepted.

Most adult-oriented ads place strong emphasis on the sexual benefits of products (whether there are any such benefits or not), usually by having them demonstrated by attractive, high-status models whose opposite-sex partners are often nearby just about to ravish them. The implication, of course, is that people just like these will be climbing into consumers' beds if only they will buy a particular brand of clothing, beer, cigar, or cosmetic.

Personality and Disease

Matt Clark

Nearly three decades ago, Dr. Caroline Bedell Thomas of Johns Hopkins University set out on an intriguing search to identify personal characteristics—both physical and emotional—that might be linked to the development of various diseases later in life. Between 1946 and 1964, she and her colleagues gave meticulous physiological and psychological examinations to more than 1,000 students as they passed through the Baltimore medical school and followed them up with detailed annual questionnaires as they went on to their careers. Now, as the participants enter middle age and illnesses start to take their toll, the investigators have begun to assemble a comprehensive picture of the interplay of mind and body in the susceptibility to heart disease, high blood pressure, cancer, mental illness and suicide.

Most studies that seek to identify factors leading to disease are retrospective; the researchers look into the past histories of persons already ill. Other studies that try to identify risk factors before a disease strikes are usually conducted on persons who have already reached middle age and thus may no longer be typical normal subjects. In choosing medical students, Thomas could study subjects who were young and, if anything, healthier than average.

The Toll

Among the participants, most of whom are men now ranging from 35 to 60 years of age, 131 have developed one of the disorders under study and 47 have died. Forty-three developed cancer, fourteen have had heart attacks, twenty have high blood pressure, 38 have experienced mental illness, and sixteen have committed suicide.

As might be expected, both the suicides and the victims of mental illness showed high test scores for depression, anxiety and nervous tension. The suicides were among the heaviest smokers in the study. They also tended to be underweight and to have skinny "ectomorphic" physiques. The victims of mental disorders were heavy coffee drinkers and tended to suffer from insomnia.

So far, the study suggests that a high level of cholesterol is not, in itself, an always accurate indicator of heart disease. True, the men who developed coronaries showed the highest cholesterol levels of any group, on the average. But they constituted only a fraction of all the men who had high cholesterols. What appeared to distinguish the coronary-prone from the rest was a distinctly different personality profile. The heart-attack victims showed high scores for depression, anxiety, and nervous tension, and anger under stress. They tended toward insomnia, were apt to be tired on awakening in the morning and had been among the poorer students in their respective classes. But the high-cholesterol group as a whole showed a low reaction to stress and was normal in most other respects. Significantly, the heart attack victims were among the heaviest smokers, a finding that was consistent with most other studies of risk factors in coronary disease.

Stress

Thomas thinks that the findings neither discount the importance of cholesterol in heart disease nor prove the recently publicized theory that the hard-driving "Type A" personality is most likely to suffer a coronary. Rather, she believes that both biological and emotional factors are intertwined and that a high cholesterol level and a vulnerability to stress are important harbingers of coronary disease, particularly in the 40s. To date, the study has confirmed that high blood pressure tends to run in families.

Most surprising, in Thomas's view, was the discovery of a link between personality patterns and cancer. The cancer victims were among the lowest scorers with respect to anxiety and depression. On the whole, they showed placid, gentle and non-aggressive dispositions. But they shared with the suicides and victims of mental illness a remarkable lack of closeness to their parents. On perusing the medical literature, Thomas has since found several retrospective studies that have disclosed a similar cancer-prone personality, characterized by alienation beginning in early childhood. . . . Most cancer experts now think that the body's immune system plays an important part in protecting against malignancies. A person with an unresolved emotional conflict from childhood, Thomas speculates, may be peculiarly susceptible to stresses involving the loss of strong relationships—spouses or jobs—and such stresses might produce hormonal changes and failure of the immune system.

Newsweek
September 15, 1975

It has been hypothesized that personality variables help to determine the kinds of illnesses to which a person is susceptible.

Personality Key to Pain Threshold Index

Pamela Avery

Perception of pain is as personal as the way you write a letter, laugh or cry. The more sensitive, emotional and creative the person, the more likely he or she will over-react to pain.

W. Lynn Smith, neuropsychologist at Porter Memorial Hospital, and colleagues at Porter and in Los Angeles, used personality as a gauge to develop a pain threshold index.

The index is being used to predict whether surgery will relieve a patient's chronic back pain. So far it's been 90 percent accurate, said Smith.

The index, a combination of personality and psychological testing, was used on 23 patients about to undergo pain-relieving back surgery at Porter and at Swedish Medical Center.

On the basis of the test results, Smith predicted that nine of the 23 patients would experience little back pain following surgery, and that 14 would continue to have chronic back problems.

Six months after surgery, eight of the 23 were relatively free from back problems and 13 continued to experience chronic pain. . . .

Smith and his colleagues determined that highly emotional, depressed individuals who tend to worry about their ailments are the worst candidates for pain-relieving surgery.

Logical individuals who have a high self-esteem are the best candidates, Smith added.

One of the tests used to determine whether a person is highly emotional or of an analytic mind is the free association test, a series of abstract pictures. Patients are asked to describe what the pictures look like to them.

"The test gives us a good handle on a person's basic personality. Creative, emotional people are quicker to correctly size up the pictures," said Smith. "The analytic type of person is very slow to pick up on what the pictures mean." . . .

Persons who are depressed, highly emotional or who worry about their ailments may be addicted psychologically to their back pain, the neuropsychologist noted. These are individuals that no amount of medication, therapy or surgery will help.

"It may be that they subconsciously would rather focus on pain rather than their emotional problems," said Smith. "Take away the pain and the person becomes unglued."

Smith said that he expects the index to be used as a diagnostic tool by surgeons.

"Surgeons may want to incorporate it into the framework of their treatment," said Smith. "If a person is a poor risk for pain-relieving surgery and the surgeon decides to go ahead with the operation anyway, he at least will know that the patient will need psychiatric coverage afterward."

Rocky Mountain News, *Denver October 19, 1977*

Research in personality and psychosomatic medicine clearly indicates that personality is a factor in illness. This article suggests the intriguing possibility that such research could be applied to determine the best candidates for costly surgical procedures.

PERSONALITY AND ILLNESS

As we shall see in Chapter 11, many physical illnesses include a psychological component. Such psychological factors as an emotional reaction to stress may bring on physical disorders resulting in such psychological consequences as depression. Some investigators have hypothesized that personality variables may help determine the particular forms of illness to which an individual is susceptible. This idea has been applied particularly to organic problems such as asthma, ulcers, high blood pressure, migraine headaches, and other illnesses thought to have a strong psychological basis. While there is little evidence that particular traits or intrapsychic conflicts cause specific physical disorders, many psychologists believe that personality-based attitudes toward life are associated with the appearance of certain disorders (see Table 9–4 for one set of hypotheses).

Other personality dimensions, such as clarity of one's body image (that is, the distinctness with which one perceives the boundaries between one's body and the rest of the world), have also been related to illness. It has been suggested, for example, that when persons

TABLE 9-4   Patient Attitudes and Psychosomatic Reactions

Disorder	Patient Attitude
Ulcers	Feels deprived of what is due him and wants to get even.
Hypertension	Feels threatened with harm and has to be ready for anything.
Asthma	Feels left out in the cold and wants to shut the person or situation out.
Colitis	Feels he is being injured or degraded and wishes he could get rid of the responsible agent.
Eczema	Feels he is being frustrated and can do nothing about it except take it out on himself.
Acne	Feels he is being picked on and wants to be left alone.
Psoriasis	Feels there is a constant gnawing at him and that he has to put up with it.
Rheumatoid arthritis	Feels tied down and wants to get free.
Low backache	Wants to run away.
Raynaud's disease	Wants to take hostile physical action.

with clear body boundaries develop stress-related psychosomatic illnesses, the disorders tend to involve outer layers of the body such as the skin and muscles; persons who perceive more diffuse body boundaries, on the other hand, tend to have disorders originating in deeper bodily sites such as the stomach and other internal organs. Research data on hypotheses of this type have so far tended to be equivocal, but future research in the area may help expand our understanding of psychosomatic illness.

THE PREJUDICIAL SIDE OF PERSONALITY

We have seen many ways in which the personality constructs arising from various theories are relevant to everyday life, but we need also to look at how personality data can func-

tion to bias our view of other people. For instance, having advance information about a person before we meet the individual (as in a computer dating situation) can strongly influence our reaction to him or her. If the prior information is accurate—for example, if a consistently hostile person is described to us as hostile—it may serve a valuable preparatory function. If the information is inaccurate, however, our reaction to the person may be prejudiced. It has been shown that interest on the part of college women in dating a known male was significantly reduced if undesirable personality traits were attributed to him, even though the traits were inaccurate.

In such cases, prejudice may not only cause a misperception of a person's behavior, it may actually influence it in the direction of the stereotype. A recent study observed the behavior of males during "get-acquainted" telephone conversations. Males who thought they were talking to physically attractive females not only *perceived* the women to be more sociable and poised than supposedly unattractive women but also *prompted* them to behave in warm, outgoing, and socially competent ways (Snyder, Tanke, and Berscheid, 1977). The authors speculated that such subtle influences may under certain circumstances serve to perpetuate racial, ethnic, and other stereotypes as well as to distort everyday interpersonal relationships.

In clinical settings similar prejudicial processes may be operative, but here the consequences of inaccuracy can be far more drastic than is usually the case in dating situations. Ideally, judgments concerning the seriousness of a person's psychological problems should be based on objective assessment information derived from interviews, tests, and observational techniques; yet there is reason to believe that casual remarks, rumors, and other unsystematic data can exert a profound influence on how a person's behavior is viewed.

In an important experiment by Temerlin (1968), an interview with an actor portraying a "completely normal" man was played for a series of audiences made up of psychiatrists, clinical psychologists, and graduate students in clinical psychology. Each member of the audience was asked to indicate whether the man was neurotic, psychotic, or normal. If the tape was characterized as an employment interview, 71 percent of the audience said the man was normal and 29 percent said he was neurotic (mildly disturbed). If the audience was told they were hearing a diagnostic interview, 57 percent still labeled the "client" healthy, while 43 percent diagnosed neurosis. In neither case, however, did anyone use the psychotic (severe disorder) label. However, when personality data were "accidentally" given before the tape was played, there were dramatic effects. If the audience heard that "this is a completely normal man," every one of them judged him to be normal; but if they were told that "he may look neurotic, but actually is quite psychotic," an average of 33 percent of the audience called the man psychotic, with judgments of normal plunging to about 8 percent.

Personality is a complex, multidimensional, and often useful concept, but we have seen that is has drawbacks. To use it to fullest advantage, we need to be aware of its limitations.

Social Psychology

10

Human beings are social animals. All culture, all language, all institutions, all social interactions are affected by social experience. We are, largely, what others have told us and taught us and what others expect of us. It is the social aspect of human identity and action that social psychologists study; they study people in groups and people as affected by social experience. Social psychology is the study of *the effect on indi-*

vidual behavior of the real or imagined behavior of others. This obviously applies to a very wide range of phenomena, some dramatic, others mundane.

Perhaps the most convincing evidence for the significance of the presence of other persons on an individual is the consequence of the absence of others. When children are raised with little or no social stimulation, the result is disastrous. Every now and then we hear about parents who have isolated their children. The children are almost always socially disturbed and retarded in language and intellectual development. More rigorous conclusions in the area of behavior are based on the work of Harry Harlow, who reared infant monkeys in complete social isolation. When returned to a normal social environment as adults, these animals exhibited a variety of psychopathological symptoms, especially in their reactions to cage mates.

AREAS OF SOCIAL PSYCHOLOGY

The various areas that constitute social psychology can be categorized into two types, more or less representative of two basic traditions in the field. The first to be discussed focuses on the relatively long-term and enduring effects of culture, society, social institutions, and social learning on individuals' attitudes. *Attitude research* has been the most popular topic in social psychology. As we consider various types of attitudes, we shall see how they enter into an individual's personality and serve as a general guide for the person's behavior toward others.

One of the major types of attitudes studied is *prejudice.* Its existence is expressed in thousands of different ways—from simple refusal to interact with specific individuals to mass murder. Prejudice patterns social relations in commonplace circumstances—who gets a job, attends a particular school, is invited to a party, or joins a club. Probably everyone reading this text is affected continuously and personally by prejudice. If you are not directly the object or agent of prejudice, then you are indirectly affected by the influence of prejudice on what classmates you will have and what persons you will meet. We all have a social environment that is more homogeneous than it would be if prejudice did not structure and restrict our social relations. The problem of prejudice—its origin, correlates, and consequences—and the search for means to reduce it have long been a central concern of social psychologists.

A related area of investigation is *interpersonal attraction*—the issue of friendship and romantic involvement. Do we like persons similar to ourselves or different from ourselves? Beauty is only skin deep, but how important is it for mate selection or for determining who gets a particular job? How can a person make friends and influence people? Social psychologists have tried to answer questions like these by formal research.

The second tradition in social psychology focuses on the behavior of individuals in groups. We shall examine why it is that a person will do one thing in the presence of others and quite a different thing when alone. Why, for example, do onlookers at the scene of an emergency often fail to help the person in trouble? Why are persons more apt to help or get involved if they are alone and not part of a group of bystanders?

When the social group becomes a crowd, individual behavior is even more noticeably altered. People seem more excitable, less rational, and much more conforming when in a crowd. Consider the violence of some crowds, for example, in race riots, at political rallies, and in burning buildings. How is it that perfectly normal, respectable citizens can be incited to form a fearsome, raging lynch mob? Why will people obey the commands of someone they perceive as being an authority, such as a gang or religious leader, to an often unbelievable extent?

RESEARCH ON SOCIAL ATTITUDES

A **social attitude** is a combination of feelings, beliefs, and action tendencies toward classes of persons or objects that are directly or indirectly social in nature. Thus an attitude has three com-

Parents Held for Keeping Diapered Teen in Isolation

AP

CALIFORNIA — Sheriff's deputies have arrested the parents of a 13-year-old girl who doctors say can't talk and has the mind of an infant because she was kept in virtual isolation since birth.

Sandy X, wide-eyed and brown-haired, spent her time inside her parents' modest two-bedroom home in a Los Angeles suburb except for the brief periods when she played in the yard or sat on the porch, deputies said.

She walks with a stooped shuffle like an aged person and her arms and bone structure are extremely thin, doctors said.

They placed her mental development as equal to that of a 12- to 18-month-old infant, said she still wore diapers, and that her size was that of a 10-year-old.

The doctors said Sandy could become physically normal after treatment but that they were unsure about possible mental progress.

Deputies said Sandy has been hospitalized since Nov. 4. The case was made public after her parents were arrested. . . .

Bill X, 70, and his estranged wife Joan, 50, were booked for investigation of child abuse and released on $1,250 bail each.

Sheriff's investigators said a social worker brought the case to their attention when Mrs. X left her husband, took Sandy to live with the girl's grandmother and applied for welfare.

No motive for the girl's alleged treatment was advanced by authorities.

Boulder (Colo.) Daily Camera
November 8, 1970

Clearly, lack of social contact has devastating, perhaps irreversible, effects on human development and functioning.

ponents: (1) beliefs or knowledge — the cognitive component; (2) feelings — the emotional-motivational component; and (3) tendencies to act in particular ways on the basis of knowledge and emotion — the performance component. For example, your attitude toward, say, the members of NOW (National Organization for Women) is a matter of what you know or believe about the functions, goals, and constituents of that group; the feelings (positive or negative) they arouse in you; and your tendency or disposition to take one or another action regarding the group or its individual members.

Social attitudes are a kind of concept. They are concepts about classes of people, concepts with a prominent evaluative character. Attitudes seem to function much like the concepts we discussed in Chapter 6. For one thing, they provide a way of responding to all members of a given class or category. You respond to a given object not on the basis of its uniqueness but according to its membership in a class of objects. This is not just a matter of economy (not having to learn a response to each individual object), it is a matter of necessity, because the human mind cannot contend with the welter of physical variations that make up the environment.

Furthermore, attitudes, like other concepts, serve as a guide to future behavior. They are an important basis for consistency, for we always respond in the same way to class members. A person who has a concept of or an attitude toward a particular class of objects or people has a basis for responding to any member of that class, even one not specifically encountered before.

Finally, attitudes, like other concepts, can be learned by direct examples (actual contact with class members), by instruction from others (being told about members of the class), or by the process of reasoning ("putting two and two together"). The similarity of attitudes and concepts has not escaped the notice of social psychologists. Some believe that the same underlying processes are involved in both and that laboratory studies of concept formation (see Chapter 6) will tell us quite a bit about how attitudes can be established or changed.

Organization of Attitudes

Most social psychologists now believe that attitudes and beliefs are organized basically according to the principle of consistency. The **consistency principle,** as applied to attitudes, states that the attitudes held by a particular individual are mutually supportive and do not conflict with one another. That is, they make sense to the person in a logical or psychological fashion. Consistency also refers to the tendency

Are There Any Faces in a Crowd?

Social psychologists have suggested that crowd violence may, to a large extent, be a function of the fact that crowd members typically lose their individual identity. They may feel less personally responsible for their behavior, less likely to be punished because they cannot be identified, and, as a result, more prone to behave violently. Phillip Zimbardo (1969) has done an ingenious experiment to demonstrate the importance of the deindividuation, or loss of personal identity, that takes place in groups. Groups of four female subjects listened to recordings of interviews with potential "victims." Some groups were given a deindividuation treatment—the women wore gowns and hoods to disguise themselves, and the experimenters never used their names. In other groups the women were not disguised; they wore name tags, and everyone referred to everyone else by name—these were the identifiable groups. Each group listened to interviews with pleasant and unpleasant "victims," and later each group member was induced to deliver shocks to the victims, whom they could now see through a one-way mirror. The victim was, of

Figure 10–1
Deindividuation treatment

The experimental group in which individuals were devoid of personal identity wore gowns and hoods and were never called by name.

course, a coinvestigator in the study, and she acted as if she were being shocked, although no shocks were delivered. The key finding was that women in the deindividuation groups delivered longer shocks than women in the identifiable group, and this was true regardless of whether they perceived the victim as a pleasant or an unpleasant person.

of individuals to segregate liked objects from disliked objects and to structure their thoughts in simple black-and-white terms. If one views one's set of attitudes as consistent, it will be difficult to change any single member of the set, because changing one attitude will make it inconsistent with all the others in the set. Finding this inconsistency unpleasant, one will resist attitude change.

Suppose, for example, that you really like Bob Hope—your attitude toward him is totally positive—you view him as warm, benevolent, happy, and funny. Now suppose you see him on a TV "talk show" and it comes out that politically he is extremely conservative. If you too are politically conservative, your attitude

toward him will be consistent with your attitude toward politics. It is as if you are saying to yourself, "I like Bob Hope, I like conservative politics, Bob Hope likes conservative politics." It makes sense to have this set of attitudes—they are consistent. But suppose instead that you are a liberal. Then you are faced with, "I like Bob Hope, I like liberal politics, Bob Hope likes conservative politics."

How can you have such admiration for a man whose politics are so different from yours, or how can you have such admiration for the kind of politics that your favorite performer dislikes so much? These attitudes are psychologically inconsistent. According to the consistency principle, you are likely to change one of them to bring about consistency. Inconsistency is seen as a primary reason for attitude change. Inconsistency must be resolved, because it is disturbing to see one's own attitudes as inconsistent with one another. You are now likely to change the attitudes in such a way as to bring about a state of consistency. You might conclude that you really do not like Bob Hope all that much, or that you really are not a political liberal, or you might even try to delude yourself into thinking that Bob Hope is really a liberal. Such delusional beliefs can happen when the other attitudes in a consistent set are extremely difficult for a person to change for other reasons (for example, if they are deeply held religious attitudes).

The basic prediction derived from this principle is that attitudes will be acquired and/or modified so as to bring about a state of mental and behavioral consistency. Attitude change can follow from a state of inconsistency. If you want to change your boyfriend's attitudes, you would create a state of inconsistency in his mind (probably by presenting him with some new evidence against his beliefs). You hope that he will resolve the inconsistency (assuming he believes what you are telling him) by modifying the attitude you wish to change. We will have more to say about attitude change later.

There are several varieties of consistency theory, two of which we will briefly review: the balance theory of Fritz Heider and the theory of cognitive dissonance developed by Leon Festinger.

Balance Theory

From an analysis of the psychological relationships expressed in everyday language, Fritz Heider (1958) formulated the first version of consistency theory. Heider's version, usually referred to as **balance theory,** states that objects perceived as belonging together will have the same dynamic quality—they will either be all liked or all disliked. Liked objects will not be associated with disliked objects.

The formulation of the theory involves the **p-o-x model.** The letters p, o, and x refer to the elements of a system where (1) p is the person having a positive or negative orientation toward o (usually another person); (2) p holds a positive or negative orientation toward x (usually an object); and (3) p perceives o as having a particular orientation toward x. Balanced (con-

sistent) relationships are represented in the following diagrams:

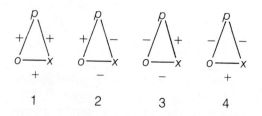

Diagram 2, for example, represents the case of a person (p) liking another (o), as is indicated by the plus sign near the line joining p and o. The two other lines with the minus signs represent the fact that p dislikes x and perceives that o dislikes x also. Thus diagram 2 could represent the fact that p likes Bob Hope, p dislikes liberal politics, and p perceives that Bob Hope also dislikes liberal politics. As an exercise, you might work out all possible combinations of p-o-x and imagine real examples for each. Note that a balanced state exists when there are two negatives or none; an imbalanced state exists when there are three negatives or only one.

Balanced states are psychologically comfortable—they are consistent. Imbalanced states are uncomfortable, motivating people to reduce or avoid the imbalance. For example, your continual disagreement with a friend (o), on some issue (x), say, an upcoming presidential election, may lead either to rejection of your friend or a change in your attitude on issue x. The case of rejecting your friend can be shown as:

$$\underset{o \underline{\quad +\quad} x}{\overset{p}{+\diagup\diagdown-}} \quad \text{changes to} \quad \underset{o\underline{\quad+\quad}x}{\overset{p}{-\diagup\diagdown-}}$$

The case of your continued friendship at the cost of changing your attitude on issue x can be shown as

$$\underset{o\underline{\quad+\quad}x}{\overset{p}{+\diagup\diagdown-}} \quad \text{changes to} \quad \underset{o\underline{\quad+\quad}x}{\overset{p}{+\diagup\diagdown+}}$$

In either case, balance is restored, but you have lost a friend or changed an attitude.

Considerable evidence has been collected supporting the general proposition that the cognitions, attitudes, opinions, and beliefs of people tend toward balance. We are motivated by states of discomfort brought on by cognitive imbalance and behave in ways designed to eliminate imbalance. Note the homeostatic character of this principle. As in other forms of motivation (see Chapter 7), the goal is to bring all operative factors into harmony, or a state of homeostasis.

Dissonance Theory

Leon Festinger's consistency theory, known as **cognitive dissonance theory,** has been particularly influential. The theory of cognitive dissonance concerns the relationship between two or more cognitive or mental elements (ideas or beliefs). A consonant relationship exists when one of the elements implies the other in some psychological sense. A dissonant relationship exists when one cognition a person holds is inconsistent with another cognition he or she also holds. If a person holds cognitions *A* and *B*, and *A* implies *not B*, the cognitions are in a dissonant relationship.

Some of the cognitive relationships said to be consonant include smoking and believing it is harmless to health, reading in a car magazine that the kind of car you just bought has been judged best by a panel of experts, and observing your chosen team winning by a landslide. On the other hand, if you smoke and know it is bad for your health, or if you bought the type of car that experts say is the most dangerous one on the road, you probably have experienced dissonance. Because dissonance, like inconsistency, is in general uncomfortable, you probably have resolved or reduced the dissonance by now. Perhaps you have said to yourself, "I like smoking and I'll quit before it starts to affect my health" or "This car was a good buy and I'm a very careful driver."

If you pay a lot for something or work hard for it, it should be of high quality. If something is cheap or free, you should not expect much. These situations are characterized by consonance. But if you work hard or pay a lot of money for something which is of very poor quality, that is dissonance. Suppose you undergo a severe initiation procedure to become a member of a fraternity or sorority, only to

"It can't be very scary."

find out that you do not like the members very much. Dissonance theory would predict that you would search for a means of reducing the dissonance, perhaps by denying that the initiation was severe or by coming to believe that the group is actually a pretty good one. Thus, we might deduce that the more severe the initiation, the greater the perceived liking of the group members. This prediction, which is not one we would make on the basis of common sense, has been verified by laboratory research (Aronson and Mills, 1959). Much of our behavior can be viewed or described as attempts to reduce dissonance that has arisen from our experiences.

The amount of dissonance is a function of the importance of a cognition and the number of dissonant elements. In general, dissonance can be reduced in two ways, either by increasing the ratio of consonant to dissonant elements or by decreasing the judged importance of the dissonant elements. Smokers, for example, could accomplish the former by adding the belief that smoking reduces tension and gives them great pleasure (increasing the consonant to dissonant ratio). Or they could reduce the importance of the problem by saying that they plan to quit or by belittling the risk of cancer.

Dissonance theory has survived extensive critical evaluation to remain a major formula-

When Prophecy Fails

What happens when you vehemently make a prediction, such as telling your friends over and over that you are going to lose weight or that the Broncos are going to win the Superbowl, only to have the prediction fail miserably? The result is dissonance that you must somehow reduce. Leon Festinger, H. W. Riecken, and Stanley Schachter did a study on this kind of problem, which we might call "when prophecy fails." (For further information see their book, *When prophecy fails: A social and psychological study of a modern group that predicted the destruction of the world.* New York: Harper & Row, 1956.)

The investigators studied a group of religious followers of a woman who, some years ago, predicted the end of the world in December of that year. She and her followers believed that only they would be saved, because a spaceship would rescue them. Some of the members made considerable financial sacrifices to join the group, and all of them were strongly committed to their belief in the woman's prophetic powers and the test of their beliefs with the impending disaster. The situation was set up for a monumental cognitive clash between prophecy and outcome. The hour was set—the world was to end, but it didn't.

The experimenters, following the situation closely (even to the point of joining the group), made a curious prediction. They said that instead of disbanding and trying to live down and forget the affair, the followers would maintain their beliefs and their group commitment and would seek even more support. The experimenters were right. As the hour of destruction passed, apprehension within the group grew. But soon the leader received a "message" that the group's devotion had been the world's salvation. Thanks to their devotion, destruction had been avoided.

At the critical moment, two facts were in dissonance. The followers believed in their prophet, and her prophecy failed. Choosing to maintain their beliefs, the followers then wholly accepted a reinterpretation of the events. That the world was not destroyed they saw as an even greater sign of the prophet's power. Now the cause was redirected. Whereas before the prophecy failed the group had avoided publicity, now they actively sought more followers. They purposely exposed themselves to public ridicule in the belief that this would increase their popular support. In short, they did what they could to increase the number of consonant elements and decrease the dissonant ones.

tion of consistency theory. It applies to any situation in which there is a cognitive conflict. Dissonance is a source of discomfort and therefore has important application to such areas as decision making and attitude change. Perhaps its more important contemporary application is in the area of the relationship of attitudes to behavior. Dissonance theory suggests that if we are induced to behave in a fashion contrary to our present attitudes (such as giving a speech or writing an essay in favor of something we are against), our attitudes will tend to move in a direction consistent with our behavior

(we begin to believe what we are saying, writing, or doing). There is considerable evidence to support this hypothesis.

The implication is that the old line "You can't legislate morality" may not always be true. If the law leads people to change their behavior —as with desegregation in the United States— at least some attitudes should follow suit.

Not all attitudes change with behavior, however. People often hold attitudes that are not consistent with their public acts. This is especially so when they feel coerced by some real or imaginary external force. The more they per-

Balance or dissonance: Can either of these theories account for Cathy's feelings?

ceive an external cause, the less they need to accept responsibility and readjust their internal views. Dissonance studies indicate that minimal external pressure or reward is most effective in achieving lasting change. The child who is threatened with a beating for eating a cookie is less likely to view the act as inherently wrong than the child who is mildly coerced into abstention; the college student who is rewarded with a large check for good grades is less likely to value study for its own sake than is the student who is simply complimented.

Prejudice

As the word itself suggests, **prejudice** is often a matter of prejudgment. It is a kind of attitude and thus consists of a combination of feelings, beliefs, and action tendencies. The implication is that one's mind has been made up too soon, before all the facts are in or have come to one's attention. This, of course, further implies that the conclusion arrived at with the inadequate set of facts is the wrong one — which means that prejudice is seen as a wrong attitude or a bad one.

There is no single, overall definition of prejudice that all social psychologists would accept. Most would agree, however, that prejudice is an attitude that is basically intergroup in character — members of one group have a particular attitude toward members of another group.

Usually, prejudice is (1) highly emotional in character, (2) rigidly or inflexibly felt and acted on by group members (meaning they will not listen to reason), and (3) negative (the object of the prejudice is disliked, and the group's tendency is to mistreat or *discriminate against* members of the disliked group).

Racial, ethnic, and religious prejudice develop at an early age. Kenneth and Mamie Clark, in a classic demonstration of the insidious nature of racial prejudice, found that black children of preschool age showed an awareness of racial identity and a markedly higher evaluation of whites than of blacks, as indicated by their characterization of white dolls as "good" and as preferable to black dolls. Originally reported in 1941, this study has been replicated several times, with the preference for white dolls expressed by both black and white children. Times are changing, however. In a later study by Hraba and Grant (1970), for the first time a majority of black children preferred a black doll. This shift undoubtedly reflects the development of racial pride among blacks, which is summed up in the phrase, "Black is beautiful."

Like attitudes in general, prejudices are learned, but usually indirectly rather than through contact with the objects of the prejudice. Prejudice has been demonstrated in persons who have no firsthand knowledge of the objects against which they are prejudiced. It has been demonstrated even against social groups that do not exist. In one study, 3 fictitious names—Danerians, Pirenians, and Wallonians—were included within a list of 32 other ethnic labels presented to a group of college students for evaluation. The students were asked to rate all groups. The fictitious groups were generally rated negatively!

Many interrelated and mutually supporting factors are involved in the development, expression, and perpetuation of prejudice; this means that modifying prejudice is not an easy job—and you do not have to be a social psychologist to know that. Let us examine the many factors that have been suggested as contributing to prejudice. For convenience we will divide these factors into two classes: (1) those that operate at the level of the specific individual who is prejudiced and (2) those that operate at the level of social institutions such as clubs, fraternities, unions, and even society in general. These are the social-cultural aspects of prejudice.

Prejudice at the Individual Level

Psychologists have been prone to interpret prejudice differently than they interpret attitudes in general, probably because in prejudice there is an implication that the belief is held in the face of overwhelming contradictory evidence. If a person believes something that to an "objective" observer is clearly false, then one tends to feel that this person is benefiting in some way from his or her false beliefs. For example, holding a prejudiced attitude may make one more popular among people who also hold the same attitude.

PREJUDICE AS A DEFENSE AGAINST ANXIETY   One way to see prejudice as benefiting an individual is to suggest that he or she is using the prejudice as a way of dealing with certain emotional problems. Such an explanation is often based on the Freudian principle of projection, one of the ego's defense mechanisms. The prejudice is seen as a means by which the prejudiced person can defend himself against the anxiety that is part of his own inner conflict. In projection, a person attributes to others the very things that he is worried about in himself. For example, the prejudiced person who believes that blacks are sloppy, dirty, and immoral might be defending himself against the realization that certain aspects of his own be-

havior suggest he is sloppy, dirty, and immoral. According to this explanation, the prejudiced person (1) is bothered by (feels anxiety about) some characteristic he perceives in himself; (2) projects this onto some other person and says that the other person possesses this characteristic; (3) emphasizes how different he is from the other person, even to the point of identifying the person as a member of various groups and then showing how he himself could not be part of these groups; and (4) denies that the "bad" characteristic applies to himself, because he now sees himself as being so different from the object of his prejudice that he could not possibly have any of the same feelings, attitudes, or characteristics as any member of these groups. By coming to this conclusion, the prejudiced person defends himself against anxiety. Thus, prejudice can be seen as an unfortunate result of the application of a defense mechanism designed basically to cope with anxiety. Appealing as this hypothesis may be, research suggests that projection is a relatively minor factor in prejudice, being limited to specific individual cases.

THE AUTHORITARIAN PERSONALITY   Another hypothesis deals with the relationship between prejudice and personality structure in general. The hypothesis is that prejudice is only one aspect of a particular personality type called the **authoritarian personality** (Adorno, Frenkel-Brunswik, Levinson, and Sanford, 1950). The hypothesis grew out of a study of anti-Semitism conducted immediately following World War II. The general conclusion was that prejudiced people tended to share a common core of attitudes. They tended to be (1) ethnocentric, having a strong identification with their in-groups and a strong dislike of out-groups; (2) politically and economically conservative; and (3) antidemocratic or authoritarian. The scores on several different measures of these factors tend to correlate with one another. For example, the prejudiced person will usually agree with all of the following statements:

1. It is wrong for Jews and gentiles to intermarry (an item from the anti-Semitism scale).
2. We are spending too much money for the pampering of criminals and the insane and for the education of inherently incapable people (an item from the ethnocentrism scale).

Copyright 1971, G. B. Trudeau. Distributed by Universal Press Syndicate.

3. Men like Henry Ford, . . who overcome all competition on the road to success, are models for all young people to admire and imitate (an item from the political and economic conservatism scale).
4. Obedience and respect for authority are the most important virtues children should learn (an item from the Implicit Anti-democratic Trends scale, known as the F scale).

The authors of the study suggest that these attitudes go together because they are rooted in some underlying personality factor. Thus, prejudice may be an outgrowth of a personality syndrome, and prejudiced people may have a lot in common in addition to their shared prejudices.

For many persons, prejudice is only one aspect of a more general attitude-belief-personality system. In such cases it may follow that reduction of prejudice will take place only when there is a change in the person's basic personality structure—meaning, of course, that prejudice in such people will be very difficult to eliminate.

Social-Cultural Aspects of Prejudice

Now we turn to the factors in prejudice that arise from the individual's membership in social groups and institutions.

CONFORMITY Often prejudice seems to be simply a matter of **conformity** to the norms of the social groups to which one belongs. Thomas Pettigrew has demonstrated a strong relationship between prejudice and conformity. The most prejudiced people are most likely to conform in other areas of behavior. They are most likely to be joiners; for example, they are typically members of a political party as opposed to being independents. This relationship between conformity and prejudice holds wherever strong social norms "dictate" that a person should be prejudiced, for example, Catholics and Protestants in Northern Ireland. This suggests that many people express overt prejudice just because it is the thing to do. The need for approval probably plays a strong role, causing people to conform to the prejudiced norms in order to be better liked by their friends and associates.

REALISTIC GROUP CONFLICT A second social factor has been called the **realistic-group-conflict theory** (Campbell, 1965). If two groups are actually in conflict with each other for some reason, members of one group will tend to develop prejudice against members of the other group. For example, if Jewish and gentile businesspeople are competing for the same business, the gentiles might develop prejudice against the Jews, and vice versa. If the United States and the Soviet Union are competing for world supremacy, we would expect prejudice to exist as a natural outgrowth of this competition. The competitor is seen as a threat, and it is only natural to feel hostile toward sources of threat against one's own security. Such a theory also implies that removing the conflict will reduce or remove the prejudice.

History supports the realistic-group-conflict theory. Anti-Russian attitudes were not prevalent during World War II when Russians and

© King Features Syndicate, Inc., 1973.

Americans were on the same side, but a good deal of prejudice was directed against the Germans and Japanese. Now there is significant anti-Russian feeling, although it is held in check somewhat by the fact that the Soviet Union and the United States tend to see a common threat in China. U.S. efforts to normalize relations with China may serve to keep things in balance, because both China and the United States see the Soviet Union as a potential threat. What would you predict about the attitudes of Americans, Russians, and Chinese if the earth were under attack by people from another planet?

Realistic-group-conflict theory has also been supported by such experimental research as the Robbers Cave study, described in detail later. In this study boys were divided into groups and put in conflict with one another; prejudice in all its forms developed. By later arranging things so that the groups had to cooperate in order to achieve a common goal, the prejudice and intergroup hostility were reduced.

INSTITUTIONAL PREJUDICE   A major source of prejudice is the opinions and actions of institutions. *Institutional prejudice* is reflected in segregated schools, houses, jobs, roles, communication patterns—in the many ethnic, religious, racial, and sexual divisions whereby one group is disadvantaged. The observer is aware of differences because differences are institutionally imposed; the ranking of groups is apparent because one group is institutionally disadvantaged.

Prejudice against blacks, for example, reflects the unfortunate facts that blacks are un-derpaid, hold inferior jobs, and are less well educated. A child seeing these harsh realities may ask why this is true and may reach the wrong conclusion. He or she may conclude that blacks must be inferior because they are black, completely failing to realize that there are other explanations for these inequities. This conclusion would be most likely to occur to a child with prejudiced parents, who would do nothing to correct the child's erroneous conclusion. And this would account for the fact that prejudiced parents have prejudiced children, without having to resort to Freudian principles about early childhood experiences. In this regard, seemingly trivial things such as making sure that black people are represented in television commercials or are given such TV roles as doctors and lawyers may be very important. These simple steps will serve to counteract the phenomenon even if the parents do not.

Race or Belief Differences?

Milton Rokeach argued in *The Open and Closed Mind* (1960) that people are prejudiced against others because of assumed differences in values, not because of ethnic or racial differences in and of themselves. Byrne and Wong (1962) found that prejudiced people indeed do assume that the targets of their dislike hold beliefs that are different from their own. According to Rokeach and his colleagues, regardless of racial or ethnic differences, people reject those who differ from themselves in basic values and like those who are similar. But prejudiced people have little contact with people who are ethnically different from themselves, and thus little opportunity to compare beliefs. These social psychologists maintain, therefore, that the source of much prejudice is the assumption of belief disparity.

Another social psychologist, Harry Triandis, believes the opposite—that prejudice does stem from differences in race or religion. It is possible, experimentally, to explore these opposing views by presenting subjects whose prejudice has been assessed independently with hypothetical persons either similar or different from themselves in basic values and similar or different in race. The subjects then indicate how intimate they would be willing to be with the target person. The results support Rokeach in part and Triandis in part. Subjects low or moderate in prejudice attend primarily to belief differences. However, highly prejudiced subjects consistently reject people on the basis of race; racial difference affected most subjects regarding intimate association. Traditional notions of prejudice survive; however, the importance of Rokeach's view on belief congruity cannot be discounted. Actual differences in beliefs, values, life-styles, or social class are also bases for rejection, and a difference on one dimension (like race) tends to generalize to assumed differences on other dimensions. Underlying the whole phenomenon of prejudice is that people prefer others who are like themselves.

Stereotypes

The final social factor to be mentioned is closely related to *social learning* and *imitation*, as discussed more fully in Chapter 9. The argument is that the prejudiced person learns, mainly through social learning principles, that all members of a particular group hold to certain beliefs or have certain attitudes or characteristics. Thus, the prejudiced person is said to hold social **stereotypes.** Social stereotypes are false generalizations about other groups. Examples include beliefs that Scots are miserly, that blacks are lazy, that the Irish are heavy drinkers. Such generalizations are usually negative, and they are almost always inadequate. Donald Campbell has identified the following kinds of inadequacies:

1. People falsely tend to assume that their view of others (the out-group) is unquestionably accurate.
2. Differences between in-groups and out-groups are much exaggerated.
3. Attributes are strongly believed to be innate ("ra-

Can Name Mean Success or Failure?

AP

ATLANTA — What's in a name? It may be the difference between success and failure at school, according to two psychologists studying the phenomenon of "loser" names.

Unpopular names such as Elmer, Otto, Percy, Gladys, Gertrude and Rhonda tend to trap pupils into stereotypes as losers among their peers, say Drs. John McDavid and Herbert Harari.

McDavid, an educational psychology professor at Georgia State University, said he and his associate stumbled onto the name phenomenon while investigating relationships among elementary school children in south Florida. . . .

The psychologist asked fourth and fifth graders to make a list of the names they felt were most desirable and then compared the lists with the students judged most popular by their peers in other classes.

"The children found to be most popular were in general the ones with the most popular names," said McDavid. "These were names like Susan, Sally, Elizabeth, David, Michael and Stephen.

"From this, we began to wonder if the teachers have the same sort of bias," he said, "and sure enough, they have the same stereotypes."

In an account of the research published recently in a professional journal, Harari noted:

"Teachers know from experience that a Hubert or an Elmer is generally a loser. Because he is taunted by other children, he reacts by becoming belligerent, aggressive and antagonistic towards others, including his teacher.

"One thing he doesn't do is study."

Rocky Mountain News, *Denver*
September 4, 1973

Stereotypes can be based upon such irrelevant factors as a person's first name.

cial") and unchangeable rather than environmentally caused.
4. Perceived differences between the out-group and the in-group are believed to cause the felt hostility toward the out-group when in fact the hostility precedes the discovering of differences.

Even when there are no differences between oneself or one's group and others, the evalua-

His Success Is Credited to Ability and Hers to Luck

Joan Beck

"He is aggressive; she is pushy;

"He is careful about details; she is picky;

"He loses his temper because he's so involved in his job; she's bitchy;

"'He makes wise judgments; she reveals her prejudices;

"He isn't afraid to say what he thinks; she is opinionated;

"He exercises authority; she's tyrannical."

Variations on this theme have been circulating lately—most recently at the Denver meeting of the American Association for the Advancement of Science—to help explain why more women are not achieving more success in various kinds of jobs.

The sum of the answers: Women are still battling upstream against subconscious prejudices about their abilities, not only on the part of males, but also by other women and themselves as well. Consciousness raising isn't enough to eliminate sex discrimination; subconsciousness raising is also essential.

What keeps holding women back besides the old weaker-sex, Adam's rib, sugar-and-nice, anatomy-is-destiny cliches? Here are findings from some of the studies discussed at the AAAS meeting:

Women are expected to do more poorly than men at numerous jobs and such expectations become self-fulfilling prophecies, according to psychologist Irene Hanson Frieze, University of Pittsburgh. One study was unable to find even one occupation—including writer, child psychologist, dancer, pediatrician, or biographer of famous women—in which women were expected to do better than men.

Men's successes are usually attributed to their abilities, while women's successes are believed more likely due to luck, according to patterns seen in several studies. Failures by women are more likely to be considered the result of lack of ability than are failures by men. And even when women do succeed—because these successes are attrib-

uted to luck—they are not expected to keep on being successful, as are men.

Achievements by women are not rated as high as similar work accomplished by men, according to Frieze. Studies show, for example, that articles are considered better when a male byline is attached than when evaluators are told they are written by women. As Frieze notes, it is "more difficult for a woman to prove her competency by a high quality performance than it would be for a man."

Females themselves do not generally expect to do as well as males, even from childhood on, research shows. "Men consistently overestimate their future performance while women tend to underestimate," says Frieze. And men generally rate their past achievements higher than do women with similar accomplishments.

Because males see themselves as more likely to be successful and act like it, and because they are so seen by males who still do most of the evaluating and promoting on the job, men generally get much better career opportunities than women with similar competence and accomplishments.

Many men are still uncomfortable with the thought that a woman might be superior in abilities or achievements and often take steps to make sure women can't demonstrate such superiority.

Women and their career goals are often not taken seriously—by teachers, employers, husband, or family, according to an AAAS report by Elske Smith, University of Maryland. A husband's career usually gets priority over his wife's. Employers generally do not give women the same kind of help, encouragement, and opportunity for career development they do comparable males.

Women must also try to succeed in an environment that is much less supportive in other ways than it is for men, notes Smith. . . .

Chicago Tribune
March 7, 1977

Society has long perpetuated prejudice through sex-role stereotypes.

tion of the in-group and out-group may differ sharply.

The content of stereotypes is relatively stable over time but it also changes in response to differing social climates. On three occasions Prince-

ton students have been questioned on their social stereotypes. Students were much more likely to make stereotyped judgments in 1931 than in 1951 or 1967; more recently they have criticized stereotypes as unreasonable. At all three times, of the 10 groups listed, the Turks were the most negatively characterized. An interesting shift has taken place in the evaluation of Americans; in 1933 and 1951 they were quite positively evaluated, but in 1967 they dropped to fifth place (the Japanese were first, the Germans second, the Jews third, and the English fourth). Dramatic reductions in stereotyping of blacks occurred between the 1931 and 1967 ratings.

Stereotypes form the cognitive component of prejudice. This component is quite complex, consisting in some cases of many beliefs that can have positive, neutral, and negative evaluative implications. There is no simple relationship between prejudice and the willingness to make a particular generalization. John Brigham (1971) has reported a positive correlation between subjects' attribution of the trait "irresponsible" to blacks and the subjects' degree of prejudice. Persons high in prejudice are more likely to say blacks are irresponsible. He found a negative correlation between attribution of the trait "intelligent" and prejudice. For many traits, there was no relationship between prejudice and stereotyping. Overall, however, there is a significant relationship between racial prejudice and the tendency to generalize about blacks.

We should note that not all stereotypes are negative, and not all generalizations are made in the service of prejudice. But the general view is that for prejudiced persons stereotypes serve to rationalize hostile opinions and feelings. These hostile views are shared with others to yield group stereotypes.

Attitude Change

Much of what we can say about attitude change follows from what we have already suggested about attitude formation. For example, if it were true that strict child rearing is the basic cause of the "authoritarian personality" and if it were true that this in turn causes prejudice, then the obvious way to change things would be to convince people to change the way they raise their children. But are you going to be successful if you tell prejudiced parents that if they raise their children differently, the children will not be prejudiced? This is just what the prejudiced persons do not want to do; they want their children to have the same values, attitudes, and beliefs that they have.

In a similar vein, we have seen that conformity to group norms is a major factor in prejudice. So you set out to convince people that they should not conform. And yet if they believe you and do not conform, they are likely to suffer somewhat for their newfound individuality; they will be cast out of their favorite social groups, lose their friends, and so on. Finally, we have emphasized realistic-group-conflict as a major source of prejudice. So you say, "Eliminate group conflict" and "Make everyone work together to achieve some superordinate goal," and theoretically this will eliminate prejudice. Easier said than done, unless you can get someone on another planet to attack us so that we all have to pull together to fight a common enemy.

Suppose we wanted to convince someone to use more permissive child-rearing practices, or we wanted to change a couple's attitude about the number of children they should have. What would we do? First, we might assume that the person in question has the wrong attitude and that if the individual knew all the facts, he or she would adopt the correct attitude. This implies that we have all the facts and the other person does not. All we have to do is present our facts and convince the person that they are true. In short, attitude change may be conceived of as a process whereby someone (the *source*) communicates the true facts (a *message*) to someone (the *recipient*), thus persuading the individual to a new point of view.

The basic process in attitude change is the familiar principle of cognitive consistency. Presumably the recipient's present attitude is consistent with facts or cognitions available to him or her. The source introduces inconsistency into the picture by communicating a new view or different position. If the recipient is persuaded that the new position is true, then a change in attitude is needed in order to achieve consistency.

Variables Influencing Attitude Change

Other than consistency many variables affect the attitude-change process. Here we will present some of these variables. Ask yourself why each of the variables changes attitudes. Does it affect whether the message is received, attended to, understood, or believed? Or does it affect the amount of inconsistency produced by the message?

Protection from Propaganda

Persuasion and propaganda are methods for bringing about attitude change. Of course, the term "propaganda" implies that the mesaage is not really true and should not cause one to change one's attitudes, but the method is often effective nonetheless. What might one do to "inoculate" oneself against propaganda? W. J. McGuire has proposed a psychological inoculation model based on the medical model of inoculation as a preventive treatment. The basic idea is to expose persons to small amounts of propaganda before they are hit with a big propaganda campaign. This, of course, is like giving someone a minute quantity of live virus in a vaccination. The assumption in medicine is that the small amount of live virus will cause the development of antibodies to fight off the disease itself at some later time. In psychological inoculation the assumption is that a lot of attitudes are learned without critical examination of the reasons why one should hold them. It is as if they are acquired and are surviving in a "germ-free" environment. If you have an attitude but are not aware of sound reasons to support it, you might be particularly vulnerable to propaganda that attacks your attitude with apparent reason. You are at a loss to produce good reasons for maintaining your attitude, and so you give in.

Suppose, however, that your views are opposed on several different occasions. Not enough information is given on any occasion to change your attitude, but you do hear enough to cause you to think of and examine your reasons for believing as you do. Now you have developed antibodies that should help you fend off propagandist attacks. This may be why hearing a two-sided presentation of an issue provides good inoculation against later counter-persuasion. Suppose you decide on the basis of a two-sided presentation (after you have heard both sides of the story) to believe A instead of B. Later you are subjected to propaganda implying that A is wrong and B is right. Because you already know the arguments in favor of B and have still chosen A, you have inoculated yourself against the arguments in favor of B. Thus propaganda favoring B should have less of an effect on you.

Figure 10–2
Propaganda

Is there a "vaccine" that will protect you from persuasion and propaganda?

In general, other things being equal, there will be more attitude change if:

1. the recipient inadvertently hears the message;
2. the person delivering the message (the source) is of high status and prestige;
3. the source begins the message by stating attitudes that are similar to the recipient's views;
4. the message gives both sides of the argument if the recipient is intelligent and gives only one side of the argument if the recipient is not very intelligent;
5. the recipient perceives that the source has nothing personal to gain by the attitude change the source is trying to produce;
6. the source clearly states the facts and the conclusions;
7. the source has a lot in common with the recipient;
8. the source is perceived as an expert on the issue;
9. the recipient does not feel compelled or forced to change but perceives that change is a matter of choice;
10. the message is repeated on several occasions;
11. the recipient is induced to express the desired attitude publicly;
12. the consequences of not changing one's attitude arouse a moderate (neither high nor low) level of fear.

These statements are, of course, subject to qualification. They do not hold in every possible instance. They are simplified conclusions from a research literature which clearly shows that attitude change is the result of very complex interactions of many such factors.

As a final variable for our list, we suggest that more attitude change will occur if you can induce behavior change in the recipient, even if his or her attitude has not yet changed. This relates to the question of "legislating morality," mentioned earlier. If you can induce someone to behave in a way that is inconsistent with his present attitude, he might change that attitude to return to a state of consistency. But you must not use extreme force to induce the behavior change because then there will be no inconsistency, and no attitude change. Getting someone to stand up and give an improvised speech on the dangers of overpopulation will change the person's attitudes against birth control more than passing a law that forces the individual to go to the family planning center.

"Some of you used to call us 'boy,' and that's why now some of us like to call you 'mother.' "

Playboy, November 1971. Reproduced by special permission of PLAYBOY Magazine; copyright © 1971 by Playboy.

When attitudes change, previously suppressed behaviors may emerge.

Interpersonal Attraction

Although psychologists have been most concerned with the study of people's unfavorable attitudes and prejudices, they have also been curious about people's favorable attitudes toward one another.

Person Perception

Our social relations are guided by the theories we have about other people. Researchers have found that we have consistent though often erroneous ideas about how people behave. In a classic study Solomon E. Asch found that changing a simple word in a complex description of a person leads to dramatic differences in observers' reactions to the person. In one instance a hypothetical individual was introduced to subjects as intelligent, skillful, industrious, *warm*, determined, punctual, and cautious. The same description was applied to another person, only the word "warm" was changed to "cold." The "warm" person was subsequently described far more favorably. While 90 percent of the subjects described the warm person as generous, only 10 percent characterized the cold person in this way. Harold Kelley actually introduced a speaker to several

Two Girls Convicted in Acid Attack on Pretty Classmate

AP

LINWOOD, Kan. — A juvenile court judge has found two 13-year-old girls delinquent in a Valentine's Day acid-throwing attack that scarred a pretty classmate at Linwood Elementary School.

Two other girls, also 13, were not found delinquent at the hearing . . . before Judge John Peters of the Leavenworth County Juvenile Court. None of the girls was identified.

Peters said . . . that a finding of delinquency brings automatic expulsion from school. School officials declined to discuss the case.

Lucy Holman, 14, a school cheerleader with a hairstyle like television star Farrah-Fawcett-Majors, suffered severe burns on her back, a shoulder and her right hand from nitric acid.

She was left with a scar on her back and had to restyle her hair.

School officials at the time attributed the attack to jealousy over Lucy's hairdo.

The girls involved have been classmates since kindergarten, and the incident has strained family relationships in this suburb of 350 people just west of Kansas City.

Rocky Mountain News, *Denver
March 25, 1977*

Incidents like the one described in this article dramatically illustrate the overemphasis on physical beauty in interpersonal relationships.

classmates. In one case the speaker was described as warm, and so on, and in the other he was introduced as cold. The speaker behaved essentially the same in both situations. However, the speaker described as cold was rated much less favorably, and class members interacted less with him.

Often the only information we have about another person is a physical impression. Physical beauty apparently influences our judgment of personality traits. Dion, Berscheid, and Walster (1972) found that attractive persons were judged to possess more desirable personality traits and to be more competent than unattractive ones. In another study of the effects of

physical attraction on impression formation, subjects rated, from photographs, attractive and unattractive persons on 17 dimensions of personality. The stimuli were rated significantly differently on 15 of the dimensions, with attractive persons being rated more favorably.

A number of researchers have now documented the observation that physical attraction is quite important to both males and females. Attractiveness affects judgments of personality, ability, and desirability for romantic relations, including dating and marriage. Even the way children are treated is a function of physical appearance—unattractive children are expected to behave badly, and the transgressions of unattractive children are judged more severely. Attractive children as young as ages four to six have been found to be more popular with other children than their unattractive peers.

Many studies seem to indicate that to be beautiful is good. Certainly physical beauty, in our culture, is often an asset. But what are the strains of physical attraction? Many attractive women complain that they do not want to be judged on their beauty alone. Apparently, beauty has its negative effects as well. Attractive women are expected to be more sociable, alluring, successful, and happy, but they are also judged as more conceited, unfaithful, materialistic, and snobbish.

Attribution Theory

How we view others—and even how we see ourselves—depends to a large extent on the intentions we ascribe to others. A behavioral sequence can have very different significance depending on our theory about why it occurred. Suppose one person jostles another. If you think the behavior was intended, you may view the act as aggression; but if you believe it was unintended, then you see the act as accidental. You may say that a child who pushes several children has an aggressive personality; but if the child is yours, you might see the other children as aggressive or rude and deserving of the treatment handed out by your well-adjusted offspring. A smile in one context may indicate friendliness and warmth, in another, contempt. **Attribution theory** concerns the bases on which we form our ideas of others' behavior. The theory contains a set of propositions that seeks to explain how the bases for attribution are developed and altered. From studies on attribution we see that we do not view the behavior of others as objectively as we like to believe we do.

ATTRIBUTION OF OTHER PERSONS Fritz Heider initiated attribution theory by observing that we attribute underlying determinants of others' behavior so that we can feel we understand them and/or will be able to predict how they will behave in the future. In our attempt to understand other people we refer to their intentions or personality or ability. These attributes are not visible; rather, they are concepts we create in order to give a pattern to observable behavior. If a person seems unpredictable to us, we might call him or her "crazy." The attributions we make, erroneous or accurate, affect how we behave toward that person.

Even though experienced psychologists and psychiatrists often have difficulty understanding the basis of a person's behavior—and, indeed, often disagree—most of us readily make instant judgments on the basis of sparse information. What are the cues? How do we know others or fool ourselves into thinking we know others so well?

Studies have suggested two important bases for attribution. First, Edward E. Jones and Keith E. Davis (1965) propose that we do not give equal weight to all of the information we have about a person. We focus instead on unusual behavior because it is informative. For example, it is more informative to know that one young girl has a pet tarantula than to know that another has a pet cat. Second, behavior that has a single apparent cause (which means we can rule out all reasonable alternative explanations) is also informative. For example, we are more likely to infer interest in a subject matter on the part of an instructor whose course is reputed to be dry and difficult than on the part of an undemanding, amusing, pleasant instructor who is known to be an easy grader.

Harold Kelly has listed three factors that determine whether we view an act as caused by a person (internal attribution) or by a situation (external attribution): (1) If an act is high in *consensus*, that is, if everyone behaves similarly, then the situation will be seen as the operating force—for example, cheering at a football game. An act low in consensus means a person behaves differently from others, and we see the act as internally caused—for example, cheering at a funeral. (2) A behavior that is highly *consistent,* meaning a person usually behaves in that way in that particular situation, is a basis for internal attribution—for example, a person is almost always quiet in class. (3) Finally, the *distinctiveness* of an act tends to determine the direction of attribution. A distinctive act is one that is quite specific to a particular situation—for example, a usually placid person suddenly becomes angry; an act low in distinctiveness means a person behaves in that way in a variety of similar circumstances—for example, is often hostile. The more distinctive the act, the more external the attribution.

SELF-ATTRIBUTION Not only do we make inferences about others, we also make inferences about ourselves. Daryl Bem has developed this idea in what he calls self-perception theory. Bem suggests that we infer our own feelings and attitudes from our behaviors—we run, therefore we infer we are afraid; we shout, therefore we decide we are angry. This relates closely to our treatment of emotions (see Chapter 7), particularly the James-Lange theory.

In a pioneering study by Schacter and Singer (1962), subjects given a drug that produced physiological arousal tended to behave and describe their emotional experience as similar to the emotions reflected by either an angry- or a happy-appearing confederate. (A confederate is a collaborator of the experimenter who poses as a subject.) Their self-ascribed mood depended not on their physiological response but on the social situation. (For a more extensive discussion of this study, see Chapter 7.)

An interesting, more recent example of self-inference is seen in a study of insomnia treatment by placebo. Storms and Nisbett (1970) gave two groups of insomniacs placebo pills (pills having no physical effects). One group was told the pills would make them more aroused; the other was told they would feel drowsy. The researchers hypothesized that emotional arousal contributes to insomnia and that sleep difficulty is partly due to associating arousal with emotionally toned cognitions, leading to heightened emotionality and difficulty in falling asleep. They predicted that if subjects could attribute their arousal to the pill, they would fall asleep more readily. As expected it

"Do you know what I like about you, Rachel? You're old, like me."

The New Yorker, July 22, 1974. Drawing by Weber; © 1974 The New Yorker Magazine, Inc.

turned out that the insomniacs who were told the pill would arouse them, increase their heart rate and body temperature, and perhaps make their minds race, got to sleep more rapidly than those who were told the pill would have a calming effect.

Nisbett and Wilson (1977) recently reviewed a large number of studies and concluded that our self-awareness is limited. We are often unaware of a stimulus that has influenced our response: sometimes we don't even know that we responded, and sometimes we don't know that a particular stimulus and response are related. Rather than through self-awareness, we often account for our own behavior by invoking "standard explanations" based on (1) what seems plausible, (2) what stands out or is most salient, and (3) previous experience with similar situations, all of which could be irrelevant. Thus people are not very accurate in indicating how they are affected by their environment. Because people tend not to be very good at explaining why they behave as they do, careful experimental investigations will be required to determine the role of self-awareness in behavior.

Individuals differ in their tendency to describe their behavior in terms of traits or situations. Some people are more likely to make self-attributions; others are more inclined to attribute behavior to the situation. A test of the generality of such attributions was reported recently. Persons were observed in restaurants to determine if they salt their food before or after tasting. These persons were then briefly interviewed to determine if they ascribed relatively few or many traits to themselves. Those that ascribed relatively many traits to themselves were particularly likely to salt their food before tasting. Further, those that salted first and tasted second explained their behavior in terms of self-characteristics, whereas the after-salters explained this act in terms of the situation.

Variables Affecting Liking

What is the primary basis for interpersonal attraction? Before you come to like someone and develop a friendship, it is obvious that you must have the opportunity to interact with that person. Thus *physical proximity* is important in determining friendship. Living near someone or working near someone is likely to produce interaction. A study of friendship patterns within a housing project for married university students showed that the closer the students lived to each other the more likely they were to become friends. Another factor appears to be *frequency of interaction*. The more frequently you interact with someone, the more likely it is that friendship will develop. Again physical proximity is likely to produce more frequent contact and thus more friendship. Indeed, any variable that increases the likelihood and the frequency of interaction between two people is likely to increase the degree of friendship between them.

But frequent interaction is not the only basis for friendship and liking. You all know individuals with whom you have interacted frequently, probably because you had to interact with them, but whom you do not like or regard as friends. Frequent interaction does not guarantee liking, although it is perhaps a starting place.

Given that two people frequently interact, what determines that a friendship will develop? Friendship is more likely if two people share the same race, sex, occupation or career objectives, socioeconomic status, age, attitudes, and so on. The evidence overwhelmingly supports

Study Shows Beauty Beats Inner Traits

Arthur J. Snider

Most people consider it vulgar to judge a person's character by physical appearance. Inner attributes are said to be much more important in determining who wins or loses our affection and esteem.

But two attractive female psychologists have concluded after a number of studies that for all the talk about inner-personality traits . . . we tend to give the best to beauty.

Prof. Ellen Berscheid of the University of Minnesota and Prof. Elaine Walster of the University of Wisconsin find in their collaborative studies that the influence of physical attractiveness begins making an impact early in life.

The teacher's pet in kindergarten is likely to be the attractive youngster. The one blamed for breaking the vase or creating the disturbance is the unattractive one. . . .

Not only is physical attractiveness the crucial standard by which we form our first impressions, the psychologists said, but also we tend to assign to pretty people attributes that may not exist.

Possible Reason

One of their studies finds students think good-looking persons generally are "more sensitive, kind, interesting, strong, poised, modest, sociable, outgoing and exciting than less attractive persons," Professors Berscheid and Walster report in Psychology Today.

"These findings suggest a possible reason for our nearly obsessive pursuit of suitably attractive mates. If we believe that a beautiful person embodies an ideal personality and that he or she is likely to garner all the world's material benefits and happiness, the substantial lure of beauty is not surprising."

What is the basis of our stereotyped image of beauty and virtue?

"It seems possible that in earlier times physical attractiveness was positively related to physical health," the authors conjecture. "It might be the instinctive nature of any species to want to associate and mate with those who are the healthiest of that species. We may be responding to a biological anachronism, left over from a more primitive age."

The Denver Post
March 29, 1972

What determines whether two people will like each other? Is it similarity in personality? Does physical beauty play a more important role than most of us care to admit?

similarity as a characteristic of friendship. We must be careful however, not to conclude that similarity causes friendship in an automatic fashion. Similarity may affect friendship indirectly by affecting physical proximity and frequency of interaction. There are likely to be people with similar attitudes near you frequently; thus the important effect on friendship could be frequency of contact, which in turn is caused by similarity. If you like to go to the library, the chances are that the people you frequently meet at the library and perhaps become friends with share this feeling about the library. *Actual* similarity may not be the *direct* cause of liking; studies show that it is *perceived* rather than actual similarity which is important. If you think that someone is similar to you even if it is not true, attitudes of liking are more likely to happen. Thus, although it is true that your friends are likely to be similar to you in many ways, this similarity is only part of the reason for your friendship.

Friendship may come about and be maintained through the satisfaction of complementary needs or the playing of complementary roles. For example, a dominant person may like people he or she can dominate, and a submissive person may like people who dominate. The needs of these two people would be described as complementary. The simplest way to see how complementary and similar needs might influence liking is to suggest that friendship is heavily determined by the mutual benefits that people can deliver to one another. In most cases, we would expect that we would benefit most from people with similar attitudes and needs (for example, we would get the most social approval from such people). However, we would also expect that in special cases two people with nearly complementary needs or who play complementary roles would gain a great deal by associating with each other, and these benefits could be the basis of their friendship.

One theory suggests that initial attraction between dating partners is based on fairly superficial characteristics like physical attraction, then proceeds to an exploration of belief, attitude, and value similarity, and continues with a concern for mutual and complementary satisfaction. Finally, some of the variables that seem related to a successful marriage include empathy with the marriage partner, open communication, and tolerance for differences.

Social Exchange Theory

Elaborating on the notion of mutual benefit as a factor in friendship, Thibaut and Kelley (1959) proposed that interpersonal attraction could be analyzed in terms of *rewards* and *costs* of each event or type of interaction. Suppose two strangers meet. They may find each other interesting, witty, helpful, and comforting. If so, they will certainly have a strong basis for friendship. Or they may find each other boring and antagonistic. At any rate, some level of satisfaction or reward results from the encounter. That reward is always at some cost, some effort expended, sacrifice made, risk taken, or obligation incurred. The attraction to each other is based on the interplay of these two factors, reward and costs.

Consider the fact that friendships are typically between similar individuals. According to social exchange theory we can understand the similarity effect by realizing that rewards in a social encounter are more likely to occur if the individuals have similar attitudes. If you encounter someone and mention in the discussion that you do not feel that abortion laws should be liberalized, what happens when the person's response is, "I wholeheartedly agree" as opposed to "I think you're all wrong"? In the first case, the response is very much like a reward, a positive reinforcer of your attitude. In the second case, you may find yourself in a heated debate (high cost factor in the encounter) with very few rewards. So similar people are likely to deliver more rewards at lower costs than dissimilar people. Social exchange theory suggests that this is one reason why similarity is such a predominant characteristic of friendships.

The costs and rewards, according to Thibaut and Kelley, are based not on any absolute level but on a comparison level. *Comparison level* refers to the standard by which persons evaluate what they feel they deserve. It is modified by experience, so that past outcomes raise or lower the comparison level depending on whether the outcomes were positive or negative. If a person has recently experienced a series of inadequate outcomes (costs are higher than rewards), he or she will lower expectations and raise evaluation of future outcomes. A future encounter for this person may be judged to be adequate, while for someone with a higher comparison level the same personal encounter would be judged inadequate.

Social exchange theory has a basis in learning theory and decision-making theory, both of which propose, in one form or another, that behavior is a function of possible reward and the probability of achieving that reward. This formulation—people choose what they like best and avoid what they dislike—has great intuitive appeal as well as empirical support. It is a quite general formulation and can encompass other simpler formulations based on single factors such as complementarity of needs, similarity of attitudes, and frequency of contact.

In its most recent form social exchange theory has decreased the emphasis on individual rewards and costs and focused on the importance of *mutual* benefits in any relationship. This is the concept of *equity*. Thus, the degree of equity in a relationship is a major factor in its survival.

INDIVIDUALS WITHIN GROUPS

In the previous section we focused on the attitudes of individuals, which are generally viewed as relatively permanent products of social experience. The major concern was with the rather pervasive effects of attitudes on an individual's treatment of or response to another person or group. This section is concerned with somewhat more immediate and probably more transitory phenomena. We will review research in a different social psychology tradition, the purpose of which is to examine how the actual presence of other people can and does influence our behavior. Research shows that the personal, social, and physical characteristics of other people who are present in a situation can forcefully affect the manner in which a person responds in that situation.

Social Influence

The mere presence of others, as audience or as coworkers without any verbal exchange, affects individual performance. This phenomenon is known as **social influence,** which can be either facilitative or inhibitory.

The first social psychological experiment, conducted by Norman Triplett in 1897, demonstrated social facilitation. Triplett, a fan of bicycle racing, noticed that when racers were bicycling against one another, their times were faster than when they raced against the clock. His observation prompted him to conduct the following experiment. He had children wind kite string under two conditions—while alone and with other children. Triplett found, as he expected, that children performed the task more slowly when they were alone.

Since Triplett's study, many other investigators have conducted experiments on social facilitation. All of them have demonstrated that the presence of others seems to enhance performance of simple, well-learned skills, such as winding string, but inhibits the acquisition of new skills, such as memorizing a list of nonsense syllables. Robert B. Zajonc (1965) has suggested that the presence of others increases arousal or drive level in such a way that the dominant (or most probable) response becomes even more dominant. Because old response patterns take precedence over new responses, new learning is inhibited. Zajonc's interpretation, diagramed below, seems to take into account most of the data.

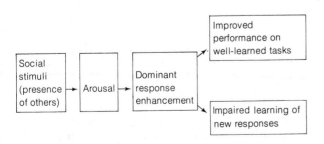

Shyness—Social Inhibition

An obvious prerequisite to effective interpersonal relationships is a willingness to engage in interaction with others at some minimal level. Socializing is an important part of our experience, and much of our lives is the product of social interaction. Nevertheless, many people are uncomfortable in social situations because they feel shy, an obvious example of inhibitory social influence. Shyness as a phenomenon has recently been studied by social psychologist Philip Zimbardo and his colleagues. Of thousands of high school and college students surveyed, 40 percent described themselves as presently shy, and 80 percent reported that they had been shy at some period in their lives. For more information on Zimbardo's shyness survey, see the article entitled, "Almost Everyone Is Shy, Sometimes."

Zimbardo has started a clinic for the treatment of shy people in which patients are taught social skills and ways of recognizing the situations that trigger the shy response. Using such techniques as role playing, videotape feedback, group discussion, and homework assignments (for example, go out and introduce yourself to a stranger), the clinic offers a pioneering effort focused on helping people deal with the shyness syndrome.

Conformity

The influence of others is more dramatic when pressure is placed on the individual to conform. People tend to feel uncomfortable when they are alone in their actions, out of step with the crowd. The effect of a conflict between individual judgment and group decisions has been cleverly studied by Solomon Asch (1956), among others. Asch required subjects to make perceptual judgments of the length of two lines in the presence of a group of confederates (see Figures 10-3 and 10-4). First the confederates reported, publicly and in turn, that what was clearly and objectively the shorter of two lines was the longer. Then it was the subject's turn to respond. He was in a state of conflict since he saw that the group was wrong. Asch found that approximately one-third of the subjects' responses were in conformity with the group, an indication of succumbing to social pressure (see Figure 10-5). Compare this with the lone jury member who disagrees with all the others.

Almost Everyone Is Shy, Sometimes

STANFORD, Calif. — Barbara Walters says, "If I'm the epitome of a woman who is always confident and in control, don't ever believe it of anyone."

Elizabeth Taylor says, "I'm basically shy. When I look in the mirror, all I see is an unmade-up face or a made-up face."

Johnny Mathis says, "For a while I thought there was no way I could get over the hangups and be able to be at ease on stage and look like I belong here. It was hell at times. I used to be genuinely petrified. But I'm still not sure what to do and how to act between songs. I feel more at ease than I used to, but shyness on stage is still a problem."

Shyness on stage and in personal life is a problem for a lot of people. Not just celebrities like Carol Burnett, Lawrence Welk and Joan Sutherland. Shyness is a problem that "affects 80 per cent of us at one point or another," says Dr. Philip G. Zimbardo, a social psychology professor at Stanford University, who has spent five years studying it.

"At any one time at least 40 per cent of the people you meet will tell you they're shy. Two-thirds of those who are shy consider it a personal problem," says Zimbardo.

Because "statistics are convincing but individuals persuade," Zimbardo likes to use celebrities as examples. He is saying to a shy person, "Here are people you admire and respect who have learned to conceal their shyness, but down deep they feel as shy as you do."

Shyness is a complex phenomenon with no one single cause, according to Zimbardo. It is a phenomenon that some people encourage because it is to their advantage.

"It's rare that parents are upset over a shy child. Shyness for many parents and teachers is preferable to assertiveness and outgoing behavior on the part of a child.

"Behavior management is the essential ingredient to the way they perceive their job. Shy people are easy to manage."

For the shy child that never grows out of it they can look forward to a life where "amost every aspect of it is diminished. They have few friends. Less sexual contact, if any. They tend not to date or marry. The kinds of jobs they take lead to positions of less authority.

"It's a minimal arrangement with life. The shy person gives little and gets little. They always sell themselves short and always settle for less than they ought to." . . .

It is a myth that men tend to be more shy than women, points out Zimbardo. But it is the man who will suffer more, because the traits of shyness stereotypically accepted in women as attractive and appealing features are not in men. . . .

"The central feeling of shyness is anxiety that other people will evaluate your performance in a negative way. Everything you do, you see as a performance. Life is a performance filled with an audience of critics like William F. Buckley Jr. ready to pounce on your every wrong move or utterance," says Zimbardo. . . .

Boulder (Colo.) Daily Camera
December 27, 1977

Have you ever worried about being shy? Just about everyone is shy in some circumstances.

Asch suggests that the subjects' conformity reflects their reasonable reliance on the judgment of others. Subjects have two sources of information, their own and others' judgments, both of which have proved reliable in the past and neither of which is necessarily superior. Asch suggests that conformity is in large part a rational process reflecting a recognition of the validity of other viewpoints. Asch's formulation is important because it points to the complexity of social influence. Social influence is not simply a blind following of others, an instinctive response to group pressure or social dominance.

Rather, it is the result of a complex set of factors, including the informational value of other responses as well as a need for social approval.

Is Asch right in asserting that conformity results from reinterpretation of perception as a result of information? If others provided only additional information, people who conformed publicly would also do so privately. However, when simple judgments of line length are given privately, conformity drops markedly. Thus it seems that expressing disagreement with others publicly is, in itself, disagreeable and is probably a major factor contributing to conformity.

Figure 10-3
To conform or not to conform?

In the classic study of conformity, Solomon Asch had seven subjects sit around a table and judge which of three lines was equal in length to a standard line they had seen earlier. The only real subject was Number 6; the others were paid confederates of Asch. Although the task was very easy, in one of the experimental conditions the confederates all lied about which line was correct. When it was Number 6's turn to respond, he usually showed signs of conflict (straining, double-checking, and so on) over whether to conform to the group judgment or give the response that he perceived was correct.

Figure 10-5
Asch's results

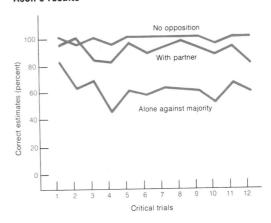

The number of correct responses of subject Number 6 under three conditions: when the group did not lie (no opposition), when they all lied together (alone against majority), and when one confederate agreed with Number 6 against the majority (with partner). Note that all it takes is one other person to counteract the conformity effect.

Figure 10-4
Asch's task

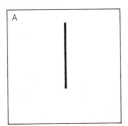
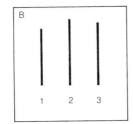

After viewing card A, the subjects must pick the line from B that matches.

Limits

The most dramatic demonstration in the social psychological literature of willingness to obey — to comply with the demands of another — has been reported by Stanley Milgram (1965). Milgram had subjects help him run an experiment in which the subjects were to administer electric shocks to another person — presumably to investigate the effect of punishment on learning. In fact, Milgram was concerned with how far subjects would go in shocking another when told to do so by an authority figure. No one actually was shocked. The shocking apparatus was disconnected, although the subjects did not know this.

The setting of the experiment was as follows. A middle-aged victim was strapped into a chair. Subjects who had been led to believe that the

The New Yorker, December 6, 1976. Drawing by Lorenz; © 1976 The New Yorker Magazine, Inc.

victim had a heart ailment, were told to give increasingly intense electric shocks, ranging from 15 to 450 volts (15 more volts with each "mistake" the victim made), labeled "mild" to "danger—severe." (The "victim" was, of course, a confederate; his "mistakes" were deliberate.) At 75 volts, the victim grunts; at 100 volts, he complains; at 150 volts, he demands release; at 285 volts, he screams and refuses to answer. When subjects objected to the continuation of the experiment, they were encouraged or ordered to go on (with phrases like "You must continue; the experiment requires you to continue"). Many subjects protested strongly, but nevertheless obeyed the experimenter. In fact, 62 percent of the subjects (20- to 50-year-old males of varied occupations, all of whom had voluntarily responded to a newspaper ad promising $4.50 to take part in a psychological experiment) obeyed completely. They went all the way to 450 volts!

The experiment clearly showed that people respond readily to the demands of authority. Milgram has pointed out the relation of his findings to the situation that prevailed in Nazi Germany when millions of Jews and others were murdered on the orders of the regime. Interestingly, a recent replication of Milgram's paradigm was undertaken in Germany. Subjects included four persons described by the author as hippies. In the structured obedience situation described above, 85 percent of the participants employed the highest level of shock.

Demonstrating that these results are not limited to Europe or North America, Shannab and Yahya (1977) repeated the study with Jordanian school-children. Again, in the standard situation, 73 percent delivered the maximum level of shock.

Milgram's results are frightening. They also raise the moral question of who is responsible for the behavior—the person behaving or the authority demanding obedience. Subsequent studies in varied conditions have confirmed the willingness of a large proportion of perfectly ordinary persons to obey authority when requested to mistreat another in cruel and potentially harmful ways. Milgram concluded that:

The results, as seen and felt in the laboratory, are to this author disturbing. They raise the possibility that human nature, or more specifically the kind of character produced in American democratic society, cannot be counted on to insulate its citizens from brutality and inhumane treatment at the direction of malevolent authority. A substantial proportion of people do what they are told to do, irrespective of the content of the act and without limitations of conscience, so long as they perceive that the command comes from a legitimate authority. If, in this study, an anonymous experimenter could successfully command adults to subdue a 50-year-old man and force on him painful electric shocks against his protests, one can only wonder what government, with its vastly greater authority and prestige, can command of its citizenry. (Milgram, 1965)

Person-Situation Interaction

A person's behavior is a function of both what the individual brings to a situation and the characteristics of the situation; either component alone is insufficient to account for the results. For a long time psychologists have recognized that attitudes are not always expressed in behavior. Bigots, for example, sometimes behave like egalitarians, and unprejudiced persons may act like bigots. When such apparent inconsistencies exist, a careful analysis of the attitudes and situations reveals consistent situational pressures toward counterattitudinal behavior.

Recently, personality and social psychologists have become more critical of a simple trait theory approach to behavior. Trait theory says that people behave in a consistent manner, that human beings have a predisposition for personality stability. The critics point out that such an approach is not valid because there are too many instances in which behavior in one situation fails to match behavior in another. The new approach views behavior as a consequence of the interaction between personal predisposition and the situation. As a consequence, predictions of behaviors must be of limited generality. For example, it has been found that authoritarian persons conform when pressured to do so by a high-status person but tend to conform less than average when confronted by a low-status person. Thus the situation influences the expression of the trait.

The implications of a reevaluation of trait theory are considerable. We may question the validity of describing people in terms of personality traits, and it may be that the psychological tests which have long been used for such purposes as job placement, academic and career counseling, and program evaluations are of questionable value. Recognition of situational bounds to behavioral tendencies is a tribute to both the complexity of human behavior and its potential for change.

Group Performance and Organization

"Too many cooks spoil the broth." But, "Two heads are better than one." These two common sayings are potentially conflicting descriptions of the relative excellence of individual versus group performance. But in the area of problem solving both statements are sometimes right. In solving some problems, a group is more effective than any individual. In dealing with others, group performance is lower. Like our evidence on leadership, the evidence here is by no means clear or straightforward.

Group Problem Solving

Although conclusions about group problem solving are far from final, it seems that group performance is particularly superior on moderately difficult problems but inferior on very difficult ones requiring a series of cumulative steps for solution. Groups have *not* been demonstrated to be clearly superior to the sum of attempts of individuals working separately, and sometimes they are clearly inferior. Furthermore, a group decision frequently takes longer and uses more total hours than individual ones. Whether the improvement in performance shown by groups in solving some problems makes up for their frequent inefficiency is an open question.

In part, group forces may inhibit a creative approach. The social facilitation literature suggests that the presence of others inhibits new and unique responses. In addition, fear of the reaction of others may inhibit the expression of unusual responses. Such self-censorship may prevent expression of very useful solutions. To counter this inhibition the technique of brainstorming has been developed. This technique requires group members to respond freely without evaluation either by themselves or others. The intent is to discover as many approaches as possible that may be productive of an original and superior solution. Systematic evaluation, however, suggests that brainstorming itself is often inferior to individuals working alone, because groups tend to concentrate on one line of thought and do not move as readily to other

TABLE 10–1   Two Sample Problems Used by Stoner

Problem A

A college senior planning graduate work in chemistry may enter University X where, because of rigorous standards, only a fraction of the graduate students manage to receive the Ph.D.; or he may enter University Y, which has a poorer reputation, but where almost every graduate student receives the Ph.D. What chance of success would you require before recommending that the student enter University X?

Problem B

Mr. M is contemplating marriage to Ms. T, a woman whom he has known for a little more than a year. Recently, however, a number of arguments have occurred between them suggesting some sharp differences of opinion in the way each views certain matters. Indeed, they decide to seek professional advice from a marriage counselor as to whether it would be wise for them to marry. On the basis of the meetings with a marriage counselor, they realize that a happy marriage, while possible, would not be assured. What chance of success would you require before recommending that the couple marry?

perspectives or themes. Moreover, when individuals are given instructions to avoid self-criticism, their creativity and problem solving improve whether or not they are part of a group.

Group Decision Making

Who will be more likely to recommend a risky course of action—an individual or a group, a brain surgeon or a committee of brain surgeons? This problem first came to the attention of social psychologists in 1961, when a student in the School of Business Administration at MIT, J. Stoner, reported in his master's thesis that group recommendations were in general more risky than the average individual recommendations. Stoner asked subjects to indicate the chances of success they would require before recommending that a risk be taken in several problem situations (see Table 10–1). He found that groups tended to require lesser chances of success than individuals did—the *risky shift*.

Several interpretations of this phenomenon have been offered. One emphasizes the diffusion of responsibility that can occur in groups. Because individuals in groups share the potential burden of being wrong, each individual has less to lose. He or she is willing to risk partial blame for an error for the chance of being right, which the individual can represent as a personal success.

But there are other factors. Some data suggest that in a group people who are naturally riskier in their decisions are also more influential. The risky person tends to talk more and louder and to be more impelled by immediate practical possiblities than the conservative person. The risk takers, then, might effectively pull the group as a whole toward the decision they favor.

Finally, Roger Brown has pointed out that most Americans evaluate themselves as being at least as risky as the average person. Even objectively conservative people tend to appraise themselves as daring and willing to take a chance in most situations. Risk appears to be a general cultural value in this country. Thus, when a person hears other members suggest riskier positions than he was thinking about, he shifts his thinking toward greater risk to prove to himself and the group that he is at least as risky and daring as the next person.

A complication with these explanations is that there are some problems for which groups are more cautious than individuals. Problem B in Table 10–1 is an example of one of the Stoner problems that consistently elicits a more cautious group response.

Any explanation of the difference between individuals and groups should apply to both greater riskiness and greater caution. Groups are not always more risky; sometimes they are more conservative than individuals. Fortunately, the risk-as-value hypothesis can be modified to fit the cases where groups are more conservative. For certain kinds of issues, there are cultural values implying that conservatism is "right." In such cases the individual values his conservatism and feels that he is at least as conservative as the next person. He may see that some group members are more conservative and so he shifts toward a greater degree of caution—the *cautious shift*.

It seems that the initial definition of the problem—that is, whether it calls for riskiness or caution—determines the relative position of the group response. By their very nature, most problems entail an element of risk, and risk is the only means of attaining a valued outcome. This fact, combined with the influence of "risky as thou" group members, means that, on the average, groups will conclude in favor of more risky action than individuals. However, when the potential payoff to a risky course of action is not seen as equivalent to the cost even by the risk takers, caution is indicated and the risky group becomes the cautious group.

Generosity Shift

An extension of the application of the risk-shift phenomenon has now been made to "the generosity shift." A shift in the direction of greater personal generosity such as helping another even at the expense of greater personal discomfort results from group discussions. This change, which is similar to the change following group discussions in the directions of greater riskiness (when risk is a value), can be seen in terms of Levinger and Schneider's conflict-compromise theory. Briefly, an individual will move in the direction of greater realization of a value after finding that his or her own position is not distinctly different from that group. The observations suggest that a generosity shift as well as a risk shift will occur in a direction seen as desirable by a person following a group discussion that reveals the individual is not distinctly different. In addition to a shift toward risk and generosity, we can expect a shift toward greater honesty, altruism, social justice, and so on.

GROUPTHINK   What happens when powerful decision makers get together to decide important courses of action potentially leading to historic events? What are the possible sources of error? How is it that brilliant people may make stupid decisions? After analyzing a number of historic decisions, Irving Janis formulated the concept of *groupthink* to describe what happens in such situations. Groupthink occurs in highly cohesive groups where the members are strongly oriented toward maintaining group unanimity, with the result that critical responses are reduced and rendered ineffective. Janis identified the characteristics of groupthink as: (1) a sense of invulnerability, (2) extensive rationalization, (3) moral self-righteousness, (4) simplistic stereotypic description of the opposition, (5) strong conformity pressures, (6) self-censorship of divergent views, (7) suppression of divergent information from others, and (8) an illusion of unanimity.

Janis analyzed in groupthink terms the decision by President Kennedy and his advisers to support the Bay of Pigs invasion of Cuba by Cuban dissidents. The events leading up to the final decision have been widely documented; important intelligence information was ignored, misinformation was attended to, and the results were disastrous. The President and his advisers formed a highly cohesive group. Everything seemed to fall right for them. Moral questions were not raised; self-censorship and the censorship of others have been documented. The Cuban government was characterized as stupid and ineffective. Because serious doubts were not expressed, the illusion of unanimity was maintained.

Many other events seem to fit Janis' model. Consider as an example the events preceding the disastrous decision of the Israeli leaders in the 1973 Arab-Israeli war not to mobilize. There are strong suggestions that elements of groupthink were operating. Can you think of any other instances? What about the Watergate affair and the White House "plumbers" unit?

Cooperation and Conflict

The problem of conflict between individuals and between groups is one of obvious importance. Psychologists have tried to analyze and understand the processes underlying it in order to find ways of reducing conflict and its accompanying hostility and to induce cooperation in its place. Perhaps the most important factor uncovered in this research is the overwhelming tendency to overvalue one's own groups (either those we belong to or those we identify with) and to undervalue others. This is perhaps the major component of the dynamics of intergroup hostility. It is clearly at the heart of the stereotypes involved in prejudice that we discussed earlier.

The Robbers Cave Experiment

A classical social psychology experiment on group conflict called the Robbers Cave experiment (named after the site of the study) was published in 1961 by Sherif, Harvey, White, Hood, and Sherif. Here are the facts of the Robbers Cave experiment.

The subjects were 12-year-old boys selected to be good examples of typical middle-class American children. They were normal, healthy, well adjusted, happy, fun-loving, and energetic. The experimenters divided the boys into two groups designed to equate the members on such attributes as intelligence and size.

Figure 10-6
The trucking game

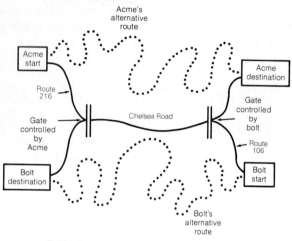

Subject's roadmap showing the long routes and the short route that both trucks had to share.

The boys understood they were going to summer camp, and each group was taken separately to an isolated Boy Scout camp.

The camp was actually being run by the experimenters, who hired the camp counselors. The counselors observed the boys' behavior and reported on it to the experimenters (the measurement was unobtrusive because the boys merely thought of the counselors as counselors). The experimenters and counselors conducted camp activities according to a preconceived experimental plan that had three stages.

In the first stage the two groups of boys were treated separately in such a way as to develop a feeling of group identification and belongingness. This was done by having the boys work on projects designed to achieve goals that they all would value and that they all would have to cooperate to attain. Sample projects were improving the swimming hole and building a rope bridge. Each group was treated so that the end result would be two groups of boys, each with a high level of within-group cohesiveness. One group of boys decided to call itself the Rattlers, and the other group took the name Eagles. At this stage each group was separated from the other and worked independently on different projects. By the end of the first stage the experimenters had succeeded in creating two real groups as opposed to just a collection of boys. Within each group there were definite feelings of belonging to the group.

In the second stage the counselors began to create conflict between the two groups, pitting one group against the other in a series of contests, such as baseball and tug-of-war. The competition between groups produced intergroup hostility, expressed in name calling, fighting, and raiding each other's camps. The Rattlers did not like the Eagles, and the feeling was mutual. Prejudice against out-group members and in favor of in-group members clearly existed.

The third stage consisted of efforts to reduce the intergroup hostility. Simply bringing the two groups together (for example, having them eat together) had no effect on the hostility. Providing the boys with a common enemy (a third group of boys) did reduce hostility between the Rattlers and the Eagles, but the boys were still hostile. The groups merely displaced their hostility to the common enemy.

What did reduce the total hostility was the same thing that was responsible for developing the feelings of group belongingness in the first stage. The experimenters set tasks that required the two groups to work together to achieve the goals, and the goals were designed to be of value to members of both groups. For example, it was arranged for the camp truck to break down while it was taking both groups on a camping trip both were looking forward to. All the boys in both groups were needed to pull the truck up a hill to get it started again. Because the goal was positive in character, hostility was not elicited. Because cooperative effort between the groups was necessary, intergroup hostility was no longer appropriate. A series of such cooperative ventures eventually led to intergroup friendliness to the point that the boys requested that they go home together in one bus. In fact, with their prize money one of the groups treated the other to milkshakes on the way home.

The Trucking Game Study

Deutsch and Krauss (1960) studied conflict in a situation analogous to the cold war arms escalation. Each of a pair of subjects was given a set of switches that controlled an imaginary truck. The two trucks were owned by competing trucking companies. Each truck could reach its destination by taking either a long route or a

Marriage Off the Tracks?

Psychotherapists who specialize in marital problems have quite an array of technical aids at their disposal. Often the standard sessions on the couch are augmented by the use of tape recorders, Rorschach ink blots, a wide range of written tests and sometimes drugs. Now a new technique is coming into widespread use: it is a deceptively simple game in which the partners in a troubled marriage act out their problems with a set of electric trains.

The Ravich Interpersonal Game-Test, as it is called, was developed six years ago by Dr. Robert Ravich, a psychiatrist at the Cornell University School of Medicine. What it does is use the way a husband and wife manipulate their respective electric trains to reveal and make clear the unconscious patterns and rules that govern their marital relationship. The test is just about impossible to outwit because the preliminary instructions tell only how the trains are to be operated; they offer no clear-cut definition of winning and losing.

To play the game, husband and wife sit at opposite sides of a large board divided by a low partition that prevents them from observing each other's moves. But they can see each other's faces over the partition and are free to discuss tactics and strategy as the game progresses. Using individual control panels, each partner directs his own train forward or backward over one of two paths to a terminal point. There are two routes, a direct one and a long, winding one. A quick trip is rewarded with imaginary pennies and a slow trip is penalized. If both partners choose the direct route, there is a "collision" (indicated by a red light) just short of the terminal point, and one or both players must back up their trains so the game may proceed. Each player also controls a barrier that prevents his partner's train from moving until he chooses to remove it.

Cost

During this confrontation, each partner has options: he can play primarily against the clock (he starts to lose pennies after 30 seconds); he can

compete heavily against his partner by employing the barrier—though this can cost him time in getting his own train through; or he may decide to cooperate with his partner to get both trains to the terminal in the least amount of time.

A typical first session of the therapy includes an extended train game that takes about an hour. All conversation during the game is tape-recorded, and each move made by the players is fed into a computer and evaluated.

A few days later, during the second session, the play is reviewed. By this time, the partners may have a distorted recollection of how they interacted. But then, confronted by the evidence of the computer, they begin to acknowledge the patterns they exhibited in the game and may spontaneously draw analogies to their real lives. When it was pointed out to one woman that neither she nor her husband had spoken throughout the entire game, she replied, "Once I thought of saying something, but then I just didn't. We hardly ever talk."

"What happens," says Ravich's colleague, psychologist Dr. Michael Rothenberg, "is that the partners have made up their own rules, based on the way they are used to behaving toward each other." . . .

Through therapy, such couples must actually be taught how to face up to and tolerate the conflicts and disagreements that are part of all marriages. . . .

To date, thousands of couples have made use of the Ravich Interpersonal Game-Test, and sets are already in use in medical centers across the country. There is one obvious question about the game that remains unanswered: how do happily married couples play it? That promises to remain something of a mystery. "The fact is," says Dr. Rothenberg, "that happily married couples just don't come to see marriage counselors."

Newsweek
February 5, 1973

Do you think a control group of happily married couples would help to clarify the meaning of this research?

short shared route (see Figure 10–6). If both persons could use the short route, by cooperating with each other they could gain the most— the faster the time, the greater the prize. In the first situation both participants controlled a gate

that would block progress of the other along the short route; in the second situation only one person had a gate; and in the third neither had a gate. Players did best when no threat existed (no gate could be closed). They did next best when only one person controlled the threat; the player with the threat gained the most. They did worst when both had the gate as a weapon. Thus when a person was faced with a threat, it was better for him in terms of personal gain to be without a weapon!

The analogy is crude. It is a long way from the Acme Trucking Company to the Kremlin or Pentagon, from gates to bombs. But the experimental results are intriguing and suggestive of possible applications in international affairs and interpersonal affairs (see the article "Marriage Off the Tracks").

Helping Victims of Accidents and Crimes

When will you help a stranger? Who can be counted on? Why in New York City were Kitty Genovese's screams, ending in her murder after a half-hour of torment, unanswered by 38 persons who heard her cries for help? Why did no one even bother to call the police?

Bibb Latané and John Darley (1968) suggest that help may be least likely when there are many possible helpers. Two experiments on the reaction of people to accidents support this idea. In one study smoke was pumped into an experimental room. When subjects were alone, 75 percent reported the smoke to a nearby experimenter within 6 minutes. When others were present, 38 percent at most (and in one condition only 10 percent) reported the smoke.

In another study an attractive young woman gave subjects some questionnaires, then went into an adjoining room, made some noises as though she had fallen, and screamed, "Oh, my God, my foot . . . I . . . can't move . . . it. Oh . . . my ankle, I . . . can't get this . . . thing . . . off me." Of the persons waiting alone, 70 percent offered help. When two subjects were waiting together, 40 percent of those in such groups offered help. When a confederate was there with a subject, and remained impassive, only 7 percent of the subjects intervened.

Who will help the victim of a crime? Latané and Darley devised an ingenious experiment to test their proposition that the more persons present when a victim needs help, the less help will come forth. They staged a robbery of a liquor store 96 times in a two-week period. The robberies were planned so that there were either one or two customers present during the robbery. The liquor store was real, the customers

---

Woman Slain in Subway; 12 Watch, Don't Help

AP

NEW YORK — Police say more than a dozen persons watched without helping as a would-be robber knifed a 34-year-old former Denver woman to death in the 66th Street IRT subway station at Lincoln Center.

Claudia Curfman Castellana, of 560 Riverside Drive, New York, was stabbed and slashed 10 times in the chest, back and arm at the bottom of the stairs of the subway station . . . , police said.

Witnesses said they heard the woman screaming, "Leave me alone. Leave me alone," just before the killer attacked.

Mrs. Castellana staggered further into the station and collapsed between the turnstiles and the change booth just as passengers began to leave a train that had pulled into the station. She was pronounced dead on arrival at Roosevelt Hospital. . . .

Police said persons who witnessed the attack apparently made no move to help the woman fight off the killer, but some of those getting off the northbound local chased a man they believed to be the assailant. The man got away.

"He got away and we don't know whether it was the right man or not," a detective said late Sunday.

Police believe the assailant followed the woman into the subway, intending to rob her. . . .

Mrs. Castellana's murder came just as Transit Authority police released a report claiming that major crime in the subways had dropped 16 per cent in the first seven months of this year.

The Denver Post
August 8, 1977

Social psychologists are grappling with the problem of bystander apathy, the refusal of bystanders to help in an emergency. One theory is that the more bystanders there are, the more everyone tends to assume that someone else in the group will take the responsibility.

---

were real customers, the robbers were experimental accomplices. The robber would enter the store and ask the manager for the most expensive beer. While the manager was in the back room, the robber would pick up a case of

"They said they don't want to get involved."

© *Punch (Rothco).*

"I find that as long as you avoid eye contact, you hardly realize there is a crowd."

© 1979 by Sidney Harris.

beer and walk out, saying, "They'll never miss this," and he would drive off. A minute later, the store manager would return to the counter, and if the customers did not report the theft spontaneously, the manager would ask, "Hey, what happened to that man who was here? Did you see him leave?" Twenty percent of the customers reported the theft without prompting; 51 percent of the remainder reported it after the manager's questions. Of the 48 single customers, 65 percent reported the theft. The theft was reported in only 56 percent of the cases when two customers were present, a significantly smaller percentage than statistically expected for two-customer groups. It seems that, in the case of a liquor store robbery at least, two customers are less likely than one customer to report a theft.

The decision to help or not to help is affected not only by the social environment. The physical environment can also reduce or facilitate altruism. K. E. Mathews, Jr., and L. K. Canon, for example, showed that noise level can influence helping. In a laboratory study they staged an event in which the experimenter appeared to accidentally drop several objects. In one condition observers were subjected to 85-decibel white noise in contrast to a quiet control condition. Helping was considerably less in the noisy condition. The experimenters replicated these results in a field study in which a passerby dropped objects in the presence of either a very noisy or quiet lawnmower. The results are interpreted by the researchers as reflecting increased arousal level, which in turn leads to reduced attention and limited cue utilization.

Social Crowding

Most Americans live or work in cities. Despite the flight to suburbia, cities continue to grow. It is impossible today for most of us to avoid almost continuous contact and interaction with other people, most of whom are strangers or at best mere acquaintances. Psychologists have become increasingly interested in the effects of crowded conditions and city life in general on the social and individual behavior of human beings.

This interest is prompted, in part, by the large number of socially pathological incidences in recent years that seem to be unique to cities. A prominent example, of course, was the slaying of Kitty Genovese in New York City while literally dozens of people sat by passively and listened to her screams. Some writers have been quick to interpret facts like these as a result of the evils of crowding and urban living. High-rise

For a large number of Americans crowded conditions are an accepted part of everyday life.

People-Crowding Not Critical, Preliminary Studies Indicate

AP

SALT LAKE CITY, Utah — Crowding people together may not be as bad psychologically as is popularly believed, a University of Utah sociologist says.

"The greater the number in the household, the less evidence there is of psychological disorder, alcoholism and use of mood-modifying drugs," said Dr. John Collette.

Basis Told

Collette recently joined the Utah university and bases his preliminary study findings on three years of research and teaching in New Zealand.

He said his study, conducted along with Dr. Stephen D. Webb at the University of Victoria in British Columbia, indicates that human psychological disorders are more frequent where there is great population density, but are less likely to occur where there is household crowding.

"There is prevalent assumption that human populations can reach critical limits as far as personal stress is concerned," said Collette, "but there is no definition of when those limits are reached. We could be there now, we may have already exceeded the limits, or they may not exist at all."

Countries Similar

He said his studies in New Zealand can be applied to American society because the two countries are similar in urbanization, industrial development and life styles.

Collette and Webb collected information from 1,200 individuals, mailed questionnaires to 5,000 others and gathered case histories from the New Zealand Department of Health on stress-related deaths and diseases.

He said some of the study's findings run counter to what are common assumptions about population density.

"Most studies of population and stress relationships have utilized animals to assess reactions, and it has been shown, for example, that crowding produced homosexuality and cannibalism in rats," he said. "But there has been nothing to document what constitutes critical limits for humans."

The Denver Post
September 2, 1974

Not all the evidence on crowding is negative. Household crowding may have different effects than general population crowding (population density).

The Stanford Prison Study

To study the social psychology of imprisonment, Phillip Zimbardo and his colleagues devised an experiment in which they could observe behavior in a simulated prison environment. The inmates were male college student volunteers, as were the guards. Members of both groups received $15 a day for their participation. The expected duration of sentence was two weeks. The simulated jail, in the basement of the psychology building at Stanford University, was divided into cells with bars on the doors and equipped with the minimum amount of furniture; the toilets were public. The mock prisoners were "arrested" in realistic manner by the local police department, booked, stripped, examined, given prison clothes and a number, and incarcerated. The guards were in uniform with silvered sunglasses, billy clubs, and handcuffs. The atmosphere was oppressive.

The results of this experiment were dramatic; seemingly typical college students began to behave in strange ways. The pseudoprisoners became increasingly disturbed; the pseudoguards became quite brutal. After three days, the first prisoner was released because he showed signs of severe emotional disturbance. Before the experiment was prematurely terminated after 6 days, 3 other prisoners of the total of 10 had to be released because they were seriously disturbed. The guards also were affected. They relied heavily on physical force and harassment. For example, one of the guards commented: "I was surprised at myself . . . I made them call each other names and clean the toilets out with their bare hands. I practically considered the prisoners cattle, and I kept thinking I have to watch out for them in case they try something."

The investigators were surprised by the relative ease with which sadistic behavior could be elicited from normal, nonsadistic people and the extent of the emotional disturbance that emerged in young men selected precisely on the basis of their emotional stability. The pathology observed in this study cannot be attributed to any preexisting personality differences of the subjects. Rather, their abnormal social and personal reactions were a product of their transaction with an environment whose norms and contingencies supported the production of behavior that would be pathological in other settings, but was "appropriate" in this prison.

Findings such as these could have considerable impact on the administration of prisons and prison-reform efforts.

---

apartments, tenements, condominiums, housing projects, and other similar living arrangements that promote crowding have been indicted as the major cause of modern social grief. The general underlying factor is said to be urbanization and the expansion of cities.

Stanley Milgram (1970) has offered a psychological interpretation for the unique social behaviors of city dwellers in terms of an information-overload hypothesis. He argues that people who live in large cities are subjected to an often overwhelming influx of stimulation and information. As a consequence, these people develop strategies to protect themselves against this overload. Among the commonly observed acquired strategies are a norm of noninvolvement in the affairs of others, respect for privacy, tolerance for diverse life-styles, and distrust.

Milgram has conducted a number of experiments to demonstrate the existence and function of these strategies. In one study, for example, experimenters attempted to gain entry to the dwellings of a selected sample of residents of New York City and to those of a similar sample from a small town outside New York

City. The results were interesting and consistent with Milgram's idea. Male experimenters could gain entry some three to five times more often in a small town than in a city. Female experimenters were more likely to gain entry than males, succeeding nearly 100 percent of the time in small towns. Still, even females could gain entry in less than half their attempts in the city. Apparently, city dwellers have a greater distrust of strangers than do residents of small towns.

Some of the findings on the effects of crowding, consistent with Milgram's overload hypothesis include: (1) the more dense the environment, the less children interact with each other; (2) violations of personal sense of space or privacy leads to withdrawal; and (3) adults in crowded situations look at each other's faces less and like others less. These studies show the dislike we have for crowded situations and for loss of privacy. (Loss of privacy, for example, is the most aversive aspect of prison life.)

SUMMARY

1. Social psychology is the study of the effects on individual behavior of the real or imagined behavior of others. As a discipline it has been concerned with two major areas of investigation: social attitudes and the behavior of individuals in groups.

2. Many social psychological phenomena demonstrate the validity of two principles—the need for consistency in behavior and the need for social approval.

3. Attitudes are believed to be organized according to the consistency principle. Two varieties of consistency theory are the balance theory and the theory of cognitive dissonance.

4. Prejudice is a learned attitude held by members of one group toward members of another. Bases for prejudice include defense against anxiety, out-group aggression, economic competition, and social limitation.

5. Social stereotypes and prejudice are closely related. Both are associated with a highly defensive, potentially fascistic, personality syndrome labeled the authoritarian personality.

6. One important basis for liking is physical attraction. How we view others also depends on the intentions we ascribe to them. Attribution theory is concerned with the bases on which we form our ideas of others' behavior.

7. We tend to attribute order and pattern in describing how others behave. The behavior of others is seen as dispositional, while we see ourselves as behaving in response to situational factors.

8. How we interpret our own behavior and the behavior of others is more important than what really occurs.

9. Social psychologists have recently devised methods to help people overcome the obstacle to effective interpersonal relationships known as shyness.

10. The presence of others and what they do—social influence—is an extremely powerful factor affecting individual behavior. We usually try to do what others do.

11. A number of experiments have shown that people respond readily to the demands of authority. These results raise the question of who is responsible for the behavior—the individual behaving or the authority.

12. Recent studies suggest that behavior is a consequence of personal predisposition and the specific situation. Thus predictions of behavior may have limited value.

13. The investigation of group dynamics has included evaluation of the relative efficiency of groups versus individuals in decision making. Which is most effective seems to depend on the nature of the problem at hand.

14. Studies of intergroup conflict have revealed the ease with which it is created and the difficulty with which it is dissolved. One effective means of conflict reduction is joint pursuit of superordinate goals.
15. Some additional problems of current interest to social psychologists include investigation of conditions that affect the likelihood that one person will help another in distress and the effect of social crowding on behavior.

RECOMMENDED ADDITIONAL READINGS

Aronson, E. *The social animal,* 2d ed. San Francisco: Freeman, 1976.
Berkowitz, L. *A survey of social psychology.* Hinsdale, Ill.: Dryden Press, 1975.
Brown, R. *Social psychology.* New York: Free Press, 1965.
Middlebrook, P. N. *Social psychology and modern life.* New York: Knopf, 1974.
Wrightsman, L. S. *Social psychology,* 2d ed. Monterey, Calif.: Brooks/Cole, 1977.

what does it mean?

Social psychology has application in many diverse areas. Consider the industrial work setting. Employee attitudes toward fellow workers and toward the company will influence production and product quality and will also play a large part in employee morale. There are group norms about how to work, how much work to do, how to behave on the job, and who to associate with. There are problems of picking and training leaders. Virtually every aspect of social psychology can be applied to the industrial setting, for the industrial setting is itself like a small society. Other areas in which social psychology has useful applications include educational institutions, mental hospitals, and prisons. There is also a social psychology of sexuality, which ranges from studies of sexual promiscuity to studies of love and platonic friendship. There is a social psychology of organizations, of the family, of prejudice, of altruism, and of many other topics. In short, because social behavior is so prevalent, social psychology has wide applicability.

THE SOCIAL PSYCHOLOGY OF JUSTICE

Social psychologists have increasingly attended to the processes of jury selection and decision making by juries. The findings of social psychology apply to the jury room as well as to the psychological laboratory. It has been found, for example, that persons with greater prestige—higher in social class—are more active participants in jury discussions and are more often chosen as jury foremen; similarity of the defendant to members of the jury also influences decision making.

Physical attraction also plays a role in jury verdicts. In several studies it was found that attractive offenders received more lenient treatment. However, in a more recent study beauty was sometimes an asset, sometimes a liability. When the crime was burglary—a crime unrelated to physical appearance—attractive defendants received more lenient sentences. When the crime was related to physical appearance—swindles—attractive defendants received more severe sentences.

The U.S. Supreme Court recently ruled that the state of Florida can use six-member juries. Two social psychologists subsequently studied the results of decisions made by simulated six-member juries in contrast to twelve-member juries. They found that jury size made no apparent difference when the guilt of the defendant was not clear; however, when the defendant's guilt was apparent, the six-member group showed a greater tendency to convict. Evidence that six- and twelve-member juries do not make equivalent decisions may affect the future structure of the jury system.

As the psychology of jurors is more clearly understood, the use of psychology for jury selection has become controversial. Social scientists have aided lawyers in jury selection in the following highly publicized cases cited in *Science* (1974):

© 1977 United Feature Syndicate, Inc.

Does TV advertising manipulate attitudes?

The trial and acquittal of Angela Davis, where five black psychologists observed the jurors during their selection.

The trial and acquittal in Camden, New Jersey, of 28 radical Catholics in connection with a draft board raid.

The trial in Gainesville, Florida, of some militant members of Vietnam Veterans Against the War, where a jury that included some men of draft age voted for acquittal.

A series of trials arising out of the Indian takeover at Wounded Knee, South Dakota, including one of Dennis Banks and Russell Means, leaders of the American Indian Movement, which is still in progress.

A civil damages suit brought on behalf of 650 survivors of the Buffalo Creek, West Virginia, dam disaster who won $13.5 million.

The trial of Daniel Ellsberg and Anthony Russo, where the case was dismissed part way through, but where a follow-up study showed that the jury was likely to have voted for acquittal.

The trial and acquittal of John Mitchell and Maurice Stans, where Long Island consultant Martin Herbst helped the defense lawyers select the jury.

The Attica trials, where more than 1000 counts are being charged against inmates of Attica prison.
(*Science,* September 20, 1974)

The use of psychology for this purpose remains highly controversial.

PERSUASIVE COMMUNICATION

Persuasive communication is a big business in the United States, and persuasion is mainly an application of the principles of attitude change. The most obvious example is advertising. An advertisement or TV commercial is basically a message designed to change your attitudes about some product or service, particularly the action tendency component of attitudes—advertisers want you to buy their product.

We can apply the principles of attitude change to advertising and see what an effective (persuasive) ad would look like. The fact that such an advertisement might not be one we would like in the esthetic sense is irrelevant, as you can well appreciate if you have ever watched television.

The effective ad, say for a new cereal, might have the following characteristics:

1. It would be catchy or lively or loud—you want your ad to stand out and be seen or heard.
2. It would be fairly simple-minded—you want your message to be clear and understandable to all who are to receive it.
3. It would repeat the message over and over, for example: "Buy Zappo! Zappo, the best cereal you ever tasted. Remember Zappo, Z-A-P-P-O, that's Zappo. Get Zappo today."
4. It might have a famous football player saying that he eats Zappo every day, implying that this is why he is such a good football player. A football player would be used, of course, only if the people you were trying to impress considered football players to be high-prestige and high-status individuals—people they would like to be like. You would adjust your choice of the actor in the ad according to the audience you wished to per-

Reprinted by permission of the Chicago Tribune-New York News Syndicate.

suade. A roller derby star would probably not help you sell a Rolls-Royce.

5. It would demonstrate for the audience the value of eating Zappo, perhaps by showing all the beautiful, rich, sexy, and completely happy people who eat Zappo.

How do you think the advertising business is doing with respect to the use of these principles? Have you ever seen a TV commercial that fits this description?

Actually, persuasive communications, such as speeches, TV commercials, and newspaper articles, sometimes fail to change attitudes, despite what seem to be optimal conditions. The best example of this is the failure of the antismoking campaign to decrease cigarette consumption in this country—despite some very clever and dramatic TV spots, a barrage of newspaper and magazine articles, warnings on cigarette packages, and a ban on TV cigarette ads. One major problem, obviously, is getting the audience to attend to the message; smokers probably pay less attention to the antismoking ads and obtain less information about the harmful effects of smoking. As for the warning on the cigarette pack, the odds are that it is perceived rarely, if at all.

With regard to cigarette smoking, one technique of persuasion that has shown some promise is *role playing.* In one study smokers were required to assume the role of a patient who had just been diagnosed as having lung cancer. The technique was similar to psychodrama (see Chapter 12), with each subject acting out the role of the dying cancer patient and with the experimenter playing the doctor role and repeatedly giving antismoking information. Role playing significantly reduced smoking in this study. Other, similar studies have shown significant attitude change resulting from giving speeches in favor of the desired attitude, especially if the subject must improvise the speech. Thus, getting a bigot to stand up before an audience and improvise a speech favoring equality, integration, and civil rights will produce more attitude change in the bigot than in the group of people who merely listen to the speech. Can you see how consistency theory would account for this? Why is it better to have a person improvise a speech as opposed to just reading a prepared speech?

The use of psychotherapy in behavior disorders is, in many cases, conceived of by the therapist as a process of attitude changes. Usually the goal of this type of therapy is self-insight, which is basically a matter of changing attitudes about oneself. Group psychotherapy obviously involves social psychology and attitude change. The sensitivity training-encounter group movement got its start in Bethel, Maine, at the National Training Laboratory, where students of the distinguished social psychologist Kurt Lewin pioneered the basic techniques. We will have more to say about this form of psychotherapy in Chapter 12.

Persuasive communication is involved in just about all aspects of our lives. Consider political campaigns and the massive advertising involved. Consider sermons delivered at churches. Consider government propaganda on drugs and alcoholism. Attitude formation and attitude change is a major aspect of education. We hope that some of your attitudes about behavior will be changed by reading this book.

SEXISM, "AGE-ISM," AND RACISM

We have already experienced the effects of psychological studies on social change in the social revolution following from the Supreme Court ruling against school segregation. In that historic case — Brown *vs.* Board of Education — social psychological studies were cited documenting the perfidious effects of racial segregation.

Social psychologists are now focusing on other forms of discrimination. Two prominent social concerns are the injustices stemming from sexism and racism. The social psychological view has consistently been that biological differences such as race have been erroneously used to explain social differences. The current extension of legislation against sexual discrimination is, in part, an extension of social psychological findings.

Currently, mandatory retirement at age 65 is being recognized as discriminatory. State and federal legislatures are in the process of raising the age of mandatory retirement or eliminating such rules altogether. The majority of adults are in favor of voluntary retirement.

Social psychologists and social gerontologists have documented the negative effects of prejudice against old persons. The social sciences, in correcting errors in social stereotypes and thereby altering our treatment of others in the direction of greater fairness, have changed our social lives in profound ways.

Figure 10-7
The social reconstruction syndrome: A benign cycle of increasing competence through social system inputs

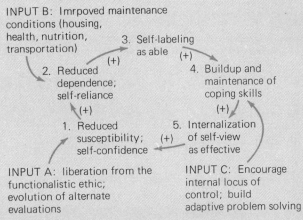

Bengston has adapted the concept of a social breakdown syndrome to the problems of aging in America. The syndrome involves a cycle of increasing incompetence based on the effects of negative stereotypes or labeling. The population at risk, in this case elderly persons, is susceptible to psychological breakdown which leads to their being labeled incompetent. Such labeling pushes individuals into the role of sick or dependent persons, so that they begin to view themselves as inadequate. This self-identification makes the person more vulnerable to breakdown, and the cycle repeats itself with increasing negative effects on the individual.

The cycle can be broken, however, by several benevolent inputs, as described in the social reconstruction syndrome (see Figure 10-7).

Liberation from a functionalistic ethic means getting persons to adopt some other evaluative criterion than productivity. Self-worth might be judged in terms of self-insight or humanitarian goods. Improving the environment in ways that enable a person to be more mobile (hence more independent) counters the effect of negative labeling. Finally, a sense of internal locus of control (perception of oneself as in control of desired outcomes) has

The Myth of Aging

The stereotypes most people hold regarding old persons are remarkably inaccurate. Erdmure Palmore has developed a short quiz for assessing knowledge about aging. How much do you know about old people? How many of the following questions can you get right? Circle "T" for True, or "F" for False.

T F 1. The majority of old people (past age 65) are senile (i.e., defective memory, disoriented, or demented).

T F 2. All five senses tend to decline in old age.

T F 3. Most old people have no interest in, or capacity for, sexual relations.

T F 4. Lung capacity tends to decline in old age.

T F 5. The majority of old people feel miserable most of the time.

T F 6. Physical strength tends to decline in old age.

T F 7. At least one-tenth of the aged are living in long-stay institutions (i.e., nursing homes, mental hospitals, homes for the aged, etc.).

T F 8. Aged drivers have fewer accidents per person than drivers under age 65.

T F 9. Most older workers cannot work as effectively as younger workers.

T F 10. About 80% of the aged are healthy enough to carry out their normal activities.

T F 11. Most old people are set in their ways and unable to change.

T F 12. Old people usually take longer to learn something new.

T F 13. It is almost impossible for most old people to learn new things.

T F 14. The reaction time of most old people tends to be slower than reaction time of younger people.

T F 15. In general, most old people are pretty much alike.

T F 16. The majority of old people are seldom bored.

T F 17. The majority of old people are socially isolated and lonely.

T F 18. Older workers have fewer accidents than younger workers.

T F 19. Over 15% of the U.S. population are now age 65 or over.

T F 20. Most medical practitioners tend to give low priority to the aged.

T F 21. The majority of older people have incomes below the poverty level (as defined by the Federal Government).

T F 22. The majority of old people are working or would like to have some kind of work to do (including housework and volunteer work).

T F 23. Older people tend to become more religious as they age.

T F 24. The majority of old people are seldom irritated or angry.

T F 25. The health and socioeconomic status of older people (compared to younger people) in the year 2000 will probably be about the same as now.

The key to the correct answer is simple: all the odd numbered items are false and all the even numbered are true.

been found to be associated with positive psychological adjustment.

PUBLIC OPINION POLLING

In order to study attitudes and opinions, psychologists have developed techniques for measuring attitudes accurately and efficiently. The development of these measurement techniques has had an enormous impact on our lives, and in the case of public opinion polling this impact has not always been beneficial. It is possible, by **sampling techniques,** to measure a small number of people and determine the attitudes of the entire group from which the small number was sampled. Thus, one could get a fairly good idea of how all people in the United States feel about a particular issue or event by **random sampling** — asking just a few hundred people.

Public opinion polls are valuable sources of data on the beliefs, opinions, attitudes, and values of representative samples of large populations. Although most psychologists recognize the importance of generalizing to a large population, seldom do they have the opportunity to collect data on more than very restricted and rather particular groups such as college sophomores or white rats. Increasingly, social psychologists are recognizing the possibilities of using poll data to test hypotheses. Being interested and involved in attitude assessment, social psychologists have contributed extensively to the design of public opinion polls.

The technique of polling public opinion is much abused, as you probably know. But when properly conducted, polls are exceedingly accurate estimators of public opinion. Their impact as a contributory factor to democratic processes has been reflected as much in their misuse as in their proper application. Two factors, which we discussed in Chapter 1, are of great importance in evaluating polls: (1) that the data are based on random selection of respondents from the appropriate population and (2) that the basis for the data collection is not biased (leading questions, for

"This survey indicates you can fool seventeen per cent of the people a hundred per cent of the time, thirty-four per cent of the people fifty-one per cent of the time, and a hundred per cent of the people twelve per cent of the time."

The New Yorker, September 19, 1977. Drawing by Stevenson; © 1977 The New Yorker Magazine, Inc.

example, are to be avoided). Few polling organizations meet these two criteria, which has led to some lack of confidence on the part of the public. Clearly, just because an organization calls itself an "independent research firm" does not ensure either its independence (lack of bias) or research competence.

APPLYING PRINCIPLES OF SOCIAL INFLUENCE

International Conflict

The problems of generalizing from psychological studies of conflict between game players or young children to studies of conflict between nations are many and difficult. Nevertheless, social psychological analysis of international conflict can be illustrated by an impressive interpretation of a partial reduction in Russian-American tension accompanying what has been called the J.F.K. experiment.

What You Can't Have, You Duz Want— A Tide Stronger Than Dirt

Kenneth Goodall

When Big Brother swoops down on Big Mama and outlaws her favorite laundry detergent, how will she react? Such, roughly, was the question investigated by social psychologist Michael B. Mazis in Miami alfter Dade County authorities banned the sale, possession or use of phosphate detergents.

Mazis saw the ban as a good opportunity to test the predictive power of psychological reactance theory in a field setting. This theory states that when a person's freedom of choice or action is restricted he or she will experience psychological reactance, a motivational state directed toward regaining the freedom. It figures. First advanced by Jack Brehm in 1966, the theory has generated much lab but little field experimentation.

When the Dade County antipollution measure went into effect, few of the popular brands of detergent were available in no-phosphate formulas, so many Miami housewives had to switch brands as well as formulas. All of them found their choices drastically reduced.

Mazis speculated that Miami housewives would be aroused and "feel an increased desire to have the forbidden detergent. . . ." This reactance, in turn, should result in "higher effectiveness attributed to phosphate detergents . . ." and "more negative attitudes toward governmental regulation of environmental matters . . ." by housewives in Miami than in a control city, Tampa, where phosphate detergents were still legal.

Pollsters interviewed 76 middle-class housewives in Miami and 45 in Tampa. All had at least one child under 16 living at home and all had depended primarily on phosphate detergents during the previous six months. Asked to rate the effectiveness of these phosphate detergents on such characteristics as whiteness, freshness, stain removal and gentleness, the now-deprived Miami housewives gave them significantly higher overall ratings than did the Tampa housewives. Miami housewives also expressed significantly less agreement with the statement that "Legal restrictions should be imposed against the sale of detergents containing phosphates." So Mazis' data supported his forbidden-fruit predictions. . . .

Mazis says that his study shows that psychological reactance is not solely a laboratory phenomenon and has public policy implications for administrative decisions and ordinances that restrict the public's freedom of choice. . . .

Psychology Today
September 1975

Social or legal pressure to change attitudes can sometimes backfire. Could dissonance theory predict this effect?

On June 10, 1963, at the American University in Washington, D.C., President Kennedy delivered an important policy speech that took a conciliatory tone toward Russia. He indicated that constructive changes had taken place that could lead to solutions to world problems, and he urged the American people to reexamine their attitudes toward Russia and the cold war. *Izvestia*, in turn, published the speech in full, and Russia reversed its objection to the Western proposal that United Nations observers be sent to war-torn Yemen. The United States then lifted its objection to full status for the Hungarian delegation to the United Nations, and Russia announced it had halted production of strategic bombers. During the course of these events there were clear signs of a cold war thaw. By November 22, 1963, additional tension-reducing events included (1) signing the limited nuclear test ban treaty, (2) discussion of joint space exploration, (3) consideration of new consular facilities, (4) sale of U.S. wheat to Russia, and (5) continuing meetings between the two sides to explore other matters of interest. The experiment slowed down with the approach of a new election campaign and ended with Kennedy's assassination.

Considerable reduction in conflict occurred largely because of improved communication, which in turn helped correct the false images both sides held of each other. This allowed them to pursue matters of mutual interest and concern. The initial friendly overture by President Kennedy reduced tension, which in turn enhanced communication, helped correct biased stereotypes (thus increasing social support for change), and initiated a decreasing cold war spiral. In addition, the improved communication and continuing reciprocity led to mutual dependence for attaining common goals. As we saw in the Robbers Cave experiment, cooperation in solving common problems is an important condition for reducing conflict.

We conclude that four factors are important in reducing international conflict: (1) a unilateral gesture toward conflict reduction, (2) increased communication, (3) heightened awareness of mutual dependence in order to identify the opportunities that exist for nations to pursue common goals, and (4) actual cooperation between nations to achieve these goals. Perhaps the joint space mission involving Soviet and American astronauts was not as trivial an event as it may have seemed at first glance.

Social Influence and Conformity

In this brief section we will mention instances of social influence and conformity in action. This is not really an application of social psychology principles but is rather a small set of illustrations of these principles.

Consider the influence of a single person over another person. How many times have you done something just because someone in authority told you to do it, even to the point (in some cases) of doing things you felt were wrong? Lying to someone is a good example, and the whole notion of a "white lie" suggests the operation of the consistency principle. There are many examples of crimes being committed by people who were "under the influence" of another person, usually a loved one. Occasionally, in rare instances, there is the accusation that hypnosis was used to make the person commit a crime, but the fact is that hypnosis is an instance of social influence between two people, and the hypnotic procedures themselves are not necessary in

"A word to the wise, Benson. People are asking why they don't see Old Glory on *your* bike."

Playboy, June 1971. Reproduced by special permission of PLAYBOY Magazine; copyright © 1971 by Playboy.

order to get people to behave in unusual, even illegal ways (see the discussion of hypnosis in Appendix D).

It is obvious that conformity is everywhere. Think about what you are wearing right now and how it fits in with the style of dress of the groups you belong to. Think of a time when you and several friends went to a movie or a lecture and all your friends said they liked it but you didn't. What did you do in this case? Have you ever been with a group of friends who wanted to do something that you found offensive, immoral, or just simply distasteful? What did you do? How do you think people get started drinking, smoking, taking drugs, stealing, and so on? Why is it that a drug addict who is cured or a paroled criminal who is rehabilitated cannot stay "clean" when he or she returns to old social habits and old friends? Why do parents so often fail to appreciate why their children can behave the way they do — wear long hair and "strange" clothes and speak a "strange" language? And why do children see their parents' behavior as equally strange? Is there a generation gap? Is it because the social norms are different for different generations?

Social Principles and Self-Understanding

The major application of social psychological literature may well be its role in increasing our understanding of ourselves as social beings.

Social Support (Love) Tied to Better Health

LOS ANGELES — Whether a high fat diet leads to a heart attack may depend on how well the person is loved, a public health authority says.

Dr. John C. Cassel wasn't scoffing at the role played by diet in causing heart disease.

Rather he was emphasizing the less well-recognized importance of warm social contacts, like love, in preventing disease.

Prevention of disease, he said, depends as much on the psychological and social climate the person lives in as it does on things like diet and housing.

Recent Study

In an interview here, Cassel, who is head of the epidemiology department at the University of North Carolina School of Public Health, told of a recent study to learn the number of complications that occurred in 200 women giving birth to their first baby.

Women who had had many recent social adjustments in addition to pregnancy—like changing residence or quitting a job—had a 90 per cent chance of complication if they had little warm social support by their husbands and families.

If they were well loved—even though they had had many recent social readjustments—the complication rate was 30 per cent, Cassel said.

Cassel believes the absence of strong, positive social support for their behavior is the true explanation for the much higher incidences of infant mortality and diseases of all kinds among ghetto dwellers.

The lack of warm social approval can result in marked alterations in hormone levels and nervous system changes which increase their susceptibility to disease, he said. . . .

The Denver Post
April 26, 1972

Social relationships play an important and intimate role in emotions. And as we know, emotions are related to physical health. Therefore the study of social relationships could give us information that would be useful in the treatment and prevention of physical illnesses.

Take as an example the implications of the social psychological findings on social prejudice and stereotyping. The insidious effects of prejudice have been extensively documented in social psychological laboratories. We have become increasingly aware of the psychologically harmful effects of the hostility of prejudice, which, when combined with the binding force of social stereotypes and the destructive force of the corresponding self-fulfilling prophecies, produces social and psychological pathology. This awareness has contributed to concrete actions, such as the 1954 ruling by the Supreme Court ordering school integration.

Along a different line, social psychologists have shown an increasing interest in the effects of sexual discrimination. Evidence is accumulating that characteristics once thought to be simply innate and characteristically female or male are really social products. From an early age females and males have different socializing experiences. They learn what is considered sex-appropriate behavior. They then tend to conform to those expectations (see Chapter 8). We do not claim that *all* sex differences are psychological. Many of them are, however, and these can lead to unfortunate and unwarranted forms of sexual discrimination.

Understanding prejudice and how it might work within us, understanding sexual differences and their source, and understanding our social motives, our capacity for social development, our morality, and our concept of social justice are important for getting along with other human beings. What insights we have at present are at least in part a product of social psychological research. It is reasonable to expect a fuller understanding of ourselves as social beings as this research continues to progress.

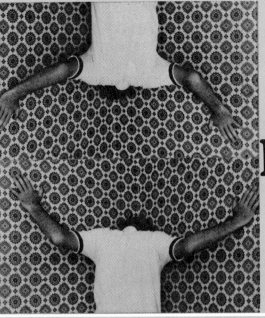

11

Psychopathology

The term **psychopathology** covers a tremendous range of behaviors. For example, it can be applied to a college student who gets violently ill before every final exam; a man who cannot quit gambling even though he does not enjoy it; a 22-year-old girl who believes she is the Virgin Mary; a woman who consumes a fifth of vodka every day; and a man in his late thirties who believes his mind is being controlled by creatures from Mars using invisible laser beams.

The extreme diversity of psychopathological behaviors, indicated by the examples above, makes it difficult to formulate a single definition to fit all cases. Some psychologists have tried to define the group of behaviors traditionally labeled psychopathological as behaviors that are characterized by *subjective discomfort,* that is, feeling anxious, depressed, or otherwise dissatisfied without apparent cause. The person's discomfort seems to be "all in the mind," as in the case of a person who claims to feel chest pains but has no physical signs of disease. However, in some cases the *lack* of discomfort may indicate psychopathology, as when a person responds to the death of a loved one or flunking out of school with no signs of grief or depression. Thus, this definition does not cover all instances.

Psychopathological behavior has also been defined as behavior that *deviates from the norm.* This definition is also unsatisfactory because it includes positive abnormalities such as great intelligence or creativity, which are seldom considered pathological. In addition, some deviant behaviors are considered more significant than others—eating peas with a knife might be more unusual than suicide in our country, but it would be considered much less pathological.

Others have defined psychopathological behavior as *maladaptive behavior,* that is, behavior which has adverse effects for either society or the individual. This definition clearly covers many of the conditions we described, such as compulsive gambling, alcoholism, and suicide, and it comes closer to what we mean by psychopathology. However, it fails to designate why the undesirable behavior occurred or how to modify it.

A DEFINITION OF PSYCHOPATHOLOGY

We shall define psychopathology as *the inability to behave in a socially appropriate way such that the consequences of one's behavior are maladaptive for oneself or society.* Thus, inability might reflect *organic deficiency* (such as brain damage), *functional deficiency* (lack of knowledge, competence, or motivation), or a combination. In short, a person might fail to behave appropriately or adaptively for any of three reasons; the individual might not have the necessary physiological equipment, knowledge, or competence, or he or she might not want to behave appropriately.

The word "appropriate" is important in our definition because labeling behavior as abnormal is necessarily a culturally determined act. A woman from a rural area who thinks she is hexed may be behaving quite appropriately in her community, although her behavior would be considered abnormal by a psychologist or psychiatrist in the city. The anthropologist Ruth Benedict notes that trances and seizures, which most cultures consider pathological, may be a sign of prestige and power in some Indian tribes of California. The daily life of the people who live on an island in northwest Melanesia is based on suspicion and paranoia. They are preoccupied with being poisoned by a neighbor, and the person who failed to be suspicious would be viewed as behaving inappropriately and maladaptively. Thus there is no single set of behaviors that is considered appropriate in all societies and cultures.

MODELS OF PSYCHOPATHOLOGY

Part of the problem of defining psychopathology is due to the fact that psychologists lack a complete understanding of maladaptive behavior and its causes and cures. Thus much of our discussion in this chapter will be based on *theories of psychopathology.* As we saw in our discussion of personality, psychological theories are typically based on a framework or structure, a

TABLE 11-1   Models of Psychopathology

Model	Theoretical Cause of Abnormality	Theoretical Cure	Therapist
Medical	A process similar to that underlying physical illness	Medication, rest, physical treatment	Physician
Dynamic	Unconscious conflicts	Insight into conflicts	Specially trained physician or mental health professional
Behavioral	Maladaptive learning	Learning or relearning	Behavior modifier
Phenomenological	Lack of meaning in life or cut off from experiencing	Development of awareness of here and now	Phenomenological therapist
Ethical	Lack of responsibility	Acceptance of responsibility	Reality therapist

The New Yorker, December 23, 1974. Reprinted by permission of S, Gross.

model, which provides a way of conceptualizing behavioral observations. A model provides the basic assumptions from which various theories are derived. We will examine five major models that serve as the basis for most theories of psychopathology: the medical model, dynamic model, behavioral model, phenomenological model, and ethical model (see Table 11–1). Like a theory, a model is neither true nor false but only useful or not useful. A model is useful if it leads to valid explanations and effective therapies.

The particular model one chooses has profound impact on how one sees others and on whether one conceptualizes feelings and behaviors as pathological or normal. The model also serves as a guide in selecting both the kind of therapy to be used for persons with emotional problems and the source of the treatment. The classification of psychopathology in this chapter is influenced by the medical and dynamic models, largely because that is the system most commonly used today. It will be apparent in the next chapter on psychotherapy, however, that different models organize or classify abnormal behavior in very different ways.

Medical Model

In the **medical model** pathological behaviors are viewed as symptoms of a disease or a process

like a disease. Hence the term *mental illness.* One basic assumption of the medical model is that emotional problems, like physical diseases, can be fitted into diagnostic categories that have implications for cause and treatment. Historically, the use of the medical model is important. During the nineteenth century people who claimed they had no control over their inappropriate behavior were seen as malingerers or fakers. They were either ignored or sent to prison. In an effort at reform, some physicians claimed that these people should be thought of as sick in the mind. Thus, people with emotional problems came to be defined as ill rather than as loafers, and they were transferred from prisons to hospitals.

The medical model is still in common use today, although many people both outside and within the medical profession are disturbed by its unfortunate consequences. If an emotional problem is truly an illness, then one might argue that physicians are the only people capable of helping the emotionally disturbed. Although such restrictions may be appropriate in cases in which there is a known organic involvement (such as psychosomatic illness), or genetic or biochemical causes (as may be true in schizophrenia), there are many other cases in which other kinds of treatment are clearly called for. A person who is anxious and cannot get along with others typically does not have a physical illness. The disorder could perhaps be viewed as analogous to physical illness, but this does not automatically make it a "medical" problem. The problem is not so much something that

The relatively high income of psychiatrists and other mental health professionals has led some people to challenge whether persons in lucrative private practices have the client's welfare as their basic concern.

Others have referred to psychotherapy as the purchase of friendship. Many mental health professionals, however, do base their fees on ability to pay.

the person *has* as it is something that the individual *is* or *does*.

Furthermore, the medical model has led people to feel no sense of responsibility for their behavior. It is common for persons to ask therapists to "cure" them of emotional problems in the same way they ask physicians to cure a cold. Typically, the therapist has no "cure"—the patient must assume some responsibility for changing his or her own behavior.

Finally, although the term "mentally ill" was thought to be a more humane label for people with emotional problems than "insane" or "lunatic," few people view the mentally ill with the same compassion they feel for the physically ill. The negative attitudes and fears associated with the irrational, unpredictable, and sometimes dangerous behaviors of the emotionally disturbed have become associated with the term "mental illness." Thus, although the medical model provided the impetus for hospital care and medical treatment of people with emotional problems, it did not lead to much attitude change, as the "jokes" about "men in white coats" perhaps indicate.

In spite of its negative consequences, the medical model has been exceedingly useful in the treatment of psychopathology. As we shall see, much of the terminology, explanation, and therapy to be discussed in this chapter reflects the conception of psychopathology as a disease process.

Dynamic Model

In the **dynamic model** the basic assumption is that abnormal behavior reflects a "dynamic" battle or conflict occurring between parts or aspects of a person's personality rather than any physical or organic deficiencies. Ironically, it was Freud, a physician by training, who pioneered the dynamic model. He found the medical model unsuitable for treatment of abnormal behavior and developed in its place the first truly dynamic theory.

Freud believed that behavior is partially determined by psychological conflicts of which the individual is totally unaware. He proposed that mental processes occur at three levels: the **conscious,** the **preconscious,** and the **unconscious.** The conscious is made up of the ideas, thoughts, and images that one is aware of at any given moment. The preconscious consists of ideas, thoughts, and images that one is not aware of at the moment but that can be brought into awareness with little or no difficulty. Finally, the unconscious is that part of the mental process that one resists being aware of—the unacceptable drives of sex and aggression, and the memories, thoughts, impulses, and ideas that were once conscious but were removed from awareness because they made the individual anxious or tense.

Freud proposed that anxiety grows out of socially unacceptable impulses, the expression of which would lead to punishment or disapproval from one's self or others. For example, a child might find that his mother is terribly hurt and disapproving of the anger he feels and expresses toward her. He might then try to forget that he has angry feelings; although he is still unconsciously angry toward his mother, he consciously tries to convince himself and others of his devotion. If the process ended here, there would be no problem—the child would have rid himself of all unpleasant or unacceptable thoughts and feelings. However, as we will see, Freud believed that these thoughts persist, causing unconscious conflicts, and that they tend to be expressed behaviorally in ways that are often socially inappropriate. According to the dynamic model, therapy should make the person aware of unconscious processes.

Theoretically, the medical model and the dynamic model are independent of one another. One can accept the basic assumptions of one of the models without accepting the assumptions of the other. Historically, however, the two models are closely related. In the United States some of the strongest proponents of the dynamic model have been psychiatrists, who are themselves trained in medicine. But recently many mental health workers have come to accept the idea that one can view humankind as functioning in a dynamic way without assuming the process is similar to physical disease.

Behavioral Model

Behaviorists, as we have seen, believe that because the unconscious is by definition unavailable for direct study, it is neither a scientific nor a useful concept. They assume, rather, that a person's observable actions determine whether he or she is normal or abnormal; one is abnormal if one *acts* abnormally. It follows that the way to treat psychopathology is to change the person's behavior.

According to the **behavioral model,** all behavior, normal or otherwise, is a product of learning about the environment. Behavior is determined by one's history of reinforcement. Thus, abnormal behavior can be changed into normal behavior by retraining (reeducating or reconditioning) individuals (that is, teaching them new and appropriate responses to environmental stimuli) and/or by changing their

Psychologist Alters Childhood Schizophrenia

Sandra Gittens

NEW YORK — Dr. Irene Kassorla claims her professional life essentially started when she was 42.

That's after she developed new techniques which enabled her to generate speech from mute, autistic children, thereby markedly altering childhood schizophrenia.

While attending the University of California at Los Angeles she was assigned hospital observation duties and says it was there she realized doctors were reinforcing psychosis.

"I went back to my school and wrote a paper saying doctors are reinforcing psychosis at such and such hospital," she said in an interview here.

After the papers were graded and handed back she recalls that her professor asked, "Who is Irene Kassorla? May I speak with you for a moment?"

"I thought he was going to do something drastic; instead he said, 'Look, what do you want?'. I told him I wanted a patient and I wanted to try out my own ideas, which of course was absurd because you don't get a patient for another 10 years—when you're close to your doctorate," she explained.

She got a patient, nevertheless, and within a week, she says, she was able to get remarkable results from a sick little girl.

By simply reversing what was done at the hospital, Dr. Kassorla said she reinforced healthy responses, ignored the bizarre, and the child got better.

"Before," she said, "doctors would see a psychotic doing something crazy and say, 'Oh, that's all right!' I wouldn't say, 'Oh, that's all right.' I'd say, 'Hey, that's crazy, what the heck are you doing? Stop it!'

"I'm never dishonest with such a person. I give him reality, and this is what is important about my techniques—treat the psychotic normally and you know what, he acts normal!" . . .

The Sunday Camera *(Boulder, Colo.)*
July 14, 1974

Perhaps a significant portion of the "abnormal" behavior of mentally ill people is inadvertently rewarded by others. Behavior therapists believe that changing these reinforcement contingencies is the best way to eliminate the undesired behaviors. This is a major principle of the behavioral model.

Theorists assume that the kinds of labels you employ to identify particular experiences that you have affect significantly the way you feel about yourself and the way life is going.

environment in certain ways. Bandura's social learning theory (see Chapter 9) is typical of the theories based on the behavioral model. The application of learning principles to emotional problems is fairly recent, but the behavioral model poses a strong challenge to the medical and dynamic models and has provided the basis for several effective therapeutic approaches generally known as behavior modification.

Phenomenological Model

Carl Rogers, Abraham Maslow, and Fritz Perls proposed a model that emphasizes the importance of the person's existence in the here and now, placing heavy stress on the individual's own efforts to actualize his or her potential. Moving away from the stimulus-response view of causation of the behaviorists, the **phenomenological model** focuses on the internal reality of the conscious mind. Feelings and intuition become a part of the phenomenological understanding of causes of behavior.

One type of phenomenological model is the *existential model,* which focuses on the need for each person to develop his or her own meaning for life, to take responsibility for guiding personal growth. *Existential anxiety* is experienced when life seems meaningless. Rather than assuming that a person's behavior is determined by past experiences, the existential model assumes that behavior is determined by the choices the individual makes in life.

Ethical Model

Thomas Szasz (1961), in an attack on the medical model, suggested that having "problems in living" is the most appropriate way of looking at those who suffer from emotional problems. He proposed that life is not essentially harmonious and satisfying but rather is filled with stresses (economic, social, biological, and political) one must cope with. Individuals who need professional help are those who cannot handle these problems by themselves.

Szasz proposed that the medical "myth" of abnormal behavior allows people to avoid the *moral* responsibility of their actions. The **ethical model** assumes that individuals are responsible for their own behavior. The same idea underlies Glasser's (1965) concept of reality therapy. For Glasser, abnormal behavior is behaving irresponsibly. Only when people are ready to accept responsibility for the consequences of their behavior can they adequately cope with their problems.

The ethical and existential models are the only ones that assume people have responsibility for their own behavior rather than attributing the behavior to illness, unresolved childhood conflicts, reinforcement, or other governing factors. The question of responsibility for individual behavior has far-reaching social implications. For example, our courts of law are currently having difficulty resolving the issue of personal responsibility. If a person's behavior is determined by his or her reinforcement history, how can the individual be held responsible for illegal behavior?

CLASSIFICATION OF PSYCHOPATHOLOGY

Psychopathology can take many and varied forms, as our examples thus far indicate. In order to simplify and make sense of these diverse forms, classification systems have been developed. There is no single classification system that all workers in this field agree on. For one thing, psychologists and other professionals usually disagree about the diagnosis (classification statement) of any one case. From their independent diagnoses, one might legitimately wonder whether two psychologists are talking about the same case. Diagnoses are usually reliable on gross classifications, such as whether a person is neurotic or psychotic, but not when a more specialized analysis is attempted. If there is no agreement on the diagnosis, of what value is it to make one in the first place?

Advantages and Disadvantages of Classification

The chief advantage of any classification system is communication. Diagnostic labels convey in a single word a lot of general information about a person's behavior and enable therapists, researchers, and others to discuss psychopathology in general or in specific cases. Knowing that an individual has symptoms similar to those of other patients also helps a psychologist form reasonable expectations about the individual's future behavior and chances for improvement. In turn, this knowledge allows the psychologist to plan and conduct the most suitable therapy. However, since no two cases are exactly alike, the gain in communication and treatment planning can be costly, for it inevitably obscures the unique features of the individual case.

Another problem is that labeling someone may have the effect of making the person behave according to what he or she thinks are the therapist's expectations (for example, suicidally). The therapist, if anxious to prove that the diagnosis is correct, may pay special attention to aspects of the person's behavior that support the diagnosis and completely fail to notice other important aspects that do not fit it. Thus, the diagnostic prophecy becomes self-fulfilling.

Classification is important for communication, and thus we spend considerable time on it in this chapter. But we should not be fooled into thinking that classification is the same as understanding and treatment. No classification system should be regarded as explanatory. There is a tendency to feel that behavior can be explained by attaching a label to it, but labeling is neither explanation nor cure.

With all these drawbacks, it is no wonder that the trend in clinical psychology today is away from an emphasis on diagnostic classification. Clinical psychologists are primarily interested in changing behavior. They use all the therapeutic tools available to them without an undue emphasis on the names they happen to apply to disorders. And given the state of the diagnostic arts, this is only appropriate.

Not all mental health professionals see diagnosis as appropriate. In particular, those who are oriented toward the behavioral, phenomenological, or ethical models will often respond to a person's problems on an individual basis without attempting to classify the behavior into a particular category.

Major Diagnostic Categories

The most common scheme for classifying abnormal behavior is based on grouping people according to similar behavioral or emotional symptoms. (Note the use of medical terminology.) The assumption is that behaviors can be grouped together in meaningful and reliable ways. Thus everyone who behaves in a certain way would be given the same label. The term symptom is commonly used because of the assumption that the behaviors classified as abnormal are indications of underlying conflicts in the way that a fever is a symptom of various illnesses, such as a cold or infection.

The classification system in wide use in the United States today is based on the medical and dynamic models. Other classification schemes could be based on such dimensions as the causes of the emotional problems, the preferred treatment, the person's reinforcement history, the social environment, or the types of life choices the person has made. However, there is presently no evidence that any of these classification schemes would be more useful than the one that is commonly accepted now.

The procedure of deciding how to classify a person is known as *diagnosis*. Several kinds of evidence are typically taken into account in making a diagnosis, including family history and biographical information, descriptions of the problem behavior, and assessments of the person's intellectual, emotional, and personality characteristics. This information is usually obtained by having a relative or friend fill out a questionnaire giving the person's medical history and other data, interviewing the person, and administering appropriate tests. Assessment techniques such as personality inventories and projective tests are discussed in detail in Appendix C.

The major diagnostic categories of the present system are neurosis, psychosomatic illness, personality disorders, and psychosis. We will briefly define each of these classifications before discussing them and the various subcategories in detail. Keep in mind throughout this discussion that most, if not all, forms of psychopathology result from or are most commonly and strongly manifested during stress. Thus, psychopathology can be seen as an abnormal or inappropriate reaction to stress.

The primary defining characteristic of **neurosis** is anxiety, which can be described as the experience of fear in the absence of, or disproportionate to, the objective danger. Neurosis refers to mental processes and behavior designed to avoid or reduce the anxiety. In neurosis there is no gross distortion of reality. The straight "A" student who is petrified of making a "B" (exaggerated fear) or who is constantly concerned about failing (unfounded fear) might very well be neurotic. (The term **nervous breakdown** is often used by lay persons to describe those whose emotional problems are so severe that they can no longer cope with a job or home responsibilities. It is not a description of the physical state of the person's nerves, nor is it synonymous with neurosis.)

The defining characteristic of a **psychosomatic illness** (the latest term is **psychophysiologic reaction**) is the presence of a physical illness in which psychological processes have played an important causative role. Asthma,

peptic ulcers, hives, arthritis, and to a lesser extent the common cold all have possible psychosomatic elements. More recently psychological factors, particularly emotional stress, have been strongly implicated in heart disease and even cancer.

The primary defining characteristic of a **personality disorder** (formerly called **character disorder**) is a dominant personality trait leading to maladaptive behavior that the individual typically has no motivation to change; examples are alcoholism, drug addiction, and sexually deviant behavior. The behavior is maladaptive from the point of view of society and not the person. The individual experiences little or no anxiety and exhibits no gross distortions of reality other than a failure in self-appraisal.

The defining characteristic of **psychosis** is gross disturbance in thought processes, distortion of reality, or loss of reality testing. Psychotic persons can no longer tell the difference between fantasy and what is actually happening, and they lose voluntary control over thoughts, feelings, and actions. Psychosis is usually accompanied by delusions and hallucinations. A **delusion** is an unshakable idea or belief that is held in the face of contradictory evidence, simple logic, or common experience. For example, a person may insist, despite all objective evidence to the contrary, that he is Jesus Christ or the President. **Hallucinations** are a form of bizarre or distorted perception without corresponding sensory stimuli. The person perceives visual images, hears voices or sounds, and feels things over the body when no such events are occurring in the objective world. Hallucinations thus differ from illusions, which are misperceptions of sensory information. In short, the primary defining characteristic of psychosis is *faulty cognition*.

Another major distinction typically made is between functional and organic disorders. A **functional disorder** refers to an emotional problem that is the result of psychological variables rather than biological ones. For example, a person who has a phobia about going outdoors may be thought of as unconsciously avoiding the anxiety associated with failure on the job or some other anxiety-provoking situation. On the other hand, **organic disorders** are those caused typically by impairment of brain functioning. There is an interesting case history of

Neurotics Lose "Standing" as Word Vanishes

AP

NEW YORK — Next year the uncounted thousands of Americans undergoing therapy to iron out their personal neurotic wrinkles are going to have a little problem: Neurosis is going to vanish.

The American Psychiatric Association is doing away with neurosis. They have decided "it doesn't mean anything."

That is what Dr. Robert L. Spitzer says. He is the same New York psychiatrist who played a central role four years ago in the APA's vote to take homosexuality off the list of mental illnesses.

Spitzer has been busy since then heading the task force that is writing the APA's third Diagnostic and Statistical Manual of Mental Disorders. It is a dictionary of mental ailments, used mainly as a guide in making diagnoses.

The manual will be published in late 1979 and, for the first time since a controversial Austrian named Freud began sorting them out, the various sorts of neuroses will not be listed.

Hysterical conversion neurosis will be gone. So will depressive neurosis. Let's not forget depersonalization neurosis or anxiety neurosis.

And what will the diagnosing doctor find listed in their place?

Disorders, mostly: somatoform disorders, major depressive disorders, anxiety disorders and, of course, dissociative disorders.

"The term neurosis has been used in so many different ways that we believe it no longer has a very precise meaning. More often it's defined by what it's not—it's not a known physical problem, for instance, or it's not psychosis." Spitzer says.

So the task force searched psychiatric literature and devised new, specific categories for ailments traditionally considered neurotic. They say the ailments and their listed symptoms will be based on data, statistics, hard evidence. Not theory.

Traditionally, Freud's followers have defined neurosis as a symptom of repressed subconscious thoughts. They believe that when you dam back such things as, say, incestuous desires, a neurotic reaction bubbles up. Depression, for instance, or wide swings in mood.

The problem, says Dr. Arthur Shapiro, a task force consultant, is that "you can't identify neuroses reliably. Even psychoanalysts don't agree. So you identify it in other, more specific, measurable, documentable ways — as anxiety reactions, for example, or depressive reactions."

Spitzer says the change is not so revolutionary as it might appear. He says the varieties of neurosis will simply be given new names and very precise definitions. . . .

Rocky Mountain News, *Denver September 10, 1978*

The technical names of the various diagnostic categories in psychopathology are agreed upon by convention and are listed in a manual published by the American Psychiatric Association. This is called the Diagnostic and Statistical Manual of Mental Disorders, or the DSM for short. In this book, we are using the second edition of the manual, known as the DSM-II. In late 1979 DSM-III will appear, and there may be some controversial changes, such as elimination of the diagnosis neurotic. Other important changes are expected in the classification of schizophrenia.

a man who drank a bottle of insect killer because he thought it would make him sick and his girl friend would feel sorry for him. His behavior would be considered *functionally* abnormal, though not necessarily psychotic. However, as a consequence of his behavior, he was poisoned and developed a psychosis that would be called *organic*. Chronic alcoholism is perhaps the most common cause of organic psychosis today. With organic psychosis the behavioral problem is usually resolved if the underlying biophysical malfunctioning can be corrected.

An assumption of this diagnostic scheme is that people whose behavior is psychopathological will fit neatly into one of the major diagnostic categories. Yet people exist on continua within all these classes of behavior, and one label is seldom an accurate description of a problem.

The diagnostic system we have described is based on the *Diagnostic and Statistical Manual, II,* of the American Psychiatric Association. This system is currently being revised and a new edition should be published by late 1979. The revision seeks to eliminate some confusing distinctions and categories that have not been demonstrated to be useful, but will retain the same basic characteristics.

NEUROSIS

The neurotic has perfect vision in one eye, but he cannot remember which. *(The Neurotic's Notebook)*

According to the dynamic model, neurosis is a special pattern of behavior that is instigated and maintained for the purpose of contending with stress and avoiding anxiety. What are the indications that a pattern of behavior is neurotic? First, if the person is prevented from performing the behavior, he or she will become anxious. Second, the behavior has a rigid, driven quality about it; the person cannot perform the behavior in a relaxed manner. Finally, the need being served by the behavior is insatiable; the person never seems to relax and give up the behavior.

Thus it is easy to see why neurosis is a problem for the individual. Defending against the anxiety takes up a tremendous amount of energy that the person could usefully spend elsewhere. In addition, the time spent avoiding the anxiety prevents the person from ever dealing effectively with its cause. Thus new behaviors are never learned that would allow the person to get out of the anxiety-provoking situation altogether. This self-perpetuating aspect of neurosis is called the **neurotic paradox.**

The paradox refers to the fact that the neurotic individual persists in the maladaptive behavior even in the face of unpleasant consequences. The behavioral model also helps explain this behavior. The unpleasantness may not occur for some time after the behavior has taken place, whereas the immediate consequence is that anxiety is reduced, providing positive reinforcement of the neurotic behavior. The immediate reduction of anxiety is called the neurotic's **primary gain.** The primary gain is so great that later negative consequences, if they arise, do not have much effect in changing the neurotic behavior.

Neurotic behavior is extremely persistent because it often has other positive consequences in addition to the relief from tension, or primary gain. The additional benefits are the **secondary gains** of neurosis. For example, the neurotic may receive sympathy and support from friends or special dispensations that allow him or her to avoid responsibilities or activities that are disliked. The fact that neurosis has both primary and secondary gains makes behavior change more difficult. In some cases the therapist may have to detect and remove the sources of secondary gain in addition to working on the neurotic's primary source of anxiety.

The various subcategories of neurosis can best be understood if they are grouped according to how people cope with anxiety. Neurotic defenses or coping behaviors will be discussed under seven classifications: (1) transient situational disturbances, (2) anxiety neurosis, (3) phobias and hypochondriasis, (4) obsessive-compulsive neurosis, (5) conversion reactions, (6) dissociative reactions, and (7) neurotic depression.

Transient Situational Disturbances: Overwhelming Stress

An individual faced with repetitive, intense stress or a single traumatic incident will sometimes fail to develop any successful defense except to withdraw. Such persons try to cope but are unable to. They react as if they were under stress at all times, even when there is no obvious stressor. A common symptom is overreaction to minor stress, irritations, and noises. In war soldiers who are under constant strain at the battle line sometimes lose their ability to cope. They develop poor appetites, are constantly nervous, and have insomnia with repetitive nightmares. This condition could be referred to as a **traumatic neurosis,** but is usually not listed as a true neurosis.

Anxiety Neurosis: Repression of Anxiety-Provoking Stimuli

One means of neurotic defense involves removing the anxiety-provoking thoughts from awareness and focusing on the anxiety, which is still

© 1977 United Feature Syndicate, Inc.

Neurotic phobias are ineffective means of controlling anxiety. The phobia tends to expand to include greater and greater aspects of a person's life until with serious phobias the person may be completely incapacitated.

present. An **anxiety reaction** is a neurotic episode in which a person has repressed the cause of the anxiety but not the anxiety itself. Such persons are anxious without knowing why. They report feeling nervous or jittery throughout the day but are unable to report anything occurring in their lives that should make them nervous. They may displace the anxiety by attaching it to a less relevant and therefore less threatening stressor. In this way they may react with overwhelming anxiety to an objectively mild stress.

Phobias and Hypochondriasis: Displacement of Anxiety

Phobias are intense, irrational fears that, according to psychoanalytic theory, arise from the displacement of anxiety onto a situation that could be mildly dangerous. Thus the woman who has a fear of heights (called acrophobia) might be symbolically expressing her anxiety over an overwhelming anger toward her parents. By displacing her fear she is prevented from acting directly on her anger, which she has repressed. Other common phobias are fear of small enclosed spaces (claustrophobia), fear of water (aquaphobia), and, for young children, school phobia.

There is a subclassification of phobias not easily conceptualized as neurotic. These phobias are best explained by learning theory and might be called *traumatic phobias*. The young girl who develops a fear of dogs after being bitten is not displacing a fear; she has learned in one trial

that dogs are dangerous. This conditioned fear response is durable. Even if the girl is not bitten again, as long as she can reduce the fear (reinforcement) by escaping from dogs, the fear will persist.

Another type of problem arising from displaced anxiety is **hypochondriasis,** a preoccupation with one's physical health. For example, a hypochondriac may read the health columns in the newspapers and magazines and rush to a doctor with all the latest symptoms. Such persons may distort the meaning of minor aches and pains, imagine discomfort in various parts of their bodies, and constantly complain of ill health, although the physician can seldom find anything physically wrong. Physicians have estimated that as many as 60 percent of their

"He was a dreadful hypochondriac."

© Punch (Rothco)

patients express anxiety about their lives in their physical symptoms. The "medical student syndrome," in which students working and studying in a hospital develop whatever illness they read about or are exposed to that day, is probably a response to the extreme pressure of medical school training. Some male students express great relief when on duty in the obstetrics ward.

The same process of displacement can occur as psychology students read about psychopathology. They too can experience the "medical student syndrome," seeing themselves described on every page and concluding that they have serious emotional problems. More likely these students are reasonably well-adjusted persons who have feelings and thoughts that are included in the diagnostic categories.

Obsessive-Compulsive Neurosis: Defenses against Anxiety by Means of Cognitive and Behavioral Activation

The obsessive or compulsive approach of neurotic defense involves behavior in which the person repetitiously thinks about or performs a behavior against his or her own wishes. Most of us have obsessions (repetitive thoughts) from time to time, such as a song that keeps running through our heads. And we frequently feel compulsive about performing some act. Obsessions and compulsions are neurotic only when the thought or action interferes with the person's ability to behave appropriately. Obsessive thoughts and compulsive behavior tend to go together in the same individual, thus the term **obsessive-compulsive syndrome.**

Obsessive-compulsive behavior functions in two major ways. First, it prevents the individual from thinking anxiety-provoking thoughts. Obsessive persons may fill their minds with constant trivial thoughts (counting their heartbeats, for example) as a way of avoiding awareness of ideas or memories that would be threatening. A person who keeps to a rigid schedule or who maintains an extremely neat home may be structuring life so as to avoid any possible upsets.

Sometimes the obsessive thinking or compulsive behavior bears a symbolic relation to the anxiety-provoking thought. In one case a woman had an obsessive fear that she would harm herself if she picked up a kitchen knife. This fear so frightened her that she was unable

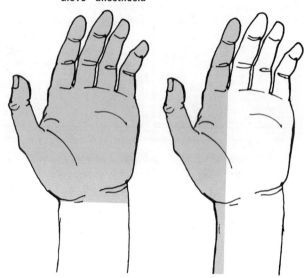

Figure 11–1
"Glove" anesthesia

In the conversion reaction known as "glove" anesthesia the person loses all feeling in the hand in a pattern that follows the outline of a glove, stopping short at the wrist. However, because the nerve pathways for the hand go up the arm, as shown on the right, it would be impossible to have a *physically* caused glove pattern of anesthesia, as depicted on the left, unless there were also anesthesia of the arm.

to prepare meals. Therapy led to the interpretation that her obsession was covering up a desire to kill her husband (felt in a primitive way at the unconscious level and consciously unacceptable to her). By obsessively avoiding knives she was also able to protect herself from overtly acting out her conflict. In addition, obsessive-compulsive behavior may be an expression of guilt and fear of punishment. The classic example of this is the compulsive hand washing of Shakespeare's Lady Macbeth. Compulsive hand washing has also been associated with conflicts over guilt and masturbation.

Conversion Reactions: Defense against Anxiety by Means of Cognitive and Behavioral Inactivation

A person can defend against anxiety-provoking thoughts by selectively cutting off certain experiences. One subclassification of this response is the **conversion reaction,** in which the person

A Case of Obsessive-Compulsive Behavior

The following case description illustrates how the obsessive-compulsive individual successfully avoids anxiety-provoking situations. His defensive behavior, however, also prevents him from trying and learning new behaviors that would enable him to cope with his anxiety.

Eliot H., a college student, went to a telephone booth to call up a wealthy girl whom he had recently met, to ask her for a date. He spent an hour there, anxious and indecisive, unable to put the coin in the slot and unable to give up and go home. Each time his hand approached the telephone he anxiously withdrew it because he felt that telephoning her might ruin his chances with her. Each time he withdrew his hand he seemed to be throwing away a golden opportunity. Every positive argument for telephoning her he matched with a negative argument for not doing so. He went into all the ramifications of his ambivalent motivations. He imagined to himself what the girl and the members of her family—whom he scarcely knew—might think of his attentions to her; and then he had to picture to himself what they would think if he neglected her.

His whole future seemed to Eliot to hang on the outcome of this little act. Had he any right to put his coin in? If he did so would the girl respond favorably? If she did, what would happen next? Eliot fantasied every conceivable consequence as he sat there sweating in the booth, conse-

quences to him and to her, on and on into remote contrasting futures. He was helplessly caught in an obsessive dilemma, as he had been caught before hundreds of times. The more he tried to be sure of what he did, the more things he imagined going wrong, any one of which might ruin everything. In the end he gave up the anxious debate and went home, exasperated and worn out. Later he became convinced that in not making the call at that particular time he had missed the chance of a lifetime for winning security and happiness.

This absurd little episode sounds like the mere exaggeration of a shy suitor's hesitancy, but it was much more than this. It was a condensed symbolic expression of an intensely ambivalent personality, one that was volatile, impulsive, and unpredictable. Almost every enterprise upon which Eliot had embarked since early adolescence had involved similar obsessive rumination. Into each decision he funneled all of his ambivalent conflicts—conscious, preconscious, and unconscious—and then he found himself unable to follow through to a decision. The same thing unfortunately happened to his search for therapeutic help. He began with despair, switched quickly to great optimism, and then got bogged down in endless doubting and rumination over whether to continue. In the end he withdrew from therapy without ever becoming really involved in it. (Cameron, 1963, page 396)

reduces the anxiety by inactivating part of the body (as in paralysis, blindness, deafness, or the like). Thus the person converts the psychological problem into a physical one that prevents him or her from behaving in a way that would be anxiety provoking. For example, the student who suddenly became "blind" would be unable to do class assignments. There are no actual

physical changes; the inactivation is due to unconscious psychological factors.

One of the most famous conversion reactions is that of "glove" anesthesia, in which the person loses all feeling in the hand. The pattern of loss of feeling follows the outline of a glove (see Figure 11–1). Physicians are immediately able to identify this symptom as nonphysical because the nerve pathways for the hand mark off narrow strips of sensitivity that go up the arm, and it would be impossible to have a glove pattern of anesthesia unless there were also anesthesia of the arm. Conversion reactions were fairly common in Freud's day (and prompted him to move from neurology to psychiatry), but today people are better informed about biophysical processes, and their reactions to anxiety usually take other forms, such as pain and simulation of bodily disease. Simply reading this chapter may prevent you from ever developing a glove anesthesia.

Dissociative Reactions: Amnesia, Fugue State, Multiple Personality

Another means of avoiding anxiety-provoking associations involves blocking off large parts of the memory. This kind of defensive behavior is referred to as **dissociative reactions.** All of the dissociative reactions are rare, but they have a dramatic flavor that results in their frequent use in books and movies. The simplest is **amnesia,** which refers to partial or total loss of memory of one's past identity. The amnesic person may forget his or her name, family, job, and home. However, the individual will retain memory for nonthreatening aspects of life. He or she will remember how to speak, how to drive, and other perceptual-motor skills unrelated to any psychological danger. Amnesia can also be caused by physical trauma such as a blow to the head, but this form differs from neurotic amnesia in that the memories of the neurotic can often be recalled under hypnosis.

More complex and much rarer is the **fugue state,** in which the person has amnesia for the past but avoids the anxiety associated with such loss of identity by developing a new one and fleeing from the situation that could not be tolerated. The individual may function as a completely new personality, remarry, have more children, and get a new job in another city, all without any memory of his or her previous (and undivorced) spouse and children. Such states may last for a long or relatively short period of time; when the old memories return, the individual may forget all of the events that occurred in the fugue state.

Finally, the rarest form of dissociative reaction is the **multiple personality.** There are

© 1979 by Sidney Harris.

fewer than 100 recorded cases of multiple personality in this century. In these cases the person has two or more complete but alternating personalities; at one point in time the individual is one personality and at another point in time a different personality. Frequently each personality expresses an aspect of a conflict the person is experiencing. One personality is usually dominant and is unaware of the existence of the other personality. In the famous case about which the book *The Three Faces of Eve* was written, Eve White was unaware of Eve Black, although Eve Black continued to be aware of what Eve White was doing. Jane, the third personality, seemed to be a more satisfactory resolution of the dissociations of aspects of personality. Later in life Eve developed other personalities in spite of psychotherapy, as we saw in the news clipping on page 3. Multiple personality is not to be confused with schizophrenia—literally, split personality—which is a much more common and more severe disorder.

Neurotic Depression

The increasing incidence of depressive neurosis in our society has led some people to suggest that we are facing an epidemic of depression. *Neurotic depression* is characterized by an exces-

Doctors Call Depression
Major Health Problem

UPI

WASHINGTON — You're depressed, down in the dumps. Is it just a passing case of the blues or something more serious?

The National Association for Mental Health, a government agency, says the answer is important for a growing number of Americans.

Depression, the NAMH says, now rivals schizophrenia as the nation's number one mental health problem. A recent survey indicates 15 per cent of Americans 18 to 74 suffer symptoms of serious depression.

Depression can be caused by chemical changes in the body, reaction to outside events, unconscious effects of behavior and personal relationships or combinations of these.

The NAMH, therefore, has issued a list of 10 "depression danger signals" that may help an individual distinguish between normal, temporary depression and a mental disability that needs professional help.

The agency emphasizes, however, that some of the signals may be normal reactions to disappointments, loss or stress, and a person should be concerned only if the signals persist without specific cause.

The 10 "danger signals" are:

A general and lasting feeling of hopelessness and despair.

Inability to concentrate, making reading, writing and conversation difficult. Thinking and activity are slowed because the mind is absorbed by inner anguish.

Changes in physical activities such as eating, sleeping and sex. Frequent physical complaints with no evidence of physical illness.

A loss of self-esteem which brings on continual questioning of personal worth.

Withdrawal from others, not by choice but from fear of rejection.

Threats or attempts to commit suicide, which is seen as a way out of a hostile environment. About one in 200 depressed persons do commit suicide.

Hypersensitivity to words and actions of others and general irritability.

Misdirected anger and difficulty in handling most feelings. Self-directed anger because of perceived worthlessness may produce general anger directed at others.

Feelings of guilt in many situations. A depressed person assumes he is wrong or responsible for the unhappiness of others.

Extreme dependency on others. Feelings of helplessness and then anger at the helplessness.

Rocky Mountain News (Denver)
September 22, 1975

---

sive reaction of depression, usually accompanied by significant anxiety feelings. The disorder usually involves feelings of fatigue, weakness, and exhaustion—and yet the individual has difficulty falling asleep. Such individuals almost always consider themselves worthless persons who have accomplished nothing in life and who expect to accomplish nothing in the future; often depressive neurotics feel guilty. Despite all these symptoms, the depressive neurotic does not suffer from loss of contact with reality, although some reality distortion is often present. Typically the person maintains a reasonable level of functioning in day-to-day life, a fact that distinguishes neurotic depression from the much more severe psychotic depression, which we will discuss later in this chapter.

Neurotic depression is often attributable to a personal loss such as the death of a loved one or a serious financial setback. Occasionally, depressive neurosis follows the achievement of an important goal in the person's life. At least four other factors have been suggested as important in neurotic depression, each having a different theoretical orientation. According to Freudian theory, depression is a result of the inability to outwardly express hostility and anger, even when this expression would be perfectly appropriate. Such persons turn their anger inward against themselves. They convince themselves that they are worthless bums who do not deserve any of the good things they have earned.

In Carl Rogers' view depression arises because the person has an image of an ideal self that he or she sees as different from the real self. The ideal self-image is so completely perfect that the real self seems impossibly far from attaining any of the qualities of the ideal self.

If, as Rogers claims, one of a person's major goals is to strive for self-actualization, such a conception of the distance between one's real and ideal selves would lead the person to be depressed and anxious about life.

Another explanation of depression, based on behavioral theory, is that a person becomes depressed because there is a lack of positive reinforcement in his or her life, a view similar to the idea of personal loss. Feelings of happiness, freedom, and self-worth are seen as basically due to consistent receipt of positive rewards for one's behavior. If persons find themselves in life situations in which their behavior is controlled mainly by negative reinforcement (they do what they do to avoid punishment), then their emotional responses will be depressive.

As we saw in Chapter 4, a different conceptualization of depression comes out of *learned helplessness* research with animals. In a typical learned helplessness experiment a dog is placed in a large box and given electric shock. There is no way for the dog to escape the shock, and after some time the animal's response to the situation appears very much like depression in human beings, with such symptoms as passivity, loss of appetite, weight loss, and loss of motivation to escape. Later, when the dog is given an opportunity to escape the shock, it does not even try. Martin Seligman has proposed that depression in people occurs in a similar manner. A person comes to believe that he or she has no personal control over life—that there is no way to escape anxiety-provoking situations—and gives up. Both the animal and person have learned to be helpless and hopeless. Not all experimental evidence supports the analogy between learned helplessness in animals and depression in human beings, but the results are sufficiently interesting to be worthy of further exploration.

In summary, there are at least five possible factors in depression: (1) personal loss, (2) anger turned inward, (3) an unusually large discrepancy between the real and ideal self, (4) the lack of positive reinforcement, and (5) learned helplessness. The depressive reaction may often be triggered by personal loss, but the other factors are probably all important in maintaining the depression. In any particular case, however, only one or two of these factors may be operating, and very likely one factor alone cannot account for all depressive reactions.

PSYCHOSOMATIC ILLNESS

For the neurotic individual stress leads to anxiety and repression. For others, however, stress may be expressed in physical illnesses such as asthma, ulcers, hypertension (high blood pressure), ulcerative colitis, headaches, arthritis, and perhaps even the common cold. (Of course, many of these illnesses have other causes as well.) Physiologically, our bodies prepare us to flee or fight when faced with danger. Heartbeat increases markedly, blood pressure rises, muscles tense, secretion of stomach acids increases, and oxygen supply is directed to large muscles and the brain. All of these physiological mechanisms are geared to enable the body to respond quickly and efficiently. While the pressure of work or the anxieties of social relationships do not pose the threat of physical danger, such as that experienced by early human beings who had constantly to fear attacks by wild animals, our bodies still respond to these "emergencies." But as part of our socialization we are discouraged from fleeing or fighting when we are scared or angry. The chronic physiological arousal continues, nevertheless, and the result in some people is physical illness. **Psychosomatic illness** refers to physical illness in which emotional factors are the cause. Typically such illnesses involve a single organ system that is controlled by the autonomic nervous system (see Chapter 2).

People tend to be insulted when they are told they have a psychosomatic illness because they assume they are being told the illness is imaginary. Yet psychosomatic illnesses are real illnesses. A person with a psychosomatic ulcer really does have a sore in the lining of the stomach or intestines, and a person can die of psychosomatic asthma. Psychosomatic illness is quite different from conversion reaction, in which there is no tissue damage but the individual is denying sensory input, and from hypochondriasis, in which the person displaces anxiety into exaggerated concern for physical health but is not truly ill.

Factors Contributing to Psychosomatic Illness

A variety of factors are believed to contribute to the development of psychosomatic illness. For

A Case of Psychosomatic Asthma

Patricia M., a Baraboo schoolgirl, fourteen years of age, was admitted to a general hospital because of severe attacks of bronchial asthma. The nurses reported that she entered the ward flanked by her frightened parents, the mother supporting her on one side and the father walking on the other side, carrying a syringe with adrenalin ready for instant use. This entrance was a dramatic representation of the attitudes all three had developed during the four months of her asthmatic attacks. At home the father, after work, had been devoting himself entirely to a task of diverting Patricia, so as to minimize her attacks. Actually, the attacks had increased in frequency and severity following his arrival at home, but neither the parents nor the child seemed to suspect that there might be some connection involved. By the time she was brought to the hospital, her activities had been restricted to those of a person in imminent danger of collapse and sudden death.

Although a respiratory hypersensitivity to bacterial protein was clearly demonstrated, it was obvious to everyone that the extreme anxiety of the child and her parents presented a major problem. At first, parental visits to the child, but not to the hospital, were limited. Both parents and the child received psychotherapy during the period of her being desensitized to her specific allergens. When Patricia had asthmatic attacks they were treated competently and without anxiety on the part of the staff. When it was observed that she had an increase of attacks on "Protein Clinic" days, the allergist made arrangements to have her treated on the psychiatric ward, and the increase disappeared. Because of her long period of inactivity, it was necessary to schedule increasing activity until Patricia had regained the confidence that she had lost because of everyone's extreme anxiety. After four months, she was well enough to go home and resume a normal life. When asthmatic attacks then occurred, which they did at infrequent intervals, both the parents and the girl were able to handle the situation without alarm. Patricia was seen in office treatment for some time after discharge so that some of her personal problems could be worked through. (Cameron, 1963, page 693)

any given individual, one or more of these factors may play a decisive role. Some of the more important ones are outlined below.

Stress

There is a close relationship between the experiencing of stress and the development of an illness. Recent research has demonstrated that many more events are stressful to people than was previously thought. While most people would agree that death of a spouse, divorce, or loss of a job is stressful, research has demonstrated that other life changes such as purchasing a house, getting married, having a child, moving, or getting a promotion also put pressure on individuals to assume new roles and meet new demands. Using a measure of stressful life events that gave various weightings to both "positive" and "negative" events (see the box on pages 16 and 17), researchers found that among physicians, 93 percent of health problems came within two years of a high number of life changes. Similar results were obtained for medical students, as well as for naval officers and enlisted men. Persons with many life changes had 90 percent more illnesses than those with few life changes. Among football players, those with more life changes are more likely to have injuries. It seems clear that stress alone can increase our susceptibility to illness and injury, perhaps by draining the energy we need to combat illness.

Jobs that repeatedly place people under great stress — such as trading gold futures on the floor of the Mid-American Commodity Exchange — may contribute to the development of both psychological and physiological problems.

Psychological Conflicts

Franz Alexander, called the father of psychosomatic medicine, proposed that specific conflicts are associated with specific psychosomatic illnesses. Table 11–2 lists examples of the types of conflicts that were thought to cause psychosomatic illnesses. Attempts to validate the relation between specific conflicts and specific psychosomatic illnesses have seldom been successful. Furthermore, in cases where the predicted relationship was found, there was often some question as to which was the cause and which the effect. Asthma has been explained as the result of excessive unresolved dependency on the mother, and it is a common finding that asthmatics are unusually dependent. It is just as possible, however, that asthma produces dependency. If a child is in chronic danger of suffocating, as the asthmatic child often is, it is understandable that he or she would become very dependent.

Some success in finding a specific conflict or personality characteristic has occurred with the identification of the *Type A* personality in the case of heart disease. Type A personalities are driving, aggressive, assertive, tense, achieving people. Such a tense life-style is likely to lead to chronic high blood pressure and heart attacks. Jenkins (1974) followed 2700 men who had never had heart attacks and identified men with high and low risk for heart attacks. Over the next four years twice as many high-risk men (Type A) experienced heart attacks than did low-risk men. However, many Type A men did not have heart attacks and some low-risk men did. The Type A personality style is only a partial predictor of heart attacks.

Attitudes

D. T. Graham and his associates proposed that attitudes determine a person's physiological responses. Table 11–2 lists some attitudes he proposed as related to psychosomatic illness. As experimental evidence to support these hypotheses, subjects were hypnotized and given the attitudes for Reynaud's disease (a circulatory disease involving cold hands and feet) or hives (a rash). The attitude proposed for Reynaud's disease was to want to take "hostile gross motor action" (fight), while for hives it was to feel one was under attack and was helpless. Physiological measures showed a decline in hand temperature for the hostile suggestion and a rise in hand temperature for the feeling of being attacked; both changes were in the direction consistent with the associated illness. Other studies with other attitudes have had mixed success in obtaining the predicted physiological changes.

More broadly conceptualized, it is clear that certain emotions lead to predictable physiological responses. When a person is angry the stomach lining becomes red, contracts, and secretes hydrochloric acid. When a person is anxious, the lining is pale, contraction decreases, and acid levels go down. Thus, if the stress a person experiences leads to chronic anxiety, the tendency will be for the person to develop problems in different physiological modalities than if he or she were chronically angry.

Conditioning

New associations between a thought, feeling, or action and a physiological response can be obtained through both classical and instrumental conditioning. If a person has experienced a severe emotional upset at the time of a physical illness, it is possible that the next time the individual is upset in that way the same physiological illness will occur. Asthmatics (who may have specific allergens to which they are sensitive) very easily associate asthma with previously neutral stimuli that then become capable of eliciting the asthma response. In a person who is allergic to cat hair, for example, the mere sight of a cat may elicit the asthma re-

TABLE 11-2   Comparison of Alexander's and Graham's Views of the Causes of Selected Psychosomatic Illnesses

Illness	Alexander's Psychological Conflict Hypothesis	Graham's Attitude Hypothesis
Asthma	Excessive unresolved dependence upon the mother, a dependence that is a wish to be encompassed or protected. Asthma occurs when there is a threat of separation of the patient from the protective mother. It represents a suppressed cry for the mother.	Feelings of being left out in the cold and wanting to shut the person or situation out.
Constipation	"I cannot expect anything from anybody, therefore I do not need to give anything. I must hold on to what I have."	Feelings of being in a situation from which nothing good could come but keeping on with it grimly.
Duodenal ulcer	Frustration of oral receptive longings leading to oral aggressive response, followed by overcompensation by successful accomplishment in responsible activities, leading to increased unconscious oral-dependent cravings as reactions to excessive effort and concentration; or, prolonged frustration of oral receptive longings, with repression of these wishes.	Feelings of being deprived of what was due and wanting to get even.
Hives	Inhibited dependent longing for a parental object, with suppression of weeping.	Feelings of taking a beating and being helpless to do anything about it.
Essential hypertension	Hostile competitive tendencies leading to intimidation, due to fear of retaliation, and failure, with consequent increase of dependent longings, leading to inferiority feelings, leading to reactivation of hostile competitiveness, leading to anxiety and aggressive hostile impulses.	Feelings of being threatened with harm and having to be ready for anything.
Migraine	Repressed hostile impulses, perhaps when the repression or inhibition occurs during the planning and preparation for a hostile attack.	Feelings that something had to be achieved and then being relaxed after the effort.
Rheumatoid arthritis	Restrictive parental influence leading to rebellion against restrictions, with repression of rebellious tendencies followed by expression of rebellion in sports and outdoor activities, followed by expression of hostility while both serving and controlling the environment in later life, together with rejection of the feminine role in women. Arthritis occurs when the successful pattern of serving and dominating the environment is interrupted.	Feelings of being tied down and wanting to get free.

sponse even before the individual comes into contact with any of the specific allergens. Strong emotions such as anger or fear could also be conditioned to elicit an asthma response.

Physiological Causes

There is ample evidence that there are individual differences among people in physiological responses. Of two people with the same stress or learning history, one might develop an ulcer and one might not. The individual, however, tends to have reliable physiological patterns of response to stress. In a stressful situation, for example, some people may characteristically exhibit significant changes in heart rate, others may breathe rapidly and perspire freely, whereas still others may reflect changes in four or five physiological modalities. Since a person tends to respond to stress in a particular physiological modality, under chronic stress the individual is likely to develop a physical illness in that modality. Some evidence suggests that these specific physiological responses are hereditary. Thus the factor of genetics plays some role in determining if you are, for example, a high risk for ulcers.

Cause and Treatment

Determining the cause of specific cases of psychosomatic illness is difficult, given all of the different pathways by which a person can develop an illness. Treatment of psychosomatic disorders may involve psychotherapy to resolve the conflict that leads to the excessive and prolonged physiological response under stress. However, if the emotional conflict and the physiological response were associated through conditioning, gaining insight into the conflicts will probably not resolve the conditioned link. Through research psychologists are now learning techniques to recondition the individual to produce a new pattern of physiological responses (such as those associated with relaxation) in the presence of the stimuli that previously provoked the physiological reaction (see Chapter 12).

PERSONALITY DISORDERS

"You agreed to fix the screen door!"

"I know, I know. I will. I just haven't had a chance to do it yet."

"But I asked you to fix it over two months ago."

"Look, I said I would do it and I will. I will get it done in the next couple of days."

(Two weeks later.)

"Dear" *(said with controlled anger)*, "I thought you said you were going to get the screen door fixed!"

"You are absolutely right, dear. I don't have time right now, but I'll get right to it. You don't have to nag about it."

That was two years ago and the screen door is not fixed yet!

You might ask what the above example has to do with abnormal psychology. Certainly the importance of getting the screen door fixed is minor compared to the distress and lack of functioning that we see in severe neurosis or psychosis. However, this interaction illustrates a maladaptive relationship that leaves one member of the couple with extreme levels of frustration and anger and the other with a self-righteous indignation over being nagged after having agreed to the reasonableness of the demands.

This section describes a class of behavior referred to as **personality disorders.** People with personality disorders are defined as individuals with *dominant personality traits that lead to behavior that is seen as maladaptive to society.*

Stress and Personality Disorders

Unlike the neuroses and psychosomatic illnesses, the personality disorders are not clearly reactions to stress. While maladaptive reactions to stress are characteristic of some personality disorders, such as the passive-aggressive personality and the alcoholic, stress reactions do not define these problems. Personality disorders occur as the result of deeply ingrained habits or personality styles, not as defense mechanisms against anxiety or as physiological expressions of tension.

There are many different types of personality disorders, but we will discuss here those that fall under the following major categories: the passive-aggressive personality, the antisocial personality, the dyssocial personality, the alcoholic, the drug addict, and the sexual deviant.

The Passive-Aggressive Personality

The procrastinating spouse we saw above is a passive-aggressive personality who illustrates an extraordinarily effective technique for manipulating other individuals. Passive aggression is typically seen in individuals with deep dependency needs that prevent the direct expression of anger because of fear that the dependency needs will no longer be met. Since overt anger or even behavior that might lead to disagreement and thus unpleasantness must be avoided, the person develops a pattern of behavior that involves *apparent* agreement and compliance, but that in fact displays passive resistance. The example demonstrates easy agreement over the assignment of chores, but *procrastination* as a way of avoiding a chore that obviously is unpleasant.

Other strategies of the passive-aggressive involve stubbornness and *passive obstructionism.* Passive-aggressives can also behave in a passive-dependent manner, acting *helpless, indecisive,* and *clinging.* The passive-aggressive strategy is effective because it blocks any discussion about the trouble that arises from its use. All the passive-aggressive person has to do is agree readily with all the criticisms, apologize profusely, and continue to avoid doing whatever is asked *or* self-righteously assume the martyr role, pointing out that he or she has always been agreeable and that the demands reflect an intolerance on the part of the other person.

Theorists of both the dynamic and behaviorist schools agree that passive-aggressive behavior is the result of faulty development rather than unconscious responses to internal or external stress. Passive-aggressive individuals frequently are quite satisfied with themselves and would be content to persist in their behavior if society would just leave them alone.

The Antisocial Personality

Antisocial individuals, often called **sociopaths,** are pleasure-oriented (hedonistic) and indifferent to the needs or concerns of others. They exploit others for their own selfish ends and do not feel guilty or anxious except when it is clear that they might be prevented from satisfying their needs for pleasure. At this point they will become anxious but will not regret their past behavior or learn from punishment to avoid this behavior in the future.

In the early twentieth century antisocial personalities were viewed as "moral imbeciles" who were incapable of differentiating right from wrong. We know now, however, that these people are above average in intelligence and especially adept at manipulating others. They also tend to be physically attractive, which gives them a head start in learning to manipulate others. Punishment seems to have less impact on these individuals than is normal. The presence of an antisocial parent within the home is one of the chief factors in the development of a sociopath. The child learns at an early age how to win social approval.

Treatment of antisocial personalities is difficult. These individuals see nothing wrong in their behavior and will seek help only to manipulate their way out of trouble. It is clear that this kind of maladaptive behavior is a failure of *motivation* to behave appropriately, and psychotherapy is seldom effective in effecting change. If it were not for the fact that many seem to "burn out" around the age of 30 and less actively pursue their manipulations of others, they would present a much more serious social problem than they already do.

The Dissocial Personality

Dissocial individuals hold values that conflict with the mores of the society. For this reason they might more appropriately be called cultural deviants. However, they do exhibit intense loyalty to one or, at most, a few subgroups, usually on the periphery of society. Some juvenile delinquent gangs and drug-oriented individuals fit into this classification.

The Alcoholic

An alcoholic is defined as an excessive drinker whose dependence on alcohol is so strong that it interferes with the performance of socially appropriate behavior. Alcoholism occurs in all social classes and occupational groups, although the incidence appears to be higher in the middle and upper socioeconomic levels. Skid-row bums are estimated to constitute only 5 percent of the over nine million alcoholics in the United States. Alcoholism is fourth among the major health problems in this country and is considered a major social problem as well. Long-term consumption of alcohol can lead to damage to the central nervous system and susceptibility to other diseases, such as tuberculosis and liver disease. Alcohol dependence may also be the cause of family disruption, poor job performance, and social isolation for the individual. Society suffers from the high crime rate associated with alcoholism and the tragic consequences of drunken driving.

Contrary to popular belief, alcohol is not a stimulant but a depressant. Its first effect is to inhibit processes in the higher levels of the brain and reduce inhibitory control over lower levels. Thus, sexual activity might increase under mild intoxication because sexual controls are reduced more than sexual drive. At more extreme levels of intoxication, however, sexual desire is also reduced. Excessive drinking invariably results in some degree of motor uncoordination and inability to make fine discriminations (see Appendix D). More important in the development of alcoholism is the fact that perception of discomfort (both physical and psychological) is dulled.

Many people are capable of restricting their intake to social drinking, but for others this is the first phase in the development of alcoholism

TABLE 11–3   Pattern of Development for Alcoholism

1. Prealcoholic phase	→ Social drinking → drinking to reduce tension → Daily drinking
2. Prodromal (beginning) phase	→ Blackouts with no memory the next day → morning drinking to offset hangover or to face a difficult day
3. Crucial phase	→ Loss of control over drinking → loss of family and job
4. Chronic phase	→ Prolonged bouts of drinking → impairment of thinking

(called the *prealcoholic phase*—see Table 11–3). In the second or *prodromal phase* the person drinks in the morning and experiences blackouts. In the *crucial phase* he or she loses control over drinking behavior. The *chronic phase* is marked by long "binges" of drinking and impairment of thought processes.

Causes of Alcoholism

There is probably no single cause of alcoholism. Although there is some evidence of a genetic component in alcoholic behavior, most psychologists still feel that the alcoholic has learned to drink to reduce anxiety generated by personal problems. There is no evidence that alcoholics are under unusual stress. They tend to be immature, impulsive individuals with low self-esteem and feelings of not living up to their own goals and standards, and they display an inability to tolerate failure.

Treatment of Alcoholism

Alcoholics are extremely difficult to treat. The dependence on alcohol is evidently a result of a deeply embedded personality trait, possibly coupled with a genetic predisposition for the effects of alcohol. Insight-oriented psychotherapy has not been successful in treating alcoholism. Alcoholics tend to see therapists as unsympathetic and lacking in understanding. Many do not return after the first session, and most have left therapy before a month has gone by.

Some drugs have been used to reduce the typically rather mild withdrawal symptoms of craving for alcohol—tremors, sweating, and nausea. **Antabuse** is a drug frequently given to alcoholics; it causes intense nausea if alcohol is consumed while the chemical is in the bloodstream. The knowledge that drinking will lead to a severe illness helps some alcoholics refrain from impulsive drinking. But because taking the drug each day requires the cooperation of the alcoholic, such a treatment program helps only the alcoholic who sincerely wants to control drinking and needs a "crutch" to eliminate impulsive drinking.

Alcoholics Anonymous (AA), a mutual aid organization with a religious orientation, has had perhaps the greatest success in treating alcoholics. AA groups provide social support and reassurance from recovered alcoholics who understand alcoholics' problems. AA members help new members withstand the trials of "drying out" and provide social events to prevent them from returning to their drinking habits, especially during nonworking hours. Alcoholics must learn new ways to spend their time in place of their drinking activities. Part of the difficulty in treating alcoholism is that alcoholics frequently do not accept the fact that they have a drinking problem, rarely seek treatment voluntarily, and in most states cannot be forced to seek treatment.

The Drug Addict

Some people cope with life's problems by the excessive use of drugs other than alcohol. Drug addiction is considered primarily a personality disorder, although like alcoholism it can occur in combination with neurosis and psychosis. Heroin, the most commonly used addictive drug in the United States, constitutes a major social problem because of the large amount of illegal behavior associated with addiction; the loss of socially appropriate behavior like working and maintaining a family; and the "contagion" effect—it is estimated that each addict introduces an average of *six* others to narcotics.

There are several differences between drug addiction and alcoholism. Psychologically, drugs frequently produce euphoria rather than just the reduction in tension that comes with the consumption of alcohol. Furthermore, while the alcoholic shows an initial slight increase in tolerance for alcohol, followed later by a decrease, the drug addict finds that an increasing amount of the drug is required in order to maintain the same "high." For this reason addiction becomes tremendously expensive, and the addict may need $50 or more a day to maintain the habit. For many people, antisocial behaviors such as stealing or prostitution are the only means for attaining the necessary funds. Because the addict cannot be sure of the quality of the drugs, overdoses (ODs) are common and often result in death.

Whereas the chronic alcoholic may experience only mild to severe illness when withdrawn from alcohol, the heroin addict becomes severely ill within two days after withdrawal from the drug. The symptoms of withdrawal may begin anywhere from 4 to 12 hours after the last dose, depending on the level of addiction. Restlessness, depression, and irritability may begin the withdrawal, followed by vomiting, diarrhea, cramps, pains, severe headaches, tremors, and possibly hallucinations and delirium. The symptoms peak in three to four days and decline after the fifth day. The tolerance built up before withdrawal disappears after the addict goes "cold turkey" (so called because of the common "goose bumps" seen during withdrawal), and people have died from taking a dose as heavy as the ones they were taking before withdrawal.

Causes of Addiction

Many drug addicts are more like the sociopathic personality than the impulsive, immature, and dependent person who becomes an alcoholic. One indication of the personality-disorder aspect of these addicts is the fact that many of them take the "cure" not to be cured but in order to start over again with a less expensive habit. Although the withdrawal symptoms are severe, it is not fear of withdrawal that maintains a drug habit, as is commonly believed. The sociopathic drug addict finds that drugs are an easy way to maintain a pleasure-oriented approach to life.

However, not all drug addicts are sociopathic. About 20 percent of the patients at the federal hospital for drug addiction in Lexington, Kentucky, used drugs originally to relieve anxiety. These people feel unsure of themselves and gain psychological support from the drug subculture. Another group of addicts come from middle-class liberal backgrounds. These addicts become users during adolescence and frequently try their first heroin out of curiosity.

Often they are rebelling against their family's life-style and start using drugs as one way of experimenting with alternative life-styles. These individuals are rarely involved in criminal activities.

Treatment of Addiction

Treating drug addiction is even more difficult than treating alcoholism. The addict's lack of motivation to behave in socially appropriate ways is a major problem. Psychotherapy is typically not successful. Enforced treatment in a government hospital has produced cure rates varying from 1 to 15 percent. Drugs have not been extensively applied, although **methadone** is increasingly being used. Maintenance on methadone prevents withdrawal symptoms from heroin addiction, and when taken orally, methadone does not produce the intense "high" that prevents the drug user from functioning in society. (Interestingly, methadone does produce a mild "high" of its own, which has led to a methadone black market.) Although methadone tends to block a heroin high, thus reducing the pleasurable (reinforcing) aspects of heroin, this treatment technique has been severely criticized because methadone itself is addictive. It is probably well to remember that years ago heroin was touted as the "cure" for morphine addiction. On the other hand, methadone is cheap and legal when used in a medically supervised treatment program. At the very least, it reduces the probability that an addict will have to steal or become a prostitute to get drugs. Methadone is not a cure-all, however, as demonstrated by the fact that when an addict withdraws from methadone, the craving for *heroin* returns. Other types of drug abuse are considered in Appendix D.

The Sexual Deviant

The final classification of personality disorders —sexual deviance—is broadly defined as any method of obtaining sexual satisfaction or participating in sexual relationships that is disapproved by the community.

The first type of deviance to be discussed involves apparently normal sexual activity carried out in extraordinary antisocial conditions. Promiscuity, prostitution, and rape are examples of this category. The rapist has a fairly

Figure 11–2
Homosexuality

Homosexuals are now militantly protesting their unequal treatment by society.

typical antisocial character structure. He seeks his own pleasure at the expense of others and feels no guilt about his behavior. He is clearly and coldly indifferent to the feelings of others. Rape is just a way of taking what he wants, and the rapist frequently rationalizes his behavior by claiming that his victim probably enjoyed it (Kopp, 1962). He learns nothing from punishment and does not cooperate with psychotherapy attempts unless the alternative is confinement.

The second form of deviance focuses on inappropriate sexual objects. This is a difficult category to discuss, mainly because of a lack of widespread agreement among experts as to what constitutes an appropriate or inappropriate object. Most people would agree, however, that a person who can achieve orgasm only when masturbating against the foot of another person is sexually deviant.

But other conditions are not so easy to categorize. Consider the **homosexual,** a person who has overt sexual interests in or receives sexual satisfaction from members of the same sex. Homosexuality was for a long time commonly categorized as a sexual deviation. In 1973, however, the American Psychiatric Association removed homosexuality from its list of mental disorders. Several other sections of society have become more accepting of homosexuality, but there is still much opposition to overt homosexuality from some groups and individuals who consider homosexual relationships distasteful.

Certain sexual problems are better described as *sexual dysfunctions* rather than deviations. These problems should not be categorized under personality disorders, but more properly ought to be classified as neuroses, psychosomatic illnesses, or transient situational disturbances. Sexual dysfunctions include deficient sexual activity or desire. The most obvious example is sexual impotence or frigidity, a loosely used term which has many different meanings. Broadly it means the inability to engage in sexual intercourse or the lack of enjoyment from this activity. Often such problems can be traced to personal (possibly unconscious) conflict with the partner that leads to remoteness, lack of emotional love, or even anger. Excessive concern with the morality of sex and situational stresses may all preclude normal sexual relationships.

PSYCHOSIS

Individuals who can no longer differentiate between reality and fantasy, who sometimes experience hallucinations and delusions, or who occasionally lose conscious control of thoughts, feelings, and actions are considered **psychotic.** These behavioral characteristics often have dramatic effects on the individual's observable behavior as well as on his or her internal processes. Such persons may lose awareness of who and where they are, talk aloud to themselves, conduct nonsensical conversations with strangers, or withdraw and say nothing for days, months, or years. The normal workaday world is usually unprepared to understand or accept the bizarre behavior of the psychotic. Indeed, psychotic behavior is apt to elicit fear, repugnance, or ridicule, because its effect is so disrupting to society.

Psychosis, unless organically caused and treatable, is most often a chronic illness that may affect the greater part of an individual's lifetime. Spontaneous recovery is rare, although a person may have psychotic episodes alternating with periods when he or she is able to function independently and maintain a somewhat normal life-style. The current emphasis in treating psychosis is to help the patient to do this, using long-term hospital care only as a last resort.

There has been a long and persistent search for physical causes of psychosis, with some suggestive findings but no definitive answers as yet. The fact that many of the symptoms of psychosis can be reduced or alleviated with drugs is also suggestive of organic causes. Indeed, it is with psychosis that the medical model is most useful. In some of the disorders there is evidence of a genetic link. However, most psychologists agree that even if there is a biochemical or genetic foundation for the psychosis, environment still plays an important role.

The Desire To Hurt Is More Important To Rapists Than Sex

Ronald Kotulak

Rapists fall into two categories, and sexual desire has nothing to do with either, according to a team of Boston College researchers.

It is a misconception to think that a man commits rape to fulfill sexual needs, they reported in the current issue of the American Journal of Psychiatry.

In a study of 133 convicted rapists and 92 rape victims, they found no rapes in which sex was the dominant issue.

All of the offenses fit into one of two categories—power rapes or anger rapes—and sexuality was always in the service of other nonsexual needs.

"Rape is a pseudo-sexual act, a pattern of sexual behavior that is concerned much more with status, aggression, control, and dominance than with sensual pleasure or sexual satisfaction," they reported.

It is important to recognize that rape is a sexual deviation and that the offender is pathologically disturbed, said Dr. A. Nicholas Groth. . . .

Chicago Tribune
November 9, 1977

Stress and Psychosis

Many people assume that anyone can be driven psychotic if put under enough stress. The relation between stress and psychosis is not clearly defined, however. Neurotics under severe stress may just quit functioning because they are anxious, but they do not necessarily become psychotic. Some individuals have a dramatic psychotic break under intense stress, while others become psychotic without any apparent stress. Still others develop a psychosis over a long period, gradually becoming more and more disturbed. The dramatic onset of psychosis under stress usually means the person has a better chance of recovery than if the onset is without apparent stress or if the psychosis develops gradually and slowly. We will discuss this process in more detail under the section on schizophrenia. The three major classifications of psychosis we will consider are the

Becoming Psychotic

A few weeks before my illness I began to regress into success daydreams somewhat similar to, though not quite as naive and grandiose as, those I had had during early adolescence. I was puzzled by this tendency, though not greatly alarmed because it hardly seemed that my daydreaming self was a part of my adult ethical self. At the onset of panic, I was suddenly confronted with an overwhelming conviction that I had discovered the secrets of the universe, which were being rapidly made plain with incredible lucidity. The truths discovered seemed to be known immediately and directly, with absolute certainty. I had no sense of doubt or awareness of the possibility of doubt. In spite of former atheism and strong antireligious sentiments, I was suddenly convinced that it was possible to prove rationally the existence of God. I remember at the time trying to write an essay on cognition. I began to write compulsively and at the same time was aware that I was developing schizophrenia. I found later among the disorganized notes which I had carefully hidden away, a number of passages that were quite lucid as well as others that were incoherent and full of symbolic sexual content. I also felt that I was embarking on a great Promethean adventure. I was filled with an audacious and unconquerable spirit. As panic mounted, I grew afraid of being alone, had an intense desire to communicate. I had for a short time a sense of exclusive mission but was able to struggle consciously against messianic delusions. These tendencies were replaced by a sense of burdensome and exclusive responsibility, which continued throughout the entire several years of illness. (Anonymous, 1955)

affective reactions, involutional melancholia, and schizophrenia.

Affective Reactions

During the nineteenth century Emil Kraepelin, the father of the present psychiatric diagnostic system, identified two emotional problems with opposite characteristics—depression and mania—as part of the same "disease" process. Deep or psychotic depression involves feelings of profound sadness, loneliness, and lack of self-worth. Thought processes are slowed down, and the person has a very low level of energy. In contrast, mania involves feelings of optimism and the speeding up of thought processes and motor behavior. The person is loud, energetic, and usually involved in all sorts of activities. The assumption is that the manic person is using a defensive mechanism, reaction formation, to escape feeling depressed.

For some individuals the mania and deep depression seem to alternate in a fairly regular pattern. These circular variations in mood, called **manic-depressive psychosis,** or *bipolar depression*, are relatively uncommon, however. Of individuals exhibiting psychotic depressions, only 10 to 15 percent show the switch to mania and back again. Those people who show only the depression are said to have *unipolar depression*.

Depression reaches psychotic proportions when the person loses contact with reality. Manics may develop delusions of grandeur or consider themselves to have unusual powers. Depressives may have hallucinations and delusions involving depressive thoughts. An example is the psychotic depressive who feels that his insides are rotting and filled with insects. There is evidence for a continuum of severity in depression from normal depression (with the normal disappointments of life) through neurotic depression to the most severe psychotic depression. All depressions, whether severe or mild, involve systems of fantasies that may become delusional. For example, it is not unusual for the depressed adolescent to have fantasies of committing suicide—an act that so upsets people that the individual imagines himself finally appreciated at his funeral. If the depression is severe, the person may "live" this fantasy.

Suicide

Most people believe that suicide occurs in the depths of depression. With severe depression, however, the person seldom has enough energy to try suicide. It is during the swing out of depression that the risk of suicide is greatest. The person is still depressed, but now is active enough to do something about it. Indeed, the lifting of the deepest depression may indicate that the person has found one solution to personal problems—death. Deep depression and suicides tend to occur during holidays, pleasant weather, and the first day of spring rather than in dreary weather. Apparently this has to do with the discrepancy between how persons feel and how they think they ought to feel. The expectation that everyone should be happy at Christmas causes depressed persons to feel even more depressed.

Suicide ranks ninth in causes of death in the United States, with about 200,000 attempts each year and about 25,000 successes. Three times as many men as women successfully complete suicide, but three times as many women attempt suicide. Suicide attempts are highest among professional groups. During national crises like war and earthquakes, suicide rates decrease, but they increase during economic depression. The prevention of suicide is discussed in Chapter 12.

Heredity

Population statistics are often used to document the role of heredity in manic-depressive psychosis. Kallman (1953) noted that 25 percent of the brothers, sisters, parents, and children of manic-depressives were also manic-depressive, whereas the expectancy rate in the general population is around 0.5 percent. In a later study (1958) Kallman compared the **concordance rate** of manic-depressives in fraternal and identical twins. The concordance rate is defined as the probability that one member of a pair of twins is manic-depressive, given that the other twin is so diagnosed. Fraternal twins have the same overlap of genes as any two brothers or sisters, whereas identical twins have identical genetic make-up. Kallman reported that the concordance rate for fraternal twins was .265 and for identical twins .957. He concluded that manic-depressive reactions result from a genetic defect in the neurohormonal mechanisms that control emotion.

These findings, while impressive, are not as conclusive as Kallman suggests. First, being from the same family, all siblings—including twins—have a much more similar environment than randomly chosen members of the population. Thus, if the nature of the environment is such as to produce depression in one family member, others subject to the same circumstances might be affected in the same way. Furthermore, identical twins, because they look alike, will have even more similar environments than fraternal twins or ordinary siblings. Because it is difficult to tell one from the other, identical twins tend to elicit the same responses from people. Thus, the higher correlations noted by Kallman among identical twins as contrasted with fraternal twins or ordinary siblings could be environmentally rather than genetically based.

In addition, there are methodological problems associated with Kallman's work. At the time of his studies techniques for distinguishing between identical and fraternal twins lacked precision. A fraternal pair might be incorrectly classified as identical if they looked and behaved enough alike—for example, if they were both depressed. Nowadays, blood serum studies make it possible to categorize twin types with little error. Furthermore, it should be noted that medical diagnoses of depression are not made blindly. A physician who finds in the family history that the identical (or fraternal) twin of a patient has been diagnosed as depressive is more likely to apply that label to his patient. These factors, too, tend to inflate the estimates of depression among family members.

Research evidence tends to support the idea that bipolar depression has a major genetic component. There is much less evidence for genetic causes in unipolar depression, however.

Biochemical Causes

Current research has led to an increasing interest in the role of biochemical factors in affective disorders. One theory proposes that a state of well-being is maintained in the body by hormones produced in the brain called *catechol-*

amines (epinephrine and norepinephrine). Deficits of these hormones may lead to severe emotional disruption and the mood swings of the manic-depressive. The evidence to support this theory is indirect. A group of drugs that lifts depression in some people is known also to increase the level of norepinephrine in the brain, while a drug that tends to produce depression reduces the amount of this hormone in the brain (see Appendix D).

Psychological Causes

Some evidence is difficult to fit into any strictly biological theory of manic-depressive psychosis. For example, a disproportionate number of manic-depressives tend to come from upper socioeconomic groups, and income is unlikely to be heavily biologically determined. Some researchers and clinicians have reached the conclusion that severe depression may be rooted in rejection in early childhood. The manic-depressive seems to be trying to win approval from parents who are constantly finding fault. Frequently, the precipitating event for the depression is loss of a loved one or loss of status. Behavior theorists have proposed that depression results from the lack of positive reinforcement within a person's life, a view that has a slightly different focus than the dynamic point of view but is consistent with it.

Treatment

A unique aspect of depression is the spontaneous remission of symptoms; that is, depression tends to lift after a period of time without the benefit of treatment. If a person in a severe depression is kept from committing suicide, the depression will lift. It may take weeks, months, or even years, but the state is self-limiting. This does not mean, however, that the person will not experience depression again in the future. Treatment is important, even though the depression is self-limiting, in order to reduce the suffering of the depressed person and his or her family.

How to understand and treat affective disorders is still very much unresolved. Many factors are involved, and no single set of circumstances has been found in the history of all manic-depressives. The treatment of psychotic depressives is difficult. Drugs are only partly successful, and psychotherapy tends to be a slow, up-hill climb. Supportive therapy, combined with drugs, with attempts to understand the causes of the depression and to help persons change their lives so as to eliminate the causes, is the most common strategy used today.

Involutional Melancholia

The depression associated with aging is referred to as **involutional** ("lack of will") **melancholia** ("depression") and is significantly different from the other forms of depression. It is relatively rare and is becoming even less frequent; in fact, today it constitutes only about 2 percent of admissions to mental hospitals. Involutional melancholia is a depressed psychotic reaction characterized by agitation and anxiety that tends to occur during the period of life when physiological and mental facilities are on the decline. Beginning with restlessness, insomnia, and excessive worrying, a person suffering from involutional melancholia may experience agitation, delusions, and ideas of persecution; in addition, the risk of suicide is quite high.

For women the age of onset is usually between 45 and 60 years and for men between 50 and 65 years. The beginning of involutional melancholia is closely associated with feelings that one has physically deteriorated and has a limited usefulness in society. Interestingly, most victims do not have a prior history of depression. In the past the disorder has been linked with menopause in women and with retirement in men. As sex roles continue to change, however, the age of onset in the future may be different for both males and females. Regardless of when the symptoms appear, the disorder is precipitated by the person's concern for his or her declining abilities and usefulness.

The role of biological factors in this disorder is not clear, although it has been suggested that genetically the disorder may be more closely akin to schizophrenia than to the manic-depressive psychosis. From a psychological point of view, pre-illness personalities are characterized as compulsive, over-conscientious, and insecure.

Unlike those who suffer from other forms of depression, persons with this disorder are not likely to recover spontaneously and will continue to be depressed if not treated. Medication and psychotherapy may be effective in reawakening these people to life.

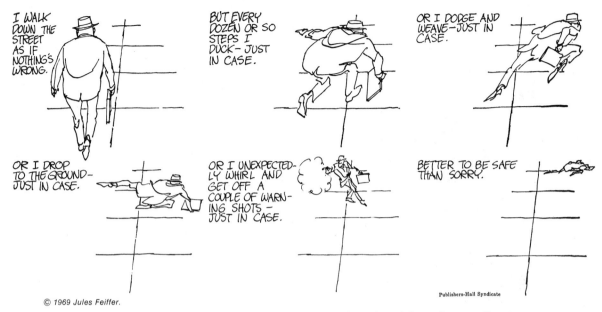

I WALK DOWN THE STREET AS IF NOTHING'S WRONG.

BUT EVERY DOZEN OR SO STEPS I DUCK – JUST IN CASE.

OR I DODGE AND WEAVE – JUST IN CASE.

OR I DROP TO THE GROUND – JUST IN CASE.

OR I UNEXPECTEDLY WHIRL AND GET OFF A COUPLE OF WARNING SHOTS – JUST IN CASE.

BETTER TO BE SAFE THAN SORRY.

© 1969 Jules Feiffer.

Publishers-Hall Syndicate

Paranoia is defined as inappropriate or irrational feelings of suspicion and persecution.

Schizophrenia

Schizophrenia refers to a group of psychotic disorders characterized by disturbances in thought processes and emotions as well as a marked distortion of reality. Conscious thought processes are often unpredictable because they usually follow a chain of free associations that is difficult for others to understand. Generally the schizophrenic withdraws from interpersonal relationships, and there is a blunting or flattening of emotional responses, which may change to extreme, inappropriate emotional responses. Another frequent symptom is depersonalization, or the loss of personal identity. The schizophrenic may become preoccupied with bodily functions, which are attributed to nonhuman causes. Such people may feel that a hand has turned to stone or that the body is full of bugs so that they are no longer human. There seems to be a preoccupation with inner fantasies. While schizophrenics are probably of normal intelligence, their lack of attention to the external environment leads to low scores on IQ tests.

In some cases schizophrenic breakdown is highly dramatic and is described by persons as something happening to them rather than something that they are doing. Schizophrenia in which there is a sudden onset of symptoms is sometimes referred to as **reactive schizophrenia;** the probability of recovery (**prognosis**) is good in such cases. Schizophrenia characterized by slow onset of symptoms over a period of years with progressive withdrawal from others, increasing deterioration of thought processes, and slow onset of hallucinations and delusions is referred to as **process schizophrenia;** in this case the prognosis is very poor. Some evidence suggests that genetics may play a greater causative role in process schizophrenia than in reactive schizophrenia.

Types of Schizophrenia

There are four main subtypes of schizophrenia: simple, hebephrenic, paranoid, and catatonic. **Simple schizophrenia** is generally a process type; the person is usually characterized by a reduction in interpersonal relationships, apathy, and indifference, but seldom has delusions and hallucinations. He or she has difficulty in focusing on anything in the outside world. Simple schizophrenics rarely cause much trouble because their symptoms do not intrude on the lives of others.

Hebephrenic schizophrenia is marked by

Figure 11–3
Catatonic schizophrenia

The patient in this picture is in a position that he might hold rigidly for long periods.

behavior that is grossly inappropriate in most situations. Such persons are given to much silliness, giggling, and childish behavior. Frequently hallucinations occur. The hebephrenic may break out laughing for no apparent reason or burst into rage without provocation. This subtype is usually a process type involving gradual symptom onset, and the prognosis is poor.

Paranoid schizophrenia is frequently a reactive problem, and there is a reasonable chance of recovery. This subtype is characterized by delusions of persecution and suspicion of others. The feeling of being singled out for persecution leads the paranoid to conclude that he or she is a special person, selected because of unusual powers or qualities. Thus, the paranoid schizophrenic is often characterized by *delusions of grandeur*. In one case, a youth attacked a total

stranger who was standing near him at a baseball game. When asked later by the police why he had done this, he responded that it was well known that he was sexually attractive to women and this man was trying to steal his sexual attractiveness by electrical waves. It is assumed that paranoids use projection, denying their unacceptable anger and ascribing it to others. Paranoid schizophrenia should not be confused with the paranoid personality, a personality disorder characterized by suspiciousness and jealousy but no loss of contact with reality.

Catatonic schizophrenia may be a reactive or a process type. The reactive catatonic probably has the best prognosis of any of the schizophrenics. The catatonic is characterized by a *waxy flexibility* of body and limbs, loss of motion, and a tendency to remain motionless for hours or days. Such persons may allow their arms to be placed in uncomfortable positions without resistance and remain in that position far longer than the normal individual would tolerate. The dynamic theorists see the catatonic as handling hostility by immobility (see Figure 11–3). The catatonic may have episodes of furious rage from time to time that alternate with the rigid withdrawal.

While these four types of schizophrenia are carefully described in diagnostic manuals and books of psychopathology, it is important to note that individuals seldom fit into such neat patterns. The two most common diagnoses made within the schizophrenic classification are *paranoid* and *chronic-undifferentiated*. The latter diagnosis is a wastebasket term indicating that the person has characteristics belonging to more than one subtype. In general, schizophrenics can be described as being either paranoid schizophrenic or undifferentiated schizophrenic and as either process or reactive. The term "schizophrenia" is often applied when a person is psychotic but not depressed. The lack of clarity in the use of the term "schizophrenia" and its different definitions from one mental institution to the next has complicated the extensive research conducted on the causes of the disorder.

Causes of Schizophrenia

We shall briefly consider research on genetic, biochemical, and environmental factors. It is clear from the research that all three of these factors are involved in causing schizophrenia.

TABLE 11-4 Schizophrenia Rates in Identical Twins

Investigator	Number of Twin Pairs Studied (One Twin Already Diagnosed as Schizophrenic)	Number of Pairs in Which the Other Member of the Pair Also Has Schizophrenia	Number of Pairs in Which the Other Member of the Pair Is Abnormal But Not Schizophrenic
Kallman	174	103	62
Essen-Moller	9	0	8
Slater	37	18	11
Tienari	16	1	12
Kringlen	45	14	17
Inouye	53	20	29
Gottesman and Shields	24	10	8
Total	358	166 (46.4%)	147 (41.1%)
		Concordance rate = .46	Concordance rate = .41

GENETIC FACTORS There is little doubt now that there is a genetic component in schizophrenia, although different investigators have found widely different concordance rates for sets of identical twins. For example, Kallman, whose research is most well known in this area, found that of 174 pairs of twins with one member who had already been diagnosed as schizophrenic, the other twin was also schizophrenic in 103 cases (see Table 11-4). On the other hand, Essen-Moller found no pairs of twins in which both members were schizophrenic.

It is generally agreed now that Kallman's data significantly exaggerate the degree of heredity involved in schizophrenia. We reviewed some of the general problems with his methods in our discussion of affective disorders, but additional questions have arisen in connection with his work on schizophrenia. For example, Kallman's sample of patients has been criticized as having involved only the most severe cases and as having a preponderance of females. There is some evidence (Gottesman and Shields, 1966) that the degree of concordance between twins is higher as the severity of the affliction increases. This in turn suggests that schizophrenia is not a unitary disorder and that process forms may be more genetically based than reactive forms.

Perhaps the best estimate of the degree of genetic determination of schizophrenia can be obtained by pooling the results of several different studies. On the basis of the results of the seven studies shown in Table 11-4, we conclude: Given that one twin is schizophrenic, the chances are 46/100 that the other twin will be schizophrenic (the probability that the other twin will be schizophrenic = .46). The value for ordinary brothers and sisters would only be around 10 to 15 percent, so these data strongly suggest a genetic component in schizophrenia. Even if the other twin is not schizophrenic, the odds are quite high that he or she will have some significant behavior abnormality. Thus, if one of a pair of identical twins is schizophrenic, about 88 percent of the other twins either will be schizophrenic or will suffer from some other behavior disorder (the sum of columns two and three in Table 11-4).

It is probably true that in all cases of schizophrenia, as in the affective disorders, both heredity and environment are important, a notion formally called the *diathesis-stress* theory of psychosis. According to this theory, schizophrenia develops because there is a genetic predisposition to the disorder (called *diathesis*) *and* because there are environmental factors (*stress*) that trigger the disorder. If either factor is missing, the disorder will not appear. This theory is a better approximation to our current knowledge than a model which suggests that one type of schizophrenia is genetic (the process type, say) and the other is environmental (the reactive type, say).

BIOCHEMICAL FACTORS Are there biochemical factors in schizophrenia? At times chemicals have supposedly been found in the blood of schizophrenics that are not found in normal blood. However, no single chemical has been consistently found by all research groups. It has also been proposed that a neural transmitter, called *serotonin*, produces the symptoms of schizophrenia, but our understanding of how neural transmitters work is still far from complete.

The Case of a Paranoid Schizophrenic

I, LPK, had a few days to spend with Long Island relatives before returning to work for the War Dept., Wash., D.C. One day I went to reconnoitre in N.Y. City's East Side. Being a stranger I was surprised to hear someone exclaim twice: "Shoot him!", evidently meaning me, judging from the menacing talk which followed between the threatener and those with him. I tried to see who the threatener, and those with him were, but the street was so crowded, I could not. I guessed that they must be gangsters, who had mistaken me for another gangster, who I coincidentally happened to resemble. I thought one or more of them really intended to shoot me so I hastened from the scene as fast as I could walk. These unidentified persons, who had threatened to shoot me, pursued me. I knew they were pursuing me because I still heard their voices as close as ever, no matter how fast I walked . . . Days later while in the Metropolis again, I was once more startled by those same pursuers, who had threatened me several days before. It was nighttime. As before, I could catch part of their talk but, in the theatre crowds, I could see them nowhere. I heard one of them, a woman, say: "You can't get away from us; we'll lay for you, and get you after a while!" To add to the mystery, one of these "pursuers" repeated my thoughts aloud, verbatim. I tried to allude [sic] these pursuers as before, but this time, I tried to escape from them by means of subway trains, darting up and down subway exits, and entrances, jumping on, and off trains, until after midnight. But, at every station where I got off a train, I heard the voices of these pursuers as close as ever. The question occurred to me: How could as many of these pursuers follow me as quickly unseen? Were they ghosts? Or was I in the process of developing into a spiritual medium? No! Among these pursuers, I was later to gradually discover by deduction, [there] evidently were some brothers, and sisters,[1] who had inherited from one of their parents, some astounding, unheard of, utterly unbelievable occult powers. Believe-it-or-not, some of them,[2] besides being able to tell a person's thoughts, are also able to project their magnetic voices—commonly called "radio voices" around here—a distance of a few miles without talking loud, and without apparent effort, their voices sounding from that distance as tho heard thru a radio head-set,[3] this being done without electrical apparatus. This unique, occult power of projecting their "radio voices" for such long distances, apparently seems to be due to their natural, bodily electricity, of which they have a supernormal amount. Maybe the iron contained in their red blood corpuscles is magnetised. The vibration of their vocal chords, evidently generates wireless waves, and these vocal radio waves are caught by human ears without rectification.[4] (Kaplan, 1964, pages 133–135)

[1] Maybe some were half brothers, or half sisters, or both.
[2] There is little doubt but what more than one of them can read minds.
[3] Hence the term "radio voices."
[4] The other day I read about a man who could hear radio broadcasts of a local station thru his teeth without a receiving set. In the plant where he worked the air was filled with tiny carborundum crystals, and some of these had collected on his teeth.

All the studies implicating biochemical factors suffer the same difficulty in interpretation—it is never clear if the biochemical change is a cause or a result of the disorder. For example, many mental hospitals are nonhygienic and overcrowded. Most patients are on medication of some kind, taking drugs that often have unknown biochemical side effects. The eating

Most research studies which find that children have problems similar to those of their parents assume that the parents' behavior led to the children's prob- lems. Yet, the possibility is frequently ignored that the parents' behavior may be a reaction to having an emotionally disturbed child.

habits of psychotics may be poor, since they often withdraw from all activity in the external world. All these factors may lead to biochemical imbalance. Although it is tempting to think of biochemical abnormalities as the cause of schizophrenia, these conditions suggest that they might really be the result.

ENVIRONMENTAL FACTORS   In an effort to isolate environmental factors, extensive research has been done on the family life of the schizophrenic. Lidz et al. (1963) have proposed that there is a *marital skew* in the family, in which serious psychopathology in one parent is accepted or supported by the other parent. In other families the problem is one of *marital schism*—there is open warfare between husband and wife. Bitter arguments are so common that the marriage is in constant danger of breaking up. There may be a serious lack of understanding and cooperation between parents, resulting in distrust and rivalry. The father is frequently seen as insecure and weak, and the mother as domineering and hostile.

Bateson et al. (1956) describe a conflict situation known as the *double bind,* in which a parent presents to the child ideas, feelings, and demands that are contradictory. At one level of communication the parent may express love and at another rejection. At the third level of communication the parent prevents the child from commenting on the paradox. The parent may say "I love you" but provide no physical con-

Schizophrenics' Blood Abnormal?

AP

ANAHEIM, Calif. — Schizophrenic patients who improved after their blood was filtered by a kidney machine appear to have abnormal quantities of a newly identified protein substance, two California researchers report. . . .

Dr. Frank Ervin of the University of California at Los Angeles and Roberta Palmour of the University of California at Berkeley reported their study at the Society for Neuroscience meeting here.

The substance removed from the blood of schizophrenics is from a group of chemicals called endorphins, which recently have been discovered in the brain and pituitary gland. Researchers have connected endorphins with a wide variety of mental states or processes, including euphoria and pain perception. . . .

The research grew out of reports by two investigators, Drs. James Cade of the University of Miami and Herbert Wagemaker of the University of Louisville, who found improvement in 18 of 21 psychotic patients treated on kidney machines. . . .

"After 16 weekly dialysis sessions, the patients' delusions disappeared, though they were left with significant problems in adjusting to society," Ervin said. They were generally younger patients belonging to the 20 percent of schizophrenics that aren't helped by antipsychotic drugs. . . .

The Denver Post
November 10, 1977

Psychotics Prefer Delusions

WASHINGTON — The delusions of grandeur entertained by some schizophrenics may be far more comforting to these patients than the stark realities they face in moments of sanity.

This is the conclusion reached by a team of psychiatric researchers after a three-year study to determine why some chronic schizophrenics persistently refuse to take drugs that alleviate their psychoses, while other patients, also suffering from schizophrenia, are unswervingly faithful in complying with their treatment regimen.

The study involved 59 patients — 29 who persistently refused drugs and 30 who just as persistently came in for medication — at the Brentwood Veterans Administration Hospital in Los Angeles.

The crucial factor that distinguished the two groups appeared to be the nature of their personal psychoses....

While the drug refusers basked in Napoleonic delusions, the schizophrenics who cooperated with the drug-treatment program were far more likely to be subject to acute attacks of anxiety and depression when they failed to take their medication and slipped back into psychosis....

"The observation that hard-core drug refusers can count on a resurgence of a florid psychosis characterized by grandiosity and relative absence of such dysphoric affects as anxiety and depression does not necessarily mean that they stop taking medication for that reason," the researchers said.

"However, three years' experience with a merry-go-round of readmissions and discharges forced us to realize that there exists a group of chronic schizophrenic patients who never become reconciled to the need for antipsychotic medications and who cannot tolerate the drug-induced increase in reality."

The researchers cited the case of a 30-year-old man who was hospitalized 19 times, harboring delusions that he was a composer, that he possessed "billions" and that he was "the greatest aeronautical engineer in the world."

While in the hospital, he spent his time sketching "satellite stations" and would demand from time to time to see his imaginary publisher.

As drugs he was given to clear up his psychosis took effect, the researchers reported, "He started to mention his loneliness and his realistic lack of any life accomplishments and developed some insight into his illness.

"At this point he demanded to leave the hospital and resumed living in a lonely hotel. He returned for only one injection (of the anti-psychotic medication) and was re-admitted three months later, psychotic as before." . . .

"The hard-core drug refusers resembled Elwood P. Dowd, the whimsical hero of the play 'Harvey'," the researchers said. In the play, Dowd's closest friend and most frequent companion is a civilized, six-foot, invisible white rabbit, who goes by the name Harvey.

"When his psychiatrist urged (Dowd) to struggle with reality," the researchers noted, "he responded, 'Doctor, I wrestled with reality for 40 years and I am happy to state that I finally won out over it'."

The authors of the study were Dr. Theodore Van Putten, Evelyn Crumpton and Coralee Yale.

The Denver Post
February 16, 1977

Some theorists have proposed that delusions serve the function of reducing anxiety for the psychotic.

tact, indicating rejection. Uncertain as to whether or not he or she should respond to the parent's expressions of affection, the child withdraws and establishes no relationships.

Still, there is a great deal of overlap between schizophrenics and normal people in family background. Also, people from completely different types of families become schizophrenics. Of two people from relatively similar backgrounds, one may be schizophrenic while the other is quite normal. Thus, as in the case of biological factors, the role of family and other social influences in schizophrenia is far from clear.

SUMMARY

1. Psychopathology is defined as the inability to behave in a socially appropriate way, with maladaptive consequences. This inability might reflect either organic or functional deficiencies.

2. The medical model views psychopathological behaviors as symptoms of an underlying process that operates like a disease.

3. The dynamic model assumes psychopathology results from a conflict between the conscious and unconscious aspects of the personality.

4. The behavioral model proposes that psychopathology is the result of positive and negative reinforcements in a person's environment.

5. The phenomenological model emphasizes the importance of the here-and-now existence and is a noncausative model.

6. The ethical model assumes that psychopathology results when an individual makes irresponsible choices in life.

7. The most widely used system for classifying abnormal behavior is to group people on the basis of similar behavioral or emotional symptoms.

8. The experience of anxiety is unpleasant, and people try to cope with the stress of being anxious. The two primary defenses against anxiety are repression and denial.

9. Neurosis develops out of attempts to avoid anxiety. The neurotic paradox refers to the fact that while people find anxiety unpleasant, their defenses prevent them from learning new ways of dealing effectively with the cause of the anxiety.

10. Neurotic defenses or coping behaviors were grouped into seven classifications: transient situational disturbances, anxiety neurosis, phobias and hypochondriasis, obsessive-compulsive neurosis, conversion reactions, dissociative reactions, and neurotic depression.

11. Psychosomatic illness is a physical illness that is caused by emotional factors.

12. Personality disorders, such as alcoholism, drug addiction, and sexually deviant behavior, are defined as failures to behave in socially appropriate ways due to lack of motivation or lack of skill in coping with the normal stresses of everyday life.

13. Psychosis refers to behavior characterized by loss of contact with reality, frequently accompanied by hallucinations and delusions.

14. A depression becomes diagnosed as psychotic when a person has lost contact with reality. Mania, with feelings of great optimism and the speeding up of thought processes, is a form of reaction formation against depression. In manic-depressive psychosis states of mania and depression occur alternately in a fairly regular cycle.

15. Involutional melancholia is the depression of aging, and unlike other depressions does not exhibit spontaneous recovery.

16. In schizophrenia there are marked distortions of reality and disturbances in thought processes and emotions. The four main subtypes of schizophrenia are: simple, hebephrenic, paranoid, and catatonic.

17. On the basis of twin studies, researchers have pretty well agreed that there is a genetic component in schizophrenia, although environment is also an important factor.

RECOMMENDED ADDITIONAL READINGS

Alvarez, A. *The savage god: A study of suicide.* New York: Bantam, 1973.

Goldstein, J. J., & Palmer, J. O. *The experience of anxiety: A casebook,* 2d ed. New York: Oxford University Press, 1975.

Kaplan, B. (ed.) *The inner world of mental illness.* New York: Harper & Row, 1964.

Martin, B. *Abnormal psychology.* New York: Holt, Rinehart and Winston, 1977.

Plath, S. *The bell jar.* New York: Harper & Row, 1971.

Schreiber, F. R. *Sybil.* Chicago: Regnery, 1973.

Wilson, L. *This stranger my son.* New York: Signet, 1968.

what does it mean?

Most of the meaning of our scientific knowledge of psychopathology is best illustrated by our discussion of psychotherapy in Chapter 12. Indeed, the techniques of psychotherapy can be seen as an outgrowth of the application of personality theory (Chapter 9) to the problems of pathological behavior described in this chapter. Therefore, this section will be somewhat briefer than comparable sections of earlier chapters. We will concentrate on only a few general issues.

HAS THE WORLD GONE MAD?

We have already made it clear that psychopathology is to some extent a culturally defined activity. Behavior that is accepted in one society may be considered seriously deviant in another. Thomas Szasz (1963) was one of the earliest psychologists to ask the important question, "Who defines the norms and hence the deviation?" On the one hand, the person himself may decide that he deviates from the norm. Alternatively, someone other than the sufferer may decide that the person is deviant in some important respect. When a psychiatrist is hired by the court to decide whether a person is sane or insane (and whether the individual should be held responsible for his or her behavior), the psychiatrist is not given the alternative to testify that the accused is normal, but the legislators are "insane" for passing the law that made

that behavior illegal (Szasz, 1963, pages 14–15)! Obviously, society's laws and rules are not infallible. With respect to psychopathology, one need only consider the decision by the American Psychiatric Association to remove homosexuality from the list of categories of abnormal behavior.

R. D. Laing (1967, 1969) has gone even further than Szasz in attacking labels and diagnostic categories. Schizophrenia is not a "mental illness" but an adaptive response to an insane world, according to Laing. Diagnostic labels are "straightjackets" that keep us from communicating with the disturbed person. Society and particularly the family in the society are destructive forces that attack the self. Laing's approach is strongly anticognitive, and he sees feelings and intuition as the hope of mankind. Yet when we look at the behavior of a suffering neurotic or psychotic, it is difficult to defend the idea that such behavior is always a creative way of adapting to a disordered world, as implied by Laing.

However extreme their positions in some respects, both Szasz and Laing remind us that societies as well as people can be disordered. Of course, all societies label some behaviors unacceptable. The range of behaviors is simply too great to permit all behaviors to exist in a society without some form of control. But societies that permit a greater range of non-harmful (a value judgment!) behaviors— behaviors that do not endanger the safety or well-being of others, for instance—can be

461

"When Jud accuses Zack, here, of hostility toward his daughter, like he seems to every session, why, it's plain to me he's only rationalizing his own lack of gumption in standing up to a stepson who's usurping the loyalty of his second wife. The way he lit into him just now shows he's got this here guilt identification with Zack's present family constellation. Calling Zack egotistical ain't nothing but a disguise mechanism for concealing his secret envy of Zack's grit and all-around starch, and shows mighty poor ego boundaries of his own, it appears to me."

The New Yorker, April 5, 1976. Drawing by Whitney Darrow, Jr.; © 1976 The New Yorker Magazine, Inc.

Psychological concepts have reached almost all corners of our society.

viewed as healthier or more adaptive. As well as being willing to confront their personal ethical and social conflicts, people must be open to recognizing when the social structure needs changing.

THE DANGER OF DIAGNOSIS

It has been demonstrated that psychologists' expectations about the results of an experiment can influence (through their own behavior) the results that are obtained. The diagnosis of an individual—assigning a label to him or her—can have the same effect.

Although it is important to recognize that behavioral problems do exist and to know which symptoms indicate significant disorder, there is a danger that diagnostic labels will become self-fulfilling prophecies of the person's behavior. There is some evidence, for example, that teachers who assume that minority students will do poorly in school lower their standards and demands for excellence, leading the students to perform at a lower level than they might otherwise. Persons who are labeled mental retardates can be treated in such a way that they are effectively no longer allowed to learn. The juvenile labeled as delinquent starts to behave in such a way as to realize society's expectations. With psychopathology, the same problem exists. There is a strong moral responsibility for the diagnostician to keep labels away from people who might misuse them. Thus, a diagnosis is seldom given to the person or family of the person who is diagnosed for fear that the diagnosis will be self-fulfilling.

THE UNRELIABILITY OF DIAGNOSIS

The relatively clear descriptions of diagnostic categories given in this chapter might lead one to assume that diagnosis is a straightforward job for clinicians. It has generally been found that there is a high level of agreement among clinicians in the assignment of patients to the major diagnostic categories such as neurosis, personality disorder, or psychosis; for the subcategories—for example, simple and hebephrenic schizophrenia—however, agreement is much lower. In one study, four experienced psychiatrists diagnosed 153 patients referred for outpatient treatment (Beck, Ward, Mendelson, Mock, and Erbaugh, 1962). Each person was interviewed by two psychiatrists. The overall rate of agreement on diagnosis averaged only 54 percent. Agreement occurred only 53 percent of the time for schizophrenia (a lower percentage than the

Study Reveals Psychiatrists Can't Tell Sane from Insane

AP

STANFORD, Calif. — Who's sane? Who's insane?

The psychiatrists and staffs of mental hospitals cannot be trusted to tell the difference, declares Prof. David L. Rosenhan, a Stanford University psychologist.

Rosenhan says he and seven other sane investigators arranged as a test to be admitted as schizophrenic patients in 12 different mental hospitals, yet none of the eight was found to be sane by hospital professionals.

But Rosenhan says it was "quite common" for actual psychiatric patients to correctly identify the "pseudopatient" imposters.

Important Questions

"The fact that patients often recognized normality when staff did not raised important questions," Roesenhan observes. . . .

Rosenhan said he and his seven colleagues eventually were released as "schizophrenics in remission," despite their best efforts to convince the hospital staff of their sanity.

"We now know that we cannot distinguish insanity from sanity," Rosenhan declared.

"We continue to label patients 'schizophrenic', 'manic-depressive', and 'insane' as if in those words we had captured the essence of understanding," he wrote.

"The facts of the matter are that we have known for a long time that our diagnoses often are not useful or reliable, but we have nevertheless continued to use them."

Rosenhan, who also teaches law at Stanford, said he and the other pseudopatients were shocked and horrified by their experiences.

But, he said, they did not blame the hospital staffs.

"By and large, they were well-intentioned people, and in no way do we want to malign them," he said.

"The hospital itself imposes a special environment in which the meanings of behavior can easily be misunderstood."

Rosenhan said the pseudopatient group included a psychiatrist, a pediatrician, a painter, a housewife, a Stanford psychology graduate student and three other psychologists.

Feigned Symptoms

He said they gained admission to hospitals in California, Oregon, Pennsylvania, New York and Delaware by feigning symptoms of schizophrenia.

"The uniform failure to recognize sanity cannot be attributed to the quality of treatment facilities. While there was considerable variability between them, several are considered excellent," Rosenhan reported.

"Nor can it be alleged that there simply was not enough time to observe the pseudopatients. Length of hospitalization ranged from seven to 52 days, with an average of 19 days."

"All pseudopatients took extensive notes publicly. Under ordinary circumstances such behavior would have raised questions in the minds of observers, as in fact it did among patients.

"Nursing records for three pseudopatients indicate that the writing was seen as an aspect of their pathological behavior."

Boulder (Colo.) Daily Camera
January 18, 1973

This article clearly demonstrates the danger of diagnosis. Once a person is labeled abnormal, any subsequent behavior is likely to be seen as additional evidence of emotional disturbance.

70 percent agreement usually found for *hospitalized* patients), 40 percent for involuntional melancholia, and 63 percent for neurotic depression. Such difficulty in reaching agreement in diagnosis makes it clear why research on the cause and cure of specific diagnostic disorders is so difficult.

THE DANGER OF DIAGNOSING YOUR OWN PROBLEMS

A little learning is a dangerous thing. It is not unusual for persons reading about abnormal behavior for the first time to raise questions about themselves and their own

Psychologists' Panel Hits Self-Help Books

AP

SAN FRANCISCO — The millions of Americans who are buying self-help books may be helping themselves to the harmful therapies of charlatans, a panel of psychologists said. . . .

The psychologists, including one who has written self-help books, suggested that a guide for consumers should be circulated to "check up in a scientific way" on authors' claims.

They were careful to say that even the most irresponsible books—such as those which promise instant happiness or a better sex life overnight—should not be banned. . . .

. . . such titles as "How to Take Control of Your Life," "Looking Out for Number 1" and "I'm OK You're OK," have been on best-seller lists all over the country. The panel did not single out any specific book for criticism.

The APA's [American Psychological Association] concern is prompted by books and tape recordings that encourage mental self-help—sidestepping the psychologist or psychiatrist.

While it might seem selfserving for psychologists to criticize the trend, many of the authors are APA members themselves. . . .

Boulder (Colo.) Daily Camera
August 28, 1977

A danger with self-help books is that one might be given poor advice or apply good advice inappropriately, and thus do more harm than good.

levels of adaptive or maladaptive functioning. The "medical student's syndrome" (where the medical student imagines he or she has every disease studied about) often occurs in students reading about abnormal psychology.

One could suffer needlessly thinking that every symptom one shows that is similar to those described here is an indication of a behavior problem. As we noted, everyone shows one or more of these symptoms from time to time.

It is best to keep in mind the definition of psychopathology given at the beginning of this chapter; psychopathology is a failure, for either organic or psychological reasons, to behave in a socially appropriate and acceptable way, such that the person or society suffers adverse consequences. Suppose you were unhappy and worried about poor school work. No one would think it unreasonable for you to feel anxious about the consequences of flunking out of school, and psychotherapy would not be indicated. However, if your poor work could be traced to a panic state you experienced before each exam, your anxiety would appear to be inappropriate and you might benefit from a therapy designed to replace fear responses with more functional behavior.

To be overly sensitive to minor anxiety or depression could lead you to worry more about the normality of feelings than about the stress that caused those feelings in the first place. Yet to ignore strong feelings of distress because of fear of being abnormal could lead you to settle for a much less rewarding life than you could obtain. All too often people are more concerned with knowing whether they can be labeled with a diagnosis of neurotic, psychosomatic, or psychotic rather than with asking and answering much more basic questions: *Am I functioning appropriately under the circumstances? Am I behaving responsibly? Am I happy or am I working toward goals that will allow me to be happy?*

12

Psychotherapy

The odds are surprisingly high that someday each of us will feel the need to seek professional help in solving a mental or emotional problem of our own or of someone close to us. Most families experience some maladjustment at some time, whether it is a psychosomatic illness such as asthma or ulcers, a neurotic depression following divorce or loss of a job, a strong dependence on alcohol or drugs, or a more serious disorder such as schizophrenia. Some people believe, in fact, that the vast majority of American adults are neurotic to some degree. Divorce rates and suicide rates are skyrocketing in some areas, as are crime and delinquency. Psychological distress and disorder are common in our society, and psychopathology constitutes a major social problem.

Indeed, serious disturbances in psychological functioning are so common that it is absurd to attach any particular stigma to them. For a long time the mentally ill were treated as criminals, witches, or worse, and even today some people "look down on" those who seek professional help for psychological problems. They are often regarded as weird, "funny," or weak in some way, although some problem behaviors, such as alcoholism, seem to be more acceptable in our society than others, such as sexual exhibitionism.

Of the many different ways of responding to psychopathological behavior, only some are therapeutic. Others, such as imprisonment, cruelty, or rejection obviously are not. When mental illness was viewed as possession by the devil, drilling holes in a person's head to allow the evil spirits to escape was perhaps an appropriate "therapy." And when mental illness was considered a symptom of character weakness or moral degeneracy, chains and whipping were attempts to correct it. But given our conception of psychopathology as the failure, for organic or psychological reasons, to behave in a socially appropriate way, how is psychotherapy conceptualized and practiced today?

A DEFINITION OF PSYCHOTHERAPY

Psychotherapy can be defined as *a corrective experience leading a person to behave in a socially appropriate, adequate, and adaptive way*. The therapy will focus on the lack of knowledge, the lack of skill, or the lack of motivation to behave appropriately, or on the abnormal behavior itself. In most cases, a combination of these factors would be involved in the pathology, and the therapy would be adjusted accordingly. When we speak of therapy we usually imply that it is delivered by a professional—a psychologist, psychiatrist, psychiatric social worker, or psychiatric nurse (see Table 12–1). This does not mean, however, that all corrective experiences are professionally arranged. Close personal friends probably do a great deal of psychotherapy unwittingly. Here, however, we will be concerned mainly with formal psychotherapy administered by professionals. Finally, it is important to note that all those concerned with correcting maladaptive behavior should be equally concerned with *preventing* it. Although in the past prevention has not been a major focus of therapists' efforts, it may be increasingly so in the future.

One of the first questions in a therapist's mind when confronted with a person seeking psychotherapy is, Why is the person here? The most common reason people seek therapy is that they are uncomfortable with the way they are handling their lives. They may be frequently anxious when interacting with others or find that they are having trouble coping successfully with their job or marriage. Other reasons may enter into the decision to seek therapy, however. A person may be blackmailed into therapy, such as when a man threatens to leave his wife unless she seeks help. Or a physician may tell the person that his ulcer or arthritis is of psychosomatic origin and that psychotherapy is recommended. Or a person may be experiencing anxiety, anger, or depression without knowing why, so that self-knowledge and control is the goal.

In general, the relationship between one's ideal self-concept and one's behavior is important in therapy. If the ideal self-concept and the behavior are consistent with each other, the symptoms (or inappropriate behaviors) are said to be *syntonic*. If the ideal self-concept and the behavior are inconsistent, the symptoms are said to be *dystonic*. If a person is comfortable with his or her behavior (a syntonic relation-

TABLE 12-1 Mental Health Professionals

Name	Degree	Specialization	Education
Clinical psychologist	Master of Arts, Doctor of Philosophy, Doctor of Psychology	Research, therapy, diagnostic testing	Graduate education in a department of psychology
Psychiatrist	Doctor of Medicine	Therapy, psychosomatics, medication	Residency training in psychiatry
Psychoanalyst	Usually, Doctor of Medicine	Psychoanalysis	Usually psychiatrist with additional training in psychoanalysis
Psychiatric social worker	Master of Social Work	Individual and family therapy and counseling, community orientation	Graduate education in school of social work
School psychologist	Master of Arts, Doctor of Philosophy, or Doctor of Education	Counseling or educational testing	Graduate work in psychology or education
Counseling psychologist	Same as school psychologist	Counseling, therapy, vocational counseling, rehabilitation	Graduate work in psychology or education
Psychiatric nurse	Registered Nurse	Counseling, therapy, care of hospitalized mental patients	Training in nursing and psychiatry
Paraprofessional	None necessary	Ability to communicate with people in own community	Short orientation in service facility

ship), there is little reason to change. The individual is likely to be brought to therapy by someone else (parents, spouse, courts) and is likely to be difficult to treat. In such cases the therapist has an ethical responsibility to make clear to the client his own goals in therapy and to indicate how they might differ from the client's. The types of psychotherapy to be discussed in this chapter can be divided into two broad categories: (1) insight-oriented therapies, which have as their focus change in motivation and knowledge, and (2) noninsight-oriented therapies (often referred to as behavior therapies), which have as their focus change in motivation, skills, and performance. We will also discuss the biological therapies (based on the medical model), group approaches to therapy, and community mental health.

INSIGHT-ORIENTED THERAPY

Insight-oriented therapy is based on the assumption, similar to that of the dynamic model of psychopathology, that emotional problems stem from the conflict between conscious and unconscious processes. To resolve this conflict persons must be made aware of their uncon-

scious processes, and thus the goal of therapy is insight or self-knowledge. The insight-oriented therapies can be divided into two types: (1) those focusing on the repressed memories of the past, such as psychoanalysis—these are based on the dynamic model of psychopathology discussed in the last chapter; and (2) those focusing on denied aspects of present feelings, such as client-centered therapy, Gestalt therapy, and transactional analysis—these are based on the phenomenological or ethical model discussed in the last chapter.

The Dynamic Model: Insight into Past Experiences

Psychoanalysis is the therapeutic technique Freud developed on the basis of his psychoanalytic theory. Freud, as we know, assumed that emotional problems are in part the result of repression of drives, feelings, and memories and that an awareness of these unconscious mental processes will resolve most emotional problems. However, the client must not only achieve insight into the cause of his or her symptoms but must also experience the emotion associated with the original memory.

"The Electra complex is always a toughie, and on top of that, you were born under Aquarius. Let's see what the 'I Ching' says."

Playboy, November 1974. Reproduced by special permission of PLAYBOY Magazine; copyright © 1974 by Playboy.

Trying to take into account too many theories of human behavior may lead one to have no real theory at all.

. . . we found, to our great surprise at first, that each individual . . . symptom immediately and permanently disappeared when we had succeeded in bringing clearly to light the memory of the event by which it was provoked and in arousing its accompanying affect (emotions), and when the patient had described that event in the greatest possible detail and had put the affect into words. Recollection without affect almost invariably produces no result. (Breuer and Freud, 1957)

Because the open expression of sexual and aggressive feelings is generally thought unacceptable for children and adults in our society, we are taught to inhibit or repress these feelings. Thus sexual and aggressive feelings are a main focus in psychoanalysis. Sexual mores are changing dramatically in the direction of greater freedom. If this is a mentally healthy change, psychoanalysis should in the future focus less on sexual feelings and more on aggressive feelings.

The aim of psychoanalysis is to help the client overcome the unconscious resistance to remembering anxiety-provoking thoughts and impulses. Freud developed a variety of tech-

niques to aid the client overcome this resistance. One of these is the use of the *couch*, the subject of numerous jokes. In psychoanalysis the patient typically lies down on the couch, looking up to the ceiling, and the analyst sits behind the client out of direct sight (see Figure 12–1). Some reasons for the use of the couch may have nothing to do with technique. First, Freud discovered the importance of recollection of repressed memories through hypnosis, and the couch is in part a carryover from the use of hypnosis as a technique. Second, it is rumored that Freud preferred sitting behind the patient because he felt uncomfortable having people look at him all day. Thus, the couch may be attributable to one of Freud's own hang-ups! Most important, however, is the fact that the couch reduces external stimulation and encourages the client to turn inward to focus on his or her own associations.

Some analysts who prefer face-to-face contact with the client want the client to be aware of their reactions on the assumption that one of the client's problems might be a lack of sensitivity to the reactions of others. However, the psychoanalyst is more interested in an inward focus of attention to facilitate the remembering of repressed memories. The following techniques are used to help patients understand the contents of their own unconscious.

Free Association

Clients are instructed to say anything and everything that comes to mind. They are told to express their thoughts as freely as possible and hold nothing back, no matter how trivial or shocking. This basic rule of psychoanalysis sounds relatively easy, but, in fact, most people find it extremely difficult to give up their concern over the impression they are making on someone else, including the analyst. Resistance to the basic rule of free association at the unconscious level will therefore often lead to blocking—the person simply cannot think of any association. Such resistance helps the analyst understand what areas of the person's memories are repressed and can then help the client overcome such resistance to remembering.

Symptomatic Acts

The behavior of the client during analysis may lead the analyst to understand areas of repression. Slips of the tongues, changes in

Psychiatric News, November 5, 1977. Reprinted by permission of Sidney Harris.

Figure 12-1
Psychoanalysis

In classical psychoanalysis the patient lies on a couch, and the therapist sits out of the client's direct line of sight.

behavior toward the therapy hour, forgetting therapy appointments, and unusual behavior during therapy may all be symptomatic of deeper and more significant unconscious processes.

Dream Analysis

In his book *The Interpretation of Dreams,* Freud maintained that it was useful to consider dreams as representing, in a symbolic way, the unconscious conflicts or desires of the dreamer (see Appendix D). The purpose of the symbolic nature of the dream message is to avoid anxiety that would wake the person up. The symbolic meaning of elements of a dream cannot easily be interpreted without knowing the associational links of the individual who had the dream. There have been "dream books" published that propose to interpret the symbols in dreams. The authors tend to interpret every pointed object in a dream as a symbol of a phallus and every open space as a symbol of a vagina because Freud believed that sexual

conflicts determined most symbols. Although Freud proposed that such general symbolism may be involved, he felt that each person tends to have idiosyncratic associations that lead to unique symbols as well. It is the therapist's task to discover the meanings of such symbols.

After the client has related a dream, the analyst asks the person to free associate to various elements of the dream. He may also ask for information about the previous day in an effort to understand the **manifest content** (the superficial story of the dream), and the **latent content** (the symbolic meaning of that story). For example, a woman reported dreaming that a man unknown to her stole her car and was killed in an accident—the manifest content. The latent content of her dream was not obvious and could be clarified only with free association and the therapist's knowledge of some of the personality dynamics of the client. However, the latent content became clear when the therapist discovered that the unknown man could be considered a symbol for her husband. The woman did not know or understand her husband very well ("unknown to her"), he frequently took advantage of her ("stole her car"), and she was very angry at him for this manipulative behavior ("he was killed"). Her anger toward him was unacceptable to her, and she feared expressing it because she felt he

"You won't save any money by talking fast, Mrs. Lewis."

Ladies Home Journal, October 1969. Reprinted by permission of Don Orehek.

One problem with psychoanalysis is the high cost of seeing a therapist four to five times a week.

would leave her. The anxiety-provoking latent content of the dream was expressed symbolically.

Interpretation

The psychoanalyst's basic job is interpretation, explaining to the client the unconscious meaning of what he or she says. The purpose of interpretation is to help the client overcome the resistance to remembering repressed memories. Not infrequently the symbolic meaning of what is being said is not obvious, and the analyst must maintain a free-floating attention for many sessions, looking for cues to the content of the unconscious mind.

Once he develops a degree of certainty about his interpretation, the analyst must decide when to present it to the client. If the interpretation is given before the client is capable of accepting it, anxiety will be generated and the repression will become more severe. It is desirable to lead clients slowly so that they can gradually arrive at their own interpretations and work at overcoming their own resistance.

A single proper interpretation does not resolve the client's problems. The repression of unconscious material shows up in various aspects of the person's life, and repeated interpretations are required to help the person give up the repression in all aspects of his or her life. The process of repeated interpretation and con-

tinued efforts on the part of the client to resolve the conflict is called *working through*.

Transference

According to the theory of psychoanalysis, the patient must **transfer** to the therapy relationship the conflicts from early life that interfere with the capacity to live normally. As a consequence, however, the analyst becomes a unique person in the client's eyes. Freud first noticed transference when he realized that patients ascribed to him characteristics of God and the devil or professed mad love for him even though their meetings were brief and infrequent. Transference is necessary and desirable, but it is only a temporary goal of psychoanalysis. As the significant unconscious processes affecting his or her behavior are made conscious to the client, he or she gives up neurotic defenses. As defenses are lowered, transference is resolved. The client comes to respond more appropriately to the analyst, no longer exhibiting a need to defend against unconscious conflicts. The problems that brought the person to analysis are resolved, and the problem of transference disappears.

Recent Changes in Psychoanalysis

Although the basic techniques of Freudian psychoanalysis have remained the same, some variations have been tried. For example, analysts who follow the school of ego psychology place less emphasis on sex and aggression and more emphasis on the rational aspects of the ego. Most analysts still use the techniques of free association and dream interpretation, although with greater caution and less frequently than did Freud. Some analysts have given up the use of the couch and have a more spontaneous face-to-face interchange with the client. Many psychoanalytically trained therapists place more emphasis on the here and now and less on what happened in the past. Chief among these therapists is Rollo May, one of the pioneers in a technique called *existential therapy*.

Disadvantages of Psychoanalysis

Psychoanalysis is inefficient by today's standards. The analyst can treat only one person at a time, and each client is seen sometimes as frequently as five days a week for a 45- or 50-minute "hour" over a period of months or even years. Because analysis takes such a long time, the analyst can treat only a very small number of people in a lifetime. Furthermore, since the analyst is so highly trained and treatment is so time-consuming, the total cost to the client is very high. The cost alone excludes many potential users of psychoanalysis. For some people, such as children, analysis is ineffective or inadequate because they are not equipped for the highly verbal nature of the technique, and some potential patients are too disordered to benefit from it. Thus most persons in psychoanalysis are from the upper or middle class, although psychoanalysts have made some attemps to broaden their scope of treatment.

The Phenomenological Model: Insight into Present Experiences

Client-centered Psychotherapy

Rather than attempting to provide insight into repressed memories of the past, the client-centered therapist tries to help clients accept all aspects of themselves in the present. Emotional problems are seen as stemming from a lack of self-knowledge, a denial of certain feelings, and an inability to experience all feelings fully. In order to describe how the therapist tries to help the client in therapy, it is necessary to outline the progress that client-centered psychotherapy has made over the years.

Carl Rogers, whose ideas we encountered in Chapter 9, first wrote about the theory of present-oriented therapy in 1942. His early views focused on recognizing and clarifying the client's expressed feelings. At that time the technique was called **nondirective therapy** because a basic rule was that the therapist should only respond to the stated feelings of the client and never direct the conversation. The purpose of clarifying clients' feelings was to facilitate the appropriate expression of feelings, to help persons understand how they felt, and to help them use feelings as a basis for action. The term "nondirective" was dropped because it became clear that the therapist was indeed directing the course of treatment with clarifying comments.

Client-centered therapy is based on Rogers' theory of personality, in which, as we know, the main concept is self. The **self-concept** is defined as *a relatively consistent and enduring framework of self-regarding attitudes.* Disturbed

The goal of client-centered psychotherapy is to help clients achieve acceptance of themselves in the present so that they can go on to lead more fulfilling and meaningful lives.

persons are those who find some of their experiences or feelings to be inconsistent with the concept they have of themselves, and so they deny that the feelings apply to them. If the person denies part of his or her own experience, these feelings and experiences cannot be used as a guide for action.

For example, one woman in therapy responded to every question about how she felt about a negative event in her life with the comment that she was "upset." When asked by the therapist what she meant by "upset," she said she did not know. Later it was discovered that in her formative years her mother had denied her the implications of any negative feelings. She would say, "You aren't angry at me, you're upset." The woman had learned to cut off feelings of anger, depression, jealousy, and anxiety. She responded to situations that would normally have elicited such feelings with vague reactions of apprehension and uneasiness. Therapy led her to understand and accept the fact that she has these feelings and to experience them in appropriate situations. Instead of being confused and disoriented in unpleasant situations, she could respond spontaneously and openly with her feelings. Openly expressing one's feelings is more apt to help resolve the situation causing the negative feelings. For example, people are likely to avoid saying things that make you angry if they know how you feel about such things.

Client-centered therapy promotes self-exploration. The therapist tries to develop an environment of acceptance in which clients can take the chance of facing their denied feelings. Clients are encouraged to move to an internal frame of reference in which they decide how worthwhile they are rather than always looking to others for evaluation. Emphasis is placed on the development of a *real* relationship in therapy rather than on role playing for the therapist.

Rogers proposed that the therapist must possess three basic characteristics before he or she can successfully use the client-centered technique: empathic understanding, unconditional positive regard, and congruence. **Empatic understanding** means that the therapist accurately understands the immediate feelings of the client. **Unconditional positive regard** means that the therapist cares about the client. He or she does not put conditions on the caring, nor does the therapist care less when clients reveal aspects of themselves about which they are ashamed and anxious. This does not mean that the therapist agrees with the view that the client presents; but it does mean that the therapist cares about the client as a person regardless of viewpoints. **Congruence** means that what the therapist is experiencing inside and how he presents himself or herself to the client are consistent. Thus the therapist is genuine.

Rogers outlined several stages of development of the integrated person in the therapeutic process. The first stage is characterized by rigidity and remoteness of experiencing, with no self-relevant communication to others. As clients come to accept their feelings. they may progress to the point where they can admit to feelings that are still removed from experience. For example, a client in therapy may be able to tell the therapist about how angry he or she was the previous week in therapy, while denying any annoyance at the present time. Eventually, through therapy or other positive experiences, the client is able to express immediate feelings and to integrate his or her self-concept with present everyday experiences.

Gestalt Therapy

As we have seen, Gestalt psychology emphasizes the perception of patterns or totalities rather than separate elements of a stimulus. **Gestalt therapy,** founded by Fritz Perls, developed from attempts to help persons look at the entirety of their immediate experience. According to Perls, people with emotional problems tend to focus their attention on only part of what they feel and on only part of what they do, especially in their communications with others. The focus of Gestalt therapy is not *why* the client is behaving in a certain way but rather *what* the person is feeling and *how* the person is behaving. The therapist helps the client overcome barriers to self-awareness. The goal is for the client to become aware of what he or she is doing from moment to moment and to accept responsibility for that behavior. Theoretically, clients will then be able to attend to all aspects of their experience. Attention and awareness become integrated.

Notice in the following excerpt of a Gestalt group therapy session (Gestalt therapy is typically practiced as a group therapy) how the therapist points out all aspects of the client's behavior—the tone of her own voice and the shaking of her leg. The client had been describing a dream in which her dead mother appeared, and the therapist, noticing that she was beginning to sound whiny and complaining, asked her if she had any "unfinished business" with her mother. The client replied:

Mrs. R: Well . . . if only she had loved me, things would be different. But she didn't and . . . and I've never had any real mother love (crying).

S (Steve Tobin): Put your mother in that chair and say that to her.

Mrs. R: If only she had cared for me, I'd be much better today.

S: I want you to say this to her, not to me. Can you imagine her sitting there in front of you?

Mrs. R: Yes, I see her as she looked when she was still alive. Mother, if you had only loved me. Why couldn't you ever tell me you loved me? Why did you always criticize me? (almost a wail, more tears)

S: Now switch over to the other chair and play your mother. (She moves over to the other chair and doesn't say anything.)

S: What do you experience as your mother?

Mrs. R: I-I-I don't know . . . I don't know what she would say.

S: Of course you don't know. She's not around any more. You're playing the part of you that is your mother. Just say whatever you experience there.

Mrs. R: Oh, I see. Well, I don't know what to say to her.

S: Say *that* to her.

Mrs. R M (Mrs. R as Mother): I don't know what to say to you. I *never* knew what to say to you. I really did love you, you know that. Look at all the things I did for you, and you never appreciated it. (voice sounds defensive and whiny)

S: Now switch back and reply as yourself.

Mrs. R S (Mrs. R as Self): Loved me! All you ever did was criticize me. Nothing I ever did was good enough! (voice beginning to sound more whiny). When I got married to J. you disapproved, you were always coming over and telling me what I was doing wrong with the kids. Oh, you never came right out and said anything, but you were always making snide remarks or saying, "Now, dear, wouldn't it be a good idea to put another blanket on the baby." You made my life *miserable;* I was always worrying about you criticizing me. And now I'm having all this trouble with J. (breaks down and starts to cry.)

S: Did you hear your voice?

Mrs. R S: Yes.

S: What did you hear in it?

Mrs. R S: Well, I guess I sounded kind of complaining, like I'm feeling sor—like I'm feeling mad.

S: You sounded more like feeling self-pity. Try this on for size: say to your mother, "Look what you've done to me. It's all your fault."

Mrs. R S: Look what you've done. Everything's your fault.

S: Now let yourself switch back and forth as you find yourself changing roles.

Mrs. R M: Come on, stop blaming me for everything. You are always complaining about something. If you had been better—if you had been a *decent* daughter, I wouldn't have had to criticize you so much.

Mrs. R S: Oh, oh, (under her breath) Damn. (She's swinging her right leg slightly.)

S: Notice your leg.

Mrs. R S: I-I'm shaking it.

S: Exaggerate that, shaking it harder.

Mrs. R S: (shakes leg harder, it begins to look like a kick)

S: Can you imagine doing that to your mother?

Mrs. R S: No, but I-I-I-I'm sure feeling pissed at her.

S: Say this to her.

Mrs. R S: I feel pissed off at you! I hate you!

S: Say that louder.

Mrs. R S: I hate you! (volume higher, but still some holding back)

S: Louder!

Mrs. R S: I HATE YOU, YOU GODDAMNED BITCH. (She sticks her leg out and kicks the chair over.)

S: Now switch back.

Mrs. R M: (voice sounds much weaker now) I-I guess I didn't show you much love. I really felt it, but I was unhappy and bitter. You know all I had to go through with your father and brother. You were the only one I could talk to. I'm sorry . . . I wanted you to be happy . . . I wanted so much for you.

Mrs. R S: You sure did! . . . I know you did love me, Mother, I know you were unhappy (voice much softer now, but sounding real, not whiny or mechanical). I guess I did some things that were ba— wrong, too. I was always trying to keep you off my back.

Mrs. R M: Yes, you were pretty sarcastic to me, too. And that hurt.

Mrs. R S: I wish you had told me. I didn't think you were hurt at all.

Mrs. R M: Well, that's all over now.

Mrs. R S: Yeah, it is. I guess there's no use blaming you. You're not around any more.

S: Can you forgive your mother now?

Mrs. R S: Mother, I forgive you . . . I really do forgive you. (Starts crying again, but not in the whiny way of before. She sounds genuinely grieving and cries for a couple of minutes.)

S: Now switch back.

Mrs. R M: I forgive you too, dear. You have to go on now. You can't keep blaming me forever. I made my mistakes but you have your own family and you're doing okay.

S: Do you feel ready to say goodbye now?

Mrs. R S: Yes. I-I think so (starts to sob). Goodbye, Mother, goodbye. (breaks down, cries for a few minutes)

S: What do you experience now?

Mrs. R: I feel better. I feel . . . kind of relieved, like a weight is off my back. I feel calm.

S: Now that you've said goodbye to her, to this dead person, can you go around and say hello to the live people here, to the group?

Mrs. R: Yes, I'd like that.

(She goes around the room, greets people, touches some, embraces others. Many in the group are tearful. When she reaches her husband, she starts crying again, and tells him she loves him, and they embrace.)

(Tobin, 1971, pages 154–155)

T.A.: Doing OK

In the 1960s it was encounter groups. In the 1970s it is transactional analysis, or T.A., the pop-psychological path to happiness charted by Sacramento Psychiatrist Thomas A. Harris in his bestseller *I'm OK—You're OK*. T.A., or close facsimiles of it, is now practiced by some 3,000 psychiatrists, psychologists, social workers and ministers in the U.S. and 14 foreign countries. In fact, it may be the most widely used and fastest-growing form of treatment for emotional distress in the world. . . .

The central thesis of T.A., as Harris teaches it, stems from Psychiatrist Alfred Adler's concept of a universal "inferiority feeling." Most people, Harris says, never stop thinking of themselves as helpless children overwhelmed by the power of adults. For that reason they go through life believing that they are inferior, or "not OK," while they view everyone else as superior, or "OK." The aim of T.A. therapy is to instill the conviction that "I'm OK—you're OK," meaning that no one is really a threat to anyone else. . . .

More specifically, transactional analysts believe that what makes a person unhappy is an unbalanced relationship between the three parts that constitute every human personality: Parent, Adult and Child. Harris rejects any suggestion that these are the equivalent of Freud's superego, ego and id. "The Parent, Adult and Child are real things that can be validated," he insists. "We're talking about real people, real times and real events, as recorded in the brain." Be that as it may, the theory is that unless the mature, rational Adult dominates the personality, or, in the language of T.A., is "plugged in," the overly restrictive Parent and the primitive, self-depreciating Child will foul up most "transactions," or relationships with others.

To put his Adult in charge, Harris says, the troubled person must "learn the language of transactional analysis and use it in examining his everyday transactions." He must also learn to diagram these transactions, using three circles to represent the personality components of each person and drawing arrows to show how two people interact. Parallel lines depict "complementary transactions," which occur,

Transactional Analysis

Transactional analysis (T.A.) is a tremendously popular form of therapy espoused in best-selling books such as Eric Berne's *Games People Play* (1964) and Thomas Harris' *I'm OK—You're OK* (1967). The focus of the therapy is the transactions that people have with one another and how those transactions express three basic aspects of the personality known as the *Child*, the *Parent*, and the *Adult*. According to T.A., in each of us there is a Child that is made up of the residuals of our childhood way of behaving and thinking; a Parent based on the controlling behaviors, judgments, and attitudes derived from our parents' treatment of us as children; and an Adult, the mature, reasoning, adaptive part of personality. The Child is the recording from early childhood of internal events: the child's reactions to what he or she sees and hears. The situation of childhood leads the child to experience feelings of frustration, rejection, or fear of abandonment, leading the child to feel "not OK." There are many positive sides to the Child as well. Creativity, curiosity, exploration, the ability to touch, feel, and experience, and the excitement of new discoveries are all stored in the recording of the Child. The Parent is the recording from early childhood of external events during the first five years of life. Much of what is recorded at this

for instance, when a husband's Adult speaks to his wife's Adult and gets a response in kind. In that type of exchange, the husband might ask, "Where are my

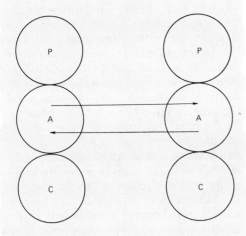

cuff links?" and his wife might reply, "In your top left dresser drawer"—or, perhaps, "I'm not sure, but I'll help you find them."

Crossed lines like this denote uncomplementary transactions, and bode trou-

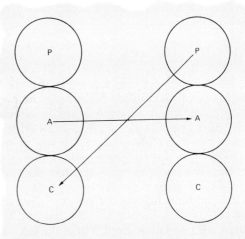

ble. For example, the Adult-to-Adult question about the cuff links might be answered with a sharp "Where you left them," a reproof that comes from the wife's Parent and is addressed to what she sees as the inept Child in her husband's personality. . . .

Time
August 20, 1973

One major reason transactional analysis has been so popular is that the theory uses language that is easy to relate to one's own experience.

time is examples and pronouncements from the child's parents. Since the child is relatively incapable of interpreting the meaning of what is happening to him or her at this age, these recordings are made without editing (or question). The source of all rules and judgments or how-to-do-it instructions is in the Parent, and the child is unable to determine whether the rule is good (don't play with that knife!) or poor (never get dirty!). The replaying of the Parent "tapes" later in life has a powerful influence on personality. The Adult is that part of the personality which gathers information, processes and files it, and makes decisions based on that information.

Transactional analysis therapy involves using the above vocabulary to analyze the types of interactions (transactions) that people have with one another and to help them understand the difficulties of inappropriate interactions. People can communicate Parent to Parent, Parent to Child, Parent to Adult, Child to Parent, Child to Child, Child to Adult, Adult to Parent, Adult to Child, and, finally, Adult to Adult. This last type of transaction is the ideal and is very difficult to achieve.

Transactional therapy allows one to understand the communication interactions one is having, to listen to and appreciate one's Child and Parent, and to train the Adult to make conscious decisions that allow the Child and Parent to be expressed in behavior in reasonable and controlled ways.

BEHAVIOR THERAPY

The insight-oriented therapies are the traditional forms of psychotherapy; indeed the popular notion of psychotherapy is of developing insight into one's behavior. Self-knowledge is certainly a worthwhile goal, but many people have worked out an adequate understanding of their behavior only to discover that they still have difficulty changing it. For example, a young man may understand that the reason he has difficulty asking girls for dates is that he had few opportunities to date in high school, he felt that he was not physically attractive, and he did not know how to ask for a date or what to say on a date. He understands perfectly well the reasons for his difficulty, but that does not change the fact that he still does not have the skill of appropriate dating behavior.

In contrast to insight-oriented therapy, behavior therapy focuses on changes in skill, motivation, and performance. **Behavior modification,** as the behavior therapies are called, uses the relatively well-established principles of learning and conditioning to help the person change (see Chapter 4). The behavior therapist makes no assumption of unconscious motivations and indeed proposes that such assumptions are irrelevant to therapy. The focus may be on the extinction of undesirable behaviors, such as compulsive eating or stuttering or the learning of alternative positive behaviors. Since the early 1920s there has been interest in the use of conditioning techniques for psychotherapy, but it is only recently that the techniques of classical and instrumental conditioning have actually been successfully applied to individuals with emotional problems.

Conditioning Therapies

Classical Conditioning

For some time the principles of conditioning have been applied to the treatment of such emotional problems as enuresis (night bedwetting) in elementary school children. For a long time enuresis was considered a sign of emotional

disturbance, but we know now that it can be treated by training children with classical conditioning techniques. An alarm is set off, waking the child so that he or she can go to the bathroom, whenever the slightest amount of urine begins to flow. The stimulus of the full bladder becomes conditioned to the response of awakening and inhibiting urination. The technique is effective, with from 75 to 90 percent of children so treated obtaining night control of the bladder in a matter of a few weeks (see Chapter 4).

Although many people now think homosexuality should not be considered abnormal (see Chapter 11), some homosexuals do wish to change. In these cases classical conditioning techniques have been used with some success. The sexual response of male homosexuals is handled in the following way. In order to reduce the positive sexual response to men, the homosexuals are shown pictures of nude males and simultaneously given an emetic to induce vomiting. The idea is that the UCS of vomiting and nausea will become conditioned to the CS of a nude male. To condition a positive sexual response to females, the homosexual is injected with testosterone, a male sex hormone (the UCS), and then shown pictures of nude females (the CS). In one study, 12 of 67 male homosexuals showed changes in the direction of relatively long-term heterosexual behavior (Freund, 1960). Although this is a small proportion, insight-oriented therapies have typically been even less successful with homosexuals.

Instrumental Conditioning

The technique of **shaping,** based on the principles of instrumental conditioning, has been applied to the problem of short attention span, a frequent cause of classroom disruption and poor academic performance. The child with a short attention span can be rewarded for paying attention to his or her studies for even short periods of time. If the longest period of time a child can attend to studying without becoming distracted is one minute, then he or she is initially rewarded at the end of every minute of actual studying. After this habit is well established (perhaps after several days), the requirements are increased. Now the child is rewarded only when the studying is for two-minute periods. The length of the study time is gradually increased until the child is able to work for a half hour or more without interruption.

Through the judicious use of reinforcement a therapist can shape the desired behavior from modest beginnings. After the new behavior is established the external rewards can be withdrawn, because new rewards will maintain the behaviors. The rewards of easier studying, increased feelings of competence, and (one hopes) better grades will all help to maintain the behaviors.

Instrumental conditioning has been surprisingly effective with some severe cases of psychopathology. Withdrawn children can be trained to speak with others if properly rewarded. The behavior of severely schizophrenic hospitalized adults can be modified by rewarding them for talking to other patients on the ward, grooming themselves, or making their beds. The hospital staff may use cigarettes and candy for rewards, or it may use tokens that can be traded for items or privileges the patient wants. As we saw in Chapter 4, some mental hospitals use treatment programs, called token economies, that are based completely on instrumental principles. Patients are put in situations in which they must use tokens they have *earned* to gain any but the barest essentials of life. Although such treatment may seem cruel, it is probably kinder to require socially acceptable behavior than it is to provide total care of individuals who are capable of developing some degree of self-care.

Institutionalism refers to the passive, dependent behavior of the "model" mental patient who bothers no one and always does what he or she is told. Some patients are so disturbed and withdrawn from the real world that they must wear diapers and be spoon fed. In one such case the nurses complained about having constantly to change a man who stayed in bed all day and was cared for like a baby. As a final attempt at therapy, the patient was told that he would no longer be cared for, and he would have to get up and go to the bathroom. For three days the man lay in bed, soiling himself, until the stench became intolerable. On the third day he got up and went to the bathroom and continued to do so from then on. There is a tendency for hospitals to be more concerned with efficient administration than with the encouragement of appropriate behaviors. The programs based on operant learning principles have shown that patients do not starve when social behaviors are required before feeding occurs.

Punishment

Although the judicious use of rewards seems to be quite effective in changing behavior, the approach is sometimes difficult to implement. What if the desired behavior never occurs? What if the maladaptive behavior that occurs is self-reinforcing? One example of self-reinforcing behavior is stealing. The only way positive reinforcement could be used to eliminate stealing is to reward the person for *not* stealing with things of greater value than the things that could be stolen. Social approval may help maintain nonstealing behavior, but people usually do not reward others for *lack* of a behavior. As almost everyone realizes, we typically ignore a child *until* he or she misbehaves, and attention at that point can increase the very behavior we would like the child to stop.

When reward does not work, punishment may be helpful. Alcoholics have been treated with some success in this way. In one such program a bar was set up in a ward for alcoholics, but the bar stools were wired for electricity. Some alcoholics were shocked if they requested a drink and had one. Other alcoholics, under a different program, were allowed to have a drink but were shocked if they asked for a drink that was not diluted with a mixer, if they drank their drink in less than 20 minutes, or if they asked for a fourth drink. The theory behind this approach is that alcoholics are not physiologically dependent on alcohol but have maladaptive drinking patterns that can be relearned. The therapy consisted of using shock to punish inappropriate drinking behavior. Some alcoholics have been helped in an enduring way with this technique.

Biofeedback

A procedure to teach people to gain control over their physiological responses to stress is biofeedback (see Chapter 2 and Appendix D). In biofeedback a person is attached to an electronic measuring device that monitors various physiological responses which are usually affected by emotion, for example, muscle tension or skin temperature. The person's physiological signal is then amplified and "fed back" to the client in the form of a tone, clicks, or various colored lights. A high tone, fast clicks, or a red light might reflect muscle tension, low skin temperature, or high heart rate. A low tone, slow clicks, or a green light might reflect low muscle

Resolute Prisoners Struggle against Behavioral Modification

William Claiborne

In a solitary confinement cell behind two locked corridor grills in a remote wing of the medical center for federal prisoners here, Forest G. is engaged in a desperate struggle of wills with the U.S. Bureau of Prisons.

But for Forest G., a 34-year-old convicted bank robber serving 15 years, solitary confinement has become a way of life. He has been sitting alone in what amounts to a walk-in closet for more than eight months, and in all likelihood he will remain there at least until next February.

From Forest's point of view, what is at stake in the struggle is his pride and his right to control of his own behavior, even if it is regarded by others as belligerent and recalcitrant.

From the prison authorities' point of view, what is at stake is the right of the state to promote change in the behavior of the most hardened inmate, even if the only alternative is to let the inmate vegetate indefinitely in maximum security incarceration.

Sunshine Street

The struggle will ultimately be resolved in a U.S. District Court in Kansas City, but for now the drama is being painfully acted out at the massive, 40-year-old prison hospital here, which is incongruously located on Sunshine Street, on the outskirts of town.

At issue in the court test brought by a group of inmates and supported by the American Civil Liberties Union (ACLU) is a year-old behavior modification program called START, an acronym for Special Treatment and Rehabilitative Training. . . .

START is based on a deceptively simple system of programmed rewards in which a prisoner begins a fixed term at the most severe level of incarceration and then "earns" some freedom of movement and a few privileges by adapting to various rules of behavior. . . .

Time Off

Gradually, the inmate is allowed more privileges, is allowed to earn money in an adjacent factory six hours daily and begins to have sentence time off for good behavior restored.

In 7½ months, he is "graduated" from the program and is returned to the general population of the penitentiary that referred him to START in the first place. If the inmate rebels, refuses to follow rules or becomes verbally abusive to staff members, he is returned to the solitary confinement level for a designated period. If he refuses to participate, he remains in solitary for a year, and is then returned to a segregation unit of his home institution.

Forest G. was in the "hole" (segregation unit) at the Leavenworth penitentiary for two years when he was notified that he was to be sent to Springfield's START program. . . .

Forest did briefly participate in the program, earning points for good behavior. Then, he said, he saw several other inmates being beaten by guards during a disturbance in the tier opposite his cell, and he decided to lay down and finish his year in solitary.

Hole with Factory

"After you look at it a while, all this is a hole with a factory, and somebody calling it behavior modification. There's nobody here who's going to modify me," said Forest.

Asked if he had considered faking a change in his behavior long enough to earn privileges and graduate from the program, Forest replied, "It wouldn't be no act, it would be for real. They're trying to get a program going smoothly by bribing guys. If you are playing a game on them, you are playing it on yourself, because they want you modified, and they don't care what makes you do it. . . .

Boulder (Colo.) Daily Camera
January 5, 1974

The use of behavior modification in corrective institutions has led to a strong controversy about the ethics of forcing people to behave in "socially appropriate" ways. Do criminals have the right to resist such treatment? Does such a program constitute "cruel and unusual" punishment?

A popular new development in biofeedback is a process teaching muscle relaxation to reduce the effects of stress and the diseases it can nurture.

trouble with the progressive muscle relaxation used in systematic desensitization can often learn very deep relaxation via biofeedback. Biofeedback is used to help people with anxiety in a broad range of areas. In addition, the technique has been helpful in treating such varied psychosomatic illnesses as migraine headaches, tension headaches, asthma, arthritis, and even epilepsy.

Cognitive Behavior Modification

One major drawback of the conditioning therapies we have just discussed is that the treatment must be administered at exactly the time and place the problem behavior occurs. The therapist must be there or have equipment there to detect the deviant behavior and deliver the reinforcements or punishments. This makes treatment cumbersome, expensive, and unnatural. As an alternative, many behaviorally oriented therapists employ techniques that can be applied by having the patient *imagine* the circumstances surrounding the behavior under treatment. Principles of learning are used to associate the thoughts (cognitions) of the patients with certain consequences. In short, behavior therapy is carried out in the imagination of the client. This general category of therapy is known as cognitive behavior modification; we will examine two examples of this type.

Systematic Desensitization

One innovation in the use of learning techniques in psychotherapy was developed by Joseph Wolpe in the late 1950s. He proposed that neurotic habits are learned in anxiety-provoking situations by the association of neutral stimuli with anxiety responses. The anxiety response is made up of subjective feelings and physiological tension. Wolpe proposed that if a response incompatible with anxiety, such as relaxation, sex, or assertiveness, occurred in the presence of the anxiety-provoking stimuli, the connection between the stimulus and the anxiety response would be weakened. He called this process **reciprocal inhibition.**

Wolpe developed the technique of therapy called **systematic desensitization** based on the process of reciprocal inhibition. The first step in desensitization therapy is to gain an understanding of the types of stimuli that lead to

tension, warm skin, or a slow heart rate. By trying various fantasies, relaxation, meditation, or other strategies, people can learn to control the feedback signal by changing their physiological responses. For example, using feedback on the amount of tension in the forehead muscle as a cue, one can learn to obtain deep muscle relaxation. These techniques can then be applied in stressful situations as a means of eliminating anxiety responses. People who have anxiety responses. Based on interviews with the client, a hierarchy of fear-provoking stimuli is constructed ranging from situations involving very mild fear to ones in which the fear is quite intense.

While the hierarchy is being constructed, **relaxation training** begins. Wolpe focuses on muscle relaxation techniques in which the client is taught to become aware of and control specific muscle groups throughout the body by successively tensing and relaxing each muscle group. Deep and slow breathing coupled with the relaxation of more and more muscle groups can lead to very deep relaxation. While deeply relaxed, the client is asked to imagine a scene involving the least threatening stimulus in the hierarchy. If any anxiety is felt while imagining the scene, the person raises a finger and is told to put the scene out of mind immediately. Deeper relaxation is induced. When the scene can be imagined without anxiety several times, the person is asked to move up the hierarchy and imagine the next most anxiety-provoking scene. The relaxation response slowly generalizes to other items on the list, making the next item less stressful. Once relaxation to the entire list of scenes is complete, the client finds that freedom from anxiety to an imagined stimulus generalizes and results in freedom from anxiety to the real event.

Systematic desensitization can be easily used for anyone who is anxious in a particular situation. Test anxiety, fear of speaking in front of large groups, and phobias have all been successfully treated with desensitization training. This type of therapy was effective with Mr. J, a talented basketball player attending college on an athletic scholarship (Katahn, 1967). Just before coming into therapy, Mr. J began to feel that his game was falling apart. He was tired and sluggish on the court. His anxiety was so great that he lost eight pounds in one month. Although the intensity of the anxiety was new, he had felt anxiety about playing for a long time. Nausea and vomiting had occurred on the day of a game since he was 12 years old. Although his father did not seem to have a heavy involvement with his playing, his mother's avid interest in his achievement made him even more nervous.

Three therapy sessions were devoted to the construction of an anxiety hierarchy and training Mr. J in muscle relaxation. The following

hierarchy, from least to most anxiety-provoking, was established:

1. Mr. J meets an assistant coach in the gym, and the coach doesn't say "hello" to him.
2. He is in the gym changing for practice, and he notices his hands are beginning to sweat.
3. He is trying to study, but he can't get the day's practice out of his thoughts.
4. He finishes practice, and the "drugstore coaches" (his term for spectators who have passes for practice) speak to the other players and ignore him.
5. He is on the court and gets a tired, draggy, no-good feeling.
6. He is on the court and notices that the coaches are keeping a record of each player's performance.
7. He is visiting at home, and his mother makes some remark about another player.
8. He is eating dinner with his mother when she asks him something about how his game is going.
9. It is time for the late afternoon pre-game dinner, and he is on the way to the cafeteria.
10. He is in the cafeteria line, and the sight of food makes him feel sick.
11. He is in the gym changing for a game, and he is sick to his stomach.

After about 14 more sessions the anxiety hierarchy had been completely worked through and the client stopped vomiting before games. The nausea and the tired, sluggish feeling during the games had also disappeared. The counseling that accompanied the desensitization focused on study habits and the role of basketball in Mr. J's life. As a result of the combined therapeutic techniques, his grades rose from a "D" to a "B" average. Basketball plays a less overwhelming (although still important) part in his life, and he has been accepted by a law school.

Covert Sensitization

The second type of therapy based on learning principles which utilizes the patient's imagination is called covert sensitization. It is most simply described as punishment training by imagination. The technique is designed for eliminating an undesired behavior and involves asking the patient to imagine first engaging in the behavior and then to imagine that very undesirable things happen as a result of the behavior. We will illustrate with the treatment of alcoholism, although the technique could be applied to any undesired behavior. The alco-

'Symptom Prescriptions' Really Work

WASHINGTON — A 61-year-old man with a distaste for housework went to a psychiatrist to alleviate the insomnia that was limiting his sleep to about two hours a night.

The doctor learned of his loathing for cleaning up and ordered his patient to stop sleeping altogether. Instead the man was to don pajamas and spend the night polishing floors.

After three nights on the prescribed regimen the patient crawled to bed exhausted and remained untroubled by insomnia from then on.

"The old gentleman would do anything to get out of polishing floors—even sleep," said his psychiatrist.

That is one example of what is known as symptom prescription in psychiatry, the gist of which might be expressed: Take pride in your paranoia and it will disappear.

It is a little-known, but fairly common therapeutic technique that has worked on everything from excessive sweating to schizophrenic delusions, according to a review of the practice by two psychiatric researchers.

In an article entitled, "Losing a Symptom Through Keeping It" published in the Archives of General Psychiatry, the official journal of the American Psychiatric Association, the two authors said the approach seems to work for several reasons.

One, well-illustrated by the case of the insomniac, is aversion—getting the patient to repeat the behavior until he is just plain sick and tired of it. Sometimes the symptom—like sleeplessness—can be linked with another distasteful chore such as scrubbing the floor.

In other cases, the symptom itself can become distasteful with enough repetition—such as the patient who takes to carrying a six-foot cross around the neighborhood. As an occasional, impulsive act it may have its charms for him, but lugging the thing around eight hours a day under doctor's orders erases its appeal.

A second reason symptom prescriptions work

may lie in the sense of self-control patients get from willing a frightening delusion or an involuntary bad habit (like stuttering or nail biting or overeating) into action.

The psychiatric researchers said a patient with a tic might be ordered to repeat the spasm willfully over and over again all day long. By learning what goes into the tic, by paying attention to the emotional and physical cues that precede it, the patient may learn how to halt it. . . .

Phobias, or intense fears of such things as height, crowds or vast open spaces, can be managed by requiring patients either to experience them in gradually increasing doses, or to fantasize about them while practicing muscle relaxation.

"The newly gained sense of control may have a powerful effect on the patient as a demonstration of . . . a new definition of the symptom—from the 'uncanny' to that which can be willed into being," the researchers said.

What is important is that the patient feels a sense of achievement, the researchers said.

A third reason for symptom prescription's effectiveness may be the sense of detachment the patient attains—from wry humor to the first realization their behavior is foolish.

A young medical doctor reported to one psychiatrist that he suffered from profuse sweating each time he confronted any of his superiors.

Rather than fight the excessive perspiration, the physician was ordered to try to sweat as much as he could. At his next encounter with a senior of the hospital where he was an intern, he did just that. The anxiety that created the symptom turned to amusement at his own efforts. The sweating stopped after the one attempt. . . .

The Denver Post
June 23, 1976

> The medical model implies that psychotherapy should be directed at a presumed underlying illness, which if cured will alleviate all symptoms. In contrast, the behavioral model directs its attack on the symptoms themselves.

holic is told to imagine he or she is about to have an alcoholic drink. The individual is then told to bring into the fantasy the sensations of nausea and vomiting. With frequent repetition of this fantasy, the person often will come to

associate the thought of drinking with nausea. This technique is used to prevent drinking altogether rather than to condition the rate of drinking. Cautela (1970), who developed this procedure, gave the following example:

You are walking into a bar. You decide to have a glass of beer. You are now walking toward the bar. As you are approaching the bar you have a funny feeling in the pit of your stomach. Your stomach feels all queasy and nauseous. Some liquid comes up your throat and it is very sour. You try to swallow it back down, but as you do this, food particles start coming up your throat to your mouth. You are now reaching the bar and you order a beer. As the bartender is pouring the beer, puke comes into your mouth. . . . As soon as your hand touches the glass, you can't hold it down any longer. You have to open your mouth and you puke. It goes all over your hand, all over the glass and the beer. You can see it floating around in the beer. . . . (Cautela, 1970, p. 87)

Covert sensitization has been demonstrated to be very effective in producing behavior change in this and similar cases.

Behavior Modification by Changing Cognitions

Behavior therapists have become increasingly convinced that the faulty cognitions (thoughts, beliefs, attitudes) people develop about themselves and about their environment are of major importance in understanding the faulty behavior these people engage in. This presents a choice point to the therapist—do you treat the behavior directly and not worry about the cognitions, assuming the cognitions will change if you can change the behavior, or do you treat the cognitions assuming that the cognitions cause the behavior and that changing the cognitions will automatically lead to changes in the behavior? Strict behavior modification has always stressed treating the behavior, but the trend is clearly toward giving the cognitions at least equal if not exclusive treatment. There is undoubtedly truth in both versions, and so modern behavior therapy is likely to involve treatment of both cognitions and behavior. Therapies designed basically to affect the cognitions of the patient are many and varied; we will briefly examine three.

Modeling

Bandura has demonstrated that behavior change can be affected by what we observe, not just by the reinforcements we receive. We are strongly influenced by the models around us. Not only do we learn to cope with stress by

"Leave us alone! I am a behavior therapist! I am helping my patient overcome a fear of heights!"

© *1975 Medical Tribune. Reprinted by permission of Sidney Harris.*

observing how others around us handle stress but we can learn new coping styles from our observations. Bandura has accumulated impressive evidence to demonstrate that observing live models (as opposed to filmed models) cope well with situations that are fearful for the person who is observing can significantly change that person's ability to cope with the situation in real life. Seeing someone cope with petting a large dog or handling a nonpoisonous snake or a difficult social situation can be an effective therapy intervention leading to behavior change.

Rational Emotive Therapy

Albert Ellis proposed that our cognitive understanding of events, when mistaken, can

John is a compulsive eater who weighs 350 pounds. Seeking help, he sees a therapist, who might approach this problem in the following ways.

Physician (Medical Model)

The therapist assumes that the behavior is the result of a physiological illness. He or she might use amphetamines to reduce appetite or tranquilizers to reduce anxiety associated with stress in John's life.

Psychoanalyst (Dynamic Model)

The therapist explores early childhood memories, the content of dreams, free association, and slips of the tongue to determine the symbolic meaning of the eating behavior. The psychoanalyst would look for the possibility that John is symbolically expressing strong needs for love and aggression.

Behavior Modifier (Behavioral or Learning Theory Model)

The therapist explores the rewarding aspects of overeating and determines whether such behavior allows John to avoid other anxiety-evoking situations. The therapist may set up a conditioning form of treatment in which John is punished for overeating or thinking about eating or is rewarded for noneating behavior. The therapist might try to increase behavior incompatible with eating or change John's eating patterns. If eating leads to anxiety reduction, relaxation techniques may be used to lower anxiety levels.

Jane is a 25-year-old graduate student with a severe stuttering problem. Seeking help, she sees a therapist, who might approach her problem in the following ways.

Physician (Medical Model)

The therapist assumes that stuttering is a neurological problem in the perceptual-motor areas of the brain. The physician might prescribe medication (tranquilizers) or recommend perceptual-motor training.

Psychoanalyst (Dynamic Model)

The therapist assumes that the stuttering behavior is an expression of an unconscious conflict associated with hostility, particularly toward Jane's parents. Therapy would involve trying to bring into awareness this underlying conflict through the interpretation of free association, dreams, slips of the tongue, and repressed memories.

Behavior Modifier (Behavioral or Learning Theory Model)

The therapist explores the possibility that the stuttering behavior was a classically conditioned response. Techniques to treat stuttering might involve negative practice, a technique requiring a person to stutter repeatedly on purpose. Rhythmic speech patterns and operant conditioning involving rewards for appropriate speech might also be used. Finally, if stuttering increases as anxiety increases, then relaxation training might be used.

Existentialist (Phenomenological Model)

In both cases, stuttering and overeating, the therapist makes no assumption about the underlying meaning of symptomatic behavior. Therapy would focus on helping the client clarify values, goals, and feelings. The client would be helped in understanding how he or she feels and would be led in a nonjudgmental, accepting atmosphere to experience those feelings in the here and now.

lead us to maladaptive behavior. These mistaken beliefs or self statements are learned early in life. People make such irrational statements as, "I must never make a mistake; if I did, it would be horrible"; or, "I should always act pleasant. I would destroy other people by being angry at them." Ellis' therapy, called *rational emotive therapy*, is based on the premise that through extensive talking with clients the therapist can lead them to see the irrational nature of their self statements and bring them to a more appropriate way of viewing the world.

Building on the work of Ellis, behavior modifiers have treated the self statements that people make by using guided fantasy or by pairing particular fantasies with relaxation. Instead of merely imagining an anxiety-provoking scene while under deep muscle relaxation, the client might be asked to fantasize *coping* with an anxiety-provoking situation. Practice with such fantasy has been demonstrated to lead to more effective coping in the actual situations.

Misconception Therapy

Victor Raimy, like Ellis, has proposed that if mistaken ideas or misconceptions about oneself could be changed to be more accurate, maladjustment would be eliminated. Raimy has explored several misconceptions in detail:

1. The phrenophobia misconception. *Phrenophobia* is the fear that one is "crazy" or losing one's mind. Raimy states that phrenophobics have the misconceptions that anxiety indicates insanity, that gaps in memory or difficulties in concentration are signs of mental breakdown, that irritability signifies severe mental problems, and that insomnia will make one "go crazy."

2. The special person misconception. According to Raimy, the exaggerated self-importance of some individuals should not be thought of as a compensation for inferiority feelings but may reflect true feelings of superiority and of being special. These cognitions include misconceptions that one has a need to control others, to be superior, to never compromise, to be perfect, and to not trust others. Such people feel that they *are* special, and they may be depressed because the world does not accord them the recognition they believe they deserve.

3. The obsessive misconception. For persons with obsessive misconceptions the world is filled with "I should" and "I must." Their misconceptions lead them to feel that they must be punctual, conscientious, orderly, and reliable at all times.

There are many ways to eliminate misconceptions. Indeed, many of the presently used therapies are particularly geared to help persons eliminate these misconceptions. The most commonly used methods are self-examination, explanation, self-demonstration, and modeling. According to Raimy, traces of these techniques are found in all therapies. One area that Raimy himself is exploring is the effect of repeated review of the misconception on the person's self-understanding.

NEW WAYS OF OBTAINING BEHAVIOR CHANGE—FADS OR EFFECTIVE TECHNIQUES?

Several forms of therapy that have elicited strong support among the general public and some mental health professionals have quite different orientations from the therapies discussed so far. These therapies have acquired a large following in a relatively short time, although many people have dismissed them as fads or sensational approaches to behavior change. Hundreds of other approaches have developed and within a few years faded without making any noticeable impact on present-day psychotherapy theory or technique. Whether these techniques are truly effective or simply enjoy a placebo effect (that is, they are effective because people *believe* they are effective) can be determined only with the test of time and additional research.

EST

EST, which stands for *Erhard Seminar Training*, was founded in 1971 by Werner Erhard. Since then, it is estimated that over 85,000 people have gone through the 60-hour, two-weekend training period. EST borrows from many therapy orientations, including scientology, psychoanalysis, Arica, transactional analysis, Dale Carnegie, Gestalt, and Eastern (such as Zen) and Western spiritualism.

The training, which is given to large groups of several hundred people, combines lectures on EST philosophy with experiential exercises in a highly stressful setting that is designed to break down defenses and lead the trainee to accept the EST orientation. During training EST rules forbid talking, smoking, taking drugs, wearing a watch, using a tape recorder, or taking notes. Eating is scheduled once a day, and restroom breaks are rare (strong bladder control seems essential). Participants sit on hard-back chairs for 15 hours at a time and are subjected to lectures on EST philosophy that sometimes go on for as long as 10 hours. The lectures are combined with attacks on participants, who are called a variety of names because of their alleged stupidity and hang-ups. Lectures are followed by exercises involving relaxation, meditation, and Gestalt principles. One may be asked to experience boredom, anger, or anxiety, to beat one's chest like Tarzan or to growl like a gorilla, or to imagine oneself a rose or climbing a 25-foot high strawberry. A common exercise involves lying on the floor and imagining danger everywhere. After continuous stress and involvement, many (but not all) people experience strong emotional reactions. Fainting, vomiting, loss of bladder control, screaming, and other violent reactions during training testify to the intense effect of the experience. The mid-training seminar and the post-training seminar are filled with testimonials of profound changes that have taken place in people's lives.

The basic philosophy of EST is oriented around an existential acceptance of whatever life brings. There are no victims in life. Our experience is our reality, and what happens is what happens. We have no control over events and we will be happy when we accept that fact. We are machines, not doers. This philosophy is reflected in such EST sayings as, "Ride the horse in the direction it is going" and "Life works when you choose what you've got." While many professionals have attacked EST as a Madison Avenue packaging of brainwashing, common sense psychology, and borrowed therapy techniques, a high percentage of participants have attested that it changed their lives. In addition, a large number of individuals express their enthusiasm for the movement by working for it on a volunteer basis, primarily recruiting new members.

Structural Integration (Rolfing)

A totally different approach to behavior change has been developed by Ida Rolf. Formally called Structural Integration, the technique is popularly called *Rolfing* after its origi-

"Don't shoot. I am Dr. Cranish, and this is my patient. I am a pioneer in excitement therapy."

© *1979 by Sidney Harris.*

We don't have excitement therapy yet, but there are so many fads in this field, based on unsupported ideas, that the appearance of something like excitement therapy would come as no surprise.

nator. Rolf assumes that physical and emotional hurts become defensively stored up in the body structure, preventing people from achieving harmony with themselves and from using their bodies efficiently and with ease. Hang-ups become literally walled up in the body. By manipulating the connective tissues and major muscle groups by deep and vigorous massage, using fingers, fist, open hand, and elbow, the Rolfer can realign the body so that it has a proper relationship to the gravitational field. As the muscles and connective tissue are loosened and lengthened in the 10 one-hour sessions involved in the Rolfing treatment, persons frequently experience relief from chronic physical ailments involving muscle pain and often experience intense childhood memories which were previously repressed. The treatment can be physically and emotionally painful. Ida Rolf does not consider her treatment a form of

The New Yorker, April 5, 1976. Drawing by Mort Gerberg; © 1976 The New Yorker Magazine, Inc.

Some individuals become samplers of all the new types of therapy.

"Oh, good Lord, no! It was just a primal scream."

The New Yorker, July 2, 1973. Drawing by Whitney Darrow, Jr.; © 1973 The New Yorker Magazine, Inc.

In primal therapy one indication that a person has experienced the pain of hurts accumulated during childhood is the expression of the primal scream, an agonizing scream of pain.

therapy but rather a means of helping persons establish a higher level of bodily functioning so that they are freed to grow and develop. While there have been few systematic evaluations of changes that have been ascribed to Rolfing, one study indicated that subjects could differentiate between Rolfed and non-Rolfed individuals on the basis of physical appearance at above-chance levels.

Bioenergetics

A third form of therapy obtaining national recognition is the *bioenergetic approach* of Alexander Lowen. Lowen developed his therapy over the last 25 years starting with Wilhelm Reich's (an early Freudian analyst) focus on muscle manipulation and breathing exercises. Lowen parted from Reich in several basic ways and used much less direct body manipulation. Instead, Lowen developed a series of do-it-yourself exercises to locate energy blockages so that a person's metabolic energy could be released as quickly as possible. The series begins with breathing exercises as a person is placed in a position of chronic muscle tension involving

stretching backward over a stool or perhaps arching backward with only the top of the head, elbows, and bottoms of the feet touching the floor. This technique, along with others—including kicking and beating on a couch while yelling for as long as can be tolerated—is said to mobilize the energy control to the breaking point. This stress makes it possible for a person to let go of the usual controls and release tremendous quantities of energy. As these exercises go on the therapist offers aloud his or her interpretation of the client's personality rigidities and explains how they are being expressed and controlled in the physiology of the body. The stresses and interpretations are designed to provoke, upset, and frighten the individual so that he or she will break up the maladaptive adjustments stored up in the body structure. Bioenergetics has many basic underlying assumptions that are similar to Ida Rolf's Structural Integration, but the procedure used to correct the structural problems is quite different.

Primal Therapy

Another recently developed therapy based on assumptions somewhat similar to psychoanalysis is **primal therapy.** Its theoretical strategy focuses on one particular conflict, the cutting off of feelings experienced as a young child in response to an accumulation of hurts and rejections on the part of the parents. The major primal scene results from the build-up of such small hurts. Eventually the hurts make sense to the child as indications that the parents do not like the child as he is. The recognition of this fact is so traumatic that the child cuts off the feelings and develops an unreal self that protects the child from knowing he or she is suffering. However, the pain associated with these hurts, the *primal pain,* still exists and continues to manifest itself in everyday life in subtle ways. The neurotic symptoms express the pain.

In primal therapy the therapist probes and attacks the defenses and confronts the client to help him or her reexperience the pain. This experience of the pain is called a *primal.* One indication that a person is experiencing a primal is the primal scream, the release of the primal pain that was stored up from childhood.

GROUP APPROACHES TO EMOTIONAL PROBLEMS

Most of the treatment approaches discussed thus far have involved a therapist trying to help an individual on a one-to-one basis. Since World War II, however, group psychotherapy has become popular. Group therapy is a more efficient use of the therapist's time and talents, and it can therefore be offered with less expense to more people. The size of a group can vary from 3 to 20, although 8 to 10 seems optimal.

Group psychotherapy, moderated by an effective leader, can frequently provide a person with experiences that are difficult to duplicate in a one-to-one setting. First, typically people feel that their problems are unique and worse than anyone else's. In a group people frequently find that others have similar problems. Second, a group member can get feedback from several points of view about how he or she affects others, and this feedback carries a weight that the therapist seldom can provide. Group members can pool their experiences and encourage a member to try new solutions to problems. Third, group members frequently fulfill the needs of other people in the group. And helping someone else is often therapeutic for the helper. Finally, the individual may try out new behaviors on others in a relatively safe, accepting environment.

Sensitivity Training

Some special therapeutic techniques have arisen from the group therapy movement. Among them is the **sensitivity training** group (sometimes called T-group for "training" group), which has increased in popularity since the mid-1940s. Sensitivity training originated as a series of group exercises designed to help business persons improve managerial skills, human relations, and productivity. People were taught in an actual group experience how interpersonal relationships work, how to understand organizational behavior, and how to facilitate group functioning. In the clinical setting these

In group therapy, finding out that other people are in the "same boat" can help a person to cope with his or her own problems. Most group leaders employ techniques that foster honest communication among members.

exercises focus on the need for interpersonal warmth and honesty and the requirement of self-disclosure for improved group functioning. T-groups serve to confront individuals with feedback about how others see them and to pressure them to exchange socially unacceptable interactions for appropriate behaviors.

Encounter Groups

In an **encounter group** the goal is not to work on specific problem areas of the members but rather to sensitize each member to the feelings of others. Members are placed in a face-to-face encounter under instructions to say what they feel and "pull no punches." Theoretically this procedure enables members to experience and express their feelings more forcefully.

The encounter group process varies tremendously from one group to the next. All encounter groups focus on here-and-now feelings, negative *and* positive feedback to each member of the group, and the removal of facades that interfere with honest, open communication. Most group leaders use a variety of techniques that are designed to make the

participants communicate honestly. Some of these techniques are:

1. Self-description. All group members write down the three adjectives most descriptive of themselves. The slips of paper are mixed, and the group discusses the kind of person that is being described.
2. Eyeball-to-eyeball. This technique involves two participants staring into each other's eyes for a minute or two, communicating as much as possible, and discussing the feelings afterward.
3. The blind walk. All group participants pair off, and with one person leading and the other blindfolded, the "blind" person walks around the room or outdoors and sensitizes himself to the environment. One variant of this exercise is for the "blind" persons to try to communicate by touch alone.
4. Trusting exercises. Participants take turns being lifted and passed around a circle formed by the group members.
5. Hot seat. One group member sits in a special chair and others give the individual honest feedback about how he or she affects them.
6. Positive and negative bombardment. In this method, similar to the hot seat technique, the group member is given feedback that focuses on only positive or only negative feedback.

Some groups may not use any formal techniques. Instead, the group is allowed to develop its own strategies for encouraging honest and open interactions.

The majority of participants in encounter groups report positive changes as a function of participation. One study, however (Yalom and Lieberman, 1971), reported that 16 of 170 students who had participated in one or another of several different encounter groups reported significant psychological damage as a result of participation. Other studies have also reported possible psychological damage. These studies indicate that anyone entering an encounter group should be careful to choose one with an experienced, nondemanding, and open leader.

Marathon Groups

A **marathon group** is an encounter group in which members meet for many consecutive hours. Weekend marathons may start on Friday night and continue until Sunday night. Short breaks for eating and sleeping may be taken, but usually only in the location of the marathon. Because the weekend defines the entire encounter for the group, there is no time for group members to be supportive and tactful toward one another. There is tremendous group pressure for self-disclosure and genuine open interactions with others. The fatigue of constant group interaction tends to break down defenses, making it more difficult to play those roles that often get in the way of honest communication and self-knowledge.

One special type of marathon therapy, *nude marathon therapy*, has received much attention from the press. The idea of a group of mixed sexes interacting in an intense interpersonal encounter without wearing clothes has been seen by many people as an excuse for perverted sexual behavior. However, those who have developed this technique are serious about its therapeutic aspects. Clothes help define the roles we tend to hide behind. In addition to the rejection of some of our experiences and feelings, many individuals tend to be ashamed and nonaccepting of the physical aspects of their being. To give up one's clothes is really to be open and defenseless!

Family Therapy

One special form of group psychotherapy has received the particular attention of prac-

"Don't be alarmed. We're an encounter group."

Ladies Home Journal, 1972. Reprinted by permission of S. Gross.

Some individuals have developed an erroneous stereotype of the encounter group as a free-for-all "love-in."

titioners for many years. Therapists were quick to discover that the problems of a troubled child are often embedded in pathological interactions within the family. Even if the therapist were able to help the child in individual psychotherapy, the child would have to return to a family life that supported old, inappropriate ways of behaving. In these cases therapists with family orientations quickly moved away from working with the identified client to working with the whole family to change ways of interacting.

The therapist's first goal is to determine what each family member sees as the problems within the family and what each hopes to achieve through family therapy. The therapist tries to determine how the problem that is presented relates to the family network and how the family maintains a homeostatic balance among members. Family rules are uncovered. Some rules are overt—such as those that state when bedtime is and who is supposed to take out the trash—and some are covert—such as "Don't take your problems to Dad. He is too mixed up." The family may make a scapegoat of one family member (often the identified

Family Sickness

A sullen twelve-year-old girl hunches over in a chair, surrounded by her father, mother, sister, brother and a child psychiatrist. Her problem: severe asthma that will not respond to medical attention. After listening to the parents discuss the asthma, the psychiatrist suddenly switches attention to the sister's ample figure. She is clearly overweight. Isn't that a family problem too? As the family starts talking about obesity, the asthmatic girl sits up in her chair.

According to the psychiatrist, Dr. Ronald Liebman, Chief of Psychiatry at Philadelphia's Children's Hospital, that shift in the discussion helped bring the asthma under control. "The patient's overprotective parents," he says, "were focusing so much concern on her that she was responding with ever more severe symptoms." The girl understood that her parents' concern was no longer focused on her alone but on two family problems. After two months of complicated family therapy, the girl's asthma symptoms subsided. . . .

The case is a classic one in family therapy, the medical movement that arose some 15 years ago from a common clinical observation: many psychiatric patients seem unable to get better because of the pressures their families put on them. Family therapists began by abandoning the one-on-one, isolated relationship of traditional psychiatry to take on a patient's whole family. Their aim: to expose and break family patterns that create individual emotional disorders. Now family therapists are increasingly finding that those patterns also help produce physical ailments, from asthma to heart attacks and — some are convinced — even cancer. . . .

Dr. Salvador Minuchin, Director of the Philadelphia Child Guidance Center, has already attracted wide attention with his work on anorexia nervosa, the "starvation disease". . . . Now Minuchin and his team are concentrating on asthma and diabetes. In one case of diabetic sisters, ages twelve and 17, doctors found a metabolic defect, but only the younger sister responded to drugs and diet changes. A therapist found out why: each parent constantly tried to get her support in fights with the other parent. The allegiance of the twelve-year-old was not sought. Once the parents stopped trapping the older sister in their struggles, she too began responding to treatment.

In many cases, family therapists argue, an outbreak of physical illness is both a symptom of high stress among family members and an attempt to cope with it. Minuchin says that anorexia nervosa victims are "saviors of the family" because they paper over parental conflicts that threaten to destroy the family. Psychiatrist Philip Guerin, director of the Center for Family Learning in New Rochelle, N.Y., finds that many fathers suffer heart attacks shortly after a grown son or daughter leaves home. His hypothesis: the child may have functioned as a buffer for parental conflict. . . .

Time
November 24, 1975

Family therapy is oriented toward more effective communication between family members.

client) as having all the problems in the family. The family therapist will try to (1) improve communication within the family, (2) encourage autonomy and empathy among family members, (3) help the family develop new ways of making decisions, and (4) facilitate conflict resolution.

Psychodrama

A technique called **role playing** is used to work through interpersonal problems in **psychodrama.** One group member agrees to be the *protagonist* (the main actor in the drama), who typically describes a problem in interpersonal relationships. Other group members (including the therapist) play other roles in the drama, play aspects of the protagonist's personality or merely observe as the audience. Because the situation is not real and the people with whom the protagonist is having trouble are not usually present, the individual feels less threatened and is capable of freer expression of feelings and greater spontaneity. Alternative solutions to problems can be tried out in the drama without danger. Not infrequently, spectators with similar problems become just as emotionally involved in the drama as the protagonist.

Group psychotherapy has become so popular that many "groups" have arisen relatively spontaneously. Individuals who have participated in a single group experience sometimes feel competent to lead another group. If nothing happens, the results may be minimally dangerous; however, the intensity of emotion experienced in groups generally requires an experienced leader to ensure that negative experiences do not occur. A person interested in participating in a group should get information about the level of competence of the leader before volunteering. The same caution, of course, applies to all forms of psychotherapy.

While ethical guidelines may provide some structure for professionals concerning appropriate behavior, individual judgment must always be involved in solving ethical problems. How a therapist handles clients whose problems involve religious or political or moral issues must always stem from the therapist's understanding of the dangers and benefits that are involved for the client. How would you weigh client benefit for a client who wants to be a more effective heroin pusher or a more effective bigot? Take the case of a male therapist who decides to date a shy, withdrawn female client. Who is benefiting from the treatment, and how can the therapist be sure that *his* welfare is not being given more importance? What would you do if you heard that a therapist is on drugs while seeing clients? Professional guidelines provide for a series of steps from a personal warning to notification of the licensing board.

BIOLOGICAL THERAPIES

Chemotherapy

Drugs to treat psychopathology have been used for at least as long as recorded history. Many of the drugs used for treatment today, however, were originally used for other purposes, and their psychological effects were discovered accidentally. Even now, in many cases, scientists have only a vague idea why some drugs work. The drugs used in **chemotherapy** can be roughly divided into four categories: sedatives, tranquilizers, antidepressants, and antipsychotics (see Table 12–2).

Sedatives and Tranquilizers

Sedatives and tranquilizers have been used to help highly anxious people under transient

TABLE 12–2   Prescription Drugs Used in Chemotherapy

Sedatives Generic Name	Trade Name
Amobarbital	Amytal
Chloral hydrate	Noctec
Flurazepam hydrochloride	Dalmane
Methaqualone	Quaalude
Phenobarbital	Luminal
Sodium secobarbital	Seconal sodium
Sodium pentobarbital	Nembutal sodium
Triclofos	Triclos

Tranquilizers (Antianxiety Drugs) Generic Name	Trade Name
Chlordiazepoxide	Librium
Clorazepate	Tranxene
Diazepam	Valium
Hydroxyzine	Atarax
	Vistaril
Meprobamate	Equanil
	Miltown
Oxazepam	Serax

Antipsychotic Drugs Generic Name	Trade Name
Acetophenazine	Tindal
Butaperazine	Repoise
Carphenazine	Proketazine
Chlorpromazine	Thorazine
Haloperidol	Haldol
Molindone	Moban
Perphenazine	Trilafon
Prochlorperazine	Compazine
Thioridazine	Mellaril
Trifluoperazine	Stelazine
Triflupromazine	Vesprin

Antidepressant Drugs Generic Name	Trade Name
Amitriptyline	Elavil
Desipramine	Norpramin
	Pertofrane
Imipramine	Presamine
	Tofranil
Isocarboxazid	Marplan
Phenelzine	Nardil
Protriptyline	Vivactil
Nortriptyline	Aventyl
Tranylcypromine	Parnate

stress or those showing early manifestations of neurosis and psychosis. Although tranquilizers have been in use only since the middle 1950s, sedatives have been known for a long time. A **sedative** is defined as a drug that reduces anxiety and tension by inducing muscle relaxa-

"I see a substantial upswing in the economy by October, but who knows? Maybe it's the Valium talking."

The New Yorker, September 9, 1974. Drawing by Weber; © 1974 The New Yorker Magazine, Inc.

One problem in the use of medications to treat emotional problems is the difficulty people have using their feelings as a guide to action.

tion, sleep, and inhibition of the cognitive centers of the brain. Although they do reduce severe anxiety responses, sedatives have a major disadvantage; sedated individuals cannot function well in activities involving complex cognition because of the sleep-inducing quality of the drugs. The most common sedative is alcohol; others include barbiturates (a common type of sleeping pill), bromides, and chloral hydrate (also known as "knock-out" drops).

In the middle 1950s, a new group of drugs — the **tranquilizers** — were introduced. They had the advantage of reducing anxiety in neurotics and psychotics (as well as people under unusual stress) without the severe sleep-inducing side effect of the sedatives. Tranquilizers have become tremendously popular. Under moderate doses a person can cope with stresses of life without debilitating anxiety.

Both sedatives and tranquilizers have a major drawback that also applies to the antidepressant and antipsychotic drugs; once the person quits taking the drug, the emotional problems return. Severe dependence on tranquilizers and sedatives is far too common in our country. How-

ever, the drugs can be used effectively to help persons under transient situational stress and to help neurotics or psychotics reduce their anxiety to the point at which they can work on their problems in therapy.

Antidepressants

Although tranquilizers do not help individuals who are depressed, a group of drugs referred to as "mood elevators" — the **antidepressants** — are useful. The first drug discovered to have this effect was iproniazid. Originally designed for the treatment of tuberculosis, iproniazid was observed to have an unexpected side effect. The patients became less depressed and happier about life. Other drugs belonging to the same chemical family or having similar biochemical properties were subsequently found to have some antidepressant function. Antidepressants apparently affect the amount of certain biochemical transmitters within the brain, which in turn affects synaptic transmission (see Appendix D). Although the manufacturers claim tremendous success with antidepressant drugs, they are generally less effective for their purpose than are tranquilizers.

Antipsychotics

The first **antipsychotic** drug was extracted from a plant, *Rauwolfia serpentina,* mentioned in Hindu writing over 2500 years ago. The root of this plant was used in India to treat snake bites (which it did not affect), epilepsy and dysentery (which it made worse), and insomnia and insanity (which it helped). Not until the late 1940s were the therapeutic effects of this plant noticed in the Western world, and the active ingredient, called reserpine, was isolated in the early 1950s.

Although reserpine markedly helps to calm agitated psychotics, it occasionally produces undesirable side effects such as severe depression. For that reason reserpine has largely been replaced by another group of drugs — the phenothiazines — that dramatically calm agitated psychotics. The first phenothiazine to be used to treat psychosis — chlorpromazine — was, like the antidepressants, discovered by accident. It was originally used in anesthesia for surgical patients, in whom it produced profound calm before the operation. Many hospitalized psychotics have been discharged under chlorpromazine

Use of Drugs for Depression Challenged

UPI

LOS ANGELES — Depression in varying degrees affects about 60 million Americans at any given time, but a University of Southern California psychiatrist believes widely used mood-elevating drugs are not the answer.

Dr. Edward J. Stainbrook, chairman of the USC Department of Human Behavior, said tranquilizers and antidepressants camouflage, rather than solve, the problems causing the condition.

"Most people feel unable to cope with anxiety and depression and become even more anxious and depressed," he said in an interview.

"Actually, such emotions give us valuable information about ourselves if we let them. If the result is action that reduces the emotional pain then these negative emotions have served their purpose."

Stainbrook said we tend to think of emotions causing behavior when, in fact, the feelings result from behavior. . . .

Rocky Mountain News (Denver)
September 10, 1976

Writer Says Drugs Lifted Depression

Bob Jain

Drugs — some new and some not so new — may prove potent weapons against severe mental depression, a former foreign correspondent who has suffered that affliction said. . . .

Percy Knauth [said] . . . that he had seriously contemplated suicide a few years ago because of a "mood of pervasive sadness" that struck him for no apparent reason.

'Saved Life'

His understanding wife, Knauth said, probably saved his life at that time, but real recovery came after he became a patient at the Depression Research Unit of the Connecticut Mental Health Center. There, he said, he received drugs that eventually brought him back to normal.

Recovery wasn't immediate, he said, because the drugs worked cumulatively, correcting a chemical imbalance in his brain. He still is taking a "maintenance dose" of those drugs, much reduced from what he took during treatment, and may have to take them the rest of his life, he said. . . .

The experience was "a terrible journey, a frightening journey, that brought me very close to death," Knauth said, but he added that he had no regrets at having experienced it. . . .

He said symptoms were sadness, "to which was added fear, hopelessness and (a feeling of) personal worthlessness" that eroded his self-confidence and hurt his ability to make even the smallest decision.

"I came out of it a better person," he said, "certainly a different person."

The Denver Post
September 12, 1974

Two very different views on the use of medications to relieve depression!

treatment, but the symptoms tend to reappear if the patient quits taking the drug.

We know relatively little about how these drugs work. However, antidepressant and tranquilizing drugs may affect a person's level of motivation by altering the process of synaptic transmission in the central nervous system. They probably also have peripheral effects, such as producing muscle relaxation. Antipsychotic drugs also affect CNS transmission and may work by inhibiting bizarre psychotic cognitions that interfere with applying more realistic knowledge and skills. Until more is known about the nature of the action of these drugs, however, we can only speculate.

Shock Therapy and Lobotomy

Two types of therapy or treatment that have become less popular since the advent of chemotherapy involve direct nervous system intervention. One of these, *frontal lobotomy*, involves cutting through nerve pathways in the frontal lobe of the brain. Different parts of the frontal lobe are cut depending on the technique. The operation usually has dramatic effects on agitated psychotics. They calm down, relax, and become more cheerful, although they still have psychotic thoughts. The main advantage of lobotomies is an administrative one. The patient is still psychotic but no longer violent,

Attack on Electroshock

Matt Clark with Gerald C. Lubenow

For three decades, electroshock therapy has been regarded as one of the most effective treatments for severe mental depression. But along with psychosurgery and behavior modification, electroshock has recently come under attack by civil libertarians and consumer groups as a hazardous and even wanton infringement on the rights of mental patients. As the result of one such legal attack, electroshock therapy has been virtually halted in mental institutions throughout California since the first of the year.

What led to the ban was the passage last fall of a state law that places severe restrictions on the use of what is more properly called electroconvulsive therapy, or ECT. . . .

The law specifies that ECT may be given only with the consent of a relative or guardian—even when the patient voluntarily requests it. It also requires written approval by a panel of three physicians and permits ECT only after all other methods of treatment have been tried first. Violation could lead to a $10,000 fine and revocation of a doctor's license.

Fear

The law sailed through the legislature almost unnoticed by the majority of California psychiatrists. But it has not yet taken effect because of a suit brought by two psychiatrists and a patient challenging its constitutionality and a subsequent court restraining order. Even so, most mental institutions have suspended the use of ECT because staff doctors fear prosecution if the law if upheld.

Critics charge that the law breaches the traditional confidentiality of the doctor-patient relationship by its provision for review by other physicians, government agencies and members of the family. What is even more objectionable to the psychiatrists is the need to use every other treatment technique before resorting to ECT. "For psychotic depression," says Dr. Francis Rigney of the San Francisco Mental Health Advisory Board, "ECT is the treatment of choice."

But Dr. John Friedberg, the leading medical advocate of the law, insists that the profession has suppressed evidence that ECT can cause brain damage and minimized the problem of memory loss occurring after treatment. . . . In reply, ECT experts argue that the amnesia is only temporary.

Still, the majority of professionals share Friedberg's concern that ECT is used too extensively and for inappropriate cases by some doctors. . . . What Rigney would like is a law that would spell out the proper indications for administering convulsive therapy, provide for informed consent and put the "shock shops" out of business.

Newsweek
March 17, 1975

Shock treatment can be an effective method of treating depressions, although many people object to the procedure because (1) it is a violent and distasteful treatment, (2) it may produce unknown changes in the brain, and (3) the reason for its effectiveness is unknown.

and is therefore easier to care for (although he or she now has irreversible brain damage). With the discovery of antipsychotic drugs, however, lobotomies were largely discontinued. Lobotomy is one type of **psychosurgery.** As we noted in Chapter 2, because drug therapy has its own weaknesses, psychosurgery may be on the upswing again, albeit in a much more sophisticated form, involving surgery in very specific areas of the brain.

Electroconvulsive therapy (ECT), or shock therapy, has been demonstrated to be effective for people with relatively severe depressions that do not respond to chemotherapy. In ECT the patient is placed on a bed, given muscle relaxants, and while lightly held by attendants, is given an electric shock across the temples of sufficient intensity to produce a convulsion. The convulsion lasts up to a minute and is followed by unconsciousness for about half an hour. Although scientists do not actually know how ECT works, both convulsion and resulting coma seem to be necessary for effective treatment. The patient cannot remember anything about the shock or convulsion. Surprisingly, ECT has been found to be effective in reducing or eliminating depression (after several treatments), but it is not effective in treating other problems.

Although the treatment may seem drastic, it can eliminate months of suffering and possibly prevent suicide. Unfortunately, ECT does not reduce the possibility of future depressions.

Hospitalization

Persons who are not competent to handle everyday requirements, who are not helped by psychotherapy and/or medication to function effectively, whose behavior might be dangerous to themselves or others, or who need more intensive treatment than can be provided by a therapist in an office setting may require hospitalization. Each year about a quarter of a million peple are admitted for the first time to mental institutions in this country. At any given time around three-quarters of a million people are hospitalized for emotional problems —at least as many as are hospitalized for all physical illnesses combined. Fortunately, the average length of confinement today is roughly two weeks, a drastic reduction from earlier years. Still, one out of five will remain hospitalized for a year or more, and about 50 percent will be hospitalized again later in life.

Most of the hospitalized mental patients have been *involuntarily committed* by civil court procedures for a specific period of days or months or perhaps for an indefinite period, to be released only at the discretion of hospital officials. Commitment is a serious step and is presently quite controversial. In most states the involuntarily committed person is denied most civil rights and may not be able to vote, marry, or obtain a divorce. Some states have put civil rights for patients into law, but in many states there is no protection. If a patient is disliked by the people in charge, there are few legal pathways available to obtain freedom. All too frequently the mentally ill are committed and "forgotten." Steps have been taken only recently to try to ensure that those who are committed to mental hospitals for treatment do in fact receive treatment.

A few years ago most state mental hospitals were little more than rest homes for the emotionally disturbed, with little or no treatment administered to patients. Frequently, the patient population numbered in the thousands while the professional staff was a mere handful. In recent years we have come to realize that it is more expensive *not* to provide treatment than it is to help individuals leave the hospitals. "Back" wards, where some people spend all their lives, are becoming less common, and antipsychotic drugs have helped reduce patient loads. Hospitalization is now seen primarily as an aid to therapy and not a therapy itself. The federal government and many states have a policy of trying to reduce the size of mental hospitals by keeping afflicted persons in their communities, functioning as best they can under drugs if necessary and with some outpatient form of treatment. Some states are experimenting with a procedure called *voluntary commitment,* in which one may sign oneself in and out of a hospital. Under this procedure, a person can be held involuntarily only for a few days at a time.

SOCIAL APPROACHES TO EMOTIONAL PROBLEMS

Community Mental Health

The field of **community mental health** has developed out of two concerns: (1) the need for more efficient and comprehensive provision of mental health services and (2) the attempt to prevent mental illness by "treating" a community or a whole social system rather than each individual in the community.

President John F. Kennedy, just before he was assassinated in 1963, proposed to Congress that comprehensive community mental health centers be set up to provide treatment for the emotionally disturbed *within* the community. By so doing, Kennedy shifted the focus away from treatment in state hospitals, which were originally built in isolated rural areas usually miles away from the home of the disturbed individual. Under President Lyndon B. Johnson, the Comprehensive Community Mental Health Centers Act was passed, providing federal aid to states for the contruction of community mental health centers. The centers were required to provide short-term hospitalization; outpatient care, usually traditional psychotherapy; 24-hour emergency service, including suicide prevention and crisis therapy; day care for people who need a structured setting during the day but can return home at night; night care for people who need a sheltered place to stay at night but can work at jobs during the day; and consultation to community agencies.

Although community mental health centers have not eliminated the need of many individuals for long-term care in a state or other hospital, they have provided more convenient treatment and a wider range of services than was previously available. Ultimately, these centers aim at broadening their activities so they can intervene in community crises before emotional disturbances occur. One center, for example, has already been able to prevent a potential race riot by sending a team of crisis workers into a school riddled by racial disturbances.

Community mental health programs tend to divide into three kinds of services: primary, secondary, and tertiary.

Primary Services

Primary services (often referred to as primary prevention) are directed toward eliminating the basic causes of a problem. The eradication of poverty and disease, of racial discrimination and injustice, and of other stresses might be taken as examples of primary prevention, because these conditions are probably significantly involved in the incidence of emotional problems. The theory of primary prevention is that by identifying potential crises in a person's life and preparing the individual in advance to handle these crises, abnormal reactions can be prevented. It is in primary prevention that the most important gains can be made in the control of psychopathology, but so far little work toward this end has been done in our society.

Secondary Services

In *secondary services* (also called secondary prevention) the focus is on existing psychopathological problems. Traditional psychotherapy is the major form of secondary treatment, although other approaches designed to help a wider group of people have evolved in the community mental health movement. **Crisis intervention** is an example of one of these more recent approaches. A **crisis** can be defined as a point in a person's life that is unusually stressful and may be handled in a maladaptive way. Crisis intervention is based on the assumption that persons can best be helped when there is an immediate crisis in their lives, when their marriage or romance has just broken up, for

example. At this time a person is more willing to accept help from a mental health worker and is able to change more in a shorter period of time. Crisis therapy involves helping the person define the immediate problem and seek alternative solutions to it, because people panic when they see no way out of the problems they are facing. Crisis therapy tends to be more directive and confrontative than traditional insight therapy. Receiving short-term psychotherapy during crisis situations can frequently prevent the need for hospitalization, medication, or psychotherapy at other times in life. Students who are in danger of flunking out of school, individuals who have lost their jobs, or people in any of a thousand other crisis situations may need a therapist for four or five sessions to help them over that crisis, although they can function normally at other times.

A specific example of crisis intervention is *suicide prevention*. In many cities across the country phone numbers are available that will connect a potentially suicidal person with a counselor at a suicide prevention center. Prevention centers are effective because people who are suicidal usually are ambivalent about dying, wanting to die but also wanting to live. It is well known that most people who are considering killing themselves communicate these feelings either in their behavior or by talking about suicide sometime before any attempt is made. Finally, suicide attempts occur when a person is in a crisis and therefore is more receptive to help.

One of the first things a suicide prevention counselor will try to do when on the phone with a suicidal person is to determine the risk. The following factors help determine how likely death is:

1. Age. The older the person, the greater the risk of death. The exception is among male blacks, for whom the greatest risk is from age 20 to 24.

2. Sex. Men are about three times as likely to commit suicide as women, although women are about three times as likely to attempt suicide as men.

3. Plan for suicide. The more specific the plan and the more deadly the method, the greater the risk. Guns are a greater danger than pills or wrist cutting.

4. Resources. People who have fewer resources to turn to for help in a crisis are a

Best Medicine for Prevention of Suicide Is 'Talk, Talk'

You—ordinary citizen—are carrying around the best medicine for prevention of suicide.

That medicine is talk, said Julie Greenblatt, of the Suicide and Crisis Control. . . .

Ms. Greenblatt said most people are dismayed or frightened when friends or family members give hints of killing themselves, and shy away from the subject.

"If the friend or relative who is approached by a potential suicidal person could just say calmly, 'You feel like committing suicide don't you,' then the subject is in the open and can be dealt with," Ms. Greenblatt explained.

Margaret Palmer, also of the control group, said lay people can recognize potential suicide victims by these characteristics:

Deep depression, particularly if it is a drastic change from the person's normal personality.

Withdrawal from normal activity.

Conversation about being a burden to family and friends, feeling worthless, not wanting to face the next day.

Giving away of possessions.

Threats of suicide, contrary to popular belief, are very serious, the women said. In fact, 80 per cent of suicide victims give clues they are planning to end their lives, Ms. Greenblatt explained.

She said anyone who knows a potential suicidal person, he or she should try to convince that person to call a preventions center, mental health clinic, family physician, clergyman or hospital.

"If the suicidal person can't be convinced to make the call, the friend or relative should," she said. . . .

The Denver Post
May 21, 1974

greater risk for suicide. Those who are isolated from family, relatives, and friends and are not in a position to turn to physicians or clergymen for support and help are a greater risk. Divorced people have a suicide rate three to four times the national average.

If the risk of death is high, the counselor will be more active in trying to intervene. If the risk is low, the counselor will first try to establish a relationship over the phone in order to maintain contact and obtain information. The counselor first tries to communicate interest and optimism about finding a solution to the crisis. The second step is to identify and clarify problems. The suicidal person is often confused and unsure as to precisely what problems he or she faces. At this point alternative solutions to the problem might be suggested. The resources of the person will be taken into account, and attempts will be made to bring the person in contact with mental health professionals within the community.

In an attempt to make mental health services more available to the poor, *storefront clinics* or outreach centers have been set up in the middle of poverty areas. These clinics are usually staffed by people from the community who act as problem solvers, sympathetic listeners, and community facilitators. Trying to obtain services from community agencies, for example, can be very frustrating if a person does not know what is available, which agency is appropriate, and what the eligibility requirements are. Sometimes mental health professionals work in conjunction with community service programs such as Model Cities.

Tertiary Services

Tertiary services (also called tertiary prevention) are concerned with the aftereffects of having emotional problems. This type of treatment is generally referred to as *rehabilitation*. People who have had severe emotional problems may have lost their job or family and need counseling to get back into the community. This may involve job training, counseling in how to get a job, and development of social skills.

Social Action

As we have seen, psychologists have strong feelings about possible changes in the structure of society that could reduce the frequency of mental disorder and mental suffering, as well as correct social wrongs. However, such changes may involve expensive programs that the taxpayer is not willing to support, and there is frequently disagreement about the types of changes needed. Not infrequently a redistribution of power is required, and those in power are not willing to give it up. Because a political activist orientation implies the direct confrontation of incompatible social values, such activities are controversial, and an activist orientation is not shared by all mental health professionals. However, almost all mental health professionals *are* concerned about social change.

Some psychologists have been active in redefining for society what is abnormal. Several states have removed or are considering removing laws pertaining to sexual behavior between consenting adults, because there is no victim and no crime. Homosexuality would then no longer be a crime. Psychologists have tried to institute changes in the punishment techniques used in prisons on the basis of modern reinforcement principles. Some have tried to remove bail as a requirement for release from prison prior to trial. The belief is that the poor should not be penalized by imprisonment simply because they cannot pay bail.

In the schools some psychologists concerned with social change have worked not to produce a better curriculum content but to change the focus of teaching from the memorization of facts to the process of problem solving. Working in such areas of concern is frustrating, however, because large institutions build up considerable inertia and change very slowly.

THE STATE OF THE ART

If you view these two chapters on psychopathology and psychotherapy superficially, you might arrive at the following oversimplified view. The clinical psychologist, confronted with a case of behavior disorder, first makes a diagnosis of the disorder, then applies a treatment or a therapy (psychotherapy) to remove the disorder or "cure" it, and finally helps his patient resume his normal activities within the community. In other words, the procedure appears quite similar to the medical model of treating physical illness (diagnosis-treatment-cure-rehabilitation)—a nice, neat, and simple picture. However, the picture is not nearly so neat in reality, and we would like to close by emphasizing that fact.

In Chapter 11 we saw that diagnostic classification is a difficult task, and clinical psychologists frequently disagree about diagnoses in

particular cases. More important, we saw that with present knowledge of psychopathology, psychologists are rarely certain of the causes of or "cure" for a particular disorder, even if they have been able to agree on what to call it. We have seen in this chapter that there are many different types of psychotherapy and that each type can be applied to a wide variety of diagnostic categories. Any particular therapist is likely to be "sold" on one school of thought in which he or she is a highly skilled and knowledgeable student. This method of therapy is then applied to just about all the cases encountered. However, the state of the psychotherapeutic art is such that mental health professionals cannot now claim that they are doing an outstanding job in treating many kinds of behavioral disorders.

But there are some promising trends emerging that we would like to highlight in this concluding comment. First, as we stated in Chapter 11, there is much less emphasis today on the problem of diagnostic classification—the psychologist now attempts to identify the client's problems and does not worry too much about being able to fit each client into a neat category of mental "illness." Second, psychotherapists are more likely today than they were 10 years ago to be trained in a variety of techniques. The hope is for more adaptable behavior on the part of the therapist in the future. Third, the new methods of behavior modification hold great promise for specific disorders, and more and more psychologists are becoming sophisticated in the application of these techniques. Fourth, we see a greater realization among psychologists of the fact that traditional psychotherapy is not the answer to every problem for several reasons—it costs too much, it cannot be given to enough people, not everyone benefits from it, and the delivery system as it now stands discriminates unfairly. As a result of all these factors, we see a fifth trend emerging—a trend away from individual psychotherapy delivered after someone has developed a disorder to a community mental health system oriented around preventive mental health, crisis intervention, short-term psychotherapy, and minimal hospitalization. We see the continuing rise of community psychology with its attempts to delineate and attack the social-cultural sources of behavioral disorders.

We do not mean to conclude that psychology

will shortly discover all the answers to mental illness. We do mean to suggest, however, that the next 20 years will result in more progress than the last 20 years. We do not believe that this progress will necessarily consist of the discovery of great new "cures" for neurosis (although we would hope that this would be the case for the psychotic disorders). Rather, we expect there to be an entirely new set of working assumptions about mental health, and we expect these assumptions to conflict dramatically with the "diagnosis-treatment-cure" model that has characterized the work of the clinical psychologist for such a long time.

SUMMARY

1. Psychotherapy is defined as a corrective experience leading a person to behave in a socially appropriate way.
2. The types of psychotherapy can be divided into two broad categories: insight-oriented therapy, focusing on change in motivation and self-knowledge, and noninsight-oriented therapy (behavior therapy), focusing on change in motivation and skill.
3. Insight-oriented therapy assumes that emotional problems stem from conflicts between conscious and unconscious processes. The two major types are those focusing on repressed memories of the past, such as psychoanalysis and primal therapy, and those focusing on denied aspects of present experiences, such as client-centered therapy, Gestalt therapy, and transactional analysis.
4. In classical psychoanalysis the patient, lying on a couch to reduce external stimuli, is asked to free associate, to say anything and everything that comes to mind. Dream interpretation and interpretation of such unusual behaviors as slips of the tongue help the therapist evaluate the contents of the unconscious mind.
5. Client-centered psychotherapy has as its focus helping the client move from denial of certain feelings and experiences to acceptance and experiencing of all feelings and thoughts in the here and now. The client-centered therapist develops an atmosphere of empathic understanding, unconditional positive regard, and congruence to encourage the client to risk facing his or her denied feelings.
6. Gestalt therapy is another therapy that focuses on insight into present experience. This form of therapy tries to help persons become aware of what they are feeling and how they are behaving from moment to moment.
7. Transactional analysis focuses on the way in which the Parent, Child, and Adult aspects of each person's personality are expressed in interactive communications.
8. The behavior modification therapist uses well-established principles of learning in order to change behavior.
9. Classical conditioning has been used in the treatment of neurosis, homosexuality, and alcoholism.
10. In instrumental conditioning therapy the client is rewarded for appropriate behavior or punished for behavior that is inappropriate. However, if the desired behavior never occurs, or if the inappropriate behavior is self-reinforcing, instrumental conditioning may be difficult to use.
11. In biofeedback people can learn to control the physiological processes that are affected by emotion, thus learning to obtain deep muscle relaxation in response to stress or to control psychosomatic illnesses.
12. Wolpe's systematic desensitization pairs relaxation training with the fantasy of feared stimuli, moving slowly from the least to the most feared.

13. In covert sensitization unpleasant images and fantasy are paired with behavior that the therapist is trying to help the client change. This paired fantasy is effective in changing behavior in situations in which punishment might be difficult or inappropriate to use.

14. Cognitive therapies use intervention techniques designed to change a person's self-understanding or understanding of the nature of the world. Bandura's modeling, Ellis' rational-emotive therapy, and Raimy's misconception therapy are examples of this approach.

15. New ways of obtaining behavior change, such as EST, Rolfing, and bioenergetics are constantly being developed. Time and research are needed to verify their effectiveness.

16. Group therapy offers group members the opportunity to understand others, get feedback, share solutions, be a therapist for others, and practice new behaviors. Forms of group therapy include sensitivity training groups, encounter groups, marathon groups, family therapy, and psychodrama.

17. Biological therapies include chemotherapy, psychosurgery, and shock therapy. Drugs used in psychiatry for the treatment of emotional problems can be divided into four categories: sedatives, tranquilizers, antidepressants, and antipsychotics.

18. Lobotomies (cutting nerves in the frontal lobe of the brain) and electroconvulsive therapy (in which a person has a convulsion induced by electric shock across the temples) are techniques that have become less common since the use of drugs in psychiatric treatment.

19. Hospitalization may be used when therapy and medication alone are not sufficient to help a person function effectively.

20. Quite often social approaches are effective in treating emotional problems. Community mental health is concerned with the more efficient delivery of mental health services, particularly to the poor, and treatment of a community or social system rather than each individual.

21. In primary services the focus is on eliminating the cause of emotional problems. Secondary services center on problems that already exist. Tertiary services deal with rehabilitation and the aftereffects of having emotional problems.

RECOMMENDED ADDITIONAL READINGS

Bandura, A. *Principles of behavior modification.* New York: Holt, Rinehart and Winston, 1969.

Duke, M. P., & Frankel, A. S. *Inside psychotherapy.* Chicago: Markham, 1971.

Freud, S. *A general introduction to psychoanalysis.* New York: Washington Square Press, 1920.

Greenwald, H. (ed.). *Great cases in psychoanalysis.* New York: Ballantine, 1959.

Moser, T. *Years of apprenticeship on the couch: Fragments of my training analysis.* New York: Urizen Books, 1977.

what does it mean?

WHAT IS IT LIKE TO BE IN THERAPY?

Once one has decided that one needs help with emotional problems, one has to do something about it. Table 12–3 presents the results of a survey concerning why people seek help. Table 12–4 indicates that relatively few people seek help from a therapist, but usually go to their clergy or physician. Unfortunately, in many cases in which the problem is severe, it is someone else who decides that the individual needs treatment, and involuntary commitment is sought. Indeed, some people have the misconception that one must be obviously psychotic or nonfunctioning before it is legitimate to ask for help. Actually, just the desire to *change* is sufficient reason to seek professional help. Dissatisfaction with his present existence was the client's motivation in the following case:

This [psychotherapy] is something I've been thinking about for a long time. I've known that it was something I've needed and wanted, but I just haven't done anything about it. Recently though, I've been realizing more than ever that I'm just not the way I want to be. I'm not sure what I am, and I'm not sure I want to know, but I sure don't like this. I'm not even sure what I want to be—sometimes it's one thing, sometimes something quite different. I don't know where I am or where I'm going, but I've at last decided to try to find out. (Fitts, 1965, page 16)

It can, of course, be frightening to ask a strange person for help with one's problems, taking a chance that the therapist will understand and not criticize or consider the problem trivial. Finally, the client must feel that he or she can trust the therapist, or openness and frankness will not be possible. The client in the following case was probably not ready to benefit from therapy until he got over some of his initial doubts about therapy and the therapist:

The first few visits I felt uneasy, tearful, embarrassed, ashamed, guilty, and depressed, and constantly reminded myself: "surely I could have done better than this; why did this have to happen to me?" What does my Doctor think of me? How could he know what I'm going through? Why should he care? Why should he spend his time with me? (Someone else maybe, but I should be capable of straightening this out myself!)
As I sat in that chair choked with emotion, and ashamed that I was, it was hard for me to say anything. When I did have a feeling and wanted to express it, it was so vague I couldn't find the words. After three sessions of saying so little, I felt like I wasn't getting anywhere, and was wasting the Doctor's time. I wanted the therapist to be proud of me. What he thought of me was always important. (Fitts, 1965, page 26)

Therapy is difficult under the best of circumstances. There are times when the process of trying to understand oneself can be almost physically painful, and the effort is always tiring. People develop feelings of anger and affection for the therapist that can get in the way of clear thinking. Sometimes people get

TABLE 12–3   Nature of Personal Problems for Which People Sought Professional Help — Survey Results

Problem Area	
Spouse; marriage	42%
Child; relationship with child	12
Other family relationships — parents, in-laws, etc.	5
Other relationship problems; type of relationship problem unspecified	4
Job or school problems; vocational choice	6
Nonjob adjustment problems in the self (general adjustment, specific symptoms, etc.)	18
Situational problems involving other people (e.g., death or illness of a loved one) causing extreme psychological reaction	6
Nonpsychological situational problems	8
Nothing specific; a lot of little things; can't remember	2
Not ascertained	1
Total	**
Number of people	(345)

** Percentages total to more than 100 percent because some respondents gave more than one response.

TABLE 12–4   Where Do People Go for Help?

Source of Help	
Clergyman	42%
Doctor	29
Psychiatrist (or psychologist): private practitioner or not ascertained whether private or institutional[a]	12
Psychiatrist (or psychologist) in clinic, hospital, other agency; mental hospital	6
Marriage counselor; marriage clinic	3
Other private practitioners or social agencies for handling psychological problems	10
Social service agencies for handling nonpsychological problems (e.g., financial problems)	3
Lawyer	6
Other	11
Total	**
Number of people	(345)

[a] Actually only six people specifically mentioned going to a private practitioner. This category should thus be looked upon as representing in the main those people who said "psychiatrist" without specifying that he or she was part of a mental hygiene agency.

** Percentages total to more than 100 percent because some respondents gave more than one response.

annoyed at the one-sided nature of the relationship, because clients learn little or nothing about the therapist. If therapy takes a long time, persons can become embittered. Their high hopes, unfulfilled, make for considerable disappointment. It is known that some therapists can never empathize with some clients. Therefore, to prevent extreme disappointment, it is best to try several therapists before giving up therapy as a way of solving one's problems.

HOW EFFECTIVE IS PSYCHOTHERAPY?

In the early 1950s, Hans Eysenck challenged psychology to demonstrate whether psychotherapy was effective or not. In summarizing 19 experimental studies involving 7000 cases of psychoanalytic and nonpsychoanalytic types of treatment (behavior modification had not become popular at that time), Eysenck concluded that people who did not receive psychotherapy (but who may have received custodial care or care by a general practitioner) improved as much as or more than those who underwent psychotherapy! Using successful social and work adjustment as the criterion, Eysenck found that 66 percent of the patients who completed psychoanalysis improved, 64 percent of those who received nonpsychoanalytic therapy improved, and 72 percent of those who received no formal psychotherapy improved (Eysenck, 1952).

As you can imagine, Eysenck's report was a blow to mental health professionals, since it seemed to demonstrate that psychotherapy was useless. Subsequently, however, it became clear that there were several things wrong with Eysenck's conclusions. First, the people who improved without formal psychotherapy were frequently receiving help from some other source. Second, people who seek help are different from those who do not, and there is some evidence to suggest that those who seek help are the kinds of people who do not improve without it. In several respects, such as severity of problems, Eysenck's treatment and nontreatment groups were not comparable. Also, he used different criteria of improvement for the two groups. Finally, some kinds of problems simply do not get better without professional intervention; for example, the symptoms of neurosis do not commonly disappear spontaneously.

Very recently, Gene Glass has reexamined the vast research literature on psychotherapy outcome, using modern statistical evaluation techniques. While no single study, including Eysenck's, is conclusive, the sum total of the evidence strongly indicates that psychotherapy is an effective treatment for psychopathology.

Despite these findings, it is apparent that many people improve without psychotherapy. Those who conclude that nearly everyone needs a therapist sometime in life are vastly underrating the ability of people to solve their own personal problems, although often with the help of relatives and of close friends.

People use different criteria for "cure" in therapy. The psychoanalyst will evaluate whether transference is resolved, the Rogerian will look at the quality of expression of feelings and experiencing, and the behavior modifier will be concerned with changes in the specific behavior that led to the request for therapy. It is difficult, therefore, to find a simple criterion for improvement for all kinds of therapy. Why not ask clients themselves whether they are better?

A common problem that shades the client's evaluation of the therapy is the *hello-goodbye effect*. When the client says "hello" to the therapist at the beginning of therapy, he presents himself as unhappy and troubled; in fact, he may exaggerate to convince the therapist he is really "sick." At the end of the therapy, the "goodbye" effect is apt to occur. The client tries to present himself as strongly improved in order to resolve any dissonance about wasting his time and money and to express appreciation to the therapist for his efforts. Thus it would be easy to mistake the hello-goodbye effect for real improvement.

The ideal situation would seem to be to determine the type of therapy that is most effective for each type of problem and refer people to the appropriate therapist, much in the same way that a physician writes a prescription for an illness. However, there is as

"Because of you, my darling, I've never had an ulcer. I've never needed a psychiatrist. When I poured out my troubles, you listened. When I ranted and raved, you listened. Thank you, my angel, for listening."

"Who listened?"

The New Yorker, June 5, 1971. Drawing by Frascino; © 1971 The New Yorker Magazine, Inc.

Many psychologists believe that much good "psychotherapy" is done by close friends and relatives who simply listen. When personal problems are not extremely serious or disturbing, such "therapy" may be helpful. Just having someone to talk to who will not be highly critical and rejecting can be comforting in times of stress. Cynics have even characterized psychotherapy as "the purchase of friendship."

yet little evidence that the various insight-oriented therapies differentially help different problems. Although there may be differences not yet found in research, present evidence suggests that all therapies tend to help the same types of problems.

Behavior modification has been demonstrated to be effective with phobias and anxiety states in which there is a specific anxiety-provoking stimulus. Typical reports suggest that as many as 90 percent of clients with such problems are helped with behavioral techniques such as systematic desensitization. As behavior modification techniques have been extended and applied to more complex problems, such as very diffuse anxiety, the improvement rate has not been as high. Be-

HERMAN

"Sorry to keep you both waiting out here. Where's your wife?"

© 1975 Universal Press Syndicate.

Psychologists do a great deal of marriage counseling. Many states, by the way, restrict the use of the word "psychologist" to licensed graduates of approved programs. As a result, many "therapists" call themselves marriage counselors. When seeking help, one should consult the local mental health association for the names of qualified practitioners.

cause of all of these uncertainties, the question of the best therapy for a particular problem is still far from being resolved.

WHAT KIND OF THERAPIST IS BEST?

For some reason there has been little research isolating the personality characteristics of good therapists. Many training programs in clinical psychology place considerable weight on intellectual attributes such as grade point averages and test scores in deciding which applicants to accept for training. But do high intelligence and outstanding grades mean that a person will make a good therapist? Most of us would agree that other personality characteristics are also crucial to the effectiveness of a therapist. Even in the case of behavior modification therapies, which in some sense seem pretty impersonal, therapist "warmth" probably plays a role in determining the effectiveness of therapy.

It is clear that therapists do differ widely in their success rates. One factor contributing to this variability is the amount of experience the therapist has. It has been found that effectiveness in establishing an ideal therapeutic relationship with the client increases with experience. In fact, experience is a much more important factor in a therapist's success than the school of therapy to which the therapist belongs.

In addition, three personality characteristics of the therapist (all derived from Rogers' theory of therapy; see Chapter 9) seem to be important for positive change in therapy: *accurate empathy, nonpossessive warmth,* and *genuineness.* Accurate empathy means that the therapist is sensitive to the feelings of the client and is able to communicate that awareness to the client. Nonpossessive warmth is basically caring for the client as a person without demanding changes in feelings and experiences as a precondition to acceptance. Genuineness is defined as a lack of defensiveness on the part of the therapist, who must present himself or herself in an uncontrived, honest way.

In one study it was shown that when therapists ranked low on the three characteristics, a 50 percent rate of improvement in their clients was found, but when therapists ranked high on the three personality characteristics, a 90 percent rate was found. The combined rate of 70 percent for the two groups is near the level of improvement found by Eysenck for untreated controls (Truax et al., 1966). This research has not gone unchallenged, however. Some researchers have questioned whether these variables are measured in an appropriate, non-biased way. Others have sug-

Females Often Ill-Advised in Mental Therapy

J. C. Barden

NEW YORK — Only a decade or so ago there were as many men as women receiving psychiatric care. Today, many more women than men are seeking relief from their emotional problems and, according to a number of feminist psychotherapists, the women are being ill-advised by tradition-bound professionals in the field.

In 1960, the number of men and women under treatment as psychiatric patients, outpatients or in private counseling was roughly the same. In 1971, at least 100,000 more women than men sought psychiatric help, and indications are that this trend is continuing.

One reason for so many women feeling troubled, according to feminists in the psychotherapeutic field, is that women trying to escape the stereotyped roles of housewife and sex object are meeting a great deal of resistance and it leaves them guilt-ridden.

Problem Is Worsened

Then the problem is worsened, the feminists say, when psychotherapists try to make them adjust to the traditional role rather than exploring options with them.

Women as well as men are among these traditional-thinking therapists, but since more than 80 per cent of the psychotherapeutic profession is male, the men bear the brunt of the feminists' anger.

One of the feminists, Dr. Freyda Zell, co-director of the Consultation Center for Women, charges that "traditional psychotherapists perpetuate the sexist, stereotype roles in terms of male assertiveness and female nurturing." . . .

And feminists cite case studies showing that women are often labeled neurotic or even psychotic if they exhibit "healthy" male traits, such as aggressiveness, competitiveness or a high degree of sexuality.

Career Conflicts

Dr. Susanne P. Schad-Somers, one of the founders and a director of the Women's Psychotherapy Referral Service Inc., here, said that the majority of the women seeking help through the service had conflicts between careers and relationships.

"They're often told by traditional psychotherapists that they can't have both," she said. "It's not that way with men. They have a career, and whether or not they get married is not that important."

The Denver Post
March 6, 1974

Many feminists argue that male therapists should not see female clients because of sex-role biases in therapy.

gested that such therapist characteristics may be important only when weak interventions are used.

Other therapist variables have been found to be significant. Not surprisingly, the more the client *likes* the therapist, the more effective the therapy—and the longer the person stays in therapy. There is also evidence to suggest that therapists who have unresolved conflicts in the areas of dependency, warmth, intimacy, and hostility are less effective in helping people with their problems. Whether or not empathy, warmth, and genuineness are critical variables in therapy is as yet unresolved, although there is supportive evidence particularly for therapist warmth. However, a likable, conflict-free therapist is more likely to be effective than a cold, neurotic one.

An interesting hypothesis regarding the relationship between personality and therapeutic effectiveness is that certain personality characteristics may make a therapist ideally suited to treat one type of behavioral disorder but poorly suited to treat other types of disorders. Many therapists realize this implicitly and will refer clients who have problems with which they have had little success to therapists who have had better results in treating such cases. The most actively researched hypothesis along these lines is

Selecting the Right Therapist Could Be Traumatic

Carol Klieman

Caution! Therapy may be hazardous to your health!

That's a warning from a therapist, Dr. Manny Silverman, associate professor of guidance and counseling at Loyola University of Chicago.

A registered psychologist with a doctorate in counseling, Silverman says selecting a therapist is a consumer problem that only the consumer can solve—cautiously, very cautiously.

"Much psychological research shows that the net effect of therapy may not be that positive," says Silverman. "Doctors, clergy, and others who try to match people with the right therapist don't always succeed. Sometimes it's effective, and sometimes it's not.

"When it comes right down to it, you are the best judge of who and what are best for you."

First, the consumer makes the decision she needs therapy. Then she must decide to whom to go.

"A decision to seek therapy is laden with further decisions that would be difficult enough in good times, let alone when things appear rotten," he says. "But it is vital to evaluate the person from whom you are seeking help."

To help people shop for therapy, Silverman holds workshops and classes at Greenerfields Unlimited and Loyola. They are attended by consumers, therapists, doctors, lawyers, and clergymen who frequently are asked to recommend someone.

"Caveat Emptor—let the buyer beware—has too long been the rule for therapy," Silverman says.

The professor, who also does private therapy, adds, "The point is not that there are bad therapists, but that there might be certain credentials that would be important to you as the client and that might make the difference in whether your therapy is successful or not."

The beauty of asking a potential therapist direct questions is that the asking is part of the answer.

Some questions:

Where did you get your training?

What is your marital status? "This is a very personal question," says Silverman, who has been married 11 years and has two children, "but if the therapist has been divorced three times it might be indicative of a mind set you should know about. And if it matters to you, ask."

How long have you been in practice?

What types of problems do you see?

What types do you like to see?

What types do you least like to see?

Do you routinely suggest a physical examination before therapy begins?

How long on the average do you see someone?

What is your fee? Do you charge for missed sessions? How far ahead can I cancel?

Any other questions that are relevant to you.

"The basic premise of therapy is trust," Silverman says. "The way these questions are answered can tell you a lot. Remember, this is someone you will want to relate to, who should be able to listen to you, and to understand." . . .

Boulder (Colo.) Sunday Camera
June 20, 1976

called the **A-B variable hypothesis,** suggested by Whitehorn and Betz in 1954. *A* therapists were operationally defined as those who had the highest "success" rates with schizophrenics, while *B* therapists were those who did poorly in treating schizophrenics. In later studies comparing the effectiveness of the two types of therapists in treating neurotic disorders, the *B*s tended to do better.

In assessing the personality characteristics of the *A*s and *B*s, the following has been suggested: *A*s are more trusting and tolerant of the client, more personally involved with the client, less coercive, and more flexible in helping the client to define acceptable behavior (they give the client more leeway). The *B* therapists are stricter in defining right and wrong, tend to see things more in black and white terms, and are more rigid about making the client conform to "socially acceptable" norms of behavior.

It is still too early to tell if the *A-B* variable is crucially important, but enough data have accumulated to suggest strongly that it is, although many methodological problems exist in these studies. It does seem fair to conclude that *A* therapists "get along" better with schizophrenic patients and may thus be better equipped to persuade them to change their behavior. The main lesson to be learned, however, is that therapist characteristics are probably very important and that different characteristics may be desirable for handling different types of disorders. A great deal of additional research must be done, however, before psychologists can conclusively advise someone to seek out a particular personality type when looking for a therapist. At the present time clients select a therapist on a rather random basis, by asking a friend or looking in the phone book, or they are assigned to the therapist who happens to be free when they come to a mental health center or hospital.

SHORTAGE OF THERAPISTS

There are simply not enough therapists to aid everyone who needs psychological help, and the population is growing faster than the number of psychologists and psychiatrists. Thus the movement toward community mental health has developed, as well as other alternative ways of providing help to those who need it. One approach that has emerged from the community mental health orientation to problems has been the use of **paraprofessionals.** Paraprofessionals are interested individuals in the community who can with a minimum of training serve as temporary therapists. Housewives, bartenders, and beauticians have successfully served this role. Individuals from poor neighborhoods, ghettos, and foreign-language-speaking areas of a city are all frequently alienated from the middle-class, traditionally trained clinician. Paraprofessionals can communicate with these people better and are more aware of the cultural pressures surrounding them. Paraprofessionals are particularly useful in crisis intervention and community action.

One of the more recent interesting attempts to compensate for the shortage of therapists is the use of computers. Although the definition of the problem usually requires a skilled clinician, once the problem is defined, many behavior modification approaches are relatively automatic. It is possible to program a computer to provide rewards and punishments in a systematic desensitization routine in much the same way that a programmed textbook or computer-assisted instruction works. A human therapist has to construct the hierarchy of anxiety-provoking situations, but the list can then be turned over to the computer, which will teach a person how to relax. Although lacking the warmth, genuineness, and empathy that may be important with the insight-oriented therapist, computers work with some people. Instrumentally and classically conditioned problems can probably also be treated with computer-assisted psychotherapy. Psychology is just beginning to explore alternative means of helping people, and many scientists are working on developing more efficient means of providing help.

Appendices

Elementary Statistics A

The single most commonly used tool in psychology is statistics. All areas of psychology rely on one or both of the two basic types of statistics: (1) *descriptive statistics*, which are used to describe and summarize the results of research, and (2) *inferential statistics*, used to infer the meaning of and to reach conclusions about the results.

DESCRIPTIVE STATISTICS

Measures of Central Tendency

Suppose a teacher gives an IQ test to 10 students. How would he or she describe the test results? One way would be to name all students and list their IQ scores—10

511

"That's the gist of what I want to say. Now get me some statistics to base it on."

The New Yorker, December 19, 1977. Drawing by Joe Mirachi; © 1977 The New Yorker Magazine, Inc.

TABLE A–1 Computation of the Mean IQ and Height of a Class of 10 Students

Student's Name	X (IQ)	Y (Height in Inches)
Rita	115	65
Norma	120	60
Lyle	105	66
Bruce	100	68
John	130	72
Jane	95	64
Linda	90	62
Ralph	110	74
Frank	85	70
Polly	125	67
	$\Sigma X = 1075$	$\Sigma Y = 668$
	$N = 10$	$N = 10$

Then, the mean of the X scores is:

$$\overline{X} = \frac{\Sigma X}{N}$$

or

$$\overline{X} = \frac{1075}{10} = 107.5$$

Likewise, the mean of the Y scores is:

$$\overline{Y} = \frac{\Sigma Y}{N}$$

or

$$\overline{Y} = \frac{668}{10} = 66.8$$

names and 10 scores. That would probably work nicely in a small class. But it would certainly be inefficient with a class of 500. Moreover, a listing of numbers does not indicate much of anything about the group as a whole. It would be helpful to know the average, typical, or more representative score. What is needed is a measure of *central tendency* in the group of scores. We will describe three commonly used measures.

The Arithmetic Mean

The **mean** is the number you arrive at when you add up all the scores and divide by the number of scores. In the above example you would add up the 10 IQ scores and divide by 10. We have made up a set of 10 scores and computed the arithmetic mean in Table A–1, which also introduces some elementary statistical symbols. Any score for an individual subject is an X. It could be an IQ score, an anxiety score, a measure of height, or anything. In Table A–1, X is an IQ score. We add up the 10 Xs. The capital Greek letter sigma (Σ) is a shorthand symbol for "add up these scores." So, Σ X means add up the X scores. Table A–1 also gives each student's height in inches. To keep height distinct from IQ scores, we signify height by Y. Very often a problem involves two scores for each subject, as in this case, and we use X and Y to keep them separate. So Σ Y tells us to add up the heights, which is also done in Table A–1.

The final step in computing the arithmetic mean is to divide by the number of scores added (symbolized by N). There are 10 IQ scores, so we divide Σ X by 10 and get the mean IQ: 107.5. Likewise, we divide Σ Y by 10 and we get the mean height: 66.8 inches. The shorthand way of indicating that a particular number is a mean and not a single score is to put a bar over the letter. Thus, the arithmetic mean of the X scores is symbolized as $\overline{X}$ (read "X bar"), and the mean of the Y scores is $\overline{Y}$ (read "Y bar"). Thus, we arrive at a shorthand formula for finding the arithmetic mean of a set of X scores:

$$\overline{X} = \frac{\Sigma X}{N}$$

And, of course, the arithmetic mean of a set of Y scores is calculated by the formula:

$$\overline{Y} = \frac{\Sigma Y}{N}$$

Now if students ask the teacher how the class performed on the IQ test, the teacher could simply report the value of $\overline{X}$; and if they ask about how tall the students are, he or she could report $\overline{Y}$. This is obviously much simpler than listing all the X and Y scores. It gives a better idea of the general level of ability of the students and a general idea of how tall they are.

TABLE A-2 Computation of the Median IQ Score of a Class of 10 Students

Name	X	
John	130	
Polly	125	
Norma	120	
Rita	115	
Ralph	110	← the middle is in here, somewhere between 105 and 110
Lyle	105	
Bruce	100	
Jane	95	
Linda	90	
Frank	85	

The median here is the mean of the 2 scores nearest the middle point, in this case, 105 and 110. We take the mean of 105 and 110:

$$\frac{105 + 110}{2} = 107.5$$

This is the median. Note that the median would not be changed if we changed John's score from 130 to, say, 160. What would the mean be in this case?

TABLE A-3 Comparison of the Mean and Median Monthly Salaries of the Zappo Cereal Company Employees

Employee Number	Monthly Salary X (in Dollars)	
1	10,000	
2	600	
3	550	
4	500	
5	450	← midpoint
6	400	
7	375	
8	375	
9	350	
10	350	
	$\Sigma X = 13,950$	
	$N = 10$	

We can see from the midpoint that the median salary is the mean of 400 and 450, which is $425.

Yet the mean salary is:

$$\overline{X} = \frac{\Sigma X}{N} = \frac{13950}{10} = \$1,395$$

Which value, the mean or the median, do you think is more representative of Zappo wages?

The Median

The arithmetic mean of the scores is not always a good way of determining what is the *most representative* score. In these cases two other measures of central tendency are often used. The **median** is the *middle-most score* in a list of scores that have been arranged in increasing order. If there is an odd number of scores, then there will be one score exactly in the middle. Thus, if the class had 11 students, the score of the 6th student in order would be the median—there would be 5 scores higher and 5 scores lower. Or if there were 27 scores, the 14th score in order would be the median.

With an even number of scores there is no single middle score. Instead there are 2 scores that determine the middle; 1 is above and 1 is below the theoretical midpoint. In a set of 10 scores arranged in order, the 5th score from the bottom is not the median—there are 5 scores above it, but only 4 below it. In the same fashion, the 6th score is not the median, because there are 4 higher scores but 5 lower scores. So we compromise and take the halfway point between the 5th and 6th scores as the median of a set of 10 scores. The median of 28 scores would be the mean of the 14th and 15th scores. Table A-2 shows the 10 IQ scores from Table A-1, but this time we have arranged them in order. The middle point is somewhere between the 5th and 6th score, somewhere between 105 and 110. So we take the mean of these 2 scores and use this as the median. The answer is 107.5. Coincidentally, this is the same score we got for the arithmetic mean in Table A-1.

The mean and the median are not always the same, however. They will be the same whenever the distribution of scores is symmetrical or equally balanced around the mean, as in Table A-1. But consider the set of "salary scores" in Table A-3. Here we note that most of the 10 people working for the Zappo Cereal Company are not making a lot of money. One employee, obviously the president, is making a bundle. This distribution of scores or values is asymmetrical and unbalanced. Technically, we call it *skewed*. The distribution in Table A-3 is skewed to the high end. The mean monthly salary for Zappo employees is $1395, which might lead you to believe that the company pays very well. But the median is only $425, which would make you think a little differently about Zappo. The median will be unaffected if the president gives himself or herself a big raise, but the mean will go up. You can see that in this case the median is more representative of the group as a whole than the mean is. Furthermore, the median is *unaffected* by extreme scores such as the salary of the president.

The Mode

The third measure of central tendency is called the **mode.** The mode is a quick but crude measure defined as the *most frequently occurring* score. In a small set of scores, as in Tables A-1, 2, and 3, there is the possibility that no score occurs more than once. Thus there is no mode. But suppose a psychologist gives an anxiety test to a group of 200 mental patients. With such a large

TABLE A–4   A Frequency Table of the Anxiety Scores of 200 Mental Patients

Score (X)	f or Frequency
20	10
19	10
18	12
17	15
16	20
15	27
14	15
13	21
12	22
11	12
10	10
9	8
8	7
7	5
6	3
5	0
4	2
3	1
2	0
1	0
	$\Sigma f = 200 = N$

The mode, the score that occurs most frequently, is equal to 15.

Figure A–1

A frequency distribution based on the data in Table A–4

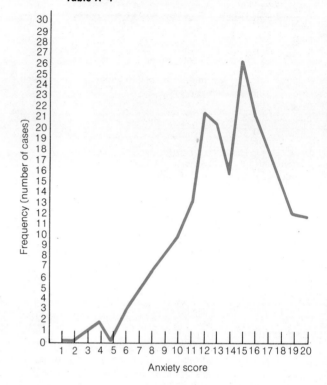

group it is convenient to set up a *frequency distribution* showing the various possible scores on the test and, for each possible score, how many people (*f* or frequency) actually got that score (see Table A–4). Suppose, for example, that 27 people got a score of 15 on the anxiety test. Looking down the frequency column in Table A–4, we see that 27 is the highest value. This means that 15 is the *mode* or the *modal score,* because it is the score that happens most frequently. Note that the sum of all the frequencies in the f column is equal to N, the number of people taking the test, in this case 200.

Frequency distributions can also appear in graphic form. Figure A–1 shows a frequency distribution using the data from Table A–4. The horizontal axis of the graph (technically, the *abscissa*) gives the value of X, the anxiety score, and the vertical axis (the *ordinate*) gives the frequency of the score.

The frequency distribution is a very important concept in statistics. More advanced techniques are heavily based on the frequency distribution principle, so make sure you understand just what it is.

Measures of Variability

People vary; not everyone gets the same score on a test or has the same height. There are **individual differences** among people. People may vary a lot when it comes to anxiety or IQ scores, but little when it comes

TABLE A–5   Two Sets of Scores That Have the Same Mean But Differ in Variability

Set A	Set B
22	36
22	32
21	28
21	24
20	20
20	20
19	16
19	12
18	8
18	4
$\Sigma X = 200$	$\Sigma X = 200$
N = 10	N = 10
$\overline{X} = \dfrac{200}{10} = 20$	$\overline{X} = \dfrac{200}{10} = 20$
Range = 22 − 18 = 4	Range = 36 − 4 = 32

to the number of fingers they have. Is there a convenient and accurate way of measuring the degree of variability in a set of scores?

TABLE A–6   Computation of the Variance and Standard Deviation for Two Sets of Scores

Set A (Ages of 10 People at a College Dance)			Set B (Ages of 10 People at the Park)		
X	$X - \overline{X}(x)$	x^2	X	$X - \overline{X}(x)$	x^2
22	2	4	36	16	256
22	2	4	32	12	144
21	1	1	28	8	64
21	1	1	24	4	16
20	0	0	20	0	0
20	0	0	20	0	0
19	−1	1	16	−4	16
19	−1	1	12	−8	64
18	−2	4	8	−12	144
18	−2	4	4	−16	256
	$\Sigma x = 0$	$\Sigma x^2 = 20$		$\Sigma x = 0$	$\Sigma x^2 = 960$

$$\sigma^2 = \text{variance} = \frac{\Sigma x^2}{N} = \frac{20}{10} = 2.00$$

$$\sigma = \text{standard deviation} = \sqrt{\sigma^2} = \sqrt{2.00} = 1.414$$

$$\text{or } \sigma = \sqrt{\frac{\Sigma x^2}{N}} = \sqrt{\frac{20}{10}} = 1.414$$

$$\sigma^2 = \text{variance} = \frac{\Sigma x^2}{N} = \frac{960}{10} = 96.0$$

$$\sigma = \text{standard deviation} = \sqrt{\sigma^2} = \sqrt{96} = 9.798$$

$$\text{or } \sigma = \sqrt{\frac{\Sigma x^2}{N}} = \sqrt{\frac{960}{10}} = 9.798$$

The quickest and least informative measure of the variability in a set of scores is the range. The **range** is defined as the *highest score minus the lowest score*. In Table A–4 we see that the anxiety scores of the patients "range" from a low of 3 to a high of 20, so the range would be $20 - 3 = 17$. The main reason for using the range as a measure of variability is that it is easy to compute. But because it is based on only two scores, it reflects very little about the distribution. A better and more commonly used measure of variability is the *standard deviation*, which reflects the degree of spread or fluctuation of scores *around the mean.*

Suppose we have a set of 10 scores with an arithmetic mean of 20. Two such sets are shown in Table A–5. The scores labeled Set A consist of only 5 different numbers that are all close to the mean of 20 (19, 19, 20, 21, and 22). Obviously, the variability in Set A is low. In Set B we have the same mean, 20, but the variability is much higher. There are 10 different scores, and some of them are a long way from the mean. If we described both sets with a central tendency measure, we would not be communicating the fact that the two sets are different in a quite basic way. To be more complete we need to provide a measure of variability.

The **standard deviation** is the *square root of the mean of the squared distance from the mean of the scores.* That's complicated, so let's analyze it in steps. First take each individual score, X, and subtract the mean from it, as we have done in Table A–6. You should be able to see that these new scores, symbolized by the lower-case x, are merely measures of the distance each score is from the mean. Now why not just calculate the average or mean of these distance scores? A glance at Table A–6 should convince you that if you add up the distance

scores to get a mean distance score, you will always get a sum of zero. For every score that is above the mean (a positive distance score) there is another score below the mean (a negative distance score) that cancels it out, meaning that the sum of the distance scores will always be zero. Instead, we square each score, which eliminates the negative numbers, and we have a new concept—the squared distance score, x^2. The x^2 scores are also shown in Table A–6. Now we can add these scores up and take the mean of them:

$$\frac{\Sigma x^2}{N}$$

This gives us the mean squared distance from the mean.

The mean squared distance from the mean has a special name, the **variance,** and a special symbol, the lower-case Greek letter sigma, squared (σ^2). The square, of course, serves to remind us that it is the mean *squared* distance score. The variance is a very good measure of variability, as you can see by comparing this value for Set A and Set B scores; σ^2 is much higher for B (96.0) than for A (2.0). This is as it should be because the Set B scores vary more (from 4 to 36) than the Set A scores (from 18 to 22).

The variance can be used by itself as the variability measure, but it is usually more convenient to take the square root of the variance. We squared the distance scores before we added them up, so now we take the square root of the variance to get back to the original scale of measurement. The square root of the variance is the standard deviation (symbolized σ). The larger the value of the standard deviation, the greater the variability in the corresponding set of scores.

Figure A–2
The normal distribution of IQ scores

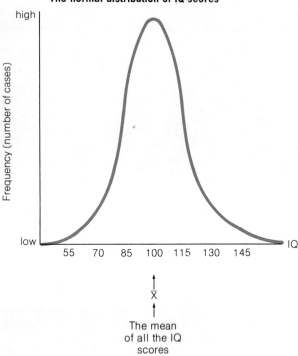

The mean
of all the IQ
scores

Figure A–3
The normal distribution divided into standard deviation units

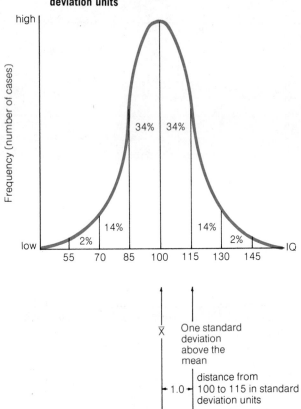

One standard
deviation
above the
mean

distance from
100 to 115 in standard
deviation units

The Normal Frequency Distribution

The frequency distribution in Figure A–2 is known as the *normal distribution*. A normal distribution is symmetric; if you fold it over at the mean, the two halves would superimpose. Moreover, it is bell-shaped; scores near the mean are most frequent, and frequency drops off smoothly as we move to the extremes. The normal distribution is the most important distribution in statistics because so many psychological factors are "normally distributed" in the population. IQ is a good example. IQ is normally distributed with a mean of 100 and a standard deviation of 15. This means that if we obtained IQ scores for everybody and took the mean of them, it would be 100, and the standard deviation would be 15. Furthermore, if we drew a graph representing the frequency of each of the possible IQ scores, it would be bell-shaped—normal—and would look like the one in Figure A–2.

If we know that a characteristic is normally distributed and if we know the mean and the standard deviation, we can use the theoretical properties of the normal distribution to deduce more information about the characteristic. We can do this because in any normal distribution the standard deviation can be used to divide the distribution into sections containing fixed percentages of the cases. Figure A–3 shows a normal distribu-

tion divided up in this way—again we have used IQ scores. The fixed percentages are printed in the various sections of the frequency distribution. For example, about 34 percent of the people lie between the mean and 115—that is, 34 percent of the people have IQs between 100 and 115. Because the standard deviation is 15, we can see that a score of 115 is one standard deviation above the mean ($115 - 100 = 15 =$ the standard deviation). Remember that the standard deviation is a distance measure, so the "distance" from 115 to the mean of 100 is one standard deviation unit. Two standard deviation units above the mean would be the distance up to 130, and three units would be to 145. Of course, we can go in the other direction also, below the mean. One unit below would be an IQ of 85, two units of standard deviation distance would be 70, and three units would be 55. From three standard deviation units *below* the mean on up to three units *above* the mean (from 55 up to 145), we cover essentially all the scores. Very few people score below 55 or above 145. So the range of scores, as measured in standard deviation units, goes from a low of −3 to a high of +3. It is very convenient to convert the IQ scores into standard deviation scores, called *z scores*.

Figure A–4
The normal distribution and z scores

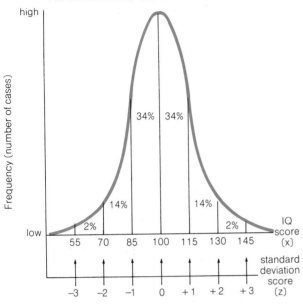

Figure A–5
The normal distribution of waist size in American men (hypothetical)

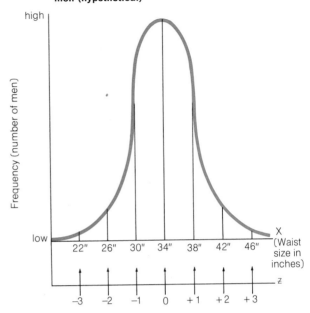

Figure A–4 again shows the IQ normal distribution, but this time we have two horizontal axes displayed. The upper one shows IQ scores and the lower one shows standard deviation scores, or z scores. Thus you can see that an IQ score of 115 is one standard deviation above the mean, so the z score corresponding to 115 is +1.0. If your friend tells you that his z score in IQ is +2.0, you can see that he has an IQ of 130. If he tells you that his z score is +4.0, he is either very brilliant or he is pulling your leg. Note that the mean of the z scores will always be equal to zero.

From Figure A–4, suppose we ask you to figure out what percentage of the people have IQs between 85 and 115, which is the same as asking how many people have z scores between −1.0 and +1.0. The answer is 68 percent; 34 percent between 85 and 100, and another 34 percent between 100 and 115.

An important thing to remember is that these percentages and the z score procedure apply to *any* normal distribution, not just the IQ distribution. The only difference between the IQ distribution and any other normal distribution is that they probably have different means and different standard deviations. But if you know that something has a normal distribution and if you know the mean and standard deviation of it, you can set up a figure like the one in Figure A–4.

Suppose, for example, that we told you that waist size in American men is normally distributed with a mean of 34 inches and a standard deviation of 4. You could now set up a normal frequency distribution, as in Figure A–5. The waist size scores run from a low of

22 inches (z score of −3; 22 is three standard-deviation units *below* the mean) up to a high of 46 (z score of +3 −3 units *above* the mean). Now you can fill in the percentages and answer the following questions:

1. What percentage of men have waist sizes less than 30 inches?

2. What percentage of men have waist sizes greater than 38?

3. If Joe's waist size is 47, is he unusual?

4. If we randomly selected one man from the American population, what is the probability (how likely is it?) that his waist size is equal to or greater than 38?

This last question brings us to the notion of probability. **Probability** refers to the *proportion of cases that fit a certain description*. In general, the probability of A (the likelihood that a randomly drawn object will be an A object) is equal to the number of A objects divided by the total number of all possible objects. The number of A objects divided by the total number of objects is, of course, the proportion of objects that *are* A, so the probability is just a proportion.

Suppose that an A is someone with a waist size equal to or greater than 38. To find the probability of selecting an A-man at random from the population, we have to know what proportion of all men are A-men. Figure A–5 tells us that 14 percent of the men are between 38 and 42 and an additional 2 percent are greater than 42, so we add 14 percent and 2 percent and we see that 16 percent of the men are A-men. In proportion terms, this becomes .16 (we move the decimal point two places to the left to translate a percentage into a proportion).

In summary, the probability of selecting a man with a waist size equal to or greater than $38 = .16$. This means that 16 out of every 100 selections would yield a man who fits this description.

Suppose that scores on an anxiety scale are normally distributed in the population of all American people with a mean of 50 and a standard deviation of 10. You should be able to calculate the probability that a randomly drawn person has an anxiety score that is equal to or *less* than 40. Can you do it?

Correlation

The final descriptive statistic to be discussed is the **correlation coefficient,** which was introduced in Chapter 1. The correlation coefficient does not describe a single set of scores as the mean or standard deviation does. Instead, it describes the degree of relationship between two sets of scores. It is basically a measure of the degree to which the two sets of scores vary together, or *covary*. Scores can vary together in one of two ways: (1) a *positive covariation,* in which high scores in one set tend to go with high scores in the other set (and low scores go with low scores), or (2) *negative covariation,* in which high scores in one set tend to go with *low* scores in the other set (and low scores go with high scores). When there is a positive covariation, we say the two sets are *positively* or *directly correlated,* and we say they are *negatively, indirectly,* or *inversely correlated* when there is a negative covariation. A common example of positive correlation is the relationship between height and weight —the taller you are the more you tend to weigh. A common example of negative correlation might be the relationship between the amount of alcohol a person has drunk in an evening and ability to drive an automobile. The more the person has drunk, the lower the ability to drive.

Note that we used "tend to go with." Correlations are almost never perfect—not all tall people are particularly heavy, and not all short people are lightweights. Of course, there is the third possibility too, namely, *no correlation* between two sets of scores, or *zero correlation.* Thus, for example, we probably would expect there to be a zero correlation between your height and your ability to learn psychology. So two variables (two sets of scores on different measures) can be *positively* or *negatively correlated* or *not correlated at all.* And the degree of correlation can be great or little. What we need is a statistic that conveniently measures the degree and the direction (positive or negative) of the correlation between two variables. This is what the coefficient of correlation does for us.

Table A–7 shows the scores of 10 people on two tests. Each person took both a test of anxiety and a test of "happiness." The possible scores on each test ranged from 1 to 10, with 1 meaning low anxiety and 10 very high anxiety for the anxiety test. For the happiness test, 1 means a low degree of happiness and 10 means a high

TABLE A–7   The Correlation between Anxiety and Happiness

Name	Anxiety (X)	Happiness (Y)
Joan	1	10
Larry	2	9
Ralph	3	8
Clint	4	7
Sue	5	6
Sharon	6	5
Sam	7	4
Bonnie	8	3
Marsha	9	2
Harry	10	1

Here we have arranged the anxiety scores in order and we see that this causes the happiness scores to be arranged in *perfect reverse order*. This is a perfect negative correlation. The coefficient of correlation would be -1.0.

degree of happiness. Intuitively we would expect a negative correlation between the two variables of anxiety and happiness; the happier you are, the less should be your anxiety, and vice versa.

For convenience we arranged the anxiety scores in order in Table A–7. What this does is to cause the happiness scores to fall in *perfect reverse order.* In other words, it is obvious in this table that there is a perfect negative correlation between anxiety and happiness. This is best displayed by making a *scatter plot* of the data, which we have done in Figure A–6. Here the horizontal axis is the anxiety score, and the vertical axis is the happiness score. Each person is represented by a point on the graph that locates him or her on the two tests. For example, Clint had an anxiety score of 4 and a happiness score of 7. So we go over (to the right) to 4 on the anxiety scale and then up to 7 on the happiness scale, and we place a dot at that point to represent Clint on the graph. All 10 people are represented in the graph. You can see that the 10 points all fall on a straight line, which means that the correlation is perfect. You can also see that the line slopes down to the right, and this means that the correlation is negative in direction— as you go up the anxiety scale the happiness scores go down.

As we have said, however, correlations are almost never perfect. This means that the points are likely to be scattered all over the graph, hence the term "scatter plot." The closer the points are to lying on a straight line, the higher the degree of correlation. So the procedure is to make a scatter plot and then try to draw a straight line that best fits the points in the plot. If all the points are close to or on this *line of best fit,* then the correlation is high. If the points are widely scattered and not close to any line you could draw, then the correlation is zero. Finally, if the line of best fit slopes downward to the right, then the correlation is negative, as we

TABLE A–8   Calculating the Pearson Product Moment Correlation Coefficient

Name	Anxiety (X)	X²	Happiness (Y)	Y²	XY (X times Y)
John	2	4	9	81	18
Ralph	5	25	6	36	30
Mary	9	81	4	16	36
Sue	1	1	3	9	3
Jim	3	9	2	4	6
Harvey	7	49	2	4	14
Jane	8	64	4	16	32
Joanne	6	36	5	25	30
N = 8 people	$\Sigma X = 41$	$\Sigma X^2 = 269$	$\Sigma Y = 35$	$\Sigma Y^2 = 191$	$\Sigma XY = 169$

$$r_{xy} \text{ (the correlation between X and Y)} = \frac{N\Sigma XY - (\Sigma X)(\Sigma Y)}{\sqrt{[N\Sigma X^2 - (\Sigma X)^2][N\Sigma Y^2 - (\Sigma Y)^2]}}$$

For these data: $r_{\text{ANXIETY·HAPPINESS}} = \dfrac{(8)(169) - (41)(35)}{\sqrt{[(8)(269) - (41)^2][(8)(191) - (35)^2]}} = \dfrac{1352 - 1435}{\sqrt{(2152 - 1681)(1528 - 1225)}}$

$$= \frac{-83}{\sqrt{(471)(303)}} = \frac{-83}{\sqrt{142713}} = \frac{-83}{377.77} = -.219$$

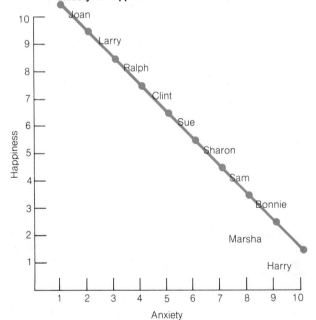

Figure A–6
"Scatter plot" of the data from Table A–7, relating anxiety to happiness

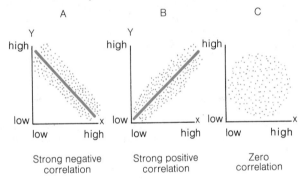

Figure A–7
Scatter plots of three correlations

A — Strong negative correlation
B — Strong positive correlation
C — Zero correlation

saw in Figure A–6. If the line slopes upward to the right, the correlation is positive. Figure A–7 shows three scatter plots. In panel A the two variables in question are highly negatively correlated; the points are all pretty close to the straight line, which slopes downward to the right. In panel B we have the case of a high positive correlation; the points are again all pretty close to the line, but this time the line slopes upward to the right. In panel C there is no correlation; the points are scattered all over, and there is no line that fits them very well.

The *Pearson product moment correlation coefficient* is the most often used of several measures of the correlation. It can take on any numerical value from −1.0 through 0.0 up to +1.0. A perfect negative product moment correlation, as in Table A–7, would be −1.0, and a perfect positive or direct correlation would be +1.0. Correlations close to zero would mean there is little or no relationship between the two variables, X and Y. The value of the correlation between 0.0 and 1 (ignoring the sign) would represent the degree of relationship. The sign of the correlation (positive or negative) does not tell you the degree of the correlation, only the direction. Thus a negative correlation of −.77 is just as strong a correlation as is a positive correlation of +.77; the only difference is the direction. Table A–8 shows the steps for calculating the Pearson product moment correlation coefficient in case you want to see exactly how it is done.

In all the examples so far, we have been correlating the scores of a person on two different tests. It does not have to be that way. We might correlate the scores of a person on the same test taken at two different times. Then we would be asking if the test is reliable — that is, does a person tend to score about the same on the test if he takes it on two different occasions? If it is a good test, it should be reliable (see Chapter 1 and Appendix C). Another common use of correlation is to determine the validity of a test — does the test measure what it is supposed to measure? If we make up a test of intelligence, we would hope that it would correlate positively with performance in school. If it did, it would help us argue that our test really did measure intelligence. (See Chapter 1 and Appendix C for a discussion of validity.)

Regression

One important use of the correlational statistics is in a procedure called **regression.** A correlation coefficient tells us the degree to which a person's score on both of two tests are related. Suppose we try to predict your weight. We have no idea what to guess, because about all we know about you is that you are reading this book. If we knew that the average person reading this book weighs 142 pounds, then that is what we would have to guess, and we would make the same guess for every reader. But if we knew your height, and we also knew the correlation between weight and height, then we could make a much more accurate guess about your weight. For example, if we knew that you were 6 feet, 6 inches tall, we would hardly guess 142 pounds. Likewise, if we knew you were 4 feet, 2 inches, 142 pounds is an inappropriate guess. We would adjust our weight guess according to what we know about your height. Regression is a fancy, complex, but accurate way of making this adjustment.

Finally, a moment's thought should convince you that the higher the correlation (in either the positive or negative direction), the better job we can do at predicting your weight — the closer we will come to your true weight. If the correlation between the two variables is perfect (+1.0 or −1.0), we can predict perfectly the value of one of the variables if we know the value of the other. But because correlations are almost never perfect, our predictions are somewhat off, and the lower the correlation, the greater the likely error.

Regression is used in many different settings. Most of you probably took the College Board examinations for getting into college. From past research we know there is a positive correlation between your score on the College Boards and your success in college. Therefore, the College Board tests can now be given to college applicants, and on the basis of their scores, we can predict approximately how a person will do in college. These predictions are used to help decide whom to admit.

Figure A–8
Scatter plots for high (A) and low (B) degrees of relationship between college GPAs and SAT scores. In the regression procedure, we try to predict what a person's score on one test will be using his or her score on another test as a basis.

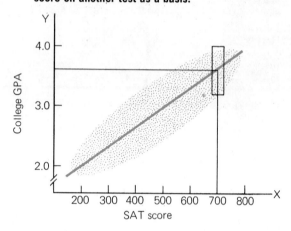

A

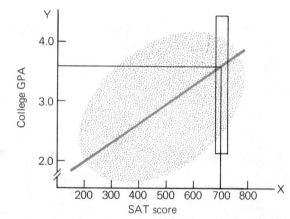

B

Similar procedures are used to process applications for law school, medical school, graduate school, or a job. Using regression techniques, the psychologist predicts the applicant's success on the job or in school, and these predictions are used to determine whether or not to hire or admit the applicant. It is a serious business, and the decisions made on this basis are extremely important to the people involved.

The simplest type of regression (technically known as *linear regression*) involves solving a mathematical equation for a straight line (hence the term "linear"), a line that "fits" the data. What we are looking for is the line that comes closest to the most points on a scatter diagram (see Figure A–8). Figure A–8 shows two different scatter plots relating scores on the College Boards (SAT scores) to grade-point average in college (GPA). Each point in the diagram represents one student; by drawing a line straight down to the X axis from any point (any particular student), we can tell the student's SAT score, and by drawing a horizontal line from the point over to the Y axis we can tell the student's GPA in college.

Once we have data relating SAT scores and college GPAs we can proceed to use regression to make predictions for future students. First we solve the equation for the best-fitting straight line (known as the *regression line*), a complex procedure we won't describe here. Then we draw the line on the scatter plot. Now we can use the line as a way to predict GPA given a student's SAT score. For example, consider a student who scores 700 on the SAT: we draw a vertical line up from 700 until it intersects the regression line, then we draw a horizontal line from this point over to the Y axis and read off the predicted GPA at the point of intersection. In this case we come up with a prediction of 3.6 for the student's GPA.

This procedure will not give us perfect predictions, as you should be able to see from Figure A–8. Not all students scoring 700 had 3.6 averages in college; some were higher than 3.6 and some lower. As we have said, the major factor in determining the accuracy of our predictions will be the degree of correlation between the two variables. If the variables are highly correlated, as depicted in panel (A), all the points will cluster close to the regression line, and none of the predictions will be far off. In fact, if the correlation were perfect, all the points would be right on the line, and there would be no error. (All students with 700 SATs would get 3.6 GPAs). On the other hand, with low correlations the points will be widely scattered, and many of them will be a long way from the regression line, as depicted in panel (B) of Figure A–8. In such a case our predictions can be way off. Take a look at the students who scored around 700 on the SATs in the two panels; these points are boxed in on the graphs. In the upper panel, which depicts a high correlation, you can see that all the students ended up with high college GPAs, and all were fairly close to 3.6, the average we would predict using the regression line. In contrast, in the lower panel the students with 700 on the SATs varied widely in their GPAs, with some as low as 2.2 and others as high as 3.95. Regression would have predicted 3.6 for all of them, and it would have been way off on many of the predictions. The lower the correlation between the two variables, the less precision we have in predicting using regression. In fact, if the correlation drops to zero, regression is useless—we might as well just guess. Given some degree of correlation, however, we can do better using regression than by simply guessing, and the higher the correlation, the better our guesses will be.

The controversy in this field comes from the fact that with low correlations predictions can still be way off. Thus people object to using tests to predict future behavior, arguing that discriminating among people on the basis of their test scores is not fair because the tests don't predict very well in the first place.

INFERENTIAL STATISTICS

Inferential statistics are used to make inferences about data or to draw conclusions and test our hypotheses about the data. Two of the basic concepts in inferential statistics are *estimation* and *hypothesis testing*.

Estimation

One use of inferential statistics is to make estimates of the actual value of some population characteristic. Suppose, for example, we wanted to know how intelligent Americans are on the average. We *could* test all 208 million Americans and compute a mean. But it would be handy to have a shortcut method, even though it is just an estimate.

In order to estimate the mean and standard deviation of a population, we take a *sample* of the population and test the members of the sample. We then compute the statistics on the sample scores and use these statistics to estimate what the mean and standard deviation would be if we *could* test every member of the population. We might sample 200 Americans and use their scores to estimate what the whole population is like. Obviously, this is what public opinion polls and the TV rating services do.

It is important to make sure that the sample is *representative* of the population. This is usually done by making the sample a random selection from all possible members of the population. **Random sampling** means that everyone in the specified population has the same chance of being in the sample. It would not be a fair sample for estimating American intelligence if we measured only white female citizens of La Mirada, California. The second factor in sampling is sample size. The larger the sample, the more accurate the estimates. If you randomly chose one person from the phone book, scheduled him or her for an IQ test, got a score, and then estimated that this IQ score was the mean IQ for all Americans, you would almost certainly be off the mark. More than one score is needed. But how many should there be in the sample? The amazing thing about sampling is that the size of the sample necessary to get a pretty accurate idea of the population is much smaller than you might guess. A sample of 30 or 40 Americans out of the 208 million, if properly drawn, would give a very accurate estimate of the entire population. There are ways of estimating how big a sample you need for a given level of accuracy. Of course, if the sample is not properly drawn, so that it is not representative, then increasing the sample size would not help our estimation much at all.

Hypothesis Testing

When we set out to do an experiment in psychology we always begin with a hypothesis. For our brief discussion we will use the example of a psychologist who wants to

Figure A-9
Three experimental outcomes differing in variability and overlap, but each with the same mean (100 and 105) and the same mean difference (105-100)

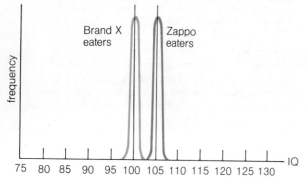

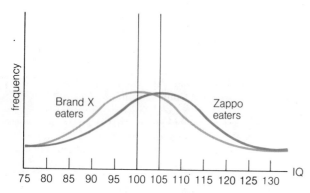

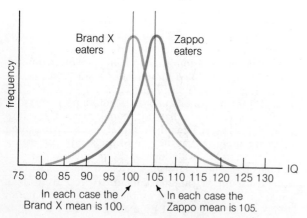

In each case the → Brand X mean is 100.   ↖ In each case the Zappo mean is 105.

know if Zappo cereal increases intelligence in people who eat it. The working hypothesis is: "People who eat Zappo will show an increase in IQ compared with people who eat Brand X." The psychologist gets 20 subjects to volunteer for the experiment and randomly assigns them to one of two groups, 10 per group. The random assignment is designed to create two groups

that at the start of the experiment are equal in IQ, scoring 100 points on the average. The Zappo group eats Zappo for one year and the Brand X group eats Brand X for one year. At the end of this time the psychologist tests all 20 subjects on intelligence and finds that the mean IQ of Zappo eaters is 105 and the mean IQ of Brand X eaters is 100. What can the psychologist conclude or infer about the initial hypothesis? If the Zappo group and the Brand X group were very close—say 99.5 and 100.1 were the means—he or she would probably conclude that Zappo does not increase intelligence. If they were very far apart—say 125 for Zappo eaters and 96 for Brand X eaters—the conclusion is that eating Zappo increases intelligence. But what do we conclude about results that fall between these extremes?

There has to be an objective way to decide whether the psychologist's hypothesis can be accepted or not. We cannot leave it up to intuition, especially not the intuition of the owner of Zappo cereal. This is where hypothesis-testing statistics come into play. There are many different kinds of these statistics. Here we will consider only one, the *t test,* which is probably the most common statistical technique for hypothesis testing.

We want to decide if the difference between 100 (the mean of the Brand X eaters) and 105 (the mean of the Zappo eaters) is a real difference. Is it a *significant difference?* A difference is said to be significant if it is very unlikely that it would happen by chance, that is, if the chance probability is small for a difference this large. The difference between Zappo and Brand X means is 5.0 IQ points. We say the *mean difference* is 5.0 (105 − 100 = 5.0). For a moment, let's assume that Zappo has no effect on intelligence. This is called the **null hypothesis** (remember that the psychologist's working hypothesis was that Zappo increases IQ). What we need to know is *if the null hypothesis is true* (Zappo does not affect IQ), what is the probability that the two groups would differ by 5 IQ points or more? If Zappo is not different from Brand X, then any difference we find between our two groups is just a chance difference. After all, we would not expect two random groups of 10 people to have exactly the same means either. Sample means will differ, and every once in a while there will be a difference of 5 or more IQ points just by chance alone, with no help from Zappo. The question is: How often will we get a difference this large? Or what is the probability of the difference occurring by chance alone?

In order to answer this question we must know not only the mean values but also the standard deviations in the two groups. We have to know how much variability there is in the IQ scores. To understand this, look at the three panels in Figure A-9. Each panel shows two frequency distributions, one for a Zappo group and one for a Brand X group. Note that in each panel the mean of the Zappo group is 105 and the mean of the Brand X group is 100. But the three panels display quite different pictures when it comes to IQ variability. In the top panel the variability is very small (all

Scientists Only 95% Sure
Cyclamate Safe

WASHINGTON — The best brains in science cannot answer the question of whether the artificial sweetener cyclamate is totally free of cancer risk, says a blue-ribbon panel that spent six months studying the problem for the government.

The committee concluded . . . that it could say with only 95 per cent probability that cyclamate, 30 to 50 times sweeter than sugar, doesn't cause cancer. The panel said there remains a nagging doubt over whether it may be a weak carcinogen.

The small degree of uncertainty seems certain to touch off a debate over what degree of safety should be required by government regulators.

The scientific panel said that not even a proposed five-year experiment costing $8 million to $10 million and using 52,000 rats and hamsters could establish, with absolute certainty, that the government was wrong in 1969 when it banned the chemical from foods and drugs.

"Science today is just not good enough to answer this question to everyone's satisfaction," said the chairman, Dr. Arnold L. Brown of Mayo Medical School. . . .

One Could Get By

Noting the relatively limited sensitivity of current scientific methods, the committee concluded, "Although no chemical can be proven unequivocally to lack carcinogenicity with these techniques, ones with a significant carcinogenic hazard for humans could escape detection" . . .

The Denver Post
January 14, 1976

Contrary to Dr. Brown's statement, it may be more a matter of statistics than of scientific methods. As long as there is variability in the data and some overlap in the distribution of scores from an experimental (in this case, the use of cyclamate) and a control (no cyclamate) group, there will be some degree of uncertainty about the effects of the experimental manipulation. Just as in the Zappo example, we need a way to measure the probability of an effect. In most experiments, being 95 percent sure of the hypothesis is an acceptable probability level. Where human health is concerned, we demand higher standards.

Zappo eaters score about the same, near 105, and Brand X eaters are all close to 100), and the two distributions do not overlap at all (all Zappo eaters have higher IQs than all Brand X eaters). In this case, it looks as though the 5-point difference between the means is a significant one.

In the middle panel the IQ scores are highly variable (Zappo eaters do not all score near the mean of 105, and Brand X scores do not cluster close to 100). This means that there is a lot of overlap in the two distributions. Some Zappo eaters are lower in IQ than some Brand X eaters, and some Brand X eaters are higher in IQ than some Zappo eaters. In fact, there is so much overlap in the two distributions that we would tend to bet that the difference between 100 and 105 (the two means) is just a chance difference. The two distributions look almost identical. In neither the top nor the middle panel would we need a statistical test to help us decide whether or not to accept the null hypothesis.

Situations like those depicted in the top panel are very rare indeed. Unfortunately, the middle panel is a more frequent outcome of an experiment—the experiment is a flop! The bottom panel represents the most common outcome of all, and the only one of the three in which the conclusion is unclear. The two distribu-

tions overlap somewhat, much more than in the top panel but much less than in the middle panel. There is a moderate amount of variability. Do we conclude that the 105 to 100 mean difference is a real one or not? Is there a significant difference between the means?

The t test is basically a ratio. It is the *ratio* of the *mean difference to an estimate* of the *variability* involved in this difference. In the top panel the difference is 5 units, but the variability is very small. So if we take 5 and divide it by this very small variability number, we will get a large number for an answer. The t ratio will be large, and we will declare the difference to be significant. In the middle panel the same difference between means, 5, will be divided by a very large variability number to give us a t ratio that will be very small. We declare the difference insignificant. In the bottom panel we have the borderline case, where we will divide 5 by a moderate variability estimate, meaning the t value obtained will be moderately large. What do we conclude? Fortunately for us, mathematical statisticians have prepared tables of the probability of various values of t happening by chance. We compute the t ratio in our experiment and then look it up in the statistical tables to find the chance probability of a t as large as the one we found. If the table tells us that our t ratio is unlikely to happen by chance, we assume that what we have is not a chance

"I'm sorry, but you've been rejected at the .05 level."

APA Monitor, September–October 1973. Copyright 1973 by the American Psychological Association. Reprinted by permission.

Principles of statistical decision theory have wide application.

effect but a real difference. Conventionally, this probability is .05. This means that if our obtained t ratio is likely to happen only 5 percent of the time or less by chance, then the odds are that this is *not* one of those times. The odds are that it is not a chance effect but a real one, which is called a significant effect.

The null hypothesis says, "There is no difference between Zappo and Brand X," and if we obtain a significant t ratio we infer or conclude that the null hypothesis is wrong. Statistical inference is basically a procedure for drawing conclusions about the null hypothesis. What the t test procedure allows us to do is to reject the null hypothesis when we get a t ratio that is very unlikely to occur by chance. If we set up the null hypothesis such that it is the opposite of our working hypothesis (Zappo improves IQ), then rejection of the null hypothesis will be evidence in support of our working hypothesis.

We will not go into the details of actually calculating a t ratio. You can find the information in any elementary statistics book (for example, Wike, 1971). Simply remember that when an experiment is done, the results will always indicate some differences between the conditions in the study. The t test as well as many other types of inferential statistics are used to help the experimenter decide if the differences are large enough, relative to the variability, to allow him to reject the null hypothesis and support his working hypothesis.

This reasoning applies to the correlation coefficient as well as to the difference between two means. If we get two sets of numbers by randomly drawing them out of a hat and correlate them, the correlation will almost never be exactly zero, even though the numbers are clearly unrelated (we drew them by chance from a hat). Suppose the correlation is very high, say, .80. It is obvious we would conclude that the correlation is significant. Suppose it is very low or close to zero, say −.07; obviously we would say there is no significant relationship or correlation. But what if it is .30 or −.42 or −.28? Where do we draw the line and say that it is highly unlikely that a correlation this high would happen by chance? At what point can we infer a real relationship between the two variables? Again, there are procedures in inferential statistics that decide objectively whether the correlation is significant or not. The null hypothesis would be that the correlation is zero, and we would then test this hypothesis to see whether it can be rejected.

ADVANCED STATISTICAL TECHNIQUES COMMONLY USED IN PSYCHOLOGY

Analysis of Variance

The t test is used when testing the difference between two groups and only two groups. But most experiments have more than two groups, and the t test is not useful in such cases. A very complex statistical procedure called the *analysis of variance* is used instead. As the name implies, the variance or variability in the data is analyzed and compared to the mean differences in much the same way as in a t test. In fact, the analysis of variance procedure reduces to a t test when there are only two groups. The test in analysis of variance is known as the *F test*, named after the famous English statistician R. A. Fisher. Basically, the procedure is just like that for the t test. It allows the experimenter to make inferences or conclusions about the differences among a set of means. It is a very common technique now, so you are likely to encounter the F test if you read any modern psychology journal.

Factor Analysis

Factor analysis is a highly sophisticated correlational procedure that is used to identify the basic factors underlying a psychological phenomenon. The technique boils down to finding clusters of tests that correlate with one another. Suppose we administer the following six tests to 100 young men: (1) vocabulary, (2) ability to play basketball, (3) ability to write an essay on philosophy, (4) speed at running the 100-yard dash, (5) ability to understand statistics, and (6) ability to climb trees. Each man takes all six tests, and then we intercorrelate the tests. We correlate test 1 with 2, 1 with 3, 1 with 4, and so on. Suppose we find that tests 1, 3, and 5 correlate highly with one another and that 2, 4, and 6 correlate highly with one another, but 1, 3, and 5 do not correlate at all with 2, 4, and 6. Why would this be the case? Look at the tests; it is easy to see that 1, 3, and 5 all involve thinking or knowledge— they all involve "mental ability." On the other hand, 2, 4, and 6 all involve physical skill. So it probably is the case that 1, 3, and 5 are all measuring something in common, which we might call Factor A. Wouldn't you guess that Factor A has something to do with intelligence? Tests 2, 4, and 6 also seem to be measuring something in common. We call it Factor B. Because 1, 3, and 5 do not correlate with 2, 4, and 6, we conclude that Factor A, which we now have decided to call intelligence, is not the same thing as Factor B. Looking at tests 2, 4, and 6, we decide to call Factor B "athletic ability."

In short, we have isolated two factors that are involved in performance on our 6 tests; one we call "intelligence" and one we call "athletic ability." Factor analysis is basically a correlational technique that allows us to analyze performance on a large number of tests into factors by isolating clusters of tests (where the clustering is not as obvious as it is in the foregoing example). Correlations are high within a cluster but low between clusters. We assume that the clusters then "represent" and measure psychological factors.

This technique has been used extensively in two areas of psychology, intelligence testing and personality assessment (see Appendix C). Intelligence consists of many factors, and so does personality. With factor analysis we can identify these factors and hope to learn from them what intelligence and personality are.

Another example of the application of factor analysis which may be of more direct relevance to you concerns the use of questionnaires to evaluate college teachers. In the typical case you as the student are asked to answer a large number of questions (each question can be thought of as a test for the professor) about your reactions to the class and the instructor. Questions such as "Was the professor well organized?" and "Was the grading system fair?" are typical of teacher-evalua-tion questionnaires. What comes out of such evaluations is an enormous amount of "raw" data—lots of answers by lots of students to lots of questions. But it may be difficult to measure teacher effectiveness from this array of answers. In fact, it is often difficult to tell what, if anything, the questionnaire is measuring. Factor analysis can help by reducing the data to factors, cutting way down on the number of scores and helping to clarify what is being measured. For example, many of the questions may all be getting at the same general factor, so we can use factor analysis to pool the answers from similar questions and come out with a score for the professor on the overall factor.

Professor Peter Frey of Northwestern University has done factor analysis on students' ratings of their professors and concludes, as many suspected earlier, that the typical questionnaire is really measuring only two factors: (1) the skill of the professor in teaching and (2) the rapport the professor establishes with the class. Think about your own professors and you will probably agree that these are two fundamental and relatively independent factors in teaching. You probably have had professors with high skill but very low class rapport, high rapport and low skill, and variations in between. Thus factor analysis can help greatly in the analysis of complex situations, reducing massive amounts of data down to a small set of basic factors.

This example points up another very important use of the factor analysis technique, namely, in test construction. Investigators attempting to construct a psychological test to measure some aspect of behavior can begin by building a test containing a very large number of items designed "by intuition" to get at the desired behavior. After administering the large test to a large group of subjects, the results are factor analyzed, the factors are identified, and then the correlation between each item on the test and the factor (this is called *the factor loading* of the item) is determined. In this way the investigator can (1) identify the factor and (2) determine which of the items are the best measures of the factors. Those items with low factor loadings can be eliminated from the test, and the investigator ends up with a short, efficient test consisting of only those items that are the best measures of the factors. In the case of the test designed by Peter Frey to measure teacher effectiveness by student ratings, Frey was able to develop a test consisting of only seven questions which measured the teacher on the two factors he identified —skill and rapport. Factor analytic techniques are crucial tools in the field of test construction, a topic we take up in Appendix C.

Neurons: The Building Blocks of the Nervous System

B

Structural Properties of the Neuron
The Nerve Cell
The Synapse

Functional Properties of the Neuron
The Resting Membrane Potential
The Action Potential
Synaptic Transmission
Neurotransmitter Substances

The human nervous system is by far the most complex component in the body. Nobody knows for sure, but it is estimated that the brain consists of approximately 10 billion nerve cells, or **neurons,** each of which is directly connected, on the average, to some 200 to 1000 other nerve cells. Most nerve cells are present at birth, although many of the connections between individual neurons are formed later during development. Until late in the nineteenth century it was believed that all of the nerve cells formed one continuous network; later it became clear that the entire nervous system consists of individual nerves that are functionally connected by so-called synaptic junctions. The complex functions of the nervous system depend on the structure and physiology of individual nerve cells and their interconnections; these functions—receiving and transmitting information—are the subject matter of this Appendix.

STRUCTURAL PROPERTIES OF THE NEURON

Neurons, like all other cells, must carry on all of those processes involved in the utilization of oxygen and the production of energy. In addition, however, nerve cells are specialized in the sense that they are excitable and that they transmit information. Excitability and the transmission of information involve two processes which are called *axonal conduction* and *synaptic transmission*. The means by which these processes take place depend on the special structural features of the neuron, as well as on the neuron's ability to alter its physical characteristics when given appropriate stimulation.

The Nerve Cell

Neurons contain most of the components found in other animal cells (see Figure B–1). The *nucleus* controls all aspects of cellular activity, and many other organelles ("little organs") maintain the structural and functional properties of the cells. For example, energy synthesis occurs in organelles that are known as *mitochondria,* and protein synthesis occurs on structures known as *ribosomes.* In addition, the neurons possess unique features; the most predominant of these are fiber extensions from the cell body. These include **dendrites,** which are generally quite short and numerous, and a single **axon.** The axon may divide into one or more branches, which are referred to as axon *collaterals.* The so-called nerves, which run throughout your body, are bundles of axons from many individual neurons. Cell division, a feature common to most other kinds of cells, does not occur in most adult nerve cells. Nerve cells lost for whatever reason are not replaced. Speculation has it that an average of 10,000 neurons die each day.

Axonal conduction originates at the *axon hillock*, the point at which the axon is connected to the nerve cell body. In some neurons the axon is covered by a sheath made of fatty material called *myelin*. This insulating myelin sheath is broken at short intervals, and the gaps are referred to as *nodes of Ranvier*. In some neurons the dendrites look virtually identical to axons and are difficult to distinguish. The most important difference between axons and dendrites is functional: axons conduct information away from the cell body, while dendrites conduct information toward the cell body. In a manner of speaking, one can think of dendrites as receiving stations and axons as transmitting stations.

As axons approach their destination—most typically these destinations are dendrites and cell bodies of other nerve cells or muscle cells or gland cells—they divide

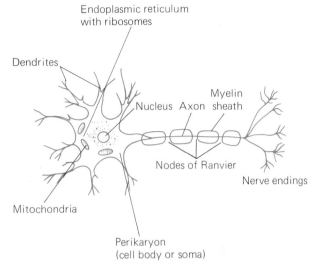

Figure B–1
Schematic illustration of a "typical" nerve cell

Endoplasmic reticulum with ribosomes

Dendrites

Nucleus Axon Myelin sheath

Nodes of Ranvier

Nerve endings

Mitochondria

Perikaryon (cell body or soma)

The diagram shows the cell body containing the nucleus, several mitochondria, and the endoplasmic reticulum, which is studded with ribosomes. Mitochondria and ribosomes are also found in other parts of the neuron, although they are not shown in this diagram.

into many small branches called *telodendria.* These telodendria terminate in small swellings which are variously referred to as *synaptic boutons, axon terminals,* or *synaptic terminals.*

The Synapse

The **synapse** is a specialized region where one nerve cell makes "contact" with another nerve cell or with a muscle or gland. It is also that region where one nerve cell transmits information to another cell. A more or less typical synapse is illustrated in Figure B–2. In this figure you should note three features. First, the synapse includes a physical space that separates two cells (the two neurons do not actually touch each other). This space is referred to as the *synaptic space* or *synaptic cleft.* Second, the synaptic region includes many small organelles referred to as *synaptic vesicles.* Third, the synaptic region is rich in mitochondria.

The portion of the axon's synaptic membrane that lines the synaptic space on the side of the axon terminal is called the *presynaptic membrane,* because it is located before the synaptic cleft. Correspondingly, the neuron that contains this membrane is referred to as the *presynaptic neuron.* That portion of the cellular membrane of the neuron lining the opposite side of the synaptic space is termed the *postsynaptic* (after the synapse) *mem-*

**Figure B-2
Schematic illustration of a synapse**

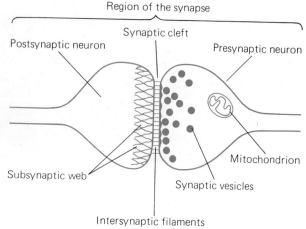

Notice that the synaptic region contains a pre- and a postsynaptic neuron. The presynaptic neuron contains the synaptic vesicles, which are the storage sites of neurotransmitter molecules.

**Figure B-3
Ion distribution**

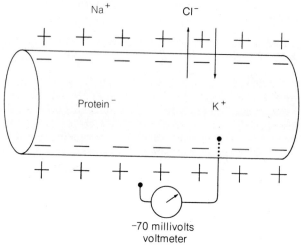

The relative distribution of ions across the cell membrane of a neuron. The membrane is almost completely permeable to potassium (K+) and chloride (Cl−), but impermeable to sodium (Na+) and the large protein molecules. The result of the electrical and diffusional forces acting on these ions is a −70 millivolt resting membrane potential, negative inside relative to outside.

brane, and this neuron is called the *postsynaptic neuron.* Information transfer across the synaptic space, *synaptic transmission,* is a chemical process. It involves the release of chemical neurotransmitter molecules by the presynaptic membrane, molecules that then produce an effect on the postsynaptic membrane. The chemical neurotransmitter molecules are believed to be stored in the *synaptic vesicles.* Synaptic transmission is a process that requires energy, and for this reason the area of the synapse is richly supplied with mitochondria, the sites of energy metabolism in all cells.

FUNCTIONAL PROPERTIES OF THE NEURON

The Resting Membrane Potential

The neuron, like all living cells, possesses across its membrane an electrical potential called the *resting membrane potential.* This potential signals that the cell is alive and functioning normally. It can be measured by means of a voltage measuring device such as a voltmeter. In making such a measurement, one lead from the voltmeter is placed outside the cell and the other lead, a fine wire called a microelectrode, is placed inside the cell. Such an arrangement is illustrated diagrammatically in Figure B-3. When this is done a voltage difference between the inside and the outside of the cell is detected. In most nerve cells this voltage difference is of the order of 70 millivolts (thousandths of a volt), the inside of

the nerve cell being electrically negative with respect to the outside. This potential difference exists only across the membrane of the cell, and this separation of charge, with relatively more negative charge inside the cell, is referred to as a state of *polarization.* In this respect the neuron can be compared to a battery cell. In this analogy the inside of the nerve cell would represent the negative pole, and the outside of the cell would represent the positive pole of the battery, with the voltage across the battery being approximately 70 millivolts. It is important to consider the mechanisms that generate and maintain the resting membrane potential before we consider perturbations in this potential, which occur when the cell becomes active. The reasons for this are that the electrical activity that characterizes neuronal functioning can be understood in terms of alterations in the resting membrane potential.

In order to understand the details of the resting membrane potential it is first necessary to deal with several physical and chemical principles. A consideration of salt water will serve to illustrate several of these important concepts. When salt, a molecule consisting of two atoms—sodium (Na) and chloride (Cl)—is dissolved in water, it breaks up into two ionic species. An ion is any molecular fragment that possesses an electrical charge. Thus, when salt (NaCl) is dissolved in water it breaks up into sodium (Na+) and chloride (Cl−) ions.

The positive and negative signs associated with the chemical symbols indicate that in a dissolved state these ions carry an electrical charge—positive in the case of sodium and negative in the case of chloride. Salt water contains many sodium and chloride ions.

Nerve cells are bathed in a fluid medium that resembles seawater rather closely. The fluid that surrounds nerve cells contains sodium (Na^+), chloride (Cl^-), potassium (K^+), calcium (Ca^{++}), and magnesium (Mg^{++}) ions, as well as more complicated molecules such as negatively charged proteins. Simply stated, the resting membrane potential results from an unequal distribution of these charged particles across the cell membrane. The net effect of this unequal distribution of charged ions across the nerve membrane is a 70-millivolt potential difference.

This unequal distribution of charged ions across the nerve cell membrane results from the fact that the membrane itself is *semipermeable,* which means that it allows certain ions, for example, potassium and chloride, to pass through it; other ions, for example, sodium, cannot pass through the membrane readily. Given a semipermeable membrane, the unequal distribution of ions across the membrane can be understood in terms of two physical-chemical principles called *diffusion* and the *attraction of charged particles,* respectively. The first of these principles, diffusion, states that substances in solution will tend to move from a region of higher concentration to one of lower concentration. The second principle determining the distribution of ions across the membrane is their electrical charge, unlike-charged particles attracting each other and like-charged particles repelling each other.

Let us now consider the situation with respect to each of the ions important in establishing the resting membrane potential. The membrane is totally impermeable to the large, negatively charged proteins; consequently, these are trapped inside the nerve cell (see Figure B–3). Similarly, the nerve cell membrane, when at rest, is impermeable to positively charged sodium (Na^+) ions, which are therefore concentrated outside the cell. However, the membrane is almost completely permeable to potassium (K^+) ions; these ions pass into the cell attracted by the negatively charged protein molecules, a movement assisted by their repulsion by the positively charged sodium (Na^+) ions on the outside of the membrane. Chloride ions are also free to move across the membrane; however, they tend to migrate out of the nerve cell because they are attracted by the positively charged Na^+ ions outside and repulsed by the negatively charged proteins inside. In keeping with the principle of diffusion, however, some chloride ions move into the cell where chloride is less concentrated, and some potassium moves out of the cell where it is less concentrated. The net effect is a slight excess of negatively charged particles inside the cell, which produces a −70-millivolt resting membrane potential, negative inside relative to outside.

The Action Potential

The **action potential** is the means by which the neuron conducts information along the axon to some destination within, or outside, the central nervous system. The action potential is a brief reversal of the resting membrane potential. It originates at the axon hillock, and it is a response to stimulus inputs to the neuron. The action potential travels down the length of the axon, finally invading the region of the telodendria and axon terminals. Here the action potential initiates those processes that result in synaptic transmission—specifically, it triggers the release of chemical neurotransmitter substances. Thus, action potentials are means of conducting information along the length of a single neuron; the action potentials do not cross the synaptic cleft.

An action potential is characterized by an initial *depolarization,* that is, a movement toward zero of the resting membrane potential. This so-called rising phase of the action potential continues past zero until a value of +40 millivolts is reached, positive inside relative to the outside of the nerve cell. Thus, the action potential is a clear reversal of the resting membrane potential. An action potential is initiated when some stimulus changes the characteristics of the nerve membrane, rendering it permeable to positively charged ions. Specifically, an action potential is initiated when the membrane becomes permeable to sodium; Na^+ now rushes into the cell.

Following this +40-millivolt peak, the voltage across the membrane begins to fall. This is brought about because potassium ions rush out of the cell. The voltage across the membrane begins to fall until it reaches a value slightly greater than its original resting value, approximately −75 millivolts, negative inside relative to outside. After a brief period the membrane returns to its normal value. The period immediately following the firing of the action potential is known as the **refractory period** because it is difficult to fire the neuron again during this period of time.

Once an action potential has been initiated in the region of the axon hillock it will continue to travel down the length of the nerve fiber. One can think of this somewhat as a wave that travels across water. However—and this is important—unlike a wave, the action potential maintains its original amplitude, shape, and speed for the entire length of the axon, because the action potential is generated anew at each stage of the process. This is referred to as the *all-or-none principle* of axonal conduction. The action potential travels down the entire length of the axon without changing any of its characteristics, somewhat like a burning fuse.

The mechanisms thought to be involved in initiating an action potential are really quite simple; they are illustrated diagrammatically in Figure B–4. The initial rising phase of the action potential, during which the membrane potential moves from approximately −70

Figure B–4
The action potential

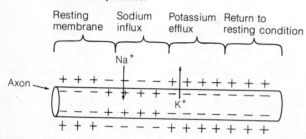

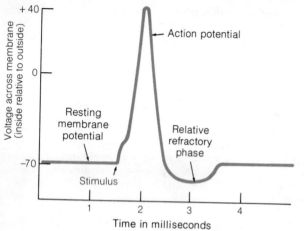

The graph (below) shows the change in voltage across the cell membrane during the rise and fall of the action potential. The voltage changes are produced by the events occurring across the membrane (illustrated above). Thus the rising phase of the action potential is caused by a brief influx of positive sodium ions, and the *hyperpolarization* (movement of the membrane potential away from zero) is produced by the efflux of positive potassium ions. Note that the entire action potential is of relatively short duration.

the permeability of the membrane to potassium. You will recall that the membrane is usually quite permeable to K+ ions; now, however, the barrier is broken completely. The resulting outward movement (efflux) of K+ ions causes the membrane potential to fall from approximately +40 to −75 millivolts, which characterizes the refractory period during which the membrane is slightly more negative than is normally the case. When the permeability to potassium is restored, the normal resting membrane potential is reestablished. All of these events are illustrated schematically in Figure B–4.

Once an action potential is initiated, it is propagated down the axon in a nondecremental fashion. This means that the action potential as it travels the length of the axon retains its original amplitude. The rate of conduction of nerve impulses varies as a function of the diameter of the axon—the thicker the nerve, the greater the rate of conduction. Conduction of nerve impulses is also much faster in myelinated nerves, as we will explain shortly. The rate of conduction of nerve impulses varies between approximately 0.5 meters per second in small unmyelinated fibers to approximately 130 meters per second in large-diameter myelinated fibers.

The propagation of the nerve impulse down the axon can be explained as follows: During the action potential Na+ rushes into the neuron. Sodium ions from adjacent regions rush to the excited area, resulting in a partial depolarization of this adjacent region. This, in turn, results in a local action potential in the adjacent region; sodium ions from the next region rush down, another action potential is initiated, and the nerve impulse is propagated down the axon.

In myelinated nerves the propagation of action potentials is slightly different. The action potentials occur only at the nodes of Ranvier, the gaps in the myelin sheath. Thus, the action potentials, instead of moving down the axon, "jump" from one node of Ranvier to another. This kind of propagation of action potential is referred to as *saltatory conduction,* and it is relatively fast. Myelination is a recent evolutionary development; its importance is that it provides large organisms, such as human beings, with rapid conduction of nerve impulses from one place to another. This, of course, is adaptive because in large animals the axons can become quite long. For example, some of your neurons extend all the way from the cortex to the lower spinal cord, a distance of several feet. Conduction of nerve impulses over such large distances would take a long time if the individual axons were not myelinated.

Synaptic Transmission

Axonal conduction, the all-or-none propagation of action potentials down the length of the axon, is the mechanism by which neurons conduct information from the region of the axon hillock to the distant reaches

to +40 millivolts, occurs because the permeability of the membrane to sodium ions suddenly increases. The temporary breakdown of the membrane barrier to sodium results in a sudden inward movement (influx) of Na+ into the interior of the neuron because of the electrical and diffusional forces acting in that direction.

This alteration of Na+ permeability is quite brief, lasting only 1 millisecond, and then the membrane permeability to sodium is restored. The sodium ions inside the neuron are "pumped out," and the resting membrane potential begins to return to −70 millivolts. This event begins the falling phase of the action potential. This phase is caused by a temporary breakdown in of the axon terminals. The transfer of information across the synaptic space is by the process of *synaptic transmission.* The sequence of events that occurs during synaptic transmission can be characterized as follows (see Figure B–5):

1. The action potential traveling down the axon invades the telodendria and axon terminals.

2. This event produces a release of chemical-transmitter substances, previously stored within the synaptic vesicles, into the synaptic cleft.

3. The neurotransmitter molecules diffuse across the synaptic space in accordance with the principle of diffusion, discussed previously.

4. The transmitter substances come into contact with the postsynaptic membrane, altering its permeability to certain classes of ions. Specifically, transmitter molecules, after they interact with receptors located on the postsynaptic membrane, alter the permeability of this membrane to either Na$^+$ or K$^+$ ions. It is commonly thought that transmitter molecules produce their effects by opening so-called sodium or potassium pores in the postsynaptic membrane.

5. Finally, the transmitter substance is neutralized or reabsorbed, thus terminating its effect.

These events are essentially the same in all nerves. However, the nature of the transmitter molecules may vary from neuron to neuron. Different kinds of nerves release different kinds of transmitter molecules, and neurons are classified on the basis of the kinds of transmitters they secrete. For example, neurons that release norepinephrine as the transmitter are called *adrenergic neurons;* those that release acetylcholine are referred to as *cholinergic neurons.* From a functional point of view there are essentially two types of synapses in the nervous system. These are the so-called *excitatory synapses,* activity in which results in excitation of the next neuron, and *inhibitory synapses,* activity in which results in inhibition of the next neuron in the circuit. In excitatory synapses the next neuron tends to become depolarized largely as a result of the influx of sodium ions into the neuron, whereas in inhibitory synapses the next neuron tends to become hyperpolarized largely because of the efflux of potassium ions out of the neuron.

Excitation

Although we have discussed the mechanisms that generate and carry action potentials down the length of the axon, we have not yet discussed how an action potential is initiated. In some cases the action potentials are generated by external stimuli. The eye, for example, has specialized cells (rods and cones) that convert *(transduce)* light energy into electrical energy, giving rise to action potentials in optic nerve fibers. Within the central nervous system, however, action potentials are generated by a process referred to as *excitatory synaptic transmission.* By this process one nerve cell, the presynaptic

Figure B–5

Diagrammatic illustration of some of the steps involved in chemical neurotransmission

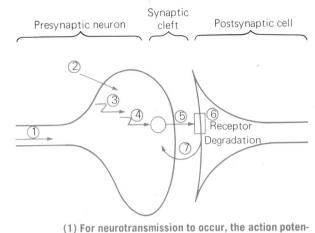

(1) For neurotransmission to occur, the action potential must first invade the region of the axon terminal. (2) The molecules from which the transmitter is manufactured must be transported into the cell. (3) The neurotransmitter must be synthesized, or made, within the nerve body. (4) The transmitter must be stored within the synaptic vesicles. (5) The transmitter must be released into the synaptic cleft. (6) The transmitter must interact with a receptor molecule located on the membrane of the postsynaptic neuron. (7) The transmitter must be removed from the region of the synapse, either by chemical degradation or by a reuptake mechanism in the presynaptic neuron. Drugs can interfere with chemical neurotransmission by acting on any of these steps.

neuron, increases the probability of an action potential in another nerve cell, the postsynaptic cell.

When an action potential reaches the region of the telodendria, synaptic transmitter molecules, previously stored in the synaptic vesicles, are released into the synaptic space and diffuse across the cleft toward the postsynaptic membrane. Here the transmitter molecules change the characteristics of the postsynaptic membrane, rendering it more permeable to sodium, potassium, and chloride ions. The ions that have the most potent effect in excitatory synaptic transmission are the sodium ions, because they are characterized by the most unequal distribution across the cell membrane when it is in the resting state. It is common to speak of excitatory synaptic transmission in terms of an opening of so-called sodium pores in the postsynaptic membrane. The result of increasing the permeability of the postsynaptic membrane to sodium ions results in depolarization, a movement of the resting membrane potential toward zero.

Figure B-6
Excitation and inhibition

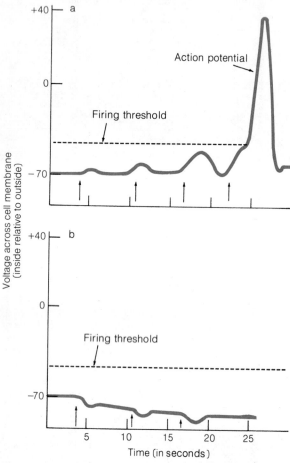

Activation of excitatory synapses results in excitatory postsynaptic potentials, shown in the top graph. Each arrow indicates activation at the synapse. Each successive activation is by a stronger stimulus. The last stimulus produces an EPSP large enough to reach the firing threshold and fire an action potential. Inhibitory postsynaptic potentials are illustrated in the bottom graph. Each arrow represents activation of an inhibitory synapse. Each activation is stronger than the preceding one. Notice that the resting membrane potential is pulled away from the firing threshold by inhibitory synaptic activation.

Unlike the depolarization that characterizes the rising phase of the action potential, the depolarization produced by excitatory synaptic transmission is graded, the extent of the depolarization depending on the strength of the stimulus, rather than being all or none, which is characteristic of action potentials. This graded change in the membrane potential is referred to as an *excitatory postsynaptic potential (EPSP)*. The relation be-

tween an EPSP and the production of an action potential is illustrated diagrammatically in Figure B-6.

An analogy is sometimes made between excitatory synaptic activation and the act of pulling the trigger of a rifle. The trigger can be pulled gently and returned to its original position without causing the rifle to discharge. The pull of the trigger represents the EPSP. If the trigger is pulled to some critical level, representing the firing threshold, the rifle will fire a single shot, which is analogous to the all-or-none discharge, or the action potential. Action potentials are initiated in the region of the axon hillock because this segment of the neural membrane has the lowest firing threshold. In the case of neurons, the firing threshold can be reached by summation of EPSPs that occur close together on the dendrites and cell body, or close together in time. In the former instance one speaks of *spatial summation*, and in the latter case of *temporal summation*. Both types of summation contribute to the triggering of action potentials.

Inhibition

Many neurons in the central nervous system perform inhibitory functions. The processes that result in inhibitory synaptic transmission are essentially similar to those outlined above with respect to excitation, except that the changes produced in the postsynaptic membrane are different. Inhibitory synaptic transmission is probably caused by a change in the membrane permeability to potassium and chloride ions. The net effect of inhibition is an outward flow of K^+ ions and an inward flow of Cl^- ions, making the inside of the membrane more negative relative to the outside. Thus, the membrane potential becomes hyperpolarized, moving farther away from zero and farther away from the firing threshold. By analogy, one can say that the trigger is now harder to pull; more precisely, one can say that a stronger stimulus (more EPSP activity) is now required to produce an action potential in the postsynaptic neuron.

The potential changes resulting from inhibitory synaptic activity are referred to as *inhibitory postsynaptic potentials (IPSPs)*. Examples of IPSPs are illustrated diagrammatically in Figure B-6.

Neurotransmitter Substances

Neurotransmitter substances are molecules that are stored in presynaptic vesicles and that produce either EPSPs or IPSPs when they come into contact with receptor molecules located on the postsynaptic membrane. Many different kinds of molecules have been identified that possess a neurotransmitter function. Some types of molecules always produce EPSPs (are always excitatory), others always produce IPSPs (are always inhibitory), whereas yet others produce both EPSPs and IPSPs depending on their site of action. Table B-1 gives a list of chemical substances that are presumed to be neurotransmitter molecules, together with their anatomical site and some of their major effects. In this section we shall describe first some of the general characteristics of neurotransmission and then in some greater detail two molecules that are believed to act as major synaptic transmitters.

General Properties of the Neurotransmitter Process

Some of the major properties of chemical neurotransmission may be summarized as follows:

1. The molecules from which chemical neurotransmitters are manufactured, the precursor molecules, must first be transported into the neurons. These processes are not passive, in the sense that they require energy and specialized transport mechanisms. Different neurons possess different kinds of transport mechanisms, and this is one way in which nerve cells acquire chemical specificity.

2. Once the precursor molecules have been transported into a nerve cell they must be assembled into the chemical that possesses transmitter properties. The manufacture of transmitters—their synthesis—requires special enzymes or organic catalysts. In some instances the synthesis of the transmitter molecule requires but a single enzymatically catalyzed reaction; in other instances many synthetic steps are required, each catalyzed by a specific enzyme. Different nerve cells contain different enzymes, and this is another way in which neurons acquire chemical specificity.

3. When the transmitter molecule has been manufactured it must be packaged and stored in vesicles, the presynaptic vesicles seen in Figure B-2. This packaging is also an active process requiring specialized mechanisms and energy. Neurotransmitter molecules are packaged to prevent their degradation in the presynaptic neuron.

4. The transmitter molecule must be released from its presynaptic storage site in response to the arrival of the action potential at the axon terminal. Very little is known about how this process works, except that it is believed that the arrival of the action potential at the terminal increases the influx of Ca^{++} ions, which somehow triggers the release of the transmitter substance.

5. The transmitter must next diffuse across the synaptic cleft, and it must interact with specialized receptor molecules located on the postsynaptic membrane. Different postsynaptic neurons contain different receptor molecules, and this also contributes to chemical specificity of synaptic units.

6. Finally, the neurotransmitter molecule must be removed from the synaptic cleft after it has produced its effect. Two different mechanisms have been identified that serve this function. These are (a) enzymatic degradation of the transmitter molecule and (b) reabsorption of the transmitter molecule into the presynaptic nerve.

As we shall discuss, different kinds of drugs produce their effects on nervous activity and, therefore, on be-

TABLE B-1   The Probable Neurotransmitters and Their Hypothesized Effects

Neurotransmitter Molecule	Effect
Acetylcholine (ACh)	Excitatory in autonomic ganglia and in the brain; both excitatory and inhibitory in the end organs of the parasympathetic nervous system.
Norepinephrine (NE)	Inhibitory in the brain; both excitatory and inhibitory in the autonomic nervous system.
Dopamine (DA)	Inhibitory in the brain.
Serotonin (5-HT)	Inhibitory in the brain.
Gamma-aminobutyric acid (GABA)	Inhibitory in the brain.
Glycine	Inhibitory in spinal cord interneurons.
Glutamic acid	Excitatory in the brain and spinal sensory neurons.

havior by potentiating or interfering with the various steps described above.

Acetylcholine

Scientists have discovered that *acetylcholine* (ACh) is the synaptic transmitter at the synapse between peripheral motor neurons, that is, those neurons that connect with muscles and muscle tissue. It is by the release of ACh that muscular activity is generated and maintained. It can safely be assumed that ACh serves as an excitatory transmitter in this instance. ACh generates EPSPs and action potentials to produce muscular contractions. There is abundant evidence that ACh is also found in the vesicles of presynaptic neurons in the central nervous system. However, it is not clear whether ACh serves as an excitatory or an inhibitory transmitter in these cases. The most probable answer is that it performs both functions in different parts of the brain, depending on the structure of the postsynaptic receptors.

ACh is produced in nerve cells from acetate and choline, a reaction catalyzed by the enzyme *choline acetylase*. Once it has produced an effect on the postsynaptic neuron it is enzymatically degraded; the destruction is catalyzed by the enzyme *acetylcholinesterase*.

ACh is often considered inhibitory with regard to *behavioral excitability* or reactivity to sensory stimulation measured, for example, as the overall activity level of an animal. Drugs that increase levels of ACh in the brain often produce a reduction in activity, while drugs that destroy or inactivate this transmitter often lead to hyperexcitability. This inhibition of activity could be entirely indirect, however. ACh might be excitatory at synapses in the central nervous system, but subsequent neurons on which it acts might be inhibitory, resulting in indirect behavioral inhibition.

Food for the Brain

Psychotic patients who take strong tranquilizing drugs often pay a dreadful price. Through long-term use of the drugs, about 40 per cent of them develop a neurological disease called tardive dyskinesia that can be almost as disabling as their psychosis. Their limbs and bodies jerk wildly, their faces contort grotesquely, their tongues dart uncontrollably. Doctors have recently discovered that a substance found in many ordinary foods seems to relieve these bizarre symptoms.

Neurologists have long suspected that tardive dyskinesia occurs because the tranquilizers create a deficiency of acetylcholine, an important brain chemical. Acetylcholine comes from choline, an amino acid derivative found in eggs, soybeans, fish and poultry. Dr. Richard J. Wurtman and Edith Cohen of the Massachusetts Institute of Technology found that they could increase the levels of acetylcholine in the brains of rats by injecting choline. Subsequently, doctors at Stanford University gave choline to a patient with tardive dyskinesia and found that it helped. More recently, an MIT team headed by Dr. John Growdon gave choline, mixed in Kool-Aid, to twenty tardive dyskinesia patients. Nine improved dramatically, ten were unchanged and one grew worse. The mixed results, Growdon suspects, may have occurred because some patients were suffering from other complications.

Investigators elsewhere are testing choline in other situations. Dr. John Davis of the University of Chicago is giving it to manic-depressives, since low levels of acetylcholine seem to develop during the manic phase of the disorder. And Dr. David Drachman of the University of Massachusetts is trying to see whether choline can improve memory in aged patients.

Newsweek
February 20, 1978

Norepinephrine

The second major transmitter substance, *norepinephrine* (NE) was first identified as acting in peripheral nerves. More recently, NE has been identified in the brain and is believed to be a synaptic transmitter there as well. The evidence suggests that NE, and several related chemicals, may play a role in behavioral excitability and reactivity increase, suggesting that it may function antagonistically to ACh.

NE is produced in nerve cells from the amino acid tyrosine. A series of enzymatically catalyzed reactions is required. Tyrosine is first metabolized to *dopa*, then to *dopamine* (DA), and then to NE. Each of these steps requires a specific enzyme. DA itself has been shown to function as a neurotransmitter molecule. Nerve cells that utilize DA as a neurotransmitter, so-called *dopaminergic neurons*, lack the enzyme that catalyzes the conversion of DA to NE. Both NE and DA seem to be inactivated by a *reuptake mechanism* rather than by enzymatic degradation. They are reabsorbed into the presynaptic terminal and probably stored again in the vesicles.

A particularly interesting theory of certain forms of behavioral pathology has arisen through work on the so-called *biogenic amines*, as NE and related compounds are called. The theory—the biogenic amine theory of mood—suggests that the biogenic amines may control or produce changes in a person's mood, even to the extreme levels of mania and depression. Although preliminary, the theory is exciting because it relates human behavior pathology to naturally occurring substances in the brain.

Drugs and Neural Transmission

Many important behavioral effects of drugs are believed to take place at the level of synaptic events. We can divide these effects into three categories.

1. Drugs may mimic the effects of transmitters. In many instances this is because the drug is similar in chemical composition to the naturally occurring transmitter molecule, so that it can "impersonate" the transmitter and produce the same effect, excitation or inhibition.

2. Second, the drug may affect the mechanisms that destroy the transmitter, thus impersonating its effects. For example, some drugs inhibit the enzyme acetylcholinesterase, the enzyme that degrades the transmitter acetylcholine, thus allowing the transmitter to have a greater effect. Other drugs prevent the reuptake of norepinephrine and dopamine, resulting in a greater effect.

3. A third way in which drugs can affect neural transmission and ultimately behavior is by directly interfering with the transmitter. Of course, the effect will be the opposite of the effect of the transmitter. Such drugs are called *blocking agents* because they block the action of the transmitter. If the transmitter is excitatory, the blocking agent will produce inhibition, and if it is inhibitory, the blocking agent will produce excitation. Thus, blocking agents are like substitutes for the inactivators of the transmitters.

With at least three different means of action, and many different kinds of transmitters, it is no wonder that many different drugs can have profound effects on the nervous system and behavior.

Psychological Tests and Assessment Techniques

C

TEST CONSTRUCTION

How are psychological tests constructed? Where do personality and behavioral assessment techniques come from? Do psychologists just sit at their desks and decide arbitrarily on what will work? How can psychologists be sure that what they make up will measure what they say it measures? Are test scores meaningful? These questions may have crossed your mind as we discussed such psychological measures as tests of intelligence, creativity, learning, perception, motivation, and personality. We consider the process of test construction in this Appendix.

SELECTING TEST ITEMS

A psychological test is made up of a set of individual items—questions, commands, or stimuli—to which the test subject must respond. The particular form of the items depends on the purpose of the test. For example, to measure verbal fluency subjects may be asked for the definitions of words; to measure short-term memory they may be asked to repeat five digits backwards; and to measure creativity they may be asked to name as many unusual uses for a brick as they can.

In many cases constructors of a new test will analyze available tests and select their items from those that have been successful in the past. If they are working in a new area, they may have no recourse but to make up items, perhaps asking colleagues and students to help. In either case test constructors must gather an abundance of various types of items, for in the process of refining the test they are bound to find many items that are poor or worthless and therefore must be discarded.

The first hurdle a test item must pass is *face validity;* that is, does the item appear on the surface as though it will correlate with the trait or variable being measured? After a large pool of items has been gathered, it is almost always found that some appear more valid than others. To measure the IQ of a 14-year-old, it seems intuitively clear (even theoretically clear, if we consider Piaget's theory discussed in Chapter 8) that defining abstract words is a better test item than building a stack of blocks. So some items in the pool are quickly rejected on grounds of appearance alone. Test constructors should be sure to have many more items than they will need in the final form of the test, because there are other reasons besides lack of face validity for eliminating items.

Trial Administration

After the test constructor has compiled an initial set of test items, the next step is to administer the test to a sample of people. The sample should be representative of those to whom the final test is meant to apply. For example, if the test is for children between 3 and 12 years old, then the sample should be likewise composed. Sometimes several samples are needed, as, for example, when there are too many items for one group to handle in a reasonable time period.

After the tests have been scored individual items are examined to see how well they performed. Suppose, for example, that a psychologist wants to develop an age scale for intelligence. He or she wants items that discriminate ages. A perfect item would be one that is failed by all up to a certain age and passed by all beyond that age. An item that is passed by roughly the same percentage of subjects at every age is a poor item and must be rejected. For example, an item that no 3-year-

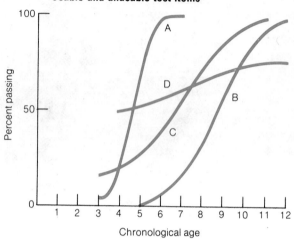

Figure C–1
Usable and unusable test items

Functions showing percentage of subjects who pass four different test items at each chronological age. Items A and B would be usable in a test to develop an age scale for intelligence. Item C could be used, although it does not discriminate as well. Item D should not be used.

old passes and no 5-year-old fails would be kept and used in the 4-year-old scale (Item A in Figure C–1). Item B in Figure C–1 is likewise very good, although at an older age level. It too would be kept. Item C is marginal and would be rejected if the psychologist had enough other items to replace it. Item D is an unusable item and must be eliminated under any circumstances.

There are two other main criteria for evaluating an item. First, is the item *reliable?* Item reliability means that a given subject will perform at the same level on the item on two different occasions. Second, is the item *valid* beyond mere face validity? Validity means that the item should measure what it is supposed to measure. The tester could rate items on reliability by correlating the scores obtained from a group of subjects who have taken the test twice and have thus been tested on the same item on two different occasions. He or she rates items on validity by correlating the item scores with some other known measure of the characteristic in question, in this case intelligence. These considerations apply not only to individual items but also to the test as a whole, and they are more easily discussed in that context.

Standardization

On the basis of an examination of individual items test constructors arrive ideally at a final form for the test. They assign items to scales according to some logical grouping. For an age test they group items according to the age of maximal discrimination. For a point scale they group items according to type, for instance, vocabulary items and current events items, and arrange them in order of difficulty within types. They keep only the best items. Then they administer the final form to a large sample of subjects for standardization purposes.

One purpose of test *standardization* is to work out the final details of the test procedure. To be fair to every individual, the test must be administered under comparable conditions and in a reasonably constant way. For example, test scores might not be comparable if the test were given under favorable conditions—good lighting, quiet room, period of alertness—to some individuals and unfavorable conditions—dark and noisy room, period of fatigue—to others. In intelligence testing particularly, even minor and seemingly unimportant variations, such as the time between items, can have significant effects. The aim is to identify the test conditions that maximize performance and then make sure that all subjects are tested under these conditions.

A second function of the standardization phase of test construction is to provide *test norms*. This is a complex issue and not easily described in general terms. The norms for a personality test are fundamentally different from the norms for an intelligence test. Establishing norms involves determining the *average* or *typical level of performance* on the test and devising a measure of score variability. Therefore, the relevant statistics are measures of central tendency, such as the mean, and measures of variability in the frequency distribution of test scores, such as the standard deviation.

Consider, for example, a point-scale IQ test. Each item passed in each subscale is awarded a certain number of points, and the total score is the sum of all earned points. In order to understand the score of any particular subject, the tester needs to know how it compares with the scores of similar people. Knowing that 16-year-old Billy earned a score of 75 points on the test is not particularly informative. To make sense of that score the tester needs to know the average score for people like him. It makes considerable difference whether that mean is 100 or 70. Likewise, it is helpful to have an idea of the variation in scores. A score of 75 in a distribution with a mean of 70 and a standard deviation of 2 is indicative of much better performance than a score of 75 in a distribution with a mean of 70 and a standard deviation of 15 (see Appendix A).

The norms of a test usually consist of means and standard deviations for all relevant subgroupings of subjects. Indeed, the better-developed tests provide this information for various classifications, such as different ages, different subscales, and so on. To simplify interpretations, many norms are converted to some standard scoring across subclassification. For example, it has become conventional to transform intelligence test scores in such a way that, regardless of age of subject or sub-

"We had intelligence tests today. Boy! Were they HARD!"

Reprinted courtesy of the Register and Tribune Syndicate

In constructing tests we must remember that a test item which everyone gets correct is not worth very much if the goal is to discriminate among people in terms of the amount of knowledge or ability or intelligence they possess. Likewise, an item that is failed by everybody taking the test is not very helpful. Try to remember this important feature of test construction the next time you have a test in your psychology class.

scale of test, the mean score is 100. For all subclassifications of the Wechsler test, the standard deviation in IQ points is 15.

Reliability

Standard test conditions and normative data are important in psychological testing, but the primary objective signs of a good test are **reliability** and **validity**. A rigorous check on reliability can be made in any of three ways, and occasionally all three are used. In the *test-retest method*, the same test is administered twice within a short time span to the same subjects. When there are two comparable forms of the test, which is especially desirable if there is the possibility of some transfer with repeated administrations of the same test, the *alternate forms method* can be used. In this method reliability is indexed by the correlation between the sets of scores obtained by subgroups of subjects who took the different forms of the same test. The *split-half method* is the easiest and most economical check. Here the items of the test are divided into two comparable groups or halves, and the resulting two sets of scores are correlated.

In any case, the higher the correlation between the two sets of scores, the more reliable is the test and, by implication, all items within it. The best-known tests of intelligence have reliability coefficients of .90 and above, which are extraordinarily high correlations. Such a high correlation indicates that a person is very likely to score approximately the same every time he or she takes the test.

Validity

Validity is the degree to which a test correlates with some accepted criterion of the behavior being measured. We shall consider briefly three kinds of validity. A test of *concurrent validity* is made when the new test is compared with existing tests designed to accomplish the same purpose. A psychologist might, for example, correlate scores on his or her IQ test with scores obtained by the same subjects on the familiar Wechsler-Bellevue test. If the correlation is high, the psychologist can conclude that the test measures what the Wechsler test measures, presumably intelligence.

Predictive validity is based on somewhat less circular reasoning. Here the tester asks if the test can predict later performance. Using subsequent school achievement to validate an IQ test is an example. If a psychologist has designed a test to select students with high engineering aptitude, later grade-point average in engineering school would be the criterion. Again, validity is measured by the magnitude of the correlation between test and the criterion it is used to predict.

Finally, when the test is designed to measure a theoretical idea or construct, its validity is judged by the extent to which it conforms to the requirements of the theory. *Construct validity* is a matter of logical analysis, not correlation. An "unusual uses" test is a valid measure of the construct of creativity according to theories that describe creativity in terms of divergent thinking and remote associative processes. But if one's theory emphasized personality traits, such as permissiveness, in creativity, a personality inventory (see Chapter 9) would be a more valid measure.

The validity of psychological tests varies with the type of behavior or construct measured. IQ tests are generally high in validity, as measured in both the concurrent and predictive sense. We find correlation coefficients up to .90. Tests of less well-known processes such as creativity are acceptable with validity correlations of .50 to .60. In some cases of personality assessment, validity might be lower or not even rigorously established. The higher the validity, the better and more useful the test, but validity should not be taken as an overriding requirement. A test with low validity is often better than none at all, especially in a new research area.

PERSONALITY ASSESSMENT

Describing the personality of friends, relatives, or strangers is one of the oldest and most popular forms of entertainment. To a psychologist, however, it is a very serious business. Over the years people have developed many different ways of arriving at statements describing a person's personality. At one time, for example, it was believed that analyzing the bumps on a person's head would reveal his or her personality. Others felt that different personality types had different body shapes. Personality has been assessed by analysis of handwriting (graphology), the planets (astrology), lines in the hands (palmistry), and tea leaves at the bottom of one's cup. Developing ways to describe other people's personalities appears to be important to everyone.

Personality assessment is the process of objectively measuring the fundamental properties of an individual's personality. To the professional psychologist, the personality assessment techniques are major tools for understanding people and for describing, predicting, and helping them change their behavior. Psychological assessment and measurement has become a highly sophisticated enterprise. Many of the assessment procedures can be administered and interpreted only by people with considerable mathematical and statistical training in addition to a thorough knowledge of personality theory, although some of the tests can be given and scored by trained assistants. The development of new assessment procedures and modification and refinement of techniques already in use is an ongoing interest of psychologists who study personality.

Uses of Personality Tests

Personality tests are used for two basic purposes: to make a diagnostic decision or to further understanding of the concept of personality. There are two distinct types of diagnostic decisions made on the basis of test results: (1) mental health decisions, that is, whether or not the person is sane, what kind of therapy to use, what aspects of the individual's personality are abnormal, and the like; and (2) prediction decisions, that is, predictions about whether or not a person will be successful in some area, say school or on the job.

The most important and most frequent use of psychological tests is to diagnose mental disorders. You probably know that psychologists and psychiatrists are often called upon by the courts to determine if someone is "legally" sane or not. But not every person with a behavior disorder is involved with the courts. Usually it is the therapist who administers psychological testing in order to understand the client's problem and develop rational ways of proceeding in therapy. For many clinical psychologists behavior or mental disorder means personality disorder, and personality measurement is the first step in diagnosis and therapy. Therapists must be able to measure personality if they are going to base treatment on the notion that something is abnormal about the personality of the clients. The decisions made on the basis of these assessment procedures have incredibly important implications for the client. The results may determine whether or not he or she is committed to a hospital, sentenced to a prison, allowed to continue on a job, keep his or her children, and so on. Thus the measures of personality, the procedures used to make these judgments, must be the best that psychologists can devise. It may be fun to read handwriting or tea leaves or palms or the stars, but these assessment techniques because they have no demonstrated validity are not acceptable means for making decisions about someone's personality.

Assessment procedures are also used to make nonclinical decisions and predictions about future behavior. In education, psychologists use the principles of psychological assessment to develop ability, aptitude, and achievement tests. Intelligence testing is used to diagnose mental retardation, reading difficulties, discipline problems, grade level, who gets into college, medical school, law school, and so on. In industry personality assessment has become an important aspect of executive hiring. There are also tests of manual ability that determine who gets hired at a factory. The military uses psychological tests in planning the training programs of new recruits and in deciding who is qualified for what service. The government uses psychological tests to make hiring decisions. Just about every area of our lives has been invaded by people using psychological tests to make decisions about us, decisions that have great impact on us.

Despite the importance of the topic, psychologists do not agree completely on what personality is or how it is to be measured. There is a lack of understanding of the concept of personality, and therefore a great deal of research effort is being devoted to the topic. In order to do research on personality it is necessary to have personality tests that can be used to test hypotheses about what personality is. For example, psychologists who believe that personality is made up of a set of traits need ways to demonstrate this in a rigorous fashion. New conceptions of personality mean developing new ways of assessing personality; thus personality tests play a crucial role in the development and refinement of the concept of personality.

Types of Personality Assessment

In addition to the behavioral observation techniques discussed in Chapter 9, there are three types of assessment procedures: interviews, objective tests, and projective tests. In an *interview* the subject is engaged in a conversation with a psychologist for the purpose of informing the psychologist about the subject's personality.

Psychologists Play Bigger Corporate Role in Placing of Personnel . . .

John Koten

Seated at student desks in a small room, prospective Delta Air Lines pilots pore over a battery of psychological tests.

"This is ridiculous," mutters one of the four applicants. "What do these tests have to do with whether I'll make a good pilot? What the hell does it matter whether I like to sing in the shower?"

It may matter a great deal.

"I tell the company, 'go or no go,'" declares Sidney Janus, a private Atlanta psychologist who gives rigorous tests to Delta's flight and management job candidates. He exaggerates somewhat, of course, but the company says his veto would jeopardize a person's chances of becoming a Delta pilot, stewardess or executive.

Many Seek Guidance

Delta is among hundreds of U.S. concerns that are turning more to psychologists for guidance in deciding who gets what job. . . .

Through testing and interviews, psychologists help screen prospective employes and select promotion candidates — occasionally all the way up the corporate ladder. Some executive-search firms have staff psychologists who advise concerns about presidential prospects.

The trend isn't new; for instance, Sears, Roebuck & Co. began its psychological-assessment program in the early 1940s. But more corporations use psychologists nowadays, partly because testing has become more sophisticated, comprehensive and objective. Increasingly, businesses believe that "promotion and hiring decisions are too important to be made solely on the basis of such things as office politics, tenure and highly subjective performance evaluations" by bosses, says Jon Bentz, Sears's director of psychological research.

The Wall Street Journal
July 11, 1978

This is an informal procedure and one of the oldest methods of finding out about a person.

The second technique, the *objective test*, is sometimes called a *personality inventory* or *self-report measure*. The procedure is to ask the person to answer, usually in writing, a number of objective questions about himself or herself. It is assumed that the person will report the true facts, or perhaps the test might be developed in such a way as to determine if he or she is being truthful. As you might suspect, this is an area of great debate—can an *accurate* measure of personality be arrived at from self-report measures?

The final technique is the *projective test,* a much less objective procedure. The "questions" on these tests are unstructured and not clearly stated. A trained psychologist is required to score and interpret projective tests, and there is considerable room for disagreement about the meaning of the responses. Those who use and defend these tests argue that their value lies in the vagueness that others criticize. The situation is so unstructured that there is no way that subjects can fake responses. For example, subjects would have no way of knowing how "sane" as opposed to "insane" persons would answer. These tests are limited primarily to clinical diagnosis of behavior disorders. In fact, the name "projective" derives from the clinical idea of projection. The test is so ambiguous that subjects have to *project* their own personality into it to provide some structure and a way of responding. The basic problem with these tests is the difficulty of developing reliable and universally accepted ways of analyzing the highly unusual and idiosyncratic responses of the subject.

Interviews

The most obvious way to assess a person's personality is to talk and interact with him or her, the technique we all use in everyday affairs. It is the most common way of "getting to know" someone else. A somewhat more formalized version of this procedure is the psychological *interview,* which can be thought of as a form of social interaction, a conversation, with the definite purpose of diagnosis and a definite agenda of issues to be covered. The interviewer wants to know some particular behavioral fact or facts about the interviewee. The interviewee, typically, does not know fully the agenda to be covered.

STRUCTURE In contrast to other personality assessment procedures, the interview is relatively informal and can be conducted in a variety of ways. A completely unstructured interview takes whatever direction the interviewee wishes to pursue. The interviewer acts merely as a sounding board and tries not to guide or direct the conversation. The classical example of an unstructured interview is that conducted by a client-centered therapist, who responds infrequently and neutrally to whatever the client says. Usually, however, the interviewer imposes some structure, for time is limited and there are particular facts that must be obtained. Interviews can be so highly structured and programmed that there may be no need for the interviewer at all; the interviewee merely fills in a questionnaire. Personality inventories are often described as completely structured interviews.

CONTROL In most cases the interviewer controls the session in fairly obvious ways. He or she has particular questions to ask, allows the interviewee to answer only in certain ways, and cuts the interview off at his or her own discretion. The interviewer's behavior also has subtle effects on the conduct of the interview. First, interviewers typically subscribe to a particular personality theory. For example, a psychoanalytically oriented psychologist might ask questions about the person's childhood or questions that are indicative of unconscious processes. An existential theorist might concentrate on the present existence of the interviewee. An interviewer with leanings toward learning theory might be curious about the important stimulus situations in a person's life and the reinforcers, especially social, that control his or her behavior. Thus the theoretical orientation of the interviewer may lend subtle structure to a session beyond any stated purpose or procedural principles that might be involved.

Research has demonstrated even more subtle effects of the interviewer's behavior. By a simple nod of the head the interviewer may greatly increase the amount of talking by the client. A frown may lead the interviewee to drop the current topic of conversation. The fact that interviewers are often unaware of their reactions to the conversation means that an interview can fail or proceed along relatively unproductive lines.

RATING SCALES Interviews and related assessment procedures sometimes move at a fast pace, and thus interviewers need a way of quickly and accurately recording responses and events for later analysis. They may try to remember everything and write it down later, but if they have many interviews to conduct during the day, memory is bound to be fuzzy for specifics at some later time. Even if they tape record every interview, the feelings or reactions they had at the time of the interview may be forgotten.

For convenience interviewers may resort to a shorthand form of note taking known as a *rating scale.* A rating scale is a device by which interviewers can rapidly and at any convenient time record their judgment of the subject according to several dimensions. The most common form is the *graphic rating scale.* Each dimension of the subject's personality that is considered critical, such as friendliness or industriousness, is represented by a segmented line. One end represents one extreme of the dimension (unusually friendly or industrious), and the other end is the opposite extreme (unusually hostile or lazy). The interviewer places a checkmark at the appropriate place on the line to represent his or her judgment of the person's position relative to other people. Ratings can be made either during or immediately after an interview. With a sufficiently complete list of scales, the interviewer can create a description of the subject's personality or some components of his or her personality in a quick and relatively reliable way.

Inventories

A personality inventory generally consists of a large number of objective questions about one's behavior. Test takers are asked about their attitudes, hobbies, personal habits, friends and family, and so on. Usually the inventory is designed to measure personality on several different scales. The test might have 10 subscales, each one presumably measuring a different aspect of personality, and for each subscale there might be 10 to 20 questions designed to get at that factor or subscale.

THE MMPI The best-known and most widely used objective personality instrument is the *Minnesota Multiphasic Personality Inventory,* known simply as the MMPI. It consists of 550 statements that subjects must judge as being either "true" of themselves, "false," or "cannot say." The items were selected because they are answered differently by normal people and psychiatric patients. The MMPI was developed by testing people with known behavior disorders and is used mainly as a diagnostic instrument for detecting psychiatric problems, although it can be used to assess individual differences in normal personality as well.

Statements on the MMPI are of this variety:

1. I have trouble making new friends.
2. I am seldom troubled by nightmares.
3. At times, my mind is very confused.
4. My parents often punished me physically.
5. I seldom get headaches.

The 550 items are usually analyzed into 10 basic "clinical" scales and 4 "validity" scales (to determine whether the subject has answered the test validly and truthfully). The 10 clinical scales are:

1. Hypochondriasis (HS)—a scale of how often the subject complains about his or her physical health.
2. Depression (D)—a scale of how depressed and pessimistic the subject is.
3. Hysteria (Hy)—a measure of neurotic reaction to stress by denial of problems with accompanying medical complaints.
4. Psychopathic deviation (Pd)—a measure of the subject's feelings about rules, laws, moral conduct, ethics, and so on.
5. Masculinity-femininity (MF)—a measure of the orientation of the subject toward the traditional masculine or feminine behavior roles.
6. Paranoia (Pa)—a measure of how suspicious the subject is, particularly in the area of interpersonal relations.
7. Psychasthenia (Pt)—a measure of how obsessed the

Figure C-2
Differentiating groups with the MMPI

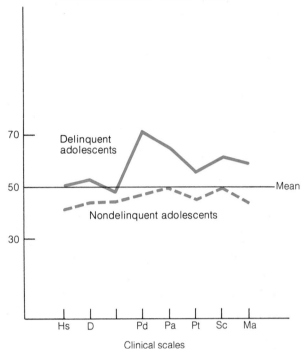

Scores for a group of delinquent adolescents and a group of nondelinquent adolescents on 8 of the 10 clinical scales of the MMPI. The largest difference between the two groups appears on the Pd (psychopathic deviation) scale.

person is with certain thoughts and how compulsive (rigid) he or she is.

8. Schizophrenia (Sc)—a measure of how withdrawn the subject is from the real world and the degree to which his or her thinking could be described as bizarre.
9. Hypomania (Ma)—a measure of how excited and active the subject is, particularly the tendency to show unusual elation and excitement.
10. Social introversion (Si)—a measure of introversion-extroversion.

As an example of how the MMPI differentiates between specified groups of individuals, consider the results of a study in which the test was administered to delinquent and nondelinquent adolescents. As you might guess, the largest difference between the two groups was on the psychopathic deviation (Pd) scale (see Figure C-2). The MMPI has proved to be a very useful clinical tool and has also contributed notably to research on behavior disorders. However, its use as a screening device, say

Figure C–3
A 16 PF test profile

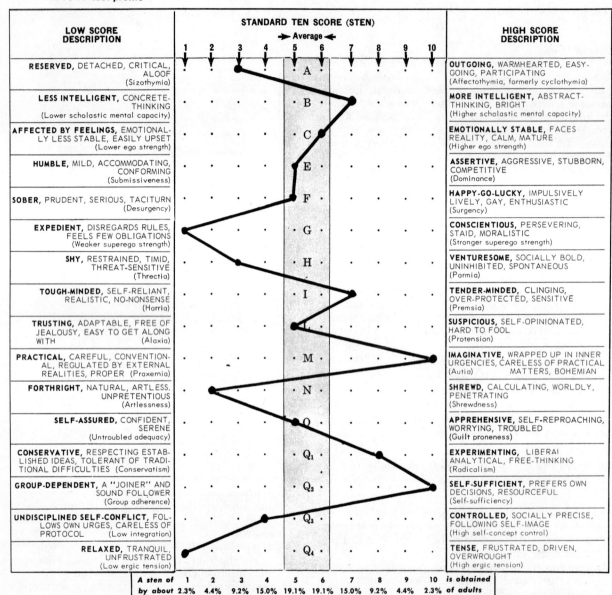

LOW SCORE DESCRIPTION	STANDARD TEN SCORE (STEN) → Average ←	HIGH SCORE DESCRIPTION
RESERVED, DETACHED, CRITICAL, ALOOF (Sizothymia)	A	**OUTGOING,** WARMHEARTED, EASY-GOING, PARTICIPATING (Affectothymia, formerly cyclothymia)
LESS INTELLIGENT, CONCRETE-THINKING (Lower scholastic mental capacity)	B	**MORE INTELLIGENT,** ABSTRACT-THINKING, BRIGHT (Higher scholastic mental capacity)
AFFECTED BY FEELINGS, EMOTIONAL-LY LESS STABLE, EASILY UPSET (Lower ego strength)	C	**EMOTIONALLY STABLE,** FACES REALITY, CALM, MATURE (Higher ego strength)
HUMBLE, MILD, ACCOMMODATING, CONFORMING (Submissiveness)	E	**ASSERTIVE,** AGGRESSIVE, STUBBORN, COMPETITIVE (Dominance)
SOBER, PRUDENT, SERIOUS, TACITURN (Desurgency)	F	**HAPPY-GO-LUCKY,** IMPULSIVELY LIVELY, GAY, ENTHUSIASTIC (Surgency)
EXPEDIENT, DISREGARDS RULES, FEELS FEW OBLIGATIONS (Weaker superego strength)	G	**CONSCIENTIOUS,** PERSEVERING, STAID, MORALISTIC (Stronger superego strength)
SHY, RESTRAINED, TIMID, THREAT-SENSITIVE (Threctia)	H	**VENTURESOME,** SOCIALLY BOLD, UNINHIBITED, SPONTANEOUS (Parmia)
TOUGH-MINDED, SELF-RELIANT, REALISTIC, NO-NONSENSE (Harria)	I	**TENDER-MINDED,** CLINGING, OVER-PROTECTED, SENSITIVE (Premsia)
TRUSTING, ADAPTABLE, FREE OF JEALOUSY, EASY TO GET ALONG WITH (Alaxia)	L	**SUSPICIOUS,** SELF-OPINIONATED, HARD TO FOOL (Protension)
PRACTICAL, CAREFUL, CONVENTION-AL, REGULATED BY EXTERNAL REALITIES, PROPER (Praxernia)	M	**IMAGINATIVE,** WRAPPED UP IN INNER URGENCIES, CARELESS OF PRACTICAL (Autia) MATTERS, BOHEMIAN
FORTHRIGHT, NATURAL, ARTLESS, UNPRETENTIOUS (Artlessness)	N	**SHREWD,** CALCULATING, WORLDLY, PENETRATING (Shrewdness)
SELF-ASSURED, CONFIDENT, SERENE (Untroubled adequacy)	O	**APPREHENSIVE,** SELF-REPROACHING, WORRYING, TROUBLED (Guilt proneness)
CONSERVATIVE, RESPECTING ESTAB-LISHED IDEAS, TOLERANT OF TRADI-TIONAL DIFFICULTIES (Conservatism)	Q_1	**EXPERIMENTING,** LIBERAL ANALYTICAL, FREE-THINKING (Radicalism)
GROUP-DEPENDENT, A "JOINER" AND SOUND FOLLOWER (Group adherence)	Q_2	**SELF-SUFFICIENT,** PREFERS OWN DECISIONS, RESOURCEFUL (Self-sufficiency)
UNDISCIPLINED SELF-CONFLICT, FOL-LOWS OWN URGES, CARELESS OF PROTOCOL (Low integration)	Q_3	**CONTROLLED,** SOCIALLY PRECISE, FOLLOWING SELF-IMAGE (High self-concept control)
RELAXED, TRANQUIL, UNFRUSTRATED (Low ergic tension)	Q_4	**TENSE,** FRUSTRATED, DRIVEN, OVERWROUGHT (High ergic tension)

A sten of	1	2	3	4	5	6	7	8	9	10	is obtained
by about	2.3%	4.4%	9.2%	15.0%	19.1%	19.1%	15.0%	9.2%	4.4%	2.3%	of adults

This is a profile of an actual male subject. Note that he is quite high on scales M and Q₂, fairly high on Q₁, fairly low on A and H, and very low on G, N, and Q₄. On the remaining scales his scores are all about average. From the verbal descriptions labeling the endpoints of the 16 scales, try writing a personality sketch of this person. What kind of a person do you think he is? Do you think this test allows you to know a lot about him? For starters, he is a 21-year-old college student at the University of Colorado.

for job applicants, has been severely criticized. Would you think it appropriate for a large company to require all its workers to take the MMPI?

THE 16 PF (16 PERSONALITY FACTORS)   Another major inventory, the *16 PF*, was developed by using only normal subjects. This is the test devised by Raymond Cattell in order to assess the basic factors of normal personality. Recall that Cattell's factor analytic studies indicated that human personality could be adequately characterized by 16 source traits. The test is called the 16 PF (16 personality factors) because it consists of separate scales for each of these traits. A sample test profile describing the 16 scales developed by Cattell is shown in Figure C–3.

Suppose a psychologist felt that something was missing from these scales, perhaps that they failed to measure how introverted or extroverted someone's personality was. He or she might devise another test of introversion-extroversion and give it along with the 16 PF to a group of subjects. Factor analysis would involve correlating the new test with each of the existing 16 tests (the 16 factors). If the new test did not correlate with any of the 16 factors, then presumably it measures something that the 16 factors had missed. Chances are, however, that the new test will correlate highly with one of the existing factors, probably factor H (Threctia-Parmia), meaning that it does not measure anything new. Through extended application of this process the personality theorist can narrow the field down to a minimal number of scales necessary to describe personality. Each of the scales would measure something different, meaning that no two scales would correlate highly with each other.

No new scales are needed unless they measure something new, that is, something the 16 existing factors fail to describe. In other words, new scales are not useful unless they fail to correlate with any of the 16 existing ones. The psychologist's description of personality would not be enriched by adding an introversion-extroversion test as a seventeenth factor if that test correlated highly with factor H or any other factor. Thus factor analysis helps to minimize the number of scales; it allows the psychologist to describe personality adequately with the fewest possible tests.

The 16 PF test (which is actually 16 tests rolled into one) consists of multiple-choice items. Four sample items are:

1. I like to watch team games:
   a. yes   b. occasionally   c. no
2. I prefer people who:
   a. are reserved   b. are in between   c. make friends quickly
3. Money cannot bring happiness:
   a. yes (true)   b. in between   c. no (false)
4. Woman is to child as cat is to:
   a. kitten   b. dog   c. boy

Figure C–4
The Rorschach Inkblot Test

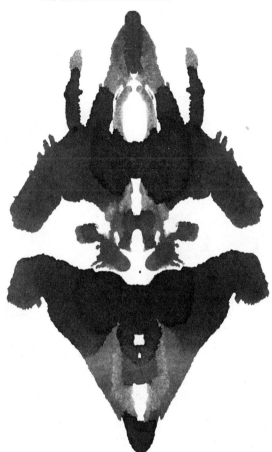

The inkblot is similar to those used in the Rorschach test. Typical responses would involve seeing animals or human beings, whereas a psychotic might respond with a bizarre comment of little relevance to the shape of the blot, such as "pools of blood pouring out of a tree."

Projective Tests

RORSCHACH INKBLOT TEST   The most famous projective test, the *Rorschach Inkblot Test*, was developed in 1921 by Hermann Rorschach. The test consists of 10 inkblots similar to the one shown in Figure C–4. Five of the blots are printed in shades of black and 5 contain varying degrees of color. The final set of 10 blots was derived from a large group of blots that was administered to psychiatric patients who had already been classified by type of disorder. Normal people were also tested. The final 10 blots were the ones that best discriminated the reactions of normal people from the

"According to your inkblots you're a compulsive thief, Mrs. Barstow."

(© Punch (Rothco)

reactions of patients and, further, showed some evidence of discriminating among the various disorders within the patient population.

The subject is shown the Rorschach cards one at a time in a specified order and is asked to describe what he or she sees. Instructions are simple in order to keep the situation as unstructured as possible and not restrict the kind of response the subject might give. In addition to recording what the subject says, the interviewer notes other features of the subject's behavior, such as the length of time it takes to respond, facial expressions, the way the subject holds the card, and so on. All descriptions are then scored on such dimensions as the form of the description, color responses, perceived movement, the figures seen, and the details of the blots that the subject responds to. Scoring is obviously a problem because it depends so much on the opinion of the psychologist, who must decide whether a response really signifies movement, animal reference, color, or whatever. Clearly, in such an ambiguous situation the psychologist's personality as well as the subject's may influence the outcome.

TAT   The other most commonly used projective test is the *Thematic Apperception Test,* the TAT. We encountered this test in Chapter 7 because it has been used successfully to measure achievement motivation. In the TAT the subject is shown a picture and is asked to tell a story about it. The story is supposed to tell what is happening in the picture, what led up to the scene in the picture, and what will happen in the future. There are 18 black and white pictures and one blank card (the subject must imagine a picture on the card and then tell

the story). A popular shortened version of the test contains only 10 cards.

The stories are scored along several dimensions. A critical one is the person in the picture whom the subject identifies as the central character. Other considerations are how the story reflects certain needs and concerns of the subject and what factors seem to be aiding or hindering the satisfaction of personal needs. There are "norms" of typical responses that may serve as guidelines for the psychologist, but the test is basically *interpreted* and not quantified. This means that the scoring procedure is highly subjective and is perhaps easily affected by extraneous variables, just like the Rorschach test.

OTHER TESTS   Other basically projective assessment techniques include dream analysis or interpretation, word association tests, analysis of subjects' artwork, and the sentence completion test. In a sentence completion test the subject is given a stem of a sentence such as "The main trouble with people is . . ." and is asked to complete the sentence in a way that indicates how he or she really feels. This test is the most objective of the projective tests, because the subject's response is structured in advance by the stem of the sentence. Subjects are also much more aware of the implications of what they say than they are when they respond to an inkblot or TAT card. As a consequence, attitudes and beliefs rather than unconscious processes (which are presumably best revealed by the Rorschach or TAT) are the focus of measurement in sentence completion. Nevertheless, as with the TAT, distortions, themes, and unusual responses can give clues to a person's thought processes.

Projective tests represent a compromise between the free-floating character of some therapeutic interviews and the rigid structure of an inventory. The stimulus materials provide some guidelines and determinants of the client's behavior, but the therapist is free to pursue, with leading questions, the various potential trouble spots as the client may reveal them. Indeed, many diagnosticians do not rely at all on standard scoring methods that have been developed for projective tests but rather use them simply as a way to get a person to speak freely about various issues that he or she might otherwise repress or disguise. Nonetheless, there are ways of scoring a person's performance and of comparing him or her with others with known psychopathology. These comparisons are then used to make a classificatory diagnosis.

RATIONALE IN TEST CONSTRUCTION

Both empirical and theoretical rationales are used in the construction of psychological tests.

Diagnosis by Drawing

"Draw a picture of everyone in your family *doing* something." Those are the simple instructions that Psychiatrist S. Harvard Kaufman and Psychologist Robert C. Burns give to children sent to them for treatment. In their new book, *Kinetic Family Drawings* (Brunner/Mazel; $8.95), the two therapists show some of the kinetic, or action, pictures drawn by their young patients and explain how the crude art reveals more fully than thousands of words what is troubling the children.

The idea of evaluating the intellectual and emotional makeup of a child by analyzing his drawings did not originate with Kaufman and Burns. Ever since the 1920s, psychologists have been measuring intelligence by asking children to draw a person (the D-A-P test). For the past two decades, clues to children's emotional problems have been found in their drawings of a house, a tree and a person (the H-T-P technique). By requiring children to draw their families in action, however, Kaufman and Burns believe they have opened new avenues of investigation. In fact, they say, kinetic family drawings "tell us more than we can decipher."

Isolated Children

What the therapists find most intriguing are some of the recurring themes that reveal how children feel about their families. Kids who feel neglected will time and again draw their mothers cleaning house and their fathers driving off to work, while "tough or castrating" fathers are often pictured mowing the lawn or chopping wood. The cat, soft and furry but armed with claws — a creature symbolizing ambivalence — turns up frequently in pictures by girls who both love and hate their mothers.

Youngsters who feel isolated, like Mike, 17, frequently draw family members doing things alone in separate rooms instead of together. Mike also showed his mother at work in the kitchen with her back turned, and he drew himself " 'stealing' food (love) from the cold refrigerator." When they first took him to Psychiatrist Kaufman, Mike's parents insisted that the family was close. But they finally admitted to Kaufman what their son's drawings made

Assessing intelligence, personality, and emotional disorders in children is difficult. A common technique is to analyze art work they have done.

painfully clear — that they "didn't give a damn what happened to Mike."

Sometimes children leave out of their pictures the very things that bother them most. Mary, 12, who had been raped by her brother, drew him sitting in a chair that concealed his body below the waist. Tim, 16, who suffered severe asthma attacks because he felt utterly unloved by his alcoholic mother, showed himself running after an elusive butterfly. On his picture he wrote: "Can't draw mother." . . .

In another drawing, Billy, 14, revealed how he felt when his mother remarried. Her new husband had children of his own, and the family was polarized into two camps. Write Kaufman and Burns: "The boy must be aware of the sexual relationship between the stepfather and the mother, as the sword between the stepfather's legs is the largest weapon in the drawing." Billy, obviously jealous, drew himself throwing darts at his stepfather. The darts were very small and could do no harm; the boy must therefore have realized how powerless he was. That feeling of impotence, the authors say, may have accounted for Billy's "bad" behavior at home and at school. . . .

Time
February 1, 1971

The Empirical Approach

Suppose a psychologist wishes to measure human anxiety. One way of proceeding would be to develop a set of *reference groups*. The psychologist might, for example, attempt to isolate one group of people high in anxiety, one medium in anxiety, and one low in anxiety. These groups might be determined by using existing tests or other available anxiety indicators. Then the psychologist would make up a set of test items, give these items to the three groups, and use their responses to eliminate items that do not discriminate. He or she would thereby supposedly arrive at a test that could tell whether any newly tested person is high, medium, or low in anxiety. Such a test would be an empirically derived test of anxiety.

Many tests have been developed in this way. The MMPI was developed by using many groups of people with different psychiatric diagnoses as the reference groups. Rorschach used a similar method in developing the inkblot test. In the most famous test of vocational interest, the Strong Vocational Interest Blank, successful doctors, lawyers, businesspersons, and so on, served as reference groups. If you take the vocational interest test, your answers are scored to see how they correlate with the answers given by various occupational reference subjects. If you answer the items in a manner similar to that of a group of successful lawyers but different from that of successful doctors, the prediction is that you would do better as a lawyer than as a doctor. The reference group approach in various forms is probably the rationale underlying most psychological tests.

Another empirical approach would be to use the statistical tool known as factor analysis (see Appendix A). This is the procedure used by Cattell to develop the 16 PF test. In this approach the psychologist who wished to develop a measure of anxiety would select a large number of existing tests, administer them to a large group of people, and then factor analyze to identify the basic underlying factors. Say, for example, that there are two clusters of tests, one more indicative of arousal and another related to compulsive movement. The last step is to select the two individual tests that best measure these factors. In this case a statistical procedure rather than a set of reference groups is used to decide on the eventual measure.

The Theoretical Approach

In the empirical approach no theoretical assumptions are made in advance about the construct (for example, anxiety) the test is attempting to measure. The theory comes later, after a description of the construct has been developed from the data of reference groups. In the theoretical approach the steps are reversed. The test constructor first develops a theory (for example, about anxiety) based on past research and already known fac-

tors, and then proceeds to design a test that will measure anxiety as defined or characterized by his or her theory. Suppose the theory says that anxiety is a drive, a motivating force which impels people to act. The implication is that people high in anxiety should show evidence of a high level of motivation. This might be called the drive theory of anxiety. Alternatively, the psychologist might theorize that anxiety has little to do with motivation level but instead is a personality trait which has to do with a person's ability to cope with or deal with stress in an adequate fashion. High-anxiety people have trouble dealing with stressful situations and low-anxiety people do not. This might be called the stress theory of anxiety. Note that the stress theory says that anxiety is independent of drive level or motivation. People can be highly anxious and still have low motivation, or they can be low in anxiety and still have high motivation.

One's theoretical conception of what anxiety really is will determine the kind of test used to measure anxiety. A person who believes in the drive theory of anxiety will obviously develop a different kind of anxiety test than one who believes in the stress theory. The stress theorist is likely to develop a test designed to measure how people handle stressful situations. It might include an item like: "Suppose you are chewed out by your boss in front of several other employees—which of the following things would you most likely do: (a) break down and start crying, (b) tell the boss off, (c) explain to the boss that you have not been feeling well lately, or (d) say nothing to the boss, but, after he leaves, tell him off behind his back." The drive theorist, on the other hand, might have a test item that aims at assessing level of motivation, such as: "Which of the following statements fits you best: (a) I am constantly on the go—I can't sit still, (b) I always take my time, (c) I work hard and I play hard, (d) I am basically a lazy person."

After a test has been constructed and found to be reliable, the psychologist must determine if the test measures what it is supposed to measure, *according to theory.* As you know, a test that measures up to its guiding theory is said to have *construct validity.* To determine if a test has construct validity, the psychologist would use the theory to deduce predictions about how people who score high and low on this test behave differently in some situations. He or she would then get a group of people who score high and another group who score low and test them in the situation to see if the prediction is supported. If it is, the test has construct validity. The idea is to make many such predictions and tests and have them heavily supported before a final conclusion about construct validy of the test is reached; establishing construct validity is a long, detailed research process.

Let us illustrate with predictions based on the two different theories of anxiety just described. The stress theorist might use the following situation to make predictions about the behavior of people who score high and low on a test of anxiety: The two groups of subjects are put in a learning situation, say memorizing a list of words. At some point in the learning process a stressful event is introduced, such as telling the subjects that they are doing so poorly that they will begin to receive shocks when they make errors. The theory of anxiety as inability to cope with stress predicts that the learning rate of the high-anxiety group will go down, whereas the low-anxiety group will be unaffected or will actually improve. If the experiment confirms the prediction, the stress theorist gains a bit of construct validity for his or her test.

The anxiety-as-drive theorist might instead make the following experimental prediction: Take two groups, one high and one low in "drive-anxiety," and put them to work sorting different-colored and different-shaped objects into compartments. Because of their higher drive, high-anxiety people will get more objects sorted than low-anxiety people. If this prediction is confirmed, then the test gains in construct validity.

Although we have divided this rationale section into two parts, empirical and theoretical, in actual practice the two approaches are almost always combined. Sometimes the psychologist does not have a formal, completely specified theory as a guide, and we say that he or she is using the empirical approach. But everyone always has personal hunches, guesses, and ideas, which serve as a theory to guide research. In the case of the theoretical approach, psychologists may have a very formal theory to go by, but they will also make great use of the empirical approaches of reference groups and factor analysis to refine their test procedures, establish construct validity, and modify their theory to account for the new facts brought out by their research.

CRITIQUE

In this final section we wish to raise two hotly debated issues about psychological testing. No simple answers are possible, but it is important that you be aware of the issues.

Behavior as Sign or Sample?

Is the behavior of a person taking a test (his or her score or answers to the test) a *sign* telling the psychologist what the person really is (really is sane or really is anxious or really is mentally retarded), or are responses on the test just a small sample of that person's behavior? We can all be anxious, crazy, or stupid at times. If a psychologist catches us at the wrong moment, we might appear worse (or better) than we really are. In fact, are we *really* anything for all time? Or does our behavior change radically with the situation such that sometimes, in some situations, we act silly or stupid, in others we are anxious, and so on? When psychologists say that a person is anxious,

"Well, frankly, no, Miss Kramer, I didn't answer all the questions honestly at the computer-mate office."

Playboy, June 1974. Reproduced by special permission of PLAY-BOY Magazine. Copyright © 1974 by Playboy.

One obvious problem with self-report measures is that the person being tested can distort his or her answers in order to appear to be different than he or she actually is.

they are using the test as a sign that the person is or has something (trait anxiety), rather than as just a sample of the way the person behaves in a particular test situation (state anxiety). "Diagnosing" a person attaches a label to him or her, and this label seems to dominate the thinking about this person in such a way that the unique features of behavior are obscured. Just because a person was anxious when he or she took the test, does this mean he or she is always and forever *an anxious person?* Who would not be "anxious" if he or she desperately needed a job and had to face a psychologist who would *determine* his or her qualifications? The tradition in psychology has been to use tests as signs, but there is a growing awareness of the sampling aspect of psychological testing and the situational determinants of test behavior, which can only lead to fairer and more appropriate test use and interpretation.

Projective versus Self-Report Measures

The final issue deals with whether or not it is better to use projective or self-report measures of personality. Projective tests usually receive the most criticism because there is a great deal of subjective judgment and interpretation involved on the part of the psychologist. The projective tests therefore have lower reliability and validity measures, which suggests that these kinds of tests are dangerous to use when crucial decisions are to be made. Self-report, inventory-type tests are objective by comparison. They can be more easily validated (although this does not mean they are necessarily more valid), more impersonally administered, and more objectively scored.

On the other hand, the self-report measures rely heavily on subjects being honest when they respond. Many of the items in some self-report measures suggest to the subject what the "best" response is, and therefore these tests can easily be faked. An honest person might be penalized by not faking. A less intelligent person might be discriminated against because he or she cannot deceive the psychologists as well as a smarter person. For this reason testers have added to many self-report tests special test items to detect faking.

Finally, even if the subject is honest and clearly understands the questions, is the person likely to be aware of all the aspects of his or her personality that are important? This is the issue of unconscious motivation — are there aspects to personality that a person is unaware of, and if so, how can that person be expected to report adequately in these areas? Projective tests presumably allow these features of personality to manifest themselves in a way that is supposed to be impossible in a self-report test. In response to this criticism, some self-report, objectively scored tests of unconscious processes have been developed. It is unfortunately too early to judge their adequacy.

We hope that you now have a better appreciation of why psychological testing is an emotional issue. It represents one area in which psychology intrudes into the lives of just about everyone in one way or another. When testing is used to decide who gets hired, who gets into a particular school, who goes to jail or to a mental hospital, then emotions are bound to run high. People who are affected by these intrusions in negative ways are bound to question the right of anybody to assess their personalities. All that psychologists can do in such cases is to develop fair tests, administer them under fair conditions, and interpret them with extreme caution. As long as decisions like these must be made by someone, then it is probably best to proceed in the light of as many facts as possible. We expect that many of these facts will come from continuing research in personality.

Altered
States of
Consciousness

D

Consciousness is that absolutely essential something—a tool or instrument—that we must use to create understanding and knowledge of the world, including all the more specialized topics we refer to as our knowledge of psychology. Indeed, psychology was defined as the study of consciousness earlier in its history, and many psychologists think it will again be defined that way in another decade. But to study consciousness we must use consciousness: how can consciousness understand itself?

Science tries to arrive at knowledge that is *objective*, so we would like to develop a scientific understanding of consciousness that is independent of the peculiarities

Figure D-1
Brain waves, sleep, and dreaming

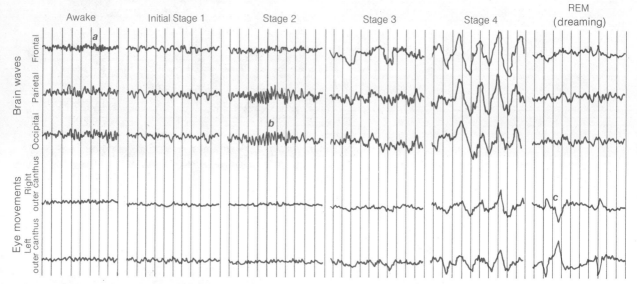

Recordings of brain waves from three cortical areas (frontal is on the forehead, parietal is over the ear, occipital is back of the head) and eye movements as a person goes to sleep. The regular alpha rhythm (a) in the awake subject is replaced by slower, irregular activity in Initial Stage 1. Spindles (b) appear in Stage 2, and delta waves are added to the irregular activity and spindles in Stage 3. The large, slow delta waves predominate in Stage 4. Rapid eye movements (REMs), measured by the electrooculogram (EOG), are associated with dreaming and occur in later Stage 1 periods of the night. They are indicated by synchronous but opposite deflections (c) on the eye-movement channels.

and subjectivity of any particular observer. The difficulty with understanding consciousness from a purely introspective position is the obvious capacity of our minds to imagine things vividly and so make them come true.

In spite of problems that may prevent us from ever having a completely objective and comprehensive knowledge of consciousness, we can learn a great deal from observing our own consciousness and behavior and from studying the behavior of others and their reports about their consciousness. Since our consciousness is the primary tool by which we cope with our world, and the ultimate reference point of our individual existence, anything we can learn about it may be of great value.

One of the most obvious things we experience about consciousness is that our experience shows great variations. We find that the totality of these variations, however, usually stays within a certain range which we have come to call *ordinary* or *normal*. Thus, you may wake up with a mild headache one morning, but you are still yourself; you can carry out your ordinary activities and experience things in pretty much the ordinary way, even though the small headache may stay with you all day. It is the experience of the many aspects of your consciousness staying within a customary range that

gives you the common sense concept of your *ordinary state of consciousness*.

But some other morning you may wake up with a high fever. Your thoughts wander about in a very strange way—you are *delirious*. Your body is not only painful but seems the wrong shape; you feel like a little child instead of your ordinary adult self. The condition or state of your consciousness has gone far beyond the usual range you call your ordinary state.

It is the experience of *radical* alterations in consciousness, of mental functioning taking on a quite different pattern than it ordinarily does, that leads to the concept of *altered states of consciousness* (altered *SoCs*). When you awaken suddenly from a dream, for example, there is an abrupt transition to a radically different style of experience and functioning. While you can find elements of commonality, such as speaking English in both the dream and in your ordinary waking state, the overall change between dream and waking is so great that it is not adequate to think of dreaming as just an extreme of the ordinary range; there was a temporary reorganization of many aspects of consciousness leading to what we call the dream. An interesting exercise is to make a list of those aspects of your experience which allow you to say, with certainty, that right now you are not dreaming but awake. Some of these will be specific elements or qualities of consciousness, such as, for some people, continuity of memory, but there is also an overall grasp of the pattern of experience such that you know instantly that you are not dreaming. Altered SoCs, then, are radical alterations of both individual elements and the overall pattern of our consciousness.

SLEEP AND DREAMS

Different stages of sleep are associated with brain waves of different frequency and amplitude, which produce distinctive electroencephalogram (EEG) patterns for each stage (see Figure D–1). The subject who is awake but resting with the eyes closed shows predominantly **alpha brain waves** (a regular rhythm of about 10 cycles per second). As sleep comes on the alpha rhythm is replaced by slower, irregular waves in what is called Initial Stage 1 EEG. With the appearance of bursts of activity of about 14 cycles per second, called *spindles,* the EEG is classified as Stage 2 sleep. When larger, slower **delta waves** (1 to 2 cycles per second) are added to the irregular activity and spindles, the pattern is called Stage 3; and when delta waves predominate, the pattern is Stage 4. The cycle of Stage 1 through Stage 4 is repeated four to six times a night.

Eugene Aserinsky found that during Stage 1 EEG periods (after the initial Stage 1), an electrooculogram (EOG) recorded rapid eye movements (REMs) in sleeping subjects, and if he awakened the subjects during these periods, they recalled a dream about 80 percent of the time. It is now generally accepted that ordinary dreaming occurs in REM sleep, although dreamlike activity is sometimes reported to occur during other stages of sleep. If the REM periods are plotted, the first one occurs about 90 minutes after going to sleep and lasts 5 to 10 minutes. At the second 90-minute mark, a somewhat longer REM period occurs, and this stage of sleep recurs and gets somewhat longer at each 90-minute cycle. The last REM dream of the night may be from half an hour to an hour long, and awakening from it is common. This last dream, of course, is the one you are most likely to remember in the morning.

Hypnagogic and Hypnopompic States

The SoC that one passes through in going from waking to sleeping is called the **hypnagogic state.** It is similar, and possibly identical to, the SoC that one passes through in going from sleeping to waking, the **hypnopompic state.** The laboratory studies that have been carried out have concentrated on the hypnagogic state, which varies tremendously from individual to individual. For some people the period of falling asleep is filled with experiences as rich as the best nocturnal

Sleep Is Crucial for Survival

PHILADELPHIA — No one knows why we sleep. But we must. Experts say we can live weeks without food. But only 10 days without sleep.

"It's not just for rest and relaxation," says noted sleep researcher Dr. Eugene Aserinsky. "That's too neat, too simple an answer.

"It may be a time when the brain circuits are organized or cause consolidation of memory," says the Jefferson Hospital doctor. "It may be like making jello — with all the activity in the day, you may need a time to allow it to solidify into memory."

"My guess is that temperature control would be a stronger reason than the others," Dr. Aserinsky said. During sleep, the body temperature drops as does the basal metabolic rate, which adds credence to the jello theory.

In animals, the amount of sleep is related to their basal metabolic rate — the higher the metabolic rate, the more sleep animals get. A mouse needs 12.8 hours compared to an elephant's 3.9 hours in a 24-hour period.

The most humans can sleep in a 24-hour period is an average of 16 hours, even though they may have been up the night before. However, they usually average between six and eight hours a night, though 10 may be more agreeable to some, according to Aserinsky.

People sleep in 90-minute cycles with 20 minutes of each cycle devoted to rapid eye movements (REM), the period when people dream, says Aserinsky, who discovered the phenomena more than two decades ago. And by counting the REM, he says, researchers can tell when a person has had enough sleep.

If a person doesn't get enough REM sleep one night, he'll make up for it the next, he says. But alcohol and sleeping pills won't help REM sleep — they depress it, which is why a person — under the influence — won't feel as refreshed. . . .

The Sunday Camera *(Boulder, Colo.)*
March 21, 1976

dreams. For others it is very dull and usually forgotten almost immediately.

Much hypnagogic experience may be identical to later dreaming, although not enough investigation of similarities and differences has been carried out to make this comparison complete. Even for the best hypnagogic "dreamers," the experiences of the hypnagogic state are usually forgotten more rapidly than ordinary dreams, especially if the dreamer continues on into sleep.

You can observe your own hypnagogic state in detail by doing the following: When lying down to sleep, balance one arm vertically, with the elbow resting on the bed. You can go fairly far into a hypnagogic state and maintain the arm in a balanced, comfortable position with little effort. When you are deep in the hypnagogic state your arm will start to fall. The action will usually startle you into wakefulness, and you can try to fix the memory of the hypnagogic experience in your mind before it fades. With the balanced arm technique the hypnagogic state can be greatly prolonged.

Ordinary Dreaming

Ordinary dreaming refers to the experience almost all of us have had of waking up and recalling scenes and events that seemed to take place in a world that often resembles the physical world, but a world we retrospectively consider to be purely imaginary. Although there have been many laboratory and home studies of dreams, most people in our culture have not learned to be good observers of their dreams. Thus much of what is known about dreams has come from piecing together the reports of poor observers.

To illustrate the flavor of ordinary dreaming, consider the following beginning of a dream, reported by a young woman.

Someone had brought a tremendous amount of LSD into town and had been dispensing it freely. The cops were frustrated because they couldn't arrest everyone and they didn't know who to pin it on. In dispensing this there seemed to be a spirit of free giving and there were no strangers. Someone said to me that if you took the LSD with fish the way the Indians (American) do, it wouldn't make you sick, but if you took it medically, it might. I took some by itself, but I knew it wouldn't make me sick anyway. I continued walking, and noticed that I wasn't wearing my clothes. The other people in town were dressed, but my unclothed state didn't seem to bother them. I went into a room where there were a lot of young people and also a man I know who is associated with young people as a teacher and counselor. (Tart, 1969, p. 173)

This dream is typical of dreams, for it seemed quite real to the dreamer. Yet from its content alone we can be sure this was a dream and not a description of a real event, because in the physical world we share American Indians do not take LSD with fish, and if you walk down a street naked people usually do get bothered! The unreality of dreams is usually a retrospective, waking state judgment: dreams are real enough at the time they occur.

Psychological Effects

PERCEPTION   Ordinary dreaming represents one of the most radical changes in perception of any altered SoC, because the external world is almost completely eliminated and replaced by an internal world. There are tremendous individual differences in how "real" the dream world is. At one extreme some people report experiencing every sensory quality that they experience in a wakeful state. They see dream scenes clearly and in color, they hear and speak with dream characters, and they may taste, touch, and smell in the dream world. At the other extreme some people report their dreams to be little more than rather hazy black and white images. The dream reported earlier was one of the more vivid types.

Occasionally stimuli from the external world make their way into the dream world, where they are usually distorted in some fashion to fit in with the action of the dream. The ringing of the alarm clock, for example, may be perceived as a church bell in the dream. Furthermore, there is selectivity in the perception of the external world during dreaming, as well as during waking (see Chapter 3). A familiar example is the parent who sleeps through and never hears the rumble of traffic outside the bedroom window, but who snaps wide awake at the slightest whimper from his or her child three rooms away.

PERFORMANCE   Motor output is virtually eliminated during dreaming. Laboratory studies have shown that there is an active inhibition in the spinal cord of nerve impulses to the muscles. Impulses corresponding to the imagery experienced during dreaming may arrive at the muscles, but the inhibitory signal keeps the muscles from reacting. Occasionally the muscles of the limbs or face may twitch slightly, and occasionally there is some vocalization during ordinary dreaming. But for the most part the dreaming person is almost totally paralyzed. The paralysis of the dream state is adaptive in a sense, because if people acted out their dreams the world would be a rather dangerous place at night, for both the dreamers and anyone near them. On occasion the paralysis may last into the waking state for a few seconds.

COGNITIVE PROCESSES   Cognitive processes in dreams are unusual in several ways. Not only do dreamers fool themselves as to whether they are awake or asleep, but they also accept all sorts of incongruities and absurdities in the dream situation without the slightest question, like walking down the street naked without attracting attention. In the ordinary SoC the person would be immediately alerted by such incongruities and consider them in detail, but the dreamer ignores errors in his or her cognitive processes until afterward, during the waking state. Freud theorized that this was because subconscious desires and emotions were actually responsible for the particular content of the dream, and not enough psychological energy was available to the "secondary processes," the intellectual functions, to allow observation of dream content. Other theorists view dream "stupidity" as a simple consequence of inadequate activation of higher brain centers during sleep.

EMOTION Emotional processes can have a greater effect on the dream experience than cognitive processes. The range of emotional experience is as great as in ordinary waking consciousness, although the emotions may be evoked by rather different stimuli than would evoke them in the waking state. Emotions may also become extremely intense, possibly because the lowered level of critical processes no longer acts to inhibit the emotional systems. Even the amount of sleep and dreaming a person does has been partially tied to emotional factors.

MEMORY Memory systems obviously function at a very high level during ordinary dreaming. Almost the entire dream world is constructed from memory images of things the dreamer has seen or otherwise sensed or from new combinations of past memories. In the example of a dream given earlier, the dreamer had to construct the experience of walking down a street naked without attracting attention from memory elements, because she had never experienced this situation in real life. The memory quality of an experience is often missing during ordinary dreaming, and the dreamer almost always mistakes an intense scene constructed from memory for a real world of experience. As is typical in altered SoCs, visual memory seems particularly strong in dreams, much stronger than a person's ability to produce a visual image from memory in the normal state. Vision is usually the dominant sense modality in dreaming, as in ordinary consciousness.

Recall that memory *for* dreams varies tremendously from person to person. Some people almost never remember a dream after waking. Other people remember many dreams practically every morning. With those who do recall their dreams on awakening, the rate at which the dream fades from memory in the normal state also varies. Some people lose the memory of the dream within a few seconds, unless they make a conscious effort to rehearse it; others may remember a dream vividly for months or years. Sometimes a dream will be forgotten, but an incident later in the day will trigger a complete memory of it. Many people who claim they never remember their dreams begin to do so in great detail if they practice taking notes on their dreams as soon as they wake up. If you are interested in your dreams, you might start keeping a "dream diary."

IDENTITY A person's sense of identity is highly variable in a dream. The dreamer can be his or her normal self, can completely identify with an entirely different character in the dream, or can identify with a version of himself or herself that is changed in a number of important ways. At times a person may have no identity at all in a dream, simply perceiving the dream as an "outside" observer might. This is a striking example of the arbitrariness of our belief in a fixed personal identity. Unique combinations of characteristics and personality elements can be grouped as "the ego" quite readily during dreams. Note too that much of the cognitive activity and emotional reaction of a dream takes place with respect to *who* the dreamer is. If he or she becomes a *different* person in a dream, then events that might be important or evoke specific plans or emotions for the individual's ordinary identity might not do so within the dream.

TIME SENSE Time in dreams generally seems to flow at about the same rate as normal waking activity. This has been established in the laboratory by timing the length of the brain-wave state associated with dreaming and then waking the person and having him or her estimate, in various ways, how long the dream lasted. Generally the subject's estimate is quite close to the actual amount of time elapsed. There still seem to be some dreams, however, in which the perceived time correlates very poorly with clock time. Thus, one might have a dream that seems to take a week, when the sleep stage associated with dreaming could not have lasted more than an hour or so. This may not mean that a week's worth of events actually occurred in the dream, but only that the *feeling* of time was of a week passing.

Physiological Correlates

As we mentioned, nearly all motor functioning is inhibited during dreaming, with two major exceptions. The first is the REMs that are characteristic of dreaming sleep. REMs have been related in some experiments (but not all) to what the dreamer reports he or she is seeing. Thus, if the dreamer reported watching objects fall from airplanes to the ground, his or her electrooculogram might register large vertical REMs. Dreams of watching a ping-pong match would probably produce large horizontal REMs. The other exception to the complete lack of motor functioning in the dream state seems to be the autonomic nervous system. Heart rate, blood pressure, and respiration show great variablity and can undergo large, sudden changes during dreaming. It is not yet clear whether this reflects the emotions of the dream or not.

In males the penis is partially erect throughout most of REM dreaming. In females there is increased vaginal blood flow. This does not necessarily represent specific, overt sexual content of the dreams so much as some sort of physiological release phenomenon. The "morning erection," previously attributed to a full bladder, is now seen to result from the last dream of the night, which frequently occurs just before awakening.

In the last two decades many drugs have been administered to subjects just before they go to bed to see what effects they have on the sleep and dream cycle. This research is particularly important because of the enormous use of sleeping medication (sedatives) in our society. Practically all drugs tested, especially the commonly used sedatives, decrease the amount of time sleepers spend in REM sleep. This deficit of REM time often carries over through a period of continuous drug use, such that when the drug is no longer taken there is a temporary increase (over normal) of REM sleep time for a few nights, although the total deficit is not made up. This has been called the *REM rebound effect*. Stimulants such as amphetamines decrease REM sleep time. There is some evidence that psychedelics, like low doses of LSD, or marijuana cause REM time to shift to earlier in the night without having much effect on total REM time.

Such disruptions of the sleep cycle are generally bad for physical health. A positive result has been the finding with a few sedatives, such as chloral hydrate, that promote sleep but do not disturb the sleep cycle.

Very little research has been done on the effects of various drugs on the content of dreams or on the quality of that altered SoC, although these psychological questions are important.

Non-REM Sleep (Dreamless Sleep?)

Dreamless sleep is a term commonly used to refer to Stages 1 (without REM), 2, 3, and 4 of the EEG sleep pattern. They are not accompanied by REMs and are therefore commonly referred to as non-REM stages or non-REM sleep. The term "dreamless sleep" should be used with caution. While there are *seldom* reports of intense, emotional episodes of dreaming from stages other than REM periods, they do occur occasionally. Researchers have not yet been able to decide whether these vivid reports are dreams recalled from an earlier REM period or whether they actually happened in non-REM sleep.

If subjects are awakened in the laboratory from non-REM sleep and asked what was going through their minds just before awakening, the usual answer is "nothing." Either there is no mental activity during this kind of sleep or memory of it is extremely poor. On rare occasions something is described by the subject that he or she labels a "dream." More frequently reports from non-REM sleep are labeled by the subject as "thinking." The impression of experiences during dreamless sleep is that they are often a sort of sporadic thinking—brief, relatively logical, and pedestrian thoughts. Perception of the external world is generally nonexistent; either stimuli are not well incorporated into the ongoing experience or the ongoing experience is forgotten. Self-awareness also seems to be nonexistent.

The major exception to the notion that only occasional vague and dull thoughts occur during dreamless sleep is the finding that most *sleep talking, sleep walking,* and what are called *night terrors* (as opposed to nightmares, which occur during REM sleep) occur during non-REM sleep. Since the person is not in a state of peripheral motor paralysis as in REM sleep, mental experiences may be expressed in physical action. The fact that most night terrors occur in non-REM sleep indicates that occasionally exceptionally intense dreamlike processes may occur, with maximal emotional arousal. Thus another altered SoC develops from non-REM sleep on these occasions.

HYPNOSIS

Hypnosis has been one of the most widely investigated SoCs in our society. We can define hypnosis as an SoC characterized by a kind of mental quiet, a lack of the ongoing thought processes usually associated with ordinary consciousness, and hypersuggestibility. In hypnosis a wide variety of specific phenomena and experiences can be brought about by suggesting them to the subject.

Hypnosis is usually induced while the subject is sitting or lying in a relaxed position. The hypnotist asks the subject to relax, to be calm and quiet, and not to worry about anything. It is usually suggested that the subject is getting drowsy or sleepy, but the subject implicitly knows that this is merely a way to let his or her mind drift and become completely relaxed. Suggestions that are responded to positively by most people are given early in the induction procedure, and the skillful hypnotist uses positive responses to these to build confidence on the subject's part that the person can go into an even deeper hypnotic state. Various types of "gadgetry" are sometimes used to induce hypnosis, such as fancy machines or crystal balls. These have no real function other than increasing the credibility of the hypnotist. The hypnotist using a machine to hypnotize a subject appears to be very "scientific," and so the subject has that much more confidence in the hypnotist.

The hypnotist's long repetition of suggestions of sleep and drowsiness may lead to a state generally termed *neutral hypnosis*, the hypnotic state without specific suggestions that anything *in particular* will happen. Subjects describe this as a state of detachment and mental quiet. They feel totally relaxed. If asked what they are thinking about, they usually answer "nothing." They describe their minds as blank, although they are alert and attentive to the hypnotist. This state contrasts markedly with our normal SoC, in which, as we discussed in Chapter 6, we are always thinking about something.

There are immense individual differences in response to hypnosis. About 5 to 10 percent of people do not respond at all, while another 10 to 20 percent can achieve very deep hypnotic states and experience almost all hypnotic phenomena. Most people fall on a normal distribution of susceptibility between these two extremes. In spite of an immense amount of research on personality characteristics of responsive and unresponsive hypnotic subjects, no solid findings have come to light. We have little knowledge of why one person is readily susceptible to hypnotic suggestion and another is not. Similarly, there has been a great deal of research on possible physiological changes during hypnosis, but no distinct changes have been identified other than those that can be attributed to physical relaxation.

There is a great deal of controversy about the nature of hypnosis. If one defines hypnosis simply in terms of hypersuggestibility, for example, some subjects will be suggestible and otherwise will behave as a hypnotized person is expected to, but will report little or no changes in their conscious experiences. Indeed, one type of hypnosis research design pioneered by psychologist Martin Orne uses *simulator control groups*—people picked because they are unresponsive to repeated attempts to hypnotize them, and then coached to *act* like hypnotized subjects. Often simulators cannot be distinguished from genuinely hypnotized subjects *on the basis of external behavior:* it is only the later, honest reports of internal experience that distinguish them.

Here we shall take the traditional view of hypnosis as an altered SoC, which is probably basically true for some subjects, but remember that some authorities do not believe that hypnosis is an altered SoC at all, only a case of involved acting or role playing.

Psychological Effects

PERCEPTION Under hypnosis many aspects of perception can be totally restructured from the subject's point of view. Perception in specific sensory modalities can be reduced to various degrees, a state called *hypoesthesia*. Subjects may be told, for example, that they cannot see clearly, and they will report that their vision is blurred or dim. Hypoesthesia can be carried to the point of total blocking of a sensory modality. Subjects may be told that they cannot smell at all, after which some will be able to take a sniff of a bottle of household ammonia, show practically no reaction to it, and report that they smelled nothing. Since the sensation of pain can be completely blocked by hypnotic suggestion, hypnosis has been used as an analgesic (pain killer) in medical and surgical treatment.

On the other hand, hyperesthesias may be created by telling subjects that one sense is exceptionally keen. Most subjects will report "feeling" an increase in sensitivity, although there is little evidence that actual sensitivity changes. Suggestion can be carried to the point of illusion, or even hallucination, in which case the subject will see things that do not really exist. A very responsive subject can be told, for example, to see a friendly polar bear walking around the room, and the person will "see" it. Note that the careful hypnotist is sure to specify a *friendly* polar bear to avoid frightening the subject.

SELF-AWARENESS Awareness in hypnosis may readily be focused on various external or internal processes. For example, subjects may feel able to become hyperaware of their internal bodily processes. Even more interesting, many processes that are ordinarily in the subject's awareness may become dissociated. Thus a subject may be told that his arm will keep moving around in circles without his awareness, and it will do so. A subject may be told that she is going completely blind, but that when the hypnotist makes a certain hand gesture the blindness will cease. The subject will report being completely blind and act appropriately, yet when

the hypnotist makes a certain hand gesture the "blindness" disappears. "Seeing" the gesture takes place outside of conscious awareness.

Awareness can be curiously split in hypnosis, as is demonstrated in a technique called the *hidden observer,* developed by Ernest Hilgard at Stanford University. A deeply hypnotized subject is told that there is some part of the mind that is always fully aware of exactly what is happening in the situation and of what he, the subject, is experiencing, and this hidden observer can report by talking in response to special cues. A subject might then be told, for example, that his arm is numb and have it placed in ice water for several minutes. This *cold pressor* test is very painful, especially if the ice water is kept circulating. The hypnotized subject will report that he feels little or no pain, and he will behave like a relaxed, pain-free person. The hidden observer, on the other hand, will report that the pain is agonizing!

EMOTION   In neutral hypnosis there are generally no emotional feelings at all. Emotions can be totally structured by suggestion; any particular emotion can be elicited at any intensity and in conjunction with any stimulus object. The stimuli can be entirely inappropriate. For example, the subject may be told, "You are about to hear an extremely funny joke"; the hypnotist then tells the person, "Pine needles are green," and the subject laughs uproariously.

The hypnotic state may allow a psychotherapist access to processes that are normally unconscious. By suggesting emotional dulling, for example, the hypnotherapist might then be able to have the patient recall and work with memories that are ordinarily too painful to deal with. Thus, hypnosis can be a useful adjunct to psychotherapy. Often when a subject is told to have a dream while in hypnosis, he or she reports material similar to that experienced in ordinary nocturnal dreams, and thus the subject's subconscious processes can be detected.

MEMORY   Memory function can be drastically altered in hypnosis. If told they cannot remember certain things, responsive subjects cannot consciously do so. They may be told that after awakening from the hypnotic state they will not be able to remember anything that went on. Or they may be told that they can remember certain parts of the hypnotic experience and not other parts. Alternatively, subjects may be told that their memory is exceptionally good for some sorts of events, and they may sometimes exhibit better memory than usual. The exact nature and size of these effects on memory are still under study. But we can say that, unfortunately, the popular myth that a student could be hypnotized and then learn exam material with little work is not true!

IDENTITY AND REGRESSION   A subject's sense of identity can be radically altered in hypnosis. It may be suggested that he or she will act like a different person, and the individual will do so. Secondary personalities, completely different from the subject's ordinary personality, have been created experimentally in the laboratory. Such secondary personalities may or may not be aware of the activities of the primary personality. Little research has been done on the creation of secondary personalities, however, because of very real dangers to the normal personality.

One interesting phenomenon of hypnosis is a talented subject's ability to **regress** to an earlier period in life. If a young man is told that he is only 5 years old, he will feel and act, in many cases, as he recalls himself to have been when he was 5. All memories of

events subsequent to that age will be temporarily unavailable to consciousness. Experts are still undecided whether a regressed subject can generally recall events of that time which are normally inaccessible to consciousness, but this seems to be possible at times. Experientially, the regressed subject *feels* as if he is 5.

Sometimes hypnotized subjects have been told to regress back to before they were conceived, to a past life or previous incarnation. A fair number of responsive hypnotic subjects will then claim to recall a past life and will tell the hypnotist all about it. This may often be a psychologically meaningful experience to the subject, but its objective truthfulness is not determined by how much the subject is impressed. In most cases of past life regression the subject gives no verifiable details of the past life that he or she could not ordinarily have known. Because reincarnation is not a generally accepted belief in Western society, it is reasonable to treat such past life recall as an interesting fantasy. In a very few cases the subject has given evidential detail. Even in these cases, however, it is not always possible to rule out normal channels of information—for example, the subject may have read a book about some historical personality but be unable consciously to recall having read it. Thus there is currently no strong scientific proof for reincarnation, although the topic deserves further research.

PERFORMANCE   The popular notion that a hypnotized subject looks rather like a zombie is partially correct; many hypnotized subjects *do* act like zombies at first because they think that is how they are *supposed* to act. What the subject expects to happen is crucial in determining what does happen. A hypnotized subject can act perfectly normal when it is suggested he or she do so, and it is frequently impossible for even an experienced hypnotist to tell whether a subject is hypnotized or not under these conditions. Thus motor functioning can be perfectly normal under hypnosis. There is some evidence that a subject may be somewhat stronger or more skillful in the hypnotic state. We have already mentioned that various kinds of motor acts can be done without conscious awareness of them, a phenomenon called *automatism*. One example is *automatic writing*. The hypnotized subject is given a pencil and paper and told that the hand will begin to write messages of one sort or another, without his or her having any idea of what the hand is doing. A talented subject may converse with someone else during this procedure and be greatly surprised by what he or she reads later.

It should be noted, however, that laboratory studies of hypnosis, done chiefly by T. X. Barber, have shown that many phenomena, which when elicited under hypnosis appear to be quite astounding, can actually be elicited readily *without* inducing hypnosis. This evidence has led Barber and others to attribute all hypnotic phenomena to motivational and social-psychological variables and to conclude that there is no unique state called hypnosis that is qualitatively different from wakefulness.

The typical experiment by Barber involves two basic groups of subjects. One group is administered a hypnotic-induction treatment, and the second group is highly motivated by the experimenter's instructions but is not hypnotized, as defined operationally by the fact that the subjects are not read the hypnotic-induction procedure. The basic finding is that many of the acts accomplished by the hypnosis group can also be accomplished by subjects in the motivated control group, such as lying stretched between two chairs, supported only by the head and ankles. Barber uses such experiments to argue that hypnosis is not a real phenomenon. Therefore, he always puts quotation marks around the word "hypnosis."

Critics have countered that Barber's results are misleading, particularly to those who have never worked with hypnosis and do not understand hypnotic behavior. They feel that defining hypnosis as reading a set of hypnotic instructions is misleading, because many subjects in the hypnosis group do not respond and thus cannot be fairly described as being hypnotized. In the control group some highly suggestible subjects might actually become hypnotized by the instructions for performing—they are so highly motivated that self-hypnosis might be induced. Furthermore, control subjects are often led to believe that everyone can perform these feats, and they might feel so compelled to perform that they would fake some of their responses.

Barber has responded to his critics' arguments, and the debate continues. It does seem clear, however, that the human mind and body are capable of doing some very strange things, with and without hypnosis, and that explanations of hypnotic phenomena will not require the invocation of mystical or magical powers on the part of the hypnotist or the subject.

Posthypnotic Effects

A particularly interesting aspect of hypnosis is what are called *posthypnotic effects*. During hypnosis the subject is told that such and such a hypnotic phenomenon will happen later, after he or she is back in normal waking consciousness. For example, the subject may be told that 15 minutes after awakening he will become extremely thirsty and need to get a glass of water. About 15 minutes later the subject does become thirsty, but he does not remember that his thirst is the result of posthypnotic suggestion. Subjects will often rationalize posthypnotic behavior even when it is very bizarre.

Uses and Dangers

Hypnosis can serve many important functions if properly used. In addition to being an experimental tool in psychology, hypnosis has important medical and psychiatric uses. As we mentioned, hypnosis was widely used as an analgesic in surgery before chemical anesthetics were available, and it is still used frequently today when chemical anesthetics are inadvisable. Hypnotic suggestions can also relieve tensions and sometimes speed the healing processes of wounds. Many special uses of hypnosis have also been developed in psychotherapy, most recently combining it with behavior modification. Indeed, practically every branch of medicine has found applications of hypnosis.

On the other hand, hypnosis can be dangerous if misused. The dangers stem from two main factors. First, many mentally ill people expect hypnotists to provide them with a magic cure, and, because of the power of hypnosis to restructure experience, they can accidentally be led into experiences that could make them worse. The second factor is that hypnosis techniques are easy to learn. People who do not have training in psychology or medicine can easily begin to practice hypnosis out of a desire to control others (sometimes rationalized as a desire to help others). A combination of these two factors can seriously upset some people. You should, of course, avoid offering yourself as a subject to improperly trained hypnotists.

DRUGS

Alcohol Intoxication

Alcohol, in the form of wine, beer, or distilled liquors, is probably the most widely known and used drug in the world. Records of its use go back to the dawn of civilization. Attitudes toward it in various cultures have ranged from acceptance to glorification to total rejection. Cultural attitudes can apparently also affect what we think of as the basic "physiological" effects of drinking alcohol. In some cultures, for example, hangovers are almost unknown in spite of heavy drinking.

Given the extent of use, alcohol intoxication is rather underresearched. There is a large literature on the effects of alcohol, but much of it seems intended to prove that "demon rum" is the devil's tool or that "a few drinks never hurt anybody." Given the ambivalent attitude toward alcohol in our own culture, this is understandable.

Not all drinking, of course, leads to an altered SoC. Degree of intoxication and the effects on behavior and functioning correlate with the concentration of alcohol in the blood (see Table D–1). With low levels of alcohol in the blood we can pretty much talk about effects on ordinary consciousness, but once the level rises to 0.01 percent or higher, we may begin to speak of drunkenness as a distinct SoC.

Psychological Effects

PERCEPTION AND SELF-AWARENESS At low levels of intoxication there actually may be a slight increase in auditory acuity. Pleasant feelings, such as warmth,

TABLE D-1 Effects of Alcohol Intoxication

Alcohol Concentration in Blood	Experiential and Behavioral Effects	Amounts of Common Beverages*
.50%	Death likely.	
.30%	Stupor likely.	1 pint whiskey
.15%	Intoxication noticeable to observers: clumsiness, unsteadiness in walking. Reduction of anxiety, fears. Impairment of mental functioning. Feelings of personal power. State-dependent memory (see Chapter 5).	5 cocktails, 28 ounces wine, or 10 bottles beer
.12%	Impairment of fine coordination, some unsteadiness in walking or standing. Feelings of social and personal power.	4 cocktails, 22 ounces wine, or 8 bottles beer
.10%	Legally defined as impaired driving in California.	
.09%	Amplified emotions, lowering of inhibitions.	3 cocktails, 1 pint wine, or 6 bottles beer
.06%	Relaxation, warmth, feeling "high," some impairment of motor acts that require a high degree of skill.	2 cocktails, 11 ounces wine, or 4 bottles beer
.03%	No obvious behavioral effects.	1 cocktail, 5½ ounces wine, or 2 bottles beer

* The alcohol concentrations in the blood for the shown quantities of beverages are based on 150 pounds of body weight. Concentrations would be higher for the same amount of beverage consumed by a lighter person and vice versa. A cocktail is specified as containing 1½ ounces of distilled liquor (whiskey, etc.). Wine refers to ordinary table wine, not fortified (dessert) wine.

may dominate perception of the body. At higher levels of intoxication sensory impairment occurs, such that a drunk person may not be able to read or otherwise perform fine visual discriminations. At very high levels the intoxicated person begins to see double. Nausea and vomiting may occur at very high levels, with a hangover the following day.

The primary effect of alcohol on self-awareness is extremely unfortunate; it tends to produce feelings of increased competence and ability rather than a realistic perception of the impairments of mental and motor functioning that occur. Such an effect is responsible for the difficulty one has in convincing a drunk that he or she is incapable of driving and for the death and destruction that the drunk driver produces.

EMOTIONS Alcohol intoxication has long been known for its effects on emotions. The relaxation and lowering of inhibitions that accompany drinking have often been cited as a plus for successful parties, allowing people to feel sociable and interact more freely. It has been found that reduction of existing anxiety does not occur until rather high levels of intoxication and that a major effect of alcohol is to induce fantasies of *power* in users. At lower levels of intoxication these tend to be feelings of "socialized power," that is, of being able to do things to save the world and the like, but at higher levels they become fantasies of purely personal power. Thus a good

deal of the aggressiveness that can result from drunkenness is understandable.

Alcohol is also widely touted as reducing sexual inhibitions, but there is some question as to how much of this (as well as other behaviors characteristic of alcohol intoxication) is actually a direct effect or simply a culturally mediated effect. That is, looser standards of conduct are applied to people defined as "drunk," and they are allowed to do things that normally they would be censured for.

Dangers

Drunken persons' feelings of confidence and ability along with their serious loss of competence make them particularly dangerous when driving. They feel they are *better* drivers than usual and so may drive faster and more recklessly than they ordinarily would. As with other SoCs, there are very wide individual differences. Highly overlearned motor actions are somewhat less vulnerable to the effects of alcohol than recently learned ones. Some people have learned to distrust feelings of increased competence and thus handle their alcohol more adequately, but most do not.

Despite its wide social use, it is clear that alcohol and the state produced by it can be very dangerous, even if we disregard the danger of the drinker becoming an alcoholic. The effects of alcohol in small quantities are not of great consequence. But when large quantities of

TABLE D–2   Factors Involved in Maximizing the Probability of a Good or Bad Trip

	Variables	Good Trip Likely	Bad Trip Likely
Drug	Quality	Pure, known	Unknown drug or unknown degree of (harmful) adulterants
	Quantity	Known accurately, adjusted to individual's desire	Unknown, beyond individual's control
Long-term factors	Culture	Acceptance, belief in benefits	Rejection, belief in detrimental effects
	Personality	Stable, open, secure	Unstable, rigid, neurotic or psychotic
	Physiology	Healthy	Specific adverse vulnerability to drug
	Learned drug skills	Wide experience gained under supportive conditions	Little or no experience, preparation; unpleasant past experience
Immediate user factors	Mood	Happy, calm, relaxed, or euphoric	Depressed, overexcited, repressing significant emotions
	Expectations	Pleasure, insight, known factors and eventualities	Danger, harm, manipulation, unknown eventualities
	Desires	General pleasure, specific user-accepted goals	Aimlessness (repressed), desires to harm or degrade self for secondary gains
Experiment or situation	Physical setting	Pleasant and esthetically interesting by user's standards	Cold, impersonal, "medical," "psychiatric," "hospital," "scientific"
	Social events	Friendly, nonmanipulative interactions overall	Depersonalization or manipulation of the user, hostility overall
	Formal instructions	Clear, understandable, creating trust and purpose	Ambiguous, deliberate lies, creation of mistrust
	Implicit demands	Congruent with explicit communications, supportive	Contradict explicit communications and/or reinforce other negative variables

alcohol are consumed and/or when alcoholism has developed, the effects constitute one of our greatest social problems (see Chapter 11 for a discussion of alcoholism).

Marijuana Intoxication

Marijuana is the name given to preparations of the flowering tops or leaves of the Indian hemp plant, *Cannabis sativa*. Slang terms for marijuana include pot, grass, shit, dope, maryjane, and hemp. Marijuana has been known as an intoxicant for thousands of years, but research into its effects has only recently begun. For example, the major active ingredient of marijuana, tetrahydrocannabinol (THC), was identified and subsequently synthesized only in the last decade. Despite the sometimes severe legal penalties for possession or sale of marijuana, which still exist in many states, a 1977 Gallup poll estimated that at least 36 million Americans have tried marijuana, and about 15 million Americans were regular users of it. About 50 percent of college students have tried the drug.

In looking at marijuana intoxication as an SoC, we must remember that the particular effects achieved at any time are greatly determined by psychological factors in addition to the pharmacological effects of the drug itself. Indeed, aside from quality and quantity of

the drug ingested, almost all other factors influencing the quality of the induced SoC—the "trip"—are psychological. These include the user's personality, expectations, mood, and desires (see Table D–2). Other nondrug factors include the physical setting and the user's physical state. We can think of marijuana intoxication or psychedelic experiences as producing two kinds of effects. The first might be called a *pure drug effect*, almost inevitably resulting from the chemical action of the drug on the human nervous system. The second is what we might call *potential effects*. The chemical action of the drug on the human nervous system creates the potential for certain kinds of experiences *if* various nondrug, psychological factors take on the appropriate values. The potential effects immensely outnumber the pure drug effects for marijuana. Taking these factors into account, we will describe the most common *experiential* characteristics of marijuana intoxication as it occurs in present-day college-educated users under ordinary social circumstances.

Psychological Effects

PERCEPTION   Marijuana intoxication has a marked effect on perceptual processes such that intoxicated persons generally feel that their perception is enhanced, that they are closer to the real, true qualities of perceptions they receive. The effects are usually very pleasing. The person may perceive new qualities in sound, taste, and touch; may get more enjoyment from eating; understand the words of songs better; find the sense of touch becoming more sensual; find new and pleasurable qualities in sexual orgasm; and be able to see patterns in visual material that is ordinarily ambiguous. New internal bodily sensations are also frequently available, and generally the intoxicated user's awareness is captivated and pleased by these interesting and pleasurable sensory enhancements. There is no evidence to date indicating an actual lowering of the threshold for any sense receptors, so these effects may be primarily a matter of how incoming stimuli are processed. The marijuana user feels that there is *less* processing; he or she feels in touch with the raw sensory data rather than with an abstract representation of it.

EMOTIONS   Experienced users of marijuana almost invariably feel good when intoxicated, but they usually find both pleasant and unpleasant emotions considerably amplified. Naive users trying marijuana may find the experience stressful and have very unpleasant emotions. Although no exact figures can be obtained, given the illegality of marijuana, rough estimates indicate that somewhere between 5 and 10 percent of people trying it have an initial bad reaction and do not go on. Even experienced users occasionally have a bad emotional reaction, particularly if they are trying to escape from unpleasant emotions by using marijuana.

COGNITIVE PROCESSES   Cognitive processes can change radically during intoxication. The user may feel that his or her thoughts are more intuitive, less bound by ordinary logic. Usually the person feels in very good control of his or her thought processes, except at very high levels of intoxication. Characteristic experiences include the ability to turn off the effects of intoxication at will if necessary, feeling more childlike and open to experience, finding it difficult to read, having feelings of psychological insights about others and about oneself, giving little thought to the future and feeling more in the here and now, appreciating very subtle humor, and being more accepting of contradictions.

MEMORY   Marijuana intoxication produces both state-dependent memory and some overall loss of memory functioning. A characteristic effect is that the span of memory may be shortened, so the user forgets the start of a conversation, although he or she may feel able to compensate for this with special effort. Memories may come back as images in various sensory modalities rather than as abstract thought. At very high levels of intoxication even the start of a sentence may be forgotten. This shortened memory span probably explains why performance on difficult tasks that require one to remember previous steps is impaired by marijuana intoxication.

IDENTITY   One's sense of identity can change radically with marijuana. Being more childlike and open to experience has already been mentioned; this may be described as perceiving stimuli more as they are instead of as they are *valued* by the ordinary ego. Other characteristic effects are being more accepting of events, feeling less need to control them, finding it hard to play ordinary social games, and having spontaneous insights about oneself.

TIME SENSE   Time usually seems to pass more slowly for the intoxicated, although occasionally the user feels that time passes more rapidly. A sense of being more in the present, more in the here and now, is also characteristic.

PERFORMANCE   Marijuana intoxication makes experienced users feel relaxed and disinclined to move about. They also report being quieter than they are in their normal state or in a state of alcohol intoxication. If they do move about, though, they usually feel very coordinated and smooth. Laboratory studies have generally found that most motor tasks are not affected by marijuana intoxication in *experienced* users, although the probability of some impairment increases with the complexity of the skill required. Naive users sometimes experience great difficulty in performing simple tasks.

Uses and Dangers

Proponents of marijuana use claim many benefits: relaxation, relief of tension, greatly enhanced sense of beauty, important psychological insights into oneself, and, sometimes, important spiritual or religious experiences. Some data collected suggest that marijuana may have value in the treatment of certain medical conditions such as high blood pressure, glaucoma, and migraine headaches. The primary proven dangers of marijuana intoxication are the adverse effects of being in jail.

The long-term effects of marijuana are still largely unknown. There is, however, no evidence that the psychological or physical effects of marijuana lead users to try more dangerous drugs, nor does any kind of addiction develop. Whether from ignorance or a desire to curb marijuana use, authorities in the past called marijuana "addicting" and today refer to it as producing "psychological dependence." Actually, the term *psychological dependence* refers to the fact that drug withdrawal produces psychological discomfort, mainly anxiety, as opposed to the real physical illness in physical addiction. Other authorities believe that psychological dependence is a meaningless concept, because in operation it simply means that people repeat behavior they find enjoyable.

Although any drug can be abused, the evidence does not suggest that marijuana is particularly dangerous in this respect. The most recent national commission on marijuana use has realized that there is a great deal of misinformation about the alleged dangers of marijuana and has recommended that private use of the drug should not be considered a crime. Certainly marijuana is no *more* dangerous than alcohol. The fact that alcohol is legally available in most places, while there are often severe penalties for marijuana use and sale, makes it appear as if we have drastically overestimated the potential dangers of pot.

The Psychedelic Experience

The term *psychedelic* is now generally applied to any drug whose primary effect is to induce an altered SoC, including LSD (lysergic acid diethylamide), mescaline (the active ingredient of peyote cactus), psilocybin, and a large number of other drugs occurring naturally in plants. Knowledge of the effects of LSD and similar psychedelics comes from several sources: the personal experiences of at least a million Americans, a large number of artistic creations (popularly known as psychedelic art) that attempt to express aspects of the experience in a nonverbal way, and finally the more than one thousand laboratory studies of this class of drugs.

Psychological factors are even more significant in the experience of psychedelics such as LSD than in marijuana intoxication. Indeed, such an immense range of variability is seen in psychedelic states that we may be dealing with many transient SoCs triggered by the drug rather than with any single uniform state. Unfortunately, many laboratory studies have been conducted under the set of psychological conditions indicated in Table D–2 that tend to maximize the probability of a "bad trip." Thus LSD was considered a *psychotomimetic* (mimicking a psychosis) drug when it was first studied. It is now clear, however, that an exceptionally wide range of experiences can be produced depending on the personality factors and the setting. Just about every effect reported for other states of consciousness has been reported at one time or another for LSD experiences.

Profundity of Experience

Certain regularities in what we might consider the profundity of the psychedelic experience have been noted by two of the leading investigators in this area, R. E. L. Masters and Jean Houston. They distinguish four levels of psychedelic experience. The first they call the *Sensory* level, in which the subject's primary experience is that of marvelous and beautiful sensory changes. Colors take on vibrant new values, rainbows may form in the air, commonplace objects become magnificent works of art, and so forth. The second and more profound level is called the *Recollective-Analytic*. Here the subject experiences very strong emotions related to his or her own personal history and, with proper guidance, may have very important therapeutic experiences, resolving personal conflicts. Without competent guidance, most subjects' experiences stay at the Sensory or Recollective-Analytic levels.

The third level of profundity is called the *Symbolic*, and here the images and hallucinations the subject experiences deal with the general history of human beings, animal evolution, rituals of passage, and so forth. If dealt with successfully, usually after successful resolution of problems at the Recollective-Analytic level, the person working at the Symbolic level can have important insights and experiences dealing with the nature of being human.

The most profound level, seldom reached, is called the *Integral* level. Experiences at this level are religious and mystical, often dealing with a confrontation with God. The individual may experience the death of his or her own ego, a union with God, and being reborn. The feeling is profoundly religious and cannot be adequately dealt with in verbal terms. Because of the experiences at the Integral level, some people have proposed that LSD be made legal for supervised religious use.

Uses and Dangers

A number of research studies have shown that LSD and other psychedelics can be used profitably in psychotherapy, and two major psychotherapeutic applications have been developed. The first, called *psycholytic therapy*, uses small doses of LSD in the course of regular psychotherapeutic work. The drug loosens associations, bypasses some defenses, and purportedly enables the analysis to proceed much faster. With prolonged therapy occasional clients begin to deal with material on the Symbolic or Integral level.

The second major therapeutic use of LSD is called *psychedelic therapy*, in which very large doses and single guided sessions are used to give the patient an overwhelming experience at the Symbolic or Integral level. The theory is that by contacting these extremely deep sources within oneself, a new sense of strength can develop, and many ordinary neurotic problems can be successfully transcended or overcome. Psychedelic therapy has also been successfully used with people suffering "existential neurosis" (that is, suffering from a sense of loss of meaning of life) even though they are otherwise successful members of society.

Considering the immense psychological power of psychedelic drugs, there are real dangers in the SoC produced. Subjects with neurotic or psychotic personality structures, or ordinary subjects who are not prepared for the drug experience, may have extremely bad reactions—sometimes, although rarely, leading to a psychosis. People who buy LSD through black market sources today also risk being poisoned by the many impurities that analyses have shown to be in black market drugs. For example, a wide variety of street drugs sold as mescaline, psilocybin, or THC (the active ingredient in marijuana) actually contain none of these substances. Often they consist either of inert ingredients or LSD, with various degrees of adulteration by highly dangerous substances like strychnine or amphetamines.

Another danger is the amateur therapist, a person

Tyrannical King Coke

The dinner party on Manhattan's fashionable East Side included all the chic refreshments. It began with perfectly mixed martinis, followed by a fine vintage French wine with the main course. With dessert, guests puffed the finest marijuana. Then, after coffee and cognac, the young hostess presented the evening's *pièce de résistance:* a glass jar filled with a white powder. "Would anybody like a hit of coke?" she inquired casually, as if offering another drink. Indeed they would. Recalls one of the guests: "I was so wrecked by the time I left that I could barely find my way to the next party. But when I got there, wow! I was really on top of it."

Not for long, of course. When a usual dose (one snort into each nostril) of cocaine wears off in about an hour, the user may have a hangover of depression. There are medical and legal hazards as well; possession of cocaine is a felony. These grim facts have not stopped some enclaves of the bored and beautiful set from making the inhaling of coke a status cult. Since cocaine for a dozen people can cost as much as $600, depending on the quality and scarcity of the drug, the hostess of that recent East Side party was showing her friends that she really cared.

Trying to keep up with ostensible trend setters, bankers, lawyers, doctors and would-be socialites have also taken to snorting coke (also called snow, freeze, flake, lady). The habit was in vogue decades ago, then fell out of style except among pop musicians, some other show-business types and the more prosperous prostitutes and procurers. Yet a recent Government study concluded that the use of coke is now more widespread than of heroin. The same survey estimated that 4.8 million Americans have sampled the drug. . . .

Medical authorities disagree over whether cocaine is physically addictive. But there is no question that steady users can become psychologically tied to the drug and have a difficult time functioning normally when they try to give it up. . . . Because the drug has a relatively short effect, cokeheads tend to keep going back for more. . . .

A frequent side effect of heavy use is bleeding from the nose, a result of injury to nasal membranes. Snow can also cause hyperactivity and damage to the nervous system. Many long-term users have suffered psychotic symptoms, such as imagining insects crawling under their skin. Still, snorting cocaine is not as bad as injecting it into a vein; a mainlined overdose can literally freeze respiration and stop the heart—permanently. Considering these hazards, the king of drugs, as cocaine is often called, is something of a tyrant. . . .

Time
April 16, 1973

who has only a little psychological knowledge and wants to cure people's hangups by giving them LSD. It is quite possible to get people into experiences that they are unprepared for and that contribute to further psychopathology instead of curing. The situation in which psychedelic drugs are taken is important too; unexpected interruptions, ugly surroundings, or being arrested can lead the user into extremely unpleasant, sometimes hellish experiences.

Although controlled studies of therapy have shown that the proper use of LSD (at *infrequent* intervals, under *trained* guidance, with lots of time devoted to *assimilating* the insights) can be valuable for personal and therapeutic growth, the frequent use of LSD generally seems to nullify any actual growth benefits and, instead, is likely to produce someone who talks about his or her great experiences but is otherwise a poorly adjusted, ineffective individual.

A good deal of propaganda about the dangers of LSD is false. First, LSD does not automatically make people go crazy. Indeed, experts have been surprised at the infrequency of psychotic breaks, given not only the impurities of the drugs generally used by individuals on their own, but even more important the uncontrolled and often poor psychological condition associated with illegal drug use. Second, experience with a psychedelic drug does not automatically lead to people "dropping out." In spite of their illegality, psychedelic drugs are used (not openly, of course) by many professional people occupying high-status positions in society. Third, there is no solid evidence that LSD causes chromosomal damage. It should be noted, however, that this statement applies to the use of pure LSD; it is not known what effects the impurities in "street" drugs might have. Finally, although the belief that using LSD during pregnancy causes birth defects has not been clearly substantiated, most physicians suggest that it is probably not a good idea for a pregnant woman to take the drug because of its exceptionally powerful psychological effects.

TABLE D–3 Some Results of Drug Abuse (X = Dangers or Symptoms of Abuse; O = Symptoms of Withdrawal)

Drug	Symptoms of Abuse and Withdrawal							Some Dangers of Abuse				
	Drowsiness	Belligerence	Anxiety	Inappropriate affect	Depression	Hallucinations	Distortion of space or time	Physical dependence	Psychological dependence	Tolerance	Psychosis	Death from overdose
Morphine	X		XO	X	O	X		X	X	X		X
Heroin	X		XO	X	O			X	X	X		X
Codeine	X		XO	X	O			X	X	X		X
Methadone	X		XO	X	O			X	X	X		X
Cocaine			X	X		X			X			
Marijuana	X		X	X	X	X	X		X			
Amphetamines			X	X		X			X	X	X	X
Methamphetamine			X	X		X			X	X	X	X
Barbiturates	X	X	O	X	X	O		X	X	X		
Lysergic acid diethylamide (LSD)			X	X	X	X	X		X	X	X	
STP				X	X	X	X		X			
Peyote			X			X			X	X		
Psilocybin			X	X	X	X	X		X	X		
Dimethyltryptamine (DMT)			X	X	X	X	X		X	X		
Alcohol	X	X	X		X	X	X		X	X	X	X

This list is taken from a publication of the Bureau of Narcotic and Dangerous Drugs. Note that the only danger common to all the drugs is labeled "Psychological Dependence." Critics have argued that all this means is that you want to repeat experiences that you have enjoyed and are unhappy when you can't.

Drug Use and Drug Abuse

The use of some drugs is automatically assumed to be detrimental to the user or society, while the use of others is casually tolerated. Indeed the topic of drug use is surrounded by much emotion and prejudice. From a "neutral" point of view we might define acceptable drug *use* as a level of use that does not significantly impair the user's functioning or cause his or her actions to be harmful to others. Drug *abuse*, on the other hand, occurs when the user's functioning or health is significantly impaired or his or her actions harm others. Occasional social drinking, in small quantities, might then be considered drug use, while alcoholism or drunken driving would be abuse.

Some individuals can abuse any drug (or anything else, for that matter). Nevertheless, there exist important differences between various drugs in their *potential* for abuse. Almost no one, for example, can experiment with injections of amphetamines ("speed") without significant damage to his or her health and drastic impairment of functioning. Many people, on the other hand, can safely use alcohol or marijuana because the abuse potential of these two drugs is less than that of injected amphetamines.

Although too much emotional bias exists to allow an "objective" ranking of the danger of various drugs, experts would probably agree that the following drugs have a dangerous potential for abuse (because of immediate impairment of body functioning or neural damage, or the possibility of addiction): alcohol, amphetamines, barbiturates, cocaine, and "hard" narcotics like morphine, opium, and heroin (see Table D–3). Major psychedelics, such as LSD or mescaline, might or might not be added to the list by various experts, but all would agree that the impurities frequently found in black market psychedelics are dangerous.

Another important source of danger from drug use comes from taking more than one drug at a time. Many drugs *potentiate* each other's action in ways that are sometimes hard to predict. Amphetamines, for example, potentiate the effects of LSD. Thus an apparently innocuous mixture may be like a far larger dose of one of the drugs than a person would want to take.

TECHNIQUES OF MIND CONTROL

Meditation

Meditation is a group of mental and physical exercises designed to produce relaxation, tranquility of thought and body, and profound insight into oneself and the meaning of worldly things. Little scientific research has been done on the wide variety of known meditative techniques and their associated SoCs. Most of our knowledge comes from religious sources, particularly Oriental. The best Western psychological approach to these techniques has been made by Ornstein and Naranjo (1971), and much of this section is drawn from their excellent analysis. We shall consider some general principles concerning meditation but will not be able to treat it in any detail.

Why do people practice meditation? A common theory underlying almost all schools of meditation is that people, because of the highly selective perception induced in the course of seeking pleasure and avoiding pain, have come to live in a world of *illusion,* called *maya* (Hindu) or *samsara* (Buddhist).

The Eastern concept that we live in a world of illusion does not mean, as is often supposed, that the world is not real. The basic idea is that our perceptions of the world are grossly distorted by our personal desires and our cultural conditioning. Our sensory receptors work well, but the final percepts, the interpretations and *meanings* of what we see, are way off. The kinds of pathologies Westerners associate with obvious neuroses and psychoses are, in the Eastern view, much more widespread, and many of them are accepted as normal in a particular culture and so are seen as realistic perceptions rather than as the distortions they are.

Persons cannot attain truth or real happiness in this view because they are out of touch with the real world and themselves. Their actions, being based on distorted information, inevitably produce undesired and pathological consequences. Thus human beings are ordinarily subject to suffering. Meditation techniques are designed ultimately to put the practitioners in a more real relationship with themselves and the world. Meditation techniques are designed to eliminate the illusions constantly being produced by the human mind and, by a nonintellectual process, allowing the person to *directly* perceive truth.

We might define meditation, then, as *a special action and/or deployment of attention designed to (1) purify the ordinary SoC by removing illusions and/or (2) facilitate the eventual production of SoCs in which truth is more directly perceived.*

Techniques of Meditation

The variety of techniques that can be used for meditation is enormous. One may, for example, sit up straight in one of the classical meditation postures and simply concentrate on being aware of the natural movements of the belly in breathing. Or, as in Yoga, the meditator may focus on complex, artificial breathing exercises *(pranayama)*. *Mantras* are sound patterns that one may meditate on; some of these are considered to have special qualities in terms of their effect on the mind, and others are regarded primarily as convenient focal points.

The sound pattern may be audibly uttered, or it may be imagined in one's own mind. The ancient Indian mantra "Om mani padme hum" is well known. *Yantras* are visual patterns to meditate on. They may be as simple as a burning candle or a religious object, or as complex as diagrams symbolizing the nature of the cosmos, called *mandalas.*

Two major classes of meditation can be distinguished. One might be called *concentrative* or *restrictive meditation,* the other *opening-up* or *widening meditation.*

Concentrative Meditation

The essence of concentrative meditation is "one-pointedness" of the mind, restricting attention to one designated object for long periods. In basic Zen meditation, for example, the meditator focuses on the movement of the belly in breathing. Whenever attention wanders away from the sensation of breathing, the meditator is to gently bring it back. He or she is not to *force* attention back or strain to keep it there, because forcing actually shifts attention to distractions.

Concentrative meditation is extraordinarily difficult. The meditator often finds that he or she has become lost in flights of fancy or "important" thoughts for long periods of time and has forgotten all about meditating. Some people achieve great success with concentrative meditation in weeks or months; others spend years before they become very good at it.

What does concentrative meditation lead to? Successful practitioners insist that only part of the experience can be expressed in words, but it seems to lead to an SoC that can be characterized by words like *emptiness, clearness,* or *voidness.* All sensory input, all perception of the world, eventually ceases temporarily. Similarly, there is no internal mental activity (fantasizing, thinking, and so on) to replace it. Yet awareness remains—pure awareness, without any particular content. This state may or may not lead to other states in which the meditator feels that he or she has a direct perception of truth.

The aftereffect of reaching a state of voidness through concentrative meditation is a feeling of greatly freshened and enhanced perception of oneself and the world, a feeling that one is perceiving things directly rather than through all the selective filters affecting normal perception. Desire for objects or personal attachments is temporarily transcended following successful concentrative meditation. This transcendence and its effect on perception has been described by a Zen master, Suzuki Roshi, in the following words: "The perfect man employs his mind as a mirror, it grasps nothing, it refuses nothing, it receives but does not keep." One is supposed to perceive with absolute clarity, in much the same way a mirror reflects everything perfectly, without distortion. Some studies of the brain waves of meditating Zen monks may be interpreted as supporting this. The monks did not show the adaptation to repeated stimuli that is considered normal, and so they may have been responding to the actual stimulus *every time* instead of "classifying" it automatically as unimportant and no longer perceiving it fully.

Opening-up Meditation

The second major style of meditation, opening-up meditation, consists basically of paying *full* attention to everything that happens to one *continuously*. Usually this is found to be rather exhausting at first, and so is done only for periods of a few minutes to a half hour. No daydreaming or drifting off into comfortable thoughts is permitted. Unpleasant thoughts and experiences must also be given full attention: it is just this tendency of our ordinary SoC to drift off into fantasies about pleasing things and avoiding full awareness of unpleasant things that is the basis of the state of illusion that meditators believe characterizes ordinary consciousness. Meditators must pay complete attention to *everything* that happens to them and to their own reactions. Opening-up meditation supposedly results in greatly clarified perception of the world and oneself immediately, rather than as an aftereffect, as in concentrative meditation.

Self-remembering

A process similar to opening-up meditation has been described by other writers as *self-remembering*. The rationale for self-remembering is the belief that ordinary persons are so *identified* with events that happen to them, including their own feelings, that they are slaves to them. They exist in a kind of "waking sleep," in which events mechanically catch them up and sweep them away. Their own needs and desires have so distorted their perceptions, even of themselves, that they live in a kind of waking dream. The only freedom they have is an ability to direct a small portion of their attention. If this small amount of attention is directed toward *being aware of being aware*, it is believed that one can enter an SoC in which one is *not identified* with the events that happen, and thus one can eventually develop genuine freedom.

The technique for dissociating oneself from events requires that one split one's attention. While part of it is observing ordinary events and thoughts, another part is aware of being aware of these events. It is as if one divided oneself into an actor and an observer. The observer is not the same thing we ordinarily think of as *conscience*, which is simply another aspect of oneself that has been mechanically programmed to approve of certain acts and disapprove of others. The observer has no characteristics other than the ability to observe. It does not approve or condemn, initiate or stop, action.

The practice of self-remembering is long and arduous, and few people succeed in it. If successful, the practice is supposed to lead to such total awareness of what is actually happening in the here and now that a person ultimately develops the genuine ability to overcome the deterministic nature of his or her behavior based on upbringing and cultural biases. One develops the freedom to choose how one will react.

Physiological Correlates

The few physiological studies that have been done on meditation suggest that there may important brain wave and other physiological changes in experienced practitioners. Studies of Zen monks, practitioners of Yoga in India, and American practitioners of Transcendental Meditation have all found increased amounts of alpha brain waves, occasional slowing of alpha waves, and occasional appearance of theta waves (4 to 7 cycles per second) in some practitioners. There are also reports of lowered metabolism and heart rate and lessened physiological responsiveness to stressful stimuli. At least some of the physiological changes associated with meditation procedures, however, are probably not unique to meditation but result from the physical relaxation associated with meditating. A noted cardiologist, for example, has claimed that a relaxation procedure of simply mentally repeating the word "one" over and over to oneself is as effective as Transcendental Meditation (a mantra meditation) in producing physical relaxation. Other researchers have found that frequent, brief periods of sleep occur during meditation in many people who practice Transcendental Meditation; some of the relaxing and beneficial effects of this meditation may partially reflect the benefits of napping!

Uses and Dangers

In addition to the use of meditation in seeking valued altered SoCs and a clearer perception of truth within various philosophical and religious contexts, there is some evidence that meditation may be therapeutic or an aid to development in ordinary people. Many people practice simplified forms of meditation and report that it calms them after a long day at work and generally keeps tension from building up. Meditation as a device for erasing tension may assume increased importance as the steadily accelerating pace of our urban society imposes increasing pressures on each person. Weekend workshops for executives, designed to help them to relax and to be more effective under stress, are now a part of American life. A number of meditative techniques have been incorporated as adjuncts to psychotherapy by various investigators.

There is some danger in meditative technique. For mentally ill or poorly balanced people, various forms of meditation may put them in contact with unacceptable parts of their mind and thus precipitate emotional crises or, in some cases, a psychotic break. Also, some techniques of meditation are extremely strenuous and may cause adverse reactions in people who are otherwise in good mental and physical health. Those who use the strenuous techniques usually point out that they are quite dangerous. They are designed for people who desire higher SoCs so much that they are willing to take severe mental and physical risks.

Meditation Machines Called Ineffective and Dangerous

Susan Fogg

WASHINGTON — Danger signals about the amateur use of bio-feedback machines sold commercially as aids to meditation are coming from a neurophysiological researcher.

The long-range physical and mental effects of altering brain wave patterns through use of the bio-feedback machines are unknown and may pose dangers, warns Dr. Michael H. Chase, director of the Brain Information Service at the University of California, Los Angeles.

Dr. Chase called for strong legal controls of bio-feedback machines in an article published in the magazine Psychology Today.

The use of bio-feedback machines should be limited to licensed practitioners, Dr. Chase said, in the same way prescription drugs or medical procedures are. . . .

The FDA is challenging the manufacturers' advertising—which promises users a short cut to enlightenment by teaching them to produce alpha waves—and the labeling and effectiveness of the machines. But the FDA's authority to regulate medical devices is much more restricted than its power over new drugs—the burden of proof is on the agency to show the devices are unsafe or improperly labeled, not on the company to prove the product is safe and effective.

Dr. Chase, who researches the use of bio-feedback machines to help patients with nervous disorders control their diseases by controlling their brain patterns, said the therapy has its dangers.

"They (brain patterns) control every system in the body, every physical and psychological state and process. If we change the electrical activity in one part of the brain, we affect almost all other areas of the brain and almost all other organ systems," Dr. Chase said. . . .

Dr. Chase, in addition to challenging the safety of such self-tinkering with brain waves, questioned whether a massive output of alpha waves is really associated with "exalted states of consciousness." . . .

The Kansas City Star
June 13, 1973

Biofeedback: Electronic Zen?

There have been reports of specially trained people, such as yogis, who have shown large degrees of control over their "involuntary" bodily functions. For example, there is a yogic practice of sitting in water and voluntarily drawing water up into the lower intestine to cleanse it. Another example is the Indian yogi, Swami Rama, who thought he could stop his heart from beating. In a laboratory at the Menninger Foundation, it was shown that what he actually did was to throw his heart into *fibrillation* for 17 seconds; that is, he made it beat about 300 beats per minute for that time. At this rate the heart will not pump any blood, and so his pulse disappeared. Reports of such unusual actions have been largely ignored in Western scientific literature but are now being looked at more intensely because of the rapidly developing field of biofeedback research.

Biofeedback research centers on the finding that if instruments are used to inform a person of exactly what some part of his or her body (normally inaccessible to consciousness) is doing, the individual may find various ways of affecting it. If the electrical activity of a single muscle fiber is electronically amplified and displayed to subjects—for example, in the form of a sound whose pitch varies with the intensity of the muscle activity—many subjects can learn to totally relax that single muscle fiber or activate it even more. Similarly, if a sound or light is used to indicate when the alpha rhythm of the brain is present, many subjects can learn to increase or decrease the amount of alpha rhythm in their brain wave pattern. The essence of biofeedback techniques is that they make available to consciousness information that ordinarily is not present; and, having the information, people can try various strategies to see what affects the involuntary process.

There are two major links of research with biofeedback to SoC. The first link is that when subjects learn an *extreme* degree of control over some things, such as producing profound muscle relaxation throughout their bodies or being able to produce very high levels of alpha or theta waves, they report strong alterations in ther states of mind, over and above that necessary for control *per se*, which suggests they may be in an altered SoC. Thus biofeedback techniques may be useful for some people in *inducing* altered SoCs, although much work remains to be done before we can adequately describe what sorts of SoCs can be induced.

The second link to altered SoCs comes from the studies of physiological changes during traditional meditation practices, such as increases in the amount of alpha rhythm and some slowing of its frequency.

Biofeedback Is Helping Self-Control

Ridder News Service

MENLO PARK, Calif. — Bizarre as it may seem, a handful of people is being treated here to use just one side of the brain at a time.

The training is taking place at Stanford Research Institute (SRI), where a psychologist hopes the subjects eventually can tell him whether they really do a different kind of thinking with each cranial hemisphere.

It is a unique application of biofeedback, the highly-publicized technique of using machines to become aware of supposedly uncontrollable body activity.

A number of laboratories across the nation is verifying that people can, indeed, exert some control, once they become aware of those activities.

But even with the widespread research going on, Erik Peper, a research psychologist who splits his time between SRI and a private education project in Berkeley, Calif., is taking an unusual tack.

Many experiments have been done in which participants get instant feedback on whether they are generating "Alpha" waves, brain waves indicating a calm inactive state of consciousness.

But Peper attaches electrodes of a brain wave (EEG) machine separately to the left and right side of the head of his subjects.

Instead of one tone indicating whether the Alpha waves are present, two distinguishable tones are heard. The participant can tell which side of his or her brain is more active.

Each hemisphere tends to control one side of the body, and so the best technique for self-control is to concentrate in a relaxed way on one side of the body, Peper says.

With that sort of active attention going on, the Alpha waves controlling that side are reduced, and those for the other half of the brain increase.

"We're teaching people to control the Alpha waves so later we can ask them what's going on" as they concentrate on one side or the other, he explains.

The unusual approach may give a subject an active role in revealing whether the left side of the brain generally controls language and analytical thought processes; the right side, spatial and creative thinking, a currently accepted theory. . . .

If the technique really proves teachable, Peper sees applications for it beyond solving the research riddle he's involved with, health, for example.

Once that sense of awareness is taught, he says, a person could possibly control his or her health to a surprising degree.

Boulder (Colo.) Daily Camera
June 21, 1975

A split brain without surgery? Maybe biofeedback techniques can be used to produce a similar experience.

It would be naive to assume that the SoC Zen monks get into is *simply* a matter of increased amount and slowed frequency of the alpha rhythm. Still, if these physiological changes are one of the components of the state Zen monks get into, perhaps that component could be taught by biofeedback techniques, and thus be learned much more rapidly and efficiently than it is ordinarily learned in Zen meditation. Conceivably, biofeedback techniques can serve as technological aids to developing certain SoCs.

Although less than a decade old, biofeedback research is an important area in psychology. Popular accounts, however, have frequently exaggerated the effects of biofeedback and often made it seem that if you learned to produce lots of alpha waves you would automatically have health, wealth, and mystical power—a kind of electronic Zen! Many nonscientific groups sprung up to sell biofeedback equipment (at high prices) to the general public with the implication of such fantastic benefits. Other groups offered expensive courses in "alpha mind control" and the like and gave training of questionable value. Some of these training programs still operate, and the old rule of "Let the buyer beware" still applies. In spite of its promise, in the actual application of biofeedback we are still a long way from electronic Zen!

Glossary

Absolute threshold   Weakest stimulus a normal person in an otherwise absolutely nonstimulating environment can detect.

A-B variable   Variable describing the effectiveness of therapists with schizophrenics or neurotics. "A" therapists work best with schizophrenics, and "B" therapists work best with neurotics.

A-B-X model   Model of consistency relationships in balance theory developed by Newcomb. Persons A and B have attitudes toward X; A perceives B's attitude toward X and B perceives A's attitude toward X; both A's system and B's system will tend toward balance.

Accommodation   In vision, a process of changing lens shape or curvature so as to focus the optic array on the retina. In Piaget's theory, a change of mental structure so as to accept new information from the environment.

Achievement motivation   Need one feels to perform successfully on any task that is undertaken.

Acrophobia   Fear of heights.

Action potential   Nerve signal in the form of an electrical impulse that travels through the axon of a neuron.

Action-specific energies   According to Lorenz, motivating energies that impel only very specific sequences of behavior; motivating energy for instinctual behaviors.

Adolescence   In human beings, the period from 11 to 18 years of age.

Adrenal cortex   Outer layer of the adrenal glands; during emotional arousal it releases hormones called corticosteroids into the circulatory system.

Adrenal glands   Produce many hormones, including adrenalin (also called epinephrine). Especially important in regulating bodily responses to stress, the adrenal glands are partially controlled by the sympathetic division of the autonomic nervous system.

Adrenalin   See "epinephrine."

Adrenal medulla   Inner core of the adrenal gland, which secretes the hormones epinephrine and norepinephrine into the circulatory system.

Adrenal steroids   Hormones secreted into the circulatory system by the adrenal cortex during emotional arousal; also called "corticosteroids."

Adulthood   In human beings, the period from the late teens or early twenties to death.

Affective reactions   Category of psychotic reactions involving emotional behavior and variations in mood.

Affective state   The positive, negative, or neutral feelings one is experiencing at a given moment.

Aggression   Behavior directed toward another person that is intended to injure or harm that person.

Alcoholic   Excessive drinker whose dependence on alcohol is so strong that it interferes with his performance of socially appropriate behavior.

Alcoholism   Disorder marked by addiction to alcohol and inability to control drinking behavior.

Algorithm   Method of problem solving in which one performs a single repetitive operation until a solution is reached. Some problems can be solved only by an algorithm procedure.

Alpha waves   Particular brain wave pattern that occurs when the subject is in a state of "relaxed wakefulness." People can be taught to control the presence of alpha waves through biofeedback training.

Altered state of consciousness   State that occurs when the overall functioning of the mind takes on a pattern that is qualitatively different from normal.

Altruism   Looking after or doing things for the benefit of others.

Amnesia   Neurotic dissociative reaction that involves partial or total loss of memory about one's past identity while retaining memory of nonthreatening aspects of life.

Amphetamines   Class of drugs characterized by presence of $C_9H_{13}N$. A characteristic effect of these drugs is stimulation of the central nervous system. They are also characterized by a high potential for abuse.

Androgyny   A perspective which asserts that, biologically, all human beings have both masculine and feminine characteristics. An androgynous person can adopt either typically feminine or typically masculine behavior patterns depending on which is most adaptive at a given time.

Angiotensin   A hormone secreted by the kidneys to signal the hypothalamus of a slowing of blood flow.

Antabuse   Drug that causes intense nausea if a person drinks alcohol while the chemical is in his bloodstream.

Antecedent-consequent research   Research strategy that studies subjects of the same age to determine how different environmental conditions affect performance.

Antidepressants   Drugs that elevate moods and counteract depression.

Antidiuretic hormone (ADH)   A hormone secreted by the pituitary gland that inhibits urine formation in the kidneys.

Antipsychotics   Drugs that calm and increase the lucidity of psychotics.

Antisocial character   Person who is pleasure oriented (hedonistic) and indifferent to the needs or concerns of others; person who exploits others for his own selfish ends and does not feel guilt or anxiety except when it is clear that he may be prevented from satisfying his need for pleasure.

Anxiety   Experience of fear in the absence of, or disproportionate to, the objective danger.

Anxiety reaction   Neurotic episode in which a person has repressed the cause of his anxiety but not the anxiety itself—a situation where he feels anxious without knowing why.

Aphagia   Condition in which an animal refuses to eat, ignores food, and starves to death unless treated. Aphagia has been produced experimentally by surgical removal of the lateral hypothalamic nucleus.

Aphasia   Loss or impairment of one's ability to use language, usually resulting from brain damage.

Aquaphobia   Fear of water.

Archetypes   Jungian concept referring to the basic elements that form the foundation for the collective unconscious and that often show up symbolically in dreams.

Arousal (activation) theory   In motivation and emotion, a theory postulating a general continuum of physiological arousal, governed by the central nervous system and varying from extremely low arousal (coma and sleep) to extremely high arousal (panic and euphoria). Variations in arousal level are thought to underlie the intensity quality of motivation and emotion.

Assimilation   In Piaget's theory, changing characteristics of new information so that it can be accepted into existing mental structures.

Associated specificity   Theory of psychosomatic illness stating that through learned mediation or accidental conditioning an association between a physiological response and an emotion, thought, or idea may become established.

Association cortex   Largest portion of the cerebral hemispheres, most highly developed in human beings. The more complex functions like perception, language, and thought are centered here.

Astral projection   See "out-of-body experience (OOBE)."

Atmosphere effect   A term referring to errors made in reasoning that are the result of the atmosphere surrounding the problem, namely, the subject's attitude or the way the problem is presented. Affirmative premises tend to create an affirmative atmosphere and, thus, imply an affirmative conclusion.

Attitude   Combination of feelings, beliefs, and tendencies to act in particular ways directed toward persons, objects, or events.

Attribution theory   A theory about the bases on which we form our ideas of other people's behavior by attributing or inferring underlying causes that make the behavior rational.

Authoritarian personality   Personality type characterized by, among other traits, high ethnocentrism, conservatism, antidemocratism, and prejudice.

Autonomic nervous system   Part of the peripheral nervous system, it contains neurons that connect to glands, smooth muscles, and the heart, and it is central to emotional behavior.

Autonomy   Sense of independence, of being an individual separate from other people.

Autoshaping   Development of a learned response under circumstances in which there is no contingency between the response and the delivery of reinforcement.

Axon   A relatively long structure extending from the cell body of a neuron, it sends messages to other cells.

Balance theory   Theory of consistency in social behavior stating that objects perceived as belonging together will have the same dynamic quality—they will be either all liked or all disliked.

Basal age   In the Binet intelligence test, the highest age level at which a subject passes all items. Used in computation of mental age.

Basal ganglia   A group of nuclei within the cerebral hemispheres that are important in the control of movement.

Basilar membrane   A flexible membrane within the inner ear or cochlea that vibrates in response to sounds in the environment.

Behavioral model   Model of psychopathology in which all behavior, normal or otherwise, is a product of learning about the environment.

Behavioral symptoms   Classes of behaviors that are indicative of underlying psychopathology.

Behaviorism   Strong American school of psychology that viewed psychology as the study of observable, objectively measurable behavior and the way in which stimulus-response relationships are formed; the objective of psychology is to predict what responses will be evoked by what stimuli.

Behavior modification   Applying the principles of learning to achieve changes in behavior. See "behavior therapy."

Behavior therapy   Type of psychotherapy that emphasizes change in motivation, skills, and performance.

Belief prejudice   See "stereotyping."

Binet test   See "Stanford-Binet Test."

Binocular disparity   Difference in optic arrays reaching each eye caused by the slightly different location of the two eyes; powerful clue for depth.

Biofeedback A technique used to teach organisms to control "involuntary" functions like blood pressure and brain waves, it involves giving the subject immediate feedback, or knowledge, of the results of bodily changes as soon as they occur.

Bipolar cells Neuron in the retina connecting rods or cones to ganglion cells.

Birth-order effects Various consistencies in personality that seem to be tied to whether a person was the first-born child in his family, the second-born, etc.

Blind spot Point in the retina, containing no receptor cells, at which the optic nerve leaves the eye.

Brainstorming Procedure used in generating new and creative ideas. Subject is encouraged to suggest any idea that has not been suggested before and might work. Evaluation of ideas is delayed until after as many suggestions as possible are made.

Brightness Psychological sensation corresponding to the physical property of intensity of light stimulation, see "intensity."

Brightness constancy Observation that objects maintain their brightness even though the amount of light reflected from them changes.

Case study Simplest and most direct type of psychological investigation; in-depth examination of a single person to find out about a certain problem, question, or issue.

Catatonic schizophrenia Subtype of schizophrenia characterized by a waxy flexibility of body and limbs, loss of motion, and a tendency to remain motionless for hours or days. See "schizophrenia."

Catecholamines Epinephrine and norepinephrine, the chemical transmitter substances in the adrenergic division of the nervous system.

Cell body The soma; the central part of a neuron, which is responsible for carrying out the cell's life processes.

Central nervous system (CNS) Includes the brain and the spinal cord and is contained within the skull and spinal column. It is the integrating center for all bodily functions and behavior.

Cerebellum Portion of the brain that controls balance, muscle tone, and motor coordination in general.

Cerebral cortex The outermost layer of the cerebral hemispheres, it contains motor, sensory, and association areas.

Cerebral hemispheres The largest parts of the brain in human beings and other higher mammals, they are the seat of the more complex functions like language, numerical ability, and abstract thought, in addition to being responsible for sensation, some aspects of bodily movement, and many other functions.

Chaining Type of instrumental conditioning whereby one learns to exhibit a series of behaviors in order to obtain reinforcement.

Character disorder See "personality disorder."

Chemical transmitter substances Chemicals that are released from the terminals of a neuron when that cell has carried a nerve impulse. The chemicals then travel to the soma or dendrites of a second, connecting neuron and may excite or inhibit activity in the second cell.

Chemotherapy Use of drugs as treatment for psychopathology.

Childhood In human beings, the period from 2 to 11 years of age.

Chromosome A structure composed of many genes found in the nucleus of cells, it contains the hereditary information of organisms. The normal human being has 23 pairs of chromosomes.

Chronological age Actual age, in years and months, of a person; used in computation of IQ.

Chunk A unit of immediate memory that may contain many bits of information.

Classical conditioning Learning of a new response to a stimulus caused by pairing this stimulus with another stimulus that already elicits the response.

Claustrophobia Fear of small enclosed spaces.

Client-centered therapy Developed by Carl Rogers, this type of psychotherapy is insight oriented and focuses on the present. Emphasis is on regaining the ability to experiencing all feelings fully. Also called "nondirective" therapy.

Closure The Gestalt principle that describes a tendency for broken or irregular figures to appear smooth or closed.

Cochlea Structure in the inner ear containing fluid that vibrates with sound stimulation and auditory receptor cells that are stimulated by vibrations in the fluid.

Codability Ease with which a stimulus can be assigned a language label.

Cognitive dissonance theory Leon Festinger's consistency theory, which states that a person acts to reduce the inconsistency between two or more ideas or beliefs.

Cognitive theory Approach to personality that emphasizes the cognitive processes such as thinking and judging and is thus highly rational in its outlook.

Collective unconscious Concept proposed by Carl Jung, referring to an inherited aspect of personality that all people share owing to their common ancestry and that has accumulated over the generations.

Color blindness Inability to experience all the colors in the spectrum.

Community mental health Approach to mental health that emphasizes the prevention of mental illness and the need for broader and more effective mental health services based within communities.

Comparison level In the social exchange theory of interpersonal attraction, the standard by which persons evaluate what they feel they deserve; similar to adaptation level.

Concentrative meditation Meditation that involves "one-pointedness" of the mind, or focusing one's attention on a specific object for some period of time.

Concept Unit of knowledge; principle for systematically responding to the objects and events that make up one's circumstances. Concepts can be classes or categories of things, sequential principles, or relational principles that specify a particular arrangement of things.

Conceptual problems Problems that can be solved by recognizing or learning the concept the solution is based on, by the use of systematic strategies.

Concordance rate Probability that one of a pair of twins will show a given characteristic, given that the other twin has the characteristic.

Concrete operational period The third stage of cognitive development as proposed by Piaget; it occurs from 7 to 11 years of age; the child learns to use the logic of classification and numbers to relate and order events.

Condensation Dream process that disguises material by having one aspect of a dream (a person, object, etc.) actually represent or be a composite of several things in real life.

Conditioned response (CR) In classical conditioning, the response that occurs after training has been completed, upon presentation of the conditioned stimulus.

Conditioned stimulus (CS) In classical conditioning, the neutral stimulus that does not elicit the desired response prior to training.

Cone Photoreceptor cell shaped like a cone, located mainly in the center of the eye, not sensitive to low light intensities, responsible for color vision.

Confederates In research, collaborators of the experimenter who pose as subjects.

Conformity Adherence to the norms of the social groups to which one belongs.

Congruence Rogerian term meaning that what is experienced inside and what is expressed outwardly are consistent.

Conjunctive concept Concept in which two or more relevant attributes must be present in a stimulus for it to be a positive instance.

Connotation Characteristic of a word; how one reacts emotionally to or feels about the word.

Conscience In Freud's theory, it is part of the superego and contains the moral values, attitudes, and rules people learn from their parents and society.

Conscious In Freudian theory, the ideas, thoughts, and images that a person is aware of at any given moment.

Consciousness State of awareness generally accompanied by thoughts in human beings.

Conservation Idea that a property remains the same despite an irrelevant transformation that may change the appearance of the object.

Conservative focusing Systematic approach to solving conceptual problems in which the subject uses a positive instance of the concept as focus and then compares it with other single instances, each differing in one and only one dimension from his focus. In this way irrelevant dimensions are eliminated one at a time until only the relevant dimension remains.

Consistency principle The idea that people strive to be consistent in their behavior. As applied to attitudes, this means that attitudes held by a particular individual are mutually supportive and do not conflict with each other. Tendency to segregate liked objects from disliked objects and to structure thoughts in simple black-and-white terms.

Consolidation theory Theory that every experience sets up a circuit in the brain that must be allowed to consolidate or strengthen in order for the experience to be stored permanently in long-term memory.

Consonance In cognitive dissonance theory, the situation where one idea or belief implies another in some psychological sense.

Context effect Ability of the surroundings to affect the ease of learning, and the idea that the more similar the recall context is to the learning context, the better recall will be.

Contour In perception, sharp discontinuity of gradients; a sharp break in stimulus characteristics.

Convergent hierarchy According to mediational theory, a hierarchy of different external stimuli all of which can elicit the same response. Seen as the basis for forming concepts.

Conversion reaction Neurotic reaction in which one reduces anxiety by inactivating part of his body; person converts psychological problem into physical one that prevents him from behaving in a way that would be anxiety provoking.

Cornea Outer coating of the front of the eye.

Corpus callosum Structure that connects the two cerebral hemispheres to each other; severing the corpus callosum prevents the hemispheres from communicating with each other.

Correlational approach Research method used to discover the degree of relationship between two or more variables.

Correlation coefficient Numerical value or statistic that represents the degree of relationship between two or more values; can vary from -1 to $+1$, with 0 meaning no relationship and $+$ or -1 indicating a perfect relationship.

Corticosteroids See "adrenal steroids."

Counterconditioning Eliminating unwanted behaviors using extinction, or punishment, while simultaneously replacing them with desirable behaviors.

Cretinism A condition that results from the underproduction of thyroxin during development and that is characterized by a brain which is smaller than normal, fewer neurons, dwarfism, and mental retardation.

Crisis Point in a person's life that is unusually stressful and could be handled in a maladaptive way.

Crisis intervention   Short-term type of therapy aimed at helping people handle crises in effective ways.

Critical period   Very brief period early in life during which imprinting is possible; any limited period in development in which the organism is especially susceptible to a given developmental process.

Cross-sectional research   Research strategy that tests subjects of different ages simultaneously in order to examine the relationships between age, experience, and behavior.

Cue-dependent forgetting   Inability to remember learned information due to retrieval failure; cues present during learning are not present during recall, see "trace-dependent forgetting."

Dark adaptation   Increase in sensitivity to light resulting from the reduction or complete absence of light energy reaching the eye, attributable to changes in the level of light-sensitive pigments in receptor cells.

Decay theory   Theory that we forget things because the memory trace for them wears out over time.

Defense mechanisms   Unconscious tactics employed by the ego in order to prevent anxiety, according to Freud.

Deindividuation   Loss of one's identity in a crowd so that a person feels he cannot be singled out by others as being personally responsible for the acts of the crowd.

Delta waves   A brain wave pattern in the EEG consisting of large amplitude but slow (1 to 2 cycles per second) waves; characteristic of deeper stages of sleep.

Delusion   Unshakable idea or belief that is held in the face of contradictory evidence, simple logic, or common experience.

Dendrites   Short structures that extend from the cell body of a neuron and pick up signals from other cells.

Denial   Removal from consciousness of an external threat; a defense mechanism.

Denotation   Characteristic of a word: the specific object, concept, or "event" to which the word refers.

Deoxyribonucleic acid (DNA)   Molecules of hereditary material that direct the growth and development of every part of the body. Genes (and thus chromosomes) contain DNA.

Dependent variable   In psychological research, the variable that the psychologist measures—some characteristic of behavior or performance.

Depersonalization   Loss of personal identity; frequent symptom in schizophrenia.

Depression   Condition marked by sadness, loneliness, and dejection. In neurosis, excessive depression is usually accompanied by anxiety, feelings of worthlessness, and fatigue, although adequate contact with reality is maintained. In psychosis, profound depression is marked by loss of contact with reality.

Deprivation   Withholding of stimulation that could satisfy a need; lack of need-satisfying stimulation. Deprivation increases motivation.

Depth perception   The ability to construct an internal representation of distance and depth.

Diagnosis   Procedure and process of deciding how to classify a person, using information gained from tests, interviews, and other observations; usually used in the context of identifying psychopathology.

Diathesis   Genetic predisposition to a particular psychotic disorder.

Diathesis-stress theory   Theory of what causes schizophrenia; states that schizophrenia develops when there is a genetic predisposition (diathesis) present *and* there are environmental factors (stress) that trigger the disorder.

Discrimination   A learned distinction between two stimuli or two responses.

Discriminative stimulus   A cue. A stimulus that, by learning, has come to control a response.

Disjunctive concept   An item must have one or more relevant attributes in order to belong to the concept. If it lacks all relevant attributes, the stimulus is a negative instance.

Displacement   Rechanneling instinctual energy from an unacceptable object to one that is of neutral value to society. Also, a dream process by which material is disguised. It involves changing the affective emphasis of something in a dream so that if it is very important in real life it is seemingly unimportant in the dream, or vice versa.

Dissocial character   Individual who has no personality disorganization but rather has values that conflict with the usual mores of the society; cultural deviant.

Dissociative reaction   Neurotic defensive behavioral inactivation in which a person blocks off large parts of his memory as a way of avoiding anxiety-provoking associations.

Double-blind experiment   An experiment in which neither the subjects nor the experimenter know which treatment is being applied until the experiment is over.

Dream   Experience that occurs during the sleeping state and that involves having an awareness of scenes and events that take place in a nonphysical, imaginary world.

Dream analysis   Technique used by Freud and other analysts based on the idea that dreams are symbolic representations of our impulses and conflicts and that by understanding the symbols we can learn about ourselves.

Dream processes   Various methods used to disguise material so that when it is presented in a dream it is not too emotionally threatening.

Drive   Energy available for behavior; psychological correlate of a physical need (for example, the hunger drive results from the need for food).

Drug abuse   The use of drugs to the point where the

user's functioning or health is significantly impaired or his actions harm others.

Dynamic model   Model of psychopathology in which abnormal behavior reflects a "dynamic" battle or conflict between parts or aspects of a person's personality rather than any physical or organic deficiencies.

Eclectic   In psychology, a psychologist who uses the theories and techniques of several approaches or models, rather than specializing in one.

Ego   One of the basic structures of the personality as proposed by Freud. The ego maintains a balance between biological impulses and society's demands; it attempts to maintain a realistic approach to life.

Egocentric speech   Speech observed in preschool children, where they seem to be talking out loud for their own sake, rather than attempting to communicate to someone else. Proposed by Piaget.

Egocentrism   Lack of differentiation between one's own point of view and that of others. As used by Piaget, it refers to the early adolescent's failure to differentiate between what he and others are thinking about.

Ego ideal   Freudial concept referring to the part of the conscience that tells us the right things to do, as learned from our parents and society.

Eidetic imagery   Ability to retain an image of a picture or a scene with great clarity for a fairly long period of time. Sometimes called "photographic memory."

Electra complex   Proposed by Freud, this is the attraction a girl has for her father and its accompanying anxiety and guilt.

Electroconvulsive therapy (ECT)   Delivering an electric shock that produces a brief coma in a patient; sometimes used to treat depression.

Electroencephalogram (EEG)   Instrument used to sense and record electrical activity originating in the brain.

Empathic understanding   Rogerian concept referring to the importance of a therapist actively understanding the immediate feelings of his client.

Enactive mode   The most primitive (or basic) way human beings convert immediate experiences into a mental model; as proposed by Bruner, it is based upon action or movement and is nonverbal.

Encounter group   Group experience aimed at increasing an awareness of emotions and an ability to communicate them accurately and effectively. Generally aimed at improving interpersonal relations.

Endocrine system   Composed of glands which produce hormones, it is central in the control and regulation of behavior. It interacts closely with the nervous system.

Enriched environment   Generally refers to an environment that contains an above-normal number of interesting and/or educational stimuli.

Enuresis   Bedwetting.

Epinephrine   Also called adrenalin, it is a hormone produced by the adrenal medulla. This chemical is especially important in mobilizing the body to meet emergencies.

Eros   Freudian concept referring to half of the id's instinctual energies—specifically those dealing with the life instincts and sexuality.

ESP   See "extrasensory perception."

Ethical model   Model of psychopathology in which psychopathology comes from guilt over immoral behavior; assumes that individual has responsibility for his own behavior.

Ethology   Study of animal behavior in the natural environment.

Existential neurosis   Feeling a loss of meaning in life even though one is a successful member of society.

Existential therapy   A type of psychotherapy developed by Rollo May and other existentialists, based on their existential model which emphasizes the here-and-now, or one's present being, and the uniqueness and separateness of each individual.

Experience   Learning, or the effects of the environment on development.

Experimental method   Research procedure in which the psychologist manipulates one variable and tests to see what effects the manipulation has on a second variable. Controls are used to eliminate the effects of all extraneous variables. This procedure can establish a cause-and-effect relationship between manipulated and unmanipulated variables.

Extinction   In classical conditioning, presenting a conditioned stimulus repeatedly without the unconditioned stimulus; gradually, the conditioned response disappears. In instrumental conditioning, eliminating a learned behavior by withholding all reinforcement of it.

Extrasensory perception (ESP)   Acquisition of knowledge about the world or another person's thoughts when no known sense modality could have picked up that information.

Extrinsic rewards   Candy, money, and similar objects that can be given to organisms and have the effect of increasing the frequency of behaviors that precede them.

Factor analysis   A statistical procedure based on correlations between tests that is used to identify the components or factors which make up or contribute to a general form of behavior such as intelligence or personality.

Factor analytic approach   One type of trait theory approach that seeks to understand personality by using various types of psychological measurement and summarizing the findings of the testing in terms of the basic factors or dimensions of personality.

Fading   Gradually introducing or taking out a stimulus so that ongoing behavior is not disrupted. An instrumental conditioning technique.

Family therapy   Psychotherapy with all members of a family meeting together with the therapist.

Fear   Response to an object or situation perceived as threatening and that the individual believes he cannot cope with; a primary emotion.

Feelings   The affective or emotional components of an experience.

Fetish   Preference for an object rather than a person as a source of sexual satisfaction.

Figure-ground   In perception, the tendency to perceive things as objects or events (figure) against a background.

Fixation   Stopping one's development at a particular stage and remaining there; a defense mechanism.

Focused attention   Attending to one aspect of a stimulus while ignoring all other parts.

Formal operational period   The fourth stage of cognitive development as proposed by Piaget, it occurs during early adolescence, 11 years and beyond, as the teenager learns to conceive of events beyond the present, imagine hypothetical situations, and develop a complex system of logic.

Formal operational thinking   Proposed by Piaget, it involves the systematic exploration and solution of problems and includes abstract thought and symbolic logic.

Fovea   The central region of the retina, containing cones but no rods. It is the area of greatest visual acuity.

Free association   Technique developed by Freud for use in psychoanalysis. It is basically saying anything and everything that comes to mind in an attempt to discover what things are being repressed and to understand the things that are being said.

Free recall   Learning some items and then trying to remember them in any order.

Frigidity   Lack of any enjoyment from sexual intercourse with an opposite-sexed partner.

Frustration   Prevention or blocking of ongoing, goal-directed behavior.

Frustration-aggression hypothesis   States that all aggressive acts are caused by frustration.

Fugue state   Neurotic dissociative reaction in which a person has amnesia for his past but avoids the anxiety associated with such loss of identity by developing a new one and fleeing from the situation he could not tolerate.

Functional disorder   Emotional or behavioral problem resulting from psychological variables rather than biological ones.

Functional fixedness   Type of mental set occurring during problem solving in which an object critical to a solution is perceived as having one and only one function different from that required by the solution.

Functionalism   Early school of psychological thought that emphasized how behavior helps one adapt to his environment and the role learning plays in this adaptive process.

Ganglion cells   Neurons in the retina connecting bipolar cells to relay areas in the brain; axons of ganglion cells from the optic nerve.

Gene   One unit, composed of DNA (deoxyribonucleic acid), that determines hereditary traits. Many genes are included within a single chromosome.

Generalization   The tendency to respond in the same way to a stimulus similar to but different from the CS or the tendency to make a similar response to the one originally learned in the presence of the CS.

Genetic counseling   Using knowledge about genetics to advise people about genetic histories and the likelihood that they will have children free of inherited abnormalities.

Gestalt psychology   German school of psychology that opposed reductionistic psychologies such as Structuralism and Behaviorism and emphasized the completeness, continuity, and meaningfulness of behavior as a whole.

Gestalt therapy   A type of psychotherapy developed by Fritz Perls, it focuses on the immediate present and helps the client increase awareness of his experiences in their totality.

Gland   Bodily structure whose function is to manufacture chemicals, called hormones, that are secreted into the bloodstream and regulate bodily activities.

Gradient of stimulus generalization   Mathematical curve that illustrates the degree of generalization between various stimuli.

Group therapy   Psychotherapy of any type conducted with 3 to 20 clients at once. Most often 8 to 10 members are in a group.

Hair cells   Auditory receptor cells located in a membrane in the cochlea that are stimulated by vibrations in the cochlear fluid.

Hallucination   Form of bizarre or distorted perception without corresponding sensory stimuli.

Harmonics   Multiples of a given frequency of sound, they combine with basic frequency to produce the psychological attribute of timbre.

Heart rate   Number of heartbeats per minute.

Hebephrenic schizophrenia   Subtype of schizophrenia characterized by silly, giggling, and childish behavior, frequent hallucinations, and grossly inappropriate behavior.

Heuristic   Principle of strategy used in problem solving that serves as a device for shortening the solution process; often used when there are many different ways to solve a problem.

High dream   Special type of dream in which the dreamer feels that his consciousness is functioning in a way similar to that experienced when under the influence of a psychedelic drug.

Higher-order conditioning   Type of classical conditioning that uses a conditioned stimulus—previously learned—as the unconditioned stimulus in a new conditioning situation.

Homeostasis Tendency of the body to react in such a way as to maintain a particular, perhaps optimal, state; process of maintaining equilibrium.

Homosexual Person who has overt sexual interests in or receives sexual satisfaction from members of the same sex.

Hormone Chemical manufactured and secreted into the bloodstream by an endocrine gland, which may then activate another gland or help to regulate bodily function and behavior.

Hue Color; property of light stimulation (wavelength) corresponding to the sensation of color.

Hyperphagia Condition in which an animal eats abnormally large amounts of food and shows no satiation of hunger, produced experimentally by destruction of the ventromedial hypothalamic nucleus.

Hypnagogic state State of consciousness experienced when passing from wakefulness to sleep.

Hypnopompic state State of consciousness experienced when passing from sleep to wakefulness.

Hypnosis State of consciousness characterized by mental quiet, lack of many normal ongoing thought processes, and a state of hypersuggestibility.

Hypochondriasis Neurotic preoccupation with one's health.

Hypothalamus Group of nuclei in the forebrain. The hypothalamus is involved in many behavioral functions, especially the emotional and motivational aspects of behavior. It controls much of the endocrine system's activities through connections with the pituitary gland.

Iconic mode Way to convert immediate experience into mental models using images in the form of sensory information. Proposed by Bruner, this mode generally involves visual images.

Id One of the basic structures of personality as proposed by Freud. The id pushes the individual to seek pleasure and avoid pain; it is the seat of human instincts.

Ideal self The way a person would like to be, which may not match the way he actually is.

Identification The incorporation into one's personality of some qualities or behaviors of another person.

Identity crisis As proposed by Erik Erikson, coming together of or clarifying one's sense of self and direction in life that is marked by much confusion, experimentation, and emotionality. It generally occurs first during adolescence and may reoccur once or more often during adulthood.

Idiosyncratic Unique to a particular person or situation.

Image Sensorylike experience in the absence of any external stimulus. May have any sensory quality — vision, audition, touch, smell, etc. — or a combination of qualities.

Implosive therapy A type of behavior therapy developed by Thomas Stampfl, it uses direct extinction to get rid of fears and anxieties.

Imprinting Formation of sexual and social attachments to members of one's own species; confined to a very brief period early in life, it depends on exposure to one's own species during the period shortly after birth.

Incentive Circumstance or stimulus situation that one attempts to obtain or avoid.

Incongruence Behaving in ways that are different from the way we see ourselves or the way we feel. This results in much anxiety and sometimes psychopathology.

Incubation stage Rest period in which one withdraws temporarily from a problem situation. Frequently, a solution is easier after an incubation period.

Independent variable In psychological research, the variable which the psychologist manipulates.

Individual differences Refers to the uniqueness of organisms, the fact that all individuals vary and are different from other individuals even though they may have some things in common.

Infancy In human beings, the period from birth to 2 years of age.

Inferiority complex Proposed by Alfred Adler, it involves setting one's life goals around overcoming the feelings of inferiority that have developed during childhood.

Information-processing theory Theory of problem solving that refers to the way a person receives information from his environment, operates on it, integrates it with other information available in memory, and uses it as a basis for deciding how to act.

Insight In Gestalt psychology, the sudden achievement of understanding that arises from a change in perspective. Insight is viewed as the most appropriate description of human problem solving.

Insight-oriented therapy Type of psychotherapy that emphasizes change in motivation and knowledge. It focuses on increasing self-knowledge or insight.

Instinct Invariant sequence of complex behaviors that is observed in all members of a species and that is released by specific stimuli in the apparent absence of learning; an innate behavior that is unaffected by practice, an innate fixed action pattern.

Instrumental conditioning Type of learning that uses reinforcers to change the frequency of a behavior. Also called operant conditioning.

Insulin A hormone secreted by the pancreas, its presence allows sugar to be used by the body.

Intellectualization Reducing anxiety in a threatening situation by turning it into an abstract problem or by explaining it in such a way as to remove the threat; a defense mechanism.

Intelligence Quotient (IQ) An index of intelligence allowing for comparison of subjects across all chronological ages. IQ is calculated by dividing mental age by chronological age and multiplying by 100.

Intensity Strength or amount of energy in a stimulus or response; in light stimuli, the amount of physical energy reaching the eye corresponds to the psychological sensation of brightness.

Interference theory The theory that we forget things because our recall of them is interfered with by other usually similar items of stored information.

Interpersonal attraction Issue of friendship and romantic involvement, and attitudes of liking; subject of social psychological research.

Intervening variable Factor that stands between and provides a relationship between some stimulus in the environment and some response on the part of an organism.

Intrinsic rewards Pleasurable internal feelings that result from accomplishments or behaviors and make it more likely that these behaviors will occur in the future.

Introspection Observing one's own private, internal state of being, including one's thoughts and feelings.

Introversion Personality dimension developed by Carl Jung and used to describe how outgoing and other-directed versus ingoing and self-directed a person is. At the two extremes are the extroverts and introverts.

Invalid conversion An error in reasoning based on the assumption that a premise means more or something different than what it really means.

Involutional melancholia A psychotic type of depression associated with aging.

Iris Part of the eye surrounding the pupil that gives the eye color; diaphragm that regulates the size of the pupil to adjust the amount of light entering the eye.

Kernel of truth hypothesis See "2 + 2 phenomenon."

Kinesthesis Sense of body position and orientation.

Lashley jumping stand Device used to study discrimination learning.

Latent content (of dreams) Unconscious wishes or impulses that seek expression through dreams; symbolic aspect of dreaming.

Law of effect The forerunner of the contemporary principle of reinforcement. Responses are learned or extinguished as a consequence of their effect on the organism.

Learned helplessness effect The consequence of exposure to aversive events that cannot be controlled leading to a failure to respond appropriately in a new situation.

Learning Relatively permanent change in behavior traceable to experience and practice.

Learning strategies Methods for forming concepts and generally for acquiring and using information about the environment. Children gradually develop more sophisticated and efficient strategies.

Lens Transparent structure in the eye that changes shape to focus the optic array on the retina at the back of the eye.

Lesion Damaged or destroyed part of the body. Lesions are often made in the nervous system by cutting out or electrically burning tissue in order to study the physical and psychological effects that occur.

Leveling Cognitive style whereby one ignores differences and emphasizes similarities in perceiving the world.

Libido According to Freudian theory, the source of instinctual motivating energy.

Light adaptation Decrease in sensitivity to light resulting from an increase in light energy reaching the eye; see "dark adaptation."

Limbic system A circuit of many structures in the midbrain and forebrain, especially important in emotions and motivation; it also contains several "pleasure centers."

Lobotomy Type of psychosurgery that involves severing the connections between the frontal lobes and the rest of the brain. It has been used to treat extremely hyperemotional mental patients but is infrequently used today.

Logical syllogism Three-step argument that consists of two premises, assumed to be true, and a conclusion that may or may not follow from these premises.

Longitudinal study Research strategy that involves observing the same subjects at repeated intervals in order to examine the influences of age and experience on behavior.

Long-term memory Memory for learned material over a relatively long retention interval (generally an hour or more). A hypothetical memory system for permanent storage of learning.

Loudness The psychological attribute corresponding to amplitude of a sound wave.

Lucid dream Special type of dream during which the dreamer is aware that he is dreaming and possesses his normal ability to think and reason.

Lysergic acid diethylamide (LSD) Psychedelic drug that can be psychotomimetic. Its primary effect is to alter one's state of consciousness.

MA See "mental age."

Mandala Complex diagram symbolizing the nature of the cosmos. It can serve as a yantra.

Mania Psychotic affective reaction involving speeding up of thought processes and motor behavior and exaggerated feelings of optimism.

Manic-depressive psychosis Circular psychotic reaction marked by fluctuation between psychotic depression and mania.

Manifest content (of dreams) Aspects of a dream that are recalled by the dreamer; concrete objects and events of the dream.

Mantra Sound pattern that can be meditated upon.

Marathon group Usually refers to an encounter group

that meets for 8 or more hours with few, if any, breaks.

Marijuana   Substance prepared from the flowers or leaves of the Indian hemp plant *Cannabis sativa.*

Marital schism   Family structure in which there is open warfare between husband and wife; common in families of schizophrenics.

Marital skew   Family structure in which serious psychopathology in one parent is accepted or supported by the other parent; common in families of schizophrenics.

Maturation   Process involving growth or change over time, with heredity being the main determinant of the change.

Mean   Arithmetic average; the sum of all scores divided by number of scores.

Means-end analysis   Problem-solving process in which one tests for difference between the present situation and a solution situation and continues to perform operations until no difference is detected. Applicable whenever there is a clearly specifiable problem situation and a clearly specifiable solution.

Median   An average, defined as the middle-most score in a set of scores; an equal number of scores are higher and lower than the median.

Mediated generalization   Generalization based upon learned similarities.

Mediational theory of thinking   Holds that as a consequence of external stimulus-response associations, the individual may form internal miniaturized versions of these stimuli (mediational stimuli) and responses (mediational responses) that serve as the connecting link between the environment and the way one responds to it.

Medical model   Model of psychopathology in which pathological behaviors are viewed as symptoms of a disease.

Meditation   Special action and/or deployment of attention designed to purify the ordinary state of consciousness by removing illusions and to facilitate the production of states of consciousness in which truth is more directly perceived.

Medulla   Part of the brain that is closest to the spinal cord, it regulates the body's vital functions, such as heart rate and breathing.

Memory span   One of four commonly used memory tasks. Tests for a subject's immediate memory capacity often include having the subject attempt to repeat some number of digits or letters.

Menarche   First menstrual period in females. In human beings, this generally occurs in the early teens.

Mental age (MA)   In the Binet intelligence test the age level at which a child can successfully pass subtests. Computed by adding basal age plus the number of age units corresponding to items the subject passes at successively higher levels. Independent of chronological age.

Mental set   Tendency to respond in a given way ir-

respective of the requirements of the situation. Sets sometimes facilitate performance and sometimes impair it.

Mescaline   A psychedelic drug derived from the peyote cactus.

Methadone   Drug used in treatment of heroin addiction that prevents withdrawal symptoms and blocks the heroin "high" but still is addictive.

Minimum principle   In perceptual organization, the organization that is perceived in an ambiguous stimulus is the one which keeps changes, discontinuities, and differences to a minimum; simplicity of organization is a determinant of what will be seen.

Mode   A measure of central tendency in a set of scores; the mode is the score that occurs most frequently.

Model   In psychological theory, a framework or structure that provides a way of conceptualizing behavioral observations.

Mongolism   Also called Down's Syndrome, it results from the presence of an extra chromosome and is characterized by mental retardation.

Monocular cues for depth   Cues for depth perception derived from information in the optic array that is available to either eye alone—interposition, size perspective, linear perspective, shading, aerial perspective, texture gradients.

Morality   Type of knowledge that involves the attitudes of human beings toward social practices and institutions.

Moro reflex   See "startle reflex."

Morpheme   The smallest meaningful unit of analysis in language; usually a syllable.

Motion parallax   A cue to depth based on the relative motion of objects at near and far locations as the head moves.

Motor   Refers to *information* being carried out from the central nervous system. *Efferent* is a synonym.

Motor cortex   Part of the cerebral cortex from which messages leading to bodily movement originate.

Motor sequence   Series of events involving the development of posture, crawling, and walking in infants. These events tend to occur in a set order and at approximately the same age in most infants of a particular culture.

Motor theory   Early stimulus-response theory of thinking espoused by behaviorists and proposing that thinking always involves muscular or glandular activity of some kind. According to this theory, most human thought is basically subvocal speech activity.

Multiple personality   Neurotic dissociative reaction in which a person has two or more complete but alternating personalities; often different personalities express different aspects of a conflict that the person is experiencing.

Naturalistic observation   Systematic method for observing and recording events as they naturally occur in the world.

Need for achievement   See "achievement motivation."

Negative afterimage   After staring at a colored stimulus for a period of time, a person sees the same stimulus in complementary colors against a neutral background.

Negative reinforcement   A reinforcement that increases the probability of a response when removal of the reinforcement is contingent on the response.

Neo-Freudian   Also called "neoanalytic." Refers to a large number of psychologists who agree with some of Freud's ideas but have modified his theory to develop their own, more modern theories.

Nerve   A bundle of axons from many neurons, it runs from one point in the body to another and carries nerve impulses.

Nervous breakdown   Commonsense term usually used to describe a person whose emotional problems are so severe that he can no longer cope with home or work responsibilities; not a description of a physical nervous condition and not synonymous with *neurosis.*

Nervous system   The brain and spinal cord, plus all of the neurons traveling throughout the rest of the body. It is a communication system, carrying information throughout the body.

Neuron   Nerve cell. The most elementary unit of the nervous system, its function is to send and receive messages.

Neurosis   Special pattern of behavior that is instigated and maintained for the purpose of contending with stress and avoiding anxiety; diagnostic category of psychopathology characterized by anxiety, rigid and unsuccessful attempts to reduce it, and an inability to totally satisfy the need being served by the behavior.

Neurotic   Person who is experiencing a neurosis.

Neurotic anxiety   In Freudian theory, anxiety or fear that occurs when there is no rational reason for it; in learning theory, conditioned fear.

Neurotic paradox   Refers to the fact that the neurotic person persists in his maladaptive behavior even in the face of unpleasant consequences.

Neurotransmitter substance   Molecules that are stored in presynaptic vesicles and that produce either an excitatory or an inhibitory potential when they come into contact with receptor molecules located on the postsynaptic membrane of an adjacent neuron.

Nondirective therapy   See "client-centered therapy."

Nonsense syllable   Three-letter syllable, consisting of two consonants separated by a vowel. It is used to study verbal learning.

Norm   A rule, established and maintained in a social context, identifying desirable behavior.

Normative developmental research   Research strategy that compares the behavior of children at different ages in one situation. It tends to be used by psychologists who stress the role of maturation in development and aims to chart behavioral norms for different ages.

Nucleus   Structure containing hereditary information and other things, found in the center of most cells. Also, a cluster of cell bodies of neurons.

Null hypothesis   Prediction that the variable being manipulated will have no effect on the behavior being measured.

Nurture   Socialization, education, training, and other environmental influences that affect the development of the organism.

Observational learning   Learning based on observation of another individual—a model—engaged in the to-be-learned behavior.

Obsession   Persistent, repetitive thought that cannot be pushed out of consciousness.

Obsessive-compulsive syndrome   Neurotic pattern in which obsessive and compulsive behavior tend to go together in the same person; the syndrome prevents a person from thinking anxiety-provoking thoughts and from doing anxiety-provoking things.

Oedipal conflict   Proposed by Freud, this is the attraction a boy has for his mother and its accompanying anxiety and guilt.

Oedipus complex ego states   Concepts coined by Eric Berne for use in transactional analysis and paralleling the superego, ego, and id of Freud.

One-shot problems   See "simple-one-shot problems."

Opening-up meditation   A form of meditation that involves paying full, continuous attention to everything that is happening to one.

Operant conditioning   See "instrumental conditioning."

Opponent process theory   In motivation and emotion, a theory proposed by Solomon and Corbit which says that for every pleasant feeling and approach tendency there is an opponent or opposing process with the opposite characteristics, i.e., an unpleasant feeling and an avoidance tendency. The net motivation or emotion at any time is the sum of the strengths of the two opposing processes.

Optic array   Pattern of light energy, reflected from the surface of an object, that enters the eye.

Optical revolving power   Ability of the lens in the eye to focus the optic array sharply on the retina and not in front of or behind it.

Organic disorder   Emotional or behavioral problem resulting from biological causes, usually from impairment of brain functioning.

Out-of-body experience (OOBE)   Experience during which a person feels that he is located at a point other than where his physical body is, and still feels he is in a normal state of consciousness.

Ovaries   Reproductive organs in females; they are also endocrine glands that secrete many hormones, regulating sexual cycles and behavior and supporting pregnancy.

Overtones   See harmonics.

Paired-associate learning   Learning a list of paired items such that one member of the pair can be recalled given the other member as a stimulus.

Pancreas   Produces the hormone insulin and thus regulates the use of sugar in the body. Below-normal production of insulin by this gland leads to diabetes mellitus, or too much sugar in the blood.

Paranoid personality   Personality disorder characterized by suspiciousness and jealousy but no loss of contact with reality.

Paranoid schizophrenia   Subtype of schizophrenia characterized by delusions of persecution, suspicion of others, and delusions of grandeur.

Paraprofessionals   Individuals from the community who are given minimum training and can then serve as temporary therapists.

Parapsychology   Study of topics that are related to psychology (such as ESP) but are not fully accepted as belonging under the heading of "psychology."

Parasympathetic nervous system   One part of the autonomic nervous system involved in controlling involuntary behavior, such as digestion; it works in opposition to the sympathetic system and conserves body energy.

Partial reinforcement   A reinforcement schedule in which less than 100 percent of all correct responses are rewarded.

Perception   The reception of information through sensory receptors and interpretation of that information so as to construct meaningfulness about one's world.

Perceptual constancy   The fact that perceptual organization remains relatively stable even though some aspects of the pattern within the optic array change: size constancy, shape constancy, brightness constancy.

Performance   One's observable responses or behavior in a given task.

Peripheral nervous system   Contains all the nerves which are the communication lines connecting muscles, glands, and sensory receptors with the central nervous system.

Personality assessment   Administering and evaluating a variety of tests (and perhaps interviews) in order to develop an understanding of an individual's personality.

Personality disorder   Diagnostic category of psychopathology marked by failure to behave in socially appropriate ways due to lack of motivation or lack of skill (competence) in coping with normal stresses of everyday life; such individuals are pathological by society's definition, not in terms of their own personal discomfort.

Perspective theory   Explanation of how physically equal stimuli are perceived as unequal by proposing that one uses perspective clues to judge depth and then uses this depth information in perceiving size.

Phenomenological model   Model of psychopathology that emphasizes current existence, perception, feel-ings, and intuition of the person in determining adjustment to the world rather than emphasizing what has happened to the person in the past.

Phi phenomenon   Apparent movement; an illusion of movement produced by the sequential illumination of two or more stationary lights, as in a theater marquee.

Phobia   Neurosis characterized by an intense, irrational fear of something; according to analytic theory, it involves displacement of anxiety onto a situation that is not dangerous or only mildly dangerous.

Phonemes   General classes of sounds common to a given language (basic sounds of a language); considered to be the conjunctive combination of several distinctive features associated with a particular language. In English, features include voiced versus voiceless and stopped (air flow interrupted) versus fricative (air flow sliding over articulator).

Phonology   Study of the sounds of a language.

Photon   A packet or quantum of visible energy or light.

Pitch   Psychological attribute corresponding to frequency of a sound wave.

Pituitary gland   The "master gland," it is activated by the hypothalamus and releases hormones that are responsible for activating many of the other glands, in addition to regulating bodily growth, water loss, and many other functions.

Placebo control group   The group of subjects in any experiment that receives a fake treatment—as, for example, a drug that contains no active ingredients.

Pleasure centers   Areas in the brain that, when electrically stimulated, produce very strong, pleasurable sensations. May be involved in determining what is rewarding for animals in everyday life.

Pleasure principle   A concept originated by Freud, it is the idea that human beings strive to avoid pain and seek pleasure.

Pons   One of the three major components of the hindbrain, lying just above the medulla and containing many ascending and descending fibers that connect higher and lower levels in the central nervous system.

Positive reinforcement   A reinforcement that increases the probability of a response when the reinforcement is contingent on the response.

Positive instances   All stimuli in a population that have the characteristics that illustrate a given concept. For instance, if *red* is the concept, objects that are red in color are positive instances.

Possession state   State in which the subject feels as if his own personality or soul has been taken over or displaced by some nonphysical entity.

Posthypnotic effects   Behavior that occurs after a subject has been brought back to normal consciousness following a hypnotic state. The behavior is caused by suggestions given to the subject while he is hypnotized.

P-O-X model   Descriptive model used to diagram relationships according to balance theory; P (person) has an orientation toward O (another person); P also has an orientation toward X (usually an object); and P perceives O as having an orientation toward X. The nature of the orientations determines whether a balanced state exists.

Prägnanz   A Gestalt principle of perceptual organization that corresponds to a "goodness of figure."

Preconscious   In Freudian theory, the ideas, thoughts, and images that a person is not aware of at a given moment but that can be brought into awareness with little or no difficulty.

Prejudice   Attitude held toward members of another group that is emotional, rigidly or inflexibly felt and acted on, and negative. The object of the prejudice is disliked and the group's tendency is to mistreat or discriminate against members of the disliked group.

Premack principle   Given two behaviors which differ in their likelihood of occurrence, the less likely behavior can be reinforced by using the more likely behavior as a reward.

Preoperational period   The second stage of intellectual development, occurring from 2 to 7 years, proposed by Piaget; it is a transitional period during which children learn to use language as a way of representing events and knowledge.

Prepared learning   A built-in conditioning system, genetically based, that quickly associates certain kinds of stimuli. For example, the special system that relates food stimuli, through taste perception, with feeling sick.

Primacy effect   Items near the beginning of a list are remembered unusually well.

Primal therapy   A type of psychotherapy developed by Arthur Janov; it focuses on the fact that people have cut off their feelings from childhood with respect to the rejection they have received from their parents, the goal being to reexperience these feelings and the associated pain.

Primary gain   For neurotic behavior, the immediate reduction of anxiety.

Primary mental abilities   According to Thurstone, the basic separate abilities that make up intelligence, including number ability, word fluency (speed of thinking of the right word at the right time), verbal meaning, memory, reasoning, spatial relations, and perceptual speed (ability to recognize similarities and differences in visual forms).

Primary reinforcer   Stimulus or event that is innately reinforcing.

Proactive inhibition   A situation where recall of learned information is made more difficult because of something learned earlier.

Probability   The proportion of cases in a population that fit a particular description; the probability of an A is equal to the number of A's divided by the total number of cases in the population.

Process schizophrenia   Schizophrenic reaction in

which there is a slow onset of symptoms over a period of years, with progressive withdrawal from others, increasing deterioration of thought processes, and slow onset of hallucinations and delusions; sometimes called *chronic schizophrenia.*

Prognosis   Probability of recovery.

Projection   Process of denying the presence of unacceptable impulses or characteristics and then seeing these qualities in another person (who may or may not actually have them); a defense mechanism.

Projective test   A test that encourages the subject to project his or her personalities and responses to ambiguous and neutral stimuli such as inkblots.

Proximity   Nearness in physical location or occurrence.

Psilocybin   Psychedelic drug derived from a certain type of mushroom.

Psychedelic   "Mind-manifesting." In reference to drugs, it denotes any drug whose primary effect is to induce an altered state of consciousness.

Psychedelic therapy   Type of psychotherapy using one or a few large doses of LSD or other psychedelic drug.

Psychoanalysis   Insight-oriented therapy developed by Freud and based upon his psychoanalytic theory.

Psychoanalytic theory   Theory of personality developed by Freud out of his work with the unhealthy personality. It is a dynamic theory that sees personality as being based in biological needs.

Psychodrama   Therapeutic technique involving the acting out of parts or roles with others, under the supervision of a therapist.

Psychology   Scientific study of behavior and systematic application of behavior principles.

Psychopathology.   Inability to behave in a socially appropriate way such that the consequences of one's behavior are maladaptive for oneself or society.

Psychopharmacology   Study of the effects of drugs on behavior and application of such knowledge in order to change behavior.

Psychophysics   Study of the relationship between physical stimulation and the conscious sensations it provokes in a person; historically, it was the first form of psychological study to appear.

Psychophysiologic reaction   See "psychosomatic illness."

Psychosexual stages   The stages of development that, according to Freud, all human beings pass through during early life. Each stage centers around a specific pleasurable area of the body. Each stage presents the opportunity for fixation.

Psychosis   Diagnostic category of psychopathology characterized by gross distortion of reality or by loss of reality testing, inability to distinguish between reality and fantasy, hallucinations, and/or delusions.

Psychosomatic illness   Physical illness that has psychological causes.

Psychosurgery   Use of lesions or surgery on the nervous system, especially the brain, for the purpose of changing behavior.

Psychotherapy   Corrective experience leading the client to behave in socially appropriate, adequate, and adaptive ways.

Psychotic   Person who is experiencing a psychosis.

Psychotic episode   Sudden experience, generally triggered by some specific stimuli in the environment, during which a person develops a psychosis.

Psychotomimetic drug   Any drug that produces a state of being similar to psychosis.

Puberty   Time of onset of sexual maturity; average age of onset for boys is 14, for girls, 12 years.

Punishment   Event of stimulus that tends to decrease the frequency of behaviors that it follows.

Random sampling   Selecting a sample in such a manner that each person in the population has an equal chance of being chosen for the sample.

Range   A statistical measure of the variability in a set of scores; the range is the highest score minus the lowest score.

Rapid eye movement (REM)   Activity of the eye muscles that occurs during one stage of sleep and that seems to indicate the occurrence of dreaming.

Rationalization   A Freudian defense mechanism that involves attempts by a person who is not conscious of the real reasons for his or her inappropriate or unacceptable behavior to justify or explain the behavior by reference to socially acceptable motives.

Reaction formation   Denial or masking of one's own unacceptable impulses by stating or emphasizing qualities that are the opposite to one's true feelings; a defense mechanism.

Reactive schizophrenias   Schizophrenic reactions in which the onset of symptoms is relatively sudden; sometimes called *acute schizophrenias.*

Realistic-group-conflict theory   Theory of prejudice stating that if two groups are in conflict with each other, members of each group will tend to develop prejudice against members of the other group.

Reality principle   A concept originated by Freud, it involves the idea that in order to exist, people must behave in ways that are consistent with the real world. The ego is the part of the personality that oversees and carries out this need.

Real self   The concept of *I, me,* or *myself* as one really is; one's own awareness of his existence.

Recency effect   The fact that items near the end of a list are remembered unusually well.

Receptive field   Area of the retina corresponding to a single cell in the visual projection of the brain.

Reciprocal inhibition   Learning to decrease the presence of a response like anxiety by increasing the presence of an incompatible response like relaxation while the original anxiety-producing stimulus occurs.

Redundancy   Presence of distinctive stimulus features or cues in each of several stimuli that differ from each other in other ways. Redundancy reduces the chance of miscommunication or misperception.

Referent   Object or thing to which a word refers.

Refractory period   Time interval, usually following a response, during which almost no stimulus will produce another response.

Regress   In relation to hypnosis it involves taking a subject back in time, until he psychologically experiences the past. It may even be possible to take a person back to a past life.

Regression   In statistics, a procedure for predicting a person's score on one variable when the person's score on another variable and the correlation between the two variables is already known.

Reinforcer   Event or stimulus that increases the frequency of a response with which it is associated.

Relational concept   See "concept."

Relaxation training   Learning to relax the body by becoming aware of and controlling the muscles of the body; one part of systematic desensitization.

Releasing stimuli   Stimuli from the environment that act as triggers for innate fixed-action patterns in behavior.

Relevant attributes   Characteristics of a stimulus that make the stimulus a positive instance of a given concept.

Relevant dimension   Stimulus dimension along which a concept is defined. For example, color is a relevant dimension along which the concept *red* is defined; size is not a relevant dimension for the concept *red.*

Reliability   The degree to which a person's score on some variable does not change on repeated testings; it is a critical characteristic of every measuring device.

Repression   Act of keeping highly threatening impulses or memories in the unconscious far away from awareness, because they are very likely to produce much anxiety or other negative consequences; a defense mechanism.

Response (R)   Any behavior that results from a stimulus.

Response discrimination   Learning to give one, and only one, particular response in a given situation.

Response generalization   Learning one response, then giving a similar but slightly different one under the same stimulus conditions.

Response integration   Several independent responses gradually become unified into a single smooth response.

Restrictive meditation   See "concentrative meditation."

Retention interval   The time between initial learning of something and its recall.

Reticular formation   Structure extending through the central core of the hindbrain and midbrain that maintains wakefulness and attentive behavior.

Retina   Photosensitive surface at the back of the eye upon which the optic array is focused; it contains visual receptor cells.

Retinal disparity   See "binocular disparity."

Retroactive inhibition   Difficulty in recalling learned information because of something learned after the information one is trying to recall.

Retrograde amnesia   Loss of memory for events just prior to the event that caused the memory loss. Long-term memory remains intact.

Reward   Stimulus or event that increases the frequency of behaviors it follows.

Rod   Photoreceptor cell shaped like a rod, located throughout the retina, with greatest concentration near its edges; it is extremely sensitive to low intensities of light—not equally sensitive to all wavelengths of light.

Role playing   Technique involving the acting out of specific roles in order to work through problems.

Sampling techniques   Procedures for selecting a small number of cases from a large population such that the sample that results is representative of the larger population.

Saturation   The dimension of color experience that corresponds to how much or how deep the hue of a light is.

Scanning   Strategy for solving conceptual problems which uses a hypothesis-testing approach. Successive scanning involves testing possible solutions one at a time. Simultaneous scanning involves testing more than one hypothesis at a time.

Scapegoat theory   Theory that prejudice serves as an outlet for personal feelings of hostility, frustration, and aggression; that it is a displacement of aggression.

Schizophrenia   Group of psychotic disorders in which there are disturbances in thought processes as well as emotions and a marked distortion of reality; often characterized by emotional blunting, disturbances in interpersonal relationships, depersonalization, and preoccupation with inner fantasies.

Secondary elaboration   Dream process that disguises material by combining separate events or objects into one cohesive unit.

Secondary gain   For neurotic behavior, other positive consequences in addition to the relief from tension or anxiety.

Secondary reinforcer   Stimulus or event that becomes a reinforcer only after being paired with a primary reinforcer.

Secondary sexual characteristics   Physical features—such as growth of beard and change of voice in males and enlarging of breasts in females—that appear during puberty and remain for most or all of one's adult life. They are indications of sexual maturity.

Sedative   Drug that reduces anxiety by inducing muscle relaxation, sleep, and inhibition of the cognitive centers of the brain.

Self-actualization   Highest-level need in Maslow's theory of motivation; the drive to develop and realize one's fullest potentialities; the need for self-fulfillment.

Self-concept   Fairly consistent and enduring framework of self-regarding attitudes.

Self-fulfilling prophecy   In research, an experimenter may have expectations about how the subjects should behave, and he may inadvertently or otherwise get his subjects to behave that way. By making a prediction one acts to insure that the prediction comes true.

Self-remembering   A process similar to opening-up meditation, it involves being aware of being aware.

Self theory   Approach to personality that focuses on the individual as a whole, unified self. It takes a fairly positive view of human beings and is a part of the humanistic approach to psychology.

Semantic differential   Procedure developed by Charles Osgood that uses the ratings that people give to words to derive the basic dimensions of meaning and the location of any given word on those dimensions. Measures word connotation.

Semantic generalization   Type of mediated generalization where language is the mediator.

Semicircular canals   Sense organs for body motion; three fluid-filled canals, in the inner ear, perpendicular to each other in three different planes, that respond to movement in any direction.

Sensations   In Structuralism, the direct products of external stimulation.

Sensitivity training   Group experience aimed at improving human relations, skills, and honesty and understanding of oneself and others; also called *T-group*.

Sensorimotor period   The first stage of cognitive development proposed by Piaget, it occurs during infancy, 0-2 years, as the infant comes to realize that objects have an existence independent of himself.

Sensory   Refers to information being brought into the central nervous system. *Afferent* is a synonym.

Sensory cortex   Areas of the cerebral cortex that are the final receiving stations for sensory information.

Sensory deprivation   Prolonged reduction of external stimulation, either in intensity or variety; produces boredom, restlessness, and disturbances of thought processes.

Serial learning   Learning a list of items in a particular order.

Sex-role identification   An organism's tendency to learn and display behaviors appropriate for males or females of the species.

Sexual deviations   Any method of obtaining sexual satisfaction or participating in sexual relationships that is disapproved of by the community; impotence, frigidity, homosexuality, fetishism.

Sexual impotence   Inability to engage in sexual intercourse with an opposite-sexed partner.

Shaman   A tribal medicine man who is thought to have extraordinary spiritual knowledge and powers.

Sham rage   Ferocious, undirected rage behavior provoked by very mild stimulation; experimental condition produced by surgical removal of the cerebral cortex.

Shape constancy   The fact that objects appear to maintain a constant shape regardless of the angle from which we observe them.

Shaping   Process that uses instrumental conditioning in gradual steps to develop an uncommon or difficult behavior.

Sharpening   Cognitive style whereby one ignores similarities and emphasizes differences in perceiving the world.

Short-term memory   Memory for learned material over a very brief retention interval. Hypothetical memory system for transient information.

Shuttle box   Device with two compartments separated by a door, used to study learning and motivation.

Sibling   Brother or sister.

Sibling rivalry   Jealousy or competition between brothers and/or sisters, which often develops in a child upon the birth of a new brother or sister.

Sign stimuli   Environmental cues that trigger instinctual behavior.

Similarity   A Gestalt principle that describes the tendency for similar or identical units to cluster together forming a larger whole.

Simple one-shot problems   Lowest level of problems studied by psychologists. All these problems have specific, known solutions that can be found relatively automatically by following a simple series of steps. May emphasize perceptual or verbal factors.

Simple schizophrenia   Subtype of schizophrenia characterized by reduction in interpersonal relationships, apathy, indifference, and difficulty in focusing on anything in the outside world; but seldom many delusions and hallucinations.

Size constancy   The observation that heights of objects do not appear to shrink as we move from them even though the size of the image on the retina does become smaller.

Skinner box   A box containing a lever that, when pushed, causes a food pellet to appear in a tray. This, and variations of it, is used to study learning.

Social attitude   Combination of feelings, beliefs, and action tendencies toward classes of persons or objects that are directly or indirectly social in nature.

Social concept   Concept about classes of people; attitude.

Social exchange theory   The idea that interpersonal attraction can be analyzed in terms of rewards and costs of each event or type of interaction.

Social facilitation   Phenomenon in which the mere presence of other persons, as an audience or as co-

workers, without any verbal exchange, affects individual performance.

Social influence   The mere presence of other persons—such as an audience or as coworkers—without any verbal exchange affects an individual's behavior, either positively or negatively.

Social learning theory   Attempt to explain personality in terms of learning, based on the assumption that much of what we call personality is learned behavior involving imitation. Albert Bandura is a social learning theorist.

Social speech   Speech with the purpose of communicating to someone else. Proposed by Piaget.

Sociobiology   A biological explanation for a social behavior based on the assumption that the primary function of behavior is to insure the survival of an organism's genes.

Sociopath   See "antisocial character."

Soma   The main cell body of a neuron, containing the nucleus of the nerve cell, which controls all cellular activities such as oxygen utilization and energy production.

Somatic nervous system   Part of the peripheral nervous system, it contains the neurons that connect to sensory organs and skeletal muscles.

Spiritual medium   Person who claims that highly evolved spirits sometimes possess him and serve as a guide to his spiritual activity.

Split-brain operation   Cutting of the corpus callosum, which connects the two halves of the cerebral hemispheres, so that the hemispheres are then unable to communicate to each other.

Spontaneous recover   Following extinction training, the return of a learned behavior even though it has not been practiced.

Standard deviation   In statistics a measure of the variability or spread of a set of scores around the mean.

Stanford-Binet test   A revision of the Binet intelligence test made by psychologists at Stanford University, it is an individual test using age-level subtests. Most widely used children's intelligence test.

Startle reflex   An automatic response shown by most normal infants to a startling stimulus, it involves throwing the arms to the side, extending the fingers, and then curving the hands back to the midline. Also called Moro reflex.

State anxiety   Momentary, consciously perceived feelings of apprehension and tension.

State-dependent learning   Ability of the learner's internal physiological state to affect learning; the more similar this state is during learning and recall, the better recall will be.

Stereopsis   A perceptual process that extracts information from the environment about depth and which operates on the fact that the two eyes are separated horizontally in the head.

Stereotyping   Adopting the belief that all members of certain groups hold to certain beliefs or have certain attitudes or characteristics; treating all members of this group in the same ways, as if they belonged to a rigidly bound conceptual class.

Stimulus (S)   Event capable of affecting an organism; specifically, anything that can activate a sensory neuron.

Stimulus control   Instrumental learning process whereby a cue in the environment comes to control the behavior of an organism.

Stimulus discrimination   Learning to respond differently to various stimuli that may have some similarities.

Stimulus generalization   Learning a response to a stimulus, then showing the same response to a similar, but slightly different, stimulus.

Stroop effect   Difficulty in attending to or responding to a given stimulus due to an inability to block responses to irrelevant features in the stimulus situation, a response competition phenomenon.

Structuralism   Early school of psychological thought that held that the subject matter of psychology was conscious experience, that the object of study was to analyze experience into its component parts, and that the primary method of analysis was introspection.

Sublimation   Rechanneling instinctual energy from an unacceptable object to one that is highly valued by society.

Subvocal activity   Behavior of speaking to oneself (that is, moving the muscles of the voice apparatus at very low levels without speaking overtly). According to the motor theory of thinking, subvocal activity is the basic behavioral component of thinking.

Superego   One of the basic structures of the personality, as proposed by Freud. The superego contains people's values, morals, and basic attitudes as learned from their parents and society.

Suppression   Act of keeping an impulse or memory just below the level of awareness, in the preconscious, because it is likely to provoke anxiety or other negative consequences.

Surface traits   The term coined by Cattell to refer to broad pervasive traits that summarize relationships found in overt behavior. For example, "honest" is a surface trait that encompasses a range of related specific behaviors.

Symbolic mode   The most sophisticated method for converting immediate experiences into mental models. As proposed by Bruner, it involves using words and sentences as symbols of objects, events, and states of affairs.

Symbolization   Dream process that disguises material in the dream so that something in the dream represents or stands for something else in real life.

Sympathetic nervous system   Part of the autonomic nervous system, it prepares the organism for emergencies, making much bodily energy available for use.

Synapse   Area where the end of one neuron connects to the next neuron in a communication chain. Speci-

fically, the axon terminals of the first cell come close to (but do not touch) the dendrites or soma of the second cell.

Systematic desensitization   Type of behavior therapy developed by Wolpe to help people overcome fears and anxiety.

Taste buds   Taste receptors, each containing taste cells, located primarily on the tongue.

Territorial instinct   An organism's innate desire for complete control of the physical area in which it lives; territoriality.

Testes   Reproductive organs in males; endocrine glands that secrete many hormones that regulate sexual behaviors and characteristics.

Tetrahydrocannabinol (THC)   Major active ingredient in marijuana.

Texture gradient   Difference in surface textures or characteristics between the area of a figure and that of the background.

Thalamus   Portion of the brain that receives information about most of the senses and relays it to the cortex. It also is involved in sleep and attention.

Thematic Apperception Test (TAT)   Projective test requiring the subject to write stories about a number of ambiguous pictures; the story content reveals unconscious motivation. Also used to measure achievement motivation.

Theory   Set of principles and statements that represent, organize, and summarize facts and suggest an explanation of what lies behind them.

Threshold   The amount of physical stimulus required to achieve a certain level of correctness in a sensory-detection task.

Thyroid gland   Produces the hormone thyroxin and thus regulates metabolism and growth.

Timbre   See "overtones."

Token economy   Reward training, based on operant conditioning, that uses tokens as rewards for certain behaviors. The tokens can be redeemed for special privileges, or primary reinforcers.

TOTE unit   Test, Operate, Test, Exit. A series of steps in problem solving, emphasizing the discrimination process. See "means-end analysis."

Trace-dependent forgetting   Loss of learned information due to the loss of memory trace, see "cue-dependent forgetting."

Tract   A bundle of axons in the central nervous system.

Trait   Relatively permanent characteristic of an individual that he tends to show in most situations.

Trait anxiety   Anxiety proneness; predisposition to respond with high anxiety when under stress.

Trait cluster   Group of traits that tend to go together, so that if a person has one of the traits he will probably have all of them.

Transcendental meditation   One type of concentrative meditation, as taught by the Maharishi Mahesh Yogi.

Tranquilizer   A drug that reduces anxiety without inducing sleep.

Transactional analysis   A type of psychotherapy originated by Eric Berne and popularized by Thomas Harris. It focuses on the transactions people have with one another and analyzes these into interactions between the various parts of each person's personality (Parent, Adult, Child).

Transference   A concept developed by Freud, it generally refers to the tendency of a person in therapy to transfer to the therapist perceptions, feelings, etc., that he has about other people in his life, rather than seeing the therapist as he really is.

Transfer of training   The effect—positive or negative—of prior learning on the subsequent performance of a different task.

Traumatic neurosis   Inability to successfully cope with stress, brought on by a single traumatic incident or by prolonged, intense stress from which there is no escape, such as battle stresses in war.

Trucking game   Decision-making game used in research on cooperation and competition. Subject is asked to make a decision between cooperating for a steady reward or competing for a large but risky reward.

2 + 2 phenomenon   Adoption of a prejudiced attitude from an erroneous conclusion about facts (for example, concluding that blacks are innately inferior because they score lower on IQ tests and overlooking the fact that often tests are biased against blacks).

Unconditioned positive regard   Rogerian concept involving the idea that a therapist must care about his client without any conditions put on the caring, even when the client reveals things that the therapist is uncomfortable about.

Unconditioned response (UCR)   In classical conditioning, the response that automatically occurs whenever the unconditioned stimulus is presented, without any training.

Unconditioned stimulus (UCS)   In classical conditioning, the stimulus that automatically elicits the desired response, without any training.

Unconscious   In Freudian theory, that part of a person's mental process that he resists being aware of; unacceptable drives and impulses and material that were once conscious but were removed from awareness because they were anxiety provoking.

Vacuum activity   Occurrence of an instinctual behavior in the absence of any releasing stimulus.

Validity   Degree to which a measuring device measures what it is supposed to measure.

Variable   Any characteristic of an object, event, or person that can take two or more values.

Variance   A measure of the variability in a set of scores; it is equal to the square of the standard deviation.

Vestibular sacs   Sense organs for perception of balance; enlargements at the base of the semicircular canals that respond to tilt.

Visual acuity   Ability to notice fine detail in a patterned stimulus.

Visual cliff   Device used to study depth perception in infants. The illusion of a cliff is built into a level glass floor, and infants are urged to crawl over the edge of the "cliff."

Wechsler-Bellevue   Intelligence test battery, in adult and children's versions, composed of tests for different abilities. Divided into performance tests and verbal tests, it yields a point score that can be converted into an IQ.

Yantra   Visual pattern that can be meditated on.

Yerkes-Dodson Law   The fact that increased motivation will improve performance up to a point, beyond which there is deterioration. The easier a task is to perform, the higher the drive level for optimal performance.

Adamson, R. E., & Taylor, D. W. Functional fixedness as related to elapsed time and to set. *Journal of Experimental Psychology*, 1954, *47*, 122–126.

Adelson, J., Green, B., & O'Neil, R. Growth of the idea of law in adolescence. *Developmental Psychology*, 1969, *1*, 327–332.

Adorno, T. W., Frenkel-Brunswik, E., Levinson, D. J., & Sanford, R. N. *The authoritarian personality.* New York: Harper & Row, 1950.

Alexander, F. Individual psychotherapy. *Psychosomatic Medicine*, 1946, *8*, 110–115.

Allbrook, R. C. How to spot executives early. *Fortune*, 1968, *78*, 106–111.

Anastasi, A. Heredity, environment, and the question "how"? *Psychological Review*, 1958, *65*(4), 197–208.

Apter, M. J. *The computer simulation of behavior.* New York: Harper & Row, 1970.

Aronson, E., & Mills, J. The effect of severity of initiation on liking for a group. *Journal of Abnormal and Social Psychology*, 1959, *59*, 177–181.

Asch, S. E. Studies of independence and conformity: I. A minority of one against a unanimous majority. *Psychological Monographs*, 1956, *70* (9, whole no. 416).

Aserinsky, E., & Kleitman, N. Regularly occurring periods of eye mobility and concomitant phenomena during sleep. *Science*, 1953, *118*, 273–274.

Atkinson, J. W., & McClelland, D. C. The projective expressions of needs. II. The effect of different intensities of the hunger drive on thematic apperception. *Journal of Experimental Psychology*, 1948, *38*, 643–658.

Atwood, M. E., & Polson, P. G. A process model for water jug problems. *Cognitive Psychology*, 1976, *8*, 191–216.

Ax, A. F. The physiological differentiation between fear and anger in humans. *Psychosomatic Medicine*, 1953, *15*, 443–452.

Azrin, N. H., Hutchinson, R. R., & Hake, D. H. Extinction-induced aggression. *Journal of the Experimental Analysis of Behavior*, 1966, *9*, 191–204.

Bach-y-rita, P. *Brain mechanisms in sensory substitution.* New York: Academic Press, 1972.

Baltes, P. B. Longitudinal and cross-sectional sequences in the study of age and generation effects. *Human Development*, 1968, *11*, 145–171.

Bandura, A. A social learning interpretation of psychological dysfunctions. In London, P., & Rosenhan, D. (Eds.), *Foundations of Abnormal Psychology.* New York: Holt, Rinehart and Winston, 1968.

Bandura, A. *Social learning theory.* New York: General Learning Press, 1971.

Bandura, A., & Walters, R. H. *Social learning and personality development.* New York: Holt, Rinehart and Winston, 1965.

Barber, T. X. *Hypnosis: A scientific approach.* New York: Van Nostrand Reinhold, 1969.

Bard, P., & Mountcastle, V. B. Some forebrain mechanisms involved in expression of rage with special reference to suppression of angry behavior. *Research Publication Association Nervous and Mental Disorders*, 1948, *27*, 362–404.

Baron, R. M., Mandel, D. R., Adams, C. A., & Griffin, L. M. Effects of social density in university residential environments. *Journal of Personality and Social Psychology*, 1976, *34*, 434–446.

Barrett, R. S. Guide to using psychological tests. *Harvard Business Review*, 1963, *41*, 139.

Bateson, G., Jackson, D. D., Haley, J., & Weakland, J. H. Toward a theory of schizophrenia. *Behavioral Science*, 1956, *1*, 251–264.

Beck, A. T., Ward, O. H., Mendelson, M., Mock, J. E., & Erbaugh, J. K. Reliability of psychiatric diagnosis: II. A study of consistency of clinical judgments and ratings. *American Journal of Psychiatry*, 1962, *119*, 351–357.

Bem, D. J. Self-perception: An alternative interpretation of cognitive dissonance phenomena. *Psychological Review*, 1967, *74*, 183–200.

Bem, S. L. The measurement of psychological androgyny. *Journal of Consulting and Clinical Psychology*, 1974, *42*, 155–162.

Bengston, V. L. *The social psychology of aging.* Indianapolis: Bobbs-Merrill, 1973.

Bexton, W. H., Heron, W., & Scott, T. H. Effects of decreased variation in the environment. *Canadian Journal of Psychology,* 1954, *8,* 70–76.

Biggs, J. B. *Information and human learning.* Glenview, Ill.: Scott, Foresman, 1971.

Bonime, W. *The clinical use of dreams.* New York: Basic Books, 1962.

Boring, E. G., Langfeld, H. S., & Weld, H. P. *Foundations of psychology.* New York: Wiley, 1948.

Bourne. L. E., Jr. *Human conceptual behavior.* Boston: Allyn and Bacon, 1966.

Bourne, L. E., Jr., Ekstrand, B. R., & Dominowski, R. L. *The psychology of thinking.* Englewood Cliffs, N.J.: Prentice-Hall, 1971.

Bourne, M. T. The nature of hypnosis: Artifact and essence. *Journal of Abnormal and Social Psychology,* 1959, *58,* 277–299.

Bower, G. H. The influence of graded reductions in reward and prior frustrating events upon the magnitude of the frustration effect. *Journal of Comparative and Physiological Psychology,* 1962, *55,* 582–587.

Brady, J. V. Ulcers in "executive" monkeys. *Scientific American,* 1958, *199,* 95–100.

Braine, M. D. S. The ontogeny of English phrase structure: The first phrase. *Language,* 1963, *39,* 1–13.

Bransford, J. D., & Franks, J. J. The abstraction of linguistic ideas. *Cognitive Psychology,* 1971, *2,* 331–350.

Bransford, J. D., & Johnson, M. K. Considerations of some problems of comprehension. In Chase, W. G. (Ed.), *Visual Information Processing.* New York: Academic Press, 1973.

Breuer, J., & Freud, S. Studies on hysteria. In Strachey, J. (Trans.), *Standard Edition of the Complete Works of Sigmund Freud.* New York: Basic Books, 1957.

Bruner, J. S. *Toward a theory of instruction.* Cambridge, Mass.: Belknap Press, 1966.

Bruner, J. S., Goodnow, J. J., & Austin, G. A. *A study of thinking.* New York: Wiley, 1956.

Butler, R. A. Discrimination learning by rhesus monkeys to visual-exploration motivation. *Journal of Comparative and Physiological Psychology,* 1953, *46,* 95–98.

Butler, R. A. Incentive conditions which influence visual exploration. *Journal of Experimental Psychology,* 1954, *48,* 19–23.

Byrne, D., & Clore, G. L., Jr. Predicting interpersonal attraction toward strangers presented in three different stimulus modes. *Psychonomic Science,* 1966, *4,* 239–240.

Byrne, D., and Wong, T. J. Racial prejudice, interpersonal attraction, and assumed dissimilarity of attitudes. *Journal of Abnormal and Social Psychology,* 1962, *65,* 246–253.

Cameron, N. *Personal development in psychopathology.* Boston: Houghton Mifflin, 1963.

Campbell, D. T. Ethnocentric and other altruistic motives. In Levine, D. (Ed.), *Nebraska Symposium on Motivation.* Lincoln, Neb.: University of Nebraska Press, 1965.

Cannon, W. B. *Bodily changes in pain, hunger, fear and rage.* New York: Appleton-Century-Crofts, 1929.

Caracena, P. F. Elicitation of dependency expressions in the initial stage of psychotherapy. *Journal of Counseling Psychology,* 1962, *9,* 329–334.

Carroll, J. B. *Language and thought.* Englewood Cliffs, N.J.: Prentice-Hall, 1964.

Casebook on ethical standards of psychologists. Washington, D.C.: American Psychological Association, 1967.

Cattell, R. B. Concepts of personality growing from multivariate experiment. In Wepman, J. M., & Heine, R. W. (Eds.), *Concepts of Personality.* Chicago: Aldine, 1963.

Cattell, R. B., & Ebel, H. W. *Handbook for the sixteen personality factor questionnaire.* Champaign, Ill.: Institute for Personality and Ability Testing, 1964.

Cautela, J. R. The treatment of alcoholism by covert sensitization. *Psychotherapy: Theory, Research and Practice,* 1970, *7,* 86–90.

Cautela, J. R., & Kastenbaum, R. A reinforcement survey schedule for use in therapy, training, and research. *Psychological Reports,* 1967, *20,* 1115–1130.

Clark, K. B., & Clark, M. P. Racial identification and preference in Negro children. In Newcomb, T. M., & Hartley, E. I. (Eds.), *Readings in Social Psychology.* New York: Holt, 1947.

Collins, A. M., & Loftus, E. F. A spreading activation theory of semantic processing. *Psychological Review,* 1975, *82,* 407–428.

Collins, A. M., & Quillian, M. R. Retrieval from semantic memory. *Journal of Verbal Learning and Verbal Behavior,* 1969, *8,* 240–247.

Cornsweet, T. N. *Visual perception.* New York: Academic Press, 1970.

Craik, F. I. M., & Lockhart, R. S. Levels of processing: A framework for memory research. *Journal of Verbal Learning and Verbal Behavior,* 1972, *11,* 671–684.

Crowne, D. P., & Marlowe, D. *The approval motive: Studies in evaluative dependence.* New York: Wiley, 1964.

Davis, H., & Silverman, S. R. *Hearing and deafness.* New York: Holt, Rinehart and Winston, 1961.

Deci, E. L. Work: Who does not like it and why. *Psychology Today,* 1972, *6,* 56–92.

Delgado, J. M. R. *Physical control of the mind.* New York: Harper & Row, 1969.

Dermer, M., & Thiel, D. L. When beauty may fail. *Journal of Personality and Social Psychology,* 1975, *31,* 1168–1176.

Deutsch, M., & Krauss, R. M. The effect of threat upon interpersonal bargaining. *Journal of Abnormal and Social Psychology,* 1960, *61,* 181–189.

DeValois, R. L., Abromov, I., & Jacobs, G. H. Analysis of response patterns of LGN cells. *Journal of the Optical Society of America,* 1966, *56,* 966–977.

Dinham, S. M. *Exploring statistics: An introduction for psychology and education.* Monterey, Calif.: Brooks/Cole, 1976.

Dion, K. L., Berscheid, E., & Walster, E. What is beautiful is good. *Journal of Personality and Social Psychology,* 1972, *24,* 285–290.

Dollard, J., Doob, L., Miller, N., Mowrer, O., & Sears, R. *Frustration and aggression.* New Haven, Conn: Yale University Press, 1939.

Dollard, J., & Miller, N. E. *Personality and psychotherapy.* New York: McGraw-Hill, 1950.

Eimas, P. D., Siqueland, E. R., Jusczyk, P., & Vigorito, J. Speech perception in infants. *Science,* 1971, *171,* 303–306.

Ellis, A. *Reason and emotion in psychotherapy.* New York: Lyle Stuart, 1961.

Engberg, L. A., Hansen, G., Welker, R. L., & Thomas, D. R. Acquistion of key-pecking via autoshaping as a function of prior experience: "Learned laziness"? *Science,* 1972, *178,* 1002–1004.

Epstein, S. Toward a unified theory of anxiety. *Progress in Experimental Personality Research,* 1967, *4,* 1–89.

Erikson, E. *Childhood and society.* New York: Norton, 1950.

Essen-Moller, E. Psychiatrische untersuchgen an einer Serie von Zwillingen. *Acta Psychiatrica et Neurologica Scandinavica,* 1941, suppl. 23.

Evans, R. M. *An introduction to color.* New York: Wiley, 1948.

Ewald, W. *Street graphics.* Washington, D.C.: American Landscape Architects Association, 1971.

Eysenck, H. J. The effects of psychotherapy: An evaluation. *Journal of Consulting Psychology,* 1952, *16,* 319–324.

Fantz, R. L. The origin of form perception. *Scientific American,* 1961, *204,* 66–72.

Fantz, R. L. Visual perception and experience in early infancy: A look at the hidden side of behavior development. In Stevenson, H. W., Hess, E. H., & Rheingold, H. L. (Eds.), *Early Behavior: Comparative and Developmental Approaches.* New York: Wiley, 1967.

Festinger, L. *A theory of cognitive dissonance.* Stanford, Calif.: Stanford University Press, 1957.

Festinger, L., Riecken, H. W., & Schachter, S. *When prophecy fails: A social and psychological study of a modern group that predicted the destruction of the world.* New York: Harper & Row, 1956.

Fitts, W. H. *The experience of psychotherapy.* Princeton, N.J.: Van Nostrand, 1965.

Ford, C. S., & Beach, R. A. *Patterns of sexual behavior.* New York: Harper & Row, 1951.

Foulkes, D. *The psychology of sleep.* New York: Scribner's, 1966.

Freedman, J., & Haber, R. N. One reason why we rarely forget a face. *The Bulletin of the Psychonomic Society,* 1974, *3,* 107–109.

French, E. G. Effects of the interaction of motivation and feedback on task performance. In Atkinson, J. W. (Ed.), *Motives in Fantasy, Action, and Society.* New York: Litton Educational Publishing Company, 1958.

Freud, S. *An outline of psychoanalysis (1940).* New York: Norton, 1949.

Freud, S. *The interpretation of dreams.* New York: Random House, 1950.

Freud, S. Some problems in the treatment of homosexuality. In Eysenck, H. J. (Ed.), *Behavior Therapy and the Neuroses.* Oxford, England: Pergamon, 1960.

Freud, S. *The interpretation of dreams.* New York: Science Editions, 1961.

Freud, S. Introductory lectures on psychoanalysis (1917). In *The Complete Introductory Lectures on Psychoanalysis.* New York: Norton, 1966.

Freud, S. New introductory lectures on psychoanalysis (1932). In *The Complete Introductory Lectures on Psychoanalysis.* New York: Norton, 1966.

Garcia, J., & Koelling, A. Relation of cue to consequence in avoidance learning. *Psychonomic Science,* 1966, *4,* 123–124.

Gardner, R. A., & Gardner, B. T. Teaching sign language to a chimpanzee. *Science,* 1969, *165,* 664–672.

Gibson, E. J. The ontogeny of reading. *American Psychologist,* 1970, *25,* 136–143.

Gibson, E. J., Gibson, J. J., Pick, A. D., & Osser, H. A. A developmental study of the discrimination of letter-like forms. *Journal of Comparative and Physiological Psychology,* 1962, *55,* 897–906.

Gibson, E. J., & Walk, R. D. The "visual cliff." *Scientific American,* 1960, *202,* 67–71.

Gibson, J. J. *The perception of the visual world.* Boston: Houghton Mifflin, 1950.

Gibson, J. J. *The senses considered as perceptual systems.* Boston: Houghton Mifflin, 1966.

Glasser, W. *Reality therapy.* New York: Harper & Row, 1965.

Goldstein, K. *The organism.* New York: American Book, 1939.

Gottesman, I. I., & Shields, J. Contributions of twin studies to perspectives on schizophrenia. In Maher, B. A. (Ed.), *Progress in Experimental Personality Research* (Vol. 3). New York: Academic Press, 1966.

Gottlieb, A. A., Gleser, G. C., & Gottschalk, L. A. Verbal and physiological responses to hypnotic suggestion of attitudes. *Psychosomatic Medicine,* 1967, *29,* 172–183.

Graham, D. T. Psychosomatic medicine. In Greenfield, N. S., & Sternbach, R. A. (Eds.), *Handbook of Psychophysiology.* New York: Holt, Rinehart and Winston, 1972.

Graham, D. T., Stern, J. A., & Winokur, G. Experimental investigation of the specificity of attitude hypothesis in psychosomatic disease. *Psychosomatic Medicine,* 1958, *20,* 446–457.

Green, R. F. Age-intelligence relationship between 16 and 64: A rising trend. *Developmental Psychology,* 1969, *1,* 618–627.

Gregory, R. L. *Eye and brain* (2d ed.). New York: McGraw-Hill, 1972.

Gregory, R. L. *The intelligent eye.* New York: McGraw-Hill, 1970.

Griffith, R. M., Miyago, O., & Tago, A. The universality of typical dreams: Japanese vs. Americans. *American Anthropologist,* 1958, *60,* 1173–1179.

Guilford, J. P. *The nature of human intelligence.* New York: McGraw-Hill, 1967.

Gulick, W. L. *Hearing: Physiology and psychophysics.* New York: Oxford, 1971.

Gurin, G., Veroff, J., & Feld, S. *Americans view their mental health.* New York: Basic Books, 1960.

Gustavson, C. R., Garcia, J., Hankins, W. G., & Rusiniak, K. W. Coyote predation control by aversive conditioning. *Science,* 1974, *184,* 581–584.

Hardy, K. R. An appetitional theory of sexual motivation. *Psychological Review,* 1964, *71*(1), 1–18.

Harlow, H. F. The nature of love. *American Psychologist,* 1958, *13,* 673–685.

Harlow, H., & Harlow, M. Learning to think. *Scientific American,* 1949, *181,* 36–39.

Harlow, H., Harlow, M. K., & Meyer, D. R. Learning motivated by a manipulation drive. *Journal of Experimental Psychology,* 1950, *40,* 228–234.

Harris, T. A. *I'm ok—you're ok.* New York: Harper & Row, 1967.

Hebb, D. O. *The organization of behavior.* New York: Wiley, 1949.

Heider, F. *The psychology of interpersonal relations.* New York: Wiley, 1958.

Held, R., & Hein, A. Movement-produced stimulation in the development of visually guided behavior. *Journal of Comparative and Physiological Psychology,* 1963, *56,* 872–876.

Held, R., & Richards, W. (Eds.). *Perception: Mechanisms and models.* San Francisco: Freeman, 1972.

Held, R., & Richards, W. (Eds.). *Recent progress in perception.* San Francisco: Freeman, 1976.

Helson, H. Adaptation level theory. In Koch, S. (Ed.), *Psychology: A Study of a Science* (Vol. 1). New York: McGraw-Hill, 1959.

Hess, E. The relationship between imprinting and motivation. In Jones, M. R. (Ed.), *Nebraska Symposium on Motivation* (Vol. 7). Lincoln, Neb.: University of Nebraska Press, 1959.

Hess, E. Ethology: An approach toward the complete analysis of behavior. In Brown, R., Galanter, E., Hess, E., & Mandler, G. (Eds.), *New Directions in Psychology.* New York: Holt, Rinehart and Winston, 1962.

Heston, L. L. The genetics of schizophrenia and schizoid disease. *Science,* 1970, *167,* 249–256.

Hilgard, E. R. Toward a neodissociation theory: Multiple cognitive control in human functioning. *Perspectives in Biology and Medicine,* 1974, *17,* 301–316.

Holmes, T. H., & Masuda, M. Psychosomatic syndrome. *Psychology Today,* 1972, *6,* 106.

Holt, J. *How children fail.* New York: Pitman, 1964.

Horney, K. *Neurotic personality of our times.* New York: Norton, 1937.

Hraba, J. G., & Grant, G. Black is beautiful: A reexamination of racial preference and identification. *Journal of Personality and Social Psychology,* 1970, *16,* 398–402.

Hubel, D. H., & Wiesel, T. N. Receptive fields of single neurons in the cat's striate cortex. *Journal of Physiology,* 1959, *148,* 574–591.

Hunt, E., Lunneborg, C., & Lewis, J. What does it mean to be high verbal? *Cognitive Psychology,* 1975, *7,* 194–227.

Isaacson, R. L., Douglas, R. J., Lubar, J. F., & Schmaltz, L. W. *A primer of physiological psychology.* New York: Harper & Row, 1971.

Janov, A. *The primal scream.* New York: Dell, 1970.

Jellinek, E. M. Phases of alcohol addiction. *Quarterly Journal of Studies on Alcohol,* 1952, *13,* 673–684.

Jenkins, C. D. Behavior that triggers heart attacks. *Science News,* 1974, *105,* 402.

Jensen, A. R. How much can we boost IQ and scholastic achievement? *Harvard Educational Review,* 1969, *39,* 1–123.

Johnson, D. M. A modern account of problem solving. *Psychological Bulletin,* 1944, *41,* 201–229.

Johnson, M. K., Bransford, J. D., & Solomon, S. Memory for tacit implications of sentences. *Journal of Experimental Psychology,* 1973, *98,* 203–205.

Jones, E. E., & Davis, K. E. From acts to dispositions: The attribution process in person perception. In Berkowitz, L. (Ed.), *Advances in Experimental Social Psychology* (Vol. 2). New York: Academic Press, 1965, pp. 219–266.

Jones, M. C. Psychological correlates of somatic development. *Child Development*, 1965, *36*, 899–911.

Jung, C. G. *Analytical psychology.* New York: Moffat, 1916.

Jung, C. G. *Psychology of the unconscious.* New York: Dodd, 1925.

Kallman, F. J. *Heredity in mental health and disorder.* New York: Norton, 1953.

Kallman, F. J. The use of genetics in psychiatry. *Journal of Mental Science*, 1958, *104*, 542–549.

Kamin, L. J. *The science and politics of I.Q.* Potomac, Md.: Erlbaum, 1974.

Katahn, M. Systematic desensitization and counseling for anxiety in a college basketball player. *Journal of Special Education*, 1967, *1*, 309–314.

Kaye, H. Infant sucking behavior and its modification. In Lipsitt, L. P., & Spiker, C. C. (Eds.), *Advances in Child Development and Behavior* (Vol. 3). New York: Academic Press, 1967.

Kelley, H. H. Interpersonal accommodation. *American Psychiatrist*, 1968, *23*, 399–441.

Kelly, G. A. *The psychology of personal constructs.* New York: Norton, 1955.

Kelly, G. A. Man's construction of his alternatives. In Lindzey, G. (Ed.), *Assessment of Human Motives.* New York: Holt, Rinehart and Winston, 1958.

Kelly, G. A. *A theory of personality: The psychology of personal constructs.* New York: Norton, 1963.

Kempler, W. Gestalt therapy. In Corsini, R. (Ed.), *Current Psychotherapies.* Itasca, Ill.: Peacock Publishers, 1973.

Kleinmuntz, B. The computer as clinician. *American Psychologist*, 1975, *30*, 379–387.

Kleinmuntz, B. Sign and seer: Another example. *Journal of Abnormal Psychology*, 1967, *72*, 163–165.

Kohlberg, L. The development of moral character and moral ideology. In Hoffman, M. L., & Hoffman, L. W. (Eds.), *Review of Child Development Research* (Vol. 1). New York: Russell Sage, 1964.

Köhler, W. *The mentality of apes.* New York: Harcourt, Brace, 1925.

Kolers, P. A. Bilingualism and information processing. *Scientific American*, 1968, *218*, 78–86.

Kopp, S. B. The character structure of sex offenders. *American Journal of Psychotherapy*, 1962, *16*, 64–70.

Krech, D., Crutchfield, R. S., & Livson, N. *Elements of psychology.* New York: Knopf, 1969.

Labov, W. The logic of nonstandard English. In Alatis, J. E. (Ed.), *20th Annual Round Table Meeting on Linguistics and Language Studies.* Washington, D.C.: Georgetown University Press, 1970.

Laing, R. D. *The divided self.* New York: Pantheon, 1969.

Laing, R. D. *The politics of experience.* New York: Pantheon, 1967.

Latané, B., & Darley, J. M. Group inhibition of bystander intervention in emergencies. *Journal of Personality and Social Psychology*, 1968, *10*, 215–221.

Laurendeau, M., & Pinard, A. *Causal thinking in the child.* New York: International Universities Press, 1962.

Lazarus, R. S., Opton, E. M., Nomikos, M. S., & Rankin, N. O. The principles of short-circuiting of threat: Further evidence. *Journal of Personality*, 1965, *33*, 622–635.

Lehman, H. C. *Age and achievement.* Princeton, N.J.: Princeton University Press, 1953.

Lidz, T., Alanen, Y., & Cornelison, A. Schizophrenic patients and their siblings. *Psychiatry*, 1963, *26*, 1–18.

Liebert, R. M., & Spiegler, M. D. *Personality: Strategies for the study of man* (rev. ed.). Homewood, Ill.: Dorsey Press, 1974.

Lilly, J. C. Mental effects of reduction of ordinary levels of physical stimuli for intact healthy persons. *Psychiatric Research Reports*, 1956, *5*, 1–9.

Lindner, R. *The fifty-minute hour.* New York: Holt, Rinehart and Winston, 1955.

Lindsay, P. H., & Norman, D. A. *Human information processing* (2d ed.). New York: Academic Press, 1977.

Loehlin, J. C., Lindzey, G., & Spuhler, J. N. *Race differences in intelligence.* San Francisco: Freeman, 1975.

Loftus, E. F., & Palmer, J. C. Reconstruction of automobile destruction. *Journal of Verbal Learning and Verbal Behavior*, 1974, *13*, 585–589.

Loftus, E. F., & Zanni, G. R. Eyewitness identification: Linguistically caused misreflections. Unpublished paper, 1973.

Logan, F. *Fundamentals of learning and motivation.* Dubuque, Iowa: Brown, 1970.

Lorenz, K. Der Kumpan in der Umwelt des Vogels. *Jour. Ornith.*, 1935, *83*, 137–213, 324–331.

Lorenz, K. Vergleichende Verhaltensforschung. *Zool. Anz. Suppl.*, 1939, *12*, 69–102.

Louis Harris and Associates, Inc. *The myth and reality of aging in America.* Washington, D.C.: National Council on the Aging, 1975.

Luchins, A. S. Mechanization in problem-solving: The effect of *Einstellung. Psychological Monographs*, 1942, *54* (whole no. 248).

MacDonald, M. L., Bernstein, D. A., & Ullmann, L. P. The reinforcing event report. Paper presented at the meeting of the Association for the Advancement of Behavior Therapy, New York, December 1976.

Maier, N. R. F. Reasoning in humans. II. The solution of a problem and its appearance in consciousness. *Journal of Comparative Psychology*, 1931, *12*, 181–194.

Maslow, A. H. A theory of human motivation. *Psychological Review*, 1943, *50*, 370–396.

Maslow, A. H. *Motivation and personality.* New York: Harper & Row, 1970.

Maslow, A. H. Some basic propositions of a growth and self-actualization psychology. In *Perceiving, Behaving, Becoming: A New Force for Education.* Washington, D.C.: Yearbook of the Association for Supervision and Curriculum Development, 1962.

Massaro, D. W. *Experimental psychology and information processing.* Chicago: Rand-McNally, 1975.

Masters, R., & Houston, J. *The varieties of psychedelic experience.* New York: Holt, Rinehart and Winston, 1966.

Mathews, K. E., Jr., & Canon, L. K. Environmental noise level as a determinant of helping behavior. *Journal of Personality and Social Psychology,* 1975, *32,* 571–577.

Mayer, R. E., & Greeno, J. G. Structural differences between learning outcomes produced by different instructional methods. *Journal of Educational Psychology,* 1972, *63,* 165–173.

McClelland, D. C., Atkinson, J. W., Clark, R. A., & Lowell, E. L. *The achievement motive.* New York: Appleton-Century-Crofts, 1953.

McClelland, D. C., & Friedman, G. A. A cross-cultural study of the relationship between child-training practices and achievement motivation appearing in folk tales. In Swanson, G. E., et al. (Eds.), *Readings in Social Psychology.* New York: Holt, 1952.

McClelland, D. C., & Winter, D. G. *Motivating economic achievement.* New York: Free Press, 1969.

McGee, M. G., & Snyder, M. Attribution and behavior: Two field studies. *Journal of Personality and Social Psychology,* 1975, *32,* 185–190.

McIntire, R. *For love of children.* Del Mar, Calif.: CRM Books, 1970.

Megargee, E. I. The prediction of violence with psychological tests. In C. D. Spielberger (Ed.), *Current Topics in Clinical and Community Psychology* (Vol. 2). New York: Academic Press, 1970.

Meichenbaum, D. H. Cognitive modification of test-anxious college students. *Journal of Consulting and Clinical Psychology,* 1972, *39,* 370–380.

Meredith, H. V. A synopsis of puberal changes in youth. *Journal of School of Health,* 1967, *37,* 171–176.

Merton, R. K. *On the shoulders of giants.* New York: Free Press, 1965.

Merton, R. K. *Social theory and social structure.* Glencoe, Ill.: Free Press, 1957.

Milgram, S. Some conditions of obedience and disobedience to authority. *Human Relations,* 1965, *18,* 57–76.

Miller, A. G. Role of physical attractiveness in impression formation. *Psychonomic Science,* 1970, *19,* 241–243.

Miller, G. A., Galanter, E., & Pribram, K. L. *Plans and the structure of behavior.* New York: Holt, Rinehart and Winston, 1960.

Miller, N. E. Learning of visceral and glandular responses. *Science,* 1969, *163,* 434–445.

Mischel, W. *Introduction to personality.* New York: Holt, Rinehart and Winston, 1971.

Money, J., & Ehrhardt, A. A. Fetal hormones and the brain: Effect on sexual dimorphism of behavior. A review. *Archives of Sexual Behavior,* 1971, *32,* 241–262.

Moore, O. K. Autotelic responsive environments and exceptional children. In Harvey, O. J. (Ed.), *Experience, Structure, and Adaptability.* New York: Springer, 1966.

Murray, H. A. *Explorations in personality.* New York: Oxford University Press, 1938.

Murray, H. A. Techniques for a systematic investigation of fantasy. *Journal of Psychology,* 1936, *3,* 115–143.

Neisser, U. Selective reading: A method for the study of visual attention. Paper presented at the 19th International Congress of Psychology, London, August 1969.

Newcomb, T. M. *The acquaintance process.* New York: Holt, Rinehart and Winston, 1961.

Nisbett, R. E. Determinants of food intake in human obesity. *Science,* 1968, *59,* 1254–1255.

Nisbett, R. E., & Wilson, T. D. Telling more than we can know: Verbal reports on mental processes. *Psychological Review,* 1977, *84,* 231–259.

Ogden, C. K., & Richards, I. A. *The meaning of meaning.* New York: Harcourt, Brace, 1923.

Olds, J., & Milner, P. M. Positive reinforcement produced by electrical stimulation of septal area and other regions of rat brains. *Journal of Comparative and Physiological Psychology,* 1954, *47,* 419–427.

Ornstein, R., & Naranjo, C. *On the psychology of meditation.* New York: Viking, 1971.

Osgood, C. E. The nature and measurement of meaning. *Psychological Bulletin,* 1952, *49,* 197–237.

Packard, V. *The hidden persuaders.* New York: Simon & Schuster, 1957.

Palermo, D. S. Language acquistion. In Reese, H. W., & Lipsitt, L. P. (Eds.), *Experimental Child Psychology.* New York: Academic Press, 1970.

Palmore, E. Facts on aging. *Gerontologist,* 1977, *17,* 315–320.

Paul, G. L. *Insight vs. desensitization in psychotherapy.* Stanford, Calif.: Stanford University Press, 1966.

Pavlov, I. P. *Conditioned reflexes.* New York: Oxford University Press, 1927.

Perls, F. S. *Gestalt therapy verbatim.* Lafayette, Calif.: Real People Press, 1969.

Pervin, L. A. *Personality: Theory, assessment, and research.* New York: Wiley, 1970.

Peterson, L. R., & Peterson, M. J. Short-term retention of individual verbal items. *Journal of Experimental Psychology,* 1959, *58,* 193–198.

Pettigrew, T. F. School desegregation. In *White House Conference on Education.* Washington, D.C.: Government Printing Office, 1965.

Piaget, J. *The language and thought of the child.* New York: Harcourt, Brace, 1926.

Pirenne, M. H. *Optics, painting and photography.* Cambridge, England: Cambridge University Press, 1970.

Pishkin, V., & Burn, J. M. Concept identification in the brain damaged: Intertrial interval and information complexity. *Journal of Abnormal Psychology,* 1971, *77,* 205–210.

Posner, M. I. *Cognition: An introduction.* Glenview, Ill.: Scott, Foresman, 1973.

Premack, D. Language in chimpanzee? *Science,* 1971, *172,* 808–822.

Premack, D. Reinforcement theory. In Levine, D. (Ed.), *Nebraska Symposium on Motivation.* Lincoln, Neb.: University of Nebraska Press, 1965.

Raimy, V. *Misunderstandings of the self.* San Francisco: Jossey-Bass, 1975.

Rebelsky, F., & Hanks, C. Father's verbal interaction with infants in the first three months of life. In Rebelsky, F., & Dorman, L. (Eds.), *Child Development and Behavior.* New York: Knopf, 1973, pp. 145–148.

Rescorla, R. A. Effect of inflation of the unconditioned stimulus value following conditioning. *Journal of Comparative and Physiological Psychology,* 1974, *86,* 101–107.

Revusky, S. H. Aversion to sucrose produced by contingent x-irradiation: Temporal and dosage parameters. *Journal of Comparative and Physiological Psychology,* 1968, *65,* 17–22.

Rodin, J., & Slochower, J. Externality in the nonobese: Effects of environmental responsiveness on weight. *Journal of Personality and Social Psychology,* 1976, *33,* 338–344.

Rogers, C. R. *Client-centered therapy.* Boston: Houghton Mifflin, 1951.

Rogers, C. R. *On becoming a person: A therapist's view of psychotherapy.* Boston: Houghton Mifflin, 1961.

Rokeach, M. *The open and closed mind.* New York: Basic Books, 1960.

Rosch, E., & Mervis, C. B. Family resemblances: Studies in the internal structure of categories. *Cognitive Psychology,* 1975, *7,* 573–605.

Rosenthal, R. *Experimenter effects in behavioral research.* New York: Appleton-Century-Crofts, 1966.

Rotter, J. B. Generalized expectancies for internal versus external control of reinforcement. *Psychological Monographs,* 1966, *80* (whole no. 609).

Runyon, R. P., & Haber, A. *Fundamentals of behavioral statistics* (3rd ed.). Reading, Mass.: Addison-Wesley, 1976.

Samuels, S. J., Dahl, P., & Archwamety, T. Effect of hypothesis/test training on reading skill. *Journal of Educational Psychology,* 1974, *66,* 835–844.

Schachter, S. Some extraordinary facts about obese humans and rats. *American Psychologist,* 1971, *26,* 129–144.

Schachter, S., & Gross L. P. Manipulated time and eating behavior. *Journal of Personality and Social Psychology,* 1968, *10,* 98–106.

Schachter, S., & Singer, J. E. Cognitive, social and physiological determinants of emotional state. *Psychological Review,* 1962, *69,* 379–399.

Schaie, K. W. A general model for the study of developmental problems. *Psychological Bulletin,* 1965, *64,* 92–107.

Schiffman, H. R. *Sensation and perception: An integrated approach.* New York: Wiley, 1976.

Schooler, C. Birth order effects: Not here, not now! *Psychological Bulletin,* 1972, *78,* 161–175.

Seeman, J. Self-exploration in client-centered therapy. In Wolman, B. B. (Ed.), *Handbook of Clinical Psychology.* New York: McGraw-Hill, 1965.

Seeman, J. *The case of Jim.* Tape recording and transcript. Nashville, Tenn.: Counselor Recordings and Tests, 1957.

Selfridge, R. G. Coding a general-purpose digital computer to operate as a differential analyzer. *Proceedings of the Western Joint Computer Conference,* Los Angeles, March 1955. New York: Institute of Electrical and Electronics Engineers, 1955.

Seligman, M. E. P. Can we immunize the weak? *Psychology Today,* June 1969, pp. 42–44.

Seligman, M. E. P. Depression and learned helplessness. In Friedman, R. J., & Katz, M. M. (Eds.), *The Psychology of Depression: Contemporary Theory and Research.* Washington, D.C.: Winston-Wiley, 1974.

Selye, H. *The stress of life.* New York: McGraw-Hill, 1956.

Shannab, M. E., & Yahya, K. A. A behavioral study of obedience in children. *Journal of Personality and Social Psychology,* 1977, *35,* 530–536.

Sherif, M., Harvey, O. J., White, B. J., Hood, W. R., & Sherif, C. W. *Intergroup conflict and cooperation: The Robbers Cave experiment.* Norman, Okla.: Institute of Group Relations, University of Oklahoma, 1961.

Shuttleworth, F. K. The adolescent period. *Monographs of the Society for Research in Child Development,* 1938, *3, 3.*

Sigall, H., & Ostrove, N. Beautiful but dangerous: Effects of offenders' attractiveness and nature of the crime on juridic judgment. *Journal of Personality and Social Psychology*, 1975, *31*, 410–414.

Siqueland, E. R., & Lipsitt, L. P. Conditioned head-turning in newborns. *Journal of Experimental Child Psychology*, 1966, *3*, 356–376.

Skinner, B. F. *The behavior of organisms.* New York: Appleton-Century-Crofts, 1938.

Slobin, D. I. *Psycholinguistics.* Glenview, Ill.: Scott, Foresman, 1971.

Smith, M. When psychology grows up. *New Scientist*, 1976, *64*, 90–93.

Snyder, M., Tanke, E. D., & Berscheid, E. Social perception and interpersonal behavior: On the self-fulfilling nature of social stereotypes. *Journal of Personality and Social Psychology*, 1977, *35*, 656–666.

Solomon, R. L., & Corbit, J. D. An opponent-process theory of motivation: II. Cigarette addiction. *Journal of Abnormal Psychology*, 1973, *83*, 158–171.

Sperling, G. The information available in brief visual presentations. *Psychological Monographs*, 1960 (74, whole no. 498).

Spock, B. *Baby and child care.* New York: Simon & Schuster, 1957.

Standing, L. G., Conezio, J., & Haber, R. N. Perception and memory for pictures: Single trial learning of 2500 visual stimuli. *Psychonomic Science*, 1970, *19*, 73–74.

Stewart, K. Dream theory in Malaya. In Tart, C. (Ed.), *Altered States of Consciousness: A Book of Readings.* New York: Wiley, 1969.

Stone, L. J., & Church, J. *Childhood and adolescence.* New York: Random House, 1968.

Stoner, J. A. F. A comparison of individual and group decisions involving risk. Unpublished master's thesis, Massachusetts Institute of Technology, 1961.

Storms, M. D., & Nisbett, R. E. Insomnia and the attribution process. *Journal of Personality and Social Psychology*, 1970, *2*, 319–328.

Strupp, H. H. *Psychotherapy and the modification of abnormal behavior.* New York: McGraw-Hill, 1971.

Strupp, H. H., Fox, R. W., & Lessler, K. *Patients view their psychotherapy.* Baltimore: Johns Hopkins University Press, 1969.

Strupp, H. H., Wallach, M. S., Wogan, M., & Jenkins, J. W. Psychotherapists' assessment of former patients. *Journal of Nervous and Mental Disease*, 1963, *137*, 222–230.

Szasz, T. S. *Law, liberty, and psychiatry.* New York: Macmillan, 1963.

Szasz, T. S. *The myth of mental illness.* New York: Harper & Row, 1961.

Tart, C. *On being stoned: A psychological study of marijuana intoxication.* Palo Alto, Calif.: Science and Behavior Books, 1971.

Tart, C. The "high" dream: A new state of consciousness. In Tart, C. (Ed.), *Altered States of Consciousness: A Book of Readings.* New York: Wiley, 1969.

Temerlin, M. K. Suggestion effects in psychiatric diagnosis. *Journal of Nervous and Mental Disease*, 1968, *147*, 349–353.

Terman, L. M., & Merrill, M. A. *Stanford-Binet intelligence scale: Manual for the third revision form L-M.* Boston: Houghton Mifflin, 1960.

Thibaut, J. W., & Kelley, H. H. *The social psychology of groups.* New York: Wiley, 1959.

Thigpen, C. H., & Cleckley, H. M. *The three faces of Eve.* New York: McGraw-Hill, 1957.

Thorndike, P. W. Cognitive structures in comprehension and memory of narrative discourse. *Cognitive Psychology*, 1977, *9*, 77–110.

Thurstone, L. L. *Primary mental abilities.* Chicago: University of Chicago Press, 1938.

Tinbergen, N. *The study of instinct.* London: Oxford University Press, 1951.

Tobin, S. A. Saying goodbye in Gestalt therapy. *Psychotherapy: Theory, Research, and Practice*, 1971, *8*, 150–155.

Triplett, N. The dynamogenic factors in pacemaking and competition. *American Journal of Psychology*, 1897, *9*, 507–533.

Trivers, R. L. The evaluation of reciprocal altruism. *The Quarterly Review of Biology*, 1971, *46*, 35–57.

Truax, C. B., Wargo, D. G., Frank, J. D., Imber, S. D., Battle, C., Hoehn-Sarie, R., Wash, E. H., & Stone, A. R. Therapist empathy, genuineness, warmth and patient therapeutic outcome. *Journal of Consulting Psychology*, 1966, *30*, 395–401.

Thorndike, P. W. Cognitive structures in comprehension and memory of narrative discourse. *Cognitive Psychology*, 1977, *9*, 77–110.

Tryon, R. C. Genetic differences in maze-learning ability in rats. In *39th Yearbook, National Society for the Study of Education.* Chicago: University of Chicago Press, 1940.

Tulving, E. Retrograde amnesia in free recall. *Science*, 1969, *164*, 88–90.

Valenti, A. C., & Downing, L. L. Differential effects of jury size on verdicts following deliberations as a function of the apparent guilt of a defendant. *Journal of Personality and Social Psychology*, 1975, *32*, 655–663.

Valins, S. Cognitive effects of false heart rate feedback. *Journal of Personality and Social Psychology*, 1966, *4*, 400–408.

van Eeden, F. A study of dreams. *Proceedings of the Society for Physical Research*, 1913, *26*, 431–461.

Wagner, A. R., Rudy, J. W., & Whitlow, J. W. Rehearsal in animal conditioning. *Journal of Experimental Psychology*, 1973, *97*, 407–426.

Wallace, W. P. Review of the historical, empirical, and theoretical status of the von Restorff phenomenon. *Psychological Bulletin*, 1965, *63*, 410–424.

Wallach, M. A., & Kogan, N. *Modes of thinking in young children*. New York: Holt, Rinehart and Winston, 1965.

Warden, C. J. *Animal motivation: Experimental studies on the albino rat*. New York: Columbia University Press, 1931.

Wason, P. C., & Johnson-Laird P. N. (Eds.), *Thinking and reasoning*. Middlesex, England: Penguin, 1968.

Wechsler, D. *Wechsler adult intelligence scale, manual*. New York: Psychological Corporation, 1955.

Werner, H., & Kaplan, E. Development of word meaning through verbal context: An experimental study. *Journal of Psychology*, 1950, *29*, 251–257.

White, R. W. Motivation reconsidered: The concept of competence. *Psychological Review*, 1959, *66*, 297–333.

Whitehead, A. N., & Russell, B. *Principia mathematica*. Cambridge, England: Cambridge University Press, 1925.

Whitehorn, J. C., & Betz, B. A study of psychotherapeutic relationships between physicians and schizophrenic patients. *American Journal of Psychiatry*, 1954, *111*, 321–331.

Whorf, B. L. *Language, thought, and reality*. New York: MIT Press—Wiley, 1956.

Wike, E. L. *Data analysis: A statistical primer for psychology students*. Chicago: Aldine-Atherton, 1971.

Wilson, E. O. *Sociobiology: The new synthesis*. Cambridge, Mass.: Belknap Press of Harvard University Press, 1975.

Winterbottom, M. R. The relation of need for achievement to learning experiences in independence and mastery. In Atkinson, J. W. (Ed.), *Motives in Fantasy*

Action and Society. Princeton, N.J.: Van Nostrand, 1958.

Wolf, M., Birnbrauer, J., Lawler, J., & Williams, T. The operant extinction, reinstatement, and re-extinction of vomiting behavior in a retarded child. In Ulrich, R., Stachnik, T., & Mabry, J. *Control of Human Behavior: From Cure to Prevention*. Glenview, Ill.: Scott, Foresman, 1970.

Wolpe, J., & Lang, P. J. A fear survey schedule for use in behavior therapy. *Behavior Research and Therapy*, 1964, *2*, 27.

Wright, R. L. D. *Understanding statistics: An informal introduction for the behavioral sciences*. New York: Harcourt Brace Jovanovich, 1976.

Yalom, I. D., & Lieberman, M. A. A study of encounter group casualties. *Archives of General Psychiatry*, 1971, *25*, 16–30.

Yarrow, M. R., Campbell, J. D., & Burton, R. V. Recollections of childhood: A study of the retrospective method. *Monographs of the Society for Research in Child Development*, 1970, *35*, (5, whole no. 138).

Zajonc, R. B. Social facilitation. *Science*, 1965, *149*, 269–274.

Zajonc, R. B. Family configuration and intelligence. *Science*, 1976, *160*, 227–236.

Zajonc, R. B., & Markus, G. B. Birth order and intellectual development. *Psychological Review*, 1975, *82*, 74–88.

Zimbardo, P. G. The human choice: Individuation, reason, and order versus deindividuation, impulse, and chaos. In *Nebraska Symposium on Motivation*. Lincoln, Neb.: University of Nebraska Press, 1969.

Zimbardo, P. G. *Shyness: What is it, what to do about it*. New York: Addison-Wesley, 1977.

Zimbardo, P. G. Pilkonis, P. A., & Norwood, R. M. The social disease called shyness. *Psychology Today*, 1975, *9*, 69–72.

Zimbardo, P. G., & Ruch, F. L. *Psychology and life* (9th Ed.). Glenview, Ill.: Scott, Foresman, 1977.

News story, p. 18, reprinted by permission of Associated Press.

Box, p. 19, data from E. G. Boring, H. S. Langfeld, and H. P. Weld, *Foundations of Psychology* (New York: Wiley, 1948). Reprinted by permission of Mrs. Lucy D. Boring.

Figure 1-2, p. 20, photo courtesy of The Bettmann Archive.

Figure 1-3, p. 21, photo courtesy of The Bettmann Archive.

Figure 1-4, p. 23, photo courtesy of James B. Watson.

Figure 1-5, p. 24, photo courtesy of United Press International.

Figure 1-6, p. 25, from *Elements of Psychology*, 2d edition, by David Krech and Richard S. Crutchfield. Copyright © 1958 by David Krech and Richard S. Crutchfield. Copyright © 1969 by Alfred A. Knopf. Reprinted by permission of the publisher.

News story, p. 27, reprinted by permission of Associated Press.

News story, p. 28, copyright 1973 by the American Psychological Association. Reprinted by permission.

Chapter 2

Photo, p. 32, by Charles Gatewood, Stock, Boston.

News story, p. 35, copyright 1977 by Newsweek, Inc. All rights reserved. Reprinted by permission.

Figure 2-2, p. 36, adapted from Fig. 3.2 (p. 63) in *A Primer of Physiological Psychology* by Robert L. Isaacson, Robert J. Douglas, Joel F. Lubar, and Leonard W. Schmaltz. Copyright © 1971 by Harper & Row, Publishers, Inc. Reprinted by permission of Harper & Row, Publishers, Inc.

Figure 2-3, p. 37, adapted from Fig. 4.6 (p. 88) in *Foundations of Physiological Psychology* by Richard F. Thompson. Copyright © 1967 by Richard F. Thompson. Reprinted by permission of Harper & Row, Pubishers, Inc.

Figure 2-4, p. 40, after William Etkin, Robert M. Devlin, and Thomas G. Bouffard: *A Biology of Human Concern*, 1972, Philadelphia, Lippincott. Reprinted by permission.

Figure 2-5, p. 41: Above, adapted from C. R. Noback and R. J. Demarest, *The Human Nervous System* (New York: McGraw-Hill, 1967). Reprinted by permission. Below, adapted from *Physiological Psychology* by Peter Milner. Copyright © 1970 by Holt, Rinehart and Winston, Inc. Reprinted by permission of Holt, Rinehart and Winston.

Figure 2-6, p. 42, adapted from *Physiological Psychology* by Peter Milner. Copyright © 1970 by Holt, Rinehart and Winston, Inc. Reprinted by permission of Holt, Rinehart and Winston.

Figure 2-7, p. 43, adapted from *Physiological Psychology* by Peter Milner. Copyright © 1970 by Holt, Rinehart and Winston, Inc. Reprinted by permission of Holt, Rinehart and Winston.

News story, pp. 44–45, copyright 1973 by Newsweek, Inc. All rights reserved. Reprinted by permission. Drawing by Roy Doty, *Newsweek.*

Figure 2-10, p. 47, adapted from H. F. Harlow et al., *Psychology* (San Francisco: Albion, 1971). Reprinted by permission.

Figure 2-11, p. 48, after William Etkin, Robert M. Devlin, and Thomas G. Bouffard: *A Biology of Human Concern*, 1972, Philadelphia, Lippincott. Reprinted by permission.

News story, p. 49, reprinted by permission from *TIME*, The Weekly Newsmagazine; Copyright Time Inc. 1978.

News story, p. 51, reprinted by permission from *TIME*, The Weekly Newsmagazine; Copyright Time Inc. 1978.

Figure 2-13, p. 53, reprinted by permission of Dr. Margery Shaw, University of Texas Health Sciences Center at Houston.

News story, p. 54, copyright 1976 by Newsweek, Inc. All rights reserved. Reprinted by permission.

News story, p. 55, reprinted by permission of United Press International.

News story, p. 59, reprinted by permission of Associated Press.

Photo, p. 59, courtesy of C. P. Hodge, Montreal Neurological Institute.

Figure 2-14, p. 61, reprinted with the permission of Charles Scribner's Sons from *The Psychology of Sleep* by David Foulkes. Copyright © 1966 David Foulkes.

News story, p. 62, copyright 1977 by the New York Times Co. Reprinted by permission.

News story, p. 64, copyright 1975 by Newsweek, Inc. All rights reserved. Reprinted by permission.

News story, p. 65, reprinted by permission of New York News, Inc.

Chapter 3

Photo, p. 66, by John T. Urban, Stock, Boston.

Figure 3-5, p. 71, adapted from *Psychology Today: An Introduction* (Del Mar, Calif.: CRM Books, 1970).

News story, p. 73, reprinted by permission from *TIME*, The Weekly Newsmagazine; Copyright Time Inc. 1972.

Figure 3-8, p. 75, adapted from S. Hecht, "Vision: II. The Nature of the Photoreceptor Process," in C. Murchison (Ed.), *A Handbook of General Experimental Psychology* (Worcester, Mass.: Clark University Press, 1934). Reprint edition by Russell and Russell, 1969. Reprinted by permission of Clark University Press.

Figure 3-16, p. 82, photo from H. L. Teuber, W. S. Battersby, and M. B. Bender, *Visual Field Defects after Penetrating Missile Wounds of the Brain* (Cambridge, Mass.: Harvard University Press, 1960), p. 36. Reprinted by permission of Harvard University Press. Photo courtesy of Massachusetts Institute of Technology.

Figure 3-17, p. 82, Part A: adapted from Julian E. Hochberg, *Perception,* © 1964. Adapted by permission of Prentice-Hall, Inc., Englewood Cliffs, N.J. Part B: adapted from D. H. Hubel and W. Torstenn, "Receptive Fields, Binocular Interaction, and Functional Architecture in the Cat's Visual Cortex," *Journal of Physiology* (Cambridge University Press), 1963, *160*, 106–154.

Figure 3-19, p. 84, adapted from Julian E. Hochberg, *Perception,* © 1964. Adapted by permission of Prentice-Hall, Inc., Englewood Cliffs, New Jersey.

Figure 3-20, p. 84, adapted from *Perception* by D. J. Weintraub and E. L. Walker. Copyright © 1966 by

Wadsworth Publishing Company, Inc. Reprinted by permission of the publisher, Brooks/Cole Publishing Company, Monterey, California 93940.

Figure 3–21, p. 85, adapted from Julian E. Hochberg, *Perception*, © 1964. Adapted by permission of Prentice-Hall, Inc., Englewood Cliffs, New Jersey.

Figure 3–22, p. 85 (except texture gradients), adapted from D. J. Weintraub and E. L. Walker, *Perception* (Monterey, Calif.: Brooks/Cole, 1966). Texture gradients adapted from James Gibson, *The Perception of the Visual World* (Boston: Houghton Mifflin, 1950), fig. 32, p. 84. Reprinted by permission.

Figure 3–23, p. 86, photos courtesy of Lou Harvey.

Figure 3–24, p. 87, adapted from *The Psychology of Visual Perception* by Ralph Norman Haber and Maurice Hershenson. Copyright © 1973 by Holt, Rinehart and Winston, Inc. Reprinted by permission of Holt, Rinehart and Winston.

Photo, p. 87, reprinted by permission of Escher Foundation.

News story, p. 88, copyright 1976 by Newsweek, Inc. All rights reserved. Reprinted by permission.

Photo, p. 90, left, from the *St. Louis Post-Dispatch*, October 29, 1977. Reprinted by permission of the Pulitzer Publishing Company.

Photo, p. 90, right, by Bohdan Hrynewych, Stock, Boston.

Figure 3–31, p. 94, adapted from *Man-Machine Engineering* by A. Chapanis. Copyright © 1965 by Wadsworth Publishing Company, Inc. Reprinted by permission of the publisher, Brooks/Cole Publishing Company, Monterey, California 93940. Also adapted from A. Chapanis, W. R. Garner, and C. T. Morgan, *Applied Experimental Psychology — Human Factors in Engineering Design* (New York: Wiley, 1949). Reprinted by permission of the authors.

Figure 3–33, p. 95, adapted from O. Stuhlman, Jr., *An Introduction to Biophysics* (New York: Wiley, 1943). Reprinted by permission of Mrs. William T. Couch.

Photo, p. 95, by Jeff Albertson, Stock, Boston.

Figure 3–34, p. 96, adapted from *Hearing and Deafness*, revised edition, edited by Hallowell Davis and S. Richard Silverman. Copyright 1947, © 1960 by Holt, Rinehart and Winston, Inc. Reprinted by permission of Holt, Rinehart and Winston.

News story, p. 100, copyright 1975 by Newsweek, Inc. All rights reserved. Reprinted by permission.

News story, p. 101, reprinted with permission from *Science News*, the weekly news magazine of science, copyright by Science Service, Inc.

Photo, p. 106, courtesy of United Airlines.

News story, p. 106, copyright 1974 by Newsweek, Inc. All rights reserved. Reprinted by permission.

News story, p. 107, reprinted by permission of United Press International.

News story, p. 108, reprinted by permission of Associated Press.

Photo, p. 108, courtesy of UPI Compix.

Figure 3–36, p. 109, adapted from *Hearing and Deafness*, revised edition, edited by Hallowell Davis and S. Richard Silverman. Copyright 1947, © 1960 by Holt, Rinehart and Winston, Inc. Reprinted by permission of Holt, Rinehart and Winston and C. C. Bunch.

Figure 3–37, p. 109, adapted from *Hearing and Deafness*, revised edition, edited by Hallowell Davis and S. Richard Silverman. Copyright 1947, © 1960 by Holt, Rinehart and Winston, Inc. Reprinted by permission of Holt, Rinehart and Winston and *Journal of Acoustic Society of America*. Data from "1954 Wisconsin State Fair Hearing Survey," by A. Glorig et al., American Academy of Opthalmology and Autolaryngology, 1937, and from Glorig, Quiggle, Wheeler, and Grings, *Journal of the Acoustic Society of America*, 28, 1110–1113 (1956). Reprinted by permission of the authors.

News story, p. 110, copyright 1975 by Newsweek, Inc. All rights reserved. Reprinted by permission.

Photo, p. 111, by Bill Saidel, Stock, Boston.

News story, p. 111, copyright © 1977 by the *Chicago Daily News*. Reprinted by permission.

News story, p. 112, reprinted by permission of Associated Press.

Chapter 3 Color Plates

Plate 2, from *Fundamentals of Child Development* by Harry Munsinger. Copyright © 1971 by Holt, Rinehart and Winston, Inc. Reprinted by permission of Holt, Rinehart and Winston.

Plate 3, left portion, standard chromaticity diagram, adapted from *Sight and Mind: An Introduction to Visual Perception* by Lloyd Kaufman. Copyright © 1974 by Oxford University Press, Inc. Reprinted by permission.

Plate 4, from R. M. Evans, *An Introduction to Color* (New York: Wiley, 1948). Reprinted by permission.

Plate 5, by permission of Inmont Corporation.

Plate 6, by permission of Inmont Corporation.

Plate 7, from AO Pseudo-Isochromatic Color Tests by American Optical Corporation. Reprinted by permission.

Plate 8, reprinted by permission of The Museum of Modern Art.

Plate 10, © Copyright 1953, 1972 CIBA Pharmaceutical Company, Division of CIBA-GEIGY Corporation. Reproduced, with permission, from *The Ciba Collection of Medical Illustrations* by Frank H. Netter, M.D. All rights reserved.

Plate 11, © Copyright 1953, 1972 CIBA Pharmaceutical Company, Division of CIBA-GEIGY Corporation. Reproduced, with permission, from *The Ciba Collection of Medical Illustrations* by Frank H. Netter, M.D. All rights reserved.

Plate 12, © Copyright 1953, 1972 CIBA Pharmaceutical Company, Division of CIBA-GEIGY Corporation. Reproduced, with permission, from *The Ciba Collection of Medical Illustrations* by Frank H. Netter, M.D. All rights reserved.

Plate 13 © Copyright 1953, 1972 CIBA Pharmaceutical Company, Division of CIBA-GEIGY Corporation. Reproduced, with permission, from *The Ciba Collection of Medical Illustrations* by Frank H. Netter, M.D. All rights reserved.

Chapter 4

Photo, p. 114, by Jill Freedman, © Magnum Photos, Inc.
Figure 4-1, p. 116, adapted from C. T. Morgan and R. A. King, *Introduction to Psychology* (New York: McGraw-Hill, 1966). Reprinted by permission. Also adapted from Pavlov, 1928.
News story, p. 117, reprinted by permission from *TIME*, The Weekly Newsmagazine; Copyright Time Inc. 1956. The authors are grateful to Bernard Spilka for drawing their attention to this article.
Photo, p. 122, courtesy of Harvard University News Office.
Figure 4-5, p. 125, photo courtesy of Yerkes Regional Primate Research Center, Emory University.
News story, p. 127, reprinted by permission of Associated Press.
Figure 4-7, p. 133, adapted from Ernest R. Hilgard and Gordon H. Bower, *Theories of Learning*, 3d edition, © 1966, p. 136. Adapted by permission of Prentice-Hall, Inc., Englewood Cliffs, New Jersey. Data from W. K. Estes, "An Experimental Study of Punishment," *Psychological Monographs*, 1944, *57*.
Table 4-6, p. 134, adapted from Frank A. Logan, *Fundamentals of Learning and Motivation*, 1970, Dubuque, Wm. C. Brown Company Publishers. Reprinted by permission.
News story, p. 134, copyright 1974 by Newsweek, Inc. All rights reserved. Reprinted by permission.
Figure 4-8, p. 136, reprinted with permission of author and publisher from: Guttman, N., "The Pigeon and the Spectrum and Other Perplexities," *Psychological Reports*, 1956, *2*, 449-460.
News story, p. 146, reprinted by permission of *The Denver Post*.
Figure 4-10, p. 147, photo courtesy of Sears, Roebuck and Co.
News story, p. 148, reprinted by permission of Knight-Ridder Newspapers.
News story, p. 151, © *The Washington Post*. Reprinted by permission.
News story, p. 153, reprinted by permission from *TIME*, The Weekly Newsmagazine; Copyright Time Inc. 1972.
News story, p. 154, copyright 1973 by Newsweek, Inc. All rights reserved. Reprinted by permission.
News story, p. 155, reprinted by permission of *The Denver Post*.

Chapter 5

Photo, p. 156, by David Seymour, "Chim," © Magnum Photos, Inc.
Photo, p. 158, by Peter Southwick, Stock, Boston.
Figure 5-2, p. 161, adapted from L. R. Peterson and M. J. Peterson, "Short-term Retention of Individual Verbal Items," *Journal of Experimental Psychology*, 1959, *58*, 193-198. Copyright 1959 by the American Psychological Association. Reprinted by permission.
Figure 5-3, p. 164, adapted from A. M. Collins and M. R. Quillian, "Retrieval Time from Semantic Memory," *Journal of Verbal Learning and Verbal Behavior*, 1969, *8*, 240-247. Copyright 1969 by Academic Press. Reprinted

by permission of Academic Press and the authors. Box, p. 167, ratings for lists of nonsense syllables from J. A. Glaze, "The Association Value of Nonsense Syllables," *Journal of Genetic Psychology*, 1928, *35*, 255-267. Reprinted by permission of The Journal Press.
Photo, p. 171, by Fredrik D. Bodin, Stock, Boston.
News story, p. 172, reprinted by permission of the *Pueblo Star-Journal* and *Pueblo Chieftain*, Pueblo, Colo. 81002.
News story, p. 175, reprinted courtesy of the *Chicago Tribune*.
Figure 5-6, p. 178, adapted from J. D. Bransford and J. J. Franks, "The Abstraction of Linguistic Ideas," *Cognitive Psychology*, 1971, *2*, 331-350. Reprinted by permission.
News story, p. 184, reprinted by permission from *Town & Country Review*, Boulder, Colorado.

Chapter 6

Photo, p. 185, by Peter Vandermark, Stock, Boston.
News story, p. 190, copyright Los Angeles Times. Reprinted with permission.
Problem of "the ages of a man and his wife," pp. 194 and 201, from D. M. Johnson, "A Modern Account of Problem Solving," *Psychological Bulletin*, 1944, *41*, 201-229.
Figure 6-2, p. 196, after W. J. McKeachie and C. L. Doyle, *Psychology*, second edition, © 1970, Addison-Wesley, Reading, Mass. Reprinted by permission.
Photo, p. 196, reprinted by permission of Wide World Photos.
Table 6-1, p. 197, adapted from p. 109 of Abraham S. Luchins and Edith H. Luchins, *Rigidity of Behavior* (Eugene: University of Oregon Press, 1959), which describes experiments that minimized and maximized Einstellung effects and recovery in arithmetic problems, anagrams, and mazes, as well as other material. Reprinted by permission of the authors.
Photo, p. 206, by Jim Harrison, Stock, Boston.
Box, p. 209, based on P. A. Kolers, "Bilingualism and Information Processing," *Scientific American*, March 1968, pp. 78-86.
Box, p. 210, drawing from J. D. Bransford and M. K. Johnson, "Considerations of Some Problems of Comprehension," in W. G. Chase (Ed.), *Visual Information Processing* (New York: Academic Press, 1973). Reprinted by permission.
News story, p. 211, reprinted by permission of United Press International.
Box, p. 213, based on C. Loehlin et al., *Race Differences in Intelligence* (San Francisco: W. H. Freeman, 1975).
Table 6-4, p. 214, adapted from D. Wechsler, *The Measurement and Appraisal of Adult Intelligence*, 4th ed., © 1958 the Williams & Wilkins Co., Baltimore. Reprinted by permission.
Table 6-5, p. 215, after a report of the President's Commission on Mental Retardation, 1963, by F. H. Sanford and L. S. Wrightsman, in *Psychology: A Scientific Study of Man*, 3d ed. (Monterey, Calif.: Brooks/Cole Publishing, 1970).
Boxes, pp. 217 and 219, adapted from F. Barron, "The

Psychology of Imagination," *Scientific American*, September 1958. Reprinted by permission of the author.

News story, p. 223, copyright 1977 by Newsweek, Inc. All rights reserved. Reprinted by permission.

Photo, p. 224, by Donald Dietz, Stock, Boston.

News story, p. 231, reprinted by permission from *TIME*, The Weekly Newsmagazine; Copyright Time Inc. 1976.

News story, p. 232, reprinted by permission from *TIME*, The Weekly Newsmagazine; Copyright Time Inc. 1977.

News story, pp. 233–234, copyright 1977 by Editorial Projects for Education, 1977. Reprinted by permission.

Chapter 7

Photo, p. 235, by Ellis Herwig, Stock, Boston.

News story, p. 240, reprinted by permission of Associated Press.

Figure 7–1, p. 240, from D. L. Hebb, *Textbook of Psychology*, 3d ed. (Philadelphia: W. B. Saunders Company, 1972), p. 199. Reprinted by permission.

Figure 7–3, p. 243, photo from R. A. Butler, "Incentive Conditions Which Influence Visual Exploration," *Journal of Experimental Psychology*, 1954, *48*, 19–23. Copyright 1954 by the American Psychological Association. Reprinted by permission. Photo courtesy of Harry F. Harlow, University of Wisconsin Primate Laboratory.

Photo, p. 245, courtesy of Wide World Photos.

Figure 7-4, p. 246, photo courtesy of Neal E. Miller.

News story, p. 246, copyright © 1978 by the *Chicago Daily News*. Reprinted by permission.

Figure 7–5, p. 252, from *A Biology of Human Concern* by William Ektin, Robert M. Devlin, and Thomas G. Bouffard. Reprinted by permission of the publisher, J. P. Lippincott Company. Copyright © 1972.

News story, p. 254, reprinted with permission from *Science News*, the weekly news magazine of science, copyright by Science Service, Inc.

News story, p. 257, reprinted by permission from *TIME*, The Weekly Newsmagazine; Copyright Time Inc. 1971.

Figure 7–7, p. 258, photo courtesy of Dorothea Lange Collection, The Oakland Museum.

Table 7–2, p. 259, from *Explorations in Personality: A Clinical and Experimental Study of Fifty Men of College Age.* By the Workers at the Harvard Psychological Clinic. Edited by Henry A. Murray. Copyright © 1938 by Oxford University Press, Inc. Renewed 1966 by Henry A. Murray. Reprinted by permission of the publisher. Also from C. S. Hall and G. Lindzey, *Theories of Personality* (New York: Wiley, 1957). Reprinted by permission.

Figure 7–8, p. 260, adapted from Abraham H. Maslow, "A Theory of Human Motivation," *Psychological Review*, 1943, *50*, 370–396.

News story, p. 262, reprinted by permission of Associated Press.

Photo, p. 263, by Peter Southwick, Stock, Boston.

Figure 7-9, p. 264, adapted from E. G. French, "Effects of the Interaction of Motivation and Feedback on Task Performance," from *Motives in Fantasy, Action, and Society*, edited by J. W. Atkinson, © 1958 by Litton Educational Publishing, Inc. Reprinted by permission of Van Nostrand Reinhold Company.

News story, p. 267, reprinted by permission of Knight-Ridder Newspapers.

News story, p. 269, reprinted by permission from *TIME*, The Weekly Newsmagazine; Copyright Time Inc. 1977.

News story, p. 273, reprinted by permission of Associated Press.

News story, p. 274, reprinted from *The Rotarian* Magazine for March 1978, with permission.

Figure 7–10, p. 275, from Hans Selye, *The Physiology and Pathology of Exposure to Stress*, 1950, ACTA, Montreal. Reprinted by permission of the International Institute of Stress.

Figure 7–11, p. 276, photos from Neal Miller, "Theory and Experiment Relating Psycho-analytic Displacement to Stimulus-Response Generalization," *Journal of Abnormal and Social Psychology*, 1948, *43*, 155–178. Photos courtesy of Neal E. Miller.

News story, p. 280, copyright © 1972 by the *Chicago Sun-Times*. Reprinted by permission.

News story, p. 285, reprinted by permission of United Press International.

News story, p. 288, reprinted by permission of Knight-Ridder Newspapers.

News story, p. 289, reprinted by permission from *TIME*, The Weekly Newsmagazine; Copyright Time Inc. 1977.

News story, p. 290, reprinted courtesy of the *Chicago Tribune*.

Chapter 8

Photo, p. 292, by Fred Weiss.

News story, p. 295, reprinted by permission of *The Denver Post*.

News story, p. 297, reprinted by permission of Associated Press.

News story, p. 298, reprinted by permission.

Chart, p. 298, reprinted courtesy of the *Chicago Tribune*.

Photo, p. 299, by Karega Kofi Moyo.

News story, p. 300, reprinted by permission from *TIME*, The Weekly Newsmagazine; Copyright Time Inc. 1972.

Figure 8-2, p. 301, adapted from R. L. Fantz, "Visual Perception and Experience in Early Infancy: A Look at the Hidden Side of Behavior Development," in H. W. Stevenson, E. H. Hess, and H. L. Rheingold (Eds.), *Early Behavior: Comparative and Developmental Approaches* (New York: Wiley, 1967). Reprinted by permission.

Figure 8–3, p. 302, from "The Origin of Form Perception" by R. L. Fantz. Copyright © 1961 by Scientific American Inc. All rights reserved. Reprinted by permission.

Figure 8-4, p. 303, photos from E. J. Gibson and R. D. Walk, "The Visual Cliff," *Scientific American*, April 1960. Photos courtesy of William Vandivert.

Figure 8–5, p. 303, adapted from E. J. Gibson, "The Ontogeny of Reading," *American Psychologist*, 1970, *25*, 136–143. Copyright 1970 by the American Psychological Association. Reprinted by permission. Taken from research by Linda Lavine.

News story, p. 304, reprinted from *Psychology Today* magazine, copyright © 1975, Ziff-Davis Publishing Company.

Figure 8-6, p. 307, photos from A. T. Jersild, *Child Psychology*, 6th ed. (Englewood Cliffs, N.J.: Prentice-Hall, 1968). Photos by George Zimbel of Monkmeyer Press.

Figure 8–7, p. 308, adapted from Figure 6 from *The Growth of Logical Thinking: From Childhood to Adolescence* by Barbel Inhelder and Jean Piaget, translated by Anne Parsons and Stanley Milgram. © 1958 by Basic Books, Inc., Publishers, New York. Reprinted by permission.

Table 8–2, p. 310, adapted from Table 1 (p. 22) in *The Acquisition of Language* by David McNeill. Copyright © 1970 by David McNeill. Reprinted by permission of Harper & Row, Publishers, Inc. Data from W. F. Leopold, *Speech Development of a Bilingual Child*, vol. 4 (Evanston, Ill.: Northwestern University Press, 1949). Reprinted by permission.

News story, p. 311, reprinted by permission from *TIME*, The Weekly Newsmagazine; Copyright Time Inc. 1976.

Table 8–3, p. 312, from Roger Brown and Ursula Bellugi, "Three Processes in the Child's Acquisition of Syntax," *Harvard Educational Review, 34*, Spring 1964, 133–151. Copyright © 1964 by the President and Fellows of Harvard College. Reprinted by permission.

News story, p. 312, reprinted by permission of United Press International.

News story, p. 315, reprinted with permission from *Science News*, the weekly news magazine of science, copyright by Science Service, Inc.

News story, p. 317, reprinted courtesy of the *Chicago Tribune*.

News story, p. 319, reprinted by permission of Associated Press.

Photo, p. 320, by Abigail Heyman, © Magnum Photos, Inc.

News story, p. 320, reprinted courtesy of the *Chicago Tribune*.

News story, p. 321, © *The Washington Post*. Reprinted by permission.

Photo, p. 322, by Ellis Herwig, Stock, Boston.

News story, p. 323, reprinted with permission from *Science News*, the weekly news magazine of science, copyright by Science Service, Inc.

Table 8–5, p. 324, table of moral development from "The Development of Moral Character and Moral Ideology," by Lawrence Kohlberg. In *Review of Child Development Research*, volume 1, edited by Martin L. Hoffman and Lois Wladis Hoffman, © 1964 by Russell Sage Foundation. Reprinted by permission.

Figure 8–10, p. 324, figure of mean percent of total moral statements of each of six moral judgment types at four ages, from, "The Development of Moral Character and Moral Ideology," by Lawrence Kohlberg. In *Review of Child Development Research*, volume 1, edited by Martin L. Hoffman and Lois Wladis Hoffman, © 1964 by Russell Sage Foundation. Reprinted by permission.

News story, p. 325, copyright 1977 by Newsweek, Inc. All rights reserved. Reprinted by permission.

Figure 8–11, p. 326, adapted from F. K. Shuttleworth, "The Adolescent Period," *Monographs of the Society for Research in Child Development, 3* (3), 1938. © The Society for Research in Child Development, Inc. Reprinted by permission.

News story, p. 328, copyright 1975 by the American Psychological Association. Reprinted by permission.

News story, p. 329, reprinted courtesy of the *Chicago Tribune*.

News story, p. 334, reprinted by permission of United Press International.

News story, p. 337, reprinted courtesy of the *Chicago Tribune*.

Figure 8–12, p. 337, adapted from J. S. Bruner, *Toward a Theory of Instruction* (Cambridge, Mass.: Belknap Press, Harvard University Press, 1966). Copyright 1966 by the President and Fellows of Harvard College. Reprinted by permission.

News story, p. 339, reprinted by permission of United Press International.

Chapter 9

Photo, p. 340, by Burk Uzzle, © Magnum Photos, Inc.

News story, p. 343, reprinted from *Psychology Today* magazine, copyright © 1977, Ziff-Davis Publishing Company.

Box, pp. 344–345, from "Fortune Tellers Never Starve," by William L. Gresham, *Esquire*, 1949. First published in *Esquire* Magazine. Copyright © 1949 by William L. Gresham; copyright © renewed 1977 by Renée Gresham. Reprinted by permission of Brandt & Brandt.

Figure 9–2, p. 351, reproduced with permission from R. M. Liebert and M. D. Spiegler, *Personality: Strategies for the Study of Man*, rev. ed. (Homewood, Ill.: The Dorsey Press, © 1974), p. 67.

Table 9–2, p. 352, reproduced with permission from R. M. Liebert and M. D. Spiegler, *Personality: Strategies for the Study of Man*, rev. ed. (Homewood, Ill.: The Dorsey Press, © 1974), p. 67.

News story, p. 352, reprinted by permission of Associated Press.

Figure 9–3, p. 353, photos (except bottom left) courtesy of Sigmund Freud Copyrights Ltd. Photo, bottom left, by Max Halberstadt, courtesy of W. E. Freud.

Table 9–3, p. 356, adapted from C. S. Hall and G. Lindzey, *Theories of Personality* (New York: Wiley, 1957). Reprinted by permission.

News story, p. 359, reprinted by permission of United Press International.

Figure 9–4, p. 360, photos from A. Bandura, D. Ross, and S. A. Ross, "Imitation of Film-Mediated Aggressive Models," *Journal of Abnormal and Social Psychology*, 1963, *66*, 3–11. Copyright 1963 by the American Psychological Association. Reprinted by permission. Photos courtesy of Albert Bandura.

Figure 9–5, p. 361, photo courtesy of Albert Bandura.

News story, p. 361, reprinted by permission of United Press International.

Figure 9–6, p. 365, photo by John T. Wood, courtesy of Carl Rogers.

News story, p. 369, reprinted by permission from *TIME*, The Weekly Newsmagazine; Copyright Time Inc. 1978.

News story, p. 370, copyright 1973 by Newsweek, Inc. All rights reserved. Reprinted by permission.

News story, p. 373, reprinted by permission of Associated Press.

News story, p. 375, reprinted by permission of Associated Press.

News story, p. 376, copyright 1975 by Newsweek, Inc.

Mental Illness (New York: Harper & Row, 1964). Reprinted by permission of Robert W. White.

News story, p. 457, reprinted by permission of Associated Press.

News story, p. 458, reprinted by permission of Newhouse News Service.

News story, p. 463, reprinted by permission of Associated Press.

News story, p. 464, reprinted by permission of Associated Press.

Chapter 12

Photo, p. 465, courtesy of Wide World Photos.

Figure 12-1, p. 469, photo by Karega Kofi Moyo.

Photo, p. 471, by Ellis Herwig, Stock, Boston.

Excerpt, pp. 472–473, from Stephan A. Tobin, "Saying Goodbye in Gestalt Therapy," *Psychotherapy: Theory, Research, and Practice,* 1971, *8,* 154–155. Reprinted by permission.

News story, pp. 474–475, reprinted by permission from *TIME,* The Weekly Newsmagazine; Copyright Time Inc. 1973. Drawings from *I'm OK—You're OK* by Thomas A. Harris. Copyright © 1967, 1968, 1969 by Thomas A. Harris, M. D. Reprinted by permission of Harper & Row.

News story, p. 478, © *The Washington Post.* Reprinted by permission.

Photo, p. 479, from "Relax! Get a Grip on Your Headaches," *Chicago Tribune,* October 8, 1975. Photo by Arthur Walker. Reprinted by permission.

Excerpt, p. 480, adapted from M. Katahn, "Systematic Desensitization and Counseling for Anxiety in a College Basketball Player," *Journal of Special Education,* 1967, *1,* 309–314. Reprinted from the *Journal of Special Education* by permission of the publisher.

News story, p. 481, reprinted by permission of Newhouse News Service.

Photo, p. 488, courtesy of the U.S. Bureau of Prisons.

News story, p. 490, reprinted by permission from *TIME,* The Weekly Newsmagazine; Copyright Time Inc. 1975.

Table 12-2, p. 491, adapted from a chart prepared by the Bureau of Narcotics and Dangerous Drugs, U.S. Department of Justice.

News stories, p. 493: (left) reprinted by permission of United Press International; (right) reprinted by permission of *The Denver Post.*

News story, p. 494, copyright 1975 by Newsweek, Inc. All rights reserved. Reprinted by permission.

News story, p. 497, reprinted by permission of *The Denver Post.*

Excerpts, p. 501, from *The Experience of Psychotherapy* by W. H. Fitts. Copyright © 1965 D. Nostrand Co., Inc. Reprinted by permission of the author.

Table 12-3, p. 502, Table 10.1 adapted from *Americans View Their Mental Health* by Gerald Gurin, Joseph Veroff, and Sheila Feld. Copyright © 1960 by Basic Books, Inc., Publishers, New York.

Table 12-4, p. 502, Table 10.3 adapted from *Americans View Their Mental Health* by Gerald Gurin, Joseph Veroff, and Sheila Feld. Copyright © 1960 by Basic Books, Inc., Publishers, New York.

News story, p. 505, copyright 1974 by the New York Times Co. Reprinted by permission.

News story, p. 506, reprinted courtesy of the *Chicago Tribune.*

Appendix A

News story, p. 523, reprinted by permission of Associated Press.

Appendix B

News story, p. 534, copyright 1978 by Newsweek, Inc. All rights reserved. Reprinted by permission.

Appendix C

News story, p. 539, reprinted by permission of The Wall Street Journal, © Dow Jones & Co., Inc., 1978. All rights reserved.

Figure C-2, p. 541, adapted from Gregory A. Kimble and Norman Garmezy, *Principles of General Psychology,* 3d edition. Copyright © 1968 The Ronald Press Company, New York. Reprinted by permission. Data from Starke R. Hathaway and Elio D. Monachesi, *Analyzing and Predicting Juvenile Delinquency with the MMPI.* University of Minnesota Press, Minneapolis, © 1953 by the University of Minnesota. Reprinted by permission.

Figure C-3, p. 542, profile sheet for the 16 PF, © 1954, 1969 by IPAT, Champaign, Ill. Reprinted by permission.

News story, p. 545, reprinted by permission from *TIME,* The Weekly Newsmagazine; Copyright Time Inc. 1971. Drawings from S. H. Kaufman and R. C. Burns, *Kinetic Family Drawings* (New York: Brunner/Mazel, Publishers, 1970). Reprinted by permission.

Appendix D

Figure D-1, p. 550, adapted from N. Kleitman, "Patterns of Dreaming," *Scientific American,* November 1960. Reprinted by permission of Dr. William Dement.

News story, p. 551, reprinted by permission of Knight-Ridder Newspapers.

Excerpt, p. 552, from Charles Tart, "The High Dream: A New State of Consciousness," in Charles Tart (Ed.), *Altered States of Consciousness: A Book of Readings* (New York: Wiley, 1969), p. 173. Reprinted by permission.

News story, p. 555, reprinted by permission of United Press International.

Table D-2, p. 559, from chart "values of variables for maximizing probability of 'good' or 'bad' trip" from Charles T. Tart, *On Being Stoned: A Psychological Study of Marijuana Intoxication* (Palo Alto, Calif.: Science and Behavior Books, 1971). Reprinted by permission.

News story, p. 562, reprinted by permission from *TIME,* The Weekly Newsmagazine; Copyright Time Inc. 1973.

Table D-3, p. 563, adapted from a chart prepared by the Bureau of Narcotics and Dangerous Drugs, U.S. Department of Justice.

News story, p. 566, reprinted by permission of Newhouse News Service.

News story, p. 567, reprinted by permission of Knight-Ridder Newspapers.

Name Index

Subject Index